International Law

International Law

Fourth Edition

Barry E. Carter
Professor of Law
Georgetown University

Phillip R. Trimble
Professor of Law
University of California, Los Angeles

Curtis A. Bradley
Professor of Law
University of Virginia

1185 Avenue of the Americas, New York, NY 10036
www.aspenpublishers.com

Permissions
Aspen Publishers
1185 Avenue of the Americas
New York, NY 10036

Printed in the United States of America

1 2 3 4 5 6 7 8 9 0

ISBN 0-7355-2706-7

Library of Congress Cataloging-in-Publication Data

Carter, Barry E.
    International law / Barry E. Carter, Phillip R. Trimble, Curtis A.
Bradley. — 4th ed.
        p.   cm.
    Includes bibliographical references and index.
    ISBN 0-7355-2706-7
        1. International law— Cases.   I. Trimble, Phillip R.   II. Bradley,
Curtis A   II. Title.
    KZ1242.5.C37   2003
        341— dc21   2003052232

877-277-9812
800-950-9259

About Aspen Publishers

Aspen Publishers, headquartered in New York City, is a leading information provider for attorneys, business professionals, and law students. Written by preeminent authorities, our products consist of analytical and practical information covering both U.S. and international topics. We publish in the full range of formats, including updated manuals, books, periodicals, CDs, and online products.

Our proprietary content is complemented by 2,500 legal databases, containing over 11 million documents, available through our Loislaw division. Aspen Publishers also offers a wide range of topical legal and business databases linked to Loislaw's primary material. Our mission is to provide accurate, timely, and authoritative content in easily accessible formats, supported by unmatched customer care.

To order any Aspen Publishers title, go to *www.aspenpublishers.com* or call 1-800-638-8437.

To reinstate your manual update service, call 1-800-638-8437.

For more information on Loislaw products, go to *www.loislaw.com* or call 1-800-364-2512.

For Customer Care issues, e-mail *CustomerCare@aspenpublishers.com*; call 1-800-234-1660; or fax 1-800-901-9075.

Aspen Publishers
A Wolters Kluwer Company

To Kathleen, Gregory, and Meghan
—Barry Carter

To Gardner, Billy, and Valeria
—Phillip Trimble

To Kathy, David, and Liana
—Curtis Bradley

Biographies

Barry E. Carter has an extensive background in law, foreign policy, and international business and trade. He is presently a professor of law at Georgetown University, where he also serves as the Director of the Program on International Business and Economic Law. Mr. Carter teaches frequently in developing and transition countries.

He returned to Georgetown in August 1996 after more than three years as the Deputy Under Secretary of Commerce for Export Administration. During 1993-1996, Mr. Carter also served as the U.S. vice chair to Secretary of Defense William Perry on bilateral defense conversion committees with Russia, Kazakhstan, Ukraine, and Belarus; as the U.S. chair of the committee with Uzbekistan; and as a member of committees with China. As a result of these responsibilities, he was involved in implementing and enforcing a variety of trade laws. Mr. Carter helped other countries strengthen their export controls, and he assisted those countries in converting some of their defense facilities to civilian production, often in joint ventures with U.S. companies. He also helped reorganize his 370-person Bureau and manage its $40+ million budget.

Before entering the government, Mr. Carter had been a Georgetown professor since 1979 and was executive director of the American Society of International Law during 1992-1993. He was a visiting law professor at Stanford in 1990. He served as a senior counsel on the Senate Select Committee on Intelligence Activities in 1975. He was a Fellow at the Institute of Politics at Harvard's Kennedy School of Government and an International Affairs Fellow at the Council on Foreign Relations in 1972. A member of Dr. Henry Kissinger's National Security Council staff during 1970-1972, he worked on U.S.-Soviet and European issues. While an Army officer, he was a program analyst in the Office of the Secretary of Defense in 1969-1970. He has also been a trial and appellate lawyer in private practice in California and Washington, D.C.

Mr. Carter, a native Californian, graduated Phi Beta Kappa from Stanford University in 1964, received a master's degree in economics and public policy from Princeton's Woodrow Wilson School of Public and International Affairs in 1966, and graduated in 1969 from Yale Law School, where he was the Projects Editor of the Yale Law Journal.

Mr. Carter's book, International Economic Sanctions: Improving the Haphazard U.S. Legal Regime (Cambridge Univ. Press 1988), received the 1989 annual award from the American Society of International Law (ASIL) for the outstanding new book on international law subjects. He has also published articles in the Yale Law Journal, California Law Review, Georgetown Law Journal, Scientific American, Daedalus, the Washington Post, and other periodicals.

He is a member of the Council on Foreign Relations, the American Law Institute, the American Bar Association, and the ASIL, and he is a Fellow of the American Bar Foundation. He is on the board of directors of an international trading company and on the advisory council of a political risk insurance company. He has been a member of two binational arbitration panels that reviewed trade matters under Chapter 19 of North American Free Trade Agreement. He has also served as chairman of the Advisory Committee of the Defense Budget Project and as the vice president of the Arms Control Association.

Phillip R. Trimble was a professor of law at the University of California, Los Angeles from 1981 through 2001. From July 1999 to January 2001 he served as the UCLA Vice-Provost for International Studies and Overseas Programs, based in the College of Letters and Science.

In the 1960s, Professor Trimble practiced tax and corporate finance law at Cravath, Swaine and Moore. His subsequent government career included service on the staff of the Senate Foreign Relations Committee under Senator Fulbright (1971-1972); Assistant Legal Adviser for Economic and Business Affairs in the Department of State in the Nixon, Ford and Carter Administrations (1973-1978); Counsel to the Mayor and then Deputy Mayor of New York City under Ed Koch (1979-1980); and American Ambassador to Nepal at the end of the Carter Administration.

During his academic career he also served as a consultant to the U.S. Arms Control and Disarmament Agency (and Counsel to the U.S. Delegation to the 1990 Nuclear Test Talks), and served on an arbitral panel under the U.S.-Canada Free Trade Agreement (settling a dispute involving the automobile industry). He was a visiting professor of law at the Stanford Law School (1988-1989) and at the University of Michigan Law School (1995-1996).

He has been a member of the Board of Editors of the American Journal of International Law; the Board of Visitors at Ohio University; the Board of Directors of the American Alpine Club; and the Southern California advisory boards of the Asia Society, the America-Nepal Friendship Society, the Himalayan Arts Council of the Pacific Asia Museum, and Human Rights Watch.

In his avocation as a mountaineer, Professor Trimble climbed on five continents, including expeditions to New Guinea, India, Pakistan, Bhutan, and both Polar Regions. In 1976 he led the successful American Expedition to Mt. Everest. Before law school he spent a year as a Fulbright scholar in Burma. More recently, he collected contemporary music for Afro Pop Worldwide during a trip to east and central Africa, and was assistant director of two music theater works in the Netherlands.

He is the author of the book, United States Foreign Relations Law (Foundation Press 2002). Other of his publications have appeared in the Harvard, Stanford, Columbia, Michigan, Pennsylvania, Northwestern, Iowa, St. Louis, and UCLA Law Reviews, the Tax Law Review, the American Alpine Journal, the Himalayan Journal,

Birding, the American Journal of International Law, Comparative Labor Law, and the Yale, Stanford, Chicago, Berkeley, and U.C. Davis Law Reviews.

Having departed the academic world in 2001, Professor Trimble Emeritus now lives full time in New York City and West Barnet, Vermont.

Curtis A. Bradley is a professor of law at the University of Virginia, where he teaches in the areas of international law and U.S. foreign relations law. He has written extensively on international law issues, with a particular focus on the relationship between international law and U.S. domestic law. His academic writings have appeared in numerous law journals, including the Harvard Law Review, Stanford Law Review, Michigan Law Review, Pennsylvania Law Review, and Virginia Law Review. He is also the co-author of a casebook on U.S. foreign relations law, published by Aspen Publishers.

Professor Bradley received his law degree magna cum laude from Harvard in 1988. He subsequently served as a law clerk for Judge David Ebel of the U.S. Court of Appeals for the Tenth Circuit and for Justice Byron White of the U.S. Supreme Court. He then practiced law for several years at the law firm of Covington & Burling in Washington, D.C., where he focused on litigation and international intellectual property law. In 1995, he began teaching at the University of Colorado law school. He joined the University of Virginia law faculty in 2000 after a one-year visit.

Professor Bradley is a member of the American Society of International Law and serves as co-chair of the Society's section on international law in domestic courts. For several years, he also served as a member of an American Bar Association working group charged with proposing amendments to the Foreign Sovereign Immunities Act.

Summary of Contents

Contents

1

What Is International Law?   1

2

The Creation of International Norms—Treaties, Customary Law, International Organizations, and Private Norm-Creation 93

3

International Law in the United States   157

4

International Dispute Resolution 271

5

States and Other Major International Entities   431

6

Foreign Sovereign Immunity and the Act of State Doctrine   547

7

Allocation of Legal Authority Among States   647

8

State Responsibility: Injuries to Aliens and International Human Rights — 743

9

Law of the Sea   835

10

International Environmental Law   911

11

Use of Force and Arms Control   961

Preface to the Fourth Edition

This casebook is designed for an introductory course in international law. It builds on the traditional theories and concepts of public international law, but it also addresses new institutions and other developments, especially the relationship between international and domestic law and the increasingly blurred line between public and private law. It analyzes as well how public international law frequently affects private activity, both individual and business. This casebook, however, does not cover in detail international trade, investment, or other economic transactions.

This Fourth Edition represents a major updating and revision of the casebook. For example, the Fourth Edition contains a case study focusing on the terrorist attacks of September 11, 2001, and the U.S. and international response to those attacks; materials on Iraq through the war there in March-April 2003; descriptions and excerpts of recent decisions by the International Court of Justice, including *Congo v. Belgium* on official immunity and the *LaGrand* decision concerning the Vienna Convention on Consular Relations; and new materials on the Alien Tort Statute (or Alien Tort Claims Act), the state sponsor of terrorism exception to the Foreign Sovereign Immunities Act, and the principle of universal jurisdiction.

Every chapter has been updated with new and fascinating issues and materials, and the Notes and Questions have been thoroughly revised throughout the casebook. We also shortened the book by deleting or editing previous materials.

Background

The United States and its people increasingly are enmeshed in international transactions and are influenced by developments abroad. The governments of the United States and more than 190 other nations deal daily with a host of issues between one another, with international institutions (like the United Nations, the International Monetary Fund, and the World Trade Organization), and with regional organizations (such as the European Union and the North Atlantic Treaty Organization). The problems range from essential, if mundane, matters (like postal agreements) to those of great economic significance (such as currency exchange rates and retaliatory tariffs). The issues even extend to matters of life and death (e.g., the use of military force and efforts to combat the proliferation of weapons of mass destruction).

Each day public and private entities move across U.S. borders billions of dollars worth of currency and goods, hundreds of thousands of people, and tens of thousands of ships, planes, and other vehicles. They also engage in a tremendous amount of communication to and from the United States, through telephones, fax machines, e-mail messages, and the Internet.

This international activity usually occurs in carefully structured ways, most often without serious incident. The structure is provided by a complex and evolving mix of international and national law. It is administered and enforced by international and national entities, both public and private.

As a result, U.S. lawyers in all parts of the country are increasingly affected. They need to understand the relevant international law and how it can affect the activities of their clients — whether the client is a government or a private party. For example, can an individual citizen invoke a treaty in domestic litigation? Does a U.S. law against terrorism or against price-fixing extend to activity outside the territory of the United States? How can individuals resort to international tribunals, such as international arbitration?

Objectives

In introducing students to international law, this casebook has five major objectives:

1. The casebook should make students think about the sources of public international law, its principal theories and concepts, and recent developments in the law. In analyzing sources, particular attention is paid to treaties and customary international law, which students probably have not studied before in depth. Traditional theories and concepts, such as the various theories for exercising prescriptive jurisdiction, the act of state doctrine, approaches to foreign sovereign immunity, and justifications for the use of military force, are then addressed in appropriate sections.

Historical materials are often used to help define the scope of a principle and to trace its development. Current materials are then extensively drawn upon to note present status, to stimulate students' interest in the issues, and to suggest what the future might hold. Excerpts from the 1987 Restatement of the Foreign Relations Law of the United States (Third), including its comments and reporters' notes, are often used because the Restatement generally represents a consensus among a wide range of U.S. international lawyers. Even when the Restatement's views are contested, they can provide a useful starting point for discussion.

2. This casebook also analyzes the supporting institutions that help public international law facilitate the burgeoning international activity. The system is addressed as it has actually developed and as it is likely to develop in the future.

The years immediately after World War II witnessed tremendous creativity and accomplishment in establishing an international system. The United Nations, International Court of Justice (or World Court), World Bank, and International Monetary Fund (IMF) were established. While the International Trade Organization never got off the ground, the General Agreement on Tariffs and Trade (GATT) was signed. This progress stimulated hopes by some observers that a new international order was at hand.

Hopes for a new order were also kindled in the 1960s and 1970s as colonialism neared its end and many new countries appeared — usually less developed economically than Europe or North America but strong in their convictions. The end of the Cold War in the 1990s then held out possibilities for greater international cooperation. Throughout these post-World War II years, the growing foreign trade and investment, accompanied by sweeping changes in technology and communications, contributed to a world that has become increasingly interconnected.

The reality of the world today is not, however, a simple structure, but rather a complex mix of international and national law, administered and enforced by a variety of entities. Some of the post-World War II institutions like the World Bank and the IMF have grown and adapted very effectively, and a weak GATT has been succeeded by a strong World Trade Organization (WTO). On the other hand, the United Nations and the International Court of Justice have not lived up to their proponents' expectations. Although the end of the Cold War and the initial U.N. response to the 1990 Iraqi invasion of Kuwait revived hopes for the U.N.'s future, these hopes were since dampened by the legal and diplomatic debate over Iraq in 2002-2003.

At the same time, other formal and informal arrangements have emerged and assumed important roles. These other arrangements include regional organizations like the European Union and the Association of Southeast Asian Nations (ASEAN), frequent use of international arbitration, and a vast array of multilateral and bilateral agreements for various purposes from protection of diplomatic personnel, to promotion of foreign investment, to the enforcement of arbitral awards.

3. The casebook recognizes and studies the interaction between public international law and national agencies and courts. It is not uncommon for such entities to look to international law on jurisdictional and interpretive questions, as well as on certain substantive issues such as human rights. The status of international law in the U.S. domestic legal system raises many issues of theoretical and practice importance.

4. Students will also be made aware of how public international law increasingly affects private activity, both individual and business.

For example, a national court might draw in part upon international human rights norms to find multinational corporations or individuals liable for large damage judgments for their activities in foreign countries. Or WTO international trade rules might allow an injured country to impose retaliatory tariffs on imports of hundreds of millions of dollars of goods produced by companies in the country that was found to be violating the rules. On a less dramatic scale, the question of sovereign immunity of foreign governments is not only of interest to governments and their diplomats, but can also be crucial to an American company dealing with a foreign supplier owned by a government.

As a result, the future lawyer should understand how the rapidly increasing body of international law — including multilateral and bilateral agreements — is made, how it can be changed, and how it can affect his or her client's interests. A student should also understand how governments make decisions and how diplomacy operates.

5. Although this casebook focuses on international law, it also aims at educating U.S. lawyers. Consequently, it often considers international law from the American perspective, including substantial sections on the U.S. Constitution and U.S. laws that have international impact. At the same time, because American lawyers must appreciate the different principles and possible strategies under foreign legal systems, materials from other legal systems are included to illustrate contrasting approaches.

Overview of the Structure of the Book

This casebook is designed primarily for an introductory course in international law that involves two to five semester hours. However, there are sufficient materials to allow professors, within limits, to select their own emphases and to choose among the materials.

Chapter 1 starts with the standard definition of international law, contrasts it with more familiar forms of domestic law, and introduces the ways in which international law is formed and enforced. A section on historical background briefly examines the development of international law and institutions. The third section considers how international law is really law. The fourth section provides some of the various scholarly approaches to international law, including international relations theory, economic analysis, critical legal studies, and feminist jurisprudence.

The chapter concludes with a new case study on the terrorist attacks of September 11, 2001, and the U.S. and world reactions to them. This case study illustrates how international law actually works.

Against this background, Chapters 2 and 3 introduce the basic building blocks of international law — treaties and custom — in the international and U.S. domestic context. In Chapter 2 students learn what a "treaty" is and some of the basic rules of treaty law. The chapter also covers the formation of customary international law, including the controversial role of the U.N. General Assembly. There is then a brief examination of the law-making role of international organizations and of non-governmental organizations — both multinational corporations and nonprofit groups. Finally, there is a section on the general principles of law of major legal systems as a further source of international law.

Chapter 3 considers the status of treaties and customary international law within the U.S. legal system. It begins by considering the scope of the U.S. treaty power and the circumstances under which treaties are enforceable by private parties in U.S. courts. It then considers the foreign relations powers of the national government more generally, and the constitutional law that governs interactions between Congress and the President in foreign relations. The chapter next discusses the status of customary international law in U.S. courts, with particular emphasis on the use of such law in international human rights litigation. The chapter concludes by examining the role of the individual U.S. states in foreign relations and the circumstances under which their foreign relations activities will be deemed to be preempted.

Chapter 4 examines the major, distinctive means by which international disputes are settled. It starts with the process of international negotiations, turns to the International Court of Justice (ICJ), and then analyzes the development of regional courts (especially the European Union's Court of Justice) and the increasingly important role of international arbitration. As recent examples of international dispute resolution systems, materials are included on the North American Free Trade Agreement (NAFTA) and the WTO. Finally, there is a section on the role of domestic courts and the enforcement of foreign court judgments.

Chapter 5 defines "state" and introduces some of the consequences of statehood, including the issue of recognition by other countries and a new government's obligation to be bound by the past agreements of prior governments. This chapter also considers the key international and regional organizations that appear as actors throughout this book, ranging from the international institutions (such as the United Nations, IMF, and World Bank) to regional economic or security organizations (such as the European Union and the North Atlantic Treaty Organization).

Chapter 6 considers the immunity that states have from suit in the domestic courts of other states, focusing especially on the immunity provided for in the U.S. Foreign Sovereign Immunities Act. The chapter also considers international and U.S. law relating to the immunity of diplomats and heads of state. Finally, the chapter discusses the "act of state doctrine," a common law doctrine applied by U.S. courts that limits their examination of actions by foreign governments.

Chapter 7 examines the international bases for a state to regulate private conduct within and outside its territory and the evolving international rules limiting extraterritorial application of law. For comparison purposes, the chapter concludes with a section that considers briefly the principles of "private" conflicts of law.

Chapter 8 considers the limitations on state activity against aliens and alien property within its territory, and the expansion of these rules to protect the state's own citizens under the regime of international human rights law. Among other things, the chapter discusses some of the most important human rights treaties and institutions, looks at the history of U.S. involvement in international human rights law, and examines regional human rights law and institutions.

Chapter 9 deals with the international law of the sea. It briefly considers the centuries-long development of customary international law and the 1958 Geneva Conventions. The focus is then on the Law of the Sea Convention, which came into force in 1994 and has been adopted by almost all the countries of the world, except for the United States, though the United States has accepted many of the Convention's provisions as customary international law.

Chapter 10 introduces the emerging international regimes covering environmental matters. The recent and limited customary international law principles are being rapidly supplemented by bilateral and multilateral treaties. The chapter addresses two situations in particular: first, the relatively successful international effort to deal with ozone depletion through the Montreal Protocol and other measures, and second, the continuing struggle to respond to global warming with the Kyoto Protocol and other approaches.

Chapter 11 explores international law regarding the use of force. After introductory historical materials, the chapter examines the justifications for the use of force that emerged in the period after World Wars I and II, especially the legal norms found in the U.N. Charter. The justifications are first considered for an individual state's use of force against another state or terrorists, and then for collective action through the United Nations and regional organizations. Various examples of uses of force are considered, including the conflicts in Vietnam, Kosovo, and Iraq. The Iraq case study is a substantial one that begins with Iraq's invasion of Kuwait in 1990 and continues through the war in Iraq in 2003. There is also a major section on individual responsibility and international humanitarian law, including materials from the Nuremberg Tribunal, the Geneva Conventions of 1949, and the new International Criminal Court. Finally, there is a brief section on U.S. domestic law (including the War Powers Resolution) and a concluding section on international efforts to combat the proliferation of weapons of mass destruction.

Each chapter contains a broad range of materials to illustrate issues and principles. As suggested by the detailed table of contents, these materials include background information, treaties and other international agreements, domestic laws, and decisions by courts and arbitral panels.

Each chapter also contains frequent questions and short problems for students, often based on recent events or reasonable hypotheticals. These questions and problems are designed to focus students' attention on the major issues and rules, and to challenge students to apply the relevant law from the perspectives of different clients and to explore alternative enforcement strategies.

While the materials in each chapter include key excerpts of important documents, the texts or excerpts of many basic documents are provided in a separate Documentary Supplement. These documents include, among others, the U.N. Charter, the ICJ Statute, the New York Convention on the Recognition and Enforcement of Foreign Arbitral Awards, the Treaty of the European Community, many other multilateral treaties (such as important human rights conventions, the Law of the Sea Convention, and the Montreal Protocol on the Protection of the Ozone Layer), the U.S. Constitution, and key U.S. laws (such as the Foreign Sovereign Immunities Act and the International Emergency Economic Powers Act). There are also many supporting documents for the substantial case studies on the terrorist attacks of September 11 and on Iraq (e.g., U.S. congressional resolutions and U.N. resolutions).

Also, to help readers keep abreast of current developments in international law, we have listed many sources (including Web sites) in the casebook and the Documentary Supplement. We would also note here the various online and hard copy materials of the American Society of International Law. Its Web site is http://www.asil.org. In addition, there will be a special Web site containing updates to this casebook, at http://www.lawinternational.org.

In short, our approach is a blend of the traditional and the new. It should provide the basis for a rigorous course in the fascinating subject of international law.

Professor Carter and Professor Trimble originally conceived this casebook and co-authored the first three editions. Having left the academic world, Professor Trimble has chosen just to comment on this Fourth Edition, while Professor Bradley has become an active co-author. For the Fourth Edition, Professor Carter has been primarily responsible for the revisions and updates to Chapters 1A-B, 1E, 2, 4, 5, 7, 9, 10, and 11. Professor Bradley has been primarily responsible for the changes in Chapters 1C-D, 3, 6, and 8. The Fourth Edition has benefited from substantial communication between Professors Carter and Bradley, with each making comments on and contributions to the other's chapters.

Our efforts on this edition and on the new Documentary Supplement were helped considerably by the comments received from many people who have used the earlier editions — faculty, students, and others. As before, we very much welcome your comments on this edition.

Barry E. Carter
Phillip R. Trimble
Curtis A. Bradley

May 2003

Acknowledgments

Many people deserve thanks for the assistance they have given us—from providing the opportunities to learn the intricacies of the subject matter to offering specific advice and comments about this casebook. Although it is impossible to mention everyone who has assisted us, we do want to acknowledge some people who have been particularly helpful.

A number of experts have read all or parts of various drafts of the book and have offered valuable comments. They include Abram Chayes, Rosa Brooks, Lee A. Kimball, David Koplow, Janet Levit, Robert J. Lieber, David Martin, and John H. McNeill, plus several anonymous reviewers.

Professor Carter would like to thank several research assistants at Georgetown who especially helped with the research on or drafts of this casebook and the companion documentary supplement. These students included, for previous editions, Eun Ah Choi, Marian Hagler, John Kliewer, Christina Paglia, Kathleen Phelps, Gwen Ponder, and Ines Radmilovic. Particularly helpful on the fourth edition were Kathryn Bisordi, Matthew Hackell, Nicholas Mitrokostas, and Sharon Yang. Others who have very ably assisted Professor Carter include Marci Hoffman and Ellen Schaffer, former Georgetown International Law Librarians. Among the supportive Georgetown Law Center staff, Brenda Moore, Sylvia Johnson, and Toni Patterson deserve special mention for helping in many ways.

Professor Trimble would like to thank John Wilson of the UCLA Law Library for his invaluable assistance in finding materials and Ellis Green and his staff, who assisted on the assembly of the first drafts of Professor Trimble's manuscript.

Professor Bradley would like to thank the staff at the University of Virginia law library for their terrific assistance. He would also like to thank his dean, John Jeffries, for his financial and other support.

Not to be forgotten are the scores of former students at Georgetown, Stanford, UCLA, and the University of Virginia, who were taught with earlier versions of this material and who helpfully offered suggestions that improved the final product.

Finally, we thank the very supportive people at Aspen Publishers, including Carol McGeehan, Melody Davies, Barbara Roth, and Troy Froebe. We also appreciate the assistance from the people at Aspen's predecessor, Little, Brown and Company, including Richard R. Heuser.

We gratefully acknowledge the permission granted by the authors, publishers, and organizations to reprint portions of the following copyrighted materials.

Abbott, Kenneth. International Relations Theory, International Law, and the Regime Governing Atrocities in Internal Conflicts, 93 Am. J. Intl. L. 361 (1999). Reproduced with permission from 93 AJIL 361 (1999), © The American Society of International Law.

Alexander, Lewis. Baseline Delimitation and Maritime Boundaries, 23 Va. J. Intl. L. 503 (1983). Copyright © Virginia Journal of International Law. Reprinted by permission of Virginia Journal of International Law.

American Law Institute, Restatement Third, Restatement of Foreign Relations Law of the United States. Copyright © 1987 by the American Law Institute. Reprinted with the permission of the American Law Institute.

Anand, Ram Prakash. International Law and the Developing Countries: Confrontation or Cooperation (1987). Copyright © Kluwer Academic Publishers. Reprinted with permission by Kluwer Law International.

Arms Control Association. US-Soviet/Russian Nuclear Arms Control, June 2002. Reprinted with permission from the Arms Control Association.

Arms Control Association. ACA FactSheet: The Nuclear NonProliferation Treaty at a Glance, Jan. 2003. Reprinted with permission from the Arms Control Association.

Aust, Anthony. Modern Treaty Law and Practice. Copyright © Cambridge University Press. Reproduced with the permission of Cambridge University Press.

Bacchus, James. Remarks at the Woodrow Wilson International Center for Scholars (May 1, 2002). Reprinted with permission of author.

Barton, John H., and Carter, Barry E. International Law and Institutions for a New Age, 81 Geo. L.J. 535 (1995). Reprinted with permission of the publisher, Georgetown Law Journal © 1995.

Basic Facts About the United Nations, United Nations (2000). Copyright © United Nations. Reprinted by permission of United Nations.

Beard, Jack. America's New War on Terror: The Case for Self-Defense under International Law, 25 Harv. J.L. & Pub. Poly. 559 (2002). Copyright © Harvard Journal of Law & Public Policy. Reprinted by permission of Harvard Journal of Law & Public Policy.

Benedick, Richard Elliot. Ozone Diplomacy: New Directions in Safeguarding the Planet. Copyright © 1991, 1998 by the President and Fellows of Harvard College. Reprinted by permission of Harvard University Press.

Bergen, Peter L. Holy War, Inc. (2001). Copyright © by Peter L. Bergen. Reprinted by permission of the author.

Bermann, George A., et al. Cases and Materials on European Union Law (2nd ed., 2002). Reprinted with permission of the West Group.

Born, Gary B. International Civil Litigation in US Courts: Commentary & Materials (1996). Reproduced with the kind permission of Kluwer Law International.

Born, Gary B. International Commercial Arbitration in the United States: Commentary and Materials (2001). Reproduced with kind permission of Kluwer Law International.

Bradley, Curtis A. and Goldsmith, Jack L. Treaties, Human Rights & Conditional Consent, 149 U. Pa. L. Rev. 399 (2000). Reproduced with permission from the University of Pennsylvania Law Review.

Bradley, Curtis A. Universal Jurisdiction and U.S. Law, 2001 U. Chi. Legal F. 323 (2001). Copyright © 2001 University of Chicago; Curtis Bradley. Reprinted by permission of the University of Chicago Legal Forum and Curtis Bradley.

Brierly, J.L. The Law of Nations (6th ed., H. Waldock ed. 1963). Copyright © Oxford University Press. Reprinted by permission of Oxford University Press.

Brownlie, Ian. International Law and the Use of Force by States. Copyright © 1981 by Clarendon Press. Reprinted by permission of Oxford University Press.

Bryk, Dale S. The Montreal Protocol and Recent Developments to Protect the Ozone Layer, 15 Harv. Envtl. L. Rev. 275 (1991). Reprinted with permission from the author.

Carter, Barry E. International Economic Sanctions: Improving the Haphazard Regime. Copyright © Cambridge University Press. Reprinted with the permission of Cambridge University Press.

Charlesworth, Hilary, et.al. Feminist Approaches to International Law, 85 Am. J. Intl. L. 613 (1991). Reproduced with permission from 85 AJIL 613 (1991), © The American Society of International Law.

Charney, Jonathan I. The Impact on the International Legal System of the Growth of International Courts and Tribunals. 31 N.Y.U. J. Intl. L. & Pol. 697 (1999). Reproduced with permission from the NYU Journal of International Law & Politics.

Charney, Jonathan I. Universal International Law, 87 Am. J. Intl. L. 529 (1993). Reproduced with permission from 87 AJIL 529 (1993), © The American Journal of International Law.

Charney, Jonathan I. International Maritime Boundaries (1993). Copyright © Kluwer Academic Publishers. Reprinted by permission of Kluwer Academic Publishers.

Chayes, Abram. The Cuban Missile Crisis (1974). Copyright © Oxford University Press. Reprinted by permission of Oxford University Press.

Chen, Lung-Chu. An Introduction to Contemporary International Law: A Policy-Oriented Perspective (2d ed. 2000). Copyright © Yale University Press. Reprinted by permission of Yale University Press.

Christenson, Gordon A., Attribution Issues in State Responsibility, 1990 Proc. Am. Socy. Intl. L. 51. Copyright © The American Society of International Law. Reproduced with permission.

Churchill, Robin R., and Lowe, A. Vaughan. Law of the Sea (3d. ed. 1999). Reprinted by permission of the authors and Juris Publishing.

Clagett, Brice M. Title III of the Helms-Burton Act is Consistent with International Law, 90 Am. J. Intl. L. 343 (1996). Reproduced with permission from 90 AJIL 343 (1996), © The American Society of International Law.

Climate Change Science: An Analysis of Some Key Questions. Copyright © 2001 by the National Academy of Sciences. Reprinted by permission of the National Academies Press, Washington, D.C.

Davies, Peter G.G. Current Developments — Public International Law — Global Warming and the Kyoto Protocol, 47 Intl. & Comp. L.Q. 446 (1998). Reprinted with permission from the Oxford University Press.

Deming, Stuart. Foreign Corrupt Practices, 33 Intl. Law. 507 (1999). Copyright © American Bar Association. Reproduced by permission of American Bar Association.

Dinstein, Yoram. War, Aggression and Self-Defence (3rd ed. 2001). Copyright 2001 by Cambridge University Press. Reprinted with the permission of Cambridge University Press.

Driscoll, David. What Is the International Monetary Fund? (1997). Reprinted with the permission of the International Monetary Fund.

Dunhoff, Jeffrey L. and Trachtman, Joel P. Economic Analysis of International Law, Yale J. Intl. L. 1 (1999). Reproduced by permission of Yale Journal of International Law.

Faure, Michael and LeFevere, Jurgen. Compliance with International Environmental Law Agreements, printed in Global Environment: Institutions, Law and Policy (Norman I. Vig & Regina S. Axelrod eds., 1999). Copyright © 1999 Congressional Quarterly Inc. Reprinted with permission from Congressional Quarterly Inc.

Feldstein, Martin. Refocusing the IMF, Foreign Affairs (March/April 1998). Copyright ©1998 by the Council of Foreign Relations Press. Reprinted with permission.

Franck, Thomas M. Legitimacy in the International System, 82 Am. J. Intl. L. 705 (1988). Reproduced with permission from 82 AJIL 705 (1988), © The American Society of International Law.

Franck, Thomas M. Recourse to Force: State Action Against Threats and Armed Attacks (2001). Copyright © 2001 by Cambridge University Press. Reprinted with the permission of Cambridge University Press.

Franck, Thomas M. Judging the World Court (1986). Reproduced with permission from Priority Press Publications.

Gerth, Jeff. Where Business Rules: Forging Global Relations That Put Industry First, N.Y. Times, Jan. 9, 1998, at D2. Copyright © by The New York Times Company. Reprinted with permission.

Glennon, Michael. The Fog of Law: Self-Defense, Inherence, and Incoherence in Article 51 of the United Nations Charter, 25 Harv. J.L. & Pub. Pol'y. 539 (2002). Copyright © Harvard Journal of Law & Public Policy. Reprinted by permission of Harvard Journal of Law & Public Policy.

Goldman, Robert K. and Tittemore, Brian D. Unprivileged Combatants and the Hostilities in Afghanistan: Their Status and Rights Under International Humanitarian and Human Rights Law, from ASIL Taskforce on Terrorism (2002). © The American Society of International Law. Reprinted with permission.

Haberman, Clyde. Japanese Fight Invading Sea for Priceless Speck of Land, N.Y. Times, Jan. 1, 1981, at A1. Copyright © by The New York Times Co. Reprinted with permission.

Hartley, T.C. Foundations of European Community Law (1998). Reprinted by permission of Oxford University Press.

Henkin, Louis, et al. eds. Right v. Might: International Law and the Use of Force (1991). Copyright © Council on Foreign Relations Press. Reprinted by permission of Council on Foreign Relations Press.

Henkin, Louis. How Nations Behave: Law and Foreign Policy (2d. ed. 1979). Copyright © Columbia University Press. Reprinted by permission of Columbia University Press.

Henkin, Louis. International Law: Politics and Values, Nijhoff Publications (1995). Reprinted by permission.

Horlick, Gary and Debusk, Amanda. Dispute Resolution under NAFTA, Journal of World Trade (1993). Reproduced with the kind permission of Kluwer Law International.

Hufbauer, Gary Clyde and Schott, Jeffrey J. NAFTA: An Assessment (1993). Copyright © by Institute for International Economics, Washington, DC. Reprinted with permission.

Jackson, John H., Davey, William J., and Sykes, Jr., Alan O. Legal Problems of International Economic Relations: Cases, Materials, and Text (4ᵗʰ ed. 2002). Reprinted with permission of the West Group.

Kalshoven, Frits. Constraints on the Waging of War (1987). Martinus Nijhoff Publishers. Reprinted with the kind permission of Kluwer Law International.

Kennedy, David. A New Stream of International Law Scholarship, 7 Wis. Intl. L. J. 1 (1988). Copyright © Wisconsin International Law Journal. Reprinted by permission of Wisconsin International Law Journal.

Kerr, Paul. North Korea Restarts Reactor; IAEA Sends Resolution to UN, March 2003. Reprinted with permission from the Arms Control Association.

Kirgis, Frederic L. North Korea's Withdrawal form the Nuclear Nonproliferation Treaty, ASIL Insights (2003). Reproduced with permission from ASIL Insights. © The American Society of International Law.

Koh, Harold Hongju. Why Do Nations Obey International Law?, 106 Yale L.J. 2599 (1997). Copyright © Yale Law Journal. Reprinted by permission of Yale Law Journal.

Lillich, Richard. The Growing Importance of Customary International Human Rights Law. 25 Ga. J. Intl. & Comp. L. 1 (1996). Copyright © Georgia Journal of International and Comparative Law. Reprinted by permission of the Georgia Journal of International Law.

Lodal, Jan. The Price of Dominance: The New Weapons of Mass Destruction and their Challenge to American Leadership (2001). Copyright © by Council on Foreign Relations Press. Reprinted with permission.

Lowe, Vaughan. Development of the Concept of the Contiguous Zone, 52 Brit. Year Book of Intl. L. 109 (1981). Reprinted with permission.

Lowenfeld, Andreas. Congress & Cuba: The Helms-Burton Act, 90 Am. J. Intl. L. 419 (1996). Reproduced with permission from 90 AJIL 419 (1996), © The American Society of International Law.

Lowenfeld, Andreas. Remedies Along with Rights: Institutional Reform of the New GATT, 87 Am. J. Intl. L. 477 (1994). Reproduced with permission from 87 AJIL 477 (1994), © The American Society of International Law.

Lowenfeld, Andreas. Remedies Along with Rights: Institutional Reform of the New GATT, 87 Am. J. Intl. Law. 477 (1994). Reproduced with permission from American Journal of International Law.

Lownfeld, Andreas F. Trade Controls for Political Ends (1983). Reprinted with the permission of Mathew Bender & Company, Inc., a member of the LexisNexis Group.

Maganza, Giorgio. The Treaty of Amsterdam's Changes, 22 Fordham Intl. L. J. 164 (1999). Reprinted with permission.

Matthews, Jessica. Power Shift, Foreign Affairs (1997). Copyright © 1997 Foreign Affairs Magazine. Reprinted by permission of Foreign Affairs Magazine.

Maynes, Charles William and Williamson, Richard S. U.S. Foreign Policy and the United Nations System (1996). Copyright © by The American Assembly. Used by permission of W.W. Norton & Company, Inc.

Menon, P.K. Law of Recognition in International Law: Basic Principles (1994). Reprinted with permission of Edwin Mellen Press.

Merrills, J.G. International Dispute Settlement (1988). Reprinted with the permission of Cambridge University Press. Copyright © 1988 Cambridge University Press.

Murphy, John. United Nations and the Control of International Violence: A Legal and Political Analysis (1983). Reprinted with permission of the author and Allanheld, Osmun Publishers.

Observations by the U.S. on GC No. 24, Human Rights Centre Newsletter (1996). Reprinted by permission of Human Rights Law Centre.

O'Connell, D.P. International Law of the Sea (1982). Copyright © Oxford University Press. Reprinted by permission of Oxford University Press.

O'Connell, Mary Ellen. The UN, NATO, and International Law After Kosovo. Human Rights Quarterly 22:1 (2000) 73-82. Copyright © The Johns Hopkins University Press. Reprinted with permission of The Johns Hopkins University Press.

Paust, Jordan J. The U.S. as Occupying Power over Portions of Iraq and Relevant Responsibilities under the Law of War, ASIL Insight (April 2003). Reproduced with permission from ASIL Insights. © The American Society of International Law.

Perry, William J., Carter, Ashton B., and Shalikashvili, John M. A Scary Thought: Loose Nukes in North Korea. Reprinted from The Wall Street Journal © 2003. Dow Jones & Company, Inc. All rights reserved.

Posner, Michael and Whittome, Candy. The Status of Human Rights NGOs, 25 Colum. Hum. Rts. L. Rev. 269 (1994). Reproduced with permission from the authors.

Ratner, Steven R. & Abrams, Jason S. Accountability for Human Rights Atrocities in International Law (2nd ed. 2001). Copyright © Oxford University Press. Reprinted by permission of Oxford University Press.

Ratner, Stephen R., and Slaughter, Anne-Marie. Appraising the Methods of International Law: A Prospectus for Readers, 93 Am. J. Intl. L. 291 (1999). Reproduced with permission from 93 AJIL 291 (1999), © The American Society of International Law.

Richman, William M. Understanding Conflict of Laws (1992). Reprinted with the permission of Matthew Bender & Company, a member of the LexisNexis Group.

Rosen, Gerald R. IMF Survey, Trade Agreement Mandates Broad Changes (1994). Reprinted with permission from the International Monetary Fund.

Rosencranz, Armin, U.S. Climate Change Policy, excerpted from Climate Change Policy: A Survey. Stephen H. Schneider, Armin Rosencranz, and John O. Niles, eds. Copyright © 2002 Island Press. Reprinted by permission of Island Press, Washington, D.C. and Covelo, California.

Roth, Kenneth. Human Rights Organizations, published in Realizing Human Rights: Moving from Inspiration to Impact (2000). Reproduced with permission from the authors.

Sadat, Leila Nadya. The International Criminal Court and the Transformation of International Law: Justice for the New Millennium (2002). Reprinted with permission form Transnational Publishers, Inc., Ardsley, NY.

Schachter, Oscar. International Law in Theory and Practice (1991). Copyright © M. Nijhoff Publishers. Reprinted by permission of Kluwer Law International.

Schwarze, Jurgen. Towards a European Foreign Policy — Legal Aspects, in Towards a European Foreign Policy (Johan K. De Vree et al. eds. 1987). Copyright © M. Nijoff Publishers. Reprinted with permission from Kluwer Law Group.

Shaw, Malcolm. International Law (4th ed. 1997). Copyright © Cambridge University Press. Reprinted with the permission of Cambridge University Press.

Shearer, I.A. Starke's International Law (1994). Copyright © Butterworths. Reprinted by permission of LexisNexis Butterworths Tolley.

Simma, Bruno and Alston, Philip. The Sources of Human Rights Law, Austl. Yearbook Intl. L. (1988). Reproduced with permission from the authors.

Simpson, J.L. and Fox, Hazel. International Arbitration: Law and Practice (Praeger Publishers, an imprint of Greenwood Publishing Group, Inc., Westport, CT 1959). Copyright © 1959 by Frederick A. Praeger, Inc. All rights reserved.

Sinclair, Ian. Vienna Convention on the Law of Treaties. Copyright © Manchester University Press. Reprinted by permission.

Sohn, Louis. Peaceful Settlement of Disputes in Ocean Conflicts, 46 L. & Contemp. Probs. 195 (1983). Reprinted by permission.

Sohn, Louis. The New International Law Protection of Rights of Individuals Rather than States, 32 Am. U.L. Rev. 1(1982). Copyright © American University Law Review. Reprinted by permission of the American University Law Review.

Solis, Gary D. The ICC and Mad Prosceutors (Remarks at Georgetown University, March 27, 2003). Reprinted by permission of the author.

Spar, Debora and James Dail. Of Measurement and Mission: Accounting, 3 Chi. J. Intl. L. 171 (2002). Reproduced with permission from the Chicago Journal of International Law.

Steiner, Henry and Alston, Philip. International Human Rights in Context (2d ed. 2000). Copyright © Oxford University Press. Reprinted by permission of Oxford University Press.

Stromseth, Jane. Iraq's Repression of Its Civilian Population: Collective Responses and Continuing Challenges, in Enforcing Restraint: Collective Intervention in Internal Conflicts (Lori F.Damrosch ed. 1993). Copyright © Council on Foreign Relations Press. Reprinted with permission.

Stromseth, Jane. Rethinking Humanitarian Intervention: The Case for Incremental Change, in Humanitarian Intervention: Ethical, Legal and Political Dilemmas (J.L. Holzgrefe & Robert O. Keohane eds., 2003). Copyright © Cambridge University Press. Reprinted with permission by Cambridge University Press.

Study Group, The International Court of Justice: Efficiency of Procedures and Working Methods. 45 Intl. & Comp. L.Q. Supplement. Report of the Study Group Established by the British Institute of International and Comparative Law as a contribution to the UN Decade of International Law (1996). Reprinted by permission of Oxford University Press.

Trimble, Phillip. Arms Control and International Negotiation Theory, 25 Stan. J. Intl. L. 543 (1989). Reprinted with the permission of the Stanford Journal of International Law. Copyright © 2002 by the Board of Trustees of the Leland Stanford Junior University.

Tutorow, Norman E. War Crimes, War Criminals, and War Crimes Trials (1986). Copyright © 1986 by Norman E. Tutorow. Reproduced with permission of Greenwood Publishing Group, Inc., Westport, CT.

Von Mehren, Arthur T. From *Vynior's Case* to *Mitsubishi:* The Future of Arbitration and Public Law, 12 Brook. J. Intl. L. 583 (1986). Reprinted by permission.

Watson, Geoffrey. The Law of State Succession, in Contemporary Practice of Public International Law (Ellen Schaffer & Randall J. Snyder eds., 1997). Oceana Publications Inc., Dobbs Ferry, NY; (1997) pgs. 115-127. Reproduced with permission from Oceana Publications, Inc.

Weiss, Edith Brown, et al. International Environmental Law and Policy (1998). Reprinted from International Environmental Law and Policy with the permission of Aspen Publishers.

Weiss, Edith Brown & Jacobson, Harold K. eds. Engaging Countries: Strengthening Compliance with International Environmental Accords (1998). Copyright © 1998 MIT Press. Reprinted with permission from The MIT Press.

Weiss, Thomas George. United Nations and Changing World Politics. Copyright © 1997 Westview Press. Reprinted by permission of Westview Press, a member of Perseus Books Group.

Wirth, David A. The Sixth Session (Part Two) and Seventh Session of the Parties to the Framework Convention on Climate Change, 96 Am. J. Intl. L. 648 (2002). Copyright © by the American Society of International Law. Reprinted with permission.

Wirth, David A. The Rio Declaration on Environment and Development: Two Steps Forward and Back, or Vice Versa?, 29 Ga. L. Rev. 599 (1995). Reproduced with permission from the Georgia Law Review.

Editorial Notice

For ease of reading, we are employing a few conventions throughout this casebook:

1. In material excerpted from other sources, additions to the material are indicated by brackets. Ellipses denote the deletion of material.

2. Throughout the book, citations and footnotes are deleted without using an ellipsis, unless an ellipsis serves a pedagogical purpose.

International Law

1

What Is International Law?

A. THE DEFINITION OF "INTERNATIONAL LAW"

We first want you to focus on the different kinds of law that an international lawyer must deal with, and on how public international law fits into the picture. You are already familiar with torts, contracts, and possibly some U.S. constitutional law. We assume, however, that you have not been exposed to much international law. Indeed, you may think of it as something entirely different from other kinds of law. You may have some notion that it exists on a higher plane, or you may have heard that international law only concerns governments. You may also be instinctively skeptical as to whether something called "international law" really exists. In this chapter, we will first introduce you to the definition of international law and present a problem showing how international law could be applied. Section B consists of materials that sketch the history of international law, which you should read as background for the course. Section C then confronts the skepticism sometimes expressed about international law and raises the following questions:

  (a) Is international law really "law"?
  (b) Why is international law binding?
  (c) What leads states to comply with international law?
  (d) What is the function of international law in the world today?
  (e) What should international law be, and what are the most compelling critiques of contemporary international law?

Section D considers some of the modern theoretical and methodological approaches to international law. Section E presents a case study of the terrorist attacks of September 11, 2001, and the U.S. and world response to them. The case study illustrates international law in action.

   Western scholars have often divided the legal universe into two parts or levels — international law and domestic law. International law prescribed rules governing the relations of nation-states (or "states," as they are called in the vocabulary of international law). It encompassed both public and private international law. Domestic law, on the other hand, prescribed rules governing everything else, mostly the conduct

1

or status of individuals, corporations, domestic governmental units, and other entities within each state.

"Public" international law was distinguished from "private" international law. Public international law primarily governed the activities of governments in relation to other governments. Private international law dealt with the activities of individuals, corporations, and other private entities when they crossed national borders. A large body of private international law consisted of choice-of-law rules (determining which state's domestic law would apply to transactions between nationals of two states, such as an international sales contract, or to controversies that had some significant connection with more than one state). Private international law also included substantive terms and conditions that had become customary in certain international practice, such as shipping terms and letters of credit. Recently the scope of private international law has expanded to encompass treaties on many subjects that were traditionally domestic law, such as the U.N. Convention on Contracts for the International Sale of Goods and the Hague Convention on Protection of Children and Co-operation in respect of Intercountry Adoption.

Moreover, norms of public international law have increasingly regulated or affected private conduct. For example, states frequently conclude treaties granting rights of trade or investment to nationals of other states, proclaiming individual human rights that are required to be protected, or establishing environmental standards to be followed by industrial plants. Those treaties, which create legally binding obligations under public international law, may also be "incorporated" into domestic law and thereby become domestic legal obligations. The lines between international law and domestic law, as well as between public law and private law, have thus become somewhat artificial. Indeed, to some commentators, the intellectual basis for the traditional conceptual structure of the old legal universe seems suspect.

One of the classic treatises, J.L. Brierly, The Law of Nations (6th ed. 1963), defined international law as

> the body of rules and principles of action which are binding upon civilized states in their relations with one another.

The 1987 revision of the American Law Institute's Restatement of Foreign Relations Law (hereinafter referred to as the Restatement) takes a limited step toward recognizing the potential importance of international law for activity traditionally within the domestic or private spheres:

Restatement Section 101

"International law," as used in this Restatement, consists of rules and principles of general application dealing with the conduct of states and of international organizations and with their relations inter se, as well as with some of their relations with persons, whether natural or juridical.

These two definitions focus on the norm or rule of law. Those norms or rules may be created by or found in different instruments or sources.

Article 38 of the Statute of the International Court of Justice, a treaty ratified by the United States and by all other members of the United Nations, contains a traditional statement of those sources. The Restatement offers an alternative exposition of basically the same idea.

Statute of the International Court of Justice

Article 38

The Court, whose function is to decide in accordance with international law such disputes as are submitted to it, shall apply:

(a) international conventions, whether general or particular, establishing rules expressly recognized by the contesting states;

(b) international custom, as evidence of a general practice accepted as law;

(c) the general principles of law recognized by civilized nations;

(d) . . . judicial decisions and the teachings of the most highly qualified publicists of the various nations, as subsidiary means for the determination of rules of law.

Restatement Section 102

(1) A rule of international law is one that has been accepted as such by the international community of states

(a) in the form of customary law;

(b) by international agreement; or

(c) by derivation from general principles common to the major legal systems of the world.

(2) Customary international law results from a general and consistent practice of states followed by them from a sense of legal obligation.

(3) International agreements create law for the states parties thereto and may lead to the creation of customary international law when such agreements are intended for adherence by states generally and are in fact widely accepted.

(4) General principles common to the major legal systems, even if not incorporated or reflected in customary law or international agreements, may be invoked as supplementary rules of international law where appropriate.

Notes and Questions

Problem. As an initial exercise, consider whether the norms or rules established by the legal instruments described below would qualify as international law under either of the two definitions above. You should focus on the norm or rule established by each of the instruments rather than on the instrument itself. (You may assume that a treaty is an agreement between states that is reached by the executive branches of the governments, often with legislative branch support.)

(a) A treaty among several countries prohibiting the use of force except in self-defense.

(b) A treaty between Mexico and the United States establishing the boundary between the two countries.

(c) A treaty between the United States and Japan under which each agrees to permit nationals of the other country to invest freely in its economy and not to expropriate property without payment of just compensation.

(d) An oil concession agreement between the government of Mexico and Texaco, under which Mexico agrees not to tax Texaco on its income from the concession for ten years. What if the concession agreement contains a clause saying that "this instrument shall have the force of law and shall be interpreted in accordance with generally recognized principles of international law"? Would it make any difference whether the concession agreement provided that disputes would be settled by international arbitration? Or if it provided that disputes would be settled exclusively in Mexican courts?

(e) A provision in the U.S. Constitution that property may not be taken except for public use and on payment of just compensation.

(f) A U.S. statute imposing licensing fees on foreign corporations.

(g) A common law rule announced by the California judiciary imposing strict liability without regard to negligence for damage caused by defective products (including those manufactured by foreign corporations).

(h) A custom long observed by all the countries of the world not to imprison properly accredited diplomats.

1. In the examples above, how was the legal norm formed? Who and/or what institutions were required for its formation?

2. Where would disputes about the validity or meaning of the norm be settled? In connection with this question, see Notes 5 and 6 below.

3. What law would govern the dispute? What difference does it make?

4. What sanctions could be imposed for violation, and who would impose them? It is important to think about sanctions other than retaliation (the normal international law sanction), and to think about why government officials comply with law, considering how factors such as judicial rebuke, adverse publicity, habitually following rules and procedures (the usual way a large bureaucracy functions), and fear of administrative sanctions or adverse effects on career development lead to compliance with international law. A relevant example occurred when two U.S. Border Patrol agents were removed from field duty because they "breached Mexico's sovereignty" by crossing the border in pursuit of two suspects. In a similar incident on the U.S.-Canadian border, the United States protested the Canadian arrest of a person 200 yards inside the United States and demanded to know what steps Canada was taking with respect to the arrested American and with respect to the arresting officer. Canada released the defendant and sought extradition under the extradition treaty between the two countries.

5. Much skepticism about international law is based on the absence of a judicial system with compulsory jurisdiction to settle disputes and the absence of a central executive authority to coerce compliance. Nevertheless, as we show in Section C, almost all rules of international law are in fact regularly complied with. Furthermore, as explored in Chapter 4, there is an International Court of Justice (ICJ),

which handles a few cases, and active regional and specialized international courts. Moreover, there are several means other than court adjudication by which disputes can be settled. For now, you should know that they include negotiation, mediation, and arbitration pursuant to a general or an ad hoc agreement. Most disputes are settled through negotiation. Consider the description of J. G. Merrills, International Dispute Settlement 2, 8 (3d ed. 1998):

> In fact in practice, negotiation is employed more frequently than all the other methods put together. Often, indeed, negotiation is the only means employed, not just because it is always the first to be tried and is often successful, but also because states may believe its advantages to be so great as to rule out the use of other methods, even in situations where the chances of a negotiated settlement are slight. . . . [The process of negotiation is] a striking reminder of the fact that states are not entities, like individuals, but complex groupings of institutions and interests [such as the various U.S. cabinet departments, like the Departments of Defense, Commerce, Labor and Agriculture, the legislative branch of the government, and regulatory and law enforcement agencies]. . . . Negotiations between states are usually conducted through "normal diplomatic channels," that is by the respective foreign offices [i.e., the Department of State in the case of the United States], or by diplomatic representatives, who in the case of complex negotiations may lead delegations including representatives of several interested departments of the governments concerned. As an alternative, if the subject matter is appropriate, negotiations may be carried out . . . by representatives of the particular ministry or department responsible for the matter in question — between trade departments in the case of a commercial agreement, for example, or defense ministries in negotiations concerning weapons' procurement.

6. Sometimes U.S. courts will look to international law and apply it, either by finding it incorporated into U.S. law or by construing statutes to avoid a violation of it. This is especially so when a treaty or other international agreement is involved to which the United States is a party. Article VI of the U.S. Constitution (the so-called Supremacy Clause) expressly makes treaties part of the "supreme Law of the Land." There are, however, questions under U.S. law about whether a treaty is self-executing or whether it needs implementing U.S. legislation. A court might also apply what is called customary international law — that is, the law that results from a general and consistent practice of states that they follow from a sense of legal obligation. One famous example of this is the decision by a U.S. court of appeals in Filartiga v. Pena-Irala (1980). There, the court determined that there was a customary international law norm against official torture, and the court held that an alien could bring suit in a U.S. court for a violation of this norm, pursuant to a U.S. statute that grants the federal courts jurisdiction to hear suits, brought by aliens, for torts "committed in violation of the law of nations. . . ." (These issues, and the *Filartiga* case, are discussed in Chapter 3.)

Litigating lawyers in the United States usually prefer to rely on constitutional and statutory arguments, rather than on international law. Does this preference reflect ignorance about international law? Parochialism? Skepticism about the perceived legitimacy of international law? Why would some people consider international law to be less legitimate than domestic law? Which of the following kinds of law would probably seem more legitimate to, or more worthy of respect by, (a) a judge, (b) a member of Congress, (c) a U.S. diplomat, and (d) an informed and concerned member of the public: the constitutional protections of free speech and privacy, a statutory protection of privacy, a treaty guaranteeing free speech and privacy that has been approved by the President and two-thirds of the Senate, a U.N. General Assembly resolution providing for rights to free speech and privacy that has been endorsed by diplomats from all countries of the world, including the United States? What contributes to respect for a legal norm?

Problem. Assume that in 1910 the United States and Mexico concluded a boundary treaty, which, in the case of the United States, was ratified by the President after receiving the advice and consent of the Senate, in accordance with Article II of the Constitution. The treaty provided that the boundary between Texas and Chihuahua would "follow the center of the normal flow channel" of the Rio Grande River "in accordance with international law." Your client is a wealthy Texas rancher who owns land on the northern bank of the river. Across the river, the land is owned by the Provincial Government of Chihuahua; this land is vacant, but the Provincial Government has plans to develop it into a bird refuge, which will stimulate local ecotourism. Assume that last spring, after an unusual spring flood, the entire river shifted 500 yards to the north, so that land formerly under water now is part of the Provincial Government's land. Moreover, the main channel of the river (which has shifted 500 yards to the north toward Texas) now covers what was formerly your client's land, and part of what he claims was his land now forms an island on the south side of the main channel. Assume that the Provincial Government has dispatched a work crew that is building a nature center on the island (this part of the river is a major migratory route for birds). Your client wants to stop the Mexican "occupation" of his land and has asked you to advise him as to (1) what the law is, (2) what remedies — judicial and non-judicial — are available, and (3) what the best strategy is for him to get "his land" back.

Your research has revealed that the treaty-established boundary has been discussed many times within the U.S.-Mexican Boundary Commission because of disputes and even fights over fishing rights in the middle of the river. The Commission and its staff are technicians and engineers who have always mediated a settlement of the problems, usually by getting the disputants to share their catches with each other, to fish on alternate days, or the like. The Commission does not have authority under the treaty to issue legal opinions. Indeed, there is no provision in the 1910 boundary treaty that specifies any judicial or other determination as to the interpretation or application of the treaty.

In 1995, the U.S. Supreme Court adjudicated a similar dispute between Louisiana and Mississippi. In such disputes between states, the Court has regularly stated that it applies general rules of international law. In Louisiana v. Mississippi, 516 U.S. 22, 24-25 (1995), the Court held:

> The controlling legal principles are not in dispute. In all four of the prior cases that have involved the Mississippi River boundary between Louisiana and Mississippi, we have applied the rule of the thalweg. Though there are exceptions, the rule is that the river boundary between States lies along the main downstream navigational channel, or thalweg, and moves as the channel changes with the gradual processes of erosion and accretion. There exists an island exception to the general rule, which provides that if there is a divided river flow around an island, a boundary once established on one side of the island remains there, even though the main downstream navigation

channel shifts to the island's other side. The island exception serves to avoid disturbing a State's sovereignty over an island if there are changes in the main navigation channel.

   The Special Master found that the disputed area derived from an island, known as Stack Island, that had been within Mississippi's boundary before the river's main navigational channel shifted to the east of the island. The Special Master found that, through erosion on its east bank and accretion on its west bank, Stack Island changed from its original location, next to the Mississippi bank of the river, to its current location, abutting the Louisiana bank. Pursuant to the island exception, then, the Special Master placed the boundary on the west side of the disputed area, confirming Mississippi's sovereignty over it.

   [The Court adopted the Special Master's decision.]

   In thinking about the advice you will give your client, consider the applicability of Texas state real property law and Article VI of the U.S. Constitution (treaties "shall be the supreme Law of the Land; and the Judges in every State shall be bound thereby, anything in the Constitution or Laws of any State to the Contrary notwithstanding"), the availability of a remedy in U.S. or Mexican courts, non-judicial remedies, international institutions, and so on. If you would like to pursue a negotiated settlement, with whom would you negotiate? If you would like to get the United States to negotiate with Mexico, or if you decide you would prefer to keep the U.S. government out of the picture, what strategy would you pursue to accomplish your objectives? How can you influence the U.S. Department of State? Can you be sure it will support your client? Should your client find it acceptable if the State Department proposes international arbitration of the dispute with Mexico?

B.   HISTORY OF PUBLIC INTERNATIONAL LAW AND ALTERNATIVE PERSPECTIVES

1.   Introduction

In the preceding section you learned that public international law deals with the activities of nation-states. The contemporary system of international relations is built on the assumption that the nation-state is the primary actor. Nevertheless, the modern nation-state is a relatively recent product of political development in Western Europe. Generally, this is traced to the Renaissance and Reformation, the expansion of trade in the fifteenth and sixteenth centuries, and the European discoveries of the New World. Intellectually, the doctrine of sovereignty and the idea of the secular, territorial state are intimately associated with the creation of the modern system.

   Of course, there had been well-organized political units in Europe before this period. And there were great empires for millennia in China, Japan, India, Africa, Southeast Asia, and the Middle East. Those empires had relations with other peoples, and hence there have been many systems of law that can be seen as predecessors to modern international law. However, even though most states today are non-European, the contemporary system of international law is based on the European model developed over the past four centuries. Some commentators have objected to what they see as a continuation of colonialism and imperialism and have urged abandonment or at least recasting the old Western system.

Throughout this course you should consider the extent to which you believe these objections are justified. As you learn the substantive rules of international law, consider what policies and interests these rules favor (and at whose expense); whether a small developing country would be likely to approve or oppose the rule (and who and what interests within that state would be likely to do so); and whether the legitimation of state authority favors Western or capitalist interests over others. In the following excerpts we introduce you to the basic history of modern international law (Starke, Shaw, and Barton and Carter). Then we present the story of contemporary international law from the perspective of developing countries (Shaw and Anand).

I. A. Shearer, Starke's International Law
7-12 (11th ed. 1994)

The modern system of international law is a product, roughly speaking, of only the last four hundred years. It grew to some extent out of the usages and practices of modern European states in their intercourse and communications, while it still bears witness to the influence of writers and jurists of the sixteenth, seventeenth, and eighteenth centuries, who first formulated some of its most fundamental tenets. Moreover, it remains tinged with concepts such as national and territorial sovereignty, and the perfect quality and independence of states, that owe their force to political theories underlying the modern European state system, although, curiously enough, some of these concepts have commanded the support of newly emerged non-European states.

But any historical account of the system must begin with earliest times, for even in the period of antiquity rules of conduct to regulate the relations between independent communities were felt necessary and emerged from the usages observed by these communities in their mutual relations. Treaties, the immunities of ambassadors, and certain laws and usages of war are to be found many centuries before the dawn of Christianity, for example in ancient Egypt and India, while there were historical cases of recourse to arbitration and mediation in ancient China and in the early Islamic world, although it would be wrong to regard these early instances as representing any serious contribution towards the evolution of the modern system of international law.

We find, for example, in the period of the Greek City States, small but independent of one another, evidence of an embryonic, although regionally limited, form of international law which one authority — Professor Vinogradoff — aptly described as "intermunicipal." This "intermunicipal" law was composed of customary rules which had crystallised into law from long-standing usages followed by these cities such as, for instance, the rules as to the inviolability of heralds in battle, the need for a prior declaration of war, and the enslavement of prisoners of war. These rules were applied not only in the relations inter se of these sovereign Greek cities, but as between them and neighbouring states. Underlying the rules there were, however, deep religious influences, characteristic of an era in which the distinctions between law, morality, justice and religion were not sharply drawn.

In the period of Rome's dominance of the ancient world, there also emerged rules governing the relations between Rome and the various nations or peoples with which it had contact. One significant aspect of these rules was their legal character, thus contrasting with the religious nature of the customary rules observed by the Greek City States. But Rome's main contribution to the development of international law was less through these rules than through the indirect influence of Roman law generally, inasmuch as when the study of Roman law was revived at a later stage in Europe, it provided analogies and principles capable of ready adaptation to the regulation of relations between modern states.

Actually, the total direct contribution of the Greeks and Romans to the development of international law was relatively meagre. Conditions favourable to the growth of a modern law of nations did not really come into being until the fifteenth century, when in Europe there began to evolve a number of independent civilised states. Before that time Europe had passed through various stages in which either conditions were so chaotic as to make impossible any ordered rules of conduct between nations, or the political circumstances were such that there was no necessity for a code of international law. Thus in the later period of Roman history with the authority of the Roman Empire extending over the whole civilised world, there were no independent states in any sense, and therefore a law of nations was not called for. During the early medieval era, there were two matters particularly which militated against the evolution of a system of international law:

a.   the temporal and spiritual unity of the greater part of Europe under the Holy Roman Empire, although to some extent this unity was notional and belied by numerous instances of conflict and disharmony; and

b.   the feudal structure of Western Europe, hinging on a hierarchy of authority which not only clogged the emergence of independent states but also prevented the Powers of the time from acquiring the unitary character and authority of modern sovereign states.

Profound alterations occurred in the fifteenth and sixteenth centuries. The discovery of the New World, the Renaissance of learning, and the Reformation as a religious revolution disrupted the façade of the political and spiritual unity of Europe, and shook the foundations of medieval Christendom. Theories were evolved to meet the new conditions; intellectually, the secular conceptions of a modern sovereign state and of a modern independent Sovereign found expression in the works of Bodin (1530-1596), a Frenchman, Machiavelli (1469-1527), an Italian, and later in the seventeenth century, Hobbes (1588-1679), an Englishman.

With the growth of a number of independent states there was initiated, as in early Greece, the process of formation of customary rules of international law from the usages and practices followed by such states in their mutual relations. So in Italy with its multitude of small independent states, maintaining diplomatic relations with each other and with the outside world, there developed a number of customary rules relating to diplomatic envoys, for example, their appointment, reception and inviolability.[1]

An important fact also was that by the fifteenth and sixteenth centuries jurists had begun to take into account the evolution of a community of independent

---

1. Cf. also the influence of the early codes of mercantile and maritime usage, e.g., the Rhodian Laws formulated between the seventh and ninth centuries, the Laws or Rolls of Oleron collected in France during the twelfth century, and the *Consolato del Mare* as to the customs of the sea followed by Mediterranean countries and apparently collected in Spain in the fourteenth century.

sovereign states and to think and write about different problems of the law of nations, realising the necessity for some body of rules to regulate certain aspects of the relations between such states. Where there were no established customary rules, these jurists were obliged to devise and fashion working principles by reasoning or analogy. Not only did they draw on the principles of Roman law which had become the subject of revived study in Europe from the end of the eleventh century onwards, but they had recourse also to the precedents of ancient history, to theology, to the canon law, and to the semi-theological concept of the "law of nature," a concept which for centuries exercised a profound influence on the development of international law. Among the early writers who made important contributions to the infant science of the law of nations were . . . Belli (1502-1575), an Italian, Brunus (1491-1563), a German, . . . Ayala (1548-1584), a jurist of Spanish extraction, Suarez (1548-1617), a great Spanish Jesuit, and Gentilis (1552-1608), an Italian who became Professor of Civil Law at Oxford, and who is frequently regarded as the founder of a systematic law of nations. The writings of these early jurists reveal significantly that one major preoccupation of sixteenth century international law was the law of warfare between states, and in this connection it may be noted that by the fifteenth century the European Powers had begun to maintain standing armies, a practice which naturally caused uniform usages and practices of war to evolve.

By general acknowledgment the greatest of the early writers on international law was the Dutch scholar, jurist, and diplomat, Grotius (1583-1645), whose systematic treatise on the subject *De Jure Belli ac Pacis* (The Law of War and Peace) first appeared in 1625. On account of this treatise, Grotius has sometimes been described as the "father of the law of nations," although it is maintained by some that such a description is incorrect on the grounds that his debt to the writings of Gentilis is all too evident and that in point of time he followed writers such as Belli, Ayala and others mentioned above. Indeed both Gentilis and Grotius owed much to their precursors.

Nor is it exact to affirm that in *De Jure Belli ac Pacis* will be found all the international law that existed in 1625. It cannot, for example, be maintained that Grotius dealt fully with the law and practice of his day as to treaties, or that his coverage of the rules and usages of warfare was entirely comprehensive. Besides, *De Jure Belli ac Pacis* was not primarily or exclusively a treatise on international law, as it embraced numerous topics of legal science, and touched on problems of theological or philosophic interest. Grotius's historical pre-eminence rests rather on his continued inspirational appeal as the creator of the first adequate comprehensive framework of the modern science of international law.

In his book, as befitted a diplomat of practical experience, and a lawyer who had practised, Grotius dealt repeatedly with the actual customs followed by the states of his day. At the same time Grotius was a theorist who espoused certain doctrines. One central doctrine in his treatise was the acceptance of the "law of nature" as an independent source of rules of the law of nations, apart from custom and treaties. The Grotian "law of nature" was to some extent a secularised version, being founded primarily on the dictates of reason, on the rational nature of men as social human beings, and in that form it was to become a potent source of inspiration to later jurists.

Grotius has had an abiding influence upon international law and international lawyers, although the extent of this influence has fluctuated at different periods. . . . While it would be wrong to say that his views were always treated as being of compelling authority — frequently they were the object of criticism — nevertheless his principal work, *De Jure Belli ac Pacis,* was continually relied upon as a work of reference and authority in the decisions of courts, and in the textbooks of later writers of standing. Also several Grotian doctrines have left their mark on, and are implicit in the character of modern international law, namely, the distinction between just and unjust war, the recognition of the rights and freedoms of the individual, the doctrine of qualified neutrality, the idea of peace, and the value of periodic conferences between the rulers of states. Nor should it be forgotten that for over three centuries Grotius was regarded as the historic standard-bearer of the doctrine of the freedom of the seas by reason of his authorship of the work, *Mare Liberum,* published in 1609.

The history of the law of nations during the two centuries after Grotius was marked by the final evolution of the modern state-system in Europe, a process greatly influenced by the Treaty of Westphalia of 1648 marking . . . the end of the Thirty Years' War, and by the development from usage and practice of a substantial body of new customary rules. Even relations and intercourse by treaty or otherwise between European and Asian governments or communities contributed to the formation of these rules. Moreover the science of international law was further enriched by the writings and studies of a number of great jurists. Side by side there proceeded naturally a kind of action and reaction between the customary rules and the works of these great writers; not only did their systematic treatment of the subject provide the best evidence of the rules, but they suggested new rules or principles where none had yet emerged from the practice of states. The influence of these great jurists on the development of international law was considerable, as can be seen from their frequent citation by national courts during the nineteenth century and even up to the present time.

. . . In the eighteenth century, there was a growing tendency among jurists to seek the rules of international law mainly in custom and treaties, and to relegate to a minor position the "law of nature," or reason, as a source of principles. . . . There were, however, jurists who at the same time clung to the traditions of the law of nature, either almost wholly, or coupled with a lesser degree of emphasis upon custom and treaties as components of international law. As contrasted with these adherents to the law of nature, writers such as Bynkershoek who attached primary or major weight to customary and treaty rules were known as "positivists."

In the nineteenth century international law further expanded. This was due to a number of factors which fall more properly within the scope of historical studies, for instance, the further rise of powerful new states both within and outside Europe, the expansion of European civilisation overseas, the modernisation of world transport, the greater destructiveness of modern warfare, and the influence of new inventions. All these made it urgent for the international society of states to acquire a system of rules which would regulate in an ordered manner the conduct of international affairs. There was a remarkable development during the century in the law of war and neutrality, and the great increase in adjudications by international arbitral tribunals following the *Alabama Claims Award* of 1872 provided an important new source of rules and principles. Besides, states commenced to acquire the habit of negotiating general treaties in order to regulate affairs of mutual concern. Nor was the nineteenth century without its great writers on international law. . . . The general tendency of these writers was to concentrate on existing practice, and to discard the concept of the "law of nature," although not abandoning recourse to reason and justice where, in the absence of custom or treaty rules, they were called upon to speculate as to what should be the law.

Other important developments have taken place in the twentieth century. The Permanent Court of Arbitration was established by the Hague Conferences of 1899 and 1907. The Permanent Court of International Justice was set up in 1921 as an authoritative international judicial tribunal, and was succeeded in 1946 by the present International Court of Justice. Then there has been the creation of permanent international organisations whose functions are . . . in the interests of peace and human welfare, such as the League of Nations and its present successor — the United Nations, the International Labour Organisation, the International Civil Aviation Organisation. . . . And perhaps most remarkable of all has been the widening scope of international law to cover by multilateral treaty or convention not only every kind of economic or social interest affecting states (e.g., patents and copyright), but also the fundamental rights and freedoms of individual human beings.

Malcolm N. Shaw, International Law

26-27 (4th ed. 1997)

The First World War marked the close of a dynamic and optimistic century. European empires ruled the world and European ideologies reigned supreme, but the 1914-18 Great War undermined the foundations of European civilisation. Self-confidence faded, if slowly, the edifice weakened and the universally accepted assumptions of progress were increasingly doubted. Self-questioning was the order of the day and law as well as art reflected this.

The most important legacy of the 1919 Peace Treaty from the point of view of international relations was the creation of the League of Nations. The old anarchic system had failed and it was felt that new institutions to preserve and secure peace were necessary. The League consisted of an Assembly and an executive Council, but was crippled from the start by the absence of the United States and the Soviet Union for most of its life and remained a basically European organisation.

While it did have certain minor successes with regard to the maintenance of international order, it failed when confronted with determined aggressors. Japan invaded China in 1931 and two years later withdrew from the League. Italy attacked Ethiopia and Germany embarked unhindered upon a series of internal and external aggressions. The Soviet Union, in a final forlorn gesture, was expelled from the organisation in 1939 following its invasion of Finland.

Nevertheless much useful groundwork was achieved by the League in its short existence and this helped to consolidate the United Nations later on.

The Permanent Court of International Justice was set up in 1921 at The Hague to be succeeded in 1946 by the International Court of Justice, the International Labour Organisation was established soon after the end of the First World War and it still exists today, and many other international institutions were inaugurated or increased their work during this period.

Other ideas of international law that first appeared between the wars included the system of mandates, by which colonies of the defeated powers were administered by the Allies for the benefit of their inhabitants rather than being annexed outright, and the attempt made to provide a form of minority protection guaranteed by the

League. This latter creation was not a great success but it paved the way for later concern to secure human rights.

After the trauma of the Second World War the League was succeeded in 1946 by the United Nations Organisation, which tried to remedy many of the defects of its predecessor. It established its site at New York, reflecting the realities of the shift of power away from Europe, and determined to become a truly universal institution. The advent of decolonisation fulfilled this expectation and the General Assembly of the United Nations today has [about 190] member-states.

Many of the trends which first came into prominence in the nineteenth century have continued to this day. The vast increase in the number of international agreements and customs, the strengthening of the system of arbitration and the development of international organisations have established the essence of international law as it exists today.

Post-World War II developments are described by Professors John Barton and Barry Carter:

John H. Barton & Barry E. Carter, International Law and Institutions for a New Age

81 Geo. L.J. 535, 535-549 (1993) [and updated by Prof. Carter through January 2003]

The years immediately after World War II witnessed tremendous creativity and accomplishment in establishing new international institutions that would play a role in the international system, in addition to the nation-state. The United Nations was created, primarily to prevent military conflict among its members and to settle international disputes. It was also intended to help spawn and oversee more specialized agencies — the International Civil Aviation Organization and the World Health Organization. It was supplemented by the International Court of Justice (I.C.J. or World Court), which was designed as the formal judicial body to resolve legal disputes among nations.

A different group of institutions, the Bretton Woods institutions, were designed to face economic issues. The International Monetary Fund (IMF) was established to promote monetary cooperation among nations and stability in foreign exchange. The International Bank for Reconstruction and Development (or World Bank) was created to help provide funds for the reconstruction of then war-ravaged nations and to promote economic development. An International Trade Organization (ITO) was envisioned as a structure to monitor and enforce rules that would regularize and encourage international trade. Opposition to the ITO, especially in the U.S. Congress, caused it to be a stillbirth. However, a subsidiary trade agreement, the GATT, was allowed to metamorphose into a skeletal institutional arrangement.

These institutions continue to exist today though they have had varied success in realizing their envisaged potential. The security-oriented entities were a disappointment. Confronted with rivalries among its veto-wielding major powers, the United Nations shifted from collective security to a new peacekeeping pattern based on the consent of the nations involved. Even so, the United Nations proved less successful at preventing war and settling disputes than its creators had hoped. Only with the end of the Cold War and the disintegration of the Soviet Union has use of the veto power in the Security Council dramatically decreased, allowing the organization to fulfill some of the dreams of its founders. . . . Additionally, the I.C.J. has been much less active and successful than was envisioned.

The institutional evolutions on the economic side have been much more far-reaching. With the admission of many new member states from the developing world in the 1960s and 1970s, developing countries increasingly dominated the U.N. General Assembly, and the United Nations itself took on a strongly economic orientation. It created, for example, the United Nations Conference for Trade and Development (UNCTAD), a group dedicated to development perspectives. In the 1970s, the IMF saw the United States go off the gold standard and the major industrial countries of the world switch to flexible exchange rates. The IMF could no longer play its original role of supporting fixed exchange rates and has instead carved out a role in assisting and supervising countries that face unreasonable debt burdens [or currency instability]. The World Bank has switched its focus from reconstructing the war-torn economies of Europe to encouraging the development of countries in Latin America, Africa, Asia, and Eastern Europe.

[Although the GATT continued to develop through the 1980s and early 1990s, it remained severely limited by the absence of an institutional structure, by its coverage of only goods and not other important matters such as services and intellectual property, and by its dispute-settlement process that was often complied with, but that lacked effective enforcement in difficult cases. Recognizing that the GATT was becoming increasingly inadequate as international trade and investment steadily grew, most of the world's nations during the so-called Uruguay Round of trade negotiations agreed to create a successor entity, the World Trade Organization (WTO). Starting in 1995, the WTO has an institutional structure, though it still is based on a one-country, one-vote system that requires unanimity on important matters. Reflecting the approximately 2,000 pages of related agreements, the WTO's scope is considerable — the agreements not only include more detailed provisions regarding trade in goods, but also cover trade in services and intellectual property, and there is the start toward regulating trade-related investment. The new WTO dispute resolution system is possibly the most influential international dispute-settlement arrangement in the world — the decisions of a WTO panel or, if appealed, of the Appellate Body, are binding on the disputing parties, except in the highly unlikely situation that all the WTO members (including the winning state in the decision) vote not to accept the report of the panel or the Appellate Body. If a country does not then bring its laws or regulations into consistency with the WTO rules as specified in the report, the complaining country may be allowed to retaliate up to the equivalent amount that it has been injured.]

While these initial institutions were growing and evolving, a wide range of other institutions developed. To deal with new, often specialized issues, entities such as the International Atomic Energy Agency in 1957, and the U.N. Environment Programme (UNEP) in 1972 were created. Countries with similar interests have combined in quasi-formal combinations, such as the Group of [Eight] (the United States, Japan, Germany, France, United Kingdom, Italy, . . . Canada [and Russia]). The finance ministers of these countries regularly discuss exchange rates among themselves and take steps that frequently have more impact on these rates than does the IMF.

At least as dramatic has been the emergence of regional entities. The European Community (EC) has achieved a high level of economic integration [and it has also expanded not only to 15 member states, but also to include several more responsibilities under the broader umbrella of the European Union (EU). Among other results are the euro, a common currency for 12 of the member states, and growing cooperation on noneconomic foreign policy issues.] Regional development banks, which substantially supplement the work of the World Bank, exist for Latin America, Asia, Africa, and now Eastern Europe. . . .

On the judicial front, the European Community's Court of Justice and the separate European Court of Human Rights are both active and effective. The . . . Law of the Sea Convention establishe[d] a new international court as well as two arbitral mechanisms.

Beyond such international and regional entities are a vast array of new bilateral and multilateral agreements that require, or at least encourage, cooperation across a nation's borders on a host of issues — from protecting the ozone layer, to combatting terrorism, safeguarding diplomatic personnel, and enforcing arbitral awards.

II.   THE CHANGES IN INTERNATIONAL LAW

Paralleling this impressive change in the international institutional order have been equally important, though often less visible, changes in international law. Most notably, (1) the international system is no longer confined to relations among nations, and the individual person has emerged as an independent and recognized actor; and (2) national and international tribunals are offering new, and much more effective, means for enforcing international law.

A.   The Emergence of the Person

The traditional concept of international law was one of law between nations. As late as 1963, a very respected English treatise defined public international law as "the body of rules and principles of action which are binding upon civilized states in their relations with one another."

Reciprocity was the critical element in ensuring that international rules and norms were observed. Formal rules about the treatment of ambassadors or about respect for a state's territorial sea, for example, were usually followed because the potential offender was also a potential victim. For reasons discussed below, only rarely would states resort to the International Court of Justice (or its predecessor, the Permanent Court of International Justice) or to formal arbitration.

In the immediate post-war era, the scope of international law expanded from nation states to the new international and regional institutions. For example, U.N. organs and agencies were allowed to seek advisory opinions from the I.C.J., which was otherwise restricted to disputes among states.

Moreover, the person (whether an individual or corporation) has become increasingly accepted as an independent actor, subject to and benefiting from international law. This has been an inevitable result of the increasing global interactions and shared interests of persons across frontiers.

Among the early steps toward the emergence of the person in international law were efforts by foreign investors and businesses to protect themselves from expropriation or other mistreatment by a host country. Under traditional international law, the investor would rely on its home country to protect its interests through diplomatic arguments and pressure. The investor, however, also wanted independent protection. Moreover, host countries wished to attract investment and all parties sought to resolve disputes quickly and reasonably. As a result, a trend developed toward arbitration between the investor and the host government by a panel that applied international principles.

This was part of a much larger phenomenon in which the traditional barriers between so-called "public" and "private" international law have come tumbling down. In contrast to the public international law of rules between states, there has long been private international law dealing with the activities of individuals, corporations, and other private entities when their activities crossed national borders. This was particularly important in the laws of admiralty, governing the maritime sector, and in choice-of-law rules, determining which country's domestic law would apply to transnational transactions between the nationals of different countries.

The distinctions between public and private international law have become increasingly artificial as many states and their instrumentalities have entered the marketplace in a major way — either as traders themselves or as guardians of industrial policy — and as commerce and foreign policy have become increasingly intertwined. For example, the Iraqi invasion of Kuwait and the resulting U.N. economic sanctions involved traditional issues of public international law; yet the implementation of the sanctions very much affected U.S. and European banks with Iraqi or Kuwaiti deposits. At much less dramatic levels, the same kinds of mixed public-private issues are posed daily by satellites broadcasting across national boundaries, by fishers in international waters, and by investors trading on foreign stock exchanges. Courts, national governments, and international organizations struggle with such issues. Thus, when the European Community developed its judicial system, it realized that it must allow individuals to appeal to, or against, Community action just as much as governments.

The independent role of individuals has probably advanced furthest in the human rights area. The tragic experience of Nazi Germany caused many to believe that citizens of a state should have some form of international protection against even their own state, a view reinforced by the recent tragic plights of the Iraqi Kurds and of the residents of [Kosovo]. There is no question that international law now defines a number of human rights, such as the right to be free from official torture. Many conventions go much further in defining rights of the individual. As discussed below, these rights can sometimes be enforced in a nation's domestic courts. In Europe, they also can be enforced before the European Court of Human Rights. . . .

B.   Enforcing International Law

Paralleling this transformation in the role of the individual in international law is an equally dramatic change in the mechanisms available to enforce international law.

The traditional, and still important, international enforcement mechanism is reciprocity. After invading Panama in December 1989, what basically kept the United States from storming the Vatican nunciature to capture General Manuel Noriega was the possibility that this would create a precedent that would endanger U.S. embassies everywhere. It would also have been a clear violation of the Vienna Convention on Diplomatic Relations of 1961, to which the United States, Panama, the Vatican, and over [175] other states are now parties. That Convention strengthens reciprocity by providing a reasonably clear definition of the rights of ambassadors and embassies.

For traditional international law, the best-known adjudicatory body was, and probably still is, the I.C.J. The Court will probably remain the principal forum for resolving certain forms of legal issues between states, especially boundary disputes. The Court has been hampered, however, by a perceived lack of bite. Under the U.N. Charter, a member "undertakes to comply with the decision" of the Court if "it is a party" to the case, and the U.N. Security Council may "decide upon measures to be taken to give effect to the [Court's] judgment." Although states have complied with the Court's judgments in many of the cases in which the judgment required an action, recalcitrant states have on occasion refused to comply. . . .

For instance, ... [in] 1980, Iran refused to comply with the Court's judgment to release the U.S. hostages. [More] recently, the United States continued its support of the Nicaraguan Contras in spite of the Court's 1986 decision that the extensive U.S. involvement with the Contras violated international law. [And, as discussed in Chapter 4, U.S. states have executed foreign nationals in recent years despite preliminary orders by the Court requesting that the United States take all measures at its disposal to stay the executions.]

This uncertain enforceability of I.C.J. judgments is one of several reasons why the Court has not emerged as an important institution for resolving international legal disputes. . . .

The Court's formal procedures have also discouraged its use. Its procedures do not yet recognize the emergence of the person in international law; only states can be parties in contentious cases, although U.N. entities can also seek advisory opinions. Moreover, a state that wants a dispute resolved promptly finds I.C.J. procedures uninviting: they are not well-adapted for fact-finding, and a long time usually passes before the Court renders a decision, even with its light caseload. Although there has been a recent surge in the number of cases brought to the Court, [the Court's 125] cases in [over 55] years average out to less than [three] new cases per year — hardly a heavy caseload. . . .

The Court has recently shown a willingness to reform itself. It adopted revised rules in 1978 to enable a state to bring cases before three- or five-judge panels, in which each country would have one of its nationals as a judge and a voice regarding the other judges. The Court's decision in 1984 to take jurisdiction in Nicaragua's case against the United States could also be seen as reflecting a new aggressiveness toward finding jurisdiction.

But these changes in the I.C.J. are minor compared with the wide variety of attractive alternative arrangements that have emerged elsewhere for formal enforcement of international rules and norms. These alternatives include international arbitration, regional and specialized courts, and transnational use of domestic courts. They amount to a revolution in international law.

1.   *Arbitration*

The 1958 New York Convention on the Recognition and Enforcement of Foreign Arbitral Awards (N.Y. Convention) has been ratified by over [130] countries, including the United States and all the other major industrialized countries. According to this treaty, subject to very narrow exceptions, a decision by an international arbitral panel sitting in a contracting state will be enforced by the domestic courts of any other contracting country as if the decision were by that domestic court. As a result, a winning party in an international arbitration can usually be assured of collecting against a recalcitrant losing party if the loser has assets — bank accounts, real estate, goods — in any one of the N.Y. Convention countries. It is only necessary to take the arbitral award to the local court for authority to have the assets seized and sold off under local law.

Libya's Colonel Qaddafi learned first-hand of this Convention in the 1970s. After his coup, Qaddafi nationalized valuable interests of foreign oil companies operating in Libya. These oil companies had entered into long-term agreements with the prior Libyan government, under which the companies were entitled to submit any dispute to arbitration and the principles of international law. Qaddafi claimed that the nationalization decree invalidated these contract provisions and that the companies had to seek redress in Libya's domestic courts. The oil companies disagreed and sought arbitration. Sole arbitrators were appointed in three separate cases. Each decided that he had jurisdiction and each ultimately entered awards against Libya. Qaddafi apparently refused initially to pay, but eventually settled for tens of millions of dollars. Had Libya not paid, the successful companies could have moved to enforce their arbitral awards against Libya in, say, Italy, Germany, Switzerland, or any of the other N.Y. Convention countries by moving to attach Libyan oil, bank accounts, airplanes, or other assets.

The N.Y. Convention gave a powerful boost to arbitration, but it is not the only reason why arbitration has grown. Arbitration already had the advantages of flexibility. Parties can choose the place of arbitration and the number, specialization, and even identity of arbitrators; they can select the procedural rules (including those governing confidentiality and the amount of discovery allowed); and they can specify the substantive rules (e.g., general principles of international law, an individual country's laws, or even specially-drafted provisions). This flexibility makes arbitration particularly useful in disputes between nations and investors or between holders of economic interests in different nations. Arbitration has also been strongly supported in a variety of U.S. Supreme Court decisions.

As a result, arbitration has been a growth industry in the last [fifty] years. For example, [566] new requests for arbitration were filed in [2001] with the International Chamber of Commerce (ICC). Although the ICC is designed to handle commercial disputes, about a fifth of its cases have involved governmental or parastatal entities, such as government-owned utilities or airlines. Similarly, the American Arbitration Association (AAA) now has over [500] cases per year involving international disputes.

The World Bank created the International Centre for the Settlement of Investment Disputes (ICSID) to resolve disputes between foreign investors and the host country through conciliation and arbitration. ICSID's own multilateral convention has enforcement provisions similar to those in the N.Y. Convention. [After getting off to a slow start, ICSID has experienced a growing number of cases, with over 45 pending as of January 2003.]

The Iran-U.S. Claims Tribunal . . . has been a pace-setting institution. It was created in 1981 as part of the arrangement for freeing the U.S. hostages and resolving a number of outstanding claims between the two countries. In spite of initial delays and wrangling, [as of January 2003, the Tribunal had nearly completed resolution of all the private claims of U.S. nationals against Iran. Its remaining focus was the arbitration of claims between the two governments. The Tribunal has rendered a total of 599 awards, the majority of which were in favor of U.S. claimants. The value of these awards to successful U.S. claimants totaled over $2.5 billion.] The awards for U.S. claimants have been paid out of an escrow account set up with Iranian funds transferred from those frozen by the U.S. government in 1979-1981 and supplemented by funds derived from Iranian oil sales. Iranians can count on directly collecting on awards in their favor because of the availability of the N.Y. Convention.

Another example of the preference for arbitration is the choice by the United States[, Canada, and Mexico to provide in the North American Free Trade Agreement (NAFTA) for arbitration as the binding method for dispute resolution of many trade disputes between any two of those countries. Since NAFTA's inception in 1994, there have been over 80 binational arbitration panels established.]

2.   *Regional and Specialized Courts*

The new regional courts of Europe — whose decisions are as effective as those of any domestic court — are among the most dramatic examples of the new mechanisms of international law. The European Community's Court of Justice [for the European Community] had [over 500] new cases brought to it in [2001]; a new court of first instance, or trial court, had to be organized in September 1989 to meet the rest of the Court of Justice's business. [The European Court of Human Rights, partly as a result of its expanding membership and institutional reforms, is now entering several hundred judgments a year.]

The Court of Justice handles a variety of appeals from [European] Community measures, and it can also be called on to interpret Community law for the benefit of national courts. It is open to individuals as well as national governments. Among its decisions are landmark opinions holding that Community law has precedence over national law — opinions very similar to the federalism decisions of the U.S. Supreme Court.

The European Court of Human Rights enforces an international bill of rights . . . — the European Convention for the Protection of Human Rights and Fundamental Freedoms. All of the [44] European states that have submitted to the compulsory jurisdiction of the court have agreed to abide by its decisions, which have normally been accepted and implemented. Such decisions have covered areas as sensitive as freedom of the press, wiretapping, and the regulation of homosexuality. In addition, some of the member states, like France and Italy, have incorporated the European Convention's bill of rights into domestic law. . . .

The success of these European courts is in large part a result of Europe's overall political moves toward integration. The European Community is obviously of vital interest to its member states. The European Court of Human Rights and the related Council of Europe enjoy widespread popular support and prestige in Europe. The courts have a focused jurisdiction and relatively easy access, unlike the I.C.J. Perhaps most important, it is very difficult to build the type of federalism being sought in Europe without a judicial institution to draw the lines between central and local authority. Judicial review, an American invention, has largely taken over in Europe, even in France, which had historically looked to a popularly-elected legislature as a defense against aristocratic judges.

A sign of the recent times is the dispute resolution system in the . . . 1982 Convention on the Law of the Sea. This Convention, drafted under U.N. auspices, [came into force in 1994 and now has over 140 parties, though the United States has not ratified this treaty. This Convention established a detailed regime for the oceans (as is discussed in Chapter 9).] Disputes under this Convention may be referred not only to the I.C.J., but also to a new International Tribunal for the Law of the Sea and two different arbitration arrangements. The choices reflect the developing countries' unhappiness with I.C.J. judgments at the time of drafting the Convention, and the drafters' hope of achieving enforceability under the N.Y. Convention. The arrangement also reflects efforts to rely more on specialized courts or on arbitration. Each country is to select the dispute resolution institution it prefers when it ratifies the Convention. If the two or more parties which are later involved in a dispute had not agreed on the institutions in their ratification documents, then the Convention directs the parties to use arbitration. Arbitration is implicitly the preferred lowest common denominator.

3.   Domestic Courts

As international trade, finance, investment, and travel have mushroomed, the domestic courts of most countries have naturally found themselves considering more and more cases that have an international impact. These courts have sometimes declined to hear such cases because of concerns about the extraterritorial impact of their decisions, and they have developed a variety of doctrines for that purpose.

The overall trend, however, is to hear more such cases and effectively to develop what amounts to an international common law that lies in between traditional domestic and traditional international law. This common law draws from a country's domestic statutes and court decisions that affect international matters, as well as international treaties and the other international legal rules generally called customary international law. These international common law doctrines are often developed further by international and regional courts and by international arbitrations. Tribunals and scholars in different nations often look to one another's work to develop the harmony needed to make the system work.

This international flow of legal ideas is especially important in human rights issues, in international economic issues, and in resolving jurisdictional conflicts. Thus, domestic courts will often entertain claims that foreign corporate conduct violated domestic . . . law, that a foreign government violated the rights of a domestic business that had contracted with it, or that a corporation should be liable for work hazards affecting foreign workers. The courts will develop rules as to when and how a foreign subsidiary is bound by the employment discrimination law or banking law of the parent corporation's home nation.

This developing role of domestic courts is evident in the human rights area. For example, U.S. federal courts allowed a suit by a Paraguayan citizen against a former Paraguayan police official who was accused of torturing and murdering the citizen in Paraguay. The U.S. courts decided the case on the basis of a U.S. law that allows tort suits by an alien for a violation of "the law of nations or a treaty of the United States." . . .

The domestic courts also have an influence beyond their specific judgments — their decisions are often cited in other national courts and in the regional courts discussed above. Thus, there is the further development of an international common law, although, discouragingly, U.S. courts tend to consider foreign decisions much less than foreign courts consider U.S. decisions.

2.   Developing Countries' Perspective

Malcolm N. Shaw, International Law

33-35 (4th ed. 1997)

In the evolution of international affairs since the Second World War one of the most decisive events has been the disintegration of the colonial empires and the birth of scores of new states in the so-called Third World. This has thrust onto the scene states which carry with them a legacy of bitterness over their past status as well as a host of problems relating to their social, economic and political development. In such circumstances it was only natural that the structure and doctrines of international law would come under attack. The nineteenth century development of the law of nations founded upon Eurocentrism and imbued with the values of Christian, urbanised and expanding Europe did not, understandably enough, reflect the needs and interests of the newly independent states of the mid and late twentieth century. It was felt that such rules had encouraged and then reflected their subjugation, and that changes were required.

It is basically those ideas of international law that came to fruition in the last century that have been so clearly rejected, that is, those principles that enshrined the power and domination of the west. The underlying concepts of international law have not been discarded. On the contrary, the new nations have eagerly embraced the ideas of the sovereignty and equality of states and the principles of non-aggression and non-intervention, in their search for security within the bounds of a commonly accepted legal framework.

While this new internationalisation of international law that has occurred in the last twenty years has destroyed its European-based homogenity, it has emphasised its universalist scope. The composition of, for example, both the International Court of Justice and the Security Council of the United Nations mirror such developments. Article 9 of the Statute of the International Court of Justice points out that the main forms of civilisation and the principal legal systems of the world must be represented within the Court, and there is an arrangement that of the ten non-permanent seats in the Security Council five should go to Afro-Asian states and two to Latin American states (the others going to Europe and other states). The composition of the International Law Commission has also recently been increased and structured upon geographic lines.

The influence of the new states has been felt most of all within the General Assembly, where they constitute a majority of the [191] member-states [in January 2003]. The content and scope of the various resolutions and declarations emanating from the Assembly are proof of their impact and contain a record of their fears, hopes and concerns.

The Declaration on the Granting of Independence to Colonial Countries and Peoples of 1960, for example, enshrined the right of colonies to obtain their sovereignty with the least possible delay and called for the recognition of the principle of self-determination. This principle . . . is regarded by most authorities as a settled rule of international law although with undetermined borders. Nevertheless, it symbolises the rise of the post-colonial states and the effect they are having upon the development of international law.

Their concern for the recognition of the sovereignty of states is complemented by their support of the United Nations and its Charter and supplemented by their desire for "economic self-determination" or the right of permanent sovereignty over natural resources. This expansion of international law into the field of economics is a major development of this century and is evidenced in myriad ways, for example, by the creation of the General Agreement on Tariffs and Trade, the United Nations Conferences on Trade and Development, and the establishment of the International Monetary Fund and World Bank.

The interests of the new states of the non-Western, non-communist Third World are often in conflict with those of the industrialised nations, witness disputes over nationalisations. But it has to be emphasised that, contrary to many fears expressed in the early years of the decolonisation saga, international law has not been discarded nor altered beyond recognition. Its framework has been retained as the new states, too, wish to obtain the benefits of rules such as those governing diplomatic relations and the controlled use of force, while campaigning against rules which run counter to their perceived interests.

While the new countries share a common history of foreign dominance and underdevelopment, compounded by an awakening of national identity, it has to be recognised that they are not a homogenous group. Widely differing cultural, social and economic attitudes and stages of development characterise them and the rubric of the "Third World" masks diverse political affiliations. On many issues the interests of the new states conflict with each other and this is reflected in the different positions adopted. The states possessing oil and other valuable natural resources are separated from those with few or none and the states bordering on oceans are to be distinguished from land-locked states. The list of diversity is endless and variety governs the make-up of the southern hemisphere to a far greater degree than in the north.

It is possible that in legal terms tangible differences in approach may emerge in the future as the passions of decolonisation die down and the western supremacy over international law is further eroded. This trend will also permit a greater understanding of, and greater recourse to, historical traditions and conceptions that pre-date colonisation and an increasing awareness of their validity for the future development of international law.

Ram Prakash Anand, International Law and the Developing Countries

17-19, 34-36, 44-45 (1987)

INDUSTRIAL REVOLUTION AND THE AGE OF IMPERIALISM

. . . With Napoleon defeated and Continental system in disarray, with no rival left in the contest for overseas dominion, and with a virtual monopoly of naval power, the British embarked on a century of world dominance.

Europe came out of the wars shaken, but not ruined. Moreover, Europe was carried on the wave of an expanding economy. The economic growth and enrichment that had resulted from the commercial expansion was so pronounced and spectacular that it is commonly called Commercial Revolution. The riches of Asia and American trade flowing to Europe, followed by numerous scientific inventions like steam engine, improved transportation facilities, railroads, steamship, harnessing of electricity and internal combustion engine, led to what is called Industrial Revolution. The industrial revolution got under way first in England. After the first quarter of the nineteenth century it started spreading gradually to the continent of Europe, and even to non-European portions of the globe. But it was not until 1870 that Britain faced any competition. The British had a virtual monopoly in textiles and machine tools. The British capitalists were accumulating surplus capital and were on the look out for investment opportunities on the continent and beyond. London became the world's clearing house and financial centre.

The needs and demands of the industrial revolution were largely responsible for the creation of huge European colonial empires in Asia and Africa. With the rapid industrialization, several European countries had developed substantial industries. The close relationship between the new imperialism and industrial revolution may be seen in the growing need and desire to obtain colonies which might serve as markets for the rising volume of manufactured goods. The several European and overseas Europeanized countries, like the United States, Canada and Australia, which had become industrialized in the nineteenth century, were soon competing with each other for markets. In the process they raised their tariffs to keep out each other's products. The only alternative was to sell their products to Asia and Africa and have colonies to provide "sheltered markets" for each industrialized country.

The industrial revolution also produced surplus capital which could not be invested in Europe and led European countries to seek colonies as investment outlets. It also created a demand for raw materials to feed the machines. Many of these materials — jute, rubber, petroleum, and various metals — could be obtained from Asia and Africa. In most cases, heavy capital outlays were needed to secure adequate production of these commodities.

There were, of course, several other factors — need for more additional manpower, influence of missionaries, and desire to strengthen national security by establishing strategic naval bases — which were responsible for the spread of imperialism which is defined as "the government of one people by another." Moreover, practically all of the Asian political systems, weakened by internal dissensions and outside pressures, were crumbling. There arose by this time an enormous difference in wealth and power between the decaying Asian empires and growing European states, enriched through commercial revolution, and bubbling with new strength provided by the industrial revolution in the form of iron and steel ships, heavier naval guns, and more accurate rifles. . . .

The net result of all these economic, political and psychological factors was the greatest land-grab in the history of the world. . . .

. . . The world as it emerged from the Second World War was a different world altogether. If a divided Asia could not withstand the pressure of an aggressive Europe, a divided and warring Europe could not continue to dominate Asia and Africa. The European Powers, which had dominated the world scene for nearly three hundred years, had been pushed aside and were no longer at the centre of the world stage. Out of the ruins of the world holocaust of 1939-1945, the United States and the Soviet Union had emerged with enough strength to dominate the international scene and seriously challenge each other. . . .

There was another significant change: With the weakening of Europe, colonialism collapsed and there emerged numerous independent countries of Asia and

Africa which for a long time had no status and no role in the formulation of international law and, as we have seen, were considered as no more than its objects. For one thing, the erstwhile "backward" China came to be recognized as a Great Power. Although in 1945, of the 51 original members of the United Nations, there were only 13 Asian-African states, their number sharply increased after 1955. Under a strong current of the principle of self-determination and aided by the unusual conditions of the cold war, most of the Asian-African and Pacific countries acquired independence and became full-fledged members of the international society. So that today Europe forms a small minority of this group and a vast majority of the UN membership consists of the thus far neglected and dominated countries of Asia, Africa, and other parts of the world. . . .

Having achieved their political independence, the "new states" of Asia and Africa naturally wanted to improve their lot and increase their political influence. The existence of an international forum, such as the United Nations, where they could make their voices heard, and where they had scope for concerted action, enhanced their power and helped them in pursuing their purposes. They were further helped by the rivalry between the big Powers. As the work of the Security Council got frozen in the chilling atmosphere of the cold war, and with the persistent use and abuse of veto its authority as well as prestige declined, the power and influence of the General Assembly began to rise. . . . With the increase in the powers of the General Assembly, the United Nations Organization changed from an instrument of the Great Powers to a forum for the smaller states to press their claims. This is a phenomenon of tremendous significance in international law. Enjoying formal legal equality with the big Powers in the new "Parliament of Mankind," and of course numerical superiority, the "new" Asian and African states, along with the equally disgruntled Latin American states — the so-called Third World as they came to be called — acquired a new influence in the post-war divided world society. . . . They could make their voices heard in the world forums and hardly lost an opportunity to air their views. Non-aligned to any of the power group as most of these countries were, they aligned themselves to take concerted action and play an important role in the international legal structure in pursuance of their interests. It was only to be expected that the new majority should try to mould the law according to their own views and for the protection of their interests. Not only colonialism, which came to be called a "form of permanent aggression," but several parts of international law of the colonial period came to be challenged. Some of the enlightened European writers themselves conceded that:

> In all positive law is hidden the element of power and the element of interest. Law is
> not the same as power, nor is it the same as interest, but it gives expression to former
> power-relation. Law has the inclination to serve primarily the interests of the powerful.
> "European" international law, the traditional law of nations, makes no exception to this
> rule. It served the interests of the powerful nations.

. . . [I]t came to be questioned if this law could be preserved "even now that the world no longer consists of European states only, does not express the unconscious desire, through rules of law, to maintain a status which can no longer be ensured by power."

Although the international society could not start with a clean slate, and indeed the "new" states did not mean to reject wholesale the existing system of international law, it was reminded afresh that law in order to remain effective must change with the changing society. Law could not be allowed to stagnate.

C.   IS INTERNATIONAL LAW REALLY LAW?

At the beginning of this chapter we anticipated a certain skepticism about the effectiveness of international law. Some believe that international law is a charade: governments comply with it only if convenient to do so and disregard it whenever a contrary interest appears. That view seems to be based on an image of global anarchy in which independent "sovereign" states selfishly contend for unilateral advantage. Some of the traditional skepticism about international law may be attributable to the extensive attention given to the highly indeterminate and often unobserved norms against the use of force, a relatively small part of international law. In addition, the most prominent institutions in this century dedicated to advancing the rule of law among states have not lived up to the expectations of their proponents. The League of Nations failed to prevent war, and the United Nations has often proved unable to take decisive action. Some people may also suspect that international law cannot really be law because there is no effective world court or international police force.

In fact, however, the image of global anarchy is not very accurate, as the abundance of international travel, economic interdependence, and transnational cooperation amply demonstrates. And the emphasis on courts and a police force is misleading. Law derives its force from sources other than those two institutions, even in industrialized societies. For example, people often comply with legal norms because of expectations of reciprocal behavior by other members of the society, or simply out of a belief that the law is legitimate and therefore ought to be obeyed. Moreover, there can be effective sanctions for breaches of international law, even without centralized adjudication and enforcement agencies, such as through arbitration or unilateral "self-help" retaliatory measures.

Professor Henkin describes the role of law in the world:

Louis Henkin, How Nations Behave

13-27 (2d ed. 1979)

As for international law, much misunderstanding is due to a failure to recognize law where it exists. That failure may be due to a narrow conception of law generally. The layman tends to think of domestic law in terms of the traffic policeman, or judicial trials for the thief or murderer. But law is much more and quite different. . . . [I]n domestic society law includes the scheme and structure of government, and the institutions, forms, and procedures whereby a society carries on its daily activities; the concepts that underlie relations between government and individual and between individuals; the status, rights, responsibilities, and obligations of individuals and incorporated and non-incorporated associations and other groups, the relations into which they enter and the consequences of these relations. Men establish families, employ one another, acquire possessions and trade them, make arrangements, join in groups for ill or good, help or hurt each other, with little thought to law and little awareness that there is law that is relevant. By law, society formalizes these relationships, creates new ones, legitimates some and forbids others, determines the content and consequences of relationships. The individual remains hardly or hazily aware that he is enmeshed and governed by "law"— laws of property, tort, contract, crimes, laws of marriage, divorce, family, inheritance, laws of employment, commerce, association; and that there are procedures and institutions and formalities which are ever there and maintain an order in society, although they may assert themselves only at critical points, when relations are established, or change, or break down.

In relations between nations, too, one tends to think of law as consisting of a few prohibitory rules (for instance, that a government may not arrest another's diplomats) or the law of the U.N. Charter prohibiting war. . . . But international law, too, is much more and quite different. Although there is no international "government," there is an international "society"; law includes the structure of that society, its institutions, forms, and procedures for daily activity, the assumptions on which the society is founded and the concepts which permeate it, the status, rights, responsibilities, obligations of the nations which comprise that society, the various relations between them, and the effects of those relations. Through what we call foreign policy, nations establish, maintain, change, or terminate myriads of relations; law — more or less primitive, more or less sophisticated — has developed to formalize these relationships, to regulate them, to determine their consequences. A major purpose of foreign policy for most nations at most times is to maintain international order so that they can pursue their national interests, foreign and domestic. That order depends on an "infrastructure" of agreed assumptions, practices, commitments, expectations, reliances. These too are international law, and they are reflected in all that governments do.

To move from the abstract, consider some of the "givens" of international relations. First, they are relations between nations (states). The nation is the principal unit. All the forms of intercourse, all the institutions, all the terms even, depend on the existence of "nations." . . . That political society is based on the nation is not commonly seen as involving either policy or law; ordinarily, nationhood is the unspoken assumption of political life. But the nation ("state") is not only a political conception; it is also a fundamental legal construct with important consequences. Statehood — who is and shall be a state — has been one of the major political issues of our day. The legal concept of statehood is crucial, of course, when the character of an entity as a state is itself in issue. . . . It was raised when Palestine was partitioned and Israel created and underlies the recent claims of Palestinians to a state of their own. It was entangled in the question of Chinese representation in the United Nations and still bedevils the future of Taiwan. The "nation" has been in issue in differences over recognition of divided countries and their membership in international organizations — China, Korea, Vietnam, Germany. The legal concept and consequences of nationhood underlie the explosion of "self-determination" which ended Western colonialism and transformed the map of the world, and have troubled even the new nations. . . . It still deeply troubles Cyprus, and also Kashmir. It has given new significance to the problem of the "micro-state" or "mini-state."

Relations between nations generally begin with "housekeeping arrangements," including recognition and establishment of diplomatic relations. That these involve law (e.g., in regard to recognition, sovereign and diplomatic immunities) is commonly known, but the importance of this law for foreign policy is commonly depreciated. In fact, this law is basic and indispensable, and taken for granted because it rarely breaks down. The newest of nations promptly adopts it and the most radical scrupulously observes it. The occasional exception confirms the obvious, that there would be no relations with a nation that regularly violated embassies and abused diplomats.

The relations of one nation with another, as soon as they begin, are permeated by basic legal concepts: nationality, national territory, property, torts, contracts, the rights and duties and responsibilities of states. These do not commonly figure in major policy doctrines, nor do they commonly occupy the attentions of diplomats. They too are taken for granted because they are rarely in issue. The concept of territory and territorial sovereignty is not prominent in foreign policy; but every foreign policy assumes the integrity and inviolability of the national territory, and any intentional violation would probably lead to major crisis.

Related to territoriality is the concept of internal sovereignty. Except as limited by international law or treaty, a nation is master in its own territory. That principle is fundamental, and commonly observed. Yet it is in issue whenever there is a claim that internal action violates international law. It figures in disputes about nationalization of alien properties and about violations of human rights. . . .

The concepts of property lie deep in international relations. Property rights are taken for granted in all international trade and finance. When a vessel plies the seas, the assumption is that others will observe the international law prohibiting interference with free navigation, recognizing rights of ownership in property, forbidding torts against persons and property. The United States went to war in 1917, in part because it thought this law was being violated to its detriment.

Contemporary international relations have seen recurrent issues as to the law of the responsibility of states, particularly in regard to the treatment of aliens and their property. But even in times when nationalizations are not everyday occurrences, even when there are no accusations that governments are denying "justice" to aliens, the law on the treatment of foreign nationals pervades relations between nations. Because there is this law (and because it is largely observed), there is tourism and foreign investment; and consular activity and "diplomatic protection" are a common, friendly, continuous part of international intercourse. . . .

Law is also essential to foreign policy and to diplomacy in that it provides mechanisms, forms, and procedures by which nations maintain their relations, carry on trade and other forms of intercourse, resolve differences and disputes. There is international law in the establishment and operation of missions and in communications between governments, in the writing of contracts and other commercial paper, in oil concessions, in tariffs and customs practices, in the registry of vessels, the shipment of goods, the forms of payment, in all the intricacies of international trade and finance. There is law in and about the variety of international conferences. International organization — from the United Nations to the Universal Postal Union — involves legal concepts, and different organizations have contributed substantial law. For settling disputes, the law provides diplomats with claims commissions, arbitration bodies, mediators and conciliators, even courts.

For foreign policy, perhaps the most important legal mechanism is the international agreement, and the most important principle of international law is *pacta sunt servanda:* agreements shall be observed. This principle makes international relations possible. The mass of a nation's foreign relations involve innumerable agreements of different degrees of formality. The diplomat promotes, develops, negotiates, implements various understandings for various ends, from establishing diplomatic relations to trade, aid, allocation of resources, cultural exchange, common standards of weights and measures, to formal alliances affecting national security, cease-fire and disengagement, arms control, and a regime for outer space. The diplomat hardly thinks of these arrangements and understandings as involving law. He does assume that, if agreement is reached, it will probably be observed; if he did not, he would not bother to seek agreement. No doubt, he thinks that nations generally observe their undertakings because that is "done" in international society and because it is generally in the interest of nations to do so. That is law, the lawyer would say. . . .

. . . Even nations that wish to escape from such arrangements are usually compelled to invoke legal principles of escape — whether by reinterpreting the agreement, by attacking its original validity, or by invoking some principle of law to claim that it permits escape or is no longer valid or binding.

In our times, there flourishes a type of international agreement that has added new dimensions to foreign policy and international law. Much of contemporary international law consists of new arrangements, often among large numbers of nations, to promote cooperation for some common aim. In this category one might place the various intergovernmental organizations and institutions, universal or regional — the United Nations, the World Bank and the Monetary Fund, the FAO, UPU, ITU and the IAEA, OECD, [WTO], the International Coffee Agreement and UNCTAD, NATO and the European Economic Community, the OAS and OAU . . . — as well as bilateral aid agreements. One might include, too, arrangements, not exclusively governmental, like the International Telecommunications Satellite Consortium (INTELSAT) or oil concessions. . . .

Law reflected in the assumptions, concepts, institutions, and procedures of international society is not the kind of international law one commonly thinks about because it does not, on its face, direct governments how to behave. But, in fact, all law is intimately related to national behavior. Even that "submerged" law molds the policies of governments. The concept of the nation determines that the United States has relations with Canada, not with Quebec. The concept of territoriality means that the United States can do largely as it likes within the United States, but is sharply restricted in what it can do outside. There are clear prohibitions in the basic legal concepts, in the rights and duties they imply: territoriality, property, tort imply that the United States cannot, at will, invade or violate the territory or seize the property of another nation. Freedom of the seas means that one nation cannot prevent the vessels of others from going their way. Contracts and agreements are not to be broken. Even organizations for cooperative welfare, though commonly distinguished from traditional law of "abstention," impose obligations on members which they must "abstain" from violating: they may not interfere with the international mails; they must pay budget assessments to the FAO. These organizations have also promoted common procedures and minimum standards of national behavior, e.g., in regard to labor, or the treatment of refugees, or basic human rights even for a nation's own citizens.

There is also the law which aims directly at controlling behavior. Governments may not arrest accredited diplomats or deny basic justice to foreign nationals. . . .

The student of foreign affairs may grant, if the lawyer insists, that the law implied in international society gives some direction to national policies and places some limitations on how nations behave. But he remains skeptical of the influence of law as it is commonly and more narrowly conceived, of that law which seeks to control the conduct of nations within the framework of the society of nations. In particular, he questions whether nations really observe the important prohibitory norms of international law or really keep their important agreements. Governments may sometimes act consistently with norms or obligations, but, he insists, only when it is in their interest to do so; and it is their interest, not the law, which governs their behavior. Such skepticism in the diplomat and the policy-maker is sometimes reflected in the foreign policies they promulgate and carry out.

The tendency to dismiss international law reflects impressions sometimes summed up in the conclusion that it is not really law because international society is not really a society: the world of nations is a collection of sovereign states, not an effective body politic which can support effective law. In this judgment are subsumed a number of alleged weaknesses and inadequacies.

The society of nations has no effective law-making body or process. General law depends on consensus: in principle, new law, at least, cannot be imposed on any state; even old law cannot survive if enough states, or a few powerful and influential ones, reject it. New universal law, then, can come about only through long, gradual, uncertain "accretion" by practice and acquiescence, or through multilateral treaties difficult to negotiate and more difficult to get accepted. Law is also slow and difficult to clarify, or amend, or repeal. The law is therefore haphazard and static. As concerns customary law in particular, there is often uncertainty and little confidence as to what it is. The law is also inadequate, for many important actions and relations remain unregulated. There are important disorders — for example, the arms race or the oil embargo — which are not subject to law. In the absence of special undertakings, nations may engage in economic warfare, may boycott, even starve each other. And law has not achieved a welfare society: there is no law requiring social and economic assistance by the very rich to the very poor, or providing community relief even to the starving.

Also lacking is an effective judiciary to clarify and develop the law, to resolve disputes impartially, and to impel nations to observe the law. The International Court of Justice does not satisfy these needs. Its jurisdiction and procedures are starkly insufficient: jurisdiction requires the consent of the parties, and few consent to it; only a minority of nations have accepted the Court's compulsory jurisdiction, some of these with important reservations. . . . The Court's justice is slow, expensive, uncertain: even nations which can invoke the Court's compulsory jurisdiction are reluctant to do so. Nations still prefer the flexibility of diplomacy to the risks of third-party judgment. In the result, few issues of substantial significance to international order ever get to the Court. No one would claim that the Court has a major influence in international affairs.

The greatest deficiency, as many see it, is that international society lacks an executive authority with power to enforce the law. There is no police system whose pervasive presence might deter violation. The society does not consider violations to be crimes or violators criminals, and attaches no stigma which might itself discourage violation. Since nations cannot be made to observe rules and keep promises, they will not do so when they deem it in their interest not to do so. . . .

In sum, to many an observer, governments seem largely free to decide whether to agree to new law, whether to accept another nation's view of existing law, whether to comply with agreed law. International law, then, is voluntary and only hortatory. It must always yield to national interest. Surely, no nation will submit to law any questions involving its security or independence, even its power, prestige, influence. Inevitably, a diplomat holding these views will be reluctant to build policy on law he deems ineffective. He will think it unrealistic and dangerous to enact laws which will not be observed, to build institutions which will not be used, to base his government's policy on the expectation that other governments will observe law or agreement. Since other nations do not attend to law except when it is in their interest, the diplomat might not see why his government should do so at the sacrifice of important interests. He might be impatient with his lawyers who tell him that the government may not do what he would like to see done.

These depreciations of international law challenge much of what the international lawyer does. Indeed, some lawyers seem to despair for international law until there is world government or at least effective international organization. But most international lawyers are not dismayed. Unable to deny the limitations of international law, they insist that these are not critical, and they deny many of the alleged implications of these limitations. If they must admit that the cup of law is half-empty, they stress that it is half-full. They point to similar deficiencies in many domestic legal systems. They reject definitions (commonly associated with the legal philosopher John Austin) that deny the title of law to any but the command of a sovereign, enforceable and enforced as such. They insist that despite inadequacies in legislative method, international law has grown and developed and changed. If international law is difficult to make, yet it is made; if its growth is slow, yet it grows. If there is no judiciary as effective as in some developed national systems, there is an International Court of Justice whose judgments and opinions, while few, are respected. The inadequacies of the judicial system are in some measure supplied by other bodies: international disputes are resolved and law is developed through a network of arbitrations by continuing or ad hoc tribunals. National courts help importantly to determine, clarify, develop international law. Political bodies like the Security Council and the General Assembly of the United Nations also apply law, their actions and resolutions interpret and develop the law, their judgments help to deter violations in some measure. If there is no international executive to enforce international law, the United Nations has some enforcement powers and there is "horizontal enforcement" in the reactions of other nations. The gaps in substantive law are real and many and require continuing effort to fill them, but they do not vitiate the force and effect of the law that exists, in the international society that is.

Above all, the lawyer will insist, critics of international law ask and answer the wrong questions. What matters is not whether the international system has legislative, judicial, or executive branches, corresponding to those we have become accustomed to seek in a domestic society; what matters is whether international law is reflected in the policies of nations and in relations between nations. The question is not whether there is an effective legislature; it is whether there is law that responds and corresponds to the changing needs of a changing society. The question is not whether there is an effective judiciary, but whether disputes are resolved in an orderly fashion in accordance with international law. Most important, the question is not whether law is enforceable or even effectively enforced; rather, whether law is observed, whether it governs or influences behavior, whether international behavior reflects stability and order. The fact is, lawyers insist, that nations have accepted important limitations on their sovereignty, that they have observed these norms and undertakings, that the result has been substantial order in international relations.

In the end, the issues do not turn on theoretical answers to theoretical questions, or on unexamined impressions or assertions about the fate and influence of law in the chancelleries of nations. We must examine as well as we can the role that law, in fact, plays in daily diplomacy, the extent to which law, in fact, affects the behavior of nations, the contribution which law, in fact, makes to order and welfare.

Questions

1. Summarize Henkin's main points. Has he convinced you that international law is "law"? That it has a significant effect on national behavior?

2. Is it accurate to describe compliance with international law as "voluntary"? Why is there compliance with law in domestic systems? Are the reasons for compliance in the international system different? What sanctions can be imposed for violations of international law?

3. What differences are there between the legal institutions in the international community and those in domestic systems, such as in the United States? What are the similarities? Is a centralized legislature necessary in order for there to be law? How about a court with general, compulsory jurisdiction? An executive agency with enforcement powers?

4. It is easy to think of examples, of course, in which nations have acted in violation of international law. Does this show that international law is not really "law"? Is it easy to think of examples of violations of domestic law?

5. Would it be accurate to say that international law is law because nations regard it as law? In what ways do nations treat international law as law? Do you think that law as such influences government decision-makers? Or just fear of sanctions? Or self-interest? Or beliefs about what is morally right? Can you separate these factors?

6. Doesn't much of international law (as described by Henkin) confer reciprocal rights on nations and therefore naturally lend itself to acceptance by government decision-makers? If so, does this disprove that international law is law? Can you think of situations in which a nation might be tempted to violate a reciprocal international legal norm — governing, for example, protection of diplomats, rights over the sea, or nonuse of force? Are there examples of international law rules that do not confer reciprocal rights?

7. Assume that you have agreed to represent an individual on death row in Texas. You find out that this individual is a citizen of Mexico who was convicted of murder several years ago in a Texas state court and sentenced to death. You do some research and discover that there is a treaty called the Vienna Convention on Consular Relations, and that both Mexico and the United States (along with many other countries) are parties to this treaty. The treaty provides that if a member country arrests and detains a citizen of another member country, the arrested person shall be informed "without delay" that they have the right to contact their country's consulate and request assistance. The treaty does not specify, however, what if any remedy is available if a nation fails to comply with this requirement. You find out that

Texas authorities never informed your client of this right and that he has not in fact communicated with the Mexican consulate.

What remedies might you seek for the apparent violation of this treaty provision? Where would you go to seek these remedies? What role, if any, will the Mexican government need to play? In terms of enforceability, how does the treaty right here compare with U.S. constitutional rights, such as the implied right under the Fifth Amendment to a *Miranda* warning? In representing your client, what additional legal or factual information would you like to have? As discussed in Chapter 4, Mexico recently brought an action against the United States in the International Court of Justice on behalf of a group of Mexican citizens on death row in various U.S. states, alleging that these citizens had not been given consular notice as required by the Vienna Convention.

Most international law is found either in international agreements or in rules based on custom. That much is not controversial. The questions that have haunted international law advocates, and that have fueled the skepticism of critics, are whether international law is properly called "law," and why it is binding on "sovereign" states. This debate has often been couched in terms of the legal theories (summarized below) known as "positivism" and "natural law."

Of course, if "sovereign state" is defined as one that is not subject to law, the definition answers the question. Some commentators (the positivists) have tried to accept that definition but then to create a theory of why sovereign states are still bound by international law based on the proposition that such states *consent* to be bound by international law. Restatement section 102, quoted above, seems to follow this path. The theory is obviously incomplete, to say the least, because it does not explain why consent is binding or why it cannot be revoked.

Other commentators have sought to base the validity of international law on some fundamental principle, like earlier natural law scholastics who appealed to the commands of God, or those who rested their arguments on right, reason, and a secular law of nature. Professor Brierly summarizes the traditional debate:

J.L. Brierly, The Law of Nations

49-56 (6th ed., Humphrey Waldock ed., 1963)

Traditionally there are two rival doctrines which attempt to answer the question why states should be bound to observe the rules of international law.

The doctrine of "fundamental rights" is a corollary of the doctrine of the "state of nature," in which men are supposed to have lived before they formed themselves into political communities or states; for states, not having formed themselves into a super-state, are still supposed by the adherents of this doctrine to be living in such a condition. It teaches that the principles of international law, or the primary principles upon which the others rest, can be deduced from the essential nature of the state. Every state, by the very fact that it is a state, is endowed with certain fundamental, or inherent, or natural, rights. Writers differ in enumerating what these rights are, but generally five rights are claimed, namely self-preservation, independence, equality, respect, and intercourse. It is obvious that the doctrine of fundamental rights is merely the old doctrine of the natural rights of man transferred to states. . . .

[Brierly then criticizes the idea of "natural" rights on the grounds that rights can only exist as part of a legal system. Moreover, the natural rights doctrine emphasizes individual rights at the expense of equally important social bonds.]

. . . [I]n the society of states the need is not for greater liberty for the individual states, but for a strengthening of the social bond between them, not for the clamant assertion of their rights, but for a more insistent reminder of their obligations towards one another. Finally, the doctrine is really a denial of the possibility of development in international relations; when it asserts that such qualities as independence and equality are inherent in the very nature of states, it overlooks the fact that their attribution to states is merely a stage in an historical process; we know that until modern times states were not regarded either as independent or equal, and we have no right to assume that the process of development has stopped. On the contrary it is not improbable, and it is certainly desirable, that there should be a movement towards the closer interdependence of states, and therefore away from the state of things which this doctrine would stabilize as though it were part of the fixed order of nature.

The doctrine of positivism, on the other hand, teaches that international law is the sum of the rules by which states have *consented* to be bound, and that nothing can be law to which they have not consented. This consent may be given expressly, as in a treaty, or it may be implied by a state acquiescing in a customary rule. But the assumption that international law consists of nothing save what states have consented to is an inadequate account of the system as it can be seen in actual operation, and even if it were a complete account of the contents of the law, it would fail to explain why the law is binding. . . . [A] customary rule is observed, not because it has been consented to, but because it is believed to be binding, and whatever may be the explanation or the justification for that belief, its binding force does not depend, and is not felt by those who follow it to depend, on the approval of the individual or the state to which it is addressed. Further, in the practical administration of international law, states are continually treated as bound by principles which they cannot, except by the most strained construction of the facts, be said to have consented to, and it is unreasonable, when we are seeking the true nature of international rules, to force the facts into a preconceived theory instead of finding a theory which will explain the facts as we have them. For example, a state which has newly come into existence does not in any intelligible sense *consent* to accept international law; it does not regard itself, and it is not regarded by others, as having any option in the matter. The truth is that states do not regard their international legal relations as resulting from consent, except when the consent is express, and that the theory of implied consent is a fiction invented by the theorist; . . . even if the theory did not involve a distortion of the facts, it would fail as an explanation. For consent cannot of itself create an obligation; it can do so only within a system of law which declares that consent duly given, as in a treaty or a contract, shall be binding on the party consenting. To say that the rule *pacta servanda sunt* is itself founded on consent is to argue in a circle. A consistently consensual theory again would have to admit that if consent is withdrawn, the obligation created by it comes to an end. . . .

There need be no mystery about the source of the obligation to obey international law. The same problem arises in any system of law and it can never be solved by a merely *juridical* explanation. The answer must be sought outside the law, and it is for legal philosophy to provide it. The notion that the validity of international law raises some peculiar problem arises from the confusion which the doctrine of sovereignty has introduced into international legal theory. Even when we do not believe in the absoluteness of state sovereignty we have allowed ourselves to be persuaded that the fact of their sovereignty makes it necessary to look for some specific quality, not to be found in other kinds of law, in the law to which states are subject. We have accepted a false idea of the state as a personality with a life and a will of its own, still living in a "state of nature," and we contrast this with the "political" state in which individual men have come to live. But this assumed condition of states is the very negation of law, and no ingenuity can explain how the two can exist together. It is a notion as false analytically as it admittedly is historically. The truth is that states are not persons, however convenient it may often be to personify them; they are merely *institutions,* that is to say, organizations which men establish among themselves for securing certain objects, of which the most fundamental is a system of order within which the activities of their common life can be carried on. They have no wills except the wills of the individual human beings who direct their affairs; and they exist not in a political vacuum but in continuous political relations with one another. Their subjection to law is as yet imperfect, though it is real as far as it goes; the problem of extending it is one of great practical difficulty, but it is not one of intrinsic impossibility. There are important differences between international law and the law under which individuals live in a state, but those differences do not lie in metaphysics or in any mystical qualities of the entity called state sovereignty.

The international lawyer then is under no special obligation to explain why the law with which he is concerned should be binding upon its subjects. If it were true that the essence of all law is a command, and that what makes the law of the state binding is that for some reason, for which no satisfactory explanation can ever be given, the will of the person issuing a command is superior to that of the person receiving it, then indeed it would be necessary to look for some special explanation of the binding force of international law. But that view of the nature of law has been long discredited. If we are to explain why any kind of law is binding, we cannot avoid some such assumption as that which the Middle Ages made, and which Greece and Rome had made before them, when they spoke of natural law. The ultimate explanation of the binding force of all law is that man, whether he is a single individual or whether he is associated with other men in a state, is constrained, in so far as he is a reasonable being, to believe that order and not chaos is the governing principle of the world in which he has to live.

In thinking about the distinction between the natural law and positivist approaches, consider the following two decisions from early in U.S. history addressing the legality under international law of the slave trade:

United States v. La Jeune Eugenie

26 F. Cas. 832 (D. Mass. 1822)

Natural Law

STORY, Circuit Justice. . . .

Now the law of nations may be deduced, first, from the general principles of right and justice, applied to the concerns of individuals, and thence to the relations and duties of nations; or, secondly, in things indifferent or questionable, from the customary observances and recognitions of civilized nations; or, lastly, from the conventional or positive law, that regulates the intercourse between states. What, therefore, the law of nations is, does not rest upon mere theory, but may be considered as modified by practice, or ascertained by the treaties of nations at different periods. It does not follow, therefore, that because a principle cannot be found settled by the consent or practice of nations at one time, it is to be concluded, that at no subsequent period the principle can be considered as incorporated into the public code of nations. Nor is it to be admitted, that no principle belongs to the law of nations, which is not universally recognised, as such, by all civilized communities, or even by those constituting, what may be called, the Christian states of Europe. Some doctrines, which we, as well as Great Britain, admit to belong to the law of nations, are of but recent origin and application, and have not, as yet, received any public or general sanction in other nations; and yet they are founded in such a just view of the duties and rights of nations, belligerent and neutral, that we have not hesitated to enforce them by the penalty of confiscation. There are other doctrines, again, which have met the decided hostility of some of the European states, enlightened as well as powerful, such as the right of search, and the rule, that free ships do not make free goods, which, nevertheless, both Great Britain and the United States maintain, and in my judgment with unanswerable arguments, as settled rules in the law of prize, and scruple not to apply them to the ships of all other nations. And yet, if the general custom of nations in modern times, or even in the present age, recognized an opposite doctrine, it could not, perhaps, be affirmed, that that practice did not constitute a part, or, at least, a modification, of the law of nations. But I think it may be unequivocally affirmed, that every doctrine, that may be fairly deduced by correct reasoning from the rights and duties of nations, and the nature of moral obligation, may theoretically be said to exist in the law of nations; and unless it be relaxed or waived by the consent of nations, which may be evidenced by their general practice and customs, it may be enforced by a court of justice, whenever it arises in judgment. And I may go farther and say, that no practice whatsoever can obliterate the fundamental distinction between right and wrong, and that every nation is at liberty to apply to another the correct principle, whenever both nations by their public acts recede from such practice, and admits the injustice or cruelty of it.

Now in respect to the African slave trade, such as it has been described to be, and in fact is, in its origin, progress, and consummation, it cannot admit of serious question, that it is founded in a violation of some of the first principles, which ought to govern nations. It is repugnant to the great principles of Christian duty, the dictates of natural religion, the obligations of good faith and morality, and the eternal maxims of social justice. When any trade can be truly said to have these ingredients, it is impossible, that it can be consistent with any system of law, that purports to rest on the authority of reason or revelation. And it is sufficient to stamp any trade as interdicted by public law, when it can be justly affirmed, that it is repugnant to the general principles of justice and humanity. Now there is scarcely a single maritime nation of Europe, that has not in the most significant terms, in the most deliberate and solemn conferences, acts, or treaties, acknowledged the injustice and inhumanity of this trade; and pledged itself to promote its abolition. I need scarcely advert to the conferences at Vienna, at Aix-la-Chapelle, and at London, on this interesting subject, as they have been cited at the argument of this cause, and authenticated by our own government, to show what may be emphatically called the sense of Europe upon this point. France, in particular, at the conferences at Vienna, in 1815, engaged to use "all the means at her disposal, and to act in the employment of these means with all the zeal and perseverance due to so great and noble a cause" (the abolition of the slave trade). And accordingly, in the treaty of peace between her and Great Britain, France, expressing her concurrence without reserve in the sentiments of his Britannic majesty with respect to this traffic, admits it to be "repugnant to the principles of natural justice, and of the enlightened age, in which we live"; and, at a short period afterwards, the government of France informed the British government, that it had "issued directions in order, that on the part of France the traffic in slaves may cease from the present time everywhere and forever." The conduct and opinions of Great Britain, honorably and zealously, and I may add, honestly, as she has been engaged in promoting the universal abolition of the trade, are too notorious, to require a pointed enumeration. She has through her parliament expressed her abhorrence of the trade in the most marked terms, as repugnant to justice and humanity; she has punished it as a felony, when carried on by her subjects; and she has recognized through her judicial tribunals the doctrine, that it is repugnant to the law of nations. Our own country, too, has firmly and earnestly pressed forward in the same career. The trade has been reprobated and punished, as far as our authority extended, from a very early period of the government; and by a very recent statute, to mark at once its infamy and repugnance to the law of nations, it has been raised in the catalogue of public crimes to the bad eminence of piracy. I think, therefore, that I am justified in saying, that at the present moment the traffic is vindicated by no nation, and is admitted by almost all commercial nations as incurably unjust and inhuman. It appears to me, therefore, that in an American court of judicature, I am bound to consider the trade an offence against the universal law of society and in all cases, where it is not protected by a foreign government, to deal with it as an offence carrying with it the penalty of confiscation. And I cannot but think, notwithstanding the assertion at the bar to the contrary, that this doctrine is neither novel nor alarming. That it stands on principles of sound sense and general policy, and, above all, of moral justice. And I confess, that I should be somewhat startled, if any nation, sincerely anxious for the abolition, and earnest in its duty, should interpose its influence to arrest its universal adoption.

The Antelope

23 U.S. (10 Wheat.) 66 (1825)

Legal positivism

Mr. Chief Justice MARSHALL. . . .

The question, whether the slave trade is prohibited by the law of nations has been seriously propounded, and both the affirmative and negative of the proposition have been maintained with equal earnestness.

That it is contrary to the law of nature will scarcely be denied. That every man has a natural right to the fruits of his own labour, is generally admitted; and that no other person can rightfully deprive him of those fruits, and appropriate them against his will, seems to be the necessary result of this admission. But from the earliest times war has existed, and war confers rights in which all have acquiesced. Among the most enlightened nations of antiquity, one of these was, that the victor might enslave the vanquished. This, which was the usage of all, could not be pronounced repugnant to the law of nations, which is certainly to be tried by the test of general usage. That which has received the assent of all, must be the law of all.

Slavery, then, has its origin in force; but as the world has agreed that it is a legitimate result of force, the state of things which is thus produced by general consent, cannot be pronounced unlawful.

Throughout Christendom, this harsh rule has been exploded, and war is no longer considered as giving a right to enslave captives. But this triumph of humanity has not been universal. The parties to the modern law of nations do not propagate their principles by force; and Africa has not yet adopted them. Throughout the whole extent of that immense continent, so far as we know its history, it is still the law of nations that prisoners are slaves. Can those who have themselves renounced this law, be permitted to participate in its effects by purchasing the beings who are its victims?

Whatever might be the answer of a moralist to this question, a jurist must search for its legal solution, in those principles of action which are sanctioned by the usages, the national acts, and the general assent, of that portion of the world of which he considers himself as a part, and to whose law the appeal is made. If we resort to this standard as the test of international law, the question, as has already been observed, is decided in favour of the legality of the trade. Both Europe and America embarked in it; and for nearly two centuries, it was carried on without opposition, and without censure. A jurist could not say, that a practice thus supported was illegal, and that those engaged in it might be punished, either personally, or by deprivation of property.

Notes and Questions

1. How does Story's view of international law in *La Jeune Eugenie* compare with Marshall's view of international law in *The Antelope?* Who is right? Should some rules of international law bind nations regardless of whether they consent to the rules? Or should international law be purely like contract law, only binding if nations agree?

2. Why is domestic law binding? What are the sources of domestic criminal law, contract law, and constitutional law? Why are those bodies of law generally followed and considered binding? Doesn't the validity of any legal norm ultimately rest on some form of myth or partial myth — for example, that a legislature reflects the will of the people or that a court applies neutral principles of law or legislative intent? Is international law any different? Is the role of sanctions significantly different in the case of international law?

3. Isn't consent an appealing myth to explain the binding nature of international law? It is used to explain the value of personal choice and the basis of contract and is not limited to Western civilization. What are the problems with maintaining that the consent of a state binds it and its people?

4. Why is international law binding under a natural law approach? If the basis of authority is religion or "reason" or "nature," does it follow that international law is based on Western cultural values and is therefore illegitimate with respect to the rest of the world?

5. Consider the following argument by the late Professor Jonathan Charney:

The international community of the late-twentieth century faces an expanding need to develop universal norms to address global concerns. Perhaps one of most salient of these concerns is to protect the earth's environment. While many environmentally harmful activities result only in local damage, others have an impact far beyond the boundaries of the states in which they take place and may cause damage to the earth's environment as a whole. For example, the discharge of some substances into the atmosphere may adversely affect the global climate or the ozone layer. Discharges that pollute the common spaces of the oceans may also have a global impact and thus raise similar concerns. Current threats to the environment highlight the importance of establishing norms to control activities that endanger all nations and peoples, regardless of where the activities take place. Acts of international terrorism, the commission of international crimes (such as genocide and war crimes), and the use of nuclear weapons pose similar global problems and have been on the international agenda for some time.

To resolve such problems, it may be necessary to establish new rules that are binding on all subjects of international law regardless of the attitude of any particular state. For unless all states are bound, an exempted recalcitrant state could act as a spoiler for the entire international community. Thus, states that are not bound by international laws designed to combat universal environmental threats could become havens for the harmful activities concerned. Such states might have an economic advantage over states that are bound because they would not have to bear the costs of the requisite environmental protection. They would be free riders on the system and would benefit from the environmentally protective measures introduced by others at some cost. Furthermore, the example of such free riders might undermine the system by encouraging other states not to participate, and could thus derail the entire effort. Similarly, in the case of international terrorism, one state that serves as a safe haven for terrorists can threaten all. War crimes, apartheid, or genocide committed in one state might threaten international peace and security worldwide. Consequently, for certain circumstances it may be incumbent on the international community to establish international law that is binding on all states regardless of any one state's disposition.

Jonathan I. Charney, Universal International Law, 87 Am. J. Int'l L. 529 (1993). Do you agree with Professor Charney's assessment? How can the international community go about creating this sort of universal international law? How would this law be enforced? When such law is invoked against them, will nations regard it as legitimate?

Professor Franck offers an explanation of the power of international law and its basis in legitimacy:

Thomas M. Franck, Legitimacy in the International System
82 Am. J. Intl. L. 705 (1988)

The surprising thing about international law is that nations ever obey its strictures or carry out its mandates. . . .

Why should rules, unsupported by an effective structure of coercion comparable to a national police force, nevertheless elicit so much compliance, even against perceived self-interest, on the part of sovereign states? Perhaps finding an answer to this question can help us to find a key to a better, yet realistic, world order. The answer, if there is one, may also incidentally prove useful in designing more widely obeyed, less coerced, laws for ordering the lives of our cities and states.

A series of events connected with the role of the U.S. Navy in protecting U.S.-fla11gged vessels in the Persian Gulf serves to illustrate the paradoxical phenomenon of uncoerced compliance in a situation where the rule conflicts with perceived self-interest. Early in 1988, the Department of Defense became aware of a ship approaching the gulf with a load of Chinese-made Silkworm missiles en route to Iran. The Department believed the successful delivery of these potent weapons would increase materially the danger to both protected and protecting U.S. ships in the region. It therefore argued for permission to intercept the delivery. The Department of State countered that such a search and seizure on the high seas, under the universally recognized rules of war and neutrality, would constitute aggressive blockade, an act tantamount to a declaration of war against Iran. In the event, the delivery ship and its cargo of missiles were allowed to pass. Deference to systemic rules had won out over tactical advantage in the internal struggle for control of U.S. policy.*

Why should this have been so? In the absence of a world government and a global coercive power to enforce its laws, why did the U.S. Government, with its evident power to do as it wished, choose to "play by the rules" despite the considerable short-term strategic advantage to be gained by seizing the Silkworms before they could be delivered? Why did preeminent American power defer to the rules of the sanctionless system? At least part of the answer to this question, quietly given by the State Department to the Department of Defense, is that the international rules of neutrality have attained a high degree of recognized legitimacy and must not be violated lightly. Specifically, they are well understood, enjoy a long pedigree and are part of a consistent framework of rules — the *jus in bello* — governing and restraining the use of force in conflicts. To violate a set of rules of such widely recognized legitimacy, the State Department argued, would transform the U.S. posture in the gulf from that of a neutral to one of belligerency. That could end Washington's role as an honest broker seeking to promote peace negotiations. It would also undermine the carefully crafted historic "rules of the game" applicable to wars, rules that are widely perceived to be in the interest of all states.

Such explanations for deferring to a rule in preference to taking a short-term advantage are the policymaker's equivalent of the philosopher's quest for a theory of legitimacy. Washington voluntarily chose to obey a rule in the Persian Gulf conflict. Yet it does not always obey all international rules. Some rules are harder to disobey — more persuasive in their pull to compliance — than others. This is known intuitively by the legions of Americans who deliberately underreport the dutiable price of goods purchased abroad, and by the aficionados who smuggle Cuban cigars into the country behind pocket handkerchiefs, but would not otherwise commit criminal fraud. That some rules *in themselves* seem to exert more pull to compliance than others is the starting point in the search for a theory of legitimacy. . . .

Most students of law, power and structure in society have sought to identify other characteristics [besides power] that conduce to the rule of law. . . .

---

* [A similar event occurred in December 2002 when U.S. and Spanish authorities stopped a North Korean freighter bound for Yemen and discovered that it was carrying Scud missiles (see Chapter 9). After a protest by Yemen's president, the Bush Administration decided to release the vessel, noting that international law did not prohibit the delivery of the missiles to Yemen. –EDS.]

Four elements — the indicators of rule legitimacy in the community of states — are identified and studied in this essay. They are *determinacy, symbolic validation, coherence* and *adherence* (to a normative hierarchy). To the extent rules exhibit these properties, they appear to exert a strong pull on states to comply with their commands. To the extent these elements are not present, rules seem to be easier to avoid by a state tempted to pursue its short-term self-interest. This is not to say that the legitimacy of a rule can be deduced solely by counting how often it is obeyed or disobeyed. While its legitimacy may exert a powerful pull on state conduct, yet other pulls may be stronger in a particular circumstance. The chance to take a quick, decisive advantage may overcome the counterpull of even a highly legitimate rule. In such circumstances, legitimacy is indicated not by obedience, but by the discomfort disobedience induces in the violator. (Student demonstrations sometimes are a sensitive indicator of such discomfort.) The variable to watch is not compliance but the strength of the compliance pull, whether or not the rule achieves actual compliance in any one case.

Each rule has an inherent pull power that is independent of the circumstances in which it is exerted, and that varies from rule to rule. This pull power is its index of legitimacy. For example, the rule that makes it improper for one state to infiltrate spies into another state in the guise of diplomats is formally acknowledged by almost every state, yet it enjoys so low a degree of legitimacy as to exert virtually no pull towards compliance. As Schachter observes, "some 'laws,' though enacted properly, have so low a degree of probable compliance that they are treated as 'dead letters' and . . . some treaties, while properly concluded, are considered 'scraps of paper.' " By way of contrast, we have noted, the rules pertaining to belligerency and neutrality actually exerted a very high level of pull on Washington in connection with the Silkworm missile shipment in the Persian Gulf.

The study of legitimacy thus focuses on the inherent capacity of a rule to exert pressure on states to comply. This focus on the properties of rules, of course, is not a self-sufficient account of the socialization process. How rules are made, interpreted and applied is part of a dynamic, expansive and complex set of social phenomena. That complexity can be approached, however, by beginning with the rules themselves. . . .

Perhaps the most self-evident of all characteristics making for legitimacy is textual *determinacy*. What is meant by this is the ability of the text to convey a clear message, to appear transparent in the sense that one can see through the language to the meaning. Obviously, rules with a readily ascertainable meaning have a better chance than those that do not to regulate the conduct of those to whom the rule is addressed or exert a compliance pull on their policymaking process. Those addressed will know precisely what is expected of them, which is a necessary first step towards compliance. . . .

Indeterminacy . . . has costs. Indeterminate normative standards not only make it harder to know what conformity is expected, but also make it easier to justify noncompliance. Put conversely, the more determinate the standard, the more difficult it is to resist the pull of the rule to compliance and to justify noncompliance. Since few persons or states wish to be perceived as acting in obvious violation of a generally recognized rule of conduct, they may try to resolve the conflicts between the demands of a rule and their desire not to be fettered, by "interpreting" the rule permissively. A determinate rule is less elastic and thus less amenable to such evasive strategy than an indeterminate one. . . .

The degree of determinacy of a rule directly affects the degree of its perceived legitimacy. A rule that prohibits the doing of "bad things" lacks legitimacy because it fails to communicate what is expected, except within a very small constituency in which "bad" has achieved a high degree of culturally induced specificity. To be legitimate, a rule must communicate what conduct is permitted and what conduct is out of bounds. These bookends should be close enough together to inhibit incipient violators from offering self-serving exculpatory definitions of the rule. When almost everyone scoffs at such an exculpation, the outer boundary of the rule's determinacy has been established.

There is another sense in which determinacy increases the legitimacy of a rule text. A rule of conduct that is highly transparent — its normative content exhibiting great clarity — actually *encourages* gratification deferral and rule compliance. States, in their relations with one another, frequently find themselves tempted to violate a rule of conduct in order to take advantage of a sudden opportunity. If they do not do so, but choose, instead, to obey the rule and forgo that gratification, it is likely to be because of their longer term interests in seeing a potentially useful rule reinforced. They can visualize future situations in which it will operate to their advantage. But they will only defer the attainable short-term gain if the rule is sufficiently specific to support reasonable expectations that benefit can be derived in a contingent future by strengthening the rule in the present instance. . . .

As determinacy is the linguistic or literary-structural component of legitimacy, so *symbolic validation, ritual* and *pedigree* provide its cultural and anthropological dimension. As with determinacy, so here, the legitimacy of the rule — its ability to exert pull to compliance and to command voluntary obedience — is to be examined in the light of its ability to communicate. In this instance, however, what is to be communicated is not so much content as *authority:* the authority of a rule, the authority of the originator of a validating communication and, at times, the authority bestowed on the recipient of the communication. The communication of authority, moreover, is symbolic rather than literal. We shall refer to these symbolically validating communications as cues.

These three concepts — symbolic validation, ritual and pedigree — are related, but not identical. The *symbolic validation* of a rule, or of a rule-making process or institution, occurs when a signal is used as a cue to elicit compliance with a command. The cue serves as a surrogate for enunciated reasons for such obedience. The singing of the national anthem, for example, is a vocal and (on public occasions) a visual signal symbolically reinforcing the citizen's relationship to the state, a relationship of rights and duties. This compliance reinforcement need not be spelled out in the actual words of the anthem (as it is not in the commonly used stanza of the American one). The act of corporate singing itself is a sufficient cue to validate the fabric of regularized relationships that are implicated in good citizenship. We are not really singing about bombs bursting in the night air, but about free and secret elections, the marketplace of ideas, the rule of valid laws and impartial judges.

Ritual is a specialized form of symbolic validation marked by ceremonies, often — but not necessarily — mystical, that provide unenunciated reasons or cues for eliciting compliance with the commands of persons or institutions. The entry of the mace into the British House of Commons is intended to call to mind the Commons's long and successful struggle to capture control of lawmaking power from the Crown. It functions as a much more direct, literal kind of symbolic validation than the "Star-Spangled Banner." Ritual is often presented as drama, to communicate to a community its unity, its values, its uniqueness in both the exclusive and the inclusive sense.

Describing past trends of decision?

All ritual is a form of symbolic validation, but the converse is not necessarily true. *Pedigree* is a different subset of cues that seek to enhance the compliance pull of rules or rule-making institutions by emphasizing their historical origins, their cultural or anthropological deep-rootedness. An example is the practice of "recognition." When a government recognizes a new regime, or when the United Nations admits a new state to membership, this partly symbolic act has broad significance. It endows the new entity with a range of entitlements and duties, the concomitants of sovereignty. The capacity of states, and, nowadays, perhaps also of the United Nations, to confer sovereignty and its incidents in this fashion derives not from some treaty or other specific agreement but from the ancient practice of states and groupings of states, which legitimizes the exercise of this power. . . .

Symbolic validation, like determinacy, serves to legitimize rules. But like determinacy, symbolic validation is not quite as simple a notion as it may initially appear. For example, ... a pedigree only confers actual rights and duties when the standards for pedigreeing are applied *coherently*. When, on the contrary, symbols, ritual and pedigree are dispensed capriciously, the desired effect of legitimization may not accrue.

Both determinacy and symbolic validation are connected to a further variable: coherence. The effect of incoherence on symbolic validation can be illustrated by reference to diplomatic practices pertaining to the ritual validation of governments and states. The most important act of pedigreeing in the international system is the deep-rooted, traditional act that endows a new government, or a new state, with symbolic status. When the endowing is done by individual governments, it is known as *recognition*. The symbolic conferral of status is also performed collectively through a global organization like the United Nations when the members vote to admit a new nation to membership, or when the General Assembly votes to accept the credentials of the delegates representing a new government. . . .

To recapitulate: an act of recognition, the symbolic validation of a state or regime, has the capacity to bestow, symbolically, rights and duties on the recognized entity when, *but only if,* it is done in accordance with the applicable principled rules and procedures. Such pedigreed recognition, and its corporate UN equivalent, is everywhere accorded great weight. On the other hand, when the rules and standards for validation are violated, or are themselves unprincipled and capricious, then symbolic validation fails in its objective of bestowing status. Moreover, when validation is seen to be capricious, a failure to validate will do more to undermine the legitimacy of the validating process than of the state or government thus deprived of symbolic validation. . . .

There is another aspect of coherence. It encompasses the further notion that a rule, standard or validating ritual gathers force if it is seen to be connected to a network of other rules by an underlying general principle. . . .

By focusing on the connections between specific rules and general underlying principles, we have emphasized the horizontal aspect of our central notion of a community of legitimate rules. However, there are vertical aspects of this community that have even more significant impact on the legitimacy of rules. . . .

According to Dworkin, a true community, as distinguished from a mere rabble, or even a system of random primary rules of obligation, is one in which the members

> accept that they are governed by common principles, not just by rules hammered out in political compromise. . . . Members of a society of principle accept that their political rights and duties are not exhausted by the particular decisions their political institutions have reached, but depend, more generally, on the scheme of principles those decisions presuppose and endorse. So each member accepts that others have rights and that he has duties flowing from that scheme. . . .

Nor are these rights and duties "conditional on his wholehearted approval of that scheme; these obligations arise from the historical fact that his community has adopted that scheme, . . . not the assumption that he would have chosen it were the choice entirely his."

Moreover, the community "commands that no one be left out, that we are all in politics together for better or worse." And its legitimizing requirement of rule integrity "assumes that each person is as worthy as any other, that each must be treated with equal concern according to some coherent conception of what that means."

Does that accurately describe the social condition of the nations of the world in their interactive mode? The description does not assume harmony or an absence of strife. According to Dworkin, an "association of principle is not automatically a just community; its conception of equal concern may be defective." What a rule community, a community of principle, does is to validate behavior in accordance with rules and applications of rules that confirm principled coherence and adherence, rather than acknowledging only the power of power. A rule community operates in conformity not only with primary rules but also with secondary ones — rules about rules — which are generated by valid legislative and adjudicative institutions. Finally, a community accepts its ultimate secondary rules of recognition not consensually, but as an inherent concomitant of membership status.

In the world of nations, each of these described conditions of a sophisticated community is observable today, even though imperfectly. This does not mean that its rules will never be disobeyed. It does mean, however, that it is usually possible to distinguish rule compliance from rule violation, and a valid rule or ruling from an invalid one. It also means that it is not necessary to await the millennium of Austinian-type world government to proceed with constructing — perfecting — a system of rules and institutions that will exhibit a powerful pull to compliance and a self-enforcing degree of legitimacy.

Professor Koh discusses why states comply with international law (going beyond self-interest and the force of legitimacy) in the context of recent developments in international law.

Harold Hongju Koh, Why Do Nations Obey International Law?

106 Yale L.J. 2599 (1997)

By the 1970s and '80s, the legal landscape had altered significantly. The growth of international regimes and institutions, the proliferation of nonstate actors, and the increasing interpenetration of domestic and international systems inaugurated the era of "transnational relations," defined by one scholar as "regular interactions across national boundaries ari[sing] when at least one actor is a non-state agent or does not operate on behalf of a national government or an intergovernmental organization." Multinational enterprises, nongovernmental organizations, and private individuals reemerged as significant actors on the transnational stage. . . . Instead of focusing narrowly on nation-states as global actors, scholars began to look as well as transnational networks among nonstate actors, international institutions, and domestic political structures as important mediating forces in international society.

The post-Cold War era has seen international law, transnational actors, decisional fora, and modes of regulation mutate into fascinating hybrid forms. International law now comprises a complex blend of customary, positive, declarative, and "soft" law, which seeks not simply to ratify existing practice, but to elevate it. As sovereignty has declined in importance, global decisionmaking functions are now executed by a complex rugby scrum of nation-states, intergovernmental organizations, regional compacts, nongovernmental organizations, and informal regimes and networks. The system has become "neomonistic," with new channels opening for the interpenetration of international and domestic law through judicial decision, legislation and executive action. New forms of dispute resolution, executive action, administrative decisionmaking and enforcement, and legislation have emerged as part of a transnational legal process that influences national conduct, transforms national interests, and helps constitute and reconstitute national identities.

In the last five years, these developments have returned the compliance question to center stage in the journals of international theory.

The compliance literature has followed three distinct explanatory pathways. . . . The first, not surprisingly, is a rationalistic instrumentalist strand that views international rules as instruments whereby states seek to attain their interests in wealth, power, and the like [and employs] sophisticated techniques of rational choice theory to argue that nation-states obey international law when it serves their short or long term self-interest to do so. Under this rationalistic account, pitched at the level of the international system, nations employ cooperative strategies to pursue a complex, multifaceted long-run national interest, in which compliance with negotiated legal norms serves as a winning long-term strategy in a reiterated "prisoner's dilemma" game. . . . [T]he more sophisticated instrumentalists are willing to disaggregate the state into its component parts, to introduce international institutions and transnational actors, to incorporate notions of long-term self-interest, and to consider the issue within the context of massively iterated multiparty games.

A second explanatory pathway follows a Kantian, liberal vein. The Kantian thread divides into two identifiable strands: one based on Franck's notion of rule-legitimacy, and another that makes more expansive claims for the causal role of national identity. . . . [T]he determinative factor for whether nations obey can be found, not at a systemic level, but at the level of domestic structure. Under this view, compliance depends significantly on whether or not the state can be characterized as "liberal" in identity, that is, having a form of representative government, guarantees of civil and political rights, and a judicial system dedicated to the rule of law. Flipping the now-familiar Kantian maxim that "democracies don't fight one another," these theorists posit that liberal democracies are more likely to "do law" with one another, while relations between liberal and illiberal states will more likely transpire in a zone of politics.

The third strand is a "constructivist" strand, based broadly on notions of both identity-formation and international society. Unlike interest theorists, who tend to treat state interests as given, "constructivists" have long argued that states and their interests are socially constructed by "commonly held philosophic principles, identities, norms of behavior, or shared terms of discourse." Rather than arguing that state actors and interests create rules and norms, constructivists argue that "[r]ules and norms *constitute* the international game by determining who the actors are, what rules they must follow if they wish to ensure that particular consequences follow from specific acts, and how titles to possessions can be established and transferred." Thus constructivists see norms as playing a critical role in the formation of national identities. . . .

[T]he norms, values, and social structure of international society . . . help . . . form the identity of actors who operate within it. Nations thus obey international rules not just because of sophisticated calculations about how compliance or noncompliance will affect their interests, but because a repeated habit of obedience remakes their interests so that they come to value rule compliance. . . . [S]tates follow specific rules, even when inconvenient, because they have a longer-term interest in the maintenance of law-impregnated international community.

Each of these explanatory threads has significant persuasive power, and strongly complements the others. Yet . . . none of these approaches provides a sufficiently "thick" theory of the role of international law in promoting compliance with shared global norms. The short answer to the question, "Why do nations obey international law?" is not simply: "interest"; "identity"; "identity-formation"; and/or "international society." A complete answer must also account for the importance of *interaction* within the transnational legal process, *interpretation* of international norms, and domestic *internalization* of those norms as determinants of why nations obey. What is missing, in brief, is a modern version of the fourth historical strand of compliance theory — the strand based on <u>*transnational legal process*</u>. . . .

[S]uch a process can be viewed as having three phases. One or more transnational actors provokes an *interaction* (or series of interactions) with another, which forces an *interpretation* or enunciation of the global norm applicable to the situation. By so doing, the moving party seeks not simply to coerce the other party, but to *internalize* the new interpretation of the international norm into the other party's internal normative system. The aim is to "bind" that other party to obey the interpretation as part of its internal value set. Such a transnational legal process is normative, dynamic, and constitutive. The transaction generates a legal rule which will guide future transnational interactions between the parties; future transactions will further internalize those norms; and eventually, repeated participation in the process will help to reconstitute the interests and even the identities of the participants in the process.

The Anti-Ballistic Missile Treaty Reinterpretation Debate represents one recent example of this phenomenon from United States foreign policy. To simplify a complex story, in 1972, the United States and the U.S.S.R. signed the bilateral Anti-Ballistic Missile Treaty (ABM Treaty), which expressly banned the development of space-based systems for the territorial defense of our country. Thirteen years later, in October 1985, the Reagan Administration proposed the Strategic Defense Initiative (SDI), popularly called "Star Wars," which amounted to a space-based antiballistic missile system for American territorial defense. To skirt the plain language of the ABM Treaty, the Reagan Administration proposed to "reinterpret" it to permit SDI, essentially amending the treaty without the consent of either the Senate or the Soviet Union. That decision triggered an eight-year battle in which numerous present and former government officials, including six former Secretaries of Defense and numerous key Senators (principally Sam Nunn, Chairman of the Senate Armed Services Committee), rallied in support of the original treaty interpretation. One key player in the fight against the ABM treaty reinterpretation was Gerard C. Smith, the chief American negotiator at SALT I and principal negotiator of the ABM Treaty, who chaired the boards of two influential nongovernmental organizations, the Arms Control Association and the National Committee to Save the ABM Treaty.

The ABM controversy raged in many fora: Senate hearings, debates over other arms control treaties, journal articles, and op-ed columns. In the end, Congress withheld appropriations from SDI tests that did not conform with the treaty; the Senate reported the ABM Treaty Interpretation Resolution, which reaffirmed its original understanding of the treaty; and in 1988 the Senate attached a condition to the Intermediate-Range Missile Treaty, which specified that the United States would interpret the treaty in accordance with the understanding shared by the President and the Senate at the time of advice and consent. In response, the Reagan and Bush Administrations maintained that their broad reinterpretation was "legally correct," but announced that they would comply with the original understanding as a matter of "policy." In 1993, the episode ended, when President Clinton repudiated the unilateral Reagan reinterpretation and announced that his administration would abide by the original ABM treaty interpretation.

None of this legal dispute reached any court. Indeed, had one stopped tracing the process of the dispute in 1987, one might have concluded that the United States had violated the treaty and gotten away with it. But in the end, the ABM Treaty Reinterpretation Debate demonstrates how the world's most powerful nation, the United States, returned to compliance with international law.

Standing alone, neither interest, identity, or international society provides sufficient explanation for why the United States government obeyed the original ABM Treaty interpretation. Presumably, the U.S. national interest in deploying SDI remained roughly the same under either legal interpretation, as did the liberal identity of the American polity. If the response of international society, in the form of allies' and treaty partners' resistance to the reinterpretation, was not enough to block the reinterpretation in 1985, it is unclear why that resistance should have become overwhelming by 1993.

In my view, a transnational legal process explanation provides the missing link.

Transnational actors such as a U.S. Senator (Sam Nunn), a private "norm entrepreneur" (Gerard Smith), and several nongovernmental organizations (the Arms Control Association and the National Committee to Save the ABM Treaty) formed an "epistemic community" to address the legal issue. That community mobilized elite and popular constituencies and provoked a series of interactions with the U.S. government in a variety of fora. They challenged the Administration's broad reinterpretation of the treaty norm with the original narrow interpretation in both public and private settings, and succeeded in internalizing the narrow interpretation into several legislative products. In the end, the executive branch responded by internalizing that interpretation into its own official policy statement. Thus, the episode proved normative . . . and constitutive of U.S. national interests supporting the original ABM treaty interpretation. In this dynamic process, the episode established a precedent for the next debate over the antiballistic missile issue. . . .

This example reveals that the various theoretical explanations offered for compliance are complementary, not mutually exclusive. In his classic statement of neorealism, *Man, the State and War,* Kenneth Waltz posited three levels of analysis, or "images," at which international relations could be explained: the international system (systemic); the state (domestic politics); and the individuals and groups who make up the state (psychological/bureaucratic).These images are not mutually exclusive, but sit atop one another like a layer cake; thus, interest and international society theorists seek to explain compliance primarily at the level of the international system, while identity theorists seek to explain it at the level of domestic political structure. Transnational legal process analysts, by contrast, seek to supplement these explanations with reasons for compliance that are found at a *transactional* level: *interaction, interpretation,* and *internalization* of international norms into domestic legal structures. While the interest, identity, and international society approaches all provide useful insights, none, jointly or severally, provides a sufficiently thick explanation of compliance with international obligations.

Questions

1. Do you agree with Professor Franck concerning the factors that make law legitimate? Based on the factors identified by Professor Franck, how can international law's legitimacy be enhanced?

2. Do you agree with Professor Koh's "transnational legal process" explanation for national compliance with international law? Can you think of recent examples of this process? Professor Koh uses the ABM reinterpretation debate as an example. In December 2001, the Bush Administration announced that it was withdrawing from the ABM treaty, effective in June 2002. (See Chapter 2, at page 120.)

D. INTERNATIONAL LAW THEORY AND METHODOLOGY

This section provides an overview of some of the modern theoretical and methodological approaches to international law. It is not expected that students will master these approaches in the basic international law course, especially at the beginning of the course. Students may find it useful, however, to have a sense of different ways of thinking about international law before evaluating the substantive international law topics in subsequent chapters.

1. Overview

Excerpted below is a brief description of some of the modern approaches to international law, prepared for a 1999 symposium on "Method in International Law." This excerpt is followed by more in-depth materials discussing some of the specific approaches.

Steven R. Ratner & Anne-Marie Slaughter, Appraising the Methods of International Law: A Prospectus for Readers

93 Am. J. Intl. L. 291 (1999)

Positivism. Positivism summarizes a range of theories that focus upon describing the law as it is, backed up by effective sanctions, with reference to formal criteria, independently of moral or ethical considerations. For positivists, international law is no more or less than the rules to which states have agreed through treaties, custom, and perhaps other forms of consent. In the absence of such evidence of the will of states, positivists will assume that states remain at liberty to undertake whatever actions they please. Positivism also tends to view states as the only subjects of international law, thereby discounting the role of nonstate actors. It remains the lingua franca of most international lawyers, especially in continental Europe.

New Haven School (policy-oriented jurisprudence). Established by Harold Lasswell and Myres McDougal of Yale Law School beginning in the mid-1940s, the New Haven School eschews positivism's formal method of searching for rules as well as the concept of law as based on rules alone. It describes itself as a policy-oriented perspective, viewing international law as a process of decision making by which various actors in the world community clarify and implement their common interests in accordance with their expectations of appropriate processes and of effectiveness in controlling behavior. Perhaps the New Haven School's greatest contribution has been its emphasis on both what actors say and what they do.

International legal process. International legal process (ILP) refers to the approach first developed by Abram Chayes, Thomas Ehrlich, and Andreas Lowenfeld at Harvard Law School in the 1960s. Building on the American legal process school, it has seen the key locus of inquiry of international law as the role of law in constraining decision makers and affecting the course of international affairs. Legal process theory has recently enjoyed a domestic revival, which seeks to underpin precepts about process with a set of normative values. Some ILP scholars are following suit.

Critical legal studies. Critical legal studies (CLS) scholars have sought to move beyond what constitutes law, or the relevance of law to policy, to focus on the contradictions, hypocrisies and failings of international legal discourse. The diverse group of scholars who often identify themselves as part of the "New Stream" have emphasized the importance of culture to legal development and offered a critical view of the progress of the law in its confrontations with state sovereignty. Like the deconstruction movement, which is the intellectual font of many of its ideas, critical legal studies has focused on the importance of language.

International law and international relations.   IR/IL is a purposefully interdisciplinary approach that seeks to incorporate into international law the insights of international relations theory regarding the behavior of international actors. The most recent round of IR/IL scholarship seeks to draw on contemporary developments and strands in international relations theory, which is itself a relatively young discipline. The results are diverse, ranging from studies of compliance, to analyses of the stability and effectiveness of international institutions, to the ways that models of state conduct affect the content and subject of international rules.

Feminist jurisprudence.   Feminist scholars of international law seek to examine how both legal norms and processes reflect the domination of men, and to reexamine and reform these norms and processes so as to take account of women. Feminist jurisprudence has devoted particular attention to the shortcomings in the international protection of women's rights, but it has also asserted deeper structural challenges to international law, criticizing the way law is made and applied as insufficiently attentive to the role of women. Feminist jurisprudence has also taken an active advocacy role.

Law and economics.   In its domestic incarnation, which has proved highly significant and enduring, law and economics has both a descriptive component that seeks to explain existing rules as reflecting the most economically efficient outcome, and a normative component that evaluates proposed changes in the law and urges adoption of those that maximize wealth. Game theory and public choice theory are often considered part of law and economics. In the international area, it has begun to address commercial and environmental issues.

2.   *International Relations Theory*

Kenneth W. Abbott, International Relations Theory, International Law, and the Regime Governing Atrocities in Internal Conflicts

93 Am. J. Intl. L. 361 (1999)

Over the last ten years, international relations (IR) theory, a branch of political science, has animated some of the most exciting scholarship in international law. If a true joint discipline has not yet emerged, scholars in both fields have clearly established the value of interdisciplinary cross-fertilization. . . .

[A]s a social science IR does not purport to be . . . a true "legal method" capable of answering doctrinal questions. . . . And like most social sciences, IR takes its "science" seriously (often too seriously), generally eschewing specific normative recommendations. An IR perspective can, however, enhance both kinds of scholarship. In general, by situating legal rules and institutions in their political context, IR helps to reduce the abstraction and self-contained character of doctrinal analysis and to channel normative idealism in effective directions. More concretely, the visions of international politics underlying theories of IR do suggest some (often implicit) preferences for particular sources of law and normative outcomes.

IR theory is most helpful in performing three different, though equally significant, intellectual tasks: *description, explanation* and *institutional design*. First, while lawyers *describe* rules and institutions all the time, we inevitably — and often subconsciously — use some intellectual template (frequently a positivist one) to determine which elements of these complex phenomena to emphasize, which to omit. The carefully constructed models of social interaction underlying IR theory remind us to choose these templates carefully, in light of our purpose. More specifically, IR helps us describe legal institutions richly, incorporating the political factors that shape the law: the interests, power, and governance structures of states and other actors; the information, ideas and understandings on which they operate; the institutions within which they interact. IR scholars are primarily concerned with *explaining* political behavior — recently, at least, including law-related behavior. Especially within those schools that favor rationalist approaches, scholars seek to identify the actors relevant to an issue, the factors (material or subjective) that affect their behavior or otherwise influence events, and the "causal pathways" by which those factors have effect. These elements are typically incorporated in a model that singles out particular factors for study. In designing research, scholars look for ways to test explanatory hypotheses, using case studies or data analysis. . . .

A scholar applying IR theory might treat legal rules and institutions as phenomena to be explained ("dependent variables"). . . . Alternatively, IR might analyze legal rules and institutions — including the processes of legal decision making — as explanatory factors ("independent variables"). . . .

Why should a lawyer care about questions like these? Analyses treating law as a dependent variable are valuable in many settings, for they help us understand the functions, origin and meaning of rules and institutions. Analyses treating law as an independent variable are also valuable (though unfortunately less common): they help us assess the workings and effectiveness of legal arrangements in the real world. Both forms of explanation, then, are valuable in their own right. But explanation is at least as important for its forward-looking applications: predicting future developments and *designing institutions* capable of affecting behavior in desirable ways. It is here — constructing law-based options for the future, as the editors put it — that lawyers can play their greatest role and IR can make its most significant contribution. . . .

Four visions of international politics are prominent in IR scholarship today. . . .

Realist theory has dominated IR since before World War II. Realists treat states as the principal actors in international politics. States interact in an environment of anarchy, defined as the absence of any central government able to keep peace or enforce agreements. Security is their overriding goal, and self-help their guiding principle. Under these conditions, differences in power are usually sufficient to explain important events. Realists concentrate on interactions among major powers and on matters of war and peace. Other issues — even related issues like war crimes — are secondary.

Realists do not conclude that international cooperation and international law are unlikely or unimportant: states will naturally cooperate when it advances their interests. They do assert, however, that political realities constrain the commitments states will accept, and that the interests of more powerful states set the terms of cooperation. As a corollary, realists believe that international rules and institutions have little, if any, independent effect on state behavior: they are mere ("epiphenomenal") artifacts of the underlying interest and power relationships, and will be changed or disregarded (at least on important issues) if those relationships change.

In analyzing legal doctrine (which they rarely do), realists would hew closely to the actual practice and unambiguous expressions of consent of major states. They would be deeply suspicious of efforts to establish customary law through mere verbal formulations, pronouncements of international institutions or scholarly writings. Since even treaties frequently obligate states to do only what they would have done anyway, or reflect political pressures rather than serious commitments, these scholars should be narrowly interpreted.

Many *institutionalist* scholars start from a similar model of decentralized state interaction. Some share with realists a conviction that states are "real" actors with clearly specified national interests. Most, however, view states as legal fictions that aggregate the interests and preferences of their citizens; these scholars rely on state-centric analysis rather than true "methodological individualism" because it allows for more parsimonious explanation. In either case, these theorists acknowledge a broad spectrum of interests, from wealth to a cleaner environment, that depend on cooperation. Drawing on game theory, economics and other disciplines, institutionalists identify conditions that prevent states from realizing potential gains from cooperation — "market failures," in economic terms — and analyze how rules and other institutions can overcome those obstacles. Regime theory, a more expansive vein of institutionalist scholarship, incorporates information and ideas as well as power and interests, and acknowledges significant roles for private and supranational actors and domestic politics.

In these accounts, institutions — broadly defined to include both norms or rules and organizations — *may* have independent effects on behavior: by changing the context of interaction, they facilitate the negotiation and implementation of agreements as well as other substantive interactions. For example, institutions can reduce the transaction costs of negotiation, provide unbiased information, create cognitive focal points to coordinate decentralized activities, insert neutral actors into situations of conflict, fill gaps in incomplete contracts, and facilitate the pooling of resources. Of course, the obstacles that create a need for institutions also hamper their formation; how are institutions created in the first place? Institutionalists have made less progress in answering these "supply side" questions.

On matters of legal doctrine, institutionalists would accept the traditional sources of international law, especially those revealing voluntary agreement among states; they would also be comfortable looking to national judicial decisions and norms promulgated by international courts and organizations. Some might even search more broadly for relevant normative expressions. In practice, though, institutionalist scholarship focuses on treaties. These are often seen as reciprocal bargains or contracts emerging from market-style interactions, a view that supports a narrow, textual mode of interpretation. But treaties are also viewed as purposive acts akin to legislation; this vision suggests the appropriateness of the kinds of teleological interpretation supported by legal process scholars.

Various forms of *liberal* IR theory have been influential for many years, but this approach has recently been given new vitality. Liberals insist on methodological individualism, viewing individuals and private groups as the fundamental actors in international (and domestic) politics. States are not insignificant, but their preferences are determined by domestic politics rather than assumed interests or material factors like relative power. This approach implies that interstate politics are more complex and fluid than realists and institutionalists assume: national preferences can vary widely and change unpredictably. It calls for careful attention to the domestic politics and constitutional structures of individual states — a daunting prospect for analysts of international relations.

Liberals, on the other hand, are developing their own theoretical generalizations, using variations in domestic governance to explain differences in international behavior. For example, scholars are exploring whether liberal democratic states — with representative institutions and a commitment to the rule of law — are more amenable to legal relationships and arguments and more prone to comply with legal rules than states with different domestic regimes. Research in this vein . . . is also helping to identify the domestic mechanisms through which international institutions affect behavior, and thus how they can be strengthened.

Transnational liberals go further, highlighting the activities of private individuals and groups across national polities and within international institutions. Traditional interest groups like business and labor, scientific communities, advocacy groups and networks concerned with issues like the rights of women or indigenous peoples, and other private organizations all play significant roles, independently of states, in creating international rules and institutions. Such institutions may in turn function most effectively by changing the terms of domestic politics. Some liberals emphasize the role of particular organs of government — national ministries, courts, legislators — which increasingly forge their own transnational relationships.

In analyzing legal doctrine, liberals would accept traditional sources of law, but would question lawyers' easy claims of universality. . . . [L]iberals might rather emphasize differences in adherence and implementation across domestic regime types. Transnational liberals, moreover, would reject doctrines that limit law creation to states. Asserting that the domestic-international distinction has broken down, they would urge the significance of transnational norms created by private actors and governmental units, as well as domestic norms.

Constructivist theory differs fundamentally from these rationalist accounts. Constructivists reject the notion that states or other actors have objectively determined interests that they can pursue by selecting appropriate strategies and designing effective institutions. Rather, international actors operate within a social context of shared subjective understandings and norms, which constitute their identities and roles and define appropriate forms of conduct. Even fundamental notions like the state, sovereignty and national interests are socially constructed. They are not objectively true, but subjective; their meaning is not fixed, but contingent. . . .

In terms of legal doctrine, for constructivists all is subjective and perpetually "in play." Constructivists would look to a variety of normative expressions, including practice, to define the subjective element of custom or the meaning of treaty commitments. In addition, normative understandings vary with historical and political context. Much as liberals see categories of states differentially amenable to law, some international society theorists see "concentric circles of commitment," with a Western core embedded in dense webs of norms and institutions, a Southern ring that participates selectively, and an outer ring on the fringes of society.

3. *Economic Analysis of International Law*

Jeffery L. Dunoff & Joel P. Trachtman, Economic Analysis of International Law

24 Yale J. Intl. L. 1 (1999)

Economics is the study of rational choice. As such, it plays a leading role in evaluating the effects of rational maximizing behavior under conditions of scarcity. Eco-

Does the image of states or their leaders as rational maximizers track with reality? Sufficiently?

nomics enjoys an advantage over other disciplines in rationality-based analysis, simply because this analysis is central to economics, and economics has developed this analysis extensively. The development has largely been in the mathematical realm, the so-called "blackboard economics." However, at this point in the development of economics — and of international law — the more mathematical models do not yet seem to engage the core issues of international law. Economics as practiced by lawyer-economists often involves complex cost-benefit analyses. This approach is often useful, but has important limitations due to problems of administrability, commensurability, and interpersonal comparison of utility.

However, the more promising economic methodologies, in terms of their capacity to generate a progressive research program that might usefully address persistent international law problems, may not be those that teach us to balance the costs and benefits of any particular policy, but rather those that focus on the balancers: international institutions (including the general international legal system). Indeed, the threshold issue in many, if not all, international legal problems is that of institutional choice. What institution — market, domestic legislature, adjudicatory body, or international rule-making body — ought to decide, for example, if one state's intellectual property standards are too low, or another's environmental standards are too high? The answers to questions like these ought to be informed by an understanding of the relative institutional competencies and capacities of the various alternatives, as well as by an appreciation of the strategic interactions among the various institutions. . . .

[T]ransactions in international relations are analogous to transactions in private markets. . . .

At its core, the relevant similarity is that international society, like any society, is a place where individual actors or groups of actors encounter one another and sometimes have occasion to cooperate, to engage in what may broadly be termed "transactions." . . . In [law and economics] literature, markets are understood to arise out of the activities of individual persons or firms. . . .

So, too, for the international system. Like economic markets, the international system is formed by the interactions of self-regarding units — largely, but not exclusively, states. . . . Actors in each system are willing — to some extent — to relinquish autonomy in order to obtain certain benefits. Both the international and the domestic systems, then, are individualist in origin, spontaneously-generated and unintended products of self-interested behavior.

The assets traded in this international "market" are not goods or services per se, but assets peculiar to states: components of power. In a legal context, power is jurisdiction, including jurisdiction to prescribe, jurisdiction to adjudicate, and jurisdiction to enforce. In international society, the equivalent of the market is simply the place where states interact to cooperate on particular issues — to trade in power — in order to maximize their baskets of preferences. To be sure, states may also trade in money or physical assets; however, the unique feature of states is their possession of governmental regulatory authority in the broad sense. International law is concerned with the definition, exchange, and pooling of this authority.

States enter the market of international relations in order to obtain gains from exchange. For present purposes, we can understand the structure of this market as follows: Beginning from the state of nature, the first level of "trade" is that which establishes constitutional rules — rules about how subsequent and subordinate rules will be made. The next level of trade is that which allows departure from the state of nature: establishment of market-organizing rules of non-coercion, property rights, and contract. These rules facilitate additional transactions among states. Finally, institutions can be established to constrain (positively or negatively) transaction choices in the future. Of course, in contexts where there are no gains from trade, there should be no trade; that is, depending on the context, no cooperation, no treaty, and/or no integration may result. . . .

A. EXTERNALITIES AND EXCHANGE

Actions or inactions of states may have positive or negative "effects" on other states. Thus, for example, the environmental law (or deficiencies therein) in one state may be associated with adverse or beneficial effects (negative or positive externalities) in other states, because (for example) the first state's law permits pollution that flows to other states. Domestic environmental laws may also "cause" adverse effects in other states by being too strict regarding the entry of foreign goods into the national market, or too lax with respect to domestic industries, resulting in competitiveness effects (pecuniary externalities). Externalization through regulation that fails to protect foreign interests, pecuniary externalization through strict regulation that has protectionist effects or through lax regulation that may be viewed as a subsidy, and subsidization itself may all be viewed as questions of prescriptive jurisdiction: which state — or international body — will have power to regulate which actions?

These external effects may cause other states to wish to alter some of these activities, through their own regulation or through changes in the first state's regulation. There are two main ways to do so: the first is bilateral persuasion; the second is through institutionalization. Bilateral persuasion may involve force, exchange, or implicit reciprocities (either specific or diffuse); it occurs in the "spot market." Institutionalization involves the transfer of power over time through a treaty or an international organization. . . .

B. ECONOMIES OF SCALE AND SCOPE

Related potential sources of gains from trade are economies of scale and economies of scope. Given the increasingly global nature of society, and of problems such as environmental degradation and trade, it seems likely that there would be economies of scale, under some circumstances, in the international or regional regulation of these matters.

Economies of scale have a number of components. First, states may enjoy economies of scale in contexts where they regulate transnational actors. For example, there may be efficiencies gained through coordinated rule-making, surveillance, and enforcement activities. In the absence of these transactions, states face heightened risks of evasion, detrimental regulatory competition (which can be driven by externalization), and unjustified regulatory disharmony, all resulting in inefficiencies. Second, there may be technological economies of scale, relating to equipment, acquisition of specialized skills, or organization. Economies of scale may provide a motivation for integration in order to capture these economies.

Economies of scope are reductions in cost resulting from centralized production of a group of products, especially where the products share a common component. Once several areas of international regulation are established, economies of scope may be realized by regulating other areas. . . .

Finally, economies of scale and scope may arise from increased frequency of transactions or from longer duration of transactions. Given greater numbers of transactions in international relations, one would expect greater economies of scale. In addition, learning curve effects may, over time, give rise to economies of experience, which are economies of scale and scope that arise from repeated activity over time.

C. TRANSACTIONS AND INSTITUTIONS

States may enter into one-off unilateral transfers of power or jurisdiction, for example, when one state's courts determine that the doctrine of forum non conveniens or another doctrine of abstention calls on them to decline adjudicative jurisdiction in favor of another forum. Alternatively, states may enter into treaties to exchange jurisdiction over time with respect to a particular subject matter. For instance, states may enter into extradition treaties whereby they agree on the circumstances under which they will transfer jurisdiction to adjudicate claims against particular individuals. In addition, states may enter into institutional arrangements — constituted by treaties — that provide for legislative capacity to agree on further exchanges of jurisdiction over time. . . .

The new institutional economics assumes a dichotomy between transactions and institutions. But between the spot market transaction and the formal organization there exist many types of formal contracts and informal arrangements, and even the formal organization is a nexus of contracts. Thus, the supposed dichotomy is, in fact, a continuum: the boundary between the transaction and the institution is blurred. The metric of this continuum is the relative scope of retained individual discretion: where the individual retains greater discretion, she is closer to the pole of the market; where the individual retains less discretion — and assigns more discretion through contract or organization — she is closer to the pole of the firm. This continuum is translated in international economic relations to the continuum running from intergovernmentalism to integration, where integration denotes a pooling of authority. . . .

These analytical perspectives allow us to understand the choices that states make in deciding how to relate to one another. There may be circumstances where it is easier (in transaction cost and strategic terms) to engage in transactions through a market-type mechanism. Alternatively, in some circumstances it may be easier to engage in transactions — to deal in power or jurisdiction — through organizational mechanisms. The recognition that these mechanisms are related and comparable allows states to compare them and to match their characteristics to particular circumstances more accurately.

Thus, states choose among varying types and locations of transactions in power. Law and economics would predict that their choice depends on factors such as transaction costs and strategic considerations.

4. *Critical Legal Studies*

David Kennedy, A New Stream of International Law Scholarship

7 Wis. Intl. L.J. 1 (1988)

Let me begin with ideas about the relationship between public international law on the one hand, and something called "society" or "political economy" or "state behavior" on the other. Images of such a relationship have preoccupied public international law scholarship. Everyone has seemed convinced that these two things were, or should be, or purported to be, or struggled to be, different from one another. Indeed, they seemed to feel public international law could only *be* law if it were independent and "normative," a word which, somewhat oddly, has been read to mean "against the state." At the same time, and equally fervently, everyone has seemed convinced that the goal, or achievement, or aspiration or project of public international law is to link law with international "society." This could be done descriptively, or theoretically, or by enacting resolutions, or signing treaties or allocating rights—but it had to be done. Otherwise public international law would seem hopelessly irrelevant to what really mattered, out of touch with the sovereign, in danger of losing touch with the source of power, glory and employment.

This conviction—that international law was not politics but struggled to be politics—has accounted for much of the discipline's eclectic insecurity. It explains the pressure to regularize international law institutionally, and to analogize international law to more familiar domestic constitutional configurations. It explains the historic preoccupation with the relationship between norm and deed, and the mountain of theory—be it naturalist or positivist—explaining how law might both emanate from and control the state. It undergirds the oscillation between Republican formalism and democratic enthusiasm and explains the doctrinal preoccupation with rights—be they rights to food, to self-determination or to asylum—which could link legislative determination to political enactment and ensure respect for public law.

Displacing—and I mean "displacing," setting aside, neither proving nor disproving but simply avoiding—such an entrenched constellation of imagery has been difficult. Doing so has meant borrowing from recent linguistic and literary theory and from the work of contemporary critical legal scholarship—which has itself drawn on the European philosophical traditions of structuralism and post-structuralism—in order to reformulate the relationship between law and politics in *rhetorical* terms.

Rather than concentrating on the relationship between a law and a society which actually *are* separate, joined or related only through the prism of the state or sovereign, I have tried to extend what has been the single most telling and controversial insight of much recent critical legal scholarship in the United States: namely, that law is nothing but a repetition of the relationship it posits between law and society. Rather than a stable domain which *relates* in some complicated way *to* society or political economy or class structure, law is simply the practice and argument about the relationship between something posited as law and something posited as society.

Mine is a relational and rhetorical image of a "law" and a "society"—invoked by a language which establishes them by positing their originality, their priority,

[margin note: Should we abandon the effort to analogize law to domestic practice—ie can we have law w/o a state?]

[margin note: might we simply understand international law in rhetorical terms as the interaction of something posited as law & something posited as society?]

their presence. My sense is that this rhetorical project — in many ways *the* rhetorical project of public international law scholarship — accounts for the doctrinal structures of "public" and "private" or "objective" and "subjective" which we find recurring throughout international public law doctrine and for the recurrent scholarly contrasts we find between theory and practice.

In this alternative picture, law is nothing but an attempt to project a stable relationship between spheres it creates to divide. As a result, the relationship between these zones is much looser than we usually think. . . .

International legal scholars have produced a large body of work about the conditions under which treaties, custom or general principles of law bind actors and the hierarchy among the various doctrinal forms which might apply in a given instance. This body of doctrine provides a good introduction to the rhetorical patterns of public international law as a whole. Contemporary analyses generally work from the sources enumerated in Article 38 of the Statute of the International Court of Justice, proceeding to examine the conditions under which norms of these types will be binding, the hierarchical relationships among them, and the extent to which potential sources not included in the list (such as U.N. resolutions) might be assimilated to one of these classic forms.

Several aspects of this literature might seem odd to a man from the moon. For one thing, the literature proceeds quite abstractly, attempting to delimit boundary conditions for each category independent of the particular content of the norms whose source is being considered. There seems a shared sense that the abstract categories will control the content of the norms, rather than merely register them. Argument about sources doctrine is similarly abstracted from the content of the norm under consideration.

Much of this argument, moreover, seems to repeat a rather simple and familiar debate between the authoritative power of sovereign consent on the one hand, and some extraconsensual norm on the other. Argument about the relative authority of various sources, about their boundaries and effects, seems to be carried out as a debate about sovereign consent. It is an odd debate. At one level, it seems that the choice between a preference for consensual and non-consensual norms will answer all questions. Either a consensual treaty beats a non-consensual custom or it does not. But somehow this question is never squarely faced in doctrinal argument — somebody always seems to muddy the waters.

The bindingness of treaties, after all, seems more than consent, prior to consent, the very condition for a consensual system. And custom might also be the product of consent. Although arguments about the authority of international norms appeal either to consent or to some norm beyond consent as if these were exclusive and definitive possibilities, in the end, each always seems to invoke the other somehow — in a subordinate interpretation, or secondary doctrine.

The basic debate about consent suggests that the discourse of sources will address a basic theoretical dilemma for international law: how can it be simultaneously independent of and enmeshed with sovereign will? The autonomy of sovereigns ensures the attractiveness of consensual sources, while their participation in a preexisting normative order encourages a non-consensual rhetorical line. In order to fulfill the desire for an autonomous system of normative law, argument about the sources of international law simply included strands associated with both visions. Sources rhetoric is interesting not because it resolves the issue, but because it transforms it

Does it help to see international law not as neutral but as a rhetoric about power?

into a debate between abstract legal forms — a debate which can manage the conflict between them interminably.

For all its abstraction, sources rhetoric is a distinctly doctrinal affair, neither theoretical nor political. Norms are legally binding which fit within one of a series of doctrinally elaborated categories, not when a persuasive argument about political interest or theoretical coherence can be made for their observance. The distinction between consensual and non-consensual sources — used to distinguish treaties from custom, to contrast various schools of thought about the nature of custom, to divide arguments for and against the application of specific norms in various situations, and in dozens of other ways throughout the materials on sources — opposes themes whose fluidity encourages a proliferation of rhetorical possibilities and strategies more than decisive identifications and differentiations.

The play between these themes gives sources discourse a doctrinal feel without ever presenting the clash between two norms — or two sovereigns — in substantive or political terms. A source discourse which operated completely within the rhetoric of either consent or systemic considerations would seem doctrinal, but it would not be able to avoid a more substantive face. A consensual rhetoric could certainly differentiate and prioritize norms in an abstract way, but in choosing among two norms, one would need to choose between the claims of two sovereigns about their autonomous consents. A purely extra-consensual rhetoric, while it would obviously avoid this problem, would have a difficult time avoiding a more substantive choice among various systemically grounded norms. By combining these two rhetorics, sources discourse can defend its independence from sovereign autonomy and from substantive legal regulation.

when we mobilize consent or the underlying inste beins for consent what are we saying about actual power and interest, Is international law ultimately international politics? Does its autonomy matter?

The question, obviously, is how do they do it? My own examination of various sources doctrines and cases suggested a number of rather obvious rhetorical strategies. The most obvious is simply repetition: differentiating various doctrines from one another as consensual and non-consensual and then repeating the distinction in distinguishing each doctrine from its exception or interpreting doctrinal strands which have once been characterized and perhaps adopted as consensual in non-consensual terms. Thus, custom might seem non-consensual when contrasted with treaty, but be measured in consensual terms, or subjected to a consent based exception — say, for persistent opposers. . .

Can law be autonomous? Or should we understand its rhetoric in critiquing its contradictions, its treatment of, political terms? interests?

For additional discussion of critical legal studies as applied to international law, see Anthony Carty, Critical International Law: Recent Trends in the Theory of International Law, 3 Eur. J. Intl. L. 66 (1992); Nigel Purvis, Critical Legal Studies in Public International Law, 32 Harv. Intl. L.J. 81 (1991); and Phillip Trimble, International Law, World Order and Critical Legal Studies, 42 Stan. L. Rev. 811 (1990).

5. *Feminist Jurisprudence* *Avenue to concretize an abstract critique*

Hilary Charlesworth, Christine Chinkin & Shelley Wright, Feminist Approaches to International Law

85 Am. J. Intl. L. 613 (1991)

The development of feminist jurisprudence in recent years has made a rich and fruitful contribution to legal theory. Few areas of domestic law have avoided the scrutiny of feminist writers, who have exposed the gender bias of apparently neutral systems of rules. A central feature of many western theories about law is that the law is an autonomous entity, distinct from the society it regulates. A legal system is regarded as different from a political or economic system, for example, because it operates on the basis of abstract rationality, and is thus universally applicable and capable of achieving neutrality and objectivity. These attributes are held to give the law its special authority. More radical theories have challenged this abstract rationalism, arguing that legal analysis cannot be separated from the political, economic, historical and cultural context in which people live. Some theorists argue that the law functions as a system of beliefs that make social, political and economic inequalities appear natural. Feminist jurisprudence builds on certain aspects of this critical strain in legal thought. It is much more focused and concrete, however, and derives its theoretical force from immediate experience of the role of the legal system in creating and perpetuating the unequal position of women. . . .

International law has thus far largely resisted feminist analysis. The concerns of public international law do not, at first sight, have any particular impact on women: issues of sovereignty, territory, use of force and state responsibility, for example, appear gender free in their application to the abstract entities of states. Only where international law is considered directly relevant to individuals, as with human rights law, have some specifically feminist perspectives on international law begun to be developed. . . .

Our approach requires looking behind the abstract entities of states to the actual impact of rules on women within states. We argue that both the structures of international lawmaking and the content of the rules of international law privilege men; if women's interests are acknowledged at all, they are marginalized. International law is a thoroughly gendered system. . . .

The structure of the international legal order reflects a male perspective and ensures its continued dominance. The primary subjects of international law are states and, increasingly, international organizations. In both states and international organizations the invisibility of women is striking. Power structures within governments are overwhelmingly masculine: women have significant positions of power in very few states, and in those where they do, their numbers are minuscule. Women are either unrepresented or underrepresented in the national and global decision-making processes.

States are patriarchal structures not only because they exclude women from elite positions and decision-making roles, but also because they are based on the concentration of power in, and control by, an elite and the domestic legitimation of a monopoly over the use of force to maintain that control. This foundation is reinforced by international legal principles of sovereign equality, political independence and territorial integrity and the legitimation of force to defend those attributes.

International organizations are functional extensions of states that allow them to act collectively to achieve their objectives. Not surprisingly, their structures replicate those of states, restricting women to insignificant and subordinate roles. Thus, in the United Nations itself, where the achievement of nearly universal membership is regarded as a major success of the international community, this universality does not apply to women. . . .

At a deeper level one finds a public/private dichotomy based on gender. One explanation feminist scholars offer for the dominance of men and the male voice in all areas of power and authority in the western liberal tradition is that a dichotomy is drawn between the public sphere and the private or domestic one. The public realm of the work place, the law, economics, politics and intellectual and cultural life, where power and authority are exercised, is regarded as the natural province of men; while the private world of the home, the hearth and children is seen as the appropriate domain of women. The public/private distinction has a normative, as well as a descriptive, dimension. Traditionally, the two spheres are accorded asymmetrical value: greater significance is attached to the public, male world than to the private, female one. The distinction drawn between the public and the private thus vindicates and makes natural the division of labor and allocation of rewards between the sexes. Its reproduction and acceptance in all areas of knowledge have conferred primacy on the male world and supported the dominance of men. . . .

What force does the feminist critique of the public/private dichotomy in the foundation of domestic legal systems have for the international legal order? Traditionally, of course, international law was regarded as operating only in the most public of public spheres: the relations between nation-states. We argue, however, that the definition of certain principles of international law rests on and reproduces the public/private distinction. It thus privileges the male world view and supports male dominance in the international legal order.

The grip that the public/private distinction has on international law, and the consequent banishment of women's voices and concerns from the discipline, can be seen in the international prohibition on torture. The right to freedom from torture and other forms of cruel, inhuman or degrading treatment is generally accepted as a paradigmatic civil and political right. It is included in all international catalogs of civil and political rights and is the focus of specialized United Nations and regional treaties. The right to be free from torture is also regarded as a norm of customary international law — indeed, like the prohibition on slavery, as a norm of *jus cogens*.

The basis for the right is traced to "the inherent dignity of the human person." Behavior constituting torture is defined in the Convention against Torture as

> any act by which severe pain or suffering, whether physical or mental, is intentionally inflicted on a person for such purposes as obtaining from him or a third person information or a confession, punishing him for an act he or a third person has committed or is suspected of having committed, or intimidating or coercing him or a third person, or for any reason based on discrimination of any kind, when such pain or suffering is inflicted by or at the instigation of or with the consent or acquiescence of a public official or other person acting in an official capacity.

This definition has been considered broad because it covers mental suffering and behavior "at the instigation of" a public official. However, despite the use of the term "human person" in the Preamble, the use of the masculine pronoun alone in the definition of the proscribed behavior immediately gives the definition a male, rather than a truly human, context. More importantly, the description of the prohibited conduct relies on a distinction between public and private actions that obscures injuries to their dignity typically sustained by women. The traditional canon of human rights law does not deal in categories that fit the experiences of women. It is cast in terms of discrete violations of rights and offers little redress in cases where there is a pervasive, structural denial of rights.

The international definition of torture requires not only the intention to inflict suffering, but also the secondary intention that the infliction of suffering will fulfill a purpose. Recent evidence suggests that women and children, in particular, are victims of widespread and apparently random terror campaigns by both governmental and guerrilla groups in times of civil unrest or armed conflict. Such suffering is not clearly included in the international definition of torture.

A crucial aspect of torture and cruel, inhuman or degrading conduct, as defined, is that they take place in the public realm: a public official or a person acting officially must be implicated in the pain and suffering. The rationale for this limitation is that "private acts (of brutality) would usually be ordinary criminal offenses which national law enforcement is expected to repress. International concern with torture arises only when the State itself abandons its function of protecting its citizenry by sanctioning criminal action by law enforcement personnel." Many women suffer from torture in this limited sense. The international jurisprudence on the notion of torture arguably extends to sexual violence and psychological coercion if the perpetrator has official standing. However, severe pain and suffering that is inflicted outside the most public context of the state — for example, within the home or by private persons, which is the most pervasive and significant violence sustained by women — does not qualify as torture despite its impact on the inherent dignity of the human person. Indeed, some forms of violence are attributed to cultural tradition. The message of violence against women, argues Charlotte Bunch, is domination:

> [S]tay in your place or be afraid. Contrary to the argument that such violence is only personal or cultural, it is profoundly political. It results from the structural relationships of power, domination, and privilege between men and women in society. Violence against women is central to maintaining those political relations at home, at work, and in all public spheres.

States are held responsible for torture only when their designated agents have direct responsibility for such acts and that responsibility is imputed to the state. States are not considered responsible if they have maintained a legal and social system in which violations of physical and mental integrity are endemic. . . .

Another example of the failure of the normative structure of international law to accommodate the realities of women's lives can be seen in its response to trafficking in women. Trafficking in women through prostitution, pornography and mail-order-bride networks is a pervasive and serious problem in both the developed and the developing worlds. These practices do not simply fall under national jurisdiction, as the ramifications of the trafficking and exploitative relationships cross international boundaries. They involve the subordination and exploitation of women, not on the simple basis of inequality or differences among individuals, but as a result of deeply engrained constructs of power and dominance based on gender. Catharine MacKinnon's observation that women's "material desperation" is connected to violence against women is even more powerful in the international context. To a large extent, the increase in trafficking in women in the Third World stems from growing economic disparities on the national and international levels. Once caught up in the trafficking networks, penniless women in foreign countries are at the mercy of those who arrange and profit from the trade.

Existing norms of international law could be invoked to prohibit at least some of the international exploitation of women and children. The international law on this issue, however, is incomplete and limited in scope. Just as the prohibition of the slave trade, and subsequently of slavery itself, did not occur until economic considerations supported its abolition, so a real commitment to the prevention of sexual trafficking in women is unlikely to be made unless it does not adversely affect other economic interests. . . .

Another example of internationally recognized rights that might affect women and men differently are those relating to the protection of the family. The major human rights instruments all have provisions applicable to the family. Thus, the Universal Declaration proclaims that the family is the "natural and fundamental group unit of society and is entitled to protection by society and the State." These provisions ignore that to many women the family is a unit for abuse and violence; hence, protection of the family also preserves the power structure within the family, which can lead to subjugation and dominance by men over women and children.

The development of rights may be particularly problematic for women in the Third World, where women's rights to equality with men and traditional values may clash. . . .

_____

For additional discussion of feminist perspectives on international law, see Hilary Charlesworth & Christine Chinkin, The Boundaries of International Law: A Feminist Analysis (2000); Barbara Stark, Women and Globalization: The Failure and Postmodern Possibilities of International Law, 33 Vand. J. Transnat'l L. 503 (2000); and Fernando R. Teson, Feminism and International Law: A Reply, 33 Va. J. Intl. L. 647 (1993).

Bibliography

Standard texts on international law include Ian Brownlie, Principles of Public International Law (5th ed. 1998); Robert Jennings & Arthur Watts, eds., Oppenheim's International Law (9th ed. 1992); Peter Malanczuk, Akehurst's Modern Introduction to International Law (7th rev. ed. 1997); I.A. Shearer, Starke's International Law (11th ed. 1994); and Malcom N. Shaw, International Law (4th ed. 1997). More summary treatments can be found in David J. Bederman, International Law Frameworks (2001); Thomas Buergenthal & Sean D. Murphy, Public International Law (2002); and Mark W. Janis, An Introduction to International Law (3d ed. 1999). For additional discussion of the reasons that nations comply with international law, see Abram Chayes & Antonia Handler Chayes, The New Sovereignty: Compliance with International Regulatory Agreements (1995).

E. INTERNATIONAL LAW IN ACTION: THE U.S. AND INTERNATIONAL RESPONSE TO THE ATTACKS OF SEPTEMBER 11, 2001

In this section we recount the events surrounding the terrorist attacks of September 11, and the U.S. and international response to them. These events have fundamentally altered the existing relations among many states and other entities, and have had a major impact on international law. This case study, designed to stimulate your thinking about the role of international law, includes many accompanying questions, questions that you will be able to answer much more knowledgeably later in the course. In subsequent chapters we also use the collective reaction to the attacks for occasional questions.

1. Introduction

September 11, 2001, started as a relatively peaceful day in the world. However, as people began arriving at work on the U.S. East Coast, the calm of a crisp, clear day was shattered. American Airlines Flight 11, out of Boston and destined for San Francisco, was hijacked in mid-air by Mohammed Atta and four accomplices. Atta then diverted the large Boeing 767 and crashed it at high speed and full of fuel into the North Tower of New York City's World Trade Center at 8:46 A.M.

As fire and police forces converged on the building and sketchy initial media reports were widely circulated, a second large passenger jet, United Airlines Flight 175, slammed into the South Tower at 9:03 A.M., making clear that the events were no accident. About 30 minutes later, American Airlines Flight 77, originating at Dulles Airport near Washington, D.C., and destined for Los Angeles, flew low along the Potomac River and initially appeared headed toward the White House. Possibly because the hijacker pilot had trouble picking out the White House, the plane veered and found a target about two miles away, hitting the highly visible Pentagon at ground level. A fourth hijacked plane, United Airlines Flight 93, crashed in western Pennsylvania about 20 minutes later. Some of its passengers, who had learned of the first attacks from family and friends over cellular phones, valiantly decided to rush the cockpit and to try to retake control of the plane, rather than let it serve as another flying bomb. In the ensuing struggle between the four trained hijackers, who were armed with box cutters (that contain razor blades), and the passengers, who apparently commandeered the food cart and tableware, the plane crashed, far from its apparent target of the U.S. Capitol or the White House.

About 3,000 innocent people were killed at the World Trade Center site, the Pentagon, and aboard the four aircraft, in addition to the 19 hijackers. The victims included 343 firefighters and 72 police officers who had rushed without hesitation to the aid of people at the World Trade Center. More Americans died in the attacks on September 11 than on any other single day in U.S. history, except during the Battles of Antietam and Gettysburg during the Civil War. The Japanese attack on Pearl Harbor, another highly destructive sneak attack, killed about 2,400 people, mostly sailors and other military personnel. But Pearl Harbor was an attack on a military target for a military purpose — to weaken or cripple the ability of the United States to fight a naval war in the Pacific — and Gettysburg and Antietam were full-fledged military battles. By contrast, the terrorists on September 11 intentionally targeted civilians as part of their attempt to inflict much symbolic and physical damage. The World Trade Center had earlier been the target of a terrorist bombing in February 1993 and stood as a visible symbol of the United States and its economic power, and the Pentagon was a symbol of the U.S. government and its military. Nationals of 83 other countries besides the United States were murdered in the attacks, including many Muslims. Great Britain alone lost at least 67 citizens, making September 11 the most deadly terrorist attack in its history as well.

2.   *Historical Background*

The attacks were deliberate and carefully planned. The United States quickly established that Osama bin Laden and his Al Qaeda organization were behind them. It helps to understand the historical background.

Bin Laden and Al Qaeda

Osama bin Laden's *jihadi* career began in the 1980s, fighting the Soviets in Afghanistan.

Peter L. Bergen, Jr., Holy War, Inc.: Inside the Secret World of Osama bin Laden
53-54, 62, 80-81, 88, 98-99 (2002)

Within weeks of the Soviet invasion [in December 1979, Osama] bin Laden, then twenty-two, voted with his feet and his wallet, heading to Pakistan to meet with Afghan [opposition] leaders. . . . He then returned to Saudi Arabia and started lobbying his family and friends to provide money to support the Afghan guerrillas and continued making short trips to Pakistan for his fund-raising work.

In the early 1980s bin Laden, already an expert in demolition from time spent working in his family's construction business, made his first trips into Afghanistan, bringing with him hundreds of tons of construction machinery, bulldozers, loaders, dump trucks, and equipment for building trenches, which he put at the disposal of the *mujahideen*. The machinery would be used to build rough roads, dig tunnels into the mountains for shelter, and construct rudimentary hospitals. Bin Laden's followers also set up mine-sweeping operations in the Afghan countryside.

Despite the fact that the United States was also supporting the mujahideen, bin Laden was already voicing anti-American sentiments during the early eighties. . . .

In 1984 bin Laden set up a guesthouse in Peshawar[, Pakistan] for Muslims drawn to the jihad. It was called *Beit al-Ansar,* or House of the Supporters, an allusion to the Prophet Muhammad's followers who helped him when he had to flee his native Mecca for Medina. Initially the house was simply a way station for those who would be sent for training with one of the Afghan factions. Later, bin Laden would form his own military operation. . . .

The Afghan war did not only move men like bin Laden spiritually; it also enabled them to meet key figures in terrorist organizations in the Arab world. In 1987 bin Laden was introduced to members of Egypt's Jihad group, the organization behind the 1981 assassination of Egyptian President Anwar Sadat. A leader of the group, Ayman al-Zawahiri, had settled in Peshawar and was putting his skills as a physician to work at a hospital for Afghan refugees. In 1989, bin Laden founded al-Qaeda, the "base" in Arabic, an organization that would eventually merge with al-Zawahiri's Jihad group. . . .

[When the Soviets finally withdrew from Afghanistan in 1989, bin Laden left as well, returning to his native Saudi Arabia at the age of 32. Bin Laden's anti-Americanism received a target in 1990, when the Persian Gulf War brought hundreds of thousands of U.S. troops to Saudi Arabia, in violation of what bin Laden saw as the prophet's command to "let there be no two religions in Arabia."]

. . . [B]in Laden had been denouncing Americans well before he was forced to put up with them in the flesh. On his return from the Afghan war . . . , he was quickly in demand as a speaker in mosques and homes, and one of his principal themes was a call for a boycott of American goods because of that country's support for Israel. Hundreds of thousands of recordings of his speeches circulated in the Saudi kingdom.

Ironically, bin Laden was sympathetic to the underlying cause of the U.S. presences in Saudi Arabia: the war against Saddam Hussein. . . .

After Hussein's forces did invade the small, oil-rich state on August 1, 1990, and threaten the security of Saudi Arabia, bin Laden immediately volunteered his services and those of his holy warriors. The Saudi army and his own men would be enough to defend the Kingdom, he reasoned; after all, hadn't his own troops been instrumental in driving the Russians from Afghanistan?

The Saudis did not take the offer seriously. Despite the tens of billions of dollars they had spent on their own army, they turned instead for help to the U.S. government and then-President Bush. . . .

Bin Laden's opposition to the presence of American troops was echoed by two prominent religious scholars, Sarar al-Hawali and Salman al-'Auda, who were subsequently jailed by the Saudis. Bin Laden, whose credentials as a religious scholar are nonexistent, often cites al-Hawali and al-'Auda to justify his own pronouncements against the United States. . . .

[By 1991 the Saudi regime was fed up with bin Laden's anti-government critiques and effectively put him under house arrest. But bin Laden was able to use his family connections to leave the kingdom, and he moved his base of operations to Sudan, then under the de facto rule of an Islamist cleric.

[From his base in Sudan, bin Laden simultaneously ran both a legitimate business operation and a terrorist organization. He plausibly claims responsibility for the deaths of 18 American soldiers in Mogadishu in 1993, which helped lead the United States to withdraw from Somalia. The 1993 bombing of the World Trade Center was carried out by a group of terrorists closely connected to the Al Qaeda network. The bomber was himself apparently trained in explosives by Al Qaeda instructors in Afghanistan.]

In 1995 the de facto ruler of Sudan . . . organized an Islamic People's Congress, during which bin Laden was able to meet with leaders of militant groups from Pakistan, Algeria, and Tunisia as well as the Palestinian Islamic Jihad and Hamas. At the same time, al-Qaeda sought to forge alliances with the Iranian-backed Hezbollah, based in southern Lebanon. Despite their disputes over religious doctrine — Hezbollah is Shia, while bin Laden espouses a conservative Sunni Islam — the two groups buried their differences to make war against their common enemy, the United States. Al-Qaeda members traveled to Lebanon, where the group maintained a guesthouse, and, with Hezbollah, learned how to bomb large buildings.

Bin Laden, meanwhile, met with Imad Mughniyeh, the secretive, Iran-based head of Hezbollah's security service. This was an important meeting. It was Mughniyeh who masterminded the suicide truck bombing of the Marine barracks in Beirut in 1983, which killed 241 American servicemen and precipitated a U.S. pullout from Lebanon within a few months.

. . . [T]he Beirut model was one bin Laden hoped to follow. . . .

[Finally, under intense U.S. pressure, Sudan expelled bin Laden in 1996. Sudan offered to send him to Saudi Arabia or the United States for detention. However, the Saudis, who had taken the unusually severe step of stripping bin Laden of his citizenship in 1994, refused to accept him. The United States determined it could not make a case against him. He went instead to Afghanistan.

[The Taliban regime treated bin Laden as an honored guest. In return, he provided money and warriors to the cash-strapped Taliban to help them in the civil war.]

On February 22, 1998, bin Laden upped the ante considerably when he announced the formation of the World Islamic Front for Jihad against the Jews and the Crusaders. Cosignatories of the agreement included Ayman al-Zawahiri of Egypt's Jihad Group, bin Laden's most trusted lieutenant; Rifia Ahmed Taha of Egypt's Islamic Group; and the leaders of Pakistani and Bangladeshi militant organizations. All were brought together under one umbrella for the first time.

Because the announcement inaugurating the World Islamic Front is the key text that set the stage for al-Qaeda's terrorist attacks, it is worth quoting at some length.

> Since Allah spread out the Arabian Peninsula, created its desert, and drew its seas, no such disaster has ever struck as when those Christian legions spread like pest, crowded its land, ate its resources, eradicated its nature, and humiliated its leaders. . . . No one argues today over three facts repeated by witnesses and agreed upon by those who are fair. . . . They are: Since about seven years ago, America has been occupying the most sacred lands of Islam: the Arabian Peninsula. It has been stealing its resources, dictating to its leaders, humiliating its people, and frightening its neighbors. It is using its rule in the Peninsula as a weapon to fight the neighboring peoples of Islam. . . . The most evident proof is when the Americans went too far in their aggression against the people of Iraq. . . . Despite major destruction to the Iraqi people at the hand of the Christian alliance and the great number of victims exceeding one million, Americans are trying once again to repeat these horrifying massacres as if they are not satisfied with the long blockade or the destruction. Here they come today to eradicate the rest of these people and to humiliate its Muslim neighbors. Although the Americans' objectives of these wars are religious and economic, they are also to serve the Jewish state and distract from its occupation of the Holy Land and its killing of Muslims therein. The most evident proof thereof is their persistence to destroy Iraq, the most powerful neighboring Arab state. . . . All those crimes and calamities are an explicit declaration by the Americans of war on Allah, His Prophet, and Muslims. . . . Based upon this and in order to obey the Almighty, we hereby give all Muslims the following judgment: The judgment to kill and fight Americans and their allies, whether civilians or military, is an obligation for every Muslim who is able to do so in any country. . . . In the name of Allah, we call upon every Muslim, who believes in Allah and asks for forgiveness, to abide by Allah's order by killing Americans and stealing their money anywhere, anytime, and whenever possible. We also call upon Muslim scholars, their faithful leaders, young believers, and soldiers to launch a raid on the American soldiers of Satan and their allies of the Devil.

A CIA analysis point out: "These *fatwas* are the first from these groups that explicitly justify attacks on American civilians anywhere in the world." . . .

On August 7, 1998, Al Qaeda operatives bombed the U.S. embassies in Nairobi, Kenya, and Dar-es-Salaam, Tanzania, killing 224 people, mostly Africans. For much of the West, this was the first time the name Osama bin Laden made headlines. The United States responded with cruise missile attacks against Al Qaeda training installations in Afghanistan, and an attack against a chemical plant in Sudan that it later appears was not connected with Al Qaeda. A U.S. grand jury subsequently indicted bin Laden in absentia for the bombing of the U.S. embassies.

On October 12, 2000, two suicide bombers exploded a bomb aboard a small boat alongside the U.S.S. Cole, which was refueling in a Yemenese port, severely damaging the destroyer and killing 17 people. This attack, which was apparently planned by Al Qaeda, drew virtually no retaliatory response from the United States. It was Al Qaeda's last attack before September 11 and might well have encouraged bin Laden to believe that the United States would not respond in any significant military way to an attack.

Bin Laden's Beliefs

Bin Laden professes a sect of Sunni Islam called Wahhabi. Professor Karen Armstrong describes the origins of this sect.

Karen Amstrong, The Battle for God
44 (2000)

On the margins of the [Ottoman] empire, where Ottoman decline was most acutely felt, people responded to the change and unrest as they had always done — in religious terms. In the Arabian Peninsula, Muhammad ibn Abd al-Wahhab (1703-92) managed to break away from Istanbul and create a state of his own in central Arabia and the Persian Gulf region. Abd al-Wahhab was a typical Islamic reformer. He met the current crisis by returning to the Koran and the Sunnah, and by vehemently rejecting medieval jurisprudence, mysticism, and philosophy. Because they diverged from this pristine Islam, as he envisaged it, Abd al-Wahhab declared the Ottoman sultans to be apostates, unworthy of the obedience of the faithful and deserving of death. Their Shariah state was inauthentic. Instead, Abd al-Wahhab tried to create an enclave of pure faith, based on the practice of the first Muslim community in the seventh century. It was an aggressive movement, which imposed itself on the people by force.

Wahhabi remains the official religion of the house of Saud today, and it remains very conservative. Reinterpretation of issues decided by the Qu'ran, *hadith,* or early jurists is forbidden, although some flexibility is permitted when new issues arise. Strict conformity with its precepts is enforced by the *mutawwiin,* who are authorized to supervise dress, public behavior, and public prayer. In recent years, the Saudi regime has taken to discouraging and even banning non-Muslim worship in the kingdom.

For bin Laden, however, his particular sect takes second place to his agenda. Not only was he closely allied with the Taliban, whose own reactionary, puritanical breed of Islam, known as Deobandi, differs in a number of ways from Wahhabi, but he has made alliances with Islamist groups from Yemen, Egypt, and various other African and Middle Eastern countries. In these countries, and especially in Egypt, the homeland of many of the top Al Qaeda leaders, Wahhabi had little influence. Bin Laden's alliance with the *shi'ite* Hezbollah organization is even more telling. Bin Laden was willing to bury a millennium of religious difference for the knowledge to make Al Qaeda more effective.

Bin Laden's ultimate goal is far grander than the mere expulsion of the infidel from Saudi Arabia. As Peter Bergen explains:

> In all the tens of thousands of words that bin Laden has uttered on the public record there are some significant omissions: he does not rail against the pernicious effects of Hollywood movies, or against Madonna's midriff, or against the pornography protected by the U.S. Constitution. Nor does he inveigh against the drug and alcohol culture of the West, or its tolerance for homosexuality. . . .
>
> Judging by his silence, bin Laden cares little about such cultural issues. What he condemns the United States for is simple: its policies in the Middle East. Those are, to recap briefly: the continued American military presence in Arabia, U.S. support for Israel, its continued campaign against Iraq, and its support for regimes such as Egypt and Saudi Arabia that bin Laden regards as apostates from Islam.
>
> Bin Laden is at war with the United States, but his is a political war, justified by his own understanding of Islam, and directed at the symbols and institutions of American power. . . .
>
> Bin Laden envisaged his own counterpoint to the mark of globalization — the restoration of the *Khalifa,* or caliphate, which would begin from Afghanistan. Not since the final demise of the Ottoman Empire after the end of World War I had there been a Muslim entity that more or less united the *umma,* the community of Muslim believers, under the green flag of Islam. In this view, the treaties that followed World War I had carved up the Ottoman Empire, "the Sick Man of Europe," into ersatz entities like Iraq and Syria. Bin Laden aimed to create the conditions for the rebirth of the *Khalifa,* where the *umma* would live under the rule of the Prophet Muhammad in a continuous swath of green from Tunisia to Indonesia, much as the red of the British empire colored maps from Egypt to Burma before World War II. As a practical matter, the restoration of the *Khalifa* had about as much chance as the Holy Roman Empire suddenly reappearing in Europe, but as a rhetorical device the call for its return exercised a powerful grip on bin Laden and his followers. (Bergen, 226-227, 20-21.)

The Taliban

It is also helpful to understand the Taliban, who provided bin Laden and Al Qaeda an important sanctuary in Afghanistan.

After the Soviet withdrawal from Afghanistan in 1989, various Afghan factions and warlords embroiled the country in a fierce power struggle. In reaction to the prevalent anarchy and warlordism, a new movement of former *mujahideen* (freedom fighters) began. This new movement, called the Taliban, took its name from the word *talib,* which means pupil. With substantial support from Pakistan, the Taliban successfully dedicated itself to removing warlords, sustaining order, and imposing an extreme interpretation of Islam on Afghanistan.

By 1994, the Taliban had captured the southern city of Kandahar, and by the fall of 1996, the regime extended its control over the capital city of Kabul and other strategic regions.

The ultra-purist version of Islam espoused by the Taliban was based in part on the rural Pashtun tradition. However, in the process of imposing this extreme interpretation of Islam, the Taliban committed grave human rights violations against the Afghan people, generating an international backlash against the rogue regime.

Some of the Taliban's most shocking policies were directed against Afghan women. Women were forced to wear a traditional body garment called a burqa, and they could not leave home without an accompanying male relative. The Taliban forbade girls from obtaining an education and prohibited women from working outside the home. Moreover, women's access to health care was restricted and women did not have the right to vote.

The Taliban also systematically opposed religious freedom. In early 2001, Mullah Omar ordered the destruction of all Buddhist statues in Afghanistan on the grounds that religious representations were un-Islamic. As a result, thousands of Buddhist statues were demolished, including some dating back to the third and fifth centuries. In particular, the Taliban blew up two giant, ancient Buddha statues outside the city of Bamiyan.

The Taliban's massive human rights violations also extended to ethnic minorities. The Taliban killed noncombatants on several documented occasions. These atrocities particularly targeted the Shi'a Hazara ethnic group, a population that was a minority in the northern and western regions of Afghanistan.

Not only were the Taliban's social and religious policies objectionable, but their economic activities stirred international concern. After the disintegration of central authority following the Soviet withdrawal, opium became the sole cash crop for many Afghans. Opium-derived revenues soon became a major source of funding for the Taliban, including nearly $40 million per year in opium taxes alone.

In part because of its human rights violations and reliance on opium exports, the Taliban were not accepted by the international community. Even though the Taliban controlled roughly 90 percent of Afghanistan from about 1998 onward, only three countries (Pakistan, Saudi Arabia, and United Arab Emirates) had formally recognized the Taliban as Afghanistan's legitimate government by September 2001. Afghanistan's seat in the U.N. General Assembly continued to be held by the Taliban's opposition, known as the Northern Alliance, even though its control over Afghan territory had dwindled.

3. Initial Reactions to the September 11 Attacks

United States

Despite the tremendous shock, confusion, and mourning on September 11 and the days immediately after, the United States responded rapidly. First to react were the brave firefighters, police officers, and other emergency personnel who rushed to the scene at the World Trade Center and the Pentagon. U.S. Air National Guard interceptors were soon scrambled, though minutes too late to prevent the attack on the Pentagon. The actions of the heroic passengers on the flight over Pennsylvania meant that a U.S. interceptor dispatched there did not have to undertake the possible mission of shooting down one of the country's own airliners. At 9:50 A.M. on September 11, the Federal Aviation Administration suspended flight takeoffs across the country and ordered all civilian planes to land at the nearest airport. Military forces were alerted and mobilized. By early afternoon, the Navy dispatched two aircraft carriers to New York harbor and scrambled five warships along the Eastern seaboard, and fighter planes were ordered to patrol over major cities.

The investigation of the attacks was underway almost immediately. Within a few days, the 19 hijackers had been identified, and attention focused on Osama bin Laden.

President George W. Bush addressed the nation the night of September 11 and ordered a number of measures that day and in the days following. Among them, on September 14, President Bush declared a national emergency under the National Emergencies Act (50 U.S.C. §1621) and called up 50,000 reservists for the purpose of "homeland defense." At the same time, both houses of Congress passed by large margins a Joint Resolution that provided in pertinent part:

> That the President is authorized to use all necessary and appropriate force against those nations, organizations, or persons he determines planned, authorized, committed, or aided the terrorist attacks that occurred on September 11, 2001, or harbored such organizations or persons, in order to prevent any future acts of international terrorism against the United States by such nations, organizations or persons. (P.L. 107-40) [1]

On September 23, President Bush invoked the International Emergency Economic Powers Act (IEEPA). IEEPA provides the President with sweeping emergency powers in the international arena. It is designed to deal "with any unusual or extraordinary threat, which has its source in whole or substantial part outside the United States, to the [U.S.] national security, foreign policy, or economy." If the President determines that such a threat exists, he can declare a national emergency as Bush did on September 14 under the National Emergencies Act (NEA). IEEPA then authorizes him to employ a wide range of economic powers, such as cutting off exports or imports with a particular country, or (especially relevant here) restricting public and private financial transactions with a particular country or particular foreign individuals or entities. (IEEPA is discussed further in Chapter 3.) The following is an excerpt of President Bush's Executive Order freezing the assets of terrorist groups.

---

1. The Joint Resolution also specifically indicated that it was intended to constitute specific statutory authorization within the meaning of section 5(b) of the War Powers Resolution of 1973. (The War Powers Resolution is discussed in Chapter 11.)

President Bush, Blocking Property and Prohibiting Transactions With Persons Who Commit, Threaten to Commit, or Support Terrorism

Exec. Order 13,224 (Sept. 23, 2001), 66 Fed. Reg. 49,079

By the authority vested in me as President by the Constitution and the laws of the United States of America, including the International Emergency Economic Powers Act (50 U.S.C. 1701 et seq.) (IEEPA), the National Emergencies Act (50 U.S.C. 1601 et seq.), section 5 of the United Nations Participation Act of 1945, as amended (22 U.S.C. 287c) (UNPA) . . . and in view of United Nations Security Council Resolution[s] . . .

I, GEORGE W. BUSH, President of the United States of America, find that grave acts of terrorism . . . by foreign terrorists, including the terrorist attacks in New York, Pennsylvania, and the Pentagon committed on September 11, 2001, acts recognized and condemned in UNSCR [U.N. Security Council Resolution] 1368 of September 12, 2001, and UNSCR 1269 of October 19, 1999, and the continuing and immediate threat of further attacks on United States nationals or the United States constitute an unusual and extraordinary threat to the national security, foreign policy, and economy of the United States, and . . . hereby declare a national emergency to deal with that threat. I also find that because of the pervasiveness and expansiveness of the financial foundation of foreign terrorists, financial sanctions may be appropriate for those foreign persons that support or otherwise associate with these foreign terrorists. . . .

I hereby order:

Section 1. Except to the extent required by section 203(b) of IEEPA (50 U.S.C. 1702(b)), or provided in regulations, orders, directives, or licenses that may be issued pursuant to this order, and notwithstanding any contract entered into or any license or permit granted prior to the effective date of this order, all property and interests in property of the following persons that are in the United States or that hereafter come within the United States, or that hereafter come within the possession or control of United States persons are blocked:

(a) foreign persons listed in the Annex to this order;

(b) foreign persons determined by the Secretary of State, in consultation with the Secretary of the Treasury and the Attorney General, to have committed, or to pose a significant risk of committing, acts of terrorism that threaten the security of U.S. nationals or the national security, foreign policy, or economy of the United States;

(c) persons determined by the Secretary of the Treasury, in consultation with the Secretary of State and the Attorney General, to be owned or controlled by, or to act for or on behalf of those persons listed in the Annex to this order or those persons determined to be subject to subsection 1(b), 1(c), or 1(d)(i) of this order; . . .

Sec. 2. Except to the extent required by section 203(b) of IEEPA (50 U.S.C. 1702(b)), or provided in regulations, orders, directives, or licenses that may be issued pursuant to this order, and notwithstanding any contract entered into or any license or permit granted prior to the effective date:

(a) any transaction or dealing by United States persons or within the United States in property or interests in property blocked pursuant to this order is prohibited, including but not limited to the making or receiving of any contribution of funds, goods, or services to or for the benefit of those persons listed in the Annex to this order or determined to be subject to this order;

(b) any transaction by any United States person or within the United States that evades or avoids, or has the purpose of evading or avoiding, or attempts to violate, any of the prohibitions set forth in this order is prohibited. . . .

Sec. 3. For purposes of this order: . . .

(c) the term "United States person" means any United States citizen, permanent resident alien, entity organized under the laws of the United States (including foreign branches), or any person in the United States; and

(d) the term "terrorism" means an activity that —

(i) involves a violent act or an act dangerous to human life, property, or infrastructure; and

(ii) appears to be intended —

(A) to intimidate or coerce a civilian population;

(B) to influence the policy of a government by intimidation or coercion; or

(C) to affect the conduct of a government by mass destruction, assassination, kidnapping, or hostage-taking. . . .

Sec. 6. The Secretary of State, the Secretary of the Treasury, and other appropriate agencies shall make all relevant efforts to cooperate and coordinate with other countries . . . to achieve the objectives of this order, including the prevention and suppression of acts of terrorism, the denial of financing and financial services to terrorists and terrorist organizations, and the sharing of intelligence about funding activities in support of terrorism. . . .

GEORGE W. BUSH, THE WHITE HOUSE, September 23, 2001.

This order froze all the assets in the United States or in possession of U.S. entities of 27 terrorists, terrorist organizations, and charitable organizations believed to fund terrorist organizations. Included in the annex to the order were bin Laden, Al Qaeda, and several allied terrorist groups and individual members of Al Qaeda. The assets of the Taliban, amounting to $265 million within the United States, had been frozen in 1999 as part of the response to the embassy bombings in Kenya and Tanzania. The Administration added an additional 39 individuals and entities to its list on October 12, and has continued to add to it since then, as new information has arisen. As of January 2003, there were over 200 individuals and entities on Bush's freeze list, including terrorist groups as wide-ranging as Palestinian Hamas, Kashmiri Lashkar-e-Tayyiba, and Basque ETA.

Most of Al Qaeda's funds are located outside the United States, so international support for the freezing of terrorist assets has been important to the effectiveness of the program. To help this process, the U.N. Security Council had decided in Resolution 1373 of September 28, 2001, that all Member States should "[f]reeze without delay funds and other financial assets or economic resources of persons who commit, or attempt to commit, terrorist acts or participate in or facilitate the commission of terrorist acts."

As of January 2003, the U.S. government reported that 161 other countries had issued their own blocking statutes. Overall, $123 million in terrorist assets had been frozen worldwide, $36 million of that had been blocked domestically in the United States, and the remaining $87 million had been blocked by other countries.

NATO

On September 12, the North Atlantic Treaty Organization (NATO) expressed its willingness to invoke Article 5 of its founding treaty for the first time in its history if it were determined that the Sept. 11 attacks were indeed directed from abroad. Article 5 states:

> The Parties agree that an armed attack against one or more of them in Europe or North America shall be considered an attack against them all and consequently they agree that, if such an armed attack occurs, each of them, in exercise of the right of individual or collective self-defence recognized by Article 51 of the Charter of the United Nations, will assist the Party or Parties so attacked by taking forthwith, individually and in concert with the other Parties, such action as it deems necessary, including the use of armed force, to restore and maintain the security of the North Atlantic area.
>
> Any such armed attack and all measures taken as a result thereof shall immediately be reported to the Security Council. Such measures shall be terminated when the Security Council has taken the measures necessary to restore and maintain international peace and security.

On October 2, the NATO Secretary General stated that NATO had determined that Al Qaeda was involved in the Sept. 11 attacks. Accordingly, "it has now been determined that the attack against the United States on 11 September was directed from abroad and shall therefore be regarded as an action covered by Article 5." Despite this rapid and heartening show of support, the role of the NATO Alliance in the ensuing military response was limited. Although some NATO members provided forces to the U.S.-led campaign (namely, Britain, Canada, and France), most members limited themselves to opening their airspace to American military flights and providing some logistical support. In part, this was because the United States did not ask some of these countries to do more. Possibly the most important role played by the Alliance as an entity was to authorize the dispatch of NATO early-warning aircraft to patrol U.S. airspace, freeing American aircraft for an offensive role in Afghanistan.

The United Nations

The United Nations has been much involved in the struggle against terrorism and quickly reacted to the attacks of September 11. Essentially all the countries of the world are members of the United Nations, with 191 member states as of January 2003.[2] The basic documents for the United Nations are its Charter (which is a

---

2. As noted earlier, Afghanistan was a U.N. member, but in September 2001 the Northern Alliance was the recognized government, not the Taliban regime. The government of Hamid Karzai gained the seat in December 2001.

treaty), and a fundamental provision of the Charter is Article 2(4). It provides: "All Members shall refrain in their international relations from the threat or use of force against the territorial integrity or political independence of any state. . . ." The only explicit exception in the Charter for a country to use force is found in Article 51:

> Nothing in the present Charter shall impair the inherent right of individual or collective self-defense if an armed attack occurs against a Member of the United Nations, until the Security Council has taken the measures necessary to maintain international peace and security. Measures taken by Members in the exercise of this right of self-defense shall be immediately reported to the Security Council and shall not in any way affect the authority and responsibility of the Security Council under the present Charter to take at any time such action as it deems necessary in order to maintain or restore international peace and security.

In response to a breach of peace or threat of aggression, the Security Council has the power under Chapter VII of the U.N. Charter, especially Articles 39-42, to decide on a wide range of economic and military measures and to call on all U.N. Member States to apply these measures. (The U.N. Charter is in the Documentary Supplement.)

The Security Council has 15 members, with five permanent, veto-wielding members (China, France, Russia, the United Kingdom, and the United States). During the Cold War, the Security Council was often hamstrung by the veto, or the threat of veto, by one or more of the five permanent members. However, with the thawing of the Cold War, the Security Council has begun cooperating in an unprecedented way. The Security Council reacted quickly and strongly to the Iraqi invasion of Kuwait in 1990, and it played a major role in the conflict in the former Yugoslavia during the late 1990s, though it was NATO that finally took the lead in using military force against Serbia over Kosovo.

Before September 11

Prior to the terrorist attacks, the U.N. Security Council passed several resolutions condemning the Taliban for harboring terrorists and protecting terrorist training camps. After the bombings of the U.S. embassies in Kenya and Tanzania in 1999, the Security Council passed Resolution 1267, which demanded that the Taliban turn over Osama bin Laden to appropriate authorities in a country where he would be arrested. Additionally, Resolution 1267 called upon all states to prevent any Taliban-operated aircraft from taking off or landing in their territory. The resolution further required states to freeze all assets derived from property owned or controlled by the Taliban.

In December 2000, the Security Council passed Resolution 1333 condemning the Taliban for its support of terrorist activity. The resolution demanded the Taliban's compliance with Resolution 1267. It also mandated additional actions against the Taliban by Member States, such as preventing the supply of arms, military equipment, and certain chemicals to the Taliban. At the same time, the resolution contained provisions designed to maintain some humanitarian aid to the Afghan people.

It was clear even before September 11 that the Taliban failed to comply with the anti-terrorism provisions of these and other resolutions.

After September 11

The day after the Sept. 11 attacks, the Security Council, operating from U.N. headquarters that are only a few miles from the World Trade Center, swiftly and unanimously passed Resolution 1368. The resolution both condemned the terrorist attacks and offered broad support for retaliation by the United States and its allies.

U.N. Security Council Resolution 1368
(Sept. 12, 2001)

The Security Council,

Reaffirming the principles and purposes of the Charter of the United Nations,

Determined to combat by all means threats to international peace and security caused by terrorist acts,

Recognizing the inherent right of individual or collective self-defence in accordance with the Charter,

1. *Unequivocally condemns* in the strongest terms the horrifying terrorist attacks which took place on 11 September 2001 . . . and *regards* such acts, like any act of international terrorism, as a threat to international peace and security;

2. *Expresses* its deepest sympathy and condolences to the victims and their families and to the people and Government of the United States of America;

3. *Calls* on all States to work together urgently to bring to justice the perpetrators, organizers and sponsors of these terrorist attacks and *stresses* that those responsible for aiding, supporting or harbouring the perpetrators, organizers and sponsors of these acts will be held accountable;

4. *Calls also* on the international community to redouble their efforts to prevent and suppress terrorist acts including by increased cooperation and full implementation of the relevant international anti-terrorist conventions and Security Council resolutions, in particular resolution 1269 (1999) of 19 October 1999;

5. *Expresses* its readiness to take all necessary steps to respond to the terrorist attacks of 11 September 2001, and to combat all forms of terrorism, in accordance with its responsibilities under the Charter of the United Nations;

6. *Decides* to remain seized of the matter.

———————————

Although Resolution 1368 was a quickly drafted response to the attacks on September 11, its language had important legal consequences. First, Resolution 1368 described the terrorist attacks as a "threat to international peace and security," thus bringing them within the scope of Chapter VII of the U.N. Charter, which raised the possibility of U.N. enforcement actions. Second, Resolution 1368 recognized the legal right of individual or collective self-defense in accordance with the Charter. In other words, the Security Council implicitly recognized that a state could respond militarily against those responsible for the attacks, even though the terrorists were not state actors. Legally, this was an unprecedented move for the United Nations. Prior to September 11, the Security Council had failed to reach a unanimous position on unilateral retaliation for terrorist attacks. Moreover, when the General Assembly spoke on the issue, it often condemned such unilateral military responses.

Although the Council's resolution suggests that a nation has a right of self-defense in response to international terrorism, according to Article 51 of the Charter, the right to individual or collective self-defense is only an interim right — "until the Security Council has taken measures necessary to maintain international peace and security." Hence, the Security Council may in future cases try to take charge, though a permanent member might use its veto power to block the Security Council.

On September 28, the Security Council followed up Resolution 1368 with an even stronger anti-terrorism declaration in Resolution 1373. Specifically, it stated that member states should implement domestic legislation that would fight the "international threat to peace and security" that terrorism had become and that all states shall take a number of other steps.

U.N. Security Council Resolution 1373
(Sept. 28, 2001)

The Security Council . . .

2. *Decides also* that all States shall:

(a) Refrain from providing any form of support, active or passive, to entities or persons involved in terrorist acts, including by suppressing recruitment of members of terrorist groups and eliminating the supply of weapons to terrorists;

(b) Take the necessary steps to prevent the commission of terrorist acts, including by provision of early warning to other States by exchange of information;

(c) Deny safe haven to those who finance, plan, support, or commit terrorist acts, or provide safe havens;

(d) Prevent those who finance, plan, facilitate or commit terrorist acts from using their respective territories for those purposes against other States or their citizens;

(e) Ensure that any person who participates in the financing, planning, preparation or perpetration of terrorist acts or in supporting terrorist acts is brought to justice and ensure that, in addition to any other measures against them, such terrorist acts are established as serious criminal offences in domestic laws and regulations and that the punishment duly reflects the seriousness of such terrorist acts;

(f) Afford one another the greatest measure of assistance in connection with criminal investigations or criminal proceedings relating to the financing or support of terrorist acts, including assistance in obtaining evidence in their possession necessary for the proceedings;

(g) Prevent the movement of terrorists or terrorist groups by effective border controls and controls on issuance of identity papers and travel documents, and through measures for preventing counterfeiting, forgery or fraudulent use of identity papers and travel documents;

3. *Calls* upon all States to:

(a) Find ways of intensifying and accelerating the exchange of operational information, especially regarding actions or movements of terrorist persons or networks; forged or falsified travel documents; traffic in arms, explosives or sensitive materials; use of communications technologies by terrorist groups; and the threat posed by the possession of weapons of mass destruction by terrorist groups; . . .

(c) Cooperate, particularly through bilateral and multilateral arrangements and agreements, to prevent and suppress terrorist attacks and take action against perpetrators of such acts;

(d) Become parties as soon as possible to the relevant international conventions and protocols relating to terrorism, including the International Convention for the Suppression of the Financing of Terrorism of 9 December 1999;

(e) Increase cooperation and fully implement the relevant international conventions and protocols relating to terrorism and Security Council resolutions 1269 (1999) and 1368 (2001);

(f) Take appropriate measures in conformity with the relevant provisions of national and international law, including international standards of human rights, before granting refugee status, for the purpose of ensuring that the asylum-seeker has not planned, facilitated or participated in the commission of terrorist acts;

(g) Ensure, in conformity with international law, that refugee status is not abused by the perpetrators, organizers or facilitators of terrorist acts, and that claims of political motivation are not recognized as grounds for refusing requests for the extradition of alleged terrorists.

The U.N. General Assembly also addressed the issue of international terrorism after the Sept. 11 attacks. Each country's U.N. permanent representative spoke in a week-long debate on the question of terrorism. Perhaps the most controversial aspect of the discussions centered on whether the U.N. should set a specific definition as to what constitutes terrorism. Both the need for such a definition and the content of such a definition produced considerable debate and disagreement. Despite the General Assembly's efforts, a general consensus on the definition of terrorism was not reached.

Notes and Questions

1. As noted above, Congress passed a resolution on September 14, 2001, authorizing the President to "use all necessary and appropriate force" against countries that had "aided the terrorist attacks that occurred on September 11, 2001." This resolution became effective on September 18 when it was signed by President Bush. Do you think that President Bush could have proceeded to conduct the major U.S. operations against the Taliban in Afghanistan that began in October 2001, even if Congress had not passed this or any similar resolution? What about Article I, Section 8, clause 11 of the U.S. Constitution, which gives Congress the power "[t]o declare War." Given this broadly phrased resolution, did Congress cede all responsibilities and authority for conducting military operations in Afghanistan? If Congress later thought that the Bush Administration and the military might be failing to take sufficient precautions to protect innocent Afghan civilians, what steps were available to Congress?

2. Did the September 14 resolution also give the President the authority to launch a major military attack on Iraq or Iran if the President determined that there was sufficient evidence to demonstrate that one of those countries had provided material support to the hijackers?

3. As noted above, President Bush's actions included issuing an Executive Order on September 23, 2001, that invoked a broad U.S. law, IEEPA, to block (or freeze) the assets of Al Qaeda and other terrorist groups and individuals when the assets are in the United States or under the control of "U.S. persons." This phrase was defined to include, among others, U.S. individual citizens and U.S. corporations even if they were abroad. What authority does a U.S. President have to regulate assets in other countries, such as Saudi Arabia, even if they are held by a "U.S. person"? Does it matter that most other countries agreed to cooperate with the U.S. order? What if Saudi Arabia disagreed with some of the Executive Order's designations of terrorist groups and individuals, and directed that a U.S. company in Saudi Arabia should not freeze the assets of those disputed entities? Whose law controls?

4. Assume that the scope of the Executive Order, issued pursuant to IEEPA, was extended to include, besides U.S. individual citizens and U.S. corporations, "any corporation, wherever organized or doing business, that is owned or controlled by a U.S. corporation"—that is, foreign subsidiaries of a U.S. corporation. Does the U.S. President have the power to order an Italian subsidiary of a U.S. corporation to freeze assets that it might have in its possession in Italy from Al Qaeda or the Taliban (e.g., a bank deposit, or advances for goods that have yet to be delivered)? Should the President have this power? What are the rights of the government of Italy?

5. NATO was created in 1949 to provide a counterweight to the Soviet Union and its satellite states in Eastern Europe. Its primary purpose was to discourage a Soviet attack on Western European democracies. With the end of the Cold War, its mission has been redefined. It has expanded in recent years to include some of its former adversaries in Eastern Europe, and has even created a system by which Russia can have a nearly equal say in its deliberations. NATO forces fought the war against Milosevic in the former Yugoslavia and then provided peacekeepers in Kosovo afterwards.

When NATO invoked Article 5 against Al Qaeda on October 2, 2001, what were the obligations of the 19 countries then in NATO? Does Article 5 require each country to assist the United States?

After invoking Article 5 for the first time in its history, NATO's most important action was to contribute five early warning aircraft to the defense of United States skies. Why did the United States and just a few allies, and not NATO, take the lead in operations against Al Qaeda and the Taliban?

6. As noted earlier, from 1998 to 2001, the Taliban controlled about 90 percent of Afghanistan, but only three countries recognized the Taliban as the legitimate government of Afghanistan, with most of the remaining countries (including those in Europe and the United States) recognizing the rival Northern Alliance. Morever, while Afghanistan is a member state of the United Nations and has signed the U.N. Charter, the United Nations continued to recognize the Northern Alliance as that state's government. What does recognition mean when a group (such as the Northern Alliance) cannot exercise effective control over its own territory? What effect does non-recognition have on a regime that is the de facto government of a state? (We return to these questions in Chapter 5.)

7. Security Council Resolution 1368 declared terrorism a threat to international peace and security. This finding is a precondition to any use by the Security Council of Chapter VII powers under the U.N. Charter, that is to say, the power to direct member states to take certain actions. Resolution 1373 exercised these powers for the first time after September 11, obligating member states to deny terrorists safe

haven in their territories, to refrain from supporting terrorists, and to bring terrorists and their supporters to justice. Was the Taliban bound by Resolution 1373?

Of course, the Taliban did not abide by Resolution 1373. Were states other than
Afghanistan obligated to use force to ensure compliance by the Taliban? Were they
authorized to do so? Could the Security Council have authorized or required the use
of force against the Taliban?

8. Resolution 1368 recognized the inherent right of individual and collective
self-defense, and called on member states to ensure that the perpetrators of the
Sept. 11 attacks are held accountable. Does this authorize the use of force by the
United States? By Great Britain? Whatever your answer about Resolution 1368, does
international law require that the United States obtain U.N. Security Council authorization to use force against those who supported the Sept. 11 terrorists? Did
Great Britain need authorization? Does "collective self-defense" include only recognized regional groups, such as NATO, or can informal coalitions be developed?
See also U.N. Charter Article 52.

4.   Building a Coalition

In his September 20, 2001, address to a joint session of Congress, President
Bush issued an ultimatum to the Taliban:

> Deliver to United States authorities all the leaders of Al Qaida who hide in your
> land. Release all foreign nationals, including American citizens, you have unjustly im-
> prisoned. Protect foreign journalists, diplomats, and aid workers in your country. Close
> immediately and permanently every terrorist training camp in Afghanistan, and hand
> over every terrorist and every person in their support structure to appropriate author-
> ities. Give the United States full access to terrorist training camps, so we can make sure
> they are no longer operating. These demands are not open to negotiation or discus-
> sion. The Taliban must act and act immediately. They will hand over the terrorists, or
> they will share in their fate.

The Taliban attempted to negotiate turning over bin Laden in the days after
September 20, but the Taliban sought to impose conditions that President Bush had
already said were unacceptable. In the meantime, the Taliban was losing what little
international support it might have had. Both Saudi Arabia and the United Arab
Emirates severed their diplomatic ties with the Taliban, leaving Pakistan as the only
country that recognized the Taliban, and this was primarily to keep open a channel
for negotiations.

Even before President Bush's September 20 speech, the United States had initiated far-ranging diplomatic negotiations with many countries to seek their understanding and possible cooperation for the military steps that the Pentagon began
planning shortly after the Sept. 11 attacks. General Pervez Musharraf of Pakistan was
crucial to this emerging coalition. Although Pakistan's intelligence services had supported the Taliban in its rise to power, Musharraf promptly condemned the attacks
and the Taliban for harboring bin Laden, and agreed to allow the United States and
its coalition to use Pakistani airspace and eventually airbases. Despite early violent
protests by Islamic groups against cooperation, Musharraf reversed what had been
an increasingly chilled U.S.-Pakistani relationship.

Also important was the agreement of the former Soviet republics of Uzbekistan, Kyrgyzstan, and Tajikistan, which faced internal threats from Al Qaeda-linked Islamist movements, to permit U.S. forces to operate from bases in their territory in exchange for increased U.S. aid and closer political and security ties. Similarly, Kuwait and Qatar, Muslim countries in the Middle East, allowed the use of existing airbases for U.S. air strikes in Afghanistan.

Although several European countries offered military support as well, the United States chose to use primarily its own forces and those of the Northern Alliance and other indigenous Afghan forces, with limited military assistance from British troops (as well as Australian and Canadian forces). Other European countries were asked to provide humanitarian aid and sometimes overflight permission for U.S. military aircraft. Turkey allowed the use of important airbases there.

President Vladimir Putin of Russia agreed to provide more Soviet-era arms and munitions to the Northern Alliance, with whom it already had existing ties. Russia also let the U.S. military operate freely in the former Soviet republics that Russia still considered to be in the Russian sphere of influence. Putin's price for this cooperation was not completely clear to observers, but aside from closer ties generally with the West, one benefit has been a freer hand in dealing with the separatist Chechens, some of whom have links to Al Qaeda.

China's support publicly and in the United Nations had considerable political value for the United States, though China also used the rhetoric of the "war on terrorism" to justify its crackdown on its own Islamic separatist minority, the Uighurs in Xinjiang province. Finally, while most of the Muslim states of the Middle East were not forthcoming with material support, several provided intelligence and law enforcement assistance in disrupting Al Qaeda networks outside of Afghanistan.

5. *The Military Campaign*

With the coalition assembled and with U.S. air, ground, and naval units moved thousands of miles into forward positions, President Bush gave the order on October 7, 2001, to begin the campaign against Afghanistan, code-named Operation Enduring Freedom. Nighttime airstrikes began on October 7 and continued for three nights, after which the United States declared that it had established air supremacy and could now bomb in daylight and, when appropriate, send in ground forces. The strikes were carried out with ship-launched cruise missiles and aircraft launched from carriers in the Arabian Sea, as well as bases in Pakistan and Uzbekistan, by B-52 and B-2 bombers flying from Diego Garcia, an island in the Indian Ocean, and by B-2 bombers flying day-long missions from bases in the United States itself. Airstrikes continued around the clock after October 9, targeting Taliban tanks, artillery, weapons and fuel depots, and command centers, as well as Al Qaeda training camps. Meanwhile, the allies dropped food rations, trying to minimize the bombing campaign's impact on civilians. By October 19, American Special Forces were able to land and to carry out raids and other missions near Taliban strongholds.

The ground war began in earnest in the closing days of October. Instead of continuing to bomb strategic targets, most of which had already been destroyed, the U.S. air campaign shifted its emphasis to supporting the ground forces of the Northern Alliance, a group of mostly Tajik and Uzbek warlords who were at that time the only effective anti-Taliban rebels. Their charismatic leader, Ahmad Shah Massood, had been assassinated just two days before the Sept. 11 attacks, almost certainly by Al Qaeda. However, his faction still controlled significant amounts of territory when Operation Enduring Freedom began. The United States began targeting Taliban troop concentrations in the north and, in particular, those forces opposing Northern Alliance fighters.

The first major successes of this coordinated campaign came in mid-November. On November 9, the northern stronghold of Mazar-e-Sharif fell to the Northern Alliance, operating in coordination with U.S. forces. After that intial victory, the rest of the country fell relatively quickly. Northern Alliance forces took the capital, Kabul, from retreating Taliban forces on November 12, and the cities of Herat, Jalalabad, and Konduz fell within weeks. U.S. forces were able to occupy Bagram Air Force Base, about 27 miles north of Kabul, and use it as a staging area for other operations. The success of the Northern Alliance and the promise of American air support encouraged rebel groups in other parts of Afghanistan to rise up against the Taliban. One of these groups, under the leadership of Hamid Karzai, accepted the surrender of the Taliban capital of Kandahar on December 6. (As discussed below, Karzai had been chosen to lead an interim post-Taliban government days earlier.) Although many top Taliban officials, including Mullah Mohammed Omar, escaped Kandahar, the fall of the city finished them as a power in Afghanistan.

Remnants of the Taliban and Al Qaeda retreated to tunnel complexes built to house *mujahideen* fighting against the Soviets, such as Tora Bora, near the Pakistani border. Tora Bora fell on December 16 to a combination of American precision bombs and local forces the Americans called the "Eastern Alliance." However, the Eastern Alliance failed to follow up its victory, and there were insufficient U.S. forces on the ground to prevent hundreds of Al Qaeda, apparently including bin Laden, from escaping into the relatively lawless tribal regions of Pakistan. Another attack on an Al Qaeda cave complex in February and March 2002 was more successful. Over 1,000 U.S. infantrymen led the attack, called Operation Anaconda, against regrouping Al Qaeda in the Shah-i-kot valley, and they were able to prevent most of the fighters from escaping.

After Operation Anaconda, the remnants of Al Qaeda mostly scattered to tribal areas of Pakistan and Afghanistan. Cooperative operations between U.S. and allied forces and some local warlords against pockets of fighters continued, but nothing on the scale of Anaconda or Tora Bora.

Notes and Questions

1. Mostly through Pakistani intermediaries, the United States apparently communicated with Taliban representatives in an attempt to capture bin Laden and his accomplices without war. How could the United States negotiate with the Taliban without recognizing them?

2. On August 2, 1990, an Iraqi army invaded and occupied Kuwait. The reaction around the world was all but instantaneous and, with very few exceptions, entirely negative. The United Nations and the governments of most nation-states condemned the invasion as a violation of international law. Yet the U.S. attack on the Taliban was criticized only by a small minority of Muslim states, most of which

dropped their objections when the invasion succeeded beyond expectations. Why did the world community condemn the Iraqi invasion, but not the U.S. attacks? Were the U.S. attacks consistent with international law? If so, what principles provided the justification for them? Besides the fact that the United States was responding to the Sept. 11 attacks on its territory that were organized by Al Qaeda, does it help that the United States was also operating in conjunction with the Northern Alliance?

3. Given that most countries and the U.N. recognized the Northern Alliance as the government of Afghanistan, were the U.S. attacks in Afghanistan an "invasion" of Afghanistan? Did the United States "declare war" or "go to war" against Afghanistan? How would you characterize the U.S. operations against the Taliban and Al Qaeda? Was the United States intervening in a civil war?

4. (Review Note 8 in the last set of Notes and Questions.) If you think that the United States might have been justified in attacking the Taliban and Al Qaeda under Article 51 of the U.N. Charter and/or pursuant to U.N. Security Council Resolutions 1368 and 1373, did the attack have to be proportional? The United States made the overthrow of the Taliban one of its explicit objectives when the U.S. offensive began. If it could have uprooted Al Qaeda without bringing down the Taliban, should it have had to?

5. One notable aspect of the conflict in Afghanistan was the increased use of high technology warfare. Perhaps the most important innovation was the widespread use of "smart bombs," guided by Global Positioning System (GPS) satellites. These GPS-guided smart bombs are significantly more accurate and dependable than the laser-guided munitions used in the Persian Gulf War in 1991, and potentially cheaper as well. As many as 70 percent of the bombs used in Afghanistan were smart bombs (versus about 9 percent in Iraq). Most were actually ordinary bombs equipped with a JDAM (for Joint Direct Attack Munitions), a kit that cost about one-fifth a Gulf War smart bomb and that allows a bomb to guide itself to within three feet of a target. Other high-tech American advances that transformed this war include infantry equipment such as night-vision goggles, as well as the "Predator" unmanned aircraft, which were used to take images and, later in the campaign, to fire missiles.

This high technology was often combined with old-fashioned low-tech warfare. There were situations when an American soldier, traveling on horseback and accompanied by Afghan forces using World War I-era rifles, would enter target coordinates into a state-of-the-art laptop computer. Within minutes, the command center in Saudi Arabia would relay the coordinates to a 1970s-era bomber, which would drop a GPS-guided bomb on Taliban or Al Qaeda troop concentrations or installations.

The use by American forces of high-tech weaponry kept both U.S. and civilian casualties relatively low. One result was that far fewer civilian targets were hit by stray bombs, although some mistakes still occurred, largely as a result of human error and equipment failure.

Despite a low ratio of civilian casualties compared to past military actions, even ones as recent as the Kosovo air campaign, the U.S. military was criticized for some operations that resulted in civilian casualties. Is the United States or its soldiers responsible when a bomb goes astray in an area of conflict? What if human error is the cause and the bomb is mistakenly programmed with the coordinates of a hospital, or a U.S. gunship fires on a wedding party? In at least one such case, the United

Nations faced pressure to perform an independent investigation. What limits should international law place on warfare? With the recent creation of an International Criminal Court, do U.S. soldiers have to worry about being criminally charged for decisions made under fire? (These questions are discussed more fully in the section on Individual Responsibility in Chapter 11.)

6.   Nation Building

The Bonn Compromise

As the United States and Britain launched their military operations in Afghanistan, President Bush called on the United Nations to help rebuild a post-war Afghanistan. However, after the very troubled experience of peacekeeping operations in Somalia, U.N. officials were wary of taking on the nation-building role in Afghanistan. Nevertheless, U.N. Secretary-General Kofi Annan appointed a former Algerian foreign minister, Lakhdar Brahimi, as U.N. envoy for the Afghan peace settlement. As discussed below, backed by the United States and other countries, Brahimi was able to successfully negotiate an agreement in Bonn, Germany, that set up an interim Afghan administration. In addition, Brahimi and a number of countries shaped the U.N. aid programs that sustained much of Afghanistan's population.

The Bonn conference brought together the leaders of the four primary Afghan factions: the Northern Alliance, representing the Uzbek and Tajik minorities, and the Rome, Peshawar, and Cyprus Groups, representing Pashtuns connected to former King Mohammed Zahir Shah, to Pakistan, and to Iran, respectively. The conference met from November 27 through December 5, 2001, and created an interim government under the leadership of Hamid Karzai, who was absent from the meeting because he was commanding the assault on Kandahar. The meeting also provided for a *loya jirga,* or "grand council," to establish a transitional government that would lead for up to two years. Elections are to be held in 2004 and a new constitution ratified. The Karzai government was sworn in on December 21, 2001.

United Nations Peacekeeping

In December 2001, after the negotiation of the Bonn agreement, the U.N. Security Council passed Resolution 1386, which authorized the establishment of an International Security Assistance Force (ISAF) to aid the Afghan Interim Authority in maintaining peace and security in Kabul. Resolution 1386 established the ISAF to take "all necessary measures" to fulfill the peacekeeping mission. Everyone recognized that this might include the use of force.

U.N. Security Council Resolution 1386
(Dec. 20, 2001)

The Security Council . . .

1. *Authorizes,* as envisaged in Annex 1 to the Bonn Agreement, the establishment for 6 months of an International Security Assistance Force to assist the Afghan

Interim Authority in the maintenance of security in Kabul and its surrounding areas, so that the Afghan Interim Authority as well as the personnel of the United Nations can operate in a secure environment;

2. *Calls upon* Member States to contribute personnel, equipment and other resources to the International Security Assistance Force, and invites those Member States to inform the leadership of the Force and the Secretary-General;

3. *Authorizes* the Member States participating in the International Security Assistance Force to take all necessary measures to fulfil its mandate;

4. *Calls upon* the International Security Assistance Force to work in close consultation with the Afghan Interim Authority in the implementation of the force mandate, as well as with the Special Representative of the Secretary-General;

5. *Calls upon* all Afghans to cooperate with the International Security Assistance Force and relevant international governmental and non-governmental organizations, and welcomes the commitment of the parties to the Bonn Agreement to do all within their means and influence to ensure security . . . ;

6. *Takes note* of the pledge made by the Afghan parties to the Bonn Agreement in Annex 1 to that Agreement to withdraw all military units from Kabul . . . ;

7. *Encourages* neighbouring States and other Member States to provide to the International Security Assistance Force such necessary assistance as may be requested, including the provision of overflight clearances and transit;

8. *Stresses* that the expenses of the International Security Assistance Force will be borne by the participating Member States concerned, *requests* the Secretary-General to establish a trust fund through which contributions could be channelled to the Member States or operations concerned, and encourages Member States to contribute to such a fund; . . .

10. *Calls on* Member States participating in the International Security Assistance Force to provide assistance to help the Afghan Interim Authority in the establishment and training of new Afghan security and armed forces;

11. *Decides* to remain actively seized of the matter.

In November 2002, the Security Council extended the mandate of the ISAF to run through December 2003. Participation in the ISAF totaled roughly 4,600 troops from 122 different countries. Originally, the force was led for six months by the United Kingdom and then by Turkey. In December 2002, Germany and the Netherlands took the lead. Primarily, the ISAF aims to develop Afghan national security structures, assist the nation's reconstruction, and aid the training of future Afghan military forces.

Unlike many of its Western allies, the United States did not contribute troops to the peacekeeping force in Kabul, though U.S. forces remained in Afghanistan trying to track down the remnants of Taliban and Al Qaeda forces. The United States helped coordinate the peacekeeping operations and provided intelligence assistance to the peacekeeping troops. In addition, the United States supplied equipment and training to Afghans who were to become part of the new Afghan national army.

Despite the vital importance of the peacekeeping forces, U.N. officials still had many concerns about the future of the peacekeeping project. A primary concern was the cost of the mission. Resolution 1386 stressed that the expenses would be borne by the nations involved; however, it also requested the Secretary-General to create a trust fund through which the U.N. funds could be channeled to the countries supplying troops. In any case, the costs of maintaining the peacekeeping force would be in addition to the estimated $10 billion needed to rebuild Afghanistan over the next five years.

Another major concern was the safety of the peacekeeping personnel. U.N. officials worried that the peacekeeping forces might find themselves caught in a battle between rival post-war factions or the peacekeepers might be attacked by Taliban hold-outs. Moreover, the ISAF has only been authorized to operate in the capital city of Kabul, yet there is need for relief and recovery operations throughout Afghanistan. Concerns for safety and expense continued to prevent the spread of peacekeeping forces into other areas of the country.

In addition to establishing the ISAF, the U.N. Security Council passed Resolution 1401 in March 2002, which approved the establishment of the United Nations Assistance Mission in Afghanistan (UNAMA). Headed by Lakhdar Brahimi, the Algerian diplomat who negotiated the Bonn Agreement, the UNAMA is a small-scale peacekeeping project initially comprised of roughly 100 international representatives. The UNAMA coordinates relief and reconstruction efforts, narcotics control, and other U.N. activities in Afghanistan.

Transitional Government

The *loya jirga* called for in the Bonn Agreement met practically on schedule in June 2002, and elected Hamid Karzai as the President of the transitional government. Many participants were disappointed with the outcome, however, because decisions appeared to have been made before the council met. Karzai was elected with 80 percent of the vote, but only after Burhanuddin Rabbani, the Tajik former president and a leader of the Northern Alliance, and the popular ex-king Mohammed Zahir Shah declared that they would not stand for election. These withdrawals were perceived by many Afghans to have been engineered by the U.S. government, which supported Karzai. Zahir Shah was given the formal title "Father of the Nation" and a series of ceremonial responsibilities, but no political role. The *loya jirga* disbanded without an agreement on the makeup or powers of a national parliament. On June 24, Karzai and his cabinet were sworn into office.

The transitional government's cabinet was more balanced between Tajik and Pashtun ministers than its predecessor, which had been dominated by members of the Northern Alliance. However, as of January 2003, it still faced serious opposition to its effective governance over Afghanistan. First, some members of the Northern Alliance felt that, having defeated the Taliban, they are being shut out of the new government in favor of Pashtuns who have only recently returned from exile. Second, the significant Uzbek and Hazara minorities were still underrepresented in the Karzai government, as were women. Third, two of Afghanistan's most powerful warlords, Ismail Khan and Abdul Rashid Dostum, refused vice presidential posts in the new regime, preferring virtually unfettered local power to a role in the central government. Drug lords who can make enormous opium profits from Afghan poppies have incentive to oppose any strong central government. And finally, pockets of Taliban and Al Qaeda fighters with an interest in overthrowing the new government remained at large in the country, still capable of destabilizing terrorist acts and assassinations.

Evidence of these difficulties was not hard to find. On July 5, 2002, the most important Pashtun in Karzai's government, vice president Abdul Qadir, was murdered in Kabul. It was not clear who was responsible for his death — Qadir was pro-Western and anti-drugs, as well as a powerful Pashtun leader — but his was the second assassination of a government minister in six months. Nor did the new government have a monopoly on the use of force, one of the essential elements of stability. An Afghan army will take time to build. In the meantime, President Karzai, who had no troops loyal to him personally, was dependent on foreigners and on the various warlords and commanders who joined the central government. In many areas outside of Kabul, the armed forces were in the hands of warlords with questionable loyalty to the central government. Karzai himself found it necessary to have American bodyguards, because Afghan soldiers, who are mostly former *mujahideen*, did not have sufficient training to protect him against possible threats.

Notes and Questions

1. As outrageous as the Taliban were and as justified as the U.S. invasion might have been, did the United States and its allies have the right or responsibility to influence the regime change that they helped initiate by toppling the Taliban? Should international law have anything to say about the concept of nation building?

2. U.N. peacekeeping forces were sent to Kabul at the request of the Bonn meeting to prevent anarchy or warlordism from filling the void left by the Taliban's totalitarian rule. The U.N. authorized peacekeeping missions dozens of times in the 1990s, and there have been both notable successes and failures. (See Chapter 11.) In Afghanistan, the *mujahideen* greatly outnumber peacekeepers, who have no presence at all outside Kabul. As U.S. forces withdraw, will peacekeepers be able to prevent Afghanistan from disintegrating until a national army can be formed? What is the obligation of the U.N. to maintain order in a country like Afghanistan, which has not known peace since 1979? What is the obligation of the United States to see through, until there is stability, a regime change that it helped initiate by defeating the Taliban?

7.   Rights of Detainees

In the course of the armed conflict in Afghanistan, the U.S. forces captured and detained, or had handed over to them by its allies, hundreds of persons associated with either the former Taliban regime or Al Qaeda. These persons were initially detained in Afghanistan and on U.S. naval vessels in the region. Beginning in January 2002, many detainees were transported to the U.S. naval base at Guantanamo Bay, Cuba. By January 2003, over 600 persons of over 30 different nationalities were being held at the base.

The U.S. detention of the Taliban and Al Qaeda led to questions about their status under the Geneva Conventions of 1949. These are four treaties concluded at the end of World War II that were intended to reduce the human suffering caused by war. The treaties provide for the amelioration of the conditions of the wounded and sick in armed forces in the field (First Geneva Convention); amelioration of the conditions of the wounded, sick, and shipwrecked members of armed forces at sea (Second Geneva Convention); humane treatment of prisoners of war (Third Geneva Convention); and the protection of the civilian persons in time of war (Fourth Geneva Convention). As of January 2003, 190 states were parties to the Geneva Conventions, including the United States, Afghanistan, Egypt, and Saudi Arabia.

Initially, "U.S. officials referred to the detainees as 'unlawful combatants,' whom the United States regarded as falling outside the protections of the Third Geneva Convention, but who would nevertheless be treated humanely. . . . [Thus,] on January 18 [, 2002,] President Bush initially decided (without making any public announcement) that the Third Geneva Convention did not apply to any of the detainees." Sean D. Murphy, Decision Not to Regard Persons Detained in Afghanistan as POWs, 96 Am. J. Intl. L. 475, 476-477 (2002).

The U.S. government's position quickly changed, however, in part because of considerable criticism from other Western countries and legal scholars. Hence, on February 7, 2002, the Bush Administration announced the U.S. government's new stance. In an official fact sheet on the status of detainees at Guantanamo, the White House outlined that the U.S. policy was "to treat all of the individuals detained at Guantanamo humanely and, to the extent appropriate and consistent with military necessity, in a manner consistent with principles of the Third Geneva Convention of 1949." However, "the President has determined that the Geneva Convention applies to the Taliban detainees, but *not* to the al-Qaida detainees." Al Qaeda members were not given the POW status because they were not "a state party to the Geneva Convention" but rather "a foreign terrorist group." As for the Taliban detainees, the President determined that, although the terms of the Geneva Convention do not grant them POW status, many POW privileges would nevertheless be provided them as a matter of policy. White House Press Secretary Ari Fleisher explained further that "under Article 4 of the Geneva Convention . . . Taliban detainees are not entitled to POW status. To qualify as POWs under Article 4, Al Qaeda and Taliban detainees would have to have satisfied four conditions: they would have to be part of a military hierarchy; they would have to have worn uniforms or other distinctive signs visible at a distance; they would have to have carried arms openly; and they would have to have conducted their military operations in accordance with the laws and customs of war." Because "the Taliban have not effectively distinguished themselves from the civilian population of Afghanistan [and] have not conducted their operations in accordance with the laws and customs of war," they are not POWs under the Geneva Convention.

Several groups in the United States have tried to litigate the issue of detention of alien in U.S. courts. Their efforts, however, have been unsuccessful as of November 2002. U.S. federal courts have held that they lacked jurisdiction because the detainees were not within the territorial jurisdiction of the courts. See Odah v. United States, 321 F.3d 1134 (D.C. Cir 2003); Coalition of Clergy v. Bush, 310 F.3d 1153 (9th Cir. 2002).[3]

3. There is also burgeoning litigation in U.S. courts about the rights of detained U.S. citizens. E.g., Hamdi v. Rumsfeld, 316 F.3d 450 (4th Cir. 2003) and Padilla v. Rumsfeld, 243 F. Supp. 2d 42 (S.D.N.Y. 2003). Given space considerations, this case study on September 11 focuses, however, on alien detainees. See the more extensive discussion of individual responsibility in Chapter 11.

Notes and Questions

1. U.N. Security Council Resolution 1368 calls on member states to "bring to justice" those involved in terrorist activity. Does the resolution authorize whatever methods and procedures a member state may deem necessary to bring a terrorist "to justice"? Does it impose any restrictions on states? Should the U.N. step in and outline the judicial machinery that should be used to "bring to justice" those suspected of terrorist activity? Does the U.N. resolution permit Saudi Arabia to torture suspected terrorists?

2. The U.S. position on the status of the Guantanamo Bay detainees poses several questions under international law. Assuming the detainees are foreign citizens, what international norms might bind the United States on how these people are treated? One of the biggest issues is who should determine the status of the detainees. Should it be the United States? The United Nations? An independent international tribunal? A domestic court? According to Article 5 of the Third Geneva Convention to which the United States is a party, "should any doubt arise as to whether persons, having committed a belligerent act and having fallen into the hands of the enemy, belong to [the category of prisoners of war], such persons shall enjoy the protections of the present Convention until such time as their status has been determined by a competent tribunal." In the official White House fact sheet outlining the U.S. position on the status of the detainees, President Bush mentioned that the treatment of detainees is "consistent with the principles of the Third Geneva Convention of 1949." Given that the decision to deny POW privileges to Al Qaeda was made by President Bush, is the U.S. treatment of detainees really consistent with the Geneva Convention? If not, does the United States stand in violation of the treaty? What are the repercussions of such violation? Who would decide that a violation occurred? Who would enforce that decision?

3. Under Article 118 of the Third Geneva Convention, "prisoners of war shall be released and repatriated without delay after the cessation of active hostilities." For a captured Afghan Taliban, when do the hostilities end? When the armed conflict in Afghanistan ended? Or does "cessation of active hostilities" have a broader meaning implying the cessation of the war on terrorism? Who determines that and how?

4. Assume that an Al Qaeda member who is a citizen of Egypt is captured in Afghanistan and is now detained in Guantanamo Bay, Cuba. The United States explicitly stated that such persons are not covered by the Geneva Conventions because they are part of a foreign terrorist group and are thus neither POWs under the Third Geneva Convention nor "nationals" that are covered under the Fourth Geneva Convention.[4] However, Article 75 of the Protocol Additional to the Geneva Conventions of 12 August 1949 (known as the Geneva Protocol), and relating to the Protection of Victims of International Armed Conflicts, guarantees certain protections to all "persons who are in the power of a Party to the conflict," including humane treatment as well as some procedural and due process rights. The United States has

---

4. According to Article 4 of the Fourth Geneva Convention, the Convention applies only to persons "who, at a given moment and in any manner whatsoever, find themselves, in case of a conflict or occupation, in the hands of a Party to the conflict or occupying power of which they are not nationals. . . . Nationals of a neutral State [such as Egypt] who find themselves in the territory of a belligerent State . . . shall not be regarded as protected persons while the State of which they are nationals has normal diplomatic representation in the State in whose hands they are."

neither signed nor ratified this Protocol. However, a vast majority of countries are now a party to it.[5] Should the Protocol be recognized as establishing norms of customary international law that might create any legal obligations for the United States? Who can decide this issue?

5. The United States has begun releasing some people who were detained at Guantanamo Bay. In October 2002, the first small group of detainees was returned to Pakistan under a reported policy that detainees can be returned to their home country if they no longer pose a threat or have no intelligence value.

6. For a category of persons who are captured outside of Afghanistan and have no direct relationship with the armed conflict, the Geneva Conventions definitely do not apply. An example of such person is a Saudi citizen captured in Spain due to links to Al Qaeda and shipped to Guantanamo Bay naval base. Because the Geneva Conventions do not apply, the "cessation of active hostilities" cannot be used as a limit to that person's detention. What should be the limit? Can the Saudi citizen be detained at Guantanamo Bay for a prolonged period of time, without any review by a judge or other person authorized to exercise judicial power? For example, for one year? Ten years? For his or her lifetime?

The International Covenant on Civil and Political Rights states in Article 9 that "[n]o one shall be subjected to arbitrary arrest or detention" and that "[a]nyone arrested or detained on a criminal charge shall be brought promptly before a judge or other officer authorized by law to exercise judicial power and shall be entitled to trial within a reasonable time or to release." The United States is a party to this Convention, as are over 145 other countries, though the U.S. ratification includes the reservation that Article 9 and other operative parts of the Convention are not self-executing in the United States. The United States, however, is bound on the international level to the treaty. By its detention of the illustrative Saudi citizen mentioned above, is the United States obeying the Covenant that it signed? Can the detention be justified under Article 4 of the Covenant, which permits derogation from Article 9 and certain other articles "[i]n time of public emergency which threatens the life of the nation"?

One might look for further guidance to the European Convention for the Protection of Human Rights and Fundamental Freedoms, to which over 40 European nations are parties. It states in Article 5 that everyone detained "shall be brought promptly before a judge or other officer . . . and shall be entitled to trial within a reasonable time or to release pending trial." Has this been done? Should the United States even pay attention to the European Convention, to which it is not a party?

7. On November 13, 2001, President George W. Bush issued a broad Order titled "Detention, Treatment, and Trial of Certain Non-Citizens in the War Against Terrorism" which called for creation of military tribunals with exclusive jurisdiction, targeted at trying members of al Qaeda, persons involved in acts of international terrorism against the United States, and those who knowingly harbored such terrorists. At a later interview, President Bush commented that the United States will "be using the tribunals if in the course of bringing someone to justice it may jeopardize or

---

5. As of January 2003, there are 161 states that are parties to the Additional Protocol I, leaving 29 states (including the United States and Afghanistan) that are parties to the Geneva Conventions but not parties to the Protocol. Canada, France, Germany, Spain, and the United Kingdom are all parties to the Protocol, as well as Egypt and Saudi Arabia.

compromise the national security interests." The President's order called for the Secretary of Defense, Donald Rumsfeld, to issue other orders and regulations required for the operation of military tribunals.

The Nov. 13 Order was criticized by U.S. allies and has been very controversial among international and constitutional law scholars. Among the criticisms was that it violated the International Covenant on Civil and Political Rights and the Geneva Conventions. Some of the important op-ed pieces on the commissions include: Harold Hongju Koh, We Have the Rights Courts for Bin Laden, N.Y. Times, Nov. 23, 2001, at A39; Anne-Marie Slaughter, Al Qaeda Should Be Tried Before the World, N.Y. Times, Nov. 17, 2001, at A23; and Ruth Wedgwood, The Case for Military Tribunals, Wall St. J., Dec. 3, 2001, at A18. Moreover, the commissions may be lawful under U.S. constitutional law only if the United States is in a "war," and this issue may turn on the international law of armed conflict. See Curtis A. Bradley & Jack L. Goldsmith, The Constitutional Validity of Military Commissions, 5 Green Bag 2d 249 (2002).

On March 21, 2002, the Department of Defense (DoD) issued "Military Commission Order No. 1" that outlined "procedures for trials by military commission of certain non-United States citizens in the war against terrorism." By specifying various procedural protections, the DoD regulations alleviated some of the concerns about what the President's Order might entail when the military tribunals are convened.

8.   *The Widening War*

Even as sporadic fighting continued in Afghanistan and the post-war nation building was just beginning, President Bush reemphasized the global nature of the war on terrorism. In his State of the Union speech on January 29, 2002, he listed U.S. military activities (including training) in the Philippines, Bosnia, and off the coast of Africa.

The speech then wove together the war on terrorism with efforts to combat the proliferation of weapons of mass destruction. President Bush set out as a goal the prevention of "regimes that sponsor terror from threatening American or our friends and allies with weapons of mass destruction." He specifically listed Iraq, Iran, and North Korea and said that they "and their terrorist allies, constitute an axis of evil, arming to threaten the peace of the world." He went on to explain:

> By seeking weapons of mass destruction, these regimes pose a grave and growing danger. They could provide these arms to terrorists, giving them the means to match their hatred. They could attack our allies or attempt to blackmail the United States. In any of these cases, the price of indifference would be catastrophic.
>
> We will work closely with our coalition to deny terrorists and their state sponsors the materials, technology, and expertise to make and deliver weapons of mass destruction. . . . And all nations should know: American will do what is necessary to ensure our nation's security.
>
> We'll be deliberate, yet time is not on our side. I will not wait on events, while dangers gather. I will not stand by, as peril draws closer and closer. The United States of America will not permit the world's most dangerous regimes to threaten us with the world's most destructive weapons.

President Bush's speech was generally well received in the United States. However, questions were raised, especially abroad, about his lumping Iraq, Iran, and North Korea together under the umbrella of "axis of evil," especially Iran where reformist groups were struggling to change the clerics' policies. Moreover, his promise "not to wait on events" raised questions about whether the United States would engage in preemptive military strikes against these or other foreign states.

In the ensuing months, particularly accelerating in August 2002, the Bush Administration's focus seemed to shift emphasis from rooting out Al Qaeda and catching bin Laden, toward changing the regime of Saddam Hussein in Iraq. In a powerful speech to the U.N. General Assembly on September 12, President Bush focused on Iraq and its failure to comply with numerous past Security Council resolutions. He squarely challenged the U.N.: "Are Security Council resolutions to be honored and enforced, or cast aside without consequence? Will the United Nations serve the purpose of its founding, or will it be irrelevant?" He then committed the United States to work with the U.N. Security Council, though he also warned that the U.N. resolutions needed to be enforced or "action will be unavoidable."

Shortly after his speech, President Bush released his National Security Strategy for the United States, which he had foreshadowed in earlier statements. The new strategy included a proactive stance against potential threats to the United States. The strategy announced that:

> We must be prepared to stop rogue states and their terrorist clients before they are able to threaten or use weapons of mass destruction against the United States and our allies and friends. . . .
>
> [T]he greater the threat, the greater the risk of inaction — and the more compelling the case for taking anticipatory action to defend ourselves, even if uncertainty remains as to the time and place of the enemy's attack. To forestall or prevent such hostile acts by our adversaries, the United States will, if necessary, act preemptively. . . .
>
> The purpose of our actions will always be to eliminate a specific threat to the United States or our allies and friends. The reasons for our actions will be clear, the force measured, and the cause just.

(See the discussion of this new strategy in Chapter 11.A.)

As the world awaited U.N. action on Iraq, President Bush sought and obtained a strong Joint Resolution from the U.S. Congress on October 16 that authorized the President to "use the Armed Forces of the United States as he determines to be necessary and appropriate in order to defend the national security of the United States against the continuing threat posed by Iraq. . . ." Then, on November 9, the U.N. Security Council unanimously passed Resolution 1441, which provided Iraq a "final opportunity" to comply with its disarmament obligations previously imposed by the Security Council, established a rigorous inspection regime, and required Iraq to provide a full and accurate accounting of its efforts to "develop chemical, biological, and nuclear weapons, ballistic missiles, and other delivery systems. . . ." (Both resolutions are in the Documentary Supplement.)

U.N. weapons inspectors arrived in Iraq in mid-November and, pursuant to U.N. Resolution 1441, Iraq submitted a voluminous report on December 7. U.S. officials were highly critical of the report, while the chief U.N. weapons inspector, Hans Blix, and the head of the International Atomic Energy Agency (IAEA), Mohamed ElBaradei, were more mixed in their assessment.

Inspections continued at an accelerating pace into March 2003. Also accelerating were major deployments of military forces from the United States and Britain, along with some support from Australia and other countries. This was accompanied by continued harsh criticism of Saddam Hussein by President Bush and Prime Minister Blair, and the reports of mixed progress from the U.N. inspectors.

By March 2003, the debate had sharpened, with the United States, Britain, Spain and a number of other countries favoring a new U.N. resolution saying that the Saddam Hussein regime had once again not complied with the U.N. resolutions and that the use of force was appropriate. On the other side, France, Germany, Russia, and many other countries thought the inspectors needed more time. When it became clear to the United States and Britain that they did not have the requisite nine votes in the Security Council to pass a second resolution and probably faced, in any event, a French veto there, efforts for a new resolution were dropped. Instead, President Bush issued an ultimatum to Saddam Hussein and his sons that they had to leave Iraq within 48 hours or "[t]heir refusal to do so will result in military conflict, commenced at a time of our choosing."

Early on March 20 in Iraq, less than two hours after the end of the ultimatum, a major coalition attack began, first with a missile and aircraft strike against a location in Baghdad where Saddam Hussein and his senior aides were thought to be meeting. What followed was a swift campaign by coalition forces that left them in control of Iraq in less than a month. The coalition's highly mobile forces possessed overwhelming firepower and employed twenty-first-century weapons and tactics, including precision-guided missiles and bombs, new surveillance methods such as low-flying drones, and rapid communications.

As of May 2003, however, the coalition was encountering problems in establishing stability in Iraq, reconstructing the economy, and moving toward the transition to a democratic Iraqi government. (A more detailed discussion of the U.S. and world's actions toward Iraq, from its invasion of Kuwait in 1990 through the 2003 war in Iraq, is found in Chapter 11.B.)

Bibliography

There is extensive literature on the September 11 attacks and the U.S. and world response. A few examples are: Bob Woodward, Bush at War (2002); Report, Joint Committee on Intelligence Activities, Report on September 11 (2002); David Cole, Enemy Aliens, 54 Stan. L. Rev. 953 (2002).

Up-to-date information on all U.N. activities regarding the attacks and Afghanistan can be found on the excellent U.N. Web site at <http://www.un.org>.

2

The Creation of International Norms— Treaties, Customary Law, International Organizations, and Private Norm-Creation

In this chapter, we first take up two traditional components of public international law, treaties and customary international law. We then examine the increasingly important law-generating work of international and regional organizations and the activities of multinational corporations and "non-governmental organizations" (NGOs), which are growing more influential in international law-making processes. Finally, we address the third traditional component of public international law, the general principles of law common to the major legal systems of the world.

A. TREATIES

Treaties have become the most important source of international law and are the means by which international organizations are created. Like most other countries, the United States is a party to literally hundreds of international agreements that are categorized as "treaties" under international law. These agreements can be bilateral (i.e., between two countries) or multilateral. They can be labeled in a variety of ways, such as a treaty, convention (often used for multilateral agreements), agreement, covenant, charter, statute, and protocol. These agreements cover a broad range of subjects, reflecting the growing complexity of international life. Bilateral agreements might deal with extradition, visas, aircraft landing rights, taxation, and investment. Multilateral agreements range from the U.N. Charter, the Agreement Establishing the World Trade Organization, the International Covenant on Civil and Political Rights, and the Law of the Sea Convention.

Whether an instrument is a treaty or not carries a number of significant legal consequences. Under international law a treaty creates international legal obligations, with corresponding duties of compliance and remedies, including rights of retaliation, in the event of a breach. A treaty may also create domestic legal obligations.

The U.S. domestic law relating to treaties is rather complicated and will be more fully explored in the next chapter. For present purposes it is important to recognize the differences in terminology used in international law and U.S. domestic law. In international parlance all international agreements are referred to as "treaties." In U.S. law only some international agreements are called "treaties," *viz.*, those agreements concluded by the President with the advice and consent, or approval, of two-thirds of the Senate. The President may also conclude other international agreements on the basis of an authorization by the Congress as a whole or on the basis of his independent constitutional authority (such as his commander-in-chief power). Those other international agreements concluded by the President are sometimes called "executive agreements," even though they are still called "treaties" for purposes of international law.

Domestically, treaties approved by two-thirds of the Senate are the "law of the land" under the Constitution and may be directly enforceable in the courts. Executive agreements may also have legal status in the United States. This domestic incorporation of treaties into U.S. law is explored in Chapter 3. Sometimes domestic law will also simply refer to "international law" or will use a concept of international law for domestic purposes. For example, the Alien Tort Statute (or Alien Tort Claims Act) confers federal court jurisdiction over certain cases involving violations of "the law of nations or a treaty of the United States." (See Chapter 3.) The federal criminal code punishes "piracy as defined by the law of nations."

Another example is the Case Act, below, which requires the Secretary of State to transmit to the Congress a copy of all international agreements concluded by the United States without the advice and consent of two-thirds of the Senate. The Case Act was enacted in 1972 as part of the congressional effort to control presidential power in foreign affairs. The perception was that the President could previously make secret commitments, leading to unfortunate consequences suffered by the nation as a whole, without the benefit of advice or review by the Senate or Congress. Consequently, by forcing disclosure, Congress might introduce a cautionary influence on presidential behavior.

Case Act
1 U.S.C. §112b

The Secretary of State shall transmit to the Congress the text of any international agreement (including the text of any oral international agreement, which agreement shall be reduced to writing) other than a treaty, to which the United States is a party as soon as practicable after such agreement has entered into force with respect to the United States but in no event later than sixty days thereafter. . . .

1. *The Formation of Treaties*

The Vienna Convention on the Law of Treaties sets forth a comprehensive set of rules governing the formation, interpretation, and termination of treaties concluded after the Vienna Convention's entry into force in 1980. As noted by a British legal expert:

> The Convention is one of the prime achievements of the International Law Commission. The Commission was established by the UN General Assembly in 1947 with the object of promoting the progressive development of international law and its codification. The law of treaties was one of the topics selected by the Commission at its first session in 1949 as being suitable for codification. A series of eminent British international legal scholars (James Brierly, Hersch Lauterpacht, Gerald Fitzmaurice and Humphrey Waldock) were appointed as Special Rapporteurs. The Commission adopted a final set of draft articles in 1966. They were considered by the United Nations Conference on the Law of Treaties in Vienna in 1968 and 1969. The Convention was adopted on 22 May 1969 and entered into force on 27 January 1980. [Anthony Aust, Modern Treaty Law and Practice 6 (2000).]

Over 90 states are now parties to the Convention. (The Convention is in the Documentary Supplement.) The United States, however, has signed but not ratified the Convention, so the United States is not a party to the Convention and not formally covered by it. Nevertheless, U.S. officials have consistently stated from the beginning that at least most of the Convention's provisions represent customary international law, and U.S. courts have frequently relied on its terms. In his 1971 letter transmitting the Vienna Convention to the President, Secretary of State William P. Rogers called it "a generally agreed body of rules to govern all aspects of treaty making and treaty observance." President Richard M. Nixon in his 1971 Message to the Senate Transmitting the Vienna Convention for the Senate's advice and consent observed:

> The growing importance of treaties in the orderly conduct of international relations has made increasingly evident the need for clear, well-defined, and readily ascertainable rules of international law applicable to treaties. I believe that the codification of treaty law formulated by representatives of the international community and embodied in the Vienna Convention meets this need.
>
> The international community as a whole will surely benefit from the adoption of uniform rules on such subjects as the conclusion and entry into force of treaties, their interpretation and application, and other technical matters. Even more significant, however, are the orderly procedures of the Convention for dealing with needed adjustments and changes in treaties, along with its strong reaffirmation of the basic principle *pacta sunt servanda*— the rule that treaties are binding on the parties and must be performed in good faith. The provisions on judicial settlement, arbitration and conciliation . . . should do much to enhance the stability of treaty relationships throughout the world.

See also Restatement, Vol. I, Part III, Introductory Note at p. 145 (documenting U.S. acceptance of the terms of the Convention).

Consequently, the rules set forth in the Vienna Convention are relevant to the work of private lawyers, as well as government officials, who must consider the impact of a treaty on a proposed course of conduct. We now turn to some of the Convention's key provisions.

Vienna Convention on the Law of Treaties

Article 2. Use of Terms

For the purposes of the present Convention . . . "treaty" means an international agreement concluded between States in written form and governed by international law, whether embodied in a single instrument or in two or more related instruments and whatever its particular designation . . . [and a "party" to a treaty] means a State which has consented to be bound by the treaty. . . .

Article 11. Means of Expressing Consent to be Bound by a Treaty

The consent of a State to be bound by a treaty may be expressed by signature, exchange of instruments constituting a treaty, ratification, acceptance, approval or accession, or by any other means if so agreed.

Article 18. Obligation not to Defeat the Object and Purpose of a Treaty Prior to Its Entry Into Force

A State is obliged to refrain from acts which would defeat the object and purpose of a treaty when:
(a) it has signed the treaty or has exchanged instruments constituting the treaty subject to ratification, acceptance or approval, until it shall have made its intention clear not to become a party to the treaty; or
(b) it has expressed its consent to be bound by the treaty, pending the entry into force of the treaty and provided that such entry into force is not unduly delayed.

Article 2 of the Convention does not tell us much about the characteristics required of these instruments because it leaves unanswered the question of the definition of "international agreement." It does, however, limit the field to some extent in that *states* must be parties, the agreement must be governed by international law, and it must be in writing. The Restatement offers some additional detail about the nature of international agreements:

Restatement Section 301

Comment

. . . The terminology used for international agreements is varied. Among the terms used are: treaty, convention, agreement, protocol, covenant, charter, statute, act, declaration, *concordat,* exchange of notes, agreed minute, memorandum of agreement, memorandum of understanding, and *modus vivendi.* Whatever their designation, all agreements have the same legal status, except as their provisions or the circumstances of their conclusion indicate otherwise.

. . . While most international agreements are in writing, written form is not essential to their binding character. The Vienna Convention specifies (Article 2(1)(a)) that it applies only to written agreements, but under customary international law oral agreements are no less binding although their terms may not be readily susceptible of proof.

. . . Since an international agreement does not require consideration . . . its obligations may be wholly unilateral, flowing from one party only, as in a peace treaty following unconditional surrender. A unilateral statement is not an agreement, but may have legal consequences and may become a source of rights and obligations on principles analogous to estoppel. It may also contribute to customary law.

. . . An international agreement, as defined, does not include a contract by a state, even with another state, that is essentially commercial in character and is intended to be governed by some national or other body of contract law. Examples include a loan agreement, a lease of a building, or a sale of goods.

[A]n international agreement is one intended to be legally binding and to have legal consequences. . . .

Reporters' Notes

. . . An example of a nonbinding agreement is the Final Act of the Conference on Security and Cooperation in Europe signed at Helsinki on August 1, 1975, which avoids words of legal undertaking, is designated as "not eligible for registration under Article 102 of the [U.N.] Charter," and was clearly intended not to be legally binding. Other examples include the various codes of conduct for multinational enterprises which are characterized as voluntary and not legally binding, with respect to both the enterprises and to the states involved.

Parties sometimes prefer a non-binding agreement in order to avoid legal remedies. Nevertheless, the political inducements to comply with such agreements may be strong and the consequences of noncompliance may sometimes be serious. . . . A non-binding agreement is sometimes used in order to avoid processes required by a national constitutional system for making legally-binding agreements. . . .

Against this background we now consider three instruments entered into by the United States addressing economic matters. Consider whether they are "international agreements" within the meaning of the Vienna Convention or the Case Act.

a. United States-Japan FCN Treaty

Since the eighteenth century a significant component of U.S. foreign economic policy has been the conclusion of treaties of Friendship, Commerce and Navigation (FCN Treaties). Those treaties established favorable terms for mutual travel, trade, shipping, and investment with other countries. Article VII of the 1953 United States-Japan FCN Treaty is a typical provision:

Article VII

1. Nationals and companies of either Party shall be . . . permitted . . . : (a) to establish and maintain branches, agencies, offices, factories and other establishments appropriate to the conduct of their business; (b) to organize companies under the general company laws of such other Party, and to acquire majority interests in companies of such other Party; and (c) to control and manage enterprises which they have established or acquired.

b. Economic Cooperation Agreement

Here is language from a different agreement.

Article I

The Parties shall use their good offices to facilitate economic, industrial, and technical cooperation in keeping with established practices and applicable laws and regulations in the respective countries. . . .

Article III

In order to assist relevant organizations, enterprises, and firms of both countries in determining the fields of cooperation most likely to provide a basis for mutually beneficial contracts, a working group of experts . . . shall meet not less frequently than once a year to exchange information and forecasts of basic economic, industrial, and commercial trends1.

Article IV

To promote the cooperation foreseen in this Agreement the Parties undertake to facilitate, as appropriate, the acquisition or lease of suitable business and residential premises by organizations, enterprises, and firms of the other party and their employees; the importation of essential office equipment and supplies; the hiring of staffs; the issuance of visas, including multiple entry visas, to qualified officials and representatives of such organizations, enterprises, and firms and to members of their immediate families; and travel by such persons for business purposes in the territory of the receiving country.

c. 2001 Declaration of G-7 Finance Ministers

The Group of 7 (now the Group of 8 and formerly the Group of 5) is composed of certain major countries that share common interests and sometimes take coordinated actions. The Heads of State regularly meet for a private session on an annual basis, and ministers might meet on other occasions. (The present membership is the United States, Canada, England, France, Germany, Italy, Japan, and most recently Russia. See discussion in Chapter 5.) After the terrorist attacks on September 11, 2001, the Group issued a condemnation of the attacks on September 19, and engaged in discussions about what steps the Group might take.

The Finance Ministers of the then Group of 7 announced an Action Plan to Combat the Financing of Terrorism on October 6, 2001. Some of its provisions are excerpted below:

Action Plan

We, the G-7 Finance Ministers, have developed an integrated, comprehensive Action Plan to block the assets of terrorists and their associates. We pledge to work together to deliver real results in combating the scourge of the financing of terrorism.

More vigorous implementation of international sanctions is critical to cut off the financing of terrorism. We are implementing [U.N. Security Council Resolution] 1333 and UNSCR 1373, which call on all States to freeze the funds and financial assets not only of the terrorist Usama bin Laden and his associates, but terrorists all over the world. Each of us will ratify the UN convention on the Suppression of Terrorist Financing as soon as possible. We will work within our Governments to consider additional measures and share lists of terrorists as necessary to ensure that the entire network of terrorist financing is addressed.

The Financial Action Task Force (FATF) should play a vital role in fighting the financing of terrorism. . . .

- Issuing special guidance for financial institutions on practices associated with the financing of terrorism that warrant further action on the part of affected institutions;
- Developing a process to identify jurisdictions that facilitate terrorist financing, and making recommendations for action to achieve cooperation from such countries.

Enhanced sharing of information among financial intelligence units (FIUs) is also critical to cut off the flow of resources to terrorist organizations and their associates. We call on all countries to establish functional FIUs as soon as possible. The G-7 countries will all join the Egmont Group, which promotes cooperation between national FIUs, and turn around information sharing requests as expeditiously as possible. . . .

We ask all governments to join us in denying terrorists access to the resources that are needed to carry out evil acts.

Notes and Questions

1. Are all the commitments quoted in subsections (a), (b), and (c) above legally binding agreements? In addition to analysis of the text, what else would you like to know in answering this question?

2. Recall that, according to the Restatement, "an international agreement is one intended to be legally binding" and the Vienna Convention refers to "consent." If the principal test is whether the parties intended to be bound, how do you know? Besides the text, what other places could you look to discern the intent of a party to an agreement?

3. Why would a state (or a negotiator) want to make an instrument sound binding but not actually be legally binding?

4. Suppose the United States and India made an agreement for the sale of aircraft and provided that it would be governed by the law of New York. Would that agreement be a "treaty"? Would it be legally binding and enforceable in accordance with its terms?

5. In the *Legal Status of Eastern Greenland* case (Denmark v. Norway), the Permanent Court of International Justice held that an oral declaration by the Norwegian foreign minister (recorded in writing by the Danish minister) was binding. The oral declaration conceded sovereignty over Greenland, a major land mass, to Denmark:

> The Court considers it beyond all dispute that a reply of this nature given by the Minister for Foreign Affairs on behalf of his Government in response to the request by the diplomatic representative of a foreign Power, in regard to a question falling within his province, is binding upon the country to which the Minister belongs. [P.C.I.J., ser. A/B, No. 53 (1933).]

The oral declaration was made in the context of a Danish concession regarding Norwegian sovereignty over the island of Spitzbergen. What if the Norwegian oral declaration were not made in the context of mutual commitments? What if the oral declaration were made by the Minister of Fisheries?

6. Suppose that the U.S. President and Japanese Prime Minister orally agree at one of the periodic economic summits that neither government will impose any trade sanctions of any sort against the other for a period of two years. Would that be an international agreement? Would it make a difference if the oral agreement were referred to in a press communique (which would not normally be signed by anyone)? What if Japan had never invoked trade sanctions against the United States and apparently has no intention to do so? Does the Vienna Convention or customary international law require valuable consideration?

7. On December 31, 2000, shortly before President Bill Clinton left office, the United States signed the Rome Statute, a treaty establishing the International Criminal Court (ICC). President Clinton noted "our concerns about the significant flaws in the treaty," but hoped that the U.S. signature might provide influence to obtain some changes in the ICC. The Bush Administration, which took office on January 20, 2001, made clear its opposition to the ICC, especially the possibility that it might try to assert jurisdiction over U.S. military personnel involved in foreign operations, including peacekeeping missions. Neither the Clinton nor Bush Administration transmitted the Rome Statute to the U.S. Senate for its advice and consent, which is required before the United States can ratify a treaty. Moreover, there are varying views about how hard the Bush Administration tried to correct the problems it perceived in the Rome Statute. (The ICC is discussed in Chapter 11.)

In any event, the required 60 ratifications needed to bring the treaty into force was reached in April 2002, with the treaty then scheduled to come into force on July 1, 2002. On May 6, a U.S. Under Secretary of State sent a brief letter to the

Secretary-General of the United Nations, stating that "the United States does not intend to become a party to the treaty. . . . Accordingly, the United States has no legal obligations arising from its signature on December 31, 2000." Some newspapers headlined that the United States had "unsigned" the treaty, but this was not technically accurate. The United States did not physically remove its original signature, but rather attempted to terminate any obligations that might be associated with the signature.

Why did the Bush Administration take this step in May 2002? The Administration repeated its opposition to some of the provisions of the ICC. However, officials indicated that the Vienna Convention was also a consideration. The Administration was concerned that under Article 18 of the Vienna Convention the United States, as a signatory of the Rome Statute, was "obliged to refrain from acts which would defeat the object and purpose" of that treaty "until it shall have made its intention clear not to become a party to the treaty." The May letter was intended, then, in part to make clear that the United States had no intention to be a party to the treaty, thus meaning that the United States would not be obliged to refrain from acts that would defeat the "object and purpose" of the treaty.

How necessary was this step? What is the "object and purpose" of the Rome Statute that created and regulated a new international entity? Did President Clinton's announced concerns at the signing provide a basis for saying the United States was not bound at the outset by the Rome Statute? Or, how long does this obligation last after a nation has signed the treaty? Could a long delay in ratifying the treaty be interpreted as a signaling a clear intent not to become a party to the treaty?

Similar questions might arise with other treaties that the United States has signed, but not ratified. For example, in July 1994, the United States signed the 1982 Convention on the Law of the Sea. President Clinton transmitted the multilateral Convention and a companion 1994 agreement to the U.S. Senate for its advice and consent in October 1994. The Convention actually came into force a month later and the agreement two years later. However, as of January 2003, the Senate Foreign Relations Committee had not held hearings on the treaties, much less sent them to the full Senate for its advice and consent. Is the United States still obliged to refrain from acts that would defeat the object and purpose of that Convention and the companion agreement? (See Chapter 9 for a discussion of the Law of the Sea Convention, especially Section I.)

Indeed, is the United States bound not to defeat the object and purpose of the Vienna Convention on the Law of Treaties, which came into force in 1980? The United States signed the Convention in 1970 and President Nixon transmitted it to the U.S. Senate in 1971, but the Senate has yet to give its advice and consent. Does the Bush Administration's letter regarding the Rome Statute provide evidence that the United States is bound by Article 18 of the Vienna Convention? Or, might the letter be further evidence that the United States accepts the Vienna Convention provisions as constituting customary international law?

Even if a commitment is not legally binding, it may still carry force as a "political commitment." Governments may develop expectations of compliance with political commitments, invoke them in public debate to marshall support, and even impose sanctions for their violation. Given the absence of a general dispute settlement and enforcement mechanism for violations of legally binding commitments, the practical significance of the distinction between legal and political commitments may be blurred in particular cases. See generally Oscar Schachter, International Law in Theory and Practice, especially 95-101 (1991). Schachter observes,

> As might be expected, non-legal agreements and declarations take many forms and are designated by various names. Many are informal: communiqués, statements by high officials, correspondence, unwritten understanding as to future conduct. Others are more formal: proclamations by Heads of State, "final acts" of conferences, written agreements signed by the highest officials. . . .
>
> [N]either the form nor name of a document is decisive of its legal or non-legal character. . . .
>
> . . . Is a breach of a purely political agreement entirely outside the domain of international law? This question, I believe, cannot be answered solely in analytical terms. It depends not so much on legal theory as on the practice and the attitudes of governments. . . . I believe it fair to say that States entering into a non-legal commitment generally view it as a political (or moral) obligation and intend to carry it out in good faith. Other parties and other States concerned have reason to expect such compliance and to rely on it. What we must deduce from this, I submit, is that the political texts which express commitments and positions of one kind or another are governed by the general principle of good faith. Moreover, since good faith is an accepted general principle of international law, it is appropriate and even necessary to apply it in its legal sense. There appears to be no justification for distinguishing the legal meaning of "good faith" from a supposed political meaning of that concept. Whether called legal or political, its meaning is essentially the same.
>
> A significant practical consequence of the "good faith" principle is that a party which committed itself in good faith to a course of conduct or to recognition of a legal situation would be estopped from acting inconsistently with its commitment or adopted position when the circumstances showed that other parties reasonably relied on that undertaking or position. We gave an example of this earlier in our discussion in respect of the voluntary codes of conduct or guidelines adopted in the United Nations. A State that voted for such a non-binding code has no obligation to comply with it. However, if another State does comply with the recommended code, the first State may not claim that such an action is illegal. In that case, the complying State may be said to have relied on the approval the code received as evidence that the approving States considered the recommended conduct as legal. The same kind of reasoning would apply to other examples of non-binding undertakings.
>
> The principle of good faith also provides a basis for concluding that a State accepting a political commitment may not reject a complaint of non-compliance made against it by another party on the ground that the matter is solely within the domestic jurisdiction of that State. When a State enters into an international engagement, even if it is avowedly political and not legal, it should follow that the subject covered is not exclusively an internal matter. That State would therefore be precluded from asserting the latter ground (i.e., domestic jurisdiction) to oppose the right of another party to raise the issue of its non-compliance. It is interesting that there appears to be no case of a non-binding agreement in which a State denied the right of another party to bring up the question of compliance on the ground that the agreement was not a legal commitment. Of course, other grounds for rejecting a complaint can be given. For example, the USSR has rejected complaints of its violation of the Helsinki Final Act on the ground that the agreement itself affirmed the domestic jurisdiction exception in respect of human rights. Whether this was so is a matter of interpretation of the Helsinki Pact: it is not, however, a rejection based on the non-binding nature of the Accords.

The conclusion that I draw is that a State assuming an international political commitment may (under the requirement of good faith) be considered to have given up its prior right under international law to declare the matter in question as purely domestic.

It is also worth noting that the violation of a political agreement justifies the victim of that violation in using all the means permissible under international law to bring about a cessation of that violation and to obtain reparation. Any dispute arising from the violation may be submitted for settlement in accord with procedures specified in Article 33 of the United Nations Charter.

These juridical effects of a political engagement are limited. They do not extend so far as to impose on the States concerned a legal responsibility to provide reparation for a breach nor do they furnish ground for judicial action on the basis of international law. Moreover they do not limit the right of the parties to terminate the non-legal undertaking when political circumstances are deemed by that State to warrant termination.

The fact that non-binding agreements may be terminated easily does not mean that they are illusory. . . . As long as they do last, even non-binding agreements can be authoritative and controlling for the parties. It would seem sensible to recognize that non-binding agreements may be attainable when binding treaties are not and to seek to reinforce their moral and political commitments when they serve ends we value.

Notes and Questions

1. Schachter argues that it would be illegal to act inconsistently with a political commitment if other parties "reasonably relied" on the political commitment. How could any state reasonably rely on a commitment that intentionally was made nonbinding? Another problem with giving much weight to political commitments is that they may not be subjected to the same domestic political process in their formation. The Secretary of State may make what other states consider to be a political commitment. But under the Constitution, the Secretary of State cannot make a law or a treaty that requires the participation of the Congress or the Senate. Consequently, the making of a political commitment has not been subjected to the same process of publicity, consensus building, and support normally accompanying the making of a law. In light of this, shouldn't a state rely on a political commitment at its peril?

2. What Professor Schachter discusses above is a component of what has increasingly come to be referred to as "soft law." Professor Michael Reisman has defined it as "international law-making that is designed, in whole or part, not to be enforceable." See W. Michael Reisman, The Supervisory Jurisdiction of the International Court of Justice, 258 Rec. des Cours 180-182 (1996). Nevertheless, as Professor Schachter analyzed, soft law may lead to some compliance with its standards. Soft law can include such diverse quasi-legal instruments as formal statements from international organizations or meetings (such as the Helsinki Final Act, discussed above) to codes of conduct from interest groups. See Commitment and Compliance: The Role of Non-Binding Norms in the International Legal System (Dinah Shelton ed. 2000). The European Union's new Charter of Fundamental Rights is a recent example of soft law. (It is discussed in Chapters 5 and 8.)

2.   *Observance and Interpretation of Treaties*

Article 26 of the Vienna Convention expresses the fundamental and widely accepted
rule of *pacta sunt servanda:* "Every treaty in force is binding upon the parties to it and
must be performed by them in good faith." As a Comment to the Restatement notes,
this rule "lies at the core of the law of international agreements and is perhaps the
most important principle of international law." The *pacta sunt servanda* rule is subject, however, to the rules concerning the validity and termination of treaties discussed below.

Perhaps the most frequently cited provisions of the Vienna Convention are
those dealing with treaty interpretation (Articles 31 and 32). The rules of interpretation contained in the Vienna Convention are somewhat different from the rules
that a U.S. court would apply to interpret a contract or a statute. The Restatement
(Third) of Foreign Relations contrasts the approach likely to be taken by U.S. courts
(and presumably by other U.S. authorities, such as the Departments of State, Defense, Treasury, or Commerce or by the Congress).

Restatement Section 325

Comment

. . . The Vienna Convention, in Article 32, requires the interpreting body to
conclude that the "ordinary meaning" of the text is either obscure or unreasonable
before it can look to "supplementary means.". . . Article 32 of the Vienna Convention reflects reluctance to permit the use of materials constituting the development
and negotiation of an agreement *(travaux préparatoires)* as a guide to the interpretation of an agreement. The Convention's inhospitality to *travaux* is not wholly consistent with the attitude of the International Court of Justice and not at all with that
of United States courts. . . .

. . . Courts in the United States are generally more willing than those of other
states to look outside the instrument to determine its meaning. In most cases, the
United States approach would lead to the same result, but an international tribunal
using the approach called for by this section might find the United States interpretation erroneous and United States action pursuant to that interpretation a violation
of the agreement.

Reporters' Notes

1. . . . Some states at the Vienna Conference objected to resort to *travaux* as contrary to their traditions, in which resort to legislative history to interpret domestic statutory questions is impermissible, or at least uncommon. Some were concerned that if resort to *travaux* were accepted, a state might be deterred from acceding to a multilateral
convention negotiated at a conference that it had not attended. Others feared that resort to *travaux* would favor nations with long-maintained and well-indexed archives. . . .

Notes and Questions

1. What is the purpose of treaty interpretation — to ascertain the meaning of
the text or the intent of the parties? Are these different? What practical difference

would it make? If the objective is to ascertain the meaning of the text (as opposed to the intent of the parties), would the negotiation history *(travaux)* be relevant? How does the Vienna Convention resolve this issue? Is the approach taken meaningful? In any given dispute, is it likely that the meaning of the text will prove to be ambiguous? On the other hand, is the *travaux* likely to be any less ambiguous? Would be it fair to use the *travaux* to interpret a term of a multilateral treaty if the parties involved were not actually present at the negotiation of the treaty?

2. Do "supplementary" means of interpretation used in Article 32 mean "subordinate"? Is there any case where the use of *travaux,* or negotiating history, would be excluded? Professor Frankowska writes:

> Obviously, article 32 is depicted inaccurately [in the Restatement comment quoted above]. No mention is made of the fact that article 32 permits recourse to the *travaux* to confirm the meaning of the terms of the treaty, a clause which changes the whole tenor of the article. In spite of what the Restatement suggests, it is possible for the courts to look to the authority of the Vienna Convention while using the *travaux* in accordance with the American judicial tradition. [Maria Frankowska, The Vienna Convention on the Law of Treaties Before United States Courts, 28 Va. J. Intl. L. 281, 335 (1988).]

Do you agree?

3. The "ordinary meaning" of a word in English can be different from its "ordinary meaning" in German or another language. If the texts of the treaties in those languages are equally authentic, as is the common practice, the interpreter must resort to context and external sources to determine the — or a — proper interpretation. Do you think that there is always a single correct interpretation?

4. Why is the definition of "context" so narrow? Should declarations and resolutions adopted at a diplomatic conference recommending a treaty, or authoritative explanations or reports prepared by drafters, be regarded as part of the "context"?

5. Professor Myres McDougal argued that the rules of interpretation should permit the use of any evidence to elucidate the shared expectations of the parties, even if this means disregarding or contravening the ordinary meaning of the text. See Myres S. McDougal, Harold D. Lasswell & James C. Miller, The Interpretation of Agreements and World Public Order: Principles of Content and Procedure (1967). What do you think of that idea? For a critique, see Sir Gerald Fitzmaurice, Vae Victus or Woe to the Negotiators! Your Treaty or Our "Interpretation" of It?, 65 Am. J. Intl. L. 358 (1971). The Vienna Convention obviously has rejected the McDougal view.

6. Why should the *travaux* not be accorded equal weight with the text and subsequent practice of the parties? What about domestic legislative history, such as the report of the delegation, a letter of transmittal of the treaty by the President, Senate or Congressional hearings and committee reports, or statements by delegates?

7. In U.S. practice, an official called on to interpret an agreement would normally look to the text, the negotiating record, subsequent practice of the parties, the purpose of the agreement, and, in the case of a treaty or an agreement approved by the Senate or the Congress, to Executive Branch submissions and the legislative record. Appeals to these sources of authority were especially prominent in the debate over the proper interpretation of the ABM Treaty regarding the legality of developing and testing space-based weapons systems using new technologies. The process is summarized by Professor Koh above at pages 44-47. For another example, a

dispute arose when the United States sought to impose otherwise permissible noise regulations on supersonic aircraft (the Concorde) under a bilateral aviation agreement. If one party believes that a specific treaty provision prohibits a particular practice but the other party believes that the practice is not prohibited, should the dispute be resolved with reference to unilateral statements made by one party to its legislature? If unilateral materials should be avoided and the negotiating record is silent or ambiguous on the point, how should an international judge decide the dispute? Or does the silence of the negotiating record mean that there is no meeting of the minds or consent, so that there is no binding obligation at all? In another situation, would the unilateral behavior or practice of a party to a treaty, which was known to and acquiesced in by the other party, amount to an "agreement" of the parties that would be appropriately used under the Vienna Convention? If so, should a state carefully follow the domestic ratification processes of its treaty partners and monitor equally carefully their behavior under the treaty? Are Articles 27 and 46 of the Vienna Convention relevant to the last two questions? See further discussion of U.S. practices in Chapter 3 at 176 and 190-191.

The Convention's rules regarding interpretation have been applied, at least rhetorically or nominally, by U.S. domestic courts (including the Supreme Court), congressional committees, bilateral trade dispute-settlement panels, the WTO Appellate Body, arbitral bodies, and the International Court of Justice.

3. Invalidity of Treaties

Articles 46-52 of the Convention are provisions dealing with the possible invalidity of a treaty. They cover a state or its representative's competence to conclude a treaty, error, fraud, corruption, and duress. (See the Documentary Supplement for their texts.) In many ways, these provisions are analogous to the contract rules found in many nations. However, Article 52 on "Coercion of a State by the Threat or Use of Force" evoked considerable debate during the drafting process. Professor Sinclair describes the background:

> Article 52 of the Convention deals with coercion of the State itself and again lays down a rule of absolute nullity. The Commission, after reviewing the history of the matter and taking into account the clear-cut prohibition of the threat or use of force in Article 2(4) of the United Nations Charter, considered that these developments "justify the conclusion that the invalidity of a treaty procured by the illegal threat or use of force is a principle which is *lex lata* in the international law of today." Discussion at the Conference on this article tended to concentrate on two issues:
>
> (a) Whether the expression "threat or use of force" could, or should, be interpreted as covering economic and political pressure.
> (b) The temporal application of the rule — that is to say, the date from which the rule invalidating a treaty procured by the threat or use of force in violation of the principles of international law embodied in the Charter may be said to operate.

The records of the Conference reveal strongly conflicting views on both these points. That the rule now embodied in Article 52 of the Convention represents the modern law on this topic is beyond serious dispute; but there are clearly uncertainties about the scope of the rule and its temporal application. . . . From this, it may be concluded that Article 52 may savour more of codification than of progressive development, at least insofar as the expression "threat or use of force" is confined to physical or armed force and no question arises as to the temporal application of the rule. . . . [Sir Ian Sinclair, The Vienna Convention on the Law of Treaties 15-17 (2d ed. 1984).]

As Professor Sinclair notes, there could be uncertainties about Article 52's scope. For example, in the midst of the Asian financial crisis in 1997, the International Monetary Fund offered much needed financial support to Indonesia, but only upon Indonesia's acceptance to change fundamental economic policies. (See Chapter 5.) Could Indonesia validly argue later that the IMF-Indonesia agreement was void?

What about the agreements that come at the end of a crisis or even after hostilities where one or more countries might have gained the upper hand over another country? For example, the Algiers Accords were an agreement reached between Iran and the United States in 1981. They provided for, among other things, the release of U.S. embassy personnel who had been held as hostages for over one year. Could the United States later claim that the agreement was invalid? (See discussion of *Dames & Moore* in Chapter 3.) Or, were the terms regarding Kosovo that the Federal Republic of Yugoslavia finally agreed to in 1999 after NATO's bombing campaign invalid? (See Chapter 11.) Are there not some benefits in the stability of relations among countries and the presumed validity of the agreements that the countries reach?

What about the so-called unequal treaties China entered in the 19th C?

4. Jus Cogens

Articles 53 and 64 introduce the idea of "peremptory norms," or *jus cogens*. This type of norm is said to be so fundamental that states cannot agree to contravene it. Professors McWhinney and Aust explain the background:

Edward McWhinney, United Nations Law Making
73-75 (1984)

The draft article represented a compromise, in legal theory terms, between positivism and natural law. The legal positivists insisted that the concept of *jus cogens* either did not exist or was too vague to be given legal meaning, and that in any case the adoption of such a specific derogation from the free will of the parties to a treaty to conclude whatever agreement they wished would impair the sanctity of the written word and the principle of *pacta sunt servanda*. The natural law lawyers insisted that the principle of a *jus cogens* limitation to the contractual power of the parties was one common to all legal systems, existing under various rubrics, "public policy" and the like, but amounting essentially to the same thing. In "regional" international law terms, it was the Anglo-Saxon common lawyers who were most unhappy about *jus cogens,* the United States in particular opposing its incorporation in the draft treaty prepared by the International Law Commission. Continental European civil lawyers, by contrast, were not nuanced in their approach and usually supportive, the idea of *jus cogens,* after all, having some classical Roman law antecedents, and certainly deriving rich support from nineteenth-century civil law pandectist teachings. . . .

. . . [T]he Anglo-Saxon intellectual resistance to *jus cogens* [can be attributed to] to the common lawyer's instinctive aversion to, and inability easily to debate and discuss, abstract general legal notions, whether "general principles of law" or any other. Such intrinsically technical-legal attitudes were reinforced, of course, by highly pragmatic considerations of the vested interest of the major Western powers in the corpus of existing treaties. . . .

Anthony Aust, Modern Treaty Law and Practice
257-258 (2000)

The concept of *jus cogens* (peremptory norm of general international law) was controversial at the time of the Vienna Conference. Now it is more the scope and applicability of the concept which is debated. *Jus cogens* is defined in Article 53 for the purposes of the Convention as:

> a norm accepted and recognised by the international community of States as a whole as a norm from which no derogation is permitted and which can be modified only by a subsequent norm of general international law having the same character.

There is no agreement on the criteria for identifying which norms of general international law have a peremptory character. Whether a norm of general international law has it depends on the particular nature of the subject matter. Perhaps the only generally accepted example is the prohibition on the use of force as laid down in the UN Charter. The prohibitions on genocide, slavery and torture may also be said to be *jus cogens.* This is so even where such acts are prohibited by treaties which parties to them can denounce. But it would be rash to assume that all prohibitions contained in human rights treaties are *jus cogens,* or even part of customary international law. Some rights, such as the freedom of association, are far from being generally accepted as customary law. Article 53 does not therefore attempt to list examples of *jus cogens,* leaving that to be worked out by state practice and in the jurisprudence of international tribunals.

If part only of a treaty conflicts with an existing *jus cogens* the whole of the treaty is void, not just the offending part (Article 44(5)).

Article 53 has no retrospective effect (Article 4). It must, however, be read with Article 64, which provides that, if a new peremptory norm of general international law emerges, any existing treaty which is in conflict with that norm "becomes void and terminates." Since this provision is not retrospective, the treaty is invalid only as from the time the new norm is established.

The vast majority of rules do not of course have the character of *jus cogens,* and states are therefore free to contract out of them; and a treaty which conflicts with general international law is not necessarily void. Similarly, if a treaty provides that no derogation from it is permitted, but later a party concludes a treaty which conflicts with it, the latter treaty is not void although the party may be liable for breach of the earlier treaty.

There are no reported instances of Articles 53 or 64, as such, being invoked.

Questions

1. What are the advantages and disadvantages in creating another doctrine that can be used by diplomats, judges, and lawyers to justify a preferred result?

2. If you think that judges (or scholars) do not make decisions that way, how do you think they would go about a disinterested search for the norms of *jus cogens*?

3. Some examples, like an agreement to enslave Cambodians or to obliterate the Czech Republic, may seem like persuasive examples of *jus cogens*. Are they realistic examples? Can you think of other examples? What about denial of the right of self-determination, violation of the law of peaceful co-existence, the international crime of apartheid, denial of human rights like torture, capital punishment of juveniles, or state terrorism?

4. Although *jus cogens* has yet to be invoked to void a treaty, the concept has appeared in discussions of what constitutes norms of customary international law and whether certain norms have greater weight. See Section B below.

5. Termination and the Suspension of the Operation of Treaties

In the event of a material breach of a treaty, it has long been recognized and generally accepted that the affected party may unilaterally terminate the treaty or suspend the performance of its own obligations. The Vienna Convention provides:

Vienna Convention

Article 60. Termination or Suspension of the Operation of a Treaty as a Consequence of Its Breach

1. A material breach of a bilateral treaty by one of the parties entitles the other to invoke the breach as a ground for terminating the treaty or suspending its operation in whole or in part.

2. A material breach of a multilateral treaty by one of the parties entitles:

   (a) the other parties by unanimous agreement to suspend the operation of the treaty in whole or in part or to terminate it either:

   (i) in the relations between themselves and the defaulting State,
or
   (ii) as between all the parties;

   (b) a party specially affected by the breach to invoke it as a ground for suspending the operation of the treaty in whole or in part in the relations between itself and the defaulting State;

   (c) any party other than the defaulting State to invoke the breach as a ground for suspending the operation of the treaty in whole or in part with respect to itself if the treaty is of such a character that a material breach of its provisions by one party radically changes the position of every party with respect to the further performance of its obligations under the treaty.

3. A material breach of a treaty, for the purposes of this article, consists in:

(a) a repudiation of the treaty not sanctioned by the present Convention; or

(b) the violation of a provision essential to the accomplishment of the object or purpose of the treaty.

4. The foregoing paragraphs are without prejudice to any provision in the treaty applicable in the event of a breach.

5. Paragraphs 1 to 3 do not apply to provisions relating to the protection of the human person contained in treaties of a humanitarian character, in particular to provisions prohibiting any form of reprisals against persons protected by such treaties.

Notes and Questions

Article 60 sets forth detailed criteria for justifiably getting out of a treaty obligation. Consider these questions.

1. Summarize in a sentence or two the standard that must be met under Article 60.

2. What can a state then do in the event of a "material breach"? For example, if Chile violated a bilateral trade agreement with the United States providing for free trade in all products by restricting trade in American exports of designer blouses (but not computers, aircraft, and grain), what remedy would be available to the United States? Could the United States terminate the entire agreement? Would your answer change if the volume of trade in designer blouses amounted to less than $5 million out of a total of $5 billion in annual trade?

3. How do the remedies under the Vienna Convention differ from those available for breach of contract under the domestic law? What are the purposes and advantages or disadvantages of the different remedies that may be available?

4. Consider this background to the negotiation of Article 60 written by American participants:

> In the debate on the article the U.S. representative noted that the text and commentary served the cause of the stability of treaty relations by providing that a material breach could be invoked by a party to terminate a treaty or suspend its operation but did not produce that effect in itself. However, the article did not clearly indicate when a party invoking breach could suspend the operation of the treaty in whole and when in part. He thought it would be helpful to introduce into the article itself an element of proportionality. Accordingly, he proposed adding at the end of paragraph one the following language: "as may be appropriate considering the nature and extent of the breach and the extent to which the treaty obligations have been performed." He also suggested a similar formulation be added at the end of subparagraph (b) of paragraph 2.
>
> The tenor of the debate in the committee of the whole made it clear that no amendment would be possible in the article in 1968. In light of this attitude the United States Delegation responded positively to the United Kingdom suggestion that the delegation withdraw its amendments to the breach article on the understanding that the principle of proportionality embodied therein would be considered in connection with the separability article, on which a vote had not then been taken. In the separability context, although attracting substantial support, the principle failed to obtain a

majority when put to the vote. [Richard D. Kearney & Robert E. Dalton, The Treaty on Treaties, 64 Am. J. Intl. L. 495, 540 (1970).]

5. Who determines whether there has been a material breach? Whether the remedy should be suspension of part of or all of the treaty? Or some other remedy?

6. Articles 65 and 66 of the Vienna Convention provide for compulsory but non-binding conciliation of disputes over the validity or interpretation of a treaty. There is a strong case that these provisions do not amount to customary international law, especially the specific provisions of the Annex regarding the establishment of a Conciliation Commission. If a state declared a material breach of a treaty (in effect relying on the terms of Article 60), do you think that it would be obligated to give formal notice and make some attempt with the offending treaty partner to settle the dispute? Or must it use some form of third-party dispute settlement? Should it be able to terminate the treaty or some other part of it? Should the U.S. government respect all, or some, of the dispute settlement provisions of Articles 65 and 66 even though it has not ratified the Vienna Convention?

7. **Problem.** The Krasnoyarsk Radar. In May 1972, the United States and the Soviet Union signed the Treaty on the Limitations of Anti-Ballistic Missile Systems (commonly known as the ABM Treaty) in an attempt to set limits on defensive missile systems. An integral part of the ABM Treaty was a limit on the deployment of large, phased-array radars (LPARs) by both countries. According to Article VI(b), both countries committed "not to deploy in the future radars for early warning of strategic ballistic missile attack except at locations along the periphery of its national territory and oriented outward." The limitations on LPARs were important because these very large radars were key to a nationwide missile defensive system and, unlike some of the other components of the system, the radars took years to construct and were easily visible to satellites. Simply prohibiting these LPARs was not possible because both countries had other legitimate purposes for these radars, principally for tracking objects in space and for gathering intelligence. Article VI's directional limitations were important to help distinguish the LPARs meant for missile defense from other LPARs. The Treaty's locational limits meant that the LPARs that were built would be vulnerable to attacks by artillery or short-range missiles from across the border, and thus less useful for missile defense purposes.

American reconnaissance satellites revealed in 1983 a LPAR under construction near Krasnoyarsk, Siberia. (These radars covered an area larger than a football field.) It was not located along the Soviet periphery (but was over four hundred miles from the nearest border), nor was it oriented outward. The radar clearly violated Article VI(b) of the ABM Treaty.

The Soviets initially stonewalled by denying there was a breach and arguing that the radar was really for space tracking. After several years of diplomatic negotiations, the United States emphasized the importance of the Soviet violation at the treaty's five-year Review Conference in 1988. In a unilateral statement, the U.S. government "reserve[d] all its rights, consistent with international law, to take appropriate and proportionate responses in the future." What could these responses have been under international law if the Soviets had not corrected the breach?

Fortunately, further U.S. steps were not required. Apparently sensing that the Krasnoyarsk radar would become an impediment to future diplomatic relations with the United States, the Soviet Union agreed to dismantle the radar in September

1989. In a noteworthy speech to the Supreme Soviet the next month, Foreign Minister Eduard Shevardnadze acknowledged that the radar was a violation of the ABM pact. "We investigated the situation for four years. . . . The whole truth did not become known to the country's leadership right away."

Besides Article 60 on material breach, the Vienna Convention contains other provisions allowing for termination or suspension of the operation of a treaty.

Article 61 deals with impossibility of performance as a basis for terminating or withdrawing from a treaty. Article 62 deals with the permissibility of terminating a treaty because of a "fundamental change in circumstances" (the doctrine of *rebus sic stantibus*). (Both articles are in the Documentary Supplement.) Sinclair traces the formulation of Article 62:

> . . . The concept that (whether by an implied term or otherwise) a treaty may become inapplicable by reason of a fundamental change in circumstances obviously presents serious dangers to the security of treaties. Nevertheless, the doctrine that a fundamental change of circumstances may operate to bring about the termination of a treaty is of ancient origin. Traces of the *rebus* principle can be found in early canon law. . . .
>
> . . . Gentili appears to have been the first to apply this private law concept in the sphere of international relations, maintaining in his *De jure belli libri tres* that a treaty need not be performed when the condition of affairs is changed, if the change could not have been foreseen. Grotius, on the other hand, took a very restrictive attitude towards the *rebus* doctrine, as did Pufendorf and Bynkershoek, the latter asserting that invocation of the doctrine was but one of the cloaks of treachery. . . . However, diplomatic practice in the nineteenth century — and, particularly, the invocation by Russia of the *rebus* doctrine to justify her assertion in 1870 that the provisions of the 1856 Treaty regarding the neutralisation of the Black Sea were no longer binding upon her . . . began to demonstrate some of the dangers inherent in the notion of the clause; and indeed the *rebus* doctrine fell into serious disrepute during the inter-war period, largely as a result of its indiscriminate invocation by States in the period immediately preceding 1914 to escape from inconvenient treaty obligations. . . .
>
> Against this background, the Commission approached the formulation of a text on *rebus sic stantibus* with considerable caution. After extensive debate, they decided to formulate it in negative terms, declaring that a fundamental change of circumstances which had occurred with regard to those existing at the time of the conclusion of a treaty might not be invoked as a ground for terminating or withdrawing from the treaty unless two conditions were met:
>
> (a) the existence of those circumstances constituted an essential basis of the consent of the parties to be bound by the treaty; *and*
> (b) the effect of the change was radically to transform the scope of obligations still to be performed under the treaty.
>
> To this the Commission proposed two exceptions:
>
> (a) a fundamental change of circumstances could not be invoked as a ground for terminating or withdrawing from a treaty establishing a boundary;
> (b) a fundamental change of circumstances could not be invoked if it was the result of a breach by the invoking party either of the treaty or of a different international obligation owed to the other parties to the treaty.

Some interesting points were made in the course of the debate. In the first place, it was suggested, and not denied, that a State would not be entitled to invoke its own acts or omissions as amounting to a fundamental change of circumstances giving rise to the operation of Article 62. Attention was also directed to the view expressed by some members of the Commission, and recorded in the commentary to the Commission's proposal, that "a subjective change in the attitude or policy of a Government could never be invoked as a ground for terminating, withdrawing from or suspending the operation of a treaty." . . .

Concern was expressed by several delegations . . . about the Commission's proposals to preclude invocation of fundamental change of circumstances in the case of a treaty establishing a boundary, but a proposal to delete what is now paragraph 2(a) of Article 62 was not pressed to a vote. [Ian Sinclair, supra, at pp.192-195.]

Case Concerning the Gabcikovo-Nagymaros Project (Hungary v. Slovakia)

Intl. Court of Justice
1997 I.C.J. 7 (Judgment)

[In this case, Slovakia asked the I.C.J., among other issues, to rule upon the validity of Hungary's termination of a 1977 Treaty with Slovakia's predecessor state (Czechoslovakia). The 1977 Treaty concerned the construction and operation of a system of locks on the Danube River which formed part of the border between the two countries. In arriving at its decision against Hungary, the ICJ relied heavily upon the 1969 Vienna Convention on the Law of Treaties. Even though the countries had not ratified the Vienna Convention at the time of their 1977 Treaty, the ICJ concluded that Articles 60 to 62 of the Vienna Convention were "declaratory of customary law."

The ICJ then applied these articles to Hungary's arguments that it should be allowed to terminate the 1977 Treaty.]

100. The 1977 Treaty does not contain any provision regarding its termination. . . . On the contrary, the Treaty establishes a long-standing and durable regime of joint investment and joint operation. Consequently, the parties not having agreed otherwise, the Treaty could be terminated only on the limited grounds enumerated in the Vienna Convention. . . .

102. Hungary also relied on the principle of the impossibility of performance as reflected in Article 61 of the Vienna Convention on the Law of Treaties. Hungary's interpretation of the wording of Article 61 is, however, not in conformity with the terms of that Article. . . .

103. Hungary contended that the essential object of the Treaty — an economic joint investment which was consistent with environmental protection and which was operated by the two contracting parties jointly — had permanently disappeared and that the Treaty has thus become impossible to perform. . . . Article 61, paragraph 2, of the Vienna Convention expressly provides that impossibility of performance may not be invoked for the termination of a treaty by a party to that treaty when it results from that party's own breach of an obligation flowing from the treaty.

104. Hungary further argued that it was entitled to invoke a number of events which, cumulatively, would have constituted a fundamental change of circumstances. In this respect it specified profound changes of a political nature, the Project's

diminishing economic viability, the progress of environmental knowledge and the development of new norms and prescriptions of international environmental law. . . .

The changed circumstances advanced by Hungary are, in the Court's view, not of such a nature, either individually or collectively, that their effect would radically transform the extent of the obligations still to be performed in order to accomplish the Project. A fundamental change of circumstances must have been unforeseen; the existence of the circumstances at the time of the Treaty's conclusion must have constituted an essential basis of the consent of the parties to be bound by the Treaty. The negative and conditional wording of Article 62 of the Vienna Convention . . . is a clear indication moreover that the stability of treaty relations requires that the plea of fundamental change of circumstances be applied only in exceptional cases.

Questions

1. In the Gabcikovo decision excerpted above, is the Court correct that "the stability of treaty relations requires that the plea of fundamental change of circumstances be applied only in exceptional cases"?

2. Why did the drafters of the Vienna Convention decide on narrow exceptions, such as Articles 61 and 62? What is the value of, and whose interests are most protected by, the approach adopted by the Convention in this respect?

3. Does the Vienna Convention seem to protect continuation of agreements and therefore the status quo? If so, does that mean that treaty regimes are inherently conservative and difficult to change?

6. Reservations

Sometimes a party to a treaty may wish to accept most of its obligations, but not all of them. There are many possible reasons for this. Sometimes the country might not agree with a particular provision, or it might not wish to accept a dispute settlement provision (such as reference of disputes to the ICJ), or it might not have the constitutional power to accept a particular provision (e.g., a federal state may not be able to bind its constituent states or provinces).

In such a case the party may seek to enter a "reservation" to the treaty. The Vienna Convention defines a "reservation" in Article 2(1)(d) as "a unilateral statement, however phrased or named, made by a State, when signing, ratifying, accepting, approving or acceding to a treaty, whereby it purports to exclude or modify the legal effect of certain provisions of the treaty in their application to that State."

Professor Edwards provides more background about the possible reasons for reservations.

Richard W. Edwards, Jr., Reservations to Treaties
10 Mich. J. Intl. L. 362, 362-364 (1989)

The subject matter of multilateral treaties has an immensely wide range, including, inter alia, rights respecting international waterways, trade and finance, alliances and military affairs, settlement of disputes, and creation of both general and highly specialized international and regional organizations. Multilateral treaties have also led to the creation and codification of legal regimes applicable to such diverse concerns as arms control, the conduct of military hostilities, educational and cultural exchanges, diplomatic and consular relations, international trade, intellectual property, the law of the sea, the use of the ratio spectrum, and the protection of human rights. The number of nation States participating in treaties has greatly expanded in the period since World War II. International and regional organizations are not only the subjects of international agreements, they are also parties to international agreements. Individuals, although not parties to treaties, may be vested with enforceable rights under them.

The difficulty of fashioning agreed rules applicable to all parties to an international agreement has inspired the use of reservations. . . . [A] reservation can be roughly defined as a unilateral statement made by a State or international organization, when signing, ratifying, acceding, or otherwise expressing its consent to be bound by an international agreement, whereby it purports to exclude or to modify the legal effect of certain provisions of the international agreement in their application to that State or organization. Reasons for reservations include:

1. A State or international organization may wish to be a party to an international agreement while at the same time not yielding on certain substantive points believed to be against its interests.
2. A State or international organization may wish to be a party to an international agreement while at the same time not binding itself to certain procedural obligations, such as compulsory settlement of disputes in the form specified in a compromissory clause.
3. A State may wish to assure that its treaty obligations are compatible with peculiarities of its local law.
4. A State may want to preclude a treaty's application to subordinate political entities in a federal system or to foreign territories for which the State would otherwise have international responsibility.

These reasons could motivate any State, regardless of its form of government, to interpose a reservation when it expresses its consent to be bound by a treaty.

Let's now consider the process for making reservations, and their implications, as provided for in Articles 19-23 on the Vienna Convention on the Law of Treaties. These Articles are excerpted below.

Vienna Convention

Article 19. Formulation of Reservations

A State may, when signing, ratifying, accepting, approving or acceding to a treaty, formulate a reservation unless:

(a) the reservation is prohibited by the treaty;

(b) the treaty provides that only specified reservations, which do not include the reservation in question, may be made; or

(c) in cases not falling under sub-paragraphs (a) and (b), the reservation is incompatible with the object and purpose of the treaty.

Article 20. Acceptance of and Objection to Reservations

1. A reservation expressly authorized by a treaty does not require any subsequent acceptance by the other contracting States unless the treaty so provides.

2. When it appears from the limited number of the negotiating States and the object and purpose of a treaty that the application of the treaty in its entirety between all the parties is an essential condition of the consent of each one to be bound by the treaty, a reservation requires acceptance by all the parties.

3. When a treaty is a constituent instrument of an international organization and unless it otherwise provides, a reservation requires the acceptance of the competent organ of that organization.

4. In cases not falling under the preceding paragraphs and unless the treaty otherwise provides:

(a) acceptance by another contracting State of a reservation constitutes the reserving State a party to the treaty in relation to that other State if or when the treaty is in force for those States;

(b) an objection by another contracting State to a reservation does not preclude the entry into force of the treaty as between the objecting and reserving States unless a contrary intention is definitely expressed by the objecting State;

(c) an act expressing a State's consent to be bound by the treaty and containing a reservation is effective as soon as at least one other contracting State has accepted the reservation.

5. For the purposes of paragraphs 2 and 4 and unless the treaty otherwise provides, a reservation is considered to have been accepted by a State if it shall have raised no objection to the reservation by the end of a period of twelve months after it was notified of the reservation or by the date on which it expressed its consent to be bound by the treaty, whichever is later.

Article 21. Legal Effects of Reservations and of Objections to Reservations

1. A reservation established with regard to another party in accordance with articles 19, 20 and 23:

(a) modifies for the reserving State in its relations with that other party the provisions of the treaty to which the reservation relates to the extent of the reservation; and

(b) modifies those provisions to the same extent for that other party in its relations with the reserving State.

2. The reservation does not modify the provisions of the treaty for the other parties to the treaty *inter se*.

3. When a State objecting to a reservation has not opposed the entry into force of the treaty between itself and the reserving State, the provisions to which the reservation relates do not apply as between the two States to the extent of the reservation. . . .

Article 23.   Procedure Regarding Reservations

1. A reservation, an express acceptance of a reservation and an objection to a reservation must be formulated in writing and communicated to the contracting States and other States entitled to become parties to the treaty. . . .

Notes and Questions

1. If State A makes a reservation (e.g., saying a particular dispute-resolution provision does not apply) to a multilateral treaty when the state is ratifying the treaty, what is the effect of the reservation on the treaty's legal obligations between State A and State B, which has earlier ratified the treaty? Assume that the treaty allows such reservations by parties. Does it matter if State B has raised no objection to the reservation? If State B has raised an objection to the reservation but does not indicate that the reservation precludes the entry into force of the treaty as between the two states, what is the effect of the reservation on the legal obligations between the two countries? If State B objects and says that the reservation is such that it should preclude the entry into force of the whole treaty between the two countries, what is the effect of the reservation?

2. Are Articles 19 through 23 essentially applicable only to multilateral treaties, and not bilateral ones? If the treaty is a bilateral treaty, can one of the two State parties make a reservation (as defined in Article 2(1)(d) of the Vienna Convention)? One expert argues no, because "there are only two possible parties, a bilateral treaty is more like a contract, *all* the terms of which must be agreed before it can bind the parties." Aust, Modern Treaty Law and Practice, *supra* at 106; see also Restatement, section 313, cmt. f. What might be the alternative to seeking to make a reservation for a state that, after initially negotiating and signing the bilateral treaty, discovers a problem with a substantive provision of the treaty or decides that a provision is ambiguous? Can this be a request for a modification in the treaty? This situation might arise during the domestic process of obtaining the advice and consent of a legislative body.

3. Should a unilateral interpretation, also sometimes referred to as an interpretative declaration, of an ambiguous provision of a treaty be treated as a reservation? In principle, is there anything wrong with treating it as a reservation? If the unilateral interpretation is made during the negotiating process on the treaty, might it also become an element in the interpretation of the treaty under Articles 31 and 32?

4. The flexible approach for reservations to multilateral conventions embodied in the Vienna Convention, especially Article 20(4), reflects the ICJ's *Advisory Opinion on Reservations to the Genocide Convention*, 1951 I.C.J. 15. As the Court observed:

> It is well established that in its treaty relations a State cannot be bound without its consent, and that consequently no reservation can be effective against any State without its agreement thereto. It is also a generally recognized principle that a multilateral convention is the result of an agreement freely concluded upon its clauses and that consequently none of the contracting parties is entitled to frustrate or impair, by means of unilateral decisions or particular agreements, the purpose and *raison d'etre* of the convention. To this principle was linked the notion of the integrity of the convention as adopted, a notion which in its traditional concept involved the proposition that no

reservation was valid unless it was accepted by all the contracting parties without exception, as would have been the case if it had been stated during the negotiations.

This concept, which is directly inspired by the notion of contract, is of undisputed value as a principle. However, as regards the Genocide Convention, it is proper to refer to a variety of circumstances which would lead to a more flexible application of this principle. Among these circumstances may be noted the clearly universal character of the United Nations under whose auspices the Convention was concluded, and the very wide degree of participation envisaged by Article XI of the Convention. Extensive participation in conventions of this type has already given rise to greater flexibility in the international practice concerning multilateral conventions. More general resort to reservations, very great allowance made for tacit assent to reservations, the existence of practices which go so far as to admit that the author of reservations which have been rejected by certain contracting parties is nevertheless to be regarded as a party to the convention in relation to those contracting parties that have accepted the reservations — all these factors are manifestations of a new need for flexibility in the operation of multilateral conventions. . . .

It has . . . been argued that any State entitled to become a party to the Genocide Convention may do so while making any reservation it chooses by virtue of its sovereignty. The Court cannot share this view. It is obvious that so extreme an application of the idea of State sovereignty would lead to a complete disregard of the object and purpose of the Convention.

5. Some multilateral treaties prohibit reservations. What are the reasons why a treaty, say, establishing a new institution or a new regime of laws should prohibit reservations? For example, the Rome Statute of the International Criminal Court, which was signed in 1998 and came into force in 2002, prohibits reservations (Article 120).

6. The 1982 Law of the Sea Convention also prohibited reservations (Article 309). However, the problems that the United States and several other countries had with the deep seabed mining provisions of the 1982 Convention led to the imaginative solution where a later companion agreement was negotiated in 1994 that has the effect of amending the objectionable provisions in the 1982 Convention. (See Chapter 9.)

7. It appears that most multilateral conventions do not have reservations, whether because they are prohibited or because countries choose not to make reservations. Reservations are particularly rare when the conventions are limited to a few states. For example, see John King Gamble, Reservations to Multilateral Treaties: A Macroscopic View of State Practice, 74 Am. J. Intl. L. 372 (1980).

8. Reservations are nevertheless often made by the United States and other countries in conventions on human rights. Indeed, the frequency of these reservations led the U.N. Human Rights Committee and the International Law Commission to study these reservations. In its General Comment No. 24, the U.N. Human Rights Committee took the position in 1994 that it had the authority "to determine whether a specific reservation is compatible with the object and purpose" of the International Covenant on Civil and Political Rights. The United States and the United Kingdom objected to the Committee's claim of authority. (See Chapter 3 for a discussion of U.S. practice and the possible reasons for the U.S. use of reservations, as well as the U.S. position on General Comment No. 24. See also Chapter 8.)

9. Do you think that a reservation that, say, rejects a prohibition on capital punishment for juvenile offenders in a human rights treaty should be regarded as

incompatible with the object and purpose of the agreement for purposes of Article 19 of the Vienna Convention? Who is entitled to make that judgment? For a simmering dispute on these questions under the International Covenant on Civil and Political Rights, see the discussion in Chapter 3 at page 183, Note 5.

7. *Withdrawal from or Denunciation of a Treaty*

Most recent treaties contain clauses providing the bases for withdrawal from, or denunciation of, the treaty. The treaties usually specify the duration or date of termination of the treaty, and/or the conditions or events that allow for termination or the right to withdraw or denounce the treaty. For example, the 1994 Agreement Establishing the World Trade Organization provided in Article XV that "Any Member may withdraw from this Agreement. Such withdrawal . . . shall take effect upon the expiration of six months from the date on which written notice of withdrawal is received by the Director-general of the WTO."

Recognizing the rights of the parties as well as this now common practice of including withdrawal clauses, Article 54 of the Vienna Convention provides that the termination of a treaty or a party's withdrawal may take place "in conformity with the provisions of the treaty" or "at any time by consent of all the parties. . . ."

If the treaty contains no such provisions regarding termination, withdrawal, or denunciation, then Article 56 of the Vienna Convention provides that the treaty "is not subject to denunciation or withdrawal unless:

(a) it is established that the parties intended to admit the possibility of denunciation or withdrawal; or

(b) a right to denunciation or withdrawal may be implied by the nature of the treaty."

The International Court of Justice addressed this situation, where a treaty failed to include provisions for termination, denunciation, or withdrawal, in the Case Concerning the Gabcikovo-Nagymaros Project (Hungary/Slovakia), 1997 I.C.J. 7, 557-559, 574-576. In that case, which is also discussed in section 5 above, Hungary attempted to terminate a 1997 bilateral treaty without the other party's consent. After several years of difficult negotiations between Hungary and Czechoslovakia (the predecessor of Slovakia), the Hungarian Government notified Czechoslovakia that it was considering the treaty terminated, effective six days later. The I.C.J. held that Hungary could not terminate the treaty in this manner. In its opinion, the I.C.J. said:

100. The 1977 Treaty does not contain any provision regarding its termination. Nor is there any indication that the parties intended to admit the possibility of denunciation or withdrawal. On the contrary, the Treaty establishes a long-standing and durable regime of joint investment and joint operation. Consequently, the parties not having agreed otherwise, the Treaty could be terminated only on the limited grounds enumerated in the Vienna Convention. . . .

109. . . . [I]t should be noted that, according to Hungary's Declaration of 19 May 1992, the termination of the 1977 Treaty was to take effect as from 25 May 1992, that is only six days later. Both parties agree that Articles 65 to 67 of the Vienna Convention . . . , if not codifying customary law, at least generally reflect customary international law and contain certain procedural principles which are based on an obligation to act in good faith. . . .

The termination of the Treaty by Hungary was to take effect six days after its notification. On neither of these dates had Hungary suffered injury resulting from acts of Czechoslovakia. The Court must therefore confirm its conclusion that Hungary's termination of the Treaty was premature.

Notes and Questions

1. Should it be difficult to withdraw from treaties? If it is difficult, what effect, if any, will this have on the ratification of treaties? Is it better to have a regime under which a country that is unhappy with a treaty can withdraw from it, rather than a regime under which the country feels compelled to breach that treaty?

2. Reflecting the development of new defensive missile technologies and the emergence of new threats from rogue states, the administration of President George W. Bush decided that it was in the U.S. interest to build a limited missile defense system. In December 2001, President Bush gave formal notice to Russia that the United States would withdraw from the nearly 30-year old ABM Treaty, effective June 2002. Article XV(2) of the treaty provides that: "Each Party shall, in exercising its national sovereignty, have the right to withdraw from this Treaty if it decides that extraordinary events related to the subject matter of this Treaty have jeopardized its supreme interests. It shall give notice of its decision prior to the withdrawal from the Treaty. . . ."

Assuming for present purposes that the emergence of new threats to the United States and the development of new technologies constituted "extraordinary events" that "jeopardized [U.S.] supreme interests," was the U.S. withdrawal a breach of the Treaty? Was it consistent with the Vienna Convention on the Law of Treaties?

3. The International Covenant on Civil and Political Rights (ICCPR), an important human rights treaty that has been ratified by over 140 nations, does not contain a withdrawal clause. In 1998, the U.N. Human Rights Committee concluded that countries are not allowed to withdraw from this treaty. The Committee reasoned that the rights under the ICCPR "belong to the people living in the territory of the State party" and that "once the people are accorded the protection of the rights under the Covenant, such protection devolves with territory and continues to belong to them, notwithstanding change in Government of the State party, including . . . any subsequent action of the State party designed to divest them of the rights guaranteed by the Covenant." Are you persuaded? (See discussion of the ICCPR in Chapter 8.)

B.   CUSTOMARY INTERNATIONAL LAW

1.   Formation of Customary International Law

I.A. Shearer, Starke's International Law
31-35 (11th ed. 1994)

Until recent times, international law consisted for the most part of customary rules. These rules had generally evolved after a long historical process culminating in their recognition by the international community. The preponderance of customary rules was diminished as a result of the large number of "law-making" treaties concluded since the middle of the last century, and must progressively decline to negligible proportions in measure as the work of the International Law Commission in codifying and restating customary rules produces results in treaties such as the Vienna Conventions of 18 April 1961, of 24 April, 1963, and of 22 May 1969, on Diplomatic Relations, Consular Relations, and the Law of Treaties respectively. Yet according to views recently expressed by some writers, international custom may still have a significant role to play as a dynamic source of fresh rules of international law where the international community undergoes change in new areas untouched by treaties, judicial decision, or the writings of jurists.

The terms "custom" and "usage" are often used interchangeably. Strictly speaking, there is a clear technical distinction between the two. Usage represents the twilight stage of custom. Custom begins where usage ends. Usage is an international habit of action that has not yet received full legal attestation. Usages may be conflicting, custom must be unified and self-consistent. *Viner's Abridgement,* referring to custom in English law, has the matter in a nutshell.

A custom, in the intendment of law, is such a usage as hath obtained the force of a law.

A customary element has, as we have seen, been a feature of the rules of international law from antiquity to modern times. In ancient Greece, the rules of war and peace sprang from the common usages observed by the Greek City States. These customary rules crystallised by a process of generalisation and unification of the various usages separately observed by each city republic. A similar process was observable among the small Italian states of the Middle Ages. When in the sixteenth and seventeenth centuries Europe became a complex of highly nationalised, independent territorial states, the process was translated to a higher and more extensive plane. From the usages developed in the intercourse of modern European states there emerged the earliest rules of international law.

Customary rules crystallise from usages or practices which have evolved in approximately three sets of circumstances:

(a) *Diplomatic relations between states.* Acts or declarations by representatives of states, opinions of legal advisers to state governments, bilateral treaties, and press releases or official statements by governments may all constitute evidence of usages followed by states. In this regard, both conduct and statements (written and oral) are on the same footing.

(b) *Practice of international organs.* The practice of international organs, again whether by conduct or declarations, may lead to the development of customary rules of international law concerning their status, or their powers and responsibilities. Thus in its Advisory Opinion holding that the International Labour Organisation had power to regulate internationally the conditions of labour of persons employed in agriculture, the Permanent Court of International Justice founded its views to a certain extent on the practice of the Organisation. In a noted Advisory Opinion, the International Court of Justice based its opinion that the United Nations had international legal personality partly on the practice of the United Nations in concluding conventions.

(c) State laws, decisions of state courts, and state military or administrative practices.
A concurrence, although not a mere parallelism, of state laws or of judicial decisions
of state courts or of state practices may indicate so wide an adoption of similar rules
as to suggest the general recognition of a broad principle of law. . . .

For evidence of state practices, it may be necessary to refer to official books or
documents, such as military, naval, and air force manuals, or the internal regulations
of each state's diplomatic and consular services. Comparison of these may indicate
the existence of a practice uniformly followed by all states.

A general, although not inflexible, working guide is that before a usage may be
considered as amounting to a customary rule of international law, two tests must be
satisfied. These tests relate to: (i) the material, and (ii) the psychological aspects involved in the formation of the customary rule.

As regards the material aspect, there must in general be a recurrence or repetition of the acts which give birth to the customary rule. A German court held in the
case of *Lübeck v. Mecklenburg-Schwerin* that a single act of a state agency or authority
could not create any rights of custom in favour of another state which had benefited
by the act; conduct to be creative of customary law must be regular and repeated.
Material departures from a practice may negative the existence of a customary rule,
but minor deviations may not necessarily have this negative consequence. Apart
from recurrence, the antiquity of the acts may be also a pertinent consideration. Yet
even a short time may be enough where the state practice has been extensive and
for all practical purposes uniform. . . .

The psychological aspect is better known as the *opinio juris sive necessitatis,* or as
one authority has termed it "the mutual conviction that the recurrence . . . is the result of a compulsory rule." This needs further explanation. Recurrence of the usage
or practice tends to develop an expectation that, in similar future situations, the
same conduct or the abstention therefrom will be repeated. When this expectation
evolves further into a general acknowledgment by states that the conduct or the abstention therefrom is a matter both of right and of obligation, the transition from
usage to custom may be regarded as consummated. In this process, there is involved,
to some extent, an element of acceptance or assent on the part of states generally.
This conviction, this opinio juris, is a convenient if not invariable test that a usage or
practice has crystallised into custom; there is, for example, an absence of opinio juris when states conform to a usage for motives of comity or courtesy only. . . .

JUDICIAL APPLICATION OF CUSTOM

Both national and international courts play an important role in the application
of custom. Often it is claimed by one of the parties before the court that a certain
rule of customary international law exists. The court must then investigate
whether or not the rule invoked before it is a validly established rule of international custom, and in the course of this inquiry it examines all possible materials,
such as treaties, the practice of states, diplomatic correspondence, decisions of
state courts, and juristic writings. In certain cases, the court's function may be
more than purely declaratory; while not actually creating new customary rules,
the court may feel constrained to carry to a final stage the process of evolution of
usages so generally recognised as to suggest that by an inevitable course of devel-

opment they will crystallise into custom. To use Mr. Justice Cardozo's words, by its *imprimatur* the Court will attest the "jural quality" of the custom. . . .

More recently, the International Law Association (ILA) adopted, as amended at its London Conference in 2000, a Statement of Principles regarding customary international law that had been prepared by a distinguished committee, mainly composed of international law professors from outside the United States. These principles help formulate a definition of customary international law.

International Law Association, Statement of Principles Applicable to the Formation of General Customary International Law

http://www.ila-hq.org/htm/layout_committee.htm (2000)

1. Working definition
     (i) Subject to the Sections which follow, a rule of customary international law is one which is created and sustained by the constant and uniform practice of States and other subjects of international law in or impinging upon their international legal relations, in circumstances which give rise to a legitimate expectation of similar conduct in the future.   *Implied consent?*
     (ii) If a sufficiently extensive and representative number of States participate in such a practice in a consistent manner, the resulting rule is one of "general customary international law." Subject to Section 15, such a rule is binding on all States.
     (iii) Where a rule of general customary international law exists, for any particular State to be bound by that rule it is not necessary to prove either that State's consent to it or its belief in the rule's obligatory or (as the case may be) permissive character.

Commentary: . . .

     (b) Certain features of this working definition should be mentioned. . . .
     (4) The definition in (i) and (ii) does not *expressly* say anything about the so-called subjective element in customary law — the element of belief or consent — though there is an indirect allusion to this in the words "in circumstances which give rise to a legitimate expectation of similar conduct in the future." Although traditional formulations often describe customary international law as a combination of the "objective" (or "material") element — State practice — and the "subjective" element (*opinion juris sive necessitatis*), it will be seen later that, in the opinion of the Committee, this would be an oversimplification. . . . [I]t is not *usually* necessary to demonstrate the existence of the subjective element before a customary rule can be said to have come into being. There are, however, circumstances where it is necessary, and the Committee also took the view that assent to a rule can create a binding obligation. But these circumstances are so varied that they need to be dealt with specifically, rather than in a working definition. Secondly, in the

context of the *formation* of general customary law (as opposed to evidencing rules which have already come into being), the main function of the subjective element is to indicate what *practice* counts (or, more precisely, does not count) towards the formation of a customary rule. . . .

15. If whilst a practice is developing into a rule of general law, a State persistently and openly dissents from the rule, it will not be bound by it.

Commentary

(a) There is in practice some overlap between two conceptually distinct situations. (i) A State or group of States which is important in a particular area of activity can, by its opposition, prevent any rule of general . . . customary law from developing. (ii) Any State whatsoever can, by its persistent objection, prevent an emerging rule of customary law becoming opposable to it. Case (i) is simply a manifestation of the rule, just discussed [earlier] . . . that for a rule of general law to come into existence, participation in the practice must be sufficiently representative. If States of sufficient importance in the area of activity in question manifest their dissent, the requisite condition is not fulfilled. Consequently, the present Section is concerned only with case (ii) — the so-called "persistent objector rule."

(b) There is fairly widespread agreement that, even if there is a persistent objector rule in international law, it applies only when the customary rule is in the process of emerging. It does not, therefore, benefit States which came into existence only after the rule matured, or which became involved in the activity in question only at a later stage. Still less can it be invoked by those who existed at the time and were already engaged in the activity which is the subject of the rule, but failed to object at that stage. In other words, there is no "subsequent objector" rule. . . .

(c) Although some authors question the existence of this rule, most accept it as part of current international law. . . . As a matter of policy, the persistent objector rule could be regarded as a useful compromise. It respects States' sovereignty and protects them from new law imposed on them against their will by a majority; but at the same time, if the support for the new rule is sufficiently widespread, the convoy of the law's progressive development can move forward without having to wait for the slowest vessel.

Notes and Questions

1. Is the practice of calling an ambassador "Your Excellency" a custom or a usage? This practice has been followed for centuries — why is it not legally binding?
2. The traditional definition of customary international law includes both an objective element (state practice) and a subjective element (*opinio juris*). The 1987 Restatement, for example, defines customary international law as resulting "from a general and consistent practice of states followed by them from a sense of legal obligation." (Section 102(2)). The Restatement explains these elements as follows:

b. Practice as customary law. "Practice of states" includes diplomatic acts and instructions as well as public measures and other governmental acts and official statements of policy. . . . Inaction may constitute state practice, as when a state acquiesces in acts of another state that affect its legal rights. The practice necessary to create customary law might be of comparatively short duration, but it must be "general and consistent." A practice can be general even if it is not universally followed; there is no precise formula to indicate how widespread a practice must be, but it should reflect wide acceptance among states particularly involved in the relevant activity. . . . A principle of customary law is not binding on a state that declares its dissent from the principle during its development.

c. Opinio juris. For a practice of states to become a rule of customary international law it must appear that the states follow the practice from a sense of legal obligation (*opinio juris sive necessitates*); a practice that is generally followed but which states feel legally free to disregard does not contribute to customary international law. A practice initially followed by states as a matter of courtesy or habit may become law when states generally come to believe that they are under a legal obligation to comply with it. It is often difficult to determine when that transformation into law has taken place. Explicit evidence of a sense of legal obligation (e.g., by official statements) is not necessary; *opinio juris* may be inferred from acts or omissions. [Comments to Restatement Section 102.]

By contrast, the International Law Association's recent Statement of Principles (excerpted above) appears to downplay the significance of the subjective element, stating: "It is not *usually* necessary to demonstrate the existence of the subjective element before a customary rule can be said to come into being." Why do you think that the ILA took this position? Might this, in part, reflect the problems of establishing the subjective belief of states? Should widespread practice be enough to establish the existence of a binding rule of international law? What are the advantages and disadvantages of the approach in the ILA's *Principles* which deemphasizes the "subjective" element in the formation of customary international law? For an article questioning how much of a change was really being proposed by the Association, see Sienho Yee, The News that Opinio Juris "Is Not a Necessary Element of Customary [International] Law" Is Greatly Exaggerated, 43 German Y.B. 227 (2000).

3. Let's assume that customary international law prohibits customs searches of diplomats in transit and that there are no relevant treaties. In light of recent acts of terrorism, could the United Kingdom start such searches? If not, how can customary law ever change? What would be the consequence if the United Kingdom violated this customary international law?

4. How would you decide whether customary international law prohibited customs searches of diplomats in transit? If you could show many statements of diplomats asserting their immunity, a U.N. conference producing a draft treaty codifying that immunity, and universal administrative directions to customs officials not to search or arrest diplomats in transit (which were almost always followed), would that be enough? Does your answer depend on whether you are a diplomat or a law enforcement official concerned about drug smuggling and terrorism? What if you could only show the first two mentioned types of evidence?

5. Professor Shearer says that "both conduct and statements (written and oral) are on the same footing" in the formulation of customary international law. Is that plausible? Should a statement of a diplomat at the United Nations regarding diplomatic immunity be regarded as equivalent to a customs regulation? How about a statement of the Saudi government that women are entitled to equal treatment within the law?

6. Is it relevant that states say they condemn torture if in fact some of them tolerate it? Remember that the definition of customary international law requires state practice as part of the definition. Don't actions speak louder than words?

7. Until the twentieth century almost all of the extensive international norms that constituted the law of the sea were provided by customary international law — such as the width of the territorial sea and freedom of navigation in the oceans. For example, the U.S. Supreme Court looked to the sources and norms of customary international law in The Paquete Habana, 175 U.S. 677 (1900) (discussed in Chapter 3). Similarly, the International Court of Justice drew heavily upon customary international law in its determination of the width of the territorial sea in the Fisheries Case (United Kingdom v. Norway), 1951 I.C. J. 116. (That case and the law of the sea generally are discussed in Chapter 9.)

8. Based on your still growing knowledge of what might constitute customary international law, do you think that any or all of the following activities are a violation of a norm of customary international law: genocide or the killing of all or part of a national, ethnic, racial, or religious group; torturing enemy soldiers or terrorists after catching them to obtain important information; substantial pollution of a major river that flows into the ocean; engaging in racial and/or sex discrimination in the workplace; and failing to obtain informed consent from a group of adults in a developing country before testing a not yet fully approved medicine on them?

9. Is it likely that some, or all, of the activities listed in the previous paragraph would be illegal under the laws of the country where the practices are occurring? Is it likely that some of these practices are covered by multilateral treaties? How would your answer to either of these questions affect your answer to whether the particular activity is a violation of a norm of customary international law?

10. How consensual is customary international law? According to the ILA's *Principles*, does a new rule bind an existing state that is a "persistent objector" to the formation of the rule? Is it binding on an existing state that was silent during the formation period? If the ILA believes there is a difference, how can this be explained? Is a rule of customary international law binding on a new state that is silent regarding a norm — for example, against official torture? Is the norm binding on a new state that explicitly rejects it — for example, by passing a domestic law contrary to the norm or by making a statement in the U.N. General Assembly? Should customary international law bind nations that have not had an opportunity to object?

11. Some U.S. courts have dealt with the consent issue in part by concluding that at least *jus cogens* norms of international law (such as rules against genocide, slavery, and official torture, as discussed above at page 107) are binding on nations even if they do not agree to them. Does categorizing some norms as *jus cogens* make it easier to conclude that all states are bound?

12. Professors Jack L. Goldsmith and Eric A. Posner wrote an influential law review article in 1999 that has sparked considerable academic debate. Titled A Theory of Customary International Law, 66 U. Chi. L. Rev. 1113 (1999), the article challenged the traditional understanding of customary international law (CIL). Goldsmith and Posner argued that: "States do not comply with norms of CIL because of a sense of moral or legal obligation; rather, CIL emerges from the states' pursuit of self-interested policies on the international stage." Id. at 1115. Using basic elements of game theory and case studies, the authors attempted to explain "how

CIL arises, why nations 'comply' with CIL as commonly understood, and how CIL changes." Id. at 1114. They conclude:

> Both the [game] theory and the case studies suggest that when states achieve joint gains, the most plausible explanation can be found in the bilateral coordination and prisoner's dilemma models. Theory and the case studies also suggest that most instances of supposed cooperation are best explained as coincidence of interest or successful coercion. In short, CIL has real content, but it is much less robust than treaditional scholars think, and it operates in a different fashion. [Id. at 1176-1177.]

For some of the academic debate on this article and its conclusions, see Mark A. Chinen, Game Theory and Customary International Law: A Response to Professors Goldsmith and Posner, 23 Mich. J. Intl. L. 143 (2001); Jack L. Goldsmith & Eric A. Posner, Further Thoughts on Customary International Law, 23 Mich J. Intl. L. 191 (2001); J. Patrick Kelly, The Twilight of Customary International Law, 40 Va. J. Intl. L. 449 (2000); Anthea Elizabeth Roberts, Traditional and Modern Approaches to Customary International Law: A Reconciliation, 95 Am. J. Intl. L. 757 (2001).

13. Might there be some convergence between the ILA's *Principles,* which deemphasize the subject element of customary international law, and the Goldsmith-Posner view that states do not comply with CIL out of a sense of moral or legal obligation? Don't both seem to place more emphasis on deriving the norms of customary international law from state practices?

2. *The Effect of Treaties on Customary International Law*

Not only do treaties serve as a primary source of international law (as discussed in Section A of this chapter), but treaties can also play a significant role in the development of customary international law.

Encyclopedia of Public International Law
(Rudolph Bernhardt ed.)
951-952 (2000)

Multilateral law-making or codification treaties have become a means of creating widespread or even universal norms of international law, of speeding up the slow process of generating customary international law and of forming conclusive evidence of an otherwise elusive or unwieldy "soft" law. To be sure, multilateral like bi- or plurilateral treaties initially reflect solely the views of their parties. They can be taken as evidence of universal customary international law only when States not parties conform their practice to them.

The International Court of Justice dealt with the problem authoritatively in the North Sea Continental Shelf Cases. For "the formation of a new rule of customary international law on the basis of what was originally a purely conventional rule," it is "an indispensable requirement" that "State practice, including that of States whose interests are specially affected, should have been both extensive and virtually uniform in the sense of the provision invoked:—and should moreover have occurred in such a way as to show a general recognition that a rule of law or legal obligation is involved". . . (1969). The Court addressed itself to the question of the customary nature of the equidistance principle for establishing boundaries between neighbouring States, as laid down in . . . the 1958 Geneva Convention on the Continental Shelf. In so doing, it pursued three different lines of inquiry by examining the customary "status of the principle [including] . . . as it resulted from the effect of the Convention, and in the light of State practice subsequent to the Convention."

The impact of multilateral law-making treaties on general international law is considerable and is likely to become even greater. Treaty law is orderly, rational, handy, clear. Participation in its creation is assured for all States. . . . The very existence of codification treaties may induce non-parties to conform their practice to some or all of their provisions.

The Restatement addresses the relationship between treaties and customary international law, including the possibility of conflict between these two sources of international law.

Restatement Section 102

Comment

f. *International agreement as source of law.* An international agreement creates obligations binding between the parties under international law. Ordinarily, an agreement between states is a source of law only in the sense that a private contract may be said to make law for the parties under the domestic law of contracts. Multilateral agreements open to all states, however, are increasingly used for general legislation, whether to make new law, as in human rights, or for codifying and developing customary law, as in the Vienna Convention on the Law of Treaties. . . .

j. *Conflict between international agreement and customary law.* Customary law and law made by international agreement have equal authority as international law. Unless the parties evince a contrary intention, a rule established by agreement supersedes for them a prior inconsistent rule of customary international law. . . . A new rule of customary law will supersede inconsistent obligations created by earlier agreement if the parties so intend and the intention is clearly manifested.

3. *The Effect of General Assembly Resolutions*

Many commentators regard positions taken at, and resolutions adopted by, the U.N. General Assembly as evidence of customary international law. For example, in the field of human rights, innumerable resolutions have been adopted following the Universal Declaration of Human Rights in 1948. In addition, the U.N. General Assembly frequently recommends the negotiation and conclusion of treaties. For example, the treaty outlawing torture was negotiated following approval by the General Assembly. Like the Universal Declaration, the Helsinki Accords also contain a series of human rights undertakings that were expressly stated to be nonbinding. Many commentators treat these collections of legally nonbinding actions as creating an emerging customary international law of human rights. The legitimacy of relying on General Assembly resolutions has been sharply contested.

Oscar Schachter, International Law in Theory and Practice

85-92 (1991)

RESOLUTIONS OF THE UNITED NATIONS GENERAL ASSEMBLY AS EVIDENCE OF LAW

Few issues of international law theory have aroused as much controversy as that engendered by resolutions and declarations of the General Assembly which appear to express principles and rules of law. Their adoption by large majorities through voting or consensus procedures has been seen by many as attempts to impose obligatory norms on dissenting minorities and to change radically the way in which international law is made.

It is, of course, true that such resolutions are not a formal source of law within the explicit categories of Article 38(1) of the Statute of the International Court of Justice. It is also clear that under the United Nations Charter the General Assembly does not have the legal power to make law or to adopt binding decisions except for certain organizational matters (such as procedural rules, regulations for the Secretariat and subsidiary bodies and financial decisions). Yet few would deny that General Assembly resolutions have had a formative influence in the development of international law in matters of considerable importance to national States.

The reasons for this are obvious enough. As the central global forum for the international community, with the competence to discuss all questions of international concern, with institutional continuity and a constitutional framework of agreed purposes and principles, the Assembly has become a major instrument of States for articulating their national interests, and seeking general support for them. The conception of Assembly resolutions as expressions of common interests and the "general will" of the international community has been a natural consequence. It also has naturally followed that in many cases the effort is made to transform the "general will" thus expressed into law. One obvious way of accomplishing that transformation is to use a resolution as a basis for the preparation of a treaty by the Assembly itself or by a diplomatic conference convened by it. The treaties are then open for adherence by member States and other States. A considerable number of such treaties have been concluded following a formative stage in which a resolution was adopted. This two-stage process presents no problems under the United Nations Charter or classic international law. States are, of course, free to adhere to such treaties or not as they choose in keeping with their constitutional procedures. There is no legal uncertainty in that process.

Legal uncertainty has, however, been created when the Assembly adopted resolutions which purported to assert legal norms without recourse to the treaty process. Such resolutions "declared the law" either in general terms or as applied to a particular case. Neither in form nor in intent were they recommendatory. Surprising as it may seem, the authority of the General Assembly to adopt such declaratory resolutions was accepted from the very beginning. . . .

What was, however, in question was the legal force of the declarations of law, whether general or particular. Could they be considered "binding" when the Assembly lacked constitutional authority to adopt mandatory decisions concerning the subjects dealt with? If not binding, were they authoritative in some other sense? Was unanimity or near-unanimity a requirement for their authority? If nearly all States agreed on what is the law, was there a sufficient reason to deny effect to that determination? . . .

. . . Let us assume . . . that the resolution is unanimously adopted (as was the case, for example, of the resolution declaring genocide an international crime). One may say (and governments have said) that the resolution, notwithstanding its formulation as a declaration, can only be regarded, in legal effect, as a recommendation to member States to accept the asserted rule of principle as legally binding. . . . However, can we stop with this analysis? When all the States in the United Nations declare that a State norm is legally binding, it is difficult to dismiss that determination as ultra vires — or reduce it to a recommendation — because it was made in the General Assembly. The fact is that the declaration purports to express the *opinio juris communis,* not a recommendation. In considering whether that *opinio juris communis* should be given legal effect, we face two questions. The first is whether the States actually "mean" to express that conviction. That question, which is essentially one of credibility, arises because a vote on a resolution in the General Assembly may be at variance with other indicators of the government's attitude (for example, States may vote for a resolution declaring nuclear weapons illegal but seek to acquire them). . . .

The second question is whether the assertion in good faith by all States that a norm is legally binding is sufficient to validate the norm as law even though State practice is negligible or inconclusive. International lawyers differ on the answer. Some maintain that at least in some matters the *opinio juris communis,* articulated in a declaration, is sufficient to qualify the norm as a customary law. Others consider that the *opinio juris* must relate to State practice as an essential element of a conclusion that the norm constitutes law. . . .

Let us take a closer look at the assumption that if all or nearly all States agree on what is the law, that is enough to constitute conclusive evidence that the declared rule or principle is law. Are there good reasons to question that assumption? One plausible reason is that a vote for a resolution may not be intended to signify agreement on the legal validity of the asserted norm. There is evidence that governments do not always have that intent when they vote for a resolution or fail to object to it. They may assume that since resolutions generally have no more than recommendatory effect, their vote should mean no more than that. They may cast their vote solely on political grounds. . . . Moreover, the difficulties of determining the intent of States with respect to declaratory resolutions are compounded by the equivocal language used in many resolutions. For example, many resolutions affirm or declare "principles" without specifying that they are principles of law. . . .

The right of a United Nations representative to "commit" his government through a vote in the United Nations merits some comment. Since governments generally do not expect or intend to be bound by Assembly resolutions, it is reasonable to assume their representatives lack authority to bind their government by their votes. If they purport to express their government's positions on a finding of applicable law, they do so by virtue of authority given to them by their government.

This is often made explicit in the statements of the representative. A somewhat different question is whether the government is sufficiently aware of the legal significance of a resolution that "merely" interprets or applies a provision of the Charter or customary law rule. If the government assumes that a resolution would not have legal significance, does that mean that the position taken by the representative on the declaration of law cannot be regarded as his government's position? . . .

It still remains important to clarify the legal force of the declaration and determinations of law. Much of the debate has focused on the choice between two polar categories: "binding" and "hortatory" (i.e., without legal force *et al.*). That categorization — however clear it may appear — seems much less appropriate than treating the law-declaring resolutions as evidence for the asserted proposition of law. This would be compatible with the basic principle that such resolutions are not binding in the sense that treaties or judicial judgments are legally binding on the parties. However, it recognizes that interpretations and declarations of law by the Assembly are official expressions of the governments concerned and consequently are relevant and entitled to be given weight in determinations of the law in question. By characterizing them as "evidentiary" we invite an assessment of the pertinent data. We would assess the degree and character of support received in the United Nations and the relation if any of the asserted rule to an underlying Charter or customary law principle. Moreover, relevant State practice and *opinio juris* manifested outside of the United Nations would be considered. . . .

. . . [I]t would be pertinent to determine whether State practice both before and after the adoption of the resolution varies so significantly from the norm asserted as to deprive it of validity as custom or agreed interpretation. This determination — namely, whether inconsistent practice should vitiate an asserted principle — may involve drawing distinctions among norms based on value judgments of their significance. For example, a norm considered essential to peace (such as the principle of non-intervention) or one that expresses a basic universally held moral principle (such as that against torture) would retain its validity despite inconsistent practice. On the other hand, a norm relating to demarcation of jurisdiction or States' rights in areas beyond national territory (for example, the declarations on sea-bed mining or outer space) should probably not be maintained as valid in the face of substantial inconsistent State conduct. I believe we cannot escape such judgments of value in appraising the effect of State practice on declared norms. . . . They require justification grounded in values accepted by the community of States as reflected in their authoritative statements and collective declarations.

THE EFFECT OF MAJORITY RESOLUTIONS FOR NON-CONCURRING STATES

Up to now, I have considered those law-declaring resolutions that were adopted unanimously. Those resolutions were regarded as authoritative because they were taken as expressions of agreement by all States on what constitutes the rule of law. . . . [S]uch resolutions [may be seen] as evidence of what States considered to be the law. When treated as evidence (rather than as a "source" of law), they are subject to rebuttal on the basis of other indicators that bear upon their authority. It may become relevant therefore to observe that, even though resolutions were adopted without dissent, sometimes governments do not practice what they preach and have few expectations that others will. Unanimous resolutions may in consequence be no more than pious hopes and therefore lacking evidentiary value as law.

There is also another side of the picture. If we treat law-declaring resolutions as evidentiary, they may have legal effect *as evidence* even if they are *not* unanimous. For how can one say that the views of a majority of States expressed formally in a resolution are not relevant in assessing the legal force of the stated norm? It is true, as we have indicated, that the size and composition of that majority must be taken into account in judging the weight to be given the resolution. One must also consider the grounds for their position: were they interpreting an existing generally accepted principle of law, were they proposing a new rule on the basis of State practice that was beginning to crystallize, were they formulating an international rule on the basis of a generally accepted principle followed in municipal law of most States or were they simply formulating a rule that only some countries followed as a matter of policy? Those questions, among others, have to be asked in order to assess the significance of that majority position.

Does this mean that dissenting or non-concurring States could be bound by a majority resolution? The short answer is "no" because no State can be bound by an Assembly resolution *per se* (other than those on internal organizational matters for which the Charter conferred authority). On the other hand, if a resolution is persuasive evidence of an *existing* obligation, then a dissenting State may be considered bound by that obligation. The clearest example we have is the case of the resolutions declaring apartheid illegal. The fact that South Africa (and one or two other States) voted against the resolution did not mean that the resolution was deprived of its evidentiary force as an interpretation of the Charter obligations applicable to all member States. Those Charter obligations, essentially in Articles 55 and 56, were already binding on South Africa. Their application to apartheid was an interpretive decision that because it received the support of nearly all States had a high degree of persuasive force. South Africa's failure to comply did not vitiate this conclusion, particularly as the other States continued to press for compliance through sanctions and other pressures.

The position of a dissenting State would be different where the declaratory resolution asserts a rule of law that can be properly challenged as applicable to the dissenting State. Thus, a resolution asserting a principle of customary law which a dissenting State has consistently opposed in the formative period would not be persuasive evidence for the application of the principle to that State. An illustration is the Assembly resolution that sought to impose a moratorium on sea-bed mining pending the establishment of an international régime. A dissenting State, such as the United States, which had opposed that resolution and denied that it expressed a valid principle of customary law, would not be considered bound by virtue of the Assembly's resolution. . . .

An interesting question is presented by a majority resolution that on its face expresses a clear belief that an alleged rule has not been or is no longer existing law. Examples of this can be seen in the several recent resolutions which are meant to deny the international legal validity of certain requirements for compensation in cases of nationalization and to assert that questions of compensation are matters exclusively of the domestic law of the nationalizing State. Can such majority decisions be taken as a decisive indication that the supposed rule of international responsibility now lacks sufficient *opinio juris* to enable it to be regarded as a rule of customary law? Would the resolution have "delegitimized" what may have been an existing rule? Two points need to be made here. One is that the views of a majority of States must be considered as relevant evidence of *opinio juris*. The fact that those views have been formally expressed in a resolution does not *deprive* them of evidentiary value. At the same time, they should not foreclose the possibility of challenging the evidentiary value of a majority decision on grounds of contrary practice and contrary *opinio juris* manifested in other contexts. For example, contrary practice has been cited to rebut an inference from the above-mentioned resolutions that compensation has now become exclusively a matter of domestic jurisdiction of the nationalizing State. It is pertinent that many bilateral treaties and negotiated settlements cast doubt on that proposition. In sum, a "delegitimizing" resolution should be subjected to criteria of evidence — namely practice and *opinio juris* — to the same degree as any resolution purporting to express the customary law in force. . . .

Some writers have suggested that on democratic principles majority approval should in itself give Assembly resolutions legal value. But there are obvious difficulties in transposing to international society a principle of democratic rule that is based on individual votes and acceptance of national solidarity. Decisions based on the principle of one-State-one-vote cannot be considered as democratic when States vary so enormously in size and composition of their populations and in their internal responsiveness to their people.

The Reporters' Notes to Section 102 of the Restatement take an expansive view of the role of "official statements" (referred to in Section 102 comment *b*, quoted above):

> The practice of states that builds customary law takes many forms and includes what states do in or through international organizations. The United Nations General Assembly in particular has adopted resolutions, declarations, and other statements of principles that in some circumstances contribute to the process of making customary law, insofar as statements and votes of governments are kinds of state practice, and may be expressions of *opinio juris*. The contributions of such resolutions and of the statements and votes supporting them to the lawmaking process will differ widely, depending on factors such as the subject of the resolution, whether it purports to reflect legal principles, how large a majority it commands and how numerous and important are the dissenting states, whether it is widely supported (including in particular the states principally affected), and whether it is later confirmed by other practice. "Declarations of principles" may have greater significance than ordinary resolutions. A memorandum of the Office of Legal Affairs of the United Nations Secretariat suggests that:
>
>> in view of the greater solemnity and significance of a "declaration," it may be considered to impart, on behalf of the organ adopting it, a strong expectation that Members of the international community will abide by it. Consequently, insofar as the expectation is gradually justified by State practice, a declaration may by custom become recognized as laying down rules binding upon States.
>
> The Outer Space Declaration, for example, might have become law even if a formal treaty had not followed, since it was approved by all, including the principal "space powers." A spokesman for the United States stated that his Government considered that the Declaration "reflected international law as accepted by the members of the

United Nations," and both the United States and the U.S.S.R. indicated that they intended to abide by the Declaration. . . .

International conferences, especially those engaged in codifying customary law, provide occasions for expressions by states as to the law on particular questions. General consensus as to the law at such a conference confirms customary law or contributes to its creation . . . e.g., as to the law of the sea. . . .

Notes and Questions

1. How does widespread ratification of a treaty contribute to the development of customary international law? Does ratification of a treaty by itself suggest that the ratifying nations believe the norms in the treaty are legally binding in the absence of a treaty? If treaties can create customary international law that is binding on non-ratifying states, does this diminish the importance of the act of ratification of treaties?

2. Should there be a negative implication drawn from the failure of a state to ratify a treaty? If most (say, 80 percent) of the countries of the world were to ratify a treaty that the United States strongly opposes, could the United States ever be bound by some of the norms of that treaty as norms of customary international law? (As discussed in Chapter 11, there is the possibility of large-scale ratification of the Rome Statute establishing the International Criminal Court, which the Bush Administration strongly opposes.) See the ILA's *Principles,* excerpted above, and Note 10 at page 126.

3. In terms of the impact of a treaty on the development of customary international law, does it matter whether the countries that have ratified a treaty fully comply with it? For example, as discussed in Chapter 8 almost all countries except for the United States have ratified the Convention on the Rights of the Child, yet many of the ratifying countries probably do not accord children all the rights specified in the Convention.

4. Doesn't the doctrine expressed in the Restatement, by which a subsequent custom supersedes a treaty, introduce great uncertainty about the continuing validity of treaties? Is that desirable? Can a custom be used to interpret a treaty under Articles 31 and 32 of the Vienna Convention? Does that affect your answer to the first two questions in this Note?

5. When nations voted for resolutions at the General Assembly did they think they would become law? Who represents a country at the United Nations? What is their authority to make law?

6. If a General Assembly resolution simply reflects a rule of customary law (as opposed to making law), why shouldn't a person who wants to establish the existence of that rule be required to show the underlying state practice independently of the General Assembly resolution? Do you think that the mere existence of a General Assembly debate (or the convening of an international conference) can stimulate the development of, or a change in, state practice? Even if this is so, shouldn't the burden be on the proponent of a new rule to show the underlying state practice?

7. Can a series of nonbinding votes and actions, like General Assembly votes and signed but unratified treaties, add up to law? Does Article 34 of the Vienna Convention affect your answer?

8. Which form of law-making, treaty or custom, is more likely to be able to adapt to new circumstances? Which is easier to change? Which is more likely to be responsive to the interests of a developing state? Or to the United States?

C. INTERNATIONAL ORGANIZATIONS AND NON-GOVERNMENTAL ORGANIZATIONS (NGOs) AS CREATORS OF LAW

International law has traditionally been made by governments, normally through the conclusion of treaties or through state practice amounting to customary law. Treaties have been especially prominent since World War II. Now, however, international law is increasingly being made by international organizations, and important international norms are being created by private actors as well. These norms are not legally binding as a matter of formal law; they do not fit the traditional process for law-making, which is largely limited to treaties and customary law. Nevertheless, these norms may in fact have a significant impact on governments, multinational corporations, and people throughout the world. Moreover, these new law-making and norm-creating processes are influenced by an explosively increasing array of private, non-governmental organizations (NGOs).

In this section, we look first at the scope, organization, and authority of international organizations. Then we examine their role in developing "soft law" and in making "recommendations" to governments, with illustrations involving (a) codes of conduct for multinational corporations (MNCs) and (b) the problems of bribery and corruption in which MNCs have been prominently involved. These illustrations show how international organizations attempt to govern conduct through non-legally-binding instruments, the interaction between international norms and domestic law, and the phenomenon of MNCs developing their own codes of conduct independently of governments and international organizations. Then we explore the increasingly important impact of NGOs on law-making and the creation of norms by governments and international organizations. We conclude by looking at the potential significance of private standard-setting in an increasingly globalized world.

1. International Organizations

States create intergovernmental organizations for the purpose of accomplishing generally shared social or economic objectives. For example, the World Health Organization was created to assist in the reduction of disease. The World Bank raises money in international capital markets and makes loans for economic development projects. And the International Civil Aviation Organization (ICAO) promotes civil aviation. These organizations serve as a forum for the exchange of information and views. They may also carry out research and other projects directly. They also play a very significant role in creating new international legal norms. See supra pages 13-15 for an overall history of international institutions since World War II. International organizations are created by treaty, and their areas of competence are quite diverse.

Their work ranges from controversial political issues (as in the United Nations) to mostly uncontroversial matters (as in the Universal Postal Union). For example, the U.N. Security Council has authority to impose legally binding economic sanctions as it has done in recent years against Iraq and Serbia. The ICAO Council has authority to impose safety regulations for aircraft and air navigation. The International Maritime Organization (IMO) establishes shipping rules, and the World Health Organization (WHO) adopts health regulations. The International Whaling Commission (IWC) establishes limits on whaling. The actions of these international organizations may be automatically legally binding on all parties (as with some Security Council decisions), or their actions can be binding on a party if it does not "opt out" of the obligation (as in the WHO, IWC, and ICAO). Other organizations (such as Organization for Economic Cooperation and Development (OECD) and the International Labor Organization (ILO)) propose standards, rules, or regulations to member states for them to consider adopting. Professor Shaw describes the basic structure that is common to many intergovernmental organizations and the practical political pressures on states to accept their law-making output.

> The usual structure of a specialised agency is based upon the plenary body [of the particular agency], in which all members are represented. This organ elects a smaller executive council in which membership may be determined not only by geographical distribution but also functional conditions.
>
> For instance, of the twenty-four members of the Council of the International Maritime Organisation, six must be governments of states with the largest interest in providing international shipping services, six must be governments of other states with the largest interest in international seaborne trade, while the remaining twelve have to be governments of states (not already elected) with special interests in maritime transport or navigation whose election will ensure an equitable geographical representation. Similarly, the composition of the Council of the International Civil Aviation Organisation is weighted in favour of those states most active in the fields of air transport and the provision of facilities for international air navigation. . . .
>
> Most of the specialised agencies have devised means whereby the decisions of the particular organisation can be rendered virtually binding upon members. This is especially so with regard to the International Labour Organisation, UNESCO and the World Health Organisation. Although such institutions are not able to legislate in the usual sense, they are able to apply pressures quite effectively to discourage non-compliance with recommendations or conventions. In the case of the ILO, treaties are submitted to member governments for ratification and within twelve or eighteen months must be laid before the state's legislative organs. The governments, in putting the convention before their parliaments, are required to outline their proposed line of action. Although no obligations are imposed, considerable pressures often build up in favour of ratifying the ILO convention and this is reinforced by the comprehensive system of reporting back to the organisation that exists. Similarly, sanctions and enforcement procedures in the specialised agencies show much subtlety and sophistication and operate, on the whole, beyond the normal confines of strict legal obligations. [Malcolm N. Shaw, International Law 836 (4th ed. 1997.)]

Notes and Questions

1. How and why do the pressures to accept international recommendations or recommendations that Shaw refers to actually work? What are the "pressures"

that Shaw refers to? Domestic or international or both? Which would be more effective?

2. Do you think the opportunity to opt out of an adopted regulation is an adequate protection of the national interest? If all aspects of a regulation except one were acceptable to a government, it might have difficulty opting out, especially if the favorable aspects were beneficial to politically influential forces and the negative aspect only affected one part of the constituency. If you represented an industry or community that had a potential stake in the ICAO process, how (and at what stage in the process) would you attempt to protect your clients' interests?

3. See generally Derek W. Bowett, The Law of International Institutions (4th ed. 1982); Frederic L. Kirgis, Jr., International Organizations in Their Legal Setting (1977) (casebook). On ICAO, see generally Thomas Buergenthal, Law-Making in the International Civil Aviation Organization (1969).

4. Perhaps the most important example of states delegating law-making authority is the Treaty of Rome that established the European Economic Community, now called the European Union (EU). The EU's Council has the power to adopt regulations, directives, and decisions on the basis of proposals by the European Commission that are directly binding on Member States or persons within Member States. (See Article 249 (ex Art. 189) of the EU Treaty in the Documentary Supplement, and see also the discussion of the EU's Court of Justice in Chapter 4 and of the EU in Chapter 5.)

2. *Multinational Corporations*

Lung-Chu Chen, An Introduction to Contemporary International Law

72-74 (2d ed. 2000)

Multinational corporations play an increasingly important role in contemporary transnational interactions. Because they are profit-oriented, multinational corporations are commonly treated as distinct from NGOs in general. Multinational corporations are those corporations and associations that operate transnationally in finance, transportation, communication, mining, fishing, agriculture, manufacturing, wholesaling, retailing, and other areas of economic life. They apply modern technologies to activities ranging from production and marketing to finance and management. Multinational corporations have grown in number, size, activities, and importance thanks to technological developments, new management techniques, and transnational networks of communication and transportation. Because they operate across many state boundaries, they serve as a global vehicle to transfer and disseminate capital, skill, and technology. . . . The larger transnational corporations negotiate directly with nation-state representatives in a new form of diplomacy: agreements with these corporate giants may surpass treaties between states in terms of values affected and the prescribing effect engendered. They have contributed greatly to the internationalization of production, finance, and ownership and to the growing integration of national economies into a world economy. According to [a U.N. organization], today the world economy is more integrated than at any other time in history, and multinationals and foreign investment are leading the globalization of trade and finance that is now reshaping business and labor markets around the world.

Because they may possess more resources than most nation-states, multinational corporations have sometimes been seen as threats to nation-states. Their impact on the shaping and sharing of values, both actual and potential, has provoked increasing alarm. Profit-oriented by nature, multinational corporations have come to be perceived variously as exploiters of the labor and physical resources of the developing countries, environmental polluters, manipulators of currencies and commodities, tax dodgers, practitioners of corrupt business practices, supporters of reactionary regimes, and instruments of their national governments. They have recently gained particular notoriety due to the exposure of the widespread business practice of bribery — corrupting and conspiring with power elites to the detriment of democratic values and the masses of the population. . . .

Though they are labeled multinational, transnational, or international, multinational corporations owe their creation to national laws. Their success in operation, however, depends greatly on the transnational recognition of such national laws. Typically, a multinational corporation is incorporated under the domestic law of a nation-state, acquiring nationality of the state of incorporation. Yet as their operations expand in geographical reach and in magnitude of impact and grow in complexity, it has become increasingly apparent that conflicting national laws are inadequate to deal with manifold problems having to do with multinational corporations. . . .

In 1972 the Economic and Social Council called together a group of eminent experts to study the role and impact of transnational corporations and to recommend measures toward international accountability, and as a follow-up in 1974 two permanent bodies were established to deal with the problems of multinational corporations. After reorganization only one body . . . remains, now called the Commission on International Investment and Transnational Corporations. . . . (The commission was retained largely because developing countries, wary of the influence of multinationals, insisted on continuing U.N. oversight.) The commission has given special attention to ways to halt corrupt practices involving multinational corporations, making it a top priority to develop a code of conduct for the activities of transnational corporations. This was an arduous task that finally collapsed under U.N. auspices but still continues in interstate discussions in bilateral, regional, and plurilateral settings. Whereas some states have undertaken exclusive, unilateral programs of investment liberalization, others have demonstrated a greater readiness to join in more inclusive, plurilateral agreements.

Notes and Questions

1. The U.N.-based effort to draft a Code of Conduct for Transnational Enterprises failed because of fundamental differences between North and South over issues like the expropriation of property and the role of multinational corporations. The threat of a U.N.-based (and Third World-dominated) Code of Conduct stimulated an effort by industrialized countries to adopt their own rules of conduct. Excerpts of the OECD Declaration on International Investment and Multinational Enterprises are in the Documentary Supplement. One of the big disputes in the United Nations was

whether its Code should be legally binding. What difference would it make whether a code is legally binding or not, since there is no international court of general jurisdiction anyway? How could such an instrument be used and by whom?

2. Corporations have sometimes adopted codes among themselves — for example, dealing with labor conditions. In the mid-1970s, many foreign firms doing business in South Africa adopted the "Sullivan Principles," which established minimum and nondiscriminatory working conditions. More recent efforts are described by James Dorsey:

> *Corporate Codes of Conduct.* . . . Reebok, Levi Strauss & Co., Liz Claiborne, J.C. Penney, and The Gap . . . have developed a global human rights policy that applies not only to their own operations, but also to their buyers, suppliers, and contractors. These voluntary standards are generally referred to as "codes of conduct" or "supplier standards" and typically cover employment conditions, forced labor, equal opportunities, and the environment. They are based on the principle that businesses have a responsibility towards the people who produce their products, for the consumers that buy them, and for the people who are affected by them.
>
> According to a recent U.S. Department of Labor child labor report:
>
>> The recent proliferation of codes can be attributed to several factors. With media reports and exposes on child labor becoming more frequent, consumers — and therefore companies — are becoming increasingly concerned about the conditions under which garments they purchase are made. Companies' adoptions of codes of conduct serve to ease consumer concerns — and their own — that they may be contributing to the exploitation of child labor. Often companies adopt codes to project a positive image and protect their brand name or quality reputation. Some are motivated by good intentions; some by bottom-line considerations; many by both.
>
> While developing a code of conduct is an important first step, the second, more challenging aspect is the enforcement of the codes of conduct. Companies find that monitoring their suppliers (often numbering in the hundreds or thousands) is a daunting task, often time-consuming, and financially burdensome. Some U.S. companies, however, are looking into working with nongovernmental or independent organizations to assist in this task. For example, The Gap, a San Francisco-based clothing chain, is working with the National Labor Committee (NLC). After the NLC found human rights violations, including child labor, forced overtime, and unsafe working conditions at a factory in El Salvador, and after religious and community groups protested the conditions, the company agreed to allow respected Salvadoran organizations, such as the Human Right's Institute of the University of Central America, to monitor the San Salvador factory for human rights abuses. A few companies have involved nongovernmental organizations for advice and consultation, while other companies conduct audits through in-house personnel or have hired accounting firms to conduct audits.
>
> While these are just a few examples of the efforts towards linking corporate responsibility and human rights, there is a general agreement that this is only the beginning. Much more work is needed to make corporate codes of conduct and their effective enforcement a priority in the human rights community. [James E. Dorsey, International Human Rights, 31 Intl. Law. 659 (1997)].

What are the advantages, apart from good public relations, to such codes? What are the corporate motivations besides public relations? Can you think of strategies to expand their acceptance by the corporate community?

3. When proposals for legislation requiring a code of conduct for American corporations are made, American corporations have argued that such legislation would put them at a competitive disadvantage vis-à-vis European or Asian corporate competitors. One way to deal with that problem is to get an international code or even a treaty mandating compliance with the matters covered by the code.

The competitive disadvantage problem became acute for American MNCs in 1977 when Congress passed the Foreign Corrupt Practices Act (FCPA). The FCPA provided criminal penalties for defined corrupt practices, such as bribery of foreign officials by American nationals, American corporations, and their subsidiaries to get business. To try to meet the problem of competitive disadvantage, the U.S. government then sought to negotiate a treaty obligating other industrialized states to do likewise. More than 20 years later, substantially aided by the advocacy of NGOs, such as Transparency International, U.S. diplomacy finally bore some fruit. This excerpt from Deming describes the extensive activity involved in this exercise.

> On May 27, 1994, the 26 OECD governments agreed to take collective action to tackle the problem of bribery in international business transactions. The OECD Recommendation on Bribery in International Business Transactions was the first multilateral agreement among governments to combat the bribery of foreign officials. The recommendation called on Member countries to take effective measures to deter, prevent, and combat bribery of foreign public officials. . . .
>
> In the fall of 1995, the fiscal and bribery committees of the OECD approved a report calling on member countries to discontinue the practice of providing tax deductions for bribes made by their companies overseas. . . . More than half of the OECD member countries consider bribery in the conduct of international business to be deductible as a business expense for tax purposes.
>
> . . . At the 1996 Summit of Industrialized Nations in Lyon, France, the "G-7" reinforced the efforts of the OECD in resolving "to combat corruption in international business transactions through supporting ongoing efforts in other multinational organizations."
>
> Finally, in May, the OECD Development Assistance Committee adopted a statement of principle to include anti-corruption provisions in bilaterally funded procurement contracts. This is representative of an effort to reduce opportunities for transnational bribery in projects funded by bilateral assistance. . . .
>
> [Recommendations and Reports of the Council of Europe and the European Parliament are omitted.]
>
> [I]n the joint report of the Transatlantic Business Dialogue Conference in . . . Spain, European and U.S. business leaders concluded that the "highest priority" should be given "to collective efforts to combat corruption and bribery, and fully support the prompt implementation of the 1994 OECD Recommendation on Bribery in International Transactions. . . ." This joint report was followed by the communiqué of the Madrid Summit, on December 3, 1995, where the European Union and the United States agreed to combat corruption and bribery by implementing the 1994 OECD Recommendation. . . .
>
> During 1996, the United States introduced a proposal for a "United Nations Declaration on Corruption and Bribery in Transnational Commercial Activities." The proposal called on member states to criminalize both domestic and international bribery and to prohibit the tax deductibility of bribes. It was adopted . . . by the General Assembly of the United Nations on December 16, 1996. . . .
>
> In May 1993, an international, nonprofit NGO known as Transparency International (TI) was established to curb corruption in international business transactions.

TI is headquartered in Germany and has chapters in almost fifty countries. TI has taken a prominent role in pressing governments and international organizations to adopt measures designed to deter corruption in the conduct of international business. Other organizations like the American Bar Association (ABA) and more recently the International Bar Association (IBA) have taken official positions to support and endorse efforts by the international community, by national governments, and by nongovernmental organizations to encourage the adoption of effective legal measures, which are actively implemented and enforced, to deter corrupt practices in the conduct of international business. . . .

To a large degree, the international action to date represents the evolution of "soft" rather than "hard" law. Only recently have the first incremental steps in the transition from "soft" law to substantive law and business practices begun to emerge. . . .

Antibribery amendments to the World Bank's loan conditions, procurement rules, and standard bidding documents were approved in July [1997]. They require disclosure of commissions and gratuities paid or to be paid to agents relating to their bids or to contract execution on World Bank-financed contracts. The Bank will reject proposals for contract awards or cancel the portion of a loan if the bidder or the borrower has engaged in fraud or corruption in the procurement or execution of the contract. . . . [Stuart H. Deming, Foreign Corrupt Practices, 31 Intl. Law. 695, 695-700 (1997).]

The OECD continued its efforts in 1994 through 1997 and produced a proposed OECD Convention on Combating Bribery of Foreign Public Officials in International Business Transactions (OECD Convention). The Convention obligates the Parties to criminalize bribery of foreign public officials in the conduct of international business. It aims to proscribe the activities of those who offer, promise, or pay a bribe.

The United States and 32 other nations signed the OECD Convention on December 17, 1997. The U.S. Senate unanimously advised and consented to ratification of the Convention, and Congress approved the implementing legislation that made minor changes to the Foreign Corrupt Practices Act (FCPA) in 1998. The OECD Convention obtained the necessary ratifications and entered into force on February 15, 1999.

The OECD Convention envisioned that the ratifying states would pass implementing national legislation. As November 2002, 34 countries have ratified the Convention. Besides the United States, they include other major industrial countries such as Japan, most European Union members, and Brazil. All but (Turkey) have passed implementing legislation, though the OECD is still working with some of the countries to improve this legislation. China, India, Indonesia, and Nigeria are not parties to the Convention.

The OECD, as well as TI, the United States, and other entities, is now working on monitoring compliance with the Convention and obtaining new signatories. There are also efforts to implement the OECD Recommendation Ending the Tax Deductibility of Bribes to Foreign Public Officials. For further information on OECD's efforts, see its Web site at <www.oecd.org>.

4. The problems of rampant bribery of public officials in some countries have not been solved, nor have the likely disadvantages encountered by the U.S. companies that are careful to comply with the FCPA. The U.S. Department of Commerce estimated that "between May, 1, 2001 and April 30, 2002, the competition for 60 contracts worth $35 billion may have been affected by bribery of foreign officials.

Of these 60 contracts, U.S. firms are believed to have lost nine contracts worth $6 billion." U.S. Department of Commerce, Addressing the Challenges of International Bribery and Fair Competition: July 2002.

5. As Transparency International (TI) succinctly notes: "Corruption is one of the greatest challenges facing the contemporary world. It undermines good government, distorts public policy, leads to the misallocation of resources and harms the private sector and private sector development. But, most of all, corruption hurts those who can afford it least." Among its efforts to build coalitions and lobby for change, TI publishes annually its Corruption Perceptions Index (CPI), which measures from numerous sources the perceptions of the corruption among public officials in many countries. The 2001 Index found that at the bottom of the list (i.e., most corrupt) were Bangladesh, Nigeria, Uganda, and Indonesia. TI has also started publishing every two years a Bribe Payers Index (BPI), which measures the levels of the perceptions of bribery in leading exporting countries in 14 emerging markets. Its May 2002 list showed very high levels of bribery in developing countries by corporations from Russia, China, Taiwan, and South Korea, as well as numerous leading industrial nations, the latter all now having laws making corrupt payments to foreign officials a crime. TI observed: "The laws are not being properly enforced." Further information can be found at the TI Web site at <www.transparency.org>.

6. For scholarly analyses of the corruption problems and the international efforts to combat it, see, for example, Peter J. Henning, Public Corruption: A Comparative Analysis of International Corruption Conventions and United States Law, 18 Ariz. J. Intl. & Comp. L. 793 (2001); Philip M. Nichols, Regulating Transnational Bribery in Times of Globalization and Fragmentation, 24 Yale J. Intl. L. 257 (1999).

3. Non-Governmental Organizations (NGOs)

In the past 25 years or so, one of the most striking developments in international affairs has been the increased prominence of NGOs. They have drafted treaties, lobbied governments, helped develop and implement "soft law," and played a critical role in forming the coalitions that have an important role in international norm formation, interpretation, and implementation. The discussion above on Transparency International's anti-corruption efforts is one example.

In the excerpt below, Dr. Jessica T. Mathews, president of the Carnegie Endowment for International Peace, explains how the emergence of NGOs has led to the blurring of traditional state lines. She provides examples of how NGOs exerted influence on the United States and Mexico during the NAFTA negotiations and on many countries in international environmental negotiations. The second excerpt then provides more numerical data on NGOs and also addresses further the issue of the accountability of NGOs.

Jessica T. Mathews, Power Shift
76 Foreign Aff. 50, 51-64 (1997)

The end of the Cold War has brought no mere adjustment among states but a novel redistribution of power among states, markets, and civil society. National governments are not simply losing autonomy in a globalizing economy. They are sharing powers — including political, social, and security roles at the core of sovereignty — with businesses, with international organizations, and with a multitude of citizens groups, known as nongovernmental organizations (NGOs). The steady concentration of power in the hands of states that began in 1648 with the Peace of Westphalia is over, at least for a while. . . .

The most powerful engine of change in the relative decline of states and the rise of nonstate actors is the computer and telecommunications revolution. . . . Widely accessible and affordable technology has broken governments' monopoly on the collection and management of large amounts of information and deprived governments of the deference they enjoyed because of it. In every sphere of activity, instantaneous access to information and the ability to put it to use multiplies the number of players who matter and reduces the number who command great authority. The effect on the loudest voice — which has been government's — has been the greatest. . . .

Above all, the information technologies disrupt hierarchies, spreading power among more people and groups. In drastically lowering the costs of communication, consultation, and coordination, they favor decentralized networks over other modes of organization. In a network, individuals or groups link for joint action without building a physical or formal institutional presence. Networks have no person at the top and no center. Instead, they have multiple nodes where collections of individuals or groups interact for different purposes. Businesses, citizens organizations, ethnic groups, and crime cartels have all readily adopted the network model. Governments, on the other hand, are quintessential hierarchies, wedded to an organizational form incompatible with all that the new technologies make possible. . . .

No one knows how many NGOs there are or how fast the tally is growing. Published figures are badly misleading. One widely cited estimate claims there are 35,000 NGOs in the developing countries; another points to 12,000 irrigation cooperatives in South Asia alone. In fact, it is impossible to measure a swiftly growing universe that includes neighborhood, professional, service, and advocacy groups, both secular and church-based, promoting every conceivable cause and funded by donations, fees, foundations, governments, international organizations, or the sale of products and services. The true number is certainly in the millions, from the tiniest village association to influential but modestly funded international groups like Amnesty International to larger global activist organizations like Greenpeace and giant service providers like CARE, which has an annual budget of nearly $400 million.

Except in China, Japan, the Middle East, and a few other places where culture or authoritarian governments severely limit civil society, NGOs' role and influence have exploded in the last half-decade. Their financial resources and — often more important — their expertise, approximate and sometimes exceed those of smaller governments and of international organizations. "We have less money and fewer resources than Amnesty International, and we are the arm of the U.N. for human rights," noted Ibrahima Fall, head of the U.N. Centre for Human Rights, in 1993. "This is clearly ridiculous." Today NGOs deliver more official development assistance than the entire U.N. system (excluding the World Bank and the International Monetary Fund). . . .

The range of these groups' work is almost as broad as their interests. They breed new ideas; advocate, protest, and mobilize public support; do legal, scientific, technical, and policy analysis; provide services; shape, implement, monitor, and enforce national and international commitments; and change institutions and norms.

Increasingly, NGOs are able to push around even the largest governments. When the United States and Mexico set out to reach a trade agreement, the two governments planned on the usual narrowly defined negotiations behind closed doors. But NGOs had a very different vision. Groups from Canada, the United States, and Mexico wanted to see provisions in the North American Free Trade Agreement on health and safety, transboundary pollution, consumer protection, immigration, labor mobility, child labor, sustainable agriculture, social charters, and debt relief. Coalitions of NGOs formed in each country and across both borders. The opposition they generated in early 1991 endangered congressional approval of the crucial "fast track" negotiating authority for the U.S. government. After months of resistance, the Bush administration capitulated, opening the agreement to environmental and labor concerns. Although progress in other trade venues will be slow, the tightly closed world of trade negotiations has been changed forever.

Technology is fundamental to NGOs' new clout. . . . The dramatically lower costs of international communication have altered NGOs' goals and changed international outcomes. Within hours of the first gunshots of the Chiapas rebellion in southern Mexico in January 1994, for example, the Internet swarmed with messages from human rights activists. The worldwide media attention they and their groups focused on Chiapas, along with the influx of rights activists to the area, sharply limited the Mexican government's response. What in other times would have been a bloody insurgency turned out to be a largely nonviolent conflict. "The shots lasted ten days," Jose Angel Gurria, Mexico's foreign minister, later remarked, "and ever since, the war has been . . . a war on the Internet."

. . . [C]ross-border NGO networks offer citizens groups unprecendented channels of influence. Women's and human rights groups in many developing countries have linked up with more experienced, better funded, and more powerful groups in Europe and the United States. The latter work the global media and lobby their own governments to pressure leaders in developing countries, creating a circle of influence that is accelerating change in many parts of the world.

OUT OF THE HALLWAY, AROUND THE TABLE

In international organizations, as with governments at home, NGOs were once largely relegated to the hallways. Even when they were able to shape governments' agendas, as the Helsinki Watch human rights groups did in the Conference on Security and Cooperation in Europe in the 1980s, their influence was largely determined by how receptive their own government's delegation happened to be. Their only option was to work through governments.

All that changed with the negotiation of the global climate treaty, culminating at the Earth Summit in Rio de Janeiro in 1992. With the broader independent base of public support that environmental groups command, NGOs set the original goal of negotiating an agreement to control greenhouse gases long before governments were ready to do so, proposed most of its structure and content, and lobbied and mobilized public pressure to force through a pact that virtually no one else thought possible when the talks began.

More members of NGOs served on government delegations than ever before, and they penetrated deeply into official decision-making. They were allowed to attend the small working group meetings where the real decisions in international negotiations are made. The tiny nation of Vanuatu turned its delegation over to an NGO with expertise in international law (a group based in London and funded by an American foundation), thereby making itself and the other sea-level island states major players in the fight to control global warming. ECO, an NGO-published daily newspaper, was negotiators' best source of information on the progress of the official talks and became the forum where governments tested ideas for breaking deadlocks.

Whether from developing or developed countries, NGOs were tightly organized in a global and half a dozen regional Climate Action Networks, which were able to bridge North-South differences among governments that many had expected would prevent an agreement. United in their passionate pursuit of a treaty, NGOs would fight out contentious issues among themselves, then take an agreed position to their respective delegations. When they could not agree, NGOs served as invaluable back channels, letting both sides know where the other's problems lay or where a compromise might be found.

As a result, delegates completed the framework of a global climate accord in the blink of a diplomat's eye — 16 months — over the opposition of the three energy superpowers, the United States, Russia, and Saudi Arabia. The treaty entered into force in record time just two years later. Although only a framework accord whose binding requirements are still to be negotiated, the treaty could force sweeping changes in energy use, with potentially enormous implications for every economy.

The influence of NGOs at the climate talks has not yet been matched in any other arena, and indeed has provoked a backlash among some governments. . . .

FOR BETTER OR WORSE?

A world that is more adaptable and in which power is more diffused could mean more peace, justice, and capacity to manage the burgeoning list of humankind's interconnected problems. At a time of accelerating change, NGOs are quicker than governments to respond to new demands and opportunities. Internationally, in both the poorest and richest countries, NGOs, when adequately funded, can outperform government in the delivery of many public services. Their growth, along with that of the other elements of civil society, can strengthen the fabric of the many still-fragile democracies. And they are better than governments at dealing with problems that grow slowly and affect society through their cumulative effect on individuals — the "soft" threats of environmental degradation, denial of human rights, population growth, poverty, and lack of development that may already be causing more deaths in conflict than are traditional acts of aggression. . . .

There are at least as many reasons, however, to believe that the continuing diffusion of power away from nation-states will mean more conflict and less problem-solving both within states and among them.

For all their strengths, NGOs are special interests, albeit not motivated by personal profit. The best of them, the ablest and most passionate, often suffer most from tunnel vision, judging every public act by how it affects their particular interest. Generally, they have limited capacity for large-scale endeavors, and as they grow, the need to sustain growing budgets can compromise the independence of mind and approach that is their greatest asset.

Debora Spar & James Dail, Of Measurement and Mission: Accounting for Performance in Non-Governmental Organizations
3 Chi. J. Intl. L. 171, 171-172 (2002)

In the last decades of the twentieth century, the world witnessed an unprecedented surge in the number and scope of non-governmental organizations ("NGOs") — formal, influence-minded groups unattached to any state. We see evidence of these NGOs scattered on our streets and our TV sets; in protests and relief activities; in solicitations and annual campaigns. . . .

Certainly, the available statistics support this anecdotal impression. NGOs registered in the Organization of Economic Cooperation and Development ("OECD") countries rose from 1,600 in 1980 to 2,970 in 1993, and spending by these groups more than doubled during this time from $2.8 billion to $5.7 billion. By 1995, a United Nations report put the number of international NGOs at nearly 29,000; while the Economist estimated that there were 2 million of these groups in the United States alone by 2000. Similar growth rates are reported in the developing world: in Nepal, for example, the number of registered NGOs rose from 220 in 1990 to 1,210 in 1993; and in Kenya, a reported 240 NGOs are created every year.

More critical than the numbers, however, is the influence that NGOs are beginning to exert over other, more established sectors of society. In the United States and European Union, for example, NGOs have become major conduits for development aid, accounting for 67 percent of the EU's relief aid in 1994 and 5 percent of the OECD's total aid budget between 1993 and 1994. In Bangladesh, Uganda, and elsewhere, they act in some instances like agents of the state, performing functions that were once reserved solely for local governments, such as education, health, and rural banking. And in the private sector, NGOs exert a strong and growing pull. Corporate giants such as Shell and Nike have altered their commercial practices in response to NGO critics, and hordes of less visible firms are paying new heed to the scruffy activists they once dismissed. In what may be seen as a watershed of nongovernmental activity, the 1999 world trade talks in Seattle were effectively paralyzed by NGO protests, causing great embarrassment (and in some cases, significant financial loss) to the firms and states involved.

We know, then, that NGOs have power. What is less clear is precisely how they got this power and how they intend to deploy it. Traditionally, power in civil society has derived from one of three sources: military prowess, social status, or elected position. Rulers rule because they can, because they are born into it, or because their citizens have willingly placed power in their hands. According to the Marxists, power can also stem from the sheer accumulation of capital and the influence that money can bring to bear on any political system. NGOs, however, do not fit neatly into any of these categories. They clearly do not employ force. Their members are not born to their posts, nor are they elected. Behind many NGOs there is money, to be sure, but it does not seem to operate in the usual profit-enhancing way. So from where does their power come? And to whom or what does it respond?

Such questions lead inevitably to the issue of accountability. As members of civil society, NGOs would seem to have a built-in proclivity towards representation: working on behalf of some group of people, or for some specific goal. Yet in practice such moments of accountability are rare. Unlike other social agents — firms, for example, or elected officials — NGOs have not yet developed customary mechanisms for reporting on their activities.

Questions

1. Given the open-ended concept of what kind of organization qualifies as an NGO, what can prevent a government from establishing a "front" organization to promote its own interests at these conferences? How can one distinguish a "fake" NGO from a real one? Who determines the agenda of a particular NGO? What law regulates that process? How democratic are NGOs? How can one find out about the financial support of a particular NGO? In liberal societies, governments are subject to the rule of law and are accountable to their constituents. How can accountability be assured for NGOs?

2. For additional reading on the role of NGOs, see Peter J. Spiro, The Democratic Accountability of Non-Governmental Organizations, 3 Chi. J. Intl. L. 161 (2002), and the sources cited there; William Pace and Mark Thieroff, Participation of Non-Governmental Organizations, in The International Criminal Court: The Making of the Rome Statute — Issues, Negotiations, and Results (Roy S. Lee ed. 1999).

One result of the increased activity by MNCs and NGOs in the international arena is the growth of international private standard-setting. The following excerpt from the New York Times provides concrete illustrations of some of the problems raised by this approach.

Jeff Gerth, Where Business Rules: Forging Global Regulations That Put Industry First

N.Y. Times, Jan. 9, 1998, at D1

The gilded Palais des Nations in Geneva is a perfect setting for the elite group of industry executives and government regulators who regularly meet there to establish worldwide auto safety regulations for the next century. A sign marked "Private" prevented anyone not part of the official 90-member delegation from entering the last gathering held in November.

As they decide public safety issues from emission standards to safety belts that will affect drivers and passengers around the world, the Geneva negotiators do not have to adhere to many of the rules requiring openness to the public and interest groups that govern similar proceedings in the United States.

In the interest of breaking down trade barriers, negotiations like these are trying to harmonize or create common regulations for products to be sold around the world. The auto negotiations in Geneva are on the cutting edge of this new regulatory world, where government agreements on everything from drug testing procedures to food safety standards are driven largely by the business interests most affected.

At the dawn of this new worldwide regulatory machinery, it is premature to predict its impact. But corporate executives are generally ecstatic, consumer advocates are increasingly critical and many regulators from the United States have mixed feelings. This reflects the tension that can sometimes arise between the expansion of trade and the retention of high standards for safety and health.

Barely noticed outside a small circle, the international rule making has sparked an underground debate over who gets to write the rules. Already, one of its creators is worried about the shape it is taking.

"This is about sovereignty, multinational corporations, the new post-cold-war world, global standards and international harmonization," said Mickey Kantor, chief trade negotiator and Commerce Secretary for President Clinton during his first term. "These are very important issues. But it is like they are being dealt with in a closet somewhere and no one's watching."

The final automobile standards agreement is expected by March but few consumer advocates will have had a say. There were 62 government regulators and 26 industry representatives who took part in the Geneva auto committee last November, under United Nations rules, but only one consumer representative from London and one auto club member from France.

Many American regulatory operations — from those designed to prevent unsanitary meatpacking plants and adulterated drugs at the turn of the century to those put in place in the 1960's in response to unsafe cars — were created to address social concerns and before global trade was so important. Now some of these rules are seen as impediments that can block markets and cause inefficiency. . . .

But since the regulation and standard setting is increasingly taking place in less open or accessible international forums, like the United Nations committee in Geneva, safety advocates worry that their concerns will be slighted. Already, David Snyder, an assistant counsel with the American Insurance Association, has criticized the "closed door" nature of the road to Geneva.

The United States wants to open up the process, but does not always get its way in international standard-setting forums. Last year, for example, Codex Alimentarius, a Rome-based group that sets global food safety standards, rejected United States efforts to cut in half the acceptable levels of lead in mineral water and to require dairy products to be pasteurized.

International business diplomacy was jump-started in 1995 with the creation of the World Trade Organization, which calls for single standards and shared regulatory systems across borders in the name of reducing barriers to trade.

Members of the W.T.O., like the United States, can theoretically retain their own higher standards, but those standards would be harder to defend before its international panels against a charge by another country that they represent a barrier to imports, according to trade experts. There are few legal precedents.

More and more standards are likely to be set in such global forums. The same week as the Geneva meeting, 70 corporate leaders from the United States and Europe gathered at the Excelsior Hotel in Rome. They drafted plans for streamlined government regulation of many industries, like chemicals and agribusiness, and acted at the behest of their respective governments. The group, the Trans Atlantic Business Dialogue, was conceived in December 1994 by Commerce Secretary Ronald H. Brown. . . .

"We should put the business 'horse' before the government 'cart,' " he told the group. The business leaders recommended that their governments create common regulations, a plan adopted by President Clinton and European leaders at the end of 1995. The industrialists also called for common auto safety regulations through a United Nations committee — the same committee that met last November in Geneva.

But the emphasis on business first bothers negotiators like Ricardo Martinez, the United States auto safety czar, who was at both the Geneva and Rome meetings. . . . [H]e is concerned that the Trans Atlantic Business Dialogue and American car makers put too much emphasis on knocking down trade barriers rather than raising safety standards. . . .

From the outset, Dr. Martinez had concerns about a lack of openness. In April 1996, he attended an industry conference in Washington where auto executives asked governments in Europe and the United States to follow their detailed road map to common international regulations.

That conference was not open to the public, either. . . .

Over the next few months the highway safety agency and car executives listened to consumer and safety advocates. The agency held a public hearing, but by then an accord for Geneva was already drafted.

Safety advocates, used to playing a significant role in Federal rule making, complained of being left out of the early planning.

"Only when the train was well down the track were the groups brought into the process," said Mr. Snyder, a safety advocate who works with a group of American insurers. By contrast, consumer groups and ordinary Americans weigh in loudly on a variety of safety issues in the United States, both at public hearings and through the public comment periods that are mandated before any new regulation is approved.

Mr. Snyder cites the recent dispute over air bag safety for children as a vivid example of the critical role advocacy groups play in shaping regulations: The public comment period lasted most of last year.

In response, the car makers say that promotion of trade by governments can improve, not lower, safety standards.

It is not easy to combine European and American standards: Europe has higher standards in some areas and lower in others. American car makers certify their own products, while governments perform that job in Europe. European regulators say the United States is asking for too much control over the process. And they complain that Washington, while pushing for more openness, is leading the charge to intimately involve Detroit in the process. French officials "don't accept that businessmen can sit down and set policy," one European regulator said.

In December 1996, as President Clinton and European Union leaders announced a deal to begin recognizing each other's regulatory systems in several product areas, he thanked "the Trans Atlantic Business Dialogue for their leadership in achieving these agreements."

Then Mr. Clinton responded to a question about the agreement by turning to Dana Mead, the chairman of Tenneco and the co-chair of the dialogue. Mr. Mead, not the President, answered the question.

Questions

1. What is the value of international, as opposed to domestic, standard-setting?

2. What institutions are involved in domestic standard-setting (e.g., for pesticides, drugs, or product safety)?

3. How are the diverse interests of business, labor, consumers, and so on taken into account and compromised in the domestic standard-setting process?

4. How could an international process be structured that would similarly take into account the varied interests that are affected by the standards involved?

D. GENERAL PRINCIPLES OF LAW

Article 38 of the Statute of the International Court of Justice (ICJ) lists the formal sources of international law to be applied by the Court. (See Chapter 1 at page 3.) In addition to treaties and customary international law, it includes "the general principles of law recognized by civilized nations." (Recall that the Restatement definition also refers to "general principles common to the major legal systems of the world.") Professor Shaw explains:

Malcolm N. Shaw, International Law
77-82 (4th ed. 1997)

GENERAL PRINCIPLES OF LAW

In any system of law, a situation may very well arise where the court in considering a case before it realises that there is no law covering exactly that point, neither parliamentary statute nor judicial precedent. In such instances the judge will proceed to deduce a rule that will be relevant, by analogy from already existing rules or directly from the general principles that guide the legal system, whether they be referred to as emanating from justice, equity or considerations of public policy. Such a situation is perhaps even more likely to arise in international law because of the relative underdevelopment of the system in relation to the needs with which it is faced.

There are fewer decided cases in international law than in a municipal system and no method of legislating to provide rules to govern new situations. It is for such a reason that the provision of "the general principles of law recognised by civilised nations" was inserted into article 38 as a source of law, to close the gap that might be uncovered in international law and solve this problem which is known legally as *non-liquet*. . . .

There are various opinions as to what the general principles of law concept is intended to refer. Some writers regard it as an affirmation of Natural Law concepts, which are deemed to underlie the system of international law and constitute the method for testing the validity of the positive (i.e. man-made) rules. Other writers, particularly positivists, treat it as a sub-heading under treaty and customary law and incapable of adding anything new to international law unless it reflects the consent of states. . . .

Between these two approaches, most writers are prepared to accept that the general principles do constitute a separate source of law but of fairly limited scope, and this is reflected in the decisions of the Permanent Court of International Justice and the International Court of Justice. It is not clear, however, in all cases, whether what is involved is a general principle of law appearing in municipal systems or a general principle of international law. But perhaps this is not a terribly serious problem since both municipal legal concepts and those derived from existing international practice can be defined as falling within the recognised catchment area.

While the reservoir from which one can draw contains the legal operations of 190 or so states, it does not follow that judges have to be experts in every legal system. There are certain common themes that run through the many different orders. Anglo-American Common Law has influenced a number of states throughout the world, as have the French and Germanic systems. There are many common elements in the law in Latin America, and most Afro-Asian states have borrowed heavily from the European experience in their efforts to modernise the structure administering the state and westernise economic and other enterprises.

Reference will now be made to some of the leading cases in this field to illustrate how this is working out in practice.

In the *Chorzow Factory* case in 1928, which followed the seizure of a nitrate factory in Upper Silesia by Poland, the Permanent Court of International Justice declared that "it is a general conception of law that every violation of an engagement involves an obligation to make reparation." The Court also regarded it as:

> a principle of international law that the reparation of a wrong may consist in an indemnity corresponding to the damage which the nationals of the injured state have suffered as a result of the act which is contrary to international law.

The most fertile fields, however, for the implementation of municipal law analogies have been those of procedure, evidence and the machinery of the judicial process. . . . The International Court of Justice in the *Corfu Channel* case, when referring to circumstantial evidence, pointed out that "this indirect evidence is admitted in all systems of law and its use is recognised by international decisions." Five years later in the *Administrative Tribunal* case the Court dealt with the problem of the dismissal of members of the United Nations Secretariat staff and whether the General Assembly had the right to refuse to give effect to awards to them made by the relevant Tribunal.

In giving its negative reply, the Court emphasized that:

> according to a well-established and generally recognised principle of law, a judgment rendered by a judicial body is res judicata and has binding force between the parties to the dispute. . . .

The Court has also considered the principle of estoppel which provides that a party that has acquiesced in a particular situation cannot then proceed to challenge it. In the *Temple* case the International Court of Justice applied the doctrine, but in the *Serbian Loans* case in 1929, in which French bondholders were demanding payment in gold francs as against paper money upon a series of Serbian loans, the Court declared the principle inapplicable. . . .

Thus, it follows, that it is the Court which has the discretion which principles of law to apply in the circumstances of the particular case under consideration, and it will do this upon the basis of the inability of customary and treaty law to provide the required solution. In this context, one must consider the *Barcelona Traction* case between Belgium and Spain. The International Court of Justice relied heavily upon the municipal law concept of the limited liability company and emphasised that if the Court were to decide the case in disregard of the relevant institutions of municipal law it would, without justification, invite serious legal difficulties. It would lose touch with reality, for there are no corresponding institutions of international law to which the Court could resort.

However, international law did not refer to the municipal law of a particular state, but rather to the rules generally accepted by municipal legal systems which, in this case, recognise the idea of the limited company.

A recent example of judges seeking to derive general principles of law is found in the 1997 opinion by two judges on the International Criminal Tribunal for the Former Yugoslavia (ICTY) in Prosecutor v. Drazen Erdemovic, at <http// www.un.org/icty/erdemovic/appeal/judgement/erd-asojmcd971007e.htm>. There, the defendant had been convicted of participating in mass executions of unarmed Bosnian Muslims. He pleaded guilty, but stated the following at his sentencing hearing:

> Your Honour, I had to do this. If I had refused, I would have been killed together with the victims. When I refused, they told me: "If you are sorry for them, stand up, line up with them and we will kill you too." I am not sorry for myself but for my family, my wife and son who then had nine months, and I could not refuse because then they would have killed me. That is all I wish to add.

In trying to determine whether duress (in the sense of "imminent threats to the life of the accused if he refuses to commit a crime") was a complete defense for the defendant, two of the five appellate judges referred to Article 38 of the ICJ and many of the cases cited in the Shaw excerpt above to indicate that it was appropriate to look for a general principle of law recognized by civilized nations. The judges then carefully reviewed the penal codes of 15 countries with civil law systems and the case law of 8 countries with common law tradition, as well as the criminal laws of some other states. Based on that survey, the judges concluded that:

> [I]t is, in our view, a general principle of law recognized by civilized nations that an accused person is less blameworthy and less deserving of the full punishment when he performs a certain prohibited act under duress. . . .
>
> The rules of the various legal systems of the world are, however, largely inconsistent regarding the specific question whether duress affords a complete defence to a combatant charged with a war crime or a crime against humanity involving the killing of innocent persons. [Id. at 48.]

Given the factual situation in this case, the judges voted as part of the majority to rule that duress did not afford a complete defense to a soldier who was charged with a crime against humanity and/or a war crime involved with the killing of innocent human beings. For additional discussion of this decision, see Rosa Ehrenreich Brooks, Law in the Heart of Darkness: Atrocity & Duress, 43 Va. J. Intl. L. ___ (2003).

Notes and Questions

1. As the Shaw excerpt indicates, the most fertile fields for the use of general principles of law of the major legal systems lies in "procedure, evidence, and machinery of due process." Besides the possible principles of res judiciata, estoppel, and the use of circumstantial evidence discussed there, what other procedural, evidentiary, and due process rules that you are familiar with from the U.S. legal system might be useful? What about statutes of limitations? Laches? Ex post facto? Exhaustion of local remedies?

2. How are general principles different than customary international law? Although general principles of law is a separate source in the ICJ Statute and the Restatement for determining international law, might there be some overlap with customary international law? For example, in looking to state practices for determining customary international law, can the civil laws and case law of states be considered relevant practices? (See the Shearer excerpt on customary international law at page 120. See also the discussion of customary international law in Chapter 3, including the *Filartiga* case and other Alien Tort Statute cases.)

At this point you should have a sense of the major sources of traditional public international law as well as the changing environment in which international norms are formed. This complements your familiarity with the various categories of domestic law, such as constitutional law, statutes, administrative regulation, and common law, that affect transnational activity. Of course, there is enormous variety of domestic law around the world. The United Kingdom does not have a written constitution. Civil law countries are often said to more generally rest law-making power in the legislature, not the courts. In Japan the right of judicial review is guaranteed by law, but Japanese companies may be "less inclined to use legal actions to cope with troubles with the government." John H. Jackson, Jean-Victor Louis & Mitsuo Matsushita, Implementing the Tokyo Round — National Constitutions and International Economic Rules 131 (1984). In many countries litigation is relatively uncommon.

It is important that you as a lawyer be aware of the potential significance of these differences. Provisions of a bilateral treaty may well mean different things in the two countries because of differences in the way in which treaties are authorized, in the way public international law is implemented, and in the roles of courts, the bureaucracy, local governments, trade associations, and individual persons whose conduct is supposed to be affected by the treaty. You may know what the treaty requires and how it should be interpreted, but until you understand the domestic thicket in which it operates you cannot advise a client about the legal implications of a course of conduct. Thus, if your client (or government) proposes a transaction involving Japan, you may raise questions and try to anticipate problems about Japanese law, but in the end you will need to call on specialized help (and may indeed be required by law to do so).

Your role will be, at least primarily, to give advice on U.S. law or international law from a U.S. perspective. This will be true whether you are in private practice, work for a corporation or a private voluntary organization, or serve as counsel to a government agency. A thorough understanding of the U.S. constitutional framework is indispensable. In the next chapter we will look at how the United States participates in the conclusion of international agreements and the creation of customary international law, and how those types of traditional public international law can affect private conduct.

Bibliography

Introduction. There are extensive sources of international law. Several helpful guides for doing research in the area are located on the Georgetown University Law Center's library Web page. For an Introduction to International Legal Research, see <http://www.ll.georgetown.edu/tutorials/intl/index.html>. For Treaty Research, see <http://www.ll.georgetown.edu/intl/guides/treaty>. For other types of international research, see <http://www.ll.georgetown.edu/intl/guides>.

Some of the basic sources for doing international law research include Edmund Jan Osmanczyk, The Encyclopedia of the United Nations and International Relations (2d ed. 1990); Clive Parry & John P. Grant, The Encyclopaedic Dictionary of International Law (1986); Encyclopedia of Public International Law (1981-1990) and the new edition (1992-); and Restatement (Third) of Foreign Relations Law of the United States (1987).

1. *Compilations of treaties.* All treaties registered with the United Nations are compiled in the U.N. Treaty Series. A subscription database located at <http://untreaty.un.org> contains most of them. There is also a League of Nations Treaty Series. United States treaties are published in the Treaties and Other International Acts Series (TIAS) and in turn compiled in the U.S. Treaties and Other International Agreements (UST) volumes. The British Treaty Series covers the period from 1892. A historical compilation was done by Clive Parry, The Consolidated Treaty Series, 1648-1919 (1969).

The State Department's annual Treaties in Force (located at <http://www.state.gov/s/l/c3431.htm>) lists each treaty and other international agreements to which the United States is a party, gives citations, and lists other parties to the agreements.

2. *Diplomatic and other practice.* There is a Digest of U.S. Practice in International Law, which used to be published by the Department of State, but is now being published by the International Law Institute. The predecessor compilations are Marjorie M. Whiteman, Digest of International Law (1963-1973); Green Haywood Hackworth, Digest of International Law (1973); and John Basset Moore, Digest of International Law (1906). These volumes contain diplomatic notes, briefs and memoranda, policy statements, judicial decisions, and other documents that may be useful in learning about events and in determining customary international law.

3. *Judicial and arbitral decisions.* Judicial decisions from all countries are collected in International Law Reports, including its predecessors, the Annual Digest of Public International Law Cases and the Annual Digest and Reports of Public International Law Cases. British and Commonwealth decisions are found in Commonwealth International Law Cases (Clive Parry & J. A. Hopkins eds., 1974-present).

The International Court of Justice (located at <http://www.icj-cjj.org>) and its predecessor, the Permanent Court of International Justice, publish official reports of decisions. See also the Yearbook of the International Court of Justice. (The ICJ is discussed further in Chapter 4.)

Some arbitral decisions are collected in United Nations Reports of Arbitral Awards. See also the Iran-U.S. Claims Tribunal Reports (1981-present).

The European Union's Court of Justice (whose Web site is at <http://europa .eu.int/cj/en/>) publishes official Reports of Cases Before the Court. See Chapters 4 and 8 for additional citations. Both the European (located at <http://www .echr.coe.int>) and the Latin American (located at <http://www. corteidh.or.cr>) Courts of Human Rights publish two series, one covering judgments, decisions, and opinions, and the other covering pleadings, oral arguments, and documents.

4. *Yearbooks.* Many yearbooks and other similar periodicals contain current judicial decisions and state practice as well as scholarly articles. They include the American Journal of International Law, the British Yearbook of International Law, the Japanese Annual of International Law, the Chinese Yearbook of International Law, the Chinese Yearbook of International Law and Affairs (Taiwan), The Indian Journal of International Law, the Canadian Yearbook of International Law, the Australian Yearbook of International Law, Annuaire Francais de Droit International, and the German Yearbook of International Law.

For other current compilations of important documents, see the American Society of International Law's International Legal Materials and International Law in Brief (located on the Web at <http://www.asil.org/ilibindx.htm>).

5. *Standard treatises on treaties.* These include Anthony Aust, Modern Treaty Law and Practice (2000); Shabtai Rosenne, Developments in the Law of Treaties, 1945-1986 (1988); and Arnold Duncan McNair, The Law of Treaties (1986). More works focusing on the Vienna Convention include Ian Sinclair, The Vienna Convention on the Law of Treaties (2d ed. 1984); and Shabtai Rosenne, The Law of Treaties — A Guide to the Legislative History of the Vienna Convention (1970).

3

International Law in the United States

In this chapter, we examine traditional public international law (treaties and customary law) in the United States context. The focus is on the U.S. constitutional structure and how it affects U.S. participation in treaty and customary international law-making, and how in turn that law-making can affect rights and duties under U.S. domestic law.

In Section A we examine the scope of the Article II treaty power, the limitations on that power, and the status of those treaties as U.S. domestic law. In Section B we take up the other sources of presidential power to conclude international agreements on behalf of the United States, and we also examine the scope of presidential power to conduct foreign affairs generally. In Section C we deal with the formation of customary international law and its status in the U.S. domestic legal system. In Section D we consider the effect of international law on the interpretation of federal statutes. Finally, in Section E we examine the constitutional limitations on the 50 states in matters touching foreign affairs.

A. ARTICLE II TREATIES

As noted in Chapter 2, the Vienna Convention uses the term "treaty" in a broader sense than does the U.S. Constitution. In U.S. practice a "treaty" is only one of four types of international agreement. Articles II and VI of the Constitution provide:

U.S. Constitution

Article II

Section 2. [2] He [the President] shall have Power, by and with the advice and consent of the Senate to make Treaties, provided two thirds of the Senators present concur. . . .

157

Article VI

[2] This Constitution and the Laws of the United States which shall be made in Pursuance thereof; and all Treaties made, under the Authority of the United States, shall be the supreme Law of the Land; and the Judges in every State shall be bound thereby, any Thing in the Constitution or Laws of any State to the Contrary notwithstanding.

In addition to Article II treaties, it is generally accepted that the President may conclude international agreements on behalf of the United States on the basis of congressional authorization, on the basis of his independent constitutional authority to conduct foreign relations, or on the basis of authorization contained in an earlier Article II treaty. We will discuss these other international agreements in Section B below. Here we will outline the scope of the Article II treaty power and the limitations on that power.

1. Scope of the Treaty Power and Limitations Thereon

The term *treaty* is not defined in the Constitution. It is possible that it encompasses any international agreement approved by two-thirds of the Senate, regardless of subject matter. It has sometimes been suggested, however, that to be valid under the Constitution, a treaty must address matters of "international" or "external" concern. For example, the Restatement (Second) of Foreign Relations, published in 1965, stated that the United States had the constitutional power to enter into international agreements as long as "the matter is of international concern." Restatement (Second) of the Foreign Relations Law of the United States Section 117(1)(a) (1965). A comment to this provision explained that an international agreement of the United States "must relate to the external concerns of the nation as distinguished from matters of a purely internal nature." Id., cmt. *b*. See also Power Authority of New York v. Federal Power Commission, 247 F.2d 538, 543 (D.C. Cir. 1957) (suggesting that the treaty power cannot be used to regulate "matters which are of purely domestic concern and do not pertain to our relations with other nations").

It is not clear what this sort of subject matter limitation would entail, although it is conceivable that it could limit U.S. participation in some modern treaty regimes. Some provisions of human rights treaties, for example, address the relationship between nations and their own citizens and thus could be described as encompassing matters of domestic rather than international concern. On the other hand, the fact that a subject such as human rights is addressed by treaty might itself show that the subject is a matter of international concern.

In any event, many commentators today reject the idea of a subject matter limitation on the treaty power. The Restatement (Third) of Foreign Relations Law, for example, states that "[c]ontrary to what was once suggested, the Constitution does not require that an international agreement deal only with 'matters of international concern.' . . . The United States may make an agreement on any subject suggested by its national interests in relations with other nations." Restatement (Third) of the Foreign Relations Law of the United States Section 302, cmt. *c* (1987). There is also Supreme Court dicta describing the treaty power in broad (although not necessarily unlimited) terms. In Geofroy v. Riggs, 133 U.S. 258 (1890), for example, the Court stated:

> The treaty power, as expressed in the Constitution, is in terms unlimited except by those restraints which are found in that instrument against the action of the government or of its departments, and those arising from the nature of the government itself and of that of the States. It would not be contended that it extends so far as to authorize what the Constitution forbids, or a change in the character of the government or in that of one of the States, or a cession of any portion of the territory of the latter, without its consent. . . . But with these exceptions, it is not perceived that there is any limit to the questions which can be adjusted touching any matter which is properly the subject of negotiation with a foreign country. [Id. at 267.]

For similarly broad descriptions, see, for example, Santovincenzo v. Egan, 284 U.S. 30, 40 (1931) ("The treaty-making power is broad enough to cover all subjects that properly pertain to our foreign relations. . . ."); Asakura v. City of Seattle, 265 U.S. 332, 341 (1924) ("The treaty-making power . . . extends to all proper subjects of negotiation with foreign governments.").

Even if the treaty power is not limited by subject matter, it is possible that it is limited by principles of U.S. federalism. The Constitution makes clear that treaties are the supreme law of the land and therefore preempt inconsistent state law. But this is also true of federal statutes, and the power to make federal statutory law has (at least sometimes) been thought to be constrained by principles of federalism. The Supreme Court addressed the relationship between the treaty power and U.S. federalism in the decision below.

Missouri v. Holland

U.S. Supreme Court
252 U.S. 416 (1920)

Mr. Justice HOLMES delivered the opinion of the Court.

This is a bill in equity brought by the State of Missouri to prevent a game warden of the United States from attempting to enforce the Migratory Bird Treaty Act of July 3, 1918, c. 128, 40 Stat. 755, and the regulations made by the Secretary of Agriculture in pursuance of the same. The ground of the bill is that the statute is an unconstitutional interference with the rights reserved to the States by the Tenth Amendment, and that the acts of the defendant done and threatened under that authority invade the sovereign right of the State and contravene its will manifested in statutes. . . . A motion to dismiss was sustained by the District Court on the ground that the act of Congress is constitutional. . . .

The State appeals.

On December 8, 1916, a treaty between the United States and Great Britain was proclaimed by the President. It recited that many species of birds in their annual migrations traversed certain parts of the United States and of Canada, that they were of great value as a source of food and in destroying insects injurious to vegetation, but were in danger of extermination through lack of adequate protection. It therefore provided for specified close seasons and protection in other forms, and agreed that the two powers would take or propose to their law-making bodies the necessary measures for carrying the treaty out. 39 Stat. 1702. The above mentioned Act of July 3, 1918, entitled an act to give effect to the convention, prohibited the killing, capturing or selling any of the migratory birds included in the terms of the treaty except as permitted by regulations compatible with those terms, to be made by the Secretary of Agriculture. Regulations were proclaimed on July 31, and October 25, 1918. 40 Stat. 1812; 1863. It is unnecessary to go into any details, because, as we have said, the question raised is the general one whether the treaty and statute are void as an interference with the rights reserved to the States.

To answer this question it is not enough to refer to the Tenth Amendment, reserving the powers not delegated to the United States, because by Article II, §2, the power to make treaties is delegated expressly, and by Article VI treaties made under the authority of the United States, along with the Constitution and laws of the United States made in pursuance thereof, are declared the supreme law of the land. If the treaty is valid there can be no dispute about the validity of the statute under Article I, §8, as a necessary and proper means to execute the powers of the Government. The language of the Constitution as to the supremacy of treaties being general, the question before us is narrowed to an inquiry into the ground upon which the present supposed exception is placed.

It is said that a treaty cannot be valid if it infringes the Constitution, that there are limits, therefore, to the treaty-making power, and that one such limit is that what an act of Congress could not do unaided, in derogation of the powers reserved to the States, a treaty cannot do. An earlier act of Congress that attempted by itself and not in pursuance of a treaty to regulate the killing of migratory birds within the States had been held bad in the District Court. United States v. Shauver, 214 Fed. Rep. 154. United States v. McCullagh, 221 Fed. Rep. 288. Those decisions were supported by arguments that migratory birds were owned by the States in their sovereign capacity for the benefit of their people, and that under cases like Geer v. Connecticut, 161 U.S. 519, this control was one that Congress had no power to displace. The same argument is supposed to apply now with equal force.

Whether the two cases cited were decided rightly or not they cannot be accepted as a test of the treaty power. Acts of Congress are the supreme law of the land only when made in pursuance of the Constitution, while treaties are declared to be so when made under the authority of the United States. It is open to question whether the authority of the United States means more than the formal acts prescribed to make the convention. We do not mean to imply that there are no qualifications to the treaty-making power; but they must be ascertained in a different way. It is obvious that there may be matters of the sharpest exigency for the national well being that an act of Congress could not deal with but that a treaty followed by such an act could, and it is not lightly to be assumed that, in matters requiring national action, "a power which must belong to and somewhere reside in every civilized government" is not to be found. Andrews v. Andrews, 188 U.S. 14, 33. What was said in that case with regard to the powers of the States applies with equal force to the powers of the nation in cases where the States individually are incompetent to act. We are not yet discussing the particular case before us but only are considering the validity of the test proposed. With regard to that we may add that when we are dealing with words that also are a constituent act, like the Constitution of the United States, we must realize that they have called into life a being the development of which could not have been foreseen completely by the most gifted of its begetters. It was enough for them to realize or to hope that they had created an organism; it has taken a century and has cost their successors much sweat and blood to prove that they created a nation. The case before us must be considered in the light of our whole experience and not merely in that of what was said a hundred years ago. The treaty in question does not contravene any prohibitory words to be found in the Constitution. The only question is whether it is forbidden by some invisible radiation from the general terms of the Tenth Amendment. We must consider what this country has become in deciding what that Amendment has reserved.

The State as we have intimated founds its claim of exclusive authority upon an assertion of title to migratory birds, an assertion that is embodied in statute. No doubt it is true that as between a State and its inhabitants the State may regulate the killing and sale of such birds, but it does not follow that its authority is exclusive of paramount powers. To put the claim of the State upon title is to lean upon a slender reed. Wild birds are not in the possession of anyone; and possession is the beginning of ownership. The whole foundation of the State's rights is the presence within their jurisdiction of birds that yesterday had not arrived, tomorrow may be in another State and in a week a thousand miles away. If we are to be accurate we cannot put the case of the State upon higher ground than that the treaty deals with creatures that for the moment are within the state borders, that it must be carried out by officers of the United States within the same territory, and that but for the treaty the State would be free to regulate this subject itself.

As most of the laws of the United States are carried out within the States and as many of them deal with matters which in the silence of such laws the State might regulate, such general grounds are not enough to support Missouri's claim. Valid treaties of course "are as binding within the territorial limits of the States as they are elsewhere throughout the dominion of the United States." Baldwin v. Franks, 120 U.S. 678, 683. No doubt the great body of private relations usually fall within the control of the State, but a treaty may override its power. . . .

Here a national interest of very nearly the first magnitude is involved. It can be protected only by national action in concert with that of another power. The subject-matter is only transitorily within the State and has no permanent habitat therein. But for the treaty and the statute there soon might be no birds for any powers to deal with. We see nothing in the Constitution that compels the Government to sit by while a food supply is cut off and the protectors of our forests and our crops are destroyed. It is not sufficient to rely upon the States. The reliance is vain, and were it otherwise, the question is whether the United States is forbidden to act. We are of opinion that the treaty and statute must be upheld.

As the Court noted in *Holland*, Article VI of the Constitution states that federal statutes must be "made in Pursuance" of the Constitution, whereas it states that treaties must be made "under the Authority of the United States." This difference in wording (and some of the Court's statements in *Holland*) might suggest that the treatymakers have the power to disregard even the individual rights protections in the Constitution. The Supreme Court addressed this issue in the decision below.

Reid v. Covert

U.S. Supreme Court
354 U.S. 1 (1957)

[Defendants were civilian dependents of armed servicemen who murdered their husbands on the overseas bases where they were stationed. Defendants were tried by court-martial under the Uniform Code of Military Justice (UCMJ), which permitted military trials of such civilian dependants. They were sentenced to death. Under the UCMJ, defendants were not entitled to a grand jury or a jury trial. An international agreement between the United States and United Kingdom conferred exclusive criminal jurisdiction on the United States over such crimes by civilian dependents, and the government argued that the UCMJ in this situation was legislation necessary and proper to carry out an international agreement of the United States.]

Mr. Justice BLACK announced the judgment of the Court and delivered an opinion, in which the Chief Justice, Mr. Justice DOUGLAS, and Mr. Justice BRENNAN join. . . .

At the beginning we reject the idea that when the United States acts against citizens abroad it can do so free of the Bill of Rights. The United States is entirely a creature of the Constitution. Its power and authority have no other source. It can only act in accordance with all the limitations imposed by the Constitution. When the Government reaches out to punish a citizen who is abroad, the shield which the Bill of Rights and other parts of the Constitution provide to protect his life and liberty should not be stripped away just because he happens to be in another land. This is not a novel concept. To the contrary, it is as old as government. It was recognized long before Paul successfully invoked his right as a Roman citizen to be tried in strict accordance with Roman law. . . . The rights and liberties which citizens of our country enjoy are not protected by custom and tradition alone, they have been jealously preserved from the encroachments of Government by express provisions of our written Constitution.

Among those provisions, Art. III., §2 and the Fifth and Sixth Amendments are directly relevant to these cases. Article III, §2 lays down the rule that:

> The Trial of all Crimes, except in Cases of Impeachment, shall be by Jury; and such Trial shall be held in the State where the said Crimes shall have been committed; but when not committed within any State, the Trial shall be at such Place or Places as the Congress may by Law have directed.

The Fifth Amendment declares:

> No person shall be held to answer for a capital, or otherwise infamous crime, unless on a presentment or indictment of a Grand Jury, except in cases arising in the land or naval forces, or in the Militia, when in actual service in time of War or public danger. . . .

And the Sixth Amendment provides:

> In all criminal prosecutions, the accused shall enjoy the right to a speedy and public trial, by an impartial jury of the State and district wherein the crime shall have been committed. . . .

The language of Art. III, §2 manifests that constitutional protections for the individual were designed to restrict the United States Government when it acts outside of this country, as well as here at home. After declaring that *all* criminal trials must be by jury, the section states that when a crime is "not committed within any State, the Trial shall be at such Place or Places as the Congress may by Law have directed." If this language is permitted to have its obvious meaning, §2 is applicable to criminal trials outside of the States as a group without regard to where the offense is committed or the trial held. From the very first Congress, federal statutes have implemented the provisions of §2 by providing for trial of murder and other crimes committed outside the jurisdiction of any State "in the district where the offender is apprehended, or into which he may first be brought." The Fifth and Sixth Amendments, like Art. III, §2, are also all inclusive with their sweeping references to "no person" and to "all criminal prosecutions." . . .

. . . While it has been suggested that only those constitutional rights which are "fundamental" protect Americans abroad, we can find no warrant, in logic or otherwise, for picking and choosing among the remarkable collection of "Thou shalt nots" which were explicitly fastened on all departments and agencies of the Federal Government by the Constitution and its Amendments. Moreover, in view of our heritage and the history of the adoption of the Constitution and the Bill of Rights, it seems peculiarly anomalous to say that trial before a civilian judge and by an independent jury picked from the common citizenry is not a fundamental right. As Blackstone wrote in his Commentaries:

> . . . the trial by jury ever has been, and I trust ever will be, looked upon as the glory of the English law. And if it has so great an advantage over others in regulating civil property, how much must that advantage be heightened when it is applied to criminal cases! . . . [I]t is the most transcendent privilege which any subject can enjoy, or wish for. . . .

II

At the time of Mrs. Covert's alleged offense, an executive agreement was in effect between the United States and Great Britain which permitted United States' military courts to exercise exclusive jurisdiction over offenses committed in Great Britain by American servicemen or their dependents. For its part, the United States agreed that these military courts would be willing and able to try and to punish all offenses against the laws of Great Britain by such persons. [This executive agreement was concluded by the President on the basis of implied authorization from a prior Article II treaty approved by the Senate. Consequently, the Court treated the executive agreement as if it had the same legal effect as an Article II treaty.]

. . . Even though a court-martial does not give an accused trial by jury and other Bill of Rights protections, the Government contends that Art. 2(11) of the UCMJ, insofar as it provides for the military trial of dependents accompanying the armed forces in Great Britain . . . can be sustained as legislation which is necessary and proper to carry out the United States' obligations under the international agreements made with those countries. The obvious and decisive answer to this, of course, is that no agreement with a foreign nation can confer power on the

Congress, or on any other branch of Government, which is free from the restraints of the Constitution.

Article VI, the Supremacy Clause of the Constitution, declares:

> This Constitution, and the Laws of the United States which shall be made in Pursuance thereof; and all Treaties made, or which shall be made, under the Authority of the United States, shall be the supreme Law of the Land. . . .

There is nothing in this language which intimates that treaties and laws enacted pursuant to them do not have to comply with the provisions of the Constitution. Nor is there anything in the debates which accompanied the drafting and ratification of the Constitution which even suggests such a result. These debates as well as the history that surrounds the adoption of the treaty provision in Article VI make it clear that the reason treaties were not limited to those made in "pursuance" of the Constitution was so that agreements made by the United States under the Articles of Confederation, including the important peace treaties which concluded the Revolutionary War, would remain in effect. It would be manifestly contrary to the objectives of those who created the Constitution, as well as those who were responsible for the Bill of Rights — let alone alien to our entire constitutional history and tradition — to construe Article VI as permitting the United States to exercise power under an international agreement without observing constitutional prohibitions. In effect, such construction would permit amendment of that document in a manner not sanctioned by Article V. The prohibitions of the Constitution were designed to apply to all branches of the National Government and they cannot be nullified by the Executive or by the Executive and the Senate combined. . . .

This Court has also repeatedly taken the position that an Act of Congress, which must comply with the Constitution, is on a full parity with a treaty, and that when a statute which is subsequent in time is inconsistent with a treaty, the statute to the extent of conflict renders the treaty null. It would be completely anomalous to say that a treaty need not comply with the Constitution when such an agreement can be overridden by a statute that must conform to that instrument.

There is nothing in Missouri v. Holland, 252 U.S. 416, which is contrary to the position taken here. There the Court carefully noted that the treaty involved was not inconsistent with any specific provision of the Constitution. The Court was concerned with the Tenth Amendment which reserves to the States or the people all power not delegated to the National Government. To the extent that the United States can validly make treaties, the people and the States have delegated their power to the National Government and the Tenth Amendment is no barrier. . . .

[Concurring opinions of Justices Frankfurter and Harlan and dissenting opinions of Justices Clark and Burton omitted.]

Notes and Questions

1. The Tenth Amendment provides that "[t]he powers not delegated to the United States by the Constitution, nor prohibited to it by the States, are reserved to the States respectively, or to the people." Article II of the Constitution clearly delegates the power to enter into treaties to the national government, and in Article I, Section 10, it expressly prohibits states from entering into treaties. Does this make

the Tenth Amendment irrelevant to the treaty power? Consider this argument from Professor Louis Henkin: "Since the Treaty Power was delegated to the federal government, whatever is within its scope is not reserved to the states: the Tenth Amendment is not material." Louis Henkin, Foreign Affairs and the United States Constitution 191 (2d ed. 1996). By contrast, consider the following analysis in an article published in 1909:

> This argument indeed proves that the states did not reserve the power to make treaties, and hence have no such power even in the exercise of their reserved powers. But it fails to prove that the federal government in the *exercise* of its undoubted treaty-making power is not limited by those restrictions which the first ten amendments have placed on the power of the federal government. It proves that the federal power to make treaties is *exclusive,* but it does not prove that it is *unlimited,* or that [it] is not limited by the tenth amendment. [William E. Mikell, The Extent of the Treaty-Making Power of the President and Senate of the United States (pt. 2), 57 U. Pa. L. Rev. 528, 539-540 (1909).]

Which view is more persuasive?

2. In recent years, the Supreme Court has imposed a number of federalism restraints on Congress's domestic law-making powers. In particular, it has imposed limits on the scope of Congress's powers under the Commerce Clause and Fourteenth Amendment, see, e.g., United States v. Lopez, 514 U.S. 549 (1995); City of Boerne v. Flores, 521 U.S. 507 (1997); United States v. Morrison, 529 U.S. 598 (2000); prohibited Congress from "commandeering" state legislatures and executive officials, see, e.g., New York v. United States, 505 U.S. 144 (1992); Printz v. United States, 521 U.S. 898 (1997); and limited the ability of Congress to override the immunity of states from private lawsuits, see, e.g., Seminole Tribe of Florida v. Florida, 517 U.S. 44 (1996); Alden v. Maine, 527 U.S. 706 (1999). To what extent should these limitations apply to the treaty power? For example, in *City of Boerne,* the Supreme Court held that the Religious Freedom Restoration Act—a 1993 statute that was being applied to override even local zoning decisions that affected the practice of religion—exceeded Congress's powers under the Fourteenth Amendment. Could Congress validly enact a similar statutory provision as an implementation of the religious freedom provision in the International Covenant on Civil and Political Rights, a treaty ratified by the United States in 1992? For an argument that it could, see Gerald L. Neuman, The Global Dimension of RFRA, 14 Const. Commentary 33 (1997).

3. The Supreme Court sometimes uses the "Tenth Amendment" as a shorthand phrase for "any implied constitutional limitations on [the national government's] authority to regulate state activities, whether grounded in the Tenth Amendment itself or in principles of federalism derived generally from the Constitution." South Carolina v. Baker, 485 U.S. 505, 511 n.5 (1988). Does *Holland* address the relationship between that broader "Tenth Amendment" and the treaty power? For example, does *Holland* immunize the treaty power from anti-commandeering restrictions? State sovereign immunity limitations? Compare, for example, Martin Flaherty, Are We to Be a Nation? Federal Power vs. "States' Rights" in Foreign Affairs, 70 U. Colo. L. Rev. 1277, 1279 (1999) (arguing that the anti-commandeering restrictions do not limit the treaty power), with Louis Henkin, Foreign Affairs and the United States Constitution 467 (2d ed. 1996) (assuming that the restrictions do limit the treaty

power), and Carlos Manuel Vazquez, Treaties and the Eleventh Amendment, 42 Va. J. Intl. L. 713 (2002) (concluding that the treaty power is subject to state sovereign immunity).

4. The central holding of *Holland* is that the treaty power can be used to regulate matters beyond the scope of Congress's legislative powers. As a textual matter, this conclusion might seem obvious: Congress's legislative powers are referred to in Article I of the Constitution, whereas the treaty power is referred to in Article II. This structure might suggest that the limitations in Article I apply only to Congress's enactments, not treaties. On the other hand, as discussed in the next Note, it is now settled that the treaty power is limited by the First Amendment, yet that Amendment refers only to Congress, not the treatymakers ("Congress shall make no law . . ."). Although the First Amendment has been held to apply to the *states* by virtue of the Fourteenth Amendment due process clause, there is no equivalent textual basis for applying the First Amendment to the federal treatymakers. Can the First Amendment be distinguished from other restrictions on Congress?

5. According to the plurality decision in Reid v. Covert, what is the relationship between the treaty power and the individual liberty provisions in the Constitution? How persuasive is the plurality's attempt to distinguish Missouri v. Holland? In Boos v. Barry, 485 U.S. 312 (1988), the Court confirmed that the treaty power is subject to individual rights limitations. There, the Court held that legislation prohibiting the display of any sign within 500 feet of a foreign embassy if that sign tends to bring that foreign government into "public odium" or "public disrepute" violated the First Amendment, notwithstanding the fact that the legislation implemented a treaty. Quoting the *Reid* plurality opinion, the Court stated that "it is well established that 'no agreement with a foreign nation can confer power on the Congress, or on any other branch of Government, which is free from the restraints of the Constitution.'" Id. at 324.

6. As we discuss in Chapter 8, one of the most important developments in international law has been the rise of international human rights law. Prior to World War II, international law did not typically regulate the relationship between nations and their citizens. Soon after the war, with the experience of the Holocaust and other atrocities fresh in mind, the international community began to develop a comprehensive body of international human rights law. Today, there are numerous multilateral human rights treaties. Probably the most important of these treaties is the International Covenant on Civil and Political Rights, which the United States ratified in 1992. The Covenant, which is reprinted in the Documentary Supplement, contains a long list of rights relating to, among other things, discrimination, criminal procedure, religious freedom, freedom of association, and marriage. Do all of these human rights protections fall within the subject matter scope of the U.S. treaty power? Is there any subject that could not be regulated by treaty?

7. The Second Optional Protocol to the ICCPR, which has been ratified by over 40 countries (but not by the United States), prohibits the use of the death penalty. Could the President and Senate validly ratify this treaty and thereby preempt U.S. states from utilizing the death penalty? In answering this question, does it matter whether Congress has the constitutional power to abolish the death penalty in the absence of a treaty?

8. In the 1950s, there were a number of proposals to amend the Constitution to limit the treaty power. One of the key supporters of these proposed amendments

was Senator John Bricker of Ohio, and the proposals are often referred to collectively as the "Bricker Amendment." In general, the proposed amendments were intended to preclude treaties from being self-executing (a concept discussed in the next section) and to make clear that treaties could not override the reserved powers of the states. One of the proposed amendments fell only one vote short of obtaining the necessary two-thirds vote in the Senate. As part of its efforts to defeat the Bricker Amendment, the Eisenhower Administration promised the Senate that it would not enter into any of the human rights treaties being developed at that time and would not attempt to use the treaty power to regulate domestic matters. What, if anything, does the Bricker Amendment controversy suggest about the scope of the treaty power? For additional discussion of this controversy, see Duane Tananbaum, The Bricker Amendment Controversy: A Test of Eisenhower's Political Leadership (1988).

9. Starting in the 1980s, the United States began ratifying some of the human rights treaties. In doing so, the United States has consistently attached a series of reservations, understandings, and declarations ('RUDs') limiting or clarifying the U.S. obligations under the treaties. These RUDs typically include a declaration that the substantive terms of the treaty will not be considered self-executing (and thus will not preempt inconsistent state law) and an understanding that the treaty "shall be implemented by the Federal Government to the extent that it exercises legislative and judicial jurisdiction over the matters covered therein, and otherwise by the state and local governments." What, if anything, do these RUDs suggest about the scope of the treaty power?

10. Article 4 of the American Convention on Human Rights provides that "[e]very person has the right to have his life protected . . . , in general, from the moment of conception." If the United States adhered to this Convention without a reservation covering Article 4, could Congress then pass a statute implementing the treaty obligation and prohibiting abortion? Is this situation distinguishable from *Reid,* because the right to privacy sanctioned by Roe v. Wade, 410 U.S. 113 (1973), is not specifically enumerated in the Bill of Rights? If Roe v. Wade were overturned so that the states could regulate abortion, could the President and Senate preempt that result through a treaty guaranteeing a woman's right to an abortion?

11. Another issue in *Reid* was whether the constitutional rights at issue applied to prosecutions conducted outside of U.S. territory. Justice Black's plurality opinion reasons that the United States "is entirely a creature of the Constitution" and thus must act, even outside U.S. territory, in "accordance with all the limitations imposed by the Constitution." In a concurring opinion, Justice Harlan disagreed "that every provision of the Constitution must always be deemed automatically applicable to American citizens in every part of the world" and stated specifically that he did not agree "with the sweeping proposition that a full Article III trial, with indictment and trial by jury, is required in every case for the trial of a civilian dependent of a serviceman overseas." 354 U.S. at 74-75. He nevertheless concurred because the case involved capital offenses for which "the law is especially sensitive to demands for the procedural fairness which inheres in a civilian trial where the judge and the trier of fact are not responsive to the command of the convening authority." Id. at 77. Several years later, however, a majority of the Court extended the holding in *Reid* to noncapital offenses. See Kinsella v. United States ex rel. Singleton, 361 U.S. 234 (1960).

In a more recent decision, United States v. Verdugo-Urquidez, 494 U.S. 259 (1990), the Supreme Court held that the Fourth Amendment did not apply to the search and seizure by U.S. agents of property owned by a nonresident alien and located abroad. The Court distinguished the Fourth Amendment, which refers to rights of "the people," from the Fifth and Sixth Amendments, which refer to the rights of a "person" and the "accused." The phrase "the people," the Court reasoned, "refers to a class of persons who are part of a national community or who have otherwise developed sufficient connection with this country to be considered part of that community." Id. at 265. The Court rejected the broad reasoning of Justice Black's plurality opinion in *Reid*, noting that the actual holding in *Reid* was simply "that United States citizens stationed abroad could invoke the protection of the Fifth and Sixth Amendments." Id. at 270. We consider the extraterritorial application of the U.S. Constitution, and other U.S. domestic law, more fully in Chapter 7.

12. For additional discussion of whether the treaty power should be subject to federalism limitations, compare Curtis A. Bradley, The Treaty Power and American Federalism, 97 Mich. L. Rev. 390 (1998) (arguing that it should), and Curtis A. Bradley, The Treaty Power and American Federalism, Part II, 99 Mich. L. Rev. 98 (2000) (same), with David M. Golove, Treaty-Making and the Nation: The Historical Foundations of the Nationalist Conception of the Treaty Power, 98 Mich. L. Rev. 1075 (2000) (arguing against federalism limitations). For additional discussion of the historical background and context of *Holland,* see Charles A. Lofgren, Missouri v. Holland in Historical Perspective, 1975 Sup. Ct. Rev. 77.

2.   *The Effect of Article II Treaties as Domestic Law*

a.   Non-Self-Execution

Article VI of the Constitution provides that "all Treaties made, or which shall be made, under the Authority of the United States, shall be the supreme Law of the Land; and the Judges in every State shall be bound thereby, any Thing in the Constitution or Laws of any State to the Contrary notwithstanding." This language could be read to suggest that every treaty ratified by the United States has the status of judicially enforceable federal law. Since early in U.S. history, however, the Supreme Court has recognized a distinction between "self-executing" and "non-self-executing" treaties, and it has held that, in the absence of implementing legislation, only self-executing treaties are judicially enforceable. The Court first relied on this distinction in Foster v. Neilson, 27 U.S. (2 Pet.) 253 (1829), a case involving a treaty with Spain in which Spain ceded Florida to the United States. In an opinion by Chief Justice Marshall, the Court concluded that a provision in the treaty preserving grants of land that had been made by Spain in the ceded territory was not self-executing. Marshall explained that the treaty provision, the English version of which provided that the grants of land "shall be ratified and confirmed to the persons in possession of the lands," was in "the language of contract," and thus would not take effect as domestic law until implemented by the legislature. Id. at 315. The Court further stated:

A treaty is in its nature a contract between two nations, not a legislative act. It does not generally effect, of itself, the object to be accomplished, especially so far as its operation is infra-territorial; but is carried into execution by the sovereign power of the respective parties to the instrument.

In the United States a different principle is established. Our constitution declares a treaty to be the law of the land. It is, consequently, to be regarded in courts of justice as equivalent to an act of the legislature, whenever it operates of itself without the aid of any legislative provision. But when the terms of the stipulation import a contract, when either of the parties engages to perform a particular act, the treaty addresses itself to the political, not the judicial department; and the legislature must execute the contract before it can become a rule for the Court. [Id. at 314.]

Interestingly, several years later the Court changed its mind about this particular treaty provision. After examining the Spanish version of the provision, the English translation of which provided that the grants of land "shall remain ratified and confirmed," the Court concluded that the provision was in fact self-executing. See United States v. Percheman, 32 U.S. (7 Pet.) 51, 88-89 (1833).

The two decisions below illustrate this distinction between self-executing and non-self-executing treaties.

Asakura v. City of Seattle

U.S. Supreme Court
265 U.S. 332 (1924)

Mr. Justice BUTLER delivered the opinion of the Court.

Plaintiff in error is a subject of the Emperor of Japan, and, since 1904, has resided in Seattle, Washington. Since July, 1915, he has been engaged in business there as a pawnbroker. The city passed an ordinance, which took effect July 2, 1921, regulating the business of pawnbroker and repealing former ordinances on the same subject. It makes it unlawful for any person to engage in the business unless he shall have a license, and the ordinance provides "that no such license shall be granted unless the applicant be a citizen of the United States." Violations of the ordinance are punishable by fine or imprisonment or both. Plaintiff in error brought this suit in the Superior Court of King County, Washington, against the city, its Comptroller and its Chief of Police to restrain them from enforcing the ordinance against him. He attacked the ordinance on the ground that it violates the treaty between the United States and the Empire of Japan, proclaimed April 5, 1911, 37 Stat. 1504. . . . It was shown that he had about $5,000 invested in his business, which would be broken up and destroyed by the enforcement of the ordinance. The Superior Court granted the relief prayed. On appeal, the Supreme Court of the State held the ordinance valid and reversed the decree. . . .

Does the ordinance violate the treaty? Plaintiff in error invokes and relies upon the following provisions: "The citizens or subjects of each of the High Contracting Parties shall have liberty to enter, travel and reside in the territories of the other to carry on trade, wholesale and retail, to own or lease and occupy houses, manufactories, warehouses and shops, to employ agents of their choice, to lease land for residential and commercial purposes, and generally to do anything incident to or necessary for trade upon the same terms as native citizens or subjects, submitting themselves to the laws and regulations there established. . . . The citizens or subjects of each . . . shall receive, in the territories of the other, the most constant protection, and security for their persons and property. . . ."

A treaty made under the authority of the United States "shall be the supreme law of the land; and the judges in every State shall be bound thereby, any thing in the constitution or laws of any State to the contrary notwithstanding." Constitution, Art. VI, §2.

The treaty-making power of the United States is not limited by any express provision of the Constitution, and, though it does not extend "so far as to authorize what the Constitution forbids," it does extend to all proper subjects of negotiation between our government and other nations.

. . . The treaty was made to strengthen friendly relations between the two nations. As to the things covered by it, the provision quoted establishes the rule of equality between Japanese subjects while in this country and native citizens. Treaties for the protection of citizens of one country residing in the territory of another are numerous, and make for good understanding between nations. The treaty is binding within the State of Washington. . . . The rule of equality established by it cannot be rendered nugatory in any part of the United States by municipal ordinances or state laws. It stands on the same footing of supremacy as do the provisions of the Constitution and laws of the United States. It operates of itself without the aid of any legislation, state or national; and it will be applied and given authoritative effect by the courts. . . .

The purpose of the ordinance complained of is to regulate, not to prohibit, the business of pawnbroker. But it makes it impossible for aliens to carry on the business. It need not be considered whether the State, if it sees fit, may forbid and destroy the business generally. Such a law would apply equally to aliens and citizens, and no question of conflict with the treaty would arise. The grievance here alleged is that plaintiff in error, in violation of the treaty, is denied equal opportunity. . . .

Decree reversed.

United States v. Postal

U.S. Court of Appeals
589 F.2d 862 (5th Cir. 1979)

TJOFLAT, Circuit Judge:

This case presents a consequential issue of international and domestic law that has been noted in this circuit but not yet authoritatively decided: whether a court of the United States can assert jurisdiction over persons arrested aboard a foreign vessel seized beyond the twelve-mile limit in violation of a particular provision of a treaty to which the United States and the foreign country are parties. We hold that such a violation does not divest the court of jurisdiction over the defendants.

The defendants in this case were convicted in a joint bench trial of conspiring to import marijuana into the United States . . . and of conspiring to possess marijuana with intent to distribute. . . . [W]e affirm as to all defendants. . . . [Defendants were U.S. nationals, arrested on board a vessel registered in the Grand Cayman Islands, 16 miles from the shore and hence outside the limits of the U.S. territorial sea.]

The treaties of concern are the Convention on the High Seas, *opened for signature* April 29, 1958, 13 U.S.T. 2312, T.I.A.S. No. 5200 (entered into force Sept. 30,

1962), and the Convention on the Territorial Sea and the Contiguous Zone, *opened for signature* April 29, 1958, 15 U.S.T. 1606, T.I.A.S. No. 5639 (entered into force Sept. 10, 1964). These treaties set forth principles of international law governing the relations of the ratifying states with respect to territorial seas, those waters adjacent to a state's coast and subject to its sovereignty, and to the high seas, those waters lying seaward of the territorial seas and subject to the sovereignty of no state. . . .

. . . The regulation of a vessel on the high seas is normally the responsibility of the nation whose flag that vessel flies, and of that nation alone. Article 6 provides, in pertinent part, "Ships shall sail under the flag of one State only and, save in exceptional cases expressly provided for in international treaties or in these articles, shall be subject to its exclusive jurisdiction on the high seas." . . .

We find that article 6 of the Convention on the High Seas was violated. This conclusion, however, does not end our inquiry; the issue remains as to the effect of the violation upon the defendants' convictions. To this important issue we now turn.

B.   The Effect of the Treaty Violation

The defendants contend that because the second boarding was in violation of a treaty obligation of the United States, the district court did not have jurisdiction over them. We would summarily dismiss the defendants' contention, under the authority of ample precedent, if it concerned a mere violation of law not embodied in a treaty binding on the United States. A defendant may not ordinarily assert the illegality of his obtention to defeat the court's jurisdiction over him. This proposition, the so-called *Ker-Frisbie* doctrine, is equally valid where the illegality results from a breach of international law not codified in a treaty.

These precedents

> rest on the sound basis that due process of law is satisfied when one present in court is convicted of crime after having been fairly apprized of the charges against him and after a fair trial in accordance with constitutional procedural safeguards. There is nothing in the Constitution that requires a court to permit a guilty person rightfully convicted to escape justice because he was brought to trial against his will.

Frisbie v. Collins, [342 U.S. 519, 522 (1952)].

Where a treaty has been violated, the rules may be quite different, as was demonstrated by the Supreme Court in the case of Cook v. United States, 288 U.S. 102, 53 S. Ct. 305, 77 L. Ed. 641 (1933). *Cook* involved a libel brought against the British vessel *Mazel Tov,* which had been seized for smuggling liquor into the United States. The Court held that the seizure had been effected in violation of a treaty between the United States and Great Britain. The Court recognized the forfeiture principle paralleling the *Ker-Frisbie* doctrine that the wrongful acquisition of property against which a libel has been filed does not affect the court's jurisdiction over the property. It went on, however, to hold this principle inapplicable because the United States "had imposed a territorial limitation upon its own authority" by entering into the treaty. "Our government, lacking power to seize, lacked power, because of the Treaty, to subject the vessel to our laws." . . . .

Cook. . . must be viewed in the fuller context of treaty law to appreciate [its] reasoning, for it is not true that every treaty to which the United States is a party acts to limit the jurisdiction of its courts. Article 6 of the United States Constitution declares treaties made "under the Authority of the United States [to] be the supreme Law of the Land," but it was early decided that treaties affect the municipal law of the United States only when those treaties are given effect by congressional legislation or are, by their nature, self-executing.

We read *Cook*. . . to stand for the proposition that self-executing treaties may act to deprive the United States, and hence its courts, of jurisdiction over property and individuals that would otherwise be subject to that jurisdiction. The law of treaties teaches, however, that treaties may have this effect only when self-executing. Therefore, the determinative issue in the case before us is whether article 6 of the Convention on the High Seas is self-executing. We hold that it is not.

The question whether a treaty is self-executing is a matter of interpretation for the courts when the issue presents itself in litigation, and, as in the case of all matters of interpretation, the courts attempt to discern the intent of the parties to the agreement so as to carry out their manifest purpose. The parties' intent may be apparent from the language of the treaty, or, if the language is ambiguous, it may be divined from the circumstances surrounding the treaty's promulgation.

The self-execution question is perhaps one of the most confounding in treaty law. "Theoretically a self-executing and an executory provision should be readily distinguishable. In practice it is difficult." A treaty may expressly provide for legislative execution. An example is found in articles 27 through 29 of the Convention on the High Seas, each of which begins with the preamble "Every State shall take the necessary legislative measures to. . . ." Such provisions are uniformly declared executory [i.e., non-self-executing]. And it appears that treaties cannot affect certain subject matters without implementing legislation. "A treaty cannot be self-executing . . . to the extent that it involves governmental action that under the Constitution can be taken only by the Congress." Restatement (Second) of Foreign Relations Law of the United States §141(3) (1965). Thus, since article 1, section 9 of the Constitution prohibits the drawing of money from the treasury without congressional enactment, it is doubtful that a treaty could appropriate moneys. The same appears to be the case with respect to criminal sanctions.

Apart from those few instances in which the language of the provision expressly calls for legislative implementation or the subject matter is within the exclusive jurisdiction of Congress, the question is purely a matter of interpretation. In carrying out our interpretative task, "we may look beyond the written words to the history of the treaty, the negotiations, and the practical construction adopted by the parties." In the specific context of determining whether a treaty provision is self-executing, we may refer to several factors:

> the purposes of the treaty and the objectives of its creators, the existence of domestic procedures and institutions appropriate for direct implementation, the availability and feasibility of alternative enforcement methods, and the immediate and long-range consequences of self- or non-self-execution.

People of Saipan v. United States Department of Interior, 502 F.2d 90, 97 (9th Cir. 1974), *cert. denied*, 420 U.S. 1003, 95 S. Ct. 1445, 43 L. Ed. 2d 761 (1975). With these principles in mind, we proceed to examine the treaty provision in issue here, article 6 of the Convention on the High Seas.

Article 6 declares the exclusivity of a nation's jurisdiction over the vessels entitled to fly its flag: "Ships shall sail under the flag of one State only and, save in exceptional cases expressly provided for in international treaties or in these articles, shall be subject to its exclusive jurisdiction on the high seas." On its face, this language would bear a self-executing construction because it purports to preclude the exercise of jurisdiction by foreign states in the absence of an exception embodied in treaty. We are admonished, however, to interpret treaties in the context of their promulgation, and we think the context of article 6 compels the conclusion that it is not self-executing.

We start with the observation that the Convention on the High Seas, as its preamble states, is intended to be "generally declaratory of established principles of international law." Indeed, that a state enjoys exclusive jurisdiction over its flag vessels, in the absence of an exception sanctioned under customary international law, is just such a principle. But the question we must answer is whether by ratifying the Convention on the High Seas the United States undertook to incorporate the restrictive language of article 6, which limits the permissible exercise of jurisdiction to those provided by treaty, into its domestic law and make it available in a criminal action as a defense to the jurisdiction of its courts. There is nothing in the circumstances surrounding the formulation and adoption of the Convention that would support the conclusion that it did.

The Convention on the High Seas is a multilateral treaty which has been ratified by over fifty nations, some of which do not recognize treaties as self-executing. It is difficult therefore to ascribe to the language of the treaty any common intent that the treaty should of its own force operate as the domestic law of the ratifying nations. This is not to say that by entering into such a multilateral treaty the United States cannot without legislation execute provisions of it, but one would expect that in these circumstances the United States would make that intention clear. The lack of mutuality between the United States and countries that do not recognize treaties as self-executing would seem to call for as much. Here there was no such manifestation. . . .

Since its inception, the United States has asserted limited jurisdiction over vessels on the high seas, generally but not always within the twelve-mile limit, to enforce a variety of interests not expressly authorized in treaties. . . .

[There have been a number of] enactments authorizing the boarding and searching of foreign vessels within twelve miles of the coast of the United States and imposing penalties for violations of customs provisions operating within that limit. Through the years the courts have had numerous occasions to address the issue of the propriety of the exercise of United States jurisdiction over foreign vessels within twelve miles but beyond three miles under these statutes and in the absence of treaty. . . .

It is clear, therefore, that the consistent attitude of the United States has been that it may assert limited jurisdiction over foreign vessels within twelve miles of its coast. Although the conventions we construe today do provide for some control within this zone, the ambit of this control is much narrower than that which the United States has customarily asserted. A self-executing interpretation, which would eviscerate many of these provisions, would, therefore, be wholly inconsonant with the historical policy of the United States.

Notes and Questions

1. The Court in *Asakura* did not use the term *self-executing,* but it found the treaty provision there to be judicially enforceable. Why? Why did the court in *Postal* find the treaty provision in that case to be non-self-executing? The court in *Postal* recites a variety of factors to be considered in determining whether a treaty is self-executing. See also Frolova v. Union of Soviet Socialist Republics, 761 F.2d 370 (7th Cir. 1985); People of Saipan v. United States Department of Interior, 502 F.2d 90, 97 (9th Cir. 1974). What is the source of these factors?

2. Redraft the treaty language involved in *Asakura* to make it non-self-executing. Redraft the treaty language in *Postal* to make it self-executing.

3. Is the distinction between self-executing and non-self-executing treaties consistent with the language of the Supremacy Clause, which provides that "all" treaties shall be supreme federal law? What purpose is served by the distinction between self-executing and non-self-executing treaties?

4. What, precisely, is a self-executing treaty? At the most general level, it is a treaty that can be enforced by courts without domestic implementing legislation. Is a self-executing treaty the same thing as a treaty that gives private parties a right to sue in U.S. courts? Can a non-self-executing treaty ever be enforced by a court — for example, as a defense to a state criminal charge? Is there a single non-self-execution "doctrine" that answers these and related questions? Consider the following analysis by Professor Vazquez:

> Bringing coherence and analytical clarity to this area of the law requires recognition that the self-execution "doctrine" addresses at least four distinct types of reasons why a treaty might be judicially unenforceable. First, a treaty might be judicially unenforceable because the parties (or perhaps the U.S. treaty makers unilaterally) made it judicially unenforceable. This is primarily a matter of intent. Second, a treaty might be judicially unenforceable because the obligation it imposes is of a type that, under our system of separated powers, cannot be enforced directly by the courts. This branch of the doctrine calls for a judgment concerning the allocation of treaty-enforcement power as between the courts and the legislature. Third, a treaty might be judicially unenforceable because the treaty makers lack the constitutional power to accomplish by treaty what they purported to accomplish. This branch of the doctrine calls for a judgment about the allocation of legislative power between the treaty makers and the lawmakers. Finally, a treaty provision might be judicially unenforceable because it does not establish a private right of action and there is no other legal basis for the remedy being sought by the party relying on the treaty. Unlike the first three categories of non-self-executing treaties, a treaty that is non-self-executing in the fourth sense will be judicially unenforceable only in certain contexts. These four issues are sufficiently distinct and require sufficiently differing analyses that they should be thought of as four distinct doctrines. [Carlos Manuel Vazquez, The Four Doctrines of Self-Executing Treaties, 89 Am. J. Intl. 695 (1995).]

Is this helpful?

5. How should U.S. courts determine whether a treaty is self-executing? Should courts attempt to discern the intent of all the parties to the treaty, or just the intent of the U.S. treatymakers? What does the excerpt from Foster v. Neilson suggest? What do *Asakura* and *Postal* suggest? In deciding whose intent to consider, does it matter whether the treaty is bilateral or multilateral? Of what significance is the fact that in many countries, such as the United Kingdom, all treaties are considered

non-self-executing? Is it likely that treaties with numerous parties will have a single intent concerning self-execution?

6. The Restatement (Third) of Foreign Relations Law states:

> In the absence of special agreement, it is ordinarily for the United States to decide how it will carry out its international obligations. Accordingly, the intention of the United States determines whether an agreement is to be self-executing in the United States or should await implementation by legislation or appropriate executive or administrative action. [Restatement (Third) of the Foreign Relations Law of the United States Section 111, cmt. *h* (1987).]

On this point, the Restatement appears to be at odds with what a number of courts have said about self-execution. See, e.g., Diggs v. Richardson, 555 F.2d 848, 851 (D.C. Cir. 1976) ("In determining whether a treaty is self-executing courts look to the *intent of the signatory parties* as manifested by the language of the instrument, and, if the instrument is uncertain, recourse must be had to the circumstances surrounding its execution.") (emphasis added). On the other hand, it is arguable that, despite what courts have said, they end up looking primarily to the actual or likely intent of the U.S. treatymakers rather than to the intent of all the ratifying parties.

Assuming the Restatement approach is correct, whose intent constitutes the intent of the United States? The intent of the approving Senators? The intent of the ratifying President? The intent of *subsequent* Senators or Presidents? What does *Postal* suggest? Whose intent counts when a court determines whether a *statute* is judicially enforceable? Are there relevant differences on this issue between a statute and a treaty?

7. After deciding whose intent counts, the next question is what must have been intended. If the relevant actors make their intent (of self-execution or non-self-execution) plain in the treaty, there is no interpretive difficulty. But what if (as is usually the case) the treaty is silent or ambiguous about self-execution? Should there be a presumption in favor of self-execution or against self-execution? There appears to be some division in the courts on this issue. Compare, for example, Goldstar (Panama) S.A. v. United States, 967 F.2d 965, 968 (4th Cir. 1992) ("International treaties are not presumed to create rights that are privately enforceable."), with Beharry v. Reno, 183 F. Supp. 2d 584, 593 (E.D.N.Y. 2002) ("Treaties are generally treated as self-executing, that is, they are enforceable in courts once signed and ratified."). What is the proper default rule? Of what significance is the fact that non-self-executing treaties are still binding on the United States on the international plane?

8. As indicated in *Postal*, the Constitution's separation of powers may affect the self-execution analysis. See also Restatement (Third) of the Foreign Relations Law of the United States Section 111, cmt. *i* and reporters' note 6 (1987). Thus, for example, treaty provisions calling for the appropriation of money have long been treated as non-self-executing in order to preserve Congress's constitutional authority over appropriations. See U.S. Const. art. I, §9, cl. 7 ("No Money shall be drawn from the Treasury, but in Consequence of Appropriations made by Law."). Similarly, treaties modifying tariff duties have generally been treated as non-self-executing to preserve the House of Representatives' role in raising revenue. See U.S. Const. art. I, §7, cl. 1 ("all Bills for raising Revenue shall originate in the House of Representatives"). For somewhat different reasons (relating to notice and the Supreme Court's rejection in the early 1800s of a federal common law of crimes), it has generally

been assumed that treaties calling for the criminalization of conduct are non-self-executing — that is, they do not themselves create criminal liability within the United States. See, e.g., Hopson v. Kreps, 622 F.2d 1375, 1380 (9th Cir. 1980); and The Over the Top, 5 F.2d 838, 845 (D. Conn. 1925). It is also often said that, because the full Congress has the constitutional power to declare war, a treaty cannot, by itself, place the United States into a state of war. See, e.g., Edwards v. Carter, 580 F.2d 1055, 1058 n.7 (D.C. Cir. 1978).

9. The Supreme Court has stated that the Executive Branch's construction of a treaty is entitled to "great weight." See, e.g., United States v. Stuart, 489 U.S. 353, 369 (1989); Sumitomo Shoji America, Inc. v. Avagliano, 457 U.S. 176, 184-185 (1982); Kolovrat v. Oregon, 366 U.S. 187, 194 (1961). At times, the Court has used somewhat different terms to describe this deference, but it is not clear that the Court has intended these terms to reflect a different standard. See, e.g., El Al Israel Airlines v. Tsui Yuan Tseng, 525 U.S. 155, 168 (1999) ("[r]espect"); Factor v. Laubenheimer, 290 U.S. 276, 295 (1933) ("of weight"). This deference can have a significant effect on the outcome of treaty decisions. Indeed, after studying numerous treaty cases, Professor David Bederman has observed that judicial deference to the Executive Branch may be "the single best predictor of interpretive outcomes in American treaty cases." David J. Bederman, Revivalist Canons and Treaty Interpretation, 41 UCLA L. Rev. 953 (1994). What are the justifications for this treaty deference? Should courts similarly defer to the views of the Executive Branch concerning whether a treaty is self-executing? See, e.g., More v. Intelcom Support Services, Inc., 960 F.2d 466 (5th Cir. 1992) (deferring to the Executive Branch on this issue). Recall from Chapter 2 that, when interpreting treaties, U.S. courts also tend to rely more heavily on drafting history than appears to be contemplated by the Vienna Convention on the Law of Treaties.

10. In two recent articles, Professor Yoo argues that as an original matter, treaties that touched on subjects within Congress's Article I powers could not be self-executing, but rather needed domestic implementing legislation before having domestic force. Treaties that regulated areas that would be beyond Congress's legislative powers, by contrast, did not impinge upon the legislative power and could apply as self-executing federal law even in the absence of implementing legislation. Professor Yoo concludes that, at the very least, the Constitution requires treaties to be non-self-executing unless the treatymakers clearly specify the contrary. See John C. Yoo, Globalism and the Constitution: Treaties, Non-Self-Execution, and the Original Understanding, 99 Colum. L. Rev. 1955 (1999); John C. Yoo, Treaties and Public Lawmaking: A Textual and Structural Defense of Non-Self-Execution, 99 Colum. L. Rev. 2218 (1999). For a challenge to Professor Yoo's views based on historical materials, see Martin S. Flaherty, History Right? Historical Scholarship, Original Understanding, and "Supreme Law of the Land," 99 Colum. L. Rev. 2095 (1999). For a challenge to his views based on structural constitutional arguments, and in particular the implications of the Supremacy Clause, see Carlos M. Vazquez, Laughing at Treaties, 99 Colum. L. Rev. 2154 (1999).

b.   Reservations

As indicated in Chapter 2, a state may under some circumstances enter a "reservation" to its full adherence to a treaty. In U.S. practice the President would communicate any U.S. reservation when he ratifies the treaty (i.e., when he takes the formal act required to indicate U.S. adherence to the treaty). Accordingly, the President may initially decide what reservations are appropriate, and he would normally indicate those views when he sends a treaty to the Senate for its advice and consent to ratification. In addition, especially in recent years, the Senate has initiated or required the entry of substantive reservations to treaties as part of its "advice and consent" role.

In addition to reservations, which constitute qualifications to particular treaty terms, the President and Senate also sometimes attach "understandings" and "declarations" to the U.S. ratification of treaties. Understandings are interpretive statements that clarify or elaborate on, rather than change, the provisions of the treaty. Similarly, declarations are statements of policy relating to the treaty that do not alter or limit its substantive provisions. Collectively, reservations, understandings, and declarations are sometimes referred to as "RUDs."

As noted earlier in this chapter, the President and Senate have often attached RUDs to the U.S. ratification of human rights treaties. For example, they attached the following RUDs to U.S. ratification of the International Covenant on Civil and Political Rights:

I. The Senate's advice and consent is subject to the following reservations:

(1) That Article 20 does not authorize or require legislation or other action by the United States that would restrict the right of free speech and association protected by the Constitution and laws of the United States.

(2) That the United States reserves the right, subject to its Constitutional constraints, to impose capital punishment on any person (other than a pregnant woman) duly convicted under existing or future laws permitting the imposition of capital punishment, including such punishment for crimes committed by persons below eighteen years of age.

(3) That the United States considers itself bound by Article 7 to the extent that "cruel, inhuman or degrading treatment or punishment" means the cruel and unusual treatment or punishment prohibited by the Fifth, Eighth and/or Fourteenth Amendments to the Constitution of the United States. . . .

II. The Senate's advice and consent is subject to the following understandings, which shall apply to the obligations of the United States under this Covenant:

(1) That the Constitution and laws of the United States guarantee all persons equal protection of the law and provide extensive protections against discrimination. The United States understands distinctions based upon race, color, sex, language, religion, political or other opinion, national or social origin, property, birth or any other status — as those terms are used in Article 2, paragraph 1 and Article 26 — to be permitted when such distinctions are, at minimum, rationally related to a legitimate governmental objective. The United States further understands the prohibition in paragraph 1 of Article 4 upon discrimination, in time of public emergency, based "solely" on the status of race, color, sex, language, religion or social origin not to bar distinctions that may have a disproportionate effect upon persons of a particular status. . . .

(5) That the United States understands that this Covenant shall be implemented by the Federal Government to the extent that it exercises legislative and judicial jurisdiction over the matters covered therein, and otherwise by the state and local governments; to the extent that state and local governments exercise jurisdiction over such matters, the Federal Government shall take measures appropriate to the Federal system to the end that the competent authorities of the state or local governments may take appropriate measures for the fulfillment of the Covenant.

III. The Senate's advice and consent is subject to the following declarations:
  (1) That the United States declares that the provisions of Articles 1 through 27 of the Covenant are not self-executing. . . .
  IV. The Senate's advice and consent is subject to the following proviso, which shall not be included in the instrument of ratification to be deposited by the President:
  Nothing in this Covenant requires or authorizes legislation, or other action, by the United States of America prohibited by the Constitution of the United States as interpreted by the United States.

The two decisions below (both of which are death penalty cases involving the execution of juvenile offenders) consider the validity and effect of the RUDs.

Domingues v. Nevada

Supreme Court of Nevada
961 P.2d 1279 (1998)

[A Nevada statute allows imposition of the death penalty on a defendant who was 16 years old or older at the time that the capital offense was committed. Michael Domingues was convicted under the statute for a murder he committed when he was 16 years old, and sentenced to death. After his appeals were exhausted, Domingues filed a motion for correction of illegal sentence, arguing that his execution would violate Article 6(5) of the ICCPR.]

By the Court, YOUNG, J. . . .
Domingues contends that pursuant to the ICCPR, imposition of the death sentence on one who committed a capital offense while under the age of eighteen is illegal. Although the United States Senate ratified the ICCPR with a reservation allowing juvenile offenders to be sentenced to death, Domingues asserts that this reservation was invalid and thus this capital sentencing prohibition set forth in the treaty is the supreme law of the land. Domingues contends that his death sentence, imposed for crimes he committed when he was sixteen years old, is thereby facially illegal. . . . We disagree.
We conclude that the Senate's express reservation of the United States' right to impose a penalty of death on juvenile offenders negates Domingues' claim that he was illegally sentenced. Many of our sister jurisdictions have laws authorizing the death penalty for criminal offenders under the age of eighteen, and such laws have withstood Constitutional scrutiny. See Stanford v. Kentucky, 492 U.S. 361 (1989). . . .

SPRINGER, C.J., dissenting:
The International Covenant on Civil and Political Rights, to which the United States is a "party," forbids imposing the death penalty on children under the age of eighteen. International treaties of this kind ordinarily become the "supreme law of the land." Under the majority's interpretation of the treaty, the United States, at least with regard to executing children, is a "party" to the treaty, while at the same time rejecting one of its most vital terms. Under Nevada's interpretation of the treaty, the United States will be joining hands with such countries as Iran, Iraq, Bangladesh,

Nigeria and Pakistan in approving death sentences for children. I withhold my approval of the court's judgment in this regard.

ROSE, J., dissenting:

Following a brief hearing, the district court summarily concluded that the death sentence was facially valid in spite of an international treaty signed by the United States which prohibits the execution of individuals who were under eighteen years of age when the crime was committed. I believe this complicated issue deserved a full hearing, evidentiary if necessary, on the effect of our nation's ratification of the ICCPR and the reservation by the United States Senate to that treaty's provision prohibiting the execution of anyone who committed a capital crime while under eighteen years of age.

The penultimate issue that the district court should have considered is whether the Senate's reservation was valid. Article 4(2) of the treaty states that there shall be no derogation from Article 6 which includes the prohibition on the execution of juvenile offenders. . . .

If the reservation was not valid, then the district court should determine whether the United States is still a party to the treaty. If the reservation was a "sine qua non" of the acceptance of the whole treaty by the United States, then the United State's ratification of the treaty could be considered a nullity. But, if the United States has shown an intent to accept the treaty as a whole, the result could be that the United States is bound by all of the provisions of the treaty, notwithstanding the reservation.

These are not easy questions and testimony about the international conduct of the United States concerning the subjects contained in the treaty, in addition to expert testimony on the effect of the Senate's reservation may be necessary. A federal court that deals with federal law on a daily basis might be better equipped to address these issues; however, the motion is before the state court and it should do its best to resolve the matter. Accordingly, I would reverse the district court's denial of Domingues' motion and remand the case for a full hearing on the effect of the ICCPR on Domingues' sentence.

Beazley v. Johnson

U.S. Court of Appeals for the Fifth Circuit
242 F.3d 248 (2001)

[Napoleon Beazley committed a capital murder three months before his eighteenth birthday. He was convicted pursuant to a Texas statute that provides that "if a person was at least age 17 when he committed a capital offense, he can receive the death penalty." He filed a federal court petition for a writ of habeas corpus, maintaining that the statute violated Article 6(5) of the ICCPR. Because Beazley did not raise this issue in either his direct appeal or his state habeas corpus petition, he was barred from raising it in his federal habeas petition unless he could show "cause" for failing to have raised the issue earlier, and "prejudice" from the failure to raise it. Beazley asserted "cause" on the ground that the novelty of his ICCPR claim made it reasonably unavailable to prior counsel; and he maintained that prejudice was "obvious" because, but for this error, he would not have received the death sentence.]

RHESA HAWKINS BARKSDALE, Circuit Judge. . . .

The Senate ratified the ICCPR in 1992; Beazley's trial was in early 1995; and he filed for state habeas relief in June 1997. Therefore, the claim was available to him throughout his state court proceedings.

Notwithstanding the Senate's 1992 ratification, Beazley asserts the claim was "novel" at the time of his trial in 1995, prior to the United Nations Human Rights Committee's (HRC's) supposedly finding the reservation "void." However, he cites *no* specific ruling that the reservation was void, but apparently piggybacks several HRC statements.

In April 1994, the HRC issued a General Comment on reservations to the ICCPR:

> The Covenant neither prohibits reservations nor mentions any type of permitted reservation. . . . Where a reservation is *not* prohibited by the treaty or falls within the specified permitted categories, a State may make a reservation provided it is *not* incompatible with the object and purpose of the treaty. . . . Reservations that offend *peremptory norms* would *not* be compatible with the object and purpose of the Covenant. . . . *Accordingly, a State may not reserve the right . . . to execute . . . children.* . . . The *normal consequence* of an unacceptable reservation is *not* that the Covenant will *not* be in effect at all for a reserving party. Rather, such a reservation will *generally* be severable, in the sense that the Covenant will be operative for the reserving party without benefit of the reservation. See General Comment 24, General Comment on Issues Relating to Reservations Made upon Ratification or Accession to the Covenant or the Optional Protocols Thereto, or in Relation to Declarations Under Article 41 of the Covenant, U.N. GAOR Human Rights Comm., 52d Sess., PP 5, 6, 8, 18, U.N. Doc. CCPR/C/21/Rev.1/Add.6 (Nov. 1994) [hereinafter *General Comment*] (emphasis added).

In October 1995, the HRC expressed its "concern[]" that the United States Senate's reservation to article 6(5) was "incompatible with the object and purpose of the Covenant," and "*recommended* . . . withdrawing . . . [that] reservation[]." See Annual General Assembly Report of the Human Rights Committee, U.N. GAOR Human Rights Comm., 50th Sess., Supp. No. 40, PP 279, 292, U.N. Doc. A/50/40 (3 Oct. 1995) (emphasis added).

Beazley's assertion of novelty fails for several reasons. First, even assuming *arguendo* the HRC's post-conviction statements in 1995 created a novel claim, state habeas counsel made *no* attempt to present the claim to the state courts two years later or to assert that the claim satisfied an exception to the procedural bar. In fact, Beazley's federal petition suggested Texas courts probably would have heard an ICCPR claim *even though* it had *not* been preserved through a contemporaneous objection at trial.

Furthermore, the claim the United States was *not* in compliance with article 6(5) was *no* more "available" following the HRC's statement in 1995 than it was in 1992, when the Senate ratified the treaty *and* created the reservation.

Finally, perhaps it is arguable that an assertion that the United States is *not in compliance* with the treaty (a claim available in 1992) is distinct from a claim that the reservation is *void* (a claim Beazley asserts became available late in 1995). However, by simply "suggesting and recommending" that the Senate withdraw the reservation, the HRC declined to attempt either to void or to sever the reservation. Therefore, we need *not* reach the question of whether an HRC pronouncement that the reservation was void would create a novel claim, and we certainly need *not* address whether such a pronouncement would bind the United States.

In the light of the above, Beazley has failed to show cause for the procedural default. . . .

In his habeas petition, Beazley asserts that the Senate's ICCPR reservation is invalid and must be severed, based on his contention that the HRC has found it "void" for the reservation's violation of ICCPR's object and purpose. As discussed, the HRC has *not* found the reservation void, and the claim is procedurally barred; however, we address the question of the reservation's validity because it further supports our procedural-bar conclusion.

Two state supreme courts have addressed whether the ICCPR supersedes state law allowing execution for a crime committed while under age 18. Most recently, the Alabama Supreme Court concluded that the Senate's reservation had *not* been demonstrated illegal. See Ex parte Pressley, 770 So. 2d 143, 148 (Ala. 2000) ("We are not persuaded that [petitioner] has established that the Senate's express reservation of this nation's right to impose a penalty of death on juvenile offenders, in ratifying the ICCPR, is illegal."). And, in Domingues v. Nevada, the Supreme Court of Nevada concluded that "the Senate's express reservation of the United States' right to impose a penalty of death on juvenile offenders negated Domingues' claim that he was illegally sentenced." 961 P.2d 1279, 1280 (1998). We agree.

Furthermore, our court has recognized the validity of Senate reservations to the ICCPR. See White v. Johnson, 79 F.3d 432, 440 & n.2 (5th Cir.) ("Even if we did consider the merits of this claim, we would do so under the Senate's reservation that the treaties [among them the ICCPR] only prohibit cruel and unusual punishment".). . . .

In claiming that the reservation is invalid, Beazley cites a declaration to the ICCPR:

> The United States declares that it accepts the competence of the Human Rights Committee to receive and consider communications under Article 41 in which a State Party claims that another State Party is *not* fulfilling its obligations under the Covenant[.] [138 Cong. Rec. S4784 (1992) (statement of presiding officer of resolution of ratification) (emphasis added).]

But, this declaration, while acknowledging the HRC, does *not* bind the United States to its decisions.

Beazley asserts that other courts have found the HRC's interpretation of the ICCPR persuasive. See, e.g., United States v. Duarte-Acero, 208 F.3d 1282, 1287 (11th Cir. 2000) (looking to HRC's guidance as "most important[]" component in interpreting ICCPR claim (brackets omitted)); United States v. Benitez, 28 F. Supp. 2d 1361, 1364 (S.D. Fla. 1998) (finding HRC's interpretation of ICCPR article 14(7) helpful). However, these courts looked to the HRC only for guidance, *not* to void an action by the Senate.

In the light of our analysis, the reservation is valid. Accordingly, we could dispense with, as moot, Beazley's contention that the ICCPR is self-executing; however, we consider it briefly. As quoted above, the Senate ratified the ICCPR with a declaration that articles 1 to 27 were *not* self-executing. Beazley claims this declaration is trumped by article 50 of the ICCPR, which states: "The provisions of the present Covenant shall extend to all parts of federal States without any limitations or exceptions."

ICCPR, art. 50. He maintains also that various statutory provisions constitute enabling statutes to allow private rights of action.

The claim that the Senate, in ratifying the treaty, voided its own attached declaration is nonsensical, to say the very least. The Senate's intent was clear — the treaty is *not* self-executing. See Duarte-Acero, 208 F.3d at 1285 ("If the language of the treaty is clear and unambiguous, as with any exercise in statutory construction, our analysis ends there and we apply the words of the treaty as written."). "'Non-self-executing' means that absent any further actions by the Congress to incorporate them into domestic law, the courts may *not* enforce them." Jama v. I.N.S., 22 F. Supp. 2d 353, 365 (D.N.J. 1998) (emphasis added).

Moreover, although Beazley cites *no* case law supporting the proposition that the treaty *is* self-executing, many courts have found it *is not*. . . . The reservation is an express exception to article 50; restated, article 50 does *not* void the Senate's express intent.

Notes and Questions

1. The ICCPR's RUDs are typical; the United States has attached similar RUDs to all the major human rights treaties it has ratified. Such RUDs were first proposed by President Carter in 1979 as a way of overcoming decades-long opposition in the Senate — including, most famously, the Bricker Amendment debate — to ratification of human rights treaties. There were many reasons for this opposition, including concerns that (a) provisions in the human rights treaties might conflict with U.S. constitutional guarantees; (b) the vaguely worded terms in the treaties would, if self-executing, sow confusion in the law by superseding inconsistent state law and prior inconsistent federal legislation; (c) even if courts ultimately decided that each of the differently worded provisions in the ICCPR did not require a change in domestic law, litigation of these issues would be costly and would generate substantial legal uncertainty; and (d) that the human rights treaties would affect the balance of power between state and federal governments. RUDs were a response to these concerns that made it possible for the Senate to ratify not only the ICCPR, but also the Genocide Convention, the Torture Convention, and the Convention on the Elimination of All Forms of Racial Discrimination.

2. Critics of the RUDs argue that that RUDs show disrespect for international law because they render the treaty obligations empty promises that require no change in U.S. practice. They claim that RUDs send a message to the international community that the United States does not take international human rights law seriously. They further argue that this message has a negative effect that, in the words of Professor Henkin, "threaten[] to undermine a half-century of effort to establish international human rights standards as international law." Louis Henkin, U.S. Ratification of Human Rights Treaties: The Ghost of Senator Bricker, 89 Am. J. Intl. L. 341, 349 (1995).

Supporters of RUDs emphasize that RUDs have had wide bipartisan support and were crucial in breaking the logjam in domestic politics that had prevented U.S. ratification of any of the major human rights treaties. They also note that RUDs are not empty promises. The United States has in fact enacted domestic criminal, civil, and immigration laws to implement the Genocide and Torture Conventions. See 18

U.S.C. §1091 (1994) (genocide); 18 U.S.C. §2340A (1994) (torture); that even with the RUDs, the United States has bound itself to almost all of the obligations in each of the four major human rights treaties it has ratified, and thus has promised not to retreat from those protections; and that the United States has opened its domestic human rights practices to official international scrutiny by filing with international bodies associated with the treaties reports that describe and defend U.S. human rights practices. Finally, supporters of RUDs note that there is no evidence linking U.S. RUDs practice with a diminution of human rights protections around the world, and indeed that international human rights law has flourished during the period that U.S. RUDs were introduced. See generally Curtis A. Bradley & Jack L. Goldsmith, Treaties, Human Rights, and Conditional Consent, 149 U. Pa. L. Rev. 399, 456-468 (2000).

Which view is right?

3. Are reservations constitutional? One potential argument is that they are in tension with separation of powers principles, either because they violate the President's constitutional prerogatives in making treaties, or because they constitute an improper "line-item veto" in that the Senate is, in effect, trying to change the terms of the treaty. Do these arguments apply to RUDs to human rights treaties, which have largely been proposed by Presidents? Assuming they do, is it relevant that the Senate must attach RUDs before, and not after, ratification, see Fourteen Diamond Rings v. United States, 183 U.S. 176, 180 (1901) ("The meaning of the treaty cannot be controlled by subsequent explanations of some of those who may have voted to ratify it"); and that the President always retains the discretion to refuse to ratify a treaty that the Senate has consented to conditionally? How about the line-item veto argument? The Supreme Court struck down a line-item veto in Clinton v. New York because it constituted an attempt by one branch or house of the legislature to alter already-enacted law. 524 U.S. 417, 447 (1998) (invalidating Line Item Veto Act because it "gives the President the unilateral power to change the text of duly enacted statutes"). Do RUDs give the Senate unilateral power to change the duly ratified treaties? Or are they analogous to a bill passed by both Houses of Congress, which the President can veto?

4. Another complaint about RUDs is that they are "antimajoritarian" because they allow a minority of senators to force limitations on treaties through their power to block the two-thirds advice and consent needed for ratification. See, e.g., Stefan A. Riesenfeld & Frederick M. Abbott, The Scope of U.S. Senate Control Over the Conclusion and Operation of Treaties, 67 Chi.-Kent L. Rev. 571, 600-601 (1991). It is true that a minority of senators can insist on a package of RUDs as a precondition of senatorial consent to the treaty. Is this minority power of conditional consent any more pernicious than Article II's super-majoritarian treatymaking procedure? Does this antimajoritarian feature of the treaty process distinguish it from other constitutional provisions designed to protect minority interests, including Article I's bicameralism and presentment process, Article II's impeachment process, Article V's constitutional amendment process, and the Bill of Rights?

5. The ICCPR establishes a Human Rights Committee ("HRC") that is charged with receiving reports submitted by nations under the ICCPR's self-reporting provisions and issuing "such general comments as it may consider appropriate." As the court notes in Beazley, the HRC technically has no official power to issue binding legal interpretations of the ICCPR. Nonetheless, the HRC has declared itself to be the

definitive interpreter of whether a reservation to the ICCPR is consistent with the international law rule that a reservation cannot violate the treaty's "object and purpose." See ICCPR Human Rights Comm., General Comment 24(52), 52d Sess., 1382d mtg. P 10, U.N. Doc. CCPR/C/21/Rev.1/Add.6 (1994), at 18. And, as the court notes in *Beazley*, the HRC has stated that the execution of juvenile murderers violates the object and purpose test, and that the remedy for this violation is that the entire treaty, including the provision to which the United States reserved, remains binding on the United States. See id.; Human Rights Committee, Comments on United States of America, U.N. Doc. CCPR/C/79/Add.50 (1995). In short, the HRC appears to maintain that the U.S. reservation with respect to the juvenile death penalty is invalid under international law and the United States is bound by the ICCPR's prohibition on the juvenile death penalty even though it specifically declined to consent to it.

In "Observations" responding to the HRC, the U.S. government has contested these conclusions. It disagreed with the legal analysis supporting the view that the reservation to the death penalty provision violated the ICCPR's object and purpose; and it maintained (along with other leading Western nations) that it was inconsistent with the principle of state consent to bind a nation to a term to which it had attached an (invalid) reservation. See Observations by the United States on General Comment 24, 3 Intl. Hum. Rts. Rep. 265 (1996).

Does this debate about the validity of reservations under international law have any implications for domestic U.S. law? Even if the reservation were invalid under international law, would the reservation nonetheless bind U.S. courts? Does the answer to this question depend on the validity of the non-self-executing declaration?

6. Why does the United States attach non-self-executing declarations to human rights treaties? The State Department's Legal Advisor to the HRC offered this answer: "[T]he decision to make the treaty 'non-self-executing' reflects a strong preference, both within the Administration and in the Senate, not to use the unicameral treaty power of the U.S. Constitution to effect direct changes in the domestic law of the United States." Statement by Conrad K. Harper, USUN Press Release #49-(95), at 3 (Mar. 29, 1995). Can you think of other reasons?

7. As noted earlier in this chapter, it has sometimes been suggested that the treaty power is limited to matters of international or external concern. One decision suggesting this limitation is Power Authority of New York v. Federal Power Commission, 247 F.2d 538 (D.C. Cir. 1957). In that decision, the court considered the effect of a reservation attached by the Senate to its ratification of a treaty with Canada concerning use of water from the Niagara River. The reservation purported to preclude the development of the U.S. share of the water until Congress specifically provided for its development, notwithstanding federal statutes giving the Federal Power Commission authority to issue licenses for water development. The court construed the Senate's reservation as merely "an expression of the Senate's desires and not a part of the treaty." Id. at 543. It adopted this construction to avoid what it perceived to be the serious constitutional question of whether the reservation exceeded the scope of the treaty power, which the court noted might be limited to matters of international concern.

What, if anything, does the *Power Authority* decision suggest about the validity of non-self-execution declarations? For an argument that these declarations are invalid under the analysis in *Power Authority*, see Malvina Halberstam, United States

Ratification of the Convention on the Elimination of All Forms of Discrimination Against Women, 31 G.W. J. Intl. L. & Econ. 49, 69 (1997); John Quigley, The International Covenant on Civil and Political Rights and the Supremacy Clause, 42 DePaul L. Rev. 1287, 1303-1305 (1993); and Stefan A. Riesenfeld & Frederick M. Abbott, The Scope of U.S. Senate Control Over the Conclusion and Operation of Treaties, 67 Chi.-Kent L. Rev. 571, 590-600 (1991). But see Bradley & Goldsmith, supra, at 452-453 (arguing that *Power Authority* and the scope of the treaty power do not affect the validity of the RUDs).

c. Last-in-Time Rule

The Constitution provides that both treaties and federal statutes are part of the supreme law of the land and thus preempt inconsistent state law. The Constitution does not specify, however, the relationship between treaties and statutes. The Supreme Court nevertheless has long held that self-executing treaties and federal statutes have essentially equal status under U.S. law, such that the later in time will prevail under U.S. law in the event of a conflict.

The Court applied this "last-in-time rule" in the decision below.

Breard v. Greene

U.S. Supreme Court
523 U.S. 371 (1998)

Per Curiam.

Angel Francisco Breard is scheduled to be executed by the Commonwealth of Virginia this evening at 9:00 P.M. Breard, a citizen of Paraguay, came to the United States in 1986, at the age of 20. In 1992, Breard was charged with the attempted rape and capital murder of Ruth Dickie. At his trial in 1993, the State presented overwhelming evidence of guilt, including semen found on Dickie's body matching Breard's DNA profile and hairs on Dickie's body identical in all microscopic characteristics to hair samples taken from Breard. Breard chose to take the witness stand in his defense. During his testimony, Breard confessed to killing Dickie, but explained that he had only done so because of a Satanic curse placed on him by his father-in-law. Following a jury trial in the Circuit Court of Arlington County, Virginia, Breard was convicted of both charges and sentenced to death. On appeal, the Virginia Supreme Court affirmed Breard's convictions and sentences, and we denied certiorari. State collateral relief was subsequently denied as well.

Breard then filed a motion for habeas relief under 28 U.S.C. §2254 in Federal District Court on August 20, 1996. In that motion, Breard argued for the first time that his conviction and sentence should be overturned because of alleged violations of the Vienna Convention on Consular Relations (Vienna Convention), April 24, 1963, [1970] 21 U.S. T. 77, T.I.A.S. No. 6820, at the time of his arrest. Specifically, Breard alleged that the Vienna Convention was violated when the arresting authorities failed to inform him that, as a foreign national, he had the right to contact the Paraguayan Consulate. The District Court rejected this claim, concluding that Breard procedurally defaulted the claim when he failed to raise it in state court and that Breard could not demonstrate cause and prejudice for this default. The Fourth Circuit affirmed. Breard has petitioned this Court for a writ of certiorari.

In September 1996, the Republic of Paraguay, the Ambassador of Paraguay to the United States, and the Consul General of Paraguay to the United States (collectively Paraguay) brought suit in Federal District Court against certain Virginia officials, alleging that their separate rights under the Vienna Convention had been violated by the Commonwealth's failure to inform Breard of his rights under the treaty and to inform the Paraguayan consulate of Breard's arrest, conviction, and sentence. In addition, the Consul General asserted a parallel claim under 42 U.S.C. §1983, alleging a denial of his rights under the Vienna Convention. The District Court concluded that it lacked subject-matter jurisdiction over these suits because Paraguay was not alleging a "continuing violation of federal law" and therefore could not bring its claims within the exception to Eleventh Amendment immunity established in Ex parte Young, 209 U.S. 123 (1908). The Fourth Circuit affirmed on Eleventh Amendment grounds. Paraguay has also petitioned this Court for a writ of certiorari.

On April 3, 1998, nearly five years after Breard's conviction became final, the Republic of Paraguay instituted proceedings against the United States in the International Court of Justice (ICJ), alleging that the United States violated the Vienna Convention at the time of Breard's arrest. On April 9, the ICJ noted jurisdiction and issued an order requesting that the United States "take all measures at its disposal to ensure that Angel Francisco Breard is not executed pending the final decision in these proceedings. . . ." The ICJ set a briefing schedule for this matter, with oral argument likely to be held this November. Breard then filed a petition for an original writ of habeas corpus and a stay application in this Court in order to "enforce" the ICJ's order. Paraguay filed a motion for leave to file a bill of complaint in this Court, citing this Court's original jurisdiction over cases "affecting Ambassadors . . . and Consuls." U.S. Const., Art. III, §2.

It is clear that Breard procedurally defaulted his claim, if any, under the Vienna Convention by failing to raise that claim in the state courts. Nevertheless, in their petitions for certiorari, both Breard and Paraguay contend that Breard's Vienna Convention claim may be heard in federal court because the Convention is the "supreme law of the land" and thus trumps the procedural default doctrine. This argument is plainly incorrect for two reasons.

First, while we should give respectful consideration to the interpretation of an international treaty rendered by an international court with jurisdiction to interpret such, it has been recognized in international law that, absent a clear and express statement to the contrary, the procedural rules of the forum State govern the implementation of the treaty in that State. This proposition is embodied in the Vienna Convention itself, which provides that the rights expressed in the Convention "shall be exercised in conformity with the laws and regulations of the receiving State," provided that "said laws and regulations must enable full effect to be given to the purposes for which the rights accorded under this Article are intended." Article 36(2), [1970] 21 U.S. T., at 101. It is the rule in this country that assertions of error in criminal proceedings must first be raised in state court in order to form the basis for relief in habeas. Claims not so raised are considered defaulted. By not asserting his Vienna Convention claim in state court, Breard failed to exercise his rights under the Vienna Convention in conformity with the laws of the United States and the

Commonwealth of Virginia. Having failed to do so, he cannot raise a claim of violation of those rights now on federal habeas review.

Second, although treaties are recognized by our Constitution as the supreme law of the land, that status is no less true of provisions of the Constitution itself, to which rules of procedural default apply. We have held "that an Act of Congress . . . is on a full parity with a treaty, and that when a statute which is subsequent in time is inconsistent with a treaty, the statute to the extent of conflict renders the treaty null." Reid v. Covert, 354 U.S. 1, 18 (1957) (plurality opinion); see also Whitney v. Robertson, 124 U.S. 190, 194 (1888) (holding that if a treaty and a federal statute conflict, "the one last in date will control the other"). The Vienna Convention — which arguably confers on an individual the right to consular assistance following arrest — has continuously been in effect since 1969. But in 1996, before Breard filed his habeas petition raising claims under the Vienna Convention, Congress enacted the Antiterrorism and Effective Death Penalty Act (AEDPA), which provides that a habeas petitioner alleging that he is held in violation of "treaties of the United States" will, as a general rule, not be afforded an evidentiary hearing if he "has failed to develop the factual basis of [the] claim in State court proceedings." 28 U.S.C.A. §§2254(a), (e)(2) (Supp. 1998). Breard's ability to obtain relief based on violations of the Vienna Convention is subject to this subsequently-enacted rule, just as any claim arising under the United States Constitution would be. This rule prevents Breard from establishing that the violation of his Vienna Convention rights prejudiced him. Without a hearing, Breard cannot establish how the Consul would have advised him, how the advice of his attorneys differed from the advice the Consul could have provided, and what factors he considered in electing to reject the plea bargain that the State offered him.

Notes and Questions

1. As illustrated by *Breard*, Congress's ability to override treaties, for purposes of U.S. domestic law, is well settled. See also, e.g., Reid v. Covert, 354 U.S. 1, 18 (1957) (plurality); Chae Chan Ping v. United States (Chinese Exclusion Case), 130 U.S. 581, 600-601 (1889); Whitney v. Robertson, 124 U.S. 190, 194 (1888); Edye v. Robertson (Head Money Cases), 112 U.S. 580, 597-598 (1884). What is the basis for this ability? Treaties and statutes are both mentioned in the Supremacy Clause, but are all types of law mentioned in the Clause equal in status? Given that two-thirds of the Senate must consent in order for the United States to enter into a treaty, why should a simple majority of Congress have the ability to override a treaty? Given that the President is given the power to make treaties (with the advice and consent of the Senate), why should Congress (if it passes a veto-proof statute) have the ability to override a treaty against the wishes of the President? In considering these questions, keep in mind that even when Congress does override a treaty as a matter of U.S. domestic law, the treaty is still binding on the United States internationally until validly terminated.

2. The last-in-time rule can work the other way as well. That is, later-in-time treaties can, at least in theory, override earlier federal statutes. See, e.g., Cook v. United States, 288 U.S. 102 (1933). This is relatively rare, however. Why are there not more decisions allowing treaties to override statutes? Are the justifications the

same for allowing later treaties to supersede earlier statutes as they are for allowing later statutes to supersede earlier treaties? What is the relationship between the self-execution doctrine and the ability of treaties to override statutes?

3. Under *Missouri v. Holland*, discussed above, the scope of the treaty power is broader than the scope of Congress's legislative powers. If the United States enters into a treaty that regulates something that cannot be regulated by Congress, does Congress have the power to override such a treaty? If not, does this mean that the treaty is immune from the last-in-time rule? Does the last-in-time rule suggest that, contrary to *Holland*, treaties should be subject to the same federalism limitations as statutes?

4. Courts ordinarily will not apply the last-in-time rule to override a treaty or statute absent a clear conflict with a subsequent treaty or statute. See, e.g., Trans World Airlines, Inc. v. Franklin Mint Corp., 466 U.S. 243, 252 (1984); Johnson v. Browne, 205 U.S. 309, 321 (1907); United States v. Lee Yen Tai, 185 U.S. 213, 222 (1902). This is a subset of the "*Charming Betsy* canon," which is discussed in more detail later in this chapter. Did the Court in *Breard* overlook this canon? Was there a clear conflict between the 1996 habeas statute and the consular notice provision in the Vienna Convention? Even if there was, why wasn't the order from the International Court of Justice the operative last-in-time rule? What, if anything, does the Court suggest about the status of such orders in U.S. courts? For discussion of these and other aspects of the *Breard* case, see Agora: *Breard,* 92 Am. J. Intl. L. 666-712 (1998); Curtis A. Bradley, *Breard,* Our Dualist Constitution, and the Internationalist Conception, 51 Stan. L. Rev. 529 (1999).

5. Since the *Breard* decision, foreign citizen defendants have brought numerous challenges to their convictions and sentences based on violations of the consular notice provision in the Vienna Convention on Consular Relations. Many of these challenges have been brought on direct appeal and thus have not been subject to the habeas corpus limitations applied in *Breard*. Nevertheless, essentially all courts have rejected the challenges. In some cases, courts have found that the treaty violation was harmless error. In other cases, courts have held that the treaty did not give the criminal defendants a right to the relief they were seeking, such as suppression of evidence. See, e.g., United States v. La Pava, 268 F.3d 157 (2d Cir. 2001); United States v. Lawal, 231 F.3d 1045 (7th Cir. 2000); United States v. Li, 206 F.3d 56 (1st Cir. 2000). If the consular notice provision of the Vienna Convention is self-executing, as most courts have assumed, why did it not provide a right to relief in these cases?

6. After the *Breard* case, the International Court of Justice was faced with a similar dispute involving German nationals on death row. Two brothers of German nationality, Walter and Karl LaGrand, were arrested in Arizona in 1982 for committing murder during an attempted armed robbery. They were convicted and sentenced to death, but they were not informed of their rights under the Vienna Convention on Consular Relations. After exhausting appellate and state post-conviction proceedings, the LaGrands filed petitions for writs of habeas corpus in the 1990s, raising for the first time the Vienna Convention violation. After these petitions were denied, and after Karl LaGrand was executed, Germany filed a suit against the United States in the ICJ, seeking, among other things, a stay of Walter LaGrand's execution. As in the *Breard* case, the ICJ issued a provisional order stating that the United States should "take all measures at its disposal" to ensure that the execution was not carried

out while the ICJ heard the case. Despite this order, neither Arizona's governor nor the U.S. Supreme Court granted a stay of execution, and Walter LaGrand was executed. Unlike Paraguay in the *Breard* case, however, Germany did not abandon its case before the ICJ at this point, and the ICJ subsequently issued a final decision in the case. In its decision, the ICJ held that the United States had violated the Vienna Convention; that the United States had also violated the ICJ's provisional order, which the Court held was legally binding; and that in future situations in which German nationals "have been subjected to prolonged detention or convicted and sentenced to severe penalties," the United States would be required "to allow the review and reconsideration of the conviction and sentence by taking account of the violation of the rights set forth in the Convention." LaGrand Case (Germany v. United States of America), ICJ, No. 104 (June 27, 2001). The ICJ also stated, however, that "[t]his obligation can be carried out in various ways" and that "[t]he choice of means must be left to the United States." It remains to be seen what if any effect the *LaGrand* decision will have on U.S. judicial enforcement of the Convention.

7. For academic discussion of the last-in-time rule, see, for example, Louis Henkin, The Constitution and United States Sovereignty: A Century of *Chinese Exclusion* and Its Progeny, 100 Harv. L. Rev. 853 (1987); Jules Lobel, The Limits of Constitutional Power: Conflicts Between Foreign Policy and International Law, 71 Va. L. Rev. 1071 (1985); Detlev Vagts, The United States and Its Treaties: Observance and Breach, 95 Am. J. Intl. L. 313 (2001); and Peter Westen, The Place of Foreign Treaties in the Courts of the United States: A Reply to Louis Henkin, 101 Harv. L. Rev. 511 (1987).

d. Treaty Termination and Reinterpretation

The above materials address, among other things, the power to *override* U.S. treaty obligations *as a matter of U.S. law.* What about the power to *terminate* U.S. treaty obligations *on the international plane?* Many treaties contain clauses specifying the circumstances under which parties to the treaty may withdraw. For example, the 1972 Anti-Ballistic Missile (ABM) Treaty between the United States and the Soviet Union (now Russia) provides that the Treaty "shall be of unlimited duration," except that each nation has the right to withdraw "if it decides that extraordinary events related to the subject matter of this Treaty have jeopardized its supreme interests." When a treaty does not specifically provide for withdrawal, the parties may still have a right to withdraw if the parties intended to allow for that possibility or if the nature of the treaty itself suggests a right of withdrawal. In addition, parties may terminate their treaty commitments if certain events occur, such as a material breach of the treaty by another party, impossibility of performance, or a fundamental change in circumstances. See Vienna Convention on the Law of Treaties, arts. 60-62.

Does the President have the constitutional authority to withdraw the United States from treaties? Article II of the Constitution requires that, in order to make a treaty, Presidents must obtain the advice and consent of two-thirds of the Senate. Does this requirement imply that Presidents must also obtain two-thirds Senate consent before they can terminate a treaty? In considering this question, of what significance is the fact that many constitutional Founders believed that it should be difficult for the United States to enter into treaties? As a practical matter, does the United States need more flexibility in the termination of its treaty commitments than in the making of such commitments?

In 1978, as part of the process of recognizing the People's Republic of China, President Jimmy Carter announced that he planned to terminate the U.S. mutual defense treaty with Taiwan, pursuant to a provision in the treaty that allowed either party to withdraw after giving a year's notice. In response, eight senators and sixteen members of the House of Representatives sued for declaratory and injunctive relief to prevent Carter from terminating the treaty. The federal district court held that the notice of termination was ineffective absent either a manifestation of the consent of the Senate to such termination by a two-thirds vote, or an approving majority vote by both houses of Congress. See Goldwater v. Carter, 481 F. Supp. 949 (D.D.C. 1979). The court of appeals reversed, holding that the President had the power to terminate the treaty. See 617 F.2d 697 (D.C. Cir. 1979). Without issuing a majority opinion, the Supreme Court granted certiorari, vacated the lower court judgment, and remanded the case with directions to dismiss the complaint. Four Justices reasoned that the issue was a "political question" not susceptible to judicial resolution. Justice Powell reasoned that the issue was not ripe because Congress had taken no official action and there was no actual confrontation between the Legislative and Executive Branches. Justices White and Blackmun believed that the issue should have been more fully considered before the Court issued any decision. Justice Brennan opined that the President had the authority to terminate the Taiwan treaty by virtue of his authority to recognize foreign governments. Justice Marshall concurred in the result. See 444 U.S. 997 (1979).

In 2001, President George W. Bush announced that the United States would withdraw from the ABM Treaty. The treaty, as modified by a 1974 protocol, prohibits both nations from testing, developing, or deploying any anti-ballistic missile system, except for a single system to protect the nation's capital or another designated site. As noted above, the treaty also allows each party to terminate the treaty if the party "decides that extraordinary events related to the subject matter of this Treaty have jeopardized its supreme interests." The Bush Administration invoked this withdrawal clause, and it also claimed that there had been a fundamental change in circumstances — namely, the collapse of the Soviet Union, the end of the Cold War, and the proliferation of nuclear weapons. For debate over the legitimacy of the Administration's action, compare Bruce Ackerman, Treaties Don't Belong to Presidents Alone, N.Y. Times, Aug. 29, 2001, at A23 (arguing that congressional consent is required for treaty termination), with Jack Goldsmith & John Yoo, Missiles Away: Bush Has Power to Clear Path for Missile Defense Shield by Scrapping Treaty, Legal Times, May 7, 2001, at 76 (defending Bush's authority to withdraw from the treaty).

Some years earlier, the ABM Treaty generated a different, but somewhat related, controversy. The controversy was over whether the President had the power unilaterally to *reinterpret* the meaning of a treaty. In the mid-1980s, the Reagan Administration adopted a new interpretation of the ABM Treaty, pursuant to which the treaty would not prohibit research and development of ABM systems using technologies not in existence in 1972. This attempt to reinterpret the treaty generated substantial criticism and debate — in Congress, among academic commentators, and in the international community. The administration subsequently announced that, while it considered its broad interpretation of the treaty "fully justified," it would follow a narrower interpretation in practice. Congress subsequently imposed conditions on Defense Department appropriations forbidding the testing of new technologies that would violate a narrow construction of the treaty. In addition, the Senate attached a reservation to its advice and consent to the Intermediate Nuclear Forces Treaty with the Soviet Union, requiring that the treaty be interpreted according to the shared understanding of the Senate and President at the time of ratification, and requiring Senate consent for any future reinterpretation. Although the Reagan Administration argued that this condition unconstitutionally infringed on the President's foreign affairs powers, it proceeded to ratify the treaty with the condition.

Are the issues of treaty termination and treaty reinterpretation constitutionally distinguishable? Might the President have one power but not the other? If the Executive Branch assures the Senate of a particular treaty interpretation when the Senate is giving its advice and consent to the treaty, should the Executive Branch be bound by that interpretation? What if the Executive Branch's new interpretation is supported by the treaty's negotiating history?

For additional discussion of the issue of treaty termination, see, for example, David Gray Adler, The Constitution and the Termination of Treaties (1986); Raoul Berger, The President's Unilateral Termination of the Taiwan Treaty, 75 Nw. U. L. Rev. 577 (1980); and Louis Henkin, Litigating the President's Power to Terminate Treaties, 73 Am. J. Intl. L. 647 (1979).

For additional discussion of the issue of treaty reinterpretation, see, for example, David A. Koplow, Constitutional Bait and Switch: Executive Reinterpretation of Arms Control Treaties, 137 U. Pa. L. Rev. 1353 (1989); Abraham D. Sofaer, The ABM Treaty and the Strategic Defense Initiative, 99 Harv. L. Rev. 1972 (1986); Phillip R. Trimble, The Constitutional Common Law of Treaty Interpretation: A Reply to the Formalists, 137 U. Pa. L. Rev. 1461 (1989); and John Yoo, Politics as Law?: The Anti-Ballistic Missile Treaty, The Separation of Powers, and Treaty Interpretation: Way Out There in the Blue, 89 Cal. L. Rev. 851 (2001).

B.   PRESIDENTIAL POWER AND OTHER INTERNATIONAL AGREEMENTS

In addition to the power conferred by Article II of the Constitution, the President has three other sources of authority to conclude international agreements on behalf of the United States: (1) authority based on a prior Article II treaty, (2) authority from the Congress, and (3) independent authority conferred directly by the Constitution. Within the third category, the President has express constitutional authority (like the commander-in-chief power) and implied constitutional authority (to conduct foreign relations). In this section we will focus on the last two categories of executive agreement (the first category is simply an extension of the basic Article II doctrine). But first we begin with a general discussion of presidential power.

As background for both the discussion of presidential power and the discussion of executive agreements, review the following constitutional grants of power to Congress and the President:

U.S. Constitution

Article I

Section 1. All legislative Powers herein granted shall be vested in a Congress of the United States, which shall consist of a Senate and House of Representatives....

Section 7. [1] All Bills for raising Revenue shall originate in the House of Representatives; but the Senate may propose or concur with Amendments as on other Bills....

Section 8. [1] The Congress shall have Power To lay and collect Taxes, Duties, Imposts and Excises, to pay the Debts and provide for the common Defence and general Welfare of the United States; but all Duties, Imposts and Excises shall be uniform throughout the United States;

[2] To borrow money on the credit of the United States;

[3] To regulate Commerce with foreign Nations, and among the several States, and with the Indian Tribes;

[4] To establish an uniform Rule of Naturalization, and uniform Laws on the subject of Bankruptcies throughout the United States;

[5] To coin Money, regulate the Value thereof, and of foreign Coin, and fix the Standard of Weights and Measures;

[6] To provide for the Punishment of counterfeiting the Securities and current Coin of the United States; ...

[10] To define and punish Piracies and Felonies committed on the high Seas, and Offenses against the Law of Nations;

[11] To declare War, grant Letters of Marque and Reprisal, and make Rules concerning Captures on Land and Water;

[12] To raise and support Armies, but no Appropriation of Money to that Use shall be for a longer Term than two Years;

[13] To provide and maintain a Navy;

[14] To make Rules for the Government and Regulation of the land and naval Forces;

[15] To provide for calling forth the Militia to execute the Laws of the Union, suppress Insurrections and repel Invasions;

[16] To provide for organizing, arming, and disciplining, the Militia, and for governing such Part of them as may be employed in the Service of the United States, reserving to the States respectively, the Appointment of the Officers, and the Authority of training the Militia according to the discipline prescribed by Congress; ...

[18] To make all Laws which shall be necessary and proper for carrying into Execution the foregoing Powers, and all other Powers vested by this Constitution in the Government of the United States, or in any Department or Officer thereof.

Section 9. . . . [7] No money shall be drawn from the Treasury, but in Consequence of Appropriations made by Law; and a regular Statement and Account of the Receipts and Expenditures of all public Money shall be published from time to time.

Article II

Section 1. [1] The executive Power shall be vested in a President of the United States of America. . . .

Section 2. [1] The President shall be Commander in Chief of the Army and Navy of the United States, . . .

[2] He shall have Power, by and with the Advice and Consent of the Senate to make Treaties, provided two thirds of the Senators present concur; and he shall nominate, and by and with the Advice and Consent of the Senate, shall appoint Ambassadors, other public Ministers and Consuls, . . .

[Section 3. [1]] . . . he shall receive Ambassadors and other public Ministers. . . .

1.   *Presidential Foreign Relations Power*

Unlike the long list of congressional foreign affairs powers in Article I of the Constitution, there are only a few presidential foreign relations powers enumerated in Article II, and even some of those powers (such as treatymaking) require senatorial consent. Nevertheless, the President has always exercised substantial foreign relations power. Indeed, the President is often described as having the dominant role in the conduct of U.S. foreign relations. The two decisions below consider the sources and scope of presidential foreign relations authority.

United States v. Curtiss-Wright Corp.

U.S. Supreme Court
299 U.S. 304 (1936)

Mr. Justice SUTHERLAND delivered the opinion of the Court.

On January 27, 1936, an indictment was returned in the court below, the first count of which charges that appellees, beginning with the 29th day of May, 1934, conspired to sell in the United States certain arms of war, namely fifteen machine guns, to Bolivia, a country then engaged in armed conflict in the Chaco, in violation of the Joint Resolution of Congress approved May 28, 1934, and the provisions of a proclamation issued on the same day by the President of the United States pursuant to authority conferred by §1 of the resolution. In pursuance of the conspiracy, the commission of certain overt acts was alleged, details of which need not be stated. The Joint Resolution (c.365, 48 Stat. 811) follows:

> *Resolved by the Senate and House of Representatives of the United States of America in Congress assembled,* That if the President finds that the prohibition of the sale of arms and munitions of war in the United States to those countries now engaged in armed conflict in the Chaco may contribute to the reestablishment of peace between those countries, and if after consultation with the governments of other American Republics and with their cooperation, as well as that of such other governments as he may deem necessary, he makes proclamation to that effect, it shall be unlawful to sell, except under such limitations and exceptions as the President prescribes, any arms or munitions of war in any place in the United States to the countries now engaged in that armed conflict, or to any person, company, or association acting in the interest of either country, until otherwise ordered by the President or by Congress. . . .

. . . [A]ppellees urge that Congress abdicated its essential functions and delegated them to the Executive.

Whether, if the Joint Resolution had related solely to internal affairs it would be open to the challenge that it constituted an unlawful delegation of legislative power to the Executive, we find it unnecessary to determine. The whole aim of the resolution is to affect a situation entirely external to the United States, and falling within the category of foreign affairs. The determination which we are called to make, therefore, is whether the Joint Resolution, as applied to that situation, is vulnerable to attack under the rule that forbids a delegation of the law-making power. In other words, assuming (but not deciding) that the challenged delegation, if it were confined to internal affairs, would be invalid, may it nevertheless be sustained on the ground that its exclusive aim is to afford a remedy for a hurtful condition within foreign territory?

It will contribute to the elucidation of the question if we first consider the differences between the powers of the federal government in respect of foreign or external affairs and those in respect of domestic or internal affairs. That there are differences between them, and that these differences are fundamental, may not be doubted.

The two classes of powers are different, both in respect of their origin and their nature. The broad statement that the federal government can exercise no powers except those specifically enumerated in the Constitution, and such implied powers as are necessary and proper to carry into effect the enumerated powers, is categorically true only in respect of our internal affairs. In that field, the primary purpose of the Constitution was to carve from the general mass of legislative powers *then possessed by the states* such portions as it was thought desirable to vest in the federal government, leaving those not included in the enumeration still in the states. Carter v. Carter Coal Co., 298 U.S. 238, 294. That this doctrine applies only to powers which the states had, is self evident. And since the states severally never possessed international powers, such powers could not have been carved from the mass of state powers but obviously were transmitted to the United States from some other source. During the colonial period, those powers were possessed exclusively by and were entirely under the control of the Crown. By the Declaration of Independence, "the Representatives of the United States of America" declared the United [not the several] Colonies to be free and independent states, and as such to have "full Power to levy War, conclude Peace, contract Alliances, establish Commerce and to do all other Acts and Things which Independent States may of right do."

As a result of the separation from Great Britain by the colonies acting as a unit, the powers of external sovereignty passed from the Crown not to the colonies severally, but to the colonies in their collective and corporate capacity as the United States of America. Even before the Declaration, the colonies were a unit in foreign affairs, acting through a common agency — namely the Continental Congress, composed of delegates from the thirteen colonies. That agency exercised the powers of war and peace, raised an army, created a navy, and finally adopted the Declaration of Independence. Rulers come and go; governments end and forms of government change; but sovereignty survives. A political society cannot endure without a supreme will somewhere. Sovereignty is never held in suspense. When, therefore, the external sovereignty of Great Britain in respect of the colonies ceased, it immediately passed to the Union. . . .

It results that the investment of the federal government with the powers of external sovereignty did not depend upon the affirmative grants of the Constitution. The powers to declare and wage war, to conclude peace, to make treaties, to maintain diplomatic relations with other sovereignties, if they had never been mentioned in the Constitution, would have vested in the federal government as necessary concomitants of nationality. Neither the Constitution nor the laws passed in pursuance of it have any force in foreign territory unless in respect of our own citizens (see American Banana Co. v. United Fruit Co., 213 U.S. 347, 356); and operations of the nation in such territory must be governed by treaties, international understandings and compacts, and the principles of international law. As a member of the family of nations, the right and power of the United States in that field are equal to the right and power of the other members of the international family. Otherwise, the United States is not completely sovereign. The power to acquire territory by discovery and occupation (Jones v. United States, 137 U.S. 202, 212), the power to expel undesirable aliens (Fong Yue Ting v. United States, 149 U.S. 698, 705 et seq.), the power to make such international agreements as do not constitute treaties in the constitutional sense (Altman & Co. v. United States, 224 U.S. 383, 600-601; Crandall, Treaties, Their Making and Enforcement, 2d ed., p. 102 and note 1), none of which is expressly affirmed by the Constitution, nevertheless exist as inherently inseparable from the conception of nationality. This the court recognized, and in each of the cases cited found the warrant for its conclusions not in the provisions of the Constitution, but in the law of nations. . . .

Not only, as we have shown, is the federal power over external affairs in origin and essential character different from that over internal affairs, but participation in the exercise of the power is significantly limited. In this vast external realm, with its important, complicated, delicate and manifold problems, the President alone has the power to speak or listen as a representative of the nation. He *makes* treaties with the advice and consent of the Senate; but he alone negotiates. Into the field of negotiation the Senate cannot intrude; and Congress itself is powerless to invade it. As Marshall said in his great argument of March 7, 1800, in the House of Representatives, "The President is the sole organ of the nation in its external relations, and its sole representative with foreign nations." Annals, 6th Cong., col. 613. The Senate Committee on Foreign Relations at a very early day in our history (February 15, 1816), reported to the Senate, among other things, as follows:

"The President is the constitutional representative of the United States with regard to foreign nations. He manages our concerns with foreign nations and must necessarily be most competent to determine when, how, and upon what subjects negotiations may be urged with the greatest prospect of success. For his conduct he is responsible to the Constitution. The committee consider this responsibility the surest pledge for the faithful discharge of his duty. They think the interference of the Senate in the direction of foreign negotiations calculated to diminish that responsibility and thereby to impair the best security for the national safety. The nature of transactions with foreign nations, moreover, requires caution and unity of design, and their success frequently depends on secrecy and dispatch." U.S. Senate, Reports, Committee on Foreign Relations, vol. 8, p.24.

It is important to bear in mind that we are here dealing not alone with an authority vested in the President by an exertion of legislative power, but with such an authority plus the very delicate, plenary and exclusive power of the President as the sole organ of the federal government in the field of international relations — a power which does not require as a basis for its exercise an act of Congress, but which, of course, like every other governmental power, must be exercised in subordination to the applicable provisions of the Constitution. It is quite apparent that if, in the maintenance of our international relations, embarrassment — perhaps serious embarrassment — is to be avoided and success for our aims achieved, congressional legislation which is to be made effective through negotiation and inquiry within the international field must often accord to the President a degree of discretion and freedom from statutory restriction which would not be admissible were domestic affairs alone involved. Moreover, he, not Congress, has the better opportunity of knowing the conditions which prevail in foreign countries, and especially is this true in time of war. He has his confidential sources of information. He has his agents in the form of diplomatic, consular and other officials. Secrecy in respect of information gathered by them may be highly necessary, and the premature disclosure of it productive of harmful results. Indeed, so clearly is this true that the first President refused to accede to a request to lay before the House of Representatives the instructions, correspondence and documents relating to the negotiation of the Jay Treaty — a refusal the wisdom of which was recognized by the House itself and has never since been doubted.

Youngstown Sheet & Tube Co. v. Sawyer

U.S. Supreme Court
343 U.S. 579 (1952)

Mr. Justice BLACK delivered the opinion of the Court.

We are asked to decide whether the President was acting within his constitutional power when he issued an order directing the Secretary of Commerce to take possession of and operate most of the Nation's steel mills. The mill owners argue that the President's order amounts to law-making, a legislative function which the Constitution has expressly confided to the Congress and not to the President. The Government's position is that the order was made on findings of the President that his action was necessary to avert a national catastrophe which would inevitably result from a stoppage of steel production, and that in meeting this grave emergency the President was acting within the aggregate of his constitutional powers as the Nation's Chief Executive and the Commander in Chief of the Armed Forces of the United States. The issue emerges here from the following series of events:

In the latter part of 1951, a dispute arose between the steel companies and their employees over terms and conditions that should be included in new collective bargaining agreements. Long-continued conferences failed to resolve the dispute. On December 18, 1951, the employees' representatives, United Steelworkers of America, C.I.O., gave notice of an intention to strike when the existing bargaining agreements expired on December 31. The Federal Mediation and Conciliation Service then intervened in an effort to get labor and management to agree. This failing, the President on December 22, 1951, referred the dispute to the Federal Wage Stabilization Board to investigate and make recommendations for fair and equitable terms of settlement. This Board's report resulted in no settlement. On April 4, 1952, the Union gave notice of a nation-wide strike called to begin at 12:01 A.M. April 9.

The indispensability of steel as a component of substantially all weapons and other war materials led the President to believe that the proposed work stoppage would immediately jeopardize our national defense and that governmental seizure of the steel mills was necessary in order to assure the continued availability of steel. Reciting these considerations for his action, the President, a few hours before the strike was to begin, issued Executive Order 10340. . . . The order directed the Secretary of Commerce to take possession of most of the steel mills and keep them running. The Secretary immediately issued his own possessory orders, calling upon the presidents of the various seized companies to serve as operating managers for the United States. They were directed to carry on their activities in accordance with regulations and directions of the Secretary. The next morning the President sent a message to Congress reporting his action. Cong. Rec., April 9, 1952, p.3962. Twelve days later he sent a second message. Cong. Rec., April 21, 1952, p.4192. Congress has taken no action. . . .

The President's power, if any, to issue the order must stem either from an act of Congress or from the Constitution itself. There is no statute that expressly authorizes the President to take possession of property as he did here. Nor is there any act of Congress to which our attention has been directed from which such a power can fairly be implied. Indeed, we do not understand the Government to rely on statutory authorization for this seizure. There are two statutes which do authorize the President to take both personal and real property under certain conditions. However, the Government admits that these conditions were not met and that the President's order was not rooted in either of the statutes. The Government refers to the seizure provisions of one of these statutes (§201(b) of the Defense Production Act) as "much too cumbersome, involved, and time-consuming for the crisis which was at hand."

Moreover, the use of the seizure technique to solve labor disputes in order to prevent work stoppages was not only unauthorized by any congressional enactment; prior to this controversy, Congress had refused to adopt that method of settling labor disputes. When the Taft-Hartley Act was under consideration in 1947, Congress rejected an amendment which would have authorized such governmental seizures in cases of emergency. Apparently it was thought that the technique of seizure, like that of compulsory arbitration, would interfere with the process of collective bargaining. Consequently, the plan Congress adopted in that Act did not provide for seizure under any circumstances. Instead, the plan sought to bring about settlements by use of the customary devices of mediation, conciliation, investigation by boards of inquiry, and public reports. In some instances temporary injunctions were authorized to provide cooling-off periods. All this failing, unions were left free to strike after a secret vote by employees as to whether they wished to accept their employers' final settlement offer.

It is clear that if the President had authority to issue the order he did, it must be found in some provision of the Constitution. And it is not claimed that express constitutional language grants this power to the President. The contention is that presidential power should be implied from the aggregate of his powers under the Constitution. Particular reliance is placed on provisions in Article II which say that "The executive Power shall be vested in a President . . ."; that "he shall take Care that the Laws be faithfully executed"; and that he "shall be Commander in Chief of the Army and Navy of the United States."

The order cannot properly be sustained as an exercise of the President's military power as Commander in Chief of the Armed Forces. The Government attempts to do so by citing a number of cases upholding broad powers in military command-ers engaged in day-to-day fighting in a theater of war. Such cases need not concern us here. Even though "theater of war" be an expanding concept, we cannot with faithfulness to our constitutional system hold that the Commander in Chief of the Armed Forces has the ultimate power as such to take possession of private property in order to keep labor disputes from stopping production. This is a job for the Na-tion's lawmakers, not for its military authorities.

Nor can the seizure order be sustained because of the several constitutional provisions that grant executive power to the President. In the framework of our Constitution, the President's power to see that the laws are faithfully executed re-futes the idea that he is to be a lawmaker. The Constitution limits his functions in the lawmaking process to the recommending of laws he thinks wise and the vetoing of laws he thinks bad. And the Constitution is neither silent nor equivocal about who shall make laws which the President is to execute. The first section of the first article says that "All legislative Powers herein granted shall be vested in a Congress of the United States. . . ." After granting many powers to the Congress, Article I goes on to provide that Congress may "make all Laws which shall be necessary and proper for carrying into Execution the foregoing Powers, and all other Powers vested by this Constitution in the Government of the United States, or in any Department or Officer thereof."

The President's order does not direct that a congressional policy be executed in a manner prescribed by Congress — it directs that a presidential policy be exe-cuted in a manner prescribed by the President. The preamble of the order itself, like that of many statutes, sets out reasons why the President believes certain policies should be adopted, proclaims these policies as rules of conduct to be followed, and again, like a statute, authorizes a government official to promulgate additional rules and regulations consistent with the policy proclaimed and needed to carry that pol-icy into execution. The power of Congress to adopt such public policies as those pro-claimed by the order is beyond question. It can authorize the taking of private prop-erty for public use. It can make laws regulating the relationships between employers and employees, prescribing rules designed to settle labor disputes, and fixing wages and working conditions in certain fields of our economy. The Constitution does not subject this lawmaking power of Congress to presidential or military supervision or control. . . .

Mr. Justice JACKSON, concurring in the judgment and opinion of the Court.

. . . A judge, like an executive adviser, may be surprised at the poverty of really useful and unambiguous authority applicable to concrete problems of executive power as they actually present themselves. Just what our forefathers did envision, or would have envisioned had they foreseen modern conditions, must be divined from materials almost as enigmatic as the dreams Joseph was called upon to interpret for Pharaoh. A century and a half of partisan debate and scholarly speculation yields no net result but only supplies more or less apt quotations from respected sources on each side of any question. They largely cancel each other. And court decisions are indecisive because of the judicial practice of dealing with the largest questions in the most narrow way.

The actual art of governing under our Constitution does not and cannot con-form to judicial definitions of the power of any of its branches based on isolated clauses or even single Articles torn from context. While the Constitution diffuses power the better to secure liberty, it also contemplates that practice will integrate the dispersed powers into a workable government. It enjoins upon its branches separateness but interdependence, autonomy but reciprocity. Presidential powers are not fixed but fluctuate, depending upon their disjunction or conjunction with those of Congress. We may well begin by a somewhat over-simplified grouping of practical situations in which a President may doubt, or others may challenge, his powers, and by distinguishing roughly the legal consequences of this factor of relativity.

1. When the President acts pursuant to an express or implied authorization of Congress, his authority is at its maximum, for it includes all that he possesses in his own right plus all that Congress can delegate[2]. In these circumstances, and in these only, may he be said (for what it may be worth) to personify the federal sovereignty. If his act is held unconstitutional under these circumstances, it usually means that the Federal Government as an undivided whole lacks power. A seizure executed by the President pursuant to an Act of Congress would be supported by the strongest of presumptions and the widest latitude of judicial interpretation, and the burden of persuasion would rest heavily upon any who might attack it.

2. When the President acts in absence of either a congressional grant or denial of authority, he can only rely upon his own independent powers, but there is a zone of twilight in which he and Congress may have concurrent authority, or in which its distribution is uncertain. Therefore, congressional inertia, indifference or quiescence may sometimes, at least as a practical matter, enable, if not invite, measures on independent presidential responsibility. In this area, any actual test of power is likely to depend on the imperatives of events and contemporary imponderables rather than on abstract theories of law.

3. When the President takes measures incompatible with the expressed or implied will of Congress, his power is at its lowest ebb, for then he can rely only upon his own constitutional powers minus any constitutional powers of Congress over the matter. Courts can sustain exclusive presidential control in such a case only by disabling the Congress from acting upon the subject. Presidential claim to a power at once so conclusive and preclusive must be scrutinized with caution, for what is at stake is the equilibrium established by our constitutional system.

Into which of these classifications does this executive seizure of the steel industry fit? It is eliminated from the first by admission, for it is conceded that no congressional authorization exists for this seizure. . . .

Can it then be defended under flexible tests available to the second category? It seems clearly eliminated from that class because Congress has not left seizure of private property an open field but has covered it by three statutory policies inconsistent with this seizure. In cases where the purpose is to supply needs of the Government itself, two courses are provided: one, seizure of a plant which fails to

---

2. It is in this class of cases that we find the broadest recent statements of presidential power, including those relied on here. United States v. Curtiss-Wright Corp., 299 U.S. 304, involved, not the question of the President's power to act without congressional authority, but the question of his right to act under and in accord with an Act of Congress. . . .

That case does not solve the present controversy. It recognized internal and external affairs as being in separate categories, and held that the strict limitation upon congressional delegations of power to the President over internal affairs does not apply with respect to delegations of power in external affairs. It was intimated that the President might act in external affairs without congressional authority, but not that he might act contrary to an Act of Congress. . . .

comply with obligatory orders placed by the Government; another, condemnation of facilities, including temporary use under the power of eminent domain. The third is applicable where it is the general economy of the country that is to be protected rather than exclusive governmental interests. None of these were invoked. In choosing a different and inconsistent way of his own, the President cannot claim that it is necessitated or invited by failure of Congress to legislate upon the occasions, grounds and methods for seizure of industrial properties.

This leaves the current seizure to be justified only by the severe tests under the third grouping, where it can be supported only by any remainder of executive power after subtraction of such powers as Congress may have over the subject. In short, we can sustain the President only by holding that seizure of such strike-bound industries is within his domain and beyond control by Congress. Thus, this Court's first review of such seizures occurs under circumstances which leave presidential power most vulnerable to attack and in the least favorable of possible constitutional postures.

I did not suppose, and I am not persuaded, that history leaves it open to question, at least in the courts, that the executive branch, like the Federal Government as a whole, possesses only delegated powers. The purpose of the Constitution was not only to grant power, but to keep it from getting out of hand. However, because the President does not enjoy unmentioned powers does not mean that the mentioned ones should be narrowed by a niggardly construction. Some clauses could be made almost unworkable, as well as immutable, by refusal to indulge some latitude of interpretation for changing times. I have heretofore, and do now, give to the enumerated powers the scope and elasticity afforded by what seem to be reasonable, practical implications instead of the rigidity dictated by a doctrinaire textualism.

The Solicitor General seeks the power of seizure in three clauses of the Executive Article, the first reading, "The executive Power shall be vested in a President of the United States of America." Lest I be thought to exaggerate, I quote the interpretation which his brief puts upon it: "In our view, this clause constitutes a grant of all the executive powers of which the Government is capable." If that be true, it is difficult to see why the forefathers bothered to add several specific items, including some trifling ones.[9]

The example of such unlimited executive power that must have most impressed the forefathers was the prerogative exercised by George III, and the description of its evils in the Declaration of Independence leads me to doubt that they were creating their new Executive in his image. Continental European examples were no more appealing. And if we seek instruction from our own times, we can match it only from the executive powers in those governments we disparagingly describe as totalitarian. I cannot accept the view that this clause is a grant in bulk of all conceivable executive power but regard it as an allocation to the presidential office of the generic powers thereafter stated.

The clause on which the Government next relies is that "The President shall be Commander in Chief of the Army and Navy of the United States. . . ." These cryptic words have given rise to some of the most persistent controversies in our

---

9. ". . . he may require the Opinion, in writing, of the principal Officer in each of the executive Departments, upon any Subject relating to the Duties of their respective Offices. . . ." U.S. Const., Art. II, §2. He " . . . shall Commission all the Officers of the United States." U.S. Const., Art. II, §3. Matters such as those would seem to be inherent in the Executive if anything is.

constitutional history. Of course, they imply something more than an empty title. But just what authority goes with the name has plagued presidential advisers who would not waive or narrow it by nonassertion yet cannot say where it begins or ends. It undoubtedly puts the Nation's armed forces under presidential command. Hence, this loose appellation is sometimes advanced as support for any presidential action, internal or external, involving use of force, the idea being that it vests power to do anything, anywhere, that can be done with an army or navy.

That seems to be the logic of an argument tendered at our bar — that the President having, on his own responsibility, sent American troops abroad derives from that act "affirmative power" to seize the means of producing a supply of steel for them. To quote, "Perhaps the most forceful illustration of the scope of Presidential power in this connection is the fact that American troops in Korea, whose safety and effectiveness are so directly involved here, were sent to the field by an exercise of the President's constitutional powers." Thus, it is said, he has invested himself with "war powers."

I cannot foresee all that it might entail if the Court should indorse this argument. Nothing in our Constitution is plainer than that declaration of a war is entrusted only to Congress. Of course, a state of war may in fact exist without a formal declaration. But no doctrine that the Court could promulgate would seem to me more sinister and alarming than that a President whose conduct of foreign affairs is so largely uncontrolled, and often even is unknown, can vastly enlarge his mastery over the internal affairs of the country by his own commitment of the Nation's armed forces to some foreign venture. . . .

The Solicitor General lastly grounds support of the seizure upon nebulous, inherent powers never expressly granted but said to have accrued to the office from the customs and claims of preceding administrations. The plea is for a resulting power to deal with a crisis or an emergency according to the necessities of the case, the unarticulated assumption being that necessity knows no law.

Loose and irresponsible use of adjectives colors all non-legal and much legal discussion of presidential powers. "Inherent" powers, "implied" powers, "incidental" powers, "plenary" powers, "war" powers and "emergency" powers are used, often interchangeably and without fixed or ascertainable meanings.

The vagueness and generality of the clauses that set forth presidential powers afford a plausible basis for pressures within and without an administration for presidential action beyond that supported by those whose responsibility it is to defend his actions in court. The claim of inherent and unrestricted presidential powers has long been a persuasive dialectical weapon in political controversy. While it is not surprising that counsel should grasp support from such unadjudicated claims of power, a judge cannot accept self-serving press statements of the attorney for one of the interested parties as authority in answering a constitutional question, even if the advocate was himself. But prudence has counseled that actual reliance on such nebulous claims stop short of provoking a judicial test.

The Solicitor General, acknowledging that Congress has never authorized the seizure here, says practice of prior Presidents has authorized it. He seeks color of legality from claimed executive precedents. . . .

The appeal, however, that we declare the existence of inherent powers *ex necessitate* to meet an emergency asks us to do what many think would be wise, although it is something the forefathers omitted. They knew what emergencies were, knew the pressures they engender for authoritative action, knew, too, how they afford a ready pretext for usurpation. We may also suspect that they suspected that emergency powers would tend to kindle emergencies. Aside from suspension of the privilege of the writ of habeas corpus in time of rebellion or invasion, when the public safety may require it, they made no express provision for exercise of extraordinary authority because of a crisis. I do not think we rightfully may so amend their work, and, if we could, I am not convinced it would be wise to do so. . . .

The Executive, except for recommendation and veto, has no legislative power. The executive action we have here originates in the individual will of the President and represents an exercise of authority without law. No one, perhaps not even the President, knows the limits of the power he may seek to exert in this instance and the parties affected cannot learn the limit of their rights. We do not know today what powers over labor or property would be claimed to flow from Government possession if we should legalize it, what rights to compensation would be claimed or recognized, or on what contingency it would end. With all its defects, delays and inconveniences, men have discovered no technique for long preserving free government except that the Executive be under the law, and that the law be made by parliamentary deliberations.

Such institutions may be destined to pass away. But it is the duty of the Court to be last, not first, to give them up.

[Concurring opinions of Justices Frankfurter, Douglas, Burton, and Clark, and dissenting opinions of Chief Justice Vinson and Justices Reed and Minton omitted.]

Notes and Questions

1. What was actually decided in *Curtiss-Wright*? Is the Court's effusive language on the subject of presidential power necessary to the decision? Wasn't this a case of congressional delegation of power rather than independent presidential power?

2. Does the Court's distinction in *Curtiss-Wright* between constitutional powers in the domestic and external realms make sense? How can courts tell whether a case raises an issue of domestic or external power? Couldn't *Curtiss-Wright* itself be characterized as a domestic case because it involved attempted sales by an American company and its U.S. citizen officers? In our increasingly globalized world, is the domestic/foreign distinction a tenable basis for such important differences in constitutional doctrine?

3. How tenable is the Court's claim in *Curtiss-Wright* that the foreign relations powers of the federal government are derived from a source other than the U.S. Constitution? Is this claim consistent with the idea of a limited national government regulated by a written Constitution? With the actual allocation of foreign relations powers in the Constitution itself? If the national government does have extra-constitutional foreign relations powers, what are they?

4. What are the implications of the Court's suggestion in *Curtiss-Wright* that international law notions of sovereignty are the source of the U.S. foreign relations power? International law might dictate that nationhood requires, for example, the ability to engage in international relations and make treaties. But does it also specify

the particular allocation of foreign relations power *within* a sovereign — for example, between political branches, or between national and sub-national governments? If international law notions of sovereignty provide the source for the national government's foreign relations powers, do they also provide limitations? For example, if nations are prohibited from engaging in certain acts, for example, waging aggressive war, does this mean that the U.S. government lacks the constitutional power to do so? In other words, does the Constitution require that the national government act as a *lawful sovereign?*

5. The steel seizure at issue in *Youngstown* took place in the midst of, and indeed in alleged furtherance of, the Korean War. Under the analysis in *Curtiss-Wright,* isn't the Korean War an "external affair" regarding which the President has plenary power? Why does the Court take such a different approach to constitutional limits in *Youngstown,* where the majority opinion does not even cite *Curtiss-Wright?* Are the holdings in *Curtiss-Wright* and *Youngstown* reconcilable, as Justice Jackson suggests in note 2 of his concurrence?

6. Justice Jackson's concurrence in *Youngstown,* especially its articulation of three categories of presidential power, has been very influential. Indeed, courts and commentators often give more weight to Jackson's concurrence than to the majority opinion. Why do you think this is so? How much guidance does Jackson's framework provide in ascertaining the scope of presidential power? Is it clear that President Truman's actions in *Youngstown* fell within the third category, as Jackson argues?

2.   *Executive Agreements*

International agreements concluded by the United States other than Article II treaties are generally referred to as "executive agreements." Those executive agreements that are based on congressionally delegated or statutory authority are often referred to as "congressional-executive agreements." Those executive agreements that are based on independent presidential constitutional authority are sometimes called "presidential executive agreements" or "sole executive agreements." The State Department has promulgated an internal regulation that describes the different kinds of executive agreement and the factors taken into account in choosing among them:

Department of State Circular 175

. . . There are three constitutional bases for international agreements other than treaties as set forth below. An international agreement may be concluded pursuant to one or more of these constitutional bases:

(1)   AGREEMENTS PURSUANT TO TREATY

The President may conclude an international agreement pursuant to a treaty brought into force with the advice and consent of the Senate, whose provisions constitute authorization for the agreement by the Executive without subsequent action by the Congress;

(2) AGREEMENTS PURSUANT TO LEGISLATION

The President may conclude an international agreement on the basis of existing leg-islation or subject to legislation to be enacted by the Congress; and

(3) AGREEMENTS PURSUANT TO THE CONSTITUTIONAL AUTHORITY OF THE PRESIDENT

The President may conclude an international agreement on any subject within his constitutional authority so long as the agreement is not inconsistent with legislation enacted by the Congress in the exercise of its constitutional authority. The constitu-tional authority for the President to conclude international agreements include:

(a) The President's authority as Chief Executive to represent the nation in for-eign affairs;

(b) The President's authority to receive ambassadors and other public ministers;

(c) The President's authority as "Commander-in-Chief"; and

(d) The President's authority to "take care that the laws be faithfully executed."

721.3   Considerations for Selecting Among Constitutionally Authorized Procedures

In determining a question as to the procedure which should be followed for any particular international agreement, due consideration is given to the following factors . . . :

a. The extent to which the agreement involves commitments or risks affecting the nation as a whole;

b. Whether the agreement is intended to affect State laws;

c. Whether the agreement can be given effect without the enactment of subse-quent legislation by the Congress;

d. Past United States practice with respect to similar agreements;

e. The preference of the Congress with respect to a particular type of agreement;

f. The degree of formality desired for an agreement;

g. The proposed duration of the agreement, the need for prompt conclusion of an agreement, and the desirability of concluding a routine or short-term agree-ment; and

h. The general international practice with respect to similar agreements.

Questions

1. How useful do you think the factors listed in Circular 175 are in actual situa-tions for selecting among the types of international agreement to use? Do these fac-tors adequately protect the constitutional powers of the Senate? Of the full congress? Can you prepare a more precise set of criteria or specify how the various factors should be balanced in particular cases?

2. What is the significance of Congress's enactment of the Case Act, excerpted in Chapter 2, for the validity of executive agreements? Is the Act constitutional? Judicially enforceable? A Senate study concludes that the Act "has been helpful in apprising Congress of executive agreements as defined by the Act," and that the Act "has contributed to improved relations between Congress and the executive branch in the area of executive agreements." See Congressional Research Service, Treaties and Other International Agreements: The Role of the United States Senate, S. Prt. 106-71, 106th Cong., 2d Sess., at 225 (2001). Between 1978 and 1999, more than 7,000 agreements were transmitted to Congress pursuant to the Act. See id. at 226-227.

The criteria for determining which agreements should or must be submitted to the Senate sometimes seem to be more political, depending on a calculation of the votes in Congress and the Senate, than legal or principled. On the other hand, precedent plays a highly significant role. The determining criteria in many cases seem to be historical: traditionally almost all agreements dealing with human rights, extradition, diplomatic and consular privileges, military alliances, war and peace, arms control, boundaries, immigration, intellectual property, taxation, and the environment have been submitted to the Senate as Article II treaties. Most, but not all, agreements to join international organizations have also been concluded under Article II. However, international agreements dealing with trade, finance, energy, fisheries, postal matters, and bilateral aviation relations have regularly been concluded as Congressional-Executive agreements. Senators have occasionally asserted that "major" agreements or "major military" agreements must be submitted to the Senate under Article II.

a. Congressional-Executive Agreements

Congressional-executive agreements are international agreements authorized in advance, or approved after the fact, by a majority of both houses of Congress. The decision below addresses a constitutional challenge to one such agreement — the North American Free Trade Agreement (NAFTA).

Made in the USA Foundation v. United States

U.S. District Court for the Northern District of Alabama
56 F. Supp. 2d 1226 (N.D. Ala. 1999), aff'd on other grounds,
242 F.3d 1300 (11th Cir. 2001)

ROBERT B. PROPST, District Judge. . . .
In 1990 the United States, Mexico and Canada initiated negotiations with the intention of creating a "free trade zone" through the elimination or reduction of tariffs and other barriers to trade. After two years of negotiations, the leaders of the three countries signed the North American Free Trade Agreement ("NAFTA" or the "Agreement") on December 17, 1992. Congress approved and implemented NAFTA on December 8, 1993 with the passage of NAFTA Implementation Act

("Implementation Act"), which was passed by a vote of 234 to 200 in the House and 61 to 38 in the Senate. The Implementation Act served two purposes, to "approve" NAFTA and to provide a series of laws to "locally" enforce NAFTA's provisions. The enactment of the Implementation Act brought to a close a lengthy period of rancorous debate over NAFTA. The instant suit seeks to reopen that debate by pulling back NAFTA's coat and demonstrating that the Agreement and Implementation Act stand on sand rather than on firm Constitutional ground. Brought to bear in this case is an almost century-long bout of Constitutional theorizing about whether the Treaty Clause, contained in Article II, Section 2 of the United States Constitution (the "Treaty Clause"), creates the exclusive means of making certain types of international agreements.

Neither NAFTA nor the Implementation Act were subjected to the procedures outlined in the Treaty Clause. The President purportedly negotiated and concluded NAFTA pursuant to his constitutional responsibility for conducting the foreign affairs of the United States and in accordance with the Omnibus Trade and Competitiveness Act of 1988, 19 U.S.C. §2901, et seq. ("Trade Act of 1988"), and the Trade Act of 1974, 19 U.S.C. §2101, et seq. ("Trade Act of 1974"), under the so-called "fast track" procedure. Congress then approved and implemented NAFTA by enacting the Implementation Act, allegedly pursuant to its power to legislate in the areas of tariffs and domestic and foreign commerce.

The plaintiffs contend that this failure to go through the Article II, Section 2, prerequisites renders the Agreement and, apparently, the Implementation Act, unconstitutional. The Government denies this . . . .

B.   THE EXCLUSIVITY OF THE TREATY CLAUSE

The Government argues that the Treaty Clause of Article II is not the exclusive means for entering into an international agreement such as NAFTA or for adopting legislation implementing such an agreement. To begin with, the Government notes that the plaintiffs concede the existence of some kinds of valid and binding international agreements that do not constitute Article II treaties. This concession, comments the Government, is unsurprising in light of the fact that there exist several types of non-Article II treaty international agreements that have been well-established as valid under United States law. Such agreements include: (1) congressional-executive agreements — agreements negotiated by the President that are either pre- or post-approved by a simple majority of Congress; (2) executive agreements authorized expressly or implicitly by an existing treaty; and (3) presidential or sole executive agreements — agreements concluded unilaterally by the President pursuant to his constitutional authority. The Government notes that nothing in the Constitutional text elevates the Article II treaty ratification process over Article I's law making powers. Plaintiffs' claims represent, according to the Government, nothing more than an attempt to engraft an artificial and illegitimate hierarchy onto the Constitution.

The plaintiffs argue that the Government's argument as to exclusivity is persuasive only to the extent that it promotes the position that some international agreements do not rise to the level of treaties and do not require approval of two-thirds of the Senate. They argue that acceptance of the executive agreement and/or the congressional-executive agreement as all-purpose alternatives to the Treaty Clause represents an acceptance of the principle that the Constitution may be amended without reference to Article V of the Constitution. They note that in the 1930's and 1940's when advocates of the congressional-executive agreement first garnered significant support for their use, there was a widespread recognition of the fact that in order to make the practice constitutional an amendment would be necessary. A movement in favor of such an amendment took place in 1943-45, but was abandoned when advocates decided that it was "ridiculous to suppose that two-thirds of the Senate would voluntarily surrender its treaty-making prerogatives by supporting a formal constitutional amendment." Thus, according to [Laurence H. Tribe, Taking Text and Structure Seriously: Reflections on the Free-Form Method in Constitutional Interpretation, 108 Harv. L. Rev. 1221 (1995)], rather than properly amending the Constitution, politicians and academics chose to ignore the intent of the Framers and historical precedent in favor of political prudence and "strategic compromise." Tribe at 1280-86.

The plaintiffs reject the Government's characterization of the broad powers of the President and Congress with respect to international agreement-making. They claim that the Government's description of the powers of the President is so broad as to leave nothing beyond the scope of unilateral executive agreements as long as such agreements deal with "foreign affairs." Similarly, the Government's characterization of Congress's power lacks any defined boundaries, and, in effect, amounts to a total interchangeability argument.

The parties' arguments addressing the extent to which the Treaty Clause represents an exclusive grant of authority can be more or less broken down into several sub-sections. The parties first address the text of the Constitution and the proper manner of examining that text. Next, they look at the intent of the Framers with respect to the relevant Constitutional provisions and the historical practices that have arisen out of those provisions. Finally, the parties examine the (allegedly) relevant federal court decisions.

1. Government's Textual Analysis with Respect to Exclusivity . . .

According to the Government, the text of the Constitution, as interpreted by the Supreme Court, allows for the utilization of executive agreements whenever there exists constitutional authority outside of the Treaty Clause allowing the President to negotiate and conclude an international agreement and allowing Congress to enact the legislation required for a given agreement's implementation. The Government, citing the Constitutional authority granted to both the President and Congress, and noting that the Supreme Court has characterized Congress's power to regulate "Commerce with foreign Nations" as "broad," "comprehensive," "plenary," "and "complete,"[267] argues that NAFTA and the Implementation Act fall squarely within the combined enumerated powers of the two political branches. Further, it argues that the Agreement and the Act stand at the intersection of Congress's and the President's power over foreign commerce and foreign affairs, respectively, and that each

---

267. United States v. 12 200-Ft. Reels of Super 8 MM. Film, 413 U.S. 123, 125-26 (1973) (citations and quotations omitted).

provision of the Implementation Act could, therefore, have been enacted in the absence of any agreement with Mexico and Canada.

While acknowledging that NAFTA could have been ratified as a treaty, the Government contends that the congressional-executive agreement process was certainly acceptable, that the Treaty Clause does not expressly prohibit the employment of an alternative procedure, and that the congressional-executive agreement method may have been the Constitutionally preferable method by which to approve of and implement NAFTA. Thus, the Supreme Court, in holding that a later act of Congress may override a treaty, stated that the House's action with respect to such legislation "does not render it less entitled to respect in the matter of its repeal or modification than a treaty . . . . If there be any difference in this regard, it would seem to be in favor of an act in which all three of the bodies [the President, House, and Senate] participate."[269]

2. Plaintiffs' Textually-Based Exclusivity Argument

The plaintiffs argue that the text of the Constitution supports their contention that international agreements that have the substance of a treaty cannot be adopted without the approval of two-thirds of the Senate. In doing so, they begin by contending that the most "natural" reading of the Treaty Clause is one that reads the clause as creating the exclusive method by which to conclude that certain class of international agreements called "treaties." They, like Tribe, argue that basic provisions of the Constitution that define the locus of power for certain governmental actions are properly construed as creating the exclusive means by which to exercise those powers. Both the plaintiffs and Tribe assert that the Treaty Clause represents such a provision. They therefore argue that any other reading of the Treaty Clause renders it a "dead letter," and allows the corruption of one of the Constitution's fundamental provisions. . . .

D. FIFTH AND FINAL CONCLUSION OF THE COURT

The most significant issue before the court is whether the Treaty Clause is an exclusive means of making an international agreement under the circumstances of this case. It is clear that there is no explicit language in the Constitution which makes the Treaty Clause exclusive as to all international agreements. On the other hand, the broad breadth of the Commerce Clause, particularly the Foreign Commerce Clause, has been repeatedly emphasized. The inability of the Congress under the Articles of Confederation to regulate commerce was one of the main weaknesses which led to the call of the Constitutional Convention. The Annapolis Convention of 1786 was called to discuss problems which had resulted from this weakness. This meeting, in turn, led to the Constitutional Convention. The Commerce Clause was clearly intended to address this concern. The "Power" to regulate commerce, foreign and interstate and with Indian Tribes, was specifically given to Congress. The Treaty Clause makes no specific reference to commerce of any type. . . .

---

269. Head Money Cases, 112 U.S. 580, 599 (1884).

Thus, while the reason(s) for the existence and adoption of the Treaty Clause and its scope are debatable, the plenary scope of the Commerce Clause is clear. There exists no reason to apply a limiting construction upon the Foreign Commerce Clause or to assume that the Clause was not meant to give Congress the power to approve those agreements that are "necessary and proper" in regulating foreign commerce. It is impossible to definitively conclude that the Framers intended the regulation of foreign commerce to be subject to the rigors of the Treaty Clause procedure when commercial agreements with foreign nations are involved. Given the Court's language in Gibbons v. Ogden, the power of Congress to regulate foreign commerce with foreign nations is so extensive that it is reasonably arguable, as earlier discussed, that no "treaty" affecting commerce with foreign nations is valid unless adopted by Congress as a whole. In the absence of specific limiting language in or relating to the Treaty Clause, I am led to conclude that the Foreign Commerce power of Congress is at least concurrent with the Treaty Clause power when an agreement, as is the case here, is dominated by provisions specifically related to foreign commerce and has other provisions which are reasonably "necessary and proper" for "carrying all others into execution." . . . Further, I note that the President, in negotiating the Agreement in connection with the fast track legislation, was acting pursuant to his constitutional responsibility for conducting the Nation's foreign affairs and pursuant to a grant of authority from Congress.[352]

The foregoing, considered in light of at least some degree of presumption of constitutionality to which the Agreement is entitled, leads me to ultimately conclude that NAFTA and the Implementation Act were made and approved in a constitutional manner.[354] One thing is clear. This court does not have jurisdiction to review the wisdom of NAFTA or to determine whether it is in the best interest of the Nation.

Notes and Questions

1. There have been congressional-executive agreements since early in U.S. history. In 1792, for example, Congress authorized the Postmaster General to conclude international agreements concerning the exchange of mail. See Act of Feb. 20, 1792, ch. 7, §26, 1 Stat. 232, 239. Additional examples are discussed by the court in

---

352. Again, according to *Youngstown*, the President's power is at its pinnacle when he acts in concert with Congress. . . .

354. In reaching my conclusion, I do not accept a theory of total interchangeability. As the Supreme Court has stated, "it is obvious that there may be matters of the sharpest exigency for the national well being that an act of Congress could not deal with but that a treaty followed by such an act could." Missouri v. Holland, 252 U.S. 416, 433 (1920). Further, the Justice Department has stated that it does not disagree with the premise that some agreements with foreign nations "may have to be ratified as treaties." Memorandum, Walter Dellinger, Asst. Atty. Gen. to Ambassador Michael Kantor, November 22, 1994. Similarly, while purportedly speaking on behalf of the Senate Judiciary Committee, Senator Dirksen, in 1956, rejected the "doctrine that treaties and executive agreements are wholly interchangeable." Senate Rep. No. 1716, 84th Congress, 2nd Session 9 (1956). Thus, there may exist circumstances where the procedures outlined in the Treaty Clause must be adhered to in order to adopt an international agreement. However, it is not entirely clear what those circumstances are. In any case, in light of Congress's enumerated powers in the areas dealt with by NAFTA, I conclude that such circumstances are not present in this case. My opinion is limited to the area of foreign commerce and related enumerated powers coupled with Presidential power(s) and the powers under the Necessary and Proper Clause.

the *Made in the USA Foundation* decision excerpted above. Most of the congressional-executive agreements before World War II, like the postal agreements, involved *ex ante* delegations of authority by Congress rather than *ex post* approval by Congress of agreements already negotiated. Since the war, however, many congressional-executive agreements have involved *ex post* approvals. Some of these agreements have been quite significant. Famous examples of congressional-executive agreements include the Bretton Woods Agreement (which established the International Monetary Fund and the World Bank), the GATT and NAFTA trade agreements, the SALT I agreement limiting offensive weapons, and the U.N. Headquarters Agreement. Is there constitutional significance in the distinction between *ex ante* and *ex post* congressional-executive agreements? Is one more legitimate than the other?

2. During the period 1789-1839, the United States entered into 60 treaties and 27 nontreaty international agreements (a category that includes congressional-executive agreements and presidential executive agreements). From 1939-1989, the United States entered into 702 treaties and 11,698 nontreaty agreements. See Congressional Research Service, Treaties and Other International Agreements: The Role of the United States Senate, S. Prt. 106-71, 106th Cong., 2d Sess., at 39 (2001). Most of these nontreaty agreements were congressional-executive agreements: one study found that 88.3 percent of the nontreaty agreements between 1946 and 1972 were congressional-executive agreements. See id. at 41. Why was there such a substantial increase in the relative use of congressional-executive agreements? Is this related to the mid-century rise in Executive Branch power in foreign affairs? Might it reflect in part the increasing number and complexity of U.S. government activities abroad? What if anything does the frequent use of congressional-executive agreements suggest about their constitutionality? Is it relevant that congressional-executive agreements have not generated significant inter-branch conflict?

3. Although the Supreme Court has never directly addressed the constitutionality of congressional-executive agreements, it has appeared to assume their validity in several decisions. In Weinberger v. Rossi, 456 U.S. 25 (1982), for example, the Court interpreted the word "treaty" in an employment discrimination statute as referring not only to Article II treaties but also congressional-executive agreements. The Court noted that the United States has entered into numerous such agreements, that they are binding on the United States, and that Congress sometimes uses the word treaty to refer to them. See also B. Altman & Co. v. United States, 224 U.S. 583 (1912) (construing the word "treaty" in a jurisdictional statute as including congressional-executive agreements); Field v. Clark, 143 U.S. 649 (1892) (upholding congressional delegation of tariff authority to the Executive Branch and citing, among other things, the history of congressional authorizations of executive trade agreements).

4. What does the text of the Constitution suggest about the validity of congressional-executive agreements? Does the Article II treaty clause indicate that all international agreements entered into by the United States must go through the two-thirds senatorial advice and consent process? Does it indicate that at least *some* international agreements must go through this process? Do Congress's Article I powers provide a basis for congressional-executive agreements? Is Congress's power to make legislation on certain subjects tantamount to a power to approve international agreements on those subjects? Of what relevance to this issue is Congress's

Necessary and Proper power? Are congressional-executive agreements more "democratic" than treaties? If so, does this matter?

5. Assuming congressional-executive agreements are valid, are they completely interchangeable with treaties? In other words, could any U.S. international agreement be entered into by either method? The Restatement (Third) of Foreign Relations Law maintains that "the prevailing view is that the Congressional-Executive agreement can be used as an alternative to the treaty method in every instance," and adds that "which procedure should be used is a political judgment, made in the first instance by the President." Restatement (Third) of Foreign Relations Law Section 303 cmt. *e* (1987). Several scholars have recently questioned this conventional wisdom, arguing in various (and not always consistent) ways that treaties and congressional-executive agreements are not, and should not be, perfectly interchangeable. See, for example, Joel R. Paul, The Geopolitical Constitution: Executive Expediency and Executive Agreements, 86 Cal. L. Rev. 671 (1998); Peter J. Spiro, Constitutional Method and the Great Treaty Debate, 79 Tex. L. Rev. 961 (2001); and John C. Yoo, Laws as Treaties?: The Constitutionality of Congressional-Executive Agreements, 99 Mich. L. Rev. 757 (2001).

6. Does interchangeability mean that if an international agreement fails to obtain the required two-thirds senatorial consent in the Article II process, the President can simply resubmit it to Congress for a majority vote? Or must the President choose one method and stick to it? Consider the fate of the Comprehensive Test Ban Treaty. In October 1999, the Senate declined to give the requisite two-thirds consent to the treaty. Fifty-one senators voted against the treaty, forty-eight in its favor. If President Clinton could have persuaded three "no" votes to switch (thereby giving him a majority of support in the Senate), could he have resubmitted the treaty to the House and Senate as a congressional-executive agreement?

7. Assuming that every type of international agreement that could be done by treaty could also be done by congressional-executive agreement, are the two forms of international agreement treated alike for other purposes? For example, does the analysis of Missouri v. Holland, excerpted above, apply to congressional-executive agreements? Do congressional-executive agreements warrant the same degree of judicial deference to Executive Branch interpretation as treaties? Do the same rules of self-execution that apply to treaties also apply to congressional-executive agreements? How about the last-in-time rule? Do the same separation of powers limitations that apply to treaties (such as the bar on treaties that proscribe criminal penalties) apply to congressional-executive agreements?

8. In 1997, President Clinton agreed to submit the Flank Agreement, an update of the Treaty on Armed Conventional Forces in Europe ('CFE Treaty'), to the Senate for its Article II consent. This action marked an abandonment of an earlier decision to seek only a congressional majority approval for the Flank Agreement. See Phillip R. Trimble & Alexander W. Koff, All Fall Down: The Treaty Power in the Clinton Administration, 16 Berkeley J. Intl. L. 55 (1998). In connection with the original CFE Treaty, the Senate had attached, as a condition of its consent, a declaration stating that international agreements that "reduce or limit the armed forces or armaments of the United States in a militarily significant manner" can be approved only pursuant to the Article II treaty process. See 137 Cong. Rec. S17846 (daily ed. Nov. 23, 1991). In a letter to the Senate, a presidential advisor noted that submission of the agreement for Senate approval was "without prejudice to its legal position

vis-à-vis the approval options we believe are available to us." Letter from Samuel R. Berger, Assistant to the President for National Security Affairs, to Trent Lott, Majority Leader of the Senate, dated March 25, 1997, quoted in The Arms Control Reporter 1997 at 603.D.45. What does this episode teach us about the validity of congressional-executive agreements? About the limits on those agreements? About how the Senate's treaty prerogatives can be enforced? About the role of courts in policing these issues?

9. The plaintiffs in the *Made in the USA Foundation* case appealed the district court's decision to the Eleventh Circuit Court of Appeals, which dismissed the appeal without reaching the merits. See 242 F.3d 1300 (11th Cir. 2001). Although the Eleventh Circuit noted that "certain international agreements may well require Senate ratification as treaties through the constitutionally-mandated procedures of Art. II, §2," id. at 1302, it declined to adjudicate the challenge to NAFTA, concluding that, at least in the context of that case, "the issue of what kinds of agreements require Senate ratification pursuant to the Art. II, §2 procedures presents a nonjusticiable political question." Id. at 1319.

10. In recent years scholars have engaged in a lively debate about the legitimacy of congressional-executive agreements. Compare, for example, Bruce Ackerman & David Golove, Is NAFTA Constitutional?, 108 Harv. L. Rev. 799 (1995), and David Golove, Against Free-Form Formalism, 73 N.Y.U. L. Rev. 1791 (1998), with Laurence H. Tribe, Taking Text and Structure Seriously: Reflections on the Free-Form Method in Constitutional Interpretation, 108 Harv. L. Rev. 1221 (1995).

b. Presidential Executive Agreements

Some of the most contentious foreign affairs cases have involved presidential executive agreements. In these situations the President has chosen not to use the procedure established in Article II of the Constitution for treaties and does not have a delegation of authority or other expression of support from Congress. Presidential executive agreements have been used infrequently (accounting for less than 10 percent of all U.S. international agreements). However, they have been used to resolve major diplomatic problems (like the Iran hostage crisis) where the President for whatever reason felt that congressional support was either not necessary or not feasible.

To date Congress has not attempted to limit this presidential power, although it has required that presidential executive agreements be reported to it after the fact (recall the Case Act). Most of these agreements deal with technical or minor matters, like consulting with other governments in specific circumstances and the many "housekeeping" aspects of government operations. Occasionally, however, the President has concluded a presidential executive agreement that affects private causes of action.

In both United States v. Belmont, 301 U.S. 324 (1937), and United States v. Pink, 315 U.S. 203 (1942), the Supreme Court upheld the validity of a presidential executive agreement against the claim that Article II required the participation of the Senate for the conclusion of such agreements. Moreover, the Court held in both cases that the executive agreement in question superseded the otherwise applicable state law.

United States v. Pink

U.S. Supreme Court
315 U.S. 203 (1942)

[In this century revolutionary governments have frequently nationalized property, including American property in the nationalizing State and property of citizens and corporations of the nationalizing State in the United States. Under the U.S. view of international law, the nationalizing State is under a duty to pay compensation to the United States to recompense the injuries done to U.S. nationals. The United States has typically reacted to confiscatory nationalizations by revolutionary governments by freezing the assets of those governments and their nationals in the United States. The United States and the revolutionary government frequently have settled the outstanding international claims and other issues through a "lump sum claims agreement" under which, inter alia, the revolutionary government agrees to pay compensation to the United States in respect of the nationalized property of U.S. citizens. The amount paid has often been the same as the amount of frozen assets held in the United States. After the 1917 Revolution, the Soviet government nationalized private property, including the First Russian Insurance Co., which had a branch in New York. Under New York law the Soviet nationalization decree arguably would not be recognized by New York State courts because it would violate New York State public policy. Therefore the Soviet government's ownership claim would not be enforced in the New York courts. In 1933 the United States agreed to grant diplomatic recognition to the Soviet government, and the Soviets assigned to the U.S. government its claims to certain nationalized assets in the United States, including the assets of the nationalized First Russian Insurance Co. The U.S. government in turn planned to use those assets to pay American nationals whose property in Russia had been seized by the Soviets. The agreement was called the Litvinov Assignment, and it was a presidential executive agreement.

In this case the U.S. government sued the insurance commissioner of New York to claim, as successor to the Soviet government, the New York assets of the First Russian Insurance Co. (even though the Soviet government presumably could not have successfully maintained such an action). The other claimants to the assets were foreign creditors of the company.]

Mr. Justice DOUGLAS delivered the opinion of the Court. . . .

At the outset, it should be noted that, so far as appears, all creditors whose claims arose out of dealings with the New York branch have been paid. Thus we are not faced with the question whether New York's policy of protecting the so-called local creditors by giving them priority in the assets deposited with the State should be recognized within the rule of Clark v. Williard, 294 U.S. 211, or should yield to the Federal policy expressed in the international compact or agreement. We intimate no opinion on that question. The contest here is between the United States and creditors of the Russian corporation who, we assume, are not citizens of this country and whose claims did not arise out of transactions with the New York branch. The United States is seeking to protect not only claims which it holds but also claims of its nationals [against the Soviet Union in respect of their nationalized property]. Such claims did not arise out of transactions with this Russian corporation; they are, however, claims against Russia or its nationals. The existence of such claims and

their non-payment had for years been one of the barriers to recognition of the Soviet regime by the Executive Department. The purpose of the discussions leading to
the policy of recognition was to resolve "all questions outstanding" between the two
nations. Settlement of all American claims against Russia was one method of removing some of the prior objections to recognition based on the Soviet policy of nationalization. The Litvinov Assignment was not only part and parcel of the new policy of recognition, it was also the method adopted by the Executive Department for
alleviating in this country the rigors of nationalization. Congress tacitly recognized
that policy. Acting in anticipation of the realization of funds under the Litvinov
Assignment, it authorized the appointment of a Commissioner to determine the
claims of American nationals against the Soviet Government. Joint Resolution of
August 4, 1939, 53 Stat. 1199 [under which Congress provided a statutory procedure for determining the value of those claims and for paying those claims out of
the Soviet assets transferred to the United States government under the Litvinov
Assignment]. . . .

If the priority had been accorded American claims by treaty with Russia, there
would be no doubt as to its validity. The same result obtains here. The powers of the
President in the conduct of foreign relations included the power, without consent
of the Senate, to determine the public policy of the United States with respect to the
Russian nationalization decrees. "What government is to be regarded here as representative of a foreign sovereign state is a political rather than a judicial question,
and is to be determined by the political department of the government." Guaranty
Trust Co. v. United States, [304 U.S. 126, 137 (1938)]. That authority is not limited
to a determination of the government to be recognized. It includes the power to determine the policy which is to govern the question of recognition. Objections to the
underlying policy as well as objections to recognition are to be addressed to the political department and not to the courts. As we have noted, this Court in the *Belmont*
case recognized that the Litvinov Assignment was an international compact which
did not require the participation of the Senate. It stated: "There are many such compacts, of which a protocol, a modus vivendi, a postal convention, and agreements
like that now under consideration are illustrations." Recognition is not always absolute; it is sometimes conditional. Power to remove such obstacles to full recognition as settlement of claims of our nationals certainly is a modest implied power of
the President who is the "sole organ of the federal government in the field of international relations." United States v. Curtiss-Wright Corp. Effectiveness in handling
the delicate problems of foreign relations requires no less. Unless such a power exists, the power of recognition might be thwarted or seriously diluted. No such obstacle can be placed in the way of rehabilitation of relations between this country
and another nation, unless the historic conception of the powers and responsibilities of the President in the conduct of foreign affairs is to be drastically revised. It
was the judgment of the political department that full recognition of the Soviet Government required the settlement of all outstanding problems including the claims
of our nationals. Recognition and the Litvinov Assignment were interdependent.
We would usurp the executive function if we held that that decision was not final and
conclusive in the courts.

"All constitutional acts of power, whether in the executive or in the judicial department, have as much legal validity and obligation as if they proceeded from the
legislature, . . ." The Federalist, No. 64. A treaty is a "Law of the Land" under the

supremacy clause (Art. VI, Cl. 2) of the Constitution. Such international compacts and agreements as the Litvinov Assignment have a similar dignity. . . .

[Concurring opinion of Justice Frankfurter and dissenting opinion of Chief Justice Stone and Justice Robert omitted.]

The legal authority of presidential executive agreements was bolstered in the following case, which grew out of the 1979 Iranian revolution.

Dames & Moore v. Regan

U.S. Supreme Court
453 U.S. 654 (1981)

[On November 4, 1979, Iranian militants seized the U.S. embassy in Tehran and began holding the U.S. diplomatic personnel there as hostages. The revolutionary Iranian government made no effort to stop the militants and soon sided with them in negotiations. The government also repudiated its predecessor government's contracts with U.S. companies. Acting pursuant to the International Emergency Economic Powers Act (IEEPA), President Carter quickly blocked the removal or transfer of Iranian assets held within the jurisdiction of the United States. Carter subsequently issued orders authorizing the initiation of judicial proceedings in U.S. courts against Iran. These orders allowed for the entry of a pre-judgment attachment in such proceedings, but not a final judgment. After the issuance of these orders, Dames & Moore filed suit against Iran and various Iranian entities seeking the recovery of money owed to its subsidiary under a service contract, and it obtained a pre-judgment attachment of the property of certain Iranian banks. On January 20, 1981, the U.S. hostages were released by Iran pursuant to the Algiers Accords, a presidential executive agreement. Under the Accords, the United States agreed to "terminate all legal proceedings in United States courts involving claims of United States persons and institutions against Iran and its state enterprises, to nullify all attachments and judgments obtained therein, to prohibit all further litigation based on such claims, and to bring about the termination of such claims through binding arbitration [before a special tribunal to be established in the Hague]." Immediately before leaving office, President Carter issued executive orders implementing the terms of the Accords. President Reagan subsequently issued an executive order in which he reaffirmed Carter's orders and "suspended" all "claims which may be presented to the . . . Tribunal" and provided that such claims "shall have no legal effect in any action now pending in any court of the United States." Dames & Moore challenged the validity of the Carter and Reagan executive orders.]

Justice REHNQUIST delivered the opinion of the Court. . . .

II

The parties and the lower courts, confronted with the instant questions, have all agreed that much relevant analysis is contained in Youngstown Sheet & Tube Co. v. Sawyer, 343 U.S. 579 (1952). . . .

Although we have in the past found and do today find Justice Jackson's classification of executive actions into three general categories analytically useful, we should be mindful of Justice Holmes' admonition, quoted by Justice Frankfurter in *Youngstown,* supra, at 597 (concurring opinion), that "[t]he great ordinances of the Constitution do not establish and divide fields of black and white." Justice Jackson himself recognized that his three categories represented "a somewhat over-simplified grouping," and it is doubtless the case that executive action in any particular instance falls, not neatly in one of three pigeonholes, but rather at some point along a spectrum running from explicit congressional authorization to explicit congressional prohibition. This is particularly true as respects cases such as the one before us, involving responses to international crises the nature of which Congress can hardly have been expected to anticipate in any detail. . . .

IV

Although we have concluded that the IEEPA [International Emergency Economic Powers Act] constitutes specific congressional authorization to the President to nullify the attachments and order the transfer of Iranian assets, there remains the question of the President's authority to suspend claims pending in American courts. Such claims have, of course, an existence apart from the attachments which accompanied them. In terminating these claims through Executive Order No. 12294, the President purported to act under authority of both the IEEPA and 22 U.S.C. §1732, the so-called "Hostage Act."[7]

We conclude that although the IEEPA authorized the nullification of the attachments, it cannot be read to authorize the suspension of the claims. The claims of American citizens against Iran are not in themselves transactions involving Iranian property or efforts to exercise any rights with respect to such property. An in personam lawsuit, although it might eventually be reduced to judgment and that judgment might be executed upon, is an effort to establish liability and fix damages and does not focus on any particular property within the jurisdiction. The terms of the IEEPA therefore do not authorize the President to suspend claims in American courts. This is the view of all the courts which have considered the question.

The Hostage Act, passed in 1868, provides:

> Whenever it is made known to the President that any citizen of the United States has been unjustly deprived of his liberty by or under the authority of any foreign government, . . . the President shall use such means, not amounting to acts of war, as he may think necessary and proper to obtain or effectuate [their] release. . . .

We are reluctant to conclude that this provision constitutes specific authorization to the President to suspend claims in American courts. Although the broad language of the Hostage Act suggests it may cover this case, there are several difficulties

---

7. Judge Mikva, in his separate opinion in American Intl. Group, Inc. v. Islamic Republic of Iran, 657 F.2d 430, 452 (1981), argued that the moniker "Hostage Act" was newly coined for purposes of this litigation. Suffice it to say that we focus on the language of 22 U.S.C. §1732, not any shorthand description of it. See W. Shakespeare, Romeo and Juliet, Act II, scene 2, line 43 ("What's in a name?").

with such a view. The legislative history indicates that the Act was passed in response to a situation unlike the recent Iranian crisis. Congress in 1868 was concerned with the activity of certain countries refusing to recognize the citizenship of naturalized Americans traveling abroad, and repatriating such citizens against their will. These countries were not interested in returning the citizens in exchange for any sort of ransom. This also explains the reference in the Act to imprisonment "in violation of the rights of American citizenship." Although the Iranian hostage-taking violated international law and common decency, the hostages were not seized out of any refusal to recognize their American citizenship — they were seized precisely *because* of their American citizenship. The legislative history is also somewhat ambiguous on the question whether Congress contemplated Presidential action such as that involved here or rather simply reprisals directed against the offending foreign country and *its* citizens.

Concluding that neither the IEEPA nor the Hostage Act constitutes specific authorization of the President's action suspending claims, however, is not to say that these statutory provisions are entirely irrelevant to the question of the validity of the President's action. We think both statutes highly relevant in the looser sense of indicating congressional acceptance of a broad scope for executive action in circumstances such as those presented in this case. . . . The IEEPA delegates broad authority to the President to act in times of national emergency with respect to property of a foreign country. The Hostage Act similarly indicates congressional willingness that the President have broad discretion when responding to the hostile acts of foreign sovereigns. . . .

. . . [W]e cannot ignore the general tenor of Congress's legislation in this area in trying to determine whether the President is acting alone or at least with the acceptance of Congress. As we have noted, Congress cannot anticipate and legislate with regard to every possible action the President may find it necessary to take or every possible situation in which he might act. Such failure of Congress specifically to delegate authority does not, "especially . . . in the areas of foreign policy and national security," imply "congressional disapproval" of action taken by the Executive. Haig v. Agee, [453 U.S. 280, 291 (1981)]. On the contrary, the enactment of legislation closely related to the question of the President's authority in a particular case which evinces legislative intent to accord the President broad discretion may be considered to "invite" "measures on independent presidential responsibility," *Youngstown*, 343 U.S., at 637 (Jackson, J., concurring). At least this is so where there is no contrary indication of legislative intent and when, as here, there is a history of congressional acquiescence in conduct of the sort engaged in by the President. It is to that history which we now turn.

Not infrequently in affairs between nations, outstanding claims by nationals of one country against the government of another country are "sources of friction" between the two sovereigns. United States v. Pink, 315 U.S. 203, 225 (1942). To resolve these difficulties, nations have often entered into agreements settling the claims of their respective nationals. As one treatise writer puts it, international agreements settling claims by nationals of one state against the government of another "are established international practice reflecting traditional international theory." L. Henkin, Foreign Affairs and the Constitution 262 (1972). Consistent with that principle, the United States has repeatedly exercised its sovereign authority to settle the claims of its nationals against foreign countries. Though those settlements have sometimes been made by treaty, there has also been a longstanding practice of settling such claims by executive agreement without the advice and consent of the Senate. Under such agreements, the President has agreed to renounce or extinguish claims of United States nationals against foreign governments in return for lump-sum payments or the establishment of arbitration procedures. To be sure, many of these settlements were encouraged by the United States claimants themselves, since a claimant's only hope of obtaining any payment at all might lie in having his Government negotiate a diplomatic settlement on his behalf. But it is also undisputed that the "United States has sometimes disposed of the claims of its citizens without their consent, or even without consultation with them, usually without exclusive regard for their interests, as distinguished from those of the nation as a whole." It is clear that the practice of settling claims continues today. Since 1952, the President has entered into at least 10 binding settlements with foreign nations, including an $80 million settlement with the People's Republic of China.

Crucial to our decision today is the conclusion that Congress has implicitly approved the practice of claim settlement by executive agreement. This is best demonstrated by Congress's enactment of the International Claims Settlement Act of 1949, 64 Stat. 13, as amended, 22 U.S.C. §1621 et seq. (1976 ed. and Supp. IV). The Act had two purposes: (1) to allocate to United States nationals funds received in the course of an executive claims settlement with Yugoslavia, and (2) to provide a procedure whereby funds resulting from future settlements could be distributed. To achieve these ends Congress created the International Claims Commission, now the Foreign Claims Settlement Commission, and gave it jurisdiction to make final and binding decisions with respect to claims by United States nationals against settlement funds. 22 U.S.C. §1623(a). By creating a procedure to implement future settlement agreements, Congress placed its stamp of approval on such agreements. . . .

Over the years Congress has frequently amended the International Claims Settlement Act to provide for particular problems arising out of settlement agreements, thus demonstrating Congress' continuing acceptance of the President's claim settlement authority. . . .

Finally, the legislative history of the IEEPA further reveals that Congress has accepted the authority of the Executive to enter into settlement agreements. Though the IEEPA was enacted to provide for some limitation on the President's emergency powers, Congress stressed that "[n]othing in this act is intended . . . to interfere with the authority of the President to [block assets], or to impede the settlement of claims of U.S. citizens against foreign countries." . . .

Petitioner raises two arguments in opposition to the proposition that Congress has acquiesced in this longstanding practice of claims settlement by executive agreement. . . .

Petitioner . . . asserts that Congress divested the President of the authority to settle claims when it enacted the Foreign Sovereign Immunities Act of 1976 (hereinafter FSIA), 28 U.S.C. §§1330, 1602 et seq. The FSIA granted personal and subject-matter jurisdiction in the federal district courts over commercial suits brought by claimants against those foreign states which have waived immunity. 28 U.S.C. §1330. Prior to the enactment of the FSIA, a foreign government's immunity to suit was determined by the Executive Branch on a case-by-case basis. According to petitioner, the principal purpose of the FSIA was to depoliticize these commercial lawsuits by taking them out of the arena of foreign affairs — where the Executive

Branch is subject to the pressures of foreign states seeking to avoid liability through a grant of immunity—and by placing them within the exclusive jurisdiction of the courts. Petitioner thus insists that the President, by suspending its claims, has circumscribed the jurisdiction of the United States courts in violation of Art. III of the Constitution.

We disagree. In the first place, we do not believe that the President has attempted to divest the federal courts of jurisdiction. Executive Order No. 12294 purports only to "suspend" the claims, not divest the federal court of "jurisdiction." As we read the Executive Order, those claims not within the jurisdiction of the Claims Tribunal will "revive" and become judicially enforceable in United States courts. This case, in short, illustrates the difference between modifying federal-court jurisdiction and directing the courts to apply a different rule of law. The President has . . . simply effected a change in the substantive law governing the lawsuit.

In light of all of the foregoing—the inferences to be drawn from the character of the legislation Congress has enacted in the area, such as the IEEPA and the Hostage Act, and from the history of acquiescence in executive claims settlement—we conclude that the President was authorized to suspend pending claims pursuant to Executive Order No. 12294. As Justice Frankfurter pointed out in *Youngstown*, 343 U.S., at 610-611, "a systematic, unbroken, executive practice, long pursued to the knowledge of the Congress and never before questioned . . . may be treated as a gloss on 'Executive Power' vested in the President by §1 of Art. II." Past practice does not, by itself, create power, but "long-continued practice, known to and acquiesced in by Congress, would raise a presumption that the [action] had been [taken] in pursuance of its consent. . . ." United States v. Midwest Oil Co., 236 U.S. 459, 474 (1915). Such practice is present here and such a presumption is also appropriate. In light of the fact that Congress may be considered to have consented to the President's action in suspending claims, we cannot say that action exceeded the President's powers.

Our conclusion is buttressed by the fact that the means chosen by the President to settle the claims of American nationals provided an alternative forum, the Claims Tribunal, which is capable of providing meaningful relief. The Solicitor General also suggests that the provision of the Claims Tribunal will actually *enhance* the opportunity for claimants to recover their claims, in that the Agreement removes a number of jurisdictional and procedural impediments faced by claimants in United States courts.* Although being overly sanguine about the chances of United States claimants before the Claims Tribunal would require a degree of naiveté which should not be demanded even of judges, the Solicitor General's point cannot be discounted. Moreover, it is important to remember that we have already held that the President has the *statutory* authority to nullify attachments and to transfer the assets out of the country. The President's power to do so does not depend on his provision of a forum whereby claimants can recover on those claims. The fact that the President has provided such a forum here means that the claimants are receiving something in return for the suspension of their claims, namely, access to an international tribunal before which they may well recover something on their claims. Because there does

---

*[In its contract Dames & Moore agreed to submit disputes to the courts of Iran. In such a case it was unclear whether it could take advantage of the arbitration in the Hague (Dames & Moore argued that the contract, including the forum selection, was void). In the end, it received a favorable settlement from the Hague Tribunal.—EDS.]

appear to be a real "settlement" here, this case is more easily analogized to the more traditional claim settlement cases of the past.

Just as importantly, Congress has not disapproved of the action taken here. Though Congress has held hearings on the Iranian Agreement itself, Congress has not enacted legislation, or even passed a resolution, indicating its displeasure with the Agreement. Quite the contrary, the relevant Senate Committee has stated that the establishment of the Tribunal is "of vital importance to the United States." S. Rep. No. 97-71, p.5 (1981). We are thus clearly not confronted with a situation in which Congress has in some way resisted the exercise of Presidential authority.

Finally, we re-emphasize the narrowness of our decision. We do not decide that the President possesses plenary power to settle claims, even as against foreign governmental entities. As the Court of Appeals for the First Circuit stressed, "[t]he sheer magnitude of such a power, considered against the background of the diversity and complexity of modern international trade, cautions against any broader construction of authority than is necessary." Chas. T. Main Intl., Inc. v. Khuzestan Water & Power Authority, 651 F.2d, at 814. But where, as here, the settlement of claims has been determined to be a necessary incident to the resolution of a major foreign policy dispute between our country and another, and where, as here, we can conclude that Congress acquiesced in the President's action, we are not prepared to say that the President lacks the power to settle such claims.

V

We do not think it appropriate at the present time to address petitioner's contention that the suspension of claims, if authorized, would constitute a taking of property in violation of the Fifth Amendment to the United States Constitution in the absence of just compensation. Both petitioner and the Government concede that the question whether the suspension of the claims constitutes a taking is not ripe for review. . . .

. . . [T]o the extent petitioner believes it has suffered an unconstitutional taking by the suspension of the claims, we see no jurisdictional obstacle to an appropriate action in the United States Court of Claims under the Tucker Act.

The judgment of the District Court is accordingly affirmed, and the mandate shall issue forthwith.

[Concurring opinion of Justice Stevens and concurring and dissenting opinion of Justice Powell omitted.]

Notes and Questions

1. Presidents have made presidential executive agreements since the beginning of the nation. See Wilfred McClure, International Executive Agreements 53 (1941); Michael D. Ramsey, Executive Agreements and the (Non)Treaty Power, 77 N.C. L. Rev. 133 (1998). These agreements bind the United States on the international plane just as would a treaty with Senate participation. Most executive agreements have concerned relatively insignificant matters such as protocols, modus vivendi,

and postal agreements. But they also have included very important matters, such as the World War II agreements at Yalta and Potsdam, the Litvinov Assignment at issue in *Pink*, and the Algiers Accords at issue in *Dames & Moore*. What is the constitutional authority for presidential executive agreements? Do they even require constitutional authority? Are there any limits on executive agreements? How would limits be discerned? How would they be enforced?

2. The asserted basis for the Litvinov Assignment was the President's power to recognize foreign governments. This power, in turn, purportedly stems from the President's power in Article II to "receive Ambassadors and other public Ministers." Does the recognition power flow from this Article II provision? If not, where else could the recognition power be found in the Constitution? Does the power to recognize include the power to make international agreements relating to recognition?

3. Even assuming that Presidents have the power to make executive agreements that bind the United States on the international plane, does it follow that these agreements preempt state law? The *Belmont* decision, referred to in *Pink*, was the first decision to hold that a presidential executive agreement preempts state law. What does the language of the Supremacy Clause suggest about the preemptive power of executive agreements? Assuming, as stated in *Belmont*, that "in respect of our foreign relations generally, . . . the State of New York does not exist," 301 U.S. at 331, does it follow that there are no limits on the power of the President to make executive agreements that preempt state law? What about separation of powers concerns, such as a concern with undermining the Senate's constitutional role in treatymaking?

4. Most of the decision in *Dames & Moore* focuses on the domestic sources of authority for President Carter's and President Reagan's executive orders nullifying and transferring attached Iranian funds, and suspending claims in U.S. courts. Why didn't the Court rely more heavily on the Algiers Accords, the executive agreement that ended the hostage crisis? After all, this agreement obligated the United States to "terminate all legal proceedings" in U.S. courts, to "nullify all attachments . . . obtained therein," and to "prohibit all further litigation based on such claims."

5. Do you draw the same inference from the IEEPA and Hostage Act as the Court? Isn't the opposite inference equally possible? Is the Court's reliance on congressional acquiescence persuasive? In what did Congress acquiesce? Was it appropriate for the Court to look at the "general tenor of Congress's legislation in this area in trying to determine whether the President is acting alone or at least with the acceptance of Congress"?

6. In which category of Jackson's concurrence in *Youngstown* do you place the *Dames & Moore* case? Do you agree with Professor Koh that the approach in *Dames & Moore* "elevat[es] the president's power from the twilight zone — Jackson's category two — to its height in Jackson's category one" and "effectively follow[s] the dissenting view in *Youngstown*, which had converted legislative silence into consent, thereby delegating to the President authority that Congress itself had arguably withheld"? Harold Hongju Koh, The National Security Constitution: Sharing Power After the Iran-Contra Affair 139 (1990).

7. In 1976, Congress enacted the Foreign Sovereign Immunities Act (which we discuss in Chapter 6). This Act, which was in effect at the time Dames & Moore filed its suit, provides for federal court jurisdiction over civil suits against foreign states. In *Dames & Moore*, did Presidents Carter and Reagan, in effect, override this statute?

Can a presidential executive agreement override federal legislation? Cf. United States v. Guy W. Capps, Inc., 204 F.2d 655, 659-660 (4th Cir. 1953) ("We think that whatever the power of the executive with respect to making executive trade agreements regulating foreign commerce in the absence of action by Congress, it is clear that the executive may not through entering into such an agreement avoid complying with a regulation prescribed by Congress."), aff'd on other grounds, 348 U.S. 296 (1955).

8. In what sense was the claim in *Dames & Moore* suspended? The Algiers Accords provided that "[t]he United States agrees to terminate all legal proceedings in United States courts involving claims of United States persons and institutions against Iran and its state enterprises." However, as the Court notes in *Dames & Moore*, the executive order implementing the Algiers Accords used the verb "suspend." Why the different language? Is the Supreme Court's explanation persuasive? After the Algiers Accords, will there be a different rule of law applicable, or simply a different tribunal, or both?

9. *Postscript.* Dames & Moore took its case to the Iran-United States Claims Tribunal, as required by the Algiers Accords. The Tribunal awarded Dames & Moore (a) $100,000, plus interest, against the Islamic Republic of Iran; and (b) $108,435, plus interest, against the National Iranian Gas Company. See Award No. 97-54-3, 4 Iran-U.S. C.T.R. 212 (1983).

3.   *National Emergency Legislation*

In the Iran hostage crisis the President attached or froze Iranian assets pursuant to a delegation of congressional authority under the International Emergency Economic Powers Act (IEEPA). The *Dames & Moore* opinion upheld the authority of the President to nullify previously issued attachments and to transfer the Iranian property back to Iran. Presidential authority under IEEPA can be vitally important to private entities that get caught up in the larger foreign policy picture.

Congress has legislated extensive powers to the President for use in a national emergency. Since 1976, the National Emergencies Act (NEA) has provided the procedures for declaring, conducting, and terminating emergencies. However, it provides no new authority to the President but leaves that to other legislation. In the international area, IEEPA is usually the statutory vehicle (in addition to the President's nonemergency powers) for major economic steps by the President during a declared national emergency. (The texts of the NEA and IEEPA are in the Documentary Supplement.)

IEEPA is designed to deal with "any unusual or extraordinary threat, which has its source in whole or substantial part outside the United States, to the [U.S.] national security, foreign policy, or economy." 50 U.S.C. §1701(e). If the President determines that such a threat exists, he can declare a national emergency under the NEA. IEEPA then authorizes him, pusuant to sweeping language in section 1702(a), to employ a very wide range of economic sanctions, such as cutting off exports or imports, or restricting private financial transactions. (Control over financial transactions was used to restrict travel to or in another country until IEEPA was amended in 1994 to exempt financial transactions ordinarily incident to travel. There are a few other exceptions at section 1702(b).)

Before exercising these authorities, the President is directed "in every possible instance" to consult with Congress. Moreover, if he does use IEEPA, he must immediately make a report to Congress explaining his actions. Id. at §1703(a) and (b). The President can continue IEEPA sanctions until he terminates the emergency or unless Congress acts to terminate it by joint resolution. Alternatively, the emergency automatically lapses after one year if the President does not renew it.

a.   A Brief History

IEEPA was passed in 1977 to replace the Trading with the Enemy Act (TWEA), which had become "essentially an unlimited grant of authority for the President to exercise, at his discretion, broad powers in both the domestic and international arena, without congressional review." H.R. Rep. No. 459, 95th Cong., 1st Sess. 7 (1977).

The statute that included IEEPA also amended TWEA to limit the President's power under TWEA to solely "[d]uring the time of war." 50 U.S.C. App. §5(b) (1982). However, rather than requiring the President to declare a new national emergency in order to continue then-existing TWEA sanctions, such as those against Cuba and North Korea, Congress included a grandfather provision.

A question arose as to whether the scope of the specific controls existing in 1977 against one of these countries could be expanded under TWEA, or whether resort to IEEPA was needed. In 1984, in Regan v. Wald, 468 U.S. 222 (1984), the Supreme Court by a 5-4 vote effectively decided that reliance on TWEA was sufficient for new controls against the countries subject to the grandfathered controls.

b.   The Past and Present Uses of IEEPA

Except for Cuba and North Korea that are still covered by TWEA, IEEPA provides the statutory basis for employing many economic tools during a declared national emergency. Presidents are increasingly resorting to the law.

Passed in 1977, IEEPA was not used until the 1979-1981 Iranian hostage crisis. Receiving reports that the government of Iran was about to withdraw its billions of dollars on deposit in U.S. banks, President Carter declared a national emergency in November 1979 and, pursuant to IEEPA, blocked the transfer of all property of the Iranian government. The order froze about $12 billion of Iranian funds in U.S. banks or in the possession of U.S. corporations, whether located in the United States or abroad. The IEEPA controls were later expanded to cut off almost all trade with Iran.

In 1981 President Carter and then President Reagan took a number of steps to implement the so-called Algiers Accords, which resulted in the release of the hostages and the termination of the U.S. sanctions. These included ordering the transfer of billions of dollars back to Iran or to trust funds and suspending claims against Iran that were pending in U.S. courts. All the Iranian sanctions and the actions to end them were upheld by U.S. courts under IEEPA, except that the Supreme Court in Dames & Moore v. Regan, looked to additional authority to uphold the suspension of the claims then pending in U.S. courts.

On May 1, 1985, President Reagan declared a national emergency and ordered a number of actions against Nicaragua. These included a ban on the import of Nicaraguan goods; a ban on the export of all goods to Nicaragua not destined for the U.S.-backed Contras; and prohibitions on Nicaraguan vessels and air carriers entering the United States. (President George H. W. Bush ended the IEEPA sanctions after the Sandinistas were defeated in elections in Nicaragua in March 1990.)

President Reagan later imposed IEEPA sanctions against South Africa, Libya, and Panama. Presidents Bush and Clinton declared national emergencies in response to the Iraqi invasion of Kuwait and troubles in the former Yugoslavia, Haiti, and Angola. President Clinton also declared a national emergency and imposed sanctions with regard to Rwanda. And Presidents Reagan, Bush, and Clinton used IEEPA to continue U.S. export controls when there were delays in Congress renewing the Export Administration Act.

President Clinton also started to use the IEEPA powers frequently to combat terrorism, the international drug traffic, and the proliferation of weapons of mass destruction — sometimes in very focused ways against individuals and non-state entities. For example, in January 1995, he froze any assets in the United States, or in the control of U.S. persons, of designated terrorist organizations and prohibited any transaction or dealing by U.S. persons or within the United States of any interests in property with these groups. In October 1995, President Clinton applied similar restrictions against four foreign individuals designated as significant narcotics traffickers, and later added more individuals. In July 1998, he imposed a variety of economic sanctions against any foreign person whom the Secretary of State might designate as having materially contributed, or attempted to do so, to the efforts of any foreign country or entity to develop weapons of mass destruction or missiles capable of delivering such weapons.

President George W. Bush continued the IEEPA sanctions existing at the start of his Administration — e.g., against Iran, Iraq and Libya, as well as designated terrorists, narcotics traffickers, and proliferators. Like his predecessors, he also used IEEPA to continue export controls when a congressionally passed export law lapsed in 2001. As discussed in Chapter 1.E., President Bush declared a new national emergency after the attacks of September 11 and froze the assets of, and imposed other financial sanctions, against Osama bin Laden, Al Qaeda, and other terrorists and terrorist organizations. The Administration's expanding list of targeted individuals and other non-state entities reflected the increased use of selective sanctions.

In March 2003, President Bush also invoked a new IEEPA provision added after the attacks of September 11, 2001. Going beyond IEEPA's existing authorization to, among other steps, freeze foreign assets, the new provision authorizes the President to "confiscate any property" of any foreign person, entity, or country that has attacked the United States or that is engaged in armed hostilities with the United States. (Section 1702(a)(1)(C).) The provision also gives the President discretion on how to use the assets. After the United States and its coalition partners began hostilities against Iraq in March 2003, President Bush directed the confiscation of the approximately $1.7 billion in Iraqi assets that had been frozen before under IEEPA (most from the time of Iraq's invasion of Kuwait in 1990). Some of these assets were to be distributed among plaintiffs who had obtained U.S. court judgments against Iraq, many stemming from the Gulf War of 1990–91. The balance was to be used for the reconstruction and development of Iraq.

Notes and Questions

1. Are the IEEPA requirements of consulting with and reporting to Congress likely to have any effect on the President's decision-making? How much consultation is required?

2. Have Presidents declared too many "national emergencies"? Are there any significant differences among the emergencies that have been declared?

3. Do you think a litigant could successfully challenge a President's determination that an "unusual and extraordinary threat" exists?

4. Should the President be required to obtain specific legislative approval, rather than resorting to IEEPA, in certain situations? If so, how could one define them? If not, what are the effective limits on a President's use of IEEPA? For example, should the sanctions against Nicaragua in 1985 have required specific congressional approval? What about the 1995 sanctions against four foreign individuals designated as significant narcotics traffickers?

5. Are the termination provisions for national emergencies and IEEPA adequate? As noted above, the President can terminate the national emergency. Alternatively, it will automatically terminate in one year unless the President renews it, but renewal is a simple matter of publishing a brief notice in the Federal Register.

The National Emergency Act as passed had a third termination provision — by a concurrent resolution of Congress (which cannot be vetoed). This was effectively invalidated by the decisions of the U.S. Supreme Court striking down "legislative vetoes" such as this. See Immigration and Naturalization Service v. Chadha, 462 U.S. 919 (1983). Congress then amended the provision to provide instead for termination by a joint resolution. See 50 U.S.C. §1622 (Supp. III 1985). Since the President can veto a joint resolution, however, the practical effect of this amendment is that a declared national emergency can probably continue at the President's pleasure. (Congress would be unlikely to muster the two-thirds vote of both houses necessary to override the veto.)

Would it be a good idea to provide for automatic termination of a declared national emergency after, say, six months or a year? In other words, should the President be required to obtain the legislative support of Congress for continuing international economic measures initially imposed pursuant to IEEPA? Would this require the President to pursue policies that have public support? Would it unnecessarily bind the President's hands?

6. For additional discussion of U.S. laws concerning economic sanctions, see the materials in Chapter 8 at page 808, and other sources at page 813.

C. CUSTOMARY INTERNATIONAL LAW

As compared with treaties, the Constitution is relatively silent about the formation and domestic status of customary international law. Indeed, the only reference in the Constitution to customary international law, which was referred to at the time of the Founding as part of the "law of nations," is a grant of power to Congress to "define and punish . . . Offenses against the Law of Nations." Art. I, §8, cl. 10. Moreover, as we learned in Chapter 2, customary international law is more diffuse than treaty law. It consists of obligations inferred from the general and consistent practice of states followed out of a sense of legal obligation *(opinio juris)*. That practice may be found in diplomatic correspondence, official statements, military and administrative practice, treaties, and judicial decisions, as well as national legislation. Consequently, all the law-making powers reflected in the Constitution — ranging from presidential foreign affairs authority, delegated legislative authority, the treaty power, the entire Article I legislative power, and Article III — are involved in the making of customary international law by the United States.

Considerable controversy surrounds the domestic legal status of customary international law. Recall that Article VI of the Constitution provides that treaties are the supreme law of the land. As a result, treaties (at least if they are self-executing) preempt inconsistent state law. In addition, under the last-in-time rule, treaties can, at least in theory, override earlier inconsistent statutes. Customary international law, however, is not mentioned in Article VI. Nor has the Supreme Court definitively resolved the relationship between customary international law and either state law, federal statutes, or Executive Branch action.

1. Part of Our Law

In several decisions, the Supreme Court has referred to customary international law as "part of our law" or part of the "law of the land." The most famous of these decisions is The Paquete Habana. It was a case in the federal courts on the basis of federal admiralty jurisdiction. In admiralty cases the courts apply admiralty or maritime law, a separate body of law that historically was part of the "law of nations" and was considered to be applicable — uniformly — throughout the seafaring world. One part of this law was prize law, dealing with the rights of persons to capture enemy vessels and cargoes during wartime.

The Paquete Habana

U.S. Supreme Court
175 U.S. 677 (1900)

Mr. Justice GRAY delivered the opinion of the court.

These are two appeals from decrees of the District Court of the United States for the Southern District of Florida, condemning two fishing vessels and their cargoes as prize of war.

Each vessel was a fishing smack, running in and out of Havana, and regularly engaged in fishing on the coast of Cuba; sailed under the Spanish flag; was owned by a Spanish subject of Cuban birth, living in the city of Havana; was commanded by a subject of Spain also residing in Havana; and her master and crew had no interest in the vessel, but were entitled to shares, amounting in all to two thirds, of her catch, the other third belonging to her owner. Her cargo consisted of fresh fish, caught by her crew from the sea, put on board as they were caught, and kept and sold alive. Until stopped by the blockading squadron, she had no knowledge of the existence of the war, or of any blockade. She had no arms or ammunition on board, and made no attempt to run the blockade after she knew of its existence, nor any resistance at the time of the capture. . . .

Both the fishing vessels were brought by their captors into Key West. A libel for the condemnation of each vessel and her cargo as prize of war was there filed in April 27, 1898; a claim was interposed by her master, on behalf of himself and the other members of the crew, and of her owner: evidence was taken, showing the facts above stated; and on May 30, 1898, a final decree of condemnation and sale was entered, "the court not being satisfied that as a matter of law, without any ordinance, treaty or proclamation, fishing vessels of this class are exempt from seizure."

Each vessel was thereupon sold by auction; the Paquete Habana for the sum of $490; and the Lola for the sum of $800. . . .

We are then brought to the consideration of the question whether, upon the facts appearing in these records, the fishing smacks were subject to capture by the armed vessels of the United States during the recent war with Spain.

By an ancient usage among civilized nations, beginning centuries ago, and gradually ripening into a rule of international law, coast fishing vessels, pursuing their vocation of catching and bringing in fresh fish, have been recognized as exempt, with their cargoes and crews, from capture as prize of war.

This doctrine, however, has been earnestly contested at the bar; and no complete collection of the instances illustrating it is to be found, so far as we are aware, in a single published work, although many are referred to and discussed by the writers on international law. . . . It is therefore worth the while to trace the history of the rule, from the earliest accessible sources, through the increasing recognition of it, with occasional setbacks, to what we may now justly consider as its final establishment in our own country and generally throughout the civilized world.

[The Court then proceeds to trace the history of the rule through an extensive examination of state practice, beginning with the issuance of orders by Henry IV to his admirals in 1403 and 1406.]

Since the English orders in council of 1806 and 1810, before quoted, in favor of fishing vessels employed in catching and bringing to market fresh fish, no instance has been found in which the exemption from capture of private coast fishing vessels, honestly pursuing their peaceful industry, has been denied by England, or by any other nation. And the Empire of Japan, (the last State admitted into the rank of civilized nations,) by an ordinance promulgated at the beginning of its war with China in August, 1894, established prize courts, and ordained that "the following enemy's vessels are exempt from detention"— including in the exemption "boats engaged in coast fisheries," as well as "ships engaged exclusively on a voyage of scientific discovery, philanthropy or religious mission." Takahashi, International Law, 11, 178.

International law is part of our law, and must be ascertained and administered by the courts of justice of appropriate jurisdiction, as often as questions of right depending upon it are duly presented for their determination. For this purpose, where there is no treaty, and no controlling executive or legislative act or judicial decision, resort must be had to the customs and usages of civilized nations; and, as evidence of these, to the works of jurists and commentators, who by years of labor, research and experience, have made themselves peculiarly well acquainted with the subjects of which they treat. Such works are resorted to by judicial tribunals, not for the speculations of their authors concerning what the law ought to be, but for trustworthy evidence of what the law really is. Hilton v. Guyot, 159 U.S. 113, 163, 164, 214, 215. . . .

This review of the precedents and authorities on the subject appears to us abundantly to demonstrate that at the present day, by the general consent of the civilized nations of the world, and independently of any express treaty or other public act, it is an established rule of international law, founded on considerations of humanity to a poor and industrious order of men, and of the mutual convenience of belligerent States, that coast fishing vessels, with their implements and supplies, cargoes and crews, unarmed, and honestly pursuing their peaceful calling of catching and bringing in fresh fish, are exempt from capture as prize of war.

The exemption, of course, does not apply to coast fishermen or their vessels, if employed for a warlike purpose, or in such a way as to give aid or information to the enemy; nor when military or naval operations create a necessity to which all private interests must give way.

Nor has the exemption been extended to ships or vessels employed on the high sea in taking whales or seals, or cod or other fish which are not brought fresh to market, but are salted or otherwise cured and made a regular article of commerce.

This rule of international law is one which prize courts, administering the law of nations, are bound to take judicial notice of, and to give effect to, in the absence of any treaty or other public act of their own government in relation to the matter. . . .

The position taken by the United States during the recent war with Spain was quite in accord with the rule of international law, now generally recognized by civilized nations, in regard to coast fishing vessels.

On April 21, 1898, the Secretary of the Navy gave instructions to Admiral Sampson commanding the North Atlantic Squadron, to "immediately institute a blockade of the north coast of Cuba, extending from Cardenas on the east to Bahia Honda on the west." Bureau of Navigation Report of 1898, appx. 175. The blockade was immediately instituted accordingly. On April 22, the President issued a proclamation, declaring that the United States had instituted and would maintain that blockade, "in pursuance of the laws of the United States, and the law of nations applicable to such cases." 30 Stat. 1769. And by the act of Congress of April 25, 1898, c.189, it was declared that the war between the United States and Spain existed on that day, and had existed since and including April 21. 30 Stat. 364.

On April 26, 1898, the President issued another proclamation, which, after reciting the existence of the war, as declared by Congress, contained this further recital: "It being desirable that such war should be conducted upon principles in harmony with the present views of nations and sanctioned by their recent practice." This recital was followed by specific declarations of certain rules for the conduct of the war by sea, making no mention of fishing vessels. 30 Stat. 1770. But the proclamation clearly manifests the general policy of the Government to conduct the war in accordance with the principles of international law sanctioned by the recent practice of nations. . . .

Upon the facts proved in either case, it is the duty of this court, sitting as the highest prize court of the United States, and administering the law of nations, to declare and adjudge that the capture was unlawful, and without probable cause; and it is therefore, in each case,

Ordered, that the decree of the District Court be reversed, and the proceeds of the sale of the vessel, together with the proceeds of any sale of her cargo, be restored to the claimant, with damages and costs.

[Dissenting opinion of Mr. Chief Justice Fuller, with whom concurred Mr. Justice Harlan and Mr. Justice McKenna, omitted.]

Customary international law has been prominently involved in the human rights area. Consider these two cases:

Filartiga v. Pena-Irala

U.S. Court of Appeals
630 F.2d 876 (2d Cir. 1980)

KAUFMAN, Circuit Judge:

Upon ratification of the Constitution, the thirteen former colonies were fused into a single nation, one which, in its relations with foreign states, is bound both to observe and construe the accepted norms of international law, formerly known as the law of nations. Under the Articles of Confederation, the several states had interpreted and applied this body of doctrine as a part of their common law, but with the founding of the "more perfect Union" of 1789, the law of nations became pre-eminently a federal concern.

Implementing the constitutional mandate for national control over foreign relations, the First Congress established original district court jurisdiction over "all causes where an alien sues for a tort only [committed] in violation of the law of nations." Judiciary Act of 1789, ch. 20, §9(b), 1 Stat. 73, 77 (1789), codified at 28 U.S.C. §1350. Construing this rarely-invoked provision, we hold that deliberate torture perpetrated under color of official authority violates universally accepted norms of the international law of human rights, regardless of the nationality of the parties. Thus, whenever an alleged torturer is found and served with process by an alien within our borders, §1350 provides federal jurisdiction. Accordingly, we reverse the judgment of the district court dismissing the complaint for want of federal jurisdiction.

I

The appellants, plaintiffs below, are citizens of the Republic of Paraguay. Dr. Joel Filartiga, a physician, describes himself as a longstanding opponent of the government of President Alfredo Stroessner, which has held power in Paraguay since 1954. His daughter, Dolly Filartiga, arrived in the United States in 1978 under a visitor's visa, and has since applied for permanent political asylum. The Filartigas brought this action in the Eastern District of New York against Americo Norberto Pena-Irala (Pena), also a citizen of Paraguay, for wrongfully causing the death of Dr. Filartiga's seventeen-year-old son, Joelito. Because the district court dismissed the action for want of subject matter jurisdiction, we must accept as true the allegations contained in the Filartigas' complaint and affidavits for purposes of this appeal.

The appellants contend that on March 29, 1976, Joelito Filartiga was kidnapped and tortured to death by Pena, who was then Inspector General of Police in Asuncion, Paraguay. Later that day, the police brought Dolly Filartiga to Pena's home where she was confronted with the body of her brother, which evidenced marks of severe torture. As she fled, horrified, from the house, Pena followed after her shouting, "Here you have what you have been looking for for so long and what you deserve. Now shut up." The Filartigas claim that Joelito was tortured and killed in retaliation for his father's political activities and beliefs.

Shortly thereafter, Dr. Filartiga commenced a criminal action in the Paraguayan courts against Pena and the police for the murder of his son. As a result, Dr. Filartiga's attorney was arrested and brought to police headquarters where, shackled to a wall, Pena threatened him with death. This attorney, it is alleged, has since been disbarred without just cause.

During the course of the Paraguayan criminal proceeding, which is apparently still pending after four years, another man, Hugo Duarte, confessed to the murder. Duarte, who was a member of the Pena household, claimed that he had discovered his wife and Joelito *in flagrante delicto,* and that the crime was one of passion. The Filartigas have submitted a photograph of Joelito's corpse showing injuries they believe refute this claim. Dolly Filartiga, moreover, has stated that she will offer evidence of three independent autopsies demonstrating that her brother's death "was the result of professional methods of torture." Despite his confession, Duarte, we are told, has never been convicted or sentenced in connection with the crime.

In July of 1978, Pena sold his house in Paraguay and entered the United States under a visitor's visa. He was accompanied by Juana Bautista Fernandez Villalba, who had lived with him in Paraguay. The couple remained in the United States beyond the term of their visas, and were living in Brooklyn, New York, when Dolly Filartiga, who was then living in Washington, D.C., learned of their presence. Acting on information provided by Dolly the Immigration and Naturalization Service arrested Pena and his companion, both of whom were subsequently ordered deported on April 5, 1979 following a hearing. They had then resided in the United States for more than nine months.

Almost immediately, Dolly caused Pena to be served with a summons and civil complaint at the Brooklyn Navy Yard, where he was being held pending deportation. The complaint alleged that Pena had wrongfully caused Joelito's death by torture and sought compensatory and punitive damages of $10,000,000. The Filartigas also sought to enjoin Pena's deportation to ensure his availability for testimony at trial. The cause of action is stated as arising under "wrongful death statutes; the U.N. Charter; the Universal Declaration on Human Rights; the U.N. Declaration Against Torture; the American Declaration of the Rights and Duties of Man; and other pertinent declarations, documents and practices constituting the customary international law of human rights and the law of nations," as well as 28 U.S.C. §1350. . . .

II

Appellants rest their principal argument in support of federal jurisdiction upon the Alien Tort Statute, 28 U.S.C. §1350, which provides: "The district courts shall have original jurisdiction of any civil action by an alien for a tort only, committed in violation of the law of nations or a treaty of the United States." Since appellants do not contend that their action arises directly under a treaty of the United States, a threshold question on the jurisdictional issue is whether the conduct alleged violates the law of nations. In light of the universal condemnation of torture in numerous international agreements, and the renunciation of torture as an instrument of official policy by virtually all of the nations of the world (in principle if not in practice), we find that an act of torture committed by a state official against one held in detention violates established norms of the international law of human rights, and hence the law of nations.

The Supreme Court has enumerated the appropriate sources of international law. The law of nations "may be ascertained by consulting the works of jurists, writing professedly on public law; or by the general usage and practice of nations; or by judicial decisions recognizing and enforcing that law." . . .

The Paquete Habana, 175 U.S. 677 (1900), reaffirmed that

> where there is no treaty, and no controlling executive or legislative act or judicial decision, resort must be had to the customs and usages of civilized nations; and, as evidence of these, to the works of jurists and commentators, who by years of labor, research and experience, have made themselves peculiarly well acquainted with the subjects of which they treat. Such works are resorted to by judicial tribunals, not for the speculations of their authors concerning what the law ought to be, but for trustworthy evidence of what the law really is.

. . . *Habana* is particularly instructive for present purposes, for it held that the traditional prohibition against seizure of an enemy's coastal fishing vessels during wartime, a standard that began as one of comity only, had ripened over the preceding century into "a settled rule of international law" by "the general assent of civilized nations." Thus it is clear that courts must interpret international law not as it was in 1789, but as it has evolved and exists among the nations of the world today.

The requirement that a rule command the "general assent of civilized nations" to become binding upon them all is a stringent one. Were this not so, the courts of one nation might feel free to impose idiosyncratic legal rules upon others, in the name of applying international law. Thus, in Banco Nacional de Cuba v. Sabbatino, 376 U.S. 398 (1964), the Court declined to pass on the validity of the Cuban government's expropriation of a foreign-owned corporation's assets, noting the sharply conflicting views on the issue propounded by the capital-exporting, capital-importing, socialist and capitalist nations.

The case at bar presents us with a situation diametrically opposed to the conflicted state of law that confronted the *Sabbatino* Court. Indeed, to paraphrase that Court's statement, id., at 428, there are few, if any, issues in international law today on which opinion seems to be so united as the limitations on a state's power to torture persons held in its custody.

The United Nations Charter (a treaty of the United States, see 59 Stat. 1033 (1945)) makes it clear that in this modern age a state's treatment of its own citizens is a matter of international concern. It provides:

> With a view to the creation of conditions of stability and well-being which are necessary for peaceful and friendly relations among nations . . . the United Nations shall promote . . . universal respect for, and observance of, human rights and fundamental freedoms for all without distinctions as to race, sex, language or religion.

Id. Art. 55. And further:

> All members pledge themselves to take joint and separate action in cooperation with the Organization for the achievement of the purposes set forth in Article 55.

Id. Art. 56.

While this broad mandate has been held not to be wholly self-executing, this observation alone does not end our inquiry. For although there is no universal agreement as to the precise extent of the "human rights and fundamental freedoms" guaranteed to all by the Charter, there is at present no dissent from the view that the guaranties include, at a bare minimum, the right to be free from torture. This prohibition has become part of customary international law, as evidenced and defined by the Universal Declaration of Human Rights, General Assembly Resolution 217 (III) (A) (Dec. 10, 1948) which states, in the plainest of terms, "no one shall be subjected to torture."[10] The General Assembly has declared that the Charter precepts embodied in this Universal Declaration "constitute basic principles of international law." G.A. Res. 2625 (XXV) (Oct. 24, 1970).

Particularly relevant is the Declaration on the Protection of All Persons from Being Subjected to Torture, General Assembly Resolution 3452 (1975), which is set out in full in the margin. The Declaration expressly prohibits any state from permitting the dastardly and totally inhuman act of torture. Torture, in turn, is defined as "any act by which severe pain and suffering, whether physical or mental, is intentionally inflicted by or at the instigation of a public official on a person for such purposes as . . . intimidating him or other persons." The Declaration goes on to provide that "[w]here it is proved that an act of torture or other cruel, inhuman or degrading treatment or punishment has been committed by or at the instigation of a public official, the victim shall be afforded redress and compensation, in accordance with national law." This Declaration, like the Declaration of Human Rights before it, was adopted without dissent by the General Assembly.

These U.N. declarations are significant because they specify with great precision the obligations of member nations under the Charter. Since their adoption, "[m]embers can no longer contend that they do not know what human rights they promised in the Charter to promote." Sohn, "A Short History of United Nations Documents on Human Rights," in The United Nations and Human Rights, 18th Report of the Commission (Commission to Study the Organization of Peace ed. 1968). Moreover, a U.N. Declaration is, according to one authoritative definition, "a formal and solemn instrument, suitable for rare occasions when principles of great and lasting importance are being enunciated." 34 U.N. ESCOR, Supp. (No. 8) 15, U.N. Doc. E/cn.4/1/610 (1962) (memorandum of Office of Legal Affairs, U.N. Secretariat). Accordingly, it has been observed that the Universal Declaration of Human Rights "no longer fits into the dichotomy of 'binding treaty' against 'non-binding pronouncement,' but is rather an authoritative statement of the international community." E. Schwelb, Human Rights and the International Community 70 (1964). Thus, a Declaration creates an expectation of adherence, and "insofar as the expectation is gradually justified by State practice, a declaration may by custom become recognized as laying down rules binding upon the States." 34 U.N. ESCOR, supra. Indeed, several commentators have concluded that the Universal Declaration has become, *in toto,* a part of binding, customary international law. . . .

Turning to the act of torture, we have little difficulty discerning its universal renunciation in the modern usage and practice of nations. The international consensus surrounding torture has found expression in numerous international treaties

---

10. Eighteen nations have incorporated the Universal Declaration into their own constitutions. 48 Revue Internationale de Droit Penal Nos. 3 & 4, at 211 (1977).

and accords. E.g., American Convention on Human Rights, Art. 5 ("No one shall be subjected to torture or to cruel, inhuman or degrading punishment or treatment"); International Convenant on Civil and Political Rights, U.N. General Assembly Res. 2200 (Dec. 16, 1966) (identical language); European Convention for the Protection of Human Rights and Fundamental Freedoms, Art. 3. The substance of these international agreements is reflected in modern municipal — i.e. national — law as well. Although torture was once a routine concomitant of criminal interrogations in many nations, during the modern and hopefully more enlightened era it has been universally renounced. According to one survey, torture is prohibited, expressly or implicitly, by the constitutions of over fifty-five nations, including both the United States and Paraguay. Our State Department reports a general recognition of this principle:

> There now exists an international consensus that recognizes basic human rights and obligations owed by all governments to their citizens. . . . There is no doubt that these rights are often violated; but virtually all governments acknowledge their validity.

Department of State, Country Reports on Human Rights for 1979. . . . We have been directed to no assertion by any contemporary state of a right to torture its own or another nation's citizens. Indeed, United States diplomatic contacts confirm the universal abhorrence with which torture is viewed:

> In exchanges between United States embassies and all foreign states with which the United States maintains relations, it has been the Department of State's general experience that no government has asserted a right to torture its own nationals. Where reports of torture elicit some credence, a state usually responds by denial or, less frequently, by asserting that the conduct was unauthorized or constituted rough treatment short of torture.[15]

Memorandum of the United States as Amicus Curiae at 16 n.34.

Having examined the sources from which customary international law is derived — the usage of nations, judicial opinions and the works of jurists — we conclude that official torture is now prohibited by the law of nations. The prohibition is clear and unambiguous, and admits of no distinction between treatment of aliens and citizens. Accordingly, we must conclude that the dictum in Dreyfus v. von Finck, supra, 534 F.2d at 31, to the effect that "violations of international law do not occur when the aggrieved parties are nationals of the acting state," is clearly out of tune with the current usage and practice of international law. The treaties and accords cited above, as well as the express foreign policy of our own government, all make it clear that international law confers fundamental rights upon all people vis-à-vis their own governments. While the ultimate scope of those rights will be a subject for continuing refinement and elaboration, we hold that the right to be free from torture is now among them. We therefore turn to the question whether the other requirements for jurisdiction are met.

15. The fact that the prohibition of torture is often honored in the breach does not diminish its binding effect as a norm of international law. As one commentator has put it, "The best evidence for the existence of international law is that every actual State recognizes that it does exist and that it is itself under an obligation to observe it. States often violate international law, just as individuals often violate municipal law; but no more than individuals do States defend their violations by claiming that they are above the law." J. Brierly, The Outlook for International Law 4-5 (Oxford 1944).

III

Appellee submits that even if the tort alleged is a violation of modern international law, federal jurisdiction may not be exercised consistent with the dictates of Article III of the Constitution. The claim is without merit. Common law courts of general jurisdiction regularly adjudicate transitory tort claims between individuals over whom they exercise personal jurisdiction, wherever the tort occurred. Moreover, as part of an articulated scheme of federal control over external affairs, Congress provided, in the first Judiciary Act, §9(b), 1 Stat. 73, 77 (1789), for federal jurisdiction over suits by aliens where principles of international law are in issue. The constitutional basis for the Alien Tort Statute is the law of nations, which has always been part of the federal common law.

It is not extraordinary for a court to adjudicate a tort claim arising outside of its territorial jurisdiction. A state or nation has a legitimate interest in the orderly resolution of disputes among those within its borders, and where the lex loci delicti commissi is applied, it is an expression of comity to give effect to the laws of the state where the wrong occurred. . . .

During the eighteenth century, it was taken for granted on both sides of the Atlantic that the law of nations forms a part of the common law. 1 Blackstone, Commentaries 263-64 (1st Ed. 1765-69); 4 id. at 67. Under the Articles of Confederation, the Pennsylvania Court of Oyer and Terminer at Philadelphia, per McKean, Chief Justice, applied the law of nations to the criminal prosecution of the Chevalier de Longchamps for his assault upon the person of the French Consul-General to the United States, noting that "(t)his law, in its full extent, is a part of the law of this state. . . ." Republica v. DeLongchamps, 1 U.S. (1 Dall.) 113, 119 (1784). . . .

[O]ne of the principal defects of the Confederation that our Constitution was intended to remedy was the central government's inability to "cause infractions of treaties or of the law of nations, to be punished." 1 Farrand, Records of the Federal Convention 19 (Rev. ed. 1937) (Notes of James Madison). . . .

As ratified, the judiciary article contained no express reference to cases arising under the law of nations. Indeed, the only express reference to that body of law is contained in Article I, §8, cl. 10, which grants to the Congress the power to "define and punish . . . offenses against the law of nations." Appellees seize upon this circumstance and advance the proposition that the law of nations forms a part of the laws of the United States only to the extent that Congress has acted to define it. This extravagant claim is amply refuted by the numerous decisions applying rules of international law uncodified in any act of Congress. . . . Federal jurisdiction over cases involving international law is clear. . . .

In the twentieth century the international community has come to recognize the common danger posed by the flagrant disregard of basic human rights and particularly the right to be free of torture. Spurred first by the Great War, and then the Second, civilized nations have banded together to prescribe acceptable norms of international behavior. From the ashes of the Second World War arose the United Nations Organization, amid hopes that an era of peace and cooperation had at last begun. Though many of these aspirations have remained elusive goals, that circumstance cannot diminish the true progress that has been made. In the modern age, humanitarian and practical considerations have combined to lead the nations of the world to recognize that respect for fundamental human rights is in their individual and collective interest. Among the rights universally proclaimed by all nations, as we have noted, is the right to be free of physical torture. Indeed, for purposes of civil liability, the torturer has become like the pirate and slave trader before him hostis humani generis, an enemy of all mankind. Our holding today, giving effect to a jurisdictional provision enacted by our First Congress, is a small but important step in the fulfillment of the ageless dream to free all people from brutal violence.

Garcia-Mir v. Meese

U.S. Court of Appeals
788 F.2d 1446 (11th Cir. 1986)

JOHNSON, Circuit Judge. . . .

This is an appeal and cross-appeal from the final decision of the trial court ordering the government to prepare and implement a plan to provide individual parole revocation hearings for unadmitted aliens. The appellees-cross appellants ["appellees" or "aliens" or "Mariels"] are a certified class of Mariel Cuban refugees who were accorded a special immigration parole status by the Refugee Education Assistance Act of 1980. The district court has broken the class into two sub-classes. The "First Group" includes those who are guilty of crimes committed in Cuba before the boat-lift or who are mentally incompetent. They have never been paroled into this country. The "Second Group" consists of all other Mariels — those who, because there was no evidence of criminal or mental defect, were paroled under the provisions of the general alien parole statute, 8 U.S.C.A. §1182(d)(5) (1985) [i.e., permitted to remain free in the United States pending resolution of their status], but whose parole was subsequently revoked. All are currently detained in the Atlanta Penitentiary. . . .

B.   INTERNATIONAL LAW

The public law of nations was long ago incorporated into the common law of the United States. The Paquete Habana, 175 U.S. 677, 700 (1900); The Nereide, 13 U.S. (9 Cranch) 388, 423, 3 L. Ed. 769 (1815); Restatement of the Law of Foreign Relations Law of the United States (Revised) §131 comment d (Tent. Draft No. 6, 1985) [hereinafter cited as "Restatement 6"]. To the extent possible, courts must construe American law so as to avoid violating principles of public international law. Murray v. The Schooner Charming Betsy, 6 U.S. (2 Cranch), 64, 102, 118 (1804); Lauritzen v. Larsen, 345 U.S. 571, 578 (1958). But public international law is controlling only "where there is no treaty and no controlling executive or legislative act or judicial decision. . . ." 175 U.S. at 700. Appellees argue that, because general principles of international law forbid prolonged arbitrary detention, we should hold that their current detention is unlawful.

We have previously determined that the general deportation statute, 8 U.S.C.A. §1227(a) (1985), does not *restrict* the power of the Attorney General to detain aliens indefinitely. Fernandez-Roque II, 734 F.2d at 580 n.6. But this does not resolve the question whether there has been an *affirmative legislative grant* of authority to detain. As to the First Group there is sufficiently express evidence of congressional intent as to interdict the application of international law [i.e., after examining the 1980 legislation, the court concluded that Congress intended to allow persons in the First Group to be detained indefinitely, even though such detention violated international law].

The trial court found, correctly, that there has been no affirmative legislative grant to the Justice Department to detain the Second Group without hearings because 8 U.S.C.A. §1227(c) does not expressly authorize indefinite detention. Thus we must look for a controlling executive act. The trial court found that there was such a controlling act in the Attorney General's termination of the status review plan and in his decision to incarcerate indefinitely pending efforts to deport. The appellees and the amicus challenge this by arguing that a controlling executive act can only come from an act by or expressly sanctioned by the President himself, not one of his subordinates. Amicus Brief at 12. They rely for that proposition upon The Paquete Habana and upon the Restatement of the Law of Foreign Relations Law of the United States (Revised) §131 comment c (Tent. Draft No. 1, 1980) [hereinafter cited as "Restatement 1"]. . . .

As to the Restatement 1, the provision upon which amicus relies [to the effect that a controlling executive act can only come from the President] has been removed in subsequent drafts. The most recent version of that provision notes that the President, "acting within his constitutional authority, may have the power under the Constitution to act in ways that constitute violations of international law by the United States." The Constitution provides for the creation of executive departments, U.S. Const. art. 2, §2, and the power of the President to delegate his authority to those departments to act on his behalf is unquestioned. Likewise, in Restatement 6, §135 Reporter's Note 3, the power of the President to disregard international law in service of domestic needs is reaffirmed. Thus we hold that the executive acts here evident constitute a sufficient basis for affirming the trial court's finding that international law does not control.

Notes and Questions

1. What is the holding of the Paquete Habana case? What is the meaning of the Court's statement that "international law is part of our law"? What is the significance of the Court's statements that customary international law applies "where there is no treaty, and no controlling executive or legislative act," and that courts must "give effect to" customary international law "in the absence of any treaty or other public act of [the] government in relation to the matter"? What would the court have held if there had been no reference to the "law of nations" in the presidential proclamation? What if Congress had provided in the declaration of war that all Spanish vessels were subject to capture?

2. In *Filartiga,* what was the rule of international law involved? What evidence did the court cite in support of that rule? What role did state practice play in the court's analysis? What is the significance of footnote 15 of the court's opinion? How

does the Supreme Court's use of international law in The Paquete Habana compare with the Second Circuit's use of international law in *Filartiga*?

3. Although the Constitution does not mention customary international law in either Article III or Article VI, those Articles do refer to the "Laws of the United States," and some scholars have argued that the Founders intended that phrase to encompass customary international law. But isn't that argument undermined by the express reference to the law of nations in Article I? Also, is it likely that the Founders would have wanted *all* of the law of nations to be included within the federal courts' jurisdiction set out in Article III or the preemptive federal law specified in Article VI? Would the Founders have considered customary international law to be "made in Pursuance [of the Constitution]," as required by Article VI for "Laws of the United States"? If not, is it likely that they intended the phrase "Laws of the United States" in Article III to be broader than the similar phrase in Article VI? For a discussion of these and related issues, compare Curtis A. Bradley, The Alien Tort Statute and Article III, 42 Va. J. Intl. L. 587 (2002) (arguing that the phrase "Laws of the United States" was not intended to encompass the law of nations in either Article III or Article VI), with William S. Dodge, The Constitutionality of the Alien Tort Statute: Some Observations on Text and Context, 42 Va. J. Intl. L. 687 (2002) (arguing that the phrase "Laws of the United States" in Article III was intended to encompass the law of nations).

4. Whatever its status at the Founding, it appears that by the late 1790s and early 1800s, customary international law was not viewed as federal law within the meaning of Articles III and VI. In Ware v. Hylton, 3 U.S. 199, 281 (1796), the Court considered whether Virginia's confiscation of debts owed to British creditors was consistent with the Treaty of Peace with Great Britain and the law of nations. As to the latter point, Justices Chase and Iredell concluded (without disagreement from the other Justices) that customary international law did not preempt inconsistent state law. See id. at 229 (Chase, J.); id. at 265-266 (Iredell, J.). In the early nineteenth century, the Supreme Court held that nonwritten common law (including, presumably, customary international law) could not serve as the basis for a criminal prosecution in the federal courts. See United States v. Hudson & Goodwin, 11 U.S. (7 Cranch) 32, 34 (1812); United States v. Coolidge, 14 U.S. (1 Wheat.) 415, 416-417 (1816).

5. In the nineteenth and early twentieth centuries, the law of nations was treated as an element of "general common law," a body of law most famously identified with Swift v. Tyson, 41 U.S. 1 (1842). General common law was a type of customary law that U.S. courts applied as "rules of decision in particular cases without insisting that the law be attached to any particular sovereign." William A. Fletcher, The General Common Law and Section 34 of the Judiciary Act of 1798: The Example of Marine Insurance, 97 Harv. L. Rev. 1513, 1517 (1984). General common law was not considered part of the "Laws of the United States" within the meaning of Articles III and VI of the Constitution; federal court interpretations of general common law were not binding on the states; and a case "arising under" general common law did not by that fact alone establish federal question jurisdiction. Fletcher, supra, at 1521-1527. The Supreme Court expressly referred to customary international law as "general law" or "common law" during this period, and in several cases it declined to review state court determinations of customary international law because of the lack of a federal question. See, e.g., Oliver Am. Trading Co. v. Mexico, 264 U.S. 440, 442-

443 (1924) (foreign sovereign immunity); New York Life Ins. Co. v. Hendren, 92 U.S. 286, 286-287 (1875) ("laws of war").

6. The Supreme Court overruled Swift v. Tyson in Erie Railroad Co. v. Tompkins, 304 U.S. 64 (1938), stating that "there is no general federal common law," and holding that "[e]xcept in matters governed by the Federal Constitution or by Act of Congress, the law to be applied in any case is the law of the State." One reason the Court in *Erie* rejected the notion of a general common law in the federal courts was the Court's belief that "law in the sense in which courts speak of it today does not exist without some definite authority behind it." Id. at 79. *Erie* did not, however, eliminate the lawmaking powers of federal courts. *Erie* ruled that federal court development of general common law was illegitimate not because it was a form of judicial lawmaking *per se,* but rather because it was *unauthorized* lawmaking not grounded in a sovereign source. Federal courts thus retain some power to make federal common law when authorized to do so in some fashion by the Constitution or a federal statute or treaty. This grounding of federal common lawmaking in a federal sovereign source makes the new federal common law, unlike the pre-*Erie* general common law, federal law within the meaning of Article II ("take care" clause), Article III (arising under jurisdiction), and Article VI (the Supremacy Clause). What are the implications of *Erie* and post-*Erie* federal common law for the domestic status of customary international law? This question is considered in the notes below.

7. *Filartiga* was the first decision in the post-*Erie* period to squarely hold that customary international law has the status of federal common law. *Filartiga* itself makes clear one implication of this holding: a case arising under customary international law "arises under" federal law for purposes of Article III federal jurisdiction. Is the court in *Filartiga* correct in stating that customary international law has "always been part of the federal common law"?

8. A second possible consequence of *Filartiga*'s holding is that customary international law binds the President under Article II, which provides that the President "shall take Care that the Laws be faithfully executed." See U.S. Const., Art. II, §3. What does The Paquete Habana suggest? Assuming the President has the authority to violate customary international law, do lower-level Executive Branch officials also have this authority? For discussion of these and other issues, see, for example, Essays, Agora: May the President Violate Customary International Law?, 80 Am. J. Intl. L. 913 (1986).

9. In *Garcia-Mir,* what was the rule of international law at issue? How did the plaintiffs want it employed? The court in *Garcia-Mir* rejects the argument that customary international law is judicially enforceable against the President or high-level Executive Branch officials. A number of other courts have similarly rejected this argument. See, e.g., Barrera-Echavarria v. Rison, 44 F.3d 1441, 1451 (9th Cir. 1995); Gisbert v. United States Attorney General, 988 F.2d 1437, 1448 (5th Cir. 1993).

10. A third possible consequence of the view that customary international law is federal common law is that it preempts inconsistent state law pursuant to the Supremacy Clause. No court has yet applied customary international law to invalidate a state law, although one state court decision could be read to support this proposition: In Republic of Argentina v. City of New York, 250 N.E.2d 698 (Ct. App. N.Y. 1969), the New York Court of Appeals held that the City of New York could not assess taxes against Argentina's consulate property because the assessment would violate customary international law. The court never explained its views about the pre-

cise status of customary international law, but the court might have implicitly been accepting Argentina's argument that customary international law had the status of preemptive federal law. Despite the lack of significant precedent, many commentators have argued that customary international law should preempt inconsistent state law. For example, a number of commentators have argued that customary international law prohibits the execution of juvenile offenders and should preempt state laws that allow such executions. What are the consequences of treating customary international law as binding on states in the absence of congressional action?

11. A final possibility is that customary international law, as federal common law, binds Congress. Lower courts have generally held that Congress can violate customary international law. See, e.g., *Garcia-Mir*, supra; United States v. Yunis, 924 F.2d 1086, 1091 (D.C. Cir. 1991). However, as discussed earlier in this chapter, the Supreme Court has held that treaties and federal statutes are essentially equal in status, such that the later in time prevails as a matter of U.S. domestic law. This invites the argument that a newly developed norm of customary international law, like a new treaty, could supersede a prior inconsistent federal statute. As the Restatement (Third) of Foreign Relations Law explains: "Since international customary law and an international agreement have equal authority in international law, and both are law of the United States, arguably later customary law should be given effect as law of the United States, even in the face of an earlier law or agreement, just as a later international agreement of the United States is given effect in the face of an earlier law or agreement." Restatement (Third), section 115, reporters' note 4. Is this argument persuasive? Can courts exercise other federal common law powers to invalidate a federal statute? For a recent controversial decision suggesting that customary international law can supersede a federal statute if it develops after the enactment of the statute, see Beharry v. Reno, 183 F. Supp. 2d 584 (E.D.N.Y. 2002).

12. There has been substantial commentary in recent years concerning the domestic status of customary international law. For the view that customary international law has the status of federal common law, see, for example, Louis Henkin, International Law as Law in the United States, 82 Mich. L. Rev. 1555 (1984); Harold Hongju Koh, Is International Law Really State Law?, 111 Harv. L. Rev. 1824 (1998). For the view that customary international law should not be treated as federal common law, see Curtis A. Bradley & Jack L. Goldsmith, Customary International Law as Federal Common Law: A Critique of the Modern Position, 110 Harv. L. Rev. 815 (1997); Curtis A. Bradley & Jack L. Goldsmith, Federal Courts and the Incorporation of International Law, 111 Harv. L. Rev. 2260 (1998); see also Phillip R. Trimble, A Revisionist View of Customary International Law, 33 UCLA L. Rev. 665 (1986) (arguing that direct incorporation of customary international law may be inconsistent with U.S. political traditions).

Filartiga v. Pena-Irala

U.S. District Court
577 F. Supp. 860 (E.D.N.Y. 1984)

NICKERSON, District Judge. . . .

Following remand Pena took no further part in the action. This court granted a default and referred the question of damages to Magistrate John L. Caden for a report. The Magistrate, after a hearing, recommended damages of $200,000 for Dr. Joel Filartiga and $175,000 for Dolly Filartiga. Plaintiffs filed objections to the report, and the matter is now here for determination. . . .

II

The Court of Appeals decided only that Section 1350 gave jurisdiction. We must now face the issue left open by the Court of Appeals, namely, the nature of the "action" over which the section affords jurisdiction. Does the "tort" to which the statute refers mean a wrong "in violation of the law of nations" or merely a wrong actionable under the law of the appropriate sovereign state? The latter construction would make the violation of international law pertinent only to afford jurisdiction. The court would then, in accordance with traditional conflict of laws principles, apply the substantive law of Paraguay. If the "tort" to which the statute refers is the violation of international law, the court must look to that body of law to determine what substantive principles to apply.

The word "tort" has historically meant simply "wrong," or "the opposite of right," so-called, according to Lord Coke, because it is "wrested" or "crooked," being contrary to that which is "right" and "straight." Sir Edward Coke on Littleton 158b; see also W. Prosser, Law of Torts 2 (1971). There was nothing about the contemporary usage of the word in 1789, when Section 1350 was adopted, to suggest that it should be read to encompass wrongs defined as such by a national state but not by international law. Even before the adoption of the Constitution piracy was defined as a crime by the law of nations. United States v. Smith, 18 U.S. (5 Wheat.) 153, 157 (1820). As late as 1819 Congress passed legislation, now 18 U.S.C. §1651, providing for punishment of "the crime of piracy, as defined by the law of nations." 3 Stat. 510 (1819). Congress would hardly have supposed when it enacted Section 1350 that a "crime," but not the comparable "tort," was definable by the law of nations. Nor is there any legislative history of the section to suggest such a limitation.

Accordingly, there is no basis for adopting a narrow interpretation of Section 1350 inviting frustration of the purposes of international law by individual states that enact immunities for government personnel or other such exemptions or limitations. The court concludes that it should determine the substantive principles to be applied by looking to international law, which, as the Court of Appeals stated, "became a part of the common law *of the United States* upon the adoption of the Constitution."

The international law described by the Court of Appeals does not ordain detailed remedies but sets forth norms. But plainly international "law" does not consist of mere benevolent yearnings never to be given effect. Indeed, the Declaration on the Protection of All Persons from Being Subjected to Torture, General Assembly Resolution 3452 (1975), adopted without dissent by the General Assembly, recites that where an act of torture has been committed by or at the instigation of a public official, the victim shall be afforded redress and compensation "in accordance with national law," art. 11, and that "[e]ach state" shall ensure that all acts of torture are offenses under its criminal law, art. 7.

The international law prohibiting torture established the standard and referred to the national states the task of enforcing it. By enacting Section 1350 Congress entrusted that task to the federal courts and gave them power to choose and develop federal remedies to effectuate the purposes of the international law incorporated into United States common law.

In order to take the international condemnation of torture seriously this court must adopt a remedy appropriate to the ends and reflective of the nature of the condemnation. Torture is viewed with universal abhorrence; the prohibition of torture by international consensus and express international accords is clear and unambiguous; and "for purposes of civil liability, the torturer has become — like the pirate and the slave trader before him — *hostis humani generis,* an enemy of all mankind." 630 F.2d at 884, 888, 890. We are dealing not with an ordinary case of assault and battery. If the courts of the United States are to adhere to the consensus of the community of humankind, any remedy they fashion must recognize that this case concerns an act so monstrous as to make its perpetrator an outlaw around the globe.

III

The common law of the United States includes, of course, the principles collected under the rubric of conflict of laws. For the most part in international matters those principles have been concerned with the relevant policies of the interested national states, and with "the needs" of the "international systems." Restatement (Second) of Conflict of Laws (1971) §6(2). The chief function of international choice-of-law rules has been said to be to further harmonious relations and commercial intercourse between states. Id., comment d.

However, where the nations of the world have adopted a norm in terms so formal and unambiguous as to make it international "law," the interests of the global community transcend those of any one state. That does not mean that traditional choice-of-law principles are irrelevant. Clearly the court should consider the interests of Paraguay to the extent they do not inhibit the appropriate enforcement of the applicable international law or conflict with the public policy of the United States.

In this case the torture and death of Joelito occurred in Paraguay. The plaintiffs and Pena are Paraguayan and lived in Paraguay when the torture took place, although Dolly Filartiga has applied for permanent asylum in the United States. It was in Paraguay that plaintiffs suffered the claimed injuries, with the exception of the emotional trauma which followed Dolly Filartiga to this country. The parties' relationships with each other and with Joelito were centered in Paraguay.

Moreover, the written Paraguayan law prohibits torture. The Constitution of Paraguay, art. 50. The Paraguayan Penal Code, art. 337, provides that homicide by torture is punishable by imprisonment for 15 to 20 years. Paraguay is a signatory to the American Convention on Human Rights, which proscribes the use of torture. Paraguayan law purports to allow recovery for wrongful death, including specific pecuniary damages, "moral damage," and court costs and attorney's fees. Thus, the pertinent formal Paraguayan law is ascertainable.

All these factors make it appropriate to look first to Paraguayan law in determining the remedy for the violation of international law. It might be objected that, despite Paraguay's official ban on torture, the "law" of that country is what it does in fact, Holmes, The Path of the Law, 10 Harv. L. Rev. 457, 461 (1897), and torture persists throughout the country. . . .

Where a nation's pronouncements form part of the consensus establishing an international law, however, it does not lie in the mouth of a citizen of that nation, though it professes one thing and does another, to claim that his country did not mean what it said. In concert with the other nations of the world Paraguay prohibited torture and thereby reaped the benefits the condemnation brought with it. Paraguayan citizens may not pretend that no such condemnation exists. If there be hypocrisy, we can only say with La Rochefoucauld that "hypocrisy is the homage which vice pays to virtue." Reflections; or Sentences and Moral Maxims 218 (1678).

To the extent that Pena might have expected that Paraguay would not hold him responsible for his official acts, that was not a "justified" expectation, so as to make unfair the application to him of the written law of Paraguay.

IV

Plaintiffs claim punitive damages, and the Magistrate recommended they be denied on the ground that they are not recoverable under the Paraguayan Civil Code. While compensable "moral" injuries under that code include emotional pain and suffering, loss of companionship and disruption of family life, plaintiffs' expert agrees that the code does not provide for what United States courts would call punitive damages. Paraguayan law, in determining the intensity and duration of the suffering and the consequent "moral" damages, takes into account the heinous nature of the tort. However, such damages are not justified by the desire to punish the defendant. They are designed to compensate for the greater pain caused by the atrocious nature of the act.

Yet because, as the record establishes, Paraguay will not undertake to prosecute Pena for his acts, the objective of the international law making torture punishable as a crime can only be vindicated by imposing punitive damages.

It is true, as plaintiffs concede, that damages designated punitive have rarely been awarded by international tribunals. As explained in M. Whiteman, Damages in International Law 716-17 (1937), the international law of damages has developed chiefly in the resolution of claims by one state on behalf of its nationals against the other state, and the failure to assess exemplary damages as such against a respondent government may be explained by the absence of malice or *mala mens* on the part of an impersonal government. Here Pena and not Paraguay is the defendant. There is no question of punishing a sovereign state or of attempting to hold the people of that state liable for a governmental act in which they played no part.

Moreover, there is some precedent for the award of punitive damages in tort even against a national government. In I'm Alone (Canada v. United States), U.N. Rep. Int. Arb. Awards, vol. 3, at 1609, the American and Canadian Claims Commissioners recommended, in addition to compensatory damages, payment of $25,000 by the United States to Canada for intentionally sinking a Canadian ship. In Re Letelier v. Republic of Chile, 502 F. Supp. 259, 266, 267 (D.D.C. 1980), the court awarded $2,000,000 in punitive damages against the Republic of Chile and various of its employees to the survivors and personal representatives of the former Chilean Ambassador to the United States and a passenger in his car, both killed by the explosion of a bomb. While the court imposed the damages under domestic laws, it mentioned that the "tortious actions" proven were "in violation of international law."

Where the defendant is an individual, the same diplomatic considerations that prompt reluctance to impose punitive damages are not present. The Supreme Court in dicta has recognized that punishment is an appropriate objective under the law of nations, saying that "an attack from revenge and malignity, from gross abuse of power, and a settled purpose of mischief . . . may be punished by all the penalties which the law of nations can properly administer." In developing common law remedies to implement the rights secured by the Constitution, the Supreme Court has stated that courts may award punitive damages in actions based on the Constitution alone, Carlson v. Green, 446 U.S. 14, 21-22 (1980), and based on 42 U.S.C. §1983, where the legislation makes no reference to the nature and extent of the damages to be awarded.

This court concludes that it is essential and proper to grant the remedy of punitive damages in order to give effect to the manifest objectives of the international prohibition against torture.

In 1992, Congress enacted a statute that gives both foreign and U.S. victims of torture and "extrajudicial killing" the right to sue for damages in U.S. courts.

Torture Victim Protection Act

Act March 12, 1992, P.L. 102-256, 106 Stat. 73

Sec. 1. Short title

This Act may be cited as the "Torture Victim Protection Act of 1991."
Sec. 2. Establishment of civil action

(a) Liability. An individual who, under actual or apparent authority, or color of law, of any foreign nation— *State action*

(1) subjects an individual to torture shall, in a civil action, be liable for damages to that individual; or

(2) subjects an individual to extrajudicial killing shall, in a civil action, be liable for damages to the individual's legal representative, or to any person who may be a claimant in an action for wrongful death.

(b) Exhaustion of remedies. A court shall decline to hear a claim under this section if the claimant has not exhausted adequate and available remedies in the place in which the conduct giving rise to the claim occurred.

(c) Statute of limitations. No action shall be maintained under this section unless it is commenced within 10 years after the cause of action arose.
Sec. 3. Definitions

(a) Extrajudicial killing. For the purposes of this Act, the term "extrajudicial killing" means a deliberated killing not authorized by a previous judgment pronounced by a regularly constituted court affording all the judicial guarantees which are recognized as indispensable by civilized peoples. Such term, however, does not include any such killing that, under international law, is lawfully carried out under the authority of a foreign nation.

(b) Torture. For the purposes of this Act—

(1) the term "torture" means any act, directed against an individual in the offender's custody or physical control, by which severe pain or suffering (other than pain or suffering arising only from or inherent in, or incidental to, lawful sanctions), whether physical or mental, is intentionally inflicted on that individual for such purposes as obtaining from that individual or a third person information or a confession, punishing that individual for an act that individual or a third person

has committed or is suspected of having committed, intimidating or coercing that individual or a third person, or for any reason based on discrimination of any kind; and

(2) mental pain or suffering refers to prolonged mental harm caused by or resulting from —

(A) the intentional infliction or threatened infliction of severe physical pain or suffering;

(B) the administration or application, or threatened administration or application, of mind altering substances or other procedures calculated to disrupt profoundly the senses or the personality;

(C) the threat of imminent death; or

(D) the threat that another individual will imminently be subjected to death, severe physical pain or suffering, or the administration or application of mind altering substances or other procedures calculated to disrupt profoundly the senses or personality.

Both the Alien Tort Statute and the Torture Victim Protection Act were at issue in the decision below.

Kadic v. Karadzic

U.S. Court of Appeals
70 F.3d 232 (2d Cir. 1995)

JON O. NEWMAN, Chief Judge:

Most Americans would probably be surprised to learn that victims of atrocities committed in Bosnia are suing the leader of the insurgent Bosnian-Serb forces in a United States District Court in Manhattan. Their claims seek to build upon the foundation of this Court's decision in Filartiga v. Pena-Irala, 630 F.2d 876 (2d Cir. 1980), which recognized the important principle that the venerable Alien Tort Act, 28 U.S.C. §1350 (1988), enacted in 1789 but rarely invoked since then, validly creates federal court jurisdiction for suits alleging torts committed anywhere in the world against aliens in violation of the law of nations. The pending appeals pose additional significant issues as to the scope of the Alien Tort Act: whether some violations of the law of nations may be remedied when committed by those not acting under the authority of a state; if so, whether genocide, war crimes, and crimes against humanity are among the violations that do not require state action; and whether a person, otherwise liable for a violation of the law of nations, is immune from service of process because he is present in the United States as an invitee of the United Nations. . . .

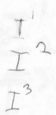

BACKGROUND

The plaintiffs-appellants are Croat and Muslim citizens of the internationally recognized nation of Bosnia-Herzegovina, formerly a republic of Yugoslavia. Their complaints, which we accept as true for purposes of this appeal, allege that they are victims, and representatives of victims, of various atrocities, including brutal acts of rape, forced prostitution, forced impregnation, torture, and summary execution, carried out by Bosnian-Serb military forces as part of a genocidal campaign conducted in the course of the Bosnian civil war. Karadzic, formerly a citizen of Yugoslavia and now a citizen of Bosnia-Herzegovina, is the President of a three-man presidency of the self-proclaimed Bosnian-Serb republic within Bosnia-Herzegovina, sometimes referred to as "Srpska," which claims to exercise lawful authority, and does in fact exercise actual control, over large parts of the territory of Bosnia-Herzegovina. In his capacity as President, Karadzic possesses ultimate command authority over the Bosnian-Serb military forces, and the injuries perpetrated upon plaintiffs were committed as part of a pattern of systematic human rights violations that was directed by Karadzic and carried out by the military forces under his command. The complaints allege that Karadzic acted in an official capacity either as the titular head of Srpska or in collaboration with the government of the recognized nation of the former Yugoslavia and its dominant constituent republic, Serbia.

The two groups of plaintiffs asserted causes of action for genocide, rape, forced prostitution and impregnation, torture and other cruel, inhuman, and degrading treatment, assault and battery, sex and ethnic inequality, summary execution, and wrongful death. They sought compensatory and punitive damages, attorney's fees, and, in one of the cases, injunctive relief. Plaintiffs grounded subject-matter jurisdiction in the Alien Tort Act, the Torture Victim Protection Act of 1991 ("Torture Victim Act"), Pub. L. No. 102-256, 106 Stat. 73 (1992), codified at 28 U.S.C. §1350 note (Supp. V 1993), the general federal-question jurisdictional statute, 28 U.S.C. §1331 (1988), and principles of supplemental jurisdiction, 28 U.S.C. §1367 (Supp. V 1993).

In early 1993, Karadzic was admitted to the United States on three separate occasions as an invitee of the United Nations. According to affidavits submitted by the plaintiffs, Karadzic was personally served with the summons and complaint in each action during two of these visits while he was physically present in Manhattan. Karadzic admits that he received the summons and complaint in the *Kadic* action, but disputes whether the attempt to serve him personally in the Doe action was effective. . . .

I. SUBJECT-MATTER JURISDICTION

Appellants allege three statutory bases for the subject-matter jurisdiction of the District Court — the Alien Tort Act, the Torture Victim Act, and the general federal-question jurisdictional statute.

A. The Alien Tort Act

1. General Application to Appellants' Claims

. . . Our decision in *Filartiga* established that [the Alien Tort Statute] confers federal subject-matter jurisdiction when the following three conditions are satisfied: (1) an alien sues (2) for a tort (3) committed in violation of the law of nations (i.e., international law).[1] 630 F.2d at 887. The first two requirements are plainly satisfied

---

1. *Filartiga* did not consider the alternative prong of the Alien Tort Act: suits by aliens for a tort committed in violation of "a treaty of the United States." See 630 F.2d at 880. As in *Filartiga*, plaintiffs in the instant cases "primarily rely upon treaties and other international instruments as evidence of an emerging norm of customary international law, rather than independent sources of law," id. at 880 n.7.

here, and the only disputed issue is whether plaintiffs have pleaded violations of international law.

Because the Alien Tort Act requires that plaintiffs plead a "violation of the law of nations" at the jurisdictional threshold, this statute requires a more searching review of the merits to establish jurisdiction than is required under the more flexible "arising under" formula of section 1331. Thus, it is not a sufficient basis for jurisdiction to plead merely a colorable violation of the law of nations. There is no federal subject-matter jurisdiction under the Alien Tort Act unless the complaint adequately pleads a violation of the law of nations (or treaty of the United States).

Filartiga established that courts ascertaining the content of the law of nations "must interpret international law not as it was in 1789, but as it has evolved and exists among the nations of the world today." Id. at 881. We find the norms of contemporary international law by "'consulting the works of jurists, writing professedly on public law; or by the general usage and practice of nations; or by judicial decisions recognizing and enforcing that law.'" *Filartiga*, 630 F.2d at 880 (quoting United States v. Smith, 18 U.S. (5 Wheat.) 153 (1820)). If this inquiry discloses that the defendant's alleged conduct violates "well-established, universally recognized norms of international law," 630 F.2d at 888, as opposed to "idiosyncratic legal rules," 630 F.2d at 881, then federal jurisdiction exists under the Alien Tort Act.

Karadzic contends that appellants have not alleged violations of the norms of international law because such norms bind only states and persons acting under color of a state's law, not private individuals. In making this contention, Karadzic advances the contradictory positions that he is not a state actor, . . . even as he asserts that he is the President of the self-proclaimed Republic of Srpska, . . . For their part, the *Kadic* appellants also take somewhat inconsistent positions in pleading defendant's role as President of Srpska, and also contending that "Karadzic is not an official of any government."

Judge Leisure accepted Karadzic's contention that "acts committed by non-state actors do not violate the law of nations," *Doe*, 866 F. Supp. at 739, and considered him to be a non-state actor. The Judge appears to have deemed state action required primarily on the basis of cases determining the need for state action as to claims of official torture, without consideration of the substantial body of law, discussed below, that renders private individuals liable for some international law violations.

We do not agree that the law of nations, as understood in the modern era, confines its reach to state action. Instead, we hold that certain forms of conduct violate the law of nations whether undertaken by those acting under the auspices of a state or only as private individuals. An early example of the application of the law of nations to the acts of private individuals is the prohibition against piracy. . . . Later examples are prohibitions against the slave trade and certain war crimes.

The liability of private persons for certain violations of customary international law and the availability of the Alien Tort Act to remedy such violations was early recognized by the Executive Branch in an opinion of Attorney General Bradford in reference to acts of American citizens aiding the French fleet to plunder British property off the coast of Sierra Leone in 1795. See Breach of Neutrality, 1 Op. Att'y Gen. 57, 59 (1795). The Executive Branch has emphatically restated in this litigation its position that private persons may be found liable under the Alien Tort Act for acts of genocide, war crimes, and other violations of international humanitarian law. See Statement of Interest of the United States at 5-13.

The Restatement (Third) of the Foreign Relations Law of the United States (1986) ("Restatement (Third)") proclaims: "Individuals may be held liable for offenses against international law, such as piracy, war crimes, and genocide." Restatement (Third) pt. II, introductory note. The Restatement is careful to identify those violations that are actionable when committed by a state, Restatement (Third) §702, and a more limited category of violations of "universal concern," id. §404, partially overlapping with those listed in section 702. Though the immediate focus of section 404 is to identify those offenses for which a state has jurisdiction to punish without regard to territoriality or the nationality of the offenders, cf. id. §402(1)(a), (2), the inclusion of piracy and slave trade from an earlier era and aircraft hijacking from the modern era demonstrates that the offenses of "universal concern" include those capable of being committed by non-state actors. Although the jurisdiction authorized by section 404 is usually exercised by application of criminal law, international law also permits states to establish appropriate civil remedies, id. §404 cmt. b, such as the tort actions authorized by the Alien Tort Act. Indeed, the two cases invoking the Alien Tort Act prior to *Filartiga* both applied the civil remedy to private action. See Adra v. Clift, 195 F. Supp. 857 (D. Md. 1961); Bolchos v. Darrel, 3 F. Cas. 810, 1 Bee 74 (D.S.C. 1795) (No. 1,607).

Karadzic disputes the application of the law of nations to any violations committed by private individuals, relying on *Filartiga* and the concurring opinion of Judge Edwards in *Tel-Oren*. *Filartiga* involved an allegation of torture committed by a state official. Relying on the United Nations' Declaration on the Protection of All Persons from Being Subjected to Torture, G.A. Res. 3452, U.N. GAOR, U.N. Doc. A/1034 (1975) (hereinafter "Declaration on Torture"), as a definitive statement of norms of customary international law prohibiting states from permitting torture, we ruled that "*official* torture is now prohibited by the law of nations." *Filartiga*, 630 F.2d at 884 (emphasis added). We had no occasion to consider whether international law violations other than torture are actionable against private individuals, and nothing in *Filartiga* purports to preclude such a result. . . .

Karadzic also contends that Congress intended the state-action requirement of the Torture Victim Act to apply to actions under the Alien Tort Act. We disagree. Congress enacted the Torture Victim Act to codify the cause of action recognized by this Circuit in *Filartiga*, and to further extend that cause of action to plaintiffs who are U.S. citizens. See H.R. Rep. No. 367, 102d Cong., 2d Sess., at 4 (1991), reprinted in 1992 U.S.C.C.A.N. 84, 86 (explaining that codification of *Filartiga* was necessary in light of skepticism expressed by Judge Bork's concurring opinion in *Tel-Oren*). At the same time, Congress indicated that the Alien Tort Act "has other important uses and should not be replaced," because

> claims based on torture and summary executions do not exhaust the list of actions that may appropriately be covered [by the Alien Tort Act]. That statute should remain intact to permit suits based on other norms that already exist or may ripen in the future into rules of customary international law. [Id.]

The scope of the Alien Tort Act remains undiminished by enactment of the Torture Victim Act.

2. *Specific Application of Alien Tort Act to Appellants' Claims*

... [I]t will be helpful to group the appellants' claims into three categories: (a) genocide, (b) war crimes, and (c) other instances of inflicting death, torture, and degrading treatment.

(a) Genocide. In the aftermath of the atrocities committed during the Second World War, the condemnation of genocide as contrary to international law quickly achieved broad acceptance by the community of nations. In 1946, the General Assembly of the United Nations declared that genocide is a crime under international law that is condemned by the civilized world, whether the perpetrators are "private individuals, public officials or statesmen." G.A. Res. 96(I). . . . The General Assembly also affirmed the principles of Article 6 of the Agreement and Charter Establishing the Nuremberg War Crimes Tribunal for punishing "'persecutions on political, racial, or religious grounds,'" regardless of whether the offenders acted "'as individuals or as members of organizations,'" In re Extradition of Demjanjuk, 612 F. Supp. 544, 555 n.11 (N.D. Ohio 1985) (quoting Article 6).

The Convention on the Prevention and Punishment of the Crime of Genocide, 78 U.N.T.S. 277, entered into force Jan. 12, 1951, for the United States Feb. 23, 1989 (hereinafter "Convention on Genocide"), provides a more specific articulation of the prohibition of genocide in international law. The Convention, which has been ratified by more than 120 nations, including the United States, . . . defines "genocide" to mean

> any of the following acts committed with intent to destroy, in whole or in part, a
> national, ethnical, racial or religious group, as such:
>
> (a) Killing members of the group;
> (b) Causing serious bodily or mental harm to members of the group;
> (c) Deliberately inflicting on the group conditions of life calculated to bring
>   about its physical destruction in whole or in part;
> (d) Imposing measures intended to prevent births with the group;
> (e) Forcibly transferring children of the group to another group. [Convention
>   on Genocide art. II.] Especially pertinent to the pending appeal, the Con-
>   vention makes clear that "persons committing genocide . . . shall be pun-
>   ished, *whether they are constitutionally responsible rulers, public officials or private
>   individuals.*" Id. art. IV (emphasis added). These authorities unambiguously
>   reflect that, from its incorporation into international law, the proscription of
>   genocide has applied equally to state and non-state actors.

The applicability of this norm to private individuals is also confirmed by the Genocide Convention Implementation Act of 1987, 18 U.S.C. §1091 (1988), which criminalizes acts of genocide without regard to whether the offender is acting under color of law, id. §1091(a) ("whoever" commits genocide shall be punished), if the crime is committed within the United States or by a U.S. national, id. §1091(d). Though Congress provided that the Genocide Convention Implementation Act shall not "be construed as creating any substantive or procedural right enforceable by law by any party in any proceeding," id. §1092, the legislative decision not to create a new private remedy does not imply that a private remedy is not already available under the Alien Tort Act. Nothing in the Genocide Convention Implementation Act or its legislative history reveals an intent by Congress to repeal the Alien Tort

Act insofar as it applies to genocide, and the two statutes are surely not repugnant to each other. Under these circumstances, it would be improper to construe the Genocide Convention Implementation Act as repealing the Alien Tort Act by implication.

Appellants' allegations that Karadzic personally planned and ordered a campaign of murder, rape, forced impregnation, and other forms of torture designed to destroy the religious and ethnic groups of Bosnian Muslims and Bosnian Croats clearly state a violation of the international law norm proscribing genocide, regardless of whether Karadzic acted under color of law or as a private individual. The District Court has subject-matter jurisdiction over these claims pursuant to the Alien Tort Act.

(b) War crimes. Plaintiffs also contend that the acts of murder, rape, torture, and arbitrary detention of civilians, committed in the course of hostilities, violate the law of war. Atrocities of the types alleged here have long been recognized in international law as violations of the law of war. Moreover, international law imposes an affirmative duty on military commanders to take appropriate measures within their power to control troops under their command for the prevention of such atrocities.

After the Second World War, the law of war was codified in the four Geneva Conventions, which have been ratified by more than 180 nations, including the United States,. . . . Common article 3, which is substantially identical in each of the four Conventions, applies to "armed conflicts not of an international character" and binds "each Party to the conflict . . . to apply, as a minimum, the following provisions":

> Persons taking no active part in the hostilities . . . shall in all circumstances be treated humanely, without any adverse distinction founded on race, colour, religion or faith, sex, birth or wealth, or any other similar criteria.

> To this end, the following acts are and shall remain prohibited at any time and in any place whatsoever with respect to the above-mentioned persons:

> (a)   violence to life and person, in particular murder of all kinds, mutilation, cruel treatment and torture;
> (b)   taking of hostages;
> (c)   outrages upon personal dignity, in particular humiliating and degrading treatment;
> (d)   the passing of sentences and carrying out of executions without previous judgment pronounced by a regularly constituted court. . . . [Geneva Convention I art. 3(1).]

Thus, under the law of war as codified in the Geneva Conventions, all "parties" to a conflict — which includes insurgent military groups — are obliged to adhere to these most fundamental requirements of the law of war.

The offenses alleged by the appellants, if proved, would violate the most fundamental norms of the law of war embodied in common article 3, which binds parties to internal conflicts regardless of whether they are recognized nations or roving hordes of insurgents. The liability of private individuals for committing war crimes has been recognized since World War I and was confirmed at Nuremberg after World War II, and remains today an important aspect of international law. The District Court has jurisdiction pursuant to the Alien Tort Act over appellants' claims of war crimes and other violations of international humanitarian law.

(c) Torture and summary execution. In *Filartiga,* we held that official torture is prohibited by universally accepted norms of international law, and the Torture Victim Act confirms this holding and extends it to cover summary execution. Torture Victim Act §§2(a), 3(a). However, torture and summary execution — when not perpetrated in the course of genocide or war crimes — are proscribed by international law only when committed by state officials or under color of law.

In the present case, appellants allege that acts of rape, torture, and summary execution were committed during hostilities by troops under Karadzic's command and with the specific intent of destroying appellants' ethnic-religious groups. Thus, many of the alleged atrocities are already encompassed within the appellants' claims of genocide and war crimes. Of course, at this threshold stage in the proceedings it cannot be known whether appellants will be able to prove the specific intent that is an element of genocide, or prove that each of the alleged torts were committed in the course of an armed conflict, as required to establish war crimes. It suffices to hold at this stage that the alleged atrocities are actionable under the Alien Tort Act, without regard to state action, to the extent that they were committed in pursuit of genocide or war crimes, and otherwise may be pursued against Karadzic to the extent that he is shown to be a state actor. Since the meaning of the state action requirement for purposes of international law violations will likely arise on remand and has already been considered by the District Court, we turn next to that requirement.

3.   The State Action Requirement for International Law Violations

In dismissing plaintiffs' complaints for lack of subject-matter jurisdiction, the District Court concluded that the alleged violations required state action and that the "Bosnian-Serb entity" headed by Karadzic does not meet the definition of a state. Appellants contend that they are entitled to prove that Srpska satisfies the definition of a state for purposes of international law violations and, alternatively, that Karadzic acted in concert with the recognized state of the former Yugoslavia and its constituent republic, Serbia.

(a) Definition of a state in international law. The definition of a state is well established in international law:

> Under international law, a state is an entity that has a defined territory and a permanent population, under the control of its own government, and that engages in, or has the capacity to engage in, formal relations with other such entities. [Restatement (Third) §201.]

Although the Restatement's definition of statehood requires the capacity to engage in formal relations with other states, it does not require recognition by other states. Recognized states enjoy certain privileges and immunities relevant to judicial proceedings . . . but an unrecognized state is not a juridical nullity. Our courts have regularly given effect to the "state" action of unrecognized states. . . .

The customary international law of human rights, such as the proscription of official torture, applies to states without distinction between recognized and unrecognized states. It would be anomalous indeed if non-recognition by the United

States, which typically reflects disfavor with a foreign regime—sometimes due to human rights abuses—had the perverse effect of shielding officials of the unrecognized regime from liability for those violations of international law norms that apply only to state actors.

Appellants' allegations entitle them to prove that Karadzic's regime satisfies the criteria for a state, for purposes of those international law violations requiring state action. Srpska is alleged to control defined territory, control populations within its power, and to have entered into agreements with other governments. It has a president, a legislature, and its own currency. These circumstances readily appear to satisfy the criteria for a state in all aspects of international law. Moreover, it is likely that the state action concept, where applicable for some violations like "official" torture, requires merely the semblance of official authority. The inquiry, after all, is whether a person purporting to wield official power has exceeded internationally recognized standards of civilized conduct, not whether statehood in all its formal aspects exists.

(b) Acting in concert with a foreign state. Appellants also sufficiently alleged that Karadzic acted under color of law insofar as they claimed that he acted in concert with the former Yugoslavia, the statehood of which is not disputed. The "color of law" jurisprudence of 42 U.S.C. §1983 is a relevant guide to whether a defendant has engaged in official action for purposes of jurisdiction under the Alien Tort Act. See Forti v. Suarez-Mason, 672 F. Supp. 1531, 1546 (N.D. Cal. 1987), reconsideration granted in part on other grounds, 694 F. Supp. 707 (N.D. Cal. 1988). A private individual acts under color of law within the meaning of section 1983 when he acts together with state officials or with significant state aid. See Lugar v. Edmondson Oil Co., 457 U.S. 922, 937 (1982). The appellants are entitled to prove their allegations that Karadzic acted under color of law of Yugoslavia by acting in concert with Yugoslav officials or with significant Yugoslavian aid.

Notes and Questions

1. Prior to *Filartiga*, only two courts had upheld jurisdiction under the Alien Tort Statute (ATS) (also sometimes called the "Alien Tort Claims Act" or the "Alien Tort Act") since the statute was enacted in 1789. See Adra v. Clift, 195 F. Supp. 857 (D. Md. 1961) (holding that a mother's concealment of her half-Lebanese child's name and nationality, resulting in the child being given a falsified Iraqi passport, was a tort in violation of the law of nations for purposes of the ATS); Bolchos v. Darrell, 3 F. Cas. 810 (D.S.C. 1795) (No. 1607) (finding jurisdiction under both an admiralty statute and the ATS in a case involving dispute about ownership of slaves on board a captured Spanish vessel). Why did the ATS not serve as a basis for jurisdiction in more cases? Part of the answer is that, before *Filartiga*, courts generally held that the law of nations did not regulate the ways in which nations treated their own citizens. See, e.g., Dreyfus v. Von Finck, 534 F.2d 24, 31 (2d Cir. 1976) ("[V]iolations of international law do not occur when the aggrieved parties are nationals of the acting state.").

2. The Second Circuit decided in *Filartiga* that the plaintiff had satisfied the ATS's jurisdictional requirement of alleging a "tort . . . committed in violation of the law of nations," and that jurisdiction over such a suit satisfied Article III. The Second Circuit did not clearly decide the separate issue of *choice of law* in an ATS suit, that is,

what substantive law governs in an ATS lawsuit. On remand, what was the district court's holding on choice of law? Did the district court apply Paraguayan law? International law? Federal common law? What law should govern in an ATS suit? How should courts decide? In this regard, what is the significance of the Second Circuit's statement that it was treating the ATS "not as granting new rights to aliens, but simply as opening the federal courts for adjudication of the rights already recognized by international law"? Was the remand decision consistent with this treatment?

3. What was the legal basis for the district court's award of punitive damages? Is it proper for a court to formulate a remedy for a violation of the law of nations when the remedy is not recognized under either the law of nations or the local law where the tortious conduct occurred? The policy rationale for the punitive damages award was punishment; was the award in fact likely to punish? Was it likely to deter future tortious conduct?

4. Even if a court has jurisdiction, and even after a court identifies the governing law, there is still a question whether the governing law provides a private cause of action. What do the *Filartiga* decisions suggest about the source of the cause of action for customary international law claims brought under the ATS? This issue arose in a case decided several years after *Filartiga*, Tel-Oren v. Libyan Arab Republic, 726 F.2d 774 (D.C. Cir. 1984), in which the D.C. Circuit dismissed an ATS suit concerning a terrorist attack in Israel. There was no opinion for the panel in that case; rather, each of the three judges wrote separate concurring opinions. Judge Bork argued in his concurrence that neither the ATS nor customary international law provided a private right to sue for human rights violations. See id. at 798 (Bork, J., concurring). Judge Edwards disagreed with Judge Bork about the lack of a private cause of action, but concluded that there was insufficient state action to support a claim under customary international law. See id. at 775 (Edwards, J., concurring). Judge Robb concluded that the case presented a nonjusticiable political question. See id. at 823 (Robb, J., concurring). Judge Bork's concurrence generated concern among supporters of international human rights litigation, and it was criticized in academic commentary. See, e.g., Anthony D'Amato, Judge Bork's Concept of the Law of Nations Is Seriously Mistaken, 79 Am. J. Intl. L. 92 (1985).

5. The original purposes of the ATS are uncertain. One historical event that many commentators believe that Congress may have had in mind was the Marbois episode. During the Articles of Confederation period in 1784, a Frenchman named De Longchamps assaulted Marbois, the French Counsel General to Pennsylvania. The incident sparked international controversy and made clear that the Continental Congress had no authority to punish the offender, who was tried in a Pennsylvania state court. Is it plausible to view the ATS as a response to this incident? If so, what does that suggest about the ATS's purposes? Is the use of the ATS today consistent with these purposes?

6. The legislative history of the TVPA expresses support for the *Filartiga* approach to human rights litigation under the ATS, and disagreement with the views of Judge Bork. For example, the Senate Majority Report states:

> The TVPA would establish an unambiguous basis for a cause of action that has been successfully maintained under an existing law, section 1350 of title 28 of the U.S. Code, derived from the Judiciary Act of 1789 (the Alien Tort Claims Act) which permits Fed-

eral district courts to hear claims by aliens for torts committed "in violation of the law of nations." Section 1350 has other important uses and should not be replaced. . . . The *Filartiga* case has met with general approval. . . . At least one Federal judge, however, has questioned whether section 1350 can be used by victims of torture committed in foreign nations absent an explicit grant of a cause of action by Congress. In a concurrence in *Tel-Oren* . . ., Judge Robert H. Bork questioned the existence of a private right of action under the Alien Tort Claims Act, reasoning that separation of powers principles required an explicit grant by Congress of a private right of action for lawsuits which affect foreign relations. The TVPA would provide such a grant, and would also enhance the remedy already available under section 1350 in an important respect: while the Alien Tort Claims Act provides a remedy to aliens only, the TVPA would extend a civil remedy also to U.S. citizens who may have been tortured abroad. Official torture and summary executions merit special attention in a statute expressly addressed to those practices. At the same time, claims based on torture or summary executions do not exhaust the list of actions that may appropriately be covered by section 1350. Consequently, that statute should remain intact. For example, outside of the torture and summary execution context, several Federal court decisions have relied on sec. 1350. [Torture Victim Protection Act of 1991, S. Rep. 102-249, 102d Cong. (Nov. 19, 1991).]

Despite this legislative history, is the text of the TVPA in fact consistent with the *Filartiga* approach to human rights litigation? Note that the TVPA, unlike the ATS, is limited to two specifically defined violations of international law, and contains a statute of limitations and an exhaustion requirement. In this light, does the TVPA narrow ATS-style human rights litigation with respect to torture and extrajudicial killing? Or could plaintiffs avoid the limitations of the TVPA by bringing their torture or extrajudicial claim under the ATS? If the TVPA narrows the scope of all claims of torture and extrajudicial killing, should it be viewed as authorizing other human rights litigation under the ATS, which provides no limitation on or definition of covered international law violations, and no procedural limitations? Does the answer depend on the legitimacy of using legislative history in statutory interpretation?

7. Some cases brought under the ATS have involved conduct that took place many years ago. For example, ATS suits were brought in 2002 against companies that had done business with South Africa's apartheid regime (which was in power between 1960 and 1993). Is there any statute of limitations for claims brought under the ATS? Should courts borrow the ten-year statute of limitations prescribed by Congress for claims brought under the Torture Victim Protection Act? See, e.g., *Pappa v. United States*, 281 F.3d 1004 (9th Cir. 2002) (borrowing the statute of limitations).

8. Why does the TVPA contain the limitations that it does? Despite these limitations, the first President Bush expressed the following concerns upon signing the legislation:

With rare exceptions, the victims of [acts covered by the TVPA] will be foreign citizens. There is thus a danger that U.S. courts may become embroiled in difficult and sensitive disputes in other countries, and possibly ill-founded or politically motivated suits, which have nothing to do with the United States and which offer little prospect of successful recovery. Such potential abuse of this statute undoubtedly would give rise to serious frictions in international relations and would also be a waste of our own limited and already overburdened judicial resources. [Statement by President George Bush upon Signing H.R. 2092, 28 Weekly Compilation of Presidential Documents 465, March 16, 1992, reprinted in 1992 U.S.C.C.A.N. 91.]

Are these concerns justified? Do you think that some of the cases in this section were politically motivated? Assuming they were, what's wrong with politically motivated lawsuits to redress gross human rights abuses?

9. What is the constitutional authority for Congress to enact the TVPA? Congress's power to define and punish offenses against the law of nations? Does that power allow Congress to create civil causes of action? Does it apply to offenses against the law of nations perpetrated by non-U.S. citizens in foreign countries? Can the TVPA be justified on some basis in Article I other than the define and punish clause? How about the Commerce Clause? Can the TVPA be justified as an implementation of the Convention Against Torture and Other Cruel, Inhuman or Degrading Treatment or Punishment, ratified by the United States in 1994, which requires that nations "prosecute or extradite" torturers found in their territory?

10. The TVPA provides a cause of action only for claims of torture and extrajudicial killing. What about other claims brought under the ATS? A number of courts, including the court in *Karadzic,* have held that the ATS itself impliedly provides a cause of action for violations of customary international law. See also, e.g., Hilao v. Estate of Marcos, 25 F.3d 1467, 1474-1475 (9th Cir. 1994); Xuncax v. Gramajo, 886 F. Supp. 162, 179 (D. Mass. 1995). By contrast, one court has held that the ATS delegates to the federal courts the task of fashioning remedies, including causes of action, to give effect to the federal policies underlying the ATS. See Abebe-Jira v. Negewo, 72 F.3d 844 (11th Cir. 1996). What is the difference between these two approaches? How do they differ from the approach in *Filartiga?* Is that the proper test of interpretation?

11. By its terms, the ATS can be invoked only by alien plaintiffs. Although the TVPA can be invoked by U.S. citizens, it applies only when the defendant has acted "under actual or apparent authority, or color of law, of any foreign nation." Thus, U.S. citizens who sue domestic defendants for violations of customary international law cannot invoke either the ATS or the TVPA. In this context, a number of courts have held that the plaintiffs lack a private right of action. See, e.g., Hawkins v. Comparet-Cassani, 33 F. Supp. 2d 1244 (C.D. Cal. 1999), rev'd on other grounds, 251 F.3d 1230; Heinrich v. Sweet, 49 F. Supp. 2d 27 (D. Mass. 1999), and White v. Paulsen, 997 F. Supp. 1380 (E.D. Wash. 1998). See generally Curtis A. Bradley, Customary International Law and Private Rights of Action, 1 Chi. J. Intl. L. 421 (2000) (discussing these decisions). Why have courts been less receptive to customary international law claims in this context? Should alien plaintiffs have greater ability to bring international law claims in U.S. courts than U.S. plaintiffs?

12. What did the court hold in *Karadzic?* Under the court's analysis there, when can a private actor violate international law? The *Karadzic* decision opened up the possibility of bringing ATS suits against non-state actors, either on the theory that they can themselves violate international law or on the theory that their involvement with foreign government actors renders their conduct state action. In effect, this aspect of *Karadzic* facilitated one of the recent waves of ATS cases — suits against private corporations. A number of lawsuits have been brought in recent years by foreign plaintiffs under the ATS against private corporations, from the United States

and abroad, with respect to alleged human rights and environmental abuses committed in foreign countries. See, e.g., Doe v. Unocal Corp., 110 F. Supp. 2d 1294 (C.D. Cal. 2000) (appeal pending) (suit by Myanmar citizens against U.S. corporations and their executives for alleged human rights abuses committed in connection with drilling of oil pipeline in Myanmar); Wiwa v. Royal Dutch Petroleum Co., 226 F.3d 88 (2000) (suit by Nigerians against non-U.S. corporation for alleged human rights abuses in Nigeria); Beanal v. Freeport McMoran, Inc., 197 F.3d 161 (5th Cir. 1999) (suit by Indonesian citizen against U.S. corporations for environmental effects of mining operations in Indonesia); Aguinda v. Texaco, Inc., 303 F.3d 470 (2d Cir. 2002) (suit by citizens of Ecuador and Peru against U.S. corporation for alleged violations of customary international law protecting the environment in connection with activities in South America). Is this a legitimate extension of *Filartiga*? Is it justified on the basis of the ATS? On the basis of customary international law?

13. In September 2000, a jury awarded the plaintiffs in the *Karadzic* case $4.5 billion in damages. As in many international human rights cases in U.S. courts (except in the recent corporate cases), the plaintiffs have little prospect of recovering this award. Does this mean the case was a waste of time? After the verdict, one of the plaintiffs said that the case "was not about monetary damages, but about gaining recognition of the acts committed by Bosnian Serb ultra-nationalists." The jury foreman added: "I hope the world gets the message. . . . What happened was reprehensible." David Rohde, Jury in New York Orders Bosnian Serb to Pay Billions, N.Y. Times, Sept. 26, 2000, at A10. Will unenforceable jury verdicts awarded in U.S. courts in fact achieve these ends?

D. THE *CHARMING BETSY* CANON

Even when international law is not directly enforceable within the U.S. legal system, it may have an effect on the interpretation of U.S. law. The Supreme Court has long sought to construe federal statutes so that they do not violate either treaties or customary international law.

One of the earliest applications of this principle was in Murray v. The Schooner Charming Betsy, 6 U.S. (2 Cranch) 64 (1804), which concerned events relating to the undeclared war between the United States and France in the late 1790s. During that war, the United States passed a statute prohibiting trade "between any person or persons resident within the United States or under their protection, and any person or persons resident within the territories of the French Republic, or any of the dependencies thereof." To enforce the statute, the U.S. Navy was under orders from President Adams to seize any vessel suspected of trading with the French. A Navy frigate subsequently seized the schooner *Charming Betsy* on the high seas, suspecting her of engaging in trade with Guadaloupe, a French dependency, in violation of the statute. The owner of the ship had been born in the United States but had moved as a child to St. Thomas, a Danish island, and had become a Danish citizen. He argued that, because he was a citizen of a neutral country, the seizure of his vessel violated international law rules of neutrality.

The Court, in an opinion by Chief Justice Marshall, recited among the "principles . . . believed to be correct" and "which ought to be kept in view in construing the act now under consideration," the following proposition: "an act of Congress ought never to be construed to violate the law of nations if any other possible construction remains. . . ." 6 U.S. at 118. The Court proceeded to construe the statute as not applying to the owner of the vessel, because he was not at the time of the seizure a resident of the United States or "under [its] protection." Id. at 120. The canon of construction invoked by the Court is today commonly referred to as the "*Charming Betsy* canon."

What, if anything, does the *Charming Betsy* canon tell us about the status of international law in U.S. courts? What is the relationship between the canon and the last-in-time rule between treaties and statutes? Should the canon apply equally to potential conflicts with treaties and customary international law? In *Filartiga v. Pena-Irala,* which we considered above, the court cited the *Charming Betsy* canon as "[t]he plainest evidence that international law has an existence in the federal courts independent of acts of Congress." See 630 F.2d 876, 887 n.20. What does this statement mean? Is it correct?

The Restatement (Third) of Foreign Relations Law describes the *Charming Betsy* canon in somewhat softer terms than the language used by Chief Justice Marshall. The Restatement (Third) states that "[w]here fairly possible, a United States statute is to be construed so as not to conflict with international law or with an international agreement of the United States." Restatement (Third) of the Foreign Relations Law of the United States Section 114 (1987). Under either formulation of the canon, what evidence will be sufficient to show that Congress intended a result contrary to international law?

Some commentators have argued that U.S. courts should take account of international law when interpreting the U.S. Constitution — for example, when interpreting "due process," "equal protection," or "cruel and unusual punishments." Does this follow from the *Charming Betsy* canon? Consider the applicability of the Eighth Amendment to the execution of juvenile offenders. Almost all nations, including almost all nations that still have the death penalty, now decline to impose capital punishment on individuals who were under the age of 18 at the time of their offense. A number of U.S. states, however, permit the imposition of capital punishment on 16- and 17-year-old offenders. In Stanford v. Kentucky, 492 U.S. 361 (1989), the Supreme Court held that this practice does not violate the prohibition on "cruel and unusual punishments" in the Eighth Amendment. In response to the evidence of international practice, the Court stated that "it is *American* conceptions of decency that are dispositive." Id. at 369 n.1. Is this approach to the Eighth Amendment too parochial? What if customary international law prohibits the execution of juvenile offenders — should that affect the Eighth Amendment analysis? If customary international law does prohibit this practice, does the Supreme Court's construction of the Eighth Amendment in *Stanford* create a conflict between the Eighth Amendment and international law? Or is the conflict only with state death penalty laws that provide for the execution of juvenile offenders?

For general discussions of the *Charming Betsy* canon, see, for example, Curtis A. Bradley, The *Charming Betsy* Canon and Separation of Powers: Rethinking the Interpretive Role of International Law, 86 Geo. L.J. 479 (1998); and Ralph G. Steinhardt, The Role of International Law as a Canon of Domestic Statutory Construction, 43 Vand. L. Rev. 1103 (1990).

E.   THE FIFTY STATES AND FOREIGN AFFAIRS

One of the perceived defects of the Articles of Confederation (the agreement among the 13 states in place prior to the Constitution) was that they did not give the federal government sufficient authority to conduct foreign relations. The Constitution addressed this problem in a variety of ways: Article I, Section 10 prohibits the states from performing certain foreign relations functions, such as treaty-making; Article I, Section 8 and Article II broadly authorize the federal political branches to conduct foreign relations through the enactment of federal statutes and treaties; the Supremacy Clause in Article VI establishes that these federal enactments are supreme over state law; Article III extends the federal judicial power to cases involving these federal enactments and to other transnational controversies; and the "take care" clause in Article II authorizes the President to enforce federal enactments.

Despite these constitutional provisions, it cannot be said that federalism is irrelevant to the conduct of U.S. foreign relations. As confirmed by the Tenth Amendment, the Constitution vests the federal government with only limited and enumerated powers, and this principle might apply even when the government is regulating foreign affairs. Further, state law has traditionally governed many aspects of a foreign national's activities in the United States. This is true, for example, of private law issues such as tort, contract, and family law, as well as issues of criminal law. In addition, states sometimes take positions on international economic and political issues, and the federal government often declines to preempt the states on these issues.

The relationship between foreign affairs and federalism has become a more significant issue in recent years, for three reasons. First, there has been increasing overlap between certain areas of international law, such as international trade law and international human rights law, and areas of traditional state regulation. Second, as discussed earlier in this chapter, the Supreme Court has imposed a number of federalism restraints on the national government in the domestic context. It is conceivable that, notwithstanding Missouri v. Holland, the Court would apply some of these limitations to the foreign affairs context. Third, states and cities increasingly are expressing their own views regarding foreign policy.

Zschernig v. Miller

U.S. Supreme Court
389 U.S. 429 (1968)

Mr. Justice DOUGLAS delivered the opinion of the Court.

This case concerns the disposition of the estate of a resident of Oregon who died there intestate in 1962. Appellants are decedent's sole heirs and they are residents of East Germany. Appellees include members of the State Land Board that petitioned the Oregon probate court for the escheat of the net proceeds of the estate under the provisions of Ore. Rev. Stat. §111.070 (1957), which provides for escheat in cases where a nonresident alien claims real or personal property unless [specified] requirements are satisfied. . . .

[O]ne of the conditions of inheritance under the Oregon statute requires "proof that such foreign heirs, distributees, devisees or legatees may receive the benefit, use or control of money or property from estates of persons dying in this state without confiscation, in whole or in part, by the governments of such foreign countries," the burden being on the nonresident alien to establish that fact.

This provision came into Oregon's law in 1951. Prior to that time the rights of aliens under the Oregon statute were defined in general terms of reciprocity, similar to the California Act which we had before us in Clark v. Allen, [331 U.S. 503, 506, n.1 (1947)].

We held in Clark v. Allen that a general reciprocity clause did not on its face intrude on the federal domain. We noted that the California statute, then a recent enactment, would have only "some incidental or indirect effect in foreign countries."

Had that case appeared in the posture of the present one, a different result would have obtained. We were there concerned with the words of a statute on its face, not the manner of its application. State courts, of course, must frequently read, construe, and apply laws of foreign nations. It has never been seriously suggested that state courts are precluded from performing that function, albeit there is a remote possibility that any holding may disturb a foreign nation — whether the matter involves commercial cases, tort cases, or some other type of controversy. At the time Clark v. Allen was decided, the case seemed to involve no more than a routine reading of foreign laws. It now appears that in this reciprocity area under inheritance statutes, the probate courts of various States have launched inquiries into the type of governments that obtain in particular foreign nations — whether aliens under their law have enforceable rights, whether the so-called "rights" are merely dispensations turning upon the whim or caprice of government officials, whether the representation of consuls, ambassadors, and other representatives of foreign nations is credible or made in good faith, whether there is in the actual administration in the particular foreign system of law any element of confiscation. . . .

The Government's acquiescence in the ruling of Clark v. Allen certainly does not justify extending the principle of that case, as we would be required to do here to uphold the Oregon statute as applied; for it has more than "some incidental or indirect effect in foreign countries," and its great potential for disruption or embarrassment makes us hesitate to place it in the category of a diplomatic bagatelle. . . .

As we read the decisions that followed in the wake of Clark v. Allen, we find that they radiate some of the attitudes of the "cold war," where the search is for the "democracy quotient" of a foreign regime as opposed to the Marxist theory. . . .

As one reads the Oregon decisions, it seems that foreign policy attitudes, the freezing or thawing of the "cold war," and the like are the real desiderata.[8] Yet they are of course matters for the Federal Government, not for local probate courts. . . .

---

8. Such attitudes are not confined to the Oregon courts. Representative samples from other States would include statements in the New York courts, such as "This court would consider sending money out of this country and into Hungary tantamount to putting funds within the grasp of the Communists," and "If this money were turned over to the Russian authorities, it would be used to kill our boys and innocent people in Southeast Asia. . . ." Heyman, The Nonresident Alien's Right to Succession Under the "Iron Curtain Rule," 52 Nw. U.L. Rev. 221, 234 (1957). In Pennsylvania, a judge stated at the trial of a case involving a Soviet claimant that "If you want to say that I'm prejudiced, you can, because when it comes to Communism I'm a bigoted anti-Communist." And another judge exclaimed, "I am not going to send money to Russia where it can go into making bullets which may one day be used against my son." A California judge, upon being asked if he would hear argument on the law, replied, "No, I won't send any money to Russia." The judge took "judicial notice that Russia kicks the United States in the teeth all the time," and told counsel for the Soviet claimant that "I would think your firm would feel it honor bound to withdraw as representing the Russian government. No American can make it too strong." Berman, Soviet Heirs in American Courts, 62 Col. L. Rev. 257, and n.3 (1962). . . .

It seems inescapable that the type of probate law that Oregon enforces affects international relations in a persistent and subtle way. The practice of state courts in withholding remittances to legatees residing in Communist countries or in preventing them from assigning them is notorious. The several States, of course, have traditionally regulated the descent and distribution of estates. But those regulations must give way if they impair the effective exercise of the Nation's foreign policy. Where those laws conflict with a treaty, they must bow to the superior federal policy. Yet, even in absence of a treaty, a State's policy may disturb foreign relations. As we stated in Hines v. Davidowitz, [312 U.S. 52, 64 (1941)]: "Experience has shown that international controversies of the gravest moment, sometimes even leading to war, may arise from real or imagined wrongs to another's subjects inflicted, or permitted, by a government." Certainly a State could not deny admission to a traveler from East Germany nor bar its citizens from going there. If there are to be such restraints, they must be provided by the Federal Government. The present Oregon law is not as gross an intrusion in the federal domain as those others might be. Yet, as we have said, it has a direct impact upon foreign relations and may well adversely affect the power of the central government to deal with those problems.

The Oregon law does, indeed, illustrate the dangers which are involved if each State, speaking through its probate courts, is permitted to establish its own foreign policy.

Reversed.

Mr. Justice Marshall took no part in the consideration or decision of this case.

[Concurring opinion of Justice Stewart, with whom Justice Brennan joined, is omitted.]

HARLAN, J., concurring in result. . . . There are several defects in [the majority's] rationale. The most glaring is that it is based almost entirely on speculation. My Brother Douglas does cite a few unfortunate remarks made by state court judges in applying statutes resembling the one before us. However, the Court does not mention, nor does the record reveal, any instance in which such an occurrence has been the occasion for a diplomatic protest, or, indeed, has had any foreign relations consequence whatsoever. The United States says in its brief as amicus curiae that it

> does not . . . contend that the application of the Oregon escheat statute in the circumstances of this case unduly interferes with the United States' conduct of foreign relations.

At an earlier stage in this case, the Solicitor General told this Court:

> The Department of State has advised us . . . that State reciprocity laws, including that of Oregon, have had little effect on the foreign relations and policy of this country. . . . Appellants' apprehension of a deterioration in international relations, unsubstantiated by experience, does not constitute the kind of "changed conditions" which might call for re-examination of Clark v. Allen.

Essentially, the Court's basis for decision appears to be that alien inheritance laws afford state court judges an opportunity to criticize in dictum the policies of foreign governments, and that these dicta may adversely affect our foreign relations.

In addition to finding no evidence of adverse effect in the record, I believe this rationale to be untenable because logically it would apply to many other types of litigation which come before the state courts. It is true that, in addition to the many state court judges who have applied alien inheritance statutes with proper judicial decorum, some judges have seized the opportunity to make derogatory remarks about foreign governments. However, judges have been known to utter dicta critical of foreign governmental policies even in purely domestic cases, so that the mere possibility of offensive utterances can hardly be the test.

If the flaw in the statute is said to be that it requires state courts to inquire into the administration of foreign law, I would suggest that that characteristic is shared by other legal rules which I cannot believe the Court wishes to invalidate. For example, the Uniform Foreign Money-Judgments Recognition Act provides that a foreign-country money judgment shall not be recognized if it "was rendered under a system which does not provide impartial tribunals or procedures compatible with the requirements of due process of law." When there is a dispute as to the content of foreign law, the court is required under the common law to treat the question as one of fact and to consider any evidence presented as to the actual administration of the foreign legal system. . . .

[Dissenting opinion of White, J., is omitted.]

Crosby v. National Foreign Trade Council

U.S. Supreme Court
530 U.S. 363 (2000)

Justice SOUTER delivered the opinion of the Court.

The issue is whether the Burma law of the Commonwealth of Massachusetts, restricting the authority of its agencies to purchase goods or services from companies doing business with Burma, is invalid under the Supremacy Clause of the National Constitution owing to its threat of frustrating federal statutory objectives. We hold that it is.

I

In June 1996, Massachusetts adopted "An Act Regulating State Contracts with Companies Doing Business with or in Burma (Myanmar)." The statute generally bars state entities from buying goods or services from any person (defined to include a business organization) identified on a "restricted purchase list" of those doing business with Burma. Although the statute has no general provision for waiver or termination of its ban, it does exempt from boycott any entities present in Burma solely to report the news, or to provide international telecommunication goods or services, or medical supplies. . . .

There are three exceptions to the ban: (1) if the procurement is essential, and without the restricted bid, there would be no bids or insufficient competition; (2) if the procurement is of medical supplies; and (3) if the procurement efforts elicit no "comparable low bid or offer" by a person not doing business with Burma, meaning an offer that is no more than 10 percent greater than the restricted bid.

To enforce the ban, the Act requires petitioner Secretary of Administration and Finance to maintain a "restricted purchase list" of all firms "doing business with Burma."

In September 1996, three months after the Massachusetts law was enacted, Congress passed a statute imposing a set of mandatory and conditional sanctions on Burma. The federal Act has five basic parts, three substantive and two procedural.

First, it imposes three sanctions directly on Burma. It bans all aid to the Burmese Government except for humanitarian assistance, counternarcotics efforts, and promotion of human rights and democracy. The statute instructs United States representatives to international financial institutions to vote against loans or other assistance to or for Burma, and it provides that no entry visa shall be issued to any Burmese government official unless required by treaty or to staff the Burmese mission to the United Nations. These restrictions are to remain in effect "until such time as the President determines and certifies to Congress that Burma has made measurable and substantial progress in improving human rights practices and implementing democratic government."

Second, the federal Act authorizes the President to impose further sanctions subject to certain conditions. He may prohibit "United States persons" from "new investment" in Burma, and shall do so if he determines and certifies to Congress that the Burmese Government has physically harmed, rearrested, or exiled Daw Aung San Suu Kyi (the opposition leader selected to receive the Nobel Peace Prize), or has committed "large-scale repression of or violence against the Democratic opposition." "New investment" is defined as entry into a contract that would favor the "economical development of resources located in Burma," or would provide ownership interests in or benefits from such development, but the term specifically excludes (and thus excludes from any Presidential prohibition) "entry into, performance of, or financing of a contract to sell or purchase goods, services, or technology."

Third, the statute directs the President to work to develop "a comprehensive, multilateral strategy to bring democracy to and improve human rights practices and the quality of life in Burma." He is instructed to cooperate with members of the Association of Southeast Asian Nations (ASEAN) and with other countries having major trade and investment interests in Burma to devise such an approach, and to pursue the additional objective of fostering dialogue between the ruling State Law and Order Restoration Council (SLORC) and democratic opposition groups.

As for the procedural provisions of the federal statute, the fourth section requires the President to report periodically to certain congressional committee chairmen on the progress toward democratization and better living conditions in Burma as well as on the development of the required strategy. And the fifth part of the federal Act authorizes the President "to waive, temporarily or permanently, any sanction [under the federal Act] . . . if he determines and certifies to Congress that the application of such sanction would be contrary to the national security interests of the United States."

On May 20, 1997, the President issued the Burma Executive Order, Exec. Order No. 13047. He certified . . . that the Government of Burma had "committed large-scale repression of the democratic opposition in Burma" and found that the Burmese Government's actions and policies constituted "an unusual and extraordinary threat to the national security and foreign policy of the United States," a threat characterized as a national emergency. The President then prohibited new investment in Burma "by United States persons," any approval or facilitation by a United States person of such new investment by foreign persons, and any transaction meant to evade or avoid the ban. The order generally incorporated the exceptions and exemptions addressed in the statute. Finally, the President delegated to the Secretary of State the tasks of working with ASEAN and other countries to develop a strategy for democracy, human rights, and the quality of life in Burma, and of making the required congressional reports. . . .

III

A fundamental principle of the Constitution is that Congress has the power to preempt state law. Art. VI, cl. 2. Even without an express provision for preemption, we have found that state law must yield to a congressional Act in at least two circumstances. When Congress intends federal law to "occupy the field," state law in that area is preempted. And even if Congress has not occupied the field, state law is naturally preempted to the extent of any conflict with a federal statute. . . . We will find preemption where it is impossible for a private party to comply with both state and federal law, and where "under the circumstances of [a] particular case, [the challenged state law] stands as an obstacle to the accomplishment and execution of the full purposes and objectives of Congress." Hines [v. Davidowitz, 312 U.S. 52, 67 (1941)]. What is a sufficient obstacle is a matter of judgment, to be informed by examining the federal statute as a whole and identifying its purpose and intended effects. . . .

Applying this standard, we see the state Burma law as an obstacle to the accomplishment of Congress's full objectives under the federal Act. We find that the state law undermines the intended purpose and "natural effect" of at least three provisions of the federal Act, that is, its delegation of effective discretion to the President to control economic sanctions against Burma, its limitation of sanctions solely to United States persons and new investment, and its directive to the President to proceed diplomatically in developing a comprehensive, multilateral strategy towards Burma.[8]

A

First, Congress clearly intended the federal act to provide the President with flexible and effective authority over economic sanctions against Burma. Although Congress immediately put in place a set of initial sanctions (prohibiting bilateral aid,

---

8. We leave for another day a consideration in this context of a presumption against preemption. Assuming, *arguendo*, that some presumption against preemption is appropriate, we conclude, based on our analysis below, that the state Act presents a sufficient obstacle to the full accomplishment of Congress's objectives under the federal Act to find it preempted. See Hines v. Davidowitz, 312 U.S. 52, 67 (1941).

Because our conclusion that the state Act conflicts with federal law is sufficient to affirm the judgment below, we decline to speak to field preemption as a separate issue, . . . or to pass on the First Circuit's rulings addressing the foreign affairs power or the dormant Foreign Commerce Clause. See Ashwander v. TVA, 297 U.S. 288, 346-347 (1936) (concurring opinion).

support for international financial assistance, and entry by Burmese officials into the United States), it authorized the President to terminate any and all of those measures upon determining and certifying that there had been progress in human rights and democracy in Burma. It invested the President with the further power to ban new investment by United States persons, dependent only on specific Presidential findings of repression in Burma. And, most significantly, Congress empowered the President "to waive, temporarily or permanently, any sanction [under the federal act] . . . if he determines and certifies to Congress that the application of such sanction would be contrary to the national security interests of the United States."

This express investiture of the President with statutory authority to act for the United States in imposing sanctions with respect to the government of Burma, augmented by the flexibility to respond to change by suspending sanctions in the interest of national security, recalls Justice Jackson's observation in Youngstown Sheet & Tube Co. v. Sawyer, 343 U.S. 579, 635 (1952): "When the President acts pursuant to an express or implied authorization of Congress, his authority is at its maximum, for it includes all that he possesses in his own right plus all that Congress can delegate." See also id. at 635-636, n.2 (noting that the President's power in the area of foreign relations is least restricted by Congress and citing United States v. Curtiss-Wright Export Corp., 299 U.S. 304 (1936)). Within the sphere defined by Congress, then, the statute has placed the President in a position with as much discretion to exercise economic leverage against Burma, with an eye toward national security, as our law will admit. And it is just this plenitude of Executive authority that we think controls the issue of preemption here. The President has been given this authority not merely to make a political statement but to achieve a political result, and the fullness of his authority shows the importance in the congressional mind of reaching that result. It is simply implausible that Congress would have gone to such lengths to empower the President if it had been willing to compromise his effectiveness by deference to every provision of state statute or local ordinance that might, if enforced, blunt the consequences of discretionary Presidential action.

And that is just what the Massachusetts Burma law would do in imposing a different, state system of economic pressure against the Burmese political regime. As will be seen, the state statute penalizes some private action that the federal Act (as administered by the President) may allow, and pulls levers of influence that the federal Act does not reach. But the point here is that the state sanctions are immediate, and perpetual, there being no termination provision. This unyielding application undermines the President's intended statutory authority by making it impossible for him to restrain fully the coercive power of the national economy when he may choose to take the discretionary action open to him, whether he believes that the national interest requires sanctions to be lifted, or believes that the promise of lifting sanctions would move the Burmese regime in the democratic direction. Quite simply, if the Massachusetts law is enforceable the President has less to offer and less economic and diplomatic leverage as a consequence. In Dames & Moore v. Regan, 453 U.S. 654 (1981), we used the metaphor of the bargaining chip to describe the President's control of funds valuable to a hostile country; here, the state Act reduces the value of the chips created by the federal statute. It thus "stands as an obstacle to the accomplishment and execution of the full purposes and objectives of Congress." *Hines,* 312 U.S. at 67.

B

Congress manifestly intended to limit economic pressure against the Burmese Government to a specific range. The federal Act confines its reach to United States persons, imposes limited immediate sanctions, places only a conditional ban on a carefully defined area of "new investment," and pointedly exempts contracts to sell or purchase goods, services, or technology. These detailed provisions show that Congress's calibrated Burma policy is a deliberate effort "to steer a middle path," *Hines*, supra.

The State has set a different course, and its statute conflicts with federal law at a number of points by penalizing individuals and conduct that Congress has explicitly exempted or excluded from sanctions. While the state Act differs from the federal in relying entirely on indirect economic leverage through third parties with Burmese connections, it otherwise stands in clear contrast to the congressional scheme in the scope of subject matter addressed. It restricts all contracts between the State and companies doing business in Burma, except when purchasing medical supplies and other essentials (or when short of comparable bids). It is specific in targeting contracts to provide financial services, and general goods and services, to the Government of Burma, and thus prohibits contracts between the State and United States persons for goods, services, or technology, even though those transactions are explicitly exempted from the ambit of new investment prohibition when the President exercises his discretionary authority to impose sanctions under the federal Act.

As with the subject of business meant to be affected, so with the class of companies doing it: the state Act's generality stands at odds with the federal discreteness. The Massachusetts law directly and indirectly imposes costs on all companies that do any business in Burma, save for those reporting news or providing international telecommunications goods or services, or medical supplies. It sanctions companies promoting the importation of natural resources controlled by the government of Burma, or having any operations or affiliates in Burma. The state Act thus penalizes companies with pre-existing affiliates or investments, all of which lie beyond the reach of the federal act's restrictions on "new investment" in Burmese economic development. The state Act, moreover, imposes restrictions on foreign companies as well as domestic, whereas the federal Act limits its reach to United States persons.

The conflicts are not rendered irrelevant by the State's argument that there is no real conflict between the statutes because they share the same goals and because some companies may comply with both sets of restrictions. The fact of a common end hardly neutralizes conflicting means, and the fact that some companies may be able to comply with both sets of sanctions does not mean that the state Act is not at odds with achievement of the federal decision about the right degree of pressure to employ. Sanctions are drawn not only to bar what they prohibit but to allow what they permit, and the inconsistency of sanctions here undermines the congressional calibration of force.

C

Finally, the state Act is at odds with the President's intended authority to speak for the United States among the world's nations in developing a "comprehensive, multilateral strategy to bring democracy to and improve human rights practices and the quality of life in Burma." Congress called for Presidential cooperation with members of ASEAN and other countries in developing such a strategy, directed the President to encourage a dialogue between the government of Burma and the democratic opposition, and required him to report to the Congress on the progress of his diplomatic efforts. As with Congress's explicit delegation to the President of power over economic sanctions, Congress's express command to the President to take the initiative for the United States among the international community invested him with the maximum authority of the National Government, cf. *Youngstown Sheet & Tube Co.*, 343 U.S. at 635, in harmony with the President's own constitutional powers, U.S. Const., Art. II, §2, cl. 2 ("[The President] shall have Power, by and with the Advice and Consent of the Senate, to make Treaties" and "shall appoint Ambassadors, other public Ministers and Consuls"); §3 ("[The President] shall receive Ambassadors and other public Ministers"). This clear mandate and invocation of exclusively national power belies any suggestion that Congress intended the President's effective voice to be obscured by state or local action.

Again, the state Act undermines the President's capacity, in this instance for effective diplomacy. It is not merely that the differences between the state and federal Acts in scope and type of sanctions threaten to complicate discussions; they compromise the very capacity of the President to speak for the Nation with one voice in dealing with other governments. We need not get into any general consideration of limits of state action affecting foreign affairs to realize that the President's maximum power to persuade rests on his capacity to bargain for the benefits of access to the entire national economy without exception for enclaves fenced off willy-nilly by inconsistent political tactics. When such exceptions do qualify his capacity to present a coherent position on behalf of the national economy, he is weakened, of course, not only in dealing with the Burmese regime, but in working together with other nations in hopes of reaching common policy and "comprehensive" strategy.

While the threat to the President's power to speak and bargain effectively with other nations seems clear enough, the record is replete with evidence to answer any skeptics. First, in response to the passage of the state Act, a number of this country's allies and trading partners filed formal protests with the National Government. . . . Second, the EU and Japan have gone a step further in lodging formal complaints against the United States in the World Trade Organization (WTO), claiming that the state Act violates certain provisions of the Agreement on Government Procurement, and the consequence has been to embroil the National Government for some time now in international dispute proceedings under the auspices of the WTO. In their brief before this Court, EU officials point to the WTO dispute as threatening relations with the United States, and note that the state Act has become the topic of "intensive discussions" with officials of the United States at the highest levels, those discussions including exchanges at the twice yearly EU-U.S. Summit. Third, the Executive has consistently represented that the state Act has complicated its dealings with foreign sovereigns and proven an impediment to accomplishing objectives assigned it by Congress. . . . This evidence in combination is more than sufficient to show that the state Act stands as an obstacle in addressing the congressional obligation to devise a comprehensive, multilateral strategy. . . .

IV

The State's remaining argument is unavailing. It contends that the failure of Congress to preempt the state Act demonstrates implicit permission. The State points out that Congress has repeatedly declined to enact express preemption provisions aimed at state and local sanctions, and it calls our attention to the large number of such measures passed against South Africa in the 1980s, which various authorities cited have thought were not preempted. The State stresses that Congress was aware of the state Act in 1996, but did not preempt it explicitly when it adopted its own Burma statute. The State would have us conclude that Congress's continuing failure to enact express preemption implies approval, particularly in light of occasional instances of express preemption of state sanctions in the past.

The argument is unconvincing on more than one level. A failure to provide for preemption expressly may reflect nothing more than the settled character of implied preemption doctrine that courts will dependably apply, and in any event, the existence of conflict cognizable under the Supremacy Clause does not depend on express congressional recognition that federal and state law may conflict, *Hines*. The State's inference of congressional intent is unwarranted here, therefore, simply because the silence of Congress is ambiguous. Since we never ruled on whether state and local sanctions against South Africa in the 1980s were preempted or otherwise invalid, arguable parallels between the two sets of federal and state Acts do not tell us much about the validity of the latter.

Notes and Questions

1. The Court in *Zschernig* applied what has been called "dormant foreign affairs preemption." The idea is that some state laws or activities relating to foreign affairs are preempted as a result of the national government's unexercised, or "dormant," foreign affairs powers. What is the scope of the prohibition on state activity announced in *Zschernig*? What matters in answering this question: Foreign relations effects? The state's purpose in engaging in the activity? Both? Neither?

2. What is the constitutional source for dormant foreign affairs preemption? Read Article I, Section 10 of the Constitution. Among other things, this Section excludes state authority in a defined set of "high" foreign relations functions, such as treatymaking and war-making. Now read the foreign relations powers conferred on the federal government in Articles I, Section 8 and in Article II, Sections 2-3. Are these powers *exclusive* (which means that they can be exercised only by the federal government)? Or are they, like most other powers conferred on the federal government, *concurrent* (which means that they can be exercised by both state and federal governments until the federal government affirmatively acts to preempt state authority)? Now consider the Tenth Amendment, which provides that the "powers not delegated to the United States by the Constitution, nor prohibited by it to the States, are reserved to the States respectively, or to the people." What implications, if any, can one draw from these textual provisions? Compare Jack L. Goldsmith, Federal Courts, Foreign Affairs, and Federalism, 83 Va. L. Rev. 1617, 1642 (1997) (arguing that the "most natural inference . . . is that all foreign relations matters not excluded by Article I, Section 10 fall within the concurrent power of the state and federal governments until preempted by federal statute or treaty"), with Brannon P. Denning

& Jack H. McCall Jr., The Constitutionality of State and Local "Sanctions" Against Foreign Countries: Affairs of State, States' Affairs, or a Sorry State of Affairs?, 26 Hastings Const. L.Q. 307, 337 (1999) ("[T]he various provisions related to foreign affairs can be read to contain a structural or 'penumbral' restriction on state actions affecting foreign affairs, even in the absence of a congressional enactment.").

3. Another justification for dormant foreign affairs preemption is a functional one. Even if federal courts are not as well suited as the federal political branches to perform the foreign relations inquiries in support of dormant preemption, the federal political branches cannot redress every state foreign relations activity. Moreover, the federal courts are at least in a better position than states to identify and police U.S. foreign relations interests. And any errors the courts might make in inappropriately preempting state law can always be corrected by subsequent federal legislation. Is this argument persuasive? Do the federal political branches need the assistance of federal courts in policing states for harmful foreign relations activity? Are courts well suited to assist in this task? What effect does dormant foreign affairs preemption have on the political branches that are primarily responsible for conducting U.S. foreign relations? Are there any other costs to dormant foreign affairs preemption?

4. In Barclays Bank v. Franchise Tax Board of California, 512 U.S. 298 (1994), the Supreme Court held that California's "worldwide combined reporting" method of taxing multinational corporations was not subject to dormant preemption, even though it was different from the federal government's method of taxation and even though it had generated significant protest from foreign governments. The Court rejected the argument that an interference by a state with the nation's ability to "speak with one voice when regulating commercial relations with foreign governments" was sufficient to trigger preemption. The Court explained:

> The Constitution does "'not make the judiciary the overseer of our government.'" Dames & Moore v. Regan, 453 U.S. 654, 660 (1981), quoting Youngstown Sheet & Tube Co. v. Sawyer, 343 U.S. at 594 (Frankfurter, J., concurring). Having determined that the taxpayers before us had an adequate nexus with the State, that worldwide combined reporting led to taxation which was fairly apportioned, nondiscriminatory, fairly related to the services provided by the State, and that its imposition did not result inevitably in multiple taxation, we leave it to Congress — whose voice, in this area, is the Nation's — to evaluate whether the national interest is best served by tax uniformity, or state autonomy. Id. at 330.

Does Barclays Bank overrule Zschernig? Is its reasoning consistent with Zschernig? Is its conception of the judicial role consistent with Zschernig?

The First Circuit Court of Appeals in the Crosby case, which held that the Massachusetts Burma statute was subject to dormant preemption, concluded that Barclays Bank did not undermine the dormant preemption doctrine applied in Zschernig. See National Foreign Trade Council v. Natsios, 181 F.3d 38 (1st Cir. 1999). The court reasoned that Barclays Bank did "not apply outside the context of Commerce Clause challenges to laws that do not target specific foreign nations or foreign commerce," that the "message of Barclays is . . . consistent with Zschernig: foreign government views, although not dispositive, are one factor to consider in determining whether a law impermissibly interferes with the federal government's foreign affairs power," and that "there is simply no indication, in Barclays or in any other post-Zschernig case, that Zschernig is not good law and is not binding on us." Id. at 54-55, 59.

The Ninth Circuit Court of Appeals expressed a somewhat different view in a decision holding that a California statute, which required insurers doing business in California to submit information relating to insurance policies sold in Europe between 1920 and 1945, was not preempted. See Gerling Global Reinsurance Corp. of America v. Low, 240 F.3d 739 (9th Cir. 2001). The court noted that, because *Zschernig* had been applied "sparingly" and because "the Supreme Court's foreign commerce cases [such as *Barclays Bank*] have taken a different approach . . . we hesitate to apply *Zschernig* to a facial challenge to state statutes involving "foreign affairs" (a) but that mainly involve foreign commerce and (b) that are not directed at a particular country." Id. at 753. Can *Gerling* and *Natsios* be reconciled? (The U.S. Supreme Court granted review of the *Gerling* decision and was expected to issue a decision in the case by early summer 2003.)

5. In In re World War II Era Japanese Forced Labor Litigation, 164 F. Supp. 2d 1160 (N.D. Cal. 2001), the court dismissed slave labor claims brought against Japanese corporations by former prisoners of war from Korea and China. Earlier in the litigation, the court had dismissed similar claims by former U.S. prisoners, on the ground that the claims were preempted by a 1951 peace treaty with Japan. Neither Korea nor China were parties to the treaty, however, so these plaintiffs' claims, unlike the claims of the U.S. prisoners, were not subject to treaty preemption. Nevertheless, relying on *Zschernig*, the court concluded that the claims, which were brought under a California reparations statute, were subject to dormant foreign affairs preemption. For a discussion of this and other World War II reparations decisions, and their relationship to U.S. federalism, see Curtis A. Bradley, World War II Compensation and Foreign Relations Federalism, 20 Berkeley J. Intl. L. 282 (2002).

This decision was affirmed in Deutsch v. Turner Corp., 317 F.3d 1005 (9th Cir. 2003). The Ninth Circuit held that the California reparations statute was preempted under *Zschernig* because the statute "intrude[d] on the federal government's exclusive power to make and resolve war." Recounting the various treaties and agreements entered into by the United States addressing resolution of claims relating to World War II, the court explained that "the federal government, acting under its foreign affairs authority, provided its own resolution to the war; California has no power to modify that resolution." The court distinguished the insurance statute at issue in *Gerling* on the ground that the insurance statute imposed "merely a reporting requirement" that did "not attempt to hold defendants liable for their wartime conduct; it therefore does not implicate the exclusive power of the federal government to make and resolve war; including the resolution of claims arising out of such actions."

6. Several states have enacted "Buy American" statutes that require private contractors with state agencies to provide goods made in the United States. Should these statutes be subject to dormant foreign affairs preemption? Lower courts have reached different conclusions. Most have upheld state Buy-American laws. For example, in upholding Pennsylvania's Buy-American law, the Third Circuit Court of Appeals reasoned as follows:

The Pennsylvania statute exhibits none of the dangers attendant on the statute reviewed in *Zschernig*, for Pennsylvania's statute provides no opportunity for state administrative officials or judges to comment on, let alone key their decisions to, the nature of foreign regimes. On its face the statute applies to steel from any foreign source, without respect to whether the source country might be considered friend or foe. Nor is there any indication from the record that the statute has been selectively applied according to the foreign policy attitudes of Commonwealth courts or the Commonwealth's Attorney General. And while it is possible that sub-national government procurement restrictions may become a topic of intense international scrutiny, and a target in international trade negotiations, that possibility alone cannot justify this court's invalidation of the Commonwealth's statute. This is especially true when Congress has recently directed its attention to such restrictions and has taken no steps to preempt them through federal legislation. Trojan Technologies, Inc. v. Pennsylvania, 916 F.2d 903 (3d Cir. 1990).

By contrast, a California appellate court invalidated the California Buy American Act. It reasoned as follows:

The California Buy American Act, in effectively placing an embargo on foreign products, amounts to a usurpation by this state of the power of the federal government to conduct foreign trade policy. That there are countervailing state policies which are served by the retention of such an act is "wholly irrelevant to judicial inquiry" (United States v. Pink, 315 U.S. 203, 233), since "[it] is inconceivable that any of them can be interposed as an obstacle to the effective operation of a federal constitutional power." (United States v. Belmont, 301 U.S. 324, 332). Foreign trade is properly a subject of national concern, not state regulation. State regulation can only impede, not foster, national trade policies. The problems of trade expansion or non-expansion are national in scope, and properly should be national in scope in their resolution. Bethlehem Steel Corp. v. Board of Commissioners, 276 Cal. App. 2d 221, 80 Cal. Rptr. 800 (Ct. App. 2d Dist. 1969).

7. Some courts have held that a case that is likely to have a substantial impact on foreign affairs falls within the statutory federal question jurisdiction of the federal courts (under 28 U.S.C. §1331), regardless of whether the plaintiff's claims are based on federal law. See, e.g., Torres v. Southern Peru Copper Corp., 113 F.3d 540 (5th Cir. 1997); Republic of Philippines v. Marcos, 806 F.2d 344 (2d Cir. 1986); Sequihua v. Texaco Inc., 847 F. Supp. 61 (S.D. Tex. 1994); see also De Perez v. AT&T Co., 139 F.3d 1368 (11th Cir. 1998) (accepting this doctrine, but finding that it was not satisfied under the particular facts of the case). The precise test for this jurisdictional "federal common law of foreign relations" is not clear, but courts have tended to place significant weight on the existence or nonexistence of protests by foreign governments. For a recent decision criticizing this doctrine, see Patrickson v. Dole Food Co., 251 F.3d 795 (9th Cir. 2001).

8. What was the basis for the Court's finding of statutory preemption in *Crosby*? Was there a conflict between the federal and state statutes? If not, what was the problem? How does the preemption holding of *Crosby* compare with the preemption holding of *Zschernig*? *Crosby* has provoked substantial academic commentary that is noteworthy for its widely differing interpretations of the opinion. See, e.g., Sarah H. Cleveland, Crosby and the "One-Voice" Myth in U.S. Foreign Relations, 46 Villa. L. Rev. 975, 1013 (2001) ("The Court's willingness to invalidate a state measure that was perceived as digressing from federal policy, however incidentally, is more akin to foreign affairs preemption in *Zschernig* than to the simple statutory preemption the Court purported to apply."); Jack L. Goldsmith, Statutory Foreign Affairs Preemption, 2001 Sup. Ct. Rev. 175 (arguing that *Crosby* rejects judicial foreign relations

effects test and reaffirms trend toward formal rules in U.S. foreign relations law); Edward Swaine, Crosby as Foreign Relations Law, 41 Va. J. Int'l L. 481 (2001) (describing *Crosby* as an effort to engage in constitutional avoidance and judicial minimalism, and criticizing this effort); Carlos Manuel Vazquez, W[h]ither Zschernig?, 46 Villanova L. Rev. 1259, 1323 (2001) ("[I]t is only a slight exaggeration to say that *Crosby* is a dormant foreign affairs case in disguise."); Ernest A. Young, Dual Federalism, Concurrent Jurisdiction, and the Foreign Affairs Exception, 69 Geo. Wash. L. Rev. 139 (2001) (arguing that *Crosby* embraces a presumption in favor of preemption for foreign relations statutes).

Bibliography

For additional discussion of the relationship between international law and U.S. law, and of U.S. foreign relations law more generally, see Curtis A. Bradley & Jack L. Goldsmith, Foreign Relations Law: Cases and Materials (2003); Michael J. Glennon, Constitutional Diplomacy (1999); Louis Henkin, Foreign Affairs and the United States Constitution (2d ed. 1996); Harold Hongju Koh, The National Security Constitution (1990); John M. Rogers, International Law and United States Law (1999); and Phillip R. Trimble, International Law: United States Foreign Relations Law (2002).

4

International Dispute Resolution

In Chapters 1 and 2 you were introduced to the ways in which the rules of public international law are formed, mostly through the conclusion of treaties and the development of customary international law. Inevitably there are disputes over the meaning of those rules and their enforcement. Those disputes can range from the classic cases of boundary disputes and expropriations of foreign investment to disagreements over the application of import laws or compliance with an environmental or arms control treaty.

In the earlier chapters you have seen some examples of international dispute resolution, such as through negotiation, arbitration, and domestic courts. This chapter will analyze the principal methods for resolving international disputes. In reality, there are a wide variety of methods and institutions for dealing with these conflicts. While these possible approaches do not add up to the relatively organized and comprehensive systems found in most countries for resolving domestic disputes, they often provide effective and reasonable avenues for resolving international disagreements and for enforcing decisions. And, as will be seen in this chapter, some international approaches — notably regional courts and arbitration — hold even greater promise for the future. Indeed, when one looks at the problems with domestic dispute resolution in many countries — such as the often overlapping jurisdiction and the backlog of cases in U.S. courts, or the limits on the powers of domestic courts — the weaknesses in the international system are not as glaring as some critics have suggested.

This chapter begins with a section on how parties often work out disagreements through negotiation, occasionally supplemented by mediation or conciliation (Section A). If a dispute is not resolved through these methods, parties often resort to more formal institutions — the International Court of Justice, regional or specialized courts, international arbitration, or domestic courts — which are discussed in the next sections of this chapter.

Section B examines the International Court of Justice, sometimes known as the World Court. It is the International Court of Justice that most people first hear about, though for a variety of reasons it has not lived up to the expectations of its creators. Section C considers the important role of regional or specialized courts. The materials there focus on the Court of Justice of the European Communities.

Additional examples are covered in later chapters, such as the European Court of Human Rights, with its increasingly important role (Chapter 8); the International Tribunal for the Law of the Sea (Chapter 9); and the International Criminal Court (Chapter 11).

Section D addresses the rapidly growing field of international arbitration. It considers briefly the history of international arbitration and then looks at its present uses and outstanding issues, with considerable focus on the enforcement of arbitral awards. The section concludes with the important new variations on arbitration in the North American Free Trade Agreement and with the dispute resolution arrangement in the World Trade Organization, which became effective in 1995 and has been very active.

Finally, Section E notes the increasing role of domestic courts in international issues. You have already begun to see in Chapter 3 how U.S. courts have applied international law, such as in cases addressing human rights issues. Other countries' domestic courts also hear and decide cases that have international implications.

A. NEGOTIATION, MEDIATION, AND CONCILIATION

Most disputes involving international law are resolved through negotiation. In some situations a negotiation is supplemented by mediation or conciliation.

J.G. Merrills, International Dispute Settlement
2-15, 27-28, 42, 62, 87 (1998)

[1.] NEGOTIATION

. . . [I]n practice, negotiation is employed more frequently than all the other methods put together. Often, indeed, negotiation is the *only* means employed, not just because it is always the first to be tried and is often successful, but also because states may believe its advantages to be so great as to rule out the use of other methods, even in situations where the chances of a negotiated settlement are slight. On the occasions when another method is used, negotiation is not displaced, but directed towards instrumental issues, the terms of reference for an inquiry or conciliation commission, for example, or the arrangements for implementing an arbitral decision.

Thus in one form or another negotiation has a vital part in international disputes. But negotiation is more than a possible means of settling differences, it is also a technique for preventing them from arising. Since prevention is always better than cure, this form of negotiation, known as "consultation," is a convenient place to begin.

Consultation

When a government anticipates that a decision or a proposed course of action may harm another state, discussions with the affected party can provide a way of heading off a dispute by creating an opportunity for adjustment and accommodation. Quite minor modifications to its plans, of no importance to the state taking the decision, may be all that is required to avoid trouble, yet may only be apparent if the other side is given a chance to point them out. The particular value of consultation is that it supplies this useful information at the most appropriate time — before anything has been done. For it is far easier to make the necessary modifications at the decision-making stage, rather than later, when exactly the same action may seem like capitulation to foreign pressure, or be seized on by critics as a sacrifice of domestic interests.

A good example of the value of consultation is provided by the practice of the United States and Canada in antitrust proceedings. Writing of the procedure employed in such cases, a recent commentator has noted that:

> While it is true that antitrust officials of one state might flatly refuse to alter a course of action in any way, it has often been the case that officials have been persuaded to modify their plans somewhat. After consultation, it may be agreed to shape an indictment in a less offensive manner, to change the ground rules of an investigation so as to require only "voluntary" testimony from witnesses, or that officials of the government initiating an investigation or action will keep their antitrust counterparts informed of progress in the case and allow them to voice their concerns.

Consultation between states is usually an ad hoc process and except where reciprocity provides an incentive, as in the cases considered, has proved difficult to institutionalise. . . .

Whether voluntary or compulsory, consultation is often easier to implement for executive than legislative decision making, since the former is usually less rigidly structured and more centralised. But legislative action can also cause international disputes, and so procedures designed to achieve the same effect as consultation can have an equally useful part to play. Where states enjoy close relations it may be possible to establish machinery for negotiating the co-ordination of legislative and administrative measures on matters of common interest. There are clear advantages in having uniform provisions on such matters as environmental protection, where states share a common frontier, or commerce, if trade is extensive. The difficulties of achieving such harmonisation are considerable, as the experience of the European Economic Community has demonstrated, though if uniformity cannot be achieved, compatibility of domestic provisions is a less ambitious alternative. In either case the rewards in terms of dispute avoidance make the effort well worthwhile.

Another approach is to give the foreign state, or interested parties, an opportunity to participate in the domestic legislative process. Whether this is possible depends on the legislative machinery being sufficiently accessible to make it practicable and the parties' relations being good enough for such participation, which can easily be construed as foreign interference, to be acceptable. When these conditions are fulfilled the example of North America, where United States gas importers have appeared before Canada's National Energy Board and Canadian officials have testified before Congressional Committees, shows what can be achieved. . . .

The difficulty of persuading states to accept consultation procedures and the ways in which they operate when established are reminders of the fact that states are not entities, like individuals, but complex groupings of institutions and interests. . . .

Forms of Negotiation

Negotiations between states are usually conducted through "normal diplomatic channels," that is by the respective foreign offices, or by diplomatic representatives, who in the case of complex negotiations may lead delegations including representatives of several interested departments of the governments concerned. As an alternative, if the subject matter is appropriate, negotiations may be carried out by what are termed the "competent authorities" of each party, that is by representatives of the particular ministry or department responsible for the matter in question — between trade departments in the case of a commercial agreement, for example, or between defence ministries in negotiations concerning weapons' procurement. Where the competent authorities are subordinate bodies, they may be authorised to take negotiations as far as possible and to refer disagreements to a higher governmental level. . . .

In the case of a recurrent problem or a situation requiring continuous supervision, states may decide to institutionalise negotiation by creating what is termed a mixed or joint commission. Thus neighbouring states commonly employ mixed commissions to deal with boundary delimitation, or other matters of common concern. . . .

Mixed commissions usually consist of an equal number of representatives of both parties and may be given either a broad brief of indefinite duration, or the task of dealing with a specific problem. An outstanding example of a commission of the first type is provided by the Canadian-United States International Joint Commission, which, since its creation in 1909, has dealt with a large number of issues including industrial development, air pollution and a variety of questions concerning boundary waters. . . .

The public aspect of negotiations which is exemplified in summit diplomacy is also prominent in the activity of international organisations. In the United Nations General Assembly and similar bodies states can, if they choose, conduct diplomatic exchanges in the full glare of international attention. This is undoubtedly a useful way of letting off steam and, more constructively, of engaging the attention of outside states which may have something to contribute to the solution of a dispute. It has the disadvantage, however, that so visible a performance may encourage the striking of attitudes which are at once both unrealistic and difficult to abandon. It is therefore probable that for states with a serious interest in negotiating a settlement, the many opportunities for informal contact which international organisations provide are more useful than the dramatic confrontations of public debate. . . .

. . . For a negotiated settlement to be possible, the parties must believe that the benefits of an agreement outweigh the losses. If their interests are diametrically opposed, an arrangement which would require one side to yield all or most of its position is therefore unlikely to be acceptable. . . .

There are a number of ways in which such an impasse may be avoided. If negotiations on the substantive aspects of a dispute are deadlocked, it may be possible for the parties to agree on a procedural solution. . . .

Another approach is to consider whether the issue at the heart of a dispute can be split in such a way as to enable each side to obtain satisfaction. A solution of this kind was recently devised to the problem of maritime delimitation between Australia and Papua New Guinea in the Torres Strait. Having identified the different strands of the dispute, the parties succeeded in negotiating an agreement which deals separately with the interests of the inhabitants of islands in the Strait, the status of the islands, seabed jurisdiction, fisheries jurisdiction, conservation and navigation rights. The virtue of this highly functional approach to the problem is underlined by the fact that earlier attempts to negotiate a single maritime boundary for the area had all ended in failure.

If splitting the dispute is not possible, a procedural agreement may be used to compensate one side for yielding on the substantive issue. In 1961 the United Kingdom and Iceland ended a dispute over the latter's fishing limits with an agreement which provided for the recognition of Iceland's claims in return for phasing out arrangements to protect British interests and an undertaking that future disputes could be referred to the International Court. . . .

It often happens that the nature of a dispute and the parties' interests are such that in any agreement one side is bound to gain at the other's expense. A possible way of providing compensation in such a situation is to give the less-favoured party control of details such as the time and place of the negotiations. The latter in particular can assume considerable symbolic importance and thus constitutes an element which may be used to good effect. A more radical solution is to link two disputes together so that a negotiated settlement can balance gains and losses overall and be capable of acceptance by both sides. Such "package deals" are particularly common in multilateral negotiations such as the recent United Nations Conference on the Law of the Sea, where the large number of states involved and the broad agenda made the trading of issues a conspicuous feature of the proceedings.

The fact that today the public dimension of diplomacy has much greater importance than in the past is another factor with a bearing on the substance of international negotiations. For if negotiation is a matter of exchanging proposals and counter-proposals in an attempt to arrive at an agreement from which both sides can derive a measure of satisfaction, the parties' awareness of an audience consisting of the general public in one or both of the states concerned, and the international community as a whole, can seriously affect the outcome. The element of give and take which is usually an essential part of a successful negotiation is likely to be inhibited if every step is being monitored by interested pressure groups at home, while the suspicion that the other side may simply be interested in eliciting a favourable audience reaction may lead serious proposals to be dismissed as mere propaganda. The difficulty of negotiating arrangements for arms limitation and disarmament in the era of the Cold War illustrates both points. . . .

[2.] MEDIATION

When the parties to an international dispute are unable to resolve it by negotiation, the intervention of a third party is a possible means of breaking the impasse and producing an acceptable solution. Such intervention can take a number of different forms. The third party may simply encourage the disputing states to resume negotiations, or do nothing more than provide them with an additional channel of communication. In these situations he is said to be contributing his "good offices." On the other hand, his job may be to investigate the dispute and to present the parties with a set of formal proposals for its solution. As we shall see . . . this form of intervention is called "conciliation." Between good offices and conciliation lies the form of third party activity known as "mediation."

Like good offices, mediation is essentially an adjunct of negotiation, but with the mediator as an active participant, authorised, and indeed expected, to advance his own proposals and to interpret, as well as to transmit, each party's proposals to the other. What distinguishes this kind of assistance from conciliation is that a mediator generally makes his proposals informally and on the basis of information supplied by the parties, rather than his own investigations, although in practice such distinctions tend to be blurred. In a given case it may therefore be difficult to draw the line between mediation and conciliation, or to say exactly when good offices ended and mediation began.

Mediation may be sought by the parties or offered spontaneously by outsiders. Once under way it provides the governments in dispute with the possibility of a solution, but without any antecedent commitment to accept the mediator's suggestions. Consequently it has the advantage of allowing them to retain control of the dispute, probably an essential requirement if negotiations are deadlocked on a matter of vital interest. On the other hand, if a face-saving compromise is what is needed, it may be politically easier to make the necessary concessions in the course of mediation than in direct negotiation. If a dispute concerns sensitive issues, the fact that the proceedings can be completely confidential is an advantage in any case. As with other means of dispute settlement, however, not every international dispute is suitable for mediation. . . .

. . . [M]ediation can only be as effective as the parties wish it to be and this is governed largely by their immediate situation. Although this is a major limitation on the usefulness of mediation, it is important to retain a sense of perspective. It would be quite wrong to think that a mediator is merely someone who lends his authority to an agreement that is already virtually made. On the contrary, by facilitating the parties' dialogue, providing them with information and suggestions, identifying and exploring their aims and canvassing a range of possible solutions, he can play a vital role in moving them towards agreement. Although success will often be incomplete and failure sometimes inevitable, the mediator's job is to do his best for the parties and trust that they will reciprocate. . . .

[3.]   CONCILIATION

Conciliation has been defined as:

> A method for the settlement of international disputes of any nature according to which a Commission set up by the Parties, either on a permanent basis or an ad hoc basis to deal with a dispute, proceeds to the impartial examination of the dispute and attempts to define the terms of a settlement susceptible of being accepted by them, or of affording the Parties, with a view to its settlement, such aid as they may have requested.

The eclectic character of the method is at once apparent. If mediation is essentially an extension of negotiation, conciliation puts third party intervention on a formal legal footing and institutionalises it in a way comparable, but not identical, to . . . arbitration. . . . [T]he search for terms "susceptible of being accepted" by the parties, but not binding on them, provides a sharp contrast with arbitration and a reminder of the link between conciliation and mediation. . . .

Currently, . . . conciliation is regularly included in provisions dealing with dispute settlement and retains a modest place among the procedures actually used by states when disputes arise. . . . [C]onciliation offers a procedure adaptable to a variety of needs and demonstrates the advantage to be derived from the structured involvement of outsiders in the settlement of international disputes.

The following materials will give you a sense of how an international negotiation works. First there is the account of former Secretary of State Henry Kissinger on how he approached a complicated negotiation. Then there is an excerpt from Professor Phillip Trimble on the process by which the U.S. government negotiates treaties. His description deals with arms control, which is more complex and more important than most negotiations. For example, the President and cabinet officers are personally involved in arms control, unlike the situation in many international claims and disputes. And arms control involves the national security side of the bureaucracy, rather than officials handling trade, financial, agricultural, business, and labor issues. Nevertheless, you should get a sense of how the foreign affairs bureaucracy operates and how complex the dynamics of a negotiation can be.

Henry A. Kissinger, Years of Upheaval

214 (1982)

The opening of a complicated negotiation is like the beginning of an arranged marriage. The partners know that the formalities will soon be stripped away as they discover each other's real attributes. Neither party can yet foretell at what point necessity will transform itself into acceptance; when the abstract desire for progress will leave at least residues of understanding; which disagreement will, by the act of being overcome, illuminate the as-yet undiscovered sense of community and which will lead to an impasse destined to rend the relationship forever. The future being mercifully veiled, the parties attempt what they might not dare did they know what was ahead.

Almost invariably I spent the first session of a new negotiation in educating myself. I almost never put forward a proposal. Rather, I sought to understand the intangibles in the position of my interlocutor and to gauge the scope as well as the limits of probable concessions. And I made a considerable effort to leave no doubt about our fundamental approach. Only romantics think they can prevail in negotiations by trickery; only pedants believe in the advantage of obfuscation. In a society of sovereign states, an agreement will be maintained only if *all* partners consider it in their interest. They must have a sense of participation in the result. The art of diplomacy is not to outsmart the other side but to convince it either of common interests or of penalties if an impasse continues.

Phillip R. Trimble, Arms Control and International Negotiation Theory

25 Stan. J. Intl. L. 543, 549-565 (1989)

I. THE PROCESS OF INTERNATIONAL NEGOTIATION[26]

We have all participated in some form of negotiation: leasing an apartment, buying a car or arranging some other personal transaction. By reading the newspaper and observing domestic political processes, we also become familiar with more complicated domestic negotiations: settlement of labor disputes, distribution of benefits under community programs or passage of congressional legislation. Drawing on this experience, we form at least some implicit model of negotiating tactics, style and behavior.

An international negotiation is significantly different from its more familiar domestic counterparts. The most important differences stem from the fact that an international negotiation is much more than an exercise between two autonomous individuals seeking to reach a compromise on mutually accepted goals, and it is also significantly more complicated than the typical labor or corporate negotiation. It involves several interlocking processes, intragovernmental as well as international. Initially, the government bureaucracies involved formulate positions through intricate interagency negotiations. In the case of the American government, an administration may pursue additional negotiations, or at least discussions, with congressional committees and affected nongovernmental interests, such as the nuclear weapons laboratories. The ensuing exchange of positions at the intergovernmental level then normally stimulates further domestic bureaucratic negotiations to produce counterproposals.

In the domestic negotiation each agency has a distinctive perspective from which it views the process and which influences the position it advocates. For example, in a negotiation regarding numbers of strategic nuclear missiles, the Pentagon and the Joint Chiefs of Staff (JCS) would likely propose a position that accommodates current production plans, especially if the United States is producing a new missile while [the other country] is not. Thus, their preferred agreement would permit the United States to carry out its plans but also place some future constraint on the [other country]. . . . The Department of State is concerned with improvement of the overall political relationship and may therefore also want to reach an agreement that can contribute to the maintenance of a good relationship. In this light they are likely to look to what *can* be negotiated and thus favor a result that accommodates both sides' interests. The Central Intelligence Agency (CIA) may want an agreement that can be monitored easily. Some members of Congress may want to assure that any proposed position does not foreclose production of a favored new system that is important to their constituencies. The weapons laboratories may favor a position that requires the development of new warheads.

---

26. Part I, the description of the international negotiation process, is based on the author's experience in international economic negotiations and on published accounts of arms control negotiations. See generally . . . McNeill, U.S.-U.S.S.R. Arms Negotiations: The Process and the Lawyer, 79 Am. J. Intl. L. 52 (1985) (an especially valuable account of the process itself).

All these interests must either be accommodated, compromised or overridden by the President before a position can even be put on the negotiating table. Moreover, since the resulting treaty must be approved by Congress or the Senate, the President would be reluctant to override a strong congressional preference or the position of the Pentagon or JCS, whose views carry great weight in the Congress. Hence, accommodation of all competing interests is frequently the order of the day, with the most powerful domestic constituencies having a particularly influential role. The complicated, bureaucratic nature of position formulation distinguishes this type of negotiation from almost all domestic counterparts.

There are, of course, many similar features. Labor and business negotiators also have multiple constituencies with differing interests to satisfy. Even a person negotiating a lease may also have to take account of the separate interests of a spouse. . . . [T]he interests within a government may include a wide range of political, military, economic and ideological preferences. . . . In the context of arms control, it is also less likely that both parties want or need an agreement. Simply appearing to negotiate may be enough to satisfy the political needs of the parties. . . .

One major consequence of these differences is that an international negotiation is likely to be a more formal and time-consuming exercise than its domestic counterpart. Carefully negotiated government positions are stated and restated in a stylized fashion. Responses and changes of position are coordinated through sometimes cumbersome national bureaucracies comprised of officials who may be slow to reach agreement on how to proceed. A variety of congressional forces and nongovernmental constituencies subject the negotiators and their supporting bureaucracies to further pressures and delays. Because of this bureaucratic process, negotiators cannot engage in the freewheeling style that one may expect in a domestic context. In international negotiations, personalities thus tend to be less important. Positions represent compromises of basic institutional interests and can be changed only by another compromise of those interests. The individual negotiator therefore normally operates under strict instructions and has much less flexibility or opportunity for creative diplomacy. . . . In addition, international agreements, especially in arms control, do not rest on trust. The personal relationships that presidents often refer to in glowing terms . . . may make a difference in a marginal situation, but those relationships do not deeply influence the outcome of the governmental decisionmaking process.

Moreover, the positions advanced generally reflect compromises with interests dedicated to the status quo, or to no agreement at all. Negotiating positions frequently embody the lowest common denominator of conflicting agency positions. Results therefore tend not to deviate radically from the status quo. Bureaucrats with differing institutional interests will often seek to accommodate all of them. Hence, in the example outlined above regarding strategic missiles, the position finally agreed upon might permit full deployment of current systems, but allow only a single new system or modernization within limits, with provisions for on-site inspection. The military gets its current system. Congress, the defense industry and the weapons labs get the opportunity to develop a new system. The JCS get some limits and some predictability. . . . The State Department would be satisfied because the proposal would seem negotiable. . . . Thus all the institutional interests are to a large degree satisfied by an approach that represents the lowest common denominator. . . . Bureaucrats also prefer to negotiate a compromise themselves, especially if they get most of what they want, rather than permitting a decision to go to a higher level where they may lose everything.

The following description is necessarily very generalized. In the real world of international politics any particular negotiation may play out quite differently, and, of course, all actual negotiations are more complicated than this model. However, this simplified sketch will demonstrate how the internal dynamics of a negotiation severely constrain the results that can be expected.

The Development of the U.S. Negotiating Position

The negotiating process, of course, starts with the decision of the two governments to negotiate. That decision, particularly in the case of major issues such as arms control, may itself be the product of bureaucratic negotiation. The President or the National Security Council (NSC) staff may activate the process in order to assess the prospects for a negotiation, or an agency . . . may initiate the proposal itself. In response, middle-level officials of each agency concerned with the subject matter of the proposed negotiation normally prepare a memorandum to their agency head discussing the objectives of and prospects for the proposed negotiation. That discussion necessarily reflects to some extent the particular perspective of their agency's interests. Then interagency meetings will be held and additional papers will be prepared for the President. . . .

[T]he status quo would be the starting point for any discussion on whether to negotiate or continue negotiating. Almost always some agency or group of agencies would prefer no change or no agreement. The burden falls on the group advocating change. . . . An agency advocating change would have to articulate a new position and a supporting rationale, and then spend time, energy and political credit in marshalling support for the new position. It is also virtually certain that some, even most, agencies . . . will have been satisfied with the existing position. . . .

The next step in the negotiation process is to formulate a negotiating position. In matters that are domestically contentious . . . the President normally determines the position to take in opening the negotiation. In making this determination, the President often relies on an options paper presented by an interagency working group. The working group is composed of representatives of all the agencies of government that the agreement concerns. The group that normally works on arms control matters includes the NSC, the Departments of State and Defense, . . . the JCS, the CIA and, on some matters, perhaps the Department of Energy and NASA. Sometimes other personnel may become involved for particular purposes, such as a White House congressional liaison, a presidential political advisor, or a representative of the scientific community. . . . Congressional committees may also hold hearings at this stage, seeking to influence the negotiating posture.

An options paper prepared by a working group typically consists of a statement of the relevant background and facts, an outline of alternative negotiating positions that the President might select, the arguments for and against each alternative, and a statement of each agency's recommendation. In addition, separate papers may be attached as appendices to an options paper (or they may be sent separately as briefing memoranda) on particular topics, such as verification capabilities and limitations, . . . evasion techniques, the existing legal framework, potential military uses of space, or the political environment and foreign policy implications of different approaches. . . . The total package may well be several hundred pages long.

The selection of the chair of the working group is obviously important in the formulation of negotiating options. Normally the President would select a representative from the NSC or from another part of the White House staff, officials at least temporarily free of parochial bureaucratic biases, to play this role. The chair has a significant advantage in shaping policy because he is responsible for shaping and drafting documents (or assigning other agencies to do so). As any lawyer knows, the person who drafts a document can influence the outcome by artfully framing the issues and fixing the terms of discussion. Moreover, the NSC has a uniquely powerful position because it controls communication with the President and may forward the option paper (under a covering memorandum not cleared by other agencies) containing its own views and recommendations.

Although initial drafting and redrafting of an options paper may be assigned by the chair of the working group to a particular agency (or may be undertaken by the chairing agency), all agencies involved must "clear" the final product. The act of "clearance" does not mean that each agency or person agrees with everything in the paper; it indicates only that he or she finds it to be an acceptable presentation of the issues to the President. Each agency may consciously or subconsciously pay special attention to its particular bureaucratic interests throughout the drafting and redrafting of the options paper and its appendices. Moreover, particular agencies may have persuasive and legitimate claims to insist upon its language in particular parts of a paper. For example, the Defense Department may claim a special role in articulating military capabilities and threats; the State Department may insist on its characterization of the political consequences of a position with the allies; and the CIA may claim priority in discussing [the other country's] intentions or verification measures. Thus the final product is frequently the result of a composite of initial drafts prepared by different agencies that have been "marked-up" or redrafted by other representatives and forged into a final, agreed-upon product through interagency meetings and negotiations among the drafters and their superiors. In this way, the necessity of clearance by all the agencies involved with the final product may mute one-sided advocacy and overstatement in any particular part of the document.

In most situations the important points to be included in the options paper are negotiated in interagency working group meetings or among the agency heads themselves. . . . In some situations all the agencies will agree on a position and will simply seek the President's concurrence with their joint recommendation. . . . Since it would be fairly unusual for a President to reject a position that the agencies have agreed upon, this process has the advantages of encouraging the President's assent and keeping control over the issue in the hands of the bureaucracy. Large differences among agencies on the objectives for or even the desirability of most proposed arms control negotiations, however, can make this kind of joint recommendation impossible. . . .

Once the President decides on the negotiating position or approach, the working group writes negotiating instructions to carry out the presidential directive. The formulation of these instructions may also be an extremely contentious process, as agencies with differing perspectives and goals inevitably construe the President's decisions narrowly or loosely to suit their interests. More interagency negotiations ordinarily follow (especially if the President's instructions address such matters as tactics or fall-back positions), and the agencies then normally seek another presidential decision with respect to the formal instructions.

The Formal Negotiation . . .

A large delegation headed by an individual with ambassadorial rank conducts an arms control negotiation. In the American case, the President appoints the ambassador to serve as his or her representative. . . . The delegation itself consists of representatives of the same (or at least most of the same) agencies represented in the interagency working group. In addition, the House and Senate have often designated representatives to negotiations. These representatives have access to some of the papers involved and sometimes sit in on plenary negotiating sessions. Although they do not normally have any impact on the day-to-day negotiations, the specter of congressional consideration of a negotiated agreement can be quite important.

Another important participant in any arms control negotiation is the working group maintained in Washington to "back-stop" the delegation. It is comprised of the same agencies that participated in the initial work on the negotiations and that are represented in the delegation, principally State, . . . Defense, JCS, CIA and the NSC. The working group is responsible for receiving daily reporting cables, reacting to proposals from the other side and drafting instructions for high-level approval. The interaction of the delegation and the backstop group is extensive. Since each daily development must normally be reported back to Washington and may elicit new instructions or guidance, a regular exchange of cables, phone calls and personal visits is generated between the delegation and the working group and between the ambassador and the White House. . . .

The result of this wealth of interchange among various governmental and non-governmental entities is an abundance of more interagency negotiation with further opportunity to shape and reshape the original negotiating position. . . .

The formality of highly stylized arms control negotiations imposes further constraints. Each ambassador normally reads an opening statement setting forth the position and making the best arguments available. . . . The responses to the opening statements tend also to be "set pieces" restating fixed positions and refuting the other side's arguments. Each delegate must follow instructions that . . . are likely to be inflexible in the beginning. . . .

The movement from formal exchanges of positions in plenary sessions to the conclusion of an agreed text — the heart of the negotiation process — can take place in a variety of other environments. Negotiators can more easily negotiate in informal settings, such as one-on-one meetings of the delegation heads, social occasions, or smaller working groups growing out of the formal session. Frequently, small working groups dealing with specialized "technical" topics or problems can make progress toward resolving disputes that would be unimaginable in a more formal and conspicuous setting. Agreements can be reached on these matters, while larger, more political differences persist until a high-level decision is made to remove those obstacles to a settlement.

While informal discussions are a central feature of international negotiations, they scarcely resemble the free-wheeling deal-making that the reader may associate with business negotiations. The international negotiator's latitude is considerably restricted by the limited authority delegated in negotiating instructions and the close supervision of working groups in the capital. . . .

The importance of individual negotiating skills and personality in the international context is frequently overstated and is certainly insufficient to change basic government positions; nevertheless, the international negotiator is not entirely without room to maneuver and bring personal skills to bear. Even detailed instructions cannot provide guidelines sufficiently specific to provide minute-by-minute guidance in actual negotiations. Items inevitably arise on which the instructions are silent or at least ambiguous. The ambassador must decide, within the parameters of the instructions, a variety of matters that eventually will determine the pace, and even the success, of the negotiations. For example, the negotiator must decide how and when to present a position, how to support it, when to resort to a fall-back position and when to seek new instructions. The negotiator must exploit ambiguity or silence in the instructions, and must decide whether and when to explore possible compromises without express authority. In doing this, the negotiator must have a sense of the process back home, a command of the interagency delegation structure, and an understanding of the positions of the other side. The negotiator may also use skillful negotiating tactics, such as claiming to lack authority actually possessed to create the appearance of having achieved a "difficult" compromise. Above all, a sound sense of timing is crucial. These skills distinguish the brilliant from the mediocre negotiator and are the most difficult to impart and articulate. . . .

Notes and Questions

1. Which agency of the U.S. government would be most inclined to stand up for the interests of farmers? Auto workers? The computer industry? The steel industry?

2. If your client has been injured by an act of a foreign government that you conclude may be a treaty violation, how would you try to stimulate an international negotiation of the matter?

3. Given the complicated interagency process discussed in the excerpt above, why might a President ask one of his closest advisers during ongoing negotiations to undertake, without resorting to the interagency process or formal negotiations, private negotiations with a high-level representative from the other country — for example, to try out a new position or to break a deadlock? This out of the normal channel approach is sometimes referred to as using the "back channel." President Nixon and Henry Kissinger used this approach at least twice in 1970-1972 during the initial Strategic Arms Limitation Talks (SALT) to break deadlocks, only informing the U.S. negotiating team and Executive Branch agencies after the back-channel negotiations had come up with a result or new position.

What are the advantages of back-channel negotiations? The disadvantages? What effect will they have on the regular negotiating team, and on the interagency process? Can the President be confident that a result achieved through back-channel negotiations will have the support of the government bureaucracies or of key figures in Congress? Might the President in some situations combine regular negotiations with occasional resort to the back channel?

4. Based on the brief descriptions in the Merrills excerpt earlier, when do you think that a state or states might be interested in supplementing negotiations with a mediator? With conciliation? For more information regarding mediation, see Mediation: Theory, Policy and Practice (Carrie Menkel-Meadow ed., 2001); see also Saadia Touval & I. William Zartman, International Mediation in the Post-Cold War Era, in Turbulent Peace: The Challenges of Managing International Conflict (Chester A. Crocker, Fen Olsen Hampson, Pamela Aall eds., 2001).

5. What are the advantages and disadvantages of negotiation, as opposed to adjudication or arbitration, of a dispute?

6. Does the fact that countries often resort to negotiations or other informal dispute-resolution mechanisms imply that international law is not really law in any binding sense?

7. During negotiations over a disputed matter, the parties might well be influenced by the relevant international legal norms. The parties are likely to realize that, if the negotiations fail, the parties might resort to a formal institution for dispute resolution — such as an arbitral tribunal or a court — and that institution will apply the international legal norms. The international legal system thus helps provide a framework for the negotiations. For a seminal study on the impact of domestic law on negotiations and bargaining that occur outside a court, see Robert H. Mnookin & Lewis Kornhauser, Bargaining in the Shadow of the Law: The Case of Divorce, 88 Yale L.J. 950 (1979).

8. Many U.S. courts have utilized with varying degrees of success a variety of alternative dispute resolution programs. These programs encompass a wide range of approaches, including mediation and conciliation. See, for example, Wayne D. Brazil, Comparing Structures for the Delivery of ADR Services by Courts: Critical Values and Concerns, 14 Ohio St. J. on Disp. Resol. 715 (1999).

B. INTERNATIONAL COURT OF JUSTICE

The International Court of Justice, often called the ICJ or the World Court, was created by the U.N. Charter in 1945 and designed to be the principal judicial organ of the United Nations. (See Articles 92 to 96 of the U.N. Charter and the separate Statute of the International Court of Justice in the Documentary Supplement.)

Located in the Netherlands at the Hague, the ICJ is the successor to the Permanent Court of International Justice (PCIJ), which was created by the League of Nations in 1920. The ICJ's Statute is substantially the same as the PCIJ's Statute, and the ICJ has frequently referred to its predecessor's precedents.

The PCIJ was most active from 1922 to 1939. During those 18 years it heard 65 cases, issued 27 advisory opinions, and rendered 32 judgments. Its efforts, for example, effected the settlement of several boundary disputes and a dispute between Denmark and Norway over the sovereignty of eastern Greenland. The PCIJ was dissolved in 1946, soon after the formation of the ICJ.

The ICJ is composed of 15 judges, who are elected to serve nine-year terms. One-third of the court is elected, or reelected, every three years. The U.N. General Assembly and Security Council are responsible for electing the judges from a list of candidates provided to the Secretary General by national groups appointed by individual governments. No two judges may be nationals of the same state. (See Articles 2 to 14 of the ICJ Statute.) Professor Thomas Franck provides a sense of the election process in the following excerpt.

Thomas M. Franck, Judging the World Court

5-8 (1986)

Article 2 of the Statute of the International Court of Justice provides: "The Court shall be composed of a body of independent judges, elected regardless of their nationality from among persons of high moral character, who possess the qualifications required in their respective countries for appointment to the highest judicial offices, or are jurisconsults of recognized competence in international law." Stipulating that the World Court shall consist of fifteen persons meeting those qualifications, article 3 adds that "no two . . . may be nationals of the same State. . . ." Article 9 makes this "geographical distribution" even more explicit in cautioning "the electors" to see to it that the bench as a whole is representative "of the main forms of civilization and of the principal legal systems of the world." The statute stipulates no lower or upper age limit for World Court judges.

The nomination and election of judges proceeds by a somewhat arcane procedure. Shabtai Rosenne, in his definitive work on the law and practice of the World Court, has shrewdly observed that the political nature of this process should not be surprising to those who understand that judicial selection in the national systems of virtually every nation is inevitably political, since the alternative would be an even more unsatisfactory arrangement by which new judges are selected by other sitting judges or by a judicial service commission — procedures that are too elitist for the tastes of most publics.

Articles 4 and 5 of the Statute of the International Court of Justice provide that candidates be nominated through "national groups." These are nominating colleges of up to four persons, chosen by the respective governments, serving for six years with the possibility of reappointment. Each "national group" may nominate up to four persons for each judicial vacancy, not more than two being of the group's own nationality.

The purpose of this, evidently, is to make the role of governments appear somewhat less intrusive. In fact, at least as far as the United States is concerned, that appearance is not wholly misleading. When President Jimmy Carter tried to offer the U.S. seat on the World Court to former Supreme Court Justice Arthur Goldberg, he was prevented from doing so by the national group's preference for Richard R. Baxter of the Harvard Law School. The process also mildly encourages judicial independence. . . .

Unlike the system of nominations, the process of election is openly political. The Statute of the International Court of Justice provides that a candidate is elected on obtaining a majority in both the UN General Assembly and Security Council. Because terms are staggered to maintain continuity, five of the fifteen judgeships are up for election or reelection every three years. Balloting continues in the two UN chambers until all vacancies have been filled. . . .

While there is nothing in the Statute of the International Court of Justice to ensure the election of judges from the "Big Five" states that occupy permanent seats in the Security Council (Britain, China, France, the United States, and Russia), and their veto does not apply to balloting for judges, their candidates usually have been elected — except in the case of China during the height of the conflict between the Communist and Nationalist regimes. But such a result is not inevitable; in 1945, the permanent members accounted for five of eleven seats in the Security Council, but since the 1963 enlargement, their role has been diluted to only five of fifteen.

While the process of electing judges is political, the Statute of the International Court of Justice seeks to guarantee the independence of a judge, once elected, by a nine-year tenure. All members are eligible for reelection and, even if not re-elected, serve on the World Court until the conclusion of the proceedings in a case before them. Every three years the judges elect a president from among their number. As it hears cases, the World Court ordinarily sits with all judges on the bench. With the agreement of the parties, however, the World Court may also constitute chambers of three or more. . . .

The Statute of the International Court of Justice does not require the judge of a state that is a party to a case to step down while it is being heard. If he or she does not do so, however, the other party is entitled to name an ad hoc judge. If neither litigant has a judge on the bench, each may make an ad hoc appointment. This procedure introduces a whiff of arbitration into what is otherwise a judicial proceeding. However, in every case so far, the balance of power has been firmly with the preponderance of judges who are nationals of neither party.

As noted above, most of the cases that have come before the ICJ have been decided by the entire Court. If one of the parties to a case has a national on the Court, the other party is allowed to choose a person to sit as a judge for that case. If the Court includes no judge of the nationality of either party, then each of the parties may proceed to choose a judge. (See Article 31 of the ICJ Statute.)

Has the ICJ been fair and impartial, given the selection process described above? In her study, Professor Edith Brown Weiss concluded:

> This chapter reports the results of a quantitative analysis of the voting behavior of judges in all contentious cases before the International Court of Justice since its inception through 1986. If the Court were according grossly unequal treatment to parties appearing before it, it should show up in the voting patterns of the judges. But the record does not reveal significant alignments, either on a regional, political, or economic basis. There is a high degree of consensus among the judges on most decisions. The most that can be discerned is that some judges vote more frequently together during certain periods than do others, and that in rare instances, notably with the Soviet and Syrian judges, they have always voted the same way. But there have not been persistent voting alignments which have significantly affected the decisions of the Court. [Edith Brown Weiss, Judicial Independence and Impartiality: A Preliminary Inquiry, in The International Court of Justice at a Crossroads 134 (Lori F. Damrosch ed., 1987).]

The Court's Statute also allows for a smaller chamber (of three or more judges) to hear a case. (Article 26.) Under the Rules of the Court, as revised in 1978, the parties are able to approve the size of the chamber. Moreover, the president of the Court is to "consult" with the parties as to the identity of the judges who are to sit on the chamber. (Rules, Article 17.) As noted earlier, each party is already allowed under Article 31 of the ICJ Statute to have a person of its choice on a panel.

The revised Rules effectively allow the parties to choose the entire composition of the chamber.

The chamber approach is seen as one way to introduce more flexibility into the Court and to make it more attractive to parties seeking formal resolution of a dispute. For example, two boundary disputes, including a disagreement between the United States and Canada over the Gulf of Maine, were decided by chambers, as was a U.S.-Italian dispute over the seizure of an Italian subsidiary of two U.S. companies.

The ICJ has jurisdiction over two types of cases: contentious cases and cases seeking an advisory opinion. Only states can be parties in contentious cases, as discussed below. The Court's advisory procedure is open only to organs or specialized agencies of the United Nations (Statute, Article 65). As of January 2003, 125 cases had been presented to the Court. Of these, 102 cases were contentious cases and 23 involved advisory opinions. The Court has issued judgments in 69 cases as well as 23 advisory opinions. For example, as noted in the Restatement:

> [The ICJ] has rendered several decisions relating to the law of the sea — Norway's maritime boundary, transit of warships through the Corfu Channel, the delimitation of the North Sea continental shelf, . . . the maritime boundary between Canada and the United States in the Gulf of Maine area, the last a decision by a panel of the Court; it dealt with several territorial disputes . . . ; claims on behalf of stockholders in a foreign company . . . ; and safety of diplomatic and consular personnel (United States-Iran). [Section 903, Reporters' Note 13, at 374.]

As of January 2003, there were 24 contentious cases pending before the Court, though eight of these involve the same issue of Yugoslavia suing various nations for alleged illegal bombing of Yugoslav territory. (For a complete listing of the cases before the Court between 1946 and January 2003, see the Documentary Supplement.)

While many of its decisions have been important, the Court has not lived up to the hopes of many of its early supporters that the Court, along with the United Nations, would evolve into an international government. To begin with, 125 cases in over 57 years is not a heavy caseload (though the Court's docket has become more active recently). Moreover, many of the cases have not been of great international importance. And, in more than 30 contentious cases, the Court's jurisdiction or the admissibility of an application (i.e., the complaint) was challenged, with the Court dismissing many of these cases. When the Court did reach a judgment on the merits, the affected parties have generally complied with it, but there have been exceptions, especially in recent years.

The reasons for the Court's limited influence are varied. This section will address some of the more important issues and problems facing the Court. These include the limits on the Court's jurisdiction, its relatively rigid procedures, the long time period most cases consume, and the enforceability of its decrees.

On enforceability of decrees, a U.N. member "undertakes to comply with the decision" of the Court if "it is a party" to the case, and the U.N. Security Council may "decide upon measures to be taken to give effect to the [Court's] judgment." (U.N. Charter, Article 94; see also the discussion below in the Restatement excerpt.) As noted above, although states have complied with the Court's judgments in many of the cases, recalcitrant states have on occasion refused to comply.

For example, in 1980, Iran refused to comply with the Court's judgment to release the U.S. hostages. And the United States continued to support the Nicaraguan Contras in spite of the Court's 1986 decision saying that this support violated international law. Moreover, in the *Breard* and *LaGrand* cases in the late 1990s, the United States did not comply with ICJ preliminary orders that directed a stay of execution for certain foreign nationals who were not provided access to consular assistance under a multilateral treaty, the Vienna Convention on Consular Relations treaties. The Court later determined that such defiance of a preliminary order constituted a violation of a binding legal obligation.

The U.N. Security Council, hampered in part by its veto-wielding members, has yet to take measures to enforce an ICJ judgment.

One result of the Court's problems is that states are turning to other approaches for formal dispute resolution. For example, even when a court is the preferred approach, states are relying more on regional and specialized courts (as discussed in Section C). Possibly the most important alternative is the increasing use of international arbitration (as discussed in Section D).

1. *Jurisdiction and Remedies of the ICJ*

Articles 34 to 36 of the ICJ Statute, excerpted below, constitute the primary jurisdictional bases for the Court.

Statute of the International Court of Justice

Article 34

1. Only states may be parties in cases before the Court. . . .

Article 35

1. The Court shall be open to the states parties to the present Statute. . . .

Article 36

1. The jurisdiction of the Court comprises all cases which the parties refer to it and all matters specially provided for in the Charter of the United Nations or in treaties and conventions in force.

2. The states parties to the present Statute may at any time declare that they recognize as compulsory *ipso facto* and without special agreement, in relation to any other state accepting the same obligation, the jurisdiction of the Court in all legal disputes concerning:

   a. the interpretation of a treaty;
   b. any question of international law;

c. the existence of any fact which, if established, would constitute a breach of an international obligation;

d. the nature or extent of the reparation to be made for the breach of an international obligation.

3. The declarations referred to above may be made unconditionally or on condition of reciprocity on the part of several or certain states, or for a certain time.

4. Such declarations shall be deposited with the Secretary-General of the United Nations, who shall transmit copies thereof to the parties to the Statute and to the Registrar of the Court.

5. Declarations made under Article 36 of the Statute of the Permanent Court of International Justice and which are still in force shall be deemed, as between the parties to the present Statute, to be acceptances of the compulsory jurisdiction of the International Court of Justice for the period which they still have to run and in accordance with their terms.

6. In the event of a dispute as to whether the Court has jurisdiction, the matter shall be settled by the decision of the Court.

Article 38

1. The Court, whose function is to decide in accordance with international law such disputes as are submitted to it, shall apply:

(a) international conventions, whether general or particular, establishing rules expressly recognized by the contesting states;

(b) international custom, as evidence of a general practice accepted as law;

(c) the general principles of law recognized by civilized nations;

(d) . . . judicial decisions and the teachings of the most highly qualified publicists of the various nations, as subsidiary means for the determination of rules of law.

2. This provision shall not prejudice the power of the Court to decide a case ex aequo et bono, if the parties agree hereto.

Article 59

The decision of the Court has no binding force except between the parties and in respect of that particular case.

The Comment to section 903 of the Restatement provides further explanation of the Court's jurisdiction and its remedies.

Restatement Section 903

Comment

a. Jurisdiction of International Court of Justice. . . . The jurisdiction of the Court in contentious cases is based on consent of the parties, either express or implied.

Under Article 36(1) of the Statute, consent may be given *ad hoc,* or by prior agreement, for example by provision in an international agreement giving the Court jurisdiction over a dispute between parties to that agreement as to its interpretation or application. Contentious cases may be brought also under the compulsory jurisdiction of the Court between states that have made declarations under Article 36(2) of the Statute. . . .

  b. Compulsory jurisdiction under Article 36(2). Under the Statute of the Court, a state may declare that it recognizes as compulsory the jurisdiction of the Court with respect to all legal disputes concerning the interpretation of a treaty, any question of international law, the existence of any fact constituting a breach of an international obligation, or the nature or extent of the reparation for such a breach. Such a declaration by a state applies only in relation to another state that has made a similar declaration. A declaration may accept the jurisdiction of the court for all legal disputes, or may exclude certain categories of disputes. A declaration is, however, subject to reciprocity, and a defendant state against which a proceeding is brought may invoke an exclusion or other reservation not stipulated in its own declaration but included in the declaration of the plaintiff state. A declaration may be of indefinite duration, or for a limited time only. A declaration for a given time is binding for the period indicated. . . .

  d. Legal disputes. The jurisdiction of the Court, pursuant to the declarations made under Article 36(2) of the Court's Statute, is expressly limited to "legal disputes." No such limitation appears in respect of the Court's jurisdiction under Article 36(1). Cases brought pursuant to prior agreement generally involve legal disputes as to the interpretation or application of an international agreement. But the Court may accept a case submitted to it by the parties even though it involves a political rather than a legal dispute. In such a case the Court is in effect asked to decide the case *ex aequo et bono.* See Article 38(2) of the Court's Statute. Under that article, the Court may decide even a legal dispute *ex aequo et bono,* rather than according to international legal principles, if the parties agree.

  e. Provisional measures. If the Court considers that circumstances so require, it may "indicate" any provisional measures for the parties to take in order to preserve their respective rights. I.C.J. Statute, Article 41. Such measures may be indicated by the Court either at the request of a party or on the Court's own initiative. The Court may indicate measures other than those requested, including measures to be taken by the requesting party. I.C.J. Rules of Court, Articles 73-75. The Court usually asks both parties to avoid any action that may aggravate the tension between them or render the dispute more difficult to resolve. . . .

  g. Enforcement of judgments. Judgments of the Court are binding between the parties. I.C.J. Statute, Article 59. Under Article 94(1) of the Charter of the United Nations, all members of the United Nations have undertaken to comply with a judgment of the Court in any case to which they are parties. If any party fails to comply with the judgment of the Court, any other party may call on the Security Council to enforce the judgment. The Council may, if it deems it necessary, make recommendations or decide upon measures (such as economic measures provided for in Article 41 of the Charter) to give effect to the judgment. Article 94(2). Members of the United Nations have agreed to accept and carry out any such decision of the Council. Article 25.

a. Declarations Accepting Compulsory Jurisdiction of the Court

As of January 2003, 64 states had declarations in force under Article 36(2) of the Statute of the Court accepting compulsory jurisdiction of the Court. As indicated in the Reporters' Notes to section 903 of the Restatement:

> Several of the declarations antedate the International Court of Justice and originally conferred jurisdiction on the Permanent Court of International Justice, but under Article 36(5) of the Statute of the International Court of Justice such declarations are deemed to be acceptances of the jurisdiction of the successor Court.
>
> Some of the declarations are without limit of time; others are for a specific period (usually five or ten years), in many instances with an automatic renewal clause. Many declarations reserve the right to terminate by a notice of withdrawal effective upon receipt by the Secretary-General of the United Nations. Some declarations specify that they apply only to disputes arising after the declaration was made or concerning situations or facts subsequent to a specified date. Seventeen declarations are without any reservation; the remaining declarations are accompanied by a variety of reservations. Many states have modified their reservations, some of them several times.
>
> The most common reservation excludes disputes committed by the parties to other tribunals or which the parties have agreed to settle by other means of settlement. Another common reservation excludes disputes relating to matters that are "exclusively" or "essentially" within the domestic jurisdiction of the declarant state; some of these reservations provide in addition that the question whether a dispute is essentially within the domestic jurisdiction is to be determined by the declaring state (a so-called "self-judging" clause). Several declarations exclude disputes arising under a multilateral treaty "unless all parties to the treaty affected by the decision are also parties to the case before the Court" or, more broadly, "unless all parties to the treaty are also parties to the case before the Court." . . . [Reporters' Note 2.]

The following are examples of declarations by states, including one by the United States (which has since been terminated), under Article 36(2) of the ICJ Statute.

Nicaragua[1]

[Translation from the French]   24 IX 29.

On behalf of the Republic of Nicaragua I recognize as compulsory unconditionally the jurisdiction of the Permanent Court of International Justice.

Geneva, 24 September 1929.

(Signed) T. F. Medina

---

1. According to a telegram dated 29 November 1939, addressed to the League of Nations, Nicaragua had ratified the Protocol of Signature of the Statute of the Permanent Court of International Justice (16 December 1920), and the instrument of ratification was to follow. It does not appear, however, that the instrument of ratification was ever received by the League of Nations.

United States of America

26 VIII 46.

I, Harry S Truman, President of the United States of America, declare on behalf of the United States of America, under Article 36, paragraph 2, of the Statute of the International Court of Justice, and in accordance with the Resolution of 2 August 1946 of the Senate of the United States of America (two-thirds of the Senators present concurring therein), that the United States of America recognizes as compulsory *ipso facto* and without special agreement, in relation to any other State accepting the same obligation, the jurisdiction of the International Court of Justice in all legal disputes hereafter arising concerning

(a) the interpretation of a treaty;
(b) any question of international law;
(c) the existence of any fact which, if established, would constitute a breach of an international obligation;
(d) the nature or extent of the reparation to be made for the breach of an international obligation;

Provided, that this declaration shall not apply to

(a) disputes the solution of which the parties shall entrust to other tribunals by virtue of agreements already in existence or which may be concluded in the future; or
(b) disputes with regard to matters which are essentially within the domestic jurisdiction of the United States of America as determined by the United States of America; or
(c) disputes arising under a multilateral treaty, unless (1) all parties to the treaty affected by the decision are also parties to the case before the Court, or (2) the United States of America specially agrees to jurisdiction; and

Provided further, that this declaration shall remain in force for a period of five years and thereafter until the expiration of six months after notice may be given to terminate this declaration.

Done at Washington this fourteenth day of August 1946.

(Signed) Harry S Truman

6 IV 84.

I have the honour on behalf of the Government of the United States of America to refer to the declaration of my Government of 26 August 1946 concerning the acceptance by the United States of America of the compulsory jurisdiction of the International Court of Justice, and to state that the aforesaid declaration shall not apply to disputes with any Central American State or arising out of or related to events in Central America, any of which disputes shall be settled in such manner as the parties to them may agree.

Notwithstanding the terms of the aforesaid declaration, this proviso shall take effect immediately and shall remain in force for two years, so as to foster the continuing regional dispute settlement process which seeks a negotiated solution to the inter-related political, economic and security problems of Central America.

(Signed) George P. Shultz,
Secretary of State of
the United States of America

The ICJ addressed the validity of reservations in a state's declaration in the following case:

Case of Certain Norwegian Loans (France v. Norway)

Intl. Court of Justice
[1957] I.C.J. Rep. 9 (Judgment)

[French nationals owned bonds issued before World War I by the Kingdom of Norway and two Norwegian banks. These bonds initially contained varying clauses that France claimed expressly promised and guaranteed payment in gold. Norway later passed legislation allowing payment of the bonds with Bank of Norway notes, which were not convertible into gold.

The French government espoused the claims of its nationals. During diplomatic negotiations, it proposed that the problem be submitted to a commission of economic and financial experts, to arbitration, or to the ICJ. The Norwegian government maintained that the bondholders' claims were within the jurisdiction of the Norwegian courts and that these claims were solely matters of domestic law.

The French government then brought the case to the ICJ, where it argued that the bonds were international loans that "cannot be unilaterally modified by [Norway] without negotiation with the holders, with the French State which has adopted the cause of its nationals, or without arbitration." The French asked that the Court stipulate the amount of the lender's obligation in gold, and that the lender then pay off this amount.]

The Application [of France] expressly refers to Article 36, paragraph 2, of the Statute of the Court and to the acceptance of the compulsory jurisdiction of the Court by Norway on November 16th, 1946, and by France on March 1st, 1949. The Norwegian Declaration reads:

I declare on behalf of the Norwegian Government that Norway recognizes as compulsory *ipso facto* and without special agreement, in relation to any other State accepting the same obligation, that is to say, on condition of reciprocity, the jurisdiction of the International Court of Justice in conformity with Article 36, paragraph 2, of the Statute of the Court, for a period of ten years as from 3rd October 1946.

The French Declaration reads:

On behalf of the Government of the French Republic, and subject to ratification, I declare that I recognize as compulsory *ipso facto* and without special agreement, in relation to any other State accepting the same obligation, that is on condition of reciprocity, the jurisdiction of the International Court of Justice, in conformity with Article 36, paragraph 2, of the Statute of the said Court, for all disputes which may arise in respect of facts or situations subsequent to the ratification of the present declaration, with the exception of those with regard to which the parties may have agreed or may agree to have recourse to another method of peaceful settlement.

This declaration does not apply to differences relating to matters which are essentially within the national jurisdiction as understood by the Government of the French Republic. . . .

After presenting the first ground of its first Preliminary Objection on the basis that the loan contracts are governed by municipal law, the Norwegian Government continues in its Preliminary Objections:

There can be no possible doubt on this point. If, however, there should still be some doubt, the Norwegian Government would rely upon the reservations made by the French Government in its Declaration of March 1st, 1949. By virtue of the principle of reciprocity, which is embodied in Article 36, paragraph 3, of the Statute of the Court and which has been clearly expressed in the Norwegian Declaration of November 16th, 1946, the Norwegian Government cannot be bound, *vis-à-vis* the French Government, by undertakings which are either broader or stricter than those given by the latter Government. . . .

It will be recalled that the French Declaration accepting the compulsory jurisdiction of the Court contains the following reservation:

This declaration does not apply to differences relating to matters which are essentially within the national jurisdiction as understood by the Government of the French Republic.

In the Preliminary Objections filed by the Norwegian Government it is stated:

The Norwegian Government did not insert any such reservation in its own Declaration. But it has the right to rely upon the restrictions placed by France upon her own undertakings.

Convinced that the dispute which has been brought before the Court by the Application of July 6th, 1955, is within the domestic jurisdiction, the Norwegian Government considers itself fully entitled to rely on this right. Accordingly, it requests the Court to decline, on grounds that it lacks jurisdiction, the function which the French Government would have it assume.

In considering this ground of the Objection the Court notes in the first place that the present case has been brought before it on the basis of Article 36, paragraph 2, of the Statute and of the corresponding Declarations of acceptance of compulsory jurisdiction; that in the present case the jurisdiction of the Court depends upon the Declarations made by the Parties in accordance with Article 36, paragraph 2, of the Statute on condition of reciprocity; and that, since two unilateral declarations are involved, such jurisdiction is conferred upon the Court only to the extent to which the Declarations coincide in conferring it. A comparison between the two Declarations shows that the French Declaration accepts the Court's jurisdiction within narrower limits than the Norwegian Declaration; consequently, the common will of the

Parties, which is the basis of the Court's jurisdiction, exists within these narrower limits indicated by the French reservation.

France has limited her acceptance of the compulsory jurisdiction of the Court by excluding beforehand disputes "relating to matters which are essentially within the national jurisdiction as understood by the Government of the French Republic." In accordance with the condition of reciprocity to which acceptance of the compulsory jurisdiction is made subject in both Declarations and which is provided for in Article 36, paragraph 3, of the Statute, Norway, equally with France, is entitled to except from the compulsory jurisdiction of the Court disputes understood by Norway to be essentially within its national jurisdiction.

The Court does not consider that it should examine whether the French reservation is consistent with the undertaking of a legal obligation and is compatible with Article 36, paragraph 6, of the Statute which provides:

> In the event of a dispute as to whether the Court has jurisdiction, the matter shall be settled by the decision of the Court.

The validity of the reservation has not been questioned by the Parties. It is clear that France fully maintains its Declaration, including the reservation, and that Norway relies upon the reservation.

For these reasons, the Court, by twelve votes to three, finds that it is without jurisdiction to adjudicate upon the dispute which has been brought before it by the Application of the Government of the French Republic of July 6th, 1955.

Questions

1. What if the Norwegian declaration did not include the reciprocity condition — that is, what if it had been made unconditional? Based on the reasoning in the opinion above, would the Court have found jurisdiction? As Professor Rosenne concludes, "[W]here two declarations are in different terms, jurisdiction exists only to the extent that they coincide." Shabati Rosenne, The Law and Practice of the International Court, 1920-1996, at 90 (3d ed. 1997).

2. If the facts in the case were reversed so that Norway sued France in the ICJ over French bonds, would France have any grounds for objecting to the jurisdiction of the Court? If France claimed that the matters were "essentially within the national jurisdiction" of France, could the Court have decided that the jurisdictional question was a matter of proper legal interpretation for the Court to address? Or should the Court always accept the French invocation of this national jurisdiction exception?

3. Do you believe there should be any limits on a state's ability to invoke a self-judging reservation? What about the provision in Article 36(6) that the Court should determine questions of its own jurisdiction?

4. What law would the Court have applied if it had decided that it had jurisdiction in this case? What legal documents or sources would the Court have looked to? Was the dispute really a political dispute? If you were counsel to Norway or France, would you recommend that the Court decide the case *ex aequo et bono*? What would be the advantages of using a chamber instead of the full Court?

5. What precedential value would an ICJ judgment on the merits have? See Article 59, which provides that "[t]he decision of the Court has no binding force except between the parties and in respect of that particular case."

6. Assume that one country, *X*, has accepted the jurisdiction of the Court unconditionally and that it has not specified any time within which it might withdraw its acceptance. Assume that a second country, *Y*, has accepted the jurisdiction of the Court subject to several reservations, including one regarding reciprocity, and that its declaration says that the declaration will remain in force until six months after notice is given of termination. *Y* gives notice on April 6 that, effective immediately, it withdraws its acceptance of jurisdiction with regard to suits brought by *X*. *X* then sues *Y* on April 9. Does *Y* have a valid argument that, because *X* could have withdrawn or modified its acceptance of jurisdiction without notice, *Y* should be able to do this as well because of its reciprocity reservation?

b. The Nicaragua Litigation

The Court faced a major challenge to its jurisdiction when Nicaragua sued the United States in 1984 over U.S. support of the Contras. (It was also a challenge, as we shall see, to respect for its judgments.) Nicaragua alleged in its Application that started the proceeding that the United States "is using military force against Nicaragua and intervening in Nicaragua's internal affairs. . . . The United States has created an 'army' of more than 10,000 mercenaries . . . installed them in more than ten base camps in Honduras along the border with Nicaragua, trained them, paid them, supplied them with arms, ammunition, food and medical supplies, and directed their attacks against human and economic targets inside Nicaragua."

Case Concerning Military and Paramilitary Activities In and Against Nicaragua (Nicaragua v. United States of America)

Intl. Court of Justice
[1984] I.C.J. Rep. 392 (Jurisdiction of the Court and Admissibility of the Application)

1. On 9 April 1984 the Ambassador of the Republic of Nicaragua to the Netherlands filed in the Registry of the Court an Application instituting proceedings against the United States of America in respect of a dispute concerning responsibility for military and paramilitary activities in and against Nicaragua. In order to found the jurisdiction of the Court the Application relied on declarations made by the Parties accepting the compulsory jurisdiction of the Court under Article 36 of its Statute. . . .

5. In the Memorial, the Republic of Nicaragua contended that, in addition to the basis of jurisdiction relied on in the Application, a Treaty of Friendship, Commerce and Navigation signed by the Parties in 1956 provides an independent basis for jurisdiction under Article 36, paragraph 1, of the Statute of the Court. . . .

11. The present case concerns a dispute between the Government of the Republic of Nicaragua and the Government of the United States of America occasioned, Nicaragua contends, by certain military and paramilitary activities conducted in Nicaragua and in the waters off its coasts, responsibility for which is attributed by Nicaragua to the United States. In the present phase the case concerns

the jurisdiction of the Court to entertain and pronounce upon this dispute, and the admissibility of the Application by which it was brought before the Court. . . .

13. Article 36, paragraph 2, of the Statute of the Court provides [see page 288, above]. The United States made a declaration, pursuant to this provision, on 14 August 1946, containing certain reservations, to be examined below, and expressed to

> remain in force for a period of five years and thereafter until the expiration of six months after notice may be given to terminate this declaration.

On 6 April 1984 the Government of the United States of America deposited with the Secretary-General of the United Nations a notification, signed by the United States Secretary of State, Mr. George Shultz, referring to the Declaration deposited on 26 August 1946, and stating that: [the notification as well as the Declaration are quoted at page 292]. This notification will be referred to, for convenience, as the "1984 notification."

14. In order to be able to rely upon the United States Declaration of 1946 to found jurisdiction in the present case, Nicaragua has to show that it is a "State accepting the same obligation" within the meaning of Article 36, paragraph 2, of the Statute. For this purpose, Nicaragua relies on a Declaration made by it on 24 September 1929 pursuant to Article 36, paragraph 2, of the Statute of the Permanent Court of International Justice. . . . Nicaragua relies further on paragraph 5 of Article 36 of the Statute of the present Court, which provides that:

> Declarations made under Article 36 of the Statute of the Permanent Court of International Justice and which are still in force shall be deemed, as between the parties to the present Statute, to be acceptances of the compulsory jurisdiction of the International Court of Justice for the period which they still have to run and in accordance with their terms.

15. [The facts regarding Nicaragua's joining the PCIJ were somewhat unique because Nicaragua had declared that it wanted to join the PCIJ, but the country's instrument of ratification never reached the depository League of Nations, possibly because the document might have been lost at sea during World War II. Nevertheless, the Court found that the absence of the formality did not exclude the operation of Article 36(5) transferring the Declaration from the PCIJ to the ICJ. The Court noted that Nicaragua had signed and ratified the U.N. Charter and thereby accepted the ICJ Statute. The Court also found that the "constant acquiescence of Nicaragua in affirmations, to be found in United Nations and other publications, of its position as bound by the optional clause constitutes a valid manifestation ¶109 of ICJ opinion.)

The Court then turned to the question of the 1984 notification by the United States that disputes with Central American states were excluded from the coverage of the 1946 U.S. declaration, effective immediately.]

59. Declarations of acceptance of the compulsory jurisdiction of the Court are facultative, unilateral engagements, that States are absolutely free to make or not to make. In making the declaration a State is equally free either to do so unconditionally and without limit of time for its duration, or to qualify it with conditions or reservations. In particular, it may limit its effect to disputes arising after a certain date; or it may specify how long the declaration itself shall remain in force, or what notice (if any) will be required to terminate it. However, the unilateral nature of

declarations does not signify that the State making the declaration is free to amend the scope and the contents of its solemn commitments as it pleases. . . .

61. . . . Although the United States retained the right to modify the contents of the 1946 Declaration or to terminate it, a power which is inherent in any unilateral act of a State, it has, nevertheless assumed an inescapable obligation towards other States accepting the Optional Clause, by stating formally and solemnly that any such change should take effect only after six months have elapsed as from the date of notice.

62. The United States has argued that the Nicaraguan 1929 Declaration, being of undefined duration, is liable to immediate termination, without previous notice, and that therefore Nicaragua has not accepted "the same obligation" as itself for the purposes of Article 36, paragraph 2, and consequently may not rely on the six months' notice proviso against the United States. The Court does not however consider that this argument entitles the United States validly to act in non-application of the time-limit proviso included in the 1946 Declaration. The notion of reciprocity is concerned with the scope and substance of the commitments entered into, including reservations, and not with the formal conditions of their creation, duration or extinction. It appears clearly that reciprocity cannot be invoked in order to excuse departure from the terms of a State's own declaration, whatever its scope, limitations or conditions. . . .

63. Moreover, since the United States purported to act on 6 April 1984 in such a way as to modify its 1946 Declaration with sufficiently immediate effect to bar an Application filed on 9 April 1984, it would be necessary, if reciprocity is to be relied on, for the Nicaraguan Declaration to be terminable with immediate effect. But the right of immediate termination of declarations with indefinite duration is far from established. It appears from the requirements of good faith that they should be treated, by analogy, according to the law of treaties, which requires a reasonable time for withdrawal from or termination of treaties that contain no provision regarding the duration of their validity. Since Nicaragua has in fact not manifested any intention to withdraw its own declaration, the question of what reasonable period of notice would legally be required does not need to be further examined: it need only be observed that from 6 to 9 April would not amount to a "reasonable time." . . .

65. In sum, the six months' notice clause forms an important integral part of the United States Declaration and it is a condition that must be complied with in case of either termination or modification. Consequently, the 1984 notification, in the present case, cannot override the obligation of the United States to submit to the compulsory jurisdiction of the Court vis-à-vis Nicaragua, a State accepting the same obligation. . . .

67. The question remains to be resolved whether the United States Declaration of 1946, though not suspended in its effects vis-à-vis Nicaragua by the 1984 notification, constitutes the necessary consent of the United States to the jurisdiction of the Court in the present case, taking into account the reservations which were attached to the declaration. Specifically, the United States has invoked proviso *(c)* to that declaration, which provides that the United States acceptance of the Court's compulsory jurisdiction shall not extend to

disputes arising under a multilateral treaty, unless (1) all parties to the treaty affected by the decision are also parties to the case before the Court, or (2) the United States of America specially agrees to jurisdiction.

This reservation will be referred to for convenience as the "multilateral treaty reservation." Of the two remaining provisos to the declaration, it has not been suggested that proviso *(a),* referring to disputes the solution of which is entrusted to other tribunals, has any relevance to the present case. As for proviso *(b),* excluding jurisdiction over "disputes with regard to matters which are essentially within the domestic jurisdiction of the United States of America as determined by the United States of America," the United States has informed the Court that it has determined not to invoke this proviso, but "without prejudice to the rights of the United States under that proviso in relation to any subsequent pleadings, proceedings, or cases before this Court."

68. The United States points out that Nicaragua relies in its Application on four multilateral treaties, namely the Charter of the United Nations, the Charter of the Organization of American States, the Montevideo Convention on Rights and Duties of States of 26 December 1933, and the Havana Convention on the Rights and Duties of States in the Event of Civil Strife of 20 February 1928. . . .

73. . . . . The Court cannot dismiss the claims of Nicaragua under principles of customary and general international law, simply because such principles have been enshrined in the texts of the conventions relied upon by Nicaragua. The fact that the above-mentioned principles, recognized as such, have been codified or embodied in multilateral conventions does not mean that they cease to exist and to apply as principles of customary law, even as regards countries that are parties to such conventions. Principles such as those of the non-use of force, non-intervention, respect for the independence and territorial integrity of States, and the freedom of navigation, continue to be binding as part of customary international law, despite the operation of provisions of conventional law in which they have been incorporated. Therefore, since the claim before the Court in this case is not confined to violation of the multilateral conventional provisions invoked, it would not in any event be barred by the multilateral treaty reservation in the United States 1946 Declaration. . . .

[FCN TREATY]

77. . . . . [I]n its Memorial [Nicaragua] invokes also a 1956 Treaty of Friendship, Commerce and Navigation between Nicaragua and the United States as a complementary foundation for the Court's jurisdiction. . . .

81. Article XXIV, paragraph 2, of the Treaty . . . , signed at Managua on 21 January 1956, reads as follows:

> Any dispute between the Parties as to the interpretation or application of the present Treaty, not satisfactorily adjusted by diplomacy, shall be submitted to the International Court of Justice, unless the Parties agree to settlement by some other pacific means.

The treaty entered into force on 24 May 1958 on exchange of ratifications. . . . The provisions of Article XXIV, paragraph 2, are in terms which are very common in bilateral treaties of amity or of establishment, and the intention of the parties in accepting such clauses is clearly to provide for such a right of unilateral recourse to the Court in the absence of agreement to employ some other pacific means of settlement (cf. *United States Diplomatic and Consular Staff in Tehran,* I.C.J. Reports 1980, p.27, para. 52). . . .

82. Nicaragua in its Memorial submits that the 1956 Treaty has been and was being violated by the military and paramilitary activities of the United States in and against Nicaragua, as described in the Application; specifically, it is submitted that these activities directly violate the following Articles:

Article XIX: providing for freedom of commerce and navigation, and for vessels of either party to have liberty "to come with their cargoes to all ports, places and waters of such other party open to foreign commerce and navigation," and to be accorded national treatment and most-favored-nation treatment within those ports, places and waters.

Article XIV: forbidding the imposition of restrictions or prohibitions on the importation of any product of the other party, or on the exportation of any product to the territories of the other party. . . .

Article XX: providing for freedom of transit through the territories of each party. . . .

83. Taking into account these Articles of the Treaty of 1956, particularly the provision in, inter alia, Article XIX, for the freedom of commerce and navigation, and the references in the Preamble to peace and friendship, there can be no doubt that . . . there is a dispute between the Parties, inter alia, as to the "interpretation or application" of the Treaty. That dispute is also clearly one which is not "satisfactorily adjusted by diplomacy" within the meaning of Article XXIV of the 1956 Treaty. . . . Accordingly, the Court finds that . . . the Court has jurisdiction under that Treaty to entertain such claims. . . .

[ADMISSIBILITY]

84. The Court now turns to the question of the admissibility of the Application of Nicaragua. The United States of America contended in its Counter-Memorial that Nicaragua's Application is inadmissible on five separate grounds, each of which, it is said, is sufficient to establish such inadmissibility, whether considered as a legal bar to adjudication or as "a matter requiring the exercise of prudential discretion in the interest of the integrity of the judicial function." Some of these grounds have in fact been presented in terms suggesting that they are matters of competence or jurisdiction rather than admissibility, but it does not appear to be of critical importance how they are classified in this respect. These grounds will now be examined. . . .

86. The first ground of inadmissibility relied on by the United States is that Nicaragua has failed to bring before the Court parties whose presence and participation is necessary for the rights of those parties to be protected and for the adjudication of the issues raised in the Application. The United States first asserts that adjudication of Nicaragua's claim would necessarily implicate the rights and obligations of other States, in particular those of Honduras, since it is alleged that Honduras has allowed its territory to be used as a staging ground for unlawful uses of force against Nicaragua. . . .

88. There is no doubt that in appropriate circumstances the Court will decline . . . to exercise the jurisdiction conferred upon it where the legal interests of a State not party to the proceedings "would not only be affected by a decision, but would form the very subject-matter of the decision" (I.C.J. Reports 1954, p.32). Where however claims of a legal nature are made by an Applicant against a Respondent in

proceedings before the Court, and made the subject of submissions, the Court has in principle merely to decide upon those submissions, with binding force for the parties only, and no other State, in accordance with Article 59 of the Statute. As the Court has already indicated (paragraph 74, above) other States which consider that they may be affected are free to institute separate proceedings, or to employ the procedure of intervention. There is no trace, either in the Statute or in the practice of international tribunals, of an "indispensable parties" rule of the kind argued for by the United States. . . .

89. Secondly, the United States regards the Application as inadmissible because each of Nicaragua's allegations constitutes no more than a reformulation and restatement of a single fundamental claim, that the United States is engaged in an unlawful use of armed force, or breach of the peace, or acts of aggression against Nicaragua, a matter which is committed by the Charter and by practice to the competence of other organs, in particular the United Nations Security Council. . . .

91. It will be convenient to deal with this alleged ground of inadmissibility together with the third ground advanced by the United States namely that the Court should hold the Application of Nicaragua to be inadmissible in view of the subject-matter of the Application and the position of the Court within the United Nations system, including the impact of proceedings before the Court on the ongoing exercise of the "inherent right of individual or collective self-defence" under Article 51 of the Charter. . . .

93. The United States is thus arguing that the matter was essentially one for the Security Council since it concerned a complaint by Nicaragua involving the use of force. However, having regard to the *United States Diplomatic and Consular Staff in Tehran* case, the Court is of the view that the fact that a matter is before the Security Council should not prevent it being dealt with by the Court and that both proceedings could be pursued *pari passu*. In that case the Court held: . . .

> Whereas Article 12 of the Charter expressly forbids the General Assembly to make any recommendation with regard to a dispute or situation while the Security Council is exercising its functions in respect of that dispute or situation, no such restriction is placed on the functioning of the Court by any provision of either the Charter or the Statute of the Court. The reasons are clear. It is for the Court, the principal judicial organ of the United Nations, to resolve any legal questions that may be in issue between parties to the dispute; and the resolution of such legal questions by the Court may be an important, and sometimes decisive, factor in promoting the peaceful settlement of the dispute. This is indeed recognized by Article 36 of the Charter, paragraph 3 of which specifically provides that:

>> In making recommendations under this Article the Security Council should also take into consideration that legal disputes should as a general rule be referred by the parties to the International Court of Justice in accordance with the provisions of the Statute of the Court. (I.C.J. Reports 1980, p.22, para. 40.) . . .

95. It is necessary to emphasize that Article 24 of the Charter of the United Nations provides that

> In order to ensure prompt and effective action by the United Nations, its Members confer on the Security Council *primary* responsibility for the maintenance of international peace and security . . .

The Charter accordingly does not confer *exclusive* responsibility upon the Security Council for the purpose. . . .

96. It must also be remembered that, as the *Corfu Channel* case (I.C.J. Reports 1949, p.4) shows, the Court has never shied away from a case brought before it merely because it had political implications or because it involved serious elements of the use of force. . . .

99. The fourth ground of inadmissibility put forward by the United States is that the Application should be held inadmissible in consideration of the inability of the judicial function to deal with situations involving ongoing conflict. . . .

101. The Court is bound to observe that any judgment on the merits in the present case will be limited to upholding such submissions of the Parties as have been supported by sufficient proof of relevant facts, and are regarded by the Court as sound in law. A situation of armed conflict is not the only one in which evidence of fact may be difficult to come by, and the Court has in the past recognized and made allowance for this (*Corfu Channel*, I.C.J. Reports 1949, p.18; *United States Diplomatic and Consular Staff in Tehran*, I.C.J. Reports 1980, p.10, para. 13). Ultimately, however, it is the litigant seeking to establish a fact who bears the burden of proving it. . . .

102. The fifth and final contention of the United States under this head is that the Application should be held inadmissible because Nicaragua has failed to exhaust the established processes for the resolution of the conflicts occurring in Central America. In the contention of the United States, the Contadora process, to which Nicaragua is party, is recognized both by the political organs of the United Nations and by the Organization of American States, as the appropriate method for the resolution of the issues of Central America. That process has achieved agreement among the States of the region, including Nicaragua, on aims which go to the very heart of the claims and issues raised by the Application. The United States repeats its contention (paragraph 89, above) that the Contadora process is a "regional arrangement" within the meaning of Article 52, paragraph 2, of the Charter, and contends that under that Article, Nicaragua is obliged to make every effort to achieve a solution to the security problems of Central America through the Contadora process. . . .

107. The Court does not consider that the Contadora process, whatever its merits, can properly be regarded as a "regional arrangement" for the purposes of Chapter VIII of the Charter of the United Nations. Furthermore, it is also important always to bear in mind that all regional, bilateral, and even multilateral, arrangements that the Parties to this case may have made, touching on the issue of settlement of disputes or the jurisdiction of the International Court of Justice, must be made always subject to the provisions of Article 103 of the Charter which reads as follows:

> In the event of a conflict between the obligations of the Members of the United Nations under the present Charter and their obligations under any other international agreement, their obligations under the present Charter shall prevail.

108. In the light of the foregoing, the Court is unable to accept either that there is any requirement of prior exhaustion of regional negotiating processes as a precondition to seising the Court; or that the existence of the Contadora process constitutes in this case an obstacle to the examination by the Court of the Nicaraguan Application and judicial determination in due course of the submissions of

the Parties in the case. The Court is therefore unable to declare the Application inadmissible, as requested by the United States, on any of the grounds it has advanced as requiring such a finding. . . .

113. For these reasons, the Court,

(1) (a) *finds,* by eleven votes to five, that it has jurisdiction to entertain the Application filed by the Republic of Nicaragua on 9 April 1984, on the basis of Article 36, paragraphs 2 and 5, of the Statute of the Court;

In Favour: President Elias; Vice-President Sette-Camara; Judges Lachs, Morozov, Nagendra Singh, Ruda, El-Khani, de Lacharrière, Mbaye, Bedjaoui; Judge ad hoc Colliard;
Against: Judges Mosler, Oda, Ago, Schwebel and Sir Robert Jennings.

(b) *finds,* by fourteen votes to two, that it has jurisdiction to entertain the Application filed by the Republic of Nicaragua on 9 April 1984, in so far as that Application relates to a dispute concerning the interpretation or application of the Treaty of Friendship, Commerce and Navigation between the United States of America and the Republic of Nicaragua signed at Managua on 21 January 1956, on the basis of Article XXIV of that Treaty;

In Favour: President Elias; Vice-President Sette-Camara; Judges Lachs, Morozov, Nagendra Singh, Mosler, Oda, Ago, El-Khani, Sir Robert Jennings, de Lacharrière, Mbaye, Bedjaoui; Judge ad hoc Colliard;
Against: Judges Ruda and Schwebel.

(c) *finds,* by fifteen votes to one, that it has jurisdiction to entertain the case:

In Favour: President Elias; Vice-President Sette-Camara; Judges Lachs, Morozov, Nagendra Singh, Ruda, Mosler, Oda, Ago, El-Khani, Sir Robert Jennings, de Lacharrière, Mbaye, Bedjaoui; Judge ad hoc Colliard;
Against: Judge Schwebel.

(2) *finds,* unanimously, that the said Application is admissible.

[Nov. 26, 1984]

Less than two months after the ICJ decision on jurisdiction and admissibility, the United States announced that it had decided not to participate in further proceedings in the case:

Statement by the U.S. Department of State, Jan. 18, 1985

The United States has consistently taken the position that the proceedings initiated by Nicaragua in the International Court of Justice (ICJ) are a misuse of the Court for political purposes and that the Court lacks jurisdiction and competence over such a case. The Court's decision of November 26, 1984, finding that it has jurisdiction, is contrary to law and fact. With great reluctance, the United States has decided not to participate in further proceedings in this case.

The Court continued its proceedings without U.S. participation. Then, less than a year after the 1984 decision in the case, the United States gave formal notice that it was terminating its 1946 declaration of acceptance of the Court's compulsory jurisdiction, with the effect to take place in six months.

Letter from U.S. Secretary of State Shultz to the U.N. Secretary General, Oct. 7, 1985

Dear Mr. Secretary-General:

I have the honor on behalf of the Government of the United States of America to refer to the declaration of my Government of 26 August 1946, as modified by my note of 6 April 1984, concerning the acceptance by the United States of America of the compulsory jurisdiction of the International Court of Justice, and to state that the aforesaid declaration is hereby terminated, with effect six months from the date hereof.

Sincerely yours,

George P. Shultz

Statement by the Legal Adviser, Abraham D. Sofaer, to the Senate Foreign Relations Committee

(Dec. 4, 1985)

REASONS FOR U.S. REVIEW

The Court's decision [on jurisdiction] also caused us to undertake a thorough evaluation of our 1946 declaration and its place in the system of compulsory jurisdiction established by Article 36(2) of the Court's Statute. . . .

We recognized, first of all, that the hopes originally placed in compulsory jurisdiction by the architects of the Court's Statute have never been realized and will not be realized in the foreseeable future. We had hoped that widespread acceptance of compulsory jurisdiction and its successful employment in actual cases would increase confidence in judicial settlement of international disputes and, thus, eventually lead to its universal acceptance.

Experience has dashed these hopes. Only 47 of the 162 states entitled to accept the Court's compulsory jurisdiction now do so.* This number represents a proportion of states that is substantially lower than in the late 1940s. The United Kingdom is the only other permanent member of the UN Security Council that accepts compulsory jurisdiction in any form. . . . Moreover, a substantial number of the states

---

*As of January 2003, 64 of the 191 states entitled to accept the Court's compulsory jurisdiction were currently doing so.—EDS.

accepting compulsory jurisdiction have attached reservations to their acceptances that deprive them of much of their meaning. The United Kingdom, for example, retains the power to decline to accept the Court's jurisdiction in any dispute at any time before a case is actually filed.

Compulsory jurisdiction cases have not been the principal part of the Court's overall jurisprudence. . . .

Another consideration we weighed is the fact that, although we have tried seven times, we have never been able successfully to bring a state before the Court. We have been barred from achieving this result not only by the fact that few other states accept compulsory jurisdiction but also by the principle of reciprocity as applied to our 1946 declaration. That principle allows a respondent state to invoke any reservation in the applicant state's declaration to seek to defeat the Court's jurisdiction. Thus, respondent states may invoke reservations in our 1946 declaration against us. . . .

The terms of our acceptance of compulsory jurisdiction contain an additional weakness. Nothing in it prevents another state from depositing an acceptance of compulsory jurisdiction solely for the purpose of bringing suit against the United States and, thereafter, withdrawing its acceptance. . . .

Several aspects of the Court's decisions in the Nicaragua case were disturbing. First, the Court departed from its traditionally cautious approach to finding jurisdiction. It disregarded fundamental defects in Nicaragua's claim to have accepted compulsory jurisdiction. This question involves more than a legal technicality. It goes to the heart of the Court's jurisdiction, which is the consent of states. . . .

Furthermore, the Court engaged in unprecedented procedural actions — such as rejecting without even a hearing El Salvador's application to intervene as of right — that betrayed a predisposition to find that it had jurisdiction and that Nicaragua's claims were justiciable, regardless of the overwhelming legal case to the contrary. The Court sought to cover itself by holding out the possibility of accepting the Salvadoran intervention at the merits stage — at which point Salvadoran objections to the Court's jurisdiction and the justiciability of Nicaragua's claims would have been too late.

Even more disturbing, for the first time in its history, the Court has sought to assert jurisdiction over a controversy concerning claims related to an ongoing use of armed force. This action concerns every state. It is inconsistent with the structure of the UN system. The only prior case involving use-of-force issues — the *Corfu Channel* case — went to the Court after the disputed actions had ceased and the Security Council had determined that the matter was suitable for judicial consideration. . . .

We carefully considered modifying our 1946 declaration as an alternative to its termination, but we concluded that modification would not meet our concerns. No limiting language that we could draft would prevent the Court from asserting jurisdiction if it wanted to take a particular case. . . .

CONCLUSION

Looked at from the standpoint of the reality of compulsory jurisdiction today, the decision to terminate our 1946 acceptance was a regrettable but necessary measure taken in order to safeguard U.S. interests. . . . We remain prepared to use the Court for the resolution of international disputes whenever possible and appropriate. . . .

At the same time that the United States was announcing its intention to terminate its acceptance of the Court's compulsory jurisdiction, it also announced that Italy and the United States were submitting a longstanding dispute to a special chamber of the Court.

Statement by the U.S. Department of State, Oct. 7, 1985

The United States and Italy have been engaged in a longstanding dispute arising from certain actions by Italian Government officials against a wholly owned subsidiary of Raytheon Company and Machlett Laboratories, Inc., both U.S. corporations.

The two governments have come to the conclusion that they are unable to resolve the diplomatic claim of the United States on behalf of Raytheon Company and Machlett Laboratories, Inc., through diplomatic negotiation or binding arbitration. Therefore, the United States, in conformity with the U.S.-Italian Treaty of Friendship, Commerce, and Navigation of 1948, has determined to approach the International Court of Justice (ICJ) with a view to submitting that dispute to a special chamber as provided by the Court's Statute and rules of procedure, subject to mutually satisfactory resolution of implementing arrangements. Italy concurs in the opinion that this is an appropriate course of action.

The case involved the 1968 seizure by Italian authorities of an electronics plant in Palermo, Italy. The plant was owned by an Italian subsidiary of two U.S. companies. In a 4-1 decision in July 1989 (with the U.S. judge dissenting), the ICJ chamber ruled that the seizure did not violate the treaty between the two countries.

Notes and Questions

1. Should the Court have overlooked Nicaragua's technical failures and taken jurisdiction in the Nicaragua v. U.S.A. case? Would there be any value in enforcing the technicalities? How could the United States find out who it was obligated to litigate with before the Court if the ICJ does not enforce technicalities?

2. Do you agree with the Court that the United States did not have the right to modify its acceptance because the six-months'-notice clause was applicable? Should that clause be effective even when Nicaragua had no notice period in its acceptance? Could Nicaragua have terminated its acceptance without advance notice? Why doesn't the reciprocity clause of the U.S. acceptance apply here?

3. Is the Court's decision consistent with its analysis in the *Norwegian Loans* case? Or, since the cases supposedly do not have precedential value, should inconsistency not matter? Would the answer to these questions affect your view as to whether a state should adhere to the ICJ?

4. Was the 1946 U.S. declaration a unilateral act? Could the Court have plausibly held that one unilateral act could be amended by another? Should unilateral acts create international legal obligations? How is that consistent with the positivist theory of international law that rests the law on consent, as discussed in Chapter 1?

5. Should the Treaty of Friendship, Commerce, and Navigation have been held to apply to the allegations here? Nicaragua had alleged that the United States had been behind attacks on Nicaragua's ports and airports. Should those incidents have the effect of bringing this whole case into the Court's jurisdiction?

6. The Court distinguishes between the questions of jurisdiction and the admissibility of Nicaragua's complaint. Do you see any difference between the issues? Is admissibility similar to "justiciability"? Should the Court be hearing a case, given the objections to admissibility raised by the United States — for example, that this was a matter before the U.N. Security Council, that there was an ongoing armed conflict, and that Nicaragua had failed to exhaust the established dispute resolution processes in Central America? Or are these provincial notions derived from U.S. constitutional law?

7. *The Connally reservation.* In paragraph 67 of the Court's opinion, it is noted that the United States did not invoke the "domestic jurisdiction" proviso in its 1946 declaration accepting the Court's compulsory jurisdiction, although the United States reserved the right to raise the matter later. (This proviso is often called the Connally reservation, after then-Senator Thomas Connally, who led the move to put the provision in the U.S. declaration.) If the United States had invoked the proviso, would the Court have had to accept it? See the language of the proviso and review the *Norwegian Loans* opinion. Why do you think the United States did not invoke the provision? How credible would it have been?

Given the result in the Court's 1984 decision, should the United States have promptly claimed "domestic jurisdiction," noting that it had reserved the right to do so at a later time?

8. *The Vandenberg reservation.* Also noted in paragraph 67 is the fact that the United States did invoke another proviso in its 1946 declaration, which said that its acceptance of the Court's compulsory jurisdiction did not extend to "disputes arising under a multilateral treaty, unless (1) all parties to the treaty affected by the decision are also parties to the case before the Court, or (2) the United States of America specially agrees to jurisdiction." (This provision is sometimes known as the Vandenberg reservation, after then-Senator Arthur Vandenberg.)

How do you think that invoking this reservation helped the United States? What multilateral treaties might have been applicable to provide jurisdiction? Because multilateral treaties could not be applicable because neither of the conditions of this reservation were met, what jurisdictional grounds were left for the Court to rely on? (Refer to your answers to Questions 2 and 5 above.) When in a later decision the Court turned to the substantive law regarding the use of force, how do you think that the invocation of the Vandenberg reservation might have limited the Court's sources for finding legal norms? (The substantive issues will be addressed in Chapter 11.)

9. When Nicaragua filed its suit in April 1984, the then-Legal Adviser to the U.S. Secretary of State reportedly predicted that the ICJ would not take jurisdiction of the lawsuit, probably because the Court had traditionally taken a cautious view of its jurisdiction. Do you read the ICJ's decision above to be a conservative approach to taking jurisdiction and deciding on admissibility? If not, why might the Court have been aggressive in asserting its jurisdiction? Could it have been based in part on a shared perception of the Court's majority that, with the Court's diminishing international stature and caseload, it was time to be more assertive? Or on a

perception by the Court's majority that the United States was so committed to the rule of law that it would accept any decision by the Court? Or do judges not think these ways? Should they?

10. If you think that the Court was trying to be more assertive, as you read about the later developments in this case and the U.S. reaction, consider whether the Court's decision bodes well for the Court in the long run. Think how a Justice John Marshall, who wisely guided the U.S. Supreme Court in its early years, might have counseled the ICJ justices.

11. Questions about the Court's jurisdiction and its 1984 decision in the Nicaragua v. U.S.A. case have generated a substantial literature. Besides the materials cited above, see also Michael J. Glennon, Nicaragua v. United States: Constitutionality of U.S. Modification of ICJ Jurisdiction, 79 Am. J. Intl. L. 682 (1985).

c. Judgment on the Merits

In 1986, the ICJ ruled against the United States on the merits in the suit brought by Nicaragua. By substantial majorities that varied slightly with the issue, the Court decided that the United States had violated customary international law and the FCN treaty between the two countries by a number of acts. The illegal acts included laying mines in Nicaraguan territorial waters; attacks on Nicaraguan ports and other facilities; and training, arming, equipping, financing, and supplying the Contra forces. (For a fuller discussion of this decision and the substantive issues, see Chapter 11 on the use of force.)

The general outlines of this decision were anticipated by many commentators after the Court's 1984 decision on jurisdiction and admissibility. Indeed, some observers noted that this expected decision was one reason that the United States had withdrawn from the proceedings and given notice of its intent to terminate its acceptance of the Court's compulsory jurisdiction.

When the Court's 1986 decision on the merits was handed down, the Reagan Administration took no steps to change U.S. activities in Central America. The Court's decision provided for further proceedings to determine the amount of damages that the United States owed Nicaragua. The United States continued to decline to participate in the case, although there were proceedings on the damage issue.

The February 1990 election in Nicaragua of the new government of President Violeta Barrios de Chamarro substantially improved the possibility for a settlement of the case. On September 25, 1991, the ICJ removed the case from its list at the request of Nicaragua after Nicaragua decided to renounce all rights of action based on the case. The United States had apparently encouraged the new Nicaraguan government to take this action.

2. The ICJ in the 1990s and Since

The caseload of the Court did become more active in the 1990s and since. Many of the cases involved boundary disputes of greater or lesser significance. (See the list of ICJ cases in the Documentary Supplement.) Some of the cases on other issues included the following.

In February 1996, a case that Iran had filed against the United States in 1989 was dismissed by the parties. A U.S. warship, the USS Vincennes, had accidentally shot down an Iranian passenger jet over the Persian Gulf in 1988 during a period of high tension between U.S. and Iranian forces during the Iran-Iraq war. All 290 people aboard the plane, including 248 Iranians, perished. Although the U.S. government stated that it still believed that the warship was taking appropriate defensive measures in the circumstances, the United States agreed to pay up to $300,000 to families of each of the Iranian passengers. The United States had already agreed to compensate families of non-Iranian victims.

In July 1996, the Court issued an advisory opinion to the U.N. General Assembly on the legality of the threat or use of nuclear weapons. As summarized by Professor John R. Schmertz, Jr., of Georgetown and Mike Meier, the Court held that:

— Neither customary nor conventional international law specifically authorizes the threat or use of nuclear weapons (unanimous). Neither customary nor conventional international law comprehensively and universally bans the threat or use of nuclear weapons as such (11 to 3).

— A threat or use of force by means of nuclear weapons that is contrary to Article 2, paragraph 4, of the United Nations Charter and that fails to meet all the requirements of Article 51, is unlawful (unanimous).

— A threat or use of nuclear weapons must comply with international law requirements applicable in armed conflicts (unanimous).

Generally, the threat or use of nuclear weapons would violate international law, particularly humanitarian law. For the most part, their destructive effects do not distinguish between civilians and combatants. The Court is unable to conclude whether or not the threat of use of nuclear weapons would be lawful in an extreme circumstance of self-defense in which the survival of a State is at stake (7 to 7, with the ICJ President casting the deciding vote). [Case Concerning the Legality of the Use by a State of Nuclear Weapons in Armed Conflict; Schmertz & Meier, International Court of Justice Gives Opinion on Legality of Threat or Use of Nuclear Weapons, International Law Update, September 1996.]

In February 1998, the ICJ declared that it had jurisdiction to deal with the merits of disputes that Libya had with the United Kingdom and United States concerning the destruction by a bomb of Pan Am flight 103 over Lockerbie, Scotland. Libya contended that the two countries did not have the right to compel it to surrender two Libyan nationals suspected of causing the crash. Libya argued that the Montreal Convention for the Suppression of Unlawful Acts Against the Safety of Civil Aviation allowed it to try the suspects itself. The United States and United Kingdom raised objections to the Court's jurisdiction and the admissibility of the Libyan claims, including their argument that resolutions of the U.N. Security Council had an overriding effect in accordance with Article 103 of the U.N. Charter. The ICJ directed that the case proceed to the merits. Case Concerning Questions of Interpretation and Application of the 1971 Montreal Convention Arising from the Aerial Incident at Lockerbie (Libyan Arab Jamahiriya v. United Kingdom).*

---

* Although this case remains on the ICJ docket as of January 2003, the matter has become nearly moot. In response, at least in part, to the world pressure reflected in the ICJ case, U.N. resolutions, and

In 1998, the ICJ issued a provisional order in a case where Paraguay alleged that local police in Virginia had violated the Vienna Convention on Consular Relations by not informing a foreign suspect in a brutal murder of his right under the Vienna Convention to consult with consular officials from Paraguay. The suspect was convicted of the murder in the Virginia courts and sentenced to death.

The ICJ order provided that "[t]he United States should take all measures at its disposal to ensure that Angel Francisco Breard is not executed pending the final decision in these proceedings." Case Concerning the Vienna Convention on Consular Relations (Paraguay v. U.S.), 1998 I.C.J. No. 99 (April 9). When Breard's lawyers tried to stop the execution, the Clinton Administration explained to the U.S. Supreme Court:

> [T]he "measures at [the government's] disposal" are a matter of domestic United States law, and our federal system imposes limits on the federal government's ability to interfere with the criminal justice systems of the States. The "measures at [the United States'] disposal" under our Constitution may in some cases include only persuasion.

(See the U.S. Supreme Court decision in the *Breard* case in Chapter 3 at page 185.) Secretary of State Albright wrote a letter to Governor Gilmore of Virginia requesting that the execution be postponed. On the night of the execution, he issued a statement that he had given serious consideration to the request of the Secretary of State but that his "first duty is to ensure that those within our borders . . . may conduct their lives free from fear of crime." He also said that it might be more difficult to disregard the ICJ's order later. Breard was executed on schedule.

In a similar case in 1999, the ICJ issued provisional measures ordering the United States to stay the execution of a German national who was tried and sentenced to death without being advised of his right to consular assistance under the Vienna Convention on Consular Relations. Walter and Karl LaGrand were German citizens convicted of murder in Arizona. Karl LaGrand was executed on February 24, 1999. However, on March 2, 1999, Germany filed a case against the United States requesting a stay of Walter's execution.

Like the provisional measure in *Breard,* the ICJ issued a preliminary order calling on the United States "to take all measures at its disposal to ensure that Walter LaGrand is not executed pending the final decision in the proceedings." LaGrand Case (F.R.G. v. U.S.), 2001 I.C.J. No. 104 (June 27). However, unlike *Breard,* the ICJ issued this provisional order before any oral hearings were held. Because Germany presented its request for provisional measures on the same day that Walter LaGrand was to be executed, the ICJ cited the urgency of the situation as a justification for hasty interim measures. Despite the last-minute provisional orders, the Governor of Arizona followed through with the execution of Walter LaGrand.

Nevertheless, the ICJ case continued. The Court's final judgment in 2001 held that the United States breached its obligation under the Vienna Convention by

---

U.N. economic sanctions, President Qaddafi turned over the two accused Libyans to be tried by a Scottish Court, meeting specially in The Hague, Netherlands. The court convicted one Libyan and his conviction was upheld on appeal. Qaddafi's actions led to a suspension of the U.N. sanctions in 1999. The United States opposed the removal of the U.N. sanctions until Libya took further steps regarding terrorism, and the United States has continued its sanctions pursuant to the President's authority under the International Emergency Economic Powers Act.—EDS.

failing to afford the LaGrand brothers their right to consular assistance. In addition, the Court ruled that the United States breached a binding legal obligation when it defied the Court's preliminary measures that ordered a stay of Walter LaGrand's execution pending final resolution of the case.

The outcomes in both *LaGrand* and *Breard* highlight the uncertain effects that ICJ decisions have on domestic, municipal proceedings. See Curtis A. Bradley, *Breard,* Our Dualist Constitution, and the Internationalist Conception, 51 Stan. L. Rev. 529 (1999). Should the U.S. government have done more to ensure compliance with the ICJ orders? See C.M. Vazquez, *Breard* and the Federal Authority to Require Compliance with ICJ Orders of Provisional Measures, 92 Am. J. Intl. L. 683 (1998).

A new chapter on other countries' complaints about U.S. compliance with the Vienna Convention on Consular Relations began in January 2003 when Mexico brought a case against the United States in the ICJ. Mexico alleged violations of Articles 5 and 36 of the Vienna Convention with respect to over 50 Mexican nationals who were awaiting execution in 10 U.S. states (Arizona, Arkansas, California, Florida, Illinois, Nevada, Ohio, Oklahoma, Oregon, and Texas.) Article 5 provides a general list of consular functions and Article 36 gives foreign detainees the right to communicate with and seek assistance from their consulate and states that they are to be advised of this right "without delay" after being arrested. In its suit, Mexico asked in effect that the cases involving the Mexican inmates be dismissed or re-tried, and that the United States provide Mexico with a guarantee that these alleged violations will not be repeated in the future. It also asked that execution of the inmates be stayed while the ICJ considered the case. See Proceedings Instituted by Mexico against the United States of America: Request for the Indication of Provisional Measures (Jan. 2003).

In October 2000, the Democratic Republic of the Congo filed proceedings before the ICJ requesting the cancellation of an international arrest warrant issued by a Belgian official. On April 11, 2000, a Belgian judge issued an arrest warrant against Mr. Abdulaye Yerodia Ndombasi for violations of the Geneva Conventions of 1949, the Additional Protocols thereto, and other crimes against humanity. At the time, Mr. Yerodia was the Minister for Foreign Affairs of the Congo.

The crimes for which Mr. Yerodia was wanted were punishable under a controversial Belgian law enacted on June 16, 1993. The 1993 version of the law provided for punishment of violations of the Geneva Convention of 1949, and the updated 1999 version also provided punishment for "serious violations of international humanitarian law." Under this law, Belgium claimed a broad power to invoke universal jurisdiction worldwide against government officials and other individuals.

In its final submissions to the court, the Congo claimed that "the non-recognition, on the basis of Article 5 of the Belgian Law, of the immunity of a Minister for Foreign Affairs in office" constituted a "violation of the diplomatic immunity of the Minister for Foreign Affairs of a sovereign State." The DRC thus presented the court with a question of the inviolability and immunity from criminal process of sitting foreign ministers.

The ICJ found in favor of the Congo. To determine the level of immunity accorded to ministers for foreign affairs, the Court looked to customary international law. Although the Vienna Convention on Diplomatic Relations and the New York Convention on Special Missions were useful in regard to certain aspects of immunity, neither treaty specifically defined the immunity accorded to ministers of foreign affairs. Nevertheless, the Court held that ministers for foreign affairs enjoy full inviolability and immunity from criminal jurisdiction. Further, contrary to Belgium's assertion, the Court failed to find a customary practice that provided an exception to immunity when a minister for foreign affairs is accused of war crimes or crimes against humanity. As a result, the ICJ held that the issuance and circulation of the international arrest warrant against Mr. Yerodia was a violation of Belgium's obligation toward the Congo to respect the immunity of an incumbent minister for foreign affairs. The ICJ ordered Belgium to cancel the warrant and notify the relevant authorities of the cancellation. See Case Concerning the Arrest Warrant of 11 April 2000 (Congo v. Belg.), 2002 I.C.J. No. 121 (February 14).

3. The Future of the ICJ

What does the future hold for the ICJ? There have been many suggestions. One of the more careful analyses was prepared by a study group established by the British Institute of International and Comparative Law. The four British experts published a 35-page report in 1996 that highlighted some of the problems of the ICJ and contained recommendations.

Study Group, The International Court of Justice: Efficiency of Procedures and Working Methods

45 Intl. & Comp. L.Q. Supplement S1 (1996)

. . . In its examination of the future of the International Court of Justice the Study Group has identified a core issue requiring consideration . . . : that of the efficient management by the Court of its case-load in the light of its resources and time. Consideration of this issue is supplemented by a consideration of the procedure of the Court in relation to both contentious proceedings and requests for advisory opinions. Finally, the Group has referred to some broader issues which would involve more radical reform of the Court's role. Such issues include the extension of standing before the Court, proposals for the extension of the Court's jurisdiction and the question whether advisory opinions might be sought by States. The Study Group has noted that these latter issues have attracted a great deal of attention in academic writing, but felt that it would be beyond its present purposes to undertake a full-scale review of all of the possibilities of reform. Instead the Group has reviewed the implications of some of these proposals for reform in the light of its findings on the core issue.

I. THE CORE ISSUE

5 Briefly put, the core issue is whether the Court as it functions at present will be able to cope with the increasing pressure of work which States are now bringing to it. The list, or "case-load," currently stands at a dozen cases. The tempo of the Court's procedures is such that it tends to complete two, or at the most three, cases each year and clearly, once cases begin to be brought before the Court at a faster

rate than two or three a year, a backlog will inevitably build up (as is already happening).... [T]here is nothing inherently unrealistic in expecting a faster work-rate from the ICJ. Moreover, if account is taken of the fact that there are now three times the number of States forming the international community, there is every reason to anticipate that the ICJ will be expected to handle more cases than its predecessor.

6   It is known that some States involved in cases are becoming restive at the delays in hearing their cases. To give [a] recent [example,] in Qatar v. Bahrain where the application was filed in July 1991 and the first phase was, by agreement between the parties, limited to jurisdiction/admissibility, and in which a second round of pleadings was requested by the Court itself and not by either of the parties, an initial judgment was given in July 1994; following that judgment, the final judgment on jurisdiction/admissibility was not given until February 1995, some three and a half years after the filing of the application. . . .

7   At the same time it must also be recognised that the Court's schedule requires some flexibility, to enable provisional measures applications (and other urgent applications), of which there has been an increasing number in recent years, to be dealt with. It should also be noted that such applications have the inevitable result of disrupting the Court's normal timetable. There are also cases in which the delays in fact suit the parties, either because this affords time to reach a political settlement or because the parties need time to prepare their pleadings.

II.   FACTORS RELEVANT TO THE DURATION OF TIME REQUIRED BY THE COURT TO DISPOSE OF CASES

A. The Quality of the Judgments

8   The argument that the Court must maintain the quality of its judgments, and therefore cannot risk "hurried" deliberations, must surely be accepted. . . .

9   . . . It is not clear that any marked change in quality has occurred over the years. . . .

B.   The Length of Written Pleadings . . .

12   It is fair to note that municipal courts are only rarely faced with the burden of translation which is the norm for the Court. It is also fair to note that it is bound to take longer to reach decisions in a court with 15 members, drawn from different legal traditions, than it is in a much smaller municipal court whose members share the same legal tradition. . . .

D.   The Length and Timetabling of Oral Arguments

18   Before dealing with the length of oral arguments, two preliminary points need to be made. The first is that the Court appears to engage in little or no forward planning of the oral hearings due to come before it, preferring to deal with one case at a time, as and when that case is ready for oral hearing. This practice would seem

to have little to commend it, while carrying with it the significant disadvantage that when the Court does come to fix the dates for oral hearings those dates may only with great difficulty, if at all, be fitted into the busy work schedules of those who need to be present for the hearings. . . .

19   The second preliminary point to be made is that, when the Court comes to fix the date of oral hearings, a significant delay between the close of written pleadings and the oral hearings may result from the Court's internal arrangements for the translation of the written pleadings. The Registry has only limited translation facilities, and it will depend on the total translation burden on the Registry at any given time as to how soon it can start translations of the written pleadings into French or English [the two working languages of the Court]. . . . Ideally cases should be scheduled for hearing as soon as they are ready to be heard, and there should in any event be a delay of, in principle, no more than six months between close of pleadings and the commencement of oral argument. . . .

20   Complaints are frequently made (and usually by the judges in private conversations) about the length of the oral arguments. Given the tendency to make the written pleadings lengthy, it might be thought that oral arguments — like those before the US Supreme Court — could be brief. . . .

23   In any event, the fact of the matter is that the public sittings of the Court devoted to listening to oral arguments take up quite a small fraction of the working year. For example, in 1991 the full Court held 21 sittings (i.e. 21 half-days) and a chamber of the Court 50. In 1992 the figures were five sittings for the full Court, and none for the chambers. Thus, the fact is that oral arguments take up only a small fraction of the Court's working time, so that whatever the reasons for the long delays, they cannot be the length of oral arguments.

E.   The Frequency and Length of Sittings . . .

25   . . . [A]s a rough rule of thumb, it looks as though one-third of the year is spent with the judges functioning as a collegiate court, and two-thirds spent by the judges otherwise. . . .

27   There is also a wider issue here, which has to be addressed. It is that over the years it has become quite usual for judges of the Court to undertake commitments outside The Hague, either of a brief and occasional kind, such as the delivery of lectures, or of a more time-consuming kind, such as participation in an arbitral tribunal. Such activities can be of undoubted value. . . . Times, however, have changed, and the Court is now much busier than it was; and it must be the case that the requirements of the Court have to be accorded priority. There is some evidence that, on a few occasions in recent years, the Court fixed the timetable for cases it was considering by reference to the personal convenience of judges rather than the wishes of the States parties. . . . The priorities ought to be, first, the needs of the case; second, the convenience of the States involved; and, last, personal commitments of members of the Court.

28   There are two further features of the Court's work that strike any observer familiar with the work-load of a busy national court. The first is the shortness of the Court's working day. The second is that the Court deals with only one case, which has reached an advanced stage (i.e. after pleadings have closed), at a time.

29   In relation to the first the Court sits for only half the day, usually in the mornings. Although the Court will occasionally sit both in the mornings and in the afternoons, this occurs rarely, and even then only because the Court itself insists that oral arguments must conclude on a certain day. Thus, a "day in Court" means 2 hours 40 minutes: that is, 10 a.m. to 1 p.m., with a 20-minute break for coffee.

30   The shortness of the Court's working day could be remedied in one of three ways. First, the Court could sit in plenary for oral hearings both mornings and afternoons; second, the afternoons could be devoted to private deliberations on a case other than that in which oral arguments had been heard in the morning; and, third, a chamber could use the afternoons to hear oral arguments in another case. . . .

F.   The Procedure for Elaborating a Judgment . . .

39   One suggestion might be that, on the basis of the written pleadings, the judges should each prepare, prior to their first meeting, a short note on the issues raised by the parties — i.e. before oral arguments began: this note would form the basis for a note to be agreed by the Court of the issues (or at least the principal issues) raised by the parties. This could have many advantages. The judges would know the case better, the parties could rely on this and shorten their oral arguments, and a long delay later after the close of oral argument for the preparation of a note . . . could be shortened. Collective discussion of these issues by the Court in advance of the oral arguments would also allow the Court to give advance notice to the parties of the points on which the Court would welcome clarification in oral argument. . . .

63   . . . Given that the "routine" parts of the judgment — the recitals of fact, the summaries of the arguments of the parties, etc. — are drafted by the Registry staff, the Court itself (even though it closely scrutinises these "routine parts") provides its judgment slowly. For example, in Qatar v. Bahrain it took three and a half months (arguments closed on 11 March 1994, judgment was given on 1 July) to provide a judgment of 21 pages, of which only seven and a half pages are reasoning. In *Libya/Chad* it took six and a half months (arguments closed on 14 July 1993, judgment was given on 3 February 1994) to give a judgment of 42 pages, of which only 17 pages are reasoning. As a current member of the Court has clearly recognised, for the Court to handle more cases each year, "reform of the deliberation procedure will become inevitable."

64   The judgments of the ICJ are also markedly longer than those of the PCIJ [Permanent Court of International Justice]. The average judgment of the PCIJ was 38.2 pages long, and that of the ICJ 60.9 pages long. . . . The same appears true of advisory opinions: 26.3 pages for the PCIJ, compared with 34.4 pages for the ICJ. . . .

H.   The Election of Judges

67   The system of election is a carefully balanced one and, coupled with the "conventions" that have arisen regarding the distribution of seats, seems to work well. Moreover, it does not affect the core issue of the time taken by the Court to deliver judgment save, perhaps, in one respect: this is the absence of any age limit. The experience that comes with age is an advantage that has to be set against the loss of energy and powers of concentration that may accompany old age. . . .

68 An age limit of 75 might seem wise. Obviously, people vary and some judges may remain vigorous and fully active beyond this age. However, a rule should cater for the average rather than the exceptional judge, and with this in mind 75 seems right. But even without amending the Statute as such, a less radical change might be achieved if the General Assembly were to indicate a general reluctance to elect judges who, at the time of election, would be older than, say, 70. The normal nine-year term would bring them to no more than 79 on retirement. . . .

I.   The Constitution of Chambers

70 The use of chambers is now well established: it has attracted favourable judicial comment, and the Court itself in 1994 established a chamber specifically to deal with environmental cases.

71 The extent to which the use of chambers assists in expediting the Court's work is very doubtful and will remain so as long as the Court insists on dealing with only one case at a time: time allocated to a chamber simply means that judges not on the chamber and not residing in The Hague can return home. It must also be remarked that Article 92 of the Rules of Court stipulates that in proceedings before chambers the written proceedings "shall consist of a single pleading by each side." Use of chambers would help the Court to deal with cases more speedily if this rule were applied: but in practice it is not.

72 Obviously, if the idea mooted above were adopted — i.e. the full Court dealing with one case in the morning, and a chamber dealing with a different case in the afternoon — there would be a beneficial impact on the work-rate. So, too, if two chambers (ideally of wholly different composition: but in practice this may be unlikely) worked on two different cases at the same time, with each chamber using half the day for oral arguments. . . .

III.   Aspects of the Jurisdiction of the Court with Implications for the Court's Resources . . .

75 . . . [T]he Group's feeling is that the basic barrier to increased acceptance of the Court's jurisdiction lies in State attitudes. No amount of legal inventiveness will change deep-rooted, political opposition to binding third-party settlement, or to the use of a standing court as opposed to carefully selected arbitrators.

76 The signs are that gradually, and perhaps more from necessity than for any other reason, States are making greater use of the Court. If they do so piecemeal, via special agreements or under the dispute-settlement provisions of treaties, rather than via acceptance of the Court's jurisdiction under the optional clause, in the end it matters little. The important point is that more and more States are using the Court, and in the Study Group's view this trend will be encouraged more by the merits — in terms of fairness, soundness and expedition — of the Court's procedures and judgments than by more ingenious schemes for widening the acceptance of the Court's jurisdiction. . . .

IV. STANDING BEFORE THE COURT (ARTICLE 34)

80   The principle reflected in Article 34 of the Court's Statute — that only States may appear before the Court in contentious cases — is long established and it has not been a main focus of criticism. Yet, since neither international personality nor the capacity to bring claims is restricted to States, as the Court itself affirmed in the *Reparations* case, the logic of excluding the United Nations and specialised agencies from using the Court as parties is not self-evident. These organisations are compelled to use arbitration in their disputes with States, or else use the device of the "binding" advisory opinion. From the perspective of the rule of law, this device is evidently inadequate. It is a significant gap in institutional arrangements that public international organisations cannot be held legally accountable to States in the principal judicial organ of the international community, nor can States be held legally accountable to such organisations. . . .

81   On the other hand, there seems to be little demand for direct standing from the organisations themselves, and there is the difficulty that such a change would require an amendment of Article 34 of the Statute. If disputes between States and international organisations were to go to the ICJ, they would, of course, add to the pressure on the Court's list, and so make it all the more important that the "core" problem identified above be effectively addressed. In addition, a number of specific issues would have to be faced. . . .

84   Although, in the past, academic criticism of the "only States" provision in Article 34 has sometimes ventured to suggest that individuals should be given *locus standi*, there is no strong support for this idea in current thinking. Indeed, if the contemporary concern is over how the Court can cope with inter-State disputes, it would be counterproductive to compound the problem by opening up the Court to individuals — and there are in any case other fora in which human rights cases by individuals can be pursued.

V. THE ADVISORY JURISDICTION

85   Advisory opinions are part of the overall problem of pressure on the Court's time and resources; but because of key differences between the procedure for advisory opinions and for contentious litigation, some separate issues arise. Usually only an initial round of "pleadings" in the form of written observations on the request is offered to interested States, and then a further round to make comments on the observations entered by other States. In the 21 opinions that the Court has handed down since 1948, the average time from request to the rendering of its opinion is 254 days. This period seems to have been lengthening in comparison with earlier periods in the Court's work, though the increasing number of UN members who may wish to submit observations, and the disproportionate effect of the *Yakimetz* case,[43] undoubtedly are an important part of the reason. . . .

87   It is important that advisory opinions continue to be handled briskly, in terms of the time limits allowed for written statements, the gap before the opening

---

43. Which took 990 days from request until opinion; see L.C.J. Rep. 1987, 18.

of oral proceedings and the length of time between the closure of oral proceedings and the giving of the opinion. Generally speaking, and even with an increasing number of States wanting to participate, it should be possible to answer a request for an advisory opinion within six to eight months. . . .

This report led to a conference in 1996 where some ICJ judges and scholars debated the report's analysis and recommendations. See D. Bowett et al., The International Court of Justice: Process, Practice and Procedure (1997).

Another important concern about the future role of the ICJ is the uncertainty and inconsistency that may result from the recent proliferation of international courts and other tribunals. In addition to the ICJ, the late twentieth century produced various other international tribunals, including the European Court of Justice, the European Court of Human Rights, the dispute settlement forums of the WTO, and the Inter-American Court of Human Rights. While the benefits of this increase in international forums probably outweigh the drawbacks of divergent interpretations of international law, the following excerpts highlight the debate over the impact that the international expansion might have on the ICJ.

Jonathan I. Charney, The Impact on the International Legal System of the Growth of International Courts and Tribunals

31 N.Y.U. J. Intl. L. & Pol. 697 (1999)

When one begins to examine the recent proliferation of international courts and other tribunals, this development must be put into its proper historical context. Obviously, the existence of a standing international court of general jurisdiction is a creation of the twentieth century. Prior to the establishment of the Permanent Court of International Justice (PCIJ) after World War I, many ad hoc tribunals had been used. Even after the PCIJ was established, a variety of international tribunals continued to provide forums for third-party settlement of international disputes. After the International Court of Justice (ICJ) was established at the conclusion of World War II, ad hoc tribunals also continued to be used, albeit with less frequency. Consequently, the International Court never has stood alone as the sole tribunal to settle disputes in accordance with international law. It always has coexisted with other third-party dispute settlement forums. Recent developments are changing the international environment as a result of the establishment of more permanent tribunals and, perhaps, the use of fewer ad hoc tribunals. In very recent years, the rate of change from ad hoc to permanent tribunals appears to be increasing dramatically.

Thus, states involved in international disputes have a greater range of third-party dispute settlement vehicles than heretofore. Many legitimate reasons help explain why states and other members of the international community could prefer to have available a variety of international tribunals to resolve their disputes. They include, but are not limited to, the desire for secrecy, control over the membership of the forum, panels with special expertise or perceived regional sensitivities, preclusion of third state intervention, and forums that can resolve disputes in which nonstate entities may appear as parties.

If states prefer a system with multiple options for third-party settlement of international disputes, the question arises as to whether a hierarchy may be established among them. It is clear to me that the international community will not and cannot establish such a hierarchy of international tribunals that would place the ICJ or any other tribunal at the apex of international law serving as the "Supreme Court of International Law." While the reasons may be many, two primary reasons are: (1) the fact that a universal, or near universal, agreement of states to anoint any particular forum with this status seems practically and politically impossible, and (2) such a Supreme Court would undermine the community's desire for diverse forums since many of the perceived advantages of such forums would become impossible to attain within such a hierarchical structure. Review by a court of general jurisdiction would compromise the very features that make the alternative forums attractive in the first place, such as the special qualities of the panel members. Thus, a significant number of independent international tribunals will remain a part of the international legal system for the foreseeable future.

Consequently, the question arises as to whether the proliferation of international tribunals threatens the coherence of the international legal system. Not only may a cacophony of views on the norms of international law undermine the perception that an international legal system exists, but if like cases are not treated alike, the very essence of a normative system of law will be lost. Should this develop, the legitimacy of international law as a whole will be placed at risk. . . .

However, an increase in the number of international law tribunals, absent an effective hierarchical system that would produce definitive answers to differences over norms of international law, means that complete uniformity of decisions is impossible. On the other hand, it is clear that ongoing international tribunals tend to follow the reasoning of their prior decisions. Furthermore, the views of the ICJ, when on point, are given considerable weight, and those of other international tribunals often are considered. Thus, the variety of international tribunals functioning today do not appear to pose a threat to the coherence of an international legal system. . . .

One strength of the multiplicity of international tribunals is that it permits a degree of experimentation and exploration, which can lead to improvements in international law. The lack of a strictly hierarchical system provides international tribunals with the opportunity to contribute collectively ideas that might be incorporated into general international law. It also facilitates the evaluation of those ideas by the international community as a whole. Ultimately, one would expect that the best ideas will be adopted widely, contributing to the body of international law. In some cases, however, unique solutions for special circumstances may be the better alternative. . . .

It is also difficult to argue that these forums have taken cases away from the ICJ, thereby denying the Court its rightful role in the adjudication of international law. Nor does it appear likely that a decline of the ICJ is on the horizon, even with the increased number of forums deciding international legal issues. Instead, in recent years, the ICJ has had the heaviest caseload in its history. Furthermore, during this period, the ICJ has been called upon to decide some of the hottest cases from the perspective of international politics that it ever has faced.

Nonetheless, it is true that a comparison of the number of cases handled by the ICJ and those handled by the highest courts of states, or even several other standing international dispute settlement tribunals shows that the ICJ's caseload is relatively low. Based on this fact, one can argue that the ICJ remains underutilized. Nevertheless, judges on the Court consider the number close to the limits of the Court's capacity. It is possible, however, for the Court to streamline its procedures in order to handle more cases. . . .

. . . It demonstrated recently, for example, that it could move quickly to issue an indication of provisional measures of protection in the Vienna Convention on Consular Relations Case. This example also demonstrates the delicacy of the ICJ's authority. The Court did move rapidly to indicate provisional measures of protection instructing the United States to take all measures at its disposal to prevent the execution of Mr. Breard by the State of Virginia. Nevertheless, the U.S. Executive Branch did not take as forceful a position as it might have taken to obtain a delay of the execution, the United States Supreme Court declined to order a stay of the execution, and the Governor of Virginia refused to delay the execution. An international culture that gives automatic and full authority to the ICJ's utterances does not exist. This suggests that substantial changes to expedite ICJ procedures in order to increase the Court's capacity may not be wise.

Indeed, the ICJ has taken steps to improve its procedures, but the international community has also implicitly resisted strengthening the Court. Thus, the Court has taken steps to increase the efficiency of its internal procedures, urged the litigating states to submit clearer, more succinct written pleadings, and made its orders and judgments quickly and easily accessible to all through its new web site. On the other hand, the U.N. has placed significant budgetary constraints on the Court, thereby hampering its ability to manage its increased caseload. The gross disparity in the funds appropriated to the ICJ ($11 million) as compared to those appropriated for the International Criminal Tribunal for the former Yugoslavia ($70 million) appears to reflect a lack of interest on the part of the international community to strengthen the ICJ to a point where it might serve as the Supreme International Court. Rather, it reflects a continuing international support for a variety of international tribunals. The overwhelming support given to the establishment of the International Criminal Court (ICC) at the 1998 Rome Conference provides further confirmation of this conclusion.

The establishment and use of various third-party forums to decide questions of international law means that more international issues are being resolved pursuant to international law. This will add to the body of decisions based on international law that are authoritative and can be relied upon by the international community. Unfortunately, the ICJ is unequipped and unable to address all of these numerous and sometimes highly specialized issues. As a whole, the other forums complement the work of the ICJ and strengthen the system of international law, notwithstanding the risk of some loss of uniformity.

Notes and Questions

1. What do you think should be the role of the ICJ in the future? Should it try to reform its procedures to hear more cases? How might it do so?

2. Should the ICJ try to hear a range of international law issues, or should it focus on certain areas, like boundary disputes? Should the advisory jurisdiction of the

ICJ be expanded and international organizations be encouraged to seek the Court's opinions? Should individuals be allowed to sue foreign states or even their own state? Should a process like the referral proceeding in the European Union (EU), where a national court refers EU law issues to the European Court of Justice (discussed in the next section), be developed so that national courts can refer international law issues to the ICJ for decision? Besides the excerpts above, see Louis B. Sohn, Important Improvements in the Functioning of the Principal Organs of the United Nations That Can Be Made Without Charter Revision, 91 Am. J. Intl. L. 652 (1997).

3. Should there be a formal hierarchy among the existing international tribunals? If so, should the ICJ act as an international supreme court? Could the ICJ fulfill such a role? Is a formal structure necessary?

4. What should the United States do? Should it accept compulsory jurisdiction again along the lines of its 1946 declaration? Or should it accept a more limited compulsory jurisdiction? Or should the United States accept ICJ jurisdiction only by special agreement in a specific dispute or for disputes under specific bilateral or multilateral treaties (such as a bilateral boundary agreement)?

5. Should the enforceability of ICJ judgments be improved? Or is it enough to depend on the voluntary acquiescence of the losing party, international pressures, or the yet-to-be-used enforcement by the U.N. Security Council under Article 94(2) of the Charter? See generally Mary Ellen O'Connell, The Prospects for Enforcing Monetary Judgments of the International Court of Justice, 30 Va. J. Intl. L. 891 (1990).

6. The ICJ maintains an up-to-date Web site at <http://www.icj-cij.org>.

You might want to keep your answers to the questions above a little tentative until you are more familiar with some of the other methods of formal dispute resolution in the international arena — notably, regional and specialized courts, arbitration, and domestic courts, which we discuss below.

C. REGIONAL AND SPECIALIZED COURTS

Since World War II, there has been an increasing growth of regional and specialized courts, notably in Europe. The similar societies there, combined with the searing experience of two world wars, has helped foster major efforts to integrate the economies and societies. One important result of these efforts was the creation of the Court of Justice for the European Communities. As discussed below, this court has broad powers, including the authority to rule invalid the national legislation of European Union Member States.

Europe also is the home of the European Court of Human Rights, which has a major role in the interpretation and application of the European Convention for the Protection of Human Rights and Fundamental Freedoms. Almost all European countries have agreed to abide by the decisions of this court. (See discussion in Chapter 8 on human rights.)

Outside Western Europe, regional and specialized courts are still rare and in their early stages. There is an Inter-American Court of Human Rights, but its jurisdiction is very limited and essentially advisory. (See also Chapter 8.)

One notable development is the new International Tribunal for the Law of the Sea, which was established in 1996 under the Law of the Sea Convention. This tribunal is available for disputes under the detailed provisions of the Convention governing the use of the seas, which cover approximately three-quarters of the world's surface. The Tribunal, however, is only one of four formal methods that states can choose to resolve disputes under the Convention. The other three approaches are international arbitration, special technical arbitral tribunals, and the ICJ. Moreover, if the states concerned have selected different methods of dispute resolution, the dispute may be submitted "only to arbitration." (See Chapter 9.)

Another major development is the International Criminal Court (ICC), which was established to try suspected war criminals and perpetrators of genocide or crimes against humanity. The ICC was a key part of the Rome Statute, a treaty that emerged in 1998 from a conference attended by representatives from 127 countries. The treaty obtained the necessary ratifications into force in July 2002, though the United States made clear its opposition to the treaty. The ICC was then established in 2003. The Court is designed to be the permanent successor to the temporary war crimes tribunals set up after World War II and the special tribunals created to handle the more recent situations in the former Yugoslavia and in Rwanda. (See Chapter 11 for a discussion of individual responsibility, war crimes tribunals, and the new International Criminal Court.)

1. The Court of Justice of the European Communities

The Court of Justice of the European Communities (ECJ) is the sole judicial organ of the European Union (EU). The EU was created by the Treaty on European Union, which provided new momentum for European integration. The Treaty was signed in the Netherlands at Maastricht in December 1991 and entered into force on November 1, 1993. European Union is the umbrella term referring to a three-"pillar" construction encompassing the existing European Community and two new pillars — Common Foreign and Security Policy (including defense) and Justice and Home Affairs (most notably cooperation on crime, terrorism, and immigration issues). The Treaty of Amsterdam, signed in June 1997 and entered into force on January 1, 1999, amended the previous treaties to prepare the European Union for the single currency and the enlargement of the Union membership. The Nice Treaty, signed in February 2001 and entered into force in early 2003, resolved several technical issues standing in the way of expansion.

The 15 members of the EU include Austria, Belgium, Denmark, Finland, France, Germany, Greece, Ireland, Italy, Luxembourg, the Netherlands, Portugal, Spain, Sweden, and the United Kingdom. Ten more states are scheduled to join the Union in May 2004, including many of the formerly Communist countries of Eastern Europe and the Mediterranean islands of Malta and Cyprus.

The EU is involved in determining a vast range of activities by its Member States or their citizens, including not only tariffs, exchange controls, and investment, but also foreign policy issues. The present role of the EU is broad, and it is growing. (For more information on the EU, see Chapter 5. Excerpts of the consolidated versions of the Treaty on European Union and of the Treaty Establishing the European Community are contained in the Documentary Supplement.)

The European Court of Justice is considered a central force in this process of European integration and is not answerable to any other entity for its decisions. The following excerpt by Professor Hartley provides a useful overview of the purposes, structure, and procedure of the court. We have added some bracketed inserts to this excerpt to reflect changes introduced by the Treaty of Nice, which came into effect in early 2003.

T.C. Hartley, The Foundations of European Community Law
52-76 (4th ed. 1998)

[T]he European Court['s] . . . main functions are to ensure that the law is enforced, irrespective of political considerations (especially against Member States); to act as referee between the Member States and the Community as well as between the Community institutions *inter se;* and to ensure the uniform interpretation and application of Community law throughout the Community. . . .

THE EUROPEAN COURT

Judges

There are fifteen judges on the Court, appointed by the common accord of the Member States. It is stated in the Treaties that judges must be "persons whose independence is beyond doubt and who possess the qualifications required for appointment to the highest judicial offices in their respective countries or who are jurisconsults of recognized competence". . . . [T]here is one judge from each Member State. This political convention is the consequence of the method of appointment: since each government must agree to every appointment, a country whose nominee was rejected could block all other candidates.

Judges are appointed for staggered terms of six years, so that every three years either seven or eight of the posts fall vacant. They are eligible for re-appointment and this frequently occurs; there is no retirement age. The Member States cannot remove a judge during his term of office, but he may be dismissed if, in the unanimous opinion of the other judges and advocates general, "he no longer fulfils the requisite conditions or meets the obligations arising from his office." So far this procedure has never been put into operation. [The Nice Treaty changes this system slightly, in anticipation of the accession of new Member States in the next decade, by simply declaring that there will be one judge per Member State (before Nice, the number was fixed at 15, and had been increased by treaty amendment with each accession). It also permits the Council to adjust the procedures for replacing judges and Advocates-General as appropriate.]

The President of the Court is elected by his brother judges for a renewable term of three years. The election is by secret ballot. The President's function is to direct the judicial and administrative business of the Court and to preside at sessions of the full Court. The Court is divided into Chambers and the President of each Chamber is appointed by the Court for a one-year term. . . .

The quorum for a full Court (plenary session) is nine. As the Court reaches decisions by a majority, and the President has no casting vote, there must always be an uneven number of judges deciding a case. If one judge has to withdraw — for example, through illness — the most junior remaining judge will abstain from taking part in the deliberations. . . .

A Chamber consists of either three or five judges. The Court may assign to a Chamber any appeal against a decision of the Court of First Instance, any reference for a preliminary ruling or any other case except one brought by a Member State or Community institution, "in so far as the difficulty or the importance of the case or particular circumstances are not such as to require that the Court decide it in plenary session." Actions brought by a Member State or Community institution are always heard by the full Court; any other action will be heard by it if a request is made to this effect by a Member State or Community institution which is a party to, or an intervener in, the proceedings or which has submitted written observations on a reference for a preliminary ruling. A Chamber may at any stage refer a case back to the full Court. . . .

It might be thought that the comparatively short terms of office, as well as the appointment procedure, would lessen the independence of the judges. . . . [On] the contrary, the Court is generally regarded as one of the most "European-minded" institutions in the Community.

The most important protection the judges have against national pressure is the fact that there is always just one "judgment of the Court" without any separate concurring or dissenting judgments. Since, moreover, the judges swear to uphold the secrecy of their deliberations, it is never known how individual judges voted. Therefore it is impossible to accuse a judge of being insufficiently sensitive to national interests or of having "let his government down"; no one outside the Court can ever know whether he vigorously defended the position adopted by his own country or was in the forefront of those advocating a "Community solution."

The background of the judges is varied: some previously held political or administrative offices; some were in private practice or were members of the national judiciary; others had academic appointments.

Advocates General

In addition to the judges, there are also eight advocates general. [The Nice Treaty allows for the Council to increase this number at the request of the Court of Justice.] . . . They have the same status as judges: the same provisions regarding appointment, qualifications, tenure, and removal apply to them as to judges; they receive the same salary, and they rank equally in precedence with the judges according to seniority in office. One advocate general is appointed First Advocate General. When administrative matters concerning the functioning of the Court are being discussed, the advocates general sit with the judges; but they play no part in the Court's deliberations regarding cases.

Their function has no parallel in the English legal system. . . . In the words of the Treaty, "It shall be the duty of the Advocate-General, acting with complete impartiality and independence, to make, in open court, reasoned submissions on cases brought before the Court of Justice, in order to assist the Court . . . ." When each new case comes to the Court, it is assigned by the First Advocate General to one of the advocates general. The advocate general to whom the case is assigned, together with his legal secretary . . . , will study the issues involved and undertake any legal research they think necessary. After the parties have concluded their submissions to the Court, the advocate general will give his opinion. This opinion is not binding on the Court, but will be considered with very great care by the judges when they make their decision. It is printed, together with the judgment, in the law reports.

Impartiality and independence are important characteristics of the advocate general's office. He represents neither the Community nor any Member State: he speaks only for the public interest. He works quite separately and independently from the judges; one could say that he gives a "second opinion" which is in fact delivered first. This opinion shows the judges what a trained legal mind, equal in quality to their own, has concluded on the matter before them. It could be regarded as a point of reference, or starting point, from which they can begin their deliberations. In many cases they follow the advocate general fully; in others they deviate from his opinion either wholly or in part. . . .

One feature of the European Court which has sometimes given rise to comment is that there is no appeal from its judgments. In most cases it may be regarded as a court of first and last resort. . . . In these circumstances, the role of the advocate general is especially important. His opinion could in fact be regarded as a judgment of first instance which is subject to instant and invariable appeal. It is, however, an appeal of a special nature, since the parties have no opportunity to comment on the opinion before the Court begins its deliberations. . . .

THE COURT OF FIRST INSTANCE

The Court of First Instance was established in 1989, following amendments to the Treaties contained in the Single European Act. The idea was to lessen the work-load of the European Court by relieving it of some of the cases with no political or constitutional importance, especially those involving complex facts. The European Court could then concentrate on the task of deciding the more important cases and maintaining the unity of Community law. A right of appeal to the European Court on points of law would ensure that the new court stayed in line.

It was hoped that the establishment of the Court of First Instance would reduce the backlog of cases pending before the European Court. The Court of First Instance has indeed relieved the European Court of a significant number of cases, but the unremitting build-up of new cases has meant that delays in getting cases heard (and decided) by the European Court have not been significantly shortened. [The Court of First Instance currently has fifteen judges, appointed for a renewable term of six years, although the Nice Treaty permits the Council to change this number as necessary, requiring only that the number be "at least one per Member State."]

JURISDICTION

This section is concerned with the jurisdiction of the European Court and the Court of First Instance. . . . [B]oth will be referred to as "the European Court."

The Treaties give the European Court only limited jurisdiction. There are a number of specific heads of jurisdiction and a case must be brought within one of them if the Court is to hear it. . . .

There are several criteria according to which the Court's jurisdiction may be classified. The most basic distinction is between judgments and advisory opinions or rulings. The latter are very much rarer than the former, but they occur in a number of situations, for example where the Council, the Commission, or a Member State requests an opinion on whether an international agreement which the Community intends to conclude with a non-member State is compatible with the EC Treaty. Though advisory, these opinions have legal consequences: if, in the above example, the opinion is adverse, the agreement may enter into force only if the EC Treaty is amended to accommodate it.

As far as judgments are concerned, the most fundamental distinction is between actions begun in the European Court (direct actions) and actions begun in a national court from which a reference for a preliminary ruling is made to the European Court. This distinction is important because, if an action is begun in the European Court, it will end in the European Court: the Court's judgment will constitute a final determination of the dispute between the parties and will grant any remedies that may be appropriate; it is not subject to appeal.

If, on the other hand, the action is begun in a national court, it will end in a national court: the European Court's ruling will be transmitted to the national court and the latter will then decide the case. Here the European Court's ruling, though binding and not subject to appeal, is merely a determination of an abstract point of law: the European Court does not decide the case as such. The national court decides any relevant questions of fact and then applies the law — including relevant provisions of Community law as interpreted by the European Court — to the facts; it also exercises any discretion it may have as to the remedy to be given.

In spite of the limited role played by the European Court, preliminary rulings are of great importance because they concern the relationship between Community law and national law. It is only to the extent that it penetrates the national legal systems and confers rights and imposes obligations directly on private citizens that Community law can be really effective. It is through its power to give preliminary rulings that the European Court has established the doctrine of direct effect and the doctrine of the supremacy of Community law over national law.

The European Court will give a preliminary ruling only when requested to do so by a national court which considers that a question of Community law is relevant to its decision: any court or tribunal *may* make such a request; a court or tribunal from which there is no appeal *must* do so. The issues which may be referred to the European Court are of three kinds: the interpretation of a provision of Community law, the effect of such a provision in the national legal system (which, in theory, is also a question of interpretation), and, in the case of a measure passed by the Community itself, the validity of such a provision.

Direct actions may be divided into two categories: those over which the Court has jurisdiction by virtue of an agreement between the parties and those where the Court's jurisdiction is conferred by direct operation of the law. The former are not very important in practice; the main example is actions arising out of a contract concluded by the Community which contains a clause giving jurisdiction to the European Court.

Direct actions where the Court's jurisdiction does not depend on consent may be classified according to whether the defendant is the Community or a Member State. A number of different kinds of action may be brought against the Community. The two most important are actions for judicial review and actions for damages for non-contractual liability (tort). Actions for judicial review may be brought either to annul a Community measure or to oblige a Community institution to pass a measure which it had previously refused to pass. Such proceedings are brought against the relevant Community institution; they may be brought by a Member State, another Community institution, or — in certain special cases — by a private individual.

Actions for damages for non-contractual liability may be brought against the Community by either a Member State or a private individual. The applicant must prove that he has suffered loss as a result of Community action.

Other proceedings in which a Community institution is the defendant include appeals against penalties imposed under Community regulations (if the regulation in question so provides), and employment disputes between the Community and its staff.

Actions against a Member State are called enforcement actions. . . . [T]hese may be brought against a Member State alleged to have violated Community law. The applicant may be either the Commission or another Member State; in practice it is almost always the Commission. There is a preliminary procedure in which an opinion is given by the Commission after the Member State has explained its position: if the Member State refuses to abide by this opinion, the Commission (or the other Member State) brings the action before the Court. . . .

[With respect to the second and third pillars of the European Union, the Court of Justice's jurisdiction is even more restricted than it is over the Community. The 1991 Maastricht Treaty gave the Court no jurisdiction at all over these areas of Union law, although the Court has attempted to construe this restriction narrowly, for example by holding that it was entitled to decide whether certain EU acts were incorrectly based on pillar two or three, and if so, to pass on their validity.

[In response to the absence of real judicial oversight in these non-Community areas, the 1997 Treaty of Amsterdam granted the Court some very limited powers of review over pillar three (police and judicial cooperation in criminal matters), in the area of "closer cooperation" between Member States, and in immigration policies (which were brought under pillar one by the new treaty). The 2001 Treaty of Nice further extended the Court's jurisdiction to cover the process of sanctioning a Member State where there is a serious breach of fundamental rights by that State. Outside these exceptions, the Court's jurisdiction is still largely limited to pillar one, that is, to Community law.

[As for the Court of First Instance (CFI), its jurisdiction was expanded by the Treaty of Nice. The CFI has been given original jurisdiction over virtually all cases except those specifically reserved to the Court of Justice or assigned to newly created "judicial panels," which will be attached to and subordinate to the CFI. The primary cases specifically reserved to the CFI are enforcement actions by the Commission against a Member State. The ECJ has jurisdiction over all appeals on points of law from the CFI.]

PRECEDENT

Does the doctrine of precedent apply in the European Court? The answer is that there is no legal doctrine of stare decisis, but the Court does follow its previous decisions in almost all cases. The case law of the European Court is just as important for the development of Community law as that of English courts is for modern English law. . . . However, though lawyers and advocates general have always cited copious precedents, the Court itself used to refer to its previous decisions only in rare instances. One almost got the impression that it was trying to disguise the extent to which it followed precedent: sometimes it would reproduce sentences, or even whole paragraphs, from previous judgments, without quotation marks or any acknowledgment of source. Today the position has changed, though the Court still cites precedents only when they support its reasoning: it does not normally cite them in order to distinguish them. The English practice of analyzing a previous case to discover its ratio decidendi is unknown.

There are a number of important instances where the Court has not followed precedent. These are the result of changing circumstances or a change of opinion among the judges, possibly following criticism by advocates general or academic writers. Where this happens, the Court does not normally overrule the earlier case as an English court would: it simply ignores it.

In 2001, according to the ECJ's Web site, 504 new cases were brought before the ECJ (including 237 references for preliminary rulings, 187 direct actions, and 72 appeals), and 434 cases were resolved. Among its 434 judgments, there were 182 preliminary rulings, 179 direct actions, and 59 appeals. The Court had a backlog of 839 cases at the end of 2001. The Court of First Instance received 345 new cases (including 110 staff cases) and gave 275 judgments (75 of which were staff cases); it had 589 cases on its register. (See Court of Justice for the European Communities Annual Report <http://curia.eu.int/en/pei/rapan.htm> (2001).)

2.   *The Sources of European Community Law and Its Relationship to National Law*

There are several sources of European Community law. Written sources can be subdivided into three categories. First, there is the "primary legislation," which is created directly by the Member States. It includes the Communities' constitutive treaties and their annexes, schedules, protocols, and amendments.

"Secondary legislation" consists of the law created by the Community institutions, which are expressly empowered by the primary legislation to make binding, juridical acts. (See, e.g., Article 249 (ex Art. 189) in the Consolidated Version of the Treaty Establishing the European Community (EC Treaty), excerpted in the Documentary Supplement. "Secondary" is used in a chronological sense and does not indicate that this legislation is somehow inferior in its legal effects to the constitutive treaties.) Finally, there are the international agreements concluded by the European Community, which is an entity with an international legal personality.

Community law also stems from unwritten sources and has a complex relationship with the laws of Member States.

Klaus-Dieter Borchardt, The ABC of Community Law

61-63, 96-97 (5th ed. 2000)

General Principles of Law

[Among t]he sources of unwritten Community law are the general principles of law. These are rules reflecting the elementary concepts of law and justice that must be respected by any legal system. Written Community law for the most part deals only with economic and social matters, and is only to a limited extent capable of laying down rules of this kind, which means that the general principles of law form one of the most important sources of law in the Community. They allow gaps to be filled and questions of the interpretation of existing laws to be settled in the fairest way.

These principles are given effect when the law is applied, particularly in the judgments of the Court of Justice, which is responsible for ensuring that "in the interpretation and application of this Treaty the law is observed." The main points of reference for determining the general principles of law are the principles common to the legal orders of the Member States. They provide the background against which Community rules can be developed.

Alongside the principles of autonomy, direct applicability and the primacy of Community law, other legal principles include the guarantee of basic rights, the principle of proportionality, the protection of legitimate expectations, the right to a proper hearing and the principle that the Member States are liable for infringements of Community law.

Legal Custom

Unwritten Community law also encompasses legal custom. This is understood to mean a practice which has been followed and accepted and thus become legally established, and which adds to or modifies primary or secondary legislation. The possible establishment of legal custom in Community law is acknowledged in principle. There are considerable limitations on its becoming established in the context of Community law, however. The first hurdle is the existence of a special procedure for the amendment of the Treaties (Article 48 EU). This does not rule out the possible emergence of legal custom, but it does make the criteria according to which a practice is deemed to have been followed and accepted for a substantial period much harder to meet. Another hurdle to the establishment of legal custom in the Community institutions is the fact that any action by an institution may derive its validity only from the Treaties, and not from that institution's actual conduct or any intention on its part to create legal relations. This means that, at the level of the Treaties, legal custom can under no circumstances be established by the Community institutions; at most, only the Member States can do this — and then only subject to the stringent conditions mentioned above. Practices followed and accepted as part of the law by Community institutions may, however, be drawn on when interpreting the legal rules laid down by them, which might alter the legal implications and scope of the legal act concerned. However, the conditions and limitations arising from primary Community legislation must also be borne in mind here. . . .

INTERACTION BETWEEN COMMUNITY LAW AND NATIONAL LAW

The interaction between Community law and national law covers those areas where the two systems complement each other. Article 10 of the EC Treaty is clear enough.

"Member States shall take all appropriate measures, whether general or particular, to ensure fulfilment of the obligations arising out of this Treaty or resulting from action taken by the institutions of the Community. They shall facilitate the achievement of the Community's tasks. They shall abstain from any measure which could jeopardise the attainment of the objectives of this Treaty."

This general principle was inspired by an awareness that the Community legal order on its own is not able to fully achieve the objectives pursued by the establishment of the EC. Unlike a national legal order, the Community legal order is not a self-contained system but relies on the support of the national systems for its operation. . . . It follows that national authorities are required not only to observe the community treaties and secondary legislation they must also implement them and bring them to life. . . .

In the judicial field, the two systems mesh through the preliminary ruling procedure of Article 234, of the EC Treaty, whereby national courts may, or sometimes must, refer questions on the interpretation and validity of Community law to the European Court of Justice, whose ruling may well be decisive in settling the dispute before them.

[While the EU legal system is independent of the legal systems of its Member States, there is a complex interaction between the two.]

3. *The Precedence of European Community Law*

The potential for conflict between the legal systems of the Member States and that of the European Union is clear. Two fundamental questions that have arisen are: (1) whether Community law creates direct rights and obligations for citizens and residents of Member States, and (2) which law takes precedence when Community law is inconsistent with the Member State's law. The ECJ directly addressed these issues in the following two landmark cases. Interestingly, the written Community law contains no express rule governing these conflicts. In reading the following cases, consider whether the ECJ was hampered by the lack of a "supremacy clause" when it encountered a conflict between the national and Community legal systems.

Van Gend en Loos v. Nederlandse Administratie der Belastingen

European Court of Justice
Case 26/62, [1963] ECR 1

[In September 1960 Van Gend en Loos imported ureaformaldehyde into the Netherlands from the Federal Republic of Germany. This product was then subject to an 8 percent import duty under a 1958 protocol between Belgium, Luxembourg, and the Netherlands. Van Gend en Loos challenged the application of the 8 percent duty by lodging an objection with the Inspector of Customs and Excise at Zaandam. The company argued that as of January 1, 1958 (the date the EEC [now European Community] Treaty came into force), this product had been subject to a 3 percent duty. The 1958 protocol, which had reclassified the product, resulted in a higher duty and was thus an infringement of Article 12 [now Art. 25] of the EEC [now EC] Treaty. Article 12 [now Art. 25] provides that Member States are to refrain from introducing new duties on imports and from increasing existing duties.

Countering Van Gend en Loos' argument, the Nederlandse Administratie de Belastingen, the Dutch customs collectors, stated that the product's classification as of January 1, 1958, had subjected it to a 10 percent duty; therefore, the protocol did not result in a higher duty. The Tariefcommissie, a Dutch court, without resolving the question of which duty the product had originally been subject to, requested a preliminary ruling from the Court of Justice on the following two questions:]

1. Whether Article 12 [now Art. 25] of the EEC [now EC] Treaty has direct application within the territory of a Member State, in other words, whether nationals of such a State can, on the basis of the Article in question, lay claim to individual rights which the courts must protect;

2. In the event of an affirmative reply, whether the application of an import duty of 8% to the import into the Netherlands by the applicant in the main action of ureaformaldehyde originating in the Federal Republic of Germany represented an unlawful increase within the meaning of Article 12 [now Art. 25] of the EEC [now EC] Treaty or whether it was in this case a reasonable alteration of the duty applicable before 1 March 1960, an alteration which, although amounting to an increase from the arithmetical point of view, is nevertheless not to be regarded as prohibited under the terms of Article 12 [now Art. 25] . . . .

[The Court answered the first question in the affirmative, giving the following reasoning:] The objective of the EEC [now EC] Treaty, which is to establish a Common Market, the functioning of which is of direct concern to interested parties in the Community, implies that this Treaty is more than an agreement which merely creates mutual obligations between the contracting states. This view is confirmed by the preamble to the Treaty which refers not only to governments but to peoples. It is also confirmed more specifically by the establishment of institutions endowed with sovereign rights, the exercise of which affects Member States and also their citizens. Furthermore, it must be noted that the nationals of the states brought together in the Community are called upon to cooperate in the functioning of this Community through the intermediary of the European Parliament and the Economic and Social Committee.

In addition the task assigned to the Court of Justice under Article 177 [now Art. 234], the object of which is to secure uniform interpretation of the Treaty by national courts and tribunals, confirms that the states have acknowledged that Community law has an authority which can be invoked by their nationals before those courts and tribunals.

The conclusion to be drawn from this is that the Community constitutes a new legal order of international law for the benefit of which the states have limited their sovereign rights, albeit within limited fields, and the subjects of which comprise not only Member States but also their nationals. Independently of the legislation of Member States, Community law therefore not only imposes obligations on individuals but is also intended to confer upon them rights which become part of their legal heritage. These rights arise not only where they are expressly granted by the Treaty, but also by reason of obligations which the Treaty imposes in a clearly defined way upon individuals as well as upon the Member States and upon the institutions of the Community. . . .

The wording of Article 12 [now Art. 25] contains a clear and unconditional prohibition which is not a positive but a negative obligation. This obligation, moreover, is not qualified by any reservation on the part of states which would make its implementation conditional upon a positive legislative measure enacted under national law. The very nature of this prohibition makes it ideally adapted to produce direct effects in the legal relationship between Member States and their subjects. . . .

. . . The fact that . . . Articles [226 (ex Art. 169) and 227 (ex Art. 170)] of the Treaty enable the Commission and the Member States to bring before the Court a State which has not fulfilled its obligations does not mean that individuals cannot plead these obligations, should the occasion arise, before a national court, any more than the fact that the Treaty places at the disposal of the Commission ways of ensuring that obligations imposed upon those subject to the Treaty are observed, precludes the possibility, in actions between individuals before a national court, of pleading infringements of these obligations.

A restriction of the guarantees against an infringement of Article 12 [now Art. 25] by Member States to the procedures under Article 169 [now Art. 226] and 170 [now Art. 22] would remove all direct legal protection of the individual rights of their nationals. There is the risk that recourse to the procedure under these Articles would be ineffective if it were to occur after the implementation of a national decision taken contrary to the provisions of the Treaty.

The vigilance of individuals concerned to protect their rights amounts to an effective supervision in addition to the supervision entrusted by Articles 169 [now Art. 226] and 170 [now Art. 227] to the diligence of the Commission and of the Member States.

It follows from the foregoing considerations that, according to the spirit, the general scheme and the wording of the Treaty, Article 12 [now Art. 25] must be interpreted as producing direct effects and creating individual rights which national courts must protect. . . .

[The Court of Justice then concluded that, regarding the second question, the Tariefcommissie was the proper court to make the determination as to whether the import duty charged was higher after January 1, 1958 or not.]

Amministrazione delle Finanze dello Stato v. Simmenthal S.p.A.

European Court of Justice
Case 106/77, [1978] ECR 629

[In July 1973, Simmenthal imported beef for human consumption from France into Italy. Pursuant to Italian domestic law, the Italian government charged the importer a fee for veterinary and public health inspection. Believing that such fees were contrary to Community law, Simmenthal sued in Italian court for a refund. The Italian court, the Pretora di Susa, referred the question of the validity of the fees under Community law to the ECJ. The Court ruled that the fees were the equivalent of a quantitative restriction and thus invalid under Article 30 [now Art. 28] of the EEC [now EC] Treaty. In light of this ruling, the Pretora di Susa ordered the Italian government to refund the fees charged. The Italian government appealed, contending that the Italian court had to apply Italian domestic law, absent repeal by the national legislature or invalidation by the Italian Constitutional Court. The case was then referred again to the ECJ.]

The Pretore, taking into account the arguments put forward by the parties during the proceedings arising out of this appeal, held that the issue before him involved a conflict between certain rules of Community law and a subsequent national law, namely the said Law No. 1239/70.

The Pretore . . . referred to the Court two questions framed as follows:

(a) Since, in accordance with Article 189 [now Art. 249] of the EEC [now EC] Treaty and the established case-law of the Court of Justice of the European Communities, directly applicable Community provisions must, notwithstanding any internal rule or practice whatsoever of the Member States, have full, complete and uniform effect in their legal systems in order to protect subjective legal rights created in favour of individuals, is the scope of the said provisions to be interpreted to the effect that any subsequent national measures which conflict with those provisions must be forthwith disregarded without waiting until those measures have been eliminated by action on the part of the national legislature concerned (repeal) or of other constitutional authorities (declaration that they are unconstitutional) especially, in the case of the latter alternative, where, since the national law continues to be fully effective pending such declaration, it is impossible to apply the Community provisions and, in consequence, to ensure that they are fully, completely and uniformly applied and to protect the legal rights created in favour of individuals?

(b) Arising out of the previous question, in circumstances where Community law recognizes that the protection of subjective legal rights created as a result of "directly applicable" Community provisions may be suspended until any conflicting national measures are actually repealed by the competent national authorities, is such repeal in all cases to have a wholly retroactive effect so as to avoid any adverse effects on those subjective legal rights?

The main purpose of the *first question* is to ascertain what consequences flow from the direct applicability of a provision of Community law in the event of incompatibility with a subsequent legislative provision of a Member State.

Direct applicability in such circumstances means that rules of Community law must be fully and uniformly applied in all the Member States from the date of their entry into force and for so long as they continue in force.

These provisions are therefore a direct source of rights and duties for all those affected thereby, whether Member States or individuals, who are parties to legal relationships under Community law.

This consequence also concerns any national court whose task it is as an organ of a Member State to protect, in a case within its jurisdiction, the rights conferred upon individuals by Community law.

Furthermore, in accordance with the principle of the precedence of Community law, the relationship between provisions of the Treaty and directly applicable measures of the institutions on the one hand and the national law of the Member States on the other is such that those provisions and measures not only by their entry into force render automatically inapplicable any conflicting provision of current national law but — in so far as they are an integral part of, and take precedence in, the legal order applicable in the territory of each of the Member States — also preclude the valid adoption of new national legislative measures to the extent to which they would be incompatible with Community provisions.

Indeed any recognition that national legislative measures which encroach upon the field within which the Community exercises its legislative power or which are otherwise incompatible with the provisions of Community law had any legal effect would amount to a corresponding denial of the effectiveness of obligations undertaken unconditionally and irrevocably by Member States pursuant to the Treaty and would thus imperil the very foundations of the Community.

The same conclusion emerges from the structure of Article 177 [now Art. 234] of the Treaty which provides that any court or tribunal of a Member State is entitled to make a reference to the Court whenever it considers that a preliminary ruling on a question of interpretation or validity relating to Community law is necessary to enable it to give judgment.

The effectiveness of that provision would be impaired if the national court were prevented from forthwith applying Community law in accordance with the decision or the case-law of the Court.

It follows from the foregoing that every national court must, in a case within its jurisdiction, apply Community law in its entirety and protect rights which the latter confers on individuals and must accordingly set aside any provision of national law which may conflict with it, whether prior or subsequent to the Community rule.

Accordingly any provision of a national legal system and any legislative, administrative or judicial practice which might impair the effectiveness of Community law by withholding from the national court having jurisdiction to apply such law the power to do everything necessary at the moment of its application to set aside national legislative provisions which might prevent Community rules from having full force and effect are incompatible with those requirements which are the very essence of Community law.

This would be the case in the event of a conflict between a provision of Community law and a subsequent national law if the solution of the conflict were to be reserved for an authority with a discretion of its own, other than the court called upon to apply Community law, even if such an impediment to the full effectiveness of Community law were only temporary.

The first question should therefore be answered to the effect that a national court which is called upon, within the limits of its jurisdiction, to apply provisions of Community law is under a duty to give full effect to those provisions, if necessary refusing of its own motion to apply any conflicting provision of national legislation, even if adopted subsequently, and it is not necessary for the court to request or await the prior setting aside of such provision by legislative or other constitutional means.

The essential point of the *second question* is whether — assuming it to be accepted that the protection of rights conferred by provisions of Community law can be suspended until any national provisions which might conflict with them have been in fact set aside by the competent national authorities — such setting aside must in every case have unrestricted retroactive effect so as to prevent the rights in question from being in any way adversely affected.

It follows from the answer to the first question that national courts must protect rights conferred by provisions of the Community legal order and that it is not necessary for such courts to request or await the actual setting aside by the national authorities empowered so to act of any national measures which might impede the direct and immediate application of Community rules.

The second question therefore appears to have no purpose.

On those grounds the Court, in answer to the questions referred to it by the Pretore di Susa by order of 28 July 1977, hereby rules:

> A national court which is called upon, within the limits of its jurisdiction, to apply provisions of Community law is under a duty to give full effect to those provisions, if necessary refusing of its own motion to apply any conflicting provision of national legislation, even if adopted subsequently, and it is not necessary for the court to request or await the prior setting aside of such provisions by legislative or other constitutional means.

Notes and Questions

1. What is the significance of the power of the European Court of Justice to render preliminary decisions on issues of Community law arising during litigation before Member State courts? Does this enhance the power of the court? Does it contribute to the overall harmonization of Community policies?

2. Given the Court's decisions in *Van Gend en Loos* and *Simmenthal* (which have been followed in later cases), has the authority of the European Union been enhanced? What is the effect on Member State legislatures?

3. In another landmark case, Costa (Flaminio) v. ENEL, Case 6/64, [1964] ECR 585, the European Court of Justice wrote:

> By contrast with ordinary international treaties, the EEC Treaty has created its own legal system which, on the entry into force of the Treaty, became an integral part of the legal systems of the Member States and which their courts are bound to apply.
>
> By creating a Community of unlimited duration, having its own institutions, its own personality, its own legal capacity and capacity of representation on the international plane and, more particularly, real powers stemming from a limitation of sovereignty or a transfer of powers from the States to the Community, the Member States have limited their sovereign rights, albeit within limited fields, and have thus created a body of law which binds both their nationals and themselves.

Besides the ECJ, the rest of the structure of the European Union will be considered in Chapter 5. Note for now, however, Article 292 (ex Art. 219) of the EC Treaty, which provides that "Member States undertake not to submit a dispute concerning the interpretation or application of this Treaty to any method of settlement other than those provided for" in the Treaty. Moreover, Article 226 (ex Art. 169) of the EC Treaty provides that the Commission can bring to the ECJ a matter where the Commission believes that a Member State "has failed to fulfill an obligation under this Treaty."

4. The ECJ has played a significant role in encouraging Member States to comply with their treaty obligations. First, in Andrea Frankovich v. Italy, Joined Cases 6 & 9/90, [1991] I ECR 5357, [1993] 2 CMLR 66, the Court held Italy liable for damages to individuals caused by its failure to implement an EU directive (an EU act that is binding on identified Member States, but leaves to the national authorities of each Member State the choice of form and methods to reach the required result). In Brasserie Du Pecheur Sa v. Germany Regina v. Secretary of State for Transport, ex parte Factortame Ltd. and Others, Joined Cases 46 & 48/93, [1996] All ER (EC) 301, [1996] 1 CMLR 889, the ECJ further clarified the criteria to help national courts

determine when a Member State should be held liable for damages to individual rights. Not surprisingly, *Frankovich* and *Factortame* prompted some Member States to call for limitations on their liabilities. Should there be a limit to a Member State's liability? Should the ECJ have the final review of the Member State's liability, as indicated in the cases, or should there be an additional appeals process?

Second, Article 226 (ex Art. 169) of the EC Treaty provides that the Commission can bring to the ECJ a matter where the Commission believes that the Member State "has failed to fulfill an obligation under this Treaty." Under Article 228 (ex Art. 171), the Commission can then ask the ECJ to fine a Member State that does not comply with the Court's judgment. The Commission is to specify the amount of the lump sum or penalty payment, and the ECJ may impose it.

In 1997, the Commission opened legal proceedings against six Member States (Belgium, France, Germany, Spain, Italy, and Greece) for fines for failing to follow the Court's decisions on wild birds and other environmental matters. The Commission opened additional proceedings against Member States in 1998, including Ireland for failing to implement an EU directive on water pollution. The EU Commission has used the threat of fines to bring recalcitrant Member States to prompt compliance. The more common procedure by far is for the Commission to bring an action under Article 226 (ex Art. 169) and use the ECJ judgment, along with the threat of action under Article 228 (ex Art. 171), to ensure compliance. However, the ECJ has handed down at least one such fine against a Member State. In Commission v. Greece, Case 387/97, [2000] ECR I-5407, the Court states that it:

1. Declares that, by failing to take the measures necessary to ensure that waste is disposed of in the area of Chania without endangering human health and without harming the environment in accordance with Article 4 of Council Directive 75/442/EEC of 15 July 1975 on waste and by failing to draw up for that area plans for the disposal of waste, pursuant to Article 6 of Directive 75/442, and of toxic and dangerous waste, pursuant to Article 12 of Council Directive 78/319/EEC of 20 March 1978 on toxic and dangerous waste, the Hellenic Republic has not implemented all the necessary measures to comply with the judgment of the Court of 7 April 1992 in Case C-45/91 Commission v. Greece and has failed to fulfil its obligations under Article 171 of the EC Treaty;

2. Orders the Hellenic Republic to pay to the Commission of the European Communities, into the account EC own resources, a penalty payment of EUR 20 000 for each day of delay in implementing the measures necessary to comply with the judgment in Case C-45/91, from delivery of the present judgment until the judgment in Case C-45/91 has been complied with. . . .

5. *The ECJ and human rights.* The ECJ's role in the areas of social policy and human rights has become significantly more active in recent years. While being careful not to expand its own jurisdiction too far beyond the strict terms of the Treaties, the ECJ has carefully asserted a role for itself in declaring a variety of fundamental human rights to be "general principles of Community law," which are enforceable by the Court. However, the ECJ has only rarely relied on those rights in issuing its judgments, preferring instead to base its judgments on principles expressly found in the EC Treaties. Fundamental rights jurisprudence has more typically served to guide its interpretation of the written Community law.

The sources and potential reach of the ECJ's human rights law can be found in its judgment in Kremzow v. Austria, Case C-299/95 [1997] ECR I-2629:

14. It should first be noted that, as the Court has consistently held . . . , fundamental rights form an integral part of the general principles of Community law whose observance the Court ensures. For that purpose, the Court draws inspiration from the constitutional traditions common to the Member States and from the guidelines supplied by international treaties for the protection of human rights on which the Member States have collaborated or of which they are signatories. The Convention has special significance in that respect. As the Court has also held, it follows that measures are not acceptable in the Community which are incompatible with observance of the human rights thus recognized and guaranteed. . . .

15. Further, according to the Court's case-law . . . , where national legislation falls within the field of application of Community law the Court, in a reference for a preliminary ruling, must give the national court all the guidance as to interpretation necessary to enable it to assess the compatibility of that legislation with the fundamental rights — as laid down in particular in the [European Convention for the Protection of Human Rights and Fundamental Freedoms] — whose observance the Court ensures. However, the Court has no such jurisdiction with regard to national legislation *lying outside the scope* of Community law.

Even so, the Court in *Kremzow* refused to apply its human rights jurisprudence to the case, on the grounds that the issue raised by the appellant fell outside the scope of Community law. This is the most significant limit to the ECJ's jurisdiction: it may review Community acts and Member State acts within the areas governed by Community law, but it does not yet have jurisdiction over acts by Member States in their Community capacity.

A further complication to the role of the ECJ in human rights jurisprudence is the existence of the European Convention on Human Rights, which has over 40 parties, most of which are not EU members. Every EU Member State is signatory to the Convention and is bound in certain specified areas by the jurisdiction of the European Court of Human Rights in Strasbourg. However, in its famous Opinion 2/94, the ECJ ruled that the EC as such lacked competence to accede to the Convention, which means the Strasbourg Court has no jurisdiction over Community actions and cannot review the rulings of the Court of Justice. Therefore, the Convention has no binding force on the ECJ; it is merely an informational source of "fundamental principles" that the Court can use to interpret Community Law.

But the ECJ has occasionally gone further and invalidated Member State or Community acts because of a human rights violation. In Krombach v. Bamberski, Case C-7/98 [2000] ECR I-1935, the Court held that a German court did not have to enforce a French judgment against a German citizen who was denied the right to present a defense in absentia, a right guaranteed by the Convention. Likewise, in X v. Commission, Case C-404/92 [1994] ECR I-4737, the Court upheld the right of a job applicant to refuse to take an AIDS test, relying on the right to a private life, granted by the Convention. Such cases are still uncommon, but they have become increasingly frequent in recent years.

The Charter of Fundamental Rights, signed at Nice in December 2000 by the Council, Commission, European Parliament, and the heads of the Member States, will surely further increase the role of human rights in the Court's future cases. As of

June 2002, the Court of Justice had yet to cite the Charter in one of its judgments, but the Court of First Instance has cited to it three times, and several Advocates General have referred to it in their opinions. The Charter is not currently binding law, but many Europeans want it to become the backbone of an EU constitution, which would be binding on the Court. This process could begin as soon as 2004, if the Member States agreed to do so at the Intergovernmental Conference that December.

For now, however, the Charter is so-called soft law. Like the European Convention on Human Rights, it is a source in which the ECJ may find principles of law to enforce against Union institutions or Member States acting on behalf of the Union. Because it has been proclaimed by the EU and the Member States, the Court is likely to invoke the Charter's principles more aggressively than it has applied human rights principles in the past. (The Charter is in the Documentary Supplement.)

6. Compare the European Court of Justice with the U.S. Supreme Court and the International Court of Justice. Consider, for example, (a) the power of these courts to enforce their rulings and (b) the sources of law to which these courts refer in rendering their decisions. Would you consider the ECJ more similar to the U.S. Supreme Court or to the ICJ? Why do you think that the ECJ has been viewed as more successful than the ICJ? In light of what you learned in Chapter 3, how does *Simmenthal* compare with what a U.S. court would do when confronted with a conflict between national legislation and a treaty?

7. Might the position of Advocate General that exists for the European Court of Justice have potential benefit for a U.S. court, such as the U.S. Supreme Court? Does any equivalent or similar position exist that provides submissions to the U.S. Supreme Court?

8. In July 1998, four U.S. Supreme Court Justices (Justices Sandra Day O'Connor, Anthony M. Kennedy, Ruth Bader Ginsberg, and Stephen G. Breyer) visited the ECJ in Luxemburg on a mission to share common legal ideas and to cultivate judicial cooperation. During this mission, the Justices emphasized the significance of the ECJ decisions. Justice O'Connor said, "We certainly are going to be more inclined to look at the decisions of [the European Court of Justice] on substantive issues . . . and perhaps use them and cite them in future decisions." Justice Breyer added, "Lawyers in America may cite an EU ruling to our court to further a point, and this increases the cross-fertilization of U.S.-EU legal ideas." (Washington Post, July 9, 1998, at A6.)

9. Why do you think the Western European states have taken the lead in the world in allowing regional courts (the ECJ, as well as the European Court of Human Rights) to have a major say regarding an individual state's economic and other policies? Do you expect that other regions might be willing to create and accept a court like the ECJ in the near future? What about the countries of North and South America, or the ASEAN countries in Asia (discussed in Chapter 5)?

Although the Amsterdam and Nice Treaties have expanded the ECJ's jurisdiction somewhat into the areas of police and judicial cooperation, immigration, and asylum, and the Court has itself increased its scrutiny of fundamental rights and free movement of persons, its jurisdiction is still heavily weighted toward economic and social issues, and the jurisdiction of the European Court of Human Rights is even more specialized. Moreover, the newest international courts, the Law of the Sea Tribunal and the International Criminal Court, are focused on the special issues, respectively, of the law of the sea and war crimes. Do you think that an international court with a specialized jurisdiction has more chance of gaining the support of states and other international entities than does a court with a theoretically broad jurisdiction such as the ICJ? If so, what other specialized areas would seem particularly appropriate for an international court whose decisions would be enforced by individual states?

Bibliography

Besides the publications cited above, for further reading on the European Court of Justice see L. Neville Brown and Tom Kennedy, The Court of Justice of the European Communities (5th ed. 2000); Jean Victor Louis, The Community Legal Order (3d ed. 1995); European Courts Practice and Precedents (Richard Plender ed., 1997); Henry Schermers and Denis Waelbroeck, Judicial protection in the European Union (6th ed. 2001); Philippe Leger, De la nature de l'avocat general à la Cour de Justice des Communautés Européennes, Mélanges en L'Honneur de Jean-Claude Soyer (1998); Walter Mattli and Anne-Marie Slaughter, Revisiting the European Court of Justice, 52 Intl. Org. 177 (Winter 1998); Dean Spielmann, Human Rights Case Law in the Strasbourg and Luxembourg Courts: Conflicts, Inconsistencies, and Complementarities, in The European Union and Human Rights (Alston ed., 1999); Bruno de Witte, The Future Role of the European Court of Justice in the Protection of Human Rights, in The European Union and Human Rights (Alston ed., 1999).

The ECJ's Web site is at <http://curia.eu.int>.

D. INTERNATIONAL ARBITRATION

Arbitration between countries or between a country and a private party (such as an investor) has had a mixed history over the centuries. In recent years it has taken on new life and led to the creation of new arrangements.

For instance, even while the United States and Iran traded insults and hostile fire during 1987-1988, the Iran-United States Claims Tribunal continued to proceed steadily (though slowly) through its caseload left over from the 1979-1981 hostage crisis. Also, the World Bank's International Centre for the Settlement of Investment Disputes (ICSID) has experienced a steady increase in its caseload of arbitrations between host countries and investors. And the North American Free Trade Agreement (NAFTA) provides for binational panels to address a wide variety of issues, including antidumping and countervailing duty cases that before would have been under the exclusive jurisdiction of Canadian, Mexican, or U.S. courts. Finally, compared to the General Agreement on Tariffs and Trade (GATT), the new World Trade Organization (WTO) has a much stronger dispute resolution system for a wide range of trade disputes among its 130-plus members. As we will see, if consultations fail, a dispute under the new WTO system first goes to a panel that is similar to arbitration, but then there is an automatic right of appeal to an Appellate Body that is similar to an appellate court. (ICSID, NAFTA, and the WTO are discussed in this section.)

In the analogous area of commercial arbitration among private parties, business is booming as the number of international transactions grows and as arbitration increasingly becomes the preferred method of formal dispute resolution for many types of business deals. Established institutions like the International Chamber of Commerce (ICC) and the American Arbitration Association (AAA) have seen their caseloads expand. New centers for international arbitration have also sprung up.

Although the focus in this casebook is about arbitration involving one or more states (and possibly private entities as well), the activity in private commercial arbitration is often relevant. Arbitral panels — whether a country is a party or not — are likely to select from among the same sets of procedural rules and face similar choice-of-law questions. Moreover, enforcement of most, though not all, arbitral awards looks to the same convention — the New York Convention on the Recognition and Enforcement of Foreign Arbitral Awards, which over 130 countries have ratified.

This section explores the history of arbitration, then analyzes the current uses and some outstanding issues in arbitration, including the question of enforcement of arbitral awards. The section then examines the interesting new uses of arbitration in NAFTA and the WTO.

1. *History of Arbitration*

Arbitration has had a long, and mixed, history. In his book, International Arbitration and Procedure (1911), Robert Morris (hereafter Morris) provides some of the earliest history.

Arbitration was used by the ancient Greeks to settle internal quarrels (e.g., between the city states). Disputes with the outside world, however, were settled through war or other means. Conditions in ancient Greece were especially favorable to arbitration — the Greeks shared a common religion, language, and an affinity for athletic games. The only thing they lacked was a unified political identity. Specific procedures were established and followed in arbitration proceedings. The Delphic oracle was often chosen as an arbitrator, as were poets, statesmen, and athletic victors. Alliances also were made between cities, which included clauses to ensure that any subsequent dispute between them would be subject to arbitration.

Early Roman history, when Italy was made up of many independent states, also contains many instances of arbitration. However, after Rome asserted sovereignty over all of Italy, arbitration became less frequent, finally ceasing with the assertion of dominion by Rome over all the world. "This conception [of Rome as the only sovereignty in the world] is necessarily antagonistic to the idea of [public] arbitration." (Morris, at 6.)

Upon the disintegration of the Roman Empire, arbitration once more became common. Unlike in ancient Greece, common procedures for arbitration proceedings were not established. Popes, monarchs, emperors, and lords all arbitrated disputes. "Perhaps the most famous instance [of Papal arbitration] was the decision of Alexander VI between Spain and Portugal in their quarrel over the newly discovered lands in the new world. . . . The Pope finally decided that Spain should hold everything west of a line somewhere between the forty-first and forty-fourth degrees of longitude, and Portugal everything east." (Morris, at 12.) That essentially limited Portugal to the eastern part of Brazil. Penalties against those entities that did not respect arbitration decisions ranged from monetary fines to excommunication.

With the appearance of (more or less) stable monarchies in Europe, arbitration between nations became less common, while arbitration of business disputes became more so. "[I]n a treaty between France and England in 1606, two arbitral courts were established, each consisting of two Englishmen and two Frenchmen, one court holding at London, the other at Paris. Aggrieved French shipowners presented their protests at London, and aggrieved Englishmen at Paris." An arbitration board was also established in 1652 to resolve "commercial disputes that had accumulated for many years" between merchants of England and Holland. (Morris, at 16-17.)

The following excerpt provides a survey of the development of public arbitration and some of its uses from 1794 through 1955.

J. L. Simpson & Hazel Fox, International Arbitration: Law and Practice

1-40 (1959)

THE EARLY ANGLO-AMERICAN ARBITRATIONS, 1794-1842

In 1794 there was concluded between the United Kingdom and the United States the General Treaty of Friendship, Commerce and Navigation, commonly called "the Jay Treaty" after John Jay, the [Chief Justice of the U.S. Supreme Court who negotiated the treaty for the United States]. It provided a new starting point for the development of international [public] arbitration, after the process, in the preceding period of a century or more, had come to be regarded as virtually in desuetude. Of the various questions which had been outstanding between the United Kingdom and the United States, since the latter proclaimed their independence in 1776, the Jay Treaty settled all but three. These were referred to arbitration. The form chosen was that of mixed commissions, consisting of one or two commissioners appointed by each party, who were together to choose a third or fifth by agreement or by drawing lots. The Commission set up under Article 5 had the task of deciding the exact position of the "Sainte Croix River," a loose expression used in the Versailles Settlement of 1783 to indicate part of the boundary between the remaining British possessions and the United States. The commissioners were able to give an agreed decision. The Commission set up under Article 6 was less successful. It had to deal with allegations of judicial obstruction in the collection of certain debts owing to British creditors by debtors, who had become citizens of the United States. The Commission broke up amid high feeling in 1799, and the question was ultimately settled by negotiation in the Treaty of 1802. The Commission set up under Article 7 of the Jay Treaty had to deal with claims arising from the seizure of ships and cargoes during the then war between the United Kingdom and France. It was ultimately able . . . to make a large number of awards. . . .

The termination, in 1804, of the Jay Treaty, in accordance with its terms, ushered in a new period of tension between the United States and the United Kingdom, which culminated in the war of 1812-14. The Treaty of Ghent of 1814, which restored peace, provided for four arbitrations on territorial questions. The form chosen was that of mixed commissions composed of one commissioner from each side; but, if the commissioners disagreed, there was to be a reference to a disinterested head of state. It cannot be said that the device of bringing in a head of state was proved to be a success. . . . The commissioners failed to agree on the question of the North-Eastern boundary, and, after some six years, there was a reference to the King of the Netherlands. His recommendatory award was not accepted, and the matter was ultimately settled by negotiation in the "Webster-Ashburton" Treaty of 1842. . . .

Later experience was to confirm that the success of a mixed commission often depended on the ability of the commissioners appointed by the parties to give agreed decisions on the questions submitted to them without recourse to the umpire or arbitrator. This in turn meant that the mixed commission worked best, where the subject-matter of the dispute allowed or encouraged the commissioners to act to some extent as negotiators rather than as judges, to temper justice with diplomacy, to give a measure of satisfaction to both sides, for example, in a territorial dispute. . . .

THE ALABAMA CLAIMS ARBITRATION, 1871-72

If the Jay Treaty of 1794 rescued arbitral process as a means of settling international disputes from desuetude, the *Alabama Claims* arbitration — also between the United Kingdom and the United States — gave the process a new impetus, and introduced a number of rules and practices which were gradually to command general acceptance. . . . The *Alabama* claims arose from the failure, real or alleged, of the United Kingdom in her duties as a neutral during the American Civil War — in particular, in permitting *Alabama* and her supply ship, *Georgia,* to be built in British yards for the use of the Southern States, whose belligerency, to the chagrin of the Northern States, had been recognised. References to heads of state had been shown to have certain disadvantages, while the issues were too large for a mixed commission of the traditional type. Accordingly, a new type of tribunal had to be constituted. This consisted of one member appointed by each side and members appointed, respectively, by the King of Italy, the President of the Swiss Confederation and the Emperor of Brazil. Thus, a collegiate international court, which was to set the pattern for many others, had emerged. The common law practice of permitting the preparation and publication of dissenting or separate judgments was allowed, and was later to become general in international litigation. Substantive international law was also enlarged, though this must be ascribed to the Treaty of Washington of 1871, under which the Tribunal was constituted, rather than to the Tribunal itself. Annexed to the Treaty were the Washington rules on the duties of neutrals. These rules imposed higher duties on neutrals than those generally accepted while the American Civil War was being fought. Thus, to authorise the Tribunal to apply the Washington rules virtually concluded all issues (except the quantum of damages) against the United Kingdom.

CONTINUANCE OF THE OLDER FORMS, 1871-89

. . . In the last two decades of the nineteenth century there were no fewer than ninety international arbitrations between various states. The mixed commission was still the form favoured for the settlement of private claims, particularly when these arose from the political upheavals endemic in South America. Thus, the United Kingdom participated in mixed commissions with Chile in 1883 and again in 1893, and with Nicaragua in 1895. Mixed commissions were also entrusted with the decision of other claims of secondary importance. . . .

INDEPENDENT EXPERTS OR COLLEGIATE COURTS, 1872-99

While, then, the mixed commission had by no means been abandoned, a tendency is also clearly discernible in the period from 1870 onwards to seek reference to wholly independent persons, preferably jurists. In 1872 the dispute between the United Kingdom and Portugal concerning Delagoa Bay was submitted to the arbitration of the President of France. The President was given power to decide in equity and to remit the question to such persons as he thought fit. He appointed a commission of five eminent Frenchmen, including a jurist as chairman. Their report, which upheld the Portuguese contentions in their entirety, was fully motivated. While heads of state hitherto had regarded the arbitral decision as their personal responsibility, taken though it usually was in the light of the advice of Ministers or experts, the French President did no more than sign the award submitted to him by the Commission. Reference to a head of state was thus treated as a request to him to appoint a commission. . . .

Before its close, the nineteenth century was to produce three major arbitrations, where the precedent of the collegiate court established in the *Alabama Claims* arbitration was followed. In 1891 France and the United Kingdom referred their dispute concerning the Newfoundland lobster fisheries to a tribunal composed of two members appointed by each party, and "three specialists or jurisconsults designated by common consent" by the two Governments. The same pattern was followed in constituting the Tribunal of 1892 to decide the *Behring Sea Seal Fishing* dispute between the United Kingdom and the United States. . . .

THE HAGUE PEACE CONFERENCES, 1899 AND 1907

By the end of the nineteenth century, arbitration had become a widely spread international custom; and it was natural that its discussion should occupy a considerable place in the deliberations of the Hague Peace Conferences of 1899 and 1907. The conclusion of the Convention for the Pacific Settlement of International Disputes was the most positive of the achievements of the Conference of 1899.

The Convention established, in Chapter II of Part IV, the misnamed Permanent Court of Arbitration. It is little more than a panel of names from which arbitrators may be selected, when the occasion arises. The Convention allows governments party to it to nominate a maximum of four persons "of known competency in questions of international law, of the highest moral reputation and disposed to accept the duties of Arbitrator." . . . When a dispute arises between parties to the Convention, which they wish to refer to a tribunal of the Permanent Court of Arbitration, each appoints two arbitrators from the panel. The four arbitrators thus chosen select an umpire. If the four arbitrators are evenly divided on the selection of the umpire, the choice of umpire is entrusted to a third Power selected by agreement between the parties. If the parties cannot agree upon the third Power, each party chooses a different Power and the choice of umpire is made by agreement between the two Powers thus chosen.

The only permanent feature of the Permanent Court of Arbitration is the Bureau established in accordance with Article 22 of the Convention. The services of the Bureau are available for tribunals formed from the Permanent Court of Arbitration, and may also be placed at the disposal of other tribunals and commissions of inquiry. Chapter III lays down the rules of procedure which apply in default of agreement to the contrary between the parties. The formulation of these rules in 1899 was a valuable corrective to the extreme informality of some of the earlier arbitrations. As amended in 1907, they are still today cited as authority when disputes arise upon points of procedure, and they have influenced the drafting of many *compromis*.

Between 1902 and 1905, recourse was had to the machinery established by the Convention of 1899 for the settlement of four disputes. . . . In all these cases, the issues were of secondary importance. They served, however, to put the provisions of the Convention of 1899 to the test, and to show where improvements might be attempted, when the second Hague Peace Conference assembled in 1907. . . .

The Convention of 1899 declared in Article 16 that:

> In questions of a legal nature, and especially in the interpretation or application of International Conventions, arbitration is recognised by the Signatory Powers as the most effective, and at the same time the most equitable, means of settling disputes which diplomacy has failed to settle.

The Conference of 1907 cautiously added to Article 16 the words:

> Consequently, it would be desirable that, in disputes regarding the above-mentioned questions, the Contracting Powers should, if the case arise, have recourse to arbitration, in so far as circumstances permit.

The Final Act of the Conference of 1907, with a magnificence of language masking the disappointment of high hopes, stated that the Conference was unanimous in admitting the principle of compulsory arbitration, in declaring that certain disputes, in particular those relating to the interpretation and application of international agreements, might be submitted to compulsory arbitration without any restriction, and in proclaiming that, although it had not yet been feasible to conclude a Convention in this sense . . . the collected Powers . . . had succeeded in the course of this long collaboration in evolving a very lofty conception of the common welfare of humanity.

Behind the formulae lay the frustration of all endeavours to reach agreement at either Conference on proposals of varying scope for the acceptance of compulsory arbitration. Each of the various proposals found considerable minorities in opposition, and it was held impossible to proceed further. . . .

"VITAL INTERESTS, INDEPENDENCE OR HONOUR"

In 1903 the United Kingdom concluded with France the Agreement providing for the settlement by Arbitration of Certain Classes of Questions which may arise between the two Governments. This Agreement envisaged reference to the Permanent Court of Arbitration of differences of a legal nature or relating to the interpretation of treaties, "provided, nevertheless, that they do not affect the vital interests, the independence, or the honour of the two Contracting States, and do not concern the interests of third Parties" (Article I). This was to become a stock formula for bilateral arbitration treaties of the period. By 1905 the United Kingdom had concluded treaties embodying it with ten other European states, and it was widely adopted by other Powers. Attempts, which had been made at various times since 1897, to negotiate an arbitration treaty with the United States had all proved unavailing, largely owing to the misgivings of the Senate in Washington. In 1908, however, it at length proved possible to conclude the Arbitration Convention between the United Kingdom and the United States. This Convention, in deference to the authority of the Senate, had to include a provision that any special agreement concluded under it should not be binding until confirmed by the Governments in an exchange of notes. It also adopted the "vital interests, independence or honour" formula of the European treaties. The formula became common form in arbitration treaties concluded by the United States, and is to be found in the Treaty between the United States and Liberia concluded as late as 1926. Under treaties of this type, the question — whether the obligation to seek arbitration in a particular dispute had arisen or not — was left largely to the subjective judgment of the states concerned.

THE MIXED ARBITRAL TRIBUNALS AND CLAIMS COMMISSIONS FOLLOWING THE WAR OF 1914-18

The Treaty of Versailles provided, in Article 304, for the establishment of mixed arbitral tribunals between each of the Allied and Associated Powers on the one hand and Germany on the other. Each tribunal consisted of one member appointed by each Government, and a president appointed by the two Governments jointly. If the two Governments failed to agree upon a president, he was selected by the Council of the League of Nations. The jurisdiction of the mixed arbitral tribunals included claims by nationals of the Allied or Associated Power arising out of exceptional war measures taken by Germany in respect of property, and also, in a large variety of contractual matters, cases between nationals of the Allied or Associated Power and nationals of Germany. Similar provision for mixed arbitral tribunals was made in the Treaties of St. Germain with Austria; Trianon with Hungary; Neuilly with Bulgaria; Sèvres and Lausanne with Turkey. The decisions of the mixed arbitral tribunals turn, to a large extent, on points of private law and of interpretation of the treaties of peace.

By an Agreement of August 10, 1922, between the United States and Germany, a Mixed Claims Commission was set up to deal with claims of U.S. citizens against Germany for damage to property, rights and interests in Germany, other claims for injury to persons or property as a consequence of war, and debts due to U.S. citizens by the German Government or German nationals. Similar claims by U.S. citizens against Austria or Hungary were referred to the Tripartite Claims Commission (consisting of a single commissioner) in pursuance of the Agreement of November 26, 1924, between the United States, Austria and Hungary. . . .

POST-WAR TRIBUNALS

Most of the peace treaties which followed the Second World War and the treaties embodying the provisional settlement with Germany made elaborate provision for the settlement of disputes.

A procedure closely resembling the older practice of appointing a mixed commission, consisting of two national commissioners, who tend in fact to be negotiators rather than arbitrators in the strict sense, and have resort to a "neutral" umpire only in the event of their disagreeing, is provided for in the Peace Treaties with Italy, Rumania, Bulgaria, Hungary and Finland, and the State Treaty with Austria. . . .

In other disputes concerning the interpretation or execution of the Peace Treaties or the State Treaty with Austria the emphasis is on diplomatic settlement. . . .

The divided state of Germany necessitated a different form of post-war settlement. . . . That settlement produced a series of tribunals, each with jurisdiction over different classes of matters. . . .

The Bonn Conventions of 1955 also provide for elaborate judicial machinery. Article 9 of the Convention on Relations between France, the United Kingdom and the United States of America ("the Three Powers") and the Federal Republic of Germany provides for the establishment of an Arbitration Tribunal with exclusive jurisdiction over disputes between the Three Powers and the Federal Republic of Germany, arising out of the provisions of the Conventions, with the exception of disputes involving the rights derived from the unconditional surrender of Germany and retained by the Three Powers under the Conventions, and with the further exception of disputes concerning certain specified sections of the Conventions. The Arbitration Tribunal, which will not be established until a dispute within its jurisdiction actually arises and proves incapable of settlement by negotiation, will consist of nine members, three appointed by the Federal Republic, one by each of the Three Powers, and three "neutral" members (who must not be nationals of any of the signatory states and will act as President and Vice-Presidents), appointed by the Three Powers and the Federal Republic jointly. . . .

AD HOC TRIBUNALS

The older practice of choosing as a sole arbitrator the head of a third state, in the knowledge that he would, in fact, be guided by the advice of his ministers or of jurists and other experts as he saw fit, is unlikely to commend itself to disputing states today. In modern practice an arbitrator is expected to give a decision on his personal and undivided responsibility. Since this is so, it is only rarely that states are willing to place the entire responsibility for a decision upon the shoulders of one man.

The collegiate court, consisting of a national member appointed by each party and an uneven number of "neutral" members, not nationals of either of the parties and appointed by agreement between the parties or by an outside authority, is the normal form in present-day practice. The pattern was set in the great arbitrations in the last three decades of the nineteenth century, confirmed by the Hague Conventions of 1899 and 1907, and again by the General Act for the Pacific Settlement of International Disputes of 1928, the Revised General Act of 1949 and the European Convention for the Peaceful Settlement of Disputes.

In a tribunal constituted on this pattern the determination of the number of "neutral" members and their selection are of crucial importance. Not only will the presidency go to a "neutral" member, but it is also a fair working assumption that the two national members of the tribunal will disagree, and that the decision will, in effect, be that of the "neutral" member or members. When large issues have arisen between states, there may be reluctance to entrust the effective decision to one "neutral" member. The tribunal of three "neutral" members offers the advantages of shared responsibility for the effective decision of large issues and detached consideration of the merits by several minds, and is the more usual form.

Recent public arbitrations. Arbitral tribunals have been used to settle disputes between nations in the last few decades, though private commercial arbitration is much more common. The following is a summary of some recent awards in public arbitrations that were recorded in the International Law Reports series, the International Arbitration Reports, or the Reports of International Arbitral Awards.

Date	Parties	Issue
February 1968	India/Pakistan	Determination of land boundry (Rann of Kutch case)
January 1972	Greece/Federal Republic of Germany	Settlement of war debts
February 1977	Argentina/Chile	Determination of maritime boundary (Beagle Channel)
June 1977	United Kingdom/France	Determination of continental shelf boundry
March 1978	United Kingdom/France	Interpretation of above decision
December 1978	United States/France	Interpretation of Air Services Agreement
May 1980	Belgium et al./Federal Republic of Germany	Interpretation of Agreement on German external debts
February 1985	Guinea/Guinea-Bissau	Maritime boundary delimitation
July 1986	Canada/France	Fish processing within the Gulf of St. Lawrence
September 1988	Egypt/Israel	Boundary dispute
April 1990	France/New Zealand	Return of two Frenchmen who bombed Greenpeace ship
January 1992	United States/Chile	Assassination of Orlando Letelier
November 1992	United States/United Kingdom	User fees at Heathrow Airport
October 1994	Argentina/Chile	Determination of land boundary (Laguna del Desierto Arbitration)
February 1997	Republika Srpska/ Federation of Bosnia and Herzegovina	Implementation of the Dayton Accords
October 1998	State of Eritrea/Republic of Yemen	Territorial sovereignty and maritime boundaries

2. *Arbitration: How It Works and Common Pitfalls*

The following excerpt by Gary Born provides a sense of how arbitration works and what common pitfalls need to be avoided. In addition to addressing the advantages and disadvantages of arbitration, the excerpt also provides an introduction to leading arbitral institutions and rules. Although the focus is on international commercial arbitration, states or state-owned entities are often parties in these arbitrations, and the procedures and enforcement methods discussed here are often relevant to public international arbitrations.

Gary Born, International Commercial Arbitration: Commentary and Materials

1-26 (2d ed. 2001)

A. WHAT IS INTERNATIONAL ARBITRATION?

International arbitration is a means by which international disputes can be definitively resolved, pursuant to the parties' agreement, by independent, non-governmental decision-makers. There are almost as many other definitions of international arbitration as there are commentators on the subject.

1. Defining Characteristics of Commercial Arbitration

Commercial arbitration is common in both international and domestic contexts. In each, it has several defining characteristics. First, arbitration is generally *consensual*— in most cases, the parties must agree to arbitrate their differences. Second, arbitrations are resolved by *non-governmental decision-makers*— arbitrators do not act as state judges or government agents, but are private persons ordinarily selected by the parties. Third, arbitration produces a *binding award*, which is capable of enforcement through national courts — not a mediator's or conciliator's non-binding recommendation. Finally, arbitration is comparatively *flexible*, as contrasted to most court procedures. . . .

3. Legal Framework for International Commercial Arbitration

Although international arbitration is a consensual means of dispute resolution, it has binding effect only by virtue of a complex framework of national and international law. As we discuss below, international conventions, national arbitration legislation, and institutional arbitration rules provide a specialized legal regime for most international arbitrations. This legal regime enhances the enforceability of both arbitration agreements and arbitral awards, and seeks to insulate the arbitral process from interference by national courts or other governmental authorities.

On the most universal level, the United Nations Convention on Recognition and Enforcement of Foreign Arbitral Awards (the "New York Convention") has been ratified by more than 120 nations, including all significant trading states and most major developing states. The Convention obliges member states to recognize and enforce both international commercial arbitration agreements and awards, subject to limited exceptions. Other international conventions impose comparable obligations on member states with respect to particular categories of disputes or with respect to particular bilateral or regional relationships.

In addition, most developed trading states (and many other countries) have enacted national arbitration legislation that provides for the enforcement of international arbitration agreements and awards, that limits judicial interference in the arbitration process, and that authorises specified judicial support for the arbitral process. National arbitration legislation typically affirms the capacity of parties to enter into valid and binding agreements to arbitrate future commercial disputes, provides mechanisms for the enforcement of such arbitration agreements (through orders to stay litigation or (less frequently) to compel arbitration), and requires the recognition and enforcement of arbitration awards. In addition, most modern arbitration legislation narrowly limits the power of national courts to interfere in the arbitration process, either when arbitral proceedings are pending or in reviewing ultimate arbitration awards. In many cases, national arbitration statutes also authorize limited judicial assistance to the arbitral process. This assistance can include selecting arbitrators or arbitral situses, enforcing a tribunal's orders with respect to evidence-taking or discovery, and granting provisional relief in aid of arbitration. . . .

4.   Institutional Arbitration Rules

International commercial arbitration frequently occurs pursuant to institutional arbitration rules, which are often incorporated by reference into parties' arbitration agreements. The leading international arbitration institutions include the International Chamber of Commerce, the London Court of International Arbitration, and the American Arbitration Association, each of which has adopted its own set of rules governing the procedural aspects of arbitration.* These institutions, as well as another several dozen or so less widely-known bodies, supervise international arbitrations when parties agree to dispute resolution under their auspices. In addition, the UNCITRAL Commercial Arbitration Rules are widely used in so-called *ad hoc* (or non-institutional) arbitrations.

5.   International Arbitration Agreements

International commercial arbitration is almost always consensual: arbitration generally occurs only pursuant to an arbitration agreement between the parties. Most arbitration agreements are included as standard clauses in commercial contracts, which provide for the arbitration of any dispute relating to the contract that may arise in the future between the parties. It is also possible, although much less common, for parties to an existing dispute to agree to settle that disagreement through arbitration (even where no pre-existing arbitration clause existed).

International arbitration agreements can, and should, address a number of potentially significant issues. These include the situs of the arbitration, the applicable

*Another leading arbitral institution is the International Centre for the Settlement of Investment Disputes (ICSID).—Eds.

institutional or other procedural rules, the method of selecting the arbitrators (or an appointing authority), the number of arbitrators, the applicable substantive law, and the language of the arbitration. A carefully-drafted arbitration agreement can address these (and other) issues, and provide the parties with a relatively efficient dispute resolution mechanism tailored to their particular needs. A poorly-drafted arbitration agreement can plant the seeds for disputes over jurisdiction and other matters, impose unworkable or undesirable procedures, and may be unenforceable.

6. Enforceability of International Arbitration Agreements

Disputes frequently arise over the validity and interpretation of international arbitration agreements. Leading international arbitration conventions and national law provide for the presumptive enforceability of arbitration agreements. Nonetheless, parties may resist enforcement of an international arbitration agreement on both familiar contract law principles and arbitration-specific grounds.

Among other things, the validity of arbitration agreements can ordinarily be challenged under generally-applicable contract law principles for defects in formation, lack of capacity, fraud or fraudulent inducement, unconscionability, illegality, and waiver. All of these grounds raise both substantive issues (i.e., is a particular agreement unconscionable) and choice of law questions (i.e., what law governs the issue of unconscionability). . . .

The enforcement of international arbitration agreements may also be resisted on certain arbitration-specific grounds. Most importantly, under virtually all national laws, certain categories of disputes or claims are "non-arbitrable"— not capable of settlement by arbitration (as opposed to litigation in national courts or before other governmental agencies). The categories of claims that are non-arbitrable vary from country to country, but generally involve claims under statutory protections (e.g., competition or antitrust law, employee or consumer protections, security laws) or matters of public policy. The New York Convention and other international arbitration conventions recognize and permit these non-arbitrability exceptions, at least within limits.

Institutional arbitration rules and national law in most developed jurisdictions (including the United States) recognize the principle that arbitration agreements are "separable" from the underlying contract in which they appear. According to the so-called separability doctrine, an arbitration agreement is presumptively distinct and independent from the parties' underlying contract, and is supported by the separate consideration of the parties' exchange of promises to arbitrate. As a consequence, challenges to the formation, validity, or legality of the underlying contract generally do not affect the validity of the arbitration agreement. The separability doctrine plays an important role in limiting the bases for challenging arbitration agreements before both national courts and arbitral tribunals.

Finally, disputes over the formation, validity or scope of international arbitration agreements present questions of competence and forum selection. Most developed national arbitration statutes and institutional arbitration rules provide that, in certain circumstances and subject to later judicial review, arbitrators may exercise the power to decide disputes over the formation, validity or interpretation of arbitration agreements; this reflects the so-called "competence-competence" or

"*Kompetenz-Kompetenz*" doctrine. Where disputes concerning international arbitration agreements are not decided by arbitral tribunals, questions arise as to which national court is competent to resolve such disputes.

B. AN OVERVIEW OF THE ADVANTAGES AND DISADVANTAGES OF INTERNATIONAL ARBITRATION

The popularity of arbitration as a means for resolving international commercial disputes has increased significantly over the past several decades. This popularity reflects important advantages of international arbitration as a means of resolving international commercial disputes. Despite these advantages, however, international arbitration also has significant shortcomings. These strengths and weaknesses are summarized below.

First, international arbitration is often perceived as ensuring a genuinely neutral decision-maker in disputes between parties from different countries. International disputes inevitably involve the risk of litigation before a national court of one of the parties, which may be biased, parochial, or unattractive for some other reason. Moreover, outside an unfortunately limited number of industrialized nations, local court systems simply lack the competence, experience, resources, and traditions of even-handedness satisfactorily to resolve many international commercial disputes.

International arbitration offers a theoretically competent decision-maker satisfactory to the parties, who is, in principle, independent of either party or any national or international governmental authority. On the other hand, private arbitrators can have financial, personal, or professional relations with one party (or its counsel). . . .

Second, a carefully-drafted arbitration clause generally permits the resolution of disputes between the parties in a single forum pursuant to an agreement that most national courts are bound by international treaty to enforce. This mitigates the expense and uncertainty of multiple judicial proceedings in different national courts.

On the other hand, incomplete or otherwise defective arbitration clauses can result in judicial and arbitral proceedings where the scope or enforceability of the provision, as well as the merits of the parties' dispute, must be litigated. Moreover, even well-drafted arbitration agreements cannot entirely exclude the expense and delay of a litigant determined to confound the arbitral process.

Third, arbitration agreements and arbitral awards are generally (but not always) more easily and reliably enforced in foreign states than forum selection clauses or foreign court judgments. As described elsewhere, some 120 nations have acceded to the New York Convention, which obliges contracting states to enforce arbitration agreements and awards (subject to specified, limited exceptions). In contrast, there are no world-wide treaties relating to either forum selection agreements or judicial judgments. The perceived ease of enforceability of arbitral awards has contributed to fairly substantial voluntary compliance with arbitral awards, although there is little empirical data comparing such compliance with that applicable to judicial judgments.

In some developing and other countries, there has been a perception that international commercial arbitration was developed by, and was biased in favor of,

Western commercial interests. As a consequence, national law in many countries was historically hostile towards international arbitration. . . . In general, this hostility has waned somewhat over the past decade, with many states acceding to the New York Convention and enacting "pro-arbitration" legislation.

Fourth, arbitration tends to be procedurally less formal and rigid than litigation in national courts. As a result, parties have greater freedom to agree on neutral and appropriate procedural rules, set realistic timetables, select technically expert and neutral decision-makers, involve corporate management in dispute-resolution, and the like. On the other hand, the lack of a detailed procedural code or decision-maker with direct coercive authority may permit party misconduct or create opportunities for an even greater range of procedural disputes between the parties.

Fifth, international arbitration typically involves less extensive discovery than is common in litigation in some national courts (particularly common law jurisdictions). This is generally attractive to international businesses because of the attendant reduction in expense, delay, and disclosure of business secrets.

Sixth, international arbitration is usually more confidential than judicial proceedings — as to submissions, evidentiary hearings, and final awards. This protects business and commercial confidences and can facilitate settlement by reducing opportunities and incentives for public posturing. On the other hand, few arbitrations are entirely confidential, with disclosures often occurring by means of judicial enforcement actions, unilateral party action, regulatory inquiries, or otherwise.

Seventh, the existence of an arbitration clause, a workable arbitral procedure, and an experienced arbitral tribunal may create incentives for settlement or amicable conciliation. The cooperative elements that are required to constitute a tribunal and agree upon a procedural framework can sometimes help foster a climate conducive to settlement. . . . On the other hand, where relations are irrevocably soured, the need for some measure of cooperation between the parties in conducting the arbitration can permit party misconduct greatly to impede dispute resolution.

Finally, arbitration is often lauded as a prompt, inexpensive means of dispute resolution. That can sometimes be the case, but international arbitration is also frequently criticized as both slow and expensive. The difficulties in scheduling hearing dates (with busy arbitrators, lawyers, and clients in different countries), the need to agree upon various procedural steps, and other factors often give international arbitrations a fairly stately pace. Nonetheless, national court proceedings are also often slow, and the existence of appellate review (and possible re-trials) introduces additional delays not ordinarily encountered in arbitration.

Likewise, although sometimes advertised on grounds of economy, even its proponents rightly acknowledge that "[i]nternational arbitration is an expensive process." Both private arbitrators (unlike judges) and arbitral institutions (unlike most courts) must be paid by the parties. And there is a perception that some institutional fees, charged for "administrative" services, are unnecessarily high. Nonetheless, these expenses generally will be less than the legal fees and other costs required for lengthy appellate proceedings or (in some jurisdictions) discovery. . . .

. . . At bottom, if generalizations must be made, international arbitration is much like democracy; it is nowhere close to ideal, but it is generally better than the existing alternatives. To those who have experienced it, litigation of complex international disputes in national courts is often distinctly unappealing. Despite the daunting procedural complexities and other uncertainties, arbitration often offers the least ineffective way to finally settle the contentious disputes that arise when international transactions go awry.

C.   AN OVERVIEW OF LEADING INTERNATIONAL ARBITRATION INSTITUTIONS AND RULES

International arbitration can be either "institutional" or "*ad hoc.*" There are important differences between these alternatives.

1.   Institutional Arbitration

A number of organizations, located in different countries, provide institutional arbitration services. As indicated above, the best-known international arbitration institutions are the International Chamber of Commerce ("ICC"), the American Arbitration Association ("AAA"), and the London Court of International Arbitration ("LCIA"). . . .

These (and other) arbitral institutions have promulgated sets of procedural rules that apply where parties have agreed to arbitration pursuant to such rules. Among other things, institutional rules set out the basic procedural framework and timetable for the arbitration process. Institutional rules also typically authorize the host arbitral institution to select arbitrators in particular disputes (that is, to serve as "appointing authority"), to resolve challenges to arbitrators, to designate the place of arbitration, to fix or influence the fees payable to the arbitrators, and (sometimes) to review the arbitrator's awards to reduce the risk of unenforceability on formal grounds. Each arbitral institution has a staff (with the size varying significantly from one institution to another) and a decision-making body. Of course, arbitral institutions charge an administrative fee, which can sometimes be substantial, for rendering these various services; this fee is in addition to compensation paid by the parties to the arbitrators.

It is fundamental that arbitral institutions do not themselves arbitrate the merits of the parties' dispute. This is the responsibility of the particular individuals selected as arbitrators. . . . If parties cannot agree upon an arbitrator, most institutional rules provide that the host institution will act as an "appointing authority," which chooses the arbitrators in the absence of the parties' agreement.

2.   Ad Hoc Arbitration

Ad hoc arbitrations are not conducted under the auspices or supervision of an arbitral institution. Instead, parties simply agree to arbitrate, without designating any institution to administer their arbitration. *Ad hoc* arbitration agreements will often choose an arbitrator or arbitrators, who is to resolve the dispute without institutional supervision or assistance. The parties will sometimes also select a preexisting set of procedural rules designed to govern *ad hoc* arbitrations. For international commercial disputes, the United Nations Commission on International Trade Law ("UNCITRAL") has published a commonly-used set of such rules.

Where *ad hoc* arbitration is chosen, parties usually will (and certainly should) designate an "appointing authority," that will select the arbitrator(s) if the parties cannot agree. If the parties fail to select an appointing authority, then the national arbitration statutes of many nations permit national courts to appoint arbitrators.

3. Relative Advantages and Disadvantages of Institutional and Ad Hoc Arbitration

Both institutional and *ad hoc* arbitration have strengths. Institutional arbitration is conducted according to a standing set of procedural rules and supervised, to a greater or lesser extent, by a professional staff. This reduces the risks of procedural breakdowns, particularly at the beginning of the arbitral process, and of technical defects in the arbitral award. The institution's involvement can be particularly constructive on issues relating to the appointment of arbitrators, the resolution of challenges to arbitrators, and the arbitrators' fees. Less directly, the institution lends its standing to any award that is rendered, which may enhance the likelihood of voluntary compliance and judicial enforcement.

On the other hand, *ad hoc* arbitration is typically more flexible, less expensive (since it avoids sometimes substantial institutional fees), and more confidential than institutional arbitration. Moreover, the growing size and sophistication of the international arbitration bar, and the efficacy of the international legal framework for commercial arbitration, have partially reduced the relative advantages of institutional arbitration. Nonetheless, many experienced international practitioners prefer the more structured, predictable character of institutional arbitration, at least in the absence of unusual circumstances arguing for an *ad hoc* approach.

4. Leading Arbitral Institutions

Different arbitral institutions offer somewhat different products. As noted above, the ICC, the LCIA, and the AAA [Eds. note: and the ICSID] are presently the leading international arbitral institutions. Each of these institutions, as well as several other important international arbitral institutions, is briefly described below.

a. *International Chamber of Commerce International Court of Arbitration*

The ICC's International Court of Arbitration was established in Paris in 1923. The ICC remains the world's leading international commercial arbitration institution, and has less of a national character than any other arbitral institution. Its annual case-load was well above 300 cases per year during the 1980s and early 1990s, and it now exceeds 500 cases per year. Most of these cases are international disputes, many involving very substantial sums. The ICC's case-load involves parties from around the world. . . .

The ICC has promulgated the ICC Rules of Arbitration ("ICC Rules"), which were most recently revised in 1998, as well as the ICC Rules of Optional Conciliation. Under the ICC Rules, the ICC is extensively involved in the administration of individual arbitrations. Among other things, the ICC is responsible for . . . appointing arbitrators if a party defaults or if the parties are unable to agree upon a presiding arbitrator or sole arbitrator; considering challenges to the independence of arbitrators; . . . reviewing a tribunal's award for formal defects, and fixing the arbitrator's compensation.

The ICC's International Court of Arbitration ("ICC Court") is responsible for most significant administrative decisions in ICC arbitrations. The ICC Court is not, in fact, a "court," and does not itself decide substantive legal disputes or act as an arbitrator. Rather, the ICC Court acts in a supervisory and appointing capacity under the ICC Rules. . . .

b.   London Court of International Arbitration

The LCIA is, by some accounts, the second most popular European arbitration institution. Its annual caseload, which is increasing, has reached about 50 disputes per year. Founded in 1892, the LCIA has made a determined, and generally successful, effort in recent years to overcome perceptions that it is an exclusively English organization. . . .

The LCIA administers a set of arbitration rules, the London Court of International Arbitration Rules ("LCIA Rules"), which were extensively revised in 1998. . . .

c.   American Arbitration Association

The AAA was founded in 1926 (three years after the ICC) and is based in New York, with nearly 40 regional offices throughout the United States. The AAA is the leading U.S. arbitral institution, and handles what it describes as the largest number of arbitral disputes in the world. It administers more than 60,000 arbitrations or other forms of alternative dispute resolution each year, with specialized rules for numerous different industries. . . . [T]he AAA claims a caseload of some 400 international disputes per year. . . .

Under the 1997 version, the AAA International Arbitration Rules provide the applicable set of AAA arbitration rules in "international" disputes (except where the parties have otherwise agreed). [Eds. note: The AAA amended these rules, effective November 2001.]

Under all versions of AAA rules, the AAA administrative staff plays a less significant supervisory role than does the ICC Secretariat. . . .

Non-U.S. parties are often reluctant to agree to arbitration under AAA rules, fearing parochial predisposition and unfamiliarity with international practice. The AAA is working to overcome this image. In addition to upgrading its approach to selecting arbitrators, the AAA has concentrated the handling of all international cases in an "International Center" in New York, staffed by specialized attorneys with language skills. It remains to be seen how these efforts will be received.

d.   International Center for Settlement of Investment Disputes

The International Center for the Settlement of Investment Disputes ("ICSID") administers arbitrations conducted pursuant to the ICSID Convention. ICSID is located in Washington, D.C., where it operates under World Bank auspices.

[T]he ICSID Convention provides a specialized arbitration regime for certain "investment disputes" between states and foreign investors. Before adopting an ICSID arbitration clause or commencing an ICSID arbitration, care should be taken to ensure that the Convention's jurisdictional limits are satisfied (e.g., that the relevant foreign state has ratified the ICSID Convention and that an "investment dispute" would be involved). If these limits are satisfied, parties must consider whether ICSID arbitration is suitable for their needs. . . .

D. AN INTRODUCTION TO INTERNATIONAL TREATIES AND CONVENTIONS CONCERNING INTERNATIONAL COMMERCIAL ARBITRATION

International businesses and industrialized trading nations have long sought to establish a stable, predictable legal environment in which international commercial arbitrations can be conducted. Because national arbitration laws have historically varied considerably from state to state, substantial uncertainties often attend the enforcement of international arbitral agreements and awards. To reduce these uncertainties, major trading nations have entered into international treaties and conventions designed to facilitate the transnational enforcement of arbitration awards and agreements. . . .

[1.] The New York Convention

. . . [T]he United Nations Convention on the Recognition and Enforcement of Foreign Arbitral Awards, [o]ften referred to as the "New York Convention," . . . is by far the most significant contemporary international agreement relating to commercial arbitration. The New York Convention is reproduced [in the Documentary Supplement].

The Convention was signed in 1958 in New York after lengthy negotiations under U.N. auspices. . . .

The Convention was designed to "encourage the recognition and enforcement of commercial arbitration agreements in international contracts and to unify the standards by which agreements to arbitrate are observed and arbitral awards are enforced in the signatory nations." In broad outline, the Convention: (a) requires national courts to recognize and enforce foreign arbitral awards, subject to specified exceptions; (b) requires national courts to recognize the validity of arbitration agreements, subject to specified exceptions; and (c) requires national courts to refer parties to arbitration when they have entered into a valid agreement to arbitrate that is subject to the Convention. . . .

. . . [T]oday some 120 nations have ratified the Convention. The Convention's parties include all major trading states and many Latin American, African, Asian, Middle Eastern, and former socialist states. . . . In ratifying the Convention, many states have attached reservations that can have significant consequences in private disputes. . . .

In virtually all countries, the New York Convention has been implemented through national legislation. The practical effect of the Convention is therefore dependent on both the content of such national legislation and the interpretation given by national courts to the Convention and national implementing legislation. . . .

An important aim of the Convention's drafters was uniformity: they sought to establish a single, stable set of international legal rules for the enforcement of arbitral agreements and awards. The fulfilment of that aim is dependent upon the willingness of national legislatures and courts, in different signatory states, to adopt uniform interpretations of the Convention. In general, however, national courts have performed adequately, but no better, in arriving at uniform interpretations of the Convention.

[2.] The Inter-American Convention on International Commercial Arbitration

. . . South American states were very reluctant to ratify the New York Convention, for the most part only beginning to do so in the 1980s.

. . . [I]n 1975 the United States and most South American nations negotiated the Inter-American Convention on International Commercial Arbitration, also known as the "Panama Convention." The United States ratified the Convention in 1990; other parties include Mexico, Venezuela, Columbia, Chile, Ecuador, Peru, Costa Rica, El Salvador, Guatemala, Honduras, Panama, Paraguay, and Uruguay. The Inter-American Convention is similar to the New York Convention in many respects. Among other things, it provides for the general enforceability of arbitration agreements and arbitral awards, subject to specified exceptions similar to those in the New York Convention. . . .

[3.] The ICSID Convention

The International Center for the Settlement of Investment Disputes ("ICSID") is a specialized arbitration institution, established pursuant to the so-called "Washington Convention" of 1965. ICSID was established at the initiative of the International Bank for Reconstruction and Development, and is based at the World Bank's Washington headquarters.

The ICSID Convention is designed to facilitate the settlement of a limited range of "investment disputes" that the parties have specifically agreed to submit to ICSID. Investment disputes are defined as controversies that arise out of an "investment" and involve a signatory state or designated state entity . . . and a national of another signatory state. As to such disputes, the Convention provides both conciliation and arbitration procedures.

The Convention contains a number of unusual provisions relating to international arbitration. First, the Convention provides that, absent agreement by the parties, ICSID arbitrations are governed by the law of the state that is party to the dispute (including its conflicts rules) "and such rules of international law as may be applicable." In contrast, neither the New York nor Panama Conventions contains comparable substantive choice of law provisions.

Second, ICSID awards are theoretically directly enforceable in signatory states, without any method of review in national courts. There has thus far been very little experience with judicial enforcement of ICSID awards.

Third, when a party challenges an ICSID award, the Convention empowers the Chairman of the Administrative Council of ICSID to appoint an *ad hoc* committee to review, and possibly annul, awards; if an award is annulled it may be resubmitted to a new arbitral tribunal. The ICSID annulment mechanism has been vigorously criticized, on the grounds that it permits politicized appellate review.

Nearly 100 countries, from all geographical regions of the world, have ratified the ICSID Convention. Until relatively recently, however, relatively few cases had been brought under the Convention. ICSID's caseload is gradually increasing, particularly as a consequence of arbitrations brought pursuant to bilateral investment treaties or investment protection legislation.

Unfortunately, the prospects for greatly-increased usage of the ICSID Convention have been threatened by the annulment of several ICSID awards by *ad hoc* panels assigned to review awards. . . .

[4.] Iran-United States Claims Tribunal

The Iran-United States Claims Tribunal is one of the most ambitious international claims commissions. The Tribunal was established pursuant to the so-called Algiers Accords [of 1981], which resolved some of the legal disputes arising from the Iranian seizure of U.S. hostages during President Carter's administration. Pursuant to the Accords, litigation in national courts concerning defined claims between U.S. and Iranian entities was suspended. A nine-person tribunal was established in the Hague, with defined jurisdiction over claims arising from U.S.-Iran hostilities; three tribunal members were appointed by the United States, three by Iran, and three from other states. The tribunal adopted the UNCITRAL Arbitration Rules (with some modifications) and has issued a substantial number of decisions (many of which are published).

[5.] Bilateral Investment Treaties or Investment Protection Agreements

Bilateral investment treaties ("BITs") or investment protection agreements ("IPAs") became common during the 1980s and 1990s, as a means of encouraging capital investment in developing markets. Capital-exporting states (including the United States, most Western European states, and Japan) have entered into numerous BITs or IPAs with countries in developing regions. A recent tally indicated that more than 1,300 BITS are presently operative.

Many BITs contain provisions dealing with the enforceability of international arbitration agreements and awards. In addition, some BITs contain provisions which permit foreign investors to require international arbitration of certain categories of disputes — including in the absence of an arbitration agreement in the contract(s) giving rise to the dispute. The possibility of "arbitration without privity" is an important option in some international commercial disputes, which counsels careful attention to applicable BITs.

Notes and Questions

1. There were 133 parties to the New York Convention on the Recognition and Enforcement of Foreign Arbitral Awards (New York Convention), as of January

2003. It is easily the most-used convention dealing with the recognition and enforcement stage of these awards. For more information on the New York Convention, visit the following Web site at <http://www.jus.uio.no/lm/un. conventions. membership.status/index.html>. See also the U.N. Web site at <http://untreaty. un.org>.

2. The ICSID Convention had been ratified by 136 countries as of January 2003. The Centre had 46 cases pending and 68 cases that had been concluded. The Centre's Web site is at <http://www.worldbank.org/icsid>.

3. In 1997, the International Chamber of Commerce (ICC) adopted amended rules, effective in 1998. (Excerpts of the amended rules are in the Documentary Supplement.) The ICC's Web site is at <http://www.iccwbo.org>.

The international arbitration business continues to boom at the ICC. Its Secretariat received 566 new arbitration requests in 2001, on top of the about 1,000 cases that were still pending at the end of 2000. During 2001, 1,492 parties from 116 different countries were involved. Of the new cases filed in 2000 with the ICC, 54 percent concerned goods contracts, 16 percent involved service contracts, 15 percent involved business structure contracts, 5 percent covered intellectual property disputes, and 10 percent concerned other issues.

In 2000, less than 50 percent of the parties involved in the new cases were from Western Europe. Parties from Asia and North America each separately represented roughly 15 percent of the total number of parties before the ICC. As for the amounts in dispute, about 61 percent of all cases were for $10 million dollars or less, with 38 percent of all new cases falling between $1 million and $10 million. About 51 percent of the new cases involved three arbitrators, and 40 percent had one arbitrator.

4. Business is also flourishing at the American Arbitration Association (AAA). Its cases are primarily domestic, but the AAA is expanding its international efforts, having established a new International Center for Dispute Resolution in 1996. From 1996 to 2000, the AAA received 1939 new international cases. Of these new cases, 510 were received in 2000.

The AAA amended its International Arbitration Rules, effective November 2001. The text can be found at the AAA's Web site: <http://www.adr.org>.

5. In recent years there has been a significant growth in the number of international commercial arbitrations in Asia. The globalization of Asian economies has led to more commercial arbitrations and stronger commercial dispute-resolution systems. For a discussion of the recent development of Asian-based arbitration, see Phillip McConnaughay, International Commercial Arbitration in Asia, Juris Press, December 2001.

6. What do you see as the advantages and disadvantages of international arbitration? In what kinds of disputes where at least one country is involved do you think it is most advantageous? In national security issues between two countries? In trade disputes between two countries? In an investment dispute between a country and a foreign private investor? Do you think the public visibility of a particular dispute or the monetary amount involved might affect the decision whether or not to arbitrate? Why, for example, do you believe that the Iran-United States Claims Tribunal has functioned in a reasonably satisfactory manner?

7. Should the U.S. government or another country's government want to allow potential private claims under that country's securities or antitrust laws to be settled by arbitration? Would the policies served by those laws be more aggressively

enforced by an international arbitrator or a judge in that country? What are the policies behind arbitration? How would you balance any conflicting policies?

8. Until the Arbitration Act of 1979, the United Kingdom permitted its courts to intervene in international arbitration carried out within its borders, and to rule on particular questions of law that might arise during arbitration. Did such judicial intervention make arbitration a more or less appealing alternative to other forms of dispute resolution?

Problem. You are the general counsel to Modern Copper, Inc. (MCI). MCI wants to invest $500 million in Chile to develop new copper mines. MCI, however, is cautious about making the investment, partly because of past expropriations of U.S. investment by Chile. As a result, MCI will take a number of actions to minimize its exposure — such as adding politically influential Chilean investors, borrowing heavily from U.S. and foreign banks, planning to locate its processing and fabricating plants in other countries, and purchasing insurance against expropriation. Nevertheless, MCI will have some of its own money tied up in the investment and is not fully protected from an expropriation.

In the negotiations between MCI and the Chilean government, Chile has refused to agree to allow disputes over the investment to be heard by U.S. courts or to have U.S. law apply. MCI does not want to rely for protection on the Chilean courts or Chilean law.

The president of MCI asks you to draft arbitration provisions that would protect MCI in case Chile tries to expropriate MCI's new copper mines. The president says she does not need the exact legal language now, but she would like to have a clear statement of the key provisions that should be included if MCI is to be adequately protected. She notes that the proposed provisions must be ones that MCI could reasonably try to get the Chilean government to accept. She also says that you should explain the rationale for the proposals.

3. *Judicial Attitudes Toward International Arbitration*

An article by Robert von Mehren provides a brief historical survey of judicial attitudes toward international arbitration. Following that is the U.S. Supreme Court's 1985 landmark opinion in Mitsubishi Motors v. Soler Chrysler-Plymouth, which provides an authoritative statement on the attitude of the U.S. judiciary toward international arbitration.

Arthur T. Von Mehren, From *Vynior's Case* to *Mitsubishi:* The Future of Arbitration and Public Law

12 Brooklyn J. Intl. L. 583 (1986)

B. UNITED STATES . . .

1. Judicial Attitudes Toward Arbitration: 1776-1920

From the early nineteenth century, the Supreme Court pursued a policy of enforcing arbitral awards rendered before a judicial proceeding was commenced.

An arbitration that was judged to be the product of collusion to defraud a ship's owners was, as would be expected, set aside, but in another case the Supreme Court assumed a position that would later shape the distinctive American statutory scheme for arbitration when it gave wide latitude not only to an arbitrator's findings of fact but also to his conclusions of law.[38] Arbitration, the Court said, should receive judicial encouragement and courts should not set aside arbitral awards for mistakes of law or of fact, so long as the award represents the "honest decision, of the arbitrators, after a full and fair hearing of the parties" and conforms to the terms of the arbitration agreement.

The positive attitude of the Supreme Court and of the state and lower federal courts, however, did not extend to clauses in agreements that mandated arbitration for future disputes under a contract. These courts simply assumed that such clauses were revocable and non-enforceable. Thus, in 1874, the Supreme Court relied on the principle of the non-enforceability of agreements to arbitrate future disputes. . . .[40] "Every citizen," the Court wrote, "is entitled to resort to all the courts of the country, and to invoke the protection which all the laws or all those courts may afford him." In a civil case, a party "may submit his *particular* suit by his own consent to an arbitration, or to the decision of a single judge." But a party "cannot . . . bind himself in advance by an agreement, which may be specifically enforced, thus to forfeit his rights at all times and on all occasions, whenever the case may be presented." Thus, although by agreement the parties to a present dispute could "oust" the courts from jurisdiction over the controversy, they could not do so in advance of the dispute. . . . It was left first to some state legislatures such as New York and then to the Congress[51] to overrule the common law courts' reluctance to give full effect to executory agreements for arbitration.

The Federal Arbitration Act was passed in 1925, to enhance "the great value of voluntary arbitrations" as well as "the practical justice in the enforced arbitration of disputes where written agreements for that purpose have been voluntarily and solemnly entered into." The Act allows both a stay of court proceedings when the issue involved in such a suit should be referred to arbitration by terms of an agreement as well as specific enforcement of a written arbitration clause in maritime contracts and contracts bearing on interstate or foreign commerce. Furthermore the Act provides some gap-filling power, judicial authority to compel the attendance of witnesses and a limited set of bases for overturning an award at the enforcement stage consistent with the policy enunciated as long ago as Karthaus v. Yllas y Ferrer of giving "every reasonable intendment" to uphold the award. . . . The statutory reform produced such a change of attitude toward arbitration agreements that in 1967 the Supreme Court ruled that an agreement to arbitrate precludes judicial cognizance before arbitration, even of a claim that the contract of which the arbitration clause is a part was fraudulently induced.

The old argument against ousting courts from their jurisdiction was briefly revived in a 1970 case involving judicial enforcement of the forum selection clause in

---

38. Burchell v. Marsh, 58 U.S. (17 How.) 344, 350 (1854). Here the Court commented, "[c]ourts should be careful to avoid a wrong use of the word 'mistake,' and, by making it synonymous with mere error of judgment, assume to themselves an arbitrary power over awards." Id.

40. Insurance Company v. Morse, 87 U.S. 445, 450 (1874).

51. See U.S. Arbitration Act, 9 U.S.C. §§1-14 (1982). The Act was first enacted in 1925, at 93 Stat. 883.

an international contract for the towing by a German corporation of an American drilling barge from the United States to Italy.[62] Relying on an earlier case that assumed the traditional association of "agreements in advance of controversy" with agreements to oust courts of their jurisdiction, the Court of Appeals for the Fifth Circuit ordered the German company to stay the proceedings it had commenced in England pursuant to the forum selection clause in the towage contract and to bring all claims before the American court. The Supreme Court reversed.[65] Chief Justice Burger characterized the "ouster" argument as "hardly more than a vestigial legal fiction" . . . :

> No one seriously contends in this case that the forum-selection clause "ousted" the District Court of jurisdiction over [the American company's] action. The threshold question is whether that court should have exercised its jurisdiction to do more than give effect to the legitimate expectations of the parties, manifested in their freely negotiated agreement, by specifically enforcing the forum clause.

Citing "compelling reasons why a freely negotiated private international agreement, unaffected by fraud, undue influence, or overweening bargaining power . . . should be given full effect," the Court concluded that courts should specifically enforce forum clauses.

The Court's decision in *The Bremen* came fast on the heels of the United States' ratification of the New York Convention on the Recognition and Enforcement of Foreign Arbitral Awards. In *The Bremen* the court supported judicial deference to private international agreements that choose the courts of one state over other states with equally valid claims to jurisdiction over a contractual dispute. As a result, the Court provided the foundation for a generous and unstinting construction of the Convention's requirement, under Article II-3, that the courts of contracting states, when seized of an action in a matter governed by an arbitration agreement, "at the request of one of the parties, [shall] refer the parties to arbitration, unless it finds that the said agreement is null and void, inoperative or incapable of being performed." [The Convention is in the Documentary Supplement.]

C. OTHER LEGAL TRADITIONS

Arbitration has become a welcome method of resolving disputes in almost all the legal systems of the world. In many countries, arbitration was actively practiced in the pre-industrial stages of social organization.

In France, the revolution of 1787 ushered in a period of extraordinary hospitality to arbitration as an alternative to the courts which were associated with the *ancien regime*. When first promulgated, the French Code of Civil Procedure contained provisions for the submission to arbitration of existing disputes only, but agreements for the arbitration of future disputes were viewed favorably by the courts in the early decades of the nineteenth century.

This attitude changed dramatically, however, in 1843, when the Court of Cassation, on the basis of a narrow construction of the French Code of Civil Procedure, showed . . . zeal for protecting the jurisdiction of the civil courts . . . and held arbitration clauses to be unenforceable unless specifically allowed by law.

---

62. Zapata Off-Shore Co. v. M/S Bremen, 428 F.2d 888 (th Cir. 1970), *aff'd on reh'g*, 446 F.2d 907 (5th Cir. 1971), *cert. granted sub. nom.*, The Bremen v. Zapata Off-Shore Co., 407 U.S. 1 (1972).
65. *The Bremen*, 407 U.S. 1.

Germany, meanwhile, developed a more positive appraisal of arbitration; the 1877 German Code of Civil Procedure established a liberal regime for arbitration whether by submission or by prospective agreement. The French Court of Cassation adopted a policy of upholding arbitration agreements around the turn of the century and the French Commercial Code was amended in 1925 to allow arbitration of disputes by prospective agreement in many business transactions. . . .

With the quickening pace of commercial activity after World War II, many countries adopted new measures to regularize and facilitate arbitration proceedings. In France, Book IV of the New Code of Civil Procedure, promulgated in 1981, established rules for domestic and international arbitration. The New Code specifically requires courts to decline jurisdiction over any cases which have been or could be submitted to an arbitral tribunal unless the court decides that the agreement to arbitrate is "manifestly null." The Code now makes judicial assistance available on an expedited basis, should difficulties arise in constituting an arbitral tribunal. In domestic cases, arbitrators are given broad procedural freedom so long as "the guiding principles of litigation" are observed, while in international cases arbitrators are able to select procedural rules from any legal source. . . .

D. TRENDS REGARDING THE DOMAIN OF ARBITRATION

Conceived largely as forums for the resolution of disputes under private law, arbitral panels are increasingly being asked to consider claims that involve substantial issues of public law and policy. As arbitration becomes a broadly sanctioned and even favored method of dispute resolution the world over, the question of the range of legal issues that may be submitted to arbitral settlement becomes more pressing. . . .

Issues arising under three areas of American public law — bankruptcy, securities trading, and antitrust — have engendered considerable litigation and debate in the context of arbitration. In all three areas, the American courts had traditionally restricted the authority of arbitrators. . . .

In the United States, however, the rise of international arbitration has limited the range of these traditional public policy exceptions to the arbitrability of disputes and even has cast doubt on their continuing validity. . . . In Scherk v. Alberto-Culver Co., the Supreme Court declined to extend the public policy exception on the arbitrability of claims under the Securities Act of 1933 to international arbitration of claims under the Securities Exchange Act of 1934. And finally, in Mitsubishi Motors Corp. v. Soler Chrysler-Plymouth, Inc., the Supreme Court held that a party to an international agreement with a general executory arbitration clause may not seek the aid of the federal courts for relief in a claim under the antitrust laws but must submit the claims to an arbitral tribunal. . . .

Mitsubishi Motors Corp. v. Soler Chrysler-Plymouth

U.S. Supreme Court
473 U.S. 614 (1985)

Blackmun, J., delivered the opinion of the Court, in which Burger, C.J., and White, Rehnquist, and O'Connor, J.J., joined. Stevens, J., filed a dissenting opinion, in which Brennan, J., joined, and in which Marshall, J., joined except as to Part II. Powell, J., took no part in the decision of the cases.

Justice BLACKMUN delivered the opinion of the Court.

The principal question presented by these cases is the arbitrability, pursuant to the Federal Arbitration Act, 9 U.S.C. §1 et seq., and the Convention on the Recognition and Enforcement of Foreign Arbitral Awards (Convention), of claims arising under the Sherman Act, 15 U.S.C. §1 et seq., and encompassed within a valid arbitration clause in an agreement embodying an international commercial transaction.

I

Petitioner-cross-respondent Mitsubishi Motors Corporation (Mitsubishi) is a Japanese corporation which manufactures automobiles and has its principal place of business in Tokyo, Japan. Mitsubishi is the product of a joint venture between, on the one hand, Chrysler International, S.A. (CISA), a Swiss corporation . . . wholly owned by Chrysler Corporation, and, on the other, Mitsubishi Heavy Industries, Inc., a Japanese corporation. The aim of the joint venture was the distribution through Chrysler dealers outside the continental United States of vehicles manufactured by Mitsubishi and bearing Chrysler and Mitsubishi trademarks. Respondent-cross-petitioner Soler Chrysler-Plymouth, Inc. (Soler), is a Puerto Rico corporation with its principal place of business in . . . Puerto Rico.

On October 31, 1979, Soler entered into a Distributor Agreement with CISA which provided for the sale by Soler of Mitsubishi-manufactured vehicles within a designated area, including metropolitan San Juan. On the same date, CISA, Soler, and Mitsubishi entered into a Sales Procedure Agreement (Sales Agreement) which . . . provided for the direct sale of Mitsubishi products to Soler and governed the terms and conditions of such sales. Paragraph VI of the Sales Agreement, labeled "Arbitration of Certain Matters," provides:

> All disputes, controversies or differences which may arise between [Mitsubishi] and [Soler] out of or in relation to Articles I-B through V of this Agreement or for the breach thereof, shall be finally settled by arbitration in Japan in accordance with the rules and regulations of the Japan Commercial Arbitration Association.

Initially, Soler did a brisk business in Mitsubishi-manufactured vehicles. As a result of its strong performance, its minimum sales volume, specified by Mitsubishi and CISA, and agreed to by Soler, for the 1981 model year was substantially increased. In early 1981, however, the new-car market slackened. Soler ran into serious difficulties in meeting the expected sales volume, and by the spring of 1981 it felt itself compelled to request that Mitsubishi delay or cancel shipment of several orders. About the same time, Soler attempted to arrange for the transshipment of a quantity of its vehicles for sale in the continental United States and Latin America. Mitsubishi and CISA, however, refused permission for any such diversion, citing a variety of reasons, and no vehicles were transshipped. Attempts to work out these difficulties failed. Mitsubishi eventually withheld shipment of 966 vehicles, apparently representing orders placed for May, June, and July 1981 production, responsibility for which Soler disclaimed in February 1982.

The following month, Mitsubishi brought an action against Soler in the United States District Court for the District of Puerto Rico under the Federal Arbitration Act and the Convention.[2] Mitsubishi sought an order, pursuant to 9 U.S.C. §§4 and 201,[3] to compel arbitration in accord with ¶VI of the Sales Agreement. Shortly after filing the complaint, Mitsubishi filed a request for arbitration before the Japan Commercial Arbitration Association.

Soler denied the allegations and counterclaimed against both Mitsubishi and CISA. It alleged numerous breaches by Mitsubishi of the Sales Agreement,[5] raised a pair of defamation claims, and asserted causes of action under the Sherman Act. In the counterclaim premised on the Sherman Act, Soler alleged that Mitsubishi and CISA had conspired to divide markets in restraint of trade. To effectuate the plan, according to Soler, Mitsubishi had refused to permit Soler to resell to buyers in North, Central, or South America vehicles it had obligated itself to purchase from Mitsubishi; had refused to ship ordered vehicles or the parts, such as heaters and defoggers, that would be necessary to permit Soler to make its vehicles suitable for resale outside Puerto Rico; and had coercively attempted to replace Soler and its other Puerto Rico distributors with a wholly owned subsidiary which would serve as the exclusive Mitsubishi distributor in Puerto Rico.

After a hearing, the District Court ordered Mitsubishi and Soler to arbitrate . . . the federal antitrust issues[. I]t recognized that the Courts of Appeals, following American Safety Equipment Corp. v. J.P. Maguire & Co., 391 F.2d 821 (CA2 1968), uniformly had held that the rights conferred by the antitrust laws were " 'of a character inappropriate for enforcement by arbitration.' " Wilko v. Swan, 201 F.2d 439, 444 (CA2 1953), *rev'd,* 346 U.S. 427 (1953). The District Court held, however, that the international character of the Mitsubishi-Soler undertaking required enforcement of the agreement to arbitrate even as to the antitrust claims. It relied on Scherk v. Alberto-Culver Co., 417 U.S. 506, 515-520 (1974), in which this Court ordered arbitration, pursuant to a provision embodied in an international agreement, of a claim arising under the Securities Exchange Act of 1934. . . .

The United States Court of Appeals for the First Circuit affirmed in part and reversed in part. . . .

2. The complaint alleged that Soler had failed to pay for 966 ordered vehicles; that it had failed to pay contractual "distress unit penalties," intended to reimburse Mitsubishi for storage costs and interest charges incurred because of Soler's failure to take shipment of ordered vehicles; that Soler's failure to fulfill warranty obligations threatened Mitsubishi's reputation and goodwill; that Soler had failed to obtain required financing; and that the Distributor and Sales Agreements had expired by their terms or, alternatively, that Soler had surrendered its rights under the Sales Agreement.

3. . . . Section 201 provides: "The Convention on the Recognition and Enforcement of Foreign Arbitral Awards of June 10, 1958, shall be enforced in United States courts in accordance with this chapter." Article II of the Convention, in turn, provides:

1. Each Contracting State shall recognize an agreement in writing under which the parties undertake to submit to arbitration all or any differences which have arisen or which may arise between them in respect of a defined legal relationship, whether contractual or not, concerning a subject matter capable of settlement by arbitration. . . .

3. The court of a Contracting State, when seized of an action in a matter in respect of which the parties have made an agreement within the meaning of this article, shall, at the request of one of the parties, refer the parties to arbitration, unless it finds that the said agreement is null and void, inoperative or incapable of being performed.

5. The alleged breaches included wrongful refusal to ship ordered vehicles and necessary parts, failure to make payment for warranty work and authorized rebates, and bad faith in establishing minimum sales volumes.

. . . [A]fter endorsing the doctrine of *American Safety,* precluding arbitration of antitrust claims, the Court of Appeals concluded that neither this Court's decision in *Scherk* nor the Convention required abandonment of that doctrine in the face of an international transaction. Accordingly, it reversed the judgment of the District Court insofar as it had ordered submission of "Soler's antitrust claims" to arbitration. Affirming the remainder of the judgment, the court directed the District Court to consider in the first instance how the parallel judicial and arbitral proceedings should go forward.

We granted certiorari primarily to consider whether an American court should enforce an agreement to resolve antitrust claims by arbitration when that agreement arises from an international transaction.

II

At the outset, we address the contention . . . that the arbitration clause at issue may not be read to encompass the statutory counterclaims stated in its answer to the complaint. . . .

. . . By agreeing to arbitrate a statutory claim, a party does not forgo the substantive rights afforded by the statute; it only submits to their resolution in an arbitral, rather than a judicial, forum. It trades the procedures and opportunity for review of the courtroom for the simplicity, informality, and expedition of arbitration. We must assume that if Congress intended the substantive protection afforded by a given statute to include protection against waiver of the right to a judicial forum, that intention will be deducible from text or legislative history. Having made the bargain to arbitrate, the party should be held to it unless Congress itself has evinced an intention to preclude a waiver of judicial remedies for the statutory rights at issue. Nothing, in the meantime, prevents a party from excluding statutory claims from the scope of an agreement to arbitrate.

In sum, the Court of Appeals correctly conducted a two-step inquiry, first determining whether the parties' agreement to arbitrate reached the statutory issues, and then, upon finding it did, considering whether legal constraints external to the parties' agreement foreclosed the arbitration of those claims.

III

We now turn to consider whether Soler's antitrust claims are nonarbitrable even though it has agreed to arbitrate them. . . . As in Scherk v. Alberto-Culver Co., 417 U.S. 506 (1974), we conclude that concerns of international comity, respect for the capacities of foreign and transnational tribunals, and sensitivity to the need of the international commercial system for predictability in the resolution of disputes require that we enforce the parties' agreement, even assuming that a contrary result would be forthcoming in a domestic context.

Even before *Scherk,* this Court had recognized the utility of forum-selection clauses in international transactions. In [The Bremen v. Zapata Off-Shore Co., 407 U.S. 1 (1972)], an American oil company, seeking to evade a contractual choice of an English forum and, by implication, English law, filed a suit in admiralty in a

United States District Court against the German corporation which had contracted to tow its rig to a location in the Adriatic Sea. Notwithstanding the possibility that the English court would enforce provisions in the towage contract exculpating the German party which an American court would refuse to enforce, this Court gave effect to the choice-of-forum clause. It observed:

> The expansion of American business and industry will hardly be encouraged if, notwithstanding solemn contracts, we insist on a parochial concept that all disputes must be resolved under our laws and in our courts. . . . We cannot have trade and commerce in world markets and international waters exclusively on our terms, governed by our laws, and resolved in our courts. 407 U.S., at 9.

Recognizing that "agreeing in advance on a forum acceptable to both parties is an indispensable element in international trade, commerce, and contracting," the decision in *The Bremen* clearly eschewed a provincial solicitude for the jurisdiction of domestic forums.

Identical considerations governed the Court's decision in Scherk, which categorized "[a]n agreement to arbitrate before a specified tribunal [as], in effect, a specialized kind of forum-selection clause that posits not only the situs of suit but also the procedure to be used in resolving the dispute." In *Scherk*, the American company Alberto-Culver purchased several interrelated business enterprises, organized under the laws of Germany and Liechtenstein, as well as the rights held by those enterprises in certain trademarks, from a German citizen who at the time of trial resided in Switzerland. Although the contract of sale contained a clause providing for arbitration before the International Chamber of Commerce in Paris of "any controversy or claim [arising] out of this agreement or the breach thereof," Alberto-Culver subsequently brought suit against Scherk in a Federal District Court in Illinois, alleging that Scherk had violated §10(b) of the Securities Exchange Act of 1934 by fraudulently misrepresenting the status of the trademarks as unencumbered. . . . This Court [enforced] the arbitration agreement even while assuming for purposes of the decision that the controversy would be nonarbitrable under the holding of *Wilko* had it arisen out of a domestic transaction. Again, the Court emphasized:

> A contractual provision specifying in advance the forum in which disputes shall be litigated and the law to be applied is . . . an almost indispensable precondition to achievement of the orderliness and predictability essential to any international business transaction. . . .
>
> A parochial refusal by the courts of one country to enforce an international arbitration agreement would not only frustrate these purposes, but would invite unseemly and mutually destructive jockeying by the parties to secure tactical litigation advantages. . . . [It would] damage the fabric of international commerce and trade, and imperil the willingness and ability of businessmen to enter into international commercial agreements.

Accordingly, the Court held Alberto-Culver to its bargain, sending it to the international arbitral tribunal before which it had agreed to seek its remedies.

The Bremen and *Scherk* establish a strong presumption in favor of enforcement of freely negotiated contractual choice-of-forum provisions. Here, as in *Scherk*, that presumption is reinforced by the emphatic federal policy in favor of arbitral dispute resolution. And at least since this Nation's accession in 1970 to the Convention,* and the implementation of the Convention in the same year by amendment of the Federal Arbitration Act,[16] that federal policy applies with special force in the field of international commerce. Thus, we must weigh the concerns of *American Safety* against a strong belief in the efficacy of arbitral procedures for the resolution of international commercial disputes and an equal commitment to the enforcement of freely negotiated choice-of-forum clauses.

At the outset, we confess to some skepticism of certain aspects of the *American Safety* doctrine. As distilled by the First Circuit, the doctrine comprises four ingredients. First, private parties play a pivotal role in aiding governmental enforcement of the antitrust laws by means of the private action for treble damages. Second, "the strong possibility that contracts which generate antitrust disputes may be contracts of adhesion militates against automatic forum determination by contract." Third, antitrust issues, prone to complication, require sophisticated legal and economic analysis, and thus are "ill-adapted to strengths of the arbitral process, i.e., expedition, minimal requirements of written rationale, simplicity, resort to basic concepts of common sense and simple equity." Finally, just as "issues of war and peace are too important to be vested in the generals, . . . decisions as to antitrust regulation of business are too important to be lodged in arbitrators chosen from the business community — particularly those from a foreign community that has had no experience with or exposure to our law and values." See *American Safety,* 391 F.2d, at 826-827.

Initially, we find the second concern unjustified. The mere appearance of an antitrust dispute does not alone warrant invalidation of the selected forum on the undemonstrated assumption that the arbitration clause is tainted. A party resisting arbitration of course may attack directly the validity of the agreement to arbitrate. Moreover, the party may attempt to make a showing that would warrant setting aside the forum-selection clause — that the agreement was "[a]ffected by fraud, undue influence, or overweening bargaining power"; that "enforcement would be unreasonable and unjust"; or that proceedings "in the contractual forum will be so gravely difficult and inconvenient that [the resisting party] will for all practical purposes be deprived of his day in court." But absent such a showing — and none was attempted here — there is no basis for assuming the forum inadequate or its selection unfair.

Next, potential complexity should not suffice to ward off arbitration. . . . The vertical restraints which most frequently give birth to antitrust claims covered by an arbitration agreement will not often occasion the monstrous proceedings that have given antitrust litigation an image of intractability. In any event, adaptability and access to expertise are hallmarks of arbitration. The anticipated subject matter of the dispute may be taken into account when the arbitrators are appointed, and arbitral rules typically provide for the participation of experts either employed by the parties or appointed by the tribunal. Moreover, it is often a judgment that streamlined proceedings and expeditious results will best serve their needs that causes parties to agree to arbitrate their disputes; it is typically a desire to keep the effort and expense required to resolve a dispute within manageable bounds that prompts them

---

*New York Convention on the Recognition and Enforcement of Foreign Arbitral Awards. See the Documentary Supplement — EDS.

16. Act of July 31, 1970, Pub. L. 91-368, 84 Stat. 692, codified at 9 U.S.C. §§201-208.

mutually to forgo access to judicial remedies. In sum, the factor of potential complexity alone does not persuade us that an arbitral tribunal could not properly handle an antitrust matter.

For similar reasons, we also reject the proposition that an arbitration panel will pose too great a danger of innate hostility to the constraints on business conduct that antitrust law imposes. International arbitrators frequently are drawn from the legal as well as the business community; where the dispute has an important legal component, the parties and the arbitral body with whose assistance they have agreed to settle their dispute can be expected to select arbitrators accordingly.[18] We decline to indulge the presumption that the parties and arbitral body conducting a proceeding will be unable or unwilling to retain competent, conscientious, and impartial arbitrators.

We are left, then, with the core of the *American Safety* doctrine — the fundamental importance to American democratic capitalism of the regime of the antitrust laws. Without doubt, the private cause of action plays a central role in enforcing this regime. . . .

The importance of the private damages remedy, however, does not compel the conclusion that it may not be sought outside an American court. Notwithstanding its important incidental policing function, the treble-damages cause of action conferred on private parties by §4 of the Clayton Act, 15 U.S.C. §15, and pursued by Soler here . . . , seeks primarily to enable an injured competitor to gain compensation for that injury.

> Section 4 . . . is in essence a remedial provision. It provides treble damages to "[a]ny person who shall be injured in his business or property by reason of anything forbidden in the antitrust laws. . . ."

. . . And, of course, the antitrust cause of action remains at all times under the control of the individual litigant: no citizen is under an obligation to bring an antitrust suit, and the private antitrust plaintiff needs no executive or judicial approval before settling one. It follows that, at least where the international cast of a transaction would otherwise add an element of uncertainty to dispute resolution, the prospective litigant may provide in advance for a mutually agreeable procedure whereby he would seek his antitrust recovery as well as settle other controversies.

There is no reason to assume at the outset of the dispute that international arbitration will not provide an adequate mechanism. To be sure, the international arbitral tribunal owes no prior allegiance to the legal norms of particular states; hence, it has no direct obligation to vindicate their statutory dictates. The tribunal, however, is bound to effectuate the intentions of the parties. Where the parties have agreed that the arbitral body is to decide a defined set of claims which includes, as in these cases, those arising from the application of American antitrust law, the tribunal therefore should be bound to decide that dispute in accord with the national law giving rise to the claim. Cf. Wilko v. Swan, 346 U.S., at 433-434.[19] And so long as

18. We are advised by Mitsubishi and *amicus* International Chamber of Commerce, without contradiction by Soler, that the arbitration panel selected to hear the parties' claims here is composed of three Japanese lawyers, one a former law school dean, another a former judge, and the third a practicing attorney with American legal training who has written on Japanese antitrust law.

19. In addition to the clause providing for arbitration before the Japan Commercial Arbitration Association, the Sales Agreement includes a choice-of-law clause which reads: "This Agreement is made in,

the prospective litigant effectively may vindicate its statutory cause of action in the arbitral forum, the statute will continue to serve both its remedial and deterrent function.

Having permitted the arbitration to go forward, the national courts of the United States will have the opportunity at the award-enforcement stage to ensure that the legitimate interest in the enforcement of the antitrust laws has been addressed. The Convention reserves to each signatory country the right to refuse enforcement of an award where the "recognition or enforcement of the award would be contrary to the public policy of that country." Art. V(2)(b). . . . While the efficacy of the arbitral process requires that substantive review at the award-enforcement stage remain minimal, it would not require intrusive inquiry to ascertain that the tribunal took cognizance of the antitrust claims and actually decided them.

As international trade has expanded in recent decades, so too has the use of international arbitration to resolve disputes arising in the course of that trade. The controversies that international arbitral institutions are called upon to resolve have increased in diversity as well as in complexity. Yet the potential of these tribunals for efficient disposition of legal disagreements arising from commercial relations has not yet been tested. If they are to take a central place in the international legal order, national courts will need to "shake off the old judicial hostility to arbitration," and also their customary and understandable unwillingness to cede jurisdiction of a claim arising under domestic law to a foreign or transnational tribunal. To this extent, at least, it will be necessary for national courts to subordinate domestic notions of arbitrability to the international policy favoring commercial arbitration.

Accordingly, we "require this representative of the American business community to honor its bargain," Alberto-Culver Co. v. Scherk, 484 F.2d 611, 620 (CA7 1973) (Stevens, J., dissenting), by holding this agreement to arbitrate "enforce[able] . . . in accord with the explicit provisions of the Arbitration Act." *Scherk*, 417 U.S., at 520.

It is so ordered. . . .

Justice STEVENS, with whom Justice BRENNAN joins, and with whom Justice MARSHALL joins except as to Part II, dissenting.

One element of this rather complex litigation is a claim asserted by an American dealer in Plymouth automobiles that two major automobile companies are parties to an international cartel that has restrained competition in the American market. Pursuant to an agreement that is alleged to have violated §1 of the Sherman Act, 15

---

and will be governed by and construed in all respects according to the laws of the Swiss Confederation as if entirely performed therein." The United States raises the possibility that the arbitral panel will read this provision not simply to govern interpretation of the contract terms, but wholly to displace American law even where *it* otherwise would apply. Brief for United States as *Amicus Curiae* 20. At oral argument, however, counsel for Mitsubishi conceded that American law applied to the antitrust claims and represented that the claims had been submitted to the arbitration panel in Japan on that basis. The record confirms that before the decision of the Court of Appeals the arbitral panel had taken these claims under submission.

We therefore have no occasion to speculate on this matter at this stage in the proceedings, when Mitsubishi seeks to enforce the agreement to arbitrate, not to enforce an award. Nor need we consider now the effect of an arbitral tribunal's failure to take cognizance of the statutory cause of action on the claimant's capacity to reinitiate suit in federal court. We merely note that in the event the choice-of-forum and choice-of-law clauses operated in tandem as a prospective waiver of a party's right to pursue statutory remedies for antitrust violations, we would have little hesitation in condemning the agreement as against public policy.

U.S.C. §1, those companies allegedly prevented the dealer from transshipping some 966 surplus vehicles from Puerto Rico to other dealers in the American market.

The petitioner denies the truth of the dealer's allegations and takes the position that the validity of the antitrust claim must be resolved by an arbitration tribunal in Tokyo, Japan. This Court's holding rests almost exclusively on the federal policy favoring arbitration of commercial disputes and vague notions of international comity arising from the fact that the automobiles involved here were manufactured in Japan. . . . I respectfully dissent. In my opinion, (1) a fair construction of the language in the arbitration clause in the parties' contract does not encompass a claim that auto manufacturers entered into a conspiracy in violation of the antitrust laws; (2) an arbitration clause should not normally be construed to cover a statutory remedy that it does not expressly identify; (3) Congress did not intend §2 of the Federal Arbitration Act to apply to antitrust claims; and (4) Congress did not intend the Convention on the Recognition and Enforcement of Foreign Arbitral Awards to apply to disputes that are not covered by the Federal Arbitration Act. . . .

II

Section 2 of the Federal Arbitration Act describes three kinds of arbitrable agreements. Two — those including maritime transactions and those covering the submission of an existing dispute to arbitration — are not involved in this case. The language of §2 relating to the Soler-Mitsubishi arbitration clause reads as follows:

> A written provision in . . . a contract evidencing a transaction involving commerce to settle by arbitration a controversy thereafter arising out of such contract . . . or the refusal to perform the whole or any part thereof, . . . shall be valid, irrevocable, and enforceable, save upon such grounds as exist at law or in equity for the revocation of any contract.

The plain language of this statute encompasses Soler's claims that arise out of its contract with Mitsubishi, but does not encompass a claim arising under federal law, or indeed one that arises under its distributor agreement with Chrysler. Nothing in the text of the 1925 Act, nor its legislative history, suggests that Congress intended to authorize the arbitration of any statutory claims.

Until today all of our cases enforcing agreements to arbitrate under the Arbitration Act have involved contract claims. . . . But this is the first time the Court has considered the question whether a standard arbitration clause referring to claims arising out of or relating to a contract should be construed to cover statutory claims that have only an indirect relationship to the contract. In my opinion, neither the Congress that enacted the Arbitration Act in 1925, nor the many parties who have agreed to such standard clauses, could have anticipated the Court's answer to that question. . . .

III

The Court has repeatedly held that a decision by Congress to create a special statutory remedy renders a private agreement to arbitrate a federal statutory claim unenforceable.

The special interest in encouraging private enforcement of the Sherman Act has been reflected in the statutory scheme ever since 1890. . . .

International Comity

It is clear then that the international obligations of the United States permit us to honor Congress' commitment to the exclusive resolution of antitrust disputes in the federal courts. The Court today refuses to do so, offering only vague concerns for comity among nations. The courts of other nations, on the other hand, have applied the exception provided in the Convention, and refused to enforce agreements to arbitrate specific subject matters of concern to them.[35]

Notes and Questions

1. Why might U.S. federal judges see international arbitration as a method of formal dispute resolution that deserves their support? As a threat to them?

2. The majority opinion suggests that as long as an agreement to arbitrate is valid and Congress has not forbidden it, any claim may be arbitrated. Is this a good policy? If not, what should be the limits on the parties' ability to agree to arbitrate?

3. Do you think that the arbitration in Japan will fully consider Soler's antitrust complaint? How will the arbitrators know about U.S. antitrust law? (See footnote 18 of the opinion.)

4. Isn't one of the purposes of international arbitration to get disputes settled by means other than parochial domestic courts? Did the arbitration provision in *Mitsubishi* accomplish that objective?

5. Suppose that the contract included a provision that "general principles of international commercial law" would apply. Would the arbitrators consider Soler's U.S. antitrust law complaint? What if the contract called for application of "the law of Switzerland, including its public law and policies," and Switzerland had no equivalent of the U.S. antitrust laws? How is that situation different from the actual case here? (See footnote 19 of the opinion.)

6. If the purpose of the U.S. antitrust laws is to protect dealers and ultimately consumers from anticompetitive acts, why should the parties here be given the right to remove or denigrate that protection? If Soler wanted to expressly exclude antitrust claims from the arbitration clause, do you think that it had the bargaining power to do so? If not, how can the public be protected?

7. The majority opinion seems to rely partly on the ability of the courts to review arbitral awards at the enforcement stage. Many of the awards, however, are often made without an extensive opinion by the arbitrator(s). How can legitimate public policy concerns be safeguarded at the enforcement stage if the court does not know the arbitrator's considerations or reasoning? For example, suppose the arbi-

---

35. For example, the Cour de Cassation in Belgium has held that disputes arising under a Belgian statute limiting the unilateral termination of exclusive distributorships are not arbitrable under the Convention in that country, Audi-NSU Auto Union A.G. v. S.A. Adelin Petit & Cie. (1979), in 5 Yearbook Commercial Arbitration 257, 259 (1980), and the Corte di Cassazione in Italy has held that labor disputes are not arbitrable under the Convention in that country, Compagnia Generale Construzioni v. Piersanti, [1980] Foro Italiano I 190, in 6 Yearbook Commercial Arbitration 229, 230 (1981).

trator issued a one-line decision denying Soler's claims. Could Soler then pursue an antitrust claim in U.S. courts? If the decision included an award of $500,000 in favor of Mitsubishi, would Soler have any defense? (The next section should shed some light on the questions in this Note.)

8. Arguably the presumption noted in *Mitsubishi* was further strengthened by the Supreme Court in Carnival Cruise Lines v. Shute, 499 U.S. 585 (1991). The Court there upheld a forum-selection clause contained in small print on a ticket that a Washington State couple (the Shutes) received after purchasing passage on a ship owned by a Florida-based cruise line. The clause designated Florida courts as the agreed-upon fora for the resolution of disputes. Mrs. Shute was injured when she slipped on a deck mat while the ship was in international waters off the Mexican coast. The Shutes filed suit in a U.S. district court in the state of Washington. The Supreme Court held that the U.S. Court of Appeals for the Ninth Circuit erred in not enforcing the forum-selection clause.

Since *Mitsubishi*, the U.S. Supreme Court has often reaffirmed its support for enforcing agreements to arbitrate, both international and domestic. For example, in May 1991, the Court held that statutory claims (i.e., that the Age Discrimination in Employment Act of 1967 (ADEA) had been violated) can be the subject of an arbitration agreement that is enforceable under the Federal Arbitration Act. The Court found no inherent conflict or inconsistency between the underlying purposes of the ADEA and arbitration. The Court also noted that "[m]ere inequality of bargaining power" is not sufficient to hold an arbitration agreement unenforceable, and it found no indication of fraud or coercion. Gilmer v. Interstate/Johnson Lane Corp., 500 U.S. 20 (1991). See also Rodriquez de Quijas v. Shearson/American Express, Inc., 490 U.S. 477 (1989).

However, in November 1998, in an employment discrimination case, the Supreme Court unanimously held that a vaguely worded arbitration clause in a collective bargaining agreement is not enforceable when it does not include a "clear and unmistakable" waiver of the individual employee's rights to bring statutory employment discrimination cases in federal court. Justice Scalia acknowledged that the Court's precedents on arbitration in the labor-management setting have been inconsistent to some degree. Wright v. Universal Maritime Service Corp., 525 U.S. 70 (1998).

4.   *Enforcement of International Arbitral Awards*

a.   In General

Gary Born, International Commercial Arbitration: Commentary and Materials

704-08 (2d ed. 2001)

Many international arbitral awards do not require either judicial enforcement or confirmation, because they are voluntarily compiled with. Nevertheless, the ultimate test of any arbitration proceeding is its ability to render an award which, if necessary, will be recognized and enforced in relevant national courts. The recognition and enforcement of international arbitral awards involve a potentially complex series of issues. In many cases, enforcement of an award implicates the national law of the state where an award is made, the national law of the state where enforcement is sought, and the provisions of applicable international conventions or treaties. This legal regime, and the vocabulary it employs, is outlined below.

1.   Avenues for Enforcing or Challenging Arbitral Awards

a.   "Confirming" and "Vacating" International Arbitral Awards in the Place Where They Are Made

After an international arbitral award is made, most national arbitration statutes provide two basic legal avenues which may be taken with respect to the award in the arbitral situs. First, the prevailing party in the arbitration may commence proceedings in the national courts of the arbitral situs to "confirm" the award (which will usually provide the basis for the entry of a judgment of a local national court). Thereafter, either the judgment can be enforced locally (like a domestic judgment) or the judgment and the award can be taken to another state for enforcement.

Second, the unsuccessful party in the arbitration may commence proceedings, also in the national courts of the arbitral situs, to "set aside," "vacate," or "annul" the award. If successful, such an action generally has the legal effect of nullifying the award, much the way that an appellate decision vacates a trial court judgment. After an award is vacated, it cannot be enforced locally and, in general, can be enforced outside the arbitral situs only with difficulty.

b.   Obtaining "Recognition" or "Enforcement" of an Arbitral Award

If an arbitral award is not vacated, then there are two principal purposes to which it may be put. First, the prevailing party may seek to "enforce" the award, either in the arbitral situs or in a foreign court. This will involve commencing legal proceedings, under local law, in which the award provides the basis for coercively appropriating money or imposing other consequences on the "award-debtor." An award which is subject to the New York or Inter-American Convention does not generally need to be confirmed in the arbitral situs before it may be confirmed and enforced in other forums. . . .

Second, a party to an arbitration may seek to have the arbitral award "recognized." This will usually occur in judicial proceedings commenced by a party which unsuccessfully pursued claims in an arbitration, seeking to relitigate claims or issues which were resolved by the award. Most typically, a respondent who successfully defended against claims in an arbitration will seek recognition of an award to preclude the disappointed claimant from relitigating its claims. . . .

2.   International Legal Framework for Enforcement of International Arbitral Awards

The enforcement of international arbitral awards is subject to a complex legal framework derived from international and national sources. On the national level, as outlined below, national arbitration statutes provide procedural mechanisms and substantive criteria for vacating, confirming, and enforcing international arbitral awards. On the international level, also outlined below, the New York Convention, the Inter-American Convention, and other bilateral and multilateral treaties address the recognition and enforcement of international arbitral awards.

a. National Arbitration Legislation

Most nations have enacted local arbitration legislation which provides for the confirmation or vacation of arbitral awards made locally. National arbitration statutes typically set forth substantive standards and procedural avenues for confirming an award, as well as the grounds for vacating awards made locally. . . .

Likewise, as summarized elsewhere, national arbitration legislation contains provisions governing the recognition and enforcement of arbitral awards. These provisions set forth the substantive grounds for enforcing, or denying enforcement to, arbitral awards. The provisions of Article 36 of the UNCITRAL Model Law are an illustrative example of this. National legislation often provides separate, somewhat differing, legal regimes for recognition of domestic and international awards.

b. International Arbitration Conventions

Equally relevant to the enforcement of international arbitral awards are international arbitration conventions. Particularly significant in this regard is the New York Convention. A principal purpose of the Convention was to make it easier to enforce an arbitral award made in one country in other nations. The drafting history of the New York Convention, and the clear thrust of national court decisions applying the Convention, emphasize the drafters' desire to make awards more readily enforceable. . . .

As discussed below, where the New York Convention is applicable (i.e., where its "jurisdictional requirements" are satisfied), it imposes a general obligation on signatory states to enforce arbitral awards. Article III of the Convention requires signatory states to recognize arbitral awards made in other countries, subject to procedural requirements no more onerous than those for domestic awards. Article III's presumption of enforceability is subject to important jurisdictional limitations, set forth in Article I, and significant exceptions, set forth in Article V.

Finally, Article V of the Convention sets forth a limited set of grounds for nonrecognition of an arbitral award. Importantly, Article V's exceptions are exclusive; outside its country of origin, recognition can be denied a Convention award only on one of the grounds contained in Article V. In light of all these features, national courts have emphasized the "general pro-enforcement bias informing the Convention. . . ."

Aside from the New York Convention, other international conventions and treaties can have important effects on the recognition and enforcement of international arbitral awards. The Inter-American Convention establishes a legal regime paralleling the New York Convention among the United States and many Latin American states. The ICSID Convention establishes a unique legal regime for the enforcement of arbitral awards involving investment disputes. Finally, bilateral treaties among many states facilitate the enforcement of foreign arbitral awards.

Note: Enforcement and Execution Against
Foreign States in the United States

In the past, there were problems in enforcing arbitral awards against foreign states and problems in executing against their property. The problems have been substantially alleviated in the United States by 1988 amendments to the Foreign Sovereign Immunity Act (FSIA).

Section 1605(a) of the FSIA was amended to remove the immunity of foreign states in actions seeking to enforce arbitration agreements or awards in a number of situations. These include agreements or awards made pursuant to the New York Convention or the ICSID Convention. As for execution, the Act was amended to provide that property of a foreign state "used for a commercial activity" in the United States shall not be immune from execution if:

> (6) the judgment is based on an order confirming an arbitral award rendered against the foreign State, provided that attachment in aid of execution, or execution, would not be inconsistent with any provision in the arbitral agreement. [28 U.S.C. §1610(a)(6).]

See Chapter 6, Section A, regarding foreign sovereign immunity of states.

b. Under the New York Convention

As noted in the Born excerpt above, most of the cases involving enforcement of an arbitral award arise under the New York Convention on the Recognition and Enforcement of Foreign Arbitral Awards. Let us look more closely at Articles I and V of that convention. (Additional excerpts from the Convention are in the Documentary Supplement.)

New York Convention

Article I

1. This Convention shall apply to the recognition and enforcement of arbitral awards made in the territory of a State other than the State where the recognition and enforcement of such awards are sought, and arising out of differences between persons, whether physical or legal. It shall also apply to arbitral awards not considered as domestic awards in the State where their recognition and enforcement are sought. . . .

3. When signing, ratifying or acceding to this Convention, or notifying extension under article X hereof, any State may on the basis of reciprocity declare that it will apply the Convention to the recognition and enforcement of awards made only in the territory of another Contracting State. It may also declare that it will apply the Convention only to differences arising out of legal relationships, whether contractual or not, which are considered as commercial under the national law of the State making such declaration.

Article V

1. Recognition and enforcement of the award may be refused, at the request of the party against whom it is invoked, only if that party furnishes to the competent

authority where the recognition and enforcement is sought, proof that:

(a) The parties to the agreement referred to in article II were, under the law applicable to them, under some incapacity, or the said agreement is not valid under the law to which the parties have subjected it or, failing any indication thereon, under the law of the country where the award was made; or

(b) The party against whom the award is invoked was not given proper notice of the appointment of the arbitrator or of the arbitration proceedings or was otherwise unable to present his case; or

(c) The award deals with a difference not contemplated by or not falling within the terms of the submission to arbitration, or it contains decisions on matters beyond the scope of the submission to arbitration, provided that, if the decisions on matters submitted to arbitration can be separated from those not so submitted, that part of the award which contains decisions on matters submitted to arbitration may be recognized and enforced; or

(d) The composition of the arbitral authority or the arbitral procedure was not in accordance with the agreement of the parties, or, failing such agreement, was not in accordance with the law of the country where the arbitration took place; or

(e) The award has not yet become binding on the parties, or has been set aside or suspended by a competent authority of the country in which, or under the law of which, that award was made.

2. Recognition and enforcement of an arbitral award may also be refused if the competent authority in the country where recognition and enforcement is sought finds that:

(a) The subject matter of the difference is not capable of settlement by arbitration under the law of that country; or

(b) The recognition or enforcement of the award would be contrary to the public policy of that country.

The leading U.S. case on the enforcement of international arbitral awards under the Convention is the *Parsons & Whittemore* opinion of the U.S. Court of Appeals for the Second Circuit.

Parsons & Whittemore Overseas Co. v. Societe Generale de L'Industrie du Papier (RAKTA)

U.S. Court of Appeals
508 F.2d 969 (2d Cir. 1974)

SMITH, Circuit Judge:

Parsons & Whittemore Overseas Co., Inc., (Overseas), an American corporation, appeals from the entry of summary judgment on February 25, 1974, by Judge Lloyd F. MacMahon of the Southern District of New York on the counterclaim by Societe Generale de L'Industrie du Papier (RAKTA), an Egyptian corporation, to confirm a foreign arbitral award holding Overseas liable to RAKTA for breach of contract. . . . Jurisdiction is based on 9 U.S.C. §203, which empowers federal district courts to hear cases to recognize and enforce foreign arbitral awards, and 9 U.S.C.

§205, which authorizes the removal of such cases from state courts, as was accomplished in this instance. We affirm the district court's confirmation of the foreign award. . . .

In November 1962, Overseas consented by written agreement with RAKTA to construct, start up and, for one year, manage and supervise a paperboard mill in Alexandria, Egypt. The Agency for International Development (AID), a branch of the United States State Department, would finance the project by supplying RAKTA with funds with which to purchase letters of credit in Overseas' favor. Among the contract's terms was an arbitration clause, which provided a means to settle differences arising in the course of performance, and a "force majeure" clause, which excused delay in performance due to causes beyond Overseas' reasonable capacity to control.

Work proceeded as planned until May, 1967. Then, with the Arab-Israeli Six Day War on the horizon, recurrent expressions of Egyptian hostility to Americans — nationals of the principal ally of the Israeli enemy — caused the majority of the Overseas work crew to leave Egypt. On June 6, the Egyptian government broke diplomatic ties with the United States and ordered all Americans expelled from Egypt except those who would apply and qualify for a special visa.

Having abandoned the project for the present with the construction phase near completion, Overseas notified RAKTA that it regarded this postponement as excused by the force majeure clause. RAKTA disagreed and sought damages for breach of contract. Overseas refused to settle and RAKTA, already at work on completing the performance promised by Overseas, invoked the arbitration clause. Overseas responded by calling into play the clause's option to bring a dispute directly to a three-man arbitral board governed by the rules of the International Chamber of Commerce. After several sessions in 1970, the tribunal issued a preliminary award, which recognized Overseas' force majeure defense as good only during the period from May 28 to June 30, 1967. In so limiting Overseas' defense, the arbitration court emphasized that Overseas had made no more than a perfunctory effort to secure special visas and that AID's notification that it was withdrawing financial backing did not justify Overseas' unilateral decision to abandon the project.[3] After further hearings in 1972, the tribunal made its final award in March, 1973: Overseas was held liable to RAKTA for $312,507.45 in damages for breach of contract and $30,000 for RAKTA's costs; additionally, the arbitrators' compensation was set at $49,000, with Overseas responsible for three-fourths of the sum.

Subsequent to the final award, Overseas in the action here under review sought a declaratory judgment to prevent RAKTA from collecting the award out of a letter of credit issued in RAKTA's favor by Bank of America at Overseas' request. The letter was drawn to satisfy any "penalties" which an arbitral tribunal might assess against Overseas in the future for breach of contract. RAKTA contended that the arbitral award for damages met the letter's requirement of "penalties" and counterclaimed to confirm and enter judgment upon the foreign arbitral award. Overseas' defenses to this counterclaim, all rejected by the district court, form the principal issues for review on this appeal. Four of these defenses are derived from the express language

---

3. RAKTA represented to the tribunal that it was prepared to finance the project without AID's assistance.

of the applicable United Nations Convention on the Recognition and Enforcement of Foreign Arbitral Awards (Convention), and a fifth is arguably implicit in the Convention. These include: enforcement of the award would violate the public policy of the United States, the award represents an arbitration of matters not appropriately decided by arbitration; the tribunal denied Overseas an adequate opportunity to present its case; the award is predicated upon a resolution of issues outside the scope of the contractual agreement to submit to arbitration; and the award is in manifest disregard of law. . . .

I. OVERSEAS' DEFENSES AGAINST ENFORCEMENT

In 1958 the Convention was adopted by 26 of the 45 states participating in the United Nations Conference on Commercial Arbitration held in New York. For the signatory states, the New York Convention superseded the Geneva Convention of 1927. . . . The 1958 Convention's basic thrust was to liberalize procedures for enforcing foreign arbitral awards: While the Geneva Convention placed the burden of proof on the party seeking enforcement of a foreign arbitral award and did not circumscribe the range of available defenses to those enumerated in the convention, the 1958 Convention clearly shifted the burden of proof to the party defending against enforcement and limited his defenses to seven set forth in Article V. Not a signatory to any prior multilateral agreement on enforcement of arbitral awards, the United States declined to sign the 1958 Convention at the outset. The United States ultimately acceded to the Convention, however, in 1970, and implemented its accession with 9 U.S.C. §§201-208. Under 9 U.S.C. §208, the existing Federal Arbitration Act, 9 U.S.C. §§1-14, applies to the enforcement of foreign awards except to the extent to which the latter may conflict with the Convention. . . .

A. Public Policy

Article V(2)(b) of the Convention allows the court in which enforcement of a foreign arbitral award is sought to refuse enforcement, on the defendant's motion or *sua sponte,* if "enforcement of the award would be contrary to the public policy of [the forum] country." The legislative history of the provision offers no certain guidelines to its construction. Its precursors in the Geneva Convention and the 1958 Convention's ad hoc committee draft extended the public policy exception to, respectively, awards contrary to "principles of the law" and awards violative of "fundamental principles of the law." In one commentator's view, the Convention's failure to include similar language signifies a narrowing of the defense. On the other hand, another noted authority in the field has seized upon this omission as indicative of an intention to broaden the defense.

Perhaps more probative, however, are the inferences to be drawn from the history of the Convention as a whole. The general pro-enforcement bias informing the Convention and explaining its supersession of the Geneva Convention points toward a narrow reading of the public policy defense. An expansive construction of this defense would vitiate the Convention's basic effort to remove preexisting obstacles to enforcement. Additionally, considerations of reciprocity — considerations given express recognition in the Convention itself[4] — counsel courts to invoke the public policy defense with caution lest foreign courts frequently accept it as a defense to enforcement of arbitral awards rendered in the United States.

We conclude, therefore, that the Convention's public policy defense should be construed narrowly. Enforcement of foreign arbitral awards may be denied on this basis only where enforcement would violate the forum state's most basic notions of morality and justice.

Under this view of the public policy provision in the Convention, Overseas' public policy defense may easily be dismissed. Overseas argues that various actions by United States officials subsequent to the severance of American-Egyptian relations — most particularly, AID's withdrawal of financial support for the Overseas-RAKTA contract — required Overseas, as a loyal American citizen, to abandon the project. Enforcement of an award predicated on the feasibility of Overseas' returning to work in defiance of these expressions of national policy would therefore allegedly contravene United States public policy. In equating "national" policy with United States "public" policy, the appellant quite plainly misses the mark. To read the public policy defense as a parochial device protective of national political interests would seriously undermine the Convention's utility. This provision was not meant to enshrine the vagaries of international politics under the rubric of "public policy." Rather, a circumscribed public policy doctrine was contemplated by the Convention's framers and every indication is that the United States, in acceding to the Convention, meant to subscribe to this supranational emphasis.

To deny enforcement of this award largely because of the United States' falling out with Egypt in recent years would mean converting a defense intended to be of narrow scope into a major loophole in the Convention's mechanism for enforcement. We have little hesitation, therefore, in disallowing Overseas' proposed public policy defense.

B. Non-Arbitrability

Article V(2)(a) authorizes a court to deny enforcement, on a defendant's or its own motion, of a foreign arbitral award when "[t]he subject matter of the difference is not capable of settlement by arbitration under the law of that [the forum] country." . . .

The court below was correct in denying relief to Overseas under the Convention's non-arbitrability defense to enforcement of foreign arbitral awards. There is no special national interest in judicial, rather than arbitral, resolution of the breach of contract claim underlying the award in this case. . . .

C. Inadequate Opportunity to Present Defense

Under Article V(1)(b) of the Convention, enforcement of a foreign arbitral award may be denied if the defendant can prove that he was "not given proper notice . . . or was otherwise unable to present his case." This provision essentially sanctions the application of the forum state's standards of due process.

---

4. "A Contracting State shall not be entitled to avail itself of the present Convention against other Contracting States except to the extent that it is itself bound to apply the Convention." (Article XIV.)

Overseas seeks relief under this provision for the arbitration court's refusal to delay proceedings in order to accommodate the speaking schedule of one of Overseas' witnesses, David Nes, the United States Charge d'Affairs in Egypt at the time of the Six Day War. This attempt to state a due process claim fails for several reasons. First, inability to produce one's witnesses before an arbitral tribunal is a risk inherent in an agreement to submit to arbitration. By agreeing to submit disputes to arbitration, a party relinquishes his courtroom rights — including that to subpoena witnesses — in favor of arbitration "with all of its well known advantages and drawbacks." Secondly, the logistical problems of scheduling hearing dates convenient to parties, counsel and arbitrators scattered about the globe argues against deviating from an initially mutually agreeable time plan unless a scheduling change is truly unavoidable. In this instance, Overseas' allegedly key witness was kept from attending the hearing due to a prior commitment to lecture at an American university — hardly the type of obstacle to his presence which would require the arbitral tribunal to postpone the hearing as a matter of fundamental fairness to Overseas. Finally, Overseas cannot complain that the tribunal decided the case without considering evidence critical to its defense and within only Mr. Nes' ability to produce. In fact, the tribunal did have before it an affidavit by Mr. Nes in which he furnished, by his own account, "a good deal of the information to which I would have testified." Moreover, had Mr. Nes wished to furnish *all* the information to which he would have testified, there is every reason to believe that the arbitration tribunal would have considered that as well.

The arbitration tribunal acted within its discretion in declining to reschedule a hearing for the convenience of an Overseas witness. Overseas' due process rights under American law, rights entitled to full force under the Convention as a defense to enforcement, were in no way infringed by the tribunal's decision.

D. Arbitration in Excess of Jurisdiction

Under Article V(1)(c), one defending against enforcement of an arbitral award may prevail by proving that:

> The award deals with a difference not contemplated by or not falling within the terms of the submission to arbitration, or it contains decisions on matters beyond the scope of the submission to arbitration. . . .

This provision tracks in more detailed form §10(d) of the Federal Arbitration Act, 9 U.S.C. §10(d), which authorizes vacating an award "[w]here the arbitrators exceeded their powers." Both provisions basically allow a party to attack an award predicated upon arbitration of a subject matter not within the agreement to submit to arbitration. This defense to enforcement of a foreign award, like the others already discussed, should be construed narrowly. Once again a narrow construction would comport with the enforcement-facilitating thrust of the Convention. In addition, the case law under the similar provision of the Federal Arbitration Act strongly supports a strict reading.

In making this defense as to three components of the award, Overseas must therefore overcome a powerful presumption that the arbitral body acted within its powers. Overseas principally directs its challenge at the $185,000 awarded for loss of production. Its jurisdictional claim focuses on the provision of the contract reciting that "[n]either party shall have any liability for loss of production." The tribunal cannot properly be charged, however, with simply ignoring this alleged limitation on the subject matter over which its decision-making powers extended. Rather, the arbitration court interpreted the provision not to preclude jurisdiction on this matter. As in United Steelworkers of America v. Enterprise Wheel & Car Corp., the court may be satisfied that the arbitrator premised the award on a construction of the contract and that it is "not apparent," 363 U.S. 593 at 598, that the scope of the submission to arbitration has been exceeded.

The appellant's attack on the $60,000 awarded for start-up expenses and $30,000 in costs cannot withstand the most cursory scrutiny. In characterizing the $60,000 as "consequential damages" (and thus proscribed by the arbitration agreement), Overseas is again attempting to secure a reconstruction in this court of the contract — an activity wholly inconsistent with the deference due arbitral decisions on law and fact. The $30,000 in costs is equally unassailable, for the appellant's contention that this portion of the award is inconsistent with guidelines set by the International Chamber of Commerce is twice removed from reality. First of all, contrary to Overseas' representations, these guidelines (contained in the Guide to ICC Arbitration . . .) do not require, as a precondition to an award of expenses, express authority for such an award in the arbitration clause. The arbitration agreement's silence on this matter, therefore, is not determinative in the case under review. Secondly, since the parties in fact complied with the *Guide's* advice to reach agreement on this matter prior to arbitration — i.e., the request by each for such an award for expenses amounts to tacit agreement on this point — any claim of fatal deviation from the *Guide* is disingenuous to say the least.

Although the Convention recognizes that an award may not be enforced where predicated on a subject matter outside the arbitrator's jurisdiction, it does not sanction second-guessing the arbitrator's construction of the parties' agreement. . . .

E. Award in "Manifest Disregard" of Law

Both the legislative history of Article V, see supra, and the statute enacted to implement the United States' accession to the Convention[6] are strong authority for treating as exclusive the bases set forth in the Convention for vacating an award. On the other hand, the Federal Arbitration Act, specifically 9 U.S.C. §10, has been read to include an implied defense to enforcement where the award is in "manifest disregard" of the law.

This case does not require us to decide, however, whether this defense stemming from dictum in *Wilko* obtains in the international arbitration context. For even assuming that the "manifest disregard" defense applies under the Convention, we would have no difficulty rejecting the appellant's contention that such "manifest disregard" is in evidence here. Overseas in effect asks this court to read this defense as a license to review the record of arbitral proceedings for errors of fact or law — a

---

6. ". . . The court shall confirm the award unless it finds one of the grounds for refusal or deferral of recognition or enforcement specified in the said Convention." (9 U.S.C. §207.)

role which we have emphatically declined to assume in the past and reject once
again. . . .

Insofar as this defense to enforcement of awards in "manifest disregard" of law
may be cognizable under the Convention, it . . . fails to provide a sound basis for vacating the foreign arbitral award. We therefore affirm the district court's confirmation of the award. . . .

Notes and Questions

1. Do you agree with the *Parsons & Whittemore* court on the public policy issue?
When do you believe that public policy should be a defense?

2. What was the strongest argument by Overseas to deny enforcement of the
award?

3. Does the $185,000 awarded for loss of production fall "within the terms of the
submission to arbitration"? Why or why not?

4. United States courts have set a high threshold for finding that an award
was made in "manifest disregard of the law." In Kanuth v. Prescott, Ball & Turben,
Inc., 949 F.2d 1175, 1179 (D.C. Cir. 1991), the court said: "Manifest disregard of the
law may be found if [the] arbitrator[s] understood and correctly stated the law
but proceeded to ignore it." See also Al-Harbi v. Citibank, 85 F.3d 680, 683 (D.C.
Cir. 1996).

5. Given the *Parsons & Whittemore* case (which reflects the state of the law in the
United States), do you believe that it is generally easy to enforce international arbitral decisions in U.S. courts? Is the enforcement situation what you think it should
be? For other cases following the *Parsons* approach, see National Oil Corp. v. Libyan
Sun Oil Co., 733 F. Supp. 800, 819-820 (D. Del. 1990) (upholding an international
arbitral award against a U.S. oil company in favor of an oil company owned by the
Libyan government); and Matter of Chromalloy Aeroservices and the Arab Republic of Egypt, 939 F. Supp. 907 (D.D.C. 1996) (granting Chromalloy's petition to recognize and enforce an international arbitral award that had been made in Egypt
against the Egyptian government, even though the Egyptian Court of Appeal said
the award was nullified because it found the arbitral panel had used the wrong
substantive law of Egypt).

6. Article I of the New York Convention states that the enforcement regime of
the Convention only applies to arbitral awards that are international. For the Convention to apply, the arbitral award in question must either have been granted outside the country where enforcement is sought or the award must be considered
"non-domestic" in the country where enforcement is sought. In 1983, the Second
Circuit held that an award granted in the United States can be "non-domestic" in
U.S. courts for purposes of the New York Convention if the award was based on foreign law. Bergesen v. Joseph Muller Corp., 710 F.2d 929 (2d Cir. 1983).

7. Some foreign courts have taken different approaches to the enforcement of
arbitral awards. For instance, in 1984, the Supreme Court of Indonesia held that In-
donesia could not enforce an arbitral award that was granted in London against an
Indonesian entity. See Navigation Maritime Bulgare v. P.T. Nizwar, XI Y.B. Comm.
Arb. 508 (1986). The court reasoned that Indonesia was not bound by the New York
Convention, even though Indonesia ratified it in 1981, because the Indonesian

government had not passed implementing legislation to set up an internal framework for dealing with foreign arbitral awards.

By contrast, in a 2001 decision, the Lam Dong People's Court in Vietnam upheld an arbitral award rendered by an ICC arbitral tribunal against a Vietnamese company. The underlying dispute related to a contract between a South Korean silk company and the Vietnam Sericulture Corporation (Viseri). The Vietnamese court confirmed the award against Viseri, holding that it "conformed to international practices, the Vietnam Trade Law, and the ordinance on international arbitration in Vietnam." For more information, see World Arbitration & Mediation Report, vol. 13. no. 2, March 2002.

8. In 1990, the United States ratified the 1975 Inter-American Convention on International Commercial Arbitration and enacted implementing legislation. The Inter-American Convention is similar in form and substance to the New York Convention, except that it usually provides for the use of the rules of the Inter-American Commercial Arbitration Commission. Supporters of the Inter-American Convention hoped that U.S. ratification would help promote Western Hemisphere economic cooperation because they expected more Latin American countries to accept this convention than the New York Convention. As of January 2003, 17 nations had ratified the convention, but all were also parties to the New York Convention.

9. Before proceeding to NAFTA and the WTO, one should note an important entity that helped influence the attitudes of the United States and other governments toward international arbitration.

The Iran-U.S. Claims Tribunal was established pursuant to the 1981 Algiers Accords, which dealt with several issues stemming from the Iranian seizure of 50 Americans, primarily diplomatic personnel, in November 1979. The Accords provided for Iran releasing the hostages and the United States lifting the freeze on about $12 billion in Iranian funds. The Claims Tribunal was designed to resolve a number of outstanding monetary claims by U.S. and Iranian citizens, as well as their governments, that arose from the events during that period. (See the *Dames & Moore* case and the discussion after that of IEEPA in Chapter 3.)

The Tribunal was established in the Hague. The United States appointed three arbitrators and the Iranians three, and these six picked three more arbitrators. After some initial delays and wrangling among the arbitrators, the Tribunal ruled on procedural matters, helped settle some claims, and ruled on the merits of other claims. The Algiers Accords provided for a $1 billion Security Account (created from some of the frozen Iranian funds) to ensure payments of awards against Iran. Iran had frequently replenished the account through accumulated interest on the original $1 billion and through sales of crude oil to U.S. companies.

As the Bush Administration reported in June 2002, "The Tribunal . . . has nearly completed resolution of all of the private claims of U.S. nationals against Iran. Its primary focus is now the arbitration of claims between the two governments. . . . [T]he total number of awards rendered by the Tribunal remains 599, the majority of which have been in favor of U.S. claimants. As of March 31, 2002, the value of awards to successful U.S. claimants paid from the Security Account held by the [settlement bank] was [$2.5 billion]."

The generally successful functioning of the Claims Tribunal demonstrates that two countries, even when faced with continuing diplomatic and military friction, could set up an arbitral system that would handle many business and property claims in a relatively businesslike manner.

5. North American Free Trade Agreement

The United States, Canada, and Mexico are parties to the important North American Free Trade Agreement (NAFTA), which came into force on January 1, 1994. NAFTA is the most comprehensive free trade agreement negotiated among regional countries, though it is not as comprehensive as a common market (such as the European Union).* It is also the first free trade agreement between industrial countries and a developing country (Mexico) where the obligations are reciprocal.

NAFTA also involves a large regional market, comparable to the European Union. The combined population of the three countries in 2001 was about 414 million (284 million for the United States, 90 million for Mexico, and 31 million for Canada). The 2001 gross domestic product of the NAFTA countries was approximately $11.4 trillion ($10,171 billion for the United States, $677 billion for Canada, and $618 billion for Mexico).

The United States and Canada are each other's largest trading partners. In 2001, total two-way trade between them equaled about $385 billion. In comparison, trade between the United States and Japan in 2001 was about $184 billion.

As a result of economic reforms in Mexico during the late 1980s and early 1990s, U.S. trade with Mexico had been growing rapidly even before NAFTA. In 2001, the United States exported about $102 billion in goods and services to Mexico, while importing $133 billion. Mexico has replaced Japan as the United States' second largest trading partner. Canada's trade with Mexico has been small, but it has increased under NAFTA. Since NAFTA came into effect, U.S. trade with Canada and Mexico has grown substantially faster in percentage terms than U.S. trade with the rest of the world. (For more data regarding the NAFTA countries, the European Union, and other countries, see Chart 5-1 at the start of Chapter 5.)

NAFTA followed upon the United States-Canada Free Trade Agreement (FTA) that became effective in January 1989. The FTA had been designed to remove most, though not all, trade barriers between the United States and Canada.

In the following excerpt, economists Gary Hufbauer and Jeffrey Schott provide a summary analysis of the basic NAFTA agreement negotiated in 1992.

Gary Clyde Hufbauer & Jeffrey J. Schott, NAFTA: An Assessment

2-6 (1993)

In essence, the NAFTA is a new, improved, and expanded version of the Canada-US FTA. In large part, the agreement involves commitments by Mexico to implement the degree of trade and investment liberalization promised between its northern

---

*A free trade agreement eliminates most, if not all, tariffs between its members, but its members retain their own external tariffs toward third countries. A common market goes at least one step further and creates equal external tariffs for its members for goods coming from third countries. The European Union is a common market and it involves a number of further steps toward regional integration. —Eds.

neighbors in 1988. However, the NAFTA goes further by addressing unfinished business from the FTA, including protection of intellectual property rights, rules against distortions to investment (local-content and export performance requirements), and coverage of transportation services.

The NAFTA provides for the phased elimination of tariff and most non-tariff barriers on regional trade within 10 years, although a few import-sensitive products will have a 15-year transition period. US-Canada bilateral tariffs will continue to be phased out according to the FTA schedule, that is, by January 1998. In addition, the NAFTA extends the innovative dispute settlement procedures of the FTA to Mexico (in return for a substantial revamping of Mexican trade laws that injects more transparency into the administrative process and brings Mexican antidumping and other procedures closer to those of the United States and Canada); contains precedent-setting rights and obligations regarding services and investment; and takes an important first step in addressing cross-border environmental issues.

The agreement contains notable commitments with regard to liberalization of trade and investment. First, the NAFTA establishes within 15 years free trade in agricultural products between the United States and Mexico. The accord immediately converts key US and Mexican agricultural restrictions into tariff-rate quotas and sets a maximum 15-year period for the phase-out of the over-quota tariffs — an impressive achievement considering the dismal track record of other trade talks in reducing long-standing farm trade barriers.

Second, the investment obligations of the NAFTA (and related dispute settlement provisions) accord national treatment to NAFTA investors, remove most performance requirements on investment in the region, and open up new investment opportunities in key Mexican sectors such as petrochemicals and financial services. The investment provisions provide a useful model for future GATT trade accords, despite the notable exceptions for primary energy and Canadian cultural industries.

Third, the pact sets important precedents for future regional and multilateral negotiations by substantially opening the financial services market in Mexico to US and Canadian participants by the year 2000 and by removing significant obstacles to land transportation and telecommunications services.

Finally, the NAFTA offers a schizophrenic result in textiles and apparel. On the one hand, the pact calls for the elimination of all tariffs and quotas on regional trade in textiles and apparel (except for a special US quota for Canadian apparel producers that do not meet the strict regional rules of origin). This is the first time in this heavily protected sector that imports from an important developing-country supplier have been significantly liberalized by the United States and Canada. However, the rules of origin established to qualify for duty-free treatment are highly restrictive. . . .

The NAFTA is a noteworthy achievement, but its implications for Mexico, Canada, and the United States should not be exaggerated. By widening the scope of the market and enlarging the range of available labor skills, the NAFTA enables North American firms and workers to compete more effectively against foreign producers both at home and in world markets. But the ability of the NAFTA partners to gain maximum benefits from the pact with minimum adjustment costs depends importantly on maintaining domestic economic policies that ensure growth. Firms will still look first and foremost at the macroeconomic climate in each country in setting their investment priorities.

IMPLICATIONS FOR MEXICO, THE UNITED STATES, AND CANADA

For Mexico, the NAFTA reinforces the extensive market-oriented policy reforms implemented since 1985. These reforms have promoted real annual growth of 3 to 4 percent in the 1990s and a falling rate of inflation. The NAFTA portends a continuation of the fast pace of change in the Mexican economy by extending the reform process to sectors such as autos, textiles and apparel, finance, telecommunications, and land transportation. Mexican exporters will also benefit in two distinct ways: the relatively unfettered access to the US market that they already enjoy under various unilateral US programs will be sustained, and the few remaining US trade barriers will be liberalized. . . .

For the United States, the NAFTA reforms should enhance an already-important export market. US exports to Mexico have grown sharply since 1986. . . . US suppliers of intermediates, capital goods, and high-technology products should continue to reap large benefits as prime suppliers of the growing Mexican market. Over time, the NAFTA should impel industrial reorganization along regional lines, with firms taking best advantage of each country's ability to produce components and assembled products and thus enhancing competitiveness in the global marketplace.

In addition, the NAFTA meets key US foreign policy objectives. The US debate often ignores the foreign policy dimension, blithely taking for granted that Mexican steps toward economic reform and political pluralism are irreversible. But Mexico's economic reforms are still vulnerable to political and financial shocks, and democratic reforms are still in their infancy. The NAFTA should anchor achievements already made in Mexico and reinforce efforts to promote economic growth and political pluralism in that country.

For Canada, the NAFTA reinforces, and in some cases strengthens, its FTA preferences in the US market. Canada achieved many of its specific objectives in the negotiations, such as clarifying the method used to calculate the regional content for autos and retaining the Canada-US FTA provision that exempts Canadian cultural industries from external competition. In addition, the NAFTA improves Canada's access to the Mexican market. . . .

NAFTA "LOWLIGHTS"

Despite its attractions, the NAFTA does contain warts and blemishes. For example, basic energy remains immune to free trade. . . .

But the main area where the NAFTA is open to criticism is its enunciation of restrictive rules of origin. These arcane trade provisions have been aptly labeled "tools of discrimination": they are used to determine which goods qualify for preferential treatment under the NAFTA and to deny NAFTA benefits to those goods that contain significant foreign-sourced components.

Rules of origin are an integral part of all free trade pacts, but the NAFTA provisions pose two distinct dangers. First, to an undue extent, they penalize regional producers by forcing them to source from less efficient suppliers located in the region, thereby undercutting the global competitiveness of the buying firms. Second, the NAFTA rules could establish an unhappy precedent for other preferential trading pacts, which may choose to emulate the restrictive practices articulated in the NAFTA to the disadvantage of the original perpetrators. . . .

During the 1992 Presidential campaign, then-Governor Clinton identified some problems with the basic NAFTA agreement that the Bush Administration had negotiated. In 1993, the Clinton Administration promptly negotiated with Canada and Mexico three "side agreements" to the basic NAFTA agreement before submitting the whole package to the U.S. Congress for approval.

The most important side agreements dealt with environmental concerns and labor problems. The environment agreement was an attempt to ensure that none of the three countries could gain a competitive advantage in trade by failing to enforce environmental laws. The agreement created a trilateral Commission on Environmental Cooperation with a broad agenda and some dispute resolution powers.

The labor agreement created a trilateral Commission for Labor Cooperation. The Commission has powers to gather and publish information and to coordinate cooperative activities. The Commission also had limited enforcement powers. For a detailed discussion of these two agreements, see, for example, Professor Thomas Schoenbaum's article, The North American Free Trade Agreement (NAFTA): Good for Jobs, for the Environment, and for America, 23 Ga. J. Intl. & Comp. L. 461 (1993).

The third side agreement dealt with the potential problem of import surges as a result of NAFTA hurting one of the member countries. The agreement established a working group that can evaluate the import surge provisions in the original NAFTA, and make recommendations for revisions if problems such as declining employment sufficiently harm a specific industry.

Even with the side agreements, the whole NAFTA package encountered heavy resistance in the U.S. Congress. The AFL-CIO and other labor groups were particularly unhappy with the arrangement. They believed that, even with the side agreement on labor standards, the whole NAFTA package provided inadequate protection for U.S. workers.

President Clinton and his Administration mounted a successful effort to obtain approval for the agreement in the House of Representatives and the Senate in the fall of 1993. Canada and Mexico encountered less legislative opposition and also obtained approval in 1993. As noted earlier, NAFTA went into force in January 1994.

Gary Hufbauer & Gustavo Vega, NAFTA: A Progress Report

5, 8-10 (2003)

Since NAFTA went into effect [in 1994], trade flows between the partners have experienced tremendous growth, surpassing the most optimistic prediction of free trade proponents. Trade among the NAFTA partners, between 1993 and 2000, increased by 128 percent, from $289 billion to $659 billion. . . .

In the case of Mexico and the United States, two-way trade boomed at an average annual growth rate of 17 percent, tripling between 1993 and 2000. . . . Two-way trade grew from 34 percent of Mexican GDP (measured at market exchange rates) to 63 percent. . . . Mexico displaced Japan as the second largest export market for the United States. . . .

NAFTA is also an investment agreement, aimed at facilitating both foreign direct investment (FDI) and portfolio investment. . . .

While other factors were [also] at work, we think [that some] crude comparisons indicate the positive impact of NAFTA on FDI flows. . . . This growth in intra-regional FDI occurred in tandem with a tremendous expansion of intra-regional trade. The obvious and well-known conclusion is that NAFTA accelerated the rationalization of North American production facilities, especially in integrated sectors like autos, computers, chemicals and pharmaceutical products.

Among the most important aspects of NAFTA are the numerous mechanisms established for dispute resolution. These are "state of the art" mechanisms that build upon the successful procedures that had existed under the United States-Canada Free Trade Agreement (FTA).

NAFTA established three principal mechanisms for resolving disputes. First, there is the procedure for disputes between an investor of one party and another party. Second, there is the special mechanism for disputes under the antidumping and countervailing duty laws. Third, there is a general mechanism for resolving many disputes among the parties that do not fall within the second category.

"Dumping" is defined under U.S. law as the sale of foreign merchandise in the United States at less than its fair value, usually measured by comparing (with adjustments) the price in the United States with that in the home market at the same stage of the production process. Such sales must cause or threaten "material injury" to a U.S. industry or materially retard the establishment of an industry. The International Trade Commission (ITC), an independent agency in the U.S. government (whose six commissioners are appointed for staggered nine-year terms), is charged with making the essential determination regarding injury. The U.S. Department of Commerce makes the initial determination regarding whether there has been dumping and, if so, by how much. If Commerce finds dumping and the ITC finds injury, then Commerce can make a determination of increased tariffs or other relief to offset the price discrimination. These determinations can usually be appealed to the U.S. federal courts. However, for sales from Mexico or Canada that are covered by NAFTA, an appropriate party can request a review by a NAFTA panel as a substitute for judicial review.

Similarly, "countervailing duties" under U.S. law can be imposed on foreign merchandise if the foreign manufacture, production, or export of that merchandise is being subsidized, directly or indirectly. For most cases, there is a requirement of real or threatened injury similar to that under the dumping laws, and the ITC is again charged with making this determination. The Department of Commerce determines the existence and amount of the subsidies. If the ITC finds injury and Commerce finds the subsidies, then Commerce determines the amount of countervailing duties that are to be imposed. Again, for cases not covered by NAFTA, these determinations can be appealed to the U.S. federal courts.

The following analysis by Gary Horlick and Amanda DeBusk provides an excellent overview of the principal dispute-resolution procedures in NAFTA.

Gary Horlick & Amanda DeBusk, Dispute Resolution Under NAFTA

27 J. World Trade 21-41 (1993)

I. INTRODUCTION

. . . NAFTA . . . contains numerous mechanisms for resolving disputes. This article focuses on the three dispute resolution mechanisms that are the most fully elaborated in the NAFTA:

(1)   the Chapter 11, Subchapter B mechanism for resolving disputes between a party and an investor in another party;

(2)   the Chapter 19 mechanism for resolving disputes under the antidumping and countervailing duty laws; and

(3)   the Chapter 20 mechanism for resolving disputes among the parties. . . .

II. INVESTOR DISPUTES

(A)   Description of Investor Dispute Resolution Mechanism

NAFTA breaks new ground with the Chapter 11 investor dispute resolution mechanism. It permits investors to resort to binding international arbitration if a host government violates the investment provisions of the NAFTA.[6] An investor may seek arbitration if a party (e.g. the United States, Mexico, or Canada) violates its commitment to afford treatment to investors of another party that is no less favourable than it accords its own investors and investors of other countries.[7] NAFTA prohibits the parties from imposing specific performance requirements such as minimum export levels, domestic content rules, preferences for domestic sourcing, trade balancing and technology transfer requirements.[8] Expropriations are prohibited unless certain conditions are met.[9] Investors are guaranteed the right to convert local currency into foreign currency at the prevailing market rate and freely transfer the currency.[10] There are various exceptions to NAFTA's investment provisions covering areas such as investment in telecommunications, maritime services, Mexico's oil industry and others. An investor may use the NAFTA to assert its own claims or those of an enterprise under its ownership or control in the host country.

---

6. NAFTA, Article 1116.

7. Ibid., Article 1102 (national treatment): Article 1103 (most-favoured-nation treatment).

8. Ibid., Article 1106.

9. Ibid., Article 1110. There is an exception for expropriations for a public purpose provided that they are done on a non-discriminatory basis in accordance with the due process of law and upon payment of fair compensation; id., Article 1110(1).

10. Ibid., Article 1109.

The NAFTA dispute resolution mechanism for investor disputes does not establish a new procedural regime but instead permits investors to seek arbitration for violations of NAFTA under:

— the ICSID Convention, provided that both the disputing party and the party of the investor are parties to the Convention;[13]
— the Additional Facility Rules of ICSID, provided that either the disputing party or the party of the investor, but not both, is a party to the ICSID Convention;[14]
— or the United Nations Commission on International Trade Law (UNCITRAL) Arbitration Rules.

ICSID panels are established under the auspices of the World Bank to hear disputes between governments and private investors. The Additional Facility Rules of ICSID are designed, inter alia, for investment arbitrations where one of the disputing parties is a member of the ICSID Convention but the other is not. The UNCITRAL Arbitration Rules are optional rules that parties can choose to use to govern disputes arising out of contracts or other disputes. . . .

There are several preconditions to use of the NAFTA investor dispute resolution mechanism. First, the investor must have incurred a loss or damage by reason of, or arising out of a breach of, certain NAFTA provisions protecting investors. Second, the claim must be timely lodged. . . . Third, the aggrieved investor must attempt consultation and negotiation prior to resorting to arbitration. Fourth, the aggrieved investor must give notice of its intent to submit a claim to arbitration to the allegedly offending party at least 90 days before actually submitting the claim. Fifth, at least six months must have elapsed since the events giving rise to a claim. This gives the disputants a chance to resolve the issue through negotiations. Sixth, the disputing investor must consent to arbitration and waive its right to initiate or continue the dispute in another forum.

(B)   No Deadlines for the Resolution of Investor Disputes

NAFTA does not impose deadlines for the investor arbitrations as it does for Chapter 19 and, to a lesser degree, for Chapter 20. This is unfortunate because none of the three arbitral regimes available to an investor provides for deadlines. The lack of deadlines has been a problem under the ICSID Convention and can make investors reluctant to choose that forum. . . .

(D)   Binding Nature of Investor Panel Decisions

NAFTA provides that the investor dispute resolution panel's decision will be binding. NAFTA Article 1135(5) states that each party undertakes to provide for the

---

13. Of the three parties, only the United States is a signatory of the ICSID Convention. Therefore, the option of arbitration under the ICSID Convention will be available only if another party becomes a signatory.

14. This provision would be applicable if the dispute involves the United States (or a U.S. investor) and another party (or another party's investor).

enforcement in its territory of an award. If a party fails to abide by or comply with the terms of a final award, a NAFTA Chapter 20 panel may be established. In addition, a disputing investor may seek enforcement of an arbitration award under the ICSID Convention, the United National Convention on the Recognition and Enforcement of Foreign Arbitral Awards (the New York Convention) or the Inter-American Convention on International Commercial Arbitration. . . .

III. RESOLUTION OF ANTIDUMPING/COUNTERVAILING DUTIES

(A) Introduction

Chapter 19 of the NAFTA provides for the resolution of trade disputes concerning antidumping and countervailing duty investigations. It is modeled very closely after Chapter 19 of the FTA [U.S.-Canada Free Trade Agreement]. In this article, the Chapter 19 panels of the NAFTA and FTA are referred to as the "AD/CVD panels." . . .

Both the NAFTA and the FTA provide for the parties to the agreement to request binational panel review of antidumping and countervailing duty (AD/CVD) decisions. The NAFTA, like the FTA, permits dispute resolution through a panel of experts from the exporting and importing nations as a substitute for judicial review of AD/CVD cases.

NAFTA panels must apply the same standard of review that a reviewing court of the country whose decision is challenged would apply. In the United States, the standard is whether the decision is: (a) unsupported by substantial evidence on the record; or (b) otherwise not in accordance with law.[70] . . .

(B) NAFTA Decisions Should Be as Timely as FTA Decisions

NAFTA has the same deadlines for panel decisions as the FTA, and since the FTA deadlines have been followed, it is likely that the NAFTA deadlines will be followed as well.

Almost all FTA panels have met the FTA's deadline of 315 days (about ten and one-half months) for the resolution of AD/CVD disputes, giving FTA and NAFTA dispute resolution an advantage over the Court of International Trade (CIT) review which typically takes about 27 months. . . .

Under the FTA, both Canada and the United States have adopted procedural rules that set additional deadlines. . . . Similar procedural rules are likely to be adopted to implement the NAFTA. . . .

(C) NAFTA Structured for Impartial Decision-Making

NAFTA provides for each of the two involved parties to select two panelists, with the fifth panelist to be selected by mutual agreement, or, failing agreement, by lot. This

70. See (NAFTA,] Article 1911 (definition of standard of review) which adopts the standard of Section 516A(b)(1)(B) of the Tariff Act of 1930.

provision is similar to that in the FTA, and the record shows that FTA panels have been impartial. . . .

The NAFTA roster-selection process . . . will encourage the selection of fair panelists. NAFTA provides for the establishment of a roster of 75 candidates. Each party selects 25 candidates. The candidates must be nationals of the parties, but they do not have to be of the nationality of the party making the selection (e.g. the United States could put a Mexican citizen on the roster). . . .

(D) NAFTA AD/CVD Panel Decisions Will Be Binding

. . . NAFTA AD/CVD panel decisions are binding. NAFTA Article 1904(9) provides: "The decision of a panel under this Article shall be binding on the involved parties with respect to the particular matter between the parties that is before the panel."[105] . . .

(E) NAFTA Decisions Should Be of High Quality

The NAFTA decisions should meet the high quality of the FTA panel decisions since the NAFTA panel system is very similar to that under the FTA.

Professor Andreas F. Lowenfeld studied panel decisions under the FTA. He concluded:

> The consideration given by panel members to the issues and the contentions of the parties has been careful, and . . . the opinions have been well thought through and well crafted. Though no one can be expected to agree with all of the opinions in every detail . . . , as a whole the opinions are of high quality, and should leave even losing parties — including the government agencies concerned — confident that they received a full and fair hearing. . . .

(F) NAFTA AD/CVD Panel Challenges Are Like FTA Challenges

NAFTA has a system for challenging AD/CVD panel decisions. . . .

NAFTA Article 1904.13 allows a party to challenge the decision of a binational panel in the following limited circumstances:

> (a)(i) a member of the panel was guilty of gross misconduct, bias, or a serious conflict of interest, or otherwise materially violated the rules of conduct;

---

105. When the FTA was being negotiated, there was considerable debate as to whether Article III of the U.S. Constitution required judicial review of antidumping and countervailing duty cases, making FTA panel reviews unconstitutional. See H.R. Rep. No. 816 Part 4, 100th Cong., 2nd Session 2 (1988). . . . To ensure that the binational panel review system would withstand a constitutional challenge, the implementing legislation created an exception for binational panel reviews for any constitutional challenges of the antidumping or countervailing duty laws. H.R. No. 216, 100th Cong., 2nd Session 264 (1988). In addition, the U.S. implementing legislation amended Section 516A of the Tariff Act of 1930 to provide for a fast-track procedure for the U.S. Court of Appeals for the D.C. Circuit to consider any challenge to the constitutionality of Chapter 19 binational panel reviews and for three judges to hear challenges to the constitutionality of specific panels. . . .

(ii) the panel seriously departed from a fundamental rule of procedure;
or
(iii) the panel manifestly exceeded its powers, authority or jurisdiction set forth in this Article, for example by failing to apply the appropriate standard of review.

In addition, under NAFTA Chapter 19, the party must show that the situation is so serious that at least one of the actions in subparagraph (a) materially affected the panel's decision *and* poses a continued threat to the integrity of the binational panel review process should the decision be allowed to stand. If an ECC [Extraordinary Challenge Court] finds that the narrow grounds for an extraordinary challenge have been established, it may vacate or remand the binational panel decision.

IV.   DISPUTES OF THE PARTIES

(A)   Introduction

NAFTA Chapter 20 establishes a dispute mechanism for disputes of the parties. It is modeled after FTA Chapter 18. It covers disputes concerning the interpretation or application of NAFTA, alleged violations of NAFTA and the nullification or impairment of the benefits of NAFTA. It also permits the parties to use Chapter 20 as a substitute for GATT dispute resolution. . . .

The NAFTA Chapter 20 panels are structured similarly to NAFTA AD/CVD panels, although there are some important distinctions. While the parties delegated to private parties the right to request Chapter 19 reviews, only the three national governments can request Chapter 20 reviews. Consultations are not required prior to requesting an AD/CVD panel, but they are a prerequisite under Chapter 20. In addition, under Chapter 20, the parties have considerable input into the panel process whereas under Chapter 19, they do not.

In contrast to Chapter 19 panels that issue a single binding decision, Chapter 20 panels produce an initial report, which includes recommendations for resolution of the dispute. Then, the panel will consider comments and issue a final report.

Whereas the AD/CVD panel's decision is binding, and must be enforced absent an extraordinary challenge, the parties can override a Chapter 20 panel's report. Upon receipt of the report, the parties "shall agree" on resolution of the dispute, which "normally" will conform with the panel's determinations and recommendations.[141] These provisions give the panel "moral" influence over resolution of the dispute.

While the AD/CVD panels may only affirm or remand agency decisions, the Chapter 20 panels have broader discretion in finding a remedy. . . . NAFTA expansively defines potential remedies as the "non-implementation or removal of a measure not conforming with this Agreement or causing nullification or impairment in the sense of Annex 2004 or, failing such a resolution, compensation."[142] NAFTA does not limit dispute resolution to these broadly-defined remedies. Rather, it provides that they are to be used "wherever possible."

---

141. [NAFTA,] Article 2018(1).
142. Ibid., Article 2018(2).

There is no ECC for Chapter 20 panels. If the parties do not agree with the recommendation of a panel and cannot resolve a dispute within 30 days after receiving the final panel report, then the final recourse for the aggrieved party is "to suspend the application to the party complained against of benefits of equivalent effect until such time as they have reached agreement on a resolution of the dispute."[144] . . .

(C)   NAFTA Improves on FTA Panel Selection Process

The NAFTA Chapter 20 panel selection process improves on the FTA process. NAFTA establishes an innovative system whereby a party selects panelists from nationals of another party. If the dispute involves two parties, they are to endeavour to agree on the chair of the panel and then each party is to select two panelists who are citizens of the other disputing party. If the parties cannot agree on the chair, the chair is to be chosen by lot. . . .

(D)   Panel Decisions on the Parties' Disputes — Not Binding

Under NAFTA, the parties make panel decisions binding under Chapter 19 but not binding under Chapter 20. . . .

The only remedy for the parties under NAFTA Chapter 20 is retaliation.[180] Whereas the FTA contains a general clause allowing the suspension of benefits, NAFTA is more specific. It provides that the complaining party should first seek to suspend benefits in the same sector as that affected by the offending measure. Then, if it is not practicable or effective to suspend benefits in the same sector, the complaining party can suspend benefits in other sectors. . . .

(E)   NAFTA's Provision for Expert Reports Should Contribute to
High Quality Decisions

. . . NAFTA provides for: (1) technical reports from experts; and (2) smaller rosters intended to result in highly-qualified panelists.

Under NAFTA, a party or a panel can request a technical report addressing information relevant to the proceeding. The inclusion of such a provision in the NAFTA will assist panels that must make decisions concerning the health, safety and environmental standards of a party. It will facilitate well-reasoned panel decisions.

NAFTA's system for roster panel selection could lead to better-quality decisions because the number of individuals on the roster is relatively small — and thus supposedly can be limited to the very top individuals. NAFTA specifies that under Chapter 20, the parties are to establish a roster of up to 30 individuals. Since the pool of panelists for the NAFTA Chapter 20 panels is smaller than for the Chapter 19 panels (where the roster lists 75 individuals), the Chapter 20 panelists could be better-qualified. The individuals are to be appointed "by consensus" for three-year terms

144. Ibid., Article 2019(1).
180. NAFTA, Article 2019.

and may be reappointed. The parties' hope is that this pool of individuals will be of such a high quality as to give credibility to Chapter 20 panel decisions. . . .

(F)   NAFTA Does Not Provide for Challenges to Panel Decisions

Unlike NAFTA Chapter 19, NAFTA Chapter 20 does not provide for challenges. Perhaps one reason is that compliance with Chapter 19 is mandatory but compliance with Chapter 20 is not. . . .

IV.   CONCLUSION

NAFTA contains various dispute mechanisms. The most fully defined are the Chapter 11 investor dispute mechanism, the Chapter 19 mechanism for the resolution of antidumping/countervailing disputes, and the Chapter 20 mechanism for disputes among the parties.

NAFTA Chapter 11 is an innovative mechanism. Under it, when an investor believes that a party has violated one of the NAFTA provisions protecting investors, the investor can request arbitration. NAFTA provides for arbitration under the rules of the ICSID Convention, the ICSID Additional Facility, or the UNCITRAL Arbitration Rules. NAFTA modifies those rules with its own requirements. The biggest advantage of arbitration under the Chapter 11 regime is that the decisions of the arbitral panels would be binding on the parties. However, Chapter 11 does not impose deadlines, and arbitrations under the three international arbitral regimes could be lengthy.

NAFTA's mechanism for resolution of AD/CVD disputes is modeled very closely after FTA Chapter 19. It should prove equally successful in resulting in prompt, high-quality, binding decisions. . . .

NAFTA Chapter 20 is similar to FTA Chapter 18. . . . NAFTA Chapter 20 . . . decisions are [not] automatically adopted. . . . [T]he ultimate remedy is retaliation.

Notes and Questions

The NAFTA dispute resolution provisions are not simple. To help you understand them, consider the following questions:

1. Under the NAFTA dispute resolution procedures for trade disputes concerning antidumping and countervailing duty (AD/CVD) investigations (Chapter 19), are the determinations of the panels binding?

2. Can a private party (e.g., a U.S. importer) challenge a U.S. antidumping duty investigation before a NAFTA panel?

3. What exactly is the standard of review under Chapter 19? What if the U.S. Executive Branch correctly applied existing U.S. law to find that Canadians were dumping timber in the United States and should face higher tariffs? Even if Canada felt that the U.S. law was wrong, does the dispute mechanism of the binational arbitration panel offer any relief?

The standard of review for U.S. cases is adopted from U.S. import laws, specifically 19 U.S.C. §1516A(b)(1). It provides:

> The court shall hold unlawful any determination, finding, or conclusion found —
>
> (A) in an action brought [against certain determinations by a government agency], to be arbitrary, capricious, an abuse of discretion, or otherwise not in accordance with the law, or
>
> (B) in an action [against agency determinations usually made at a later point in the fact-finding process], to be unsupported by substantial evidence on the record, or otherwise not in accordance with law.

4. How is, say, Canada protected against new U.S. laws regarding antidumping or countervailing duties that might further limit Canada's ability to sell goods in the United States? (See NAFTA, Article 1903, in the Documentary Supplement.) Does it matter whether the new laws are consistent with the General Agreement on Tariffs and Trade (GATT), with the GATT Antidumping or Subsidies Codes, or successor agreements? As indicated in Article 1903, the panel's decision here is declaratory and there is an involved process that follows. Besides reflecting a compromise among the negotiating positions of the three countries during the draft of the FTA and then NAFTA, could this approach also be designed to encourage the countries to resolve major disputes over new laws without resorting to binding arbitration?

5. Note footnote 105 in the Horlick and DeBusk article about the constitutionality of the Chapter 19 provisions. One of the arguments was that it was unconstitutional to allow arbitrators who were not appointed by the President with the advice and consent of the U.S. Senate (i.e., the Canadian and fifth arbitrators) to apply U.S. law without U.S. judicial review. Do you agree? If so, how is it distinguishable from arbitration awards, premised on U.S. law, that are enforced under the New York Convention on the Recognition and Enforcement of Foreign Arbitral Awards? Also, Congress has the authority to determine the jurisdiction of U.S. courts under Article III of the Constitution. When Congress approved NAFTA, did this not constitute a congressional decision that U.S. courts would not hear appeals from certain administrative determinations?

6. Turn to the general dispute resolution procedures of NAFTA under Chapter 20. Does a dispute go directly to a panel, or are prior consultations required between the disputing parties? Once the matter is before the panel, does it proceed directly to rendering a decision or are there interim steps? What if a Chapter 20 panel issues a final report that a party does not implement? What are the remedies of the other party? (See Articles 2018-2019.)

7. Why do you think that the Chapter 20 panel's findings were not simply made binding? Why is the Chapter 20 process more drawn out than the Chapter 19 panels for AD/CVD cases? Could it turn upon the potential importance, sensitivity, or uniqueness of issues that fall under the general dispute resolution chapter?

8. Additional dispute-resolution procedures are available through the North American Commission for Environmental Cooperation (CEC) for environmental disputes. As discussed above, the CEC was established to implement the objectives of one of NAFTA's side agreements — the North American Agreement on Environmental Cooperation (NAAEC). The CEC's dispute-settlement procedures, however, are different from those of Chapter 20; they make a CEC procedure longer, more

expensive, and more difficult to initiate. As of October 2002, although there have been environmentally oriented arbitrations under NAFTA under Chapter 11, no disputes have been resolved through the CEC procedures. In addition, some critics have noted that the dispute-resolution system of the CEC is less concerned about enforcing environmental laws than it is about dealing with the unfair trade advantage that occurs when a country has weak environmental enforcement. For further analysis of the NAAEC, see Gary Hufbauer, et al., NAFTA and the Environment: Seven Years Later, Institute for International Economics, Washington, D.C., 2000.

9. The NAFTA countries also negotiated a labor side agreement known as the North American Agreement on Labor Cooperation (NAALC). The main objectives of the NAALC are (1) to monitor national labor laws in each member country, (2) to promote joint programs to improve labor practices, and (3) to establish a dispute-resolution forum for labor cases when domestic procedures are insufficient. Although modest improvements have been made under NAALC, political pressure in all three NAFTA countries has made enforcement difficult. Specifically, the NAFTA parties continue to be reluctant to surrender authority on labor issues to a supranational institution. Instead, under NAALC, a National Administrative Office (NAO) has been set up within each county's department or ministry of labor. These national offices then decide whether a labor dispute requires international consultation with other NAFTA members. As a result, labor issues continue to be primarily a national matter. For an in-depth discussion of the NAALC, see Gary Hufbauer & Jeffrey Schott, NAFTA: An Eight Year Appraisal, Institute for International Economics (2003).

10. The new dispute-resolution systems in the U.S.-Canada FTA and then under Chapters 19 and 20 of the NAFTA have seen frequent use. During the five-year life of the FTA (1989 through 1993), 59 cases were brought under its procedures, 54 of those under the FTA's Chapter 19, which was similar to NAFTA's. From 1994 through September 2002, there were 83 binational panels created under Chapter 19 and three under Chapter 20. Of the Chapter 19 panels, 53 have been reviews of U.S. agencies' determinations, and two of the Chapter 20 filings were to review U.S. measures. For further details about NAFTA cases under these chapters, see <www.nafta-sec-alena.org>.

11. Investment disputes brought under NAFTA's Chapter 11 have been some of the most interesting and controversial developments under the agreement. Here are some examples of these cases.

In January 1997, Metalclad Corporation, a U.S. company, filed a Chapter 11 claim against Mexico. Early in the 1980s, Metalclad bought an existing waste disposal site in Mexico with the intentions of building a new hazardous waste facility. However, in 1995, local governments in Mexico passed environmental regulations that denied Metalclad permission to operate the hazardous waste landfill. The arbitral tribunal ruled in August 2000 that Mexico's actions constituted an unjustified expropriation and that such behavior denied Metalclad national treatment and the minimum standard of treatment required for investors under international law. The tribunal awarded Metalclad $16.7 million in damages.

In July 1998, a Canadian funeral conglomerate called The Loewen Group initiated an arbitration against the U.S. government for $725 million, claiming that a Mississippi jury verdict violated its investor rights under Chapter 11. In 1995, Loewen was sued by a small Mississippi funeral home operator and funeral insurance provider over the terms of an insurance contract. After Loewen refused to settle the routine contract dispute that probably was worth less than $20 million, the local company sued in state court. After being allowed to hear, among other allegations, that Canadians were racist, the rural Mississippi jury returned a $500 million verdict against Loewen, of which $400 million was for punitive damages. Loewen was prevented from filing an appeal in the Mississippi courts because Mississippi required that defendant post a bond of 125 percent of the total award, which was beyond Loewen's resources. As a result, Loewen chose to settle the case with the Mississippi plaintiff for about $175 million.

Loewen, however, then filed a case with ICSID against the United States for violations of Chapter 11. Specifically, Loewen claimed that the Mississippi trial violated international norms of fairness and amounted to an expropriation and denial of justice under Chapter 11. In January 2001, the ICSID arbitration panel determined that it had jurisdiction to hear the issues in the case. As of January 2003, however, the case was still pending. Nevertheless, if Loewen succeeds on its claim, will that success encourage investors to use Chapter 11 to challenge punitive damages awarded by U.S. courts? (U.S. courts more frequently allow punitive damages, and for larger amounts, than do the courts of other countries.)

Also, should NAFTA's expropriation provisions be comparable to, or more or less restrictive than, the U.S. domestic law on government takings? And, based on the examples above, how should NAFTA balance investment protection with environmental and labor concerns? For more information about the Chapter 11 arbitrations, consult <www.state.gov/s/1/c3439.htm>. See also, for example, Vicki Been & Joel Beauvais, The Global Fifth Amendment: NAFTA's Investment Protections and the Misguided Quest for an International "Regulatory Takings" Doctrine, 78 N.Y.U. Rev. 30 (2003).

6. Dispute Resolution Under the World Trade Organization (WTO) and the General Agreement on Tariffs and Trade (GATT)

The World Trade Organization (WTO), which was the result of the Uruguay Round negotiations, came into being in 1995 and includes a major dispute resolution system. This system represents a substantial strengthening of what existed under the General Agreement on Tariffs and Trade (GATT), which came into effect in 1947.

As an introduction, the following excerpt provides an overview of the Uruguay Round agreement and the new WTO. (The WTO is discussed in more detail in Chapter 5 at page 499.)

IMF Survey, Trade Agreement Mandates
Broad Changes
Jan. 10, 1994, at 2-3

The Final Act would, after ratification . . . , cut tariffs on industrial goods by an average of more than one third, progressively liberalize trade in agricultural products, and convert the GATT from a provisional agreement into a formal international organization, to be called the World Trade Organization (WTO).

The WTO will serve as a single institutional framework encompassing the GATT and all the results of the Round. It will be directed by a Ministerial Conference that will meet at least once every two years, and its regular business will be overseen by a General Council. Countries must accept all of the results of the Uruguay Round, without exception, to become WTO members.

The Final Act's 550 pages include about 15 separate agreements, annexes, decisions, and understandings that would, among other things, bring trade in agricultural products, services, textiles and clothing, and intellectual property within the ambit of the WTO. The agreement would also discipline the use of subsidies and countervailing measures, and technical barriers; tighten antidumping rules and eliminate certain restrictive trade-related investment measures; strengthen existing measures to open up government procurement to foreign suppliers; regulate the use of restrictive safeguard actions; strengthen and clarify procedures for the settlement of trade disputes among WTO members; and increase the transparency of national trade policies by confirming and widening the scope of the Trade Policy Review Mechanism.

Of special interest here is the WTO's dispute-resolution system. Compared to the GATT system, the new arrangement is more centralized and its streamlined procedures are set out with greater specificity. Moreover, under GATT, a panel decision had to be adopted by the consensus of the contracting parties, which meant that the losing party could oppose its adoption. In the WTO, there must be a consensus against the adoption of the report of the panel or the Appellate Body — a complete reversal. The following excerpt outlines the WTO's dispute resolution mechanism. (The Documentary Supplement includes Articles XXII and XXIII of the original GATT agreement and excerpts from the Uruguay Round agreement regarding the new dispute-resolution system.)

John H. Jackson, William J. Davey & Alan O. Sykes, Jr., Legal Problems of International Economic Relations

256-267, 270 (4th ed. 2002)

Section 7.2   Dispute Settlement in the GATT System

There are 19 clauses in the General Agreement which obligate GATT parties to consult in specific instances. These provisions cover such varied subjects as customs valuation and invocation of the Escape Clause. Likewise, there are sprinkled throughout the General Agreement at least seven different provisions for compensatory withdrawal or suspension of concessions.

While Article XXIII is GATT's . . . principal dispute settlement provision, it contains very little procedural detail. Consequently, the GATT parties had to improvise and develop procedures through practice over the years. Initially, the Contracting Parties considered disputes at their regular meetings. In some cases, working parties were used. A working party is understood in the GATT context to mean a body whose members are "nations," so that each nation may send a representative of its own choice. In the 1950's, . . . it became the practice to use panels to consider disputes. A panel is composed of individuals acting in their individual capacities, and not as national representatives. Interestingly, this shift early on in GATT's history shows a desire in GATT to emphasize adjudication by independent decision makers as opposed to negotiated settlements of differences by national representatives. The panel members, usually three in number, were in fact often chosen from available national representatives to GATT. Their reports were then (usually) adopted by consensus in the GATT Council.

The procedures used in the GATT system were codified in a 1979 Tokyo Round understanding. There were also two further declarations on dispute settlement in the mid 1980's and then a series of improvements agreed upon at the Uruguay Round midterm review session in 1989. These procedures were largely carried over in the WTO procedures.

The GATT system experienced some problems with delays and failures to adopt reports because of blocking tactics by losing parties that prevented a consensus in the GATT Council. We will see how the WTO system addresses those problems in the next section. Generally, however, the GATT dispute settlement system can be viewed as relatively successful. . . .

SECTION 7.3   THE WTO DISPUTE SETTLEMENT UNDERSTANDING

The WTO Agreement provides that one of the principal functions of the WTO is the administration of the Understanding on Rules and Procedures Governing the Settlement of Disputes, which is Annex 2 to the WTO Agreement and which is set out in the Documents Supplement. Indeed, the Dispute Settlement Understanding (DSU) states that the dispute settlement system "is a central element in providing security and predictability to the multilateral trading system" (art. 3.2). The DSU sets forth a comprehensive statement of dispute settlement rules and, while it builds on the past GATT practices, it makes several fundamental changes in the operation of the system. The DSU is administered by the Dispute Settlement Body (DSB), which is the WTO General Council acting in a specialized role under a separate chair. The DSU regulates dispute settlement under all covered WTO agreements, although under some agreements special rules and procedures will be applicable.

The general philosophy of WTO dispute settlement is set out in Article 3 of the DSU. Among the principles that are enshrined in that article are the following:

First, it is recognized that the system serves to preserve the rights and obligations of Members and to clarify the existing provisions of the WTO agreements in accordance with the customary rules of interpretation of public international law. . . .

Second, it is agreed that the results of the dispute settlement process cannot add to or diminish the rights and obligations provided in the WTO agreements. . . .

Third, several provisions highlight that the aim of dispute settlement is to secure a positive solution to a dispute and that a solution that is acceptable to the parties and consistent with the WTO agreements is clearly to be preferred.

Fourth, although the DSU provides for the eventuality of non-compliance, it is explicitly stated in DSU Article 3.7 that "the first objective of the dispute settlement mechanism is usually to secure the withdrawal of the measures concerned if these are found to be inconsistent with the provisions of any of the covered agreements." Retaliatory action is described as the last resort.

(A)   The DSU Procedures

The key stages in a WTO dispute settlement proceeding are outlined and explained below. There are four major phases of WTO dispute settlement: First, the parties must attempt to resolve their differences through consultations. Second, if that fails, the complaining party may demand that a panel of independent experts be established to rule on the dispute. Third, and new under the DSU, is the possibility of an appeal by any party to the dispute to the Appellate Body. Finally, if the complaining party succeeds, the DSB is charged with monitoring the implementation of its recommendations. If the recommendations are not implemented, the possibility of negotiated compensation or authorization to withdraw concessions arises. . . .

(1)   Consultations

The requirement that disputing parties consult with a view toward satisfactorily adjusting the matter is contained in Article XXIII itself. The hope is that the parties will resolve their dispute without having to invoke the formal dispute settlement procedures. The rules regarding consultations are set out in article 4 of the DSU. The manner in which the consultations are conducted is up to the parties. The DSU has no rules on consultations beyond that they are to be entered into in good faith and are to be held with 30 days of a request. . . . Despite the fact that the structure of consultations is undefined and there are no rules for conducting them, a significant number of cases end at the consultations stage (either through settlements or abandonment of a case). If consultations fail to settle a dispute within 60 days after the request therefor, the complaining party may request the establishment of a panel. Art. 4.7. In fact, consultations often go on for more than 60 days.

(2)   Panel Process

Under the DSU, the right of party to have a panel established is clearly set out in article 6.1. If consultations fail to resolve a dispute within the 60-day time frame specified in article 4, a complainant may insist on the establishment of a panel and, at the meeting following that at which the request first appears on the DSB's agenda, the DSB is required to establish a panel unless there is a consensus in the DSB not to establish a panel. Since the complaining party may prevent the formation of this "reverse" consensus, there is effectively a right to have a panel established. This is in contrast to the GATT system. Although persistent complainants virtually always succeeded in getting the GATT Council to establish a panel, their success sometimes came only after long periods of delay.

(a)   Setting Up the Panel

Once a panel is established, it is necessary to select the three individuals who will serve as panelists. DSU article 8 provides for the Secretariat to propose potential panel members to the parties, who are not to object except for compelling reasons. In practice, parties are relatively free to reject proposed panelists, but if the parties do not agree on panel members within 20 days of establishment, any party may request the WTO Director-General to appoint the panel on his or her own authority. Art. 8.7. In recent years, the Director-General has appointed some members of almost one-half of the panels composed.

Article 8.1 of the DSU provides [the criteria for membership on a panel]. . . . These criteria could be roughly summarized as establishing three categories of panelists: government officials (current or former), former Secretariat officials and trade academics or lawyers. It is specifically provided that panelists shall not be nationals of parties or third parties, absent agreement of the parties. It is also specified that in a case involving a developing country, one panelist must be from a developing country (if requested). Of the individuals actually chosen for panel service, it appears that the vast majority (over 80%) are current or former government officials.

The DSU provides that panelists serve in their individual capacities and that Members shall not give them instructions or seek to influence them. In addition, the DSB has adopted rules of conduct applicable to participants in the WTO dispute settlement system. The rules require that panelists "be independent and impartial, shall avoid direct or indirect conflicts of interest and shall respect the confidentiality of proceedings." . . .

(b) The Task of Panels

The DSU provides in article 7.1 for standard terms of reference (absent agreement to the contrary). The standard terms direct a panel "To examine, in the light of the relevant provisions in (name of the covered agreement/s cited by the parties to the dispute), the matter referred to the DSB by (name of party) in document DS/ . . . and to make such findings as will assist the DSB in making the recommendations or in giving the rulings provided for in that/those agreement/s." . . .

More generally, DSU Article 11 provides that a panel shall make an objective assessment of the matter before it, including an objective assessment of the facts of the case and the applicability of and conformity with the relevant WTO agreements. . . .

(c) Panel Procedures

A panel normally meets with the parties shortly after its selection to set its working procedures and time schedule. The DSU's standard proposed timetable for panels makes provision for two meetings between the panel and the parties to discuss the substantive issues in the case. Each meeting is preceded by the filing of written submissions. The DSU permits other WTO members to intervene as third parties and present arguments to the panel. Otherwise, the panel proceedings are not open to the public. It was firmly established by the Appellate Body in the *Bananas* case, however, that a party is free to choose the members of its delegation to hearings. Thus, parties may be assisted, and often are, by private counsel.

Among the most fundamental issues that arises in assessing a complaint is the assignment of the burden of proof. Generally speaking, the decisions of the Appellate Body have held that the burden of proof rests upon the party who asserts the affirmative of a particular claim or defense. If that party adduces sufficient evidence to raise a presumption that what is claimed is true, then the burden shifts to the other party to rebut the presumption. The Appellate Body has also spoken in terms of the need for a claimant to establish a *prima facie* case.

In GATT dispute settlement, it was often the case that factual issues were not that important. The basic issue was typically whether a particular governmental measure violated GATT rules. To date, comparatively more WTO disputes have involved disputed factual issues. In order to establish facts, panels normally ask oral and written questions to which the parties are expected to respond. The parties often bring government experts versed in the relevant field to panel meetings. Some parties have submitted affidavit evidence to establish facts. By and large, the fact-finding procedures of panels are relatively less sophisticated tha[n] those of national courts, although it can be expected that more sophisticated fact-finding techniques will develop as the need for fact-finding becomes more acute.

One area in which panels have already become more sophisticated is in the use of experts in scientific matters. In this regard, the DSU provides that if a panel deems it appropriate, it may consult either individual[] experts or form an expert review group to advise it on technical and scientific issues. . . .

One basic issue faced by panels is what sort of standard of review should be applied in reviewing challenged measures. Of course, in some cases that issue is not particularly significant. The only issue is whether the measure violates a WTO rule. But in an increasing number of cases, the assessment of a measure's consistency with WTO rules involves an assessment of the justification for a measure, for example, of whether a measure is "necessary" within the terms of an exception contained [in] GATT Article XX or whether a measure is "based on" or rationally related to a risk assessment in the case of an SPS (health) measure. In such a case, to what extent should a panel or the Appellate Body defer to the challenged government's assessment of necessity or rationality? The DSU gives no guidance on this issue beyond directing panels to make an objective assessment of the matter before them. . . .

After hearings and deliberations, the panel prepares a report detailing its conclusions. Traditionally, the panel has submitted its description of the dispute and of the parties' arguments to the parties for comment. Under the DSU, panels are required to submit an interim report containing their legal analysis for comment as well. Art. 15. Appendix 3 of the DSU specifies time limits for implementations of the various stages in the panel process. Those time limits suggest that the panel report should normally be issued within six to eight months of the establishment of the panel. In practice, cases typically take more time than that.

(d) Consideration and Adoption of Panel Reports

Under GATT dispute settlement practice prior to conclusion of the Uruguay Round, after a panel issued its report, it was considered for adoption by the GATT Council. Traditionally, decisions in the Council were made by consensus, which meant that any party — including the losing party — could prevent the Council from adopting a panel report. If unadopted, a report would represent only the view of the individual panel members. While parties did not often permanently block adoption of reports, some reports were never adopted (even when the underlying dispute was resolved) and others were adopted only after months of delay. Many commentators felt that this was a major failing in what was otherwise a fairly successful GATT dispute settlement system. Indeed, it is difficult to explain to some-one new to the subject why the losing party by itself should be able to prevent adoption of a panel report.

The DSU fundamentally changed this procedure. It eliminates the possibility of blockage by providing in Article 16 that a panel report shall be adopted unless there is an appeal (see below) or a "reverse consensus," i.e., a consensus *not* to adopt the report. This switch from requiring a consensus for adoption to requiring a consensus to block adoption is a very significant change. It appears that it was adopted in hopes that it would satisfy U.S. complaints about weaknesses in the GATT system and thereby result in the United States using the system in the future instead of taking unilateral action as it had done sometimes in the past. Basically, other GATT parties were willing to make the change as a way to rein in U.S. unilateralism in trade matters. Indeed, article 23.1 of the DSU requires WTO members to use the WTO dispute settlement system exclusively if they "seek the redress of a violation of obligations or other nullification or impairment of benefits under the covered agreements." . . .

(3)   The Appellate Body

The change in the consensus rule described above was paired with the introduction of a right to appeal a panel decision. The DSU creates a standing Appellate Body with seven members, appointed for four-year terms and representative of WTO membership. Only one reappointment is permitted. The Appellate Body is authorized to draw up its own working procedures, in consultation with the Chairman of the DSB and the Director-General. These procedures regulate the operation of the Appellate Body and process by which appeals are made and considered. They are available at the WTO website.

The Appellate Body hears appeals of panel reports in divisions of three, although its rules provide for the division hearing a case to exchange views with the other four Appellate Body members before the division finalizes its report. The members of the division that hears a particular appeal are selected by a secret procedure that is based on randomness, unpredictability and the opportunity for all members to serve without regard to national origin. The Appellate Body is required to issue its report within 60 (at most 90) days from the date of the appeal, and its report is to be adopted automatically by the DSB within 30 days, absent consensus to the contrary (as explained above). The appealed panel report is also adopted at that time, as modified by the Appellate Body report.

The Appellate Body's review is limited to issues of law and legal interpretation developed by the panel. However, the Appellate Body has taken a broad view of its power to review panel decisions. It has the express power to reverse, modify or affirm panel decisions, but the DSU does not include a possibility of remanding a case to a panel. Partly as a consequence, the Appellate Body has adopted the practice, where possible in light of a panel's factual findings, of completing the analysis of particular issues in order to resolve cases where it has significantly modified a panel's reasoning. This avoids requiring a party to start the whole proceeding over as a result of those modifications.

There had been 58 WTO dispute settlement cases where reports had been adopted by the DSB as of September 1, 2001 (including compliance cases). In 40 of those cases, there was an Appellate Body report. In seven cases, panels were upheld;

in one case, the panel was reversed. In the remaining 32 cases, the Appellate Body modified, sometimes extensively, the panel's findings. In all but one of those 32 cases, however, the basic finding of a violation reached by the panel was upheld, albeit sometimes to a different degree and/or on the basis of quite different reasoning. Eighteen panel reports had been adopted without an appeal. Thus, slightly more than two-thirds of the cases had been appealed.

It is probably much too early to judge an institution that has been in operation for only five and one-half years. Yet a number of points may be made. First, although the Appellate Body has never articulated a standard of review that it will apply on appeals of panel reports, it has engaged in fairly intensive review of such reports. In doing so, it has in general left its stamp clearly on most areas of WTO law that have been appealed. . . . While strict notions of "stare decisis" do not apply in the WTO, it is clear that prior cases do play an important role in dispute settlement, especially those considered to be well-reasoned and persuasive. Indeed, the Appellate Body noted early on that adopted GATT panel reports created "legitimate expectations" that similar matters would be handled similarly, and both panels and the Appellate Body frequently support their decisions by extensive citation and quotation of prior decisions. Thus, it is appropriate to speak of the Appellate Body's effect on "WTO law."

Generally speaking, the Appellate Body tends to rely heavily on close textual interpretation of the WTO provisions at issue, stressing that a treaty interpreter must look to the ordinary meaning of the relevant terms, in their context and in light of the object and purpose of the relevant agreement (a requirement of Article 31 of the Vienna Convention of the Law of Treaties) and must not interpret provisions so as to render them devoid of meaning. The Appellate Body has expressed the need to respect due process and procedural rights of Members in the dispute settlement process, but by and large it has recognized considerable discretion on the part of panels, which has led it in the end to reject most procedural/due process challenges. On the whole, it is difficult to characterize the Appellate Body as being more or less deferential to Member discretion than panels. While it has significantly cut back on the scope of panel rulings in some cases, it has significantly expanded the scope of liability in others.

(4) Implementation and Suspension of Concessions

If it is found that a complaint is justified, the panel/Appellate Body report typically recommends that the offending member cease its violation of WTO rules, normally by withdrawing the offending measure. After it adopts a report, the DSB monitors whether or not its recommendations are implemented. The DSU requires a losing respondent to indicate what actions it plans to take to implement the panel's recommendations. If immediate implementation is impracticable, then implementation is required within a reasonable period of time. Art. 21.3. The reasonable period of time is normally set by agreement of the contending parties, or, absent agreement, by arbitration. Normally, the period is not to exceed 15 months; a range of 8–10 months is average.

If the recommendations are not implemented, the prevailing party is entitled to seek compensation from the non-complying member or request DSB authority to suspend concessions previously made to that member (sometimes referred to as "retaliation"). Art. 22.1. In this regard, the DSU modifies past GATT practice. Article XXIII permitted GATT contracting parties to authorize the prevailing party to retaliate if the losing party failed to end its violation of GATT rules. Such authorization was granted only once, however, and that was in 1955 to allow the Netherlands to suspend concessions made to the United States in a case involving GATT-inconsistent U.S. quotas on Dutch agricultural products. The Netherlands apparently never utilized the authorization. Attempts to obtain authorizations in the 1980's failed because of the consensus rule, with the target country opposing the authorization. Now, under the DSU, suspension of concessions is to be authorized automatically in the absence of implementation or compensation, absent a consensus in the DSB to the contrary. Art. 22.6. There are specific arbitration procedures for determining the level of such a suspension if no agreement can be reached.

The DSU provides: "Prompt compliance with recommendations or rulings of the DSB is essential in order to ensure the effective resolution of disputes to the benefit of all Members" (art. 21.1). The DSB will normally recommend the withdrawal of any measure found to be inconsistent with a member's obligations, and the DSU explicitly provides that withdrawal of a nonconforming measure is preferred to compensation or suspension of concessions. Art. 22.1. Compensation and suspensions of concessions are viewed as "temporary measures," to be used when a report is not implemented in a reasonable time. The preference for withdrawal is also found in the WTO Agreement itself, where article XVI:4 provides that "[e]ach Member shall ensure the conformity of its laws, regulations and administrative procedures with its obligations as provided in the annexed Agreements." Thus, there would appear to be an international law obligation to implement recommendations to withdraw inconsistent measures.

The application of the foregoing procedures on implementation and retaliation has been controversial. . . .

The WTO system has had a reasonably good overall implementation record. As of September 1, 2001, panel and/or Appellate Body reports had been adopted in 52 cases (not including compliance proceedings). In 8 cases, no implementation was required; in 7 cases the period for implementation had not expired. Of the remaining 37 cases, implementation had occurred in 30, or approximately 75% of the cases. In some of these cases implementation was not completely accepted by the complaining party, but no further proceedings were initiated. In addition, implementation was not always timely; nonetheless it ultimately occurred in these cases. Of the seven remaining cases, four were in compliance proceedings to determine whether implementation had taken place. In the other three cases, where non-compliance had been found or admitted, retaliatory measures had been authorized. . . . These cases were the exceptions to an otherwise strong record in compliance. The existence of these cases (and cases where complainants have not obtained timely or complete satisfaction) has raised the question, however, of whether the remedies available under WTO rules need to be improved. It can be argued that the current structure of compliance proceedings encourages foot-dragging and that the ultimate WTO remedy for compliance — "retaliation" through trade sanctions — may not always be effective.

The Chairman of the WTO Appellate Body provided some insight and humanity into this dispute-resolution process in a 2002 speech excerpted below.

James Bacchus, Remarks at the Woodrow Wilson
International Center for Scholars

(May 1, 2002)

I am often asked:

What is it like to be one of the "faceless foreign judges" of the World Trade Organization in Geneva, Switzerland? Today, I will try to answer that question, or at least part of it. . . .

We are seven around the table. We are from seven different countries. We are from seven different regions of the world. We are from seven different legal traditions. We are, in the words of the WTO treaty, "broadly representative of membership in the WTO." . . .

We are aided in our work by the Appellate Body "Secretariat," which is a fancy way of describing our very fine staff. . . . Through the years, numerous bright young lawyers on our Secretariat have worked with us and joined with us from time to time in the discussions around our table.

The subject of these discussions is what we call the "covered agreements." The "covered agreements" are the more than 27,000 pages of international concessions and obligations that comprise the WTO treaty and that bind all WTO members.

We seven are, according to the WTO treaty, "persons of recognized authority, with demonstrated expertise in law, international trade and the subject matters of the covered agreements generally." As such, our job is to help the Members of the WTO implement, interpret, and enforce the terms of the "covered agreements." . . .

We do not even have titles. The WTO treaty speaks only of a "standing Appellate Body." The treaty does not say what the seven "persons" who are members of the Appellate Body should be called. So we call ourselves simply "Members of the Appellate Body." . . .

And we may be called "judges" because, whatever we may call ourselves, that word may best describe what we do. For our job is to "judge" appeals in international trade disputes affecting the lives of five billion people in the 95 percent of all world commerce conducted by the 144 countries and other customs territories that are — currently — Members of the WTO.

Technically, the Appellate Body is rightly described as "quasi-judicial." To have legal effect, our rulings must be adopted by the Members of the WTO. But a ruling by the Appellate Body in an international trade dispute will *not* be adopted only if *all* the Members of the WTO decide "by consensus" that it should *not* be — including the Member or Members in whose favor we may have ruled. Thus far, this has never happened.

But whether our work is described as "judicial" or "quasi-judicial," and whatever we may be called, we have much to do around our table in Geneva. We have much to do because, among all the international tribunals in the world, and, indeed, among all the international tribunals in the *history* of the world, the Appellate Body of the WTO is unique in two important ways.

The first way in which we are unique is that we have what we lawyers call "compulsory jurisdiction." All WTO Members have agreed in the WTO treaty to resolve all their disputes with other WTO Members involving matters that are covered by the WTO treaty in the WTO dispute settlement system.

The second way in which the Appellate Body is unique is that we make judgments that are enforced. Our judgments are enforced, not by us, but by the Members of the WTO themselves through the power of economic suasion.

The Members of the WTO are sovereign countries and customs territories. No Member of the WTO can ever be required to comply with any judgment in WTO dispute settlement. Yet, under the WTO treaty, if a Member chooses not to comply, it pays an economic price. That price is what the treaty describes as "compensation and the suspension of concessions."

This is a form of "damages" to the other Member injured in that trade dispute. These "damages" consist of either additional access for the injured Member to the market of the "non-complying" Member in other sectors of trade, or reduced access for the "non-complying" Member to the market of the injured Member in other sectors of trade. As this can sometimes be a very high price to pay, WTO Members have considerable economic incentive to choose to comply with WTO judgments. And they almost always do.

These two ways in which we are unique help keep us busy around our round table in Geneva in an effort to help provide what the WTO treaty calls "security and predictability to the multilateral trading system." Our jurisprudential uniqueness is, of course, the culmination of more than half a century of building the multilateral trading system, first under the GATT, and now under the Dispute Settlement Understanding that is the legal linchpin of the WTO treaty.

We are also kept busy because WTO Members know that, when they bring a case in WTO dispute settlement that eventually reaches the Appellate Body, they will receive a *legal* judgment, and not a *political* judgment. They know they will receive a judgment that will, in the words of the treaty, "address" the "issues of law" that are "raised . . . during the appellate proceeding." Nothing more. And nothing less. For, in addressing issues of law in WTO appeals, we seven have always been, and we will always be, as one observer for the *New York Times* has put it, "impartial and unflinching."

For all these reasons, in the seven years since we began working together around our table, the WTO has become by far the busiest international dispute settlement system in history. As the treaty says, "The aim of the dispute settlement system is to secure a positive solution to a dispute" involving WTO Members. And, as the system has grown, ever-increasing numbers of trade disputes have been brought to the WTO by WTO Members in search of a "positive solution."

The parties to the proceedings in WTO dispute settlement that arise from these trade disputes are exclusively the countries and other customs territories that are Members of the WTO. No one else is entitled under the WTO treaty to participate in WTO dispute settlement. But, of course, the WTO Members that are parties to these proceedings are always of the view that they are asserting and defending important domestic interests.

In these first few years of the WTO, numerous trade disputes among the Members of the WTO have been settled "out of court," so to speak, by virtue of the very existence of a compulsory dispute settlement system that can make enforceable judgments. Many of the other disputes that have been brought to the WTO in its brief history have resulted in rulings by the *ad hoc* three-judge panels that are the WTO equivalent of trial courts. And about fifty of these disputes have resulted in rulings by the Appellate Body that have been adopted by the Members of the WTO.

Almost all these disputes have been resolved with what the parties to the disputes have viewed as a "positive solution."

Not without reason has Director General Mike Moore of the WTO frequently described the dispute settlement system as the "crown jewel" of the multilateral trading system. Peter Sutherland, the former Director General of the WTO's predecessor, the GATT, has gone so far as to say that the WTO dispute settlement system "is the greatest advance in multilateral governance since Bretton Woods" at the conclusion of World War II.

Given the broad scope and sway of the WTO treaty, the disputes that are resolved in WTO dispute settlement can involve manufacturing, agriculture, services, intellectual property, investment, taxation, and virtually every other area of world commerce. The appeals we have judged thus far have involved everything from apples to computers, from automobiles to semiconductors, from shrimp to satellites, and from bananas to chemicals to oil to aerospace. Ever more varied kinds of disputes are resulting in WTO dispute settlement as more agreements enter into force, more agreements are concluded, and more concessions are made. . . .

We do not render advisory opinions on the Appellate Body. We render opinions only when there are specific trade disputes. By treaty, all WTO Members that are parties to a dispute have the automatic right to appeal "issues of law covered in the panel report and legal interpretations developed by the panel" to the Appellate Body. On appeal, we seven "shall address each of the issues raised . . . during the appellate proceeding." We "may uphold, modify or reverse the legal findings and conclusions of the panel."

Thus, we cannot choose the disputes that are appealed to us. Unlike the Supreme Court of the United States, we have no discretionary jurisdiction. Further, we have no power to remand a dispute to a panel for further consideration. We have no authority whatsoever to decline to hear an appeal. Moreover, we have no authority whatsoever to refrain from "addressing" a legal issue that has been properly raised in an appeal. The WTO treaty says that we "shall address" every legal issue raised in an appeal. So we do.

And we do so within strict deadlines established by the treaty. Most other international tribunals have no deadlines. But, no matter how complicated the issues may be that are raised on appeal, generally we have no more than 90 days in which to hear and decide an appeal. As our record reflects, we take seriously the need to "address" the legal issues raised in each appeal both thoroughly and appropriately within the treaty deadlines. We have met our treaty deadlines consistently, and I am persuaded that this, too, has contributed to the success thus far of the WTO dispute settlement system.

By treaty, we have been granted the authority to establish our own "working procedures" within our deadlines. Seven years ago, we sat down together at our table with a blank legal pad and began writing our procedures. It took three weeks. Since then, we have made only two, minor changes. Using these working procedures, in each appeal, we review the panel record and the panel report, we review submissions by the WTO Members that are interested parties and third parties, we conduct an oral hearing on the legal issues that have been raised, and we deliberate and write a final report containing our judgment. And generally we do all this within no more than 90 days. (My colleagues would no doubt urge me to add that this is, actually, no more than 75 days, as we must allow two weeks for mandatory translation.)

For translation and other purposes, there are three official languages of the WTO — English, Spanish, and French. As a matter of practice, the seven of us generally work in our common language — English. . . .

We have been able to meet our deadlines in part because we have shared our growing workload among the seven. By treaty, three of us sit as a "division" to hear and decide each appeal. Those three sign the report of the Appellate Body in that appeal. Before a decision is reached, the three on the "division" in the appeal engage in an "exchange of views" with the four others who are not on the "division." One of the three serves as "Presiding Member" of the "division." By treaty, all seven of us "serve in rotation" in all these roles, and, by rule, we do so on an anonymous and random basis that tends to equalize our individual workloads.

Whatever our individual role may be in any particular appeal, each of us strives always to reach a "consensus" in every appeal. We are not required to do so. The treaty does not prohibit dissents. The treaty provides only that "opinions expressed" by individuals serving on the Appellate Body must be "anonymous." But, thus far, in all our years of working together, and in about fifty appeals, there has not been even one dissent to the conclusions in any report of the Appellate Body. Thus far, all our decisions have been by "consensus."

I do not believe that I betray the "confidentiality" of our table talk in any way by saying that the "consensus" we have achieved in the many appeals that have been made, thus far, to the Appellate Body has not always been achieved easily. . . .

In our time together around our table, we have learned that the issues that are raised on appeal are rarely clear cut. Even seven years on, there are many important provisions of the "covered agreements" and, in fact, some entire agreements that are part of the overall WTO treaty that have yet to be construed even once by the Appellate Body. Moreover, issues are raised in almost every appeal that are, in legal parlance, issues of "first impression." In truth, it might be said of the entirety of the ruled-based WTO multilateral trading system that, in many ways, it poses a *world* of "first impression." Given this, we seven are very much of the view that we owe it to the Members of the WTO to examine every last shade of nuance of every single legal issue that is raised in every single appeal. And we always do.

That is why our hearings sometimes last for days, our deliberations sometimes last for weeks, and our drafting sometimes lasts for draft after draft after draft. That is why we meet, day after day, around our round table. . . . That is why we work together to forge a "consensus" up until the very limits of our ever-present and ever-pressing deadlines. . . .

The disputes that are appealed to us and are discussed around the table are about the meaning of the obligations that are contained in the "covered agreements" that comprise the WTO treaty. These obligations are found in the words of the treaty. The meaning of the words of the treaty is thus our constant focus in rendering our judgments. As we noted in our very first appeal, this focus is in keeping with the international rules of treaty interpretation found in the Vienna Convention on the Law of Treaties.

Our focus on the words of the WTO treaty is as it should be. The WTO treaty contains WTO rules. The Appellate Body exists to construe WTO rules in WTO dispute settlement. Yet, as we also noted in our very first appeal, WTO rules cannot, in WTO dispute settlement, be viewed in "clinical isolation" from other international law.

Our responsibility in every appeal is to say everything about the meaning of the words of the treaty that must be said in order to "address" the legal issues "raised" in that appeal and thus assist the WTO Members in resolving that dispute in a "positive solution." Our aim in every appeal is to do that, only that, and no more. . . .

. . . [S]ome may say as well that some decisions have been made in appeals in WTO dispute settlement that should, ideally, have been made instead by the Members of the WTO through multilateral negotiations leading to WTO rulemaking. Here, too, in some instances, I might agree. Yet it is neither my role nor my place to make suggestions to the Members of the WTO about their rulemaking. The Members of the WTO have established an effective system for settling disputes about existing rules. It is for the Members of the WTO to decide how best to establish an effective system for making new rules.

You tell me. Which makes better sense? Should the Members of the WTO unravel an effective system for settling disputes about existing rules because they have not yet established an effective system for making new rules? Or, should the Members of the WTO try instead to establish a system for making new rules that will be as effective as the system they already have for settling disputes about existing rules? To intone one of the many truisms of which we sometimes seem so enamored in international law, but without the usual, obligatory Latin phrasing: don't fix what ain't broke; fix only what needs fixing.

In sum, I will say this to the critics of the various outcomes of various cases thus far in WTO dispute settlement. . . . I will trust *every* Member of the WTO to remember that the entire national interest of *no* Member is to be found in the outcome of any one, single case. Rather, the overriding and abiding national interest of *every* Member of the WTO is to be found instead in the shared international interest of *all* Members in the continued success and strengthening of the WTO dispute settlement system. And, because I am an American, I will be so bold as to add: This is especially true of the largest economy in the world and the largest trading nation in the world — the United States of America. And we Americans must never forget it.

From the conclusion of the Jay Treaty, to the settlement of the Alabama Claims, to the establishment of the Hague court, to the agreement on the GATT, to the creation at long last of the WTO, we Americans have always been in the forefront of international efforts to achieve peace and prosperity in a better world through the international rule of law. Together with others of like mind around the world, we must always be in the forefront of those seeking and serving the rule of law — whatever the political pressures or the passing sentiments of any one case or any one day. . . .

This will not always be easy. . . . [I]n 1990, . . . I happened to read a column by the journalist Michael Kinsley in *The New Republic*. . . . What Kinsley wrote then is good advice for all Members of the WTO, and for all of us who support the work of the WTO, as, together, we seek and serve the international rule of law: . . . "Law that need not be obeyed if you disagree with it is not law. If we want meaningful international law to be available when we find it useful, we must respect it even when we don't." . . .

By far the most rewarding experience for me as a Member of the Appellate Body has been the intellectual communion in which I have shared around our table. For, time after time, around our table, we have, after exhaustive mutual effort, made seven minds into one. In between sips of *renversé*, we have shaped a "consensus" that has helped the Members of the WTO shape a better world.

The Appellate Body is still new. WTO dispute settlement is still new. The WTO itself is still new. All these are institutions still in their infancy internationally, and still very much in the making as ways of serving a global economy and an increasingly "globalized" world.

Ours is very much a work *in* progress in the work *of* progress that is the WTO. Even now, the Members of the WTO are looking for ways to improve WTO dispute settlement. I would be the first to say that it can be improved.

Yet, whatever our inevitable human failings and frailties may be, I do, passionately, believe this: Our work around our table in Geneva is making an historic contribution to international trade, to international law, and to the establishment of the international rule of law. And, for this reason, our work at the WTO is an important part of the work for human freedom. . . .

Notes and Questions

1. How similar were the old GATT panels to arbitration (i.e., where the panel's decision is binding)? How similar are the new WTO panels to arbitral panels?

2. The WTO system provides for a new layer for appeals. Given the membership and standing nature of the Appellate Body, it should help ensure consistency in panel decisions. If a case is appealed and the appellate panel makes its decision, how similar is that decision to an arbitration? Or to the highest appellate court in a jurisdiction?

3. Some Uruguay Round negotiators thought that the appeal mechanism also provided a little more "political cover" to a losing party back home. The losing state could appeal an adverse panel decision. Even if it lost again, the state could argue to legislators and various interest groups back home that it had fought the matter as hard as possible, that it had "gone the extra mile." This would be part of the justification for changing practices or laws that had been found in violation of the WTO agreements.

4. What are the allowed time periods for the panel and Appellate Body proceedings under the DSU? See Article 20. In the WTO's first seven years (1995-2002), the panels and Appellate Body generally adhered to the allowed time periods. How long then is the losing party allowed to take to comply with the panel's or Appellate Body's recommendations? See Article 21.

5. Does the panel or Appellate Body have the authority to rule a country's law or regulation void because it is inconsistent with a WTO agreement? How would their decisions differ in language and effect from those of the U.S. Supreme Court if the Supreme Court found the law of a U.S. state (e.g., California) inconsistent with the U.S. Constitution? How would they differ from the decision of the European Court of Justice if it found the law of a Member State (e.g., France) inconsistent with the EC Treaty? See DSU, Article 19.

6. What are the remedies under the WTO? Review GATT Articles XXII and XXIII and Articles 21 and 22 of the WTO's new dispute procedure in the Documentary Supplement. Are punitive damages allowed? Are the remedies limited to a decision that the offending practice be changed or to steps by the injured party to obtain compensation or suspension of concessions or other obligations? Is compensation limited to the amount of harm suffered (see Article 22.4)?

7. How effective are these remedies for a small country that is being injured by the illegal practices of a much larger trading partner? What if the large trading partner decides that it is upset enough with the other country (possibly for foreign policy reasons) that it is willing to accept an equivalent suspension of concessions or other obligations rather than change its practices?

8. Near the end of the excerpt from Professors Jackson, Davey, and Sykes, the authors contend: "Thus, there would appear to be an international law obligation to implement recommendations to withdraw inconsistent measures." And, as both these authors and Chairman Bacchus point out, countries have generally complied with the panel/Appellate Body reports.

However, what if a country (or countries) feels strongly that its national interests do not justify changing its laws or regulations to make them consistent with the WTO agreements as interpreted by the panel/Appellate Body? For example, in the *Beef Hormone* case, after the Appellate Body found in 1998 that the European Union did not have the requisite scientific basis for preventing the importation of American beef that had been fed hormones, the EU continued to refuse to allow the importation of the American beef, even after the WTO had authorized the United States to retaliate by imposing new tariffs on a variety of EU imports worth over $100 million. The EU countries apparently continued to resist, in part because of political pressures in their countries from various groups that were genuinely concerned about the health effects of consuming beef that had once been treated with hormones, even though the scientific basis for their fears might not have been sufficient for the WTO panel and Appellate Body. This decision took place in the context also of England's troubles with mad-cow disease in its cattle and an outbreak of hoof-and-mouth disease in livestock in England and some other EU countries. Should we expect the EU leaders to ignore these domestic concerns and accept the WTO decision as its legal obligation, thus allowing the importation of the American beef clean? Or, in certain special cases, should we recognize that the WTO members have the sovereign right essentially to decide not to comply and to accept the retaliatory measures indefinitely?

Note that a situation that might well raise similar issues are attempts by countries to prohibit or limit the importation of food that has been grown with genetically modified seed. This seed has been developed to grow strains of corn and other crops that are more resistant to disease and/or have higher yields. Critics question whether the effects, if any, on the health of people who consume these GMO crops are completely known.

9. The frequent and diverse use of the WTO dispute-resolution system continues. From June 1995 through December 2002, there were 279 complaints filed with the WTO regarding about 180 distinct matters. There were over 20 active cases pending.

10. To get a sense of the diversity of the WTO cases, here are some of the first cases for which the whole process has been completed and the report of the Appellate Body adopted: a complaint by Venezuela against the U.S. standards for imported gasoline; a complaint by the United States and EU against Japan's discriminatory internal taxes on alcoholic beverages; a complaint by Costa Rica against U.S. restrictions on imports of cotton and man-made fiber underwear; a complaint by the Philippines against Brazil for measures affecting desiccated coconut; a complaint by the United States against Canada regarding certain measures on periodicals;

a complaint by the United States and several Latin American countries against the European Union's regime for the importation, sale, and distribution of bananas; and a complaint by the United States against India's patent protection for pharmaceutical and agricultural chemical products.

11. As the incomplete list above suggests, the United States has brought more cases than any other country. It has also been sued frequently. The United States has lost some cases, such as the one regarding existing U.S. standards for imported gasoline, one involving an import ban on shrimp that were caught in a way that endangered certain sea turtles, and one involving billions of dollars in tax benefits for U.S. corporations who formed special foreign sales corporations. Nevertheless, more often than not, the United States has been successful in the WTO cases, reflecting in part its relatively open domestic market.

From what you know now, do you think that it is generally in the interest of the United States to have a strong WTO (with rules, an institutional framework, and a strong dispute resolution system) that is designed to open markets for goods and services, to encourage foreign investment, and to protect intellectual property rights? What concerns might you have regarding a strong WTO vis-à-vis other international institutions, the U.S. government, or other entities? (The institutional structure and role of the WTO will be discussed further in Chapter 5.)

12. In November 2001, the Fourth Ministerial Conference on the WTO was held in Doha, Qatar. The Conference issued the Doha Declaration, which calls for negotiations on various aspects of WTO structure and implementation procedure, specifically including negotiations to revise the Dispute Settlement Understanding. (In the late 1990s, the Dispute Settlement Body started an informal review of the DSU; however, member states were unable to reach a consensus regarding the proposed changes.)

13. The WTO has an excellent, up-to-date Web site at <www.wto.org>. In addition, there is now a voluminous array of books, journals, and articles about the WTO. For example, besides the sources cited above, see Robert E. Hudec, Enforcing International Trade Law: The Evolution of the Modern GATT Legal System (1993); John H. Jackson, The Jurisprudence of GATT and the WTO (2000); The WTO as an International Organization (Anne O. Krueger ed. 1998).

E. DOMESTIC COURTS

1. The Role of International Law

Federal and state courts in the United States and courts in other countries often adjudicate cases involving international issues. These cases might range from a claim of violation of internationally recognized human rights to the enforcement of a contract for the sale of goods across national boundaries.

In determining these cases, U.S. courts might apply state law, a federal statute or common law, the law of another country, or international law. International treaties to which the United States is a party are part of U.S. law. Moreover, as seen earlier with the *Paquete Habana* and *Filartiga* cases (pages 253 and 256), U.S. courts sometimes apply customary international law as part of U.S. law. Indeed, U.S. courts seem to be encountering such international law questions more frequently in recent decades. (See Chapter 3. Questions of choice of law and of the applicability of another nation's laws are discussed further in Chapter 7.)

Similarly, another nation's domestic courts might decide cases by applying that nation's laws, the law of another state, or international law. As discussed in the following excerpt, the role of international law in other countries varies. As in the United States, there are often important differences between the role of treaties and customary international law. Notwithstanding the variations, both treaties and customary international law appear to play an important role in many countries.

I.A. Shearer, Starke's International Law

67, 76-77 (11th ed. 1994)

The object of the present discussion is to ascertain in what manner and to what extent municipal courts do apply a rule of international law. How far do they give effect to it automatically, and how far is some specific municipal measure of statutory or judicial incorporation required before that rule can be recognised as binding within the municipal sphere? A further question is, how far a rule of international law will be applied by a municipal court if it actually conflicts with a rule of municipal law judge-made or statutory rule. The answers to these questions will be found to require distinctions to be made, on the one hand, between customary and treaty rules of international law; and on the other between statutory and judge-made municipal law. . . .

PRACTICE OF STATES OTHER THAN GREAT BRITAIN AND THE UNITED STATES

The practice of states other than Great Britain and the United States reveals wide variations both in the requirements of constitutional law, and in the attitudes of municipal courts concerning the application therein of customary international law and of treaties.

So far as one can sum up this practice, and despite the hazard of generalisation on so complex a matter, the following propositions may be ventured:

1. In a large number of states, customary rules of international law are applied as part of internal law by municipal courts, without the necessity for any specific act of incorporation, provided that there is no conflict with existing municipal law.
2. Only a minority of states follow a practice whereby, without the necessity for any specific act of incorporation, their municipal courts apply customary rules of international law to the extent of allowing these to prevail in case of conflict with a municipal statute or municipal judge-made law.
3. There is no uniform practice concerning the application of treaties within the municipal sphere. Each country has its own particularities as regards promulgation or publication of treaties, legislative approval of treaty provisions, and so on. Moreover, certain treaties, such as informal administrative arrangements, are never submitted to the legislature. Also the courts in

some countries, for example the German Federal Republic, will, like American courts, give effect to self-executing treaties, that is to say, those capable of application without the necessity of legislative implementation. In other countries, for example, Belgium, legislative enactment or legislative approval is necessary for almost all treaties, particularly those which affect the status of private citizens. As to conflicts between the provisions of treaties and earlier or later statutes, it is only in relatively few countries that the superiority of the treaty in this regard is established. France is a case in point, for if a treaty has been duly ratified in accordance with law, French tribunals, both judicial and administrative, will give effect to it, notwithstanding a conflict with internal legislation. But in most countries, for example, Norway, treaties do not per se operate to supersede state legislation or judge-made law. Exceptionally, however, there are some countries the courts of which go so far as to give full force to treaties, even if contrary to the provisions of the constitution of the country concerned.

4.   In general, there is discernible a considerable weight of state practice requiring that in a municipal court, primary regard be paid to municipal law, irrespective of the applicability of rules of international law, and hence relegating the question of any breach of international law to the diplomatic domain.

Reference should be made in this connection to certain modern constitutions, containing far-reaching provisions to the effect that international law shall be treated as an integral part of municipal law. A current example is article 25 of the Basic Law for the Federal Republic of Germany which lays down that the general rules of public international law shall form part of federal law, and shall take precedence over the laws of and create rights and duties directly for the inhabitants of the federal territory.[6] It has been claimed that this and similar constitutional provisions reflect a growing tendency among states to acknowledge the supremacy of international law within the municipal sphere. Be that as it may, it is none the less curious that these constitutional provisions appear to support the positivist thesis that before international law can be applicable by municipal courts some specific adoption by municipal law is required, since it is only in virtue of these provisions of municipal constitutional law that the rules of international law are valid and applicable within the municipal sphere. . . .

Questions

1. Based on your knowledge of practice in the United States and other countries, do you think that domestic courts should recognize an increased role for customary international law? Should customary international law take precedence over acts by a country's chief executive or his delegates? Over acts that a country recognizes

6. Cf. art. 4 of the German Republican Constitution of 1919, which provided that "the universally recognised rules of international law are valid as binding constituent parts of German Federal law." Art. 25 of the Basic Law does not operate to confer supremacy on treaties concluded by the Federal Republic over municipal law, or to enable international law to prevail over fundamental provisions of the Basic Law; cf. Case 11/70: Internationale Handelsgesellschaft . . . [1972] CMLR 255. . . .

as exclusively or primarily the responsibility of the chief executive — for example, recognition of new governments or moving military units in a crisis? Should newly developed customary international law have precedence over a country's prior statutes? Should later domestic statutes override a rule of customary international law?

2. Why do you think that the practice regarding international treaties varies so much among states? Might this reflect the relative roles of the chief executive and the national legislature in law-making? Should each state have a presumption that any treaty (or certain types of treaties) are self-executing? Or should the presumption be that a treaty is non-self-executing? What effect might such a presumption have on the relative roles of the chief executive and the national legislature?

3. Should domestic courts be the arbiters of the role of customary international law? Similarly, should domestic courts have the final say on whether a treaty is self-executing or not? Or should the courts defer to the chief executive or the legislature on various matters?

2. Enforcement of Another State's Civil Judgments

Once you have a judgment, you must enforce it. Another way in which domestic courts participate in the international arena is through the enforcement of foreign court judgments.

United States courts are required by the full faith and credit clause of the Constitution to recognize and enforce the judgments of sister states (e.g., New York, California, Virginia). Article VI, section 1 provides: "Full Faith and Credit shall be given in each State to the public Acts, Records, and Judicial Proceeding of every other State."

Foreign judgments, however, do not have the support of the constitutional command. The usual starting point for analysis of the duty of U.S. courts to enforce judgments is the principle of comity among nations, enunciated in the old case of Hilton v. Guyot, 159 U.S. 113, 202-203 (1895).

The following excerpt from the Restatement briefly notes the diversity of practice among foreign states regarding recognition and enforcement and then focuses on U.S. law and practice.

Restatement Chapter 8: Foreign Judgments and Awards

Introductory Note

. . . There are no agreed principles governing recognition and enforcement of foreign judgments, except that no state recognizes or enforces the judgment of another state rendered without jurisdiction over the judgment debtor. . . .

State practice varies widely. Some states require a treaty or proof of reciprocity (e.g., the Federal Republic of Germany), some have no such requirement (e.g., France), and some do not enforce foreign judgments at all in the absence of a treaty (e.g., The Netherlands). Some states (e.g., the United States) treat default judgments and contested judgments substantially alike for purposes of enforcement;

others (e.g., Great Britain) enforce default judgments in limited circumstances only. Some states distinguish sharply between civil judgments ordering the payment of money and other judgments, such as those determining status of persons; others treat different types of judgments substantially alike. Some states recognize foreign judgments directly, others require "validation" by local courts (e.g., Italy). Some states (e.g., France) permit intermediate provisional measures, such as attachment of the judgment debtor's assets, prior to decision on enforcement. All states decline to recognize some judgments on the basis of conflict with their public policy or *ordre public*, but these terms have different meaning from state to state. Courts of some states (e.g., France) recognize a foreign judgment only if they would have applied the same law to the controversy as that chosen by the rendering court, or if the choice of law did not affect the result. Some states (e.g., Belgium) reserve the right to review the merits of a foreign judgment, though they do not always do so. It appears that the country most receptive to recognition of foreign judgments is the United States, in which the principles and practices engendered by the Full Faith and Credit clause in the United States Constitution in respect of sister-State judgments have to a large extent been carried over to recognition and enforcement of judgments of foreign states.

Numerous bilateral and multilateral treaties, especially among the European states, mitigate the diversity suggested above and tend to promote the recognition and enforcement of foreign judgments. Since 1968, the member states of the European Community have been parties to the Brussels Convention on Jurisdiction and the Enforcement of Judgments in Civil Matters, which, where it applies, functions much like the Full Faith and Credit clause of the United States Constitution. As of 1987, the United States was not a party to any treaty concerning recognition or enforcement of foreign judgments, and no negotiations looking to such a treaty were in progress.[1]

In view of the diversity in the law and practice of states, Subchapter A of this Chapter focuses on the law and practice of the United States. . . .

Subchapter A. Foreign Judgments: Law of the United States

§481.   Recognition and Enforcement of Foreign Judgments

(1) Except as provided in §482, a final judgment of a court of a foreign state granting or denying recovery of a sum of money, establishing or confirming the status of a person, or determining interests in property, is conclusive between the parties, and is entitled to recognition in courts in the United States.

(2) A judgment entitled to recognition under Subsection (1) may be enforced by any party or its successors or assigns against any other party, its successors or assigns, in accordance with the procedure for enforcement of judgments applicable where enforcement is sought.

---

1. In the mid-1970's, the United States and Great Britain held negotiations on a proposed Convention Providing for the Reciprocal Recognition and Enforcement of Judgments in Civil Matters, but agreement could not be reached and the negotiations were terminated.

Comment

a. Recognition and enforcement of judgments as State law. This section sets forth the prevailing common and statutory law of States of the United States, not rules of federal or international law. Since Erie v. Tompkins, 304 U.S. 64 (1938), it has been accepted that in the absence of a federal statute or treaty or some other basis for federal jurisdiction, such as admiralty, recognition and enforcement of foreign country judgments is a matter of State law, and an action to enforce a foreign country judgment is not an action arising under the laws of the United States. Thus, State courts, and federal courts applying State law, recognize and enforce foreign country judgments without reference to federal rules. . . .

b. Recognition and enforcement distinguished. The judgment of a foreign state may not be enforced unless it is entitled to recognition. Whether a foreign judgment should be recognized, may be in issue, however, not only in enforcement (see §482), but in other contexts, for example where the defendant seeks to rely on a prior adjudication of a controversy *(res judicata)*, or where either side in a litigation seeks to rely on prior determination of an issue of fact or law. A proceeding to enforce a foreign judgment normally takes the form of an action by the judgment creditor to collect a sum due from the judgment debtor under a judgment rendered in another state. Recognition of a foreign judgment may also be at issue in proceedings before bodies other than courts, for example in administrative proceedings.

Judgments granting injunctions, declaring rights or determining status, and judgments arising from attachments of property, are not generally entitled to enforcement, but may be entitled to recognition under this and the following sections.

c. Effect of foreign judgment. A foreign judgment is generally entitled to recognition by courts in the United States to the same extent as a judgment of a court of one State in the courts of another State. As in the case of a sister-State judgment, a judgment of a foreign country ordinarily has no greater effect in the United States than in the country where the judgment was rendered. . . .

Reporters' Notes

1. *Reciprocity generally not required.* In Hilton v. Guyot, 159 U.S. 113 (1895), the United States Supreme Court treated the enforceability of foreign country judgments as a matter of the "comity of nations," and concluded that comity called for enforcement of judgments rendered in a foreign state in favor of a citizen of that state against a non-citizen only on the basis of reciprocity. Accordingly, the Court declined to enforce the judgment of a French court in favor of a French citizen against two United States citizens, on the ground that French courts, if the facts were reversed, would not enforce the judgment of a court in the United States. Notwithstanding that decision, the great majority of courts in the United States have rejected the requirement of reciprocity, both in construing the Uniform Foreign Money Judgments Recognition Act, and apart from the Act. . . .

§482.   Grounds for Nonrecognition of Foreign Judgments

(1) A court in the United States may not recognize a judgment of the court of a foreign state if:

        (a) the judgment was rendered under a judicial system that does not provide impartial tribunals or procedures compatible with due process of law; or

(b) the court that rendered the judgment did not have jurisdiction over the defendant in accordance with the law of the rendering state and with the rules set forth in §421.

(2) A court in the United States need not recognize a judgment of the court of a foreign state if:

(a) the court that rendered the judgment did not have jurisdiction of the subject matter of the action;

(b) the defendant did not receive notice of the proceedings in sufficient time to enable him to defend;

(c) the judgment was obtained by fraud;

(d) the cause of action on which the judgment was based, or the judgment itself, is repugnant to the public policy of the United States or of the State where recognition is sought;

(e) the judgment conflicts with another final judgment that is entitled to recognition; or

(f) the proceeding in the foreign court was contrary to an agreement between the parties to submit the controversy on which the judgment is based to another forum.

Comment

a. Mandatory or discretionary denial of recognition. If one of the defenses listed in Subsection (1) is established, the court where recognition is sought is required to deny recognition. If one of the defenses listed in Subsection (2) is established, the court is not required to deny recognition, but may do so in the interests of justice. The distinction between mandatory and discretionary denial of recognition follows §4 of the Uniform Act. . . .

§483. Recognition and Enforcement of Tax and Penal Judgments

Courts in the United States are not required to recognize or to enforce judgments for the collection of taxes, fines, or penalties rendered by the courts of other states.

Comment

a. Nonrecognition not required but permitted. This section states a principle that has long been accepted both in international and in United States practice. However, the rationale for the rule has been questioned, particularly with respect to tax judgments. No rule of United States law or of international law would be violated if a court in the United States enforced a judgment of a foreign court for payment of taxes or comparable assessments that was otherwise consistent with the standards of §§481 and 482.

b. Penal judgments defined. A penal judgment, for purposes of this section, is a judgment in favor of a foreign state or one of its subdivisions, and primarily punitive rather than compensatory in character. A judgment for a fine or penalty is within this section; a judgment in favor of a foreign state arising out of a contract, a tort, a loan guaranty, or similar civil controversy is not penal for purposes of this section. Nor is a judgment for damages rendered in an action combining claims of civil and criminal responsibility, as is possible in some states, for example in respect of vehicle accidents or nonsupport of dependents. Actions may be penal in character, however, and therefore governed by this section, even if they do not result from judicial process, for example when a government agency is authorized to impose fines or penalties for violation of its regulations. . . .

   c. Tax judgment defined. For purposes of this section, a tax judgment is a judgment in favor of a foreign state or one of its subdivisions based on a claim for an assessment of a tax, whether imposed in respect of income, property, transfer of wealth, or transactions in the taxing state. Judgments arising out of failure to pay license fees or for violation of exchange controls or similar laws are not tax judgments, but they may be treated similarly. . . .

   e. Recognition and enforcement of public law judgments distinguished. Judgments not entitled to enforcement under this section may nevertheless be recognized for certain purposes. For instance, a foreign conviction of a crime may be recognized for purposes of denying the convicted person a visa or naturalization; a conviction for extortion or blackmail may be recognized as a defense to an action by the convicted person on the debt in question; a conviction in a foreign bastardy or paternity proceeding may be recognized in an action for child support.

   The next excerpt expands on U.S. practice regarding the recognition and enforcement of foreign civil judgments and then discusses in some detail the practices of Germany, Japan, and England.

Gary Born, International Civil Litigation in United States Courts

935-943 (3d ed. 1996) [Bracketed text are editors' updates]

A. INTRODUCTION

In most circumstances, the judgment of a national court has no independent force outside the forum's territory. Thus, most courts will (and can) enforce their own money judgments only against assets located within their territorial jurisdiction; likewise, most courts will only infrequently attempt to preclude relitigation in foreign forums already decided in a domestic proceeding. As a general rule, therefore, a judgment will operate in foreign states only if the courts of those states are willing to provide assistance by recognizing or enforcing the judgment. . . .

1.   Recognition and Enforcement Distinguished

"Recognition" and "enforcement" of foreign judgments are related but distinct concepts. The "recognition" of a foreign judgment occurs when a U.S. court relies upon a foreign judicial ruling to preclude litigation of a particular claim, or issue, on the ground that it has been previously litigated abroad. Recognition is akin to the domestic U.S. doctrines of *res judicata* and collateral estoppel. In contrast, the "enforcement" of a foreign judgment occurs when a court affirmatively uses its coercive powers to compel a defendant ("judgment debtor") to satisfy a judgment rendered abroad. The enforcement of foreign judgments is typically sought by a plaintiff ("judgment creditor") who has obtained a money judgment in foreign proceedings that the judgment debtor refuses to satisfy.

2.   Recognition and Enforcement of Sister State Judgments Under the U.S. Full Faith and Credit Clause

Before examining the recognition and enforcement of "foreign" judgments, it is useful to consider briefly the treatment of this issue in domestic U.S. litigation, where the judgments of one state's courts are routinely enforced in sister states. . . . Article IV, §1 of the U.S. Constitution requires that "Full Faith and Credit shall be given in each State to the public Acts, Records, and Judicial Proceedings of every other State." The full faith and credit clause *requires* state courts, as a matter of federal constitutional law, to recognize any valid final judgment rendered in another state of the Union.

The general enforceability of state court judgments under the full faith and credit clause is subject to limited exceptions. These permit nonenforcement only where a state judgment was rendered by a court without personal or subject matter jurisdiction, where the defendant did not receive adequate notice or an opportunity to be heard, or where the state judgment was obtained by fraud. . . . Recognition or enforcement of a sister state judgment is required even where the underlying claim is contrary to the public policy of the state where enforcement is sought.

The full faith and credit clause reflects fundamental national policies. The clause rests on the belief that national unity will be promoted by requiring individual states to give effect to the judicial decisions of other states. . . . The clause also reflects the public interest in judicial finality.

B.   RECOGNITION AND ENFORCEMENT OF FOREIGN JUDGMENTS BY U.S. COURTS

1.   No Express Federal Law Governing Recognition and Enforcement of Foreign Judgments

There is presently no federal standard governing the enforcement of judgments rendered by foreign courts in the United States.[19] Unlike sister state judgments, foreign judgments are not governed by the full faith and credit clause. Nor is there any federal statute generally applicable to the enforcement of foreign court judgments in U.S. courts.

Unlike many foreign states, the United States is not a party to any international agreement regarding the mutual recognition of judgments. In contrast, the United States is a party to the New York Convention, dealing among other things with the recognition and enforcement of foreign arbitral awards. The United States has made

---

19. This distinguishes the recognition and enforcement of foreign court judgments from the enforcement of international arbitral awards, where most issues are governed by federal statute (the Federal Arbitration Act) or by treaty (the New York Convention).

few attempts to conclude treaties with other countries on the reciprocal recognition and enforcement of judgments, and those attempts have failed. . . . The United States is currently involved in discussions within the Hague Conference of Private International Law regarding a multilateral judgments convention. It appears, however, that progress on any such convention will slow.

Thus, for the present and foreseeable future, there is no direct source of federal law governing the recognition of foreign judgments. Although it has been urged that federal common law standards may properly be developed to govern the recognition of foreign judgments, few courts have actually done so. According to most authorities, the recognition and enforcement of foreign judgments in the United States is therefore governed by the laws of several states.

2.   Contemporary Approaches to Enforceability of Foreign Judgments in the United States

Although the United States lacks a uniform nationwide standard for enforcing foreign judgments, there are surprisingly few fundamental differences in the approaches taken by the various states. In [about 20] states, the recognition of foreign judgments is governed by state common law, derived from the Supreme Court's 1895 decision in Hilton v. Guyot.[27] [About 30 states and the District of Columbia] have adopted the Uniform Foreign Money Judgments Recognition Act (the "UFMJRA"), which is modelled largely on *Hilton*'s standards.

a.   *Hilton v. Guyot: International Comity and the Presumptive Enforceability of Foreign Judgments*

[Many] state courts have adopted the basic approach to foreign judgments taken almost a century ago in Hilton v. Guyot. There, a French citizen sought to enforce in the United States a judgment of a French court against two New York residents arising out of the New Yorkers' business in France. The Supreme Court reviewed a New York federal court's enforcement of the judgment.

Writing for the Court, Justice Gray began by suggesting that the enforceability of a foreign judgment required looking to international law, citing the familiar *Paquete Habana* rule that international law "is part of our law, and must be ascertained and administered by the courts of justice, as often as such questions are presented in litigation between man and man." With this explanation, Justice Gray turned to prevailing territorial limits on national jurisdiction as a ground for denying the French judgment any independent effect in the United States: "No law has any effect, of its own force, beyond the limits of the sovereignty from which its authority is derived."

The Court went on to consider what rationale would justify a U.S. court in giving effect to a foreign court's judgment. It reasoned that international comity was the relevant source of authority:

> . . . "Comity," in the legal sense, is neither a matter of absolute obligation, on the one hand, nor of mere courtesy and good will, upon the other. But it is the recognition which one nation allows within its territory to the legislative, executive or judicial acts of

27. 159 U.S. 113 (1895).

another nation, having due regard both to international duty and convenience, and to the rights of its own citizens or of other persons who are under the protection of its laws.[32]

Based upon this principle of comity, *Hilton* fashioned a rule of general common law governing when U.S. federal courts should enforce foreign judgments:

> [W]here there has been opportunity for a full and fair trial abroad before a court of competent jurisdiction, conducting the trial upon regular proceedings, after due citation or voluntary appearance of the defendant, and under a system of jurisprudence likely to secure an impartial administration of justice between the citizens of its own country and those of other countries, and there is nothing to show either prejudice in the court, or in the system of laws under which it was sitting, or fraud in procuring the judgment, or any other special reason why the comity of this nation should not allow it full effect, the merits of the case should not, in an action brought in this country upon the judgment, be tried afresh, as on a new trial or an appeal, upon the mere assertion by the party that the judgment was erroneous in law or in fact.[34]

The Court rejected earlier U.S. (and other) authorities which had concluded that foreign judgments were only prima facie evidence of the defendant's liability and were subject to rebuttal in the court where recognition was sought. On the facts in *Hilton,* the Court found that the French decree satisfied the above requirements, but nonetheless refused to enforce the judgment, citing a "reciprocity requirement." In a 5-4 decision, Justice Gray reasoned that international comity did not require enforcement of the French judgment because French courts would not reciprocally enforce a U.S. judgment in reverse circumstances.

Hilton's basic rule continued to be followed in the United States, with various modifications, for the next century. . . .

b. Statutory Mechanism for the Enforcement of Foreign Judgments: Uniform Foreign Money Judgments Recognition Act

Although [many] states follow *Hilton*'s common law approach, [most] have instead enacted statutes setting forth the circumstances in which their courts will enforce foreign money judgments. Each of these states has adopted some form of the UFMJRA, which is based closely on Hilton v. Guyot.[41] . . .

For the most part, the UFMJRA codifies existing U.S. case law concerning recognition of foreign judgments. As with the common law, foreign judgments are presumptively entitled to recognition under the UFMJRA if they are "final and conclusive and enforceable where rendered even though an appeal therefrom is pending or it is subject to an appeal."[42] If a foreign judgment does satisfy this standard, then it is "conclusive between the parties to the extent that it grants or denies recovery of a sum of money."[43] Again like *Hilton,* however, the Act sets forth a number of specific exceptions to the general enforceability of foreign money judgments.

---

32. 159 U.S. at 163-64.

34. 159 U.S. at 202-03.

41. The Uniform Act was developed in 1962 by the National Conference of Commissioners on Uniform State Laws and the American Bar Association. *See* 13 Unif. Laws Annot. 263 (1980 & 1991 Supp.).

42. Uniform Foreign Money-Judgments Recognition Act, §2.

43. Uniform Foreign Money-Judgments Recognition Act, §3.

3. Foreign Approaches to the Enforceability of U.S. and Other Judgments

There is no uniform practice among foreign states regarding the recognition and enforcement of foreign judgments. In many states (particularly civil law jurisdictions), the recognition of foreign judgments has been dealt with by bilateral or multilateral international agreements. Where no international agreement exists (as is the case where United States judgments are concerned), recognition of foreign judgments is often difficult.

In Germany, the recognition of foreign judgments is generally governed by §328 of the German Code of Civil Procedure. Section 328 provides:

> Recognition of a judgment of a foreign court shall not be permitted:
>
> 1. if the courts of the relevant foreign state would not have jurisdiction pursuant to German law;
> 2. if the defendant, who did not appear in the proceeding and objects on that basis, was not properly served or served in sufficient time to allow him to defend himself;
> 3. if the judgment is inconsistent with a German judgment or with a prior foreign judgment whose recognition is sought or with a pending proceeding concerning the same facts;
> 4. if recognition of the judgment would manifestly lead to a result which is incompatible with fundamental principles of German law (ordre public), particularly, if recognition would be incompatible with constitutional principles;
> 5. if reciprocity is not assured. . . .

In Japan, the recognition and enforcement of foreign judgments is, in the absence of an international agreement, generally subject to §200 of the Japanese Code of Civil Procedure. Section 200 provides:

> A foreign judgment which has become final and conclusive shall be valid only upon the fulfillment of the following conditions:
>
> (i) that the jurisdiction of the foreign court is consistent with Japanese laws or treaties;
> (ii) that the unsuccessful defendant, if a Japanese national, received service of process necessary to commence the foreign proceedings by public notice or has appeared without receiving service;
> (iii) that the judgment of the foreign court is not contrary to the public order or good morals of Japan;
> (iv) that reciprocity is assured.

In England, the recognition and enforcement of foreign judgments is, in the absence of an international agreement, generally subject to common law standards. These standards can be summarized as follows:

> The basic rule under English law is that any foreign judgment for a debt or definite sum of money (not being a sum payable in respect of taxes, or other charges of a like nature, a fine or other penalty) which is final and conclusive on the merits, may be enforced at Common Law in the absence of fraud or some other overriding consideration of public policy provided that the foreign court had jurisdiction over the defendant in accordance with conflict of law principles.

In cases involving default judgments, English law imposes strict jurisdictional limits. In particular, a foreign court will be found to have properly exercised jurisdiction only if the defendant was physically present in the foreign state at the time of the action, or if the defendant voluntarily appeared in the action, or if the defendant contractually submitted to the jurisdiction of the foreign court.

Questions of the enforceability of a judgment can affect the choice of the forum where a party might be inclined to bring an action that involves international issues. As discussed in Section B, there is little assurance that judgments by the ICJ are enforceable in many jurisdictions. Enforcement is through the U.N. Security Council, which can be hamstrung by a veto by one of its five permanent members. There is no comprehensive arrangement for enforcement of ICJ decisions through the domestic courts of U.N. members.

In contrast, decisions by an international arbitral panel can be enforced relatively easily in the many states that have ratified the New York Convention on the Recognition and Enforcement of Foreign Arbitral Awards or the International Convention for the Settlement of Investment Disputes. However, as is also true of foreign court judgments, if the recalcitrant party is a state (and if it has not waived its immunity), there still might be problems executing on specific assets because of the doctrine of sovereign immunity. (See page 375 above and Chapter 6 at page 599.)

Notes and Questions

1. As of early 2002, about 31 states, the District of Columbia, and the Virgin Islands had adopted some version of the Uniform Foreign Money Judgments Recognition Act. Among the states were Alaska, California, Colorado, Connecticut, Delaware, Florida, Georgia, Hawaii, Idaho, Illinois, Maryland, Massachusetts, Michigan, Minnesota, Montana, New Jersey, New Mexico, New York, North Carolina, Ohio, Oklahoma, Oregon, Pennsylvania, Texas, Virginia, and Washington.

2. Looking to the empirical evidence, whether it be under common law or under the UFMJRA, it appears that U.S. courts generally uphold foreign court civil judgments, though there have been exceptions. At the same time, although it has been said that the *Hilton* reciprocity requirement "is no longer followed in the great majority of State and federal courts in the United States" (Restatement Section 481, cmt. *d*), some common law decisions have refused to abandon the reciprocity requirement. Gary B. Born, International Civil Litigation in United States Courts 955, 963 (3d ed. 1996). Moreover, the UFMJRA has a discretionary provision on reciprocity; some eight U.S. states that have adopted the Uniform Act did so with a provision concerning reciprocity.

3. In March 2002, the American Law Institute produced a discussion draft of a proposed federal act relating to the enforcement and recognition of foreign-country judgments. This proposal is called the Foreign Judgments Recognition and Enforcement Act. The ALI Reporters indicated that the reasons for a uniform federal law included the fact that the UFMJRA is not "uniform" in all respects, "most

notably on the issue of reciprocity." The ALI draft of a proposed federal law would go beyond the scope of the Uniform Foreign Money Judgments Recognition Act in its coverage of issues such as claim preclusion, lis pendens, reciprocity, injunctions, and provisional measures in aid of foreign proceedings.

4. Would you favor a uniform rule in the United States for the enforcement of foreign court judgments? Should states be encouraged to adopt uniform acts like the Uniform Foreign Money Judgments Recognition Act? Or should Congress, pursuant to the commerce clause and other constitutional provisions, pass a statute establishing uniform standards as it did with the statute implementing the New York Convention? Or should matters be left as they are?

5. In addition to the Uniform Money Judgments Recognition Act and the proposal for a federal act on the enforcement of foreign judgments, the United States has been involved in negotiations seeking a multinational convention on the subject. Since 1993, roughly 35 countries, including the United States, have been negotiating drafts of a Convention on Jurisdiction and the Recognition of Foreign Judgments. The negotiations have occurred under the auspices of the Hague Convention on Private International Law. The target date for completion of the proposed Convention has been delayed several times and, as new issues crop up, it does not appear likely that a multilateral convention acceptable to the United States will be agreed upon in the next few years.

6. On the other hand, the European Union countries have had since 1978 an important agreement dealing with jurisdiction and enforcement of foreign judgments. The Convention on Jurisdiction and Enforcement of Judgments in Civil and Commercial Matters, also known as the Brussels Convention, deals with the recognition of foreign judgments and the permissible bases for establishing jurisdiction among member states of the EU. The Convention first outlines the permissible bases for establishing jurisdiction in Articles 2, 5, and 6. However, Article 3 of the Convention forbids member states from using "exorbitant" bases to establish jurisdiction over persons domiciled in a member state.

Additionally, the Brussels Convention provides for mutual recognition of the judgments of member state courts, with only limited exceptions. How is the Brussels Convention similar in this respect to the Full Faith and Credit Clause in U.S. practice?

7. The Internet poses complex problems for the enforcement of foreign court judgments. In November 2001, the U.S. District Court for the Northern District of California granted a declaratory judgment against enforcing a French judgment against Yahoo!, Inc., an Internet service provider based in California. Several French associations had sued Yahoo in France for failing to prevent the sale of Nazi memorabilia on an automated auction Web site. Because the sale of Nazi propaganda is a violation of the French Criminal Code, on May 2000, the High Court of Paris ordered Yahoo to eliminate French citizens' access to any Yahoo auction site advertising such products. The court also ordered Yahoo to post warnings alerting French citizens to the illegal content on the auction site.

Among Yahoo's concerns was that it was technologically impossible to block French citizens from accessing Yahoo.com without banning Nazi-related material from Yahoo.com altogether. Before the French plaintiffs brought an action to enforce the French order in U.S. courts, Yahoo sought a declaratory judgment in the U.S. district court on grounds that abiding by the French order would infringe impermissibly upon the rights of U.S. citizens under the First Amendment of the U.S. Constitution. In finding for Yahoo, the U.S. district court held:

> [T]he French order's content and viewpoint-based regulation of web pages and auction site on Yahoo.com, while entitled to great deference as an articulation of French law, clearly would be inconsistent with the First Amendment if mandated by a court in the United States. What makes this case uniquely challenging is that the Internet in effect allows one to speak in more than one place at the same time. Although France has the sovereign right to regulate what speech is permissible in France, this court may not enforce a foreign order that violates the protections of the United States Constitution by chilling protected speech that occurs simultaneously within our borders. Yahoo! Inc. v. La Ligue Contre Le Racisme et L'Anti-semitisme, 169 F. Supp. 2d 1181, 1192 (N.D. Cal. 2001).

Do you agree with the U.S. court's decision? What should the French courts now do? In addition to enforcement problems, are there potential issues arising from the ubiquitous nature of the Internet with respect to ISPs such as Yahoo or AOL now being subject to service in most countries of the world, where libel and censorship laws might well differ from those in the United States?

8. What current justifications are there for the rule stated in section 483 of the Restatement? If a court enforces other foreign judgments out of a sense of comity, why should it not enforce a tax or penal judgment? Wouldn't that please the foreign government plaintiff?

9. Why should tax judgments be treated differently from any other money judgment?

10. Even if the rule in section 483 still seems right for hard-core crime, aren't there good arguments for applying some foreign criminal laws (as distinct from enforcing foreign judgments), at least for purposes of collecting a fine, in areas like fraud and antitrust? Why shouldn't a U.S. court enforce the antitrust laws of Japan, particularly against an American national? Or would it be easier to apply those laws to a Japanese national? Wouldn't that relieve some of the impetus for extraterritorial application of U.S. law?

11. Given the possible problems of enforcing a foreign court's judgment, should a potential plaintiff be advised to sue in a jurisdiction where the defendant has assets sufficient to satisfy a judgment?

12. What impact, if any, do you think that there will be on a party's selection of a particular forum by possible concerns over whether a U.S. court will recognize and enforce a foreign court's judgment? Do these questions about foreign court judgments encourage the use of international arbitration? If so, do you favor this tendency? Do you think that the decision of an international arbitral panel should be more easily enforceable in the United States than the decision of the highest court of another country (say, France or West Germany), even when the arbitral panel might have consisted only of, say, one arbitrator acting under relatively simple procedures and subject to no right of appeal? What policies underlie U.S. support for international arbitration?

13. If the defendant has assets in the United States, do concerns over the possible enforcement of foreign court judgments encourage the initial resort to U.S. courts rather than to foreign courts? As you will see, the answer to this question

might turn on some issues addressed in later chapters — for example, the status of foreign sovereign immunity and the act of state doctrine in U.S. courts (discussed in Chapter 6), as well as the problems of obtaining evidence from abroad (treated in Chapter 7).

14. On the question of whether the United States should seek a multilateral Convention on the Recognition and Enforcement of Civil Monetary Judgments, see Russell J. Weintraub, How Substantial Is Our Need for a Judgments-Recognition Convention and What Should We Bargain Away to Get It?, 24 Brook. J. Intl. L. 167 (1998).

Problem. Much has been happening in the area of formal resolution of international disputes — ranging from new proposals for the International Court of Justice, to major new decisions by regional courts, to increased use of international arbitration.

You are the new Legal Adviser to the U.S. Secretary of State. He is trying to determine priorities and goals in foreign policy for the Administration. The Secretary of State asks you what the U.S. emphases should be in approaches to international dispute resolution. For example, in discussions with the European Union over the effects of its further integration, or with Russia over future arms control treaties, or with various states in the world over enforcement of possible new environmental conventions to combat the greenhouse effect or other environmental problems, how might disputes be best handled if diplomacy is unable to resolve an issue?

The Secretary asks you to prepare a memorandum that analyzes possible approaches to dispute resolution and that proposes some specific steps. The more comprehensive your proposals, the better. However, although you should try to develop some general recommendations or principles, you should recognize how and when different situations might require different approaches.

Bibliography

For materials on dispute resolution generally, see the sources cited in the preceding sections. Other useful sources include Lawrence R. Helfer & Anne-Marie Slaughter, Toward a Theory of Effective Supranational Adjudication, 107 Yale L.J. 273 (1997); Ronald A. Brand, Enforcing Foreign Judgments in the United States and U.S. Judgments Abroad (1992); Thomas E. Carbonneau, Alternative Dispute Resolution: Melting the Lances and Dismounting the Steeds (1989); Andreas F. Lowenfeld, International Litigation and Arbitration (1993); W. Michael Reisman, Systems of Control in International Adjudication and Arbitration (1992); World Arbitration and Mediation Reporter (Juris) (looseleaf service).

5

States and Other Major International Entities

States, international organizations, individuals, corporations, and other entities have varying legal status under international law. Each may be a "person" in some sense or another, with recognized rights and duties.

States are the principal persons under international law. As we saw in Chapter 2, states can create international law by entering into international agreements or through practice that can lead to customary international law. A state also has considerable rights and duties under international law, including the right to regulate its territory and nationals as well as the duty to accord internationally recognized fair treatment to its nationals and to aliens within its territory.

In this chapter we initially focus on what a "state" is and who determines this status. We also consider groups that fall short of being states, such as territories. We then turn to entities other than states that can also be persons under international law. An international or regional organization, such as the United Nations or the European Union,

> has the legal capacity and personality and the rights and duties given it by the international agreement that is its charter and governs its activities. Other capacities, rights and duties may be given it by particular international agreements, by agreements applicable to international organizations generally or by customary international law. International organizations, when they act within their constitutional authority, sometimes make and often contribute to international law. [Restatement, Introductory Note to Part II, at 70.]

We briefly examine the major international and regional organizations — such as the United Nations, the World Bank, the International Monetary Fund, the European Union, and the Association of Southeast Asian Nations — and some of the current issues surrounding them.

Individuals and corporations also have some status under international law.

> In the past it was sometimes assumed that individuals, [as well as] corporations, companies or other juridical persons created by the laws of a state, were not persons under (or subjects of) international law. In principle, however, individuals and private juridical entities can have any status, capacity, rights or duties given them by international law or agreement, and increasingly individuals and private entities have been

accorded such aspects of personality in varying measures. For example, international law and numerous international agreements now recognize human rights of individuals and sometimes give individuals remedies before international bodies. Individuals may be held liable for offenses against international law, such as piracy, war crimes or genocide. Corporations frequently are vehicles through which rights under international economic law are asserted. [Id. at 70-71.]

Chapter 4 analyzes the alternative forums where private entities, as well as states, can seek to protect their rights. Chapter 8 will focus on the internationally recognized rights that individuals and corporations have to fair treatment within a state.

A.   STATES AND THEIR GOVERNMENTS

1.   *What Is a "State"?*

A "state" in international law is what we often refer to as a country (like the United States of America or Japan), and is not one of the 50 U.S. states (such as California). As illustrated in Table 5-1 on pages 434-435, states come in all sizes and shapes, with great variations among them in population and in their level of economic development. States also vary tremendously in their cultures, political systems, educational levels, natural resources, and many other attributes. There are now over 190 states in the world.

Whether an entity is a state or not is a question that arises only occasionally, such as in the case of "associated territories" (entities without full control over their foreign relations) or in the event of secession. However, how would you characterize the European Union? Taiwan? The Vatican and the Holy See? Antarctica?

The 1933 Montevideo Convention on the Rights and Duties of States, ratified by 16 Western Hemisphere countries (including the United States), provided in Article I: "The state as a person of international law should possess the following qualifications: (a) a permanent population; (b) a defined territory; (c) government; and (d) capacity to enter into relations with other states."

The Restatement essentially repeats these qualifications, and its Comment elaborates on them:

Restatement Section 201

Comment

b. Defined territory. An entity may satisfy the territorial requirement for statehood even if its boundaries have not been finally settled, if one or more of its boundaries are disputed, or if some of its territory is claimed by another state. An entity does not necessarily cease to be a state even if all of its territory has been occupied by a foreign power or if it has otherwise lost control of its territory temporarily.

c. Permanent population. To be a state an entity must have a population that is significant and permanent. Antarctica, for example, would not now qualify as a state even if it satisfied the other requirements of this section. . . .

d. *Government.* A state need not have any particular form of government, but there must be some authority exercising governmental functions and able to represent the entity in international relations.

e. *Capacity to conduct international relations.* An entity is not a state unless it has competence, within its own constitutional system, to conduct international relations with other states, as well as the political, technical and financial capabilities to do so. An entity that has the capacity to conduct foreign relations does not cease to be a state because it voluntarily turns over to another state control of its foreign relations, as in the "protectorates" of the period of colonialism, the case of Liechtenstein, or the "associated states" of today. States do not cease to be states because they have agreed not to engage in certain international activities or have delegated authority to do so to a "supranational" entity, e.g., the European Communities. Clearly, a state does not cease to be a state if it joins a common market.

Notes and Questions

1. What should be the minimum population for an entity to be a state? Are the 278,000 people in Iceland (in the North Atlantic) sufficient? The 67,000 inhabitants of Andorra, a mountainous co-principality between France and Spain? The 11,000 inhabitants of Tuvalu, a group of South Pacific islands best known for leasing out the rights to its Internet domain name (.tv) for $4 million a year, effectively doubling its GDP?

2. How permanent must the population be? Does the Vatican qualify with about 900 residents and perhaps 3,000 more day workers who are non-residents?

3. Is the European Union a state because it conducts some international activities on behalf of its members — for example, setting external tariffs and negotiating with non-Union members on certain economic issues? Alternatively, are England and France still states despite their participation in the Union?

4. On October 3, 1990, Germany was formally reunified. Essentially what happened was that the government of the German Democratic Republic (East Germany) dissolved, and East Germany was absorbed as new states (laender) into the Federal Republic of Germany (FRG). The reunited nations acceded to the name, constitution, political structure, parties, parliamentary system, and administrative system of the FRG. The expanded FRG continued to respect the FRG's existing treaty obligations, including its membership in the European Union and the North Atlantic Treaty Organization (NATO). (See discussion of these entities later in this chapter.)

5. If you and your classmates could find an uninhabited, unclaimed island in the middle of the ocean (perhaps formed by recent volcanic activity), could you form a new state? Could it be in your interest to do this, rather than claim the island for the country where you are a citizen?

6. Review Table 5-1, which provides some useful geopolitical facts. Which are the five biggest states listed in the table in terms of population? GDP? Imports? If the European Union is treated as one entity, where does it rank relative to non-Union states in terms of population, GDP, and imports?

TABLE 5-1 Illustrative States and Other Entities*

	Population (Millions)	Land Area (Thousand Sq. Km.)	Gross Domestic Product (Billion U.S.$)	Exports (Billion U.S.$)	Imports (Billion U.S.$)
North and Central America					
United States	283.9	9,159	10,171	731	1,180
Canada	31.0	9,221	677	260	245[a]
Mexico	99.4	1,909	618	159	183[a]
Guatemala	11.7	108	21	3	6
Europe					
European Union (EU)	377.4	3,140	7,884	855[1]	959[1]
France	59.2	550	1,303	293	293
Germany	82.2	357	1,874	571	486
Italy	57.7	294	1,091	238[a]	237[a]
United Kingdom	59.9	241	1,406	267	321
Other EU States**	118.4	1,698	2,210	877	859
Poland	38.7	304	175	36	50
Russia	144.8	16,889	310	103	59
Turkey	66.2	770	148	27[a]	53[a]
Ukraine	49.1	579	38	12[b]	12[b]
Asia					
China, P.R.***	1,271.9	9,327	1,159	424[a]	421[a]
India	1,033.4	2,973	478	44	50
Indonesia	213.6	1,812	145	62[a]	34[a]
Japan	127.1	365	4,245	403	349
Pakistan	141.5	771	60	9[a]	11[a]
South Korea	47.6	99	422	150	141
Taiwan	22.4[2]	32[2]	357[3]	123	107
South America					
Argentina	37.5	2,737	269	27	20
Brazil	172.6	8,457	503	58	59[a]

(continued)

TABLE 5-1 (*continued*)

	Population (Millions)	Land Area (Thousand Sq. Km.)	Gross Domestic Product (Billion U.S. $)	Exports (Billion U.S. $)	Imports (Billion U.S. $)
Colombia	43.0	1,039	83	12	13
Venezuela	24.6	749	125	32[a]	18
Africa					
Egypt	65.2	995	98	4	13
Libya	5.4	1,760	39[3]	7[c]	5[c]
Nigeria	129.9	911	41	21[a]	9[a]
South Africa	43.2	1,221	113	29	28
Middle and Near East					
Iran	64.7	1,622	119[a]	28[a]	14[a]
Iraq	23.8	437	60[3]	13[3]	9[3]
Israel	6.4	21	110[a]	31[a]	31[a]
Saudi Arabia	21.4	2,150	173	78[a]	31
Syria	16.6	184	18	19[a]	17[a]
World Total	6,133.6	130,100	31,284	6,008	6520

*The figures for population, gross domestic product, and land area are from World Bank, World Development Indicators 2002 <http://www.worldbank.org/data/wdi2002/index.htm>, unless otherwise indicated. The data for population and GDP are from 2001. The data for land area are from 1999. The figures for exports and imports are for 2001 and are from International Monetary Fund, International Financial Statistics (June 2002), unless otherwise indicated.

**The IMF data for exports and imports for Denmark, Finland, Ireland, Italy, Luxembourg, and Portugal are from 2000. The IMF data for exports and imports for Greece is from 1999.

***The figures for China include Hong Kong and Macao, but not Taiwan.

[a] 2000 data.
[b] 1999 data.
[c] 1998 data.

Additional Sources:

[1] 2000 statistics from Facts and Figures on the European Union and the United States at <http://www.eurunion.org/profile/facts.htm>. These statistics do not include trade within the EU.

[2] Data are from CIA, The World Factbook 2001. The data for population and land area are from July 2001. The data for GDP are from July 2000.

[3] 1999 estimate from World Almanac and Book of Facts 2002.

2. *Who Decides What Is a State?*

Restatement Section 201

Comment h

Whether an entity satisfies the requirements for statehood is ordinarily determined by other states when they decide whether to treat that entity as a state. Ordinarily, a new state is formally recognized by other states, but a decision to treat an entity as a state may be manifested in other ways. Since membership in the principal international organizations is constitutionally open only to states, admission to membership in an international organization such as the United Nations is an acknowledgement by the organization, and by those members who vote for admission, that the entity has satisfied the requirements of statehood.

While there is some dispute, many believe that a state is under no duty to recognize another entity as a state. Professor Brownlie writes:

> Recognition, *as a public act of state,* is an optional and political act and there is no legal duty in this regard. However, in a deeper sense, if an entity bears the marks of statehood, other states put themselves at risk legally if they ignore the basic obligations of state relations. . . . Even recognition is not determinant of diplomatic relations, and absence of diplomatic relations is not in itself non-recognition of the state. [Ian Brownlie, Principles of Public International Law 90 (5th ed. 1998).]

Even if a state does not formally recognize another state, the Restatement agrees that the state is required to treat an entity as a state if it meets the standards of section 201. The Restatement does include the important caveat that the requirement does not apply if the entity "has attained the qualifications for statehood as a result of a threat or use of armed force in violation of the United Nations Charter." (Id. §202.)

The Reporters' Note to section 202 indicates:

> 1. *Statehood and recognition.* The literature of international law reflects disagreement as to the significance of the recognition of statehood. Under the "declaratory" theory, an entity that satisfies the requirements of §201 is a state with all the corresponding capacities, rights and duties, and other states have the duty to treat it as such. Recognition by other states is merely "declaratory," confirming that the entity is a state, and expressing the intent to treat it as a state. Another view has been that recognition by other states is "constitutive," i.e., that an entity is not a state in international law unless it is generally recognized as such by other states. Some writers, . . . while adopting the "constitutive" theory, argued that states had an obligation to recognize an entity that met the qualifications set forth in §201.
>
> This section tends towards the declaratory view, but the practical differences between the two theories have grown smaller. Even for the declaratory theory, whether an entity satisfies the requirements for statehood is, as a practical matter, determined by other states. On the other hand, the constitutive theory lost much of its significance when it was accepted that states had the obligation to treat as a state any entity having

the characteristics set forth in §201. . . . Delays in recognizing or accepting statehood have generally reflected uncertainty as to the viability of the new state, or the view that it was created in violation of international law, in which case there is a duty not to recognize or accept the entity's statehood.

In the past, when a state treated an entity as a state without formal recognition it was sometimes said to be extending "de facto" as opposed to "de jure" recognition. Those terms, used with varying and uncertain meaning, are avoided in this Restatement.

In U.S. law, the President has the exclusive authority to recognize or not to recognize a foreign state (and, as will be discussed later, the particular government of that state). This is implied in the President's express constitutional powers under Article II to appoint and to receive ambassadors. In addition, the President has authority to conclude international agreements related to recognition without participation of the Senate or both houses of Congress. United States v. Belmont, 301 U.S. 324 (1937) (upholding executive agreement that recognized the new government of the Soviet Union).

The President can recognize a foreign state (or its government) either expressly or by implication. As indicated in the Restatement:

> Recognition of a state has been effected by express official declaration, by the conclusion of a bilateral agreement with the state, by the presentation of credentials by a United States representative to the authorities of the new state, and by receiving the credentials of a diplomatic representative of that state. The fact that the United States is a member of an international organization of which a state it does not recognize is also a member does not imply recognition of that state by the United States. . . . [Section 202, Reporters' Note 2.]

3.   What Is the Effect of Being a State?

Statehood entails certain rights and duties. The Restatement says:

Restatement

Section 206. Capacities, Rights and Duties of States

Under international law, a state has:

(a) sovereignty over its territory and general authority over its nationals;

(b) status as a legal person, with capacity to own, acquire and transfer property, to make contracts and enter into international agreements, to become a member of international organizations, and to pursue, and be subject to, legal remedies;

(c) capacity to join with other states to make international law, as customary law or by international agreement.

These capacities, rights, and duties that derive from statehood are significant. This will become more clear as you study later materials in this chapter (such as the materials in Section 5) and those in Chapter 6 on foreign sovereign immunity and the act of state doctrine and in Chapter 7 on jurisdictional issues. It is worth pausing, however, to consider an arguably special case that highlights some of the problems of classifying an entity as a state.

Note on the International Legal Status of the Holy See and the State of Vatican City

Over 170 countries now recognize and maintain diplomatic relations with the Holy See and the State of Vatican City. In January 1984, the United States government and the Holy See established reciprocal diplomatic relations at the level of an embassy and of a nunciature, respectively.

In 1989-1990, Poland, Hungary, and Czechoslovakia restored diplomatic relations with the Holy See. (John Paul II was a Polish cardinal when he was elected Pope in 1978.) Also, the Holy See reestablished limited diplomatic ties with the Soviet Union, although they fell short of full diplomatic relations. Diplomatic ties between the two countries had been broken after the 1917 Russian revolution. Following the breakup of the Soviet Union, the individual republics went on to establish diplomatic relations with the Holy See.

Bringing to an end a long history of distrust, Israel and the Holy See established full diplomatic relations in June 1994.

In international relations, the Pope is the head of the Roman Catholic Church, the Holy See is its government and diplomatic agent, and its independent territory is the State of Vatican City. This State of Vatican City is surrounded by Italy, possesses 0.325 square miles of territory, has a resident population of about 900 people, is a full member of several United Nations specialized agencies, participates in international conferences, and is a party to treaties with many states.

The Holy See and the State of Vatican City do not readily fit into any established category of international legal status.

> Traditionally, the Pope's sovereign rule over the Papal States provided a basis for the secular authority of the Holy See. However, following the annexation of the Papal States by the Kingdom of Italy in 1870, the secular position of the Pope assumed an uncertainty that the Holy See and the State of Italy only settled in 1929 under the terms of the Lateran Treaty and the Concordat. The Treaty re-established within the city of Rome an independent State of the Vatican City, governed absolutely by the Holy See, which like all other states exercises a sovereign right to engage in foreign relations. . . .
>
> As both the sovereign of the State of the Vatican City and the spiritual authority of the Church, the Holy See joins the separate secular and ecclesiastical personalities established by these two documents. The status of the Vatican in international law thus remains difficult to define in practical terms, since most states conduct foreign relations not with the State of the Vatican City, but with the Holy See. [Note, Diplomatic Relations, 25 Harv. Intl. L.J. 445-446 (1984).]

The Holy See and some analysts have taken the position that its international personality is derived from its religious and spiritual authority, rather than from Vatican City's small territory. See Robert John Araujo, S.J., The International Personality and Sovereignty of the Holy See, 50 Cath. U. L. Rev. 291 (2001). Others highlight the effect of territorial holdings on the Holy See's status in international law. In his testimony before a House appropriations hearing in February 1984, then U.S. Deputy Secretary of State Kenneth Dam expressed the views of the Reagan Administration regarding its recognition of the Holy See:

> [T]here is a distinction in diplomatic practice in international law between the Holy See and the Vatican. The Vatican, itself, has the physical territory.
>
> The Vatican City has many of the same attributes that you would find in any country. . . .
>
> The Holy See is the government of Vatican City, but it also has activity which is disproportionately large obviously to the size of Vatican City, in the sense of a nation or a country. . . .
>
> I think that the reason that there has been some debate about whether it is really a nation under international law is because of its size. . . . [T]hat is the major problem that has troubled international legal scholars when they have approached this as a kind of academic issue. . . . [T]he reason we have an Ambassador in England is because England is an international entity with which other nations maintain relations, and that is the sole reason why we are planning to have diplomatic relations with the Vatican.

A 1987 decision by Italy's highest court, the Supreme Court of Cassation, helped clarify the status of Vatican City vis-à-vis Italy. In a victory for the Vatican, the Italian court annulled Italian arrest warrants accusing an American archbishop and two other Vatican bank executives of fraudulent complicity in the billion dollar collapse of a Milan-based bank. The three officials had lived behind Vatican walls for almost five months. The court reasoned that, pursuant to the Lateran Treaty of 1929, the affairs of the Vatican Bank were outside Italian jurisdiction.

Questions

1. What prompts states to establish diplomatic relations with the Holy See? Because it meets the traditional criteria, cited earlier, for a state? Because of its ecclesiastical influence? Political influence? A combination of all these factors? Why, for example, do you think the Polish government of General Jaruzelski made considerable efforts in the 1980s to become the first communist government to establish diplomatic relations with the Vatican?

2. Is discussion concerning recognition of the Holy See in part a question regarding the status of micro-states, such as Monaco (0.73 square miles) and Nauru (8 square miles)?

4. Who Governs the State?

Recognition of a state, as noted above, is a formal acknowledgment by another state that the entity qualifies for statehood. But who governs that state? Recognizing a specific government is "formal acknowledgment that a particular regime is the effective government of a state." Restatement, section 203, comment *a*.

There are no agreed international guidelines for determining when a government should be recognized. Usually no problems are raised when a change of government occurs in accord with the domestic law of a state. For example, when a new U.S. President is elected, relations with other countries are unaffected. Other countries do not go through the formalities of recognizing the new U.S. government.

Questions of recognition do arise, however, when a new government assumes power in a manner that violates domestic law. The change can occur in a variety of ways, including a revolution or a military coup d'état. Sometimes it is not so clear that there has been an extraconstitutional switch in government. For example, a government or the chief executive may resign under military duress, and be replaced by leadership that the military prefers. In such situations, the decision to recognize the new foreign government often involves an interesting combination of international law and international politics.

In recent years, there have been two major approaches to recognition — the traditional approach and the Estrada Doctrine — and a less well-accepted approach called the Tobar Doctrine.

P.K. Menon, The Law of Recognition in International Law
65-79 (1994)

(1) THE TRADITIONAL APPROACH

Under the traditional approach, a State considering recognition seeks to determine

    (a) Effectiveness of control;
    (b) Stability and permanence;
    (c) Popular support; and
    (d) Ability and willingness to fulfill obligations;

(a) Effectiveness of Control

The principle of effectiveness of control is a fundamental concept and uncontroverted. Recognition of a Government which is not in effective control of the territory would constitute premature recognition and would be considered intervention with domestic affairs of the State. . . .

(b) Stability and Permanence

Next to effectiveness of control, stability and permanence is another important requirement of a political body to confer upon it the legal quality of Government. The rationale of this requirement is the need for a certain measure of continuity in Inter-State relations.

The quality of stability is taken in a broad sense. It is difficult to quantify it. Lauterpacht refers to a "reasonable prospect of permanency." The decision of third States as to stability is influenced by political conditions prevailing in the particular country when the change of Government has taken place. . . .

(c) Popular Support

Another requirement for recognition of a Government is the popular support for it, otherwise known as the consent of the governed. . . .

"Popular support" does not necessarily suggest that the new Government should command the voluntary and positive support of the people. It may suffice to have "the ability to exact habitual, thought not willing, obedience." . . .

Popular support, in this context, means apparent acquiescence of the people. . . .

(d) Ability and Willingness to Fulfill Obligations . . . .

The ability to fulfill international obligations . . . is implied in the ability to govern. As Chen remarks, "A government which is unable to represent the will of the nation internationally and to compel the enforcement of its international obligations is no government."

The test of willingness to fulfill international obligations is of comparatively recent origin. . . .

. . . One of the reasons for the refusal of the United States to recognize the Soviet Government of Russia after 1917 was its unwillingness to fulfill what the United States regarded as its international obligations in the matter of certain treaties and financial commitments of the Czarist Government.

(2) THE TOBAR DOCTRINE

In 1907, Carlos R. Tobar, former Minister of Foreign Affairs of Ecuador, proposed the following which has since become known as the Tobar Doctrine:

> The American republics, for the good name and credit of all of them, if not for other humanitarian and "altruistic" considerations should intervene, at least mediately and indirectly, in the internal dissensions of the republics of the continent. This intervention might be, at least, by denying recognition to governments *de facto* born or revolutions against the constitutional order. . . .

The above general declaration was supplemented with a more categorical statement [in a 1907 Treaty among five Central American states]:

> The governments of the High Contracting Parties shall not recognize any other Government which may come into power in any of the five Republics as a consequence of a *coup d'etat* or of a revolution against the recognized Government, so long as the freely elected representatives of the people thereof have not constitutionally reorganized the Country. . . .

. . . [T]he Tobar Doctrine has never enjoyed widespread acceptance.

(3) The Estrada Doctrine

. . . [The Estrada Doctrine] is contained in a declaration of Senor Don Genaro Estrada, Secretary of Foreign Relations of Mexico, on September 27, 1930 in which it was stated that, the granting of recognition being an insulting practice implying judgment upon the internal affairs of foreign States, the Mexican Government would henceforth confine itself to the maintenance or the non-maintenance of diplomatic relations with foreign governments without pronouncing judgment upon the legality of those governments. . . .

In effect, the Doctrine is an extreme form of *de factoism.* It discards the distinction between changes of Government by peaceful ballots and changes of Government by blood-thirsty bullets.

In accordance with the Estrada Doctrine, the recognition of Governments that come to power through extra constitutional means is eliminated. Only new States are recognized; when a new Government comes to power either through constitutional means or otherwise, its relations with other States remain unchanged. Thus, the Doctrine "is in accord with the principles of the continuity of the state and of the juridical equality of states." It brushes aside all issues of a political, legal or moral character as irrelevant to the right of a Government to be the representative of the State; rejects intervention in the internal affairs of other States, and eliminates the practice of granting recognition to Governments. A good number of States have adopted the Doctrine either officially or in practice. . . .

See also Restatement section 203. The Reporters' Notes provide a succinct history of the U.S. practice on recognition:

1. *United States practice as to recognizing governments.* United States practice long reflected the view that recognition of governments was not a matter of international obligation but could be granted or withheld at will, to further national policy. United States policy has varied as to whether recognition should be withheld from a regime that has obtained power other than through constitutional processes. The case for withholding recognition was classically stated by President Wilson on March 11, 1913 after General Huerta overthrew the government of President Madero in Mexico. Based on the premise that a "just government rests always upon the consent of the governed," Wilson's view was that a regime taking control by force should not be dealt with on equal terms by other governments. . . .

At other times, however, United States policy has been to recognize the government in power despite distaste for the way it acceded to power, or for its ideology, policies, or personnel. The constitutionality of a regime's coming to power was often legally and factually difficult to determine and, in any event, the inquiry might seem improper and insulting to the country involved. It could also become awkward to continue to refuse to deal with a regime that was thriving in spite of non-recognition. . . .

Since 1970 . . . "U.S. practice has been to deemphasize and avoid the use of recognition in cases of changes of governments and to concern ourselves with the question of whether we wish to have diplomatic relations with the new governments." . . . In some situations, however, the question cannot be avoided, for example, where two regimes are contending for power, and particularly where legal consequences within the United States depend on which regime is recognized or accepted. . . .

2. *Government established in violation of international law.* In 1979-80, many governments, including the United States, withheld recognition of the regime established in Afghanistan by the U.S.S.R. following invasion in violation of Article 2(4) of the United Nations Charter. . . . Similarly, the United States refused to recognize the Heng Samrin regime imposed upon Kampuchea (Cambodia) by the armed forces of Vietnam; a majority of the General Assembly has voted against treating the Heng Samrin delegation as the representative of Kampuchea.

5.   *What Is the Significance of Recognition?*

An unrecognized regime lacks some of the important benefits of a recognized government. In the United States, Restatement section 205 says:

Restatement Section 205

Under the law of the United States:

(1) an entity not recognized as a state, or a regime not recognized as the government of a state, is ordinarily denied access to courts in the United States;

(2) a regime not recognized as the government of a state is not entitled to property belonging to that state located in the United States;

(3) courts in the United States ordinarily give effect to acts of a regime representing an entity not recognized as a state, or of a regime not recognized as the government of a state, if those acts apply to territory under the control of that regime and relate to domestic matters only.

For example, before it was recognized by the United States in 1933, the communist regime of the Soviet Union was regularly denied access to U.S. courts. See also Republic of Vietnam v. Pfizer, 556 F.2d 892 (8th Cir. 1977) (upholding dismissal of suit by the Republic of Vietnam, which was not then recognized by the United States), although see National Petrochemical Co. of Iran v. M/T Stolt Sheaf, 860 F.2d 551 (2d Cir. 1988), *cert. denied,* 489 U.S. 1081 (1989) (allowing an Iranian corporation wholly owned by Iran to bring a diversity suit even though the U.S. government had not yet formally recognized the Khomeini government of Iran). The courts are, however, open to recognized governments with which the United States does not maintain diplomatic relations, such as that of Cuba. See, e.g., Banco Nacional de Cuba v. Sabbatino, 376 U.S. 398, 408-412 (1964) (severance of diplomatic relations, commercial embargo, and freezing of Cuban assets in the United States did not bar Cuban state-owned corporation from U.S. courts).

Non-recognition was used in 1988 by the Reagan Administration as a legal tool to help impose economic sanctions against the regime of General Manuel Antonio Noriega of Panama. In late February 1988, the then President of Panama, Eric Arturo Delvalle, tried to force General Noriega to step down as commander of the armed forces. Noriega refused and obtained a vote in the legislature that ousted Delvalle instead and installed a new president acceptable to Noriega. Delvalle went into hiding at a U.S. military base in Panama.

Nevertheless, in March 1988 the Reagan Administration certified that Delvalle was still the legitimate president of Panama. As a result, under a World War II statute, U.S. banks could not release to the Noriega regime about $60 million that were on deposit in the accounts of the government of Panama (12 U.S.C. §632 (1982)). Rather, the deposits were blocked by the U.S. government, which approved payments to Delvalle's representatives for governmental activities. In April 1988 the financial sanctions against the Noriega regime were made more extensive when President Reagan declared a national emergency and invoked his powers under the International Emergency Economic Powers Act (IEEPA). (See Chapter 3.) When Delvalle's term of office expired in 1989 under Panamanian laws, the U.S. government ended his representatives' access to the blocked accounts.

A more recent case is that of the Taliban regime in Afghanistan. After the Taliban had fought and effectively obtained control of about 90 percent of Afghanistan in the late 1990s, the Taliban was only recognized as the government of Afghanistan by three countries: Pakistan, Saudi Arabia, and the United Arab Emirates. The United States and other countries objected to many of the policies of the very fundamentalist Taliban (e.g., their treatment of prisoners, women, and other religious groups) and the Taliban's refusal to accept some of the obligations of the predecessor governments. Throughout the period of Taliban control, Afghanistan's seat at the United Nations and in other international organizations was held by the previous government of Burhanuddin Rabbani. The United States closed the Afghan embassy in Washington to the Taliban government and denied it access to approximately $217 million in frozen assets.

After September 11, 2001, even two of the countries that had recognized the Taliban withdrew their recognition, with Pakistan maintaining relations primarily as a channel for negotiations. Opposition forces led by other Afghan leaders, as well as military from the United States, Britain, and other countries, routed the Taliban in late 2001. The United States and other countries soon recognized Hamid Karzai's interim authority as the government of Afghanistan in 2002, and the United States released the frozen assets to the new government.

Looking at recognition from another perspective, a state often effectively withdraws recognition from one regime when it recognizes another regime as the government. A somewhat unique example of this was the 1979 U.S. recognition of the People's Republic of China as the Chinese government. As a result, the regime on Taiwan, called the Republic of China, lost its recognition.

Note on the Special Status of Taiwan

In 1978, President Jimmy Carter announced that the United States would normalize diplomatic relations with the government of the People's Republic of China (PRC) and that present diplomatic relations with the government of the Republic of China (ROC or Taiwan) would end as of January 1, 1979. The withdrawal of recognition from the Republic of China in favor of the PRC ended nearly 30 years of a complicated relationship between the United States, Taiwan, and the PRC, but also began the problem of the "special status of Taiwan" that continues to the present.

The China policy of the United States after World War II reflected the U.S. historic ties to the Nationalist ROC regime over a communist PRC regime. Thus, the Republic of China was recognized as a sovereign state representing all the people in mainland China as well as on Taiwan. However, beginning with President Richard Nixon's 1972 visit to Beijing, the United States began a process of normalizing U.S.–PRC relations. A joint U.S.-PRC communique, known as the Shanghai Communique, was one of the results of this visit and represented the basis for future U.S.-PRC relations. The Communique stated in part:

> The two sides reviewed the long-standing serious disputes between China and the United States. The Chinese reaffirmed its position: The Taiwan question is the crucial question obstructing the normalization of relations between China and the United States; the Government of the People's Republic of China is the sole legal government of China; Taiwan is a province of China which has long been returned to the motherland; the liberation of Taiwan is China's internal affair in which no other country has the right to interfere; and all U.S. forces and military installations must be withdrawn from Taiwan. The Chinese Government firmly opposes any activities which aim at the creation of "one China, one Taiwan," "one China, two governments," "two Chinas," and "independent Taiwan" or advocate that "the status of Taiwan remains to be determined."
>
> The U.S. side declared: The United States acknowledges that all Chinese on either side of the Taiwan Strait maintain there is but one China and that Taiwan is a part of China. The United States Government does not challenge that position. It reaffirms its interest in a peaceful settlement of the Taiwan question by the Chinese themselves. With this prospect in mind, it affirms the ultimate objective of the withdrawal of all U.S. forces and military installations from Taiwan. In the meantime, it will progressively reduce its forces and military installations on Taiwan as the tension in the area diminishes.

But the normalization process stalled for awhile. The PRC maintained that it was the sole government of all China, of which Taiwan was a province; the United States continued to recognize the ROC as the government of all China. The disagreement was finally resolved under the Carter Administration by the "Joint Communique on the Establishment of Diplomatic Relations Between the United States of America and the People's Republic of China," pursuant to which the two governments mutually recognized one another. The United States concurrently withdrew its recognition of the Republic of China on Taiwan.

Since withdrawing its recognition of Taiwan, the United States has maintained "nonofficial ties" with "the people of Taiwan." These ties are extensive — in 2001 the United States exported about $18.1 billion worth of goods to Taiwan and imported about $33.4 billion in Taiwanese goods. (In comparison, the United States exported about $19.2 billion to the much larger PRC in 2001, and imported about $102.3 billion.)

The Taiwan Relations Act, 22 U.S.C. §§3301 et seq., is the statutory basis for maintaining these ties. Under the act Taiwan receives all the privileges and immunities normally extended to an officially recognized government and its diplomatic representatives.

Taiwan Relations Act

Application of Laws: International Agreements

Sec. 4. (a) The absence of diplomatic relations or recognition shall not affect the application of the laws of the United States with respect to Taiwan, and the laws of the United States shall apply with respect to Taiwan in the manner that the laws of the United States applied with respect to Taiwan prior to January 1, 1979.

(b) The application of subsection (a) of this section shall include, but shall not be limited to, the following:

(1) Whenever the laws of the United States refer or relate to foreign countries, nations, states, governments, or similar entities, such terms shall include and such laws shall apply with respect to Taiwan. . . .

(7) The capacity of Taiwan to sue and be sued in courts in the United States, in accordance with the laws of the United States, shall not be abrogated, infringed, modified, denied, or otherwise affected in any way by the absence of diplomatic relations or recognition. . . .

(c) For all purposes, including actions in any court in the United States, the Congress approves the continuation in force of all treaties and other international agreements, including multilateral conventions, entered into by the United States and the governing authorities on Taiwan recognized by the United States as the Republic of China prior to January 1, 1979, and in force between them on December 31, 1978, unless and until terminated in accordance with law. . . .

The American Institute in Taiwan

Sec. 6. (a) Programs, transactions, and other relations conducted or carried out by the President or any agency of the United States Government with respect to Taiwan shall, in the manner and to the extent directed by the President, be conducted and carried out by or through —

(1) The American Institute in Taiwan, a nonprofit corporation incorporated under the laws of the District of Columbia. . . .

Sec. 10. . . . (c) Upon the granting by Taiwan of comparable privileges and immunities with respect to the Institute and its appropriate personnel, the President is authorized to extend with respect to the Taiwan instrumentality and its appropriate personnel, such privileges and immunities (subject to appropriate conditions and obligations) as may be necessary for the effective performance of their functions.

In October 1980, the American Institute in Taiwan and the Coordination Council for North American Affairs (CCNAA), the Taiwanese instrumentality, entered an agreement whereby both unofficial organizations are given diplomatic privileges and immunities that are similar to the privileges and immunities given to official diplomats. In October 1994, the CCNAA was renamed as the Taipei Economic and Cultural Representative Office in the United States (TECRO).

Notes and Questions

1. Since the Taiwan Relations Act treats Taiwan in essentially the same way as it was treated before January 1979, should Taiwan be considered a state with a recognized government under U.S. domestic law?

2. The ROC moved away from its claim over mainland China during the 1990s and began to focus on the status of Taiwan and some nearby islands. All of the ROC's statements about its international character have been heavily nuanced. Taiwan's leaders have increasingly claimed that Taiwan is already a de facto "independent sovereign state . . . called the Republic of China," as its President Chen Shui-bian said in a May 2002 interview with Newsweek, but Taiwan has never gone so far as to declare its independence. The PRC has indicated that such a declaration would trigger military action and forcible reunification. If an entity has not declared its own statehood, can it be treated by other states as being a state? How is Taiwan similar to a sovereign state? Comment *f* of Restatement section 201 takes the view that "[w]hile the traditional definition does not formally require it, an entity is not a state if it does not claim to be a state."

3. How important are international legal principles of the recognition of governments if the ROC enjoys many benefits normally accorded to recognized governments? Taiwan has used economic grants and loans to developing countries to gain their recognition of Taiwan as an independent state. However, China's growing economy, vast potential market, and military technology have given the PRC an edge in its efforts to limit recognition of Taiwan by such nations. Thus, the competition between Taiwan and China has "set off a diplomatic bidding war in Africa, with some countries shifting relations back and forth between Beijing and Taipei to raise revenue from both sides." Charles W. Freeman, Jr., Preventing War in the Taiwan Strait, 77 Foreign Aff. 6, 9 (July/Aug. 1998). As of mid-2000, Taiwan had 29 diplomatic ties, mostly with countries in Central America, the Caribbean islands, the Pacific island-states, and Africa.

4. As part of its progress toward democracy, Taiwan held its first parliamentary elections in December 1995 and its first direct presidential election in March 1996. The voters reelected President Lee-Teng Hui with 54 percent of the vote. In the ROC's second direct presidential election, in 2000, Chen Shui-bian of the Democratic Progressive Party (DPP) defeated the incumbent Kuomintang (KMT) party, which had held power since 1949, marking the first democratic transition of power in Taiwanese history. In the 2001 legislative elections the DPP picked up 17 seats to become the largest party in the legislature for the first time. Although this peaceful transition indicates that Taiwan has become a functioning democracy, it also means that the KMT's historic support for "One China" has become less popular than the DPP's state-to-state approach to relations with China.

5. In recent years, the relationship between the PRC and the ROC has varied greatly. In the early 1990s, the PRC increased its efforts to expand relations with other countries (such as the United States and Japan). One result was the PRC's willingness to accept ROC participation in regional groups such as the Asia-Pacific Economic Cooperation (APEC) forum, which is taking on increasing importance in the region. (See discussion of APEC *infra*.)

The PRC, however, has not renounced the possibility of military force to achieve reunification with the island, and has threatened to do so if Taiwan rejects the "One China" policy. The PRC has conducted military exercises in the straits, including the launching of missiles over Taiwan shortly before the 1996 presidential election, and it raised the prospect of war in an attempt to influence the 2000 elections. Despite the political tension between the PRC and Taiwan, the two states are developing substantial economic links. In 2001, bilateral trade reached $32.3 billion, and Taiwanese companies had invested about $140 billion in the PRC.

6. From the Shanghai Communique of 1972 through the Clinton Administration, the U.S. policy toward Taiwan was generally unchanged. For example, during his major visit to China in June 1998, President Clinton reaffirmed that the United States does not "support independence for Taiwan, or two Chinas; or one Taiwan-one China. And we don't believe that Taiwan should be a member in any organization [such as the U.N.] for which statehood is a requirement." President Clinton added that matters should be handled peacefully. 34 Weekly Comp. Pres. Doc. 1272 (July 6, 1998). The Clinton Administration, however, did expand official ties and visits with Taiwan. Moreover, it backed Taiwan's as well as China's entry into the World Trade Organization in 2001 because the WTO allows "custom areas" (e.g., Taiwan), as well as states, to be members. (See WTO section later in this chapter.)

As for military support to Taiwan, officially the U.S. "acknowledges" China's claim that Taiwan is a part of China, but it has traditionally maintained a policy of "strategic ambiguity" on the question of whether it would come to Taiwan's assistance militarily if the PRC attempted to take the island by force. This policy has deterred China from using force, while leaving Taiwan hesitant to rely on the availability of the American deterrent if Taiwan were to consider a declaration of independence.

7. In April 2001, President George W. Bush appeared to break with this longstanding U.S. policy when he said that the United States would do "whatever it took to help Taiwan defend herself." 38 Weekly Comp. Pres. Doc. 965 (April 12, 2001). Others in the Bush Administration claimed that this statement did not represent a change in policy and a tilt toward Taiwan, even though Bush himself has reiterated the statement. Taiwan did not take the Bush statement as encouraging it to provoke the PRC with more explicit statements about its independence, but Beijing objected to the Bush formulation. In September 2002, President Bush's much-heralded publication of the National Security Strategy of the United States of America included a substantial section on China and the statement that "[t]he United States seeks a constructive relationship with a changing China." But the strategy statement went on to say: "There are, however, other areas in which we have profound disagreements [with China]. Our commitment to the self-defense of Taiwan under the Taiwan Relations Act is one." The strategy statement leaves ambiguous the exact scope of that commitment.

8. *Hong Kong.* After approximately 150 years of British colonial rule, Hong Kong was returned to China on July 1, 1997. Britain had formally leased the territory from China in 1898 for a period of 99 years. In 1984, as the lease was nearing its expiration, Britain and China signed a Joint Declaration on Hong Kong in preparation for the transfer. The Declaration propounds a "one country, two systems" standard, preserving a degree of freedom for Hong Kong. The Chinese incorporated the principles of the Declaration into the 1990 Basic Law, which provides the framework for the future status of Hong Kong.

The Basic Law allows Hong Kong to remain a semiautonomous Special Administrative Region for 50 years. Hong Kong will continue as a free-market economy, although the Beijing government will assume exclusive control of international relations and defense. The region will be considered a "free port" and will direct its own monetary and fiscal policies. In addition, Hong Kong will retain the British common law legal system, and a supreme appeals court will be established for the region.

Five years after the transfer, democrats in Hong Kong have been disappointed. In July 2002, Beijing effectively reappointed as chief executive Tung Chee-hwa, who has shown little inclination toward democracy in the province. Despite the Basic Law's promise of universal suffrage as the "ultimate aim," Chinese leaders have opposed major changes to the present system, in which the chief executive and most legislators are elected indirectly, allowing Beijing to intervene in the process. While the Hong Kong media remain under private control, self-censorship has increased, notably in the English-language South China Morning Post. In addition, the last five years have seen China overrule Hong Kong court decisions, the expulsion of dissidents, and the passage of anti-sedition acts. Hong Kong still retains much more freedom than the Chinese mainland, a benefit from the end of British rule there, but the trend is discouraging.

The Chinese have regained much more than an additional 365 square miles of land. Hong Kong has about 6.5 million residents, and it ranks as the world's tenth-largest trading economy. The two entities were already bound together economically; China was Hong Kong's largest trading partner.

6. And Then the Recognized Government Changes: Who Is Responsible for What?

Governments often change, through normal processes like elections and through extraconstitutional means.* Assuming that the new government is recognized, what are its international rights and obligations that stem from the rights and duties of the preceding government? Is the state bound by commitments entered into by governments that have ceased to exist? For some concrete examples, will the U.S. government after President George W. Bush be liable for the U.S. debt caused by the deficits during the Bush Administration? Was the Iranian government of Ayatollah Khomeini liable for the contracts with foreigners made by the Shah of Iran when he was in power?

The traditional international law theory has been that changes in the government or ideology of a state do not change the state or affect its international rights and obligations. See Restatement Section 208, cmt. *a* and Reporters' Note 2. However, does it matter how the new government came to power? Or how much of a change the new government represents? Or what was the nature of the past commitments?

In a 1982 case, 240 U.S. citizens sued in a class action the PRC government to recover the principal and interest on bearer bonds issued in 1911 by the Imperial Chinese Government and sold in the United States.

> These bonds were issued as part of a larger Manchu modernization program aimed at constructing the Hukuang Railway, still an important part of the transportation system of the People's Republic of China.

---

*A separate, though less frequently occurring, situation is when a state succeeds another state. The new state might have totally absorbed the first (through conquest, for example), or might have taken only a part of the territory of another state, or might have become independent of the first state (as with former colonies). There is considerable debate and uncertainty over the capacities, rights, and duties of the successor state. The disintegration of the Soviet Union and Yugoslavia are recent examples of this. See the next section.—EDS.

Interest payments were to be made on the bonds twice yearly. At the earliest, the principal was due in 1951. The face of the bond expressly stated that "[t]he Imperial Government of China pursuant to an Imperial Edict . . . engages that the principal moneys and interest hereby secured shall duly be paid in full. . . ."

In 1912, the Imperial Chinese government was overthrown and replaced by the Republic of China. Up to 1930, timely interest payments were made on the bonds. After 1930, only two fractional interest payments were made to the bondholders.

Before mid-1937, Chiang Kai-Shek's Republican government attempted to salvage the debt instruments, proposing the extension on the payment of principal of 1976. The Sino-Japanese War, in 1937, preempted further attempts at settlement. The domestic tumult continued until the end of World War II.

As late as 1947, the Chinese government, long defaulting on interest payments, reaffirmed its continuing debt. However, in 1949, history intervened. The Republic of China was overthrown in favor of the People's Republic of China. The former government fled to Taiwan; the bonds were never paid. [Note, Defaulting of Foreign States and an Expansive Role for the Act of State Doctrine, 6 Whittier L. Rev. 177, 177-178 (1984).]

The U.S. district court concluded:

It is an established principle of international law that "[c]hanges in the government or the internal policy of a state do not as a rule affect its position in international law. A monarchy may be transformed into a republic, or a republic into a monarchy; absolute principles may be substituted for constitutional, or the reverse; but, though the government changes, the nation remains, with rights and obligations unimpaired." Lehigh Valley R. Co. v. State of Russia, 21 F.2d 396, 401 (2d Cir. 1927) (quoting Moore, Digest of International Law, vol. 1, p.249). The People's Republic of China is the successor government to the Imperial Chinese Government and, therefore, the successor to its obligations. The People's Republic of China has made no provision for payment of the principal due on the Hukuang bonds. . . . [Jackson v. People's Republic of China, 550 F. Supp. 869, 872 (N.D. Ala. 1982), *rev'd on other grounds*, 596 F. Supp. 386 (1984), *aff'd*, 794 F.2d 1490 (11th Cir. 1986), *cert. denied*, 480 U.S. 917 (1987).]

The district court ruled for the plaintiffs, entering a $41 million default judgment against the PRC because the PRC had received proper service of process, and it had failed to appear or plead within the requisite time. (This decision was later reversed on foreign sovereign immunity grounds, a subject treated in Chapter 6.)

Despite its reiteration in this *Jackson* case, the theory of universal succession of governments to the international obligation of their predecessors is not always followed in the face of pragmatic modern state practice.

Perhaps more acceptable from a modern point of view are equitable theories which call for a concrete look at the benefits and burdens of successor states. Under such theories, a successor state's liability (or degree of liability) for a loan to a predecessor turns upon whether the successor government would be "unjustly enriched" if it did not assume a debt. In the case of the Huguang bonds, for instance, the benefit accruing to the Chinese from the construction of railways in China due to the Huguang loan could be material to a determination of the PRC's liability. [Eugene A. Theroux & Thomas Peele, China and Sovereign Immunity: The Huguang Railway Bonds Case, 2 China Law Reporter 129, 147 (1982-83).]

The position of the Chinese government throughout the *Jackson* case was that it did not recognize and had no obligation to repay "debts incurred by the defunct Chinese governments." *Aide memoire* to the Ministry of Foreign Affairs, reprinted in 22 I.L.M. 81 (1983). However, Theroux and Peele, supra at 133-134, note that:

> The Chinese position . . . does not appear to be that a successor government can never, or even rarely, be liable for the debts of predecessor governments. Instead, their position appears to be that obligations incurred by former Chinese regimes belong to the category of "odious debts," which successor governments may (the *aide memoire* implies) decline to assume. The *aide memoire* avers that the Huguang bonds were "one of the means" which the Qing Government, "in collusion with the imperialist powers who were carving out spheres of influence in China," used "to bolster its reactionary rule and repress the people." . . .
>
> [Two historical instances illustrate the principle of repudiation of odious debts.] One of these instances was the American refusal to assume, after the War of 1898, the Cuban debt, which arose from the sale of bonds on the international market. During negotiations, Spain argued that the debts were Cuban, and that as part of the transfer of sovereignty from Spain to the United States, the United States was bound to assume those obligations. The Americans regarded the debts as "a mass of Spanish obligations and charges . . . the burden of which, imposed upon the people of Cuba without their consent and by force of arms, was one of the principal wrongs for the termination of which the struggles for Cuban independence were taken."
>
> Another example . . . is that of the repudiation by Soviet Russia of the debts of previous Russian governments, including the debts of the former Tsarist regime. . . .

The Soviet actions are elaborated on in Restatement section 208, Reporters' Note 2:

> The new regime insisted that it was not merely a new government but represented a new state, and that therefore the U.S.S.R. was not responsible for the international obligations assumed by the previous regime, including its debts. Other states rejected that position and continued to call on the U.S.S.R. to carry out the obligations of the previous regime. The Soviet government itself frequently claimed rights belonging to Czarist Russia and accepted treaties to which Czarist Russia had adhered as effective, even if it sometimes invoked the defense of *rebus sic stantibus* to escape obligations under them.

In July 1986, the Soviet Union and Britain signed an agreement that ended a 60-year dispute over the liability of the communist government for bonds issued internationally by the Czarist government that preceded it. The agreement did not result in large amounts of money chansging hands, because both countries essentially waived the claims against each other and retained what they previously had of each other's property. As a result, the British bondholders were not expected to recover much of the Czarist bonds' $75 million face value. This agreement was, however, of practical significance to the U.S.S.R.:

> . . . Moscow's borrowing needs are increasing. In European financial markets, there have been persistent rumors recently that Moscow, through its foreign trade bank . . . wants to raise money in the international credit markets.
>
> "If the Soviets do want to issue bonds, this agreement should clear the way for them to do it," said Michael Gough, director of Britain's Council of the Corporation for Foreign Bondholders. . . ." [N.Y. Times, July 16, 1986, at D2, col. 5.]

In fall 1990, the Soviet Union agreed with France to settle a similar dispute over Czarist bonds. As Theroux and Peele conclude, "the history of . . . government succession issues illustrates 'an almost Bismarckian *Realpolitik:* expediency is the international "principle" which determines whether a successor will or will not assume the debts of a predecessor.' " (Supra at 148.)

Notes and Questions

1. Some commentators note that the *Jackson* court failed to consider the potential liability of the government of the Republic of China on Taiwan for the railway bonds. If the court had considered this issue, how should it be decided? How does it fit with the international legal principles of succession of governments?

2. After a period of turmoil in 1978-1979, the conservative religious government of Ayatollah Khomeini took control in Iran without any formal elections, displacing a moderate interim government that had come into power after the self-imposed exile of the Shah of Iran. Should private U.S. corporations be able to enforce long-term contracts entered into with the Shah's government?

3. In late 2001, a new interim government under Hamid Karzai came into power in Afghanistan and was recognized immediately by most countries. The new government replaced the defeated Taliban government, which had taken control in the late 1990s of about 90 percent of the territory of Afghanistan during a civil war, but had only been recognized by three countries. Most countries and the United Nations had continued to recognize the Northern Alliance during the late 1990s until 2002. Should the Karzai government be responsible for the debts of the Taliban? Or of the Northern Alliance?

4. As you review the preceding materials in this chapter, why do you think there should be a difference between recognition of states, recognition of governments, and establishment of diplomatic relations?

5. If you were advising a new government of a new state, what would you say are the most practical consequences of recognition and diplomatic relations? Which are the most important? Are those consequences legal or political?

6. Would you favor an objective determination of statehood (based on the facts) and a subjective determination for recognizing a government? Given the criteria for statehood, is an objective determination possible? Is an objective determination possible with respect to a set of criteria for recognition of governments?

7. In view of the recent trend toward democratic governments, should the United States revive the Tobar Doctrine (at page 441)? If so, should it do so unilaterally or seek multilateral recognition, such as through a treaty or a General Assembly resolution? (See also the European Community Declaration after the break up of the Soviet Union, at page 460.)

8. Reflecting on recent trends, Professor Henkin concluded:

> An entity that is a state in fact is a state in law. A regime that is a government in fact is a government in law. A very different question is whether other governments must establish relations with a new state or a new regime. Maintaining relations with other governments is normal behaviour within the international system, but there is no legal obligation to maintain diplomatic relations with another government. Some governments

refrain from maintaining relations with particular governments because they see no need for such relations, or find it too costly; some because they wish to show their disapproval of those governments. [Louis Henkin, International Law: Politics and Values 15-16 (1995).]

7. State Succession

Succession of states is one state replacing another state with respect to the territory, capacities, rights, and duties of the predecessor state. A clear distinction must be drawn between a state succeeding another and the changing of governments within a state. For example, the United States succeeded to the former thirteen colonies, whereas President Bush's election changed the government of the United States.

State succession raises important questions as to the ownership of public property, obligations for public debts, and burdens and privileges under international agreements. The answers to these questions are uncertain and subject to considerable debate.

Three competing theories attempt to provide an answer. The theories of universal succession, "clean slate," and partial succession respectively provide for the new state succeeding to all, none, or part of the preceding state's rights and responsibilities. Often the theory used in practice depends on the type of succession or, in the case of international agreements, the type of treaty involved.

Types of succession can include a new state totally absorbing the first (e.g., through conquest, annexation, or merger), becoming independent of the first state (as with former colonies), or taking only part of the territory of another (including both secession and movement of boundaries) or a state dissolving into two or more states (as with the former Soviet Union and Yugoslavia). Thus, the total number of states can decrease, increase, or remain constant. Types of treaties can include bilateral or multilateral agreements that relate to trade, military, or other affairs, international organizations, or boundaries.

The succession of states has historically tended to occur in waves. Most modern analysis is based on the wave of decolonization following World War II. The more recent reunification of Germany and the breakup of the Soviet Union, Czechoslovakia, and Yugoslavia created a modern wave of state successions that caught many by surprise. In reaction Professor Detlev Vagts, associate reporter of the Restatement (Third) of the Foreign Relations Law of the United States, wrote:

> [T]he impact on those of us who played a role in the Restatement process was rather humbling. We stated, in relation to the decolonization movement, that "[a] comparable wave of emerging states in the years ahead is unlikely." Obviously we had not foreseen that the former Soviet Bloc would simply disintegrate at such precipitate speed; nor had we foreseen the types of treaties that would be involved nor the types of issues about the continuing authority of those treaties that would plague both the foreign policymakers of the successor states and the states that maintain relations with them. [State Succession: The Codifiers' View, 33 Va. J. Intl. L. 274, 274-275 (1993).]

The Restatement adopted the view that succession had varying effects on the rights and duties of states. Some of the applicable Restatement provisions follow.

Restatement

Section 209.   State Succession: State Property and Contracts

(1) Subject to agreement between predecessor and successor states, title to state property passes as follows:

(a) where part of the territory of a state becomes territory of another state, property of the predecessor state located in that territory passes to the successor state;

(b) where a state is absorbed by another state, property of the absorbed state, wherever located, passes to the absorbing state;

(c) where part of a state becomes a separate state, property of the predecessor state located in the territory of the new state passes to the new state.

(2) Subject to agreement between predecessor and successor states, responsibility for the public debt of the predecessor, and rights and obligations under its contracts, remain with the predecessor state, except as follows:

(a) where part of the territory of a state becomes territory of another state, local public debt, and the rights and obligations of the predecessor state under contracts relating to that territory, are transferred to the successor state;

(b) where a state is absorbed by another state, the public debt, and rights and obligations under contracts of the absorbed state, pass to the absorbing state;

(c) where part of a state becomes a separate state, local public debt, and rights and obligations of the predecessor state under contracts relating to the territory of the new state, pass to the new state.

Comment

a. Public and private property distinguished. Subsection (1) deals with property belonging to a state. In general, private property rights are not affected by a change in sovereignty over the territory in which the property is located or in which its owner resides.

Section 210.   State Succession: International Agreements

(1) When part of the territory of a state becomes territory of another state, the international agreements of the predecessor state cease to have effect in respect of that territory and the international agreements of the successor state come into force there.

(2) When a state is absorbed by another state, the international agreements of the absorbed state are terminated and the international agreements of the absorbing state become applicable to the territory of the absorbed state.

(3) When part of a state becomes a new state, the new state does not succeed to the international agreements to which the predecessor state was party, unless, expressly or by implication, it accepts such agreements and the other party or parties thereto agree or acquiesce.

(4) Pre-existing boundary and other territorial agreements continue to be binding notwithstanding Subsections (1)–(3).

———————————

The following excerpt provides an overview of different theories and possible legal norms. Consider how each theory balances the international community's interest in stability against the new state's interest in sovereignty.

Geoffrey Watson, The Law of State Succession

Contemporary Practice of Public International Law, 115-127
(Ellen Schaffer & Randall J. Snyder eds., 1997)

When one state succeeds to part or all of the territory of another state, a number of practical problems arise. One set of questions relates to succession in respect of treaties. . . . A second set of succession questions relates to state property and debt. . . . Yet another problem is state succession in respect of international organizations. . . . With the breakup of the Soviet Union and Yugoslavia, these last questions have recently taken on new urgency. . . .

I. STATE SUCCESSION IN RESPECT OF TREATIES

This section considers two important sources on treaty succession: the 1978 Vienna Convention on State Succession in Respect of Treaties, and customary international law. The Vienna Convention is a useful starting point for analysis. The Convention is [now in force with 17 states as parties as of January 2003.] [T]he Convention [also] has importance as a codification of customary law; for example, the Legal Adviser to the U.S. Department of State has said that the Convention's provisions are "generally regarded as declarative of existing customary law by the United States." . . .

The preliminary articles of the Convention define its terms and scope of application. Article 1 provides that the Convention applies to the "effects of a succession of States in respect of treaties between States." Several other provisions, however, significantly limit the Convention's sphere of application. For example, Article 2 defines a "treaty" in the same way as the Vienna Convention on the Law of Treaties, as a written international agreement between States. Thus the convention does not apply to oral international agreements, or to treaties between states and international organizations. Article 6 makes clear that the Convention applies only to state succession "occurring in conformity with international law," in particular the U.N. Charter. This provision is apparently intended to ensure that the Convention does not bestow any legitimacy on conquest or other acquisition of territory by the unlawful use of force. . . .

Much of the Convention favors continuity in treaty relations. That is, the Convention often provides that a successor state continues to be bound by the treaties of its predecessor. For example, Article 11 provides flatly that state succession "does not as such affect" a boundary treaty. Similarly, Article 12 takes the position that succession does not affect certain rights and obligations pertaining to the use of territory. Article 31 provides that when two or more states unite, the newly-united successor state is bound by the treaties of all the predecessor states with respect to the territory formerly covered by those treaties, and potentially with respect to the entire territory of the new state if it and its treaty partners agree. Conversely, Article 34 provides for continuity when a state splits apart; in that case, the new, smaller successor states are presumptively bound by the treaties of the predecessor state. Similarly, Article 35 provides that a state loses territory remains bound by its treaties unless they apply only to the lost territory.

Still, some provisions of the Convention reject continuity in treaty succession. In particular, the Convention envisions a "clean slate" for a "newly independent State." Article 16 of the Convention provides: "A newly independent state is not bound to maintain in force . . . any treaty by reason only of the fact that at the date of the succession of States the treaty was in force in respect of the territory to which the succession of States relates." A "newly independent state" is defined as "a successor State the territory of which immediately before the date of the succession of States was a dependent territory for the international relations of which the predecessor State was responsible." The "clean slate" rule for such states is apparently designed to acknowledge that former colonies may not have consented to the predecessor treaty in any meaningful sense. . . . [However,] the rules make clear that a newly independent state may consent to be bound by a predecessor treaty, either multilateral or bilateral. Thus even the rules for "newly independent states" leave room for continuity in treaty relations. This accommodation for continuity is plainly consistent with state practice. . . .

Taken as a whole, the Convention is a useful contribution to the law of succession in respect of treaties, but it hardly represents the only source of law on the matter. Even [where it is in] force, the Convention would permit states to opt out of many of its substantive provisions, for example by permitting newly independent states to continue in force treaties of their predecessors. . . . Inevitably, then, customary law is an indispensable source of law in this area.

The customary international law of state succession, like the Vienna Convention, generally supports continuity in treaty relations. Just as the Convention supports continuity in boundary treaties, customary international law has traditionally adhered to the rule of *uti possidetis*.* Just as the Vienna Convention contemplates some continuity when two or more states unite, state practice also seems to recognize that the new larger state is bound by treaties of all its predecessors. . . . The practice on this point is somewhat variegated, however. In the most prominent recent case, the reunification of Germany, the Federal Republic of Germany did not flatly consent to be bound by all treaties applicable to East Germany. The German case is confounded by some uncertainty as to whether the reunification was a merger, with its presumption of continuity, or an absorption, as to which the "moving boundary rule" might apply. In any event, the Vienna Convention's endorsement of continuity in cases of merger has a solid foundation in state practice.

The same can be said of the Vienna Convention's emphasis on continuity of treaty relations in connection with the dismemberment of states (as opposed to the creation of "newly independent" states). A preference for continuity has

---

*"A phrase used to signify that the parties to a treaty are to retain possession of what they have acquired by force during the war." Black's Law Dictionary 1546 (6th ed. 1990).—Eds.

characterized much commentary and at least some state practice relating to the dissolution of states. Thus it is often said that the former Soviet Republics are bound by the arms-control and other agreements of their predecessor state, the Soviet Union. Likewise, it has been argued that the former Yugoslav republics are bound by Yugoslavia's treaties. Interestingly, the third U.S. Restatement of Foreign Relations Law rejects a rule of continuity in such circumstances. It has instead endorsed a "clean slate" for all new states that have broken off from a larger state, regardless of whether the new states are ex-colonies. . . .

The Vienna Convention's "clean slate" rule for "newly independent" states seems as much an exercise in progressive development as codification of customary law. To be sure, there have been instances in which new states have claimed a clean slate. . . . [E]xamples include Poland and Czechoslovakia, which claimed a clean slate upon seceding from the Austro-Hungarian Empire, and Pakistan, which claimed a clean slate when leaving India in 1947.

But many new states have foregone a clean slate and have consented to be bound by some or all of the treaties of the predecessor state. [Examples include] the dissolution of the union of Sweden and Norway in 1905, the separation of Austria and Hungary, and the separation of Syria and Egypt following the dissolution of the United Arab Republic. Moreover, this type of continuity has not been limited to new states born out of the dismemberment of a larger state. It has also extended to so-called "newly independent" states, as when a new state and its former colonial master enter into a devolution agreement. . . . In any event, state practice does not uniformly support the Vienna Convention's distinction between newly-independent states, which get a clean slate, and other new states, which do not. Not surprisingly, the reporters of the U.S. Restatement have rejected such a distinction, concluding that it "does not reflect consistent practice." . . .

. . . This area does not lend itself well to codification because states tend to resolve succession questions on an *ad hoc*, case-by-case basis, in which practical concerns outweigh theoretical ones, giving rise to divergent solutions. When resolving questions of state succession, states may make reference to the Vienna Convention, but it rarely seems to dictate final decisions on succession.

II. Succession of State Property and Debt

If a state inherits its predecessors treaties, does it also inherit the predecessors property — and debt? As with treaty succession, analysis of the succession of state property begins with a multilateral convention, in this case the Vienna Convention on Succession of States in Respect of State Property, which was concluded in 1983. . . . [T]he Property Convention is not in force. [As of January 2003, only six] states are party to it, well short of the fifteen parties required before the Convention enters into force. . . . [T]he Property Convention rarely seems to dictate states' decisions in questions of property succession, but again it is a useful starting place for analysis. . . .

The Property Convention's substantive provisions begin with twelve articles on succession in respect of state property. Article 16 provides that when two or more states unite, the successor inherits the state property of the predecessors. . . . When part of the territory of a state is transferred to another, Article 14(1) provides that succession of state property should be accomplished by agreement between the predecessor and successor states. In the absence of such agreement, Article 14(2) provides that immovable state property in the transferred territory should pass to the successor, and that movable state property should pass if it is "connected with the activity of the predecessor State in respect of the territory" in question. Articles 17 and 18 establish similar but not identical rules for separating and dissolving states, respectively. Like Article 14, these Articles provide that successor states in such circumstances do succeed to . . . movable property connected with the "activity" of the predecessor state in respect of that territory. But they also provide, more vaguely, that other movable property should pass to the successors "in equitable proportion."

Like the Treaty Convention, the Property Convention establishes different rules on the property of "newly independent" states. Article 15 reverses the presumptions established in Article 14. A newly independent state is entitled to immovable state property in the transferred territory unless the new state and its predecessor otherwise agree, and even then such agreement "shall not infringe the principle of the permanent sovereignty of every people over its wealth and natural resources." . . .

The Property Convention also establishes interesting rules relating to succession of debt. Again, the easy case is that in which two or more states unite. In such circumstances, the new, larger state simply inherits the debts of its predecessors. Otherwise, the debt is to be settled by agreement or, failing that, split in "equitable proportion." . . .

Again, the Convention's rules on succession of debt contain a striking (and controversial) exception for "newly-independent states." Under the Convention, such states are liberated from debt, just as they are liberated from their colonial masters. Article 38(1) provides: "[N]o State debt of the predecessor State shall pass to the newly independent State, unless an agreement between them provides otherwise. . . ." Any such agreement must not infringe on the "permanent sovereignty" of such a state, and its implementation may not "endanger the fundamental economic equilibria" of the new state. This exception doubtless helps explain why so few developed states have adhered to the Property Convention. . . .

The Property Convention is a helpful expression of the law of state succession, but it has had less influence than its companion, the Treaty Succession Convention. . . . [T]he Property Convention does not seem likely to enter into force soon.

III. SUCCESSION IN RESPECT OF INTERNATIONAL ORGANIZATIONS

In recent years, the most widely-publicized succession problems have involved successor states' efforts to claim the U.N. seats of their predecessors. These questions are governed primarily by the Charter and practice under the Charter, not by the Vienna Convention on Treaty Succession. The Vienna Convention by its terms applies to the "constituent instrument[s]" of international organizations, but "without prejudice to the rules concerning acquisition of membership" in international organizations."

It is now clear that a new state can sometimes succeed to its predecessor's seat in the United Nations without applying for readmission. Russia's succession to the Soviet seat in the United Nations is the most prominent example. Russia inherited the Soviet seat on the Security Council with surprisingly little fuss, and without any amendment of the U.N. Charter, which identifies the USSR — not "Russia" — as one of the five permanent members of the Council. This was possible in part because the other members of the Commonwealth of Independent States acquiesced in the outcome.* Supporters of this result can point to some U.N. precedent for it. When India and Pakistan emerged from British India, for example, the new Republic of India was permitted to assume the U.N. membership of the former Indian Union, though the new state of Pakistan was required to apply for U.N. membership. But this result also comported with a devolution agreement among Britain, India, and Pakistan, providing that India would inherit the Indian Union's membership in international organizations.

But other recent state practice makes it equally clear that new states do not *always* succeed to the U.N. seats of their predecessors. The most prominent example is the new "Federal Republic of Yugoslavia," the rump Yugoslavia composed of Serbia and Montenegro. The Federal Republic of Yugoslavia was denied full rights of succession to the seat of the former Yugoslavia in the U.N. General Assembly. Other examples point in the same direction. The new Czech and Slovak republics were not permitted to succeed automatically to Czechoslovakia's seat in the United Nations, even though the two new states had entered into a devolution agreement calling for them to "alternate the continuity of Czechoslovakia for purposes of membership in international organizations. . . ." Even so, the two new states were required to apply for admission as new Members of the United Nations, and both were admitted on January 19, 1993. . . .

Can these cases be reconciled? . . . One explanation is that a successor state is more likely to succeed to the U.N. seat of its predecessor if other successors acquiesce in or otherwise consent to the succession. In the Soviet case, the Alma Ata Declaration — signed by the leaders of the former Soviet republics — formally endorsed Russia's continuance in the Soviet seat at the United Nations. In the India case, a devolution agreement bequeathed the Indian Union's membership on the new Republic of India. By contrast, the former Yugoslav republics did not concede that the new rump Federal Republic of Yugoslavia of Serbia and Montenegro should succeed to the former Yugoslavia's U.N. seat.

Second, a successor state is more likely to inherit a predecessor's U.N. seat if the successor was the "dominant" part of the predecessor state in size or population or both. By this test, Russia was the dominant member of the Soviet Union, just as India was the dominant member of the Indian Union. By contrast, Serbia constituted only about "40% of the area and 44% of the population of the former Yugoslavia."

Third, a successor state is more likely to succeed to a U.N. seat if other states acquiesce. Again, most states acquiesced in the Russian case, whereas many objected in the Yugoslav case. This last factor may ultimately be the decisive one. A formerly "dominant" state is not as likely to succeed to its predecessor's U.N. seat if a majority of states in the General Assembly or the Security Council oppose that result — even if its fellow successors support its succession. Conversely, a less

---

*The other permanent Member States of the Security Council supported this outcome. Giving Russia the seat and the accompanying veto in December 1991 avoided problems of re-opening the Charter, thus effectively postponing action on demands by Germany, Japan, and several large developing countries for permanent membership on the Security Council. — EDS.

"dominant" state, or one that does not enjoy the support of its co-successors, may nonetheless step into a U.N. seat if it garners enough votes in the General Assembly and the Security Council.

Thus it appears that the law in this area will unfold on a case-by-case basis, and that it will be influenced at least as much by state practice as by Charter norms or either of the Vienna Conventions on state succession. . . .

Notes and Questions

1. The issues of state succession are often governed by international agreements. Examples include the 1842 agreement in which the German states that succeeded the Kingdom of Westphalia decided how to divide public debts, and the 1991 agreement establishing the Commonwealth of Independent States in which Belarus, Ukraine, and Russia divided the responsibility for the results of the Chernobyl accident.

2. Although Quebec separatists maintain a persistent voice within Canada, an issue of state succession may be helping to keep Canada together. Any agreement for the secession of Quebec would need to address Canada's large public debt. Negotiating a division of a public debt of this magnitude would be a major task. What are possible approaches to dividing the debt? Having created such a large negotiating hurdle, has the federal government in Ottawa spent its way to a stabler union?

3. As discussed in the Watson excerpt, in practice, successor states never start with a "clean slate." History shows that most successor states acknowledge some obligations of the prior state. New states find that the value of the preexisting state's rights and duties outweighs their cost, or they succumb to pressure from the other contracting states. For example, before the formal dissolution of the Soviet Union, the need to bolster the credit of the ailing Soviet Union and the promise of assistance from industrialized nations was sufficient pressure for eight of the republics to agree to take responsibility for a portion of the Soviet Union's public debt. Further, President George H. W. Bush linked U.S. formal diplomatic recognition of Ukraine to its acceptance of preexisting arms control commitments.

4. If you were the leader of a new state created from a part of the former Soviet Union or Yugoslavia, what would be your attitude toward assuming the past rights and obligations of the predecessor state for its embassies abroad? Public debts? Treaties regarding the protection of diplomatic and consular personnel? Trade agreements? Arms control agreements?

If you were the U.S. Secretary of State, what would be your attitude toward the rights and obligations of this new state on the same types of matters?

5. The disintegration of the Soviet Union and Yugoslavia led to statements by U.S. officials and a European Community Declaration establishing additional guidelines for the recognition of states. The EC Declaration "affirm[ed] their readiness to recognize, subject to the normal standards of international practice and the political realities in each case, those new states which . . . have constituted themselves on a democratic basis, have accepted the appropriate international obligations and have committed themselves in good faith to a peaceful process and to negotiations." The declaration went on to require, among other matters, "respect . . . for the rule of law, democracy and human rights." 31 I.L.M. 1486 (1992). On the other hand,

the United States and the EC Member States quickly recognized the new states, including countries like Kazakhstan, Turkmenistan, and Ukraine where observers questioned the commitment to democracy and human rights.

6. Russia's commitment to assume the bulk of the former Soviet Union's debt ran into trouble in mid-1998 when the country encountered a collapse of its currency and a deteriorating economy. In November 1998, Russia informed Western bankers that it would renege on the terms of repaying $28 billion in debt to creditors and hence would default on interest payments due the next month. As usually happens in situations in which a country has trouble paying its debts, the debts were renegotiated to stretch out the payments of interest and principal. Sometimes the principal of the loans is even reduced. The international financial organizations (e.g., the IMF and World Bank) and the so-called Paris Club of creditors (made up of most states that are creditors) often take the lead in the negotiations, but consortia of multinational banks also are regularly involved. At the beginning of 2001, Russia's debts to international financial organizations totaled $16.1 billion. It also owed $67 billion to foreign governments (including $47 billion to the Paris Club creditors) and $6.6 billion to foreign commercial banks and firms. In recent years, Russia's economy has rebounded, in part because of growing exports of petroleum, so debt repayments should be less of a problem.

7. As discussed above regarding Russia, one issue in state succession is a new state's membership in international organizations such as the U.N. In May 1992, the United States objected to the rump of Yugoslavia (the Federal Republic of Yugoslavia consisting of Serbia and Montenegro) succeeding to the U.N. seat of Yugoslavia after the secession of Slovenia, Bosnia and Herzegovina, and Croatia. U.S. objections helped result in U.N. General Assembly Resolution 47/1, which declared that the Federal Republic of Yugoslavia could not automatically continue the U.N. membership of the former Socialist Federal Republic of Yugoslavia and that it should apply for membership in the United Nations. Given the case of Russia, is this a double standard? Is requiring the new Yugoslavia to reapply consistent with the standard for membership established when India and Pakistan separated?

After the successful U.S. and NATO operations in 1999 against the Federal Republic of Yugoslavia (Serbia and Montenegro) over its repression of Albanians in Kosovo and the FRY's beginning cooperation with the International Criminal Tribunal for Yugoslavia for war crimes, the United States and other countries agreed to allow the Federal Republic of Yugoslavia to be admitted to the United Nations, the World Bank, the IMF, and the Organization for Security and Cooperation in Europe (OSCE) in 2000-2001. In early 2003, the people of the FRY voted to change the country's official name to Serbia and Montenegro.

See generally Paul R. Williams, State Succession and the International Financial Institutions: Political Criteria v. Protection of Outstanding Financial Obligations, 43 Intl. & Comp. L.Q. 776 (1994).

8. Although European colonial rule essentially ended in Africa by 1980, the succession of states continues. In 1993, after 30 years of armed struggle and a U.N. supervised referendum, Eritrea achieved independence from Ethiopia. Future state succession seems inevitable. Whether Somaliland will succeed from Somalia, southern Sudan from Sudan, or an Oromo state be created out of Ethiopia cannot be predicted. Yet, throughout Africa and the world, succession of states will continue to occur and will remain a basic staple of international law.

B. TERRITORIES AND PEOPLES

The substantial territorial holdings of the United Kingdom, France, the United States, and other Western industrialized countries shrunk during the past century as their former territories and colonies became independent. Besides new states being created, a variety of other new entities were formed. Although not precisely fitting the traditional definition of a state, they are capable of acting and interacting on the international level.

At the end of World War II, the British Empire encompassed 62 dependencies. Today, only tiny possessions containing 5.4 million people are left. Since the beginning of the twentieth century, Britain started most of its colonies evolving toward self-rule. This process has produced several interesting ties between the British monarchy and her former dependencies, such as Australia and Canada, but almost all these former dependencies are considered independent states.

For the United States, perhaps most interesting is the status of Puerto Rico and the former Trust Territory of the Pacific Islands.

1. *Puerto Rico*

Puerto Rico, a four-island chain with a population of 4 million, was ceded by Spain to the United States in 1898 at the end of the Spanish-American War. During the first half of the twentieth century, Puerto Rico and the United States managed, not without difficulty, to define the former's status as a U.S. territory. In 1952 Congress passed Public Law 600, which authorized Puerto Rico to draft its own constitution. The law was approved by the Puerto Rican people as well as by Congress and established the Commonwealth of Puerto Rico.

> [The Commonwealth] acquired the type of local governmental autonomy associated with the States in the United States federal structure. Presently, Puerto Rico has its own Constitution, pursuant to which it elects the Governor and legislature; appoints judges, cabinet officials, and lesser officials in the executive branch; sets its own educational policies; determines its own budget; and amends its own civil and criminal codes. [Arnold H. Leibowitz, The Commonwealth of Puerto Rico: Trying to Gain Dignity and Maintain Culture, 11 Ga. J. Intl. & Comp. L. 211, 232 (1981).]

Puerto Rico has had a Resident Commissioner in the House of Representatives since 1904. While he may speak in Congress and in committee, introduce legislation, and vote in the committees to which he is elected, he cannot vote on the House floor. Although U.S. citizens since 1917, Puerto Ricans cannot vote in presidential elections. Under the commonwealth relationship, the foreign and defense affairs of Puerto Rico are subordinate to the desires of the United States.

For several decades, political parties in Puerto Rico have questioned the concept of "commonwealth" as the final status for Puerto Rico, with some instead seeking either statehood or independence. The official U.S. position remains that the people of Puerto Rico are self-governing and that the decision to alter their present status rests with them alone.

Puerto Rico's international status is ambiguous partly because the parameters of its association with the United States remain uncertain. Puerto Rico is often treated as one of the U.S. states in U.S. judicial opinions as well as by the Executive Branch. At other times, its commonwealth status sets it apart from the federal states. For example, Puerto Rico is exempt from federal income taxes and from full-scale application of minimum wage laws. Puerto Rico is also the recipient of substantial federal assistance.

Notes and Questions

1. Is the Commonwealth of Puerto Rico more like one of the federal states than like a sovereign nation? Is Puerto Rico's lack of capacity in foreign affairs enough to deny it the classification of a sovereign nation?

2. A plebiscite was held in Puerto Rico on November 14, 1993, allowing Puerto Ricans to express their preferences for statehood, independence, or a continuation of commonwealth status. None of the three alternatives received a majority vote. The vote was split between statehood with 46.2 percent, independence with 4.4 percent, and commonwealth status with 48.4 percent.

3. On December 13, 1998, Puerto Ricans again voted in a plebiscite on status. The results were interpreted as a majority again rejecting the statehood idea. The results were 50.2 percent for "none of the above," the option favored by supporters for Puerto Rico remaining a U.S. commonwealth. Another 46.5 percent backed a measure to seek statehood status through the U.S. Congress. Options offering full or partial independence received less than 3 percent of the vote. Hence, despite a considerable minority in favor of statehood, Puerto Rico remains a commonwealth of the United States.

4. One recent point of friction between the United States and Puerto Rico was over the U.S. Navy's use of part of the small Puerto Rican island of Vieques for aircraft bombing drills, invasion practices, and other military exercises. The island has about 9,500 inhabitants and is located eight miles off Puerto Rico's coast. Protestors on Vieques began seeking an end to the Navy's activities after a Puerto Rican security guard was killed by an errant bomb in 1999. Vieques held a nonbinding referendum in July 2001, in which 68 percent of the voters favored an immediate military withdrawal. The governor of Puerto Rico also strongly supported a withdrawal. The U.S. Navy initially resisted, citing the scarcity of available areas in the region for military exercises. However, President Bush directed the Navy to end its exercises there and withdraw from the island, which the Navy indicated that it would do by May 2003.

5. As noted earlier, the British Commonwealth still has its interesting ties. In September 1990, Britain's Queen Elizabeth II, who is nominally Canada's sovereign as well, approved a request from Canada's Prime Minister to add eight new seats to its appointive Senate. Prime Minister Brian Mulroney was seeking to ensure passage of a controversial sales tax that might have been blocked by the appointed Senate, even though passed in the popularly elected House of Commons.

The Queen's authority stemmed from a provision of the 1867 British North America Act. Royal assent to the Prime Minister's request can only be given if the Senate is deadlocked on an important issue and if there is no other way to break the impasse. The last time a Canadian Prime Minister attempted to use a British monarch to change the Senate's membership was in 1874, when a similar request was turned down by Queen Victoria.

In Australia, 54 percent of Australians voted in 1999 against replacing Queen Elizabeth as their head of state with a president elected by parliament. Australia would have still remained in the Commonwealth if the proposal had succeeded. Many commentators saw the result not as a vote in favor of the monarchy, but as expressing a preference for a president elected directly by the people rather than indirectly by parliament.

2. *Trust Territory of the Pacific Islands*

The former Trust Territory of the Pacific Islands (Micronesia) was administered by the United States beginning in 1947, pursuant to a U.N. Strategic Trusteeship Agreement. The Trust Territory had been administered by Japan under a League of Nations mandate after World War I. The Pacific Islands Trust was established after the United States wrested the islands from Japanese occupation during World War II.

The Trust Territory encompassed an area of considerable strategic importance, including over 2,000 islands with a total population of about 140,000. While the total land area of the islands is only about 716 square miles, the islands are scattered over an ocean area as large as the continental United States. The number of islands and their location entitle the state(s) that have sovereignty over them to claim large amounts of adjoining ocean area, particularly under the new boundary lines accepted under the Law of the Sea Convention. (See Chapter 9.) Moreover, important ship and aircraft routes between Asia and the United States traverse the region.

Although relying on the United States for military and economic assistance, the Micronesians moved toward self-government beginning in the mid-1960s. In 1969 the United States started negotiations with the peoples of Micronesia in order to redefine the relationship between itself and the Trust Territory. The extensive and complex negotiations resulted in two distinct results — commonwealth status for the Northern Mariana Islands and free association for Palau, the Marshall Islands, and Federated States of Micronesia.

The Covenant to Establish a Commonwealth of the Northern Mariana Islands in Political Union with the United States of America was signed in 1975 and became U.S. law one year later. As a result, the people of the Northern Marianas became U.S. citizens (though they do not receive all of the constitutional rights of mainland citizens), and the Northern Marianas obtained self-governing commonwealth status under U.S. sovereignty.

Unlike Puerto Rico, the Mariana Islands have no representative in Congress. Designated provisions of the U.S. Constitution and certain federal laws, including income tax laws, apply to the Marianas by virtue of the covenant.

In 1982 representatives of the other three Trust Territory components and the United States signed the Compact of Free Association. In U.N.-observed plebiscites conducted in 1983, the peoples of the Republic of the Marshall Islands and the Federated States of Micronesia (FSM) approved the compact and in 1986 gained independence. Palau approved its compact in 1993, and became independent in 1994, bringing to an end the Trust Territory. U.S. financial support has remained a mainstay of these islands' economies, although aid to Micronesia is being gradually phased out since 1996. Under the free association arrangements, the United States maintains major defense rights, including the right to deny access there to any nation that the United States considers a threat.

Free association is relatively unique in international practice. Two other examples are the Cook Islands and Niue. They have free association status with New Zealand, since 1965 and 1974 respectively.

> Free association differs from independence in that one of the parties to the bilateral agreement willingly binds itself, by its own constitutional process — whether by delegation or otherwise — to cede to the other a fundamental sovereign authority and responsibility for the conduct of its own affairs. Specifically, this distinction is exemplified by the reservation to the United States of plenary defense authority (as contrasted with treaty rights to exercise certain defense functions), and the ensuing limitation on Micronesian freedom of action. Free association is distinguished from integration into a metropolitan power by the retention by the freely associated government of the power to assert itself domestically and internationally without reference to the legal authority of another state. [Arthur John Armstrong, Strategic Underpinnings of the Legal Regime of Free Association: The Negotiations for the Future Political States of Micronesia, 7 Brook. J. Intl. L. 179, 182 (1981).]

Notes and Questions

1. The ability of the FSM, Marshall Islands, and Palau to act in the international realm could potentially bring the freely associated states into conflict with U.S. national security interests in the Pacific. How might this potential conflict be resolved, given that the United States retains control over the security and defense affairs of the FSM and the Marshall Islands, while these entities retain authority over their foreign affairs? To what extent might "foreign affairs" be subsumed by "security and defense matters"? Is the United States being given a de facto voice in the foreign affairs of these states?

2. Consider the issue of succession to and effects on those international treaties that the United States formerly applied to the Trust Territories. (See the section on succession of states at page 453.) Given the compact, do the freely associated states succeed to these treaties? Are the freely associated states to be considered sovereign entities, such that one should consider the issues of state succession?

3. Under Article 4(1) of the U.N. Charter, an entity applying for U.N. membership must be a state that is willing to accept the obligations of the Charter and is able and willing to carry out these obligations. Under this standard should the Micronesian freely associated states qualify for membership? Are these entities be able to carry out their U.N. obligations if the United States retains control over their defense and security affairs?

In 1994, Palau became a member of the U.N., as FSM and the Marshall Islands had become earlier.

C. INTERNATIONAL AND REGIONAL ENTITIES

International and regional organizations, such as the United Nations or the European Union, can also be persons under international law. Indeed, their role in international activities and in the making of international law is growing rapidly. Organizations that have been in existence for decades have often continued to evolve, and new entities are coming into being in response to new needs.

To discuss all of these organizations in depth is beyond the scope of this book. In this section we briefly describe the principal international and regional entities and highlight a few of the major contemporary issues. Other chapters also contain considerable material on some of these entities. For example, the International Court of Justice is discussed in Chapter 4 on dispute resolution. Also, there are often references to these entities because of their major impact on international law.

1. An Overview

Even before the end of World War II in 1945, the Allies and other countries were actively discussing the creation of international institutions that would provide more security and stability in the world.

The central institution was to be the United Nations. The name was devised by President Franklin D. Roosevelt and was first used in the Declaration of the United Nations of January 1942, when representatives of 26 nations pledged to continue fighting together against the Axis powers. In a real sense the origins of the United Nations can be traced far back in history to several attempts — from the Achaean League in ancient Greece to the League of Nations after World War I — to create an organization that would prevent military conflict among its members and settle international disputes. The International Court of Justice (ICJ) was designed as the formal judicial body to resolve legal disputes.

Other key international institutions included the International Monetary Fund (IMF), which was designed to promote international monetary cooperation and stability in foreign exchange. The period prior to World War II had experienced tremendous financial instability, caused in part by rapid changes in the value of individual nations' currencies and numerous currency restrictions. The International Bank for Reconstruction and Development (or World Bank) was created to help provide funds for the reconstruction of war-ravaged nations and to promote economic development.

The International Trade Organization (ITO) was envisioned as an institution to provide a structure and enforcement for rules that would regularize and encourage international trade. The worldwide economic problems of the 1930s had been caused in part by the protectionist policies adopted by the United States and other countries. United States congressional opposition to the ITO, however, caused it to be a stillbirth. A subsidiary agreement, the General Agreement on Tariffs and Trade (GATT), was left to fill the void.

The creators of these international institutions also assumed that regional organizations might develop to supplement the efforts of the international entities. For example, the U.N. Charter specifically assumes the active existence of regional groups (Articles 52-54), as does the GATT for customs unions and free trade areas (Article XXIV).

In establishing the international institutions, the planners and policy-makers tried to avoid the mistakes of the past. There was a consensus that the United States would have to be a member. The U.S. failure to join the League of Nations had clearly not been helpful for the health of that institution. Similarly, the majority view that emerged in the early years of these institutions was that the defeated Axis powers — Germany, Japan, and Italy — had to be given a role. Indeed, many believed that it was important that those countries be thoroughly entwined in international and regional groups. The policy after World War I of extracting heavy reparations from Germany and slating it for harsh treatment for future decades was one of the justifications that Adolf Hitler had used to gain the support of the German people and to break the World War I agreements.

The post-World War II institutions continue to exist today, except for the ITO. They have failed, however, to achieve some of their original objectives. Although the successful U.N. response to the Iraqi invasion of Kuwait in 1990 has helped revive hopes for the future of the institution, the United Nations has been much less successful at preventing war and settling disputes than its creators had hoped. Also, as discussed in Chapter 4, the ICJ has been much less active and successful as the judicial body to help resolve disputes than was envisioned.

In the decades since World War II each of the institutions has also evolved, some much more than others. In the 1970s the IMF saw the United States go off the gold standard and the major industrial countries of the world switch to flexible exchange rates. The World Bank has switched its focus from reconstructing the war-torn economies of Europe to encouraging the development of countries in Latin America, Africa, Asia, and Eastern Europe. The GATT has been transformed into the World Trade Organization (WTO), a formal international trade institution that has become very active.

While the initial set of institutions was growing and evolving, a wide range of other institutions and separate agreements has developed. These include regional organizations like the European Union and Asia-Pacific Economic Cooperation (APEC); regional courts such as the European Union's Court of Justice and the European Court of Human Rights; international arbitration, either through institutions like the the International Chamber of Commerce (ICC) or on an ad hoc basis; the quasi-formal operations of countries with similar interests, such as the Group of 8 (G-8) countries (the United States, Japan, Germany, France, United Kingdom, Italy, Canada, and Russia); and a vast array of multilateral and bilateral agreements for various purposes — from combatting terrorism, to protecting diplomatic personnel, to enforcement of arbitral awards.

These new institutions and agreements have often supplemented the work of the older institutions. For example, the regional development banks (such as the Inter-American Development Bank and the Asian Development Bank) have helped to increase the availability of public development funds and to target them on specific regions.

For some problems and activities, the newer entities have essentially supplanted the older institutions. For instance, the finance ministers of the G-8 countries discuss exchange rates among themselves and take steps that sometimes have more impact on these rates than the IMF. Also, the active caseload of the two European regional courts include some cases that might well have gone to the ICJ.

Often the role of the newer entities vis-à-vis the older institutions is complicated. For example, the European Union (EU) helps further the aim of the WTO by reducing trade barriers among the Member States of the Union. However, to the extent that the EU might be slower to reduce barriers against non-Member States (e.g., to protect the EU's farmers) than one of the individual Member States might otherwise have been, the EU is delaying progress in the WTO. Another example is the Law of the Sea Convention. Although it provides for resort to the ICJ on disputes, it also established a new international court (the International Tribunal for the Law of the Sea) as well as two arbitral mechanisms.

2.   *International Institutions*

a.   The United Nations: Its Structure, Purposes, and Future

The United Nations, which formally came into existence in 1945, is the principal international organization designed to prevent military confrontations among its members and to help resolve international disputes. It has also embarked on numerous other tasks, from simplifying international air travel to the eradication of malaria and smallpox. The following excerpt provides a useful introduction to the U.N.'s structure and activities.

United Nations, Basic Facts About the United Nations

4-21 (2000)

The United Nations Charter is the constituting instrument of the Organization, setting out the rights and obligations of Member States, and establishing the United Nations organs and procedures. An international treaty, the Charter codifies at the international level the major principles of international relations — from the sovereign equality of States to the prohibition of the use of force in international relations. . . .

Membership

Membership of the United Nations is open to all peace-loving nations which accept the obligations of the Charter and are willing and able to carry out these obligations. [As of January 2003, there were 191 Member States in the United Nations. This number includes the 2002 admission of Switzerland and Timor-Leste. Tuvalu and also the Federal Republic of Yugoslavia (since renamed Serbia and Montenegro) joined in 2000, and Kiribati, Nauru, and Tonga became members in 1999.]

The General Assembly admits new Member States on the recommendation of the Security Council. The Charter provides for the suspension or expulsion of a Member for violation of the principles of the Charter, but no such action has ever been taken. . . .

STRUCTURE OF THE ORGANIZATION

The Charter established six principal organs of the United Nations, which are the: General Assembly, Security Council, Economic and Social Council, Trusteeship Council, International Court of Justice and Secretariat. The United Nations family, however, is much larger, encompassing 15 agencies and several programmes and bodies. . . .

General Assembly

The General Assembly is the main deliberative organ. It is composed of representatives of all Member States, each of which has one vote. Decisions on important questions, such as those on peace and security, admission of new Members and budgetary matters, require a two-thirds majority. Decisions on other questions are by simple majority.

Functions and Powers

Under the Charter, the functions and powers of the General Assembly include:

- to consider and make recommendations on the principles of cooperation in the maintenance of international peace and security, including the principles governing disarmament and arms regulation;
- to discuss any question relating to international peace and security and, except where a dispute or situation is being discussed by the Security Council, to make recommendations on it;[1]
- to discuss and, with the same exception, make recommendations on any question within the scope of the Charter or affecting the powers and functions of any organ of the United Nations;
- to initiate studies and make recommendations to promote international political cooperation, the development and codification of international law, the realization of human rights and fundamental freedoms for all, and international collaboration in economic, social, cultural, educational and health fields;
- to make recommendations for the peaceful settlement of any situation, regardless of origin, which might impair friendly relations among nations;
- to receive and consider reports from the Security Council and other United Nations organs;
- to consider and approve the United Nations budget and to apportion the contributions among Members;

1. Under the "Uniting for peace" resolution adopted by the General Assembly in November 1950, the Assembly may take action if the Security Council, because of lack of unanimity of its permanent members, fails to act where there appears to be a threat to international peace, breach of the peace or act of aggression. The Assembly is empowered to consider the matter immediately with a view to making recommendations to Members for collective measures, including, in case of a breach of the peace or act of aggression, the use of armed forces when necessary to maintain or restore international peace and security.

- to elect the non-permanent members of the Security Council, the members of the Economic and Social Council and those members of the Trusteeship Council that are elected; to elect jointly with the Security Council the Judges of the International Court of Justice; and, on the recommendation of the Security Council, to appoint the Secretary-General.

Sessions

The General Assembly's regular session usually begins each year in September. The 2000-2001 session, for example, is the fifty-fifth regular session of the General Assembly. . . .

At the beginning of each regular session, the Assembly holds a general debate, often addressed by heads of state and government, in which Member States express their views on the most pressing international issues. Most questions are then discussed in its six Main Committees. . . .

Some issues are considered only in plenary meetings, rather than in one of the Main Committees. All issues are voted on through resolutions passed in plenary meetings, usually towards the end of the regular session, after the committees have completed their consideration of them and submitted draft resolutions to the plenary Assembly. . . .

While the decisions of the Assembly have no legally binding force for governments, they carry the weight of world opinion, as well as the moral authority of the world community.

The work of the United Nations year-round derives largely from the decisions of the General Assembly — that is to say, the will of the majority of the Members as expressed in resolutions adopted by the Assembly. That work is carried out:

- by committees and other bodies established by the Assembly to study and report on specific issues, such as disarmament, peace-keeping, development and human rights;
- in international conferences called for by the Assembly; and
- by the Secretariat of the United Nations — the Secretary-General and his staff of international civil servants.

Security Council

The Security Council has primary responsibility, under the Charter, for the maintenance of international peace and security.

The Council has 15 members: 5 permanent members — China, France, the Russian Federation, the United Kingdom and the United States — and 10 elected by the General Assembly for two-year terms.

Each member has one vote. Decisions on procedural matters are made by an affirmative vote of at least 9 of the 15 members. Decisions on substantive matters require nine votes, including the concurring votes of all five permanent members. This is the rule of "great Power unanimity," often referred to as the "veto" power. If a permanent member does not agree with a decision, it can cast a negative vote, and this act has power of veto. All five permanent members have exercised the right of veto at one time or another. If a permanent member does not fully agree with a decision but does not wish to cast its veto, it may abstain.

Under the Charter, all Members of the United Nations agree to accept and carry out the decisions of the Security Council. While other organs of the United Nations make recommendations to governments, the Council alone has the power to take decisions which Member States are obligated under the Charter to carry out.

Functions and Powers

Under the Charter, the functions and powers of the Security Council are:

- to maintain international peace and security in accordance with the principles and purposes of the United Nations;
- to investigate any dispute or situation which might lead to international friction;
- to recommend methods of adjusting such disputes or the terms of settlement;
- to formulate plans for establishing a system to regulate armaments;
- to determine the existence of a threat to the peace or act of aggression and to recommend what action should be taken;
- to call on Members to apply economic sanctions and other measures not involving the use of force to prevent or stop aggression;
- to take military action against an aggressor;
- to recommend the admission of new Members; . . .
- to recommend to the General Assembly the appointment of the Secretary-General and, together with the Assembly, to elect the Judges of the International Court of Justice.

The Security Council is so organized as to be able to function continuously, and a representative of each of its members must be present at all times at United Nations Headquarters. The Council may meet elsewhere: in 1972, it held a session in Addis Ababa, Ethiopia; in 1973 it met in Panama City, Panama; and in 1990 it [met] in Geneva, Switzerland.

When a complaint concerning a threat to peace is brought before it, the Council's first action is usually to recommend that the parties try to reach agreement by peaceful means. The Council may set forth principles for a peaceful settlement. In some cases, the Council itself undertakes investigation and mediation. It may dispatch a mission, appoint special representatives or request the Secretary-General to use his good offices.

When a dispute leads to fighting, the Council's first concern is to bring it to an end as soon as possible. The Council may issue ceasefire directives that can be instrumental in preventing wider hostilities.

The Council may also dispatch military observers or a peacekeeping force to help reduce tensions, keep opposing forces apart and create conditions of calm in which peaceful settlements may be sought. Under Chapter VII of the Charter, the Council may decide on enforcement measures, including economic sanctions (such as trade embargoes), arms embargoes or collective military action. . . .

The Council has established two International Criminal Tribunals to prosecute crimes against humanity in the former Yugoslavia and in Rwanda. . . . The Tribunals are subsidiary organs of the Council.

After the Gulf War, to verify the elimination of Iraq's weapons of mass destruction, the Council established the United Nations Special Commission (UNSCOM). Its responsibilities have been taken over by the United Nations Monitoring, Verification and Inspection Commission (UNMOVIC), which the Council established in 2000. . . .

A working group of the General Assembly has been considering Council reform since 1993, including equitable representation and expansion of membership.

[There have been recent proposals for changing the membership and voting structure of the Security Council, and growing momentum behind the proposals. The only time the Security Council's composition has been changed was in 1965, when it was enlarged from 11 to 15 members by the addition of four more rotating members, which serve two-year terms. Supporters of change contend that the present five permanent members (the United States, Great Britain, France, Russia, and China) still reflect the world powers in 1945.

[Reflecting their economic power (and also considerable military power), Germany and Japan want to have permanent seats rather than act as occasional rotating members. (Unless there is an expansion in the Council's total membership of 15 states, this would reduce the opportunities for other nonpermanent members to occasionally sit on the Council.) Germany and Japan would also prefer to have a veto.

[Eliminating the veto for permanent members as part of a change in voting structure seems highly unlikely, at least for the time being. At least some of the permanent members (very likely including the United States) would be opposed to it and would have their vetoes available to prevent the change.

[Note that the use of vetoes has been rare since 1990. There have been only ten vetoes between May 1990 and June 2002 — including one by Russia over the cost of U.N. peacekeeping in Cyprus and four by the United States on resolutions against Israel. However, the veto remains a powerful tool — for example, China used the threat of one in order to obtain watered-down resolutions and delays in sanctions during the situations in Haiti and North Korea in 1994. Moreover, during the efforts led by the United States and United Kingdom against Iraq in 2002-2003 for Iraqi breaches of previous resolutions, the text and actual passage of new resolutions was very much affected by the possibility of vetoes by France, Russia, and China.

[The United States, Britain, and several other states have announced in the past their support for Germany's and Japan's bids for permanent seats on the Security Council. The Clinton Administration had also said that it was ready to consider admitting regional powers to permanent membership. Although the United States mentioned no specific nations, large developing nations such as India, Indonesia, Egypt, and Brazil could hope to fill any permanent seats given on a regional basis.

[Overall, the United States has supported five additional permanent seats, but has not made a recommendation about extending the veto power to those candidates. The United Nations has not set a timetable regarding a decision on expansion.]

Economic and Social Council

The Charter established the Economic and Social Council as the principal organ to coordinate the economic and social work of the United Nations and the specialized agencies and institutions — known as the United Nations family of organizations . . . . The Council has 54 members, who serve for three-year terms. Voting in the Council is by simple majority; each member has one vote. . . .

Relations with Non-Governmental Organizations

Under the Charter, the Economic and Social Council may consult with non-governmental organizations (NGOs) concerned with matters within the Council's competence. Over 1,600 NGOs have consultative status with the Council. The Council recognizes that these organizations should have the opportunity to express their views, and that they possess special experience or technical knowledge of value to its work. . . .

Trusteeship Council

The Trusteeship Council . . . was established by the Charter in 1945 to provide international supervision for 11 Trust Territories placed under the administration of 7 Member States, and ensure that adequate steps were taken to prepare the Territories for self-government or independence. The Charter authorized the Trusteeship Council to examine and discuss reports from the Administering Authority on the political, economic, social and educational advancement of the peoples of Trust Territories; to examine petitions from the Territories; and to undertake special missions to the Territories.

By 1994, all Trust Territories had attained self-government or independence, either as separate States or by joining neighbouring independent countries. The last to do so was the Trust Territory of the Pacific Islands (Palau), which became the 185th Member State.

Its work completed, the Trusteeship Council — consisting of the five permanent members of the Security Council, China, France, the Russian Federation, the United Kingdom and the United States — has amended its rules of procedure to meet as and where occasion may require.

International Court of Justice

Located at The Hague, the Netherlands, the International Court of Justice . . . is the principal judicial organ of the United Nations. It settles legal disputes between states and gives advisory opinions to the United Nations and its specialized agencies. Its Statute is an integral part of the United Nations Charter. [See Chapter 4.] . . .

Secretariat

The Secretariat — an international staff working in duty stations around the world — carries out the diverse day-to-day work of the Organization. It services the other principal organs of the United Nations and administers the programmes and policies laid down by them. At its head is the Secretary-General, who is appointed by the General Assembly on the recommendation of the Security Council for a five-year, renewable term....

The Secretariat has a staff of about 8,900 under the regular budget, drawn from some 160 countries. As international civil servants, staff members and the Secretary-General answer to the United Nations alone for their activities, and take an oath not to seek or receive instructions from any government or outside authority. Under the Charter, each Member State undertakes to respect the exclusively international character of the responsibilities of the Secretary-General and the staff, and to refrain from seeking to influence them improperly.

The United Nations, while headquartered in New York, maintains a significant presence in Addis Ababa, Bangkok, Beirut, Geneva, Nairobi, Santiago and Vienna, and has offices all over the world.

Secretary-General

Equal parts diplomat and advocate, civil servant and CEO, the Secretary-General is a symbol of United Nations ideals and a spokesman for the interests of the world's peoples, in particular the poor and vulnerable. The current Secretary-General, and the seventh occupant of the post, is Mr. Kofi Annan, of Ghana, who took office on 1 January 1997.

The Charter describes the Secretary-General as "chief administrative officer" of the Organization, who shall act in that capacity and perform "such other functions as are entrusted" to him or her by the Security Council, General Assembly, Economic and Social Council and other United Nations organs. The Charter also empowers the Secretary-General to "bring to the attention of the Security Council any matter which in his opinion may threaten the maintenance of international peace and security." These guidelines both define the powers of the office and grant it considerable scope for action....

One of the most vital roles played by the Secretary-General is the use of his "good offices"—steps taken publicly and in private, drawing upon his independence, impartiality and integrity, to prevent international disputes from arising, escalating or spreading....

Each Secretary-General also defines his role within the context of his particular time in office. Mr. Annan's efforts have focused on:

Reform. Shortly after taking office, Mr. Annan presented a sweeping reform package aimed at helping the United Nations to change with the times and adapt to a new era of global affairs.

Reform measures falling under the authority of the Secretary-General have been largely implemented or set in motion. They have been both administrative — such as a zero-growth budget and rigorous efforts to upgrade management practices....

The General Assembly, meanwhile, has continued to consider several questions of institutional change that fall under its authority, including the size and composition of the Security Council, methods of financing the Organization and bringing greater coherence to the wider United Nations system of specialized agencies....

Budget of the United Nations

The regular budget of the United Nations is approved by the General Assembly for a two-year period. The budget is initially submitted by the Secretary-General. . . .

The budget approved for the two years 2000-2001 is $2,535 million, $2 million higher than the 1998-1999 budget. The budget covers the costs of the United Nations programmes in areas such as political affairs, international justice and law, international cooperation for development, public information, human rights and humanitarian affairs. . . .

The main source of funds for the budget is the contributions of Member States. These are assessed on a scale approved by the Assembly on the recommendation of the Committee on Contributions, made up of 18 experts who serve in their personal capacity and are selected by the General Assembly. . . .

The fundamental criterion on which the scale of assessments is based is the capacity of countries to pay. This is determined by considering their relative shares of total gross national product, adjusted to take into account a number of factors, including their per capita incomes. . . . In 2000, the Assembly fixed a maximum of 22 percent of the budget for any one contributor.

The overall financial situation of the United Nations has been precarious for several years because of the continuing failure of many Member States to pay, in full and on time, their assessed contributions. The United Nations has managed to continue to operate thanks to voluntary contributions from some countries and to its Working Capital Fund (to which Member States advance sums in proportion to their assessed contributions), and by borrowing from peacekeeping operations.

For 2000, Member States' unpaid contributions to the regular budget totalled $222 million at 31 December 2000. Out of this amount, Member States owed $200 million for 2000 and $22 million for previous years. Out of 187 assessed Member States, 142 had paid their assessments in full, while the remaining 45 had failed to meet their statutory financial obligations to the Organization.

In addition to the regular budget, Member States are assessed for the costs of the International Tribunals . . . , and, in accordance with a modified version of the basic scale, for the costs of peacekeeping operations. . . .

Peacekeeping costs peaked at $3 billion in 1995, reflecting in particular the expense of operations in Somalia and the former Yugoslavia. . . . For 2000, costs were expected to total at least $2 billion in view of major new missions approved for Kosovo, East Timor, Sierra Leone, the Democratic Republic of the Congo, and Eritrea and Ethiopia. . . .

United Nations funds and programmes — such as the United Nations Children's Fund (UNICEF), the United Nations Development Programme (UNDP) and the High Commissioner for Refugees — have separate budgets. The bulk of their resources is provided on a voluntary basis by governments, and also by individuals, as in the case of UNICEF.

The United Nations specialized agencies also have separate budgets. . . .

The United Nations Family of Organizations

The United Nations family of organizations (the "United Nations system") is made up of the United Nations Secretariat, the United Nations programmes and funds (such as UNICEF and UNDP) and the specialized agencies. The programmes and funds are subsidiary bodies of the General Assembly. The specialized agencies, linked to the United Nations through special agreements, report to the Economic and Social Council and/or the General Assembly. They have their own governing bodies and budgets, and set their own standards and guidelines. Together they provide technical assistance and other forms of practical help in virtually all areas of economic and social endeavour. . . .

[The 14 specialized agencies related to the United Nations include: International Labour Organization (ILO); Food and Agriculture Organization of the United Nations (FAO), United Nations Educational, Scientific and Cultural Organization (UNESCO), World Health Organization (WHO), the World Bank Group, International Monetary Fund (IMF), International Civil Aviation Organization (ICAO), Universal Postal Union (UPU), International Telecommunication Union (ITU), World Meteorological Organization (WMO), International Maritime Organization (IMO), World Intellectual Property Organization (WIPO), International Fund for Agricultural Development (IFAD), United Nations Industrial Development Organization (UNIDO).]

Notes

1. The United Nations has been under increasing pressure, particularly from the United States, to tighten its budget and personnel policies and to implement cost-cutting measures. As noted in the excerpt above, for the 2000-2001 biennium, the proposed U.N. budget totaled $2,535 million, only $2 million higher than the 1998-1999 budget. These funds supported a staff of roughly 8,900, down from a staff of about 12,000 in the mid-1980s.

2. Also, as noted above, the financial difficulties in the United Nations come not only from increased demands for its services but in part also from the continuing failure of many Member States to pay their assessed contributions to the regular budget or to peacekeeping operations. In 2000, out of 187 Member States, 142 had paid their assessments in full, while the remaining 45 had failed to meet their financial obligations to the U.N.

Throughout the 1980s and 1990s, the U.S. Congress regularly withheld much of the dues owed to the United Nations on the grounds that the organization was inefficient and poorly managed. At one point, the United States had a $1.3 billion debt to the U.N., which comprised 65 percent of the total debt by Member States. Besides creating problems for U.N. operations, the U.S. arrears also threatened to cost the United States its vote in the General Assembly. Under Article 19 of the U.N. Charter, if a country owes the equivalent of two years' worth of assessed dues, the country loses its right to vote in the General Assembly, though this sanction is not automatically enforced.

In 1999, Congress passed the Helms-Biden Act, which required the U.N. to accept $926 million in full satisfaction of the U.S. debt, a reduction in the U.S. share of the regular budget from 25 percent to 22 percent, and an additional reduction to 20 percent by 2002. Moreover, the law required a reduction in the U.S. peacekeeping share from 31 to 25 percent by 2001. The goal of the Helms-Biden Act was also to make U.S. payment of dues contingent upon U.N. reforms, including the revision of the assessment scale.

Such unilateral action by the United States encountered criticism from abroad. As a result, the then Ambassador to the U.N., Richard C. Holbrooke, spent many months negotiating a deal for the reduction of U.S. dues to the U.N. The resulting agreement was adopted by the General Assembly in December 2000 and it called for the reduction of the U.S. share of the general budget from 25 to 22 percent. Also, the deal reduced the U.S. share of peacekeeping costs to 26 percent by 2003.

The agreement, however, did not end the U.S. budgetary problems with the U.N. The deal fell just short of the requirements set forth in the Helms-Biden Act because the agreement only reduced expenses to 26 percent instead of the 25 percent required by the legislation. Also, the reduction in peacekeeping expenses would only be effective as of 2003. As a result, an amendment to the Helms-Biden Act reflecting the differences between the original statute and the Holbrooke agreement was required before the United States could pay its outstanding debt to the U.N. The amendment was enacted into law in 2001 and the debt was paid.

With this introduction, you can begin to consider what the role of the United Nations has been in the past and what it should be in the years to come. In the first excerpt below, two former senior officials in the U.S. Department of State provide a brief historical overview and then highlight some of the important reasons for a country to participate in the United Nations. The second excerpt is from the executive summary of a recent report by a task force composed of knowledgeable Americans with a very wide range of views.

Charles William Maynes & Richard S. Williamson, U.S. Foreign Policy and the United Nations System

252-260 (1996)

Over its first fifty years the United States. . . . had a checkered relationship with the United Nations. In the 1940s and 1950s the West had an overwhelming majority within the organization, and its policy toward the United Nations reflected this advantage. . . .

However, by the late 1950s and into the 1960s the United Nations changed dramatically. It became the midwife for the new nations emerging from European colonies in Africa and Asia. These new nations were militarily weak and irrelevant and economically poor and aggrieved. The United Nations was one of the few venues in which they could express their frustrations. . . . [They] spoke out to the discomfort of their former colonial rulers and their allies, which included the United States. During this period American engagement in the United Nations became less central to U.S. foreign policy, and to some it was a hostile forum. But because of the cold war, it always remained an important forum. . . .

Within the United Nations the Soviet Union worked studiously to develop new alliances of convenience with both the East and the South. It exploited the issues of Israel and South Africa. By 1974 the Arabs and Africans had joined together to pass a resolution labeling "Zionism as racism," which caused American support for the

United Nations to plummet. Many in the United States came to see the United Nations as an environment hostile to U.S. interests. . . .

During the 1980s the environment at the U.N. General Assembly became one of confrontation and rhetorical brinkmanship. Congress exacerbated this by withholding the U.S. contribution pending significant budgetary and administrative reforms. But this "cold shower" set the stage for a major improvement in U.S. relations with the U.N. toward the end of the Reagan administration and throughout the Bush administration. A foundation was laid for the Bush administration to go to the U.N. for support in the effort to force Saddam Hussein to disgorge Kuwait.

Now a new cycle at the United Nations has begun. With the collapse of the Soviet Union and the elimination of the Communist system as an alternative model, the United Nations has become a forum of consensus on the issues of free markets, democracy, and the rule of law. That is not to say that all members adopt these desirable practices, but there is no longer any sustained ideological challenge to them. . . .

Our own belief is that the United Nations is a vital institution that is in great need of improvement. We would like to see that improvement take place. We would like to see both parties support it and the institution at large. . . . [T]he United Nations does matter for at least the following reasons.

1.   The United States is a global power with security and commercial interests on every continent. By its very nature, such a power must remain concerned with international rules, norms, and regimes that are relevant to American interests. . . . Establishing and maintaining international rules, norms, and regimes is one of the principal functions of the United Nations and its specialized agencies.

2.   The United States sees itself as an international leader. Every administration aspires to this role. But it is hard to be a leader if one is absent from international fora or constantly on the defensive there. It is also hard to be a leader if the United States is always saying no. It is hard to be a leader if the United States threatens not to do its fair share. It is not possible to be a leader if the United States does not take into account the concerns of its closest allies, which are anxious for the United States to play a constructive role in the United Nations.

      The bipolar ballast of the cold war is gone. . . . [N]ow there is a far greater margin for maneuver within the community of nations. There is a dispersal of power centers. . . .

3.   We are *not* members of a global village and are unlikely to reach that position for decades, if not centuries, to come. But the world's politics and economics are increasingly globalized. It is hard to believe that the world's business can be globalized and adequately managed if there are not also global institutions that assist nation states in managing the new international reality. There are many multilateral fora that can be used to advance U.S. interests. . . . Each has its special characteristics, but the United Nations itself offers many advantages. Thus the record of the U.N., while it should be better, is one of considerable benefit to humanity in general and Americans in particular. Many U.N. critics overlook such contributions as the following.

- The U.N. promotes peace. Through the office of the secretary-general the U.N. has helped to negotiate an end to the Iran-Iraq war, to persuade the Soviet Union to withdraw its troops from Afghanistan, and to end the civil war in El Salvador.
- The U.N. buys needed time for diplomacy and accommodation. U.N. peace-keepers at a cost of 1,000 dead and thousands wounded have monitored ceasefires in South Asia, the Middle East, and Cyprus for decades, providing states in conflict with the assurance that agreements were being respected and that actions by their rivals were not placing them in danger. . . .
- The U.N. heals nations. Through peacekeeping and peace-building efforts the U.N. has been able to restore a degree of civil society to Cambodia, El Salvador, Mozambique, Namibia, and Nicaragua, where hundreds of thousands of people have died in civil wars.
- The U.N. promotes democracy. U.N. missions have provided electoral assistance and advice to more than forty-five countries. . . . [T]he number requesting assistance is constantly growing.
- The U.N. has provided legitimacy to several critical U.S. foreign policy concerns—the American led intervention in the Korean War, the American led intervention in the Gulf, the Nonproliferation Treaty, and most recently the American led intervention in Haiti.
- U.N. agencies provide the indispensable institutional underpinning for a number of international regimes that are of enormous value to the United States and other major participants in the international economy. Examples are the International Atomic Energy Agency's safeguards program, which is central to America's nonproliferation effort; . . . the Food and Agriculture Organization's Codex Alimentarius, which protects the health and safety standards of foods traded internationally; . . .
- The U.N. promotes sound economic policy: U.N. development agencies, including the U.N. Development Programme (UNDP), the World Bank, and the International Monetary Fund, have promoted the kind of market oriented economic policies that the United States believes are most suitable for democratic societies. This trend has been particularly pronounced since the late 1970s when the evidence that state directed economic activity was providing diminishing returns became overwhelming.
- The U.N. saves lives. Agencies like the World Health Organization, the U.N. International Children's Emergency Fund (UNICEF), and the UNDP have saved millions of people from sickness and disease. It is estimated that in recent years 20 million people would have died from smallpox had WHO not eradicated it in 1981. . . .
- The U.N. promotes human rights. Despite the many tempestuous ideological disputes that have raged in the U.N., which were particularly dominant in the 1970s and part of the 1980s, overall the organization has promoted the ideas of democracy and human rights on which the American experiment is based. The end of the cold war has made the U.N.'s efforts to promote democracy and human rights less controversial and contested.

This recitation of the strengths of the United Nations is not to suggest that the organization lacks its weaknesses. It has many that have troubled several administrations, Republican and Democratic, in recent years.

Independent Task Force Sponsored by the Council on Foreign Relations and Freedom House, Enhancing U.S. Leadership at the United Nations (David Dreier & Lee H. Hamilton, co-chairs)
1-4 (2002)

Enhanced American leadership at the United Nations is beneficial for U.S. interests and can help strengthen the U.N. and the international system. For many years, however, the United States has not been nearly as effective at the U.N. as it can or should be.

With this in mind, the members of the Council on Foreign Relations and Freedom House Independent Task Force recommend strengthening U.S. effectiveness at the United Nations around an agenda focused on better cooperation among the U.N.'s democratic member states, on the promotion of more vigorous human rights initiatives, and on more rigorous counterterrorism efforts. The group believes a precondition for making the U.N. truly effective is to reduce the leverage of a minority of repressive regimes, which skillfully blocks many American objectives, particularly in the areas of democracy promotion and advancing fundamental human rights principles.

The U.N. system has given rise to an array of essential and effective programs in the areas of health, education, refugees, food, and development. Moreover, the Security Council has effectively addressed key threats to peace when its five permanent members have been able to work together. The same, however, has not always been true of the General Assembly and other U.N. structures where politics has made the institution an inconsistent voice for democracy and human rights. Over the years, this has produced a mixed record on efforts to promote peace and security and to deepen international cooperation on counterterrorism. The U.N. Commission on Human Rights —where many of the world's most repressive regimes escape criticism and investigation — and such highly publicized conferences as the World Conference Against Racism have been particularly disappointing.

In this context, the members of the Task Force recommend a U.S. policy toward the U.N. focused on building deeper and more effective cooperation among the democracies. Such an initiative, the Task Force concludes, can strengthen the U.N.'s credibility, enhance American leadership within the body, and bring greater effectiveness to U.N. counterterrorism efforts.

Contrary to expectations, the end of the Cold War's East-West divide has not ushered in a new period of more effective international cooperation. Indeed, several serious obstacles remain, and the United States is frequently outmaneuvered and overmatched at the U.N. First, the U.N.'s regional group structure often benefits repressive regimes because democratic governments tend to be concentrated in only a handful of groups. Second, the nonaligned movement (NAM) — created during the Cold War as a counterweight to the East and West blocs — remains an obstacle to effective action within the U.N. Its sixty-four members cooperate on substantive and procedural votes, binding the organization's many democratic nations to the objectives and blocking tactics of its remaining tyrannies. A third factor is the need for more effective coordination and cooperation between the United States and the European Union.

The Task Force also identifies several obstacles to U.S. effectiveness at the U.N. These include frequent U.S. reluctance to support international agreements without adequate explanation of U.S. objections; the U.S. practice of withholding or threatening to withhold treaty obligated dues; and long-term gaps in the confirmation of a permanent U.S. representative to the U.N. Understaffing in the political section of the U.S. U.N. Mission and the related fact that the United States rarely has engaged in the extensive outreach and lobbying practiced by other delegations are additional problems.

To address these factors, the Task Force makes a series of specific recommendations for enhancing American leadership.

The Task Force recommends that the president and the secretary of state enunciate a comprehensive U.S. view of the U.N. and the parameters for effective multilateral cooperation. In addition, the Task Force urges the United States to practice the vigorous outreach and lobbying for which American democracy is famous. To counter impressions that the United States is interested only in its own agenda, the Task Force calls on the United States to support worthy initiatives of its allies and other friendly nations. The Task Force further calls on the administration to address understaffing at the political section of the U.S. Mission to the United Nations, and enhance the prestige and rewards within the Foreign Service for serving in a U.N. posting. Moreover, the Task Force report concludes that enhanced U.S. effectiveness at the U.N. requires avoiding long gaps between appointments of the U.S. ambassador to the U.N.

Finally, the Task Force recommends a series of specific initiatives in the areas of democracy, human rights, and counterterrorism.

DEMOCRACY

The report calls on the United States to work with other democracies to institutionalize a "democracy caucus" at the U.N. as a forum for building cooperation on issues of human rights and democracy. Such a caucus could ensure that democracies operating in regional blocs work together to advance common objectives and promote the candidacies of countries that follow the best practices on issues of democracy and human rights. Members of the democracy caucus would also endeavor to block the election of undemocratic states to U.N. bodies that focus on democratic development.

The report also recommends that the United States work to establish the right to multiparty democracy as a core right within the International Covenant on Civil and Political Rights.

Lastly, the Task Force urges enhanced support for the efforts of the United Nations Development Programme to strengthen legislatures, electoral systems, and other dimensions of democratic governance. It also recommends strengthening the U.N. Electoral Assistance Division.

HUMAN RIGHTS

The Task Force calls for coordination by the democracies on significant human rights resolutions and on elections to key rights-monitoring bodies. It recommends that the United States work to move the United Nations away from broadly declarative statements on human rights to practical implementation of existing standards.

The Task Force calls for comprehensive reform of the U.N. Human Rights Commission and the office of the U.N. High Commissioner for Human Rights to ensure that they focus on the world's most egregious and massive rights violations, many of which now regularly escape investigation and censure. The Task Force also calls on the United States to work with the U.N.'s democracies to ease pressure on U.N.-accredited nongovernmental organizations, which are routinely under review and attack by an array of repressive regimes.

COUNTERTERRORISM

The Task Force calls on the United States to vigorously and publicly support the work of the U.N.'s Counter-Terrorism Committee (CTC) and recommends that the United States evaluate the need for an independent body to carry out the CTC's functions over the long term. It recommends that the United States seek broad endorsement of counterterrorism principles and benchmarks through regional and international bodies like the G-8, the Organization for Economic Cooperation and Development (OECD), the Association of Southeast Asian Nations (ASEAN), the African Union, and the Organization of American States (OAS). It also recommends that resources be allocated for building up the capacity of the U.N.'s poorer states to implement the counterterrorism measures mandated by U.N. Resolution 1373. The report concludes that given the politicization of the debate at the U.N. on a definition of terrorism, the United States should focus on building consensus around acts that are generally accepted as terrorist activities rather than awaiting the elaboration of a precise, internationally accepted definition of terrorism.

Questions

1. What should be the role of the United Nations? First, do you think that the United Nations can successfully play the role initially envisioned for it of preventing military conflict among its members and of settling international disputes? How does the voting system in the Security Council help or hurt these efforts? Can we expect the Security Council to be more effective when none of the permanent members has a vital interest that U.N. action in a dispute might threaten? Might the United Nations be particularly useful when there are regional crises or conflicts that the permanent members would prefer to have resolved? (See Chapter 11 for further discussion of U.N. peacekeeping efforts.)

2. How does the growing threat of international terrorism change the role of the United Nations? What should the U.N. be doing about counterterrorism? Should terrorism affect the definition of "self-defense" under Chapter 51 of the U.N. Charter? How should the U.N. and the international community of nations define terrorism? Given the nebulous character of many terrorist organizations, what level of connection should the U.N. seek to establish for allowing a state that has been attacked by terrorists to retaliate against another state for sponsoring terrorist activity?

3. What other roles should the United Nations have besides peacekeeping? Encouraging worldwide efforts to preserve the environment? Stopping drug traffic? Dealing with international health problems, such as AIDS? Acting as a meeting place

when new problems arise? Does the organization have greater potential in these other areas compared to peacekeeping, particularly peacekeeping among the major powers? Why or why not?

4. Why do you think that the United Nations has spawned so many specialized agencies? Are there benefits to having complex, continuing problems handled by a permanent agency with an expert staff? Or is this bureaucracy running amok?

5. As we continue through the list of other international and regional entities, consider what the alternatives are to an active United Nations. Depending on the problem or issue, do the other entities have the necessary breadth of membership and resources? Are some problems or issues better handled by the whole international community (i.e., through the United Nations), while other problems or issues are better addressed by regional entities (such as the European Union) or by groups of countries with similar interests (e.g., the G-8)?

6. What should be the approach of the United States toward the U.N.? Should the United States continue to pay its dues promptly? On what terms should the United States support the enlargement of the Security Council? Should the United States lend combat forces to U.N. peacekeeping missions? If so, under whose command?

Bibliography

The literature on the United Nations and its specialized agencies is vast. Besides the sources already cited in this section and the many official publications of the United Nations, recent studies include Combatting Terrorism: Does the U.N. Matter . . . and How (Jeffrey Laurenti ed. 2002); The United Nations and International Law (Christopher C. Joyner ed., 1997); The United Nations at Age Fifty (Christian Tomuschat ed., 1995); UNA-USA Policy Report, The Preparedness Gap: Making Peace Operations Work in the 21st Century (2001); Thomas G. Weiss, David P. Forsythe, & Roger A. Coate, The United Nations and Changing World Politics (2d ed. 1997); N.D. White, Keeping the Peace: The United Nations and the Maintenance of International Peace and Security (2d ed. 1997); Anthony Arend, The United Nations and the New World Order, 81 Geo. L.J. 491 (1993).

The U.N. has an excellent Web site at <http://www.un.org>.

b.   The International Monetary Fund and the World Bank Group

In a 1944 wartime conference in Bretton Woods, New Hampshire, representatives of 44 countries formed two international organizations to promote economic cooperation and development, the International Monetary Fund (IMF or Fund) and the International Bank for Reconstruction and Development (World Bank). Now, about 60 years later, each institution has more than 180 members, including all the major countries. In the past decades, both institutions have changed as the monetary system went off the gold standard and fixed exchange rates and as the focus of development aid shifted from post-war destruction in Europe to the Third World. The recent economic problems in Asia, Russia, and Latin America are requiring further changes.

Both the IMF and the World Bank are supposed to be apolitical. The World Bank charter, for example, provides that the Bank and its officers "shall not interfere in the political affairs of any member; nor shall they be influenced in their decisions by the political character of the member or members concerned. Only economic considerations shall be relevant to their decisions." (IBRD Articles of Agreement, art. IV, §10.)

(1) IMF: Purpose and Function

The IMF is the world's central monetary institution and in recent years has been at the forefront of the cooperative international debt strategy. The IMF's primary purpose is to promote international monetary cooperation and stability in foreign exchange. The IMF provides its member countries with assistance on balance-of-payment problems, including "structural adjustment" assistance. It does not extend assistance simply for economic development.

Specifically, the IMF has three functions: to administer the funds in various accounts and financial arrangements, which provide an asset pool that members can draw on to finance deficits in their balance of payments (discussed later); to administer special drawing rights (SDRs), an international reserve asset created by the IMF; and to administer rules of good conduct, which concern exchange rate arrangements, currency controls, and consultations regarding domestic and international policies.

Each nation has a quota, which determines how much it needs to contribute (or subscribe) to the IMF's General Reserve Account (GRA). Quotas are reviewed every five years and are based loosely on a nation's economic strength. The size of a nation's quota determines not only the amount of its subscription, but also its drawing rights in the GRA, its share of SDR allocations, and its voting power within the IMF. Members pay in their quotas using both SDRs and other currencies.

As indicated above, the SDR, or special drawing right, is an international monetary reserve asset created by the IMF in 1969 to supplement existing reserve assets and provide a common unit of account. Its value is set using a basket of four currencies: the U.S. dollar, Japanese yen, British pound sterling, and the euro. As of February 14, 2003, one SDR was equal to approximately $1.37.

When a country joins the IMF, its main obligation is to cooperate with both the Fund and with other members to assure orderly exchange arrangements. It is also required to promote exchange rate stability and to avoid exchange rate restrictions that would harm national and international prosperity. Another "rule of good conduct" requires a member to provide the Fund with financial and economic information about itself. The Fund monitors the compliance of member countries with these obligations through surveillance over members' exchange rate policies and over the international monetary system.

(2) The World Bank Group: Purpose and Function

Formed as a sister organization to the IMF, the initial goal of the International Bank for Reconstruction and Development (IBRD, or World Bank) was to provide long-term financing to those countries in need of reconstruction after World War II. Its purpose now is to promote economic and social progress in developing nations, bringing poor nations to a point of self-sustaining development. The World Bank

Group is now composed of the IRBD and its affiliates, the International Development Association (IDA), which is sometimes grouped in with the IBRD as the World Bank; the International Finance Corporation (IFC); the International Centre for the Settlement of Investment Disputes (ICSID); and the Multilateral Investment Guarantee Agency (MIGA).

The IBRD finances its lending operations primarily by borrowing money in the private international capital markets, backed by guarantees of its member governments. The IBRD makes loans only to creditworthy borrowers and only for those projects demonstrating high real rates of economic return. Loans are generally repayable over 12-15 years, and carry a near-market interest rate (commensurate with that paid by the Bank on its borrowings). Each loan must be made to or guaranteed by the government concerned.

The IDA was established in 1960 to provide assistance to the poorest countries on softer terms than those of IBRD loans. Funds lent by the IDA come principally from contributions by its richer members but also from transfers of net earnings from the IBRD. Loans generally require repayment in 35 to 40 years.

The IBRD and the IDA share the same staff, and they use the same criteria for funding projects. Together they provide more development assistance than any other single agency, multilateral or bilateral, in the world. In fiscal year 2002, they approved new loans of $19.6 billion, which financed over 220 new projects.

In financing a project, the Bank does not compete with other sources of funding. Rather, it is a "lender of last resort": it funds only those projects for which the necessary capital is not available from other sources on reasonable terms. However, once the Bank is involved, most projects then receive financial support from other multilateral or bilateral agencies or commercial banks, which reflects the Bank's role as a catalyst for capital funding.

The IFC was established in 1956. Its function is to assist the economic development of less developed countries by promoting growth in their economies' private sectors via both direct lending and encouragement of private investment. The IFC is a separate entity from the Bank and has its own operating and legal staff; however, it uses the Bank for administrative and other services. Membership in the IFC totals about 175 members.

The IFC complements the work of the Bank. It is required to make loans without a government guarantee. The IFC and the Bank have jointly financed projects, and it is not uncommon for IFC projects to be dependent on infrastructure projects financed by the Bank.

ICSID, which was created by the Convention on the Settlement of Investment Disputes Between States and Nations of Other States in 1965, provides a voluntary mechanism for settling disputes between governments and foreign investors. As of January 2003, 136 nations were parties to the Convention. (See discussion in Chapter 4.)

MIGA, established in 1988, has a specialized mandate: to encourage equity investment and other direct investment flows to developing countries through the reduction of noncommercial investment barriers. As reported in the World Bank's 1989 Annual Report:

> To carry out this mandate, MIGA offers investors guarantees [political risk insurance] against noncommercial risks; advises developing member governments on the design and implementation of policies, programs, and procedures related to foreign

investments; and sponsors a dialogue between the international business community and host governments on investment issues.

In January 2003, 160 countries were members of MIGA.

(3)   The IMF and the World Bank: Structure

The IMF and the World Bank possess similar membership and structures. Only states may be members of the IMF or the World Bank Group. A state need not be a member of the United Nations in order to join the IMF, but membership in the Fund is a prerequisite to joining the World Bank. Within the World Bank Group, most members of the IBRD are members of the IDA and the IFC as well.

The two institutions are each governed by a board of governors and an executive board. The board of governors is the senior organ and is composed of one governor and one alternate governor from each member. In practice, the executive board is the most important organ. It meets in continuous session and is responsible for general operations.

The World Bank executive board has 24 executive directors in addition to a president (traditionally an American). The IMF has 21 executive directors, three deputy managing directors, and a managing director (usually a European). Those five members with the largest quotas each appoint its own executive director. As of January 2003, the United States had the largest voting bloc at the IBRD with 16.41 percent, followed by Japan (7.87 percent), Germany (4.49 percent), France and the United Kingdom (4.31 percent each). In the IMF, the United States also had the largest voting power, with 17.10 percent. Japan and Germany followed with 6.14 percent and 6.00 percent respectively, and France and Britain with 4.95 percent each. The remaining executive directors are elected by groups of the remaining countries. Also, the two largest creditor members may also appoint a director (if they don't have one already).

The IMF and the Bank use a weighted voting system based on members' quotas. However, Fund and Bank organs rarely resort to formal votes except when required to do so. Rather, most work is done by consensus.

Although the IMF and World Bank are primarily state-centric organizations, in recent years they have become more responsive to the concerns of non-state actors.

(4)   The Changing Roles and Relationship of the IMF and the World Bank in the 1970s and 1980s

In August 1971 the United States ended the convertibility of the U.S. dollar into gold at an official fixed price. A few months later the United States devalued the dollar, and the Smithsonian Agreement attempted to reestablish fixed parities between the major currencies, with wider bands of variation allowed among these currencies. This effort to stabilize the world monetary system failed, and by March 1973 most major currencies were floating in value. The system that emerged was one of flexible exchange rates.

During the decade following the collapse of fixed exchange rates, the IMF was occupied with adapting to the new system. It created for itself a supervisory role over the floating system as monitor of members' economic policies. It also continued to lend to countries experiencing temporary balance-of-payments deficits. These deficits were severely aggravated by the sharp increases in oil prices during the late 1970s. Many oil-importing countries needed much more foreign exchange than envisioned in their existing development plans in order to adjust to higher-priced energy.

In 1982 the IMF stepped in with short-term funds to enable Mexico to meet its debt repayment obligations. That step opened the door to a new role — providing funds and encouraging new private bank lending to heavily indebted countries in exchange for IMF-supervised economic restructuring within those counties. An Economist article in February 1988 reported that the IMF lent more than $22 billion between 1982 and 1984, each dollar of which encouraged an estimated four to seven dollars in new commercial loans or refinancing.

The task of restoring creditworthiness to these countries was a more difficult task than first envisioned, however, and required more than the short-term loans then offered by the IMF. It prompted the IMF to alter its offerings to include longer-term lending.

During this same period of the 1970s and 1980s, the World Bank found that with floating exchange rates, currency exchange risks had a greater impact than before on the profitability of proposed development projects. The Bank's concern with domestic currency values increased. Likewise, its involvement in the general economic health of developing countries grew, as many oil-importing countries encountered major financial shocks from the sharp oil price rises.

Although the Articles of Agreement for both the World Bank and the IDA specify that loans made or guaranteed by these organizations shall be for specific projects, "except in special circumstances" (see IBRD art. III, §4(vii) and IDA art. V, §1(b)), the Bank Group has interpreted "specific projects" and "special circumstances" broadly. The steady growth in the breadth of their interpretation allowed the Bank in 1980 to begin offering "structural adjustment" loans. Rather than for a specific project, such as a dam or a factory, these loans can be for general macro-economic or structural programs that will have a more widespread impact on the economy or a segment of it. They are similar in both form and function to extended arrangements offered by the IMF.

Thus floating exchange rates and the growing debt burden of the developing countries caused the formerly clear delineation between the functions of the IMF and World Bank to become shadowy.

(5) U.S. Influence over International Financial Institutions

The United States was an important participant in the negotiations leading to the Bretton Woods agreement. It strongly supported the creation of the IMF and the World Bank. Although the international economy has changed since that time, the United States continues to support exchange rate stability and development efforts in less developed countries.

However, as much as the United States promotes and supports their goals, the IMF and World Bank have not been very instrumental in promoting specific U.S. foreign policy objectives. This is due to two factors: first, these institutions are apolitical in nature and focus only on economic realities within the borrowing countries; second, the U.S. quota does not give the United States even close to a majority position in either organization. Although U.S. legislation requires U.S. directors at the IMF and World Bank to oppose loans to countries that (among other things) are guilty of serious human rights violations or expropriate property without just compensation, the actual impact of this opposition is negligible. Rather, the United States must rely on informal lobbying to further its objectives, a method that has generally not proven effective.

(6) The Demanding 1990s

Both the World Bank and the IMF encountered new challenges in the 1990s as a result of the breakup of the Soviet Union, instability in Eastern Europe, the 1995 economic crisis in Mexico, and then the Asian and Russian financial crises of 1997-1998.

For the World Bank, these challenges led to record lending and raised questions about the Bank's lending practices. With the breakup of the Soviet Union and the attempts at market and social reform in former communist countries, the World Bank made large loans to Russia and other countries. In 1996, the World Bank created a trust fund to meet emergency needs in Bosnia and Herzegovina. In 1998, the Asian financial crisis pushed the Bank's lending to record levels, which included assistance in the areas of financial reforms, social security, technology, education, and health. The events in Asia also led to questions about the Bank not having imposed stricter lending conditions in prior years on countries with institutional problems, like a weak banking structure and corruption in Indonesia.

The IMF was also very active. For example, recognizing the problems that former communist countries had in transitioning to market economies, the IMF established a temporary systemic transformation facility in 1993. It loaned funds to countries so that they could institute policies that would then allow them to borrow under the other permanent IMF programs.

The challenges for the IMF — and questions about its performance — were probably even more demanding than for the World Bank. The situation might best be understood by delving further into how IMF lending occurs and then analyzing how the IMF initially reacted to the 1997-1998 Asian financial crisis. In an IMF publication, David Driscoll explains the Fund's basic lending process.

David D. Driscoll, What Is the International Monetary Fund?
14-17 (1997)

Although the IMF was founded primarily as a cooperative institution to oversee the international monetary system, it also supports that system by occasionally injecting into it sums of money, sometimes on a very large scale, through loans to its members. Indeed, the IMF is perhaps best known to the general public for pumping billions of dollars into the system during the debt crisis of the 1980s and for the vast amounts it committed to Mexico and to Russia during the 1990s. . . . In 1995, it extended to Mexico a credit of over $17 billion and to Russia more than $6.2 billion to help tide these countries over a difficult period of reform. . . .

The quota subscriptions . . . constitute the largest source of money at the IMF's disposal. Quotas are now in theory worth about [$280 billion in 2002], although in practice this sum is deceptively large. Because member countries pay 75 percent of their quotas in domestic money, and because most national currencies are rarely in demand outside the countries issuing them, approximately half of the money on the IMF's balance sheets cannot be used. . . . [M]ost potential borrowers from the IMF want only the major convertible currencies: the U.S. dollar, the Japanese yen, . . . the pound sterling, and [now the euro].

As each member has a right to borrow from the IMF several times the amount it has paid in as a quota subscription, quotas might not provide enough cash to meet the borrowing needs of members in a period of great stress in the world economy. To deal with this eventuality, the IMF has had since 1962 a line of credit, now worth about $24 billion, with a number of governments and banks throughout the world. This line of credit, called the General Arrangements to Borrow, is renewed every five years. The IMF pays interest on whatever it borrows under these arrangements and undertakes to repay the loan in five years. These arrangements have been strengthened by a decision on the New Arrangements to Borrow, which [totaled about $45 billion in 2002].

In addition to these arrangements, the IMF also borrows money from member governments or their monetary authorities for specific programs of benefit to its members. Over the past decade, using its good credit rating, the IMF has borrowed to provide needy members with more money for longer periods and under more favorable terms than they could obtain on their own. Borrowing these large amounts has to a certain extent changed the nature of the IMF, making it more like a bank, which is essentially an institution in the business of borrowing from one group and lending to another. . . .

The IMF lends money only to member countries with payments problems, that is, to countries that do not take in enough foreign currency to pay for what they buy from other countries. The money a country takes in comes from what it earns from exports, from providing services (such as banking and insurance), and from what tourists spend there. Money also comes from overseas investment and, in the case of poorer countries, in the form of aid from better-off countries. Countries, like people, however, can spend more than they take in, making up the difference for a time by borrowing until their credit is exhausted, as eventually it will be. When this happens, the country must face a number of unpleasant realities, not the least of which are commonly a loss in the buying power of its currency and a forced reduction in its imports from other countries. A country in that situation can turn for assistance to the IMF, which will for a time supply it with sufficient foreign exchange to allow it to put right what has gone wrong in its economic life, with a view to stabilizing its currency and strengthening its trade.

A member country with a payments problem can immediately withdraw from the IMF the 25 percent of its quota that it paid in gold or a convertible currency. If the 25 percent of quota is insufficient for its needs, a member in greater difficulty may request more money from the IMF. . . .

As a country draws increasingly on these funds, conditions might be attached. This conditionality is part of the IMF's attempts to stabilize the financial situations in borrowing countries and thereby reduce their need for Fund resources. The conditions might include such items as new taxes, reductions in government employment, reductions in subsidies, sale of government enterprises, devaluation of the currency, and limitations on the importation of luxury goods. Although these conditions are intended to eliminate the country's balance-of-payments deficits without imposing unnecessarily harsh restrictions on trade or causing adverse effects on economic growth, the measures sometimes prove to be unpopular domestically. These conditions have made the Fund — and the leaders who accept its austerity measures — the targets of criticism.

This general description of the IMF lending process can be put in recent context with the Asian financial crisis of 1997-1998. The excerpt from Steven Pearlstein of the Washington Post incisively sketches the dynamics that led to the crisis. It is followed by an analysis of the IMF's reaction to the situation, especially in Korea, by Professor Martin Feldstein. Although Feldstein is a respected economist, not everyone, including IMF officials, would agree with his analysis.

Steven R. Pearlstein, Background: Understanding the Asian Economic Crisis

Washington Post, Jan. 18, 1998, at A32

The basic story of the Asian bubble economics varied only slightly from country to country: Foreign investment — lured by high returns, stable government and currencies pegged tightly to the dollar — began pouring in during the early '80s. The foreign money financed factories and power plants, skyscrapers and airports for a booming export economy. Wages rose and a middle class emerged with a taste for the finer things, most of them imported. Success begat success — and then overbuilding, overlending, overconsumption.

The first signs of serious trouble appeared when the supercharged Thai economy began to slow last spring, triggering a speculative run against the baht by currency traders hoping to profit from a devaluation. In a vain attempt to defend its currency, the Thai central bank depleted its reserves of foreign currency. When the devaluation finally came in July, foreign investors fled — breaking the speculative cycle.

The Thai crisis was like a pinprick, bursting bubbles across Asia. Stock prices fell, real estate prices plummeted, local currencies went into free falls. Banks and corporations, which had borrowed heavily in dollars, yen and marks, found they could not repay. In one country after another, foreign investors came to realize that what was true in Thailand was true in many of the other Asian Tigers. . . .

The call went out to Financial 911 — the International Monetary Fund in Washington. . . .

Martin Feldstein, Refocusing the IMF

See also

Foreign Affairs, Mar./Apr. 1998, at 20-33

Joseph Stiglitz

OVERDOING IT IN EAST ASIA

In the Asian currency crisis, the International Monetary Fund is risking its effectiveness by the way it now defines its role as well as by its handling of the problems of the affected countries. The IMF's recent emphasis on imposing major structural and institutional reforms as opposed to focusing on balance-of-payments adjustments will have adverse consequences in both the short term and the more distant future. The IMF should stick to its traditional task of helping countries cope with temporary shortages of foreign exchange and with more sustained trade deficits. . . .

[Most Southeast Asian countries in financial crisis] clearly need to shrink their current account deficits by increasing exports and reducing imports.* That in turn requires reductions in public and private consumption and investment. The proper remedy is a variant of the traditional IMF medicine tailored specifically to each country — some combination of reduced government spending, higher taxes, and tighter credit. Even in those countries where government budgets are already in surplus, an increase in taxes or a reduction in government spending will shrink the current account deficit. The experience in Latin America provides a useful model of what can be done.

But the IMF's role in Thailand and Indonesia went far beyond the role that it played in Latin America. Instead of relying on private banks and serving primarily as a monitor of performance, the IMF took the lead in providing credit. In exchange, it has imposed programs requiring governments to reform their financial institutions and to make substantial changes in their economic structures and political behavior. . . . In Indonesia, for example, in exchange for a $40 billion package (more than 25 percent of Indonesia's GDP), the IMF has insisted on a long list of reforms, specifying in minute detail such things as the price of gasoline and the manner of selling plywood. The government has also been told to end the country's widespread corruption and curtail the special business privileges used to enrich President Suharto's family and the political allies that maintain his regime. Although such changes may be desirable in many ways, past experience suggests that they are not needed to maintain a flow of foreign funds.

The Korean situation is different from that of the [other Asian countries] and is more important because its economy is the 11th-largest in the world. Korea's problem did not stem from an overvalued exchange rate and an excessive current account deficit. The value of the Korean won had not been fixed in recent years but had gradually adjusted to maintain Korea's competitiveness. . . .

The Korean economy was performing well: real GDP grew at eight percent per year in the 1990s, as it had in the 1980s, inflation was below five percent, and the unemployment rate was less than three percent. . . . Korea got in trouble in mid-1997 because its business and financial institutions had incurred short-term foreign debts that far exceeded Korea's foreign exchange assets. By October, U.S. commercial banks estimated that Korea's short-term debts were $110 billion — more than three times Korea's foreign exchange reserves. With investors nervous about emerging markets in general and Asia in particular, it is not surprising that the Korean won came under attack.

Since Korea's total foreign debt was only about 30 percent of GDP (among the lowest of all developing nations), this was clearly a case of temporary illiquidity rather than fundamental insolvency. Moreover, since the current account deficit was very small and rapidly shrinking, there was no need for the traditional IMF policy of

---

*Current account deficit is the sum of a country's trade deficit and the interest on its foreign obligations. — Eds.

reduced government spending, higher taxes, and tight credit. Yet something needed to be done to stop the loss of foreign exchange and to maintain bank lending to the country and its healthy businesses. . . .

What Korea needed was coordinated action by creditor banks to restructure its short-term debts, lengthening their maturity and providing additional temporary credits to help meet the interest obligations. . . . The IMF could have helped by providing a temporary bridge loan and then organizing the banks into a negotiating group. . . .

Instead, the IMF organized a pool of $57 billion from official sources — the IMF, the World Bank, the U.S. and Japanese governments, and others — to lend to Korea so that its private corporate borrowers could meet their foreign currency obligations to U.S., Japanese, and European banks. In exchange for those funds, the IMF demanded a fundamental overhaul of the Korean economy and a contractionary macroeconomic policy of higher taxes, reduced spending, and high interest rates. . . .

EVALUATING THE STRATEGY

The fundamental issue is the appropriate role for an international agency and its technical staff in dealing with sovereign countries that come to it for assistance. It is important to remember that the IMF cannot initiate programs but develops a program for a member country only when that country seeks help. The country is then the IMF's client or patient, but not its ward. . . .

The IMF should provide the technical advice and the limited financial assistance necessary to deal with a funding crisis and to place a country in a situation that makes a relapse unlikely. It should not use the opportunity to impose other economic changes that, however helpful they may be, are not necessary to deal with the balance-of-payments problem and are the proper responsibility of the country's own political system.

In deciding whether to insist on any particular reform, the IMF should ask three questions: Is this reform really needed to restore the country's access to international capital markets? Is this a technical matter that does not interfere unnecessarily with the proper jurisdiction of a sovereign government? If the policies to be changed are also practiced in the major industrial economies of Europe, would the IMF think it appropriate to force similar changes in those countries if they were subject to a fund program? The IMF is justified in requiring a change in a client country's national policy only if the answer to all three questions is yes.

The Korean case illustrates the need for this test very well. Although many of the structural reforms that the IMF included in its early-December program for Korea would probably improve the long-term performance of the Korean economy, they are not needed for Korea to gain access to capital markets. They are also among the most politically sensitive issues: labor market rules, regulations of corporate structure and governance, government-business relations, and international trade. The specific policies that the IMF insists must be changed are not so different from those in the major countries of Europe: labor market rules that cause 12 percent unemployment, corporate ownership structures that give banks and governments controlling interests in industrial companies, state subsidies to inefficient and loss-making industries, and trade barriers that restrict Japanese auto imports to a trickle and block foreign purchases of industrial companies. . . .

. . . Korea's outstanding performance combining persistently high growth, low inflation, and low unemployment suggests that the current structure of the Korean economy may now be well suited to Korea's stage of economic and political development. . . . Even if it were desirable for Korea to shift toward labor, goods, and capital markets more like those of the United States, it may be best to evolve in that direction more gradually and with fewer shocks to existing businesses. . . .

ENCOURAGING EXCESSIVE RISK

The IMF faces a serious dilemma whenever it deals with a country that cannot meet its obligation to foreign creditors. The IMF can encourage those creditors to roll over existing loans and provide new credit by promising them that they will be repaid in full. That type of guarantee was implicit in the IMF's $57 billion credit package for Korea. But promising creditors that they will not lose in the current crisis also encourages those lenders and others to take excessive future risks. Banks that expect loans to be guaranteed by governments do not look as carefully as they should at the underlying commercial credit risks. And when banks believe that the availability of dollars to meet foreign exchange obligations will be guaranteed by the IMF, they will not look carefully at the foreign exchange risk of the debtor countries.

There is no perfect solution to this "moral hazard" problem. In principle, the IMF and the Korean government should provide the guarantees needed to keep current creditors engaged while swearing that it is the last time that such guarantees will be provided. Although there may be no way to make such a promise persuasively, the IMF may have encouraged future lenders too much by the speed with which it took control — without waiting for lenders and borrowers to begin direct negotiations with each other. The call by IMF Managing Director Michel Camdessus for member governments to provide an additional $60 billion in IMF resources, on top of the $100 billion increase requested last September, just after announcing the Korean program in December also encourages banks and other lenders to believe they will be bailed out in the future.

At the same time, the message to emerging-market countries sent by painful and comprehensive reform programs was that they should avoid calling in the IMF. . . . More generally, the tough program conditions make it difficult to get a country to work with the IMF until it is absolutely necessary. . . .

When the foreign exchange crisis hit Korea, the primary need was to persuade foreign creditors to continue to lend by rolling over existing loans as they came due. The key to achieving such credit without an IMF guarantee of outstanding loans was to persuade lenders that Korea's lack of adequate foreign exchange reserves was a temporary shortage, not permanent insolvency. By emphasizing the structural and institutional problems of the Korean economy, the fund's program and rhetoric gave the opposite impression. . . .

As a result, by late December Korea's reserves were almost gone, shrinking at a rate of $1 billion a day. The U.S. government and the IMF recognized that the original strategy had failed and agreed to accelerate $10 billion of the committed loans as a bridge to prevent a default. More important, the U.S. Federal Reserve and the other major central banks called in the leading commercial banks and urged them to create a coordinated program of short-term loan rollovers and longer-term debt restructuring. The banks agreed to roll over the loans coming due immediately, and the crisis was averted. The banks are now meeting with the Korean government to develop plans for longer-term restructuring. The situation in Korea might have been much better and the current deep crisis avoided had such negotiations begun much earlier.

Several features of the IMF plan are replays of the policies that Japan and the United States have long been trying to get Korea to adopt. These included accelerating the previously agreed upon reductions of trade barriers . . . and opening capital markets so that foreign investors can have majority ownership of Korean firms, engage in hostile takeovers opposed by local management, and expand direct participation in banking and other financial services. Although greater competition from manufactured imports and more foreign ownership could in principle help the Korean economy, Koreans and others saw this aspect of the plan as an abuse of IMF power to force Korea at a time of weakness to accept trade and investment policies it had previously rejected.

The IMF would be more effective in its actions and more legitimate in the eyes of emerging-market countries if it pursued the less ambitious goal of maintaining countries' access to global capital markets and international bank lending. Its experts should focus on determining whether the troubled country's problem is one of short-term liquidity and, if so, should emphasize that in its advice and assistance. The IMF should eschew the temptation to use currency crises as an opportunity to force fundamental structural and institutional reforms on countries, however useful they may be in the long term, unless they are absolutely necessary to revive access to international funds. . . .

The IMF should remember that the borrowers and the lending bankers or bondholders should bear primary responsibility for resolving the problems that arise when countries or their corporations cannot meet their international debt obligations. The IMF should provide technical assistance on how the debtors can improve their current account balances and increase their foreign exchange. It should act as a monitor of the success that the country is making in moving toward self-sustainable liquidity, providing its own funds as an indication of its confidence in the country's progress rather than as a bailout of international lenders and domestic borrowers. . . .

As reflected in Professor Feldman's article, after its failure to resolve the East Asian financial crisis in 1997, the IMF was substantially criticized. Among the critics was a blue-ribbon, independent task force created by the Council on Foreign Relations, whose purpose was to take a fresh look at the need for reform of the international financial architecture. The executive summary of this group, which includes seven recommendations, is excerpted below.

Report of an Independent Task Force Sponsored by the Council on Foreign Relations, Safeguarding Prosperity in a Global Financial System: The Future International Financial Architecture

1-5 (1999)

When Thailand was forced to devalue its currency in July 1997, no one could have foreseen the turmoil that would follow. Over the succeeding two years, *financial crises swept through the developing world like a hurricane.** Indonesia, South Korea, Malaysia, the Philippines, Hong Kong, Russia, and Brazil were among the hardest hit, but few developing countries emerged unscathed. *In the crisis countries, currencies and equity prices plummeted, economic growth turned into recession, wealth evaporated, jobs were destroyed, and poverty and school dropout rates soared.* Private capital flows to emerging economies nose-dived, while industrial countries saw their export markets shrink. Last fall, after Russia's debt default and devaluation and the near collapse of a large hedge fund (Long Term Capital Management, LTCM), international financial markets seized up for nearly all high-risk borrowers, including those in the United States. *Global growth slowed sharply.* In some quarters, doubts arose about the market as the engine of prosperity. Confidence in the official institutions that manage financial crises was shaken. No wonder, then, that *President Clinton . . . characterized the Asian/global crisis as "the greatest financial challenge facing the world in the last half century."*

Financial crises are nothing new. In the past 20 years alone, more than 125 countries have experienced at least one serious bout of banking problems. . . . And *in more than a dozen cases, the cost of resolving the crisis was at least a tenth — and sometimes much more — of the crisis country's annual national income. . . . And in the recent Asian crisis, economies accustomed to annual growth rates of 6-8 percent suffered severe depressions, with output falling 5 to 14 percent last year.* In the past six months, a number of the crisis countries have returned to positive economic growth and the functioning of global financial markets has improved. But the *global recovery is still in its early stages and remains fragile*— not least because most of the underlying vulnerabilities have been only partly addressed.

We cannot eliminate banking, currency, and debt crises entirely, but it would be a counsel of despair to argue that little can be done to make them less frequent and less severe. *Strengthening crisis prevention and management — that is, the international financial architecture ("the architecture" for short) — is also very much in our national interest. The US economy is connected much more closely to the rest of the world than it was 20 or 30 years ago.* The average share of exports and imports in our national output now stands at about 15 percent — twice as high as in 1980 and three times as high as in 1960. Two-fifths of our exports go to developing countries. US firms active in global markets are more productive and more profitable than those that serve only domestic customers. *Exporting firms pay their workers better and have expanded jobs faster than firms that do not export.* More than $2.5 trillion of US savings is invested abroad. Borrowing costs, including the monthly payments US households make for their home mortgages, are lower because of our participation in international capital markets.

But why worry, some might ask. . . . In the recent emerging-market crisis, *US exports to the most affected areas fell 40 percent. The Asian crisis struck when domestic spending in the United States was robust and when inflationary pressures were low. . . . Next time we might not be so well positioned to weather the storm. . . .*

The United States is not immune to financial crises abroad. There have been enough losses, close calls, and "might-have-beens" over the past few decades to remind us that international capital markets — despite their important contribution to our standard of living — can at times be risky places. . . .

---

*Certain passages in the executive summary are italicized to highlight the task force's main findings and recommendations.

Our Approach

If we are *to make real headway in improving crisis prevention and management in the developing world, we must put the primary responsibility back where it belongs: on emerging economies themselves and on their private creditors, which dominate today's international capital markets.* If the behavior of debtors and creditors does not change, the poor track record on financial crises will continue. But wishing for change will not make it happen. *Better incentives — including the prospect of smaller and less frequent official bailouts — can facilitate desirable changes in lender and borrower behavior.*

. . . [W]e *offer seven key recommendations:*

Recommendation 1. Greater rewards for joining the "good housekeeping club." The IMF should lend on more favorable terms to countries that take effective steps to reduce their crisis vulnerability and should publish assessments of these steps for each country so the market can take note.

Recommendation 2. Capital flows — avoiding too much of a good thing. Emerging economies with fragile financial systems should take transparent and nondiscriminatory tax measures to discourage short-term capital inflows and encourage less crisis-prone, longer-term ones, such as foreign direct investment.

Recommendation 3. The private sector: promote fair burden-sharing and market discipline. To encourage more orderly and timely rescheduling of private debt where it is needed, all countries should include "collective action clauses" in their sovereign bond contracts. In extreme cases where rescheduling of private debt is needed to restore a viable debt profile, the IMF should require as a condition for its own emergency assistance that debtors be engaged in "good faith" (serious and fair) discussions on debt rescheduling with their private creditors. The IMF should also be prepared to support a temporary halt in debt repayments.

To reduce moral hazard at the national level, the IMF should encourage emerging economies to implement a deposit insurance system that places the primary cost of bank failures on bank shareholders and on large, uninsured private creditors of banks — and not on small depositors or taxpayers.[1]

Recommendation 4. Just say no to pegged exchange rates. The IMF and the Group of Seven (G − 7) should advise emerging economies against adopting pegged exchange rates and should not provide funds to support unsustainable pegs.

Recommendation 5. IMF crisis lending: less will do more. For country crises, the IMF should adhere consistently to normal lending limits. This will help to reduce moral hazard at the international level. . . .

Recommendation 6. Refocus the IMF and the World Bank: back to basics. The IMF should focus on monetary, fiscal, and exchange rate policies plus financial-sector surveillance and reform and stay out of longer-term structural reforms. The World Bank should focus on the longer-term structural and social aspects of development, including the design of social safety nets. It should stay out of crisis lending and management.

Recommendation 7. Generate political support for and ownership of financial reforms. Convene a global conference of finance ministers to reach a consensus on actions,

---

1. By "moral hazard," we mean situations in which the availability of insurance from the official sector weakens investors' and borrowers' sense of responsibility for their own actions.

priorities, and timetables for actions nations will take to strengthen national financial systems.

Notes and Questions

1. What are the advantages of developed countries banding together to form apolitical international financial institutions rather than acting independently or bilaterally to achieve the same goals?

2. Should the United States (or other nations) use the Fund and the World Bank to advance its own international political/economic agenda? Did actions such as U.S. opposition to loans to the Sandinista government in Nicaragua, partly on ideological grounds, threaten the effectiveness of the institutions? Should U.S. policymakers ignore the effects that the institutions' actions might have on specific U.S. interests when making decisions on U.S. contributions? (See also the discussion in Chapter 8 regarding the use of these institutions to promote human rights.)

3. Do you think that the IMF pursued appropriate policies during the Asian financial crisis in Indonesia and Korea? Did the IMF have the right emphasis on major structural and institutional reforms versus balance of payments adjustments?

4. Professor Feldman and the task force suggest above that the IMF loan guarantees may encourage creditors to invest excessively in high-risk projects and countries. Should some of the major international private lenders have been required to "take a haircut" in, say, Korea — this is, should they be required to absorb some losses on their loans — or should they essentially be made whole through government loan guarantees and other provisions? Why or why not?

5. If you were a U.S. Senator asked to approve increased U.S. contributions to the IMF (in order to increase the size of our quota), would you want to add any conditions to the authorization?

6. Learning from its experience in Asia and hearing the criticism, such as from Professor Feldstein and the task force, the International Monetary Fund allowed Ecuador to go into default on some of its outstanding debt in 1999. In part, this appeared to be a warning to the international private lenders that the IMF would not always protect them. On a much larger scale, the IMF was limited in its support of Argentina when that country had a severe financial crisis starting in 2001.

Bibliography

The annual reports of the institutions discussed in this section are very informative, as are their Web sites: <http://www.imf.org> and <http://www.worldbank.org>. See also International Finance, the annual report of the National Council on International Monetary and Financial Policies, which provides a wealth of information about these institutions and U.S. international economic activities. Other useful sources besides those excerpted above include Joseph Gold, Interpretation: The IMF and International Law (1996); The World's Monetary System: Toward Stability and Sustainability in the Twenty-First Century (Jo Marie Griesgraber & Bernard G. Gunter eds., 1996); The World Bank in a Changing World (Ibrahim F.I. Shihata, Franziska Tschofen & Antorio R. Parra eds., 1995); Jessica Einhorn, The World Bank Mission Creep, 80 Foreign Affairs 22 (2001).

c.   The World Trade Organization (WTO) and the General Agreement on Tariffs and Trade (GATT)

The substantial growth of international trade and its related economic benefits can be attributed in part to the World Trade Organization (WTO) and its predecessor, the General Agreement on Tariffs and Trade (GATT). Indeed, the WTO has become one of the most dynamic and influential international institutions. For example, see the discussion in Chapter 4 of the frequency and diversity of cases brought before its dispute resolution system. What follows is a brief history of the GATT and an analysis of the WTO.

(1)   The GATT

The GATT continues in the new WTO framework as an important trade agreement with key principles and provisions. Moreover, when the proposed International Trade Organization (ITO) died a stillbirth after World War II because of opposition in the U.S. Senate, the GATT also metamorphosed then into an international organization that administered the GATT agreement and that provided the forum where nations could promote trade liberalization. It continued to play that role as an institution until the WTO came into being in January 1995.

The purpose of GATT was to promote trade liberalization through the elimination of both tariff barriers and non-tariff barriers (such as quotas or quantitative trade restrictions). Members had four fundamental obligations. On joining GATT, they undertook to (1) apply trade barriers on a nondiscriminatory basis; (2) limit tariffs on items at the levels set forth in the GATT tariff schedules; (3) refrain from circumventing trade concessions through the use of other barriers to trade; and (4) settle trade conflicts via consultation and a special dispute resolution process.

Central to nondiscrimination are two principles: most-favored-nation treatment (MFN) and national treatment obligation (NTO). The GATT agreement starts with an unconditional most-favored-nation provision: "[A]ny advantage, favour, privilege or immunity granted by any contracting party to any product originating in or destined for any country shall be accorded immediately and unconditionally to the like product originating in or destined for the territories of all other contracting parties." (Article I, para. 1.) In short, it prohibits discrimination between goods from different foreign countries. As for national treatment obligation, this principle tries to impose nondiscrimination between goods that are domestically produced and those that are imported. (See Article III.)

Exceptions to these GATT rules and principles, however, do exist. They can be obtained, for instance, by granting of a waiver by the Contracting Parties; by using safeguard measures that allow a nation under certain conditions to impose restrictions or increase a tariff in order to prevent or limit serious injury to domestic producers (although the other country retains a right to claim redress); or by claiming a balance-of-payments crisis. The formation of a customs union or free trade area also allows some exceptions to GATT. Additionally, developing countries are exempted from many GATT obligations.

To further their stated goals, GATT members held periodic rounds of trade negotiations. Eight rounds of negotiations took place between 1947 and 1994. The first six rounds focused primarily on the reduction of tariff barriers to trade. They were quite successful: the average level of tariffs on products in major industrial countries fell to about 13 percent by the early 1960s, and then to about 4 percent in 1986.

As tariffs were successfully reduced in the 1970s, non-tariff barriers (NTBs) became more prominent as impediments to free trade. The Tokyo Round, which lasted from 1973 to 1979, resulted in a series of "Codes" on subsidies, technical barriers to trade, and government procurement, but the Round did not fully resolve these issues.

By the mid-1980s, changes in the international economy, coupled with frustration over the continued prevalence of NTBs, threatened the international trade system. The prospect of increased use of protectionist national trade policies and bilateral trade agreements prompted GATT members to call for a new round of multilateral trade negotiations.

In September 1986, the trade ministers of GATT's member nations opened the Uruguay Round of trade negotiations (named for the location where the opening declaration was issued). The Round, which was completed in December 1993, resulted in the most comprehensive agreements ever completed under the GATT. The Final Act of the Uruguay Round was signed on April 15, 1994, in Morocco.

The Uruguay Round had many major achievements. Tariffs on industrial goods were reduced on average by more than one-third, barriers to agricultural trade were eased, and the provisional GATT institutional arrangements were changed into a formal international institution, the WTO. Previously uncovered areas (e.g., services, textiles and clothing, and intellectual property) were brought under the auspices of the WTO. New or strengthened rules were developed for a number of areas of trade and investment.

(2)   *The World Trade Organization*

The creation of the WTO was the most significant result of the Uruguay Round. The WTO is designed to help implement the agreements negotiated during the Round. It will continue to work toward the objectives of GATT—most notably, the expansion of world trade. The WTO will be the forum for future trade negotiations and will also administer the dispute resolution system.

The following excerpt from a GATT publication provides some essential data about the WTO:

What Is the WTO?

GATT Focus, May 1994, at 11-12

The World Trade Organization (WTO) will facilitate the implementation and operation of all the agreements and legal instruments negotiated in connection with the Uruguay Round, . . . ; it will provide a forum for all negotiations; and it will administer the Understanding on Rules and Procedures Governing the Settlement of Disputes. . . .

In its Preamble, the Agreement establishing a World Trade Organization reiterates the objectives of the GATT, namely raising standards of living and incomes, ensuring full employment, expanding production and trade, and optimal use of the world's resources, while at the same time extending them to services and making them more precise:

- it introduces the idea of "sustainable development" in relation to the optimal use of the world's resources . . . ;
- it recognizes that there is a need for positive efforts designed to ensure that developing countries, and especially the least-developed among them, secure a better share of the growth in international trade.Chart

DECISION-MAKING

The WTO will continue the decision-making practice followed under the GATT: decision by consensus which is deemed to exist if no member formally objects. Recourse to voting, where a decision cannot be reached by consensus, is institutionalized, whereas previously it was exceptional. Decisions will still be taken by a majority of the votes cast, on the basis of "one country, one vote."

However, in two cases—*interpretation* of the provisions of the agreements and *waiver* of a member's obligations—conditions imposed by the Agreement are more severe. The majority required is then three quarters of the members, whereas under the GATT it was only two thirds of the votes cast representing at least half of the members. Moreover, the granting of waivers will be more strictly controlled (justification, time-limits, possibility of recourse to dispute settlement). . . .

ORIGINAL AND NEW MEMBERS

The member countries of the GATT as of the date of entry into force of the WTO Agreement will become original members of the WTO. However, the least-developed countries recognized as such by the United Nations will only be required to undertake commitments and concessions to the extent consistent with their individual development.

The accession procedures and the majority of two thirds of the members required remain the same as under the GATT.

STATUS AND BUDGET

The WTO will have legal personality and will be accorded privileges and immunities similar to those accorded to the specialized agencies of the United Nations. The status of the GATT was relatively ambiguous because of the failure to set up an International Trade Organization in 1947. . . .

The establishment of the World Trade Organization will reinforce the status and the image of the principal institution with responsibility for international trade, by placing it on the same footing as the IMF and the World Bank.

The Director-General of the WTO will be appointed by the Ministerial Conference which will also adopt regulations setting up his powers and duties. . . .

Professor Andreas Lowenfeld highlights some of the more significant implications of the WTO.

WTO Structure. All WTO members may participate in all councils, committees, etc., except Appellate Body, Dispute Settlement panels, Textiles Monitoring Body, and Plurilateral committees

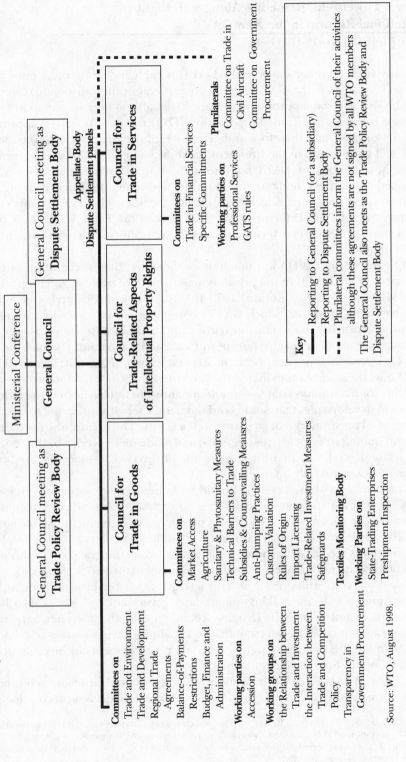

Ministerial Conference

General Council meeting as Trade Policy Review Body

General Council

General Council meeting as Dispute Settlement Body

Appellate Body
Dispute Settlement panels

Council for Trade in Goods

Council for Trade-Related Aspects of Intellectual Property Rights

Council for Trade in Services

Committees on
Trade and Environment
Trade and Development
Regional Trade Agreements
Balance-of-Payments Restrictions
Budget, Finance and Administration

Working parties on
Accession

Working groups on
the Relationship between Trade and Investment
the Interaction between Trade and Competition Policy
Transparency in Government Procurement

Committees on
Market Access
Agriculture
Sanitary & Phytosanitary Measures
Technical Barriers to Trade
Subsidies & Countervailing Measures
Anti-Dumping Practices
Customs Valuation
Rules of Origin
Import Licensing
Trade-Related Investment Measures
Safeguards

Textiles Monitoring Body

Working Parties on
State-Trading Enterprises
Preshipment Inspection

Committees on
Trade in Financial Services
Specific Commitments

Working parties on
Professional Services
GATS rules

Plurilaterals
Committee on Trade in Civil Aircraft
Committee on Government Procurement

Key
—— Reporting to General Council (or a subsidiary)
------- Reporting to Dispute Settlement Body
•••••• Plurilateral committees inform the General Council of their activities although these agreements are not signed by all WTO members
The General Council also meets as the Trade Policy Review Body and Dispute Settlement Body

Source: WTO, August 1998.

501

Andreas Lowenfeld, Remedies Along with Rights: Institutional Reform in the New GATT

88 Am. J. Intl. L. 477, 478-479 (1994)

For many years member states of the GATT, notably including the United States, have pretended that the GATT is only an agreement, not an organization. This make-believe had some purpose in the late 1940s, after it became apparent that the proposed International Trade Organization (ITO) was not likely to be approved by the U.S. Congress, and therefore authority for U.S. participation in a free-standing GATT had to be found in the President's authority to enter into trade agreements. Gradually, of course, the GATT built up staff, occupied a building in Geneva, and developed committees, budgets, internal rules and other attributes of an organization. It even had the courage, in 1965, to change the title of the principal officer from Executive Secretary to Director-General. As part of the Final Act of the Uruguay Round, the member states determined to recognize reality, and to establish . . . a World Trade Organization (WTO).[1]

Agreement on a WTO was much more, however, than recognition of the de facto status of the GATT. In the previous major round of trade negotiations, known as the MTN or the Tokyo Round (1973-1979), a series of separate agreements or codes had been produced, which GATT contracting parties could join or not join without jeopardizing their status as parties to the GATT. Thus, thirty-eight states (counting the members of the European Community separately) joined the Standards Code, twenty-four states (with the EC signing as a single unit) signed the Subsidies Code, twenty-five states joined the Anti-Dumping Code, and so on. This made it possible for like-minded states — predominantly but not exclusively the industrial states — to develop rules that would bind them inter se, without having to obtain the consent of all one hundred or so parties to the GATT. The disadvantage was that the universal trading rules, at least as amplified and made more precise by the codes, became less universal, and that the golden rule of the GATT — most-favored-nation treatment — was not fully honored.

The architects of the Uruguay Round took the opposite approach. To join the new WTO, states will be required to adhere to nearly all of the agreements embraced by what is to be called "GATT 94." More precisely, the Agreement Establishing the World Trade Organization states (in Art. II) that the "agreements and associated legal instruments included in Annexes 1, 2, and 3 . . . are integral parts of this Agreement, binding on all Members." Only four agreements (listed in Annex 4) are optional — those concerning trade in civil aircraft, government procurement, dairy products and bovine meat. This undertaking covers not only the Tokyo Round agreements, as amended in the Uruguay Round, but also the many new agreements, including agreements or understandings on trade in services, on trade-related aspects of intellectual property rights, on trade-related aspects of investment measures, and on trade in textiles and clothing.

. . . The World Trade Organization will start out with a major achievement: bringing uniformity back to the law of international trade. It is no secret that many

---

1. Throughout the Uruguay Round, the proposed new organization was referred to as Multilateral Trade Organization or MTO, apparently because of resistance by the United States to the word "world" in the title. At the last moment "world" triumphed and "multilateral," which sounded too technical and even technocratic, was abandoned.

observers have been skeptical about the future of GATT in light of the proliferation of regional trading arrangements. Notwithstanding the many ambiguities and compromises in the four hundred pages of agreed text, it is not unfair to view the commitment to universality and the rejection of side agreements as a statement by the international community that GATT is here to stay — not at the margin but at the center of the international law of international trade.

The WTO has met with wide acceptance. As of January 2003, the WTO had 145 members. (China and "Chinese Taipei" became members in 2001-2002.) Another 27 states had applied for membership, and accession talks were ongoing in many cases. All the large countries are members, except for Russia, which is involved in accession talks.

Joining the WTO requires a commitment to adhere in the future to all the WTO agreements, except for the four plurilateral ones (see Lowenfeld above). Moreover, an applicant usually will need to make substantial changes in its existing tariffs and other economic regulations (e.g., market access), rather than being allowed to maintain high tariffs and closed markets. For example, the WTO talks with China occupied several years because China resisted undertaking the market-opening steps that the United States, European Union countries, and other WTO members thought were necessary. The final accession agreement reflected a hard-fought compromise.

Present WTO members have been quick to resort to the powerful new WTO dispute system, as noted in Chapter 4.

The WTO has been busy not only implementing the hundreds of pages of new agreements but also breaking new ground. At the initiative of the Asia-Pacific Economic Cooperation (APEC) (discussed later), many of the WTO countries entered into an International Technology Agreement (ITA) in 1997, further reducing or eliminating tariffs on many information technology products. Moreover, the WTO parties negotiated a new Financial Services Agreement.

In a major speech to the WTO in May 1998, President Clinton noted the impact already of the Uruquay Round and the WTO. He pointed out that, because of the tariff cuts and other market-opening measures: "The Uruguay Round that founded the WTO amounted to the biggest tax cut in history — $76 billion a year when fully implemented. Since that event [in 1995], world trade has increased by 25 percent." However, President Clinton cautioned:

> In order to build a trading system for the 21st century that honors our values and expands opportunity, we must do more to ensure that spirited economic competition among nations never becomes a race to the bottom — in environmental protections, consumer protections, or labor standards. We should be leveling up, not leveling down. Without such a strategy, we cannot build the necessary public support for continued expansion of trade. Working people will only assume the risks of a free international market if they have the confidence that the system will work for them.

At the WTO's Fourth Ministerial Conference in Doha, Qatar, in fall 2001, the WTO members agreed on the Doha Declaration that called for new negotiations aimed to make progress on a wide range of matters, ranging from agriculture to intellectual property to services. The declaration sets January 1, 2005, as the date for completing all but two of the negotiations. Those involving the Dispute Settlement Understanding were to end in May 2003 and those regarding a register for geographical indications for wines and spirits were to be completed by the Fifth Ministerial Conference. Overall progress was also to be reviewed at that Ministerial Conference in Cancun, Mexico, in September 2003.

As of January 2003, these negotiations, which some have labeled the Doha Development Round, generally have gotten off to a slow start, even after taking into account that trade negotiations often do not have major breakthroughs until the closing days of the negotiations. Some of the resistance came from developing countries that believed, with some empirical evidence supporting them, that most of the initial benefits of the WTO had accrued to the more developed countries.

Moreover, even with the broad range of issues being considered, the opposition of developing countries and others effectively blocked two contemporary issues from being on the table: (1) the relationship between trade and the environment and (2) the relationship between trade and labor standards.

Notes and Questions

1. Why is a more open, nondiscriminatory trading system (i.e., free trade) beneficial? If it is beneficial, why do countries maintain trade barriers?

2. Do nations need international trading agreements and institutions like the GATT and WTO? Why? Why not enter into bilateral agreements with various countries?

3. Note that there has been a tendency toward free trade areas and customs unions. The European Union is the largest example (although it involves more than just free trade, as discussed later in this chapter). The North American Free Trade Agreement, effective in 1994, is another example. (See Chapter 4.) There are also a number of bilateral free trade agreements in existence, with more being negotiated. As of January 2003, for example, the EU had a free trade agreement with Mexico. Besides NAFTA, the United States also had free trade agreements with Israel and Jordan, and U.S. negotiators had reached bilateral agreements with Chile and Singapore, though Congressional approval was still pending. The U.S. Trade Representative, Robert Zoellick, was talking of other possible bilateral free trade agreements.

Although the GATT articles specifically recognize the possibility of free trade areas and customs unions, do you see how there might be some tension between an international system of open, nondiscriminatory trading and several bilateral or regional free trade arrangements? Should the United States give priority to negotiating further reductions in tariffs and NTBs in the WTO, or should it try to work out special arrangements with individual countries, such as Chile or even Japan?

4. WTO membership is open as follows:

> A government not party to this Agreement, or a government acting on behalf of a separate customs territory possessing full autonomy in the conduct of its external commercial relations and of the other matters provided for in this Agreement, may accede to this Agreement, on its own behalf or on behalf of that territory, on terms to be agreed between such government and the Contracting Parties. Decisions of the Contracting Parties under this paragraph shall be taken by a two-thirds vote. [GATT, Art. XXXIII.]

In 1990 Taiwan applied for GATT membership as the "Separate Customs Territory of Taiwan, Penghu, Kinmen and Matsu." In a carefully negotiated and choreographed process that took into account the strong views of China regarding Taiwan (see discussion earlier in this chapter), China was admitted to membership in the WTO on December 11, 2001, and Taiwan (under the name "Chinese Taipei") become a member on January 1, 2002. Chinese Taipei joined another customs territory, Hong Kong, which has been a longstanding and active member of the GATT and then WTO, even after its transfer to China.

5. Besides the voluminous GATT and WTO documents themselves and the documents cited in Chapter 4 on dispute resolution, basic sources on the GATT and WTO include Robert E. Hudec, The GATT Legal System and World Trade Diplomacy (1975); John H. Jackson, The Jurisprudence of GATT and the WTO (2000); John H. Jackson, World Trade Law and the Law of GATT (1969); and The WTO as an International Organization (Anne O. Krueger ed. 1998). The WTO's excellent Web site is at <http://www.wto.org>.

d. The Group of Eight (and sometimes Seven)

Besides the formal international institutions like the United Nations, World Bank, IMF, and WTO, there are more informal international groupings or coalitions that have a major impact on international life. The two most important are the Group of Eight and the Group of 77 (the latter now actually has over 130 members). Although their exact legal status is hazy, one should be aware of their existence.

The Group of Eight (G-8) refers in a general sense to eight major industrialized countries — Canada, France, Germany, Italy, Japan, Russia, the United Kingdom, and the United States. The heads of state of these eight countries, plus the President of the European Union's Commission, have taken to meeting in annual summits to discuss issues of common concern and to develop cooperative approaches. The emphasis is on economic matters, although the international environment emerged as a new major issue at the July 1989 summit in Paris.

Starting in 1991, the then-Group of Seven began to edge toward becoming the Group of Eight, at least for summits, as the leader of Russia was invited to some parts of the summit meetings, despite the weak Russian economy. During the 1994 summit in Naples, for example, Russia participated in several political discussions on international issues, including the conflicts in the former Yugoslavia and Rwanda. At the 1998 summit in Birmingham, England, the seven major industrialized nations and Russia formally became the Group of Eight. Finally, at the 2002 summit in Kananaskis, Canada, the G-8 announced that Russia would host the summit for the first time in 2006, marking its equal membership in the group.

However, the G-7 still exists as well because the seven members are still free to meet without Russia to consider certain issues such as international finance. For example, the deputy finance officials from G-7 countries met without Russia in June 1998 to discuss the Asian financial crisis.

At least as important as the discussions, as well as the pomp and circumstance at the G-8 summits, are the arrangements that the G-7 has developed for the coordination of economic policies. Key to this coordination are discussions and formal meetings among the finance ministers and central bank governors of the G-7 countries.[2] This intergovernmental coalition often meets to work out positions ahead of IMF meetings or whenever the leaders believe that developments require a meeting.

The nations work to achieve consistent and mutually compatible economic policies and accept considerable multilateral surveillance of their economies. Coordination has helped to change the pattern of exchange rates and to change interest rates. The negotiations have also helped reduce international trade barriers. At their 1993 summit, the nations worked together to iron out several difficult GATT issues, thereby helping to make a successful Uruguay Round conclusion possible. The nations hope this coordination will maintain and stimulate the economic stability and growth in their countries and the rest of the world.

Although these nations are aware of the advantages of intergovernmental economic cooperation, competing domestic demands pose formidable obstacles to the success of this approach. For example, when lower interest rates in the United States might be viewed by the other members as conducive to a better exchange rate between the U.S. dollar and other currencies, the U.S. government might hesitate to move in this direction because of fears of increasing domestic inflation, with the resulting political repercussions.

Because of these competing considerations, the record of the group is mixed. Its greatest success probably came in 1986-1987 when the group reached major agreements affecting interest rates and the exchange rate (bringing the U.S. dollar substantially down in value).

The financial muscle of the G-8 and its approach of making policy privately and often in advance of larger international meetings have generated criticism from other nations. They argue that their influence is diminished and that the broader consultations envisioned in the IMF are being undercut by the secret negotiations of a few beforehand.

e.   The Group of 77

The Group of 77 is a coalition of about 133 countries now that have bound together to coordinate their efforts and to protect the interests of the developing African, Asian, and Latin American countries. The organization was the first major effort at Third World unity in the economic area.

> [O]ur coming together in the Group of 77 has the purpose of enabling us to deal on terms of greater equality with an existing Centre of Power. Ours is basically a unity of opposition. And it is a unity of nationalism. . . .
>
> The Group of 77 does not share an ideology. . . . We are not necessarily friendly with each other. . . .
>
> What we have in common is that we are all, in relation to the developed world, dependent, not interdependent, nations. . . . We are not the prime movers of our own destiny.

---

2. The G-7 meetings of finance ministers and central bank governors replaced the so-called Group of Five meetings in late 1987. Originally Italy and Canada were not in the coalition and objected, stating that their economic strength justified their participation. (See the table at the start of this chapter.)

The unity of the entire Third World is necessary for the achievement of fundamental change in the present world economic arrangements. . . .

For the object is to complete the liberation of the Third World countries from
external domination. That is the basic meaning of the New International Economic
Order. And unity is our instrument — our only instrument — of liberation. [Mwalimu
Julius K. Nyerere, former President of Tanzania, in a 1979 speech, quoted in Karl P.
Sauvant, The Group of 77: Evolution, Structure, Organization 132-135 (1981).]

The "Caucus of 75" signaled the birth of the Group of 77 when it convened in
Geneva in 1964 to prepare for the first United Nations Conference on Trade and
Development (UNCTAD I). Following UNCTAD I, the caucus evaluated the work of
the conference in a Joint Declaration of 77 Developing Countries. The Group has
since continued to function as a caucus for the developing countries on both economic and political concerns before various U.N. bodies.

The group has expanded to include about 133 members. Although most of the
countries are poor, there are a few members, such as the United Arab Emirates and
Qatar, whose per capita incomes probably exceed that of the United States.

The grievances of the Group of 77 are varied. The group, however, has developed some objectives and policies that enjoy broad consensus among its members.
Many of these appear in the program for change that has been labeled the New
International Economic Order (NIEO). The NIEO, which has been enunciated in
various statements by the Group of 77 and in some U.N. documents, includes calls for
a country's right to expropriate property subject only to its own domestic law; less protection for patents, copyrights, and other intellectual property; greater protection for
the prices of raw materials through commodity agreements and buffer stocks; and
special tariff treatment by the developed countries for the products of developing
countries. Many of these policies reflect the fact that the developed countries possess
most of the world's capital, including the intellectual property, and are heavily industrialized. The developing countries often are dependent on the export of raw or partially finished materials, and they want to reduce that dependence. The NIEO also envisions procedural changes, including reform of the voting procedures in the IMF,
World Bank, and other world economic institutions so that the developing nations
have greater representation.

The Group of 77 achieved some success, notably in the 1960s and 1970s, in
making their views known and effecting some changes. Part of the strength of the
coalition lay in the ability of its members to work out their differences and develop
a consensus within the Group. With few exceptions, the Group would vote as a bloc
in the meetings and conferences of international institutions, thus giving the Group
of 77 a clear majority on most votes, unless the voting was weighted (as it is in the
IMF and World Bank, discussed earlier).

The Group of 77 often found institutional staff support for its ideas in a
U.N. agency called the United Nations Conference on Trade and Development
(UNCTAD). In many ways, UNCTAD became a counter-balance to the Organization
for Economic Cooperation and Development (OECD), the Paris-based organization that includes most of the industrialized nations and works to develop a consensus among its members on issues of common concern.

Recently, the focus of the Group of 77 has shifted somewhat. Although still pursuing a relationship with the developed countries to help their economic growth,

G-77 leaders have also called for greater "South-South" cooperation. The economic problems of the early 1990s created an atmosphere that made it difficult for the G-77 nations to stand united against developed nations. As a result, the Group struggled in its attempts to pressure the North, as many G-77 nations opted for bi-lateral negotiations with the industrialized states.

However, at a conference in 1997, the G-77 updated its 1981 Caracas Action Program, which was designed to help the developing nations coordinate their ef-forts in eight key areas: energy, finance, food and agriculture, industrialization, raw materials, technical cooperation, trade, and technology. Moreover, at the 1997 U.N. Framework Convention on Climate Change in Kyoto, the G-77 (led by the Organi-zation of Petroleum Exporting Countries) actively participated in the treaty negoti-ations to prevent mandatory controls on carbon dioxide emissions. Since 1997, the G-77 has continued to help represent developing countries in U.N. conferences on financing for development, food security, sustainable development, and on many other issues of interest to these countries. The G-77 has a Web site at <http://www.G77.org>.

3. *Regional Institutions*

A wide variety of regional entities exist, with different purposes and in varying stages of institutional development. This section first looks to Europe, where it discusses the European Union and its impressive progress, and also briefly considers the North Atlantic Treaty Organization (NATO) and the Organization on Security and Cooperation in Europe (OSCE). The section then addresses two regional economic entities that continue to develop, the Association of Southeast Asian Nations (ASEAN) and the Asia-Pacific Economic Cooperation (APEC). Lastly, two of the more traditional regional political organizations—the Organization of American States (OAS) and the Organization of African Unity (OAU)—are briefly described. Although not discussed, it should be noted that there are regional development banks for Latin America, Africa, Asia, and recently Eastern Europe, that are mod-eled on the World Bank, although their assets are substantially less. The member-ship of these banks typically includes many of the industrialized countries in addi-tion to the countries in the bank's region. There are also emerging free trade areas and common markets such as Mercosur in South America.

a. **The European Union**

Emerging from the rubble and memories of World War II, the European Union today is a vibrant, vital entity on the international scene. It not only maintains com-mon external trade policies, but succeeded by 1993 in implementing an internal market among its Member States. Four fundamental freedoms within the Union are generally recognized: (1) the free movement of goods, (2) the free movement of capital, (3) freedom of movement of persons, and (4) the right of establishment and to provide services.

Also, in November 1993, the Treaty on European Union, or Maastricht Treaty, went into force. As noted in Chapter 4, the Maastricht Treaty added two so-called pillars to the first pillar of then European Community's largely economic activities, and it adopted the all-encompassing term of "European Union" for the three pillars. The new pillars dealt with Common Foreign and Security Policy (including defense) and Justice and Home Affairs (including cooperation on crime, terrorism, and immigration issues).

The Treaty of Amsterdam, which was signed in 1997 and came into force in 1999, laid the groundwork for enlarging the Union membership and reconfirmed January 1, 1999, as the launch date for the single European currency. Then the Treaty of Nice, which was signed in 2001 and came into force in early 2003, resolved a number of outstanding issues left unresolved in Amsterdam, especially the issues of voting practices and the representation of the existing and new member states after the Union's expansion. It also laid the groundwork for further expansion of the Union's role by adopting a Convention on Fundamental Rights. As a result, since Maastricht, the Union has expanded its scope to include monetary union (the euro), cooperation on human rights, cultural cooperation, the environment, space exploration, a common foreign and security policy (CFSP), and even a military "rapid reaction force" for use in humanitarian and peacekeeping operations and crisis management. As a result, the Union today is a comprehensive, multifaceted institution, far more than merely an economic entity. All these treaties have been consolidated into the Treaty on European Union (EU Treaty) and Treaty Establishing the European Community (EC Treaty). (Excerpts of the consolidated versions of the treaties are contained in the Documentary Supplement. Note that the articles have been renumbered as a result of the Amsterdam Treaty amendments.)

As of 2003, the European Union included 15 Member States: Austria, Belgium, Denmark, the Federal Republic of Germany, Finland, France, Greece, Ireland, Italy, Luxembourg, Netherlands, Portugal, Spain, Sweden, and the United Kingdom. As an economic force, it rivals the United States. Considered as a unified economic entity, the EU's population is about 379 million, or about 105 million more than the United States and 253 million more than Japan. While the U.S. gross domestic product is about 130 percent greater than the Union's, Japan's is only about 60 percent as large. Moreover, estimates indicate that the Union's external trade (i.e., other than between Member States) accounts for approximately 19 percent of all world trade (compared to the similar U.S. figure of 21 percent). In addition, Europe has a greater share of world exports (18 percent) than the United States (16 percent). Adding Canada's and Mexico's statistics to the U.S. figures — that is, NAFTA — has the three NAFTA countries exceeding the EU in all categories, though that situation will change when the EU expands its membership in 2004 to include such countries as Poland. (For additional data, see Table 5-1 at the beginning of this chapter.)

Besides the EU member states, since January 1994 the EU has been a party to the European Economic Area (EEA) Agreement, which also includes Norway, Iceland, and Lichtenstein in the four freedoms of the European Union — that is, movement of goods, capital, and persons, and the right of establishment.

In addition to assuming additional functions and responsibilities, the European Union continues to expand its geographic scope. In December 2002, the EU concluded accession negotiations with Cyprus, the Czech Republic, Estonia, Hungary, Latvia, Lithuania, Malta, Poland, Slovakia, and Slovenia. This means that these ten states are expected to become EU members in time for the EU's parliamentary elections in 2004. Hence, the EU is expected to have 25 member states by 2004.

Moreover, Romania and Bulgaria are also in line for EU membership, perhaps by 2007, and the European Union has expressed some interest in admitting Turkey as well in the future.

The following materials examine the structure of the Union and its function within the international system.

(1)   History and Background

Although the dream of a unified Europe had existed for centuries, the events of World War II created new reasons for steps toward a Community.

> If we cast our minds back to the early post-war days we will realise that a Commu-
> nity approach was the practical answer to many problems. Europe was in ruins politi-
> cally and economically; the European colonial empires faced liquidation; the impor-
> tance of the single European states which dominated the League of Nations was
> diminished; the "dollar-gap" resulted in great influence of the USA not only as a be-
> nevolent saviour but also as a potential master; an "iron curtain" was drawn across Eu-
> rope and the world cowered in the shadows of great powers: the USA and Soviet Russia
> facing each other menacingly across Europe. Only rapid recovery in concert could re-
> store Europe's self-respect. . . . As for grand designs, the architects of the Community
> soon realised that great ideologies and elaborate blueprints were of little practical use
> and that nothing could be achieved at one stroke. [K.P.E. Lasok & D. Lasok, Law and
> Institutions of the European Union 5 (7th ed. 2001).]

Definitely in the minds of the European architects of the Community was the perception that the new Federal Republic of Germany had to be entwined in economic
and political arrangements with the rest of Western Europe. The goal was to make
war among these nations impossible and unthinkable. The other countries did not
want a repeat of World Wars I and II.

Although collectively referred to as the "European Community" from 1978 until 1993, there were three European Communities within the pre-Maastricht structure: the European Coal and Steel Community (ECSC), the European Economic
Community (EEC), and the European Atomic Energy Community (Euratom).

Trevor Hartley, The Foundations of European Community Law

3-4 (4th ed. 1998)

The ECSC is the oldest. The ECSC Treaty was signed on 18 April 1951 and entered into
force on 25 July 1952. The signatories were the six original Member States: Germany,
Belgium, France, Italy, Luxembourg, and the Netherlands. The United Kingdom was
invited to take part, but declined to do so. . . . Four principal institutions were created;
the Council (representing the Member States), the Commission (a supranational
executive, which was originally called the "High Authority"), the Assembly, and the
Court. . . .

The EC Treaty, then known as the EEC Treaty, and the Euratom Treaty were
both signed in Rome on 25 March 1957 and entered into force on 1 January 1958.
The United Kingdom was again invited to participate but dropped out of

the preliminary discussions. The signatories were therefore the same six States. . . . Separate Commissions and Councils were created for each of the new Communities but all three shared the same Assembly and Court. . . .

It was . . . illogical and inconvenient for the two most important Community institutions to be triplicated; so a Merger Treaty (officially known as the Treaty Establishing a Single Council and a Single Commission of the European Communities) was signed in Brussels on 8 April 1965 and entered into force on 1 July 1967. This Treaty did not merge the Communities themselves but merged the three Commissions to form a single Commission and merged the three Councils to form a single Council.*

---

(2) The Single European Act and 1992

Progress in the three Communities bogged down in the late 1970s and early 1980s. To break down the roadblocks and enhance European integration and cooperation, the Commission submitted in 1985 its "White Paper on Completing the Internal Market by 1992." It called for the removal of all internal barriers to an integrated common market by December 31, 1992. The European Parliament also encouraged the Member States to sit around the negotiating table.

The solution was the Single European Act (SEA), which was signed in February 1986 and came into force July 1, 1987, after ratification by all the Member States. It amended the three original treaties. Some of the Act's more notable amendments provided for changes in the decision-making processes of the Community and brought areas such as the environment within the scope of the previous treaties. The amendments also provided for the establishment of a court of first instance for the Court of Justice (discussed in Chapter 4) and furnished a legal basis for foreign policy cooperation by the members. Additionally, the amendments formally adopted the name "European Parliament" for the originally named Assembly, a switch that the Assembly had made by itself in 1962.

(3) The Treaty on European Union (Maastricht Treaty)

When the Member States signed the Treaty on European Union at Maastricht in December 1991, they took a major step toward greater economic and political integration. The Maastricht Treaty changed the framework of the existing treaties in five significant ways. First, it set a goal of 1999 for the implementation of a common European currency. Second, it established EU citizenship, in theory giving a Union citizen the right to live anywhere within the Union and to vote in local and European elections.

Third, the Maastricht Treaty gave the Commission greater authority to regulate, among other areas, education, the environment, and health and consumer protections. Fourth, the powers of the EU's democratically elected body, the European Parliament, were expanded to give it a greater voice in the appointments process and proposals for new EU directives. Fifth, the Treaty added two new pillars to the Communities, which now comprise the first pillar of the European Union. These new pillars are provisions for a Common Foreign and Security Policy (including defense)

*The ECSC treaty expired under its terms on July 23, 2002. Under the Treaty of Nice, its subjects — specifically the coal and steel sectors — are now included within the EC regime.— EDS.

(CFSP), as well as cooperation between Member States on several volatile issues such as immigration and terrorism through the Justice and Home Affairs institution.

There were, and continue to be, many stumbling blocks to a true union of Europe. In June 1992, Danish voters narrowly rejected the Maastricht Treaty in a national referendum. A watered-down version that did not require Denmark to accept a single currency, joint defense or justice and immigration policy, or EU citizenship was eventually ratified in May 1993. Britain eliminated the commitment to a single currency and the charter on labor rights in its own version of the Treaty. The Maastricht Treaty was ratified in all the Member States and went into force in November 1993 (subject to the limitations in Denmark and Britain).

(4) *The Treaty of Amsterdam*

In 1997, the leaders of Member States met in Amsterdam with the goal of setting a target date for a unified currency and making institutional reforms to allow for the inclusion of new members. The resulting Treaty of Amsterdam scheduled the euro, the single European currency, for initial accounting use in 1999 and began the negotiation process with the ten Eastern European nations applying for the EU membership. However, conflicting interests of the Member States and their reluctance to forego national sovereignty stalled deeper political integration, including some institutional reforms necessary for the expansion of the EU membership. Resolution of these further reforms was put off, in the hope that they could be resolved at a later intergovernmental conference (IGC).

After the Amsterdam Treaty survived a ratification referendum in Denmark in 1998, where the opposition to the Treaty was the strongest, it was ratified by all the Member States and came into force on 1999.

The Nice IGC in 2000 resolved many of the so-called Amsterdam leftovers, changes on which the members had been unable to agree at Amsterdam but that had to be made before new members could be admitted. These included renegotiating the makeup of Union institutions and modifying voting procedures to take into account the larger number of Member States, and increasing the power of the European Parliament and Commission President vis-à-vis the Council. In addition, the Treaty called for a conference on the future of the Union, discussed below, to propose further changes for the next IGC. After an initial "no" vote in 2001, Ireland — the only member to put the treaty to a referendum — approved the treaty in 2002, paving the way for the Nice Treaty to go into effect in early 2003.

(5) *Political Structure*

The "Constitution" of the European Union. The three original treaties that established the Communities, plus the Merger Treaty, the Single European Act, the Maastricht Treaty, the Amsterdam Treaty, the Nice Treaty, and various protocols and annexes attached to these documents are not only the primary source of Union law, but they represent the Union's "constitution." This concept stems in part from the *van Gend en Loos case* (excerpted in Chapter 4), in which the European Court of Justice construed the "EEC Treaty not as an international agreement but as a constitutional instrument, and as treating the enforceability of the EEC Treaty by private individuals as if it were a question of domestic constitutional law in a federal system." (Jacques Bourgeois, Effects of International Agreement in European Community Law: Are the Dice Cast?, 82 Mich. L. Rev. 1250, 1251 (1984).) Delineating the Union's political system, these documents outline the relationship of the Union institutions to one another and to the Union as a whole, and establish rules that render Union juridical decisions binding on Member States.

Institutions of the European Union. Besides the Court of Justice (discussed in Chapter 4), three institutions make and administer Community law. These are the Commission, the Council, and the European Parliament. In addition, the European Council (distinct from the Council) meets several times a year at the head-of-state level to resolve issues on a government-to-government basis that the institutions lack either the authority or the political will to resolve.

George A. Bermann, Roger J. Goebel, William J. Davey & Eleanor M. Fox, Cases and Materials on European Union Law

42-46, 32-39 (2d ed. 2002)

THE COMMISSION

The European Commission bears a striking but imperfect resemblance to a Government in the usual European sense of the term. Often referred to as the Community's executive organ, the Commission in fact performs tasks commonly identified with the executive: formulating a general legislative program, initiating the legislative process by drafting specific pieces of legislation, exercising the powers delegated to it by the Council, making the decisions and carrying out the administrative tasks assigned to it, and overseeing (and if need be enforcing) compliance with the law. . . .

Despite its close affinity to a modern Government in the European sense, the Commission has certain structural features that set it apart. The term and mode of appointment of the Commission has changed over time. Under the amended EC Treaty Article 214 (ex 158), the Commission is appointed for a five-year renewable term. The Member State governments nominate by common accord a Commission President, whose appointment is subject to Parliamentary assent. In concert with the nominee, the Member States then nominate the other members of the Commission. (As amended at Nice, the Treaty [gives] the Council, acting by qualified majority, the power to nominate both the Commission President and the body of Commissioners. . . . The Commission's total membership is fixed at present by Article 213 (ex 157) of the EC Treaty at 20, with the understanding that each smaller State may nominate one member apiece, while the five larger States nominate two. (As indicated below, the Nice Treaty [brings] a change.)

Before assuming office, the Commission must, as a body, receive a "vote of approval" by the Parliament. In January 1995, the Parliament made conspicuous use of this then-new power, by expressing reservations about certain individual Commission nominees before approving the Commission as a whole. . . .

The President's authority within the Commission has been progressively strengthened. As noted, he or she participates in the designation of the other Commissioners. Under the EC Treaty, as amended by the Treaty of Nice, the President appoints from among the Commissioners, with the Commission's collective approval, an unstated number of Vice-Presidents. By virtue of the same amendment, the President is given the power to allocate and reallocate portfolios among the Commission's members, to dismiss a Commissioner (with the Commission's collective approval), to determine the Commission's internal organization, and more generally to give the Commission its "political guidance."[14] . . . As of January 2003, the Commission President is Romano Prodi.

As its functions suggest, the Commission may be considered the Community's primary engine of integration. Although its members are effectively selected by nationality, the Commission is expected to act so as to promote the Community's interests and development rather than those of any of its Member States. The Commission's record of performance largely bears out this expectation. The independence of the Commission from the Member States is forcefully guaranteed: Commissioners are required to be "completely independent in the performance of their duties," to "neither seek nor take instructions from any Government or from any other body" and to "refrain from any action incompatible with their duties." The Commission acts by a simple majority of its members and its deliberations are secret. . . .

. . . Parliament is entitled to ask questions of the Commission, to receive from it an annual report on Community activities, and to censure the Commission as a body and thus force its resignation. . . .

With prospects of further EU enlargement, the growing size of the Commission has also become a serious preoccupation. The Amsterdam IGC failed to resolve the "numbers" issue. Only at Nice in December 2000 did the Member States agree on changes in the composition of the Commission, to be reflected in EC Treaty Article 213 (ex 157) as of January 1, 2005. From that date, every State — large and small — would name only a single Commissioner. Then, at the point when the EU has 27 Member States, the number of Commissioners would be set by the Council, acting unanimously, at a number less than the number of States. From then, Commissioners would be chosen according to a rotation system likewise to be decided upon by the Council acting unanimously. While based on the principle of equality[17] the rotation system would also be required "to reflect satisfactorily the demographic and geographical range" of Member States. . . .

In terms of functions, the Commission is in part a legislative and in part a regulatory body. In a few areas, the EC Treaty gives the Commission certain powers of "primary" or "original" legislative authority. . . . More generally, though, the Commission enjoys the very significant monopoly on the proposal of legislation to the Council, which means that it essentially sets the Community's legislative agenda and initially drafts its legal texts.

In addition to exercising original legislative authority under the EC Treaty, the Commission has been delegated extensive rulemaking powers by the Council. Agriculture is a sector in which such delegation occurs with particular regularity. . . .

The Commission's other institutional tasks include drafting the initial annual budget for review and adoption by the Council and Parliament, and administering

14. Article 217, as amended at Nice, further requires the Commissioners to "carry out the duties devolved upon them by the President under his authority."

17. Protocol on the Enlargement of the European Union, agreed upon at Nice in December 2000, art. 4. The Protocol, in art. 4(3)(a), specifies by way of equality that the difference between the total number of terms of office held by any pair of Member States may never be more than one.

the Community's finances. . . . The Commission also brings enforcement actions against Member States under Article 226 (ex 169) for their violations of Community law, such as maintaining barriers to trade or failing to adopt the legislation or regulations that Community directives require. Enforcement actions against Member States . . . constitute a significant part of the Commission's business. . . .

Certainly not to be overlooked are the myriad specific administrative decisions (typified by rulings on competition law violations or violation of the prohibition on state aids) that the Commission, as the Community's chief executive arm, is called upon to make on a daily basis. . . . Another prime area of Commission activity is, of course, external relations and trade. Under Article 300 (ex 228), the Commission, upon authorization by the Council, opens and conducts negotiations over international agreements for eventual conclusion by the Council. The Commission also represents the Community in the WTO and other international organizations and enforces the Community's protective trade legislation. . . .

To help discharge its far-ranging responsibilities, the Commission has, as of the year 2000, a permanent staff of over 16,400, divided into 24 large sections known as Directorates General (or "DGs"), as well as a number of other services and offices. As recently re-titled, the DGs are named by subject (e.g. competition, agriculture, internal market, enlargement) rather than number I, II, etc. Each DG is further subdivided into subdirectorates and the latter into divisions along policy lines. Most Community activities fall within the portfolio of one of the Directorates General, whether the matter is agriculture, external relations, the internal market, competition, or budget and finance. Each DG is headed by a Director General who in turn reports to one of the Commissioners. Since each Commissioner supervises one or two DGs, he or she has authority over a broad field of action. . . .

The Commission Legal Service, consisting of some 125 lawyers, reviews the texts of all draft legislation and decisions, renders legal advice, and represents the Commission in litigation before the Court of Justice. Translation of documents and interpretation at meetings alone require a Commission staff of over 1900 in the Translation Service. All measures (including drafts), as well as major reports and studies, must be translated into all eleven official Community languages, and all official meetings require simultaneous translation. These are daunting tasks for the Commission no less than for the other institutions, and they have noticeably slowed the legislative and decisionmaking processes.

THE COUNCIL . . .

Within the framework of the European Community, the Council functions as a kind of collective head of state of the European Community, deciding external trade policies and concluding international agreements. The Council also exercises primary legislative power within the Community, although it now shares that power with the European Parliament through the introduction into the EC Treaty of legislative procedures requiring the participation of both bodies. . . . Viewed structurally, the Council consists of representatives of the governments of the Member States, voting in the name of their State and (to the extent qualified majority voting obtains) with a voting strength crudely weighted according to the State's relative population size. The Council thus resembles in some degree a head of state in status, a legislature in function and an assembly of constituent states in structure. . . .

The Presidency of the Council is held for a six-month term, typically rotating among the Member States in a substantially modified alphabetical order. Article 203 empowers the Council to decide upon the order by unanimous decision. Recently, the order has been drawn up to ensure that a large state — France, Germany, Italy, Spain or the UK — holds the Presidency at least once in every third six-month period. . . .

The Council meets when convened by its President, whether on the latter's own initiative or at the request of a Member State or the Commission. It meets frequently, over 80 times a year on the average, usually in Brussels. In recent years, the Presidency has assumed increased importance as each Member State in succession uses its term to advance certain agenda items. In the interest of continuity, a "troika" staff has been established, consisting in part of representatives of the immediate past and future Presidents.

As a legislator, the Council operates under special constraints. In the first place, the Commission has exclusive authority to initiate legislation. Thus, a Commission proposal is required before the Council may consider and adopt virtually any legislative measure. . . . Further, the Single European Act and the Maastricht, Amsterdam and (prospectively) Nice Treaties have brought the European Parliament into the legislative process in decisive ways. . . . Finally . . . the Council does not enjoy plenary legislative power, the scope of its legislative authority being specified in various articles of the EC Treaty.

In international affairs, the Council plays a leading role. As amended, Article 300 (ex 228) authorizes the Council to approve most international agreements between the Community and other states or international organizations. . . .

The EC Treaty specifies the manner of Council voting. On certain matters, such as the procedure for accession of new states or the harmonization of tax legislation, unanimity is still required. In rare non-legislative instances (notably in adopting internal rules of procedure), a simple majority vote suffices. Today, by far the most widespread manner of voting is by qualified majority. Qualified majority voting (QMV) originally applied in a relatively small number of sectors, such as agriculture, transport, competition law and commercial policy. However, every major Treaty amendment starting with the Single European Act (in the area of harmonizing national laws in aid of the internal market) has expanded the scope of application of QMV to the point that it is now the decidedly preponderant voting formula in the Council.

Qualified majority voting is outlined in Article 205 (ex 148) as follows:

1. Save as otherwise provided in this Treaty, the Council shall act by a majority of its members.

2. Where the Council is required to act by a qualified majority, the votes of its members shall be weighted as follows:

Belgium	5
Denmark	3
Germany	10
Greece	5
Spain	8
France	10

                    Ireland 3
                    Italy 10
                    Luxembourg 2
                    Netherlands 5
                    Austria 4
                    Portugal 5
                    Finland 3
                    Sweden 4
                    United Kingdom 10

For their adoption, acts of the Council shall require at least:
—62 votes in favour where this Treaty requires them to be adopted on a proposal
   from the Commission,
—62 votes in favour, cast by at least 10 members, in other cases.

Under qualified majority voting all of a Member State's votes must be cast as a bloc. Since the total number of votes in the Council under qualified majority voting is now 87, the "blocking minority" is set at 26. The formula is designed in part to secure the interests of the larger states. Simple calculation shows that the opposition of three large states will defeat a proposal in a qualified majority vote, but that the opposition of the five smallest ones will not. On the other hand, the support of the five largest states is not sufficient for the passage of legislation; at least three of the smaller states must also support it. Significantly, each time the Community's membership has grown, the numbers in the qualified majority formula have been changed to produce a similar sort of equilibrium. What are the logical premises of the qualified majority voting system? Are they sound? How does the system compare with state representation rules in the US Congress?

Among the Member States' main objectives at the Nice Intergovernmental Conference was to decide upon the future re-weighting of votes in the Council in anticipation of expanded EU membership. The Treaty of Nice provides that, as of January 1, 2005, the weighting of votes among the current Member States should be as follows:

                    Belgium 12
                    Denmark .7
                    Germany 29
                    Greece 12
                    Spain 27
                    France 29
                    Ireland 7
                    Italy 29
                    Luxembourg 4
                    Netherlands 13
                    Austria 10
                    Portugal 12
                    Finland 7
                    Sweden 10
                    United Kingdom 29

Of this total of 237 votes, at least 170 would be required for the passage of legislation by qualified majority. In addition, where the EC Treaty requires measures to be adopted upon proposal by the Commission, a majority of Member States would have to have cast their votes in favor of the measure. (In the case of all other measures, the fraction rises to ⅔ of the Member States.) Finally, any State could demand verification that the total population among the States supporting the measure constitutes 62% of the total EU population; if verification is demanded and cannot be shown, the measure could not be enacted. In short, adoption would require a *triple* majority: a qualified majority of total Member State votes, a majority (or in some cases a qualified majority) of Member States, and a qualified majority of the EU population.

By increasing the vote allocation of each current Member State, the IGC cleared the way for assigning smaller vote allocations to new Member States having small populations. A Declaration on Enlargement, while keeping vote numbers for the current Member States at the levels prescribed for January 1, 2005, assigns Council votes to the applicant States as follows:

Poland	27
Romania	14
Czech Republic	12
Hungary	12
Bulgaria	10
Slovakia	7
Lithuania	7
Latvia	4
Slovenia	4
Estonia	4
Cyprus	4
Malta	3

Upon the accession of all twelve, the combined total of Council votes would be 345. Passage of legislation by qualified majority would require at least 258 votes. . . .

. . . The Council's highest staff level is known as COREPER, an acronym for the French term for "Committee of Permanent Representatives." As its name suggests, COREPER, whose existence is recognized in EC Treaty Article 207 (ex 151), consists of permanent representatives of the Member States. These representatives conduct a preliminary review of all legislative measures before they go to the Council. COREPER in turn is assisted by both standing and ad hoc working groups of a technical and/or policy character. The advice of these national officials, as well as of ministry staff in the home capitals, informs the permanent representatives and, through them, the ministers who on any given occasion constitute the Council. In many instances, COREPER is able to work out an agreement and forward a proposal for routine approval by the Council; in other cases, COREPER isolates the major unsettled issues and sends them to the Council for their specific resolution if possible. Through their expertise, COREPER and the Council staff enable the Council to scrutinize the technical and policy proposals of the Commission, and their input understandably strengthens the Council in its dealings with the Commission. . . .

The European Parliament. The European Parliament, as noted by Article 189 (ex Art. 137) of the EC Treaty, is intended to consist of "representatives of the peoples of the States brought together in the Community." Since 1979, members of the European Parliament have been elected directly by the Community population. The Amsterdam Treaty limited the number of European Parliament members to 700, and the Nice Treaty expands this to 732 (which will be reached when all 12 candidates have joined the Union), reducing the representation for the present Member States as necessary.

> MEPs [Members of the European Parliament], elected for five-year terms, are supposed to represent the European people rather than a Member State government as such. Consistent with this view, they are elected on the basis of political party affiliation, and sit together in Parliament according to that affiliation rather than nationality. Recognized groups span the political spectrum. . . . The largest bloc in the Parliament elected in 1999 is (for the first time) the European People's Party (or EPP), largely Christian Democrats, numbering 233. The next largest group is the Socialists, occupying 180 seats, followed at some distance by the Liberals with 51. Some MEPs are unaffiliated. The MEPs elect their own President and twelve vice-presidents for 2½ year terms. . . . These officers comprise the Bureau, responsible for the organization of parliamentary business, including the appointment of committee chairs and members.
>
> In addition to holding an annual session, the European Parliament meets at the request of a majority of its members or at the request of the Council or Commission. Unless otherwise provided, it votes by an absolute majority of votes cast.
>
> The European Parliament has multiple seats. . . . Parliament holds its plenary sessions in Strasbourg and its committee meetings in Brussels, while its Secretariat is based in Luxembourg. [Bermann et al., supra, at 53.]

Originally, many of the functions of the Parliament were merely advisory and served as means of gathering information or expressing public opinion. However, the Parliament's role is steadily increasing. One significant increase in the European Parliament's power is its co-decision power, discussed below, with the Council in a number of important areas. The Maastricht and the Amsterdam Treaties also gave Parliament power in the appointment of the Commission, and it has the final say on most of the non-agricultural spending in the EU budget. It also has the power to dismiss the entire Commission by a two-thirds vote, and monitors the Commission's day-to-day activities. Parliamentary approval is also required for the accession of new Member States and for the EU to enter into international agreements. One characteristic feature of the European Parliament is its large number of committees, which prepare reports on issues that come before the Parliament for debate. Under the Amsterdam Treaty, the new responsibilities of the Parliament include drafting a proposal for a uniform electoral procedure for all Member States and recommending regulations governing the performance of the duties of the Parliament members (which will need unanimous approval vote from the Council).

The European Council. As Professor Bermann and his co-authors describe further:

> . . . [T]he heads of state or government of the Member States began as early as the 1960s the custom of holding summit meetings to discuss Community policy issues. This

body, supplemented by the President of the Commission, has come to be known as the European Council. Since 1974, European Council meetings have been held regularly — at least twice or three times a year. . . .

The European Council is not properly speaking an "institution." [The Treaty of the European Union (TEU)] Article 4 (ex D) merely identifies it as "bring[ing] together the Heads of State or Government of the Member States and the President of the Commission," and it does not figure among the institutions authorized by TEU Article 5 (ex E) to exercise powers under the TEU. While it sets policies and guidelines — notably under the EC Treaty provisions on EMU and under pillars two and three — the European Council does not take legally binding decisions; such legally binding decisions as are taken will be taken by the Council. The European Council is nevertheless politically vital.

Among the European Council's most prominent functions has been coordinating Member State foreign policy. . . . The Single European Act gave this activity a firm — if intergovernmental — treaty foundation, and the Treaties of Maastricht, Amsterdam and Nice expanded and strengthened it. (For example, the European Council may now unanimously establish guidelines which enable the Council of Ministers itself to take foreign policy decisions on a qualified majority basis.) . . .

Over the years, the European Council has resolved difficult political issues that the Council lacked authority under the Treaties or lacked the political ability to resolve. The European Council, for example, has set long-term policy guidelines for the Community, agreed on the accession of new Member States, endorsed institutional reforms, embraced the idea of an Economic and Monetary Union (EMU), supported German reunification within the Community, set the criteria for accession of central and eastern European states, scheduled successive intergovernmental conferences in contemplation of treaty amendments, and commissioned and eventually endorsed the EU's Charter of Fundamental Rights. Of course the European Council has also provided a convenient forum for discussing non-Community matters of interest to the Member States.

. . . TEU Article 4 (ex D) calls on the European Council to "provide the Union with the necessary impetus for its development and [to] define the general political guidelines thereof." It requires the European Council to meet at least twice a year (with, as chair, the head of state or government of the Member State then holding the Presidency of the Council) and to submit to Parliament annual progress reports on the Union and reports after each of its meetings. . . . [Id. at 40-42.]

EU agencies. In addition to these principal institutions, a few specialized agencies also are involved in the decision-making process. For example, the Economic and Social Committee is an EU agency that is consulted by the Commission and the Council in various categories of economic and social activity. The Court of Auditors supervises EU legislation and has extensive powers to examine the legality of EU expenditures. The Committee of the Regions must be consulted before the adoption of decisions affecting regional interests.

Juridical acts of the Union's political institutions. The constitutive treaties list several types of juridical acts that Union institutions may utilize in carrying out the tasks conferred on them. These juridical acts, which Professor Hartley details below, fall under the category of "secondary legislation."

Trevor Hartley, The Foundations of European Community Law
99-101 (4th ed. 1998)

Article [249 (ex Art. 189)] lists five different kinds of act that may (if other provisions confer the power) be adopted by the European Parliament and the Council acting jointly, by the Council, or by the Commission. These are:

1. Regulations;
2. Directives;
3. Decisions;
4. Recommendations;
5. Opinions.

Article [249 (ex Art. 189)] also contains a short statement of the characteristics each kind of act is supposed to have. Thus a regulation is essentially legislative (normative): it lays down general rules which are binding both at the [Community] level and at the national level. Directives and decisions differ from regulations, in that they are not binding generally: they are binding only on the person (or persons) to whom they are addressed. Directives may be addressed only to Member States but decisions may also be addressed to private citizens. According to Article [249 (ex Art. 189], another characteristic of directives is that they are binding only "as to the result to be achieved" and leave to the national authorities "the choice of form and methods." This suggests that directives lay down an objective and allow each national government to achieve it by the means it regards as most suitable. A decision, on the other hand, is binding in its entirety. Recommendations and opinions are not binding at all. [The former suggest that the addressee take a specific course of action; the latter lay the groundwork for subsequent legal proceedings.] . . .

These provisions appear to form a neat and tidy system in which formal designations correspond to differences in function. The differences suggest a hierarchy. . . .

Unfortunately, things are not as simple as this. The first complication is that the formal designation of an act — the label given to it by its author — is not always a reliable guide to its contents. An act may be called a regulation but bear all the characteristics of an EC decision; or it may be called a directive but leave very little choice as to form and methods. Faced with this situation, the European Court has sometimes rejected the formal designation and looked instead at the substance of the act. If an act in the form of a regulation does not lay down general rules but is concerned with deciding a particular case, the Court may call it a "disguised decision" and treat it for certain purposes as an EC decision. It is not, however, clear how far the Court will go in this "relabelling" process. . . .

A second complication is that in practice the difference between the various kinds of act are not as great as might appear from the Treaty provisions. In particular, judgments of the European Court have had the effect of up-grading directives so that they are now much closer to regulations: even if they have not been implemented by the Member State to which they are addressed, they can directly confer rights on private citizens which may be invoked against public authorities.

A third complication is that the European Court has ruled that the list in Article [249 (ex Art. 189)] is not exhaustive: it is possible to have a legally binding act which does not fall into any of the categories enumerated in the Treaty. Acts falling into this residual category are usually called, for want of a better name, acts *sui generis*.

The decision-making process. The path of legislation in the Union varies from the straightforward to the Byzantine. It depends on the legal basis for the legislation (i.e., the provision under which it is being proposed). The legislative process has also become more complex as a result of the SEA, Maastricht and Amsterdam Treaties. Under the Treaty of Rome, EU legislation was generally formulated through a three-way process. First, the Commission would make a proposal, then the Council would consult with the Parliament (on most issues), and then pass some variation of the original proposal. Under this process, while the Council and Commission each possessed considerable power over the final result, Hartley claims, "in practice, the Commission will usually amend its proposals in order to secure the agreement of the Council." (Hartley, supra, at 38.)

The 1986 SEA increased the powers of the European Parliament by introducing a "co-operation procedure." Where applicable, this procedure added an additional review by Parliament at the point where the Council would have previously adopted the act. At the second reading, Parliament would have three months to reject, approve, or propose amendments to the original proposal. If Parliament rejected the Council's recommended position, the act could only be adopted by a unanimous Council.

The power of co-decision. In addition to extending the co-operation procedure to almost all areas in which the Council acts by qualified majority, the Maastricht Treaty further increased the legislative role of the Parliament by introducing a "co-decision" procedure, outlined in Article 251 (ex Art. 189b). The Amsterdam Treaty simplified the co-decision procedure and extended its use to all areas where qualified majority voting applies and in a few areas where unanimous voting is required. The Nice Treaty applied qualified majority voting to seven new areas and expanded the co-decision procedure to cover the same areas. The co-decision power applies most notably to the internal market and the new EU topics included in the recent treaties — e.g., consumer protection, education, culture, transportation, employment, protection against fraud, and public health. It does not apply, however, to decisions on agriculture or matters relating to economic and monetary union. As an EU publication explains, the co-decision procedure "give[s] the European Parliament the possibility, in the event of a difference of opinion with the Council, of seeking a compromise via a conciliation committee and thus place it on an equal footing with the Council." (Office for Official Publications of the European Communities, European Union (1994), at 28.) If no compromise can be found, Parliament may propose amendments that may be adopted by the Council or again compromised in a conciliation committee, or Parliament may flatly reject the Council's common position. (See Chart on the Co-Decision Procedure: Amsterdam Treaty, Assessing European Union Information 49 (1998), reproduced here on page 523.)

Compared to the co-operation procedure, the co-decision power substantially increases Parliament's role. In effect, the co-operation procedure increased Parliament's power only if it could form an alliance with a Member State so as to block the

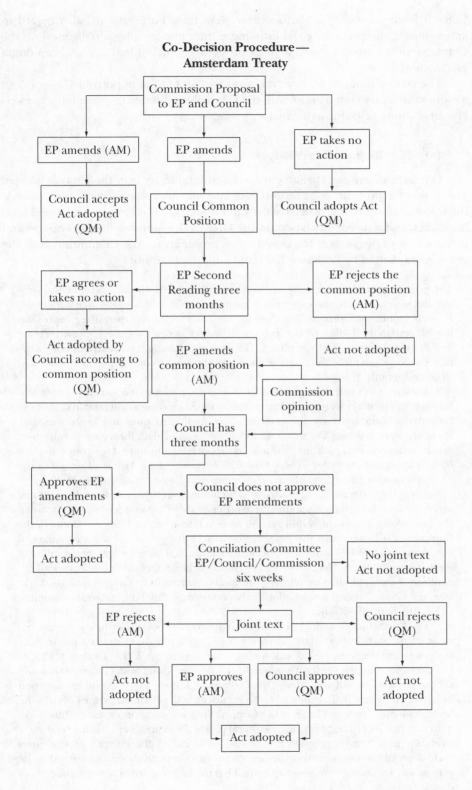

Co-Decision Procedure— Amsterdam Treaty

Commission Proposal to EP and Council

EP amends (AM)

EP amends

EP takes no action

Council accepts Act adopted (QM)

Council Common Position

Council adopts Act (QM)

EP agrees or takes no action

EP Second Reading three months

EP rejects the common position (AM)

Act adopted by Council according to common position (QM)

EP amends common position (AM)

Act not adopted

Commission opinion

Council has three months

Approves EP amendments (QM)

Council does not approve EP amendments

Act adopted

Conciliation Committee EP/Council/Commission six weeks

No joint text Act not adopted

EP rejects (AM)

Joint text

Council rejects (QM)

Act not adopted

EP approves (AM)

Council approves (QM)

Act not adopted

Act adopted

Council from overriding a Parliamentary rejection. Furthermore, with regard to amendments, the procedure did little more than impose a legal obligation on the Commission to consider Parliamentary proposals (which it had already been doing as a matter of practice).

The co-decision power, however, gives Parliament the opportunity to work out a more satisfactory compromise with the Council or, if it desires, the ability to exercise an absolute veto through a majority vote.

(6) The European Union's Budget

One area where the Parliament has considerable say is in the Union's budget. The Union's main sources of revenue are customs duties on imports from outside the Union, a portion of proceeds of the value added tax (VAT) imposed by the Member States, and a direct levy based on the GNP of the Member States. The size and composition of the budget has posed many problems for the Community over the years. As explained by Professor Bermann and his co-authors:

> The greatest part of Community revenue by far is spent to support the common agricultural policy. In 1991, this expenditure came to . . . about 55% of the total budget. . . . In the Commission's proposed budget for 2002, agricultural expenditure represents the biggest share (46%) of the proposed budget and shows the highest increase (+5.0% in relation to 2001 spending). The agriculture budget currently faces a particular challenge, namely meeting the financial burden of combating "mad cow" and "foot-and-mouth" disease.
>
> Assistance to central and eastern European countries is another major expenditure factor. The majority of candidate countries for EU accession will remain far behind the current Community average in terms of economic structures and levels of income for many years to come. The Community institutions decided, therefore, to introduce pre-accession aid for applicant countries to support the adjustment programs they will have to implement in order to adopt the *aquis communautaire*. This is all set out in the EU's program for financing enlargement, commonly known as Agenda 2000.
>
> Since 1988, decisions on budgetary discipline, together with inter-institutional agreements on budgetary discipline, have brought about a stable relationship between the European Union's commitments and its own resources. In 1999, the Council, the European Parliament and the Commission reached agreement on a new financial framework for 2000-06 to implement on a multi-annual basis budgetary discipline at the Community level. The agreement stresses that budgetary discipline covers all expenditures and is binding on all the institutions involved in its implementation. Likewise, the Council issued a regulation on September 26, 2000 on budgetary discipline (O.J. L 244, Sept. 29, 2000). . . .
>
> The Community's budget planning and approval process is complex, in part because of the institutions' shared involvement. The Commission drafts a preliminary budget, submitting it to the Council no later than September 1 (EC Treaty art. 272, ex 203), and in practice during the month of July. The draft budget is reviewed and adopted by the Council and then by the Parliament, followed by a second examination by both institutions. By December 31, the President of the Parliament must declare the budget adopted. Article 272 gives the Council the final decision on expenditures required by the Treaty, notably the agricultural policy. The Parliament has the final voice (within a fixed "maximum rate of increase") on so-called discretionary expenditures such as certain administrative expenses. Since most expenditures are deemed to be compulsory for these purposes, the Council has the larger share of power in budgetary decisionmaking.

The Community's awkward budgetary process both reflects and contributes to contention between the Council and the Parliament over their respective shares of power in the process and over substantive budgetary issues. As early as 1980 (its first year as a directly elected body), the Parliament sought to reject the draft budget in its entirety, and twice in the early 1980s and once again in the early 1990s the two institutions went before the Court of Justice to resolve their differences. One of the Parliament's principal substantive claims of recent years is that agricultural spending should be reduced and amounts spent on regional development and research and development funding increased.

Budgetary politics also produce divisions along Member State lines. In the early 1980s, the UK, under the leadership of Prime Minister Thatcher, strongly contended that the budget should be adjusted to reflect the fact that Britain (not being a major agricultural producer) paid much more into Community revenues than it received. The European Council finally agreed at its 1984 Fontainebleau meeting to give the UK a rebate of a portion of the amount by which its contribution to Community revenue exceeded its receipts. . . .

Once the budget is adopted, the Commission has responsibility under Article 274 (ex 205) for administering the receipt of revenues, the control of cash flow and the disbursement of expenditures. Its administration of Community finances is reviewed by the Court of Auditors, whose composition and role are described in Articles 246-48 (ex 188a-188c). Court of Auditors in effect carries out an annual audit and reports to the Council and the Parliament.

Fraud, especially in payments under the Common Agricultural Policy, has become a serious problem and EC Treaty Article 280 (ex 209a) enjoins the Member States and the Community to make serious efforts to combat it. The Commission's annual reports count many thousands of incidents entailing hundred of millions of euros implicated, mostly in connection with agricultural supports under the Common Agricultural Policy and in regional aid. A significant portion of the EU budget is now devoted to detecting and preventing fraud. [Bermann, et al., supra, at 102-103.]

(7) What Does It All Add Up To?

The preceding overview of the Union's structure should indicate that the Union is a unique, still-developing entity. Comparisons between it and other international and national entities are difficult. For example, look again at the three political institutions and consider what interests each institution represents. In the Council the interests of Member States are represented. In the Commission those of the Union as a whole, somehow defined, take precedence. And in the European Parliament the concerns of the peoples of the Union are considered.

Additionally, the Member States have given up certain aspects of their sovereignty to Union institutions. However, the Amsterdam Treaty introduced the concept of variable-speed integration, called "Closer Cooperation," which allows (with a number of conditions) some Member States to cooperate closely with other members to move toward greater integration, while allowing other Member States the option to join them at a later stage. Under the Union treaties, the EU institutions have express and implied powers to act within their specified fields of competence. As one Union publication states:

The EC and the EU have, by their very nature, certain features in common with the usual kind of international organisation or federal-type structure, and a number of differences.

The EU is itself not yet a "finished product"; it is in the process of evolving and the form it finally takes still cannot be predicted.

The only feature that the EU has in common with other international organisations is that it, too, came into being as a result of an international treaty. However, the anchoring of the EC within the EU's organisational structure has in itself made the EU a considerable departure from the traditional kind of international ties. This is because, although the Treaties establishing the EC were based on international treaties, they led to the creation of independent Communities with their own sovereign rights and responsibilities. The Member States have ceded some of their sovereign powers to these Communities. In addition, the tasks which have been allotted to the EC are very different from those of other international organisations. While the latter mainly have clearly defined tasks of a technical nature, the EC has areas of responsibility which together constitute essential attributes of statehood.

Through these differences between the EC and the normal type of international organisation, the EC and thus also the EU, is in the process of acquiring a status similar to that of an individual State. In particular, the Member States' partial surrender of sovereign rights was taken as a sign that the EU was already structured along the lines of a federal State. However, this view fails to take into account that the EU's institutions only have powers in certain areas to pursue the objectives specified in the Treaties. This means that they are not free to choose their objectives in the same way as a sovereign State; nor are they in a position to meet the challenges facing modern States today. The EU has neither the comprehensive jurisdiction enjoyed by sovereign States nor the powers to establish new areas of responsibility ("jurisdiction over jurisdiction").

The EU is therefore neither an international organisation in the usual sense nor an association of States, but rather an autonomous entity somewhere in between the two. In legal circles, the term "supranational organisation" is now used. [The ABC of Community Law 25 (5th ed. 2000).]

Notes and Questions

1. Is the Union a very democratic entity? Consider how Commission members are selected. Who are the delegates to the Council? What institution is the most democratic? Do you believe it beneficial that the Maastricht Treaty and the Amsterdam Treaty have given the Parliament a somewhat expanded role? Is it relevant that the governments of all the Member States are democratically elected and hence in theory are subject to the people?

2. How would you categorize the Union? Is it a state? A supranational entity? Is the Union more similar to a federal system like the United States, a regional organization like the Organization of American States (discussed below), or an international organization such as the United Nations? As you try to describe the Union, how would you define "Member States"—are they still states? Have they become something less? For example, is France still a state?

3. To what extent can the Union institutions—the Council, Commission, European Parliament, and Court of Justice—be analogized to the tripartite structure of the U.S. government? How clearly delineated are the executive and legislative functions of the Union?

4. Examining the problem from a slightly different angle, to what extent might the representatives of one Member State use Union institutions to pass legislation that is unpopular in that country? Are there any safeguards within the Union institutions

to prevent a Member State's representatives from doing so? (These questions are especially significant in light of the supremacy of Union law over national laws, discussed in Chapter 4.)

5. The general budget in 2002 for the European Union was about €99 billion euros (approximately $93 billion U.S. then). As noted above, the Common Agricultural Policy (CAP) takes by far the largest share, totaling about 45 percent of total expenditures, though this was down from about 55 percent in 1991. Expenditures for military forces and many entitlement programs, such as the equivalent of social security, unemployment compensation, and Medicaid in the United States, are not included in the Union budget, but are in the budgets of the member states. This helps explain the small budget relative to, say, that of the United States. (The U.S. federal budget for FY 2002 was about $1.7 trillion U.S.)

6. The more limited size of the EU government compared to the U.S. federal government can also be appreciated by the relative employment numbers. The U.S. government has about 2.9 million employees (including military). The EU government employees number about 29,000. This is less than the state government employment in West Virginia (about 35,000) or Maryland (about 80,000) and less than the city employment in major U.S. cities.

Moreover, the EU total includes a substantial number of interpreters because of the EU's 11 official languages. Many official proceedings and documents require interpretation in most, if not all, of the languages.

Besides not having an EU military or social security system, the EU is able to operate with much smaller numbers than the U.S. government because of much greater reliance on the government bureaucracies of Member States. The EU will often issue a directive, which the Member State governments are expected to implement. This reflects in part history. The Member State governments were well established even before the creation of the European Community and then the European Union. It also reflects the considerable political pressures in the Union against the growth of a large bureaucracy in Brussels; indeed, in 1998, the pressures from Germany and elsewhere were to downsize the EU bureaucracy.

7. The EU's size and method of operation are in part reflected in the principle of subsidiarity, which was first introduced in the Maastricht Treaty. Subsidiarity means that in areas where the EU does not have exclusive jurisdiction, the EU takes action only when the Member States have insufficient means to reach the objectives of the proposed action. (See Article 5 (ex Art. 3b) of the EC Treaty.) The principle of subsidiarity assigns decision-making to national, regional, or local levels as much as possible. It is supposed to be taken into account at every stage of the EU legislative process.

Under the principle of subsidiarity, EU directives on issues such as the environment also allow the Member States to apply standards or laws that are even stricter than those provided for by the directives.

However, the principle of subsidiarity is often confusing because the definition provided in the Treaty does not set forth a clear criteria for areas where the EU has exclusive jurisdiction. Because of this confusion, the Commission has identified the following areas as under the exclusive jurisdiction of the EU: removal of barriers to the free movement of goods, services, persons, and capital; the common commercial policy; the general rules on competition; and the common organization of agricultural markets, conservation of fisheries, and certain elements of transport policy.

However, this list is not exhaustive and debate over the responsibility of decision-making has occurred with respect to issues such as whether there should be unified tolls for EU roads. Because of such confusion, the Amsterdam Treaty added a protocol that further clarifies the criteria and the process of applying the concept of subsidiarity to actions taken by the EU institutions. However, the debate over when to apply the principle of subsidiarity will likely continue.

8. *Harmonization and mutual recognition.* The EU's method of operation and size are also affected by the principle of harmonization and the related concept of mutual recognition. The principle of harmonization was first introduced in the EC's Treaty of Rome in an effort to create an open internal market that was free from competition. The principle seeks to coordinate national legislation of the Member States in order to remove trade barriers. The establishment of common external tariffs and the prohibition of import quotas within the union are examples of methods used to achieve a single European market. (See Article 27 (ex Art. 29) and Article 28 (ex Art. 30).) The adoption of uniform environmental standards in the areas of automobile emissions, chemical substances, and pesticides also facilitates free movement of goods.

However, in line with the principle of subsidiarity, the EC Treaty allows the Member States to implement stricter national standards in order to protect the environment. (See Art. 95 (ex Art. 100a).)

Also, in a significant movement away from attempts to overharmonize national legislation, the Court of Justice introduced the concept of mutual recognition. Mutual recognition allows a product that is legally produced and sold in one Member State to move freely in all other Member States. The case that established this concept, Rewe v. Bundesmonopolverwaltung fur Branntwein, Case 120/78, [1979] E.C.R. 649, [1979] 3 C.M.L.R. 494 [hereinafter referred to by its common name, *Cassis de Dijon*], was brought to the court by a company that wanted to import a French liqueur into the Federal Republic of Germany. The company could not import the French liqueur, Cassis de Dijon, into the country because its alcohol content was lower than the German requirement of 25 percent. Even though the alcohol content requirement was applied equally to German liqueurs, the court found Germany to be in violation of Article 28 (ex Art. 30), which prohibits "any national measure capable of hindering, directly or indirectly, actually or potentially, intra-Community trade."

The ruling in *Cassis de Dijon* facilitated the EU's movement toward a single market and reduced the need for a large EU administrative bureaucracy because it allowed for free movement of goods without having to wait for harmonization directives from the EU institutions. The concept of mutual recognition is limited by the national need to impose restrictions for the protection of consumers, health, and the environment as well as for the maintenance of fair commercial transactions. However, the effects of the court's decision have been far-reaching. In 1998, Austria, Belgium, France, Greece, Ireland, Italy, the Netherlands, and Sweden faced infringement proceedings (which may subject Member States to fines) for creating trade barriers for a range of products, including alcoholic beverages, car spare parts, chocolate, diet supplements, margarine, precious metals, road tankers, salami, telecommunications equipment, and vitamin-enriched foods. Specifically in the case of the Italy, the national legislation restricted imports of chocolate that contains vegetable fats other than cocoa butter. Italy allowed those chocolates to be sold only if they were labeled as a chocolate substitute. The Commission determined that the

Italian legislation violated the concept of mutual recognition and went beyond the consumer protection exception under *Cassis de Dijon,* since the consumers can be informed by less restrictive labeling.

(8)   *The European Economic and Monetary Union (EMU)*

Perhaps the most prominent recent symbol of European integration is the adoption between 1999 and 2002 of a single currency — the euro. Although some commentators had doubted whether a close monetary union would ever be possible, the euro was introduced for bookkeeping purposes on January 1, 1999, among 11 Member States: Austria, Belgium, Finland, France, Germany, Ireland, Italy, Luxembourg, the Netherlands, Portugal, and Spain. Greece became the twelfth state to join the EMU when it met the criteria for membership in June 2000, but the United Kingdom, Denmark, and Sweden opted to remain outside, at least for the time being. New EU members will be expected to adopt the euro when they are economically prepared to do so, but not immediately upon joining.

With the new monetary union, a European Central Bank (ECB) was created in 1998. On January 1, 1999, responsibility for monetary policy among the 11 countries passed to the ECB. There was a fixing of the conversion rates (to the sixth decimal point) between those countries' currencies and the new euro. Relative to the U.S. dollar, the euro was initially worth about $1.167. By 2002, its value fluctuated between 86 cents and one dollar. In May 2003, however, its value had climbed back to about $1.18.

On January 1, 2002, euro coins and notes were introduced for the first time, and on February 28, national currencies were taken out of circulation, making the euro the sole official currency in 12 European states comprising over 300 million persons.

In a political sense, the EMU is a significant step toward the goal of a unified Europe, as the Member States have ceded a significant amount of their sovereignty in monetary and fiscal policy to the ECB for the benefits of a common currency. The euro is expected to save people and entities in the EU about €20-25 billion yearly in the transaction costs that multiple currencies caused. The additional savings from the improved ability to compare prices easily across borders will probably save even more. Moreover, in an economic sense, the size and wealth of the EMU will have important implications for the world economy.

(9)   *The External Activities of the European Union*

The provisions of the Treaty on European Union establishing a common foreign and security policy were the result of a gradual process of greater Union action outside its own economic area. Since the 1960s, the Union has been involved in international economic issues. In conjunction with its role in setting common external trade barriers and reducing internal trade barriers, the Community acted as the negotiator for its Member States in the GATT negotiating rounds.

The Union had also been involved in the international political arena. For example, the European Union is one of four entities, together with the United States, the U.N., and Russia, that attempted during the second half of 2002 to broker an Israeli-Palestinian agreement. The EC also warned Iraq during the Persian Gulf crisis of 1990 that, if an EC citizen were harmed, a unified reaction would follow.

The structure of the EU's unified foreign policy is still very much under development, but the following articles from Professor Jurgen Schwarze and Giorgio Maganza address the legal basis of this authority. Professor Schwarze discusses the bases of the European Community's foreign policy prior to the Treaty of European Union, and Mr. Maganza discusses that authority in the aftermath of the Amsterdam Treaty.

Jurgen Schwarze, Towards a European Foreign Policy — Legal Aspects

Towards a European Foreign Policy 70-71 (Johan K. De Vree et al. eds., 1987)

2.   External Competence of the European Communities

. . . In the context of foreign relations Art. [281 (ex Art. 210)] of the EEC Treaty, which provides that the "Community shall have legal personality," forms a key provision. The comparison of this provision with Art. [282 (ex. Art 211)] of the Treaty, which stipulates that the Community shall enjoy legal capacity under municipal law, leaves no legal doubt that Art. [281 (ex Art. 210)] expressly declares the Community to be a subject of international law. Within the law of nations this qualification includes the capacity to possess international rights and duties. In relation to the "classical" subjects of international law, namely the nation States, quite naturally this legal characteristic also implies complete and extensive foreign policy powers.

However, there is a vital difference between a nation State and an international organisation in this respect. The legal capacity of a nation State is original, not derived from anyone. Thus the international lawyer refers to a nation State as a "primary legal person." In contrast, the [Union] as an international organisation is not an original legal person, but was created by the Member-States. Thus the legal capacity of such an international organisation "must depend on its purposes and functions, as expressed or implied by its constituent instruments and as developed in practise," as the International Court of Justice has held.

Although the European Court in its judgment COSTA v. E.N.E.L. has concluded that international capacity is one characteristic feature of the EEC, its competences in the field of international relations are limited, contrary to the unlimited powers of nation States. In particular, the principle of *"compétence d'attribution"* has to be maintained, meaning that the Community only holds those powers which have been conferred upon it by the Treaty. Thus, Community powers in the field of foreign relations must be identified on the basis of Treaty. . . .

In this respect, Art. [133 ex Art. 113)] EEC . . . deals in its para. 3 with the conclusion of international agreements in the field of a common commercial policy. It is commonly accepted that the Community power under this Article is exclusive. However, the precise scope of this power still remains undetermined and controversial. Thus, the key problem is the exact definition of the principal term "common commercial policy," which is not explained in the Treaty. Nevertheless, [133 (ex Art. 113)] EEC contains a list of commercial policy measures, which is not exhaustive. The Court has given indications of its willingness to interpret [133 (ex Art. 113)] broadly. . . .

The *compétence d'attribution* of the EC in foreign relations was limited primarily to trade and economic relations, however, and any cooperation in other realms took place on an intergovernmental level, outside the scope of the treaties. The European Political Cooperation, established in 1970 and codified in the Single European Act, created a framework by which the Member States could coordinate their foreign policy when appropriate, but it provided no basis for a unified European policy.

The Treaty of European Union made a Common Foreign and Security Policy (CFSP) the second pillar of the new Union. Unlike the EC, however, the EU was not explicitly given an international legal personality. Although the Union was created to allow its Member States to speak with a single voice in areas of foreign policy other than trade relations, the parties to Maastricht were unwilling to cede it initially the power to conclude treaties in their names. The CFSP was a compromise: foreign policy was brought within the EU institutions, but unanimity was required for the EU to act. Under Maastricht, therefore, the Union had the ability to speak with one voice, but lacked the autonomy to establish foreign policy at a supranational level.

The Treaty of Amsterdam expanded the ability of the Union to act as an institution in implementing foreign policy, while reserving to the Member States control over its direction and, importantly, over military and defense.

Giorgio Maganza, The Treaty of Amsterdam's Changes to the Common Foreign and Security Policy Chapter and an Overview of the Opening Enlargement Process
22 Fordham Intl. L.J. 164 (1999)

The European Union ("Union" or "EU") is an important actor in the international arena. The Union behaves and acts as a political entity towards the outside world and it is perceived as such. That is certainly the case for international economic relations, where the European Community ("EC" or "Community") has played a significant role as a major partner in multilateral negotiations for several years now. It is more frequently the case with respect to foreign policy matters, as a result of the choice made by the signatories to the Maastricht Treaty ("Treaty on European Union" or "TEU") in which the signatories decided to give the Union the means to speak with one voice in world affairs and to conduct effective external action that would not be limited to economic and trade relations. The provisions of Title V of the Treaty on European Union accordingly set out the objectives of the Union's common foreign and security policy [CFSP] and provided the instruments to carry this policy out. . . .

The Treaty of Amsterdam . . . improves upon the mechanisms available to the Union to act effectively in foreign policy matters. Clearly, such mechanisms, however developed they may be, cannot by themselves create a policy that requires a political will to act in common. . . . In considering possible amendments to the provisions on the CFSP, the main concerns have been that of improving the decision-making and the implementation of the CFSP and that of allowing greater effectiveness and visibility to the Union's action.

The Treaty of Amsterdam provides for an enhanced role of the European Council. It will be for the European Council not only to define the principles of and general guidelines for the CFSP, but also to "decide on common strategies to be implemented by the Union in areas where the Member States have important interests in common." Decision-making power is thus conferred upon the European Council.

Under the new provisions, the Council is to act by a qualified majority whenever it makes a decision on the basis of a common strategy previously decided by the European Council. This requirement should allow for greater use of qualified majority voting for implementing decisions whereas unanimity would remain the rule for the main policy decisions. . . .

The maintaining of unanimity as the voting rule for all main CFSP decisions has been combined with the possibility of constructive abstention, allowing a Member State to let a decision be taken while not being obliged to apply it. This combination is intended to reduce the risk of deadlock. Unanimity will remain the rule for decisions having military or defense implications.

While the Presidency will continue to play its role of representing the Union in matters coming within the CFSP and to be responsible for the implementation of CFSP decisions, the visibility of the Union will be strengthened through the establishment of a High Representative, who will be the Secretary-General of the Council and will have the task of assisting the Council in matters coming within the scope of the CFSP, "in particular through contributing to the formulation, preparation, and implementation of policy decisions.". . .

On security and defense, the Treaty of Amsterdam amendments do not involve major changes in respect of the present situation, but they do reflect developments since the signing of the Maastrict Treaty. In particular, the so-called "Petersberg tasks"— humanitarian and rescue tasks, peace-keeping tasks, and tasks of combat forces in crisis management, including peace-making — are now specifically mentioned as aspects of the Union's security policy, which all Member States, including the neutral ones, will contribute to implementing. The CFSP includes the "progressive framing of a common defense policy": a door thus remains open to a common defense, although any decision in this respect, to be taken by the European Council, would require ratification by all Member States. . . .

Last but not least, the possibility has been explicitly recognized for the Union to negotiate and to conclude international agreements when necessary to implement the CFSP. Such agreements are to be negotiated by the Presidency and concluded by the Council acting unanimously. It is worth emphasizing the importance of this provision, which will put an end to the present unsatisfactory situation under which the Union cannot enter into legally binding international commitments in areas where Title[s] V and VI of the TEU give it powers to act and where its partners expect it to act. This provision also provides further evidence for the existence of legal personality of the Union, as it may be derived from the Treaty provisions, although not explicitly conferred by them upon the Union, as well as from the continuing and convergent behavior of third parties vis-à-vis the Union itself. . . .

The Treaty of Nice extended the principle of "enhanced cooperation" that allows some, but not all, Member States to act in the field of foreign policy, except where military or defense is implicated. The Council can permit such enhanced cooperation by qualified majority voting, although each Member State has an "emergency brake" that allows it to send the issue to the European Council for a unanimous decision.

Questions

1. Professor Schwarze notes the early importance of Article 133 (ex Art. 113), and how the Court of Justice has interpreted it broadly. Can you think of a similar provision in the U.S. legal system?

2. What seem to be the relative roles of the Union's political institutions in making and implementing international agreements on behalf of the Union?

3. Why do you think the Member States believe there are benefits in jointly developing and implementing a European foreign policy? Is there something to the old adage about "strength in numbers"?

4. To what extent will the composition of the EU affect plans for a common foreign and security policy? What limits do you see on the benefits of CFSP from the standpoint of the individual Member States? Do they all share the same views and policies — for example, toward Turkey or the Middle East?

5. Foreign policy has been one of the major issues debated at the Convention on the Future of Europe (discussed below). One consensus is that the legal personality of the Union should be recognized, as discussed in Mr. Maganza's article. This would enable it to speak with one voice in a greater range of international matters. Questions remain, however, as to how Union procedures for making foreign policy decisions will be changed.

(10) Expanding the European Union

Where is the European Union headed? The EU has been adding new Member States, while also further integrating many activities. Some experts have worried whether widening and deepening can occur simultaneously. However, the Amsterdam and then Nice Treaties appear to be attempts to do just that — to welcome new Member States into the Union while further integrating the current Members, and perhaps the new Members as well, into a more closely knit Union. The Nice IGC in 2000 produced not only the Nice Treaty, which resolved many of the details of adjusting the EU institutions for an expanded Union of up to 27 Member States, but the IGC also adopted a Charter of Fundamental Rights and called for a Convention on the Future of Europe, to propose a new round of reforms for the 2004 IGC.

Whatever the Convention on the Future of Europe proposes, it is very likely that there will be more than 15 Member States represented at the intergovernmental conference in 2004. At the European Council meeting in December 2002, the Union concluded its accession negotiations with 10 of the 13 applicant countries — namely Cyprus, the Czech Republic, Estonia, Hungary, Latvia, Lithuania, Malta, Poland, the Slovak Republic, and Slovenia — with the objective that this group join the EU on May 1, 2004. This means that, in the Commission's determination, these 10 states have met the required political and economic criteria, that is:

> The stability of institutions guaranteeing democracy, the rule of law, human rights and respect for and protection of minorities (the *political criterion*);
> The existence of a functioning market economy as well as the capacity to cope with competitive pressure and market forces within the Union (the *economic criterion*);

and that they will be able to enact and implement the *acquis communitaire*— the Union's legislation — by 2004. The October 2002 meeting of the European Council in Brussels resolved the remaining issues of allocating EU farm subsidies and the costs of expansion, clearing the last obstacles in the way of final accession negotiations.

The Commission also indicated that 2007 was a realistic target date for the accession of Bulgaria and Romania, who meet the political criterion but are not yet economically prepared for membership. It determined that Turkey had not yet met the political criteria for beginning negotiations, but noted progress and recommended increasing its financial support for Turkey's preparations.

(11) A More Integrated Union

Simultaneously with the ongoing expansion process, groups within the Union have been pressing for further integration, in politics and foreign policy as well as economics. Other forces, in particular Great Britain and Denmark, have attempted to put the brakes on further transfers of sovereignty from the Member States to Brussels. However, the success of the euro and the reforms introduced at Amsterdam led the heads of state meeting at Nice to attach a declaration on the future of the Union to the treaty. The declaration called for considering the EU's future direction and it suggested questions for the debate, including the simplification of the constitutive treaties, solutions to the so-called democracy deficit, and the status of the Charter of Fundamental Rights. The declaration also called for a new IGC in 2004 to amend the treaties appropriately. In December 2001, the European Council meeting at Laeken in the Netherlands called for the establishment of a year-long Convention on the Future of Europe to meet in March 2002 to answer these and other questions. The Convention is to present its conclusions to the European Council in June 2003, for use in writing a new treaty at the next IGC, which will be held in 2004.

It is impossible to predict what the treaty to be written in 2004 will look like, but the Convention has assumed a very broad mandate to debate possible changes. Its most ambitious achievement has been the creation of a draft Constitution of the European Union, fusing the Treaty of European Union, the Euratom Treaty, and the Treaty of the European Community into a single instrument. A draft Constitution presented in December 2002 as a feasibility study suggests one form that the Union might take in the future.

This treaty would replace the present system of renegotiating the Union's treaties on a state-to-state basis — dependent on unanimous ratification — with an amendment process similar to that of the U.S. Constitution. The power of an individual state to limit the sovereignty of the Union would be greatly reduced, although a Member State could withdraw unilaterally if it fundamentally disagreed with the rest of the Union. The draft constitution would define the key principles of the Union and incorporate the Charter of Fundamental Rights and create a high bar to amending these, as well as defining policies and the legal bases for implementing them.

The Constitution would also reorganize the government of the EU, defining its institutions in terms of functions rather than powers. The Commission would become the executive organ of the new Union, although the Council would remain the ultimate decision-maker, especially in the area of external relations. The Commission would cede its legislative powers to the Council and the Parliament, which would essentially become a two-house legislature, representing the people of the Union and its Member States, respectively. The assent of both bodies, by qualified majority, would be required to pass legislation, and the Parliament, as the most democratic Union institution, would control the budget. This reorganization, proponents argue, would greatly reduce the Union's democracy deficit.

Finally, the Constitution would create a clear legal personality for the Union, enabling it to enter into international agreements on its Members' behalf. The Union, and not the individual states, would be responsible for such matters as admitting new Member States and interacting with foreign states and international institutions. It is still too early to tell at this point whether something like this Constitution will be adopted by the European Union in 2004. However, some degree of increasing integration, at the expense of the sovereignty of Member States, is likely.

Notes and Questions

1. The Amsterdam Treaty introduced the concept of variable-speed integration, called "Closer Cooperation," to allow (with a number of conditions) pro-integration Member States to proceed toward that goal at a faster pace than other states desire. Is this approach preferable to generally requiring each Member State to proceed at the same pace? What problems would a variable-speed EU create? See generally Philippe Manin, The Treaty of Amsterdam, 4 Colum. J. Eur. L. 1 (1998).

2. As noted earlier, the ratification process for the Treaty of European Union (or Maastricht Treaty) included exemptions being obtained by Britain, Denmark, and Luxembourg on certain matters. Is this evidence of the need for flexibility?

3. Is there a potential tension between "widening" (enlarging the number of members) or "deepening" the institutions (greater integration)? Can these two goals exist coextensively? If not, is one more desirable than the other in the case of the European Union? For example, as the Union expands to include as many as 12 new states in the next five years, many of them relatively poor, will the wealthier Member States be amenable to further diluting their sovereignty to a Union that includes states with which they have much less common history? Will the new Member States be able to participate in the EMU and other European institutions as equals, or will the EU end up with two tiers of integration? Should the Union slow down its integration process to allow the new members to catch up?

4. Who is eligible to become a member of the European Union? Article 49 of the TEU says "Any European State which respects the principles set out in Article 6(1)"—liberty, democracy, respect for human rights and fundamental freedoms, and the rule of law—"may apply to become a member of the Union." By 2007, a Union that began with six of the wealthiest Western European nations will include some of the poorest states of the former Warsaw Pact. If these can join a unified Europe, who else can? Is Russia a European State, as the Union uses the term? Is Ukraine? Turkey? What defines "European?" (Russia, Ukraine, and Turkey are all members of the Council of Europe and parties to the related European Convention for the Protection of Human Rights and Fundamental Freedoms, as discussed in Chapter 8.)

The candidacy of Turkey has raised the most questions about the meaning of "Europe." Although 90 percent of Turkey's territory is outside Europe, the EU has recognized it as an applicant country. However, at the October 2002 meeting where the Commission encouraged the Union to admit the Eastern European applicants, the Commission once again found that Turkey did not meet the criteria for membership. The Commission cited Turkey's failure to ensure the rule of law and protection of its Kurdish minority. Others in the EU have noted that Turkey has a large agricultural sector (when the cost of agricultural subsidies are a major EU problem) and have warned of the harm that an influx of Turkish laborers might do to the European economy. However, many commentators believe that at least one obstacle to Turkish membership in the Union is its Muslim population. The majority of European citizens are Christian, and some political figures have asserted that, as a Muslim state, Turkey is not "European" enough to join the Union. While no Union official has made such a statement in a public capacity, many Turkish politicians are beginning to doubt if Turkey will ever be admitted. Does the Union have a right to reject Turkey, or a responsibility to admit it? Should geography, or religion, or culture be a disqualifying criterion?

5. Will the current Union continue to deepen to include other aspects of state sovereignty? The draft Constitution, discussed above, provides one possible answer, but it is not the only one. Will the European Union come to have even more integration of Member States' trade, financial, monetary, and foreign policies? Will it become a two-tiered structure, comprising a closely integrated 12-member euro zone with another dozen or so more loosely associated Member States? Will it become a federal state like the United States, but with more autonomy for the individual states? Will it become a new, unified state?

6. What role will a European Union, with a greater or lesser degree of "federalism," have in the larger world? Will it be primarily an economic superpower only, unable to turn its financial strength into foreign policy and defense leverage because of internal divisions? Or, will the European Union increasingly speak with one powerful voice across the international stage, as it does now in the World Trade Organization?

7. In addition to the works cited in this section and in Chapter 4, a few of the many other useful materials on the European Union include The Treaty of Amsterdam (Andrew Duff ed., 1997); Alain A. Levasseur et al., The Law of the European Union: A New Constitutional Order (2001); The Expanding European Union: Past, Present, Future (John Redmond & Glenda G. Rosenthal eds., 1998); Jurgen Schwarze, The Implementation of Community Law: Studies in the Legislative and Administrative Policies of the European Community and Its Member States (1994); Diane Wood, The Emerging European Union (1996); Francesca E. Bignami, The Democratic Deficit in European Community Rulemaking: A Call for Notice and Comment in Comitology, 40 Harv. J. Intl. 451 (1999); Elizabeth Shaver Duquette, The European Union's Common Foreign and Security Policy: Emerging from the U.S. Shadow?, 7 U.C. Davis J. Intl. L. & Poly. 169 (2001); Peter L. Lindseth, Democratic Legitimacy and the Administrative Character of Supranationalism: The Example of the European Community, 99 Colum. L. Rev. 628 (1999). The European Union also has a number of its own publications, including the monthly magazine the Bulletin of the European Union, and its comprehensive Web site, <http://www.europa.eu.int>, which provide updates on current events.

b. North Atlantic Treaty Organization (NATO)

The North Atlantic Treaty Organization originally was the security organization designed to provide for the defense of Western Europe. NATO was formed in 1949 in response to growing concern over actions taken by the Soviet Union, including its consolidation of communist rule in Eastern Europe after World War II.

As of January 2003, NATO had 19 full members, including the United States, Canada, Norway, Turkey, Greece, and most of the countries of Western Europe (Austria and Switzerland are not members). Poland, Hungary, and the Czech Republic had joined the Alliance in 1999. In November 2002, NATO invited seven additional countries (Bulgaria, Estonia, Latvia, Lithuania, Romania, Slovakia, and Slovenia) to begin accession talks, with the aim of their becoming members in May 2004. Other countries could be later asked to join.

The original purpose of NATO was collective self-defense. The North Atlantic Treaty, however, does not obligate a member to come to the aid of any other member if an attack occurs. Article 5, which authorizes collective self-defense in the event of an armed attack, requires only that a member take "such action as it deems necessary" to restore and maintain the security of the North Atlantic area. Each state's response must be in accord with its own constitutional processes. Nevertheless, there has been a substantial measure of integration of military forces and military planning, including unified commands (Supreme Allied Commander in Europe and Supreme Commander for the North Atlantic) and regional planning groups.

Article 5 has only been invoked once in NATO's history, namely after the events of September 11, 2001, when NATO demonstrated its support for the United States. (See discussion in the case study in Chapter 1.D.) Similarly, only invoked once has been the Treaty's Article 4, which provides in part that "the Parties will consult whenever, in the opinion of any of them, the territorial integrity, political independence or security of any of the Parties is threatened." In February 2003, Turkey formally requested consultations under Article 4 because of concerns about a possible Iraqi attack if there were to be hostilities in the region. After France blocked a consensus in NATO's North Atlantic Council because France was opposed to the U.S. and British-led efforts against Saddam Hussein, NATO moved the discussion to an alternative forum, its Defence Planning Committee (DPC), where France alone was not a member because President Charles de Gaulle had withdrawn from it in the 1960s. The DPC agreed to begin consultations and in the words of the NATO Secretary General to "integrate our collective solidarity with Turkey."

With the fall of the Berlin Wall in late 1989 and the falling apart of the Soviet Union in 1991-92, the Cold War thawed and geopolitics changed in Europe. NATO began its own transformation from just being a collective self-defense entity for Western Europe. NATO began opening its door to new members from the former Warsaw Pact, making major changes in its military and political structures, and increasing cooperation with non-member states in a wide range of areas.

First, to deepen its engagement with the neutral and formerly communist states of Central and Eastern Europe, NATO instituted the Partnership for Peace (PFP) program in 1991. While the PFP program is aimed at enhancing cooperation between NATO and non-NATO states, it does not provide full NATO membership or security guarantees. In 1997, NATO created the Euro-Atlantic Partnership Council (EAPC) to establish political and military cooperation between NATO members and

PFP states. The EAPC membership is open to all members of PFP and the Organization on Security and Cooperation in Europe (OSCE) (discussed below). The EAPC currently includes all 19 NATO members and all 27 PFP countries.

Also, in May 2002, NATO and Russia replaced the NATO-Russia Permanent Joint Council, set up in 1997 to allow bilateral consultation, with a new NATO-Russia Council. Russia now sits as an equal with the 19 NATO members and participates in the consensus, although it lacks veto power. With this new system, cooperation is being intensified in a number of new key areas, including antiterrorism, crisis management, arms control, missile defense, military cooperation, and civil emergencies.

Second, future plans are to have NATO military capability become more flexible, and focus primarily on "out-of-area" capability. Because an invasion of Western Europe is no longer a concern, NATO forces will now be adapted to address security problems in other volatile areas. Indeed, it was NATO that conducted the military efforts, which were largely an air campaign, in 1999 against Serbia over its repression of the Albanians in Kosovo. (See the Chapter 11 section on Kosovo.) More recently, at its November 2002 Summit, NATO agreed to create a NATO Response Force (NRF) consisting of technologically advanced, flexible, deployable, and sustainable military forces "to move quickly wherever needed, as decided by the Council." The NRF was to have initial operational capability as soon as possible, but not later than October 2004.

In other areas, NATO in 2002 endorsed an agreed military concept and package of measures for defense against terrorism. NATO also endorsed the implementation of five initiatives for nuclear, biological and chemical weapons defense.

Although there has been and is certain to be more overlap and tension between NATO, the EU, and the OSCE, the United States has indicated its desire to have NATO remain as the primary European security institution. NATO has an excellent Web site at <http://www.nato.int>.

c.   The Organization on Security and Cooperation in Europe (OSCE)

As a new Europe emerges, one important question is which regional organizations will play major roles? Besides the institutions already discussed in this chapter or elsewhere — the European Union, NATO, and the European Court of Human Rights — other regional entities exist. One that seems likely to play a continuing role is the Organization on Security and Cooperation in Europe (OSCE).

The OSCE membership now consists of all the European states (including the former republics of the Soviet Union), plus the United States and Canada. An OSCE Fact Sheet provides basic background information:

From CSCE to OSCE

The OSCE traces its origins back to the detente phase of the early 1970s, when the Conference on Security and Cooperation in Europe (CSCE) was created to serve as a multilateral forum for dialogue and negotiation between East and West. . . . [T]he

CSCE reached agreement on the Helsinki Final Act . . . signed on 1 August, 1975. This document . . . established fundamental principles (the "Decalogue") governing the behaviour of States towards their citizens as well as towards each other.

Until 1990, the CSCE functioned mainly as a series of meetings and conferences that built on and extended the participating States' commitments, while periodically reviewing their implementation. However, with the coming to an end of the Cold War, the Paris Summit of November 1990 set the CSCE on a new course. In the Paris Charter for a New Europe, the CSCE was called upon to play its part in managing the historic change taking place in Europe and responding to the new challenges of the post-Cold War period, acquiring permanent institutions and operational capabilities.

A major arms control agreement — the Treaty on Conventional Armed Forces in Europe (CFE) — was also concluded on the margins of the Paris Summit. A number of other important military security treaties, including the 1992 Treaty on Open Skies . . ., as well as the key Document on Small Arms and Light Weapons (2000), now form part of the CSCE/OSCE politico-military dimension acquis.

In the early 1990s, offices and institutions were set up, meetings became more regular, missions were established and the Conference's work became more structured. Recognizing that the CSCE was no longer simply a Conference, in 1994 the Budapest Summit agreed to change its name to the [OSCE]. As well as being a reflection of its institutional development following the end of the Cold War, this also gave the Organization a new political impetus.

The Lisbon Summit of 1996 strengthened the key role of the OSCE in fostering security and stability in all their dimensions. It stimulated the development of an OSCE Charter for European Security, eventually adopted at the Istanbul Summit, in November 1999. This was instrumental in improving the operational capabilities of the Organization and cooperation with its partners. A revised CFE Treaty was also signed at the Istanbul Summit by 30 OSCE participating States.

Today, the OSCE occupies a unique place among European security institutions. This is attributable to several factors: its broad membership; its co-operative and comprehensive approach to security; its conflict prevention instruments; its well-established tradition of open dialogue and consensus building; its network of field missions; and a well-developed pattern of co-operation with other international organizations. . . . [What is the OSCE? Factsheet, <http://www.osce.org/> (February 2003).]

The 1994 transition from "conference" to regional security organization has made the OSCE a more active participant in European affairs. Now comprising 55 countries, the OSCE views itself as "the primary instrument in the OSCE region for early warning, conflict prevention, and crisis management in Europe." The OSCE maintains missions in several states, including high-profile missions to Bosnia-Herzegovina, Kosovo, and Chechnya. Among the tasks of these missions is overseeing elections and helping to ensure the rule of law and protection of minorities.

In the 21st century, the OSCE's greatest contribution is likely to be in conflict prevention and de-escalation. By acting quickly and quietly, OSCE missions and field operations have defused conflicts in Ukraine and Macedonia at a fraction of the cost of its peacekeeping missions to Bosnia and Kosovo. OSCE mediators were also critical to achieving the 1997 ceasefire in Chechnya, notwithstanding its eventual collapse in 1999. Where conflict prevention has failed, OSCE missions have been helpful in rebuilding war-torn societies, particularly in the former Yugoslav and Soviet republics.

Notes and Questions

1. Would the OSCE, with its greater membership than NATO, provide a more comprehensive framework for the security of the entire continent? The United States has opposed such a belief as unworkable at the present time. It has rebuffed an independent security role for the OSCE, preferring to have it act in concert with the United Nations or NATO.

2. The Western European Union (WEU) is a security organization that has developed primarily as a purely West European version of NATO. It was largely inactive during the Cold War, but in recent years it has been called upon to be the defense arm of the European Union and to act as a bridge between the EU and NATO. The Maastricht Treaty called for a role for the WEU in the so-called Petersburg tasks — mostly peacekeeping and humanitarian missions. At subsequent conferences, the Union has begun the work of bringing the WEU within the EU political framework.

Of the EU's members, all are full members of the WEU except for Austria, Denmark, Finland, Ireland, and Sweden. These exceptions, however all have observer status within the WEU. As for non-EU members, the Czech Republic, Hungary, Iceland, Norway, Poland, and Turkey are associate members of the WEU, and associate partner status is held by seven Eastern European nations (including the Baltic states but not the other former Soviet republics). While the United States and Canada belong to NATO, they are not members of the WEU. The WEU has no geographical limitations on its activities. More information on the WEU can be found at its Web site: <http://www.weu.int>.

There is considerable interest in European and North American capitals over how the WEU will develop its relationship with the European Union, and how the WEU and NATO will interact.

3. Besides those regional institutions mentioned in the preceding sections, Europe has a number of other regional entities of varying scope and purpose. These include the Council of Europe and the Economic Commission for Europe.

The Council of Europe is a parliamentary organization aimed at furthering democracy and human rights. It had a role to play in the establishment of the European Court of Human Rights and membership in it is a precondition for participation in that court. The Council of Europe had 44 member states, including Russia, as of January 2003. With its expanded membership encompassing a large number of different nationalities, the Council has turned its attention to such issues as migration, the right to citizenship, social exclusion, and minorities. More information on the Council is available at its Web site: <http://www.coe.int>. While the United States is not a member, the Council has extended an invitation for the United States to participate in some of its functions. Several other nonmember states, such as Canada, Japan, Mexico, and the Holy See, have a similar relationship with the Council.

The Economic Commission for Europe (ECE) is one of the more active regional commissions under the United Nations, covering both Europe and North America. Headquartered in Geneva, the Council has helped develop common policies and programs in trade, in scientific and technological cooperation, and for environmental problems such as acid rain and air pollution. Its membership includes the European countries plus the United States, Canada, and most of the former Soviet republics.

There is also the Organization of Economic Cooperation and Development (OECD), but its scope has expanded beyond Western Europe and North America to include other industrial democracies, such as Japan, Korea, Australia, and New Zealand. It works toward developing policies on a range of economic, scientific, and social issues. (See, e.g., the OECD Convention on Combatting Bribery of Foreign Officials in International Business Transactions in Chapter 2 at page 141.) Its Web site is at <http://www.oecd.org>.

4. Which regional entity or entities should have the major role in helping develop coordinated policies toward regional issues in Europe — such as the movement of people or transboundary air and water pollution? Which entity(ies) should have the major role in helping resolve disputes between two or more European countries, such as the ethnic dispute between Hungary and Rumania over the treatment of minorities? How should issues of trade and investment be handled? Does it matter what the particular problem is? Do international institutions and bilateral agreements as well as regional entities have a role to play?

5. From the U.S. standpoint, which regional entities should it encourage to develop further? Should the United States especially encourage those entities of which it is a member?

6. In sharp contrast to the many regional entities in Europe, including some very strong ones, the situation in the rest of the world is more spotty. However, in the rapidly developing Pacific Rim, two major organizations — the Association of Southeast Asian Nations (ASEAN) and the broadly based Asia-Pacific Economic Cooperation (APEC) coalition — are playing an increasingly important role.

d. The Association of Southeast Asian Nations (ASEAN)

The Association of Southeast Asian Nations is a coalition of 10 rapidly developing countries in Southeast Asia. Its membership includes Brunei, Cambodia, Indonesia, Laos, Malaysia, Myanmar (formerly Burma), the Philippines, Singapore, Thailand, and Vietnam. As of 2002, these countries had a combined population of about 500 million and a gross domestic product of about $550 billion.

As stated in the Bangkok Declaration of 1967 announcing the group's creation, ASEAN was designed to

> accelerate the economic growth, social progress and cultural development in the region through joint endeavour . . . ; to promote regional peace and stability . . . ; to promote active collaboration and mutual assistance . . . in the economic, social, cultural, technical, scientific and administrative fields; . . . to collaborate more effectively for the greater utilization of their agriculture and industries, the expansion of their trade . . . and the raising of the living standards of the peoples.

History. In July 1961, Malaysia, the Philippines, and Thailand established the Association of South-East Asia, an institution designed to promote cordial relations among the newly independent countries of the region. The group, however, was limited in purpose and proved ineffective.

ASEAN was created in 1967 to replace that association. The three founding members of the ASEAN were joined by Indonesia and Singapore. (Brunei joined the five in 1984, and Vietnam, Laos, Cambodia, and Myanmar joined in the 1990s.)

ASEAN lay dormant between 1967 and 1975. The fall of Saigon to North Vietnam in 1975 prompted the Bali Summit of February 1976 and marked the emergence of the entity as a functional institution. The Summit yielded the establishment of a modest but permanent ASEAN secretariat in Jakarta, the capital of Indonesia, and the signing of two key documents, the Treaty of Amity and Cooperation in Southeast Asia and the Declaration of ASEAN Concord.

The Treaty of Amity and Cooperation established the general principles for relations among ASEAN countries. It states the importance of strengthening the national security and resiliency of the ASEAN countries to preserve their respective national identities. The Treaty also includes a procedure for the settlement of disputes.

The Declaration of ASEAN Concord mandated the elevation of economic matters to the same status as political and social concerns and thus attempted to increase the economic role of ASEAN. It also called for meetings of economic ministers on a regular basis. Furthermore, the Summit document adopted an economic program that included cooperation on basic commodities such as food and energy, support for industrial projects in each of the ASEAN countries, and promotion of intra-ASEAN trade. In this regard, ASEAN introduced preferential trading arrangements (PTAs) to reduce tariffs on selected products of Member States. In January 1992, ASEAN members made significant progress by entering into a trade agreement that set a goal of gradually dismantling intra-regional trade barriers and forming an Asia Free Trade Area (AFTA) within 15 years.

Until 1997, ASEAN members averaged impressive annual growth rates. During the 1960s and 1970s, the average growth rates of these countries were among the highest in the world, substantially buttressed by the rapidly growing U.S. import market. The growth ebbed somewhat in the 1980s and varied among the members, but by 1996 the average growth rate had risen to 7 percent, with Vietnam leading the way with a growth rate of 9 percent. Besides increasing intra-ASEAN trade, ASEAN's primary trade policy goals were to maintain access to the U.S. market and to improve access to the Japanese market, both of which are vital to the economic well-being of the region.

To varying degrees, the ASEAN countries encountered serious economic problems in 1997-1998 with the Asian economic crisis. In 1998, in response to the crisis, ASEAN established an economic surveillance group to monitor economic and financial data within the bloc and exert peer pressure for corrective measures as necessary. Since 1999, the region has rebounded economically and accelerated its integration among its members and with Northeast Asia.

Although improving its members' economic well-being is a major goal, ASEAN has broader objectives as well. Some have compared it to the European Union at a much earlier stage of development. In addition to its economic programs, ASEAN has become an important entity where Asia-Pacific security is discussed. Moreover, in the mid-1990s, the ASEAN members cooperated on a variety of political and general welfare issues. The countries signed in 1995 a treaty declaring Southeast Asia a Nuclear Free Zone. Since 1997 the group has cooperated on a number of environmental issues to ensure sustainable development in the region. In 2001, ASEAN adopted a program to combat the spread of AIDS in the region.

The past several years has seen increased integration both within Southeast Asia and increasingly with China, Japan, and South Korea (known as ASEAN +3). Barriers to trade in the ASEAN Free Trade Area (AFTA) have come down ahead of schedule — the original six members plan to eliminate tariffs by 2010, eight years earlier than planned. Since the 1990s, ASEAN meetings have frequently included China, Japan, and Korea. Japan has long been ASEAN's largest external trade partner, and trade with Korea and China is increasing rapidly. Senior officials of ASEAN +3 countries meet several times a year to discuss a variety of economic and financial matters, and there is a strong force for expanding some parts of AFTA to include these three regional giants.

While internal integration appears to be proceeding remarkably well, especially considering the 1998 crisis, many challenges face ASEAN in its global role. The importance of the United States, at present still the Association's second-largest trading partner, is in question as regional trade begins to diminish the importance of American commerce. In addition, India and China, more competitive internationally as a result of internal reforms, may compete with Southeast Asia in attracting foreign investment and trade. Finally, ASEAN's relationship with other international institutions, particularly APEC (discussed below) needs to be developed further.

The ASEAN Web site is at <http://www.aseansec.org>.

e. Asia-Pacific Economic Cooperation (APEC)

The organization for Asia-Pacific Economic Cooperation, which convened for the first time in 1989, consists of 21 Pacific members — seven ASEAN members (Brunei, Indonesia, Malaysia, the Philippines, Singapore, Thailand and Vietnam), plus Australia, Canada, Chile, China, Hong Kong, Japan, Mexico, New Zealand, Papua New Guinea, Peru, Russia, South Korea, the United States, and Taiwan. These members account for about 57 percent of the world's gross domestic product, over 47 percent of all the world's trade, 40 percent of the world's population, and 48 percent of the earth's land area, thus giving them a substantial impact on the international arena.

APEC's stated goals are to fight global protectionism, increase regional economic cooperation, and preserve the world's liberal trading system. APEC conducts annual ministerial meetings, and working groups exist to try and develop solutions to the world's trade problems. These groups address issues such as energy, telecommunications, technology transfer, transportation, and investment. Between annual ministerial meetings in such areas as the environment, trade, and finance, a group of senior officials from each member meets to oversee the forum's programs.

At the December 1996 summit meeting in the Philippines, the United States and most of the other major APEC members agreed to eliminate tariffs on information technology equipment. Their agreement was then broadened to include other countries in the WTO to create a major International Technology Agreement (ITA) that removed among those countries all tariffs on computers, software, semiconductors, and telecommunications equipment by 2000. The ITA covers over $600 billion in world trade and benefits consumers and companies through lower prices on information technology products. Similarly, the 1998 Ministerial meeting in Malaysia proposed an Accelerated Tariff Liberalization (ATL) initiative, which would eliminate tariffs in eight sectors, including forest products, chemicals, and energy. ATL too was transferred to the WTO, where it could achieve a critical mass of participating economies. These experiences have led many to hope that APEC would be not only a force for liberalized trade in the region, but also a model for the rest of the world. APEC's Web site is <http://www.apec.sec.org.sg>.

f.   The Organization of American States (OAS)

The Organization of American States was envisioned to allow the countries of the Western Hemisphere collectively to pursue economic cooperation, human development, and hemispheric security. The OAS is considered a regional organization under Article 52 of the U.N. Charter. The OAS had 35 members as of January 2003. The essential purposes of the OAS are stated in the OAS Charter, which was signed in 1948 and came into force in 1951. Specifically, the entity exists

> to strengthen the peace and security of the continent; to . . . to insure the pacific settlement of disputes that may arise among the Member States; to provide for common action on the part of those States in the event of aggression; to seek the solution of political, juridical and economic problems that may arise among them; and to promote, by cooperative action, their economic, social and cultural development.

The OAS owes its formation largely to the cold war. The United States foresaw that a mutual defense pact embracing the United States and Latin American nations would contain Soviet expansionism. Furthermore, the United States predicted that a strong regional organization of the Western Hemisphere would act as an opposing force against the Soviet bloc in the United Nations and in other strategically relevant contexts.

Although the Latin American states were less worried about the Soviet threat, they welcomed the OAS Charter as a means to inhibit the interventionist impulses of their North American neighbor. Indeed, the United States has historically acted unilaterally in the Latin American region, due to perceived threats to national security interests and to feelings that Latin America was properly within the U.S. sphere of influence. The principle of non-intervention embodied in the Charter has consequently become the cardinal doctrine of Latin Americans in their dealings with the United States.

Human rights. One area in which the OAS has made some progress has been its effort to improve human rights within the region. In 1959, the OAS created the Inter-American Commission on Human Rights. In 1969, the OAS adopted the American Convention on Human Rights, which led to the establishment of the Inter-American Court of Human Rights. (See Chapter 8 at page 827.) During the Haitian crisis of the 1990s, discussed below, the OAS and the United Nations set up a joint observer mission in Haiti to monitor human rights abuses by the military government.

Hemispheric security. The OAS role in ensuring stability in the Americas has varied. The OAS played a major role in demonstrating hemispheric opposition to the location of Soviet missiles in Cuba in 1962. (See the discussion in Chapter 11.) It authorized a peacekeeping force (including U.S. troops) for the Dominican Republic after the United States intervened there in 1965, and provided a forum for debates over the U.S. intervention in Grenada in 1983. In May 1989 after sham elections and bloodshed in Panama, the OAS adopted a resolution calling on leader Manuel

Noriega to resign. Although the resolution demonstrated that Noriega was unpopular with more nations than just the United States, it had little immediate impact. Moreover, when the United States invaded Panama in December 1989, the OAS voted 20-1 to express "regret" over the intervention and urge the United States to withdraw. The vote had little practical effect.

OAS action concerning Haiti. The September 1991 coup in Haiti focused attention on the role of the OAS as a regional peacekeeper and negotiator. The OAS quickly denounced the military ouster of Jean-Bertrand Aristide, the democratically elected President, and followed the condemnation with a trade embargo in October 1991. The sanctions, combined with similar actions from the United Nations, appeared to bring a solution to the crisis in July 1993 when the Governors Island Agreement was signed between Aristide and the military leader. However, the military government later refused to comply with the plan to return Aristide to power.

The OAS and United States continued to call for greater sanctions. In June 1994, the OAS passed a resolution banning all commercial flights and financial transactions to and from Haiti. However, the problem for the OAS was ensuring compliance with its resolutions. In fact, the June resolution contained sanctions that the OAS had approved four previous times, but had been unable to enforce.

More recent activities. In recent years, the OAS has continued to send electoral observation missions to monitor elections, helping to ensure transparency and integrity in the voting process. Special OAS missions have also worked to support the peace process in various local disputes and the OAS has taken a leading role in an effort to remove thousands of land mines in Central America. The OAS carries out technical cooperation programs to promote sustainable development and particular needs such as river basin management and natural disaster mitigation. The OAS has also adopted conventions against corruption, illegal arms trafficking, and violence against women.

The OAS Web site is located at <http://www.oas.org>.

g. The African Union (AU)

The African Union came into operation in July 2002, in Durban, South Africa, replacing the discredited Organization of African Union (OAU). The OAU was seen in much of Africa as a "President's Trade Union," with little relevance to most Africans in a continent where many of its presidents ruled dictatorially.

The OAU, although a peacekeeping and unifying force, lacked disciplinary powers. Indeed, the only power implicit in the system was that of the opinion of Member States, a power that could conceivably influence compliance.

The OAU Charter emerged as a compromise between two factions. The radicals, who desired a unified Africa with a powerful, continent-wide organization, obtained agreement on an all-Africa organization. The moderates, however who opposed any surrender of sovereignty, ensured that the Charter gave scant powers to the new organization; thus, although an instrument of unity, the Charter sanctified each state's individuality.

Although the OAU had helped promote African unity at various conferences and on some issues, its peacekeeping record was mixed at best. For instance, the OAU helped calm a 1963 border dispute between Algeria and Morocco. On the other hand, it has frequently taken no action in the face of aggression (Libya-Chad) and genocide (Burundi, Rwanda, Uganda). Further, the OAU has been very reluctant to condemn undemocratic actions by the leaders of its member states.

The Constitutive Act of the African Union is intended to restore the credibility that the OAU lacked. Article 4(h) gives the Union the right to intervene in a member state in cases of war crimes, genocide, and crimes against humanity. It also stresses the importance of human rights and democratic principles, and includes peer review mechanisms that require adherence to principles of good governance and transparency to participate in the benefits of the Union.

At the suggestion of Colonel Qadaffi, the heads of state of Africa met in Sirte, Libya in 1999, where they called for the establishment of an African Union. The Constitutive Act was completed in July 2000. As of October 2002, all 53 member states of the OAU had signed it and 51 had ratified it. It remains to be seen whether the AU will avoid the pitfalls of its predecessor, and even if it does, whether it will be the powerful unifying force or force for democracy that some hope it will. The Web site of the African Union is at <http://www.africa-union.org>.

Although most of the major international and regional organizations are discussed above, there are many others covering a wide range. These others will be noted as they appear elsewhere in the text.

Questions

1. What are the relative advantages of regional versus international organizations? Do they depend on the entity's objectives?

2. For international or regional organizations, is there a greater chance of success if the objectives are kept narrow or specialized — for example, military security, economic growth, or protection of the environment? Or, again, does it depend on what objectives are being sought?

3. Which international organization or organizations seem to have been the most successful? Which the least successful? Can we draw some lessons for the future from their experience?

4. Similarly, which regional organization or organizations seem to have been the most successful? Which the least successful? Are there lessons that we can draw from their experience?

5. Are there any compelling problems that present international and regional organizations should become active in tackling? Which organization? And are there any compelling problems that could better be handled by a new organization?

6

Foreign Sovereign Immunity and the Act of State Doctrine

This chapter explores two especially significant consequences of statehood. They are the rules in international and domestic law regarding (a) the immunity of a state from the jurisdiction of the domestic courts of another state (called foreign sovereign immunity) and (b) the legal effect of certain acts of a foreign state (called the act of state doctrine). These rules exist to varying degrees in many countries, although we will study them primarily from a U.S. perspective.

In the section on foreign sovereign immunity, we address briefly the related issues of the legal status of embassies and consulates. We also discuss personal immunity for diplomats and consuls and for present and former heads of state.

A. THE IMMUNITY OF FOREIGN STATES

Under both international and domestic law a state is immune in many situations from the jurisdiction of foreign courts. The immunity of foreign states was particularly broad throughout the world until the twentieth century, and then it began to erode in various states. The United States was slow to adjust, generally adhering to the broader, or "absolute," theory of immunity until 1952. Now existing in the United States, and generally elsewhere, is a limited scope for state immunity, often termed the "restrictive" theory.

1. Absolute Immunity

Joseph M. Sweeney, The International Law of Sovereign Immunity

20-21 (U.S. Dept. of State Publication (1963))

Until about 1900, the immunity of a state from the judicial process of another — or immunity from jurisdiction as it is frequently called for convenience — was broad, but not without limitations. It was not granted when the litigation involved ownership or other interests in immovables in the territory or when it involved an interest in an estate locally administered. Even though these limitations were well recognized, the immunity was usually stated in terms giving it an absolute character.

In Spanish Government v. Lambège et Pujol, decided in 1849, the Supreme Court of France stated the rule thus:

> The reciprocal independence of states is one of the most universally respected principles of international law, and it follows as a result therefrom that a government cannot be subjected to the jurisdiction of another against its will, and that the right of jurisdiction of one government over litigation arising from its own acts is a right inherent to its sovereignty that another government cannot seize without impairing their mutual relations. [1849] D, 1, 5, 9.

The British courts expressed the rule in equally broad terms. In The Parlement Belge, decided in 1880, the court stated:

> As a consequence of the absolute independence of every sovereign authority, and of the international comity which induces every sovereign state to respect the independence and dignity of every other sovereign state, each and every one declines to exercise by means of its courts any of its territorial jurisdiction over the person of any sovereign. . . . (1880) 5 P.D. 197, 217.

About 1900, a judicial practice developed in some states of denying immunity from jurisdiction to a foreign state when it was made a respondent with respect to an act of a commercial or so-called private nature. The courts involved reasoned that the traditional rule of immunity from jurisdiction covered only litigation arising from public acts of a foreign state and did not extend to litigation arising from other types of acts. The courts of other states did not draw this distinction and extended immunity from jurisdiction to a foreign state irrespective of the nature of the act involved.

In Société Anonyme des Chemins de Fer Liègeois Luxembourgeois v. the Netherlands, decided in 1903, the Supreme Court of Belgium stated the distinction between public and commercial or private acts as follows:

> Sovereignty is involved only when political acts are accomplished by the state. . . . However, the state is not bound to confine itself to a political role, and can, for the needs of the collectivity, buy, own, contract, become creditor or debtor, and engage in commerce. . . . In the discharge of these functions, the state is not acting as public power, but does what private persons do, and as such, is acting in a civil and private capacity. When after bargaining on a footing of equality with a person or incurring a responsibility in no way connected with the political order, the state is drawn in litigation, the litigation concerns a civil right, within the sole jurisdiction of the courts, . . . and the foreign state as civil person is like any other foreign person amenable to the Belgian courts. [1903] Pas. 1, 294, 301.

. . . Thus two concepts of sovereign immunity from jurisdiction came to coexist by the late 1930's: the one termed "absolute" because of its broader scope, and the other termed "restrictive" because of its narrower scope. . . .

Until 1952, the U.S. Executive Branch and courts generally accepted the absolute theory of immunity. The seminal case was The Schooner Exchange v. M'Faddon, 11 U.S. (7 Cranch) 116 (1812). There, the question was whether U.S.

citizens could lay claim to a French warship that had been seized in U.S. waters. The citizens claimed that they had earlier been the owners of the ship when it had been seized on the high seas by the French and that they were entitled to have the vessel restored to them through a proceeding in admiralty.

The Supreme Court unanimously decided that the French government should be immune from the jurisdiction of U.S. courts and should therefore be able to retain the vessel. Justice Marshall presumed a "perfect equality and absolute independence of sovereigns, and [a] common interest impelling them to mutual intercourse, and an interchange of good offices with each other." Id. at 136. He further noted that

> the Exchange being a public armed ship, in the service of a foreign sovereign, with whom the government of the United States is at peace, and having entered an American port open for her reception, on the terms on which ships of war are generally permitted to enter the ports of a friendly power, must be considered as having come into the American territory, under an implied promise, that . . . she should be exempt from the jurisdiction of that country. [Id. at 147.]

In the twentieth century, the absolute theory came under some attack in the lower court proceedings in Berizzi Bros. Co. v. The Pesaro, 271 U.S. 562 (1926). The Pesaro was a merchant ship owned and operated by the Italian government and was used to carry merchandise for hire. While so employed, the vessel allegedly failed to deliver artificial silk picked up at a port in Italy for delivery to New York. A "libel in rem" proceeding in admiralty was begun in the U.S. courts for damages for the failure to deliver.

The Italian government asked the U.S. Department of State to intercede in the suit to get it dismissed. The U.S. response was "The Department is of the opinion that vessels owned by a state and engaged in commerce are not entitled . . . to the immunity accorded vessels of war." (2 Hackworth, Digest of International Law 437 (1941).) A U.S. district court then denied immunity, relying in part on the Department of State's position. The Pesaro, 277 F. 473, 479-480 n.3 (S.D.N.Y. 1921). However, this decision was vacated because of a Supreme Court decision in an unrelated case dealing with the procedures for claiming immunity. Another U.S. district court judge then granted immunity to the ship.

The Supreme Court unanimously affirmed the grant of immunity. After quoting extensively from its opinion in *The Schooner Exchange,* the Court stated:

> We think the principles [for immunity enunciated in *The Schooner Exchange*] are applicable alike to all ships held and used by a government for a public purpose, and that when, for the purpose of advancing the trade of its people or providing revenue for its treasury, a government acquires, mans and operates ships in the carrying trade, they are public ships in the same sense that war ships are. We know of no international usage which regards the maintenance and advancement of the economic welfare of a people in time of peace as any less a public purpose than the maintenance and training of a naval force. [Berizzi Bros. Co. v. The Pesaro, 271 U.S. at 574.]

As the *Pesaro* litigation illustrates, although courts sometimes considered the views of the Executive Branch in making sovereign immunity determinations, they did not feel obligated to accept those views. They deferred to the Executive Branch's decisions as to which governments should be recognized, but they felt free to make their own determinations regarding sovereign immunity. This changed starting in the late 1930s. In Compania Espanola de Navegacion Maritima, S.A. v. The Navemar,

303 U.S. 68, 74 (1938), the Supreme Court stated for the first time that Executive Branch suggestions of immunity were binding on the courts. Subsequently, in Ex parte Peru, 318 U.S. 578 (1943), and Mexico v. Hoffman, 324 U.S. 30 (1945), the Court made clear that, if the Executive Branch expressed its views regarding whether immunity should be granted, courts were bound to accept those views. Thus, the Court stated in *Hoffman* that "[i]t is therefore not for the courts to deny an immunity which our government has seen fit to allow, or to allow an immunity on new grounds which the government has not seen fit to recognize." Id. at 35. Under this regime, "if the Executive announced a national policy in regard to immunity generally, or for the particular case, that policy was law for the courts and binding upon them, regardless of what international law might say about it." Louis Henkin, Foreign Affairs and the United States Constitution 56 (2d ed. 1996); see also id. at 351 n.68 (noting that the Court "was apparently giving effect not to Executive views of international law but to 'national policy' on immunity even if it was contrary to, or not based on or related to, international law").

2. *Restrictive Immunity*

A number of states had begun to shift toward restrictive immunity in the period prior to World War II, as noted earlier. Thus, the United States increasingly found itself subject to the restrictive theory of immunity in foreign courts, even though U.S. courts would grant absolute immunity to these same foreign nations. In addition, as an increasing number of nations engaged in international commerce through state-controlled enterprises, the absolute theory of immunity was perceived as undermining U.S. business interests. In response to these developments, the State Department began negotiating bilateral treaties requiring nations to waive sovereign immunity for state-controlled enterprises engaged in business activities within the territory of the other party. Between 1948 and 1958, the Department of State negotiated 14 such treaties.

Absolute immunity also was perceived as inconsistent with limitations that had been imposed by Congress on the U.S. government's immunity from suit in its own courts. These statutes included the 1887 Tucker Act, which gave the Court of Claims (now the United States Claims Court) jurisdiction over a variety of contract and other commercial claims against the U.S. government, and the 1946 Federal Tort Claims Act, which allowed the federal courts to hear certain suits against the U.S. government for common law torts committed by its employees.

The Department of State reexamined its policy toward foreign sovereign immunity in 1952. The importance of this rethinking reflected the State Department's major role since World War II in determining whether a foreign country should receive immunity. The result was the well-known "Tate Letter" by the acting Legal Adviser, Jack B. Tate. He set forth the Department's position in future cases.

May 19, 1952

My Dear Mr. Attorney General:

The Department of State has for some time had under consideration the question whether the practice of the Government in granting immunity from suit to foreign governments made parties defendant in the courts of the United States without their consent should not be changed. The Department has now reached the conclusion that such immunity should no longer be granted in certain types of cases. In view of the obvious interest of your Department in this matter I should like to point out briefly some of the facts which influenced the Department's decision.

A study of the law of sovereign immunity reveals the existence of two conflicting concepts of sovereign immunity, each widely held and firmly established. According to the classical or absolute theory of sovereign immunity, a sovereign cannot, without his consent, be made a respondent in the courts of another sovereign. According to the newer or restrictive theory of sovereign immunity, the immunity of the sovereign is recognized with regard to sovereign or public acts (*jure imperii*) of a state, but not with respect to private acts (*jure gestionis*). There is agreement by proponents of both theories, supported by practice, that sovereign immunity should not be claimed or granted in actions with respect to real property (diplomatic and perhaps consular property excepted) or with respect to the disposition of the property of a deceased person even though a foreign sovereign is the beneficiary.

The classical or virtually absolute theory of sovereign immunity has generally been followed by the courts of the United States, the British Commonwealth, Czechoslovakia, Estonia, and probably Poland.

The decisions of the courts of Brazil, Chile, China, Hungary, Japan, Luxembourg, Norway, and Portugal may be deemed to support the classical theory of immunity if one or at most two old decisions anterior to the development of the restrictive theory may be considered sufficient on which to base a conclusion.

The position of the Netherlands, Sweden, and Argentina is less clear since although immunity has been granted in recent cases coming before the courts of those countries, the facts were such that immunity would have been granted under either the absolute or restrictive theory. However, constant references by the courts of these three countries to the distinction between public and private acts of the state, even though the distinction was not involved in the result of the case, may indicate an intention to leave the way open for a possible application of the restrictive theory of immunity if and when the occasion presents itself.

A trend to the restrictive theory is already evident in the Netherlands where the lower courts have started to apply that theory following a Supreme Court decision to the effect that immunity would have been applicable in the case under consideration under either theory.

The German courts, after a period of hesitation at the end of the nineteenth century have held to the classical theory, but it should be noted that the refusal of the Supreme Court in 1921 to yield to pressure by the lower courts for the newer theory was based on the view that that theory had not yet developed sufficiently to justify a change. In view of the growth of the restrictive theory since that time the German courts might take a different view today.

The newer or restrictive theory of sovereign immunity has always been supported by the courts of Belgium and Italy. It was adopted in turn by the courts of Egypt and of Switzerland. In addition, the courts of France, Austria, and Greece, which were traditionally supporters of the classical theory, reversed their position in the 20's to embrace the restrictive theory. Rumania, Peru, and possibly Denmark also appear to follow this theory.

Furthermore, it should be observed that in most of the countries still following the classical theory there is a school of influential writers favoring the restrictive theory and the views of writers, at least in civil law countries, are a major factor in the development of the law. Moreover, the leanings of the lower courts in civil law countries are more significant in shaping the law than they are in common law countries where the rule of precedent prevails and the trend in these lower courts is to the restrictive theory.

Of related interest to this question is the fact that ten of the thirteen countries which have been classified above as supporters of the classical theory have ratified the Brussels Convention of 1926 under which immunity for government owned merchant vessels is waived. In addition the United States, which is not a party to the Convention, some years ago announced and has since followed, a policy of not claiming immunity for its public owned or operated merchant vessels. Keeping in mind the importance played by cases involving public vessels in the field of sovereign immunity, it is thus noteworthy that these ten countries (Brazil, Chile, Estonia, Germany, Hungary, Netherlands, Norway, Poland, Portugal, Sweden) and the United States have already relinquished by treaty or in practice an important part of the immunity which they claim under the classical theory.

It is thus evident that with the possible exception of the United Kingdom little support has been found except on the part of the Soviet Union and its satellites for continued full acceptance of the absolute theory of sovereign immunity. There are evidences that British authorities are aware of its deficiencies and ready for a change. The reasons which obviously motivate state trading countries in adhering to the theory with perhaps increasing rigidity are most persuasive that the United States should change its policy. Furthermore, the granting of sovereign immunity to foreign governments in the courts of the United States is most inconsistent with the action of the Government of the United States in subjecting itself to suit in these same courts in both contract and tort and with its long established policy of not claiming immunity in foreign jurisdictions for its merchant vessels. Finally, the Department feels that the widespread and increasing practice on the part of governments of engaging in commercial activities makes necessary a practice which will enable persons doing business with them to have their rights determined in the courts. For these reasons it will hereafter be the Department's policy to follow the restrictive theory of sovereign immunity in the consideration of requests of foreign governments for a grant of sovereign immunity.

It is realized that a shift in policy by the executive cannot control the courts but it is felt that the courts are less likely to allow a plea of sovereign immunity where the executive has declined to do so. There have been indications that at least some Justices of the Supreme Court feel that in this matter courts should follow the branch of the Government charged with responsibility for the conduct of foreign relations.

In order that your Department, which is charged with representing the interests of the Government before the courts, may be adequately informed it will be the Department's practice to advise you of all requests by foreign governments for the grant of immunity from suit and of the Department's action thereon.

Sincerely yours,

For the Secretary of State:
Jack B. Tate
Acting Legal Adviser

Notes and Questions

1. What explains the worldwide shift toward the restrictive theory of immunity in the early to mid-twentieth century? Was the United States advantaged or disadvantaged by adhering to the absolute theory of immunity until 1952?

2. What seemed to be the principal reasons leading to the shift in the U.S. position to the restrictive theory? Was it just that most other countries adhered to that position? Or did it have practical implications, notably the exposure of the United States in foreign courts versus the exposure of other states in U.S. courts?

3. What states would have benefited most if the United States had continued its policy of absolute immunity? Those states with large private sectors or those states with state trading companies and socialist economies? Do you think it was relevant that the Cold War was at its height in 1952, with the Soviet Union having installed friendly governments in Eastern Europe and U.S. troops fighting in Korea?

4. The status of customary international law in the U.S. legal system is considered in Chapter 3. Like other aspects of customary international law, U.S. courts in the nineteenth and early twentieth centuries treated the law of foreign sovereign immunity as "general common law" rather than as federal law. Both federal and state courts felt free to apply this law even in the absence of political branch authorization. But federal court interpretations of this law were not viewed as binding on the state courts. Nor did state court interpretations of this law raise federal questions for purposes of Supreme Court review of state court decisions. See Wulfsohn v. Russian Socialist Federated Republic, 266 U.S. 580, 580 (1924); Oliver American Trading Co. v. Mexico, 264 U.S. 440, 442-443 (1924); New York Life Ins. Co. v. Hendren, 92 U.S. 286, 286-287 (1875). See also Julian G. Ku, Customary International Law in State Courts, 42 Va. J. Intl. L. 265 (2001) (describing state court applications of customary international law during the nineteenth and early twentieth centuries).

With this history in mind, what explains the Supreme Court's shift, evident in decisions such as *Peru* and *Hoffman*, toward giving the Executive Branch absolute deference on sovereign immunity issues? Did this shift mean that the Court was no longer applying customary international law regarding foreign sovereign immunity? Is it a coincidence that the Court's first suggestion of absolute deference — in the 1938 *Navemar* decision mentioned above — came the same year as Erie Railroad v. Tompkins, which held that federal courts could no longer apply general common law? For a discussion of this point, see Curtis A. Bradley & Jack L. Goldsmith, *Pinochet* and International Human Rights Litigation, 97 Mich. L. Rev. 2129, 2161-2165 (1999). Might the Court's increased deference toward the Executive Branch also be related to the period of emergency brought on by World War II?

5. When the Executive Branch is allowed to determine foreign sovereign immunity for the courts, is it engaged in law-making? Adjudicating? If it is engaged in either law-making or adjudicating, does this law-making or adjudication violate the separation of powers structure of the Constitution, which assigns legislative power to Congress and adjudicatory power to the federal courts? Or does deference to the Executive Branch actually follow from the Constitution's division of authority? What, if anything, does this deference suggest about the status of customary international law in U.S. courts? For discussion of these questions, see Curtis A. Bradley, *Chevron* Deference and Foreign Affairs, 86 Va. L. Rev. 649, 709-713 (2000). For discussions of the propriety of this deference, compare Philip C. Jessup, Has the

Supreme Court Abdicated One of Its Functions?, 40 Am. J. Intl. L. 168 (1946) (criticizing it), with Michael H. Cardozo, Judicial Deference to State Department Suggestions: Recognition of Prerogative or Abdication to Usurper?, 48 Cornell L.Q. 461 (1963) (defending it).

For a few years after the Tate Letter, the State Department usually made decisions on sovereign immunity claims by a foreign state on the basis of the foreign government's submission. Criticism of this procedure, however, led the Department's Office of Legal Adviser to conduct quasi-judicial hearings on whether a particular claim of immunity was within the Tate Letter's criteria. Here is a summary of the procedures by which a foreign state would present its claim of immunity to the State Department:

> The state's ambassador would address a note to the Secretary of State or State Department, setting forth the name of the case and the extent of immunity requested. Usually the note was accompanied by a memorandum of facts and supporting argument. The State Department then notified the plaintiff of the request and sent him a copy of the foreign state's memorandum. The plaintiff was permitted to make a written submission of his own. On the request of either party, an informal public hearing was held, usually lasting no more than two hours, before a panel composed of the Legal Adviser or Deputy Legal Adviser and two Assistant Legal Advisers. At the hearing, only oral presentations by the parties' representatives were permitted; no witness testimony was allowed. Some time after the hearing, the Legal Adviser made a decision and sent it to the parties. If the decision was to recognize and allow the claim to immunity, the substance of the decision was relayed to the Attorney General with a request that he order the United States attorney for the district in which the action was filed to submit a suggestion of immunity to the court. There was no appeal from the decision of the Legal Adviser. Often no statement of reasons accompanied the decision. [Frederic Alan Weber, The Foreign Sovereign Immunities Act of 1976: Its Origins, Meaning, and Effect, 3 Yale J. World Pub. Order 1, 12-13 (1976).]

This regime, under which the State Department made some immunity determinations and the courts made others, did not always produce consistent decisions. A pair of Second Circuit cases, Victory Transport, Inc. v. Comisaria General de Abastecimientos y Transportes, 336 F.2d 354 (2d Cir. 1964), and Isbrandtsen Tankers v. President of India, 446 F.2d 1198 (2d Cir. 1971), illustrates this point. In *Victory Transport,* a shipowner sued a department of the Spanish government for damages sustained in connection with the department's charter of the ship to transport wheat to Spain. Because the State Department did not take a position in the case, the court made its own determination of whether immunity was warranted. After considering the purposes of the restrictive theory of immunity, international practice, and past State Department positions, the court concluded that the governmental actions in question were properly considered private and commercial and thus not entitled to immunity.

By contrast, in *Isbrandtsen Tankers,* the Second Circuit granted immunity in a similar situation. There, a shipowner sued the Indian government for damages associated with the government's detention of vessels being used to ship grain to India. The key difference from *Victory Transport* was that here the State Department submitted a suggestion of immunity. The court noted that, if it proceeded to make its own determination of immunity, "we might well find that the actions of the Indian government were, as appellant contends, purely private commercial decisions." Id. at 1200. Instead, it accepted the State Department's suggestion, stating that "once the State Department has ruled in a matter of this nature, the judiciary will not interfere." Id. at 1201. The court reached this conclusion even though the Indian government had arguably waived its immunity in its transportation contract with the shipowner. The court stated that "[t]he potential harm or embarrassment resulting to our government from a judicial finding of jurisdiction, in the face of an Executive recommendation to the contrary, may be just as severe where the foreign sovereign had initially contracted to waive its claim of sovereign immunity as where it had not done so." Id.

Unhappiness with the process for deciding immunity under the Tate Letter and a desire for greater predictability led private lawyers, scholars, and the Department of State to push for legislation establishing more precise criteria. Some of the reasons are set out in the following testimony by the Legal Adviser.

Testimony of the Legal Adviser of the U.S. Department of State on the Foreign Sovereign Immunities Act of 1976

Hearings on H.R. 11315, 94th Cong., 2d Sess. 24, 26-27 (1976)

[Monroe Leigh:]

The Tate letter was based on a realization that the prior absolute rule of sovereign immunity was no longer consistent with modern international law.

The Tate letter, however, has not been a satisfactory answer. From a legal standpoint, it poses a devil's choice. If the Department follows the Tate letter in a given case, it is in the incongruous position of a political institution trying to apply a legal standard to litigation already before the courts.

On the other hand, if forced to disregard the Tate letter in a given case, the Department is in the self-defeating position of abandoning the very international law principle it elsewhere espouses.

From a diplomatic standpoint, the Tate letter has continued to leave the diplomatic initiative to the foreign state. The foreign state chooses which case it will bring to the State Department and in which case it will try to raise diplomatic considerations.

Leaving the diplomatic initiative in such cases to the foreign state places the United States at a disadvantage. This is particularly true since the United States cannot itself obtain similar advantages in other countries. In virtually every other country in the world, sovereign immunity is a question of international law decided exclusively by the courts and not by institutions concerned with foreign affairs.

For this reason, when we and other foreign states are sued abroad, we realize that international law principles will be applied by the courts and that diplomatic relations will not be called into play.

Moreover, from the standpoint of the private citizen, the current system generates considerable commercial uncertainty. A private party who deals with a foreign government entity cannot be certain of having his day in court to resolve an ordinary legal dispute. He cannot be entirely certain that the ordinary legal dispute will not be artificially raised to the level of a diplomatic problem through the government's intercession with the State Department.

The purpose of sovereign immunity in modern international law is not to protect the sensitivities of 19th-century monarchs or the prerogatives of the 20th-century state. Rather, it is to promote the functioning of all governments by protecting a state from the burden of defending law suits abroad which are based on its public acts.

However, when the foreign state enters the marketplace or when it acts as a private party, there is no justification in modern international law for allowing the foreign state to avoid the economic costs of the agreements which it may breach or the accidents which it may cause.

The law should not permit the foreign state to shift these everyday burdens of the marketplace onto the shoulders of private parties.

Notes and Questions

1. What were the drawbacks to the Tate Letter regime for determining foreign sovereign immunity? That the Executive Branch was exercising a judicial function? That the Executive Branch was being too political? The lack of concrete standards? The lack of adequate procedures? All of the above? What were the advantages of addressing foreign sovereign immunity in the case-by-case, Executive Branch-dominated process of the Tate Letter regime? Keep these questions in mind when we consider head-of-state immunity, which is still treated to some extent the way that foreign sovereign immunity in general was treated under the Tate Letter regime.

2. As indicated in the testimony excerpted above, the U.S. Legal Adviser supported the then-proposed Foreign Sovereign Immunities Act. Since his office usually had the day-to-day responsibility then for deciding whether to recommend to courts that a foreign state or its agencies be granted immunity, the Legal Adviser was effectively giving up considerable power. Does this suggest that the problems the Legal Adviser mentioned in his testimony had become truly vexing ones?

3. For additional discussion of the history of foreign sovereign immunity in the United States, see, for example, Gary B. Born, International Civil Litigation in United States Courts 199-210 (3d ed. 1996).

3. The Foreign Sovereign Immunities Act: An Overview

In 1976, after years of discussion and debate, Congress enacted the Foreign Sovereign Immunities Act (FSIA), the current text of which is in the Documentary Supplement. The House Report on the bill that became the FSIA states that the bill "would codify the so-called 'restrictive' principle of sovereign immunity, as presently recognized in international law." It also states that the bill was designed "to transfer the determination of sovereign immunity from the executive branch to the judicial branch, thereby reducing the foreign policy implications of immunity determinations and assuring litigants that these often crucial decisions are made on purely legal grounds and under procedures that insure due process."

Under the FSIA, issues of personal jurisdiction, subject matter jurisdiction, and immunity from suit are intertwined. If proper service is made on a foreign state defendant, personal jurisdiction exists with respect to any claim for which there is federal subject matter jurisdiction. Federal subject matter jurisdiction exists "as to any claim for relief in personam with respect to which the foreign state is not entitled to immunity." 28 U.S.C. §1330(a). And the FSIA in turn specifies various exceptions to sovereign immunity. Under this structure, a court must determine whether the foreign state defendant is immune from suit in order to determine whether the court has personal and subject matter jurisdiction. If the court finds that the defendant is immune, the court lacks personal and subject matter jurisdiction. Conversely, if the court finds that there is an exception to immunity, and that proper service has been made, the court automatically has personal and subject matter jurisdiction (assuming no violation of due process requirements). See generally Working Group of the American Bar Association, Reforming the Foreign Sovereign Immunities Act, 40 Colum. J. Transnatl. L. 489, 500-506 (2002) (discussing the FSIA's structure).

In the following decision, the Supreme Court considered the structure of the FSIA in addressing a constitutional challenge to the statute.

Verlinden B.V. v. Central Bank of Nigeria

U.S. Supreme Court
461 U.S. 480 (1983)

[In 1975, Verlinden, B.V., a Dutch corporation, entered into a contract with the Federal Republic of Nigeria to provide it with 240,000 metric tons of cement. The parties agreed that the contract would be governed by Dutch law and that disputes would be resolved by arbitration under the auspices of the International Chamber of Commerce in Paris. Under the contract, the Nigerian government was obligated to establish an irrevocable, confirmed letter of credit through a bank in Amsterdam. Instead, the government's instrumentality, the Central Bank of Nigeria, established an unconfirmed letter of credit through a bank in New York.

Meanwhile, the ports of Nigeria became clogged with hundreds of ships carrying cement, sent by numerous other cement suppliers with whom Nigeria also had entered into contracts. Central Bank then unilaterally directed its correspondent banks, including the New York bank, to adopt a series of amendments to all letters of credit issued in connection with the cement contracts. Central Bank also directly notified the suppliers that payment would be made only for those shipments approved by Central Bank two months before their arrival in Nigerian waters.

Verlinden subsequently sued Central Bank in the U.S. District Court for the Southern District of New York, alleging that Central Bank's actions constituted an anticipatory breach of the letter of credit. Verlinden alleged jurisdiction under the Foreign Sovereign Immunities Act. The bank moved to dismiss for, among other reasons, lack of subject-matter and personal jurisdiction. The district court dismissed the complaint, finding no applicable exception to immunity. The court of appeals affirmed, holding that the FSIA exceeded the scope of federal court jurisdiction allowed under Article III of the Constitution.]

Chief Justice BURGER delivered the opinion of the [unanimous] Court. . . .

II

For more than a century and a half, the United States generally granted foreign sovereigns complete immunity from suit in the courts of this country. . . .

As [The Schooner Exchange v. M'Faddon, 7 Cranch 116 (1812)] made clear, however, foreign sovereign immunity is a matter of grace and comity on the part of the United States, and not a restriction imposed by the Constitution. . . .

In 1976, Congress passed the Foreign Sovereign Immunities Act in order to free the Government from the case-by-case diplomatic pressures, to clarify the governing standards, and to "assur[e] litigants that . . . decisions are made on purely legal grounds and under procedures that insure due process," H.R. Rep. No. 94-1487, p.7 (1976). To accomplish these objectives, the Act contains a comprehensive set of legal standards governing claims of immunity in every civil action against a foreign state or its political subdivisions, agencies, or instrumentalities.

For the most part, the Act codifies, as a matter of federal law, the restrictive theory of sovereign immunity. A foreign state is normally immune from the jurisdiction of federal and state courts, 28 U.S.C. §1604, subject to a set of exceptions specified in §§1605 and 1607. Those exceptions include actions in which the foreign state has explicitly or impliedly waived its immunity, §1605(a)(1), and actions based upon commercial activities of the foreign sovereign carried on in the United States or causing a direct effect in the United States, §1605(a)(2).[11] When one of these or the other specified exceptions applies, "the foreign state shall be liable in the same manner and to the same extent as a private individual under like circumstances," §1606.[12]

The Act expressly provides that its standards control in "the courts of the United States and of the States," §1604, and thus clearly contemplates that such suits may be brought in either federal or state courts. However, "[i]n view of the potential sensitivity of actions against foreign states and the importance of developing a uniform body of law in this area," H.R. Rep. No. 94-1487, supra, at 32, the Act guarantees foreign states the right to remove any civil action from a state court to a federal court, §1441(d). The Act also provides that any claim permitted under the Act may be brought from the outset in federal court, §1330(a).[13] If one of the specified exceptions to sovereign immunity applies, a federal district court may exercise subject-matter jurisdiction under §1330(a); but if the claim does not fall within one of the exceptions, federal courts lack subject-matter jurisdiction.[14] In such a case, the foreign state is also ensured immunity from the jurisdiction of state courts by §1604.

---

11. The Act also contains exceptions for certain actions "in which rights in property taken in violation of international law are in issue," §1605(a)(3); actions involving rights in real estate and in inherited and gift property located in the United States, §1605(a)(4); actions for certain noncommercial torts within the United States, §1605(a)(5); certain actions involving maritime liens, §1605(b); and certain counterclaims, §1607.

12. Section 1606 somewhat modifies this standard of liability with respect to punitive damages and wrongful death actions.

13. "[T]o encourage the bringing of actions against foreign states in Federal courts," H.R. Rep. No. 94-1487, p.13 (1976), the Act specifies that federal district courts shall have original jurisdiction "without regard to amount in controversy." §1330(a).

14. In such a situation, the federal court will also lack personal jurisdiction.

III

The District Court and the Court of Appeals both held that the Foreign Sovereign Immunities Act purports to allow a foreign plaintiff to sue a foreign sovereign in the courts of the United States, provided the substantive requirements of the Act are satisfied. We agree.

On its face, the language of the statute is unambiguous. The statute grants jurisdiction over "any nonjury civil action against a foreign state . . . with respect to which the foreign state is not entitled to immunity," 28 U.S.C. §1330(a). The Act contains no indication of any limitation based on the citizenship of the plaintiff.

The legislative history is less clear in this regard. The House Report recites that the Act would provide jurisdiction for *"any* claim with respect to which the foreign state is not entitled to immunity under sections 1605-1607," H.R. Rep. No. 94-1487, supra, at 13 (emphasis added), and also states that its purpose was "to provide when and how *parties* can maintain a lawsuit against a foreign state or its entities," id., at 6 (emphasis added). At another point, however, the Report refers to the growing number of disputes between "American citizens" and foreign states, id., at 6-7, and expresses the desire to ensure *"our citizens* . . . access to the courts," id., at 6 (emphasis added).

Notwithstanding this reference to "our citizens," we conclude that, when considered as a whole, the legislative history reveals an intent not to limit jurisdiction under the Act to actions brought by American citizens. Congress was aware of concern that "our courts [might be] turned into small 'international courts of claims[,]' . . . open . . . to all comers to litigate any dispute which any private party may have with a foreign state anywhere in the world." Testimony of Bruno A. Ristau, Hearings on H.R. 11315, at 31. As the language of the statute reveals, Congress protected against this danger not by restricting the class of potential plaintiffs, but rather by enacting substantive provisions requiring some form of substantial contact with the United States. See 28 U.S.C. §1605.[15] If an action satisfies the substantive standards of the Act, it may be brought in federal court regardless of the citizenship of the plaintiff.[16]

IV

We now turn to the core question presented by this case: whether Congress exceeded the scope of Art. III of the Constitution by granting federal courts subject-matter jurisdiction over certain civil actions by foreign plaintiffs against foreign sovereigns where the rule of decision may be provided by state law.

---

15. Section 1605(a)(1), which provides that sovereign immunity shall not apply if waived, may be seen as an exception to the normal pattern of the Act, which generally requires some form of contact with the United States. We need not decide whether, by waiving its immunity, a foreign state could consent to suit based on activities wholly unrelated to the United States. The Act does not appear to affect the traditional doctrine of forum non conveniens.

16. Prior to passage of the Foreign Sovereign Immunities Act, which Congress clearly intended to govern all actions against foreign sovereigns, state courts on occasion had exercised jurisdiction over suits between foreign plaintiffs and foreign sovereigns. . . . Congress did not prohibit such actions when it enacted the Foreign Sovereign Immunities Act, but sought to ensure that any action that might be brought against a foreign sovereign in state court could also be brought in or removed to federal court.

This Court's cases firmly establish that Congress may not expand the jurisdiction of the federal courts beyond the bounds established by the Constitution. Within Art. III of the Constitution, we find two sources authorizing the grant of jurisdiction in the Foreign Sovereign Immunities Act: the Diversity Clause and the "Arising Under" Clause. The Diversity Clause, which provides that the judicial power extends to controversies between "a State, or the Citizens thereof, and foreign States," covers actions by citizens of States. Yet diversity jurisdiction is not sufficiently broad to support a grant of jurisdiction over actions by foreign plaintiffs, since a foreign plaintiff is not "a State, or [a] [Citizen] thereof." See Mossman v. Higginson, 4 Dall. 12 (1800). We conclude, however, that the "Arising Under" Clause of Art. III provides an appropriate basis for the statutory grant of subject-matter jurisdiction to actions by foreign plaintiffs under the Act.

The controlling decision on the scope of Art. III "arising under" jurisdiction is Chief Justice Marshall's opinion for the Court in Osborn v. Bank of United States, 9 Wheat. 738 (1824). In *Osborn*, the Court upheld the constitutionality of a statute that granted the Bank of the United States the right to sue in federal court on causes of action based upon state law. There, the Court concluded that the "judicial department may receive the power of construing every law" that "the Legislature may constitutionally make." The rule was laid down that

> it [is] a sufficient foundation for jurisdiction, that the title or right set up by the party, may be defeated by one construction of the constitution or [laws] of the United States, and sustained by the opposite construction.

Osborn thus reflects a broad conception of "arising under" jurisdiction, according to which Congress may confer on the federal courts jurisdiction over any case or controversy that might call for the application of federal law. The breadth of that conclusion has been questioned. It has been observed that, taken at its broadest, *Osborn* might be read as permitting "assertion of original federal jurisdiction on the remote possibility of presentation of a federal question." Textile Workers v. Lincoln Mills, 353 U.S. 448, 482 (1957) (Frankfurter, J., dissenting). We need not now resolve that issue or decide the precise boundaries of Art. III jurisdiction, however, since the present case does not involve a mere speculative possibility that a federal question may arise at some point in the proceeding. Rather, a suit against a foreign state under this Act necessarily raises questions of substantive federal law at the very outset, and hence clearly "arises under" federal law, as that term is used in Art. III.

By reason of its authority over foreign commerce and foreign relations, Congress has the undisputed power to decide, as a matter of federal law, whether and under what circumstances foreign nations should be amenable to suit in the United States. Actions against foreign sovereigns in our courts raise sensitive issues concerning the foreign relations of the United States, and the primacy of federal concerns is evident. See, e.g., Banco Nacional de Cuba v. Sabbatino, 376 U.S. 398, 423-425 (1964); Zschernig v. Miller, 389 U.S. 429, 440-441 (1968).

To promote these federal interests, Congress exercised its Art. I powers[19] by enacting a statute comprehensively regulating the amenability of foreign nations to suit in the United States. The statute must be applied by the district courts in every

___

19. In enacting the legislation, Congress relied specifically on its powers to prescribe the jurisdiction of federal courts, Art. I, §8, cl. 9; to define offenses against the "Law of Nations," Art. I, §8, cl. 10;

action against a foreign sovereign, since subject-matter jurisdiction in any such action depends on the existence of one of the specified exceptions to foreign sovereign immunity, 28 U.S.C. §1330(a).[20] At the threshold of every action in a district court against a foreign state, therefore, the court must satisfy itself that one of the exceptions applies — and in doing so it must apply the detailed federal law standards set forth in the Act. Accordingly, an action against a foreign sovereign arises under federal law, for purposes of Art. III jurisdiction. . . .

[I]n enacting the Foreign Sovereign Immunities Act, Congress expressly exercised its power to regulate foreign commerce, along with other specified Art. I powers. See n.19, supra. As the House Report clearly indicates, the primary purpose of the Act was to "se[t] forth comprehensive rules governing sovereign immunity," H.R. Rep. No. 94-1487, p.12 (1976); the jurisdictional provisions of the Act are simply one part of this comprehensive scheme. The Act thus does not merely concern access to the federal courts. Rather, it governs the types of actions for which foreign sovereigns may be held liable in a court in the United States, federal or state. The Act codifies the standards governing foreign sovereign immunity as an aspect of substantive federal law, see Ex parte Peru, 318 U.S., at 588; Mexico v. Hoffman, 324 U.S., at 36; and applying those standards will generally require interpretation of numerous points of federal law. Finally, if a court determines that none of the exceptions to sovereign immunity applies, the plaintiff will be barred from raising his claim in any court in the United States — manifestly, "the title or right set up by the party, may be defeated by one construction of the . . . laws of the United States, and sustained by the opposite construction." Osborn v. Bank of United States, 9 Wheat., at 822. That the inquiry into foreign sovereign immunity is labeled under the Act as a matter of jurisdiction does not affect the constitutionality of Congress' action in granting federal courts jurisdiction over cases calling for application of this comprehensive regulatory statute.

Congress, pursuant to its unquestioned Art. I powers, has enacted a broad statutory framework governing assertions of foreign sovereign immunity. In so doing, Congress deliberately sought to channel cases against foreign sovereigns away from the state courts and into federal courts, thereby reducing the potential for a multiplicity of conflicting results among the courts of the 50 States. The resulting jurisdictional grant is within the bounds of Art. III, since every action against a foreign sovereign necessarily involves application of a body of substantive federal law, and accordingly "arises under" federal law, within the meaning of Art. III.

V

A conclusion that the grant of jurisdiction in the Foreign Sovereign Immunities Act is consistent with the Constitution does not end the case. An action must not only

---

to regulate commerce with foreign nations, Art. I, §8, cl. 3; and to make all laws necessary and proper to execute the Government's powers, Art. I, §8, cl. 18.

20. The House Report on the Act states that "sovereign immunity is an affirmative defense which must be specially pleaded," H.R. Rep. No. 94-1487, p.17 (1976). Under the Act, however, subject-matter jurisdiction turns on the existence of an exception to foreign sovereign immunity, 28 U.S.C. §1330(a). Accordingly, even if the foreign state does not enter an appearance to assert an immunity defense, a district court still must determine that immunity is unavailable under the Act.

satisfy Art. III but must also be supported by a statutory grant of subject-matter jurisdiction. As we have made clear, deciding whether statutory subject-matter jurisdiction exists under the Foreign Sovereign Immunities Act entails an application of the substantive terms of the Act to determine whether one of the specified exceptions to immunity applies.

In the present case, the District Court, after satisfying itself as to the constitutionality of the Act, held that the present action does not fall within any specified exception. The Court of Appeals, reaching a contrary conclusion as to jurisdiction under the Constitution, did not find it necessary to address this statutory question.[23] Accordingly, on remand the Court of Appeals must consider whether jurisdiction exists under the Act itself. If the Court of Appeals agrees with the District Court on that issue, the case will be at an end. If, on the other hand, the Court of Appeals concludes that jurisdiction does exist under the statute, the action may then be remanded to the District Court for further proceedings.

It is so ordered.

Notes and Questions

1. The "core question" presented in *Verlinden* was whether the FSIA, as applied in that case, violated Article III of the Constitution. Article III sets forth the cases and controversies that can be heard in the federal courts. These cases and controversies include cases arising under federal law and disputes between U.S. citizens and foreign citizens. What was the potential Article III problem in *Verlinden*? Do the federal courts have diversity jurisdiction over a suit between a foreign company and a foreign government? Was the plaintiff's claim in *Verlinden* based on federal law? On what basis does the Supreme Court find federal court jurisdiction? Do you think Congress intended to confer federal court jurisdiction over suits such as this one?

2. The Supreme Court has not determined the precise bounds of Article III "arising under" jurisdiction. In one decision from the early 1800s, the Court suggested that this jurisdiction might extend to any case in which there is even a potential federal law question, regardless of whether the federal law question is actually litigated. See Osborn v. Bank of the United States, 22 U.S. (9 Wheat.) 738 (1824). As the Court notes in *Verlinden*, the reasoning of *Osborn* has been questioned by some judges and commentators, and it is not clear that the modern Supreme Court would construe Article III as broadly as the *Osborn* reasoning might allow. How was the Court in *Verlinden* able to avoid determining the scope of Article III?

3. Whatever the bounds of Article III's arising under jurisdiction, it is well established that Congress's grant of federal statutory jurisdiction cannot by itself serve

---

23. In several related cases involving contracts between Nigeria and other cement suppliers, the Court of Appeals held that statutory subject-matter jurisdiction existed under the Act. In those cases, the court held that Nigeria's acts were commercial in nature and "cause[d] a direct effect in the United States," within the meaning of 28 U.S.C. §1605(a). Texas Trading & Milling Corp. v. Federal Republic of Nigeria, 647 F.2d, at 310-313. Each of those actions involved a contract with an *American* supplier operating *within the United States*, however. In the present case, the District Court found that exception inapplicable, concluding that the repudiation of the letter of credit "caused no direct, substantial, injurious effect in the United States." 488 F. Supp., at 1299-1300.

as the federal law question for purposes of this jurisdiction. See, e.g., Mesa v. California, 489 U.S. 121, 136-137 (1989). Indeed, if it were enough, there would be no limit on Congress's ability to confer jurisdiction on the federal courts. Do you see why? Did the Supreme Court in *Verlinden* ignore this rule? What are the implications of the Supreme Court's statement in *Verlinden* that immunity under the FSIA concerns "substantive" federal law?

4. The *Verlinden* case was remanded to determine if it fell within any of the FSIA's specified exceptions to immunity. Given the facts as stated, what should be the result on remand? What connections did the case have to the United States? The facts in *Verlinden* indicate that the contract provided for the use of a "letter of credit." A letter of credit is a bank's commitment that it will, under certain circumstances, make a payment to a designated beneficiary, typically the seller or its bank. A letter of credit may be either "confirmed" or "unconfirmed." These terms refer to the presence or absence of a guarantee of the letter of credit by a second bank. Of what significance is it that the letter of credit in *Verlinden* was "uncomfirmed," which meant that the U.S. bank "acted solely as an advising bank; it undertook no independent responsibility for guaranteeing the letter of credit," 461 U.S. at 482 n.1? (The *Verlinden* case was settled before any further decisions in the lower courts. Nigeria apparently paid Verlinden an undisclosed sum of money.)

5. Should foreigners be allowed to sue foreign states in U.S. courts? In what cases? What are the benefits? The dangers? (In thinking about this question, recall the Alien Tort Statute litigation discussed in Chapter 3.)

6. What safeguards exist to protect U.S. courts from being opened up to claims that have no connection to the United States? What safeguards exist under the FSIA? What safeguards exist otherwise?

7. Under the *forum non conveniens* doctrine, U.S. courts have the discretion to dismiss a case if they determine that there is an adequate alternate forum and various private and public interest factors weigh in favor of adjudicating the case in that forum. See Piper Aircraft Co. v. Reyno, 454 U.S. 235 (1981). The Court in *Verlinden* observed in note 15 of its opinion that the FSIA "does not appear to affect the traditional doctrine of forum non conveniens." Since then, most courts have accepted the proposition that FSIA cases can, at least in theory, be dismissed under the *forum non conveniens* doctrine. See, e.g., Proyecfin de Venezuela, S.A. v. Banco Indus. de Venezuela, 760 F.2d 390, 394 (2d Cir. 1985). Such dismissals appear to be relatively infrequent, however, in part because of the requirement under the *forum non conveniens* doctrine that there be an adequate alternate forum. For a rare example of an FSIA case dismissed under the *forum non conveniens* doctrine, see Bank of Credit and Commerce International v. State Bank of Pakistan, 46 F. Supp. 2d 231 (S.D.N.Y. 1999).

8. Does the FSIA apply retroactively to conduct that took place before the statute's enactment? A number of courts had held, prior to 1994, that the FSIA did not operate retroactively with respect to events prior to 1952. See, e.g., Carl Marks & Co. v. Union of Soviet Socialist Republics, 841 F.2d 26, 27 (2d Cir. 1988); Jackson v. People's Republic of China, 794 F.2d 1490, 1497-1498 (11th Cir. 1986). These decisions, though, were all issued before the Supreme Court's decision in Landgraf v. USI Film Products, Inc., 511 U.S. 244 (1994), in which the Court clarified the standards for determining whether a statute operates retroactively.

In *Landgraf,* the Court held that the Civil Rights Act of 1991, which granted the right to a jury trial in cases brought under Title VII of the Civil Rights Act of 1964, did not apply retroactively to a case pending on appeal at the time of the statute's enactment. In its decision, the Court reaffirmed a general presumption against statutory retroactivity. It stated, however, that:

> A statute does not operate "retrospectively" merely because it is applied in a case arising from conduct antedating the statute's enactment, . . . or upsets expectations based on prior law. Rather, the court must ask whether the new provision attaches new legal consequences to events completed before its enactment.

Id. at 269. The Court further suggested that changes in jurisdictional rules will not typically meet this test because "[a]pplication of a new jurisdictional rule usually 'takes away no substantive right but simply changes the tribunal that is to hear the case.'" Id. at 274. As a result, the Court indicated that courts generally should apply the jurisdictional law that exists at the time of the case rather than the jurisdictional law that existed at the time of the events in question.

Based on the reasoning in *Landgraf,* some courts have held recently that the FSIA does apply to pre-1952 events. For example, in Altmann v. Republic of Austria, 317 F.3d 954 (9th Cir. 2002), the court allowed a U.S. citizen to sue Austria and an Austrian government-owned art gallery to recover paintings allegedly seized by the Nazis, with Austria's assistance, during the 1940s. (The suit was brought under Section 1605(a)(3) of the FSIA, which allows claims for the taking of property in violation of international law.) Relying on *Landgraf,* the court reasoned that Austria could not have expected to receive immunity for assisting in the seizure of the paintings because, among other things, (a) such seizures explicitly violated both Austria's and Germany's obligations under the 1907 Hague Convention on the Laws and Customs of War on Land, (b) Austria had adopted the restrictive theory of immunity by the 1920s, and (c) Austria's post-World War II government had officially repudiated all Nazi transactions. Are these reasons persuasive? If the suit had been brought in a U.S. court before 1952, wouldn't it have been dismissed? See also Abrams v. Societe Nationale des Chemins de Fer Francais, 175 F. Supp. 2d 423 (E.D.N.Y. 2001) (discussing the retroactivity issue in detail); Adam K.A. Mortara, The Case Against Retroactive Application of the Foreign Sovereign Immunities Act of 1976, 68 U. Chi. L. Rev. 253 (2001) (same). Note that the 1996 "state sponsor of terrorism" amendments to the FSIA, discussed below, expressly operate retroactively.

9. For general discussions of the FSIA and its origins, see Joseph W. Dellapenna, Suing Foreign Governments and Their Corporations (2d ed. 2003); Mark B. Feldman, The United States Foreign Sovereign Immunities Act of 1976 in Perspective: A Founder's View, 35 Intl. & Comp. L.Q. 302 (1986); Frederic Alan Weber, The Foreign Sovereign Immunities Act of 1976: Its Origins, Meaning, and Effect, 3 Yale J. World Pub. Order 1 (1976).

The decision below considers the relationship between the FSIA and other jurisdictional statutes.

Argentine Republic v. Amerada Hess Shipping Corp.

U.S. Supreme Court
488 U.S. 428 (1989)

Rehnquist, C.J., delivered the opinion of the Court, in which Brennan, White, Stevens, O'Connor, Scalia, and Kennedy, JJ., joined. Blackmun, J., filed an opinion concurring in part, in which Marshall, J., joined.

Chief Justice REHNQUIST delivered the opinion of the Court.

Two Liberian corporations sued the Argentine Republic in a United States District Court to recover damages for a tort allegedly committed by its armed forces on the high seas in violation of international law. We hold that the District Court correctly dismissed the action, because the Foreign Sovereign Immunities Act of 1976 (FSIA), 28 U.S.C. §1330 et seq., does not authorize jurisdiction over a foreign state in this situation.

Respondents alleged the following facts in their complaints. Respondent United Carriers, Inc., a Liberian corporation, chartered one of its oil tankers, the Hercules, to respondent Amerada Hess Shipping Corporation, also a Liberian corporation. The contract was executed in New York City. Amerada Hess used the Hercules to transport crude oil from the southern terminus of the Trans-Alaska Pipeline in Valdez, Alaska, around Cape Horn in South America, to the Hess refinery in the United States Virgin Islands. On May 25, 1982, the Hercules began a return voyage, without cargo but fully fueled, from the Virgin Islands to Alaska. At that time, Great Britain and petitioner Argentine Republic were at war over an archipelago of some 200 islands — the Falkland Islands to the British, and the Islas Malvinas to the Argentineans — in the South Atlantic off the Argentine coast. On June 3, United States officials informed the two belligerents of the location of United States vessels and Liberian tankers owned by United States interests then traversing the South Atlantic, including the Hercules, to avoid any attacks on neutral shipping.

By June 8, 1982, after a stop in Brazil, the Hercules was in international waters about 600 nautical miles from Argentina and 500 miles from the Falklands; she was outside the "war zones" designated by Britain and Argentina. At 12:15 Greenwich mean time, the ship's master made a routine report by radio to Argentine officials, providing the ship's name, international call sign, registry, position, course, speed, and voyage description. About 45 minutes later, an Argentine military aircraft began to circle the Hercules. The ship's master repeated his earlier message by radio to Argentine officials, who acknowledged receiving it. Six minutes later, without provocation, another Argentine military plane began to bomb the Hercules; the master immediately hoisted a white flag. A second bombing soon followed, and a third attack came about two hours later, when an Argentine jet struck the ship with an air-to-surface rocket. Disabled but not destroyed, the Hercules reversed course and sailed to Rio de Janeiro, the nearest safe port. At Rio de Janeiro, respondent United Carriers determined that the ship had suffered extensive deck and hull damage, and that an undetonated bomb remained lodged in her No. 2 tank. After an investigation by the Brazilian Navy, United Carriers decided that it would be too hazardous to remove the undetonated bomb, and on July 20, 1982, the Hercules was scuttled 250 miles off the Brazilian coast.

Following unsuccessful attempts to obtain relief in Argentina, respondents commenced this action in the United States District Court for the Southern District of

New York for the damage that they sustained from the attack. United Carriers sought $10 million in damages for the loss of the ship; Amerada Hess sought $1.9 million in damages for the fuel that went down with the ship. Respondents alleged that petitioner's attack on the neutral Hercules violated international law. They invoked the District Court's jurisdiction under the Alien Tort Statute, 28 U.S.C. §1350, which provides that "[t]he district courts shall have original jurisdiction of any civil action by an alien for a tort only, committed in violation of the law of nations or a treaty of the United States." Amerada Hess also brought suit under the general admiralty and maritime jurisdiction, 28 U.S.C. §1333, and "the principle of universal jurisdiction, recognized in customary international law." The District Court dismissed both complaints for lack of subject-matter jurisdiction, 638 F. Supp. 73 (SDNY 1986), ruling that respondents' suits were barred by the FSIA.

A divided panel of the United States Court of Appeals for the Second Circuit reversed. 830 F.2d 421 (1987). The Court of Appeals held that the District Court had jurisdiction under the Alien Tort Statute, because respondents' consolidated action was brought by Liberian corporations, it sounded in tort ("the bombing of a ship without justification"), and it asserted a violation of international law ("attacking a neutral ship in international waters, without proper cause for suspicion or investigation"). . . . The dissenting judge took the view that the FSIA precluded respondents' action. . . . We granted certiorari, and now reverse.

We start from the settled proposition that the subject-matter jurisdiction of the lower federal courts is determined by Congress, "in the exact degrees and character which to Congress may seem proper for the public good." Cary v. Curtis, 44 U.S. (3 How.) 236, 245 (1845). . . . In the FSIA, Congress added a new chapter 97 to Title 28 of the United States Code, 28 U.S.C. §§1602-1611, which is entitled "Jurisdictional Immunities of Foreign States." Section 1604 provides that "[s]ubject to existing international agreements to which the United States [was] a party at the time of the enactment of this Act[,] a foreign state shall be immune from the jurisdiction of the courts of the United States and of the States except as provided in sections 1605 to 1607 of this chapter." The FSIA also added §1330(a) to Title 28; it provides that "[t]he district courts shall have original jurisdiction without regard to amount in controversy of any nonjury civil action against a foreign state . . . as to any claim for relief in personam with respect to which the foreign state is not entitled to immunity under sections 1605-1607 of this title or under any applicable international agreement." §1330(a).[2]

We think that the text and structure of the FSIA demonstrate Congress' intention that the FSIA be the sole basis for obtaining jurisdiction over a foreign state in our courts. Section 1604 and §1330(a) work in tandem: §1604 bars federal and state courts from exercising jurisdiction when a foreign state *is* entitled to immunity, and §1330(a) confers jurisdiction on district courts to hear suits brought by United States citizens and by aliens when a foreign state is *not* entitled to immunity. As we said in *Verlinden,* the FSIA "must be applied by the district courts in every action against a foreign sovereign, since subject-matter jurisdiction in any such action

___

2. Respondents did not invoke the District Court's jurisdiction under 28 U.S.C. §1330(a). They did, however, serve their complaints upon petitioner's Ministry of Foreign Affairs in conformity with the service of process provisions of 28 U.S.C. §1608(a) of the FSIA, and the regulations promulgated thereunder by the Department of State, 22 C.F.R. pt. 93 (1986).

depends on the existence of one of the specified exceptions to foreign sovereign immunity." Verlinden B.V. v. Central Bank of Nigeria, 461 U.S. 480, 493 (1983).[3]

The Court of Appeals acknowledged that the FSIA's language and legislative history support the "general rule" that the Act governs the immunity of foreign states in federal court. The Court of Appeals, however, thought that the FSIA's "focus on commercial concerns" and Congress' failure to "repeal" the Alien Tort Statute indicated Congress' intention that federal courts continue to exercise jurisdiction over foreign states in suits alleging violations of international law outside the confines of the FSIA. The Court of Appeals also believed that to construe the FSIA to bar the instant suit would "fly in the face" of Congress' intention that the FSIA be interpreted pursuant to "'standards recognized under international law.'"

Taking the last of these points first, Congress had violations of international law by foreign states in mind when it enacted the FSIA. For example, the FSIA specifically denies foreign states immunity in suits "in which rights in property taken in violation of international law are in issue." 28 U.S.C. §1605(a)(3). Congress also rested the FSIA in part on its power under Art. I, §8, cl. 10, of the Constitution "[t]o define and punish Piracies and Felonies committed on the high Seas, and Offenses against the Law of Nations." From Congress' decision to deny immunity to foreign states in the class of cases just mentioned, we draw the plain implication that immunity is granted in those cases involving alleged violations of international law that do not come within one of the FSIA's exceptions.

As to the other point made by the Court of Appeals, Congress' failure to enact a *pro tanto* repealer of the Alien Tort Statute when it passed the FSIA in 1976 may be explained at least in part by the lack of certainty as to whether the Alien Tort Statute conferred jurisdiction in suits against foreign states. . . . The Court of Appeals did not cite any decision in which a United States court exercised jurisdiction over a foreign state under the Alien Tort Statute, and only one such case has come to our attention — one which was decided after the enactment of the FSIA.[4] . . .

Having determined that the FSIA provides the sole basis for obtaining jurisdiction over a foreign state in federal court, we turn to whether any of the exceptions enumerated in the Act apply here. . . . We agree with the District Court that none of the FSIA's exceptions applies on these facts.[6] . . .

We hold that the FSIA provides the sole basis for obtaining jurisdiction over a foreign state in the courts of this country, and that none of the enumerated exceptions to the Act applies to the facts of this case. The judgment of the Court of Appeals is therefore reversed.

---

3. . . . Our conclusion here is supported by the FSIA's legislative history. See, e.g., H.R. Rep. No. 94-1487, p.12 (1976) (H.R. Rep.); S. Rep. No. 94-1310, pp.11-12 (1976) (S. Rep.), U.S. Code Cong. & Admin. News 1976, pp.6604, 6610 (FSIA "sets forth the sole and exclusive standards to be used in resolving questions of sovereign immunity raised by sovereign states before Federal and State courts in the United States," and "prescribes . . . the jurisdiction of U.S. district courts in cases involving foreign states").

4. See Von Dardel v. Union of Soviet Socialist Republics, 623 F. Supp. 246 (DC 1985) (alternative holding). The Court of Appeals did cite its earlier decision in Filartiga v. Pena-Irala, 630 F.2d 876 (CA2 1980), which involved a suit under the Alien Tort Statute by a Paraguayan national against a Paraguayan police official for torture; the Paraguayan Government was not joined as a defendant.

6. The Court of Appeals majority did not pass on whether any of the exceptions to the FSIA applies here. It did note, however, that respondents' arguments regarding §1605(a)(5) were consistent with its disposition of the case. 830 F.2d, at 429, n.3. The dissent found none of the FSIA's exceptions applicable on these facts. Id., at 430 (Kearse, J. dissenting).

Justice BLACKMUN, with whom Justice MARSHALL joins, concurring in part.

I join the Court's opinion insofar as it holds that the FSIA provides the sole basis for obtaining jurisdiction over a foreign state in federal court.

I, however, do not join the latter part of the Court's opinion to the effect that none of the FSIA's exceptions to foreign sovereign immunity apply in this case. As the majority notes, the Court of Appeals did not decide this question, and, indeed, specifically reserved it. Moreover, the question was not among those presented to this Court in the Petition for Certiorari, did not receive full briefing, and is not necessary to the disposition of the case. Accordingly, I believe it inappropriate to decide here, in the first instance, whether any exceptions to the FSIA apply in this case. . . . I would remand the case to the Court of Appeals on this issue.

Questions

1. Do you agree with the U.S. Supreme Court or with the majority opinion in the Second Circuit? Which is more consistent with the comprehensive scheme that Congress had created in the FSIA?

2. If the case had been remanded (as Justices Blackmun and Marshall urged), is it likely that the plaintiffs would have been able to establish that one of the FSIA's exceptions applied? If so, which one? (These exceptions will be discussed in more detail in the rest of this section.)

3. Did the plaintiffs in *Amerada Hess* meet the requirements for jurisdiction under the Alien Tort Statute? If so, why did the Court nevertheless order dismissal of their suit? What is left of Alien Tort Statute litigation (which we considered in Chapter 3) after this decision? Can a foreign citizen still maintain an action against a private citizen for a tort that violates the law of nations? Can a foreign citizen maintain such an action against a former foreign official? On the last question, why haven't cases such as Filartiga v. Pena-Irala been dismissed under the FSIA? See generally David J. Bederman, Dead Man's Hand: Reshuffling Foreign Sovereign Immunities in U.S. Human Rights Litigation, 25 Ga. J. Intl. & Comp. L. 255 (1995-1996).

4. Entities Covered by the FSIA

The FSIA covers suits against three types of entities: foreign states proper, their political subdivisions, and their agencies and instrumentalities. See 28 U.S.C. §1603(a). While all of these entities qualify as "foreign states" for purposes of FSIA immunity, the statute treats foreign states proper and their political subdivisions differently than agencies and instrumentalities for purposes of service of process, venue, punitive damages, and execution of judgments. With respect to each of these issues, foreign states proper and their political subdivisions receive more protection than do their agencies and instrumentalities.

It is thus sometimes important to distinguish between political subdivisions and agencies and instrumentalities. In making this distinction, courts have applied two basic tests. Some courts have applied a "legal characteristics" test, which looks at whether the entity displays legal characteristics signifying its independence from the foreign state, such as an ability to contract, sue and be sued, and hold property in its own name. See, e.g., Hyatt Corp. v. Stanton, 945 F. Supp. 675 (S.D.N.Y. 1996). Other courts have applied a "core functions" test, which looks at whether the functions of the entity are governmental. See, e.g., Transaero, Inc. v. La Fuerza Aera Boliviana, 30 F.3d 148 (D.C. Cir. 1994).

To qualify as an agency or instrumentality of a foreign state, an entity must, among other things, be either "an organ of a foreign state or a political subdivision thereof," or have a majority of its shares or other ownership interests "owned by a foreign state or political subdivision thereof." 28 U.S.C. §1603(b). Thus, corporations that are majority owned by a foreign state qualify as agencies or instrumentalities.

What if a corporation is not directly majority owned by a foreign state but instead is majority owned by another corporation that, in turn, is directly majority owned by a foreign state? In Dole Food Co. v. Patrickson, 123 S. Ct. 1655 (2003), the U.S. Supreme Court (in an opinion authored by Justice Kennedy) held that a foreign state must itself own a majority of a corporation's shares if the corporation is to be deemed an instrumentality of the state under the FSIA. Among other things, the Court reasoned that Congress had corporate formalities in mind when it drafted the definition of instrumentalities, and that "[a] basic tenet of American corporate law is that the corporation and its shareholders are distinct entities." Justices Breyer and O'Connor dissented on that issue, arguing that the FSIA was designed to offer legal protection to a foreign state "not only when it acts directly in its own name but also when it acts through separate legal entities," and that the majority's decision was inconsistent with this purpose.

What if an entity qualified as an agency or instrumentality at the time the claim arose, but does not qualify at the time of the suit? Conversely, what if an entity did not qualify as an agency or instrumentality at the time the claim arose, but does qualify at the time of the suit? In *Patrickson,* supra, the Supreme Court held that instrumentality status under the FSIA is to be determined at the time of the suit. The Court reasoned, among other things, that foreign sovereign immunity "is not meant to avoid chilling foreign states or their instrumentalities in the conduct of their business but to give foreign states and their instrumentalities some protection from the inconvenience of suit as a gesture of comity between the United States and other sovereigns."

To what extent are the actions of an agency or instrumentality attributable to the foreign state, or vice versa? The Supreme Court addressed this attribution question in First National City Bank v. Banco Para El Comercio Exterior de Cuba, 462 U.S. 611 (1983), also known as the "*Bancec*" case. In that case, the Cuban government had expropriated Citibank's assets in Cuba. Subsequently, Bancec, a Cuban government-owned bank, sued Citibank in a U.S. court to collect on a letter of credit. Citibank filed a counterclaim, seeking a setoff for the value of its expropriated assets. The issue was whether the Cuban government's expropriation could be attributed to Bancec for purposes of the setoff. The Court first concluded that the FSIA does not itself address this question. The Court also declined to apply state law, concluding that a uniform federal standard was desirable. Instead, the court looked to internationally recognized principles of corporate law and equity as "informed both by international law principles and by articulated congressional policies." Id. at 623.

Applying these principles, the Court in *Bancec* adopted a presumption that government instrumentalities that are established as separate entities should be treated as such, something the Court said was supported by "[d]ue respect for the actions taken by foreign sovereigns and for principles of comity between nations." Id. at 626. The Court further held that this presumption could be overcome in two situations: first, "where a corporate entity is so extensively controlled by its owner that a relationship of principal and agent is created"; and, second, where treating the entity as separate from the foreign state "would work fraud or injustice." Id. at 629. Under the facts of that case, the Court held that the presumption was overcome because Bancec had been dissolved early in the litigation and its capital divided between Cuba's central bank and other government enterprises, such that "the Cuban Government and [Cuba's central bank], not any third parties that may have relied on Bancec's juridical identity, would be the only beneficiaries of any recovery [under the letter of credit]." Id. at 631.

The presumption of separateness adopted in *Bancec* has barred recovery in a number of FSIA cases. For example, in the *Letelier* case, discussed below in subsection 8 where the U.S. district court had found the Republic of Chile liable for political assassination in Washington, D.C., the plaintiffs were not able to execute successfully against the assets of the Chilean government-owned airline because the airline was found to be a separate entity. See Letelier v. Republic of Chile, 748 F.2d 790 (2d Cir. 1984).

The FSIA does not expressly address the immunity of individual foreign officials. Rather, it covers suits against "foreign states." Although it defines foreign states to include agencies and instrumentalities of foreign states, such agencies and instrumentalities are described as "any *entity* . . . which is a separate *legal* person." 28 U.S.C. §1603(b) (emphasis added). That language does not appear to include natural persons. If individual foreign officials were not entitled to immunity, however, plaintiffs might be able to plead around the limitations of the FSIA by simply proceeding against a foreign state's officials rather than the foreign state itself. In addition, suits against high-level foreign officials, especially foreign heads of state, might create foreign relations problems for the United States. For these reasons, a number of courts have held that the FSIA extends to suits against foreign officials acting within their official capacity. These courts have also held, however, that the FSIA does not apply when the official is acting outside the scope of his or her authority. See, e.g., Jungquist v. Nahyan, 115 F.3d 1020 (D.C. Cir. 1997); Chuidian v. Philippine National Bank, 115 F.3d 1020 (9th Cir. 1997). (Courts treat suits against heads of state somewhat differently. We discuss such suits below in subsection 12.)

5. *Waiver Exception*

Under the FSIA's waiver exception, a foreign state is not immune from suit if it "has waived its immunity either explicitly or by implication." 28 U.S.C. §1605(a)(1). Explicit waivers of immunity, such as a waiver in a treaty or contract, present relatively few problems. Such waiver provisions are very common in the legal documents when a foreign state borrows money from a bank or purchases goods or services from a sophisticated company.

But what constitutes a waiver "by implication"? The legislative history of the FSIA states as follows:

> With respect to implicit waivers, the courts have found such waivers in cases where a foreign state has agreed to arbitration in another country or where a foreign state has agreed that the law of a particular country should govern a contract. An implicit waiver

would also include a situation where a foreign state has filed a responsive pleading in an action without raising the defense of foreign sovereign immunity. [H.R. Rep. No. 94-1487, at 18.]

What does this statement suggest about the scope of the implicit waiver exception? In general, courts have construed the FSIA's implicit waiver exception narrowly, limiting it to situations in which the foreign state defendant has indicated a willingness to be sued in U.S. courts. The selection of U.S. law to govern a contract is generally treated as a waiver of FSIA immunity. See, e.g., Eckert Intl., Inc. v. Fiji, 32 F.3d 77 (4th Cir. 1994). But a selection of foreign law is generally not viewed as a waiver. See, e.g., Maritime Intl. Nominees Establishment v. Republic of Guinea, 693 F.2d 1094, 1102 n.13 (D.C. Cir. 1982). Nor is an agreement to submit to the jurisdiction of a foreign state generally viewed as a waiver of FSIA immunity. See, e.g., Ohntrup v. Firearms Center, 516 F. Supp. 1281, 1285 (E.D. Pa. 1981), aff'd, 760 F.2d 259 (3d Cir. 1985).

Does a foreign state implicitly waive its immunity by engaging in egregious conduct — for example, by violating *jus cogens* norms of international law? Despite an argument to this effect by one judge, see Princz v. Federal Republic of Germany, 26 F.3d 1166, 1176 (D.C. Cir. 1984) (Wald, J., dissenting), courts have uniformly held that egregious conduct does not itself constitute a waiver. In addition to the majority opinion in *Princz*, see, for example, Sampson v. Federal Republic of Germany, 250 F.3d 1145 (7th Cir. May 23, 2001); Smith v. Socialist People's Libyan Arab Jamahiriya, 101 F.3d 239, 344-345 (2d Cir. 1996); and Siderman de Blake v. Republic of Argentina, 965 F.2d 699, 718-719 (9th Cir. 1992). There have been a number of proposals presented to Congress to create a *jus cogens* exception to immunity, but so far none of those proposals has been enacted. Should Congress create such an exception? If so, how should it be worded? What problems might courts encounter in applying such an exception?

6. Counterclaim Exception

The FSIA also has an exception to immunity for counterclaims. See 28 U.S.C. §1607. If a foreign state brings a lawsuit in a U.S. court, it is denied immunity under this section for (a) any claim that falls within an exception to immunity; (b) any claim that arises out of the same transaction or occurrence as the sovereign's claim; and (c) any claim up to the amount of the foreign state's claim. The FSIA's legislative history indicates that Congress intended by this exception to codify the Supreme Court's decision in National City Bank v. Republic of China, 348 U.S. 356 (1955), which held that the *Schooner Exchange* decision did not apply to counterclaims because such claims do not involve "an attempt to bring a recognized foreign government into one of our courts as a defendant and subject it to the rule of law to which nongovernmental obligors must bow." Id. at 361.

7. Commercial Activity Exception

One of the most widely invoked exceptions to immunity under the FSIA is the commercial activity exception in 28 U.S.C. §1605(a)(2). A suit can satisfy this exception in three different ways: either the suit must be "based upon a commercial activity carried on in the United States by the foreign state," based upon "an act performed in the United States in connection with a commercial activity of the foreign state elsewhere," or based upon "an act outside the territory of the United States in connection with a commercial activity of the foreign state elsewhere and that act causes a direct effect in the United States."

The 1976 House Report for the FSIA notes the following regarding the FSIA's definition of "commercial activity":

House Report No. 94-1487

Paragraph [(d)] of section 1603 defines the term "commercial activity" as including a broad spectrum of endeavor, from an individual commercial transaction or act to a regular course of commercial conduct. A "regular course of commercial conduct" includes the carrying on of a commercial enterprise such as a mineral extraction company, an airline or a state trading corporation. Certainly, if an activity is customarily carried on for profit, its commercial nature could readily be assumed. At the other end of the spectrum, a single contract, if of the same character as a contract which might be made by a private person, could constitute a "particular transaction or act."

As the definition indicates, the fact that goods or services to be procured through a contract are to be used for a public purpose is irrelevant; it is the essentially commercial nature of an activity or transaction that is critical. Thus, a contract by a foreign government to buy provisions or equipment for its armed forces or to construct a government building constitutes a commercial activity. The same would be true of a contract to make repairs on an embassy building. Such contracts should be considered to be commercial contracts, even if their ultimate object is to further a public function.

By contrast, a foreign state's mere participation in a foreign assistance program administered by the Agency for International Development (AID) is an activity whose essential nature is public or governmental, and it would not itself constitute a commercial activity. By the same token, a foreign state's activities in and "contacts" with the United States resulting from or necessitated by participation in such a program would not in themselves constitute a sufficient commercial nexus with the United States so as to give rise to jurisdiction (see sec. 1330) or to assets which could be subjected to attachment or execution with respect to unrelated commercial transactions (see sec. 1610(b)). However, a transaction to obtain goods or services from private parties would not lose its otherwise commercial character because it was entered into in connection with an AID program. Also public or governmental and not commercial in nature, would be the employment of diplomatic, civil service, or military personnel, but not the employment of American citizens or third country nationals by the foreign state in the United States.

The courts would have a great deal of latitude in determining what is a "commercial activity" for purposes of this bill. It has seemed unwise to attempt an excessively precise definition of this term, even if that were practicable. Activities such as a foreign government's sale of a service or a product, its leasing of property, its borrowing of money, its employment or engagement of laborers, clerical staff or public relations or marketing agents, or its investment in a security of an American corporation, would be among those included within the definition.

. . . As paragraph [(e)] of section 1603 indicates, a commercial activity carried on in the United States by a foreign state would include not only a commercial transaction performed and executed in its entirety in the United States, but also a commercial transaction or act having a "substantial contact" with the United States. This definition includes cases based on commercial transactions performed in whole or in part in the United States, import-export transactions involving sales to, or purchases from, concerns in the United States, business torts occurring in the United States (cf. §1605(a)(5)), and an indebtedness incurred by a foreign state which negotiates or executes a loan agreement in the United States, or which receives financing from a private or public lending institution located in the United States — for example, loans, guarantees or insurance provided by the Export-Import Bank of the United States. It will be for the courts to determine whether a particular commercial activity has been performed in whole or in part in the United States. This definition, however, is intended to reflect a degree of contact beyond that occasioned simply by U.S. citizenship or U.S. residence of the plaintiff.

The Supreme Court first considered the scope of the commercial activity exception in Republic of Argentina v. Weltover, Inc., 504 U.S. 607 (1992). In that case, Argentina attempted, pursuant to a presidential decree, to reschedule the payments that were due on debt instruments (called "Bonods") that it had issued to foreign creditors. These Bonods provided for payment of interest and principal in U.S. dollars, and also provided that payment was to be made in London, Frankfurt, Zurich, or New York, at the election of the creditor. The plaintiffs, two Panamanian corporations and a Swiss bank, collectively held $1.3 million of Bonods, and the plaintiffs refused to accept the rescheduling and insisted on full payment, specifying New York as the place where payment should be made. Argentina did not pay, and the plaintiffs brought a breach-of-contract action in federal court in New York, relying on the third clause of the commercial activity exception, which applies if the suit is based upon "an act outside the territory of the United States in connection with a commercial activity of the foreign state elsewhere and that act causes a direct effect in the United States."

In an opinion written by Justice Scalia, the Court first held that Argentina's issuance of the bonds was "commercial activity." The Court explained that, "when a foreign government acts, not as a regulator of a market, but in the manner of a private player within it, the foreign sovereign's actions are 'commercial' within the meaning of the FSIA." Id. at 614. The Court also emphasized that it is the nature of the foreign government's actions, not their purpose, that determines whether they are commercial. "[T]he issue," said the Court, "is whether the particular actions that the foreign state performs (whatever the motive behind them) are the *type* of actions by which a private party engages in 'trade and traffic or commerce.'" Id. (quoting Black's Law Dictionary 270 (6th ed. 1990)). In this case, the Court reasoned that "[t]he commercial character of the Bonods is confirmed by the fact that they are in almost all respects garden-variety debt instruments: They may be held by private parties; they are negotiable and may be traded on the international market (except in Argentina); and they promise a future stream of cash income." Id. at 615.

Second, the Court concluded that Argentina's unilateral rescheduling of the Bonods had a "direct effect" within the United States as required by the third clause of section 1605(a)(2). The Court rejected the argument, which had some support in the legislative history, that the effect must be "substantial" and "foreseeable." All that is required, said the Court, is that the effect be direct — that is, that it "follow[] as an immediate consequence of the defendant's activity." Id. at 618. Because the plaintiffs in this case had designated New York as the place of payment under the Bonods, the Court reasoned, Argentina's rescheduling of the obligations had a direct effect in New York: "Money that was supposed to have been delivered to a New York bank for deposit was not forthcoming." Id.

The Supreme Court considered other aspects of the commercial activity exception in the following decision.

Saudi Arabia v. Nelson

U.S. Supreme Court
507 U.S. 349 (1993)

Justice SOUTER delivered the opinion of the Court.

The Foreign Sovereign Immunities Act of 1976 entitles foreign states to immunity from the jurisdiction of courts in the United States, 28 U.S.C. §1604, subject to certain enumerated exceptions. §1605. One is that a foreign state shall not be immune in any case "in which the action is based upon a commercial activity carried on in the United States by the foreign state." §1605(a)(2). We hold that respondents' action alleging personal injury resulting from unlawful detention and torture by the Saudi Government is not "based upon a commercial activity" within the meaning of the Act, which consequently confers no jurisdiction over respondents' suit.

I

Because this case comes to us on a motion to dismiss the complaint, we assume that we have truthful factual allegations before us, though many of those allegations are subject to dispute. Petitioner Kingdom of Saudi Arabia owns and operates petitioner King Faisal Specialist Hospital in Riyadh, as well as petitioner Royspec Purchasing Services, the Hospital's corporate purchasing agent in the United States. The Hospital Corporation of America, Ltd. (HCA), an independent corporation existing under the laws of the Cayman Islands, recruits Americans for employment at the Hospital under an agreement signed with Saudi Arabia in 1973.

In its recruitment effort, HCA placed an advertisement in a trade periodical seeking applications for a position as a monitoring systems engineer at the Hospital. The advertisement drew the attention of respondent Scott Nelson in September 1983, while Nelson was in the United States. After interviewing for the position in Saudi Arabia, Nelson returned to the United States, where he signed an employment contract with the Hospital, satisfied personnel processing requirements, and attended an orientation session that HCA conducted for Hospital employees. In the course of that program, HCA identified Royspec as the point of contact in the United States for family members who might wish to reach Nelson in an emergency.

In December 1983, Nelson went to Saudi Arabia and began work at the Hospital, monitoring all "facilities, equipment, utilities and maintenance systems to insure the safety of patients, hospital staff, and others." He did his job without significant incident until March 1984, when he discovered safety defects in the Hospital's oxygen and nitrous oxide lines that posed fire hazards and otherwise endangered patients' lives. Over a period of several months, Nelson repeatedly advised Hospital officials of the safety defects and reported the defects to a Saudi Government commission as well. Hospital officials instructed Nelson to ignore the problems.

The Hospital's response to Nelson's reports changed, however, on September 27, 1984, when certain Hospital employees summoned him to the Hospital's security office where agents of the Saudi Government arrested him.[1] The agents transported Nelson to a jail cell, in which they "shackled, tortured and bea[t]" him, and kept him four days without food. Although Nelson did not understand Arabic, Government agents forced him to sign a statement written in that language, the content of which he did not know; a Hospital employee who was supposed to act as Nelson's interpreter advised him to sign "anything" the agents gave him to avoid further beatings. Two days later, Government agents transferred Nelson to the Al Sijan Prison "to await trial on unknown charges."

At the Prison, Nelson was confined in an overcrowded cell area infested with rats, where he had to fight other prisoners for food and from which he was taken only once a week for fresh air and exercise. Although police interrogators repeatedly questioned him in Arabic, Nelson did not learn the nature of the charges, if any, against him. For several days, the Saudi Government failed to advise Nelson's family of his whereabouts, though a Saudi official eventually told Nelson's wife, respondent Vivian Nelson, that he could arrange for her husband's release if she provided sexual favors.

Although officials from the United States Embassy visited Nelson twice during his detention, they concluded that his allegations of Saudi mistreatment were "not credible" and made no protest to Saudi authorities. It was only at the personal request of a United States Senator that the Saudi Government released Nelson, 39 days after his arrest, on November 5, 1984. Seven days later, after failing to convince him to return to work at the Hospital, the Saudi Government allowed Nelson to leave the country.

In 1988, Nelson and his wife filed this action against petitioners in the United States District Court for the Southern District of Florida seeking damages for personal injury. The Nelsons' complaint sets out 16 causes of action, which fall into three categories: [1] various intentional torts, including battery, unlawful detainment, wrongful arrest and imprisonment, false imprisonment, inhuman torture, disruption of normal family life, and infliction of mental anguish. [2] [N]egligently failing to warn Nelson of otherwise undisclosed dangers of his employment, namely, that if he attempted to report safety hazards the Hospital would likely retaliate against him and the Saudi Government might detain and physically abuse him without legal cause. [3] Vivian Nelson sustained derivative injury resulting from petitioners' actions. Presumably because the employment contract provided that Saudi courts would have exclusive jurisdiction over claims for breach of contract, the Nelsons raised no such matters. . . .

---

1. Petitioners assert that the Saudi Government arrested Nelson because he had falsely represented to the Hospital that he had received a degree from the Massachusetts Institute of Technology and had provided the Hospital with a forged diploma to verify his claim. The Nelsons concede these misrepresentations, but dispute that they occasioned Scott Nelson's arrest.

. . . For there to be jurisdiction in this case . . . the Nelsons' action must be "based upon" some "commercial activity" by petitioners that had "substantial contact" with the United States within the meaning of the Act. Because we conclude that the suit is not based upon any commercial activity by petitioners, we need not reach the issue of substantial contact with the United States.

We begin our analysis by identifying the particular conduct on which the Nelsons' action is "based" for purposes of the Act. Although the Act contains no definition of the phrase "based upon," and the relatively sparse legislative history offers no assistance, guidance is hardly necessary. In denoting conduct that forms the "basis," or "foundation," for a claim, see Black's Law Dictionary 151 (6th ed. 1990) (defining "base"); Random House Dictionary 172 (2d ed. 1987) (same); Webster's Third New International Dictionary 180, 181 (1976) (defining "base" and "based"), the phrase is read most naturally to mean those elements of a claim that, if proven, would entitle a plaintiff to relief under his theory of the case. See Callejo v. Bancomer, S.A., 764 F.2d 1101, 1109 (5th Cir. 1985) (focus should be on the "gravamen of the complaint").

What the natural meaning of the phrase "based upon" suggests, the context confirms. Earlier, we noted that §1605(a)(2) contains two clauses following the one at issue here. The second allows for jurisdiction where a suit "is based . . . upon an act performed in the United States in connection with a commercial activity of the foreign state elsewhere," and the third speaks in like terms, allowing for jurisdiction where an action "is based . . . upon an act outside the territory of the United States in connection with a commercial activity of the foreign state elsewhere and that act causes a direct effect in the United States." Distinctions among descriptions juxtaposed against each other are naturally understood to be significant, and Congress manifestly understood there to be a difference between a suit "based upon" commercial activity and one "based upon" acts performed "in connection with" such activity. The only reasonable reading of the former term calls for something more than a mere connection with, or relation to, commercial activity.[4]

In this case, the Nelsons have alleged that petitioners recruited Scott Nelson for work at the Hospital, signed an employment contract with him, and subsequently employed him. While these activities led to the conduct that eventually injured the Nelsons, they are not the basis for the Nelsons' suit. Even taking each of the Nelsons' allegations about Scott Nelson's recruitment and employment as true, those facts alone entitle the Nelsons to nothing under their theory of the case. The Nelsons have not, after all, alleged breach of contract, but personal injuries caused by petitioners' intentional wrongs and by petitioners' negligent failure to warn Scott Nelson that they might commit those wrongs. Those torts, and not the arguably commercial activities that preceded their commission, form the basis for the Nelsons' suit.

Petitioners' tortious conduct itself fails to qualify as "commercial activity" within the meaning of the Act, although the Act is too " 'obtuse' " to be of much help in reaching that conclusion. We have seen already that the Act defines "commercial activity" as "either a regular course of commercial conduct or a particular commercial transaction or act," and provides that "[t]he commercial character of an activity

---

4. We do not mean to suggest that the first clause of §1605(a)(2) necessarily requires that each and every element of a claim be commercial activity by a foreign state, and we do not address the case where a claim consists of both commercial and sovereign elements. We do conclude, however, that where a claim rests entirely upon activities sovereign in character, as here, jurisdiction will not exist under that clause regardless of any connection the sovereign acts may have with commercial activity.

shall be determined by reference to the nature of the course of conduct or particular transaction or act, rather than by reference to its purpose." 28 U.S.C. §1603(d). If this is a definition, it is one distinguished only by its diffidence; as we observed in our most recent case on the subject, it "leaves the critical term 'commercial' largely undefined." Republic of Argentina v. Weltover, Inc., 504 U.S. 607 (1992). We do not, however, have the option to throw up our hands. The term has to be given some interpretation, and congressional diffidence necessarily results in judicial responsibility to determine what a "commercial activity" is for purposes of the Act.

We took up the task just last Term in *Weltover*, supra, which involved Argentina's unilateral refinancing of bonds it had issued under a plan to stabilize its currency. . . . In the course of holding the refinancing to be a commercial activity for purposes of the Act, we observed that the statute "largely codifies the so-called 'restrictive' theory of foreign sovereign immunity first endorsed by the State Department in 1952." We accordingly held that the meaning of "commercial" for purposes of the Act must be the meaning Congress understood the restrictive theory to require at the time it passed the statute.

Under the restrictive, as opposed to the "absolute," theory of foreign sovereign immunity, a state is immune from the jurisdiction of foreign courts as to its sovereign or public acts (jure imperii), but not as to those that are private or commercial in character (jure gestionis). We explained in *Weltover* that a state engages in commercial activity under the restrictive theory where it exercises " 'only those powers that can also be exercised by private citizens,' " as distinct from those " 'powers peculiar to sovereigns.' " Put differently, a foreign state engages in commercial activity for purposes of the restrictive theory only where it acts "in the manner of a private player within" the market. [S]ee Restatement (Third) of the Foreign Relations Law of the United States §451 (1987) ("Under international law, a state or state instrumentality is immune from the jurisdiction of the courts of another state, except with respect to claims arising out of activities of the kind that may be carried on by private persons").

We emphasized in *Weltover* that whether a state acts "in the manner of" a private party is a question of behavior, not motivation. . . . We did not ignore the difficulty of distinguishing " 'purpose' (i.e., the reason why the foreign state engages in the activity) from 'nature' (i.e., the outward form of the conduct that the foreign state performs or agrees to perform)," but recognized that the Act "unmistakably commands" us to observe the distinction. . . .

Unlike Argentina's activities that we considered in *Weltover*, the intentional conduct alleged here (the Saudi Government's wrongful arrest, imprisonment, and torture of Nelson) could not qualify as commercial under the restrictive theory. The conduct boils down to abuse of the power of its police by the Saudi Government, and however monstrous such abuse undoubtedly may be, a foreign state's exercise of the power of its police has long been understood for purposes of the restrictive theory as peculiarly sovereign in nature. Exercise of the powers of police and penal officers is not the sort of action by which private parties can engage in commerce. . . .

The Nelsons and their amici urge us to give significance to their assertion that the Saudi Government subjected Nelson to the abuse alleged as retaliation for his persistence in reporting Hospital safety violations, and argue that the character of the mistreatment was consequently commercial. One amicus, indeed, goes so far as to suggest that the Saudi Government "often uses detention and torture to resolve commercial disputes." But this argument does not alter the fact that the powers allegedly abused were those of police and penal officers. In any event, the argument is off the point, for it goes to purpose, the very fact the Act renders irrelevant to the question of an activity's commercial character. Whatever may have been the Saudi Government's motivation for its allegedly abusive treatment of Nelson, it remains the case that the Nelsons' action is based upon a sovereign activity immune from the subject-matter jurisdiction of United States courts under the Act.

In addition to the intentionally tortious conduct, the Nelsons claim a separate basis for recovery in petitioners' failure to warn Scott Nelson of the hidden dangers associated with his employment. The Nelsons allege that, at the time petitioners recruited Scott Nelson and thereafter, they failed to warn him of the possibility of severe retaliatory action if he attempted to disclose any safety hazards he might discover on the job. In other words, petitioners bore a duty to warn of their own propensity for tortious conduct. But this is merely a semantic ploy. For aught we can see, a plaintiff could recast virtually any claim of intentional tort committed by sovereign act as a claim of failure to warn, simply by charging the defendant with an obligation to announce its own tortious propensity before indulging it. To give jurisdictional significance to this feint of language would effectively thwart the Act's manifest purpose to codify the restrictive theory of foreign sovereign immunity. . . .

Justice WHITE, with whom Justice BLACKMUN joins, concurring in the judgment. . . .

To run and operate a hospital, even a public hospital, is to engage in a commercial enterprise. The majority never concedes this point, but it does not deny it either, and to my mind the matter is self-evident. By the same token, warning an employee when he blows the whistle and taking retaliatory action, such as harassment, involuntary transfer, discharge, or other tortious behavior, although not prototypical commercial acts, are certainly well within the bounds of commercial activity. . . . Nelson alleges that petitioners harmed him in the course of engaging in their commercial enterprise, as a direct result of their commercial acts. His claim, in other words, is "based upon commercial activity."

Indeed, I am somewhat at a loss as to what exactly the majority believes petitioners have done that a private employer could not. As countless cases attest, retaliation for whistle-blowing is not a practice foreign to the marketplace. . . . On occasion, private employres also have been known to retaliate by enlisting the help of police officers to falsely arrest employees. . . . More generally, private parties have been held liable for conspiring with public authorities to effectuate an arrest, . . . and for using private security personnel for the same purposes. . . .

Nevertheless, I reach the same conclusion as the majority because petitioners' commercial activity was not "carried on in the United States." The Act defines such conduct as "commercial activity . . . having substantial contact with the United States." 28 U.S.C. §1603(e). Respondents point to the hospital's recruitment efforts in the United States, including advertising in the American media, and the signing of the employment contract in Miami. As I earlier noted, while these may very well qualify as commercial activity in the United States, they do not constitute the commercial activity upon which respondents' action is based. Conversely, petitioners' commercial conduct in Saudi Arabia, though constituting the basis of the Nelsons' suit, lacks a sufficient nexus to the United States. Neither the hospital's employment practices, nor its disciplinary procedures, has any apparent connection to this country. On that basis, I agree that the Act does not grant the Nelsons access to our courts.

Justice KENNEDY, with whom Justice BLACKMUN and Justice STEVENS join as to Parts I-B and II, concurring in part and dissenting in part.

I join all of the Court's opinion except the last paragraph of Part II, where, with almost no explanation, the Court rules that, like the intentional tort claim, the claims based on negligent failure to warn are outside the subject-matter jurisdiction of the federal courts. These claims stand on a much different footing from the intentional tort claims for purposes of the Foreign Sovereign Immunities Act (FSIA). In my view, they ought to be remanded to the District Court for further consideration. . . .

B

. . . The Nelsons' claims alleging that the Hospital, the Kingdom, and Royspec were negligent in failing during their recruitment of Nelson to warn him of foreseeable dangers are based upon commercial activity having substantial contact with the United States. As such, they are within the commercial activity exception and the jurisdiction of the federal courts. Unlike the intentional tort counts of the complaint, the failure to warn counts do not complain of a police beating in Saudi Arabia; rather, they complain of a negligent omission made during the recruiting of a hospital employee in the United States. . . .

Omission of important information during employee recruiting is commercial activity as we have described it. See Republic of Argentina v. Weltover, Inc., 504 U.S. 349 (1992).

II

Having met the jurisdictional prerequisites of the FSIA, the Nelsons' failure to warn claims should survive petitioners' motion under Federal Rule of Civil Procedure 12(b)(1) to dismiss for want of subject-matter jurisdiction.

Notes and Questions

1. In light of *Weltover* and *Nelson,* how would you define "commercial activity"? Is changing the currency exchange rates by a central bank a commercial activity? Is purchasing a pistol for the police a commercial act?

2. As the Supreme Court emphasized in *Weltover* and *Nelson,* the FSIA requires courts, in determining whether foreign state conduct is commercial, to look to the nature of the conduct rather than to the foreign state's purpose. See 28 U.S.C. §1603(d). Why do you think the FSIA requires this? Is the nature of an activity completely separate from its purpose? Can the nature of an activity be affected by who is

doing it? Compare the sale by Martin-Marietta Corporation to the government of Germany of 100 screwdrivers versus 100 missiles with a range of over 300 miles and capable of carrying nuclear warheads. Are both commercial acts?

What if a government engages in activity that involves the exchange of money but which, under that nation's laws, only the government is allowed to engage in? In addressing this issue, some courts have held (in decisions prior to *Weltover*) that a government's regulation of its natural resources is not a commercial activity. See, e.g., MOL, Inc. v. People's Republic of Bangladesh, 736 F.2d 1326 (9th Cir. 1984) (issuance of license to capture and export monkeys held not to be a commercial activity); In re Sedco, 543 F. Supp. 561 (S.D. Tex. 1982) (drilling for oil by government-owned company held not to be commercial activity); International Assn. of Machinists v. Organization of Petroleum Exporting Countries (OPEC), 477 F. Supp. 553, 567-569 (C.D. Cal. 1979) (participation in a cartel among nations to regulate the price and supply of oil held not to be a commercial activity), aff'd on other grounds, 649 F.2d 1354 (9th Cir. 1981). Does this "natural resource" limitation on the commercial activity exception survive *Weltover* and *Nelson*?

3. In *Nelson*, why didn't the plaintiffs sue for breach of Mr. Nelson's employment contract, which would have made their case seem more commercial? Why didn't they sue under the third clause of §1605(a)(2), which reaches foreign acts "in connection with" foreign commercial activities as long as the act "causes a direct effect in the United States"? Alternatively, why didn't they sue under the FSIA's noncommercial tort exception (discussed below)?

4. According to the majority in *Nelson,* how do we know whether a suit is "based upon" commercial activity? What activities, according to the majority, was the plaintiff's suit based upon? Weren't those activities at least *connected to* commercial activity? If so, why was that not sufficient? What about Justice White's argument that private businesses sometimes engage in similar activities? Does the argument improperly look to the purpose, as opposed to the nature, of the activity? Why, according to the majority, should the activities in *Nelson* be characterized as an abuse of police power rather than a retaliation for whistleblowing?

5. Why did the majority in *Nelson* reject the failure-to-warn claim? Note that the suit was dismissed on the pleadings, so the Court was supposed to presume the correctness of the plaintiffs' allegations. Nevertheless, did the Court implicitly make some judgments about Mr. Nelson's credibility? In any event, was the majority right that the failure-to-warn claim was just a "semantic ploy"? Is it relevant to your resolution of these questions that the Nelsons had already brought a failure-to-warn claim against the agent, HCA, and that claim had been dismissed by the trial court on the merits?

6. The *Weltover* test for "direct effects," which does not require that the effects be either substantial or foreseeable, has generated some confusion and discord in the lower courts. Some courts, relying on the broad language of *Weltover,* have allowed cases with limited connections to the United States to proceed. See, e.g., Hanil Bank v. P.T. Bank Negara Indonesia, 148 F.3d 127 (2d Cir. 1998) (failure of Indonesian bank to make payment on a letter of credit used to finance sale of parts from a Korean company to an Indonesian company in Indonesia, where the Korean company had designated New York City as the place of payment). By contrast, some courts have attempted to limit the application of the *Weltover* test. See, e.g., United World Trade, Inc. v. Mangyshlakneft, 33 F.3d 1232 (10th Cir. 1994) (mere requirement that

payments under contract be made in U.S. dollars not a direct effect even though U.S. bank happened to be involved in the conversion); Antares Aircraft v. Nigeria, 999 F.2d 33 (2d Cir. 1993) (mere fortuity that money paid to foreign state came from a U.S. bank account was not a direct effect because the contract did not specify the United States as the required source of payment). There is also a division in the courts over whether a "legally significant act" (i.e., an action in the United States giving rise to the cause of action) must occur in the United States for there to be a direct effect. Compare Keller v. Central Bank of Nigeria, 277 F.3d 811 (6th Cir. 2002) (not requiring a legally significant act); Voest-Alpine Trading USA Corp. v. Bank of China, 142 F.3d 887 (5th Cir. 1998) (same), with Adler v. Republic of Nigeria, 107 F.3d 720, 727 (9th Cir. 1997) (requiring a legally significant act); and *Antares Aircraft,* supra (same).

7. The FSIA provides that there is a personal jurisdiction whenever an exception to immunity is satisfied and the foreign state defendant is properly served. In some cases, the contacts with the United States required by the exceptions to immunity might not be enough to satisfy the requirements of due process. For suits based upon a defendant's contact with the forum, due process requires "minimum contacts" with the forum "such that maintenance of the suit does not offend 'traditional notions of fair play and substantial justice.'" International Shoe Co. v. Washington, 326 U.S. 310, 316 (1945). This requires that the defendant have "purposefully availed" itself of the benefits and protections of the forum and that the exercise of jurisdiction be "reasonable." See, e.g., World-Wide Volkswagen Corp. v. Woodson, 444 U.S. 286 (1980). The Supreme Court has held that these due process requirements must be met in order for a U.S. court to exercise personal jurisdiction over a *private* foreign defendant. See Asahi Metal Industry Co. v. Superior Court, 480 U.S. 102 (1987). In *Weltover,* the Court reserved judgment on whether these requirements must be met in suits against foreign state defendants.

Should suits against foreign states be subject to due process requirements? Note that the Supreme Court has held that *U.S. states* are not "persons" for purposes of the Due Process Clause of the Constitution. See South Carolina v. Katzenbach, 383 U.S. 301, 323-324 (1966). Should foreign states be treated the same for due process purposes as U.S. states? Many lower courts have assumed that the due process requirements for personal jurisdiction must be met in suits against foreign states. In *Weltover,* however, the Court treated this as an open question. See 504 U.S. at 619. Recently, the U.S. Court of Appeals for the D.C. Circuit held that a foreign state is *not* a person under the Due Process Clause and that, therefore, the Constitution imposes no limitation on the exercise of personal jurisdiction by a federal court over a foreign state. See Price v. Socialist People's Libyan Arab Jamahiriya, 294 F.3d 82 (D.C. Cir. 2002). A federal district court in Washington, D.C., had reached this conclusion several years earlier. See Flatow v. Islamic Republic of Iran, 999 F. Supp. 1, 19-21 (D.D.C. 1998). Both of these decisions involve the FSIA's exception for state sponsors of terrorism, which is discussed below in subsection 9.

The contacts required by the FSIA's exceptions to immunity will meet the due process requirements in most cases. There are at least three situations, however, where this might not be true. First, the waiver exception to immunity, 28 U.S.C. §1605(a)(1), does not require any contacts with the United States. This should not raise due process concerns in situations in which the foreign state has *expressly* waived its immunity from suit in U.S. courts because defendants are normally permitted to waive the due process requirements for personal jurisdiction. The waiver exception, however, also allows for *implicit* waivers. If the implict waiver provision were construed broadly, basing personal jurisdiction on it could raise due process concerns. See, e.g., Proyecfin de Venezuela, S.A. v. Banco Industrial de Venezuela, 760 F.2d 390, 393 (2d Cir. 1985). Second, as illustrated by *Weltover*, the Supreme Court has interpreted the reach of the "direct effect" requirement in the commercial activity exception broadly, such that it reaches foreign activities that have little connection to the United States. Third, as discussed below, Congress amended the FSIA in 1996 to allow suits against "state sponsors of terrorism," and the only U.S. connection it specified was that the victim or plaintiff must have U.S. citizenship.

8.   Noncommercial Tort Exception

Section 1605(a)(5) provides that there shall not be immunity in an action, not otherwise encompassed within the commercial activity exception, "in which money damages are sought against a foreign state for personal injury or death, or damage to or loss of property, occurring in the United States and caused by the tortious act or omission of that foreign state or of any official or employee of that foreign state while acting within the scope of his office or employment." This exception does not apply, however, to "(A) any claim based upon the exercise or performance or the failure to exercise or perform a discretionary function regardless of whether the discretion be abused, or (B) any claim arising out of malicious prosecution, abuse of process, libel, slander, misrepresentation, deceit, or interference with contract rights." The House Report for the FSIA states that this exception was directed "primarily at the problem of traffic accidents but is cast in general terms as applying to all tort actions for monetary damages, not otherwise encompassed by section 1605(a)(2) relating to commercial activities."

By its terms, this exception requires that the injury or damage occur in the United States. A number of courts have held that the tortious act or omission must also occur in the United States. See, e.g., Persinger v. Islamic Republic of Iran, 729 F.2d 835 (D.C. Cir. 1984); Frolova v. USSR, 761 F.2d 370, 379-380 (7th Cir. 1985); In re SEDCO, Inc., 543 F. Supp. 561, 567 (S.D. Tex. 1982). These courts have emphasized the legislative history, which not only refers to traffic accidents but also states that "the tortious act or omission must occur within the jurisdiction of the United States." The Restatement (Third), by contrast, has construed the noncommercial tort exception to apply whenever the injury occurs in the United States, "regardless of where the act or omission causing the injury took place." Restatement (Third) of the Foreign Relations Law of the United States §454, cmt. *e* (1987).

As noted above, the noncommercial tort exception does not apply to claims based upon the exercise or failure to exercise a discretionary function. The following decisions consider the scope of this limitation.

Letelier v. Republic of Chile

U.S. District Court
488 F. Supp. 665 (D.D.C. 1980)

[In 1976, Orlando Letelier, a former ambassador from Chile, and Ronni Moffitt were killed by a car bomb in Washington, D.C. Their families brought suit against the Republic of Chile, its intelligence agency, and various Chilean officials, alleging that they were responsible for the bombing.]

GREEN, District Judge. . . .

In the instant action, relying on section 1605(a)(5) as their basis for combatting any assertion of sovereign immunity, plaintiffs have set forth several tortious causes of action arising under international law, the common law, the Constitution, and legislative enactments, all of which are alleged to spring from the deaths of Orlando Letelier and Ronni Moffitt. The Republic of Chile, while vigorously contending that it was in no way involved in the events that resulted in the two deaths, further asserts that, even if it were, the Court has no subject matter jurisdiction in that it is entitled to immunity under the Act, which does not cover political assassinations because of their public, governmental character.

. . . It is clear from [the legislative history], the Chilean government asserts, that the intent of Congress was to include only private torts like automobile accidents within the exclusion from immunity embodied in section 1605(a)(5).

Prominently absent from defendant's analysis, however, is the initial step in any endeavor at statutory interpretation: a consideration of the words of the statute. . . . Subject to the exclusion of these discretionary acts defined in subsection (A) and the specific causes of action enumerated in subsection (B), neither of which have been invoked by the Republic of Chile, by the plain language of section 1605(a)(5) a foreign state is not entitled to immunity from an action seeking money damages "for personal injury or death . . . caused by the tortious act or omission of that foreign state" or its officials or employees. Nowhere is there an indication that the tortious acts to which the Act makes reference are to only be those formerly classified as "private," thereby engrafting onto the statute, as the Republic of Chile would have the Court do, the requirement that the character of a given tortious act be judicially analyzed to determine whether it was of the type heretofore denoted as *jure gestionis* or should be classified as *jure imperii*. Indeed, the other provisions of the Act mandate that the Court not do so, for it is made clear that the Act and the principles it sets forth in its specific provisions are henceforth to govern all claims of sovereign immunity by foreign states. 28 U.S.C. §§1602, 1604 (1976).

Although the unambiguous language of the Act makes inquiry almost unnecessary, further examination reveals nothing in its legislative history that contradicts or qualifies its plain meaning. The relative frequency of automobile accidents and their potentially grave financial impact may have placed that problem foremost in the minds of Congress, but the applicability of the Act was not so limited, for the committees made it quite clear that the Act "is cast in general terms as applying to all tort actions for money damages" so as to provide recompense for "the victim of a traffic accident or other noncommercial tort." . . .

Examining then the specific terms of section 1605(a)(5), despite the Chilean failure to have addressed the issue, the Court is called upon to consider whether either of the exceptions to liability for tortious acts found in section 1605(a)(5) applies in this instance. It is readily apparent, however, that the claims herein did not arise "out of malicious prosecution, abuse of process, libel, slander, misrepresentation, deceit, or interference with contract rights," 28 U.S.C. §1605(a)(5)(B) (1976), and therefore only the exemption for claims "based upon the exercise or performance or the failure to exercise or perform a discretionary function regardless of whether the discretion be abused," id. §1605(a)(5)(A), can be applicable.

As its language and the legislative history make apparent, the discretionary act exemption of subsection (A) corresponds to the discretionary act exception found in the Federal Tort Claims Act. As defined by the United States Supreme Court in interpreting the Federal Tort Claims Act, an act that is discretionary is one in which "there is room for policy judgment and decision." Dalehite v. United States, 346 U.S. 15, 36 (1953). Applying this definition to the instant action, the question becomes, would the alleged determination of the Chilean Republic to set into motion and assist in the precipitation of those events that culminated in the deaths of Orlando Letelier and Ronni Moffitt be of the kind in which there is "room for policy judgment and decision."

While it seems apparent that a decision calculated to result in injury or death to a particular individual or individuals, made for whatever reason, would be one most assuredly involving policy judgment and decision and thus exempt as a discretionary act under section 1605(a)(5)(A), that exception is not applicable to bar this suit. As it has been recognized, there is no discretion to commit, or to have one's officers or agents commit, an illegal act. Whatever policy options may exist for a foreign country, it has no "discretion" to perpetrate conduct designed to result in the assassination of an individual or individuals, action that is clearly contrary to the precepts of humanity as recognized in both national and international law. Accordingly there would be no "discretion" within the meaning of section 1605(a)(5)(A) to order or to aid in an assassination and were it to be demonstrated that a foreign state has undertaken any such act in this country, that foreign state could not be accorded sovereign immunity under subsection (A) for any tort claims resulting from its conduct. As a consequence, the Republic of Chile cannot claim sovereign immunity under the Foreign Sovereign Immunities Act for its alleged involvement in the deaths of Orlando Letelier and Ronni Moffitt.

Risk v. Halvorsen

U.S. Court of Appeals
936 F.2d 393 (9th Cir. 1991)

BRUNETTI, Circuit Judge....

In 1977 Plaintiff Larry Risk married Elisabeth Antonsen Risk, a native and citizen of Norway. In 1983 the Risk family — Larry, Elisabeth and their two children — moved to Norway for a period. After an attempt by Larry to remove the children to the United States, Elisabeth received a temporary order from a Norwegian County Court providing ordinary visitation rights for the father. During the first visitation period Larry returned with the children to the United States.

In 1984 Elisabeth filed a petition in the Superior Court of San Francisco seeking custody of the two children. The parties were awarded joint custody and the superior court order prohibited the parents from removing the children from the five San Francisco Bay Area counties. In addition, the parties were required to surrender their children's passports and their own to Larry Risk's attorney, and were prohibited from applying for replacement passports without a court order. In July 1984, apparently with the assistance of various Norwegian government officials, Elisabeth Risk returned to Norway with her children.

Larry Risk filed this action in April, 1988, alleging that the Norwegian government and its consular officials conspired to violate and in fact violated the 1984 California custody order by suggesting to Elisabeth Risk that she return to Norway with the children; by providing travel documentation for Elisabeth and the children; by providing financial assistance to Elisabeth to make the trip; and, finally, by obstructing Larry Risk in his effort to locate and contact his children. . . .

The district court rejected jurisdiction over Norway under the FSIA because of an exception to the general jurisdiction provision, section 1605(a)(5), which excludes claims based on the exercise or performance, or failure to exercise or perform, a discretionary function.

Whether the acts of the Norwegian officials are within the discretionary function exception to the FSIA is controlled by principles developed under the Federal Tort Claims Act ("FTCA"). First, we "must determine whether the government employee had any discretion to act or if there was an element of choice as to appropriate conduct." Liu v. Republic of China, 892 F.2d 1419, 1431 (9th Cir. 1989), cert. dismissed, 497 U.S. 1058 (1990) (citing Berkovitz v. United States, 486 U.S. 531, 535 (1988)). Second, we consider "whether the decisions were grounded in social, economic, and political policy," concentrating on "the nature of the conduct, rather than the status of the actor. . . ." MacArthur Area Citizens Ass'n v. Peru, 258 U.S. App. D.C. 77, 809 F.2d 918, 922 (D.C. Cir. 1987), vacated on other grounds, 823 F.2d 606 (1987) (quoting United States v. Varig, 467 U.S. 797, 813, 814 (1984)).

In *MacArthur,* a neighborhood association sued the Republic of Peru for occupation and use of a building in violation of a zoning ordinance. The circuit court for the District of Columbia held that the discretionary function exception to the FSIA applied because the establishment of a chancery in a particular building, and modification of that building for security purposes, is a discretionary act of public policy, both political and economic in nature.

In Joseph v. Nigeria, [830 F.2d 1018, 1026 (9th Cir. 1987)], we declined to apply the discretionary function exception to acts of officials of the Nigerian government which lead to a tort suit. In that case, the government officials were accused of destruction of the property in which the Nigerian Consulate was located. We held that while acquisition and operation of the property was a discretionary function, purely destructive acts are not part of the policy decision to establish the consulate and thus fall outside the scope of the discretionary function exception.

The acts of the agents of the Norwegian government are closer to those of the officials in *MacArthur* and thus the discretionary function exception applies.

The Norwegian officials are accused of advising and assisting a Norwegian citizen and her children in leaving the United States. There can be no doubt the officials here were exercising discretion. . . .

Appellant argues that because the acts of the Norwegian officials may constitute a violation of California criminal law,[3] the acts should fall outside the scope of the discretionary function exception to the FSIA, and thus that the district court should have retained jurisdiction over Norway. . . .

---

3. Intentional violation of a custody order, or of the rights of a parent under such an order is a felony in California. Cal. Penal Code §278.5 (West 1988).

[Among other things], appellant relies on Letelier v. Republic of Chile, 488 F. Supp. 665 (D.D.C. 1980). In that case, members of the families of a Chilean national and his assistant who were ordered assassinated by members of the Chilean government brought a tort action against Chile in federal court. The district court refused to apply the discretionary function exception to the FSIA, stating that "there is no discretion to commit, or to have one's officers or agents commit, an illegal act. . . . Whatever policy options may exist for a foreign country, it has no 'discretion' to perpetrate conduct designed to result in the assassination of an individual or individuals." Id. at 673.

While the *Letelier* court apparently considered "action that is clearly contrary to the precepts of humanity" outside the scope of the discretionary function exception, id., the nature of the act in that case obviously influenced the court. In this case, the most that can be said is that Norwegian officials issued travel documents to a Norwegian citizen and her children, also citizens of Norway; that they provided funds for her travel; and that they protected her from contact by her former husband. Although these acts may constitute a crime under California law, it cannot be said that every conceivably illegal act is outside the scope of the discretionary function exception. *MacArthur*, 809 F.2d at 922 n.4.

The district court correctly held that the discretionary function exception to the FSIA applies in this case and that it has no jurisdiction to hear the claims against Norway.

Notes and Questions

1. What should a court do when some of the tortious conduct occurs in the United States and some of it occurs outside the United States? This was the situation in Olsen ex rel. Sheldon v. Government of Mexico, 729 F.2d 641 (9th Cir. 1984), in which an airplane owned and operated by the Mexican government was flying from Monterrey, Mexico, to Tijuana, Mexico, but crashed inside the United States. A number of acts and omissions were alleged to have contributed to the crash, some occurring in Mexico and others occurring in the United States. Mexico argued that, for the situs requirement to be met, *all* of the tortious acts or omissions must occur in the United States. The Ninth Circuit rejected this argument, reasoning that it would be unjust to confer immunity on foreign state defendants for tortious acts or omissions in the United States simply because they could show that some of their tortious conduct happened to occur outside the United States. Did the Ninth Circuit reach the right conclusion?

2. The FSIA's discretionary function limitation was modeled on a similar provision in the Federal Tort Claims Act ("FTCA"), which governs tort suits against the U.S. federal government. As a result, in applying the FSIA's discretionary function provision, courts often have looked to decisions from the FTCA area. The Supreme Court has held that the FTCA's discretionary function limitation does not apply "when a federal statute, regulation, or policy specifically prescribes a course of action for an employee to follow" because in this situation "the employee has no rightful option but to adhere to the directive." Berkovitz v. United States, 486 U.S. 531, 536 (1988). Lower courts have interpreted this holding to mean that conduct by a federal official that is prohibited under federal constitutional, statutory, or regulatory

law does not fall within the FTCA's discretionary function limitation. In this circumstance, courts have reasoned, the official engaged in the conduct is acting outside of his or her discretionary authority. By analogy, one might conclude that conduct by a foreign state's official that is prohibited by the foreign state's domestic law should not fall within the FSIA's discretionary function exception. Are there nevertheless reasons to be cautious before applying the FTCA precedent on legality of conduct to the FSIA? Is it more difficult or problematic for U.S. courts to assess the legality of foreign government conduct than it is for them to assess the legality of U.S. government conduct?

3. In applying the discretionary function limitation, the court in *Letelier* states that "there is no discretion to commit, or to have one's officers or agents commit, an illegal act." If this is true, what is left of the discretionary function limitation on the noncommercial tort exception? The court in *Risk* is probably right, is it not, that "it cannot be said that every conceivably illegal act is outside the scope of the discretionary function exception"? How do these decisions compare with *Nelson*, excerpted above, in which a majority of the Supreme Court described the alleged wrongful arrest, imprisonment, and torture of Mr. Nelson as "peculiarly sovereign in nature"?

4. In addition to the discretionary function limitation, certain torts are exempted from the noncommercial tort exception: "any claim arising out of malicious prosecution, abuse of process, libel, slander, misrepresentation, deceit, or interference with contract rights." 28 U.S.C. §1605(a)(5)(B). Why do you think Congress exempted these claims from the exception? Why might it be more problematic for U.S. courts to adjudicate these claims against a foreign government as compared with other tort claims? Can plaintiffs bring these claims, or claims concerning discretionary functions, under *other* exceptions to immunity, such as the commercial activity exception? The plain language of the noncommercial tort exception suggests that these limitations apply only to the noncommercial tort exception and do not restrict the scope of other exceptions. The limitations apply to "this paragraph," which seems clearly to be a reference to the paragraph containing the noncommercial tort exception. Moreover, the noncommercial tort exception as a whole applies to cases "not otherwise encompassed [by the commercial activities exception]." In large part because of this language, most courts have concluded that other exceptions to immunity, such as the commercial activity exception, are not subject to the limitations listed in the noncommercial tort exception. See, e.g., El-Hadad v. United Arab Emirates, 216 F.3d 29 (D.C. Cir. 2000); Southway v. Central Bank of Nigeria, 198 F.3d 1210 (10th Cir. 1999); Export Group v. Reef Industries, Inc., 54 F.3d 1466, 1473-1476 (9th Cir. 1995).

5. Under what law should courts determine whether conduct is within an individual's "scope of employment" for purposes of the noncommercial tort exception? In Liu v. Republic of China, 892 F.2d 1419 (9th Cir. 1989), the court applied a federal common law choice-of-law rule to determine that California law — which was the place where the injury occurred, and the place of the plaintiff's domicile — governed the "scope of employment" question. Most courts agree that state law ultimately governs this question. See, e.g., Moran v. Kingdom of Saudi Arabia, 27 F.3d 169 (5th Cir. 1994); Rodriguez v. Republic of Costa Rica, 99 F. Supp. 2d 157 (D.P.R. 2000). Should state law have this sort of influence on the application of foreign sovereign immunity? Should the scope of employment determination vary from state

to state? Does this follow from 28 U.S.C. §1606, which states that, for any claim for which a foreign state is not entitled to immunity, the foreign state "shall be liable in the same manner and to the same extent as a private individual under like circumstances"?

9. *Terrorist Acts*

In 1996, as part of the Antiterrorism and Effective Death Penalty Act, Congress added a new exception to immunity in the FSIA for "state sponsors of terrorism." See 28 U.S.C. §1605(a)(7). Under this exception, foreign states designated as state sponsors of terrorism do not have immunity from civil suits for damages

> for personal injury or death that was caused by an act of torture, extrajudicial killing, aircraft sabotage, hostage taking, or the provision of material support or resources . . . for such an act if such act or provision of material support is engaged in by an official, employee, or agent of such foreign state while acting within the scope of his or her office, employment, or agency.

The terms *torture* and *extrajudicial killing* are defined by reference to the Torture Victim Protection Act, which we considered in Chapter 3. The terms *hostage taking* and *aircraft sabotage* are defined by reference to relevant treaties. The phrase *material support or resources* is defined by reference to a federal criminal provision.

The exception to immunity in §1605(a)(7) applies only if the claimant or the victim was a U.S. national when the act upon which the claim is based occurred. In addition, if the act complained of occurred within the foreign state being sued, the state must first be given a "reasonable opportunity to arbitrate the claim in accordance with accepted international rules of arbitration."

This exception was expressly made retroactive, such that it applies to "any cause of action arising before, on, or after" 1996. However, the state must have been designated a state sponsor of terrorism when the act occurred "unless later so designated as a result of such act." The designation of state sponsors of terrorism is made by the Department of State on an annual basis. As of July 2002, seven nations were designated state sponsors of terrorism: Cuba, Iran, Iraq, Libya, North Korea, Sudan, and Syria. See 31 C.F.R. §596.201 (2002). This list is the same one that the State Department had in effect in 1996. Actions brought under §1605(a)(7) are subject to a ten-year statute of limitations, but this limitations period can be extended based on principles of equitable tolling.

After enacting §1605(a)(7), Congress enacted a Civil Liability Act that creates a statutory cause of action for suits against agents of state sponsors of terrorism. This Act, which was codified as a note to §1605 of the FSIA, is often referred to as the "Flatow Amendment" after the name of the victim in one of the cases discussed below. Under the Act, U.S. citizens are allowed to sue an "official, employee, or agent of a foreign state designated as a state sponsor of terrorism" for acts covered by §1605(a)(7). Plaintiffs under this statute may recover money damages, "which may include economic damages, solatium, pain, and suffering, and punitive damages."

The decision excerpted below was the first decision relying on the (a)(7) exception.

Alejandre v. Republic of Cuba

U.S. District Court
996 F. Supp. 1239 (S.D. Fla. 1997)

KING, District Judge.

The personal representative of three of the deceased instituted this action against the Republic of Cuba ("Cuba") and the Cuban Air Force to recover monetary damages for the killings [described below].

. . . One of the victims was not a U.S. citizen and his family therefore could not join in the suit. This is the first lawsuit to rely on recent legislative enactments that strip foreign states of immunity for certain acts of terrorism. Neither Cuba nor the Cuban Air Force has defended this suit, asserting through a diplomatic note that this Court has no jurisdiction over Cuba or its political subdivisions. A default was thus entered against both Defendants on April 23, 1997 pursuant to Rule 55(a) of the Federal Rules of Civil Procedure. Because this is a lawsuit against a foreign state, however, the Court may not enter judgment by default. Rather, the claimants must establish their "claim or right to relief by evidence that is satisfactory to the Court." 28 U.S.C. §1608(e)(1994).[1] These three consolidated cases proceeded to trial on November 13, 14, and 20, 1997, on the issues of liability and damages. Because the Court finds that neither Cuba nor the Cuban Air Force is immune from suit for the killings, and because the facts amply prove both Defendants' liability and Plaintiffs' damages, the Court will enter judgment against Defendants.

II. FINDINGS OF FACT

At trial, Plaintiffs presented extensive testimonial and documentary evidence in support of their claims. Because Cuba has presented no defense, the Court will accept as true Plaintiffs' uncontroverted factual allegations. . . .

Alejandre, Costa, and De la Peña were all members of a Miami-based humanitarian organization known as *Hermanos al Rescate*, or Brothers to the Rescue. The organization's principal mission was to search the Florida Straits for rafters, Cuban refugees who had fled the island nation on precarious inner tubes or makeshift rafts, often perishing at sea. Brothers to the Rescue would locate the rafters and provide them with life-saving assistance by informing the U.S. Coast Guard of their location and condition.

On the morning of February 24, 1996, two of Brothers to the Rescue's civilian Cessna 337 aircraft departed from Opa Locka Airport in South Florida. Costa piloted one plane, accompanied by Pablo Morales, a Cuban national who had once been a rafter himself. De la Peña piloted the second plane, with Alejandre as his passenger. Before departing, the planes notified both Miami and Havana traffic controllers of their flight plans, which were to take them south of the 24th parallel. The

---

1. The Congressional purpose behind this section was to protect foreign states from "unfounded default judgments rendered solely upon a procedural default." *Compania Interamericana*, 88 F.3d at 950-51. As detailed more fully below, the abundant evidence offered at trial more than satisfies the Court that Plaintiffs are entitled to relief. Moreover, it bears mention that Cuba's default has been willful, as evidenced by its diplomatic note rejecting this Court's jurisdiction, further bolstering the entry of a default judgment.

24th parallel, well north of Cuba's twelve-mile territorial sea, is the northernmost boundary of the Havana Flight Information Region. Commercial and civilian aircraft routinely fly in this area, and aviation practice requires that they notify Havana's traffic controllers when crossing south through the 24th parallel. Both Brothers to the Rescue planes complied with this custom by contacting Havana, identifying themselves, and stating their position and altitude. . . .

As the civilian planes flew over international waters, a Russian built MiG 29 of the Cuban Air Force, without warning, reason, or provocation, blasted the defenseless planes out of the sky with sophisticated air-to-air missiles in two separate attacks. . . .

The missiles disintegrated the Brothers to the Rescue planes, killing their occupants instantly and leaving almost no recoverable debris. Only a large oil slick marked the spot where the planes went down. The Cuban Air Force never notified or warned the civilian planes, never attempted other methods of interception, and never gave them the opportunity to land. The MiGs' first and only response was the intentional and malicious destruction of the Brothers to the Rescue planes and their four innocent occupants. Such behavior violated clearly established international norms requiring the exhaustion of all measures before resort to aggression against any aircraft and banning the use of force against civilian aircraft altogether.[3] . . .

III.   CONCLUSIONS OF LAW

A.   Jurisdiction and Liability

District courts have original jurisdiction to hear suits, not barred by foreign sovereign immunity, that are brought against foreign states. See 28 U.S.C. §1330 (1994). Under the Foreign Sovereign Immunities Act of 1976 ("FSIA"), 28 U.S.C.A. §§1602-1611, a federal court lacks subject matter jurisdiction to hear a claim against a foreign state unless the claim falls within one of the FSIA's enumerated exceptions, id. §1605. . . . Most recently, Congress crafted an additional, narrow exception to foreign sovereign immunity through the Anti-Terrorism and Effective Death Penalty Act of 1996 ("AEDPA"), Pub.L. No. 104-132, §221, 110 Stat. 1214. AEDPA amended the FSIA to allow suits in U.S. courts against a foreign state that engages in acts of terrorism under certain specified circumstances. As a result, the FSIA now provides that a foreign state shall not be immune from the jurisdiction of U.S. courts in any case

> in which money damages are sought against a foreign state for personal injury or death that was caused by an act of torture, extrajudicial killing, aircraft sabotage, hostage taking, or the provision of material support or resources . . . for such an act if such act or

---

3. These norms have been codified in various international instruments. See, e.g., Convention on International Civil Aviation, Dec. 7, 1944, 61 Stat. 1180, 15 U.N.T.S. 295 (both the United States and Cuba are parties to the Convention). The proscription on using force against civilian planes attaches even if they penetrate foreign airspace. See, e.g., Kay Hailbronner, Freedom of the Air and the Convention on the Law of the Sea, 77 Am. J. Int'l L. 490, 514 (1983) ("Even if an order to land is deliberately disregarded, a civil unarmed aircraft that intrudes into foreign airspace may not be fired upon."). Common sense dictates that the negligible threat civilian planes may pose does not justify the possible loss of life.

provision of material support is engaged in by an official, employee, or agent of such foreign state while acting within the scope of his or her office, employment, or agency.

28 U.S.C.A. §1605(a)(7).[4] In addition, section 1605(a)(7) imposes the following requirements: (1) the U.S. must have designated the foreign state as a state sponsor of terrorism pursuant to section 6(j) of the Export Administration Act of 1979; (2) the act must have occurred outside the foreign state;* and (3) the claimants and victims must have been U.S. nationals at the time the acts occurred.[5] Id. §1605(a)(7)(A)-(B).

The record of this trial clearly establishes that all of these requirements have been met. First, the unprovoked firing of deadly rockets at defenseless, unarmed civilian aircraft undoubtedly comes within the statute's meaning of "extrajudicial killing." That term is defined in reference to its use in the Torture Victim Protection Act of 1991 ("TVPA"), which states that "the term 'extrajudicial killing' means a deliberated killing not authorized by a previous judgment pronounced by a regularly constituted court affording all the judicial guarantees which are recognized as indispensable by civilized peoples." 28 U.S.C. §1350 note (1994). Cuba's actions in this case easily come within this definition. The occupants of the two civilian, unarmed planes received no warning whatsoever of their imminent destruction, much less the judicial process contemplated by the TVPA.

Second, the Cuban Air Force was acting as an agent of Cuba when it committed the killings.[6] The evidence adduced at trial demonstrated how the pilots of the Cuban MiGs obtained authorization from state officials prior to the shootdown of each plane and hearty congratulations from those officials after the planes were destroyed.

Third, section 1605(a)(7)'s requirement that the foreign state have been designated as a state sponsor of terrorism has also been satisfied. Cuba was one of only seven states so designated at the time pursuant to the authority of the Export Administration Act of 1979.

Fourth, the act occurred outside of Cuban territory. Plaintiffs have presented undisputed and competent evidence that the planes were shot down over international waters. . . .

Having established an exception to foreign sovereign immunity, Plaintiffs base their substantive cause of action on a different statute, also enacted in 1996, entitled Civil Liability for Acts of State Sponsored Terrorism, Pub.L. 104-208, §589, 110 Stat. 3009 (codified at 28 U.S.C.A. §1605 note) ("Civil Liability Act" [also known as the Flatow Amendment]). The Civil Liability Act creates a cause of action against agents of a foreign state that act under the conditions specified in FSIA section 1605(a)(7).

---

4. The Court notes that it may retroactively apply AEDPA's amendments to the FSIA in this case. As part of AEDPA, the new exception to immunity was enacted on April 24, 1996. Yet the acts in question occurred in February 1996, two months before the FSIA was amended. AEDPA itself, however, addresses when its provisions are to become effective. It provides that the amendments to the FSIA "shall apply to any cause of action arising before, on, or after the date of the enactment of this Act." Pub. L. 104-132, §221(c), 110 Stat. 1214. Therefore, the plain language of the statute evidences a clear Congressional intent to have section 1605(a)(7) apply retroactively. . . .

*Section 1605(a)(7) provides that, if the acts occurred within the foreign state, the state must be given a reasonable opportunity to arbitrate before the suit is brought—Eds.

5. It is this last requirement that prevents the family of Pablo Morales, the fourth Brothers to the Rescue member who was killed, to take part in this suit. Pablo Morales was a Cuban national at the time of the incident.

6. The Cuban Air Force is clearly an agent of the Cuban State, as it acts on Cuba's behalf and subject to Cuba's control.

It thus serves as an enforcement provision for acts described in section 1605(a)(7). If Plaintiffs prove an agent's liability under this Act, the foreign state employing the agent would also incur liability under the theory of respondeat superior. Because, as detailed above, Plaintiffs have presented compelling evidence that all of the relevant statutory requirements have been met, the Court finds that both the Cuban Air Force and Cuba are liable for the murders of Alejandre, Costa, and De la Peña.

B.   Damages

The amount of damages that Plaintiffs may recover in this case is specified in the Civil Liability Act. It provides that an agent of a foreign state who commits an extrajudicial killing as described in FSIA section 1605(a)(7) shall be liable for "money damages which may include economic damages, solatium, pain and suffering, and punitive damages." 28 U.S.C.A. §1605 note. Thus, the Cuban Air Force is liable for both compensatory and punitive damages. Under the theory of respondeat superior, Cuba is liable for the same amount of damages as its agent, with the exception of punitive damages, which the FSIA prohibits against foreign states. 28 U.S.C. §1606.[8] . . .

Accordingly, after a careful review of the record, and the Court being otherwise fully advised, it is

ORDERED and ADJUDGED that judgment is hereby entered on behalf of Plaintiffs and against Defendants the Republic of Cuba and the Cuban Air Force for total compensatory damages of $49,927,911. Further, judgment is hereby entered for Plaintiffs and against the Defendant the Cuban Air Force (only) as punitive damages, the sum of One Hundred Thirty Seven Million, Seven Hundred Thousand Dollars ($137,700,000).

The total compensatory and punitive damages herewith awarded to Plaintiffs are $187,627,911, for which sum execution may issue forthwith against the Defendants Cuba and the Cuban Air Force and against any of their assets wherever situated.

Notes and Questions

1. Since the *Alejandre* decision, there have been numerous cases brought under §1605(a)(7), and many of them have resulted in large damage awards. These cases have concerned, among other things, the 1995 suicide bombing of a bus in Israel, see Flatow v. Islamic Republic of Iran, 999 F. Supp. 1 (D.D.C. 1998); the bombing of Pan Am Flight 103 over Lockerbie, Scotland in 1988, see Rein v. Socialist People's Libyan Arab Jamahiriya, 162 F.3d 748 (2d Cir. 1998); and the 1979-1981 Iran hostage crisis, see Roeder v. Islamic Republic of Iran, 195 F. Supp. 2d 140 (D.D.C. 2002). This exception to immunity has taken on additional significance after the September 11, 2001, terrorist attacks. See, e.g., Smith v. Islamic Emirate of Afghan-

---

8. Section 1606 of the FSIA, which determines the extent of liability in suits against a foreign state, provides in pertinent part: "[T]he foreign state shall be liable in the same manner and to the same extent as a private individual under like circumstances; but a foreign state *except for an agency or instrumentality thereof* shall not be liable for punitive damages." 28 U.S.C. §1606 (emphasis added). Thus, although punitive damages may not be assessed against the Republic of Cuba, they may be assessed against the Cuban Air Force.

istan, 2003 U.S. Dist. LEXIS 7629 (S.N.D.Y. May 7, 2003) (relying in part on the (a) (7) exception in entering a default judgment against Iraq for providing material support to Al Qaeda and in awarding millions of dollars in damages against Iraq and other defendants).

2. The damage awards in the §1605(a)(7) cases often include large amounts — sometimes hundreds of millions of dollars — for punitive damages. As the court notes in *Alejandre,* the FSIA normally precludes punitive damage awards against foreign states, although it allows such awards against their agencies and instrumentalities. See 28 U.S.C. §1606. Congress enacted legislation in 1998 expressly allowing punitive damages against foreign states in cases brought under §1605(a)(7), but it repealed this legislation in 2000. The Civil Liability Act, however, specifically provides for punitive damage awards against officials, employees, and agents of terrorist states. Does this statute implicitly allow punitive damage awards against terrorist states themselves? Most courts have held that it does not. Punitive damages are nevertheless common in §1605(a)(7) cases because the plaintiffs typically sue government departments and officials as well as the foreign state, and courts have concluded that such departments and officials qualify as an "agencies or instrumentalities" for purposes of the FSIA's punitive damage provision. This is what the court concluded in *Alejandre* concerning the Cuban Air Force. See also, e.g., Weinstein v. Islamic Republic of Iran, 184 F. Supp. 2d 13, 23-24 (D.D.C. 2002) (holding that Iranian Ministry of Information and Security was an agency or instrumentality of Iran and therefore subject to punitive damages); Hill v. Republic of Iraq, 175 F. Supp. 2d 36 (D.D.C. 2001) (treating Saddam Hussein as an instrumentality of Iraq and thus subject to punitive damages).

3. Receiving a damages award from a court does not guarantee recovery of money from the defendant. If the defendant does not voluntarily pay the judgment, the plaintiff must find assets of the defendant that he or she can enforce the judgment against. When it enacted §1605(a)(7), Congress attempted to facilitate execution by making clear that in cases brought under this exception, the property executed against need not be "involved in the act upon which the claim is based." 28 U.S.C. §1610(b)(2). Nevertheless, the only property owned by state sponsors of terrorism within the United States tends to be either frozen assets or diplomatic property, neither of which is ordinarily subject to execution.

In 1998, Congress amended the execution provisions to allow plaintiffs in cases brought under §1605(a)(7) to attach and execute on frozen assets, including frozen diplomatic property. The amendment also directed the Executive Branch to assist prevailing plaintiffs in "identifying, locating, and executing against the property of that foreign state or any agency or instrumentality of such state." See 28 U.S.C. §1610(f). But a provision in the amendment also gave the President the authority to waive the implementation of at least part of the amendment "in the interest of national security," and President Clinton immediately invoked this authority upon signing the legislation. He explained his action as follows:

I am concerned about section 117 of the Treasury/General Government appropriations section of the Act, which amends the Foreign Sovereign Immunities Act. If this section were to result in attachment and execution against foreign embassy properties, it would encroach on my authority under the Constitution to "receive Ambassadors and other public Ministers." Moreover, if applied to foreign diplomatic or consular property, section 117 would place the United States in breach of its international treaty obligations. It would put at risk the protection we enjoy at every embassy and consulate throughout the world by eroding the principle that diplomatic property must be protected regardless of bilateral relations. Absent my authority to waive section 117's attachment provision, it would also effectively eliminate use of blocked assets of terrorist states in the national security interests of the United States, including denying an important source of leverage. In addition, section 117 could seriously affect our ability to enter into global claims settlements that are fair to all U.S. claimants, and could result in U.S. taxpayer liability in the event of a contrary claims tribunal judgment. To the extent possible, I shall construe section 117 in a manner consistent with my constitutional authority and with U.S. international legal obligations, and for the above reasons, I have exercised the waiver authority in the national security interest of the United States. [Statement by President William J. Clinton upon Signing H.R. 4328, 34 Weekly Comp. Pres. Doc. 2108 (Nov. 2, 1998).]

The plaintiffs in *Alejandre* nevertheless attempted to enforce their judgment against monies owed by AT&T and other U.S. telecommunications companies to the Cuban state telecommunications company. A 1992 statute and implementing regulations authorized payments to Cuba on a case-by-case basis for telecommunications services, notwithstanding the general freeze on Cuban assets. The district court allowed the plaintiffs to enforce the judgment against such payments, despite the Executive Branch's claim that the President had effectively waived the 1998 execution provisions. See Alejandre v. Republic of Cuba, 42 F. Supp. 2d 1317 (S.D. Fla. 1999). That decision was vacated on appeal, however, on the ground that the Cuban telecommunications company was a separate entity from the defendants involved in the case and thus could not be held liable for the defendants' wrongdoing. See Alejandre v. Republic of Cuba, 183 F.3d 1277 (11th Cir. 1999). (The court relied on the *Bancec* decision concerning separate state entities, discussed above in subsection 4.) Another district court, in a case against Iran, subsequently held that the President had effectively waived the enforcement of the execution provisions. See Flatow v. Islamic Republic of Iran, 76 F. Supp. 2d 16 (D.D.C. 1999).

In response to these decisions, Congress, in a section of the Victims of Trafficking and Violence Protection Act of 2000, amended the execution provisions again. This time Congress provided for payment by the U.S. government of the compensatory damage judgments already awarded in the cases against Cuba and about a dozen of the first cases brought against Iran. Under this scheme, plaintiffs were given a choice of taking 110 percent of their compensatory damages and waiving all other damage claims or taking 100 percent of their compensatory damages and preserving their right to seek recovery of punitive damages. The statute substitutes the U.S. government as the claimant in these actions, so that it can seek recovery of this money from the foreign government in the future if it so chooses. In early 2001, the federal government liquidated $96.7 million in frozen Cuban assets and paid that amount to the plaintiffs in the *Alejandre* case. As for the covered cases against Iran, the U.S. Treasury has paid out over $350 million in U.S. funds.

Is Congress's latest approach a good solution to the execution problem? Should this scheme be limited to suits against Cuba and select suits against Iran? To judgments already awarded? What should happen after the frozen assets are exhausted? Recognizing these concerns, Congress in 2001 directed President Bush to submit "a legislative proposal to establish a comprehensive program to ensure fair, equitable, and prompt compensation for all United States victims of international terrorism . . .

that occurred or occurs on or after November 1, 1979." As of January 2003, the Bush Administration had yet to make a proposal.

Congress's latest effort to facilitate the collection of compensation awards against state sponsors of terrorism occurred in November 2002. In a statute otherwise focusing on terrorism insurance, Congress included a section providing that

> in every case in which a person has obtained a judgment against a terrorist party on a claim based upon an act of terrorism, or for which a terrorist party is not immune under section 1605(a)(7) of title 28, United States Code, the blocked assets of that terrorist party (including the blocked assets of any agency or instrumentality of that terrorist party) shall be subject to execution or attachment in aid of execution in order to satisfy such judgment to the extent of any compensatory damages for which such terrorist party has been adjudged liable. [Pub. L. No. 107-297, Title II, §201(a), (b), (d), 116 Stat. 2337, 2339.]

Congress granted the President only a limited ability to waive this provision:

> (b) Presidential Waiver.—
>   (1) In general.— Subject to paragraph (2), upon determining on an asset-by-asset basis that a waiver is necessary in the national security interest, the President may waive the requirements of subsection (a) in connection with (and prior to the enforcement of) any judicial order directing attachment in aid of execution or execution against any property subject to the Vienna Convention on Diplomatic Relations or the Vienna Convention on Consular Relations.
>   (2) Exception.— A waiver under this subsection shall not apply to —
>   (A) property subject to the Vienna Convention on Diplomatic Relations or the Vienna Convention on Consular Relations that has been used by the United States for any nondiplomatic purpose (including use as rental property), or the proceeds of such use; or
>   (B) the proceeds of any sale or transfer for value to a third party of any asset subject to the Vienna Convention on Diplomatic Relations or the Vienna Convention on Consular Relations. [Id.]

The section contains special provisions for judgments against Iran, allowing for proportional distribution of Iranian-blocked assets in the likely event that those assets are insufficient to fully cover the judgments.

The Bush administration was opposed to this section, and the State Department lobbied against it. Nevertheless, the administration supported the insurance provisions in the remainder of the statute, and President Bush decided to sign the statute into law.

4. Outstanding judgments under §1605(a)(7) against a country might well come to exceed the country's assets now frozen in the United States, as has already occurred with the outstanding judgments against Iran. Pending cases could also lead soon to this situation occurring against Iraq and Libya. If U.S. diplomatic and commercial relations were then to improve with regard to one of these countries, possibly because of a change of government there, could the successful plaintiffs still go after that country's assets were they to come under U.S. jurisdiction? For example, if an Iraqi government-owned oil company in a moderate Iraq were to do business with U.S. customers, would the customers' payments awaiting transfer from U.S.

banks be attachable? (See Chapter 5 regarding the obligations of successor governments.) If these assets were vulnerable, would this not put a damper on improving business relations between the United States and new, moderate governments? Would it put the United States at a disadvantage with other Western countries seeking to do business with new governments in the former terrorist states? Might §1605(a)(7) be amended so that judgments against a terrorist state would be conditioned to lapse upon a major change in the government of the state? Or should the law be amended so that the suits could only be brought against individuals (including government officials) and not against states? See generally Anne-Marie Slaughter & David Bosco, Plaintiff's Diplomacy, Foreign Affairs, Sept.-Oct. 2000, at 102.

5. Section 1605(a)(7) does not itself determine which nations lose their immunity by virtue of their involvement in terrorism. Instead, as noted above, that determination is delegated to the Executive Branch. Is this delegation of authority consistent with the separation of powers structure of the Constitution, which assigns the power to regulate the jurisdiction of the federal courts to Congress rather than to the Executive? In Rein v. Socialist People's Libyan Arab Jamahiriya, 162 F.3d 748 (2d Cir. 1998), the court held that there was no violation of separation of powers in a suit against Libya, because Libya was listed as a state sponsor of terrorism in 1996, when §1605(a)(7) was enacted. The court expressed no opinion about whether it would be constitutional to apply §1605(a)(7) to a nation that was not listed as a state sponsor of terrorism in 1996.

6. Unlike most of the other exceptions to immunity, §1605(a)(7) does not require any link between the defendant's actions and the United States, other than the requirement that the victim or claimant be a U.S. national. Is this exception consistent with constitutional requirements of due process? As discussed earlier in this chapter, due process normally requires certain minimum contacts between the defendant and the United States in order for a U.S. court to exercise personal jurisdiction over the defendant. But courts have held that §1605(a)(7) does not violate this requirement, either because the U.S. nationality of the victim or claimant provides a sufficient connection to the United States, because the defendants have adequate notice that they can be held accountable in a U.S. court for the egregious acts covered by §1605(a)(7), or because foreign states are not persons for purposes of the Due Process Clause. See, e.g., Price v. Socialist People's Libyan Arab Jamahiriya, 2002 U.S. App. LEXIS 12838 (D.C. Cir. Feb. 8, 2002); Daliberti v. Republic of Iraq, 97 F. Supp. 2d 38 (D.D.C. 2000); Flatow v. Islamic Republic of Iran, 999 F. Supp. 1 (D.D.C. 1998).

7. What should a court do if faced with a conflict between §1605(a)(7) and a treaty or executive agreement? As noted above, there have been a number of lawsuits brought against Iran relating to the 1979-1981 hostage crisis. The Algiers Accords (which were concluded by the United States as a presidential executive agreement) are a potential obstacle to these suits because they purport to settle claims against Iran relating to the hostage crisis. Under these Accords, the United States promised to "terminate all legal proceedings in United States courts involving claims of United States persons and institutions against Iran," "prohibit all further litigation based on such claims," and bring about the resolution of these claims through binding arbitration before the Iran-United States Claims Tribunal in the Hague.

In November 2001, Congress enacted an appropriations bill, §626(c) of which purported to exempt cases relating to the Iran hostage crisis from the requirement in §1605(a)(7) that the foreign state defendant have been designated a sponsor of terrorism at the time of the act complained of or have been subsequently designated a sponsor of terrorism based on that act. The legislative history of this provision (and of a technical correction of the amendment enacted a month later) could be read as suggesting that Congress may have intended to allow claims against Iran based on the hostage crisis and that it disapproved of efforts by the Executive Branch to have these cases dismissed. In signing this legislation, however, President Bush stated that the Executive Branch would act, and encourage courts to act, "in a manner consistent with the obligations of the United States under the Algiers Accords that achieved the release of U.S. hostages in 1981."

In Roeder v. Islamic Republic of Iran, 195 F. Supp. 2d 140 (D.D.C. 2002), the court held that suits against Iran based on the hostage crisis continue to be barred by the Algiers Accords because Congress has not clearly expressed its intent to abrogate those Accords. In effect, the court applied the *Charming Betsy* canon of construction (discussed in Chapter 3), whereby courts attempt to construe federal statutes so that they do not violate international law. The court explained:

> The Court agrees that it is *possible* to read [§626(c) and other enactments], in the context of legislative history and intent, to provide for a cause of action against Iran. . . . However, the fact that an interpretation of these statutory provisions, when considered in the context of legislative intent and purpose, allowing plaintiffs to proceed against Iran is possible, does not end the Court's inquiry. Because these statutory provisions are at best ambiguous with respect to whether plaintiffs can sue Iran, if Congress has not expressed a sufficiently clear intent to abrogate the Algiers Accords, this Court *must* construe the statutes at issue to preclude such a suit. [Id. at 174–175]

Did the court properly apply the *Charming Betsy* canon? Why did the President sign the bill containing §626(c) if he did not want suits against Iran relating to the hostage crisis to proceed? Why did Congress not state its intent more clearly?

8. In most of the cases brought under §1605(a)(7), the defendants have refused to show up for the case, and the courts have proceeded to enter default judgments. As noted in *Alejandre*, the FSIA requires that, before a default judgment can be entered against a foreign state, the claimant must "establish[] his claim or right to relief by evidence satisfactory to the court." 28 U.S.C. §1608(e). Even with this requirement, what effect might these default judgments have on the case law of foreign sovereign immunity?

9. The State Department opposed the enactment of an exception to immunity for state sponsors of terrorism. In testimony before a Senate subcommittee in 1994, a representative from the State Department explained:

> Consistency of the FSIA with established international practice is important. If we deviate from that practice and assert jurisdiction over foreign states for acts that are generally perceived by the international community as falling within the scope of immunity, this would tend to erode the credibility of the FSIA. We have made substantial efforts over the years to persuade foreign states to participate in our judicial system — to appear and defend in actions against them under the FSIA. That kind of broad participation serves the interests of all. If we expand our jurisdiction in ways that causes other states to question our statute, this could undermine the broad participation we

seek. It could also undermine our ability to influence other states to abandon the theory of absolute immunity and adopt the restrictive view of sovereign immunity, which the United States has followed for over forty years. . . .

This bill could also lead to other undesirable consequences for our foreign relations. Current U.S. law allows the U.S. Government to fine-tune the application of sanctions against state-sponsors of terrorism, increasing or decreasing them when in the national interest. In addition, the U.S. Government frequently coordinates closely with other nations at the UN and elsewhere on the imposition of sanctions and the development of joint positions vis-à-vis acts of terrorism. The possibility of civil suits and potential judgments against state-sponsors of terrorism would inject a new unpredictable element in these very delicate relationships. Such proceedings could in some instances interfere with U.S. counter-terrorism objectives. They could also raise difficult issues involving sensitive intelligence and national security information. . . .

. . . Restrictions on immunity have a reciprocal dimension. If the United States extends the jurisdiction of its courts to embrace cases involving alleged wrongdoing by a foreign state outside the United States, we would have to expect that some other states could do likewise. However, there is of course no guarantee that any action taken by other states would precisely mirror our own. If other states were to expand the jurisdiction of their own courts, they might not limit such action to terrorism, for example, but could seek to include as well other kinds of alleged wrongdoing that could be of concern to us. [The Foreign Sovereign Immunities Act, Hearings on S. 825 before the Subcommittee on Courts and Administrative Practice of the Senate Committee on the Judiciary, 103d Cong., 2d Sess. 14-15 (June 21, 1994) (Statement of Jamison S. Borek).]

Are these concerns valid? Have subsequent events supported or undermined these concerns? Are there ways that §1605(a)(7) could be amended to address these concerns?

10. In November 2000, Iran's Parliament enacted a law that allows Iranian "victims of US interference since the 1953 coup d'etat" to sue the United States in Iranian courts. This law was enacted as a "measure of reciprocity" in response to the recent suits allowed in U.S. courts against Iran. See Agence France Presse, Iran MPs Cry "Down with America," Approve Lawsuits Against United States, Nov. 1, 2000. In February 2003, it was reported that a court in Iran had entered a $500 million judgment against the U.S. government. The case was brought by an Iranian businessman who was apprehended in the early 1990s by undercover U.S. customs agents, after he allegedly violated U.S. sanctions laws by attempting to buy oil-field equipment from a Florida company and have it shipped to Libya. The businessman brought the suit in Iran after unsuccessfully attempting to recover damages against the U.S. government in a Florida court. Commentators immediately drew a connection between Iran's allowance of this suit and the recent suits allowed against Iran in U.S. courts. Should the United States be concerned about such "reciprocal" actions?

11. Section 1605(a)(7) and the Civil Liability Act are not the only statutory provisions relevant to suits involving terrorism. Foreign plaintiffs may be able to use the Alien Tort Statute (discussed in Chapter 3) to sue nonstate actors and foreign government officials acting outside their authority for acts of terrorism, if the plaintiffs can establish that such acts violate customary international law or a U.S. treaty. In addition, both foreign and domestic plaintiffs may be able to use the Torture Victim Protection Act (also discussed in Chapter 3) to sue foreign government officials who commit acts of torture or extrajudicial killing "under actual or apparent authority, or color of law, of any foreign nation." In addition, in the early 1990s, Congress enacted a statute that provides a civil cause of action for U.S. nationals injured by an

"act of international terrorism." See 18 U.S.C. §2333. The cause of action, however, does not include suits against states or against an officer or employee of a state who is acting "within his or her official capacity or under color of legal authority." 18 U.S.C. §2337. (This statute is discussed further in Chapter 7.)

12. For additional discussion of the state sponsor of terrorism exception, see Barry E. Carter, Terrorism Supported by Rogue States: Some Foreign Policy Questions Created by Involving U.S. Courts, 36 New Eng. L. Rev. 933 (2002); Joseph W. Dellapenna, Civil Remedies for International Terrorism, 12 DePaul Bus. L.J. 169 (2000); and Joseph W. Glannon & Jeffrey Atik, Politics and Personal Jurisdiction: Suing State Sponsors of Terrorism Under the 1996 Amendments to the Foreign Sovereign Immunities Act, 87 Geo. L.J. 675 (1999).

13. Besides the FSIA exceptions discussed above, Section 1605 also includes: subsection (a) (6) involving the enforcement of some arbitration agreements and awards (see page 376 above); subsection (a) (3) for certain situations involving property taken in violation of international law; subsection (a) (4) for certain rights in property in the United States; and subsection (b) for certain admiralty suits.

10.   *Immunity from Attachment or Execution*

The FSIA also contains important provisions regarding immunity from attachment or execution. As described in the House FSIA Report:

House Report No. 94-1487

Section 1609.   Immunity from Attachment and Execution of Property of a Foreign State

As in the case of section 1604 of the bill with respect to jurisdiction, section 1609 states a general proposition that the property of a foreign state, as defined in section 1603(a), is immune from attachment and from execution, and then exceptions to this proposition are carved out in sections 1610 and 1611. Here, it should be pointed out that neither section 1610 nor 1611 would permit an attachment for the purpose of obtaining jurisdiction over a foreign state or its property. For this reason, section 1609 has the effect of precluding attachments as a means for commencing a lawsuit.

Attachment of foreign government property for jurisdictional purposes has been recognized "where under international law a foreign government is not immune from suit," and where the property in the United States is commercial in nature. Weilamann v. Chase Manhattan Bank, 21 Misc. 2d 1086, 192 N.Y.S.2d 469 (Sup. Ct. N.Y. 1959). Even in such cases, however, it has been recognized that property attached for jurisdictional purposes cannot be retained to satisfy a judgment because, under current practice, the property of a foreign sovereign is immune from execution.

Attachments for jurisdictional purposes have been criticized as involving U.S. courts in litigation not involving any significant U.S. interest or jurisdictional contacts, apart from the fortuitous presence of property in the jurisdiction. Such cases frequently require the application of foreign law to events which occur entirely abroad.

Such attachments can also give rise to serious friction in United States' foreign relations. In some cases, plaintiffs obtain numerous attachments over a variety of foreign government assets found in various parts of the United States. This shotgun approach has caused significant irritation to many foreign governments.

At the same time, one of the fundamental purposes of this bill is to provide a long-arm statute that makes attachment for jurisdictional purposes unnecessary in cases where there is a nexus between the claim and the United States. Claimants will clearly benefit from the expanded methods under the bill for service on a foreign state (sec. 1608), as well as from the certainty that section 1330(b) of the bill confers personal jurisdiction over a foreign state in Federal and State courts as to every claim for which the foreign state is not entitled to immunity. The elimination of attachment as a vehicle for commencing a lawsuit will ease the conduct of foreign relations by the United States and help eliminate the necessity for determinations of claims of sovereign immunity by the State Department.

Section 1610.   Exceptions to Immunity from Attachment or Execution

Section 1610 sets forth circumstances under which the property of a foreign state is not immune from attachment or execution to satisfy a judgment. Though the enforcement or judgments against foreign state property remains a somewhat controversial subject in international law, there is a marked trend toward limiting the immunity from execution.

A number of treaties of friendship, commerce and navigation concluded by the United States permit execution of judgments against foreign publicly owned or controlled enterprises (for example, Treaty with Japan, April 2, 1953, art. 18(2), 4 UST 2063 . . .). The widely ratified Brussels Convention for the Unification of Certain Rules relating to the Immunity of State-Owned Vessels, April 10, 1926, 196 L.N.T.S. 199, allows execution of judgments against public vessels engaged in commercial services in the same way as against privately owned vessels. Although not a party to this treaty, the United States follows a policy of not claiming immunity for its publicly-owned merchant vessels, both domestically, 46 U.S.C. 742, 781, and abroad, 46 U.S.C. 747. . . . Articles 20 and 21 of the Geneva Convention on the Territorial Sea and the Contiguous Zone, April 29, 1958, to which the United States is a party, recognize the liability to execution under appropriate circumstances of state-owned vessels used in commercial service.

However, the traditional view in the United States concerning execution has been that the property of foreign states is absolutely immune from execution. Even after the "Tate Letter" of 1952, this continued to be the position of the Department of State and of the courts. . . . Sections 1610(a) and (b) are intended to modify this rule by partially lowering the barrier of immunity from execution, so as to make this immunity conform more closely with the provisions on jurisdictional immunity in the bill. . . .

Section 1611.   Certain Types of Property Immune from Execution

Section 1611 exempts certain types of property from the immunity provisions of section 1610 relating to attachment and execution.

Questions

1. Do the FSIA provisions increase or decrease the use of attachment of assets to obtain jurisdiction against a foreign state?

2. From the plaintiff's standpoint, is the FSIA system for obtaining jurisdiction usually preferable? Why or why not?

3. Do the FSIA provisions increase or decrease the use of attachment or execution to satisfy a judgment against a foreign state? How?

4. If a plaintiff obtains a judgment for damages against a foreign state in the U.S. courts, is the plaintiff likely to be able to execute successfully against that sovereign's assets in the United States? See Letelier v. Republic of Chile, 748 F.2d 790 (2d Cir. 1984), *cert. denied,* 471 U.S. 1125 (1985) (plaintiffs were unable to execute against a commercial passenger jet of the state-owned Chilean airline, in part because the airline was deemed a separate entity and plaintiffs had failed to name it as a defendant in the initial suit on liability).

11. The Current Status of Foreign Sovereign Immunity Outside the United States

As noted in the 1952 Tate Letter above, with the exception of the Soviet Union and its allies, most other industrial countries had adopted the restrictive theory of sovereign immunity even before the United States. The trend toward reduced immunity by foreign sovereigns continued in a large number of jurisdictions, including Great Britain, France, Germany, and Italy. Moreover, the FSIA rules on attachment and execution draw on and have many similarities with the European Convention on State Immunity and Additional Protocol, adopted in 1972, and the United Kingdom's State Immunity Act of 1978.

Professor Dellapenna describes these and other developments in the following excerpt.

Joseph W. Dellapenna, Suing Foreign Governments and Their Corporations

(2d ed. 2003)

§1.2 The Emergence of Restrictive Immunity Internationally. . . .

While the immunity of foreign states in common law jurisdictions today is determined by a statute which purportedly codifies the whole law of the topic, in civil law countries foreign state immunity (and the immunities of the domestic sovereign as well) largely remains, as it nearly always has been in the civil law tradition, a judicial construct discoverable only from study of the "*jurisprudence*" (caselaw) of the relevant courts. Thus one must examine the cases in civil law countries if one is to predict how a current case will come out — despite the fact that civil law courts generally are not bound by a rule of precedent. Considerable debate emerged, first regarding domestic sovereign immunity and only later mirrored in debates over foreign state immunity, over how to determine when state acts in a private capacity or in a public capacity. The theories coalesced around two approaches hinging on the purpose or on the nature of the act. Gradually most [civil law countries] accepted the nature of the act as dispositive, but without universal agreement on what acts were by their nature public or private. Courts in each particular state have generally followed the more developed domestic immunity jurisprudence to determine the nature (or the purpose) of the act in question. . . .

French jurisprudence long leaned toward the purpose test for public acts, but more recent decisions have accepted the nature test. French courts have not been troubled by the private nature of state contracts relating to the development of natural resources, such as exploration for oil. On the other hand, French courts classify the expropriation of property without compensation as a public act. Such decisions further support the conclusion that French courts now classify acts as public or private according to their nature rather than their purpose.

French courts have consistently treated operation of national railroads by foreign states as private activities. In both of these cases, the courts announced that the nature of the act determined immunity, and not the status of the entity that performs it. This principle has been applied to uphold immunity for a foreign national bank carrying out exchange controls, and in a suit against an Algerian state-owned corporation holding property expropriated without compensation. . . .

Even though French courts applied a restrictive theory to immunity from suit, until recently they adhered to absolute immunity from execution. Perhaps as a result, French courts developed a somewhat peculiar approach to immunity from execution, sharply distinguishing between granting an *exequatur* against a foreign state (recognizing the foreign judgment) and enforcement measures. The grant of an *exequatur* was consistently seen as determined by the rules governing immunity from suit. Only when enforcement measures were sought did the question of immunity from execution arise.

French courts now generally limit the property of the foreign state subject to execution according to whether the foreign state holds the property for public or private uses. On this basis, some courts have refused execution in the absence of proof of the precise purpose for which the assets are held. . . .

The German Law on the Constitution of Courts (*Gerichtsverfassungsgesetz*) declares that German courts cannot exercise jurisdiction over entities immune by virtue of general rules of international law. This provision became the basis for adopting the restrictive theory in Germany, although German courts have found little in international law to prescribe the detailed application of the restrictive theory. Thus, Germany's highest courts — the *Bundesgerichtshof* (Supreme Court) and the *Bundesverfassungsgericht* (Constitutional Court) — have consistently declared that the nature of an act must be determined according to domestic legal principles as there is no basis in international law for distinguishing between public and private acts.

German courts are definitely committed to the nature test for determining whether the specific act that is the basis for the suit is public or private. By this approach, the German courts have seldom sustained claims of immunity. Unlike courts in most other countries, German courts do not even require that the nonimmune acts have a significant contact with Germany before permitting the proceeding to go forward. The major class of cases for which German courts have upheld immunity are instances involving the expropriation of property. The provision of information by New Scotland Yard to German police has also been held to be a public act.

The one perhaps surprising decision in this jurisprudence was a decision that the performance of ordinary secretarial duties in a consulate was a public act.

German courts also held the USSR immune from claims for the loss of agricultural crops due to contamination from fallout from Chernobyl. The court held that German courts lacked jurisdiction because there was no nonimmune property in Germany from which the court could derive jurisdiction, the USSR's regulatory responsibilities were a sovereign activity that did not in themselves give rise to liability, and the USSR did not itself operate the plant. Presumably suit could have been brought against the agency or instrumentality that operated the plant based on injuries in Germany, but how one would ever be able to enforce any resulting judgment remained highly unlikely.

The German practice regarding whether a secondary entity shares the immunity of a foreign state is in stark contrast with the French practice. While the French practice is functional, the German practice is structuralist, generally rejecting any claim of immunity on behalf of any juridically separate entity. The court in which most of these cases were decided, however, later conceded that a separate entity might share the state's immunity if it were performing public functions. The Federal Constitutional Court declined to consider the question, however, because the funds in question would not have been immune in any event.

The German practice is similarly straightforward towards immunity from execution, a matter which German courts have declared to be entirely derivative from immunity from suit. Possible future use of the funds for public purposes is simply irrelevant. . . .

§1.3 The British State Immunity Act

The acceptance of the restrictive theory of foreign state immunity came more slowly in common law nations. A transition from an absolute theory to a restrictive theory was even more difficult in common law countries than to in the civil law countries, owing to the doctrine of *stare decisis*. By the beginning of the twentieth century courts in the United States and other common law countries were firmly committed to absolute immunity from suit for foreign states. Change in this regard generally required a statute rather than the development of the caselaw. The British State Immunity Act exemplifies the common law approach to the problem of state immunity outside the United States. . . .

The British State Immunity Act provides that states are "immune from the jurisdiction of the courts of the United Kingdom" except as provided elsewhere in the Act. Furthermore, the Act precludes jurisdiction if the action is between states regardless of the nature of the claim. The Act provides further that the immunity is to apply even if the foreign state does not appear in the proceeding. The State Immunity Act goes on to provide exceptions to immunity based upon (listed alphabetically):

(1) arbitrations involving foreign states and private parties;

(2) business associations issues;

(3) commercial transactions and contracts linked to the United Kingdom;

(4) damage or loss to tangible property caused by an act or omission in the United Kingdom;

(5) employment contracts made and to be at least partly performed in the United Kingdom;

(6) intellectual property rights perfected in the United Kingdom;

(7) maritime claims arising from the commercial use of a ship;

(8) personal injuries or death;

(9) property claims;

(10) submission to the jurisdiction of the courts of the United Kingdom; and

(11) tax claims arising from British taxes.

While the substantive core of the British State Immunity Act resembles our own Foreign Sovereign Immunities Act, in several respects the British Act is different and might even be superior. Most significantly, it provides a relatively clear definition of "commercial transaction":

(1) any contract for the supply of goods or services;

(2) any loan or other transaction for the provision of finance and any guarantee or indemnity in respect of any such transaction or of any other financial obligation; and

(3) any other transaction or activity (whether of a commercial, industrial, financial, professional or other similar character) into which a state enters or in which it engages otherwise than in the exercise of sovereign authority.

The definition, while leaving some residual uncertainty in its last clause, would have prevented some of the considerable difficulties our courts encountered under the "definition" provided in our Foreign Sovereign Immunities Act, although those problems can resurface when the residual clause "any other transaction or activity . . . into which a state enters or in which it engages otherwise than in the exercise of sovereign authority" applies. . . .

. . . Arbitration agreements are enforceable unless the agreement is solely between states or if the parties have, in writing, agreed otherwise. The bringing of an action in the United Kingdom is taken to be a submission to the court for the resolution of the dispute, and thus allows counterclaims growing out of the same transaction or event. . . .

Torts, whether commercial or otherwise, pose some particular problems. The British State Immunity Act excludes torts arising out of nuclear injuries or the activities of foreign armed forces in the United Kingdom. The territorial requirement that injury or loss of property is actionable only if caused by an act or omission in the United Kingdom presumably precludes suits based on transboundary pollution directly affecting Britain. . . .

The Act expansively defines a "State" as including:

(1) the sovereign or other head of the State;

(2) the government of the State;

(3) any department of the government without a separate juridical personality; and

(4) juridically separate entities when exercising sovereign authority.

The Secretary of State for Foreign and Commonwealth Affairs has the authority to grant a conclusive certificate on such questions as whether a particular country is a "State" or whether a person is a head or state or government . . . . Absent a certification by the Secretary of State, the courts will decide the question through a factual inquiry into the actual status of the claimed state. . . .

§1.4 International Conventions on State Immunity

As the foregoing discussion indicates, the patterns regarding the immunity of foreign states found in the different states spread across Europe are not uniform.

Even within the civil law tradition, courts from the different states disagree whether the proper test is the nature or the purpose of the act, as well as over how the selected test is to be applied. They tended simply to follow the same patterns regarding the immunity of their own sovereigns in proceedings before courts of law. Add into the mix the common law statutes and precedents from England and Wales and from Ireland, and there could only be considerable uncertainty among the states of the emerging European Union as well as across Europe generally. To respond to this concern, the member-states of the Council on Europe completed the drafting of the European Convention on State Immunity in 1972. [As of January 2003, it had been ratified by only eight nations: Austria, Belgium, Cyprus, Germany, Luxembourg, the Netherlands, Switzerland, and the United Kingdom.] In part, this slow acceptance reflects the willingness of many European states to await the completion of a treaty based on the work of the International Law Commission.

Superficially, the European Convention appears to have had even less impact than the handful of ratifications might suggest. According to British practice, for example, the British State Immunity Act controls over any inconsistent provisions of the Convention even though the Convention was ratified about a year after the Act was adopted. The Convention, however, had a significant impact on the drafting of the British State Immunity Act, and in fact the goal of making British law on the topic consistent with the Convention was one of the stated purposes for enactment of the statute.

Structurally, the European Convention takes the opposite approach from both the Foreign Sovereign Immunities Act and the British State Immunity Act, both of which start from a presumption of state immunity. The European Convention begins in fourteen articles by declaring that foreign states are not immune, and leaves the rule of immunity as a residual rule for cases not covered by the provisions precluding immunity. This perhaps suggests that the presumption is to be against immunity, but there are no precedents to settle the question.

With only a few exceptions, immunity is precluded for claims under the same circumstances as provided in the British Act. . . .

The European Convention has no general rule precluding immunity for commercial activities, although it does preclude immunity when the litigation concerns "industrial, commercial, or financial activity" which the state conducts through an "an office, agency, or other establishment" created on the territory of the forum state for such purposes. The Convention's provision on non-immunity for torts adds a requirement that the tortfeasor must have been in the forum state when the facts giving rise to the litigation occurred. . . .

Alongside the European Convention, the International Law Commission of the United Nations developed a set of Draft Articles on a Convention on Jurisdictional Immunities of States and Their Property ("International Law Commission Draft Articles"). . . .

The ILC Draft Articles . . . ha[ve] not yet been approved by the General Assembly or in any other fashion submitted to the member states for ratification, now being subject to study by an "open-ended working group" of the Sixth Committee of the General Assembly. It nonetheless remains the closest we have to a universal restatement of the principles of foreign state immunity.

The principles embraced in the ILC Draft Articles are remarkably ordinary, given the slowness of governments to embrace the Convention. Thus the Convention begins with a presumption of immunity, and allows that national courts can exercise jurisdiction over foreign states notwithstanding the presumption based upon (listed alphabetically):

(1) arbitral agreements or awards;

(2) certain business associations issues;

(3) commercial transactions by the foreign state;

(4) consent of the foreign state to the exercise of jurisdiction;

(5) contracts of employment to be carried out in the forum state;

(6) intellectual property rights created under the law of the forum state where ownership is in dispute or the rights are infringed in the forum state;

(7) maritime claims of a commercial nature;

(8) ownership, possession, or use of property located in the forum state;

(9) participation by the foreign state in the particular proceedings; and

(10) personal injuries or property damage occurring in the forum state.

In addition, the International Law Commission Draft Articles provides protections against "measures of constraint," such as attachment, arrest, and execution against any property of a foreign state unless the property is used for commercial purposes, is in the forum state, and is connected in some way to the claim for which the judgment was entered. Even then, the Convention absolutely exempts from "measures of constraint" diplomatic property, property of a central bank or other monetary authority, property that forms part of the national cultural heritage, and objects forming part of a scientific, cultural, or historical exhibition and not intended for sale. Finally, the Convention would establish rules governing the service of process, default judgments, the compulsion of evidence, and the resolution of disputes regarding the application of the Convention.

The major points of contention regarding the International Law Commission Draft Articles, from the beginning and continuing today, are the concept of a "state" for purposes of the Convention, the criteria for determining the commercial character of an act, the relation of state enterprises to the Convention, the applicability of the convention to contracts of employment, and the extent of allowable measures of constraint against state property.

For a discussion of sovereign immunity in China, which still purports to follow the absolute theory of immunity, see James V. Feinerman, Sovereign Immunity in the Chinese Case and Its Implications for the Future of International Law, in Essays in Honour of Wang Tieya 251 (R. St. John MacDonald ed., 1993).

12. The Legal Status of Embassies and Consulates

Related to the issue of foreign sovereign immunity and the FSIA is the question of the legal status of embassies and consulates. These premises are generally immune under U.S. law from attachment or execution. Even more than that, these premises often enjoy a special status in the United States as well as in other countries.

Contrary to popular belief, however, diplomatic mission and consular post properties are not extensions of the sending state's territory. Both in fact and in law, diplomatic premises are within the territory of the receiving state. Nevertheless, as section 463 of the Restatement states: "The premises . . . of a state's accredited diplomatic mission or consular post in the territory of another state are inviolable, and are immune from any exercise of jurisdiction by the receiving state that would interfere with their official use."

This summary is drawn from the Vienna Convention on Diplomatic Relations of April 18, 1961 (23 U.S.T. 3227; see Documentary Supplement), and the Vienna Convention on Consular Relations of April 24, 1963 (21 U.S.T. 77). Both Conventions have been widely adopted, including by the United States. The United States has also adopted statutes extending key provisions of the Convention on Diplomatic Relations to the diplomatic missions of non-ratifying countries.

The Conventions' concept of "inviolability" imposes two separate obligations on the receiving, or host, state. The first is to refrain from acting within the diplomatic premise. Diplomatic missions are immune from searches, seizures, attachment, execution, or any other form of enforcement jurisdiction that might interfere with the premise's official use. In practical terms, the receiving state can rarely exercise enforcement jurisdiction within a diplomatic premise. See, e.g., 767 Third Avenue Associates v. Permanent Mission of the Republic of Zaire to the United Nations, 988 F.2d 295 (2d Cir. 1993) (holding that the Zaire mission to the United Nations could not be evicted from its property in New York, despite having failed to pay its rent).

The second duty imposed on receiving states is protecting diplomatic premises from private interference. In the United States, the District of Columbia and the federal government have enacted statutes for this purpose, curtailing permissible activity within 500 feet of diplomatic premises. The statutes are aimed at preventing private group interference with diplomatic property. Violation of any of the statutes can result in a fine or imprisonment. See Boos v. Barry, 485 U.S. 312 (1988). (The Supreme Court upheld one clause of the statute that makes it unlawful "to congregate" within 500 feet of an embassy "and refuse to disperse after having been ordered to do so by the police." The Court, however, struck down as violating the First Amendment another clause of the statute that made it unlawful to display any sign that tends to bring the foreign government into "public odium" or "public disrepute.")

While a number of underlying theories have been offered for granting these immunities (e.g., respect for an equal sovereign, reciprocity, or ancient custom), the most common justification is functional necessity. Diplomats and consuls carry out functions that are often highly confidential, sensitive, or unpopular. Diplomatic premises are necessary for these functions. If diplomatic premises were subject to the receiving state's enforcement jurisdiction and not protected, diplomats would encounter additional obstacles to fulfilling their responsibilities.

Inviolability does not, however, exempt diplomatic premises from legislative jurisdiction. While the laws of the receiving state cannot be enforced, these laws apply with equal force within diplomatic premise walls. Whether an action triggers criminal or civil liability is determined by the receiving state's law.

For example, when criminal acts occur on diplomatic premises and inviolability either does not apply or is not invoked, those acts may be prosecuted under local law. In Fatemi v. United States, 192 A.2d 525 (D.C. 1963), for example, protestors refused to leave the Iranian embassy in Washington. The head of the mission authorized local police to arrest the demonstrators. In defense, the protestors contended that the local court lacked jurisdiction because the crime occurred in the Iranian embassy and therefore in Iranian territory. In rejecting this claim, the D.C. Court of Appeals held that diplomatic premises are part of the territory of the receiving state and when inviolability is not invoked, prosecution under municipal law is permissible.

When inviolability is invoked or applicable, the conflict between municipal law violations and the receiving state's inability to prosecute can result in dispute. For instance, diplomatic missions in Washington are required to conform to District of Columbia building and fire codes; conformance, however, cannot be enforced due to diplomatic premise inviolability. As a result, there is a continuing tension between municipal authorities and resident diplomatic missions. Under the Foreign Missions Act of 1982, 22 U.S.C. §§4301 et seq., the Secretary of State is authorized to withhold "benefits" (e.g., utilities, construction permits, American workers) from missions that violate local law.

While there is a firm consensus on the core issues of diplomatic premise inviolability, a number of issues remain in dispute. No consensus has been reached regarding either the propriety of grants of diplomatic asylum on diplomatic premises or about entry by receiving state officials in the event of an emergency. Both Vienna Conventions expressly avoided these issues.

Notes and Questions

1. Why is it so important to make diplomatic premises inviolable? If the United States fails to respect diplomatic inviolability or immunity, what consequences is it likely to suffer abroad? Does the protection and effective functioning of U.S. diplomats abroad depend on the United States' respect for inviolability and immunity for foreign diplomats in this country? What degree of immunity is needed to ensure the effective functioning of diplomatic missions?

2. *A*, a diplomat from country *X* to country *Y*, is caught stealing documents from country *X*'s embassy. Country *X* waives any personal diplomatic immunity *A* might enjoy and does not invoke its premise inviolability. May *A* avoid prosecution for theft in country *Y* by asserting that the crime was committed on "foreign soil"? See Rex v. A. B., 1 K.B. 454 (1941) (United Kingdom). *No*

3. After the American hostages in Iran were released, a number of former hostages and their families attempted to obtain compensation from the Islamic Republic of Iran based in part on the FSIA's noncommercial tort exception. (This was before Congress enacted the exception for state sponsors of terrorism.) This act denies the sovereign immunity defense with respect to certain injuries or other damages occurring within United States territory. Could the former hostages maintain their action under the FSIA? See Persinger v. Islamic Republic of Iran, 729 F.2d 835 (D.C. Cir. 1983), and McKeel v. Islamic Republic of Iran, 722 F.2d 582 (9th Cir. 1983) (U.S. embassy was not part of U.S. territory for FSIA purposes.)

4. After the United States invaded Panama in December 1989, General Manuel Noriega, the Panamanian leader, took refuge from U.S. troops in the Vatican embassy (or nunciature) in Panama City. For a day or two while Noriega was inside the

embassy, U.S. soldiers outside directed speakers at the embassy and played rock music at very high decibel levels. Was that activity consistent with the Vienna Convention on Diplomatic Relations? Should the U.S. soldiers have insisted on entering the Vatican embassy to capture Noriega, or was the United States legally correct in not forcibly entering? Noriega left the Vatican embassy voluntarily, surrendered to U.S. officials, and was flown to the United States to stand trial on charges of drug smuggling. (For a discussion of the U.S. invasion of Panama, see Chapter 11.)

13. Personal Immunity for Diplomats and Consuls

At least as well protected as the embassies and consulates are the diplomats themselves. Diplomatic personal inviolability in some form has been universally recognized. Ancient civilizations, both Western and Eastern, accorded envoys personal inviolability.

Personal inviolability in ancient Greece and Rome included immunity from the receiving sovereign's jurisdiction and a duty to protect the diplomat's person. Immunity from jurisdiction encompassed all jurisdictions, both criminal and civil. A diplomat, even one plotting the overthrow of the receiving sovereign, could not be prosecuted, detained, or punished. The only acceptable response was to oust him from the country. Sovereigns who violated a diplomat's inviolability were required to make immediate reparation or risk war. More than one war began because an envoy was detained or punished by the receiving sovereign without reparation. The duty to protect the diplomat's person was incorporated into the municipal law. Both the Greeks and Romans harshly punished private persons who violated a diplomat's inviolability.

By the end of the Middle Ages, diplomatic personal immunity from criminal and civil liability was entrenched in international law. Although occasionally criticized by commentators and violated by sovereigns, this personal inviolability has remained essentially unchanged. One justification for this inviolability was put forward by Grotius in the seventeenth century. Known as "extraterritoriality," it created the fiction that a diplomat (and his residence) legally remained in the sending state. This theory remained popular until the late nineteenth century.

Personal inviolability was recently codified in the Vienna Convention on Diplomatic Relations. Rather than using the word "extraterritoriality," the preamble to the Convention couched the diplomatic privileges and immunities in terms of functional necessity — that is, helping the diplomat perform his duties. (See Documentary Supplement.) However, personal immunity is very broad. For example, Article 29 provides: "The person of a diplomatic agent shall be inviolable. He shall not be liable to any form of arrest or detention. The receiving State shall treat him with due respect and shall take all appropriate steps to prevent any attack on his person, freedom or dignity."

Article 31 then provides, in part, that "[a] diplomatic agent shall also enjoy immunity from [the receiving State's] civil and administrative jurisdiction, except in the case of . . . an action relating to any professional or commercial activity exercised by the diplomatic agent in the receiving State outside his official functions." Courts have interpreted the commercial activity exception in this article narrowly to cover only trade or business engaged in for personal profit, not business relationships that are incidental to the daily life of a diplomat. See, e.g., Tabion v. Mufti, 73 F.3d 535 (4th Cir. 1996) (holding that diplomatic immunity extended to suit brought by diplomat's domestic servant concerning her employment relationship with the diplomat).

Consular immunity can be substantially different from diplomatic immunity. The modern consul derives from the practice of thirteenth- and fourteenth-century Venetian merchants in foreign ports choosing one of their number to represent them. Consuls were gradually given other responsibilities, such as adjudicating disputes between countrymen abroad. While this practice declined during the sixteenth century, it reemerged at the end of the seventeenth century and became very popular as trade between nations increased during the late eighteenth and throughout the nineteenth centuries.

Consuls were rarely granted any immunity, although they were accorded a great amount of respect. This was primarily due to the nature of the consuls themselves; they were merchants who carried out their duties as consuls in addition to carrying out their trade. Professional or career consuls are a relatively recent phenomena, first becoming common in the nineteenth century.

As more career consuls appeared, specific immunities were negotiated between nations as part of their consular agreements. Normally, career consuls were considered inviolable, while honorary or nonprofessional consuls were immune from liability for official acts. This dichotomy is continued in the Vienna Convention on Consular Relations. Like diplomats, career consuls are generally inviolable. Honorary consuls are accorded immunity for their official acts but remain liable for their acts not related to consular business.

Notes and Questions

1. In 1997, a Georgian diplomat, Gueorgui Makharadze, killed an American teenager in a car accident in Washington, D.C. The diplomat was very drunk and driving at a high rate of speed on a city street. Under diplomatic immunity, Makharadze could have escaped prosecution in the United States. However, Georgia's president, Eduard Shevardnadze, decided to waive his immunity. The Georgian diplomat was convicted and sentenced by a D.C. court to 7 to 21 years for involuntary manslaughter.

The waiver of the Georgian diplomat's immunity extended only to criminal prosecution and not to civil litigation. The D.C. District Court held that Georgia's waiver of Makharadze's immunity was limited to criminal prosecution because neither the Department of State's request to Georgia for a waiver of immunity nor the actual waiver expressly mentioned civil litigation. The court reasoned that "Article 31 of the Convention does not confer immunity in a single blanket statement, but confers criminal immunity in one sentence and civil and administrative immunity separately, in another sentence. This suggests that the Convention considers immunity from criminal jurisdiction and immunity from civil and administrative jurisdiction to be distinct privileges." The court also stated that although Makharadze was no longer a diplomat when the civil suit was filed, he nevertheless had "residual immunity" because he was attending a business dinner at the time of the crash. Should there be distinctive civil and criminal immunities? Do you think that express waiver of civil immunity was necessary in Makharadze's case? See Knab v. Republic of Georgia, Civ. No. 97-3118, 1998 U.S. Dist. LEXIS 8820 (D.D.C. May 29, 1998).

2. If a foreign state refuses to waive a diplomat's immunity, does this mean that injured parties in the United States are left without a remedy? What about diplomatic remedies? Remedies in the courts of the foreign state?

3. A tragic accident in Italy focused great attention on foreign immunity there. While on a low-altitude training mission, a U.S. military jet severed the cable of a ski-lift at an Italian resort in the Alps, causing the deaths of 20 people. Under the NATO treaty, military personnel on NATO missions are granted immunity from local prosecution and are allowed to be tried in their home country. Initially, facing a public outcry in Italy, the Italian government requested jurisdiction, but the United States declined to waive immunity. Although the Italian national government acquiesced in that decision, a local Italian prosecutor tried to bring a manslaughter case against the crew of the U.S. jet.

The Italian prosecutor argued that the plane should have been considered on a U.S. mission because the plane violated NATO's mandated flight patterns. Apparently, Italy would have had jurisdiction if the plane had not been on a NATO mission. The Italian judge, however, ruled that the Italian court lacked jurisdiction because the crew's flight was covered under the NATO treaty.

Back in the United States, a Marine general ordered two of the crewmen, including the pilot, to be tried on manslaughter charges in a U.S. military court. The other two crewmen were cleared of criminal charges.

14.   Head-of-State Immunity

Related to the doctrines of foreign sovereign immunity and diplomatic immunity is the question of immunity for heads of state and other high-level foreign officials. This question is not specifically addressed in either the FSIA or in the treaties and statutes governing diplomatic immunity. In the decision below, the court considered a defense of head-of-state immunity raised on behalf of General Manuel Noriega of Panama, whom the U.S. government had seized in Panama and brought back to the United States for trial on drug trafficking charges.

United States v. Noriega

U.S. Court of Appeals
117 F.3d 1206 (11th Cir. 1997)

KRAVITCH, Senior Circuit Judge:

Manuel Antonio Noriega appeals: (1) his multiple convictions stemming from his involvement in cocaine trafficking; and (2) the district court's denial of his motion for a new trial based on newly discovered evidence. In attacking his convictions, Noriega asserts that the district court should have dismissed the indictment against him due to his status as a head of state. . . .

I.

On February 4, 1988, a federal grand jury for the Southern District of Florida indicted Manuel Antonio Noriega on drug-related charges. At that time, Noriega served as commander of the Panamanian Defense Forces in the Republic of Panama. Shortly thereafter, Panama's president, Eric Arturo Delvalle, formally discharged Noriega from his military post, but Noriega refused to accept the dismissal. Panama's legislature then ousted Delvalle from power. The United States, however, continued to acknowledge Delvalle as the constitutional leader of Panama. Later, after a disputed presidential election in Panama, the United States recognized Guillermo Endara as Panama's legitimate head of state.

On December 15, 1989, Noriega publicly declared that a state of war existed between Panama and the United States. Within days of this announcement by Noriega, President George Bush directed United States armed forces into combat in Panama for the stated purposes of "safeguard[ing] American lives, restor[ing] democracy, preserv[ing] the Panama Canal treaties, and seiz[ing] Noriega to face federal drug charges in the United States." United States v. Noriega, 746 F. Supp. 1506, 1511 (S.D. Fla. 1990). The ensuing military conflagration resulted in significant casualties and property loss among Panamanian civilians. Noriega lost his effective control over Panama during this armed conflict, and he surrendered to United States military officials on January 3, 1990. Noriega then was brought to Miami to face the pending federal charges.

Following extensive pre-trial proceedings and a lengthy trial, a jury found Noriega guilty of eight counts in the indictment and not guilty of the remaining two counts. The district court entered judgments of conviction against Noriega upon the jury's verdict and sentenced him to consecutive imprisonment terms of 20, 15 and five years, respectively. . . .

Noriega first argues that the district court should have dismissed the indictment against him based on head-of-state immunity. He insists that he was entitled to such immunity because he served as the de facto, if not the de jure, leader of Panama. The district court rejected Noriega's head-of-state immunity claim because the United States government never recognized Noriega as Panama's legitimate, constitutional ruler.

The Supreme Court long ago held that "[t]he jurisdiction of courts is a branch of that which is possessed by the nation as an independent sovereign power. The jurisdiction of the nation within its own territory is necessarily exclusive and absolute. It is susceptible of no limitation not imposed by itself." The Schooner Exchange v. McFaddon, 11 U.S. (7 Cranch) 116, 136 (1812). The Court, however, ruled that nations, including the United States, had agreed implicitly to accept certain limitations on their individual territorial jurisdiction based on the "common interest impelling [sovereign nations] to mutual intercourse, and an interchange of good offices with each other. . . ." Id. at 137. Chief among the exceptions to jurisdiction was "the exemption of the *person of the sovereign* from arrest or detention within a foreign territory." Id. (emphasis added).

The principles of international comity outlined by the Court in *The Schooner Exchange* led to the development of a general doctrine of foreign sovereign immunity. . . . As this doctrine emerged, the "Court consistently [] deferred to the decisions of the political branches — in particular, those of the Executive Branch — on

whether to take jurisdiction over actions against foreign sovereigns and their instrumentalities." *Verlinden B.V.,* 461 U.S. at 486.

In 1976, Congress passed the Foreign Sovereign Immunities Act ("FSIA"). The
FSIA "contains a comprehensive set of legal standards governing claims of immunity
in every *civil action* against a *foreign state or its political subdivisions, agencies, or instrumentalities." Verlinden B.V.,* 461 U.S. at 488, (emphasis added). . . . Because the FSIA
addresses neither head-of-state immunity, nor foreign sovereign immunity in the
criminal context, head-of-state immunity could attach in cases, such as this one,
only pursuant to the principles and procedures outlined in *The Schooner Exchange*
and its progeny. As a result, this court must look to the Executive Branch for direction on the propriety of Noriega's immunity claim.

Generally, the Executive Branch's position on head-of-state immunity falls into
one of three categories: the Executive Branch (1) explicitly suggests immunity; (2)
expressly declines to suggest immunity; or (3) offers no guidance. Some courts have
held that absent a formal suggestion of immunity, a putative head of state should receive no immunity. See, e.g., In re Doe, 860 F.2d 40, 45 (2d Cir. 1988). In the analogous pre-FSIA, foreign sovereign immunity context, the former Fifth Circuit accepted a slightly broader judicial role. It ruled that, where the Executive Branch
either *expressly* grants or denies a request to suggest immunity, courts must follow
that direction, but that courts should make an independent determination regarding immunity when the Executive Branch neglects to convey clearly its position on
a particular immunity request. See Spacil v. Crowe, 489 F.2d 614, 618-19 (5th Cir.
1974) (granting petition for writ of mandamus directing district court to follow government's suggestion of immunity in civil case).

Noriega's immunity claim fails under either the *Doe* or the *Spacil* standard. The
Executive Branch has not merely refrained from taking a position on this matter; to
the contrary, by pursuing Noriega's capture and this prosecution, the Executive
Branch has manifested its clear sentiment that Noriega should be denied head-of-
state immunity. . . . Moreover, given that the record indicates that Noriega never
served as the constitutional leader of Panama, that Panama has not sought immunity for Noriega and that the charged acts relate to Noriega's private pursuit of personal enrichment, Noriega likely would not prevail even if this court had to make an
independent determination regarding the propriety of immunity in this case. Accordingly, we find no error by the district court on this point. . . .

Notes and Questions

1. Most courts have concluded that, even if the FSIA applies to lower-level foreign officials, it does not apply to heads of state. Nevertheless, every court to address
the issue has recognized a doctrine of "head-of-state immunity," and they have generally looked to the Executive Branch for guidance in applying this doctrine. When
the Executive Branch has suggested immunity, courts have almost always followed
the suggestion. For decisions in which courts have granted head-of-state immunity,
see, for example, Tachiona v. Mugabe, 169 F. Supp. 2d 259 (S.D.N.Y. 2001) (granting immunity to president and foreign minister of Zimbabwe); Lafontant v. Aristide,
844 F. Supp. 128 (E.D.N.Y. 1994) (granting immunity to exiled president of Haiti);
Alicog v. Kingdom of Saudi Arabia, 860 F. Supp. 369, 382 (S.D. Tex. 1994) (granting

immunity to king of Saudi Arabia); and Saltany v. Reagan, 702 F. Supp. 319, 320 (D.D.C. 1988) (granting immunity to prime minister of Great Britain).

As the court explains in *Noriega,* it is less clear what courts should do in the absence of an Executive Branch suggestion of immunity. Some courts have indicated that an Executive Branch suggestion is a prerequisite for immunity. See, e.g., Jungquist v. Nahyan, 940 F. Supp. 312, 321 (D.D.C. 1996). Other courts have relied on the lack of an Executive Branch suggestion simply as a factor weighing against immunity. See, e.g., First American Corp. v. Al-Nahyan, 948 F. Supp. 1107, 1121 (D.D.C. 1996). At least one court has suggested, in dicta, that "when lacking guidance from the executive branch, . . . a court is left to decide for itself whether a head-of-state is or is not entitled to immunity." In re Doe, 860 F.2d 40, 45 (2d Cir. 1988). Which of these approaches is preferable? What should be inferred from the Executive Branch's failure to file a suggestion of immunity? Why was Noriega denied head-of-state immunity?

2. Should head-of-state immunity extend to high-level officials other than the head of state? To the head of state's family members? In cases in which the Executive Branch has suggested extending head-of-state immunity to these additional individuals, courts have generally (but not always) done so. See, e.g., Kline v. Keneko, 535 N.Y.S.2d 303 (N.Y. Sup. Ct. 1988) (granting immunity to president's wife), aff'd mem. sub nom. Kline v. Cordero de la Madrid, 546 N.Y.S.2d 506 (N.Y. App. Div. 1989); Kilroy v. Windsor, No. C-78-291, slip op. (N.D. Ohio, Dec. 7, 1978) (unpublished) (granting immunity to Prince Charles of England); Chong Boon Kim v. Kim Yong Shik, 58 Am. J. Intl. L. 186 (Haw. Cir. Ct., Sept. 9, 1963) (granting immunity to foreign minister). But see El-Hadad v. Embassy of the U.A.E., 60 F. Supp. 2d 69, 82 n.10 (D.D.C. 1999) (reasoning that head-of-state immunity is limited to heads of state); Republic of Philippines v. Marcos, 665 F. Supp. 793, 797 (N.D. Cal. 1987) (refusing to grant immunity to Philippine Solicitor General despite suggestion of immunity from State Department).

3. What if a *former* head of state seeks immunity in U.S. courts? As with the immunity of current heads of state, most courts look to the Executive Branch for guidance about former-head-of-state immunity. But most former-head-of-state immunity claims have been resolved on the basis of a waiver by the ex-head of state's new government. See, e.g., In re Doe, 860 F.2d 40, 45-46 (2d Cir. 1988); In re Grand Jury Proceedings, 817 F.2d 1108, 1110-1111 (4th Cir. 1987); Paul v. Avril, 812 F. Supp. 207, 211 (S.D. Fla. 1993). Some courts have suggested in dicta that former-head-of-state immunity does not extend to private (as opposed to official) acts. See, e.g., In re Doe, 860 F.2d at 44; Republic of the Philippines v. Marcos, 806 F.2d 344, 360 (2d Cir. 1986); United States v. Noriega, 746 F. Supp. 1506, 1519 n.11 (S.D. Fla. 1990). At least one court has questioned the availability of any immunity for former heads of state. See Roxas v. Marcos, 969 P.2d 1209, 1252 (Haw. 1998).

4. It is generally accepted that a foreign government may waive the immunity of its former head of state. Why do courts allow this? What if there were a good and wise leader who was overthrown by an evil and corrupt military junta and who then fled to the United States for the safety of her and her family's. Should the new government be able to waive the former leader's head-of-state immunity? Of course, why would the former leader need immunity? On the other hand, does not immunity provide an easy defense against baseless litigation?

5. There are no applicable treaties governing head-of-state immunity. Hence, any international law norms on the subject are ones that might be found in customary international law. As discussed in Chapter 3, some courts view customary international law as federal common law that applies in U.S. courts even in the absence of any political branch authorization. Why, then, do almost all courts look for Executive Branch authorization before applying head-of-state immunity? What do the head-of-state immunity cases suggest about the status of customary international law in U.S. courts? By looking for Executive Branch authorization for head-of-state immunity, are courts implying that they lack independent authority to convert customary international law into federal law?

6. In Flatow v. Islamic Republic of Iran, referred to earlier in this chapter in connection with suits against state sponsors of terrorism, the court stated:

> The Flatow Amendment [concerning civil liability for agents of terrorist states] overrides the common law doctrine of head of state immunity, as it expressly provides for the application of 28 U.S.C. §1605(a)(7)'s exception to immunity to "[a]n official, employee, or agent of a foreign state . . . acting within the scope of his or her office, employment, or agency." This provision was directed at those individuals who facilitate terrorist acts which cause the injury or death of American citizens. The provision does not qualify or in any way limit its application only to non-heads of state. Given that state sponsorship of terrorism is a decision made at the highest levels of government, unless the Flatow Amendment is interpreted as abrogating head of state immunity under the limited circumstances of 28 U.S.C. §1605(a)(7), the provisions cannot give full effect to Congressional intent, and the federal cause of action created by the two amendments would be irreparably and unreasonably hobbled. This Court therefore concludes that the defense of head of state immunity is not available in actions brought pursuant to 28 U.S.C. §1605(a)(7) and 28 U.S.C. §1605 note. [999 F. Supp. 1, 24 (D.D.C. 1996).]

Do you agree with the court's reasoning? How, if at all, should the *Charming Betsy* canon affect this analysis?

7. In a case that received worldwide attention, the British House of Lords held that the former president of Chile, Augusto Pinochet, was not entitled to immunity from criminal extradition proceedings relating to charges of torture. The House of Lords decision is difficult to summarize, because, as is typical, each of the Law Lords issued their own opinion. A majority of the Law Lords, however, appeared to conclude that whatever customary international law immunity Pinochet possessed with respect to acts of torture had impliedly been abrogated in 1988 by a treaty outlawing torture. See Regina v. Bow Street Magistrate, Ex Parte Pinochet, [1999] 2 W.L.R. 827 (H.L.). Note that most of these Law Lords indicated that they would have granted Pinochet immunity even on the post-1988 charges of torture if he had still been a sitting head of state. Should sitting heads of state be entitled to absolute immunity? Even with respect to the most serious human rights violations? Conversely, should heads of state lose their absolute immunity once they are out of office? What incentives might such an immunity regime create?

8. For a recent and thorough examination of the history and domestic status of head-of-state immunity, see Tachiona v. Mugabe, 186 F. Supp. 2d 259 (S.D.N.Y. 2002). In *Mugabe,* a group of Zimbabwean citizens brought a class action suit against

the president of Zimbabwe, Zimbabwe's foreign minister, and the Zimbabwe government's ruling political party, alleging that the defendants had carried out a campaign of violence to suppress political opposition. The plaintiffs served the pleadings on the president and foreign minister while they were in New York attending a United Nations conference. After the suit was filed, the State Department submitted a suggestion of immunity on behalf of the president and foreign minister, and the Department also advised the court that these individuals were absolutely immune from service of process and thus could not properly be served with process for the political party defendant.

The court began its opinion by observing that there had been a shift in recent years, both internationally and domestically, away from absolute official immunity. Citing to the international criminal tribunals for former Yugoslavia and Rwanda, the establishment of the permanent international criminal court, the *Filartiga* decision, and the Torture Victim Protection Act, the court stated that there has been "some breach in the theoretical walls that once absolutely impeded the exercise of national jurisdiction against heads-of-state and other foreign officials for private conduct that violates clear and unambiguous norms of established international law." Id. at 279. Nevertheless, the court noted that "many of these developments are incipient and still relatively modest." Id.

After reviewing the various U.S. decisions that have considered head-of-state immunity (including the *Noriega* decision excerpted above), the court noted that "several issues have surfaced which have yet to be conclusively resolved." Id. at 289. These open questions, according to the court, are:

> (1) Who is entitled to assert head-of-state immunity? While the courts uniformly have accepted the claim as to heads-of-state and heads-of-government recognized by the United States, questions remain as to how far down the hierarchical chain the protection could legitimately extend. (2) What are the extent and circumstances under which head-of-state immunity may be waivable? (3) To what degree are acts of individuals rather than governmental offices covered? (4) Is there a distinction between private and governmental acts to which immunity may extend? (5) Is there a difference in the degree of immunity conferred as between sitting and former heads-of-state? (6) What is the exact weight to be accorded by the courts to the State Department's suggestions of immunity, and indeed whether . . . this role survived the FSIA at all? [Id.]

With respect to the last question, the court concluded that "until otherwise definitively settled by Congress, the Executive Branch's role in determinations of head-of-state immunity was not affected by the passage of the FSIA." Id. at 291. As a result, the court accepted the suggestion of immunity submitted by the State Department on behalf of Zimbabwe's president and foreign minister, and dismissed the charges against them. The court also determined that, because they were visiting the United Nations, these individuals were protected by diplomatic immunity.

Contrary to the advice of the State Department, however, the court entered judgment against the political party defendant. The court noted that the State Department had not suggested that this defendant was entitled to immunity from suit. The court also concluded that this defendant had been properly served with process through the personal service on the president and foreign minister. The court thus rejected the State Department's argument that these individuals were absolutely immune from service of process. The court reasoned that head-of-state immunity does not "confer absolute immunity from service of process where a head-of-state or diplomat would not be subjected personally to a foreign court's jurisdiction nor exposed to liability in that court." Id. at 308. The U.S. government sought reconsideration of this part of the court's decision, but the court denied the motion. See Tachiona v. Mugabe, 186 F. Supp. 2d 383 (S.D.N.Y. 2002).

9. In February 2002 (the same month the court in *Mugabe* denied reconsideration), the International Court of Justice issued an important decision concerning official immunity. See Case Concerning the Arrest Warrant of 11 April 2000 (Democratic Republic of the Congo v. Belgium), at http://www.icj-cij.org. In that case, an investigating judge in Belgium had issued an arrest warrant directed at Congo's Minister for Foreign Affairs, charging him with war crimes and crimes against humanity. The warrant was based on a controversial Belgian statute allowing for "universal jurisdiction" over certain egregious violations of international law committed anywhere in the world. (The universal jurisdiction basis for legislative jurisdiction is discussed in Chapter 7.) The International Court of Justice held that Belgium had violated Congo's rights under customary international law by issuing the arrest warrant.

The Court began by noting that "in international law it is firmly established that, as also diplomatic and consular agents, certain holders of high-ranking office in a State, such as the Head of a State, Head of Government and Minister for Foreign Affairs, enjoy immunities from jurisdiction in other States, both civil and criminal." The Court next examined the functions of a Minister of Foreign Affairs and concluded that these functions were such that "throughout the duration of his or her office, [a Minister of Foreign Affairs] when abroad enjoys full immunity from criminal jurisdiction and inviolability." The Court rejected any distinction for these purposes between acts performed in an official capacity and acts performed in a personal capacity, reasoning that "[t]he consequences of such impediment to the exercise of [the Minister's] official functions are equally serious" regardless of whether the official is charged in his or her official or personal capacity.

The Court further held that the Minister's immunity extended even to charges of war crimes and crimes against humanity. The Court considered state practice and the decisions of national courts, including the *Pinochet* decision, as well as treaties establishing international criminal tribunals, and said that it was "unable to deduce from this practice that there exists under customary international law any form of exception to the rule according immunity from criminal jurisdiction and inviolability to incumbent Ministers for Foreign Affairs, where they are suspected of having committed war crimes or crimes against humanity." In reasoning at odds with some of the reasoning in the *Pinochet* decision, the Court also noted that the existence of treaties calling for the extension of national jurisdiction over international crimes "in no way affects immunities under customary international law." The Court's decision may be distinguishable from the *Pinochet* decision, however, in that it involved the immunity of a *sitting* minister, whereas *Pinochet* involved the immunity of a *former* head of state. Indeed, the Court specifically observed that a foreign state could prosecute a former minister for acts "committed . . . in a private capacity" without violating the former minister's immunity.

What implications, if any, does the International Court's decision have for U.S. law concerning head-of-state immunity?

10. For additional discussion of head-of-state immunity, see Curtis A. Bradley & Jack L. Goldsmith, *Pinochet* and International Human Rights Litigation, 97 Mich.

L. Rev. 2129 (1999); and Joseph W. Dellapenna, Head of State Immunity—Foreign Sovereign Immunities Act—Suggestion by the State Department, 88 Am. J. Intl. L. 528 (1994).

B. THE ACT OF STATE DOCTRINE

Besides the question of whether a foreign sovereign is immune from the jurisdiction of the court, statehood can raise special questions when a court begins to address the substantive issues in the dispute. A defendant foreign sovereign or other party can argue that the plaintiff has no basis for its claims because the challenged acts of the foreign sovereign are valid, and the plaintiff thereby loses.

As detailed below, the act of state doctrine, which is frequently invoked in U.S. courts, provides that certain acts of a foreign state will be presumed to be valid, and the court will not sit in judgment on them. The doctrine can arise in a surprisingly wide variety of situations. Note, for example, that unlike foreign sovereign immunity, private parties can seek to rely on the doctrine.

1. Historical Background

The U.S. act of state doctrine has its roots in early decisions granting foreign governments and their leaders immunity from suit. See, e.g., The Schooner Exchange v. M'Faddon, 11 U.S. (7 Cranch) 116 (1812); Hatch v. Baez, 7 Hun. 596 (N.Y. Sup. Ct. 1876). The doctrine also has connections to the English common law. The earliest English case usually cited for the doctrine is Blad v. Bamfield, 36 Eng. Rep. 992 (Ch. 1674), in which the court refused to consider the validity of a patent issued by the King of Denmark to a Danish trader. The court there stated that it would be "monstrous and absurd" for an English court to judge the validity of a foreign patent. Another English decision often cited for the doctrine is Duke of Brunswick v. King of Hanover, 9 Eng. Rep. 993 (H.L. 1848). In that case, the former Duke of Brunswick (a German principality) sued the then Duke of Brunswick (who also was King of Hanover and a British subject), alleging that the latter had improperly seized property in Brunswick belonging to the plaintiff. The British House of Lords rejected the claim on both sovereign immunity and act of state grounds, stating that "a foreign Sovereign, coming into this country, cannot be made responsible here for an act done in his sovereign character in his own country" and that "the Courts of this country cannot sit in judgment upon an act of a Sovereign, effected by virtue of his Sovereign authority abroad." Id. at 998-999.

The first U.S. Supreme Court decision that clearly relied on the act of state doctrine was Underhill v. Hernandez, 168 U.S. 250 (1897). In that case, Underhill, an American citizen, had been living in Bolivar, Venezuela, where he had constructed a waterworks system for the city and was carrying on a machinery repair business. A revolutionary army seized control of the city and, for a time, the commander of the army refused to let Underhill leave, in an effort to coerce Underhill to operate the waterworks system and continue his repair business. Underhill eventually was allowed to leave, and he subsequently sued the commander in a U.S. federal court, seeking damages for the detention. In the meantime, the U.S. government recognized the revolutionary government as the legitimate government of Venezuela. In affirming a dismissal of Underhill's suit, the Supreme Court stated:

> Every sovereign State is bound to respect the independence of every other sovereign State, and the courts of one country will not sit in judgment on the acts of the government of another done within its own territory. Redress of grievances by reason of such acts must be obtained through the means open to be availed of by sovereign powers as between themselves. [Id. at 252.]

The Supreme Court reaffirmed this doctrine in a number of decisions in the early 1900s. For example, in two cases decided the same day in 1918, the Court applied the act of state doctrine to bar challenges to expropriations of property by the Mexican government. See Oetjen v. Central Leather Co., 246 U.S. 297 (1918); Ricaud v. American Metal Co., 246 U.S. 304 (1918). In the first case, the expropriation was carried out by military forces working for a government that was subsequently recognized by the United States. Citing *Underhill* and *American Banana,* the Court held that "the action, in Mexico, of the legitimate Mexican government when dealing with a Mexican citizen . . . is not subject to reexamination and modification by the courts of this country." *Oejten,* supra, at 303. The Court explained that the act of state doctrine "rests at last upon the highest considerations of international comity and expediency." Id. at 303-304. In the second decision, the Court applied the same principle to a case involving expropriation of a U.S. citizen's property, stating that "the act within its own boundaries of one sovereign State cannot become the subject of reexamination and modification in the courts of another." *Ricaud,* supra, at 310. The Court also explained in that decision that the act of state doctrine does not deprive a court of jurisdiction, but rather "requires only that, when it is made to appear that a foreign government has acted in a given way on the subject-matter of the litigation, the details of such action or the merit of the result cannot be questioned but must be accepted by our courts as a rule for their decision." Id. at 309.

The Court invoked the doctrine almost 20 years later in another Mexican expropriation case. See Shapleigh v. Mier, 299 U.S. 468 (1937). During that same Term, the Court also invoked the doctrine in a case involving an expropriation of property by the Soviet Union. See United States v. Belmont, 301 U.S. 324 (1937). Several years later, the Court invoked the doctrine in another Soviet expropriation case. See United States v. Pink, 315 U.S. 203 (1942). (The *Belmont* and *Pink* decisions also considered the validity and effect of executive agreements, a topic discussed in Chapter 3.)

2. *The* Sabbatino *Decision*

The Supreme Court's most important decision concerning the act of state doctrine is Banco Nacional de Cuba v. Sabbatino, excerpted below. In reading *Sabbatino,* it is important to keep in mind the historical context. The decision was issued in 1964, during the height of the Cold War. The relations between the United States and Cuba were extremely strained. Fidel Castro's Communist government had assumed power in Cuba in 1959 and, shortly thereafter, proceeded to expropriate U.S. property. The United States supported the attempted invasion of Cuba at the Bay of Pigs in 1961, and it imposed a trade embargo against Cuba in 1962. The Cuban missile crisis also occurred in 1962, during which the United States Navy blocked Soviet ships from reaching Cuba in order to compel the Soviet Union to remove nuclear missiles that it had placed there. (This crisis is discussed in Chapter 11.) This was also a time during which the customary international law rules of state responsibility, especially rules relating to the expropriation of foreign citizen property, were being challenged by Communist and newly independent third world countries.

Banco Nacional de Cuba v. Sabbatino, Receiver

U.S. Supreme Court
376 U.S. 398 (1964)

[As relations grew increasingly hostile between the United States and Cuba in 1960, the United States reduced the sugar quota* for Cuba on July 6. In response, on the same day Cuba adopted Law No. 851, which denounced the U.S. action and authorized the Cuban leaders to expropriate any property or enterprise in which American nationals had an interest. "Although a system of compensation was formally provided, the possibility of payment under it was deemed illusory," according to the Court.

Among the companies that were nationalized was Compania Azucarera Vertientes-Camaguey de Cuba (C.A.V.), a Cuban corporation whose stock was owned principally by U.S. residents. Its wholly owned subsidiary had contracted to sell Cuban sugar to Farr, Whitlock & Co., a U.S. commodities broker. After nationalization of C.A.V.'s sugar (on the day it was being loaded onto the ship), Farr, Whitlock entered into a second contract, identical to the one with C.A.V., with an instrumentality of the Cuban government.

The ship then sailed for Morocco. Farr, Whitlock received payment for the sugar from its customers. The company refused to pay the representative of the Cuban government, however; rather, it turned over the proceeds to the receiver for C.A.V.'s assets (Sabbatino), who had been appointed by a New York court. The court also ordered Farr, Whitlock not to take any step that would allow the funds to leave the state. C.A.V. made it easy for Farr, Whitlock by agreeing to indemnify the company for any loss in the ensuing litigation.

Banco Nacional de Cuba, which had been assigned the Cuban government's right to payment under the second contract, filed suit in the U.S. District Court against Farr, Whitlock and Sabbatino. The defendants responded that title to the sugar had never passed to the Cuban government because the expropriation violated international law.]

Mr. Justice HARLAN delivered the opinion of the Court [for himself and Justices Warren, Black, Douglas, Clark, Brennan, Stewart, and Goldberg]. . . .

---

*Sugar quotas limit the amount of sugar that a foreign country can sell to the United States. The US. price is generally well above the world price because the U.S. price is set in part to help higher-cost U.S. domestic producers. — EDS.

While acknowledging the continuing vitality of the act of state doctrine, the [district] court believed it inapplicable when the questioned foreign act is in violation of international law. Proceeding on the basis that a taking invalid under international law does not convey good title, the District Court found the Cuban expropriation decree to violate such law in three separate respects: it was motivated by a retaliatory and not a public purpose; it discriminated against American nationals; and it failed to provide adequate compensation. Summary judgment against petitioner was accordingly granted.

The Court of Appeals, 307 F.2d 845, affirming the decision on similar grounds, relied on two letters (not before the District Court) written by State Department officers which it took as evidence that the Executive Branch had no objection to a judicial testing of the Cuban decree's validity. The court was unwilling to declare that any one of the infirmities found by the District Court rendered the taking invalid under international law, but was satisfied that in combination they had that effect. We granted certiorari because the issues involved bear importantly on the conduct of the country's foreign relations and more particularly on the proper role of the Judicial Branch in this sensitive area. For reasons to follow we decide that the judgment below must be reversed. . . .

alleged viol of I law

Ct of App used Bernstein exception

II

It is first contended that this petitioner, an instrumentality of the Cuban Government, should be denied access to American courts because Cuba is an unfriendly power and does not permit nationals of this country to obtain relief in its courts. . . .

Under principles of comity governing this country's relations with other nations, sovereign states are allowed to sue in the courts of the United States. This Court has called "comity" in the legal sense "neither a matter of absolute obligation, on the one hand, nor of mere courtesy and good will, upon the other." Hilton v. Guyot, 159 U.S. 113, 163-164. . . .

Respondents, pointing to the severance of diplomatic relations, commercial embargo, and freezing of Cuban assets in this country, contend that relations between the United States and Cuba manifest such animosity that unfriendliness is clear, and that the courts should be closed to the Cuban Government. We do not agree. This Court would hardly be competent to undertake assessments of varying degrees of friendliness or its absence, and, lacking some definite touchstone for determination, we are constrained to consider any relationship, short of war, with a recognized sovereign power as embracing the privilege of resorting to United States courts. Although the severance of diplomatic relations is an overt act with objective significance in the dealings of sovereign states, we are unwilling to say that it should inevitably result in the withdrawal of the privilege of bringing suit. . . .

IV . . .

In deciding the present case the Court of Appeals relied in part upon an exception to the unqualified teachings of *Underhill, Oetjen,* and *Ricaud* which that court had earlier indicated. In Bernstein v. Van Heyghen Freres Societe Anonyme, 163 F.2d 246, suit was brought to recover from an assignee property allegedly taken, in effect, by the Nazi Government because plaintiff was Jewish. Recognizing the odious nature of this act of state, the court, through Judge Learned Hand, nonetheless refused to consider it invalid on that ground. Rather, it looked to see if the Executive had acted in any manner that would indicate that United States Courts should refuse to give effect to such a foreign decree. Finding no such evidence, the court sustained dismissal of the complaint. In a later case involving similar facts the same court again assumed examination of the German acts improper, Bernstein v. N. V. Nederlandsche-Amerikaansche Stoomvaart-Maatschappij, 173 F.2d 71, but, quite evidently following the implications of Judge Hand's opinion in the earlier case, amended its mandate to permit evidence of alleged invalidity, 210 F.2d 375, subsequent to receipt by plaintiff's attorney of a letter from the Acting Legal Adviser to the State Department written for the purpose of relieving the court from any constraint upon the exercise of its jurisdiction to pass on that question.[18]

This Court has never had occasion to pass upon the so-called *Bernstein* exception, nor need it do so now. For whatever ambiguity may be thought to exist in the two letters from State Department officials on which the Court of Appeals relied, is now removed by the position which the Executive has taken in this Court on the act of state claim; respondents do not indeed contest the view that these letters were intended to reflect no more than the Department's then wish not to make any statement bearing on this litigation.[19]

The outcome of this case, therefore, turns upon whether any of the contentions urged by respondents against the application of the act of state doctrine in the premises is acceptable: (1) that the doctrine does not apply to acts of state which violate international law, as is claimed to be the case here; (2) that the doctrine is inapplicable unless the Executive specifically interposes it in a particular case; and (3) that, in any event, the doctrine may not be invoked by a foreign government plaintiff in our courts.

18. The letter stated:

1. This government has consistently opposed the forcible acts of dispossession of a discriminatory and confiscatory nature practiced by the Germans on the countries or peoples subject to their controls. . . .

3. The policy of the Executive, with respect to claims asserted in the United States for the restitution of identifiable property (or compensation in lieu thereof) lost through force, coercion, or duress as a result of Nazi persecution in Germany, is to relieve American courts from any restraint upon the exercise of their jurisdiction to pass upon the validity of the acts of Nazi officials. State Department Press Release, April 27, 1949.

19. Abram Chayes, the Legal Adviser to the State Department, wrote on October 18, 1961, in answer to an inquiry regarding the position of the Department by Mr. John Laylin, attorney for *amici*:

The Department of State has not, in the *Bahia de Nipe* case or elsewhere, done anything inconsistent with the position taken on the Cuban nationalizations by Secretary Herter. Whether or not these nationalizations will in the future be given effect in the United States is, of course, for the courts to determine. Since the *Sabbatino* case and other similar cases are at present before the courts, any comments on this question by the Department of State would be out of place at this time. As you yourself point out, statements by the executive branch are highly susceptible of misconstruction.

A letter dated November 14, 1961, from George Ball, Under Secretary for Economic Affairs, responded to a similar inquiry by the same attorney:

I have carefully considered your letter and have discussed it with the Legal Adviser. Our conclusion, in which the Secretary concurs, is that the Department should not comment on matters pending before the courts.

V

Preliminarily, we discuss the foundations on which we deem the act of state doctrine to rest, and more particularly the question of whether state or federal law governs its application in a federal diversity case.

We do not believe that this doctrine is compelled either by the inherent nature of sovereign authority, as some of the earlier decisions seem to imply, see *Underhill,* supra; or by some principle of international law. If a transaction takes place in one jurisdiction and the forum is in another, the forum does not by dismissing an action or by applying its own law purport to divest the first jurisdiction of its territorial sovereignty; it merely declines to adjudicate or makes applicable its own law to parties or property before it. . . .

That international law does not require application of the doctrine is evidenced by the practice of nations. Most of the countries rendering decisions on the subject fail to follow the rule rigidly.[21] No international arbitral or judicial decision discovered suggests that international law prescribes recognition of sovereign acts of foreign governments. . . . If international law does not prescribe use of the doctrine, neither does it forbid application of the rule even if it is claimed that the act of state in question violated international law. The traditional view of international law is that it establishes substantive principles for determining whether one country has wronged another. Because of its peculiar nation-to-nation character the usual method for an individual to seek relief is to exhaust local remedies and then repair to the executive authorities of his own state to persuade them to champion his claim in diplomacy or before an international tribunal. . . . Although it is, of course, true that United States courts apply international law as a part of our own in appropriate circumstances, Ware v. Hylton, 3 Dall. 199, 281; The Nereide, 9 Cranch 388, 423; The Paquete Habana, 175 U.S. 677, 700, the public law of nations can hardly dictate to a country which is in theory wronged how to treat that wrong within its domestic borders.

Despite the broad statement in *Oetjen* that "The conduct of the foreign relations of our Government is committed by the Constitution to the Executive and Legislative . . . Departments," 246 U.S., at 302, it cannot of course be thought that "every case or controversy which touches foreign relations lies beyond judicial cognizance." Baker v. Carr, 369 U.S. 186, 211. The text of the Constitution does not require the act of state doctrine; it does not irrevocably remove from the judiciary the capacity to review the validity of foreign acts of state.

The act of state doctrine does, however, have "constitutional" underpinnings. It arises out of the basic relationships between branches of government in a system of

21. In English jurisprudence, in the classic case of Luther v. James Sagor & Co., [1921] 3 K.B. 532, the act of state doctrine is articulated in terms not unlike those of the United States cases. But see Anglo-Iranian Oil Co. v. Jaffrate, [1953] 1 Weekly L.R. 246, [1953] Intl. L. Rep. 316 (Aden Sup. Ct.) (exception to doctrine if foreign act violates international law). Civil law countries, however, which apply the rule make exceptions for acts contrary to their sense of public order. See, e.g., *Ropit* case, Cour de Cassation (France), [1929] Recueil Général Des Lois et Des Arrêts (Sirey) Part I, 217; 55 Journal Du Droit International (Clunet) 674 (1928), [1927-1928] Ann. Dig., No. 43; Graue, Germany: Recognition of Foreign Expropriations, 3 Am. J. Comp. L. 93 (1954); Domke, Indonesian Nationalization Measures Before Foreign Courts, 54 Am. J. Intl. L. 305 (1960) . . . ; Anglo-Iranian Oil Co. v. S.U.P.O.R. Co., [1955] Intl. L. Rep. 19 (Ct. of Venice), 78 Il Foro Italiano Part I, 719. . . . See also Anglo-Iranian Oil Co. v. Idemitsu Kosan Kabushiki Kaisha, [1953] Intl. L. Rep. 312 (High Ct. of Tokyo).

separation of powers. It concerns the competency of dissimilar institutions to make and implement particular kinds of decisions in the area of international relations. The doctrine as formulated in past decisions expresses the strong sense of the Judicial Branch that its engagement in the task of passing on the validity of foreign acts of state may hinder rather than further this country's pursuit of goals both for itself and for the community of nations as a whole in the international sphere. Many commentators disagree with this view. . . . Whatever considerations are thought to predominate, it is plain that the problems involved are uniquely federal in nature. If federal authority, in this instance this Court, orders the field of judicial competence in this area for the federal courts, and the state courts are left free to formulate their own rules, the purposes behind the doctrine could be as effectively undermined as if there had been no federal pronouncement on the subject.

We could perhaps in this diversity action avoid the question of deciding whether federal or state law is applicable to this aspect of the litigation. . . .

However, we are constrained to make it clear that an issue concerned with a basic choice regarding the competence and function of the Judiciary and the National Executive in ordering our relationships with other members of the international community must be treated exclusively as an aspect of federal law.[23] It seems fair to assume that the Court did not have rules like the act of state doctrine in mind when it decided Erie R. Co. v. Tompkins. . . . We conclude that the scope of the act of state doctrine must be determined according to federal law.[25]

VI

If the act of state doctrine is a principle of decision binding on federal and state courts alike but compelled by neither international law nor the Constitution, its continuing vitality depends on its capacity to reflect the proper distribution of functions between the judicial and political branches of the Government on matters bearing upon foreign affairs. It should be apparent that the greater the degree of codification or consensus concerning a particular area of international law, the more appropriate it is for the judiciary to render decisions regarding it, since the courts can then focus on the application of an agreed principle to circumstances of fact rather than on the sensitive task of establishing a principle not inconsistent with the national interest or with international justice. It is also evident that some aspects of international law touch much more sharply on national nerves than do others; the less important the implications of an issue are for our foreign relations, the weaker the justification for exclusivity in the political branches. The balance of relevant considerations may also be shifted if the government which perpetrated the challenged act of state is no longer in existence, as in the Bernstein case, for the political interest of this country may, as a result, be measurably altered. Therefore,

23. At least this is true when the Court limits the scope of judicial inquiry. We need not now consider whether a state court might, in certain circumstances, adhere to a more restrictive view concerning the scope of examination of foreign acts than that required by this Court.

25. Various constitutional and statutory provisions indirectly support this determination, see U.S. Const., Art. I, §8, cls. 3, 10; Art. II, §§2, 3; Art. III, §2; 28 U.S.C. §§1251(a)(2), (b)(1), (b)(3), 1332(a)(2), 1333, 1350-1351, by reflecting a concern for uniformity in this country's dealings with foreign nations and indicating a desire to give matters of international significance to the jurisdiction of federal institutions.

rather than laying down or reaffirming an inflexible and all-encompassing rule in this case, we decide only that the Judicial Branch will not examine the validity of a taking of property within its own territory by a foreign sovereign government, extant and recognized by this country at the time of suit, in the absence of a treaty or other unambiguous agreement regarding controlling legal principles, even if the complaint alleges that the taking violates customary international law.

There are few if any issues in international law today on which opinion seems to be so divided as the limitations on a state's power to expropriate the property of aliens. There is, of course, authority, in international judicial and arbitral decisions, in the expressions of national governments, and among commentators for the view that a taking is improper under international law if it is not for a public purpose, is discriminatory, or is without provision for prompt, adequate, and effective compensation. However, Communist countries, although they have in fact provided a degree of compensation after diplomatic efforts, commonly recognize no obligation on the part of the taking country. Certain representatives of the newly independent and underdeveloped countries have questioned whether rules of state responsibility toward aliens can bind nations that have not consented to them and it is argued that the traditionally articulated standards governing expropriation of property reflect "imperialist" interests and are inappropriate to the circumstances of emergent states.

The disagreement as to relevant international law standards reflects an even more basic divergence between the national interests of capital importing and capital exporting nations and between the social ideologies of those countries that favor state control of a considerable portion of the means of production and those that adhere to a free enterprise system. It is difficult to imagine the courts of this country embarking on adjudication in an area which touches more sensitively the practical and ideological goals of the various members of the community of nations.[34]

When we consider the prospect of the courts characterizing foreign expropriations, however justifiably, as invalid under international law and ineffective to pass title, the wisdom of the precedents is confirmed. While each of the leading cases in this Court may be argued to be distinguishable on its facts from this one — *Underhill* because sovereign immunity provided an independent ground and *Oetjen, Ricaud,* and *Shapleigh* because there was actually no violation of international law — the plain implication of all these opinions . . . is that the act of state doctrine is applicable even if international law has been violated. . . .

The possible adverse consequences of a conclusion to the contrary of that implicit in these cases is highlighted by contrasting the practices of the political branch with the limitations of the judicial process in matters of this kind. Following an expropriation of any significance, the Executive engages in diplomacy aimed to assure that United States citizens who are harmed are compensated fairly. Representing all claimants of this country, it will often be able, either by bilateral or multilateral talks, by submission to the United Nations, or by the employment of economic and political sanctions, to achieve some degree of general redress. Judicial determinations of invalidity of title can, on the other hand, have only an occasional impact, since they depend on the fortuitous circumstance of the property in question being brought

---

34. There are, of course, areas of international law in which consensus as to standards is greater and which do not represent a battleground for conflicting ideologies. This decision in no way intimates that the courts of this country are broadly foreclosed from considering questions of international law.

into this country. Such decisions would, if the acts involved were declared invalid, often be likely to give offense to the expropriating country; since the concept of territorial sovereignty is so deep seated, any state may resent the refusal of the courts of another sovereign to accord validity to acts within its territorial borders. Piecemeal dispositions of this sort involving the probability of affront to another state could seriously interfere with negotiations being carried on by the Executive Branch and might prevent or render less favorable the terms of an agreement that could otherwise be reached. Relations with third countries which have engaged in similar expropriations would not be immune from effect.

The dangers of such adjudication are present regardless of whether the State Department has, as it did in this case, asserted that the relevant act violated international law. If the Executive Branch has undertaken negotiations with an expropriating country, but has refrained from claims of violation of the law of nations, a determination to that effect by a court might be regarded as a serious insult, while a finding of compliance with international law, would greatly strengthen the bargaining hand of the other state with consequent detriment to American interests.

Even if the State Department has proclaimed the impropriety of the expropriation, the stamp of approval of its view by a judicial tribunal, however impartial, might increase any affront and the judicial decision might occur at a time, almost always well after the taking, when such an impact would be contrary to our national interest. Considerably more serious and far-reaching consequences would flow from a judicial finding that international law standards had been met if that determination flew in the face of a State Department proclamation to the contrary. When articulating principles of international law in its relations with other states, the Executive Branch speaks not only as an interpreter of generally accepted and traditional rules, as would the courts, but also as an advocate of standards it believes desirable for the community of nations and protective of national concerns. In short, whatever way the matter is cut, the possibility of conflict between the Judicial and Executive Branches could hardly be avoided. . . .

Another serious consequence of the exception pressed by respondents would be to render uncertain titles in foreign commerce, with the possible consequence of altering the flow of international trade.[38] If the attitude of the United States courts were unclear, one buying expropriated goods would not know if he could safely import them into this country. Even were takings known to be invalid, one would have difficulty determining after goods had changed hands several times whether the particular articles in question were the product of an ineffective state act.[39]

Against the force of such considerations, we find respondents' countervailing arguments quite unpersuasive. Their basic contention is that United States courts could make a significant contribution to the growth of international law, a contribution whose importance, it is said, would be magnified by the relative paucity of decisional law by international bodies. But given the fluidity of present world conditions, the effectiveness of such a patchwork approach toward the formulation of an

38. This possibility is consistent with the view that the deterrent effect of court invalidations would not ordinarily be great. If the expropriating country could find other buyers for its products at roughly the same price, the deterrent effect might be minimal although patterns of trade would be significantly changed.

39. Were respondents' position adopted, the courts might be engaged in the difficult tasks of ascertaining the origin of fungible goods, of considering the effect of improvements made in a third country on expropriated raw materials, and of determining the title to commodities subsequently grown on expropriated land or produced with expropriated machinery. . . .

acceptable body of law concerning state responsibility for expropriations is, to say the least, highly conjectural. . . .

It is contended that regardless of the fortuitous circumstances necessary for United States jurisdiction over a case involving a foreign act of state and the resultant isolated application to any expropriation program taken as a whole, it is the function of the courts to justly decide individual disputes before them. Perhaps the most typical act of state case involves the original owner or his assignee suing one not in association with the expropriating state who has had "title" transferred to him. But it is difficult to regard the claim of the original owner, who otherwise may be recompensed through diplomatic channels, as more demanding of judicial cognizance than the claim of title by the innocent third party purchaser, who, if the property is taken from him, is without any remedy.

title problems not persuasive

Respondents claim that the economic pressure resulting from the proposed exception to the act of state doctrine will materially add to the protection of United States investors. We are not convinced, even assuming the relevance of this contention. Expropriations take place for a variety of reasons, political and ideological as well as economic. When one considers the variety of means possessed by this country to make secure foreign investment, the persuasive or coercive effect of judicial invalidation of acts of expropriation dwindles in comparison. The newly independent states are in need of continuing foreign investment; the creation of a climate unfavorable to such investment by wholesale confiscations may well work to their long-run economic disadvantage. Foreign aid given to many of these countries provides a powerful lever in the hands of the political branches to ensure fair treatment of United States nationals. Ultimately the sanctions of economic embargo and the freezing of assets in this country may be employed. Any country willing to brave any or all of these consequences is unlikely to be deterred by sporadic judicial decisions directly affecting only property brought to our shores. . . .

doubts deterrent effect

It is suggested that if the act of state doctrine is applicable to violations of international law, it should only be so when the Executive Branch expressly stipulates that it does not wish the courts to pass on the question of validity. . . . We should be slow to reject the representations of the Government that such a reversal of the *Bernstein* principle would work serious inroads on the maximum effectiveness of United States diplomacy. Often the State Department will wish to refrain from taking an official position, particularly at a moment that would be dictated by the development of private litigation but might be inopportune diplomatically. . . . We do not now pass on the *Bernstein* exception, but even if it were deemed valid, its suggested extension is unwarranted.

However offensive to the public policy of this country and its constituent States an expropriation of this kind may be, we conclude that both the national interest and progress toward the goal of establishing the rule of law among nations are best served by maintaining intact the act of state doctrine in this realm of its application. . . .

The judgment of the Court of Appeals is reversed and the case is remanded to the District Court for proceedings consistent with this opinion.

It is so ordered.

Mr. Justice WHITE, dissenting.

abdicates judicial role to determine int'l law

I am dismayed that the Court has, with one broad stroke, declared the ascertainment and application of international law beyond the competence of the courts of the United States in a large and important category of cases. I am also disappointed in the Court's declaration that the acts of a sovereign state with regard to the property of aliens within its borders are beyond the reach of international law in the courts of this country. However clearly established that law may be, a sovereign may violate it with impunity, except insofar as the political branches of the government may provide a remedy. This backward-looking doctrine, never before declared in this Court, is carried a disconcerting step further: not only are the courts powerless to question acts of state proscribed by international law but they are likewise powerless to refuse to adjudicate the claim founded upon a foreign law; they must render judgment and thereby validate the lawless act. . . . [T]he Court expressly extends its ruling to all acts of state expropriating property. . . . No other civilized country has found such a rigid rule necessary for the survival of the executive branch of its government; the executive of no other government seems to require such insulation from international law adjudications in its courts; and no other judiciary is apparently so incompetent to ascertain and apply international law.[1]

I do not believe that the act of state doctrine, as judicially fashioned in this Court, and the reasons underlying it, require American courts to decide cases in disregard of international law and of the rights of litigants to a full determination on the merits. . . .

VII

The position of the Executive Branch of the Government charged with foreign affairs with respect to this case is not entirely clear. As I see it no specific objection by the Secretary of State to examination of the validity of Cuba's law has been interposed at any stage in these proceedings, which would ordinarily lead to an adjudication on the merits. Disclaiming, rightfully, I think, any interest in the outcome of the case, the United States has simply argued for a rule of nonexamination in every case, which literally, I suppose, includes this one. If my view had prevailed I would have stayed further resolution of the issues in this Court to afford the Department of State reasonable time to clarify its views in light of the opinion. In the absence of a specific objection to an examination of the validity of Cuba's law under international law, I would have proceeded to determine the issue and resolve this litigation on the merits.

Notes and Questions

1. Prior to *Sabbatino*, the Supreme Court had indicated that the act of state doctrine was derived from principles of international law and international comity.

---

1. The courts of the following countries, among others, and their territories have examined a fully "executed" foreign act of state expropriating property:

England: Anglo-Iranian Oil Co. v. Jaffrate, [1953] Intl. L. Rep. 316 (Aden Sup. Ct.). . . .

Germany: N.V. Verenigde Deli-Maatschapijen v. Deutsch-Indonesische Tabak-Handelsgesellschaft m.b.H. (Bremen Ct. App.), excerpts reprinted in Domke, supra, at 313-314 (1960). . . .

Japan: Anglo-Iranian Oil Co. v. Idemitsu Kosan Kabushiki Kaisha, [1953] Intl. L. Rep. 305 (Dist. Ct. of Tokyo), *aff'd*, [1953] Intl. L. Rep. 312 (High Ct. of Tokyo). . . .

The Court does not refer to any country which has applied the act of state doctrine in a case where a substantial international law issue is sought to be raised by an alien whose property has been expropriated. This country and this Court stand alone among the civilized nations of the world in ruling that such an issue is not cognizable in a court of law.

Is that the way the Court conceives of the doctrine in *Sabbatino*? If not, what, according to the Court, is the source of the doctrine? Was it required by the constitution? Why does the Court in *Sabbatino* conceive of the doctrine in this way? For a thoughtful consideration of these and other questions relating to the decision, see Louis Henkin, The Foreign Affairs Power of the Federal Courts: *Sabbatino*, 64 Colum. L. Rev. 805 (1964).

2. One could describe the holding of *Sabbatino* in choice-of-law terms: Normally, in determining title to property, choice-of-law principles would call for applying the law of the place where the property was located. In *Sabbatino*, this presumably would mean applying the Cuban law that existed at the time of the sale of the sugar, including the Cuban expropriation decree. Courts often decline to apply foreign law, however, if it offends some fundamental public policy of the forum. See Restatement (Second) of Conflict of Laws section 90 (1971) ("No action will be entertained on a foreign cause of action the enforcement of which is contrary to the strong public policy of the forum."). In *Sabbatino*, the respondents argued that Cuba had violated customary international law in expropriating the sugar, and that it would therefore violate public policy to give legal effect to the expropriation. Why does the Court reject such a public policy limitation?

3. The Cuban bank's claim in *Sabbatino* (for conversion of bills of lading) was not governed by federal law. Normally, under the *Erie* doctrine, the choice-of-law principles in such a case would be decided by the law of the state in which the federal court sits. See Klaxon Co. v. Stentor Elec. Mfg. Co., 313 U.S. 487 (1941). In *Sabbatino*, however, the Court holds that the act of state doctrine is a rule of federal common law that displaces the state choice-of-law rule. What justifications does the Court give for this holding? What are the implications of this holding? Does *Sabbatino* authorize the creation of federal common law rules to govern other foreign affairs issues?

4. The court of appeals in *Sabbatino*, in declining to apply the act of state doctrine, relied heavily on the letters quoted in footnote 19 of the Supreme Court's opinion, stating that, although the letters "are somewhat ambiguous, perhaps intentionally so[,] . . . they express a belief on the part of those responsible for the conduct of our foreign affairs that the courts here should decide the status here of Cuban decrees." 307 F.2d 845, 858 (2d Cir. 1962). Did the court of appeals misconstrue these letters? Note that the Justice and State Departments submitted an *amicus curiae* brief to the Supreme Court in *Sabbatino* urging the Court to apply the act of state doctrine. Among other things, the brief argued that "executive diplomatic action may be seriously impeded or embarrassed by American judicial decisions which undertake, in domestic lawsuits, to pass upon the validity of foreign acts." The brief also disputed the court of appeals' finding that the Executive Branch had supported judicial resolution of the expropriation issue. The letters referred to by the court of appeals, the brief argued, were mere refusals to comment, not an endorsement of the litigation. Finally, the brief argued that Executive Branch approval of the litigation should not be inferred from mere Executive Branch silence.

5. The Supreme Court had stated in prior decisions that international law is part of U.S. law. See, for example, The Paquete Habana, 175 U.S. 677, 700 (1900), which is excerpted in Chapter 3. Does the Court in *Sabbatino* reject that proposition? If not, how does it justify its refusal to apply customary international law principles governing the expropriation of foreign citizen property? Note that courts have held that a government's confiscation, within its territory, of the property of *its own*

[handwritten margin note:] State Dept had rejected Bernstein in amicus brief ask to apply the act of S Doctrine

citizens does not violate customary international law. See, e.g., FOGADE v. ENB Revocable Trust, 263 F.3d 1274 (11th Cir. 2001); Bank Tejarat v. Varsho-Saz, 723 F. Supp. 516, 520 (C.D. Cal. 1989).

6. In response to *Sabbatino*, Congress enacted the Amendment to the Foreign Assistance Act of 1964 (also called the "Second Hickenlooper Amendment"), which provides as follows:

> Notwithstanding any other provision of law, no court in the United States shall decline on the ground of the federal act of state doctrine to make a determination on the merits giving effect to the principles of international law in a case in which a claim of title or other right to property is asserted by any party including a foreign state (or a party claiming through such state) based upon (or traced through) a confiscation or other taking after January 1, 1959, by an act of that state in violation of the principles of international law, including the principles of compensation and the other standards set out in this subsection: *Provided,* That this subparagraph shall not be applicable (1) in any case in which an act of a foreign state is not contrary to international law or with respect to a claim of title or other right to property acquired pursuant to an irrevocable letter of credit of not more than 180 days duration issued in good faith prior to the time of the confiscation or other taking, or (2) in any case with respect to which the President determines that application of the act of state doctrine is required in that particular case by the foreign policy interests of the United States and a suggestion to this effect is filed on his behalf in that case with the court. [22 U.S.C. §2370(e)(2).]

The "principles of compensation" referred to above had been set forth in an earlier statute (the First Hickenlooper Amendment), which required "speedy compensation for [expropriated] property in convertible foreign exchange, equivalent to the full value thereof, as required by international law."

This statute was applied retroactively to the *Sabbatino* case and, as a result, Cuba's claim was ultimately dismissed. See 383 F.2d 166 (2d Cir. 1967). Since then, some courts have interpreted the statute narrowly, such that it applies only when (a) there are claims of *title to property* (rather than mere breach of contract claims), and (b) the property or its proceeds is presently *located in the United States*. See, e.g., Compania de Gas de Nuevo Laredo, S.A. v. Entex, Inc., 686 F.2d 322 (5th Cir. 1982); Banco Nacional de Cuba v. First National City Bank of New York, 431 F.2d 394 (2d Cir. 1970), rev'd on other grounds, 406 U.S. 759 (1972); Hunt v. Coastal States Gas Producing Co., 583 S.W.2d 322 (Tex. 1979).

Are these limitations supported by the language of the statute? Why do you think courts have interpreted the statute narrowly? With or without these limitations, is the statute constitutional? For an affirmative answer, see Banco Nacional de Cuba v. Farr, 383 F.2d 166 (2d Cir. 1967). The Second Hickenlooper Amendment is not the only statutory restriction imposed by Congress on the act of state doctrine. In the controversial Helms-Burton Act, enacted in 1996, Congress authorized lawsuits against individuals or companies trafficking in property confiscated by Cuba from U.S. citizens, and it expressly precluded application of the act of state doctrine to these lawsuits. See 22 U.S.C. §6082(a)(6). (This Act allows the President to suspend these lawsuit provisions for six-month terms, and to date Presidents have repeatedly done so.) See also 9 U.S.C. §15 (act of state doctrine is inapplicable to enforcement of arbitration agreements and awards).

7. The act of state doctrine has been criticized by a number of international law scholars because, among other things, it reduces the opportunities for U.S. courts to apply customary international law. See, e.g., Michael J. Bazyler, Abolishing the Act of State Doctrine, 134 U. Pa. L. Rev. 325 (1986); Harold Hongju Koh, Transnational Public Law Litigation, 100 Yale L.J. 2347, 2362-2364 (1991). However, the *Sabbatino* decision is sometimes invoked to support the argument that customary international law has the status in U.S. courts of supreme federal law. Can you see how the decision might be used in this way? What reasons did the Court give for treating the act of state doctrine as a rule of federal law? Do those reasons also apply to customary international law?

8. For additional discussion of the act of state doctrine, see Henkin, The Foreign Affairs Power of the Federal Courts, supra; Anne-Marie Burley, Law Among Liberal States: Liberal Internationalism and the Act of State Doctrine, 92 Colum. L. Rev. 1907 (1992); and Daniel C.K. Chow, Rethinking the Act of State Doctrine: An Analysis in Terms of Jurisdiction to Prescribe, 62 Wash. L. Rev. 397 (1987).

3.   *Limitations and Exceptions*

The materials below consider some of the limitations on, and possible exceptions to, the act of state doctrine.

First National City Bank v. Banco Nacional de Cuba

U.S. Supreme Court
406 U.S. 759 (1972)

Mr. Justice REHNQUIST announced the judgment of the Court, and delivered an opinion in which The Chief Justice and Mr. Justice White join.

In July 1958, petitioner loaned the sum of $15 million to a predecessor of respondent. The loan was secured by a pledge of United States Government bonds. The loan was renewed the following year, and in 1960 $5 million was repaid, the $10 million balance was renewed for one year, and collateral equal to the value of the portion repaid was released by petitioner.

Meanwhile, on January 1, 1959, the Castro government came to power in Cuba. On September 16, 1960, the Cuban militia, allegedly pursuant to decrees of the Castro government, seized all of the branches of petitioner located in Cuba. A week later the bank retaliated by selling the collateral securing the loan, and applying the proceeds of the sale to repayment of the principal and unpaid interest. Petitioner concedes that an excess of at least $1.8 million over and above principal and unpaid interest was realized from the sale of the collateral. Respondent sued petitioner in the Federal District Court to recover this excess, and petitioner, by way of setoff and counterclaim, asserted the right to recover damages as a result of the expropriation of its property in Cuba.

The District Court recognized that our decision in Banco Nacional de Cuba v. Sabbatino, 376 U.S. 398 (1964), holding that generally the courts of one nation will not sit in judgment on the acts of another nation within its own territory would bar the assertion of the counterclaim, but it further held that congressional enactments since the decision in *Sabbatino* had "for all practical purposes" overruled that case. Following summary judgment in favor of the petitioner in the District Court on all issues except the amount by which the proceeds of the sale of collateral exceeded the amount that could properly be applied to the loan by petitioner, the parties stipulated that in any event this difference was less than the damages that petitioner could prove in support of its expropriation claim if that claim were allowed. Petitioner then waived any recovery on its counterclaim over and above the amount recoverable by respondent on its complaint, and the District Court then rendered judgment dismissing respondent's complaint on the merits.

On appeal, the Court of Appeals for the Second Circuit held that the congressional enactments relied upon by the District Court did not govern this case, and that our decision in *Sabbatino* barred the assertion of petitioner's counterclaim. We granted certiorari and vacated the judgment of the Court of Appeals for consideration of the views of the Department of State which had been furnished to us following the filing of the petition for certiorari. Upon reconsideration, the Court of Appeals by a divided vote adhered to its earlier decision. We again granted certiorari.

We must here decide whether, in view of the substantial difference between the position taken in this case by the Executive Branch and that which it took in *Sabbatino,* the act of state doctrine prevents petitioner from litigating its counterclaim on the merits. We hold that it does not.

The separate lines of cases enunciating both the act of state and sovereign immunity doctrines have a common source in the case of The Schooner Exchange v. M'Faddon, 7 Cranch 116, 146 (1812). There Chief Justice Marshall stated the general principle of sovereign immunity: sovereigns are not presumed without explicit declaration to have opened their tribunals to suits against other sovereigns. Yet the policy considerations at the root of this fundamental principle are in large part also the underpinnings of the act of state doctrine. The Chief Justice observed:

> The arguments in favor of this opinion which have been drawn from the general inability of the judicial power to enforce its decisions in cases of this description, from the consideration, that *the sovereign power of the nation is alone competent to avenge wrongs committed by a sovereign,* that the questions to which such wrongs give birth are rather *questions of policy than of law,* that they are for diplomatic, rather than legal discussion, are of great weight, and merit serious attention. (Emphasis added.)

Thus, both the act of state and sovereign immunity doctrines are judicially created to effectuate general notions of comity among nations and among the respective branches of the Federal Government. The history and the legal basis of the act of state doctrine are treated comprehensively in the Court's opinion in *Sabbatino,* supra. . . .

The act of state doctrine represents an exception to the general rule that a court of the United States, where appropriate jurisdictional standards are met, will decide cases before it by choosing the rules appropriate for decision from among various sources of law including international law. The Paquete Habana, 175 U.S. 677 (1900). The doctrine precludes any review whatever of the acts of the government of one sovereign State done within its own territory by the courts of another sovereign State. It is clear, however, from both history and the opinions of this Court that the doctrine is not an inflexible one. Specifically, the Court in *Sabbatino* described the act of state doctrine as "a principle of decision binding on federal and state courts alike but compelled by neither international law nor the Constitution," and then continued:

> [I]ts continuing vitality depends on its capacity to reflect the proper distribution of functions between the judicial and political branches of the Government on matters bearing upon foreign affairs.

In *Sabbatino,* the Executive Branch of this Government, speaking through the Department of State, advised attorneys for *amici* in a vein which the Court described as being "intended to reflect no more than the Department's then wish not to make any statement bearing on this litigation." The United States argued before this Court in *Sabbatino* that the Court should not "hold, for the first time, that executive silence regarding the act of state doctrine is equivalent to executive approval of judicial inquiry into the foreign act."

In the case now before us, the Executive Branch has taken a quite different position. The Legal Adviser of the Department of State advised this Court on November 17, 1970, that as a matter of principle where the Executive publicly advises the Court that the act of state doctrine need not be applied, the Court should proceed to examine the legal issues raised by the act of a foreign sovereign within its own territory as it would any other legal question before it. His letter refers to the decision of the court below in Bernstein v. N.V. Nederlandsche-Amerikaansche, 210 F.2d 375 (CA2 1954), as representing a judicial recognition of such a principle, and suggests that the applicability of the principle was not limited to the *Bernstein* case. The Legal Adviser's letter then goes on to state:

> The Department of State believes that the act of state doctrine should not be applied to bar consideration of a defendant's counterclaim or set-off against the Government of Cuba in this or like cases.

The question that we must now decide is whether the so-called *Bernstein* exception to the act of state doctrine should be recognized in the context of the facts before the Court. In *Sabbatino,* the Court said:

> This Court has never had occasion to pass upon the so-called *Bernstein* exception, nor need it do so now. 376 U.S., at 420.

... The line of cases from this Court establishing the act of state doctrine justifies its existence primarily on the basis that juridical review of acts of state of a foreign power could embarrass the conduct of foreign relations by the political branches of the government. ...

The Court in *Sabbatino* throughout its opinion emphasized the lead role of the Executive in foreign policy, particularly in seeking redress for American nationals who had been the victims of foreign expropriation, and concluded that any exception to the act of state doctrine based on a mere silence or neutrality on the part of the Executive might well lead to a conflict between the Executive and Judicial

Branches. Here, however, the Executive Branch has expressly stated that an inflexible application of the act of state doctrine by this Court would not serve the interests of American foreign policy.

The act of state doctrine is grounded on judicial concern that application of customary principles of law to judge the acts of a foreign sovereign might frustrate the conduct of foreign relations by the political branches of the government. We conclude that where the Executive Branch, charged as it is with primary responsibility for the conduct of foreign affairs, expressly represents to the Court that application of the act of state doctrine would not advance the interests of American foreign policy, that doctrine should not be applied by the courts. In so doing, we of course adopt and approve the so-called *Bernstein* exception to the act of state doctrine. We believe this to be no more than an application of the classical common-law maxim that "[t]he reason of the law ceasing, the law itself also ceases" (Black's Law Dictionary 288 (4th ed. 1951)).

Our holding is in no sense an abdication of the judicial function to the Executive Branch. The judicial power of the United States extends to this case, and the jurisdictional standards established by Congress for adjudication by the federal courts have been met by the parties. The only reason for not deciding the case by use of otherwise applicable legal principles would be the fear that legal interpretation by the judiciary of the act of a foreign sovereign within its own territory might frustrate the conduct of this country's foreign relations. But the branch of the government responsible for the conduct of those foreign relations has advised us that such a consequence need not be feared in this case. The judiciary is therefore free to decide the case without the limitations that would otherwise be imposed upon it by the judicially created act of state doctrine.

It bears noting that the result we reach is consonant with the principles of equity set forth by the Court in National City Bank v. Republic of China, 348 U.S. 356 (1955). . . .

We therefore reverse the judgment of the Court of Appeals, and remand the case to it for consideration of respondent's alternative bases of attack on the judgment of the District Court.

Reversed and remanded.

Mr. Justice DOUGLAS, concurring in the result.

Banco Nacional de Cuba v. Sabbatino, 376 U.S. 398, does not control the central issue in the present case. Rather, it is governed by National City Bank v. Republic of China, 348 U.S. 356. . . .

Cuba sues here to recover the difference between a loan made by petitioner and the proceeds of a sale of the collateral securing the loan. The excess is allegedly about $1.8 million. Petitioner sought to set off against that amount claims arising out of the confiscation of petitioner's Cuban properties. How much those setoffs would be, we do not know. The District Court ruled that the amount of these setoffs "cannot be determined on these motions," 270 F. Supp. 1004, 1011, saying that they represented "triable issues of fact and law." Ibid. . . .

. . . I would allow the setoff to the extent of the claim asserted by Cuba because Cuba is the one who asks our judicial aid in collecting its debt from petitioner and, as the *Republic of China* case says, "fair dealing" requires recognition of any counterclaim or setoff that eliminates or reduces that claim. It is that principle, not the *Bernstein* exception, which should govern here. Otherwise, the Court becomes a mere errand boy for the Executive Branch which may choose to pick some people's chestnuts from the fire, but not others'.

Mr. Justice POWELL, concurring in the judgment.

Although I concur in the judgment of reversal and remand, my reasons differ from those expressed by Mr. Justice Rehnquist and Mr. Justice Douglas. While Banco Nacional de Cuba v. Sabbatino technically reserves the question of the validity of the *Bernstein* exception as Mr. Justice Brennan notes in his dissenting opinion, the reasoning of *Sabbatino* implicitly rejects that exception. Moreover, I would be uncomfortable with a doctrine which would require the judiciary to receive the Executive's permission before invoking its jurisdiction. . . .

Nor do I find National City Bank v. Republic of China, 348 U.S. 356 (1955), to be dispositive. . . .

I nevertheless concur in the judgment of the Court because I believe that the broad holding of *Sabbatino* was not compelled by the principles, as expressed therein, which underlie the act of state doctrine. As Mr. Justice Harlan stated in *Sabbatino,* the act of state doctrine is not dictated either by "international law [or] the Constitution," but is based on a judgment as to "the proper distribution of functions between the judicial and the political branches of the Government on matters bearing upon foreign affairs."

I do not disagree with these principles, only with the broad way in which *Sabbatino* applied them. . . . The balancing of interests, recognized as appropriate by *Sabbatino,* requires a careful examination of the facts in each case and of the position, if any, taken by the political branches of government. . . .

Unless it appears that an exercise of jurisdiction would interfere with delicate foreign relations conducted by the political branches, I conclude that federal courts have an obligation to hear cases such as this. . . .

In this case where no such conflict has been shown, I think the courts have a duty to determine and apply the applicable international law. I therefore join in the Court's decision to remand the case for further proceedings.

Mr. Justice BRENNAN, with whom Mr. Justice STEWART, Mr. Justice MARSHALL, and Mr. Justice BLACKMUN join, dissenting.

The Court today reverses the judgment of the Court of Appeals for the Second Circuit which declined to engraft the so-called *"Bernstein"* exception upon the act of state doctrine as expounded in Banco Nacional de Cuba v. Sabbatino. The Court, nevertheless, affirms the Court of Appeals' rejection of the *"Bernstein"* exception. Four of us in this opinion unequivocally take that step, as do Mr. Justice Douglas and Mr. Justice Powell in their separate opinions concurring in the result or judgment.

The anomalous remand for further proceedings results because three colleagues, Mr. Justice Rehnquist, joined by The Chief Justice and Mr. Justice White, adopt the contrary position, while Mr. Justice Douglas finds National City Bank v. Republic of China, 348 U.S. 356 (1955), dispositive in the circumstances of this case and Mr. Justice Powell rejects the specific holding in *Sabbatino,* believing it was not required by the principles underlying the act of state doctrine.

Mr. Justice Rehnquist's opinion reasons that the act of state doctrine exists primarily, and perhaps even solely, as a judicial aid to the Executive to avoid embarrassment to the political branch in the conduct of foreign relations. Where the Executive expressly indicates that invocation of the rule will not promote domestic foreign policy interests, his opinion states the view, adopting the *"Bernstein"* exception, that the doctrine does not apply. This syllogism — from premise to conclusion — is, with all respect, mechanical and fallacious. Moreover, it would require us to abdicate our judicial responsibility to define the contours of the act of state doctrine so that the judiciary does not become embroiled in the politics of international relations to the damage not only of the courts and the Executive but of the rule of law.

Mr. Justice Rehnquist's opinion also finds support for its result in *National City Bank,* and Mr. Justice Douglas would remand on the authority of that case alone. In his view, "[f]air dealing" requires that a foreign sovereign suing in our courts be subject to setoffs, even though counterclaims are barred by the act of state doctrine for amounts exceeding the state's claim. I believe that *National City Bank* is not at all in point, and that my Brother Douglas' view leads to the strange result that application of the act of state doctrine depends upon the dollar value of a litigant's counterclaim. . . .

My Brother Rehnquist's opinion asserts that the act of state doctrine is designed primarily, and perhaps even entirely, to avoid embarrassment to the political branch. Even a cursory reading of *Sabbatino,* this Court's most recent and most exhaustive treatment of the act of state doctrine, belies this contention. . . .

In short, *Sabbatino* held that the validity of a foreign act of state in certain circumstances is a "political question" not cognizable in our courts. Only one — and not necessarily the most important — of those circumstances concerned the possible impairment of the Executive's conduct of foreign affairs. Even if this factor were absent in this case because of the Legal Adviser's statement of position, it would hardly follow that the act of state doctrine should not foreclose judicial review of the expropriation of petitioner's properties. To the contrary, the absence of consensus on the applicable international rules, the unavailability of standards from a treaty or other agreement, the existence and recognition of the Cuban Government, the sensitivity of the issues to national concerns, and the power of the Executive alone to effect a fair remedy for all United States citizens who have been harmed all point toward the existence of a "political question." The Legal Adviser's letter does not purport to affect these considerations at all. In any event, when coupled with the possible consequences to the conduct of our foreign relations explored above, these considerations compel application of the act of state doctrine, notwithstanding the Legal Adviser's suggestion to the contrary. The Executive Branch, however extensive its powers in the area of foreign affairs, cannot by simple stipulation change a political question into a cognizable claim.

W.S. Kirkpatrick & Co. v. Environmental Tectonics Corp.

U.S. Supreme Court
493 U.S. 400 (1990)

Justice SCALIA delivered the opinion of the [unanimous] Court.

In this case we must decide whether the act of state doctrine bars a court in the United States from entertaining a cause of action that does not rest upon the asserted invalidity of an official act of a foreign sovereign, but that does require imputing to foreign officials an unlawful motivation (the obtaining of bribes) in the performance of such an official act.

I

The facts as alleged in respondent's complaint are as follows: In 1981, Harry Carpenter, who was then Chairman of the Board and Chief Executive Officer of petitioner W.S. Kirkpatrick & Co., Inc. (Kirkpatrick) learned that the Republic of Nigeria was interested in contracting for the construction and equipment of an aeromedical center at Kaduna Air Force Base in Nigeria. He made arrangements with Benson "Tunde" Akindele, a Nigerian citizen, whereby Akindele would endeavor to secure the contract for Kirkpatrick. It was agreed that, in the event the contract was awarded to Kirkpatrick, Kirkpatrick would pay to two Panamanian entities controlled by Akindele a "commission" equal to 20% of the contract price, which would in turn be given as a bribe to officials of the Nigerian Government. In accordance with this plan, the contract was awarded to petitioner W.S. Kirkpatrick & Co., International (Kirkpatrick International), a wholly owned subsidiary of Kirkpatrick; Kirkpatrick paid the promised "commission" to the appointed Panamanian entities; and those funds were disbursed as bribes. All parties agree that Nigerian law prohibits both the payment and the receipt of bribes in connection with the award of a government contract.

Respondent Environmental Tectonics Corporation, International, an unsuccessful bidder for the Kaduna contract, learned of the 20% "commission" and brought the matter to the attention of the Nigerian Air Force and the United States Embassy in Lagos. Following an investigation by the Federal Bureau of Investigation, the United States Attorney for the District of New Jersey brought charges against both Kirkpatrick and Carpenter for violations of the Foreign Corrupt Practices Act of 1977, 91 Stat. 1495, as amended, 15 U.S.C. §78dd-1 et seq., and both pleaded guilty.

Respondent then brought this civil action in the United States District Court for the District of New Jersey against Carpenter, Akindele, petitioners, and others, seeking damages under the Racketeer Influenced and Corrupt Organizations Act, 18 U.S.C. §1961 et seq., the Robinson-Patman Act, 49 Stat. 1526, 15 U.S.C. §13 et seq., and the New Jersey Anti-Racketeering Act, N.J. Stat. Ann. §2C:41-2 et seq. (West 1982). The defendants moved to dismiss the complaint under Rule 12(b)(6) of the Federal Rules of Civil Procedure on the ground that the action was barred by the act of state doctrine.

The District Court, having requested and received a letter expressing the views of the legal advisor to the United States Department of State as to the applicability of the act of state doctrine, treated the motion as one for summary judgment under Rule 56 of the Federal Rules of Civil Procedure, and granted the motion. The District Court concluded that the act of state doctrine applies "if the inquiry presented for judicial determination includes the motivation of a sovereign act which would result in embarrassment to the sovereign or constitute interference in the conduct of foreign policy of the United States." . . . Applying that principle to the facts at hand, the court held that respondent's suit had to be dismissed because in order to prevail respondents would have to show that "the defendants or certain of them intended to wrongfully influence the decision to award the Nigerian Contract by payment of a bribe, that the Government of Nigeria, its officials or other representatives knew of the offered consideration for awarding the Nigerian Contract to Kirkpatrick, that the bribe was actually received or anticipated and that 'but for' the payment or anticipation of the payment of the bribe, ETC would have been awarded the Nigerian Contract."

The Court of Appeals for the Third Circuit reversed. . . . [I]t found application of the doctrine unwarranted on the facts of this case. The Court of Appeals found particularly persuasive the letter to the District Court from the legal advisor to the Department of State, which had stated that in the opinion of the Department judicial inquiry into the purpose behind the act of a foreign sovereign would not produce the "unique embarrassment, and the particular interference with the conduct of foreign affairs, that may result from the judicial determination that a foreign sovereign's acts are invalid." The Court of Appeals acknowledged that "the Department's legal conclusions as to the reach of the act of state doctrine are not controlling on the courts," but concluded that "the Department's factual assessment of whether fulfillment of its responsibilities will be prejudiced by the course of civil litigation is entitled to substantial respect." In light of the Department's view that the interests of the Executive Branch would not be harmed by prosecution of the action, the Court of Appeals held that Kirkpatrick had not met its burden of showing that the case should not go forward; accordingly, it reversed the judgment of the District Court and remanded the case for trial. We granted certiorari.

II

Discusses history

This Court's description of the jurisprudential foundation for the act of state doctrine has undergone some evolution over the years. We once viewed the doctrine as an expression of international law, resting upon "the highest considerations of international comity and expediency," Oetjen v. Central Leather Co., 246 U.S. 297, 303-304 (1918). We have more recently described it, however, as a consequence of domestic separation of powers, reflecting "the strong sense of the Judicial Branch that its engagement in the task of passing on the validity of foreign acts of state may hinder" the conduct of foreign affairs, Banco Nacional de Cuba v. Sabbatino, 376 U.S. 398, 423 (1964). Some Justices have suggested possible exceptions to application of the doctrine, where one or both of the foregoing policies would seemingly not be served: an exception, for example, for acts of state that consist of commercial transactions, since neither modern international comity nor the current position of our Executive Branch accorded sovereign immunity to such acts, see Alfred Dunhill of London, Inc. v. Republic of Cuba, 425 U.S. 682, 695-706 (1976) (opinion of White, J.); or an exception for cases in which the Executive Branch has represented that it has no objection to denying validity to the foreign sovereign act, since then the courts would be impeding no foreign policy goals, see First National City Bank v. Banco Nacional de Cuba, 406 U.S. 759, 768-770 (1972) (opinion of Rehnquist, J.).

The parties have argued at length about the applicability of these possible exceptions, and, more generally, about whether the purpose of the act of state doctrine would be furthered by its application in this case. We find it unnecessary, however, to pursue those inquiries, since the factual predicate for application of the act of state doctrine does not exist. Nothing in the present suit requires the court to declare invalid, and thus ineffective as "a rule of decision for the courts of this country," Ricaud v. American Metal Co., 246 U.S. 304, 310 (1918), the official act of a foreign sovereign.

In every case in which we have held the act of state doctrine applicable, the relief sought or the defense interposed would have required a court in the United States to declare invalid the official act of a foreign sovereign performed within its own territory. In Underhill v. Hernandez, 168 U.S. 250, 254 (1897), holding the defendant's detention of the plaintiff to be tortious would have required denying legal effect to "acts of a military commander representing the authority of the revolutionary party as government, which afterwards succeeded and was recognized by the United States." In Oetjen v. Central Leather Co., supra, and in Ricaud v. American Metal Co., supra, denying title to the party who claimed through purchase from Mexico would have required declaring that government's prior seizure of the property, within its own territory, legally ineffective. In Sabbatino, upholding the defendant's claim to the funds would have required a holding that Cuba's expropriation of goods located in Havana was null and void. In the present case, by contrast, neither the claim nor any asserted defense requires a determination that Nigeria's contract with Kirkpatrick International was, or was not, effective.

Petitioners point out, however, that the facts necessary to establish respondent's claim will also establish that the contract was unlawful. Specifically, they note that in order to prevail respondent must prove that petitioner Kirkpatrick made, and Nigerian officials received, payments that violate Nigerian law, which would, they assert, support a finding that the contract is invalid under Nigerian law. Assuming that to be true, it still does not suffice. The act of state doctrine is not some vague doctrine of abstention but a *"principle of decision* binding on federal and state courts alike." Sabbatino (emphasis added). As we said in Ricaud, "the act within its own boundaries of one sovereign State . . . becomes . . . a rule of decision for the courts of this country." Act of state issues only arise when a court *must decide*—that is, when the outcome of the case turns upon — the effect of official action by a foreign sovereign. When that question is not in the case, neither is the act of state doctrine. That is the situation here. Regardless of what the court's factual findings may suggest as to the legality of the Nigerian contract, its legality is simply not a question to be decided in the present suit, and there is thus no occasion to apply the rule of decision that the act of state doctrine requires. Cf. Sharon v. Time, Inc., 599 F. Supp. 538, 546 (SDNY 1984) ("The issue in this litigation is not whether [the alleged] acts are valid, but whether they occurred"). . . .

Petitioners insist, however, that the policies underlying our act of state cases — international comity, respect for the sovereignty of foreign nations on their own territory, and the avoidance of embarrassment to the Executive Branch in its conduct of foreign relations — are implicated in the present case because, as the District Court found, a determination that Nigerian officials demanded and accepted a bribe "would impugn or question the nobility of a foreign nation's motivations," and would "result in embarrassment to the sovereign or constitute interference in the conduct of foreign policy of the United States." The United States, as amicus curiae, favors the same approach to the act of state doctrine, though disagreeing with petitioners as to the outcome it produces in the present case. We should not, the United

States urges, "attach dispositive significance to the fact that this suit involves only the 'motivation' for, rather than the 'validity' of, a foreign sovereign act," Brief for United States as Amicus Curiae 37, and should eschew "any rigid formula for the resolution of act of state cases generally." In some future case, perhaps, "litigation . . . based on alleged corruption in the award of contracts or other commercially oriented activities of foreign governments could sufficiently touch on 'national nerves' that the act of state doctrine or related principles of abstention would appropriately be found to bar the suit," id., at 40 (quoting *Sabbatino*) and we should therefore resolve this case on the narrowest possible ground, viz., that the letter from the legal advisor to the District Court gives sufficient indication that, "in the setting of this case," the act of state doctrine poses no bar to adjudication, ibid.*

These urgings are deceptively similar to what we said in *Sabbatino*, where we observed that sometimes, even though the validity of the act of a foreign sovereign within its own territory is called into question, the policies underlying the act of state doctrine may not justify its application. We suggested that a sort of balancing approach could be applied — the balance shifting against application of the doctrine, for example, if the government that committed the "challenged act of state" is no longer in existence. But what is appropriate in order to avoid unquestioning judicial acceptance of the acts of foreign sovereigns is not similarly appropriate for the quite opposite purpose of expanding judicial incapacities where such acts are not directly (or even indirectly) involved. It is one thing to suggest, as we have, that the policies underlying the act of state doctrine should be considered in deciding whether, despite the doctrine's technical availability, it should nonetheless not be invoked; it is something quite different to suggest that those underlying policies are a doctrine unto themselves, justifying expansion of the act of state doctrine (or, as the United States puts it, unspecified "related principles of abstention") into new and uncharted fields.

The short of the matter is this: Courts in the United States have the power, and ordinarily the obligation, to decide cases and controversies properly presented to them. The act of state doctrine does not establish an exception for cases and controversies that may embarrass foreign governments, but merely requires that, in the process of deciding, the acts of foreign sovereigns taken within their own jurisdictions shall be deemed valid. That doctrine has no application to the present case because the validity of no foreign sovereign act is at issue.

The judgment of the Court of Appeals for the Third Circuit is affirmed.

It is so ordered.

Notes and Questions

1. What was the basis for the Supreme Court's decision in *City Bank*? The *Bernstein* exception? A counterclaim exception? To the extent that there were different rationales by the majority, how many Justices supported each rationale?

---

*Even if we agreed with the Government's fundamental approach, we would question its characterization of the legal advisor's letter as reflecting the absence of any policy objection to the adjudication. The letter, which is reprinted as an appendix to the opinion of the Court of Appeals (CA3 1988), did not purport to say whether the State Department would like the suit to proceed, but rather responded (correctly, as we hold today) to the question whether the act of state doctrine was applicable.

2. Is a *Bernstein* exception supported or undermined by the reasoning of the Court in *Sabbatino*? Would such an exception promote or undermine the proper separation of powers between the federal branches? Notwithstanding the rejection of the *Bernstein* exception by most members of the Court in *City Bank*, lower courts have continued to give some weight (but not conclusive weight) to the views of the Executive Branch in deciding whether to apply the act of state doctrine. See, e.g., Environmental Tectonics v. W.S. Kirkpatrick, Inc., 847 F.2d 1052, 1062 (3d Cir. 1988), aff'd on other grounds, 493 U.S. 400 (1990); Kalamazoo Spice Extraction Co. v. Provisional Military Government of Socialist Ethiopia, 729 F.2d 422, 427-428 (6th Cir. 1984). Is such deference warranted? For a discussion of this issue, see Curtis A. Bradley, Chevron Deference and Foreign Affairs, 86 Va. L. Rev. 649, 716-721 (2000).

3. How persuasive is the Court's conclusion in *Kirkpatrick* that the act of state doctrine had no application there because the "validity of no foreign sovereign act is at issue"? What about Kirkpatrick's argument that Environmental Tectonics could prevail only if it proved that Nigerian officials had received payments that violated Nigerian law?

4. What limitation, precisely, does the *Kirkpatrick* decision place on the act of state doctrine? After *Kirkpatrick*, is it ever appropriate for courts to engage in case-by-case balancing in deciding whether to apply the act of state doctrine? If so, when? Note that, since *Kirkpatrick*, a number of courts have concluded that, even when the requirements for the act of state doctrine are technically satisfied, the doctrine need not be applied if the foreign relations and other concerns underlying the doctrine are not implicated. See, e.g., Bigio v. Coca-Cola Co., 239 F.3d 440 (2d Cir. 2000); Grupo Protexa, S.A. v. All American Marine Slip, 20 F.3d 1224 (3d Cir. 1994). Is this approach consistent with *Kirkpatrick*? Should courts be making these foreign relations judgments?

5. What did the Court in *Kirkpatrick* mean by the statement that the "act of state doctrine is not some vague doctrine of abstention but a '*principle of decision*'" (citing *Sabbatino*)? Was the Court saying that the doctrine is not a variant on the political question doctrine, but is rather a conflict-of-laws principle? If so, what is the significance of this statement?

6. In *Kirkpatrick*, the Justice and State Departments filed an *amicus curiae* brief with the Supreme Court arguing that the act of state doctrine should not be applied in that case. The analysis suggested in the brief, however, was substantially different from that adopted by the Supreme Court. The brief argued that, in deciding whether to apply the act of state doctrine, courts should consider a variety of "comity" factors, avoid any absolute distinction between validity and motivation, and give substantial deference to the Executive Branch's views regarding "whether foreign policy concerns, together with considerations made relevant by other components of the act of state doctrine, require that the court give effect to the act of a foreign state." Why did the Court reject that approach?

7. The Supreme Court has indicated that only official, public acts qualify as "acts of state" for purposes of the act of state doctrine. Thus, in Alfred Dunhill of London, Inc. v. Republic of Cuba, 425 U.S. 682 (1976), the Court refused to give effect to a repudiation of a quasi-contract obligation, noting that "[n]o statute, decree, order, or resolution of the Cuban Government itself was offered in evidence indicating that Cuba had repudiated its obligations in general or any class thereof or that it had as a sovereign matter determined to confiscate the amounts due." Id.

at 695. (Note, however, that there were apparently no formal, official acts in some earlier act of state cases, such as *Underhill.*) How formal must the government act be to qualify as an act of state? If government officials engage in *illegal* activities, can those activities constitute acts of state? What if the activities violate treaties? Rules of customary international law? *Jus cogens* norms? Compare The Republic of the Philippines v. Marcos, 818 F.2d 1473, 1483 (9th Cir. 1987) ("Since the act of state doctrine prohibits inquiry into the legality of official governmental acts, such acts surely cannot be official only if they are legal."), opinion withdrawn, 832 F.2d 1110 (9th Cir. 1987), with Sharon v. Time, Inc., 599 F. Supp. 538, 544 (S.D.N.Y. 1984) ("The actions of an official acting outside the scope of his authority as an agent of the state are simply not acts of state. In no sense are such acts designed to give effect to a State's public interests."). See generally Lynn E. Parseghian, Note, Defining the "Public Act" Requirement in the Act of State Doctrine, 58 U. Chi. L. Rev. 1151 (1991).

8. Another limitation on the act of state doctrine is that it covers only acts by a foreign government taken within its own territory. What is the basis for this limitation? Does this territorial restriction still make sense in today's era of globalization? Note that this limitation can pose some difficult "situs" questions, especially in cases involving intangible property, such as intellectual property and debt obligations. For debt cases, courts often find that the situs is the agreed-upon place of payment. See, e.g., Braka v. Bancomer, S.N.C., 762 F.2d 222 (2d Cir. 1985); Allied Bank Intl. v. Banco Credito Agricola de Cartago, 757 F.2d 516 (2d Cir. 1985); Garcia v. Chase Manhattan Bank, N.A., 735 F.2d 645 (2d Cir. 1984). See generally Margaret E. Tahyar, Note, The Act of State Doctrine: Resolving Debt Situs Confusion, 86 Colum. L. Rev. 594 (1986).

9. In the *Dunhill* case, cited above in Note 7, four Justices argued for a commercial activity exception to the act of state doctrine, whereby courts could adjudicate the validity of "purely commercial" acts by foreign governments. To date, courts have not adopted such an exception, although they sometimes consider the commercial character of a foreign government act in deciding whether the policies of the doctrine are implicated in a particular case. See, e.g., Honduras Aircraft Registry Ltd. v. Government of Honduras, 129 F.3d 543, 550 (11th Cir. 1997) ("[T]here is no commercial exception to the act of state doctrine as there is under the [Foreign Sovereign Immunities Act]. The factors to be considered, as recited in *Kirkpatrick,* may sometimes overlap with the FSIA commercial exception, but a commercial exception alone is not enough."). As discussed earlier in this chapter, there is a broad commercial activity exception to the sovereign immunity of foreign government defendants. See 28 U.S.C. §1605(a)(2). Should a similar exception apply in the act of state context? For discussion of this issue, see Michael D. Ramsey, Acts of State and Foreign Sovereign Obligations, 39 Harv. Intl. L.J. 1 (1998).

10. There is also an exception to foreign government immunity for counterclaims. As discussed earlier in this chapter, the Supreme Court adopted such an exception when sovereign immunity (like the act of state doctrine) was treated as a common law doctrine, see National City Bank of New York v. Republic of China, 348 U.S. 356, 363 (1955), and Congress codified this exception in 1976 when it enacted the Foreign Sovereign Immunities Act. See 28 U.S.C. §1607. The Court in *Sabbatino,* however, in a portion of the opinion not excerpted above, rejected a counterclaim exception. The Court reasoned that (a) foreign governments could attempt to get around this exception by assigning their claims; (b) if the exception applied to

assignees it could undermine the security of titles; (c) the exception would encourage claimants to engage in self-help remedies in an effort to cause the foreign government to become the plaintiff; and (d) the act of state doctrine rests on different policies than foreign sovereign immunity. See 376 U.S. at 437-439. Are these points persuasive? In the *City Bank* case, the State Department supported a counterclaim exception to the doctrine. Four Justices in *City Bank* indicated at least some support for such an exception. Justice Douglas clearly endorsed the exception, and three other Justices (in the opinion authored by then-Justice Rehnquist) noted that their position was "consonant" with the principles of equity expressed in the *Republic of China* decision regarding a counterclaim exception to foreign sovereign immunity.

11. In *Sabbatino,* the Court stated that the act of state doctrine should be applied "in the absence of a treaty or other unambiguous agreement regarding controlling legal principles." The Court also stated that "the greater the degree of codification or consensus concerning a particular area of international law, the more appropriate it is for the judiciary to render decisions regarding it." Consistent with these statements, courts generally have not applied the act of state doctrine to bar treaty claims. See, e.g., Kalamazoo Spice Extraction Co. v. Provisional Military Government of Socialist Ethiopia, 729 F.2d 422 (6th Cir. 1984); American Intl. Group, Inc. v. Islamic Republic of Iran, 493 F. Supp. 522 (D.D.C. 1980), vacated on other grounds, 657 F.2d 430 (D.C. Cir. 1981); see also Ramirez de Arellano v. Weinberger, 745 F.2d 1500, 1540 (D.C. Cir. 1984) ("[T]he doctrine was never intended to apply when an applicable bilateral treaty governs the legal merits of the controversy."), vacated and remanded, 471 U.S. 1113 (1985). But cf. Callejo v. Bancomer, S.A., 764 F.2d 1101 (5th Cir. 1985) (suggesting that act of state doctrine might bar some treaty claims). Should some *customary international law* claims be exempt from the act of state doctrine? What if there is a high degree of international consensus regarding the customary international law rule? What if the rule is considered a *jus cogens* norm?

12. We discussed international human rights litigation in U.S. courts in Chapter 3. This litigation typically involves suits by foreign victims of human rights abuses against foreign officials. The act of state doctrine is a potential barrier to this litigation because it challenges the validity of foreign governmental conduct. A number of these suits have survived dismissal under the act of state doctrine, however, because courts have either (a) applied a case-by-case approach to the doctrine and concluded that adjudication of these cases would not undermine U.S. foreign relations, (b) found that the human rights abuses were not officially authorized by the foreign government and thus did not qualify as acts of state, or (c) concluded that the customary international law prohibiting such abuses was sufficiently clear to satisfy *Sabbatino.* See, e.g., Hilao v. Estate of Ferdinand Marcos, 25 F.3d 1467, 1471 (9th Cir. 1994); Liu v. Republic of China, 892 F.2d 1419, 1431-1434 (9th Cir. 1989); Doe v. Unocal Corp., 963 F. Supp. 880 (C.D. Cal. 1997), later dismissed, 27 F. Supp. 2d 1174 (C.D. Cal. 1998); Forti v. Suarez-Mason, 672 F. Supp. 1531, 1546 (N.D. Cal. 1987). To date, however, courts have not adopted a categorical exception to the act of state doctrine for human rights abuses. Would such an exception be consistent with *Sabbatino?* Would it be good policy? For arguments in favor of such an exception, see Jeffrey M. Blum & Ralph G. Steinhardt, Federal Jurisdiction over International Human Rights Claims: The Alien Tort Claims Act after Filartiga v. Pena-Irala, 22 Harv. Intl. L.J. 53, 108-109 (1981); Daniel C.K. Chow, Rethinking the Act of State Doctrine: An Analysis in Terms of Jurisdiction to Prescribe, 62 Wash. L. Rev. 397,

445-446 (1987). See also Restatement (Third) of the Foreign Relations Law of the United States section 443 cmt. *c* (1987) ("A claim arising out of an alleged violation of fundamental human rights — for instance, a claim on behalf of a victim of torture or genocide —would (if otherwise sustainable) probably not be defeated by the act of state doctrine, since the accepted international law of human rights is well established and contemplates external scrutiny of such acts.").

13. From the plaintiff's standpoint, what is the difference between a court's dismissal of a case based on foreign sovereign immunity and a court's dismissal of a case based on its application of the act of state doctrine? Consider res judicata and collateral estoppel. For an example of a case in which the court found that it had jurisdiction under the commercial activity exception to the Foreign Sovereign Immunities Act, but then dismissed the case based on its application of the act of state doctrine, see Callejo v. Bancomer, 764 F.2d 1101 (5th Cir. 1985).

4.   *The Act of State Doctrine in Other States*

Oppenheim's International Law
365-376

(Robert Jennings & Arthur Watts eds., 9th ed. 1992)

§112 State equality and recognition of foreign official acts: 'act of state'. . . .

This restraint upon the questioning of foreign state acts, known especially in the United States of America as the act of state doctrine, may be known differently in other states. In particular, English law uses that term in a somewhat different sense; nevertheless, substantively the same general rule of judicial restraint is applied by English courts although perhaps more restrictively than in the United States.

It is not clear how far this doctrine may properly be regarded as a rule of public international law or whether it belongs essentially to the province of private international law. Considerations of public policy have often prevented a full recognition of the validity of foreign legislation. There is probably no international judicial authority in support of the proposition that recognition of foreign official acts is affirmatively prescribed by international law. . . .

The Italian Court of Cassation has, however, held the non-justiciability of acts of foreign states to be a principle of international law, forming part of the Italian legal system.

§113 Foreign legislation contrary to international law

Whatever may be the rule of international law as to the duty of states (and their courts) to recognize the effects of foreign legislation within the foreign country concerned, it would appear that there is no such obligation with respect to foreign legislation, whatever the place of its purported effect, which is in itself contrary to international law.

The matter most frequently arises in connection with the seizure of property without compensation, and courts have varied in their approach and their conclusions. Sometimes the foreign expropriation law is denied effect on grounds which may have little, if anything, to do directly with its violation of international law. Thus irrespective of its compatibility with international law, it may be held that the law does not have extra-territorial effect, or that to give effect to it would be contrary to the public policy of the forum. Similarly, where effect is given to the law, the court may not have expressly considered its possible incompatibility with international law, or may have inquired into the matter and concluded that the law, or at least its application in the case before the court, did not involve any violation of international law. However, in *Banco Nacional de Cuba v. Sabbatino* the United States Supreme Court denied the permissibility even of making such an inquiry, thus precluding any possible finding that a foreign law in violation of international law should be denied effect. . . .

Other courts have not held themselves inhibited from inquiring into the extent to which a foreign expropriation law is contrary to international law, and their conclusions justify the assertion that foreign legislation which is contrary to international law may properly be treated as a nullity and, with regard to rights of property, as incapable of transferring title to the state concerned either within its territory or outside it. Where courts have expressly reached the conclusion that the law (or the action taken under it) was contrary to international law, they have in most cases declined to give effect to it. However, some courts, while not expressly deciding that the foreign legislation in question violated international law (and thus not actually giving effect to it despite such a violation) have suggested that even if it were contrary to international law effect should nevertheless be given to it; or, having found the law contrary to international law, have said that on that ground alone it should not be denied effect, although going on to deny it effect on some other ground. In such cases the court has tended to regard questions of the violation of international law, and suitable redress therefore, as an inter-governmental rather than a judicial matter, particularly since the international remedy for a taking of property pursuant to legislation in breach of international law is not necessarily invalidity of that law or non-recognition of a private law title to property, but more often the payment of damages to the injured state.

Courts may be under a constitutional compulsion to give effect to the law of their own sovereign legislature even if violative of international law — although they will not lightly impute to it the intention to violate international law and although in some countries courts have in fact the power to refuse to give effect to national legislation contrary to international law — but there is no compelling reason why they should assist in giving effect to violations of international law by a foreign legislature. In the absence of compulsory jurisdiction of international tribunals and having regard to the prohibition, under the Charter of the United Nations and elsewhere, of compulsive means of enforcement of international law by national action, municipal courts may on occasions provide the only means for securing respect for international law in this and other spheres. Principle does not countenance a rule which, by reference to international law, obliges courts to endow with legal effect legislative and other acts of foreign states which are in violation of international law; and in practice no such international obligation is regarded as existing. However, in view of the practice of states as revealed by the actions of their courts, some of which have been prepared to acknowledge legal effects of foreign acts in violation of international law, it probably cannot be said that international law forbids courts to give effect to such a foreign act when to do so is in accordance with their own national laws. It is in any case consistent with principle that such violations of international law on the part of foreign states ought not to be assumed in the absence of evidence of a cogent character. Any complaint, on account of a judgment based on any such allegation, of the foreign state concerned is a suitable subject, at the request of that state, for international judicial determination.

Notes and Questions

1. Do the practices of other states suggest U.S. courts should continue at least some applications of the act of state doctrine?

2. What are the strongest arguments for the doctrine? The strongest arguments against?

3. Related to the act of state doctrine in the United States is the doctrine of foreign sovereign compulsion. It protects from liability under U.S. law certain actions by individuals or entities that are compelled by foreign governments. See Restatement sections 441-442; Don Wallace Jr. & Joseph P. Griffin, The Restatement and Foreign Sovereign Compulsion: A Plea for Due Process, 23 Intl. Law. 593 (1989).

Problem. Assume you are a clerk for a U.S. Supreme Court Justice. He is a thoughtful moderate. He calls you into his office and presents you with the following project:

The Court has before it a case involving the act of state doctrine. In the past the Court has heard arguments on whether to reconsider *Sabbatino* and eliminate the act of state doctrine but decided against the step. This Justice wants you to prepare a memorandum that addresses whether the Court might use this case or others on which certiorari could be granted to eliminate or make substantial modifications in the act of state doctrine. For now, the Justice is not concerned with the particulars of the specific case that is pending; rather, he wants to develop a constructive analysis of what should be done with the doctrine.

He asks that your memorandum address in detail whether or not the doctrine should be eliminated or substantially modified. Although he expects you to identify and address a range of issues, he says that you should (among other matters) include the following issues: What kind of cases would be affected by a change in the law? What types of parties would be benefited or hurt? What would be the likely impact on U.S. foreign policy and on the effective diplomacy of the U.S. Executive Branch?

The Justice asks that you give him *your* recommendation on whether the doctrine should be eliminated or not. If not, then do you have recommendations on how the doctrine should be modified? If you do propose elimination or changes, what would be the legal theory (or theories) that could be used to justify these changes?

7

Allocation of Legal Authority Among States

To advise a client on the legal implications of a course of action involving more than one country, a lawyer must obviously focus on the government or governments that may authorize, regulate, or prohibit the conduct. Even in those parts of the world where no government asserts sovereignty, such as Antarctica and outer space, there are international agreements concluded by governments that define the applicable legal regime. Moreover, while individuals and corporations as well as governments may "create" law through contract, and while international organizations may exercise law-making authority, those acts are supported by the authority of governments. A contract is valid and enforceable because some national legal system says so. Arbitral awards, even those applying international law or general principles of law, have force in part because they are enforceable under national legal systems. International organizations take their power from international agreements entered into by governments. In short, we still work in a world dominated by the power of the territorial state. States control borders, regulate conduct, and claim power over access to resources.

Consequently, an international lawyer is centrally concerned with the allocation of power and authority among states in the world. Much of this casebook can be viewed as an examination of the bases for exercise of authority by governments and the limitations expressed in legal norms on the exercise of that authority. Law performs both functions. It legitimates claims of authority, such as the right of a government to regulate all conduct within its territory, as well as the conduct of its nationals anywhere in the world. It also limits that authority. Thus, for example, a state may claim the authority to tax its nationals on their worldwide income, but the state may have limited itself from taxing their foreign income by norms established in a treaty or a statute.

The legal universe is frequently divided into public and private spheres. Public law concerns the relationship of government and its subjects, such as criminal law, tax law, and other economic regulation such as the antitrust and securities laws. By contrast, private law, such as contract, tort, and property law, concerns the relationships of persons, natural and juridical, among themselves. There are also rules that define which state's law applies to transactions having a relationship to more than one state. Thus public international law is concerned with whether a state has authority to apply its drug laws, tax laws, or antitrust laws to conduct by persons in another state (e.g., a U.S. criminal prosecution of French and German companies that agree in the Bahamas to fix prices of goods to be exported to the United States). Private international law (or conflict of laws), on the other hand, is concerned with whether a state may apply its tort, contract, or property rules to events or transactions that have significant connections with it and another state (e.g., a California court deciding which jurisdiction's law applies to determine the validity of a contract between Mitsubishi of Japan and Chrysler to sell cars manufactured in Korea for delivery in Hong Kong).

In Sections A and B of this chapter we examine public international law—first, the permissible bases on which a state may justify application of its law and the limitations imposed by international law on that application, and, second, the much stricter rules dealing with the authority of a state to enforce its law. In Section C we outline the principal approaches of private international law (or conflict of laws) in choosing applicable private law. The types of analysis sometimes used in resolving conflicts of private law are similar to those used in the public international law materials dealing with limitations on a state's ability to apply its law.

In its sphere, public international law traditionally distinguishes between two different types of authority (or "jurisdiction," as it is usually called)—a state's *right to prescribe* or apply law to certain persons or activities, and a state's *right to enforce* that law by applying sanctions to a violator. The 1987 Restatement of Foreign Relations Law adds a third category, the *right to adjudicate* the legality of conduct. An example will help illustrate the difference: A terrorist kills three pedestrians when he explodes by remote control a bomb he has placed in a parked car just outside a shopping mall in Chicago. He flees to Syria, where the Syrian authorities claim that they cannot find him. The United States has prescriptive jurisdiction regarding the terrorist's conduct in its territory. Hence, under accepted principles of international law, the United States has jurisdiction to outlaw the killings in its territory. However, under the Restatement approach, it does not have adjudicatory jurisdiction to try him, or enforcement jurisdiction to compel compliance with the law or to punish him, because he is not present in U.S. territory and is beyond the reach of U.S. officials. Further, the Restatement argues that all three bases of jurisdiction are limited by an international law principle of reasonableness, in addition to whatever limitations may be found in constitutional or statutory law.

For background, consider the following excerpt:

Restatement

Part IV—Introductory Note

Statements of the international law of jurisdiction traditionally have tended to distinguish between jurisdiction to prescribe — the authority of a state to make its substantive laws applicable to particular persons and circumstances — and jurisdiction to enforce law against particular persons or in particular circumstances. Since jurisdiction to prescribe was seen principally as a function of national legislation, it was sometimes referred to as legislative jurisdiction. Since enforcement was often thought of as exercised essentially by judicial process, jurisdiction to enforce was often equated with jurisdiction to adjudicate.

Increasingly, however, it has become clear that the identification of prescription with legislation, and of enforcement with adjudication, is too simple. In principle, substantive regulation derives its authority from legislation, in developed legal systems, such as that of the United States, but much regulation is effected through administrative rules and regulations, through executive acts and orders, and sometimes by court decree. Enforcement is often carried out through executive or administrative rather than judicial action; enforcement is thus not merely an aspect of adjudication, and the rules of jurisdiction applicable to nonjudicial enforcement are different in several respects from those that govern judicial enforcement. At the same time, adjudication is often used for purposes that are not strictly "enforcement," but rather for declaration of rights and vindication of private interests. The process of adjudication, whatever the purposes for which it is used, is a significant category in the foreign relations law of the United States.

Accordingly, this Restatement deals with jurisdiction under the following headings: (a) *jurisdiction to prescribe,* i.e., the authority of a state to make its law applicable to persons or activities; (b) *jurisdiction to adjudicate,* i.e., the authority of a state to subject particular persons or things to its judicial process; and (c) *jurisdiction to enforce,* i.e., the authority of a state to use the resources of government to induce or compel compliance with its law. See §401.

These categories of jurisdiction are often interdependent, and their scope and limitations are shaped by similar considerations. Jurisdiction to prescribe may be more acceptable where jurisdiction to adjudicate or to enforce is plainly available; jurisdiction to adjudicate may be more acceptable where the state of the forum also has jurisdiction to prescribe by virtue of its links to the persons, interests, relations, or activities involved. However, the purposes and consequences of the different categories of jurisdiction are not necessarily congruent, and balancing the competing interests in the different contexts can lead to different results.

A. JURISDICTION TO PRESCRIBE PUBLIC LAW

Typically, five bases of prescriptive jurisdiction are recognized:

(1) territory (including conduct having effects in territory)
(2) nationality
(3) protective
(4) passive personality
(5) universal

Professor Starke's treatise summarizes the five:

I.A. Shearer, Starke's International Law
183-212 (11th ed. 1994)

The practice as to the exercise by states of jurisdiction over persons, property, or acts or events varies for each state, and these variations are due to historical and geographical factors which are nonetheless coming to play a less important role in measure as, by reason of technological developments, countries have become geographically more knit together. Historically, states, such as Great Britain, in which sea frontiers predominated, paid primary allegiance to the *territorial* principle of juris-diction, according to which each state might exercise jurisdiction over property and persons in, or acts or events occurring within its territory; this was because the free or unrestricted movement of individuals or of property to or from other countries did not in the past occur so readily or frequently as between states bounded for the most part by land frontiers. On the other hand, most European states took a much broader view of the extent of their jurisdiction precisely because the continent is a network of land or river frontiers, and acts or transactions of an international character were more frequent owing to the facility and rapidity of movement across such frontiers.

However, with the increasing speed of communications, the more sophisticated structure of commercial organisations or enterprises with transnational ramifi-cations, and the growing international character of criminal activities (e.g. in the fields of narcotic drugs and currency transactions) there has been a noticeable trend towards the exercise of jurisdiction on the basis of criteria other than that of territorial location.

. . . [In] the much discussed *Lotus* Case (1927), . . . the Permanent Court of In-ternational Justice [decided] there is no restriction on the exercise of jurisdiction by any state unless that restriction can be shown by the most conclusive evidence to exist as a principle of international law. In that case the Permanent Court did not ac-cept the French thesis — France being one of the parties — that a claim to jurisdic-tion by a state must be shown to be justified by international law and practice. In the Court's opinion, the onus lay on the state claiming that such exercise of jurisdiction was unjustified, to show that it was prohibited by international law.

There is one practical limitation on the exercise of wide jurisdiction by a par-ticular state. . . . "[N]o State attempts to exercise a jurisdiction over matters, persons or things with which it has absolutely no concern." . . . [G]enerally, it will be found that the territorial basis of jurisdiction is the normal working rule.

2. Territorial Jurisdiction

The exercise of jurisdiction by a state over property, persons, acts or events occur-ring within its territory is clearly conceded by international law to all members of the society of states. The principle has been well put by Lord Macmillan:

> It is an essential attribute of the sovereignty of this realm, as of all sovereign indepen-dent States, that it should possess jurisdiction over all persons and things within its ter-ritorial limits and in all causes civil and criminal arising within these limits. . . .

For the purposes of the exercise of territorial jurisdiction, it has been customary to assimilate to state territory: (a) the maritime coastal belt or territorial sea; (b) a ship bearing the flag of the state wishing to exercise jurisdiction; and (c) ports. . . .

Technical Extensions of the Territorial Jurisdiction

Apart from the assimilation to territory of the territorial sea, of ships at sea, and of ports, certain technical extensions of the principle of territorial jurisdiction became necessary in order to justify action taken by states in cases where one or more constituent elements of an act or offence took place outside their territory. These extensions were occasioned by the increasing facilities for speedy international communication and transport, leading to the commission of crimes in one state which were engineered or prepared in another state. Some states in whose territory such ancillary acts took place, declined to prosecute or punish the offenders responsible on the ground that, as the acts were accessory to a principal offence committed elsewhere, the territorial jurisdiction did not apply. But several states met the new conditions by technically extending the territorial jurisdiction:

a. Applying the *subjective territorial principle,* these states arrogated to themselves a jurisdiction to prosecute and punish crimes commenced within their territory, but completed or consummated in the territory of another state. Although this principle was not so generally adopted by states as to amount to a general rule of the law of nations, particular applications of it did become a part of international law as a result of the provisions of two international conventions, the Geneva Convention for the Suppression of Counterfeiting Currency (1929), and the Geneva Convention for the Suppression of the Illicit Drug Traffic (1936). Under these conventions, the states parties bound themselves to punish, if taking place within their territory, conspiracies to commit and intentional participation in the commission of counterfeiting and drug traffic offences wherever the final act of commission took place, as also attempts to commit and acts preparatory to the commission of such offences, and in addition agreed to treat certain specific acts as distinct offences and not to consider them as accessory to principal offences committed elsewhere. . . .

b. Pursuant to the *objective territorial principle,* certain States applied their territorial jurisdiction to offences or acts commenced in another state, but:— (i) consummated or completed within their territory, or (ii) producing gravely harmful consequences to the social or economic order inside their territory. The objective territorial theory was defined by Professor Hyde as follows:

> The setting in motion outside of a State of a force which produces as a direct consequence an injurious effect therein justifies the territorial sovereign in prosecuting the actor when he enters its domain.

Illustrations of the theory were given in an official League of Nations report concerned with the criminal jurisdiction of states over offences committed outside their territory; these were:

a. a man firing a gun across a frontier and killing another man in a neighbouring state;
b. a man obtaining money by false pretences by means of a letter posted in Great Britain to a recipient in Germany.

The objective territorial principle was applied in the provisions of the two international conventions just referred to, and has also been recognised in decisions of English, German, and American courts. But the most outstanding example of its application has been the decision of the Permanent Court of International Justice in 1927 in the *Lotus* Case. The facts in that case were shortly, that a French mail steamer, the *Lotus,* collided on the high seas with a Turkish collier, due allegedly to the gross negligence of the officer of the watch on board the *Lotus,* with the result that the collier sank and eight Turkish nationals on board perished. The Turkish authorities instituted proceedings against the officer of the watch, basing the claim to jurisdiction on the ground that the act of negligence on board the *Lotus* had produced effects on the Turkish collier, and thus according to the rule mentioned above, on a portion of Turkish territory. By a majority decision, the Permanent Court held that the action of the Turkish authorities was not inconsistent with international law.

The objective territorial principle plays a recognised role in respect to the exercise of jurisdiction as to multinational corporations. . . . The difficulties in applying to these enterprises traditional notions of jurisdiction have been well expressed as follows:

> The multi-national corporation, by definition, is established and has activities in more than one State. If a strict territorial approach is adopted, each State may regulate only those activities within its borders. Such an approach could have serious effects. It might make it impossible for the corporation to do business by subjecting it to contradictory or confusing legal regimes, or on the other hand, it might allow the corporation to escape liability for conduct whose components are legal in each of the States in which they take place but which, taken as a whole, is illegal under the laws of some or all of the States concerned.

One approach for which there is authority is that the country in the territory of which the effects or results are felt of action taken by the head office (in another country) of the multinational corporation is entitled to exercise jurisdiction, e.g. against the servants or assets of branches or subsidiaries locally situated. It is true that the head office's action may have concurrent effects in a large number of countries, the jurisdiction of all of which could then be attracted without being debarred by international law, so that ultimately it will be necessary to work out some appropriate code or the exercise of jurisdiction under international law over multinational corporations in order to avoid jurisdictional conflicts.

Apart from the application of the objective territorial principle, another possibility has been to treat the subsidiary as notionally an alter ego of the foreign parent corporation, so that jurisdiction may be exercised over the parent corporation by the state where the subsidiary is located, this being deemed the same as the exercise of jurisdiction over the subsidiary. This, of course, is an extension of the nationality principle of jurisdiction considered below in this chapter, involving the attribution of what may be described as a "notional" nationality to the subsidiary, thus allowing the exercise of extra-territorial jurisdiction over it; as applied by the Court of Justice of the European Communities, the approach is based on the doctrine of a "single enterprise" theory of the nationality of related trans-national corporations, therefore discarding for this purpose the concept of separate identity of each member corporation of an integrated group of these.

Reference should be made to what apparently purports to be an extension by way of degree of the objective territorial principle, namely, the "effects" doctrine adopted by American federal courts under which, especially in anti-trust proceedings, jurisdiction is exercised extra-territorially on the basis of the effects or consequences, however remote, within the United States and which are deemed to be of so reprehensible a nature (provided that they are *direct*), economic or otherwise, as to attract or necessitate such jurisdiction. Having regard to the possible serious results for their trading interests which the awards of American federal courts may involve (triple damages may be awarded), this "effects" jurisdiction has been objected to by the United Kingdom, Australia and other countries, and has led to the passage of local legislation to preclude the enforcement in the objecting countries of any element, evidentiary, procedural or otherwise of the American proceedings or judgments. It is claimed that the "effects" jurisdiction, as asserted by American courts, is contrary to international law, and that the local protective legislation [sometimes called blocking statutes] is validly opposable to such American extra-territorial process.

Territorial Jurisdiction over Aliens

Territorial jurisdiction is conceded by international law as much over aliens as over citizens of the territorial state. As Judge J. B. Moore pointed out in the *Lotus* Case, no presumption of immunity arises from the fact that the person against whom proceedings are taken is an alien: an alien can claim no exemption from the exercise of such jurisdiction except so far as he may be able to show either: (i) that he is, by reason of some special immunity, not subject to the operation of the local law, or (ii) that the local law is not in conformity with international law. . . .

3. [NATIONALITY] JURISDICTION . . .

According to present international practice, [nationality] jurisdiction may be exercised on the basis of one or other of the following principles:

(A) Active nationality principle. Under this principle, jurisdiction is assumed by the state of which the person, against whom proceedings are taken, is a national. The active nationality principle is generally conceded by international law to all states desiring to apply it. There is indeed a correlative principle of the law of extradition that no state is bound to extradite from its territory a national guilty of an offence committed abroad.

(B) Passive [personality or] nationality principle. Jurisdiction is assumed by the state of which the person suffering injury or a civil damage is a national. International law recognises the passive [personality or] nationality principle only subject to certain qualifications. Thus it would appear from the *Cutting* Case that a state which does not admit the passive nationality principle is not bound to acquiesce in proceedings on this basis brought against one of its nationals by another state. The justification, if any, for exercising jurisdiction on this principle is that each state has a perfect right to protect its citizens abroad, and if the territorial state of the locus delicti neglects or is unable to punish the persons causing the injury, the state of which the victim is a national is entitled to do so if the persons responsible come within its power. But as against this, it may be urged that the general interests of a state are scarcely attacked "merely because one of its nationals has been the victim of an offence in a foreign country." The passive nationality principle is embodied in several national criminal codes. . . .

4.　Jurisdiction According to the Protective Principle

International law recognizes that each state may exercise jurisdiction over crimes against its security and integrity or its vital economic interests. Most criminal codes contain rules embodying in the national idiom the substance of this principle, which is generally known as the *protective* principle. . . .

The rational grounds for the exercise of this jurisdiction are two-fold:

i.　the offences subject to the application of the protective principle are such that their consequences may be of the utmost gravity and concern to the state against which they are directed;

ii.　unless the jurisdiction were exercised, many such offences would escape punishment altogether because they did not contravene the law of the place where they were committed (lex loci delicti) or because extradition would be refused by reason of the political character of the offence.

The serious objection to the protective principle is that each state presumes to be its own judge as to what endangers its security or its financial credit. Thus in many cases, the application of the protective principle tends to be quite arbitrary.

5.　Jurisdiction According to the Universal Principle: Piracy

An offence subject to universal jurisdiction is one which comes under the jurisdiction of all states wherever it be committed. Inasmuch as by general admission, the offence is contrary to the interests of the international community, it is treated as a delict jure gentium and all states are entitled to apprehend and punish the offenders. Clearly the purpose of conceding universal jurisdiction is to ensure that no such offence goes unpunished.

There are probably today only two clear-cut cases of universal jurisdiction, namely the crime of piracy jure gentium, and war crimes. Other cases do not necessarily involve the exercise of universal jurisdiction by *all* states. All states are entitled to arrest pirates on the high seas, and to punish them irrespective of nationality, and of the place of commission of the crime. . . .

———————————

The Restatement summarizes the international law principles of prescriptive jurisdiction as follows:

Restatement

Section 402. Bases of Jurisdiction to Prescribe

Subject to §403, a state has jurisdiction to prescribe law with respect to
(1)(a) conduct that, wholly or in substantial part, takes place within its territory;
(b) the status of persons, or interests in things, present within its territory;

(c) conduct outside its territory that has or is intended to have substantial effect within its territory;

(2) the activities, interests, status, or relations of its nationals outside as well as within its territory; and

(3) certain conduct outside its territory by persons not its nationals that is directed against the security of the state or against a limited class of other state interests.

See also Comment *g* to this section (excerpted at page 691 below) (passive personality) and section 404 (excerpted at page 698 below) (universal jurisdiction).

Notes and Questions

1. In the case of the *S.S. Lotus* (France v. Turkey), 1927 P.C.J.J. (Ser. A) No. 10, before the Permanent Court of International Justice (the predecessor of the ICJ), Turkey applied its criminal law to the conduct of a French merchant ship officer (Lieutenant Demons) on the high seas. His ship collided with a Turkish ship, killing eight Turkish nationals. France argued that Turkey violated international law by applying Turkish law in this situation. The court opined:

> The French Government contends that [Turkey] should be able to point to some title to jurisdiction recognized by international law in favour of Turkey. . . . The Turkish Government takes the view that [international law] allows Turkey jurisdiction whenever such jurisdiction does not . . . conflict with a principle of international law. . . .
>
> International law governs relations between independent States. The rules of law binding upon States therefore emanate from their own free will as expressed in conventions or by usages generally accepted as expressing principles of law and established in order to regulate the relations between these co-existing independent communities or with a view to the achievement of common aims. Restrictions upon the independence of States cannot therefore be presumed.
>
> Now the first and foremost restriction imposed by international law upon a State is that — failing the existence of a permissive rule to the contrary — it may not exercise its power in any form in the territory of another State. In this sense jurisdiction is certainly territorial; it cannot be exercised by a State outside its territory except by virtue of a permissive rule derived from international custom or from a convention.
>
> It does not, however, follow that international law prohibits a State from exercising jurisdiction in its own territory, in respect of any case which relates to acts which have taken place abroad, and in which it cannot rely on some permissive rule of international law. Such a view would only be tenable if international law contained a general prohibition to States to extend the application of their laws and the jurisdiction of their courts to persons, property and acts outside their territory, and if, as an exception to this general prohibition, it allowed States to do so in certain specific cases. But this is certainly not the case under international law as it stands at present. Far from laying down a general prohibition to the effect that States may not extend the application of their laws and the jurisdiction of their courts to persons, property and acts outside their territory, it leaves them in this respect a wide measure of discretion which is only limited in certain cases by prohibitive rules; as regards other cases, every State remains free to adopt the principles which it regards as best and most suitable.

This discretion left to States by international law explains the great variety of rules which they have been able to adopt without objections or complaints on the part of other States; . . . to remedy the difficulties resulting from such variety . . . efforts have been made for many years past, both in Europe and America, to prepare conventions the effect of which would be precisely to limit the discretion at present left to States in this respect by international law, thus making good the existing lacunae in respect of jurisdiction or removing the conflicting jurisdictions arising from the diversity of the principles . . . [in] various States.

In these circumstances, all that can be required of a State is that it should not over-step the limits which international law places upon its jurisdiction; within these limits, its title to exercise jurisdiction rests in its sovereignty.

It follows from the foregoing that the contention of the French Government to the effect that Turkey must in each case be able to cite a rule of international law au-thorizing her to exercise jurisdiction, is opposed to the generally accepted interna-tional law. . . .

Thus, the *Lotus* decision suggests that there is a presumption that an extrater-ritorial (or any other) assertion of prescriptive jurisdiction by a state is legal unless the target can show that a rule of international law prohibits that assertion. Do you think that this presumption is based on an outmoded celebration of state sover-eignty that is inappropriate today?

On the other hand, the court noted that Turkey was "exercising jurisdiction in its own territory"— the trial was in Turkey and the effects of the negligent act in question were felt on board a Turkish vessel. What was the prescriptive jurisdictional basis for the application of Turkish law to the controversy? What was France's claim? Which state had the burden of demonstrating the existence of a rule of interna-tional law to support its position? Would international law be strengthened if the rule were the opposite? Whose interests would be advanced, and whose hampered, by the approach taken in the *Lotus* case?

How would you show that international law prohibited a particular extraterri-torial assertion of prescriptive jurisdiction? Tax treaties provide an obvious source of such limitations in that they set forth in considerable detail limitations on a state's taxing authority. Limitations based on customary international law seem more difficult to establish. In the materials that follow, describing common foreign reac-tions to expansive U.S. assertions of prescriptive jurisdiction, consider whether such limitations can be inferred. How would you show that customary international law limits a state's prescriptive jurisdiction in the field of, say, securities regulation? Also consider what is at stake in these controversies. Which states and what interests benefit from strict territorial limits or at least robust customary international law-based limits on prescriptive jurisdiction?

2. Why should a Connecticut larceny statute not apply to larceny in Massachu-setts? Or France?

3. If Congress passes a law criminalizing the possession of heroin in Malaysia by Malaysian nationals, should a U.S. court apply that law (assuming the defendant was properly before the court)? Would your response be different in the case of a Swiss court applying Swiss law that criminalized the adulteration of chocolates by anyone anywhere in the world? Or a Pakistani court applying to college students drinking in Florida a Pakistani law prohibiting the consumption of alcohol (again assuming the defendants were properly before the court)?

4. Which of the bases of prescriptive jurisdiction summarized by Starke seem most appropriate to you? What are the sources of your thinking on this question? If territorial jurisdiction seems natural, why is that so?

5. Consider now the implications of the Internet. Would China violate international law if it criminalized the posting of material on the Web about certain religious groups, such as the Falun Gong? Would Saudi Arabia be in violation of international law if it criminalized the posting of photos of unveiled women on the Web? Does it matter, in the examples above, whether the individuals posting the information were in China, Iran, or the United States? Similarly, does it matter if the servers that contained the posted information were in China, Iran, or the United States?

To take an actual case, did France violate international law when it prohibited the sale of Nazi paraphernalia over the Internet? In fact, such items were for sale at the time on the Yahoo Web site. Does it matter that Yahoo's headquarters and servers were in California? Or, does it matter than Yahoo apparently could not identify and screen out all the users in France who tried to access the part of its Web site that had the Nazi items for sale? Moving for a moment beyond issues of prescriptive jurisdiction, assuming that France made these sales of Nazi items illegal under French law and a French court held that Yahoo had violated the law, how could France enforce the judgment? The Yahoo case is discussed in Chapter 4 at page 428.

Should a country's laws (statutory or common law) regarding defamation or libel apply to Internet material? Australia's highest court held that Australia's courts had jurisdiction to hear a defamation claim under Australian law (specifically the law of the plaintiff's home state of Victoria) by an Australian businessman against Dow Jones & Co. for a story published on Barron's Online. Mr. Joseph Gutnick claimed that an article defamed him by saying that he had been involved with two Americans in a money-laundering scheme. The challenged material had been edited in New York City and uploaded by Dow Jones onto its server in New Jersey. Barrons Online had an estimated 1,700 subscribers in Australia out of a total of 550,000 subscribers. The Australian High Court unanimously held that "ordinarily, defamation is to be located at the place where the damage to reputation occurs. . . . In the case of material on the World Wide Web, it is not available in comprehensible form until downloaded on to the computer of a person who has used a web browser to pull the material from the web server. It is where that person downloads the material that the damage to reputation may be done." (Para. 44.)

While recognizing the uniquely broad reach of the World Wide Web, the High Court noted that "those who make information accessible by a particular method do so knowing of the reach that their information may have." (Para. 39.) Rejecting the argument that its approach would make a publisher liable to the defamation laws of every country from "Afghanistan to Zimbabwe," the High Court said this concern was "unreal when it is recalled that in all but the unusual cases, identifying the person about whom material is to be published will readily identify the defamation law to which that person may resort." (Para. 54.) Dow Jones & Co. v. Gutnick [2002] HCA 56 (10 Dec. 2002) (High Court of Australia).

What should be the result if a repressive regime tried to prescribe strict rules regarding libel against authors and publishers on the Internet — e.g., limiting any negative comments about that country's government? Its national religion? Its citizens? Its occasional visitors? Any company doing business there?

In the *Dow Jones* case above, which of the jurisdictional principles discussed by Professor Starke is the basis for the Australian court determining that it had jurisdiction? Territorial? Objective territorial? Nationality? Passive nationality or passive personality principle?

1. Territory

In the United States legislation is normally considered to be territorial in scope. In other words, a California statute would normally be construed to apply throughout California, and a U.S. federal statute would normally be construed to apply throughout the United States. However, the California statute would not normally be interpreted to apply to California citizens elsewhere in the world, or to all people throughout the world who may later stray into California and thus be subject to the in personam jurisdiction of its courts. Nor would the U.S. federal statute normally be construed to apply to U.S. citizens elsewhere in the world or to all persons who may in the future be subject to the personal jurisdiction of U.S. courts.

Under a strict application of the territorial theory, each state would have the exclusive right to regulate within its territory and no authority to regulate outside that territory, a neat division of power in the world. The basis for this territorial limitation was found in natural law, international law (or the "law of nations" as it was often styled in the nineteenth century), or just an assumption inherent in the natural order of things. Thus, considering the question of whether the U.S. antitrust laws applied to conduct by American nationals in a foreign country, Justice Holmes remarked:

> [T]he general and almost universal rule is that the character of an act as lawful or unlawful must be determined wholly by the law of the country where the act is done. . . . For another jurisdiction, if it should happen to lay hold of the actor, to treat him according to its own notions rather than those of the place where he did the acts, not only would be unjust, but would be an interference with the authority of another sovereign, contrary to the comity of nations, which the other state concerned justly might resent. . . .
>
> The foregoing considerations would lead in case of doubt to a construction of any statute as intended to be confined in its operation and effect to the territorial limits over which the lawmaker has general and legitimate power. "All legislation is prima facie territorial." . . . We think it entirely plain that what the defendant did in Panama or Costa Rica is not within the scope of the statute so far as the present suit is concerned. . . .
>
> For again, not only were the acts of the defendant in Panama or Costa Rica not within the Sherman Act, but they were not torts by the law of the place and therefore were not torts at all. [American Banana Co. v. United Fruit Co., 213 U.S. 347, 356-357 (1909).]

To him it was inconceivable that an act of Congress would apply outside the territory of the United States. He referred to the "comity of nations" as a limiting restraint on the extraterritorial application of law. In Hilton v. Guyot, 159 U.S. 113, 163-164 (1895), the Court defined that concept:

> "Comity" . . . is neither a matter of absolute obligation, on the one hand, nor of mere courtesy and good will, upon the other. But it is the recognition which one nation allows within its territory to the legislative, executive, or judicial acts of another nation, having due regard both to international duty and convenience, and to the rights of its own citizens or of other persons who are under the protection of its laws.

The principle of comity has sometimes been treated as a principle of international law, but more often has been regarded as something short of a legal limitation, more like an act of altruistic deference or an acknowledgment of superior foreign interest (or lesser U.S. interest) in the matter at hand. Comity also refers to two types of limitation: first, the limitations that are self-imposed by a legislature in adopting a statute (or limitations placed by a court in applying the statute); and, second, limitations adopted by a court in fashioning a decision that affects foreign interests. We first examine the international law or comity limitations on application of law, and then look at those limitations on enforcement of law. Then we take up the problem of international law limitations on a state's jurisdiction to adjudicate.

Since *American Banana,* and especially in the past few decades, U.S. law enforcement agencies and U.S. courts have increasingly applied U.S. law extraterritorially, that is, to persons acting abroad, when their acts have a substantial effect on the United States. For example, if foreign nationals perpetrate fraud in sales on the New York Stock Exchange, U.S. securities legislation has been held to apply to these activities, even though they were entirely by foreigners outside the United States. Similarly a foreign price-fixing conspiracy undertaken abroad, but having an impact on prices in the U.S. market, has been held to be covered by the antitrust laws (the same laws that Justice Holmes discussed in the *American Banana* case quoted above). This tendency of U.S. courts to apply U.S. law extraterritorially has often been sharply resisted by foreign courts, governments, and scholars, and continues to generate controversy. For example, the EU, Canada, the United Kingdom, and several other states have retaliated by passing so-called blocking statutes making it illegal to comply with certain extraterritorial laws and regulations, and forbidding enforcement of certain judgments based on them. These blocking laws have sometimes even included "claw back" provisions — that is, remedies with which their nationals could seek to recover the damages imposed by U.S. enforcement efforts.

Many commentators as well as the Restatement have advanced the argument that extraterritorial application of law is limited by an international law rule of "reasonableness." The Restatement states that when a statute applied to conduct abroad that was legal where the conduct occurred, a court applying that statute should balance a long list of factors.

Restatement

Section 403. Limitations on Jurisdiction to Prescribe

(1) Even when one of the bases for jurisdiction under §402 [page 654 above] is present, a state may not exercise jurisdiction to prescribe law with respect to a person or activity having connections with another state when the exercise of such jurisdiction is unreasonable.

(2) Whether exercise of jurisdiction over a person or activity is unreasonable is determined by evaluating all relevant factors, including, where appropriate:

(a) the link of the activity to the territory of the regulating state, i.e., the extent to which the activity takes place within the territory, or has substantial, direct, and foreseeable effect upon or in the territory;

(b) the connections, such as nationality, residence, or economic activity, between the regulating state and the person principally responsible for the activity to be regulated, or between that state and those whom the regulation is designed to protect;

(c) the character of the activity to be regulated, the importance of regulation to the regulating state, the extent to which other states regulate such activities, and the degree to which the desirability of such regulation is generally accepted;

(d) the existence of justified expectations that might be protected or hurt by the regulation;

(e) the importance of the regulation to the international political, legal, or economic system;

(f) the extent to which the regulation is consistent with the traditions of the international system;

(g) the extent to which another state may have an interest in regulating the activity; and

(h) the likelihood of conflict with regulation by another state.

(3) When it would not be unreasonable for each of two states to exercise jurisdiction over a person or activity, but the prescriptions by the two states are in conflict, each state has an obligation to evaluate its own as well as the other state's interest in exercising jurisdiction, in light of all the relevant factors, Subsection (2); a state should defer to the other state if that state's interest is clearly greater.

Comment

a. Reasonableness in international law and practice. The principle that an exercise of jurisdiction on one of the bases indicated in §402 is nonetheless unlawful if it is unreasonable is established in United States law, and has emerged as a principle of international law as well. There is wide international consensus that the links of territoriality or nationality, §402, while generally necessary, are not in all instances sufficient conditions for the exercise of such jurisdiction. Legislatures and administrative agencies, in the United States and in other states, have generally refrained from exercising jurisdiction where it would be unreasonable to do so, and courts have usually interpreted general language in a statute as not intended to exercise or authorize the exercise of jurisdiction in circumstances where application of the statute would be unreasonable.

This approach was endorsed in the dissenting opinion by Justice Scalia and three other Justices in Hartford Fire Ins. Co. v. California, which follows. One of the issues in that case was whether the Sherman Act covered a conspiracy by a group of London reinsurance companies to limit the terms of insurance offered in the United States by forcing certain U.S. primary insurers to change the terms of their standard domestic liability insurance policies to conform with the policies that the defendants wanted.*

It is important to understand that there can be several different concepts of "ju-

---

*The Sherman Act makes illegal, among other matters, every contract, combination, or conspiracy in unreasonable restraint of interstate or foreign commerce. 15 U.S.C. §1. Its broad language includes conspiracies by competitors to fix prices or the terms of sale or purchase. Passed in 1890, the Sherman Act constitutes an important part of U.S. federal antitrust laws.—Eds.

risdiction" involved in a case, including personal jurisdiction of the court over the defendant, subject matter jurisdiction of the court over the type of case presented, and the international law-based concepts of jurisdiction to prescribe, jurisdiction to enforce, and jurisdiction to adjudicate (introduced above). Keep them separate in your mind.

In the *Hartford* case, the London reinsurance companies did not contest personal jurisdiction of the U.S. federal courts. Justice Scalia in his dissent noted the analytical distinction between subject matter jurisdiction of the court, which was based on the federal law conferring federal court jurisdiction over cases "arising under federal law," and the international law concept of prescriptive jurisdiction. The question whether the Sherman Act applied to defendants' foreign conduct can be framed as a question of prescriptive jurisdiction — that is, does the United States have authority under international law to apply its law (the Sherman Act) to defendants' foreign activities? Of course, you recall from Chapter 3 that an act of Congress may trump an inconsistent rule of international law, so the international law issue may seem moot. However, as Justice Scalia points out, it is a settled rule of statutory construction that an act of Congress is construed to be consistent with international law whenever possible. Because the Sherman Act is arguably ambiguous as to its coverage of acts by foreigners abroad, international law may effectively limit the scope of the Sherman Act through this technique of statutory interpretation. If the law — properly construed to be consistent with international law — does not apply to defendants' foreign conduct, then they have not violated the law. In addition, the basis for the court's subject matter jurisdiction — which depends on the case arising under federal law — disappears.

Justice Souter's majority opinion adopted a different approach. He did not use international law to construe the Sherman Act; he did not even refer to international law. Instead, he referred to possible limits required by "comity," which, as noted above, is less binding than international law. Some commentators have criticized his approach for sharply limiting the situations in which comity would be employed.

Hartford Fire Insurance Co. v. California

U.S. Supreme Court
509 U.S. 764 (1993)

[Justice SOUTER authored the opinion for the majority of five Justices:]

At the outset, we note that the District Court undoubtedly had jurisdiction of these Sherman Act claims, as the London reinsurers apparently concede. See Tr. of Oral Arg. 37 ("Our position is not that the Sherman Act does not apply in the sense that a minimal basis for the exercise of jurisdiction doesn't exist here. Our position is that there are certain circumstances, and that this is one of them, in which the interests of another State are sufficient that the exercise of that jurisdiction should be restrained"). . . . I[t] is well established by now that the Sherman Act applies to foreign conduct that was meant to produce and did in fact produce some substantial effect in the United States. . . .[22] Such is the conduct alleged here: that the London

22. Justice SCALIA believes that what is at issue in this litigation is prescriptive, as opposed to subject-matter, jurisdiction. . . . The parties do not question perspective jurisdiction, however, and for good reason: it is well established that Congress has exercised such jurisdiction under the Sherman Act.

reinsurers engaged in unlawful conspiracies to affect the market for insurance in the United States and that their conduct in fact produced substantial effect.

According to the London reinsurers, the District Court should have declined to exercise such jurisdiction under the principle of international comity. The Court of Appeals agreed that courts should look to that principle in deciding whether to exercise jurisdiction under the Sherman Act. This availed the London reinsurers nothing, however. To be sure, the Court of Appeals believed that "application of [American] antitrust laws to the London reinsurance market would lead to significant conflict with English law and policy," and that "[s]uch a conflict, unless outweighed by other factors, would by itself be reason to decline exercise of jurisdiction." But other factors, in the court's view, including the London reinsurers' express purpose to affect United States commerce and the substantial nature of the effect produced, outweighed the supposed conflict and required the exercise of jurisdiction in this litigation.

. . . [E]ven assuming that in a proper case a court may decline to exercise Sherman Act jurisdiction over foreign conduct (or, as Justice Scalia would put it, may conclude by the employment of comity analysis in the first instance that there is no jurisdiction), international comity would not counsel against exercising jurisdiction in the circumstances alleged here.

The only substantial question in this case is whether "there is in fact a true conflict between domestic and foreign law." Societe Nationale Industrielle Aerospatiale v. United States District Court, 482 U.S. 522, 555 (1987) (Blackmun, J., concurring in part and dissenting in part). The London reinsurers contend that applying the Act to their conduct would conflict significantly with British law, and the British government, appearing before us as amicus curiae, concurs. They assert that Parliament has established a comprehensive regulatory regime over the London reinsurance market and that the conduct alleged here was perfectly consistent with British law and policy. But this is not to state a conflict. . . . No conflict exists, for these purposes, "where a person subject to regulation by two states can comply with the laws of both." Restatement (Third) Foreign Relations Law 403, Comment e. Since the London reinsurers do not argue that British law requires them to act in some fashion prohibited by the law of the United States, or claim that their compliance with the laws of both countries is otherwise impossible, we see no conflict with British law. We have no need in this case to address other considerations that might inform a decision to refrain from the exercise of jurisdiction on grounds of international comity.

[Justice SCALIA wrote a dissenting opinion, which was joined by three other Justices.]

. . . The petitioners . . . various British corporations and other British subjects, argue that certain of the claims against them constitute an inappropriate extraterritorial application of the Sherman Act. It is important to distinguish two distinct questions raised by this petition: whether the District Court had jurisdiction, and whether the Sherman Act reaches the extraterritorial conduct alleged here. On the first question, I believe that the District Court had subject-matter jurisdiction over the Sherman Act claims against all the defendants (personal jurisdiction is not contested). The respondents asserted nonfrivolous claims under the Sherman Act, and 28 U.S.C. §1331 vests district courts with subject-matter jurisdiction over cases "arising under" federal statutes. As precedents such as Lauritzen v. Larsen, 345 U.S. 571 make clear, that is sufficient to establish the District Court's jurisdiction over these claims. . . . The second question — the extraterritorial reach of the Sherman Act — has nothing to do with the jurisdiction of the courts. It is a question of substantive law turning on whether, in enacting the Sherman Act, Congress asserted regulatory power over the challenged conduct. See EEOC v. Arabian American Oil Co., 499 U.S. 244 (1991) *(Aramco)* ("It is our task to determine whether Congress intended the protections of Title VII to apply to United States citizens employed by American employers outside of the United States"). If a plaintiff fails to prevail on this issue, the court does not dismiss the claim for want of subject-matter jurisdiction — want of power to adjudicate; rather, it decides the claim, ruling on the merits that the plaintiff has failed to state a cause of action under the relevant statute.

There is, however, a type of "jurisdiction" relevant to determining the extraterritorial reach of a statute; it is known as "legislative jurisdiction," or "jurisdiction to prescribe," I Restatement (Third) of Foreign Relations Law of the United States 235 (1987) (hereinafter Restatement (Third)). This refers to "the authority of a state to make its law applicable to persons or activities," and is quite a separate matter from "jurisdiction to adjudicate," see id., at 231. There is no doubt, of course, that Congress possesses legislative jurisdiction over the acts alleged in this complaint: Congress has broad power under Article 1, 8, cl. 3 "[t]o regulate Commerce with foreign Nations," and this Court has repeatedly upheld its power to make laws applicable to persons or activities beyond our territorial boundaries where United States interests are affected. But the question in this case is whether, and to what extent, Congress has exercised that undoubted legislative jurisdiction in enacting the Sherman Act.

Two canons of statutory construction are relevant in this inquiry. The first is the "long-standing principle of American law 'that legislation of Congress, unless a contrary intent appears, is meant to apply only within the territorial jurisdiction of the United States.' " Applying that canon in *Aramco,* we held that the version of Title VII of the Civil Rights Act of 1964 then in force, did not extend outside the territory of the United States even though the statute contained broad provisions extending its prohibitions to, for example, " 'any activity, business, or industry in commerce.' " We held such "boilerplate language" to be an insufficient indication to override the presumption against extraterritory. The Sherman Act contains similar "boilerplate language," and if the question were not governed by precedent, it would be worth considering whether that presumption controls the outcome here. We have, however, found the presumption to be overcome with respect to our antitrust laws; it is now well established that the Sherman Act applies extraterritorially. See Matsushita Elec. Industrial Co. v. Zenith Radio Corp., 475 U.S. 574, 582, n.6 (1986); Continental Ore Co. v. Union Carbide & Carbon Corp., 370 U.S. 690, 704, (1962); see also United States v. Aluminum Co. of America, 148 F.2d 416 (CA2 1945).

But if the presumption against extraterritoriality has been overcome or is otherwise inapplicable, a second canon of statutory construction becomes relevant: "[A]n act of congress ought never to be construed to violate the law of nations if any other possible construction remains." Murray v. The Charming Betsy, 2 Cranch 64, 118, 2 L. Ed. 208 (1804) (Marshall, C.J.). This canon is "wholly independent" of the presumption against extraterritoriality. It is relevant to determining the substantive reach of a statute because "the law of nations," or customary international law, includes limitations on a nation's exercise of its jurisdiction to prescribe. See Restatement (Third) §§401-416. Though it clearly has constitutional authority to do so, Congress is generally presumed not to have exceeded those customary international-law limits on jurisdiction to prescribe.

Consistent with that presumption, this and other courts have frequently recognized that, even where the presumption against extraterritoriality does not apply, statutes should not be interpreted to regulate foreign persons or conduct if that regulation would conflict with principles of international law. [Justice Scalia then summarized three cases where statutes were held inapplicable to the case presented in part because to do so would violate the international law of the sea or more important foreign interests.]

Lauritzen, Romero, and *McCulloch* were maritime cases, but we have recognized the principle that the scope of generally worded statutes must be construed in light of international law in other areas as well. See, e.g., Sale v. Haitian Centers Council, Inc., 113 S. Ct. 2549, 2562, n.35; Weinberger v. Rossi, 456 U.S. 25, 32 (1982). More specifically, the principle was expressed in United States v. Aluminum Co. of America, 148 F.2d 416 (CA2 1945), the decision that established the extraterritorial reach of the Sherman Act. In his opinion for the court, Judge Learned Hand cautioned "we are not to read general words, such as those in [the Sherman] Act, without regard to the limitations customarily observed by nations upon the exercise of their powers; limitations which generally correspond to those fixed by the 'Conflict of Laws.' " Id., at 448.

More recent lower court precedent has also tempered the extraterritorial application of the Sherman Act with considerations of "international comity" [citing four court of appeals cases from four different circuits]. The "comity" they refer to is not the comity of courts, whereby judges decline to exercise jurisdiction over matters more appropriately adjudged elsewhere, but rather what might be termed "prescriptive comity": the respect sovereign nations afford each other by limiting the reach of their laws. That comity is exercised by legislatures when they enact laws, and courts assume it has been exercised when they come to interpreting the scope of laws their legislatures have enacted. It is a traditional component of choice-of-law theory. Comity in this sense includes the choice-of-law principles that, "in the absence of contrary congressional direction," are assumed to be incorporated into our substantive laws having extraterritorial reach. Considering comity in this way is just part of determining whether the Sherman Act prohibits the conduct at issue.

In sum, the practice of using international law to limit the extraterritorial reach of statutes is firmly established in our jurisprudence. In proceeding to apply that practice to the present case, I shall rely on the Restatement (Third) of Foreign Relations Law for the relevant principles of international law. Its standards appear fairly supported in the decisions of this Court construing international choice-of-law principles *(Lauritzen, Romero,* and *McCulloch)* and in the decisions of other federal courts, especially *Timberlane.* Whether the Restatement precisely reflects international law in every detail matters little here, as I believe this case would be resolved the same way under virtually any conceivable test that takes account of foreign regulatory interests.

Under the Restatement, a nation having some "basis" for jurisdiction to prescribe law should nonetheless refrain from exercising that jurisdiction "with respect to a person or activity having connections with another state when the exercise of such jurisdiction is unreasonable." Restatement (Third) §403(1). The "reasonable-ness" inquiry turns on a number of factors including, but not limited to: "the extent to which the activity takes place within the territory [of the regulating state]," id., §403(2)(a); "the connections, such as nationality, residence, or economic activity, be-tween the regulating state and the person principally responsible for the activity to be regulated," id., §403(2)(b); "the character of the activity to be regulated, the impor-tance of regulation to the regulating state, the extent to which other states regulate such activities, and the degree to which the desirability of such regulation is generally accepted," id., §403(2)(c); "the extent to which another state may have an interest in regulating the activity," id., §403(2)(g); and "the likelihood of conflict with regula-tion by another state," id., §403(2)(h). Rarely would these factors point more clearly against application of United States law. The activity relevant to the counts at issue here took place primarily in the United Kingdom, and the defendants in these counts are British corporations and British subjects having their principal place of business or residence outside the United States. Great Britain has established a comprehen-sive regulatory scheme governing the London reinsurance markets, and clearly has a heavy "interest in regulating the activity," id., §403(2)(g). Finally, §2(b) of the McCarran-Ferguson Act allows state regulatory statutes to override the Sherman Act in the insurance field, subject only to the narrow "boycott" exception set forth in §3(b) — suggesting that "the importance of regulation to the [United States]," id., §403(2)(c), is slight. Considering these factors, I think it unimaginable that an asser-tion of legislative jurisdiction by the United States would be considered reasonable, and therefore it is inappropriate to assume, in the absence of statutory indication to the contrary, that Congress has made such an assertion.

It is evident from what I have said that the Court's comity analysis, which pro-ceeds as though the issue is whether the courts should "decline to exercise . . . juris-diction," rather than whether the Sherman Act covers this conduct, is simply misdi-rected. I do not at all agree, moreover, with the Court's conclusion that the issue of the substantive scope of the Sherman Act is not in the case. To be sure, the parties did not make a clear distinction between adjudicative jurisdiction and the scope of the statute. Parties often do not, as we have observed (and have declined to punish with procedural default) before. . . . In any event, if one erroneously chooses, as the Court does, to make adjudicative jurisdiction (or, more precisely, abstention) the vehicle for taking account of the needs of prescriptive comity, the Court still gets it wrong. It concludes that no "true conflict" counseling nonapplication of United States law (or rather, as it thinks, United States judicial jurisdiction) exists unless compliance with United States law would constitute a *violation* of another country's law. That breath-takingly broad proposition, which contradicts the many cases discussed earlier, will bring the Sherman Act and other laws into sharp and unnecessary conflict with the le-gitimate interests of other countries — particularly our closest trading partners.

Notes and Questions

1. What position does Justice Souter and the majority take in *Hartford Fire* con-cerning the role of comity analysis in limiting the application of U.S. antitrust analy-sis? What position does Justice Souter take concerning the likelihood of conflict with foreign law or policy (see Restatement section 403(2)(g) and (h))? Note that many

commentators have read *Hartford Fire* as precluding the use of comity analysis in cases absent what the Court calls a "true conflict" between U.S. law and foreign law. Others have questioned that interpretation. Compare, for example, Roger P. Alford, The Extraterritorial Application of Antitrust Laws: A Postscript on Hartford Fire Insurance Co. v. California, 34 Va. J. Intl. L. 212, 220 (reading the decision that way), and Robert C. Reuland, *Hartford Fire Insurance Co.,* Comity, and the Extraterritorial Reach of United States Antitrust Laws, 29 Tex. Intl. L.J. 159, 161 (1994) (same), with Curtis A. Bradley, Territorial Intellectual Property Laws in an Age of Globalism, 37 Va. J. Intl. L. 505, 557–560 (1997) (arguing against that reading of the decision). See also Gary B. Born, International Civil Litigation in United States Courts 604–605 (3d ed. 1996) (presenting alternative interpretations). Courts are divided on this issue. Compare In re Maxwell Communication Corp. PLC, 93 F.3d 1036, 1049 (2d Cir. 1996) (citing *Hartford Fire* for proposition that "[i]nternational comity comes into play only when there is a true conflict between American law and that of a foreign jurisdiction") and United States v. Nippon Paper, 109 F.3d 1 (1st Cir. 1997) (even extending the *Hartford Fire* decision to include criminal prosecution under the Sherman Act based wholly on extraterritorial conduct, so long as there were intended and substantial effects in the United States), with Metro Industries, Inc. v. Sammi Corp., 82 F.3d 839, 846 n.5 (9th Cir. 1996) ("While Hartford Fire Ins. overruled our holding . . . that a foreign government's encouragement of conduct which the United States prohibits would amount to a conflict of law, it did not question the propriety of the jurisdictional rule of reason or the seven comity factors . . ."). On the other hand, possibly reflecting the close vote in *Hartford Fire,* or the weight of academic commentary, or the ambiguous nature of Justice Souter's analysis, some courts have ignored the decision and gone directly to the section 403 analysis. See, for example, United States v. Usama Bin Laden, excerpted below.

2. Which is more persuasive — Justice Souter's majority opinion or Justice Scalia's dissenting opinion? Souter's opinion superficially seems less respectful of international law: he refers to comity, not law, and many think he would require an irreconcilable conflict of legal commands directed at the defendant before invoking comity. Scalia's opinion squarely applies customary international law to limit the U.S. legislative reach, as advocated by Restatement section 403. The differing approaches raise basic issues of the role of the judiciary vis-à-vis the political branches.

3. Do you agree with the position that many believe Justice Souter adopted — that is that there is no conflict here and that comity should apply only if a person is compelled by two sovereigns to take inconsistent action? Or is Justice Scalia's point more persuasive — that there is clearly a conflict in government policy: the United Kingdom tolerates the conduct; the United States condemns it, so a court should choose which policy should prevail. What interests should comity protect? On what basis can a court weigh the conflicting policies?

4. Professor Andreas Lowenfeld, who was one of the Reporters of the Restatement, wrote an article taking issue with the majority's reading of the Restatement:

One cannot tell, merely from the fact that state B does not prohibit or punish a given activity, whether it has a strong interest in continuance of that activity, or in non-interference in the activity by state.

The question remains whether there is a conflict — a conflict of state interests — which under international law needs to be evaluated. While I am not as certain as

Justice Scalia how such an evaluation comes out, I am clear that to say that the Insurance Antitrust Case presented no conflict at all is quite mistaken, and certainly at odds with the scheme of the Restatement. . . .

. . . My point is that there is a significant space between such indifference of state B to a given activity carried on its territory as to remove all doubt about the reasonableness of the exercise of jurisdiction by state A, and such compulsion by state B as would be required to create a "true conflict" as defined by the majority in Insurance Antitrust. . . .

In determining whether state A should exercise jurisdiction over an activity significantly linked to state B, one important question, in my submission, is whether B has a demonstrable system of values and priorities different from those of state A that would be impaired by the application of the law of A. . . . [C]onflict is not just about commands: it is also about interests, values and competing priorities. All of these need to be taken into account in arriving at a rational allocation of jurisdiction in a world of nation-states. [Andreas F. Lowenfeld, Comment: Conflict, Balancing of Interests, and the Exercise of Jurisdiction to Prescribe: Reflections on the Insurance Antitrust Case, 89 Am. J. Intl. L. 42, 50-51 (1995).]

For further discussion, see, for example, Philip R. Trimble, Comment: The Supreme Court and International Law: The Demise of Restatement 403, 89 Am. J. Intl. L. 53 (1995) (questioning whether section 403's reasonableness requirement is in fact reflected in customary international law) and Larry Kramer, Note: Extraterritorial Application of American Law After the Insurance Antitrust Case: A Reply to Professors Lowenfeld and Trimble, 89 Am. J. Intl. L. 750 (1995).

5. Here are three situations where there are serious conflicts in fundamental policy: (a) U.S. condemnation of cartels and price fixing that may be encouraged, or tolerated by, foreign governments, or (b) U.S. condemnation of securities practices that are considered acceptable in other markets, or (c) U.S. economic boycotts that undercut other governments' policy preferences (e.g., trading with Cuba). Should the federal courts take it upon themselves to limit application of an act of Congress (and thereby, at least partially, frustrate congressional policy) on grounds of customary international law? In other words, do you agree with Scalia's premise that customary international law (which he finds in Restatement section 403) can effectively limit an act of Congress? If Restatement section 403 were embodied in a treaty that were subsequent-in-time to the statute, it would (if self-executing) modify the statute. Should customary international law be different?

6. Justice Scalia identified and discussed two important U.S. canons of statutory construction:

The first is the "long-standing principle of American law 'that legislation of Congress, unless a contrary intent appears, is meant to apply only within the territorial jurisdiction of the United States.'" . . .

But if the presumption against extraterritoriality has been overcome or is otherwise inapplicable, a second canon of statutory construction becomes relevant: "An act of congress ought never to be construed to violate the law of nations if any other possible construction remains." Murray v. The Charming Betsy. . . .

We consider these two canons below.

7. As Justice Scalia cited, a leading case that invokes the first canon (which creates a rebuttable presumption against extraterritoriality) is Equal Employment

Opportunity Commission (EEOC) v. Arabian American Oil Company (Aramco), 499 U.S. 244 (1991). There the plaintiff, a U.S. citizen of Lebanese descent, was an engineer for an Aramco subsidiary. While working in Saudi Arabia, he was fired. He sued Aramco under Title VII of the Civil Rights Act of 1964, claiming that he had been discriminated against on the basis of race, religion, and national origin. The EEOC intervened on his behalf. Although, as Justice Scalia notes above, the statute contained some broad provisions and the parties offered competing interpretations, the Court in *Aramco* reasoned: "We need not choose between these competing interpretations as we would be required to do in the absence of the presumption against extraterritorial application . . . Each is plausible, but no more persuasive than that. . . . [I]t is [the plaintiff] who must make the affirmative showing. . . ." The Court then went through a careful analysis of the language of the statue as well as of other statutes that had been held to have extraterritorial effect. The Court concluded: "Thus [the plaintiff's] argument based on the jurisdictional language of Title VII fails both as a matter of statutory language and of our previous case law." Id. at 253.

8. What are the justifications for the judge-made presumption against extraterritoriality? To comply with congressional wishes? To avoid foreign relations controversy? To defer to the Executive? To comply with international law? To keep courts out of foreign affairs? Some combination of these? Something else? Should the Court abandon the presumption and simply attempt to discern legislative intent? (Legislative history might make the intention clear in some cases, but some Justices, including Justice Scalia, disfavor reference to legislative history.) Why not apply a presumption *in favor* of extraterritoriality? Or a presumption that statutes extend to the limits of Congress's powers?

9. Congress quickly overturned the specific holding of *Aramco* concerning the scope of Title VII. In the Civil Rights Act of 1991, Congress amended the definition of "employee" in Title VII to provide that, "[w]ith respect to employment in a foreign country, [the term *employee*] includes an individual who is a citizen of the United States." 42 U.S.C. §2000e(f). Congress also added the following provisions, in 42 U.S.C. §2000e-1:

> (b) It shall not be unlawful under [this statute] . . . for an employer (or a corporation controlled by an employer), labor organization, employment agency, or joint labor-management committee controlling apprenticeship or other training or retraining (including on-the-job training programs) to take any action otherwise prohibited by such section, with respect to an employee in a workplace in a foreign country if compliance with such section would cause such employer (or such corporation), such organization, such agency, or such committee to violate the law of the foreign country in which such workplace is located.
>
> (c)(1) If an employer controls a corporation whose place of incorporation is a foreign country, any practice prohibited by [this statute] engaged in by such corporation shall be presumed to be engaged in by such employer.
>
> (2) [This statute] shall not apply with respect to the foreign operations of an employer that is a foreign person not controlled by an American employer.

Does this statute show that the Court in *Aramco* erred in its original interpretation of Title VII? Or does it show the system of separation of powers working well, and that Congress is now expressing its position on the extraterritorial application of the law? Also, note subsection (b) above. How does Congress deal with the possibility of conflict between Title VII and a foreign law? Is this provision controlling with respect to Title VII instead of the majority opinion in *Hartford Fire* or Restatement section 403?

10. The Supreme Court has reaffirmed the presumption in two decisions after *Aramco*. See Sale v. Haitian Centers Council, 509 U.S. 155 (1993); Smith v. United States, 507 U.S. 197 (1993). In both of those decisions, the Court noted that the presumption applies even when there is no serious risk of conflict with the laws of another nation. In the absence of such a risk of conflict, what purpose does the presumption serve?

11. A number of academic commentators have criticized the presumption, arguing that it is inconsistent with modern international law, which allows for some extraterritorial regulation; with modern state choice-of-law rules, which generally employ a multifactored balancing analysis rather than a strict territorial presumption; and with the modern legislative focus of Congress, which they contend is often international in scope. See, e.g., Gary B. Born, A Reappraisal of the Extraterritorial Reach of U.S. Law, 24 Law & Poly. Intl. Bus. 1 (1992); Larry Kramer, Vestiges of *Beale:* Extraterritorial Application of American Law, 1991 Sup. Ct. Rev. 179. For a modest defense of the presumption, grounded in separation of powers principles, see Curtis A. Bradley, Territorial Intellectual Property Rights in an Age of Globalism, 37 Va. J. Intl. L. 505, 550-561 (1997). For an argument that the presumption should be applied only to situations in which the extraterritorial conduct does not have effects within the United States, see William S. Dodge, Understanding the Presumption Against Extraterritoriality, 16 Berkeley J. Intl. L. 85 (1998).

12. Justice Scalia also discussed the second well-established canon of statutory interpretation — that is, that a statute should be construed, if possible, not to violate international law. What is the relationship between the two canons? Is the second canon sufficient to address concerns associated with extraterritoriality? Or, in other words, is customary international law clear enough in all situations involving extraterritorial jurisdiction?

13. In discussing the second canon, besides citing *The Charming Betsy* decision (discussed in Chapter 3), Justice Scalia discussed maritime cases, in which U.S. labor and tort legislation was held not to apply to foreign flag vessels carrying cargo from foreign ports to U.S. ports. The contact with U.S. territory would arguably have been sufficient to legitimize U.S. prescriptive jurisdiction, but international law provides that the law of the foreign state whose flag the vessel flies controls and supersedes the territorial principle. Often foreign flag vessels are indirectly owned by U.S. individuals or corporations. In these cases there clearly are conflicts (or at least sharp differences) between the relevant U.S. and foreign laws. Imposition of U.S. labor and tort standards, for example, is more likely to protect the employees on board the ships and make the ships' operations more costly. Should a U.S. corporation be allowed to avoid U.S. legal requirements by conducting operations through foreign subsidiaries?

14. Whose interests would be served by a rigid territorial division of law-prescribing authority? The interests of developing states? Industrialized states? Multinational corporations? Consumers? Human rights advocates? Should the federal courts take it upon themselves to interpret laws in this way? Is a judicial holding that a statute does not apply to extraterritorial conduct because of international law more threatening to congressional prerogative than when a court construes statutes not to apply to other fact situations?

15. Although the United States is certainly among the most active countries in asserting extraterritorial jurisdiction, it is by no means the only one. For example, the European Union, with its 15 Member States, has been very active in antitrust enforcement, even when it has extraterritorial impact. In recent years, the EU has challenged several mergers between non-European companies, and has been successful in preventing them or obtaining concessions. The most notable EU challenge effectively blocked the proposed merger of two very large U.S. corporations, GE and Honeywell, after U.S. antitrust authorities had indicated that the U.S. government would not oppose the merger.

16. Would it be better to limit extraterritorial application of antitrust law or other laws by treaties and executive agreements, rather than by judicially employed presumptions and comity analysis?

17. The well-regarded authors of a leading antitrust law casebook have observed:

> Perhaps the most important recent development in the area of international comity has been the expansion of the . . . agreements [on procedural cooperation] that exist among some of the major antitrust enforcement authorities of the world. The United States is now a party to a number of such agreements. [These include Germany (1976), Australia (1982), the European Community (1991, supplemented by a 1998 agreement on "positive comity"), and Canada (1994, revised in 1995).] In one, the Treaty with Canada . . . the U.S. Department of Justice and the Canadian Bureau of Competition Policy are empowered actually to conduct joint investigations, including the sharing of confidential information. . . .
>
> The more recent cooperation agreements, such as the U.S.-EC agreement and the 1995 U.S.-Canada agreement, emphasize both traditional comity and so-called positive comity. . . . The concept of positive comity . . . allows the enforcement agency to seek action from the foreign authority in whose territory the alleged anticompetitive conduct is taking place, if that conduct would also violate the foreign country's law[, rather than the enforcement agency initially taking action]. In its present form, positive comity has not been made mandatory . . . . Instead, it is an option that is encouraged under the cooperation agreement. [Milton Handler, Robert Pitofsky, Harvey J. Goldschmid, & Diane P. Wood, Trade Regulation: Cases and Materials 1209-1210 (4th ed. 1997).]

2. *Nationality*

The right of a state to regulate the conduct of its citizens or nationals anywhere in the world is, like territorial jurisdiction, usually noncontroversial. Congress can thus legislate with respect to the conduct of a U.S. national anywhere in the world. (Note, though, that the Restatement states that jurisdiction to prescribe is limited by a reasonableness requirement with respect to a person or activity having connections with another state. Restatement §403(1).)

For example, in Blackmer v. United States, 284 U.S. 421 (1932), the defendant was a U.S. national living in France who failed to obey a subpoena ordering him to appear as a witness at a criminal trial in the United States. The Court upheld a contempt fine (which was executed against Blackmer's assets in the United States). It rejected the argument that serving notice of the subpoena in France violated France's rights under international law. Although no one would seriously question the nationality basis for prescriptive jurisdiction, the service of judicial process in a foreign country, and certainly the execution, may violate that state's sensitivities about sovereignty as well as domestic and international law. See the materials below in the section on enforcement and adjudication.

Moreover, the normal practice is to allow each state to determine who its nationals are, for example, a child of a national, no matter where the child is born, or a child born in the state's territory, no matter what the nationality of the child's parents.

The definition of "corporate nationality," however, presents particularly difficult problems. Under U.S. practice, a corporation normally has the nationality or citizenship of the state where it is incorporated. Nevertheless, the Internal Revenue Code taxes foreign source income of certain foreign corporations when they are *owned or controlled* by U.S. citizens, thereby treating those corporations as if they are U.S. nationals for this limited purpose.

More controversially, some U.S. laws apply to all individuals and corporations that are "subject to the jurisdiction of the United States," a phrase that the U.S. government sometimes interprets, through regulations, to include foreign corporations owned or controlled by U.S. persons. This would include a French subsidiary of a U.S. corporation. The claimed basis for the authority is the nationality principle. For example, one major statute authorizing international economic sanctions is the International Emergency Economic Powers Act (IEEPA). It applies to "any person, or . . . any property, subject to the jurisdiction of the United States." The Treasury regulations implementing the IEEPA provide:

> The term, person subject to the jurisdiction of the United States, includes:
> (a) Any individual, wherever located, who is a citizen or resident of the United States. . . .
> (c) Any corporation organized under the laws of the United States or of any state, territory, possession, or district of the United States; and
> (d) Any corporation, partnership, or association, wherever organized or doing business, that is owned or controlled by persons specified in paragraph (a) or (c) of this section. [31 C.F.R. 500.329 (2003).]

This form of extraterritorial application of U.S. law has long rankled foreign governments, precipitating protests and stimulating countermeasures. For example, in 1965 a French court appointed a temporary administrator to manage Fruehauf-France, a French subsidiary that was 70 percent owned by a U.S. parent, in order to carry out a contract with China that was prohibited under the then applicable U.S. regulations. The controversy is described by Professor Lowenfeld:

Andreas F. Lowenfeld, Trade Controls for Political Ends
92-93 (1983)

Fruehauf had been organized in 1918 in Detroit, had opened a Canadian plant in 1928, and had spread after the War to Europe, Brazil, Australia, and Japan. By 1965, Fruehauf had factories in 10 countries, and 80 distributors sold and serviced Fruehauf products in nearly all parts of the world other than communist countries. . . .

S.A. Fruehauf-France, located about 15 miles south of Paris, was owned 70 percent by Fruehauf Detroit, and 30 percent by French interests. Five of the directors were appointed from Detroit, including the Chairman and the Vice President/International of the parent company, and two other American citizens, all represented by one United States citizen resident in France who carried a permanent proxy from the senior officials of Fruehauf Detroit. The three other directors, all French citizens, were appointed by the holders of the 30 percent interest in the enterprise. One of the French directors, Raoul Massardy, served as President-General Manager.

In early October, 1964 Fruehauf-France was invited to bid on a contract to supply a large order of semi-trailers to the French truck company Berliet. Berliet advised that the transaction would involve exports from France, but no destination was named. Fruehauf-France submitted its bid on October 16, 1964, subject only to the condition that the unknown destination not be one in which another Fruehauf distributor had exclusive rights. Between the middle of October and the end of November a variety of communications flowed between Berliet and Fruehauf-France, dealing with specifications, price, and delivery terms. Three other French firms bid on the order, but by November 30, Berliet informed Fruehauf-France that its offer was the most attractive, and that it should begin procuring the necessary materials with a view to commencing delivery by February 15, 1965. The final signed order was received by Fruehauf-France on December 24, 1964, with a contract price of about Fr. 1,800,000 (U.S. $360,000).

At some time during the fall, Fruehauf-France learned that the trailers, together with tractors to be manufactured by Berliet, were destined for the People's Republic of China. It is not clear when or whether this fact was called to the attention of Fruehauf Detroit, but in any case the latter did not notify the United States government or apply for a license.

Early in January, 1965, the U.S. Treasury learned of the proposed transaction, and called in Fruehauf Detroit's top management. Fruehauf Detroit was instructed to cause Fruehauf-France to cancel the Berliet contract forthwith, as execution of the contract would be a violation of the Foreign Assets Control Regulations [promulgated under the predecessor statute to the IEEPA] punishable by heavy criminal penalties. Following several weeks of meetings and telephone calls, Fruehauf Detroit complied with the order of the U.S. Treasury; it formally instructed Fruehauf-France to cancel the contract, and to seek to minimize the damages vis-à-vis Berliet. When Berliet refused to release Fruehauf-France and threatened suit, Massardy resigned as president, and the three French directors petitioned the local commercial court for the appointment of a temporary administrator who would manage the company and carry out the contract. The court granted the petition on February 16, 1965. The corporation, on the basis of a resolution adopted by the five American directors, appealed.

The Court of Appeals of Paris upheld the appointment of the temporary administrator. Societe Fruehauf Corp. v. Massardy, [1968] D.S. Jur. 147 (Ct. App. Paris, May 22, 1965). Among other reasons, the court noted that the damage liability of Fruehauf-France would

> ruin the financial equilibrium and the moral credit of Fruehauf-France, S.A. and provide
> its disappearance and the unemployment of more than 600 workers; . . . in order to

name a temporary administrator the judge-referee must take into account the interests of the company rather than the personal interests of any shareholders even if they be the majority. [The opinion was translated and appeared in 5 Intl. L. Matl. 476 (1966).]

The decision of the French courts to appoint a temporary administrator to take control of a functioning French company created a new precedent in French corporate law. See William Lawrence Craig, Application of the Trading with the Enemy Act to Foreign Corporations Owned by Americans: Reflections on Fruehauf v. Massardy, 83 Harv. L. Rev. 579, 582 (1970).

The U.S. Department of Treasury did not take any further action against the U.S. parent company. This might have reflected, in part, the great French sensitivity at the time to the U.S. effort to extend its laws to a French subsidiary.

Another U.S.-European trade dispute arose in the 1980s over the construction of a Soviet pipeline to carry natural gas from large fields in Siberia to Western Europe. In June 1982, President Reagan announced an unprecedented broadening of trade controls against the Soviet Union. These controls were on exports of oil and gas equipment and technology and were designed at least in part to hamper Soviet construction of the pipeline.

Barry E. Carter, International Economic Sanctions: Improving the Haphazard Legal Regime

83-85 (1988)

Two controls went beyond any previous assertion of extraterritorial jurisdiction under the foreign policy provisions of the EAA [Export Administration Act]. First, the controls prevented foreign subsidiaries of U.S. firms from exporting equipment and technology even though it was of wholly foreign origin. Second, the controls restricted independent foreign companies from exporting foreign-origin products that were made with technology acquired through licensing agreements with U.S. companies. These controls covered, for example, compressors built by a French Company (e.g. Creusot-Loire) under a licensing agreement with a U.S. company (e.g. General Electric).

The U.S. policy against the pipeline clashed with that of major European countries that were not opposed to its construction—indeed, some were signing contracts to buy gas from the pipeline and many countries were encouraging their companies to participate in its construction. The attempt by the United States to impose its antipipeline policy on companies operating in, say, France, West Germany, England, and Italy drew a strong reaction. The European Economic Community and others argued that the extraterritorial extension of the controls was contrary to international law. Governments in some European countries encouraged companies within their borders to honor their contracts with the Soviets. France even issued formal orders directing businesses to continue to perform. As a result, several companies in Europe, including some U.S. subsidiaries such as Dresser-France, found themselves subject to conflicting orders from the United States and from the country where they were located. Several of these companies complied with the directives from their resident countries and performed under their contracts. The United States reacted swiftly by placing the companies that did not comply with the U.S. orders on a "temporary denial" list, which essentially cut these companies off from *all* exports from the United States.

Although no U.S. court ruled definitively on the extraterritorial reach of the controls, at least one European court ruled against it. In Compagnie Européenne des Petroles S.A. v. Sensor Nederland B.V., a Dutch district court decided that Sensor, a Dutch subsidiary of a U.S. corporation, could not be excused from performing a sales contract under Dutch law because of the U.S. export regulations. The court determined that the U.S. regulations had no jurisdictional basis under international law that required the court to take the regulations into account.

The President's decision to rescind the regulations was apparently caused by the strong allied reaction, pressures from the U.S. business community and Congress, and the apparent ineffectiveness of the controls since work on the pipeline continued and companies in Europe generally continued to perform under their contracts. Possibly chastened by the pipeline experience, the Reagan Administration [did not assert] such broad extraterritorial jurisdiction since, not even in . . . recent controls pursuant to IEEPA against Nicaragua, South Africa, and Libya. Nevertheless, the broad statutory authority remains unchanged at this point.

European Communities: Comments on the U.S. Regulations Concerning Trade with the U.S.S.R.

21 I.L.M. 891 (1982)

I. INTRODUCTION

1. On June 22, 1982, the Department of Commerce at the direction of President Reagan and pursuant to Section 6 of the Export Administration Act amended Sections 376.12, 379.8 and 385.2 of the Export Administration Regulations. These amendments amounted to an expansion of the existing U.S. controls on the export and re-export of goods and technical data relating to oil and gas exploration, exploitation, transmission and refinement.

The European Community believes that the U.S. regulations as amended contain sweeping extensions of U.S. jurisdiction which are unlawful under international law. Moreover, the new Regulations and the way in which they affect contracts in course of performance seems to run counter to criteria of the Export Administration Act and also to certain principles of U.S. public law. . . .

3. The following comments will discuss *firstly* the international legal aspects of the U.S. measures, including (a) the generally recognized bases on which jurisdiction can be founded in international law and (b) other bases of jurisdiction which might be invoked by the U.S. Government; *secondly* the rules and principles as laid down in U.S. law, in particular the Export Administration Act. . . .

II. THE AMENDMENTS UNDER INTERNATIONAL LAW

A. Generally Accepted Bases of Jurisdiction in International Law

The U.S. measures as they apply in the present case are unacceptable under international law because of their extra-territorial aspects. They seek to regulate companies not of U.S. nationality in respect of their conduct outside the United States and particularly the handling of property and technical data of these companies not within the United States.

They seek to impose on non-U.S. companies the restriction of U.S. law by threatening them with discriminatory sanctions in the field of trade which are inconsistent with the normal commercial practice established between the U.S. and the E.C.

In this way the Amendments of June 22, 1982, run counter to the two generally accepted bases of jurisdiction in international law: the territoriality and the nationality principles.

The *territoriality principle* (i.e. the notion that a state should restrict its rule-making in principle to persons and goods within its territory and that an organization like the European Community should restrict the applicability of its rules to the territory to which the Treaty setting it up applies) is a fundamental notion of international law, in particular insofar as it concerns the regulation of the social and economic activity in a state. The principle that each state — and *mutatis mutandis* the Community insofar as powers have been transferred to it — has the right freely to organize and develop its social and economic system has been confirmed many times in international fora. The American measures clearly infringe the principle of territoriality, since they purport to regulate the activities of companies in the E.C., not under the territorial competence of the U.S.

The *nationality principle* (i.e. the prescription of rules for nationals, wherever they are) cannot serve as a basis for the extension of U.S. jurisdiction resulting from the Amendments, i.e. (i) over companies incorporated in E.C. Member States on the basis of some corporate link (parent-subsidiary) or personal link (e.g. shareholding) to the U.S.; (ii) over companies incorporated in E.C. Member States, either because they have a tie to a U.S.-incorporated company, subsidiary or other "U.S. controlled" company through a licencing agreement, royalty payments, or payment of other compensation, or because they have bought certain goods originating in the U.S.

The Amendments in two places purport to subject to U.S. jurisdiction companies, wherever organized or doing business, which are subsidiaries of U.S. companies or under the control of U.S. citizens, U.S. residents or even persons actually within the U.S. This implies that the United States is seeking to impose its corporate nationality on companies of which the great majority are incorporated and have their registered office elsewhere, notably in E.C. Member States.

Such action is not in conformity with recognized principles of international law. In the Barcelona Traction Case, the International Court of Justice declared that two traditional criteria for determining the nationality of companies, i.e. the place of incorporation and the place of the registered office of the company concerned, had been "confirmed by long practice and by numerous international instruments." The Court also scrutinized other tests of corporate nationality, but concluded that these had not found general acceptance. The Court consequently placed primary emphasis on the traditional place of incorporation and the registered office in deciding the case in point. This decision was taken within the framework of the doctrine of diplomatic protection, but reflects a general principle of international law.

The notion inherent in the subjection to U.S. jurisdiction of companies with no tie to the U.S. whatsoever, except for a technological link to a U.S. company, or through possession of U.S. origin goods, can only be that this technology or such goods should somehow be considered as unalterably "American" (even though many of the patents involved are registered in the Member States of the European

Community). This seems the only possible explanation for the U.S. Regulations given the fact that national security is not at stake here. . . .

Goods and technology do not have any nationality and there are no known rules under international law for using goods or technology situated abroad as a basis of establishing jurisdiction over the persons controlling them. . . .

The practical impact of the Amendments to the Export Administration Regulations is that E.C. companies are pressed into service to carry out U.S. trade policy towards the U.S.S.R., even though these companies are incorporated and have their registered office within the community which has its own trade policy towards the U.S.S.R.

The public policy ("ordre public") of the European Community and of its Member States is thus purportedly replaced by U.S. public policy which European companies are forced to carry out within the E.C., if they are not to lose export privileges in the U.S. or to face other sanctions. This is an unacceptable interference in the affairs of the European Community. . . .

The Netherlands: District Court at the Hague Judgment in Compagnie Européenne des Pétroles S.A. v. Sensor Nederland B.V.

22 Intl. Legal Materials 66 (1983)

1.   THE FACTS

From the documents before the Court and the proceedings at the sitting of September 3, 1982, the following facts can so far be taken as having been established between the parties:

— Compagnie Européenne des Pétroles S.A. (C.E.P.) is a company organized and existing under French law and domiciled in Paris.
— Sensor Nederland B.V. (Sensor) is, according to its Articles of Association, domiciled at The Hague and has its business address at Voorschoten.
— The management of Sensor is entirely in the hands of Pierson Trust B.V., domiciled at Amsterdam.
— Sensor is a 100% subsidiary of Geosource International (Nederland) B.V., which is domiciled at Amsterdam and is a 100% subsidiary of Geosource, Inc., a corporation organized and existing under the laws of one of the United States of America and domiciled at Houston, Texas.
— Around February 1982 C.E.P. entered into negotiations with Sensor about the supply of 2,400 strings of geophones with spare parts.
— By telex of May 19, 1982, C.E.P. placed an order with Sensor for the supply of 2,400 strings of geophones with spare parts for the price of Nfls 2,249,369.60. The delivery time was to be 14-16 weeks.
— By telex of May 19, 1982, Sensor confirmed the order placed with it.
— C.E.P.'s official purchase order of June 3, 1982, includes the following terms:

  Price: FOB Understood Rotterdam, packing for Seashipment and delivery included

> *Delivery:* Within 14-16 weeks
> *Payment:* By letter of credit to be opened 8 weeks before delivery
> *Ultimate Destination:* U.S.S.R.

— On June 18, 1982, Sensor confirmed the purchase order in writing; mention
   was made of delivery before September 20, 1982.
— By telex and letter of June 28, 1982, C.E.P. . . . confirmed its order [with-
   out spare parts] to the 2,400 strings of geophones for the price of Nfls
   2,103,264.00.
— On July 1, 1982, Sensor confirmed to C.E.P. the receipt of the (revised)
   order placed by C.E.P. on June 28, 1982.
— On July 27, 1982, Sensor informed C.E.P. that it would not be able to meet
   its delivery obligation in good time, now that, as a subsidiary of an American
   corporation, it had to respect the export embargo of June 22, 1982, imposed
   by the President of the United States.
— On August 11, 1982, C.E.P. reminded Sensor that it had been agreed that
   the goods would be delivered f.o.b. Rotterdam not later than on September
   20, 1982.
— On that day—August 11—C.E.P. drew Sensor's attention to the consequences of failure to deliver on time.
— On August 12, 1982, Sensor again informed C.E.P. that as a subsidiary of an
   American corporation it had to respect the President's embargo.

2. THE CLAIM

After modifying its original claim, C.E.P. is now asking that Sensor be ordered to
deliver to C.E.P. by October 18, 1982, at the latest, in the agreed manner, the 2,400
strings of geophones ordered by C.E.P., on pain of a penalty of Nfls 100,000, payable
forthwith to C.E.P., for each day after October 18, 1982, that Sensor fails to deliver
the said 2,400 strings of geophones. . . .

4. APPLICABLE LAW

The international contract of sale was concluded by telex; the parties made no
choice of law.
    In the event of failure by the parties to make such a choice, an international
contract is governed by the law of the country with which it is most closely
connected.
    This is presumed to be the country where the party who is to effect the per-
formance which is characteristic of the contract has its principal place of business at
the time of conclusion of the contract.
    This principle is embodied in Article 4 of the Convention on the Law applica-
ble to Contractual Obligations, which convention was signed by the Netherlands on
June 19, 1980.
    Although this Convention has not (yet) been ratified by the Netherlands, its
Article 4 should already be applied as valid Netherlands private international law.

Applicability of Netherlands law implies in the present case that the Uniform Act governing the International Sale of Goods (Neth. O.J. 1971 No. 780) is also applicable to the contract.

5.   THE DEFENCE

Sensor has submitted that it is subject to the [U.S.] Export Administration Regulations and that by virtue of §385.2(c) of those Regulations it cannot fulfill its obligations towards C.E.P.

According to Sensor, the sanctions with which Sensor and Geosource are threatened in the event of infringement of the Export Administration Regulations constitute *force majeure* and justify a reliance on the "exonerating circumstances" of section 74 of the Uniform Act governing the International Sale of Goods.

6.   §385.2(C) OF THE EXPORT ADMINISTRATION REGULATIONS

6.1   The text of §385.2(c) of the Export Administration Regulations [would prohibit this sale].

6.2   Under Section 11 of the Export Administration Act, any infringement of the regulation reproduced above is punishable by a fine of up to $100,000, by a term of imprisonment of up to ten years and by withdrawal of export licenses.

7.   ASSESSMENT OF THE EXTRA-TERRITORIAL JURISDICTION RULE OF §385.2(C)(2)(IV)

7.1   In what follows, it will be assumed that an export transaction such as that agreed upon between C.E.P. and Sensor falls within the scope of section (1) of §385.2(c) and that the U.S. authorities have not granted an export license for that transaction.

It will also be assumed that Sensor is a "corporation" within the meaning of paragraph (iv) of section (2) of the American regulation [which provided that any corporation, wherever it was incorporated or doing business, was subject to U.S. jurisdiction if it were owned or controlled by a U.S. corporation].

7.2   Under point 4 above it has been found that the contract between C.E.P. and Sensor is governed by Netherlands law. To what extent, therefore, is it necessary to take into account a measure under U.S. law that operates in restraint of trade?

In answering that question, the first consideration must be that that measure extends to the transaction between C.E.P. and Sensor simply and solely via the jurisdiction rule of section (2)(iv). The object of that rule is manifestly to endow the [sanctions] measure with effects vis-à-vis corporations located outside the United States which conclude contracts outside the United States with non-American corporations.

That is the situation that arises in the present case. What particularly merits attention is the fact that, under international law as commonly interpreted, Sensor

Nederland B.V. has Netherlands nationality, having been organized in the Netherlands under Netherlands law and both its registered office and its real centre of administration being located within the Netherlands. In accordance with this interpretation, the Treaty of Friendship, Commerce and Navigation between the Kingdom of the Netherlands and the United States of America of March 27, 1956, provides in Article XXIII, third paragraph:

> Companies constituted under the applicable laws and regulations within the territories of either Party shall be deemed companies thereof and shall have their juridical status recognized within the territories of the other Party.

7.3   The circumstance that the trade embargo imposed by the American authorities has been endowed with extra-territorial effects as hereinbefore described raises the question as to whether the jurisdiction rule that brings about such effects is compatible with international law.

7.3.1   The starting point for answering such questions is the universally accepted rule of international law that in general it is not permissible for a State to exercise jurisdiction over acts performed outside its borders. Exceptions to this rule are, however, possible, for instance under the so-called "nationality principle" or the "protection principle" (the "universality principle" can be disregarded here).

7.3.2   The American jurisdiction rule would not appear to be justified by the nationality principle in so far as that rule brings within its scope companies of other than U.S. nationality.

The position would be different if, in the first place, the criterion "owned or controlled by persons specified in paragraphs (i), (ii), or (iii) of this section" were . . . a yardstick for the (U.S.) nationality of the corporation . . . but in general, according to the views held outside the United States, this has to be regarded as in itself dubious, and in the relations between the United States and the Netherlands it is out of the question, having regard to the treaty provision hereinbefore cited under 7.2. The consequence of this is that the nationality principle offers insufficient basis for the jurisdiction rule here at issue.

7.3.3   Under the protection principle, it is permissible for a State to exercise jurisdiction over acts — wheresoever and by whomsoever performed — that jeopardize the security or creditworthiness of that State or other State interests. Such other State interests do not include the foreign policy interest that the U.S. measure seeks to protect. The protection principle cannot therefore be invoked in support of the validity of the jurisdiction rule here at issue.

7.3.4   It is also of importance to examine whether the acts of exportation covered by the American embargo, in so far as they are performed outside the United States, have direct and illicit effects within the territory of the United States. If that is the case, then those acts can be regarded as having been performed within the United States and on that ground brought within the jurisdiction of the United States under generally accepted rules of international law.

It cannot, however, be seen how the export to Russia of goods not originating in the United States by a non-American exporter could have any direct and illicit effects within the United States. Via this route too, therefore, the jurisdiction rule cannot be brought into compatibility with international law.

7.3.5   The foregoing does not entail that, measured by international law standards, the jurisdiction rule has to be denied all effects.

It is not unacceptable, for instance, that its effects should extend to American citizens who, wishing to evade the American embargo, to that end set up a non-American corporation outside the United States.

There is, however, no evidence to suggest that this has occurred in the present case. . . .

8. CONCLUSION

It follows from the foregoing that Sensor's reliance on the American embargo fails and that the claim . . . must be allowed, Sensor being ordered to pay costs.

The imposition of economic sanctions has become a regular feature of U.S. foreign policy. Congress continues frequently to authorize a wide variety of sanctions against a number of target countries and against a great number of individual groups and entities (such as terrorists and drug traffickers). In turn, the Executive Branch continues to act to impose sanctions on countries, groups, and individuals through executive orders and other determinations. Many of these sanctions have been imposed in connection with measures authorized by the U.N. Security Council, such as those against Iraq. Others are unilateral, as with the Soviet pipeline case and, more recently, with the sanctions against Cuba under the Helms-Burton legislation and those against Iran and Libya under the Iran-Libya Sanctions Act (ILSA). Sanctions have also been imposed under general legislation such as IEEPA and the Export Administration Act, often with extraterritorial effect. (For further discussion of economic sanctions, see the Chapter 3 section on national emergency legislation at page 222 above and the section on U.S. human rights sanctions in Chapter 8 at page 808.)

There are two different types of situations where foreign governments have vigorously resisted the extraterritorial application of U.S. rules: first, where foreign operations of foreign-incorporated subsidiaries of U.S. parent corporations are covered by the rule and, second, where foreign operations of independent foreign corporations with only tenuous connections to the United States are involved — for example using technology originating in the United States, doing business through a separate subsidiary in the United States, or taking advantage of property once owned by U.S. nationals.

European judicial reaction has been hostile (as the *Fruehauf* and *Sensor* cases demonstrate). Another example involved a U.S. attempt to freeze Libyan bank deposits in a London branch of a U.S. bank. A U.K. trial court ruled that Bankers Trust Company was obligated to pay the Libyan Arab Foreign Bank $292.5 million in funds that the Libyan bank had deposited with Bankers Trust and that the U.S. bank claimed had been frozen. About half of the money had been in the London branch of Bankers Trust, and the other half was money the U.S. bank had failed to transfer, as directed by the Libyan bank, to its London branch prior to the freeze. In reaching its decision, the trial court concluded that law of the place (i.e., U.K. law) applied to accounts in the United Kingdom, even in the branch of a U.S. bank. Libyan Arab Foreign Bank v. Bankers Trust Co., 26 I.L.M. 1600 (Q.B. Comml. Ct. Sept. 2, 1987). Rather than appeal this unfavorable opinion, Bankers Trust paid the Libyan bank the $292.5 million, plus $28 million in interest. The U.S. Treasury Department granted the necessary license for Bankers Trust to make the payment to a Libyan entity.

As discussed earlier in Chapter 6 (at page 619), the United States has strongly opposed the government of Fidel Castro since shortly after he took power through a revolution in 1959. Extensive limits on trade and other economic transactions were first imposed in 1962 and have continued to varying degrees. A recent controversy was sparked by the Helms-Burton Act of 1996. Consider the following exchange of views on Helms-Burton.

Andreas F. Lowenfeld, Congress and Cuba: The Helms-Burton Act

90 Am. J. Intl. L. 419 (1996)

On March 12, 1996, President Clinton signed the Cuban Liberty and Democratic Solidarity (Libertad) Act of 1996, generally known by the names of its principal sponsors as the Helms-Burton Act. . . .

Title III of the Act, which embodies the threat to nationals of third countries — Canadians, Spaniards, Argentines or whatever — has drawn the most comment, both because it raises once again the issue of economic sanctions through exercise of extraterritorial jurisdiction, and because it explicitly rejects the act of state doctrine and empowers United States courts to adjudicate claims arising from expropriations carried out in Cuba more than three decades ago. . . .

III. PROPERTY IN CUBA, LITIGATION IN AMERICA

The issue of compensation for property of United States nationals . . . is the focus of title III. The scheme of the Act is to create a right of action in United States courts on behalf of any U.S. national who has a claim for property confiscated by Cuba since January 1, 1959, against any person who "traffics" in such property. . . . Whoever "traffics" in property that once belonged to U.S. nationals is to be confronted with the prospect of litigation in the United States, and of exposure to damages equal in the first instance to the value of the property in question, and if the trafficking continues, to treble damages (section 302(a)). "Trafficking," a word heretofore applied in legislation almost exclusively to dealing in narcotics, is defined to include not only selling, transferring, buying, or leasing the property in question, but also "engag[ing] in a commercial activity using or otherwise benefiting from confiscated property" (section 4(13)). Thus the Act contemplates that if an English company purchases sugar from a Cuban state enterprise and the English company also does business in the United States and accordingly is amenable to the judicial jurisdiction of a U.S. court, it would be liable to a U.S. national who could show that some of the

English company's purchases consisted of sugar grown on the plantation that the plaintiff once owned. There is no necessary connection between the value of the property on which the claim is based and the value of the transaction on which the assertion of "trafficking" rests. . . .

[T]he President is authorized to suspend the effectiveness of title III for a period of six months if he determines and reports to Congress that the suspension "[i] is necessary to the national interests of the United States and [ii] will expedite a transition to democracy in Cuba" (section 306(b)(1)). The suspension may be extended for additional periods of six months upon further determinations by the President to the same effect. . . . This compromise, which was not contained in either the House or the Senate bill, was accepted, according to the Conference Report, at the request of the executive branch "in order to afford the President flexibility to respond to unfolding developments in Cuba." The Report goes on to say that in the committee's judgment the President could not under "current circumstances" in good faith make the two determinations required for suspension, in particular because suspension would remove a significant deterrent to investment in Cuba, "thereby helping prolong Castro's grip on power." . . .

. . . It is clear that a suit of the kind contemplated in title III of Helms-Burton would run up against the doctrine as set out in *Sabbatino* and succeeding cases; and since the focus of the legislation is dealing in property abroad and not in the United States, the Second Hickenlooper or Sabbatino Amendment, which partly reverses the decision in the *Sabbatino* case, would not be applicable to an action under Helms-Burton. The authors of the Helms-Burton Act dealt with this problem head-on. They provided (in section 302(a)(6)) that the act of state doctrine shall not be applicable to actions brought under the Act. . . .

The *pièce de résistance* of the Cuban Liberty and Democratic Solidarity (Libertad) Act, evidently, is the linkage between exposure to litigation in the United States and conduct abroad. The conduct may be in Cuba itself, such as building a hotel or operating a cement works; or it may be in Canada, France, Mexico — anywhere that an embargo against Cuba is not in effect.

The sanction is not quite a prohibition, as now prevails with respect to foreign companies linked by ownership or control to United States firms. But virtually all commercial enterprises in Cuba were taken over by the Government in the years after Fidel Castro came to power, whether they previously belonged to U.S. nationals, Cuban nationals or third-country nationals. It follows that any person that deals with an enterprise that existed prior to January 1, 1959 (by whatever name), or with an enterprise that could be regarded as a successor to such an enterprise, stands exposed to litigation in the United States, if it does business or otherwise can be found in the United States. Of course, not all such litigation, if it took place, would result in a final judgment against the defendant. Plaintiffs would, it seems, have the burden of proving that defendants were dealing in *their* confiscated property, and there might well be different interpretations of what that meant. But no one likes to face a lawsuit with high potential damages, least of all in the United States. And just in case the potential defendant's calculation might come out to prefer continuing the commercial relation with Cuba, even at the risk of litigation in the United States, Helms-Burton provides that . . . damages are to be trebled. In case that deterrent is still not sufficient, section 401 requires that the Secretary of State shall not grant a visa to, and the Attorney General shall not admit into the United States, any person who after the enactment of the Act has confiscated property or traffics in property a claim to which is owned by a U.S. national. This provision by its terms applies also to a corporate officer, principal or shareholder with a controlling interest in such a person, and — I think for the first time in the not always honorable history of U.S. alien exclusion laws — to the spouse, minor child or agent of a person excludable under any of the preceding categories. It is hard to believe that Ms. Jones, the daughter of a corporate executive from Toronto, might be stopped at the border when she returns from her summer vacation for her junior year at Vassar, but that is what the statute says.

In short, for any firm that does business in the United States or is amenable to suit in the United States, the choice is between an ice cream sundae and a root canal treatment. Given the doubtful prospects of business in Cuba in any event, and the huge potential of the American market, the proponents of Helms-Burton are fairly confident that persons who contemplate investment in Cuba or transactions with Cuba will change their minds, and that those who have already made such deals will look for ways to unload their investments or terminate their contracts.

Helms-Burton as a Secondary Boycott

As I see it, the Helms-Burton Act is thus in intent — and probably in effect — a classical secondary boycott, much like the Arab boycott of Israel. State *A* may prohibit trade with (or investment by its nationals in) state *B*. That is the typical embargo or *primary boycott* — the United States vis-à-vis Cuba, Syria (and others) vis-à-vis Israel, many countries against South Africa until 1994. Putting aside the (not insignificant) issue of applying such a boycott to subsidiaries established abroad, a primary boycott does not usually raise issues of international law, because the boycotting state is exercising its jurisdiction in its own territory or over its own nationals.

In a *secondary boycott*, state *A* says that if *X*, a national of state *C*, trades with state *B*, *X* may not trade with or invest in *A*. In other words, *X* is required to make a choice between doing business with or in *A*, the boycotting state, and doing business with or in *B*, the target state, although under the law of *C* where *X* is established, trade with both *A* and *C* is permitted.

After some hesitation, the United States strongly condemned the boycott of Israel maintained by the League of Arab States. U.S. law has prohibited American firms from complying with the Arab boycott, and even from filling out forms supplied by the Boycott Office or otherwise answering questions designed to disclose whether or not the firm has done business with Israel. . . . Imagine if Canada took a position similar to that of the United States, and punished one of its companies for giving information to a U.S. court about its activities — or rather about its steps to end those activities — in or with Cuba.

It is true that the sanctions imposed by the Helms-Burton Act are distinguishable from the Arab boycott of Israel, in that the sanction for violation under Helms-Burton is not a prohibition, only exposure to litigation and exclusion. But the litigation, as we have seen, may result in damages equal not to defendants' gain but to plaintiffs' loss, plus interest for some thirty-five years, all subject to trebling if the potential defendants do not exercise their Hobson's choice quickly. The objective, in any case, is the same. *X*, a national of state *C* (say Canada), is being coerced by state *A* (the United States) to stop trading with *B* (Cuba) or handling merchandise containing products of state *B*, although the law of *C* makes such trade perfectly legal and may even encourage it. I believe that (in time of peace) the exercise of jurisdiction by the United States for these purposes, to impose a secondary boycott on Cuba, like the exercise of jurisdiction by members of the Arab League to impose a secondary boycott on Israel, is contrary to international law, because it seeks unreasonably to coerce conduct that takes place wholly outside of the state purporting to exercise its jurisdiction to prescribe.

Helms-Burton and the Effects Doctrine

The authors of the Helms-Burton Act were prepared for criticism that they were engaged in extraterritorial legislation. They included in the Findings on which the operative portions of the Act are based, the statement:

> International law recognizes that a nation has the ability to provide for rules of law with respect to conduct outside its territory that has or is intended to have substantial effect within its territory. (Section 301(9)) . . .

I submit that the effort by the authors of Helms-Burton to build on the *Restatement* is flawed — fundamentally flawed — in two respects. *First,* the effect against which the legislation is directed — even if one can locate it in the United States — was caused by the Government of Cuba, not by the persons over whom jurisdiction is sought to be exercised. Thus, even leaving aside the thirty-six-year interval between conduct and effect on the one hand, . . . the effort to place Helms-Burton within the effects doctrine is no more than a play on words. It does not withstand analysis, and it would carry the effects doctrine farther than it has ever been carried before.

Second, the effort to impose United States policy on third countries or their nationals in the circumstances here contemplated is unreasonable by any standard. I need not here go through the criteria for evaluating reasonableness set out in the *Restatement;* different writers and courts have formulated or understood the criteria in different ways. I think for present purposes the most persuasive way to look at the legislation is to ask how Americans would react if the tables were turned.

Suppose, for instance, Iran were to adopt a law stating that anyone who invests in the Great Satan U.S.A. will be subject to suit in Iran for up to the value of the assets that the former Shah robbed from the Iranian people, as determined by the Majlis. BMW, calculating its litigation exposure in Iran and the value of its investments in the United States, cancels operations about to begin at its new plant in Spartansburg, South Carolina; at the same time, Mercedes Benz cancels its plan to build a sports vehicle plant in Vance, Alabama. I believe all Americans would be outraged, both at Iran for adopting the law I have suggested, and at the German manufacturers for having capitulated. I do not believe we would be hearing Iran's exercise of jurisdiction characterized as reasonable. . . .

Diversion from the Situation in Cuba

In the first few days after the passage of the Cuban Liberty and Democratic Solidarity Act, the press was full of reports of opposition to the Act from America's best friends. . . . [T]here is a real danger that Helms-Burton will have the same effect that President Reagan's famous pipeline regulations had in 1982.

. . . The reaction in Europe was loud, quick, all negative, and much of it invoked international law. . . .

Brice M. Clagett, Title III of the Helms-Burton Act Is Consistent with International Law

90 Am. J. Intl. L. 434 (1996)

. . . Several governments — notably Canada, Mexico and those of the European Union, whose corporate citizens are the principal "traffickers"— have denounced the legislation as an exercise of extraterritorial jurisdiction that violates customary international law. These governments apparently see nothing wrong with permitting — even encouraging — their nationals to use and profit from property that rightfully belongs to others. The United States not only commands the moral high ground on this issue; it also has the better of the legal argument. . . .

A state has jurisdiction to prescribe rules of law with respect to "conduct outside its territory that has or is intended to have substantial effect within its territory," at least when the exercise of that jurisdiction is reasonable in all the circumstances. Congress frequently legislates in reliance on the "substantial effect" basis of jurisdiction. The antitrust laws furnish well-known examples, although they are far from the only ones.

Under the *Restatement* scheme, international law is said to require that a state, even if it has jurisdiction to prescribe based on "substantial effects," must balance its interests against those of other states, and refrain from applying its laws when the legitimate and reasonable interests of another state are greater. The appropriate question thus becomes: what other state is entitled to complain? What state can accuse the United States of an international delinquency against it?

If the "other state" is Cuba, Cuba has no legitimate interest, which other states need or should respect, in confiscating property without compensation and profiting from foreign investment in that property. Cuba's comprehensive violations of international law fully justify U.S. countermeasures such as title III, even if those measures would otherwise be unlawful.

If the "other state" is the state of which the trafficker is a national, that state's interest in protecting its national's ability to traffic in confiscated property in a third country is, at the most, no greater (let alone more legitimate) than the United States' interest in protecting the ability of *its* national — the rightful owner — to prevent further interference with his property and perhaps ultimately to recover it. The interests of both states are equally "extraterritorial," since the activity with which both are concerned is taking place in a third country, Cuba. Thus, title III does not fail a balancing test, even if such a test is deemed part of international law. Title III is well within the right of the United States to prescribe rules for application by its own courts, against defendants subject to its jurisdiction, in a matter with a demonstrable impact on the United States and its residents.

A further reason for title III is the notorious weakness and ineffectiveness of international enforcement mechanisms. Because the jurisdiction of international tribunals is consensual, it is only rarely that a confiscation case can be brought in such a forum. Espousal of claims by the victims' government can take generations to bear any fruit at all and, even when it does, typically results in recovery by the victims of only a pathetically inadequate fraction of the just compensation to which international law entitles them. In these conditions, there is every reason for an aggrieved state to supply effective remedies on its own if it can. Cuba has given the United States that opportunity by peddling confiscated property to traffickers who may be subject to U.S. jurisdiction. Creation of such a remedy, far from violating international law, works toward rescuing that law from relative impotence.

Enactment of title III does no injustice to the "traffickers" who may become defendants. That Castro's confiscations were made without compensation, and also typically involved discrimination against U.S. nationals or political persecution of Cubans, is not one of the world's best-kept secrets. Traffickers are fully aware that they are dealing in tainted property. It can be presumed that the culpability of dealing in stolen goods is a familiar concept to them from their own legal systems. Traffickers are knowingly taking the risk that the dispossessed owners or aggrieved states might take action against them. . . .

The courts might well have recognized a remedy against trafficking many years ago were it not for the judge-made act of state doctrine, which was applied in *Sabbatino* to defeat a claim by owners of confiscated Cuban property. Title III appropriately includes a provision that the act of state doctrine shall not be applicable to any lawsuit brought under its authority. . . .

Notes and Questions

1. Obviously there is great potential for conflict in these situations where the states involved have fundamentally different foreign and economic policies. Should those conflicts be resolved through a political process (such as a diplomatic negotiation) or judicially? If a political agreement cannot be reached, is it unfair to subject a defendant to inconsistent commands of the criminal law? If you were counsel to the corporate entities involved, what arguments would you make, and to whom, to prevent that from happening?

2. If you were a Senator from a state, such as California, with many exporting multinational companies, would you favor amending these laws to limit extraterritorial application? How? Does your opinion vary according to whether the sanctions are applied to Libya, Iran, Myanmar (Burma), China, or Nigeria?

3. What would be your attitude toward such an amendment if you were counsel to the State Department? Defense? Commerce? Agriculture? Would it matter to these government agencies (or to multinational companies affected by the sanctions) whether the extraterritorial elements of the sanctions were codified in the sanctions law or were implemented through an Executive Order or other regulation? Which approach is easier to change when relations between the United States and the target country change?

4. Should a U.S. corporation be able to avoid U.S. law by simply incorporating a foreign subsidiary? Was that the situation in the Fruehauf-France case?

5. What would be the result in *Sensor* if there were no FCN Treaty? Apply the Restatement section 403 factors. What result?

6. In the complicated and subtle world of assertions of extraterritorial jurisdiction, might the United States adopt, and generally support, a prohibition on

imposing secondary boycotts, as in Title III of Helms-Burton? If not, what is our justification for opposing the Arab boycott of Israel, which Professor Lowenfeld discusses above?

7. As a general rule, should U.S. sanctions legislation passed by Congress have some type of Presidential waiver provision that allows the President some flexibility in applying economic pressure and adjusting to changed circumstances? (Note the waiver added to Title III of Helms-Burton.) How hard or easy should Congress make the waiver provision? Should it just require the President to make a determination of "national interest" or "national security," or should it have additional conditions and reporting requirements?

8. The foreign reaction to the Helms-Burton Act was swift and negative, with foreign governments saying that the Act interfered with their national policies for their companies on trade with Cuba. By 1997, so-called blocking or antidote legislation had been passed by Canada, the European Union, Mexico, and Argentina. Each of these laws prohibits private or public cooperation with U.S. implementation of Helms-Burton and establishes sizeable penalties for doing so. They also bar their courts from enforcing judgments awarded under Helms-Burton.

The more innovative element of some of these blocking laws is their "claw back" provisions. These create a cause of action in the foreign state on behalf of a national or corporation of that state who has a judgment rendered against it in U.S. courts under Helms-Burton. That person can sue in his own court for an equivalent amount of damages, enforceable against the assets of the U.S. plaintiff in the defendant's home state. This has the effect both of dissuading potential U.S. litigants, who may lose as much as they gain, even with treble damages, and of indemnifying the EU, Canadian, or other foreign citizens who wish to continue trading with Cuba. For more on these blocking laws, see Jorge F. Perez-Lopez and Matias F. Travieso-Diaz, The Helms-Burton Law and Its Antidotes: A Classic Standoff?, 7 Sw. J.L. & Trade Am. 95 (2000).

9. It is in part because of these strong foreign reactions that the Clinton Administration negotiated an agreement with the EU pursuant to which the President exercised his waiver authority every six months until the end of his presidency to prevent lawsuits under Title III, and to use discretion in banning foreign nationals under Title IV. In turn, the EU made some critical statements about Castro's government in Cuba. As of May 2003, President Bush has so far similarly continued to waive the lawsuit provisions of Title III, despite political pressure from anti-Castro groups in the United States. However, the Act still remains on the books.

10. The Helms-Burton law not only has provoked diplomatic protest and retaliation but also has been condemned by the OAS Inter-American Juridical Committee as not "conforming" to international law. See 35 I.L.M. 1322 (1996).

11. The literature on extraterritoriality is extensive. See, e.g., Gary B. Born, International Civil Litigation in United States Courts 493-544 (3d ed. 1996); Andreas F. Lowenfeld, International Litigation and Arbitration 39-143 (2d ed. 2002); Barry E. Carter, International Economic Sanctions: Improving the Haphazard Legal Regime 85, 253-254 (1988).

The territorial and nationality principles support most legislation a government is likely to want to adopt. However, there are a few situations in which these principles do not cover matters that governments have often felt compelled to regulate such as currency counterfeiting and visa fraud (conduct that may well be by aliens acting outside national territory). Moreover, some states have considered it desirable to protect their nationals working or traveling abroad by extending their law to offenses against such nationals committed by foreigners on foreign territory. The protective principle and passive personality are the legal doctrines that justify these assertions of prescriptive jurisdiction.

3. *Protective Principle*

Restatement

Section 402(3). Bases of Jurisdiction to Prescribe

Subject to §403, a state has jurisdiction to prescribe law with respect to . . .
(3) certain conduct outside its territory by persons not its nationals that is directed against the security of the state or against a limited class of other state interests.

Comment

f. The protective principle. Subsection (3) restates the protective principle of jurisdiction. International law recognizes the right of a state to punish a limited class of offenses committed outside its territory by persons who are not its nationals — offenses directed against the security of the state or other offenses threatening the integrity of governmental functions that are generally recognized as crimes by developed legal systems, e.g., espionage, counterfeiting of the state's seal or currency, falsification of official documents, as well as perjury before consular officials, and conspiracy to violate the immigration or customs laws. The protective principle may be seen as a special application of the effects principle, but it has been treated as an independent basis of jurisdiction. The protective principle does not support application to foreign nationals of laws against political expression, such as libel of the state or of the chief of state.

United States v. Romero-Galue

U.S. Court of Appeals
757 F.2d 1147 (11th Cir. 1985)

TJOFLAT, Circuit Judge:
Section 955a(c) of Title 21 of the United States Code makes it a crime "for any person on board any vessel within the customs waters of the United States to knowingly or intentionally . . . possess with intent to . . . distribute" marijuana. This appeal questions whether the Congress, in enacting this statute, intended to reach the possession of marijuana by foreigners aboard a foreign vessel on the high seas.[1] The

---

1. The high seas lie seaward of a nation's territorial sea, which is the band of water that extends up to three miles out from the coast. No nation may assert sovereignty over the high seas. [The United States and almost all other countries now recognize a territorial sea of twelve rather than three nautical miles. (See Chapter 9.)—EDS.]

district court held that Congress did not so intend and dismissed the indictment. We reverse.

I

On January 7, 1984, the U.S. Coast Guard cutter *Escape,* while patrolling an area in the Caribbean Sea known as the Mysteriosa Bank of the Yucatan Pass [about 350 miles from any U.S. territory], a thoroughfare used to transport marijuana from Colombia, South America to the United States, sited a shrimp boat, the *El Don,* lying dead in the water, apparently having engine trouble. The Coast Guard suspected that the *El Don* was a smuggling vessel; she was not rigged for fishing, flew no flag, and bore no markings indicating her home port. Exercising the "right of approach,"[3] the *Escape* pulled alongside the *El Don,* and several Coast Guardsmen boarded her to examine her registration papers and determine her identity. In the course of accomplishing this, the Coast Guardsmen discovered a cargo in excess of four and one-half tons of marijuana in the vessel's hold.

The Coast Guardsmen determined that the *El Don* was of Panamanian registry. This information was relayed to the U.S. State Department which, in turn, communicated with the Panamanian government. Thereafter, the Coast Guard, presumably with Panama's approval, instructed the *Escape* to seize the *El Don* and its crew and to take them to Key West, Florida for prosecution. The *Escape* followed this instruction.

On January 20, 1984, in the Southern District of Florida, the *El Don*'s crew, the appellees here, were indicted under the Marijuana on the High Seas Act of 1980. . . . The District Court found that count II failed to state an offense because the defendants' possession of marijuana had taken place on a foreign vessel located on the high seas, i.e., beyond the territorial waters of the United States, and section 955a(c) did not reach such conduct. The government now appeals.

Section 955a(c) states:

> It is unlawful for any person on board any vessel within the customs waters of the United States to knowingly or intentionally . . . possess with intent to . . . distribute [marijuana].

The "customs waters of the United States" are defined as:

> The term "customs waters" means, in the case of a foreign vessel subject to a treaty or other arrangement between a foreign government and the United States enabling or permitting the authorities of the United States to board, examine, search, seize, or otherwise to enforce upon such vessel upon the high seas the laws of the United States, the waters within such distance of the coast of the United States as the said authorities are or may be so enabled or permitted by such treaty or arrangement and, in the case of every other vessel, the waters [within 12 miles]. . . .

---

3. The "right of approach" is a doctrine of international maritime common law that bestows a nation's warship with the authority to hail and board an unidentified vessel to ascertain its nationality. If suspicions as to the vessel's nationality persist, as they well may even after the captain has declared her nation of registry, the inquiring nation may board the vessel and search for registration papers or other identification in order to verify the vessel's nationality. The "right of approach" is codified by article 22 of the Convention on the High Seas. . . .

Congress' goal when it enacted section 955a(c) of the Marijuana on the High Seas Act was not unlike the one Congress had in mind when it passed the Anti-Smuggling Act; both statutes authorize the prosecution of smugglers hovering on the high seas beyond the twelve mile limit. Under section 955a(c), the government can now reach narcotics smugglers aboard vessels of nontreaty nations within twelve miles of our coast and those aboard vessels of treaty nations within the area on the high seas designated by treaty or other arrangement. Whether such a treaty or other arrangement existed between the United States and Panama concerning the *El Don* is a mixed question of fact and law which the government should be entitled to address at trial.

The defendants argue Congress did not intend that "customs waters" be established in areas as remote as the one in which the *El Don* was seized, because this would transgress principles of international law. It is true that Congress did not intend to transgress international law, it limited the reach of the Marijuana on the High Seas Act, declaring that the Act was "designed to prohibit all acts of illicit trafficking in controlled substances on the high seas which the United States can reach under international law." This limitation, however, would not have precluded the designation, by treaty or other arrangement, of the place where the *El Don* was seized as "customs waters."

Nothing in international law prohibits two nations from entering into a treaty, which may be amended by other arrangement, to extend the customs waters and the reach of the domestic law of one of the nations into the high seas. . . Even absent a treaty or arrangement, the United States could, under the "protective principle" of international law, prosecute foreign nationals on foreign vessels on the high seas for possession of narcotics. The protective principle permits a nation to assert jurisdiction over a person whose conduct outside the nation's territory threatens the nation's security or could potentially interfere with the operation of its governmental functions. The defendants' argument is thus without merit. Count II of the indictment stated a section 955a(c) offense, and the district court erred in dismissing it.

Notes and Questions

1. Traditionally the protective principle justified the extraterritorial application of visa fraud and counterfeiting laws. How is *Romero* different? Is it significantly different from *Postal* (above, page 170)?

2. Note the last paragraph of the *Romero* opinion. Even accepting the protective principle, what is the basis in the statute for upholding the indictment? Should the indictment stand even if a defendant's possession of marijuana was outside 12 miles and there were no treaty or other arrangements with the flag state? Or, more generally, is the court in effect allowing criminal liability to be imposed on a defendant in the absence of a governing statute? Since early times, the U.S. Supreme Court has held that there cannot be federal crimes in the absence of a statute, for example, United States v. Hudson & Goodwin, 11 U.S. (7 Cranch) 32, 34 (1812); United States v. Coolidge, 14 U.S. (1 Wheat) 415, 416-417 (1816).

3. Can exterritorial application of antitrust laws be justified under the protective principle? Can U.S. laws against foreign terrorists acting abroad be justified under the protective principle? Should there be some requirement that the terrorists

are intending to have an effect within the United States and/or that the effect needs to be more than a trivial one — that is, substantial? If so, does the protective principle differ from the effects test under the territorial principle? See Restatement section 402, cmt. *f*: "The protective principle may be seen as a special application of the effects principle, . . . but it has been treated as an independent basis of jurisdiction."

4. Does the dictum in the last paragraph of *Romero* show that Professor Starke is correct to assert that there is no limit imposed by international law on prescriptive jurisdiction?

5. The history of international law-based efforts to control drugs dates back at least to the 1912 International Opium Convention. In 1988 the U.N. General Assembly recommended by consensus the U.N. Convention Against Illicit Traffic in Narcotic Drugs and Psychotropic Substances, reproduced at 28 I.L.M. 493 (1989). The United States adhered to the Convention in 1990. As of January 2003, 167 countries were parties to the Convention. The Convention requires each signatory to adopt domestic law criminalizing a defined list of offenses, including money laundering; to provide for confiscation of assets and extradition; and to prohibit trade in prescribed chemicals.

4. Passive Personality

The comment to section 402 of the Restatement of Foreign Relations Law states:

Restatement Section 402

Comment

g. The passive personality principle. The passive personality principle asserts that a state may apply law — particularly criminal law — to an act committed outside its territory by a person not its national where the victim of the act was its national. The principle has not been generally accepted for ordinary torts or cimes, but it is increasingly accepted as applied to terrorist and other organized attacks on a state's nationals by reason of their nationality, or to assassination of a state's diplomatic representatives or other officials.

United States v. Columba-Collela

U.S. Court of Appeals
604 F.2d 356 (5th Cir. 1979)

WISDOM, Circuit Judge:

In this case, unfortunately, the legally correct result produces something like declaring an open season on motor vehicles in American border towns — provided that the recipient of the stolen vehicles escapes the clutches of Mexican and Canadian law. Nevertheless, for lack of jurisdiction, we must reverse the district court's judgment entering defendant Francesco Columba-Colella's plea of guilty to the offense of receiving a stolen vehicle in foreign commerce in violation of 18 U.S.C. §2313. The criminal offense occurred in Mexico.

I

On the evening of August 21, 1978, Francesco Columba-Colella met a young man named Keith in Curley's Bar in Juarez, Mexico. The two struck up a conversation and became casual friends. Two days later they met again by chance at five-thirty in the afternoon on a Juarez street. Keith told Francesco he wanted to sell a car, and Francesco, who had lived in Juarez for at least two years, responded that he knew someone who might be interested in buying it. Keith then informed him for the first time that the car had been stolen in El Paso, Texas, and offered Francesco half the proceeds of any sale he could arrange. Francesco assented, took the keys to the car, a Ford Fairmont, and agreed to meet Keith the next day at 2:00 P.M. in The Kentucky Bar in Juarez. The meeting was not to take place. Later, the same evening, as Francesco was approaching the car with his wife, he was arrested by Mexican police.

The defendant, who was nineteen years old, resided in Juarez, where he lived with the Mexican woman whom he had married in 1976. He is a British citizen who was not employed in the United States and did not own property in the United States. He intended to reside permanently in Mexico and become a Mexican citizen.

After the defendant's motion to dismiss was denied, Columba-Colella pleaded guilty, but reserved the right to appeal the jurisdictional issue. The trial court committed him to the custody of the Attorney General for five years.

II

The only question raised on appeal is whether the lower court had jurisdiction over the case. Had the defendant been a United States citizen, there would be no jurisdictional problem, for a country may supervise and regulate the acts of its citizens both within and without its territory.

When an allegedly criminal act is performed by an alien on foreign soil courts in the United States have long held that if jurisdiction is to be extended over that act, it must be supported by either the *protective* or the *objective territorial* theory. Under the protective theory, which does not bear on the resolution of the case before us, a country's legislature is competent to enact laws and, assuming physical power over the defendant, its courts have jurisdiction to enforce criminal laws wherever and by whomever the act is performed that threatens the country's security or directly interferes with its governmental operations. A state/nation is competent, for example, to punish one who has successfully defrauded its treasury, no matter where the fraudulent scheme was perpetrated.

The objective territorial theory looks not to interference with governmental interests but to objective effects within the sovereign state. The theory requires that before a state may attach criminal consequences to an extraterritorial act, the act must be intended to have an effect within the state. As Mr. Justice Holmes announced the theory, in the context of an interstate extradition:

> Acts done outside a jurisdiction, but intended to produce and producing effects within it, justify a state in punishing the cause of the harm as if he had been present at the effect, if the state should succeed in getting him within its power.

Strassheim v. Daily, 1911, 221 U.S. 280, 284-85. Assume, for example, that persons or their agents conspire to rent a boat in Miami, sail it beyond United States coastal waters, and load it with a cargo of illegal drugs. Then, en route to a United States port but while still on the high seas, the conspirators are apprehended. This country may under the objective territorial theory apply its drug laws to punish them if it can establish intent to violate those laws.

III

There is no basis for jurisdiction over the defendant in the present case. He is not a United States citizen. He has not threatened the security of this country or interfered with its governmental function. Although the objective territorial theory applies, the fact that no conspiracy has been alleged means that the theory does not support jurisdiction in the case.

Had a conspiracy been demonstrated, the defendant could be said to have been engaged in a criminal enterprise, an essential element of which, the theft, occurred in the United States. Had Columba-Colella's intent anticipated and embraced the car theft in Texas, that act could be imputed to him. And since the United States is competent to proscribe the theft of property within its borders, it would then have had the jurisdiction it asserts in this case.

The defendant did not conspire to steal the car, and the theft in no way depended on any act or intent of the defendant. Whatever injury the owner of the car suffered was complete before Columba-Colella's chance meeting with Keith on the street in Juarez on the afternoon of August 22, 1978, and the agreement their meeting produced. To put it differently, though Columba-Colella's agreement to fence the car followed Keith's crime, his act, which may have been a crime under Mexican law, is legally unrelated to the prior crime. His act was no constituent element of Keith's act and is not made so by the coincidence that the property subject to their agreement belonged to a citizen of the jurisdiction in which the theft occurred.

The district judge relied on United States v. Fernandez, 5 Cir. 1974, 496 F.2d at 1294, in finding he had jurisdiction over the case. In *Fernandez,* the defendant was charged with possessing, forging, and uttering stolen United States Treasury checks. The defendant argued that this Court lacked jurisdiction because all the criminal acts involved were alleged to have taken place not in the United States but in Mexico. In finding that there was jurisdiction, we noted that the defendant's acts "prevent[ed] the normal disbursement of Social Security Funds to those lawfully entitled to receive such funds." 496 F.2d at 1296. . . . The district court's reliance on *Fernandez* is misplaced in this case, for here there was no interference with a governmental function, and therefore no reason to invoke the protective theory.

IV

There is no question, of course, that Columba-Colella's conduct somehow affected a United States citizen. Had he been successful in his enterprise, he would have prevented the stolen car from finding its way back to its owner. But that an act affects the citizen of a state is not a sufficient basis for that state to assert jurisdiction over the act. It is difficult to distinguish the present case from one in which the defendant had attempted not to fence a stolen car but instead to pick the pockets of American tourists in Acapulco. No one would argue either that Congress would be competent to prohibit such conduct or that the courts of the United States would have jurisdiction to enforce such a prohibition were the offender in their control. Indeed, Congress would not be competent to attach criminal sanctions to the murder of an American by a foreign national in a foreign country, even if the victim returned home and succumbed to his injuries.

These hypothetical cases involve criminal conduct that takes place wholly within a country, and whose character must therefore be determined by the law of the place where the act was done. The present case is similar. We therefore follow the method set out in American Banana Co. v. United Fruit Co., 1909, 213 U.S. 347, 357. We find that because the defendant's act in this case is beyond its competence to proscribe, Congress did not intend to assert jurisdiction here under 18 U.S.C. §2313. . . .

V

The practical problem we face is that our decision may encourage car thefts in border towns. Two facts limit this encouragement. In the ordinary case, as the United States Attorney averred in oral argument before this Court, a conspiracy will be charged and proved. When this is possible, there is no jurisdictional problem. And even where a conspiracy cannot be shown, each sovereign may punish the wrongful act committed in its territory: when we release Columba-Colella, he will be subject to whatever sanctions are applicable under the law of Mexico.

The result we reach is part of the price a nation must pay to support mutuality of comity between sovereign nations.

The judgment is reversed and the charge is dismissed.

Notes and Questions

1. If Congress passes a statute without ascertainable legislative intent on extraterritorial application, making it a felony to murder an American citizen, would the courts apply it in cases involving murders abroad? Which crime is more prevalent — hostage murder, ordinary murder, or fencing stolen cars? Does it make any sense to conclude that Congress may legitimately punish the first crime (which Congress has done, as discussed below), but not the more common last two?

2. Do you agree with Judge Wisdom's fatalism ("unfortunately, the legally correct result produces something like declaring an open season on motor vehicles in American border towns")? Is that what Congress intended?

3. Why did Mexico not protest in this case? In the absence of such a protest, why should a criminal defendant be able to raise this supposed violation of international law?

4. As enacted in 1948 and continuing through 1984, the applicable statute (18 U.S.C. §2313) in the case above provided:

> Whoever receives, conceals, stores, barters, sells, or disposes of any motor vehicle or aircraft, moving as, or which is a part of, or which constitutes interstate or foreign

commerce, knowing the same to be stolen, shall be fined not more than $5,000 or imprisoned not more than five years, or both.

Could the court have interpreted the statute to cover the alleged offense under the passive personality principle? Should such a principle extend to receipt in a foreign country by an alien of a car stolen in the United States?

5. In 1984 Congress amended the statute to read:

> Whoever receives, *possesses*, conceals, stores, barters, sells, or disposes of any motor vehicle or aircraft, *which has crossed a State or United States boundary after being stolen*, knowing the same to have been stolen, shall be fined. . . . [Emphasis indicates 1984 changes.]

Given the same set of facts as in *Columba-Collela* but assuming they occur in 1985, should the court uphold the jurisdiction of the trial court? Must it? Note that U.S. law requires that:

> Each justice or judge of the United States shall take the following oath or affirmation before performing the duties of his office: "I, _____ _____, do solemnly swear (or affirm) that I will administer justice without respect to persons, and do equal right to the poor and to the rich, and that I will faithfully and impartially discharge and perform all the duties incumbent upon me as _____ under the Constitution and laws of the United States. So help me God." [21 U.S.C. §453.]

6. In 1984, in order to implement the Convention Against the Taking of Hostages, Congress passed legislation, which provides (as amended through 2002):

18 U.S.C. §1203. Hostage Taking

(a) Except as provided in subsection (b) of this section, whoever, whether inside or outside the United States, seizes or detains and threatens to kill, to injure, or to continue to detain another person in order to compel a third person or a governmental organization to do or abstain from doing any act as an explicit or implicit condition for the release of the person detained, or attempts (or conspires) to do so, shall be punished by imprisonment for any term of years or for life and, if the death of any person results, shall be punished by death or life imprisonment.

(b)(1) It is not an offense under this section if the conduct required for the offense occurred outside the United States unless —

(A) the offender or the person seized or detained is a national of the United States;

(B) the offender is found in the United States; or

(C) the governmental organization sought to be compelled is the Government of the United States.

(2) It is not an offense under this section if the conduct required for the offense occurred inside the United States, each alleged offender and each person seized or detained are nationals of the United States, and each alleged offender is found in the United States, unless the governmental organization sought to be compelled is the Government of the United States.

(a) What theories of prescriptive jurisdiction are reflected in section 1203(b)? Note the two different theories reflected in subsection (b)(1)(A).

(b) What interest does the U.S. government have in criminalizing acts wholly outside the United States solely on the basis that the offender is "found" in the United States? (The Hostages Convention provides for this assertion of prescriptive jurisdiction.)

(c) Could Congress have deleted subsection (b) consistent with international law? U.S. constitutional law?

(d) Would there be any international or constitutional law problems with extending prescriptive jurisdiction by making it a crime to kill an American anywhere in the world?

7. Would the *Columba-Collela* case, if correct, mean that the Hostage Act is not applicable outside the United States? Does the Hostage Act clearly intend to cover crimes outside the United States?

8. See also section 1605 (a) (7) of the FSIA and the *Alejandre* case, supra, page 588.

9. In a 2002 case, the U.S. court of appeals affirmed the conviction of a foreign citizen who, while working as an employee aboard a foreign cruise ship, engaged in sexual contact with a 12-year-old passenger, who was an American citizen, while the ship was in Mexican territorial waters. The cruise ship departed from and returned to one of California's harbors. Upon her return, the young female victim missed several days of school and underwent psychological counseling. The defendant had argued that the United States did not have extraterritorial jurisdiction over the crime.

The applicable U.S. statute, 18 U.S.C. §2344(a), makes it a criminal offense to "knowingly engage in a sexual act with another person who has attained the age of 12 years but has not attained the age of 16 years." This statute applies in the "special maritime and territorial jurisdiction of the United States," which is defined elsewhere as including, "[t]o the extent permitted by international law, any foreign vessel during a voyage having a scheduled departure from or arrival in the United States with respect to an offense committed by or against a national of the United States" [18 U.S.C. §7(8)]. The court of appeals found that international law supported extraterritorial jurisdiction in this case under the territorial principle and the passive personality principle. United States v. Neil, 312 F.3d 419 (9th Cir. 2002).

What would the court's reasoning likely have been? Do you agree? (For further discussion on the law of the sea rules regarding ships, see Chapter 9 at 839.)

10. In 1992, as part of a law making acts of international terrorism federal crimes, Congress enacted provisions allowing U.S. nationals to recover treble damages and attorneys' fees for injury to person, property, or business by reason of an act of international terrorism. As amended through 2002, the relevant provisions read:

18 U.S.C. §2331.   Definitions

As used in this chapter . . .—

(1) the term "international terrorism" means activities that—

(A) involve violent acts or acts dangerous to human life that are a violation of the criminal laws of the United States or of any State, or that would be a criminal violation if committed within the jurisdiction of the United States or of any State;

(B) appear to the intended—

(i) to intimidate or coerce a civilian population;

(ii) to influence the policy of a government by intimidation or coercion; or

(iii) to affect the conduct of a government by mass destruction, assassination, or kidnapping; and

(C) occur primarily outside the territorial jurisdiction of the United States, or transcend national boundaries in terms of the means by which they are accomplished, the persons they appear intended to intimidate or coerce, or the locale in which their perpetrators operate or seek asylum. . . .

(4) the term "act of war" means any act occurring in the course of—

(A) declared war;

(B) armed conflict, whether or not war has been declared, between two or more nations; or

(C) armed conflict between military forces of any origin; and

(5) the term "domestic terrorism" means activities that—

(A) involve acts dangerous to human life that are a violation of the criminal laws of the United States or of any State;

(B) appear to be intended—

(i) to intimidate or coerce a civilian population;

(ii) to influence the policy of a government by intimidation or coercion; or

(iii) to affect the conduct of a government by mass destruction, assassination, or kidnapping; and

(C) occur primarily within the territorial jurisdiction of the United States.

18 U.S.C. §2333. Civil Remedies

(a) Action and jurisdiction.—Any national of the United States injured in his or her person, property, or business by reason of an act of international terrorism, or his or her estate, survivors, or heirs, may sue therefore in any appropriate district court of the United States and shall recover threefold the damages he or she sustains and the cost of the suit, including attorney's fees. . . .

18 U.S.C. §2336. Other Limitations

(a) Acts of war. No action shall be maintained under section 2333 of this title for injury or loss by reason of an act of war.

18 U.S.C. §2337. Suits against Government Officials

No action shall be maintained under section 2333 of this title against—

(1) the United States, an agency of the United States, or an officer or employee of the United States or any agency thereof acting within his or her official capacity or under color of legal authority; or

(2) a foreign state, an agency of a foreign state, or an officer or employee of a foreign state or an agency thereof acting within his or her official capacity or under color of legal authority.

(a) What theories of prescriptive jurisdiction are reflected in section 2333 above?

(b) Were the attacks of September 11, 2001, an act of international terrorism (for which a civil remedy is available under section 2333) or of domestic terrorism?

(c) Do the attacks of September 11 come under the limitation for acts of war under section 2336?

(d) The scope of this statute was considered in Boim v. Quranic Literacy Institute, 219 F.3d 1000 (7th Cir. 2002). There, the parents of an American citizen killed in Israel allegedly by Hamas terrorists sued various organizations and individuals who supported Hamas. (Hamas has been designated a foreign terrorist organization by the U.S. government.) Among the organizations sued were two U.S.-based charitable organizations.

The court held that merely making financial contributions to a terrorist organization does not by itself give rise to a civil cause of action under section 2333. The court nevertheless held that such financial contributions could result in civil liability under section 2333 under certain circumstances. The court noted that Congress had criminalized the knowing provision of material support or resources to terrorist organizations (see 18 U.S.C. §§2339A and 2339B, not quoted above), and that "it would be counterintuitive to conclude that Congress imposed criminal liability [in those two sections] on those who financed international terrorism, but did not intend to impose civil liability on those same persons through section 2333." Id. at 1014. The court also reasoned that Congress had implicitly incorporated common law tort principles allowing for aiding and abetting liability. Liability under the statute for financial contributions does not violate the First Amendment, the court concluded, "so long as the plaintiffs are able to prove that the defendants knew about the organization's illegal activity, desired to help that activity succeed and engaged in some act of helping." Id. at 1028.

5. *Universal Jurisdiction*

Restatement

Section 404. Universal Jurisdiction to Define and Punish Certain Offenses

A state has jurisdiction to define and prescribe punishment for certain offenses recognized by the community of nations as of universal concern, such as piracy, slave trade, attacks on or hijacking of aircraft, genocide, war crimes, and perhaps certain acts of terrorism, even where none of the bases of jurisdiction indicated in §402 is present.

Comment

a. Expanding class of universal offenses. This section, and the corresponding section concerning jurisdiction to adjudicate, §423, recognize that international law permits any state to apply its laws to punish certain offenses although the state has no links of territory with the offense, or of nationality with the offender (or even the victim). Universal jurisdiction over the specified offenses is a result of universal condemnation of those activities and general interest in cooperating to suppress them, as reflected in widely-accepted international agreements and resolutions of international organizations. These offenses are subject to universal jurisdiction as a matter of customary law. Universal jurisdiction for additional offenses is provided by international agreements, but it remains to be determined whether universal jurisdiction over a particular offense has become customary law for states not party to such an agreement. A universal offense is generally not subject to limitations of time.

There has been wide condemnation of terrorism but international agreements to punish it have not . . . been widely adhered to, principally because of inability to agree on a definition of the offense. . . . Universal jurisdiction is increasingly accepted for certain acts of terrorism, such as assaults on the life or physical integrity of diplomatic personnel, kidnapping, and indiscriminate violent assaults on people at large.

b. Universal jurisdiction not limited to criminal law. In general, jurisdiction on the basis of universal interests has been exercised in the form of criminal law, but international law does not preclude the application of non-criminal law on this basis, for example, by providing a remedy in tort or restitution for victims of piracy.

Curtis A. Bradley, Universal Jurisdiction and U.S. Law
2001 U. Chi. Legal F. 323, 326-333 (2001)

[G]iven well-settled doctrines governing the relationship between international law and U.S. law, Congress, rather than international law or the federal courts, has ultimate control over the exercise of universal jurisdiction by the United States. . . .

There are a number of federal criminal statutes that rely, at least in part, on the universal jurisdiction concept. As one might expect, there is a federal piracy statute, which states simply that "whoever, on the high seas, commits the crime of piracy as defined by the law of nations, and is afterwards brought into or found in the United States, shall be imprisoned for life.". . .

Of more contemporary relevance are a number of terrorism and human rights-related statutes that invoke a form of universal jurisdiction. These statutes criminalize certain acts, such as hostage-taking, aircraft hijacking, and aircraft sabotage, committed outside the United States by citizens of other countries, as long as the offender is "found" within the United States. There is also a statute, enacted in 1994, that criminalizes acts of official torture committed in foreign nations by foreign citizens, although there are not yet any reported decisions applying that statute. Perhaps surprisingly, the federal genocide statute does not assert universal jurisdiction; rather, the offense must occur in the United States or the offender must be a U.S. national. Nor does the federal war crimes statute, enacted in 1996, assert universal jurisdiction. Rather, it requires that the person committing the war crime or the victim of the war crime be a member of the U.S. armed forces or a U.S. national.

In considering Congress's reliance on universal jurisdiction, another relevant statute is the Maritime Drug Law Enforcement Act, which comes close to asserting universal jurisdiction and which has generated a number of decisions addressing Congress's authority to regulate extraterritoriality. The Act makes it "unlawful for any person . . . on board a vessel subject to the jurisdiction of the United States . . . to possess with intent to manufacture or distribute, a controlled substance." The Act includes in its definition of a "vessel subject to the jurisdiction of the United States" both "a vessel without nationality" and "a vessel registered in a foreign nation where the flag nation has consented or waived objection to the enforcement of United States law by the United States." There is no express requirement in these situations of a nexus with the United States, and most courts have declined to read such a requirement into the statute. . . .

It is not clear that all of the above exercises of jurisdiction by Congress are consistent with international law. For example, the degree to which universal jurisdiction applies to acts of terrorism is still contested and uncertain. Conversely, international law may in some instances authorize more jurisdiction than is currently reflected in federal statutes — with respect to genocide, for example. Ultimately, however, the exercise of prescriptive jurisdiction by the United States is determined by Congress, not international law or the federal courts. This is so for several reasons.

First, since the early 1800s, it has been settled in the United States that there is no federal common law of crimes. Rather, federal criminal liability can be created in the United States only by a domestic enactment. . . . Nor, as a matter of public policy, will U.S. courts apply foreign criminal law.

Second, courts and scholars have long assumed that, for separation-of-powers and accountability reasons, treaties may not create domestic criminal liability. Thus, even when a treaty calls for the criminalization of conduct or for the exercise of jurisdiction over offenders, the treaty does not by itself create criminal liability under U.S. law. The treaty provisions, in other words, are "non-self-executing" and take effect domestically only when Congress implements them. As a result, a treaty granting universal jurisdiction to prosecute certain crimes does not by itself allow such prosecutions in the United States.

Finally, U.S. law has long allowed federal statutes to supersede earlier inconsistent international law. The Supreme Court has held that when there is a conflict between a federal statute and a treaty, the later in time prevails as a matter of U.S. law. And the lower courts uniformly have held that when there is a conflict between a federal statute and customary international law, the statute prevails, apparently without regard to timing. As a result, Congress is free to override the limitations of international law, including the international law of prescriptive jurisdiction, when enacting a criminal statute. Congress, not international law or the federal courts, ultimately controls the exercise of universal criminal jurisdiction in the United States. . . .

Despite Congress's control over U.S. exercises of universal jurisdiction, the international law of universal jurisdiction may be relevant to the interpretation of federal criminal statutes. Under the *Charming Betsy* canon of construction, courts attempt to construe federal statutes, where reasonably possible, so that they do not violate international law. For a variety of reasons, including a desire to avoid conflicts with international law, courts also generally presume that federal statutes do not apply extraterritorially.

These interpretive principles were applied recently in the United States v. Bin Laden embassy bombing case in New York [discussed below]. The defendants in that case challenged the extraterritorial application of numerous criminal statutes. In evaluating their challenge, the district court considered both the *Charming Betsy* canon and the presumption against extraterritoriality and ultimately dismissed several charges on the ground that Congress did not intend to apply the statutes in question extraterritorially. In particular, the court concluded that federal statutes authorizing criminal jurisdiction over acts committed within "the special maritime and territorial jurisdiction of the United States" did not authorize the United States to exercise concurrent criminal jurisdiction over U.S. embassy premises in other countries, in part because the court believed such jurisdiction would violate both international law and the presumption against extraterritoriality.

The influence of these interpretive rules should not be overstated. The *Charming Betsy* canon does not apply when the reach of a statute is clear. As one court explained in rejecting a prescriptive jurisdiction challenge to a broad anti-terrorism statute, "our duty is to enforce the Constitution, laws, and treaties of the United States, not to conform the law of the land to norms of customary international law." Nor does the *Charming Betsy* canon require the harmonization of U.S. law and international law; it requires simply the avoidance of conflict. As a result, it is not a mandate for extending a statute to the fullest reaches allowed by the international law of universal jurisdiction. In addition, courts are likely to give deference to the views of the executive branch regarding the content of international law.

As for the presumption against extraterritoriality, its effect is limited because it is not applied to all federal statutes. The Supreme Court has not applied it, for example, in the area of antitrust law. More importantly, the Court suggested, in United States v. Bowman, [260 U.S. 94 (1922)], that the presumption against extraterritoriality does not apply to criminal statutes that are, by their nature, focused on extraterritorial matters. As the Court explained, some criminal statutes "are, as a class, not logically dependent on their locality for the government's jurisdiction, but are enacted because of the right of the government to defend itself against obstruction, or fraud wherever perpetrated." [Id. at 98.] Exercises of universal criminal jurisdiction may be especially likely to fall within this exception. Indeed, the district court in *Bin Laden* relied on this exception as a basis for upholding many of the charges. In any event, the presumption against extraterritoriality, like the *Charming Betsy* canon, can be overcome by clear legislative intent.

In sum, the exercise of universal jurisdiction by the United States is ultimately determined by Congress, not international law or the federal courts. While international law may play some role in the interpretation of congressional enactments, its influence is likely to be modest in this area, and, in any event, it cannot be used to override clear legislative intent. . . .

United States v. Usama Bin Laden

U.S. District Court
92 F. Supp. 2d 189 (S.D.N.Y. 2000)

The sixth superseding indictment in this case ("the Indictment") charges fifteen defendants with conspiracy to murder United States nationals, to use weapons of mass destruction against United States nationals, to destroy United States buildings and property, and to destroy United States defense utilities. The Indictment also charges defendants Mohamed Sadeek Odeh, Mohamed Rashed Daoud al-'Owhali, and Khalfan Khamis Mohamed, among others, with numerous crimes in connection with the August 1998 bombings of the United States Embassies in Nairobi, Kenya, and Dar es Salaam, Tanzania, including 223 counts of murder. . . . Six of the Defendants are presently in the custody of the Bureau of Prisons: Mamdouh Mahmud Salim, Ali Mohamed, Wadih El Hage, Mohamed Rashed Daoud Al-Owhali, Khalfan Khamis Mohamed, and Mohamed Sadeek Odeh ("Odeh"). Presently before the Court is Odeh's Motion to Dismiss Counts 5-244 for Lack of Jurisdiction, in which the other defendants join. For the reasons given below, we grant Odeh's Motion as to Counts 234, 235, 240, and 241, but deny it as to Counts 5-233, 236-239, and 242-244.

DISCUSSION

Odeh argues that most of the counts charged in the Indictment must be dismissed by this Court because they are based on statutes that are inapplicable to the acts he is alleged to have performed. In support of this position, Odeh advances six arguments, which we address seriatim.

1. EXTRATERRITORIAL APPLICATION

Odeh argues that Counts 5-8, 11-237, and 240-244 must be dismissed because (a) they concern acts allegedly performed by Odeh and his co-defendants outside United States territory, yet (b) are based on statutes that were not intended by Congress to regulate conduct outside United States territory. More specifically, Odeh argues that "the following statutes that form the basis for the indictment fail clearly and unequivocally to regulate the conduct of foreign nationals for conduct outside the territorial boundaries of the United States: (1) 18 U.S.C. §930; (2) 18 U.S.C. §844; 18 U.S.C. §1111; 18 U.S.C. §2155; 18 U.S.C. §1114; [18 U.S.C. §924(c);] and 18 U.S.C. §114." Odeh's Memo. at 7. Whether Congress intended several of these provisions (viz., Sections 844(f), (h), and (n); 930(c), and 2155) to apply extraterritorially present issues of first impression.

A. General Principles of Extraterritorial Application

It is well-established that Congress has the power to regulate conduct performed outside United States territory. See EEOC v. Arabian Am. Oil Co., 499 U.S. 244, 248 (1991) ("Congress has the authority to enforce its laws beyond the territorial boundaries of the United States."). It is equally well-established, however, that courts are to presume that Congress has not exercised this power — i.e., that statutes apply only to acts performed within United States territory — unless Congress manifests an intent to reach acts performed outside United States territory. See Sale v. Haitian Ctrs. Council, Inc., 509 U.S. 155 (1993) ("Acts of Congress normally do not have extraterritorial application unless such an intent is clearly manifested."). . . . This "clear manifestation" requirement does not require that extraterritorial coverage should be found only if the statute itself explicitly provides for extraterritorial application. Rather, courts should consider "all available evidence about the meaning" of the statute, e.g., its text, structure, and legislative history. *Sale,* 509 U.S. at 177. . . .

Furthermore, the Supreme Court has established a limited exception to this standard approach for "criminal statutes which are, as a class, not logically dependent on their locality for the Government's jurisdiction, but are enacted because of the right of the Government to defend itself against obstruction, or fraud wherever perpetrated, especially if committed by its own citizens, officers, or agents." United States v. Bowman, 260 U.S. 94, 98 (1922). As regards statutes of this type, courts may infer the requisite intent "from the nature of the offense" described in the statute, and thus need not examine its legislative history. Id. The Court further observed that "to limit the [] locus [of such a statute] to the strictly territorial jurisdiction [of the United States] would be greatly to curtail the scope and usefulness of the statute and leave open a large immunity for frauds as easily committed by citizens on the high seas and in foreign countries as at home." Id. *Bowman* concerned a statute making it illegal knowingly to "present[] a false claim against the United States, . . . to any officer of the civil, military or naval service or to any department. . . ." Id. at 101. In concluding that Congress intended this statute to apply extraterritorially, the Court reasoned that it "cannot [be] supposed that when Congress enacted the statute or amended it, it did not have in mind that a wide field for such frauds upon the Government was in private and public vessels of the United States on the high seas and in foreign ports beyond the land jurisdiction of the United States. . . ." Id. at 102.

Odeh argues that *Bowman* is "not controlling precedent" because it "involved the application of [a] penal statute[] to United States citizens," i.e., not to foreign nationals such as himself. This argument is unavailing for three reasons. First, . . . [g]iven that foreign nationals are in at least as good a position to perform extraterritorial conduct as are United States nationals, it would make little sense to restrict such statutes to United States nationals. To paraphrase *Bowman,* "to limit [a statute's coverage to United States nationals] would be greatly to curtail the scope and usefulness of the statute and leave open a large immunity for frauds as easily committed [by foreign nationals] as [by United States nationals]." *Bowman,* 260 U.S. at 98.

Second, the Courts of Appeals—focusing on *Bowman*'s general rule rather than its peculiar facts—have applied this rule to reach conduct by foreign nationals on foreign soil. For example, the Court of Appeals for this Circuit has held that 18 U.S.C. §1546, which criminalizes the making of false statements with respect to travel documents, was intended by Congress to apply extraterritorially to the conduct of foreign nationals. See United States v. Pizzarusso, 388 F.2d 8, 9 (2d Cir.), cert. denied, 392 U.S. 936 (1968). . . . Correlatively, no court, to date, has refused to apply the *Bowman* rule on the ground that the defendant was a foreign national.

Third, the irrelevance of the defendant's nationality to the *Bowman* rule is reinforced by a consideration of the relationship between this rule and the principles of extraterritorial jurisdiction recognized by international law.[8] Under international

---

8. As Odeh correctly points out, the question whether "Congress intended that [a] statute have extraterritorial effect," is distinct from and precedent to the question of whether extraterritorial application of the statute accords with international law. Odeh's Memo. at 7 n.3. Our purpose here is merely to explain why the lower federal courts have viewed the extension of the *Bowman* rule to foreign nationals as unproblematic.

law, the primary basis of jurisdiction is the "subjective territorial principle," under which "a state has jurisdiction to prescribe law with respect to . . . conduct that, wholly or in substantial part, takes place within its territory." Restatement (Third) of the Foreign Relations Law of the United States §402(1)(a) (1987) . . . . International law recognizes five other principles of jurisdiction by which a state may reach conduct outside its territory: (1) the objective territorial principle; (2) the protective principle; (3) the nationality principle; (4) the passive personality principle; and (5) the universality principle. See id. at 50-81. . . . Because Congress has the power to override international law if it so chooses, see United States v. Yunis, 288 U.S. App. D.C. 129, 924 F.2d 1086, 1091 (D.C. Cir. 1991); . . . Restatement §402, cmt. i, none of these five principles places ultimate limits on Congress's power to reach extraterritorial conduct. At the same time, however, "in determining whether a statute applies extraterritorially, [courts] presume that Congress does not intend to violate principles of international law . . . [and] in the absence of an explicit Congressional directive, courts do not give extraterritorial effect to any statute that violates principles of international law." United States v. Vasquez-Velasco, 15 F.3d 833, 839 (9th Cir. 1994) (citing McCulloch v. Sociedad Nacional de Marineros de Honduras, 372 U.S. 10, 21-22 (1963)). Hence, courts that find that a given statute applies extraterritorially typically pause to note that this finding is consistent with one or more of the five principles of extraterritorial jurisdiction under international law. See, e.g., . . . Vasquez-Velasco, 15 F.3d at 841 (objective territoriality principle, protective principle, and universality principle); Benitez, 741 F.2d at 1316 (protective principle and passive personality principle) . . . .

The *Bowman* rule would appear to be most directly related to the protective principle, which, as noted, explicitly authorizes a state's exercise of jurisdiction over "conduct outside its territory by persons not its nationals." Restatement §402(3). Hence, an application of the *Bowman* rule that results in the extraterritorial application of a statute to the conduct of foreign nationals is consistent with international law. Therefore, it is not surprising that the lower courts have shown no hesitation to apply the *Bowman* rule in cases involving foreign defendants. . . .

B. 18 U.S.C. §§844, 924, 930, 1114, and 2155

In light of the preceding general principles, we find that Congress intended each of the following statutory provisions to reach conduct by foreign nationals on foreign soil: 18 U.S.C. §844(f)(1), (f)(3), (h) and (n); 18 U.S.C. §924(c); 18 U.S.C. §930(c); 18 U.S.C. §1114; and 18 U.S.C. §2155. We consider each in turn. . . .

[The court then undertakes a statutory analysis of each of the statutes under which Odeh is charged, using the *Bowman* rule. The court concludes that, with two exceptions, Congress unambiguously intended the statutes to apply extraterritorially against non-nationals. In the other two statutes, the court found that Congress expressly limited their reach to the territory of the United States, and therefore dismissed those indictments.]

II. FIFTH AMENDMENT DUE PROCESS

Odeh argues that application of several of the statutes relied on in the Indictment to the extraterritorial conduct of a foreign national such as himself violates his rights under the Due Process Clause of the Fifth Amendment. See *Larsen*, 952 F.2d at 1100 ("Congress is empowered to attach extraterritorial effect to its penal statutes so long as the statute does not violate the due process clause of the Fifth Amendment."). More specifically, Odeh argues that "there are several, related norms of due process" that would be violated by such application: (1) the rule of lenity, (2) the right to fair warning, and (3) the requirement of a sufficient nexus between his alleged conduct and the United States. We consider his arguments regarding each of these three aspects of due process seriatim. . . .

C. Sufficient Nexus

Odeh contends that, "as [he] is Jordanian, and the acts alleged in the indictment all took place on foreign soil, the connection between [him] and the United States is weak," Odeh's Reply Memo. at 18-19, i.e., the nexus between him and the United States is insufficient.

. . . The most extensive discussion of the issue appears in United States v. Davis, 905 F.2d 245 (9th Cir. 1990), cert. denied, 498 U.S. 1047 (1991). *Davis* announced that, "in order to apply extraterritorially a federal criminal statute to a defendant consistently with due process, there must be a sufficient nexus between the defendant and the United States, so that such application would not be arbitrary or fundamentally unfair." Id. at 248-49; see also United States v. Klimavicius-Viloria, 144 F.3d 1249, 1257 (9th Cir. 1998), cert. denied, 120 S. Ct. 110 (1999) (quoting World-Wide Volkswagen Corp. v. Woodson, 444 U.S. 286, 297 (1980)) ("The nexus requirement serves the same purpose as the 'minimum contacts' test in personal jurisdiction. It ensures that a United States court will assert jurisdiction only over a defendant who 'should reasonably anticipate being haled into court' in this country."). . . . *Davis* concerned the prosecution of a foreign national—arrested on the high seas—for attempting to smuggle marijuana into the United States under the Maritime Drug Law Enforcement Act, 46 U.S.C. app. §§1903 (a, j). See 905 F.2d at 247. After observing (i) that "international law principles [of extraterritorial jurisdiction] may be useful as a rough guide of whether a sufficient nexus exists between the defendant and the United States so that application of the statue in question would not violate due process," and (ii) that "where an attempted transaction is aimed at causing criminal acts within the United States, there is a sufficient basis for the United States to exercise jurisdiction," the Court held that a sufficient nexus existed because "the facts found by the district court . . . support the reasonable conclusion that [the defendant] intended to smuggle contraband into United States territory," id. (It is evident that this holding was "roughly guided" by the objective territoriality principle.)

. . . We agree that if the extraterritorial application of a statute is justified by the protective principle, such application accords with due process. Therefore, given that the extraterritorial application of Sections 844, 924, 930, and 2155 to Odeh's alleged extraterritorial conduct is justified by the protective principle, see Subsection I.B, supra, we conclude that the extraterritorial application of these statutes to Odeh's conduct satisfies due process. 707 F.2d 663, 667-68 (2d Cir.), cert denied, 463 U.S. 1215 (1983). . . .

IV.   The Passive Personality Principle

Odeh argues that (i) because, in enacting Sections 2332 and 2332a, Congress relied solely on the passive personality principle of jurisdiction and (ii) because the United States has "traditionally rejected" this principle, the counts based on these statutes should be dismissed.

There are two problems with this argument. First, the argument is a non sequitur. Given (i) that Congress clearly had the authority to enact Sections 2332 and 2332a (as established . . . above), and (ii) that the passive personality principle is "increasingly accepted as applied to terrorist and other organized attacks on a state's nationals by reason of their nationality, or to assassination of a state's diplomatic representatives or other officials," Restatement §402, cmt. g . . . it matters not that the United States "traditionally" rejected the principle.

Second, it is simply not the case that Congress predicated Sections 2332 and 2332a solely on the passive personality principle. Rather, as established [above], Congress also relied — indeed, relied primarily — on the protective principle.

For the foregoing reasons, we deny Odeh's motion to dismiss the counts based on Section 2332 and 2332a . . . insofar as this motion depends on his "passive personality" argument.

V.   Application of 18 U.S.C. §930(c) to Foreign Victims

Odeh argues that interpreting Section 930(c) to reach "the deaths of Kenyan and Tanzanian citizens [as opposed to United States citizens] would be contrary to established principles of international law." More specifically, Odeh advances the following two arguments. First, given (i) that "under 18 U.S.C. §930(c), the only arguable basis for jurisdiction over the deaths of foreign citizens is the principle of universality," (ii) that "universal jurisdiction results where there is universal condemnation of an offense, and a general interest in cooperating to suppress them, as reflected in widely accepted international agreements," and (iii) that "the universality principle does not encompass terrorist actions resulting in the deaths of individuals who are not diplomatic personnel," it follows that applying Section 930(c) to the deaths of "ordinary" foreign nationals on foreign soil would constitute a violation of international law.

There are two problems with this argument. First, because "universal jurisdiction is increasingly accepted for certain acts of terrorism, such as . . . indiscriminate violent assaults on people at large," Restatement §404, cmt. a, a plausible case could be made that extraterritorial application of Section 930(c) in this case is supported by the universality principle.

Second, it is not the case that the universality principle is the "only arguable basis for jurisdiction over the deaths of foreign citizens." As indicated by our conclusion (in Subsection I.B.3 above) that Section 930(c) is designed to protect vital United States interests, the protective principle is also an "arguable basis" for the extraterritorial application of Section 930(c). Hence, the only question is whether a statute of general application — the extraterritorial application of which is acknowledged to be justified by the protective principle — is nevertheless restricted to victims who are citizens of the nation that enacted the statute. We are aware of no authority for this proposition. Nor is such a limitation consistent with the purposes the protective principle is designed to serve. Such a limitation could only weaken the protective function of a statute designed to protect United States interests. In providing for the death penalty where death results in the course of an attack on a Federal facility, Section 930(c) is clearly designed to deter attacks on Federal facilities. Given the likelihood that foreign nationals will be in or near Federal facilities located in foreign nations, this deterrent effect would be significantly diminished if Section 930(c) were limited to the deaths of United States nationals. To paraphrase *Bowman*, "to limit [the reach of Section 930(c) to the deaths of United States nationals] would be greatly to curtail the scope and usefulness of the statute and leave open a large immunity for [attacks against Federal facilities]." 260 U.S. at 101.

Odeh argues, second, that, even if the universality principle (or one of the four other principles) did authorize the application of Section 930(c) to the deaths of ordinary foreign nationals on foreign soil, such application would violate international law nevertheless, because (i) "even where one of the principles authorizes jurisdiction, a nation is nevertheless precluded from exercising jurisdiction where jurisdiction would be 'unreasonable,'" and (ii) application of Section 930(c) to the deaths of ordinary foreign nationals on foreign soil would be unreasonable.

According to the Restatement, the following factors are to be taken into account for the purpose of determining whether exercise of extraterritorial jurisdiction is reasonable:

> (a) the link of the activity to the territory of the regulating state, i.e., the extent to which the activity takes place within the territory, or has substantial, direct, and foreseeable effect upon or in the territory;
> (b) the connections, such as nationality, residence, or economic activity, between the regulating state and the person principally responsible for the activity to be regulated, or between that state and those whom the regulation is designed to protect;
> (c) the character of the activity to be regulated, the importance of regulation to the regulating state, the extent to which other states regulate such activities, and the degree to which the desirability of such regulation is generally accepted;
> (d) the existence of justified expectations that might be protected or hurt by the regulation;
> (e) the importance of the regulation to the international political, legal, or economic system;
> (f) the extent to which the regulation is consistent with the traditions of the international system;
> (g) the extent to which another state may have an interest in regulating the activity; and
> (h) the likelihood of conflict with regulation by another state. [Restatement §403(2).]

Given that factor (a) alludes to the subjective territorial principle and the objective territorial principle, it is not especially relevant to a statute, such as Section 930(c), based primarily on the protective principle. Much the same can be said of factor (b), as it alludes to the nationality principle, the subjective territorial principle and the objective territorial principle. Factor (c), in contrast, is highly relevant to Section 930(c). It is important both to the United States and other nations to prevent the destruction of their facilities—regardless of their location; and such regulation is accordingly widely accepted among the nations of the world. As for factor (d), Section 930(c) protects the expectation of foreign nationals that they will be free of harm while on the premises of United States facilities. We can think of no "justified" expectation, however, that would be hurt by the extraterritorial application of Section 930(c). As for factor (e), in light of the prominent role played by the United States in "the international political, legal, and economic systems," the protection of United States facilities—regardless of their location—is highly important to the stability of these systems. Turning to factor (f) . . . most, if not all, nations are concerned about protecting their facilities, both at home and abroad. Hence, Section 930(c) is highly consistent "with the traditions of the international system." As for (g), it must be acknowledged that when the United States facility is on foreign soil, and when the victims of the attack are nationals of the host nation, the host nation "has a keen interest in regulating and punishing [the] offenders." Odeh's Memo. at 34. This is not to say, however, that the host nation has a greater interest than does the United States. Furthermore, even if it were the case that the host nation had a greater interest than the United States, this single factor would be insufficient to support the conclusion that application of Section 930(c) to the bombings of the two Embassies is unreasonable. Coming, finally, to factor (h), Odeh does not argue that application of Section 930(c) to the bombings would conflict with Kenyan and/or Tanzanian law, nor are we otherwise aware of such conflict. On the contrary, the Government informs the Court that "the Kenyan Government voluntarily rendered Odeh (and [co-defendant] al-'Owhali) to the United States, and neither the Kenyan nor the Tanzanian Government has asserted any objection to the United States' exercise of jurisdiction in this case." Factor (h) thus counts in favor of the reasonableness of applying Section 930(c) to the bombings.

In light of the foregoing, we conclude that the application of Section 930(c) to the deaths of foreign nationals on foreign soil is reasonable. . . .

CONCLUSION

In light of the foregoing, Odeh's motion to dismiss Counts 5-233, 236-239, and 242-244 for lack of jurisdiction is denied; whereas, his motion to dismiss Counts 234, 235, 240, and 241 for lack of jurisdiction is granted.

Notes and Questions

1. Odeh and three other defendants were sentenced in October 2001 to life in prison for their roles in the embassy bombings. As of January 2003, three more defendants have plead guilty to conspiracy charges and three others are in the U.K., continuing to fight extradition. Thirteen more are fugitives, although at least one of these is believed to have been killed during the war in Afghanistan.

2. Which prescriptive principles from international law did the court use to help justify the exercise of the court's jurisdiction over Odeh? What principles of domestic law did the court rely on? Were international or domestic law principles more important to the court's decision? What role did the international law principles play?

3. The court in *Bin Laden* invokes Restatement section 403 in assessing whether its exercise of jurisdiction over foreign nationals for acts committed abroad is "unreasonable," in part because the countries where the acts occurred might have the greater interest in regulating and punishing the offenders. However, isn't it unnecessary to resort to section 403 because, as the court notes, Kenya voluntarily turned

over Odeh to the United States, and neither Kenya nor Tanzania asserted any objection to the U.S. exercise of jurisdiction in this case? Wouldn't this essentially be an explicit or implicit acknowledgment by those countries that the United States could reasonably exercise jurisdiction?

Even if this might be the occasion to consider competing jurisdictional claims, shouldn't the court have begun with reference to *Hartford Fire Insurance* (see page 661) rather than section 403? Or, might the court's resort to section 403 reflect the possible ambiguity in *Hartford Fire* toward section 403, or the fact that some courts appear to ignore *Hartford Fire* and go directly to a section 403 analysis?

4. Does the principle of universal jurisdiction extend to support Israel's prosecution of German Nazi officials, such as Adolph Eichmann, who committed war crimes during World War II, even though those crimes were committed at a time when the state of Israel did not yet exist? (Israel became a state in 1948; Germany surrendered in 1945.) See Attorney General of Israel v. Eichmann, 36 Intl. L. Rep. 277, 298-304 (Sup. Ct. Israel 1962).

5. Some European countries have laws allowing for universal criminal jurisdiction. In the late 1990s, British courts famously had to decide whether to allow the extradition of Augusto Pinochet, former President of Chile, to Spain. In that case, Spain was seeking to try Pinochet, under a universal jurisdiction statute, for human rights abuses committed in Chile. The British House of Lords upheld Spain's extradition request with respect to some of the charges, but the British government decided not to extradite Pinochet due to his ill health, and he was allowed to return to Chile. The House of Lords' decision is discussed in more detail in Chapter 6, in connection with head-of-state immunity.

In 1993, Belgium enacted a law allowing for jurisdiction over certain egregious violations of international law committed anywhere in the world. In June 2001, four Rwandan Hutus were convicted, in a Belgian court, of committing genocide in Rwanda, in violation of the statute. A group of Palestinians subsequently initiated an investigation in Belgium seeking to have Israeli Prime Minister Ariel Sharon tried for his involvement in the alleged massacre of Palestinian refugees in Lebanon in 1982. In February 2003, Belgium's highest court, the Court of Cassation, ruled that customary international law prevented sitting heads of state (e.g., Prime Minister Sharon) from criminal proceedings in Belgium while they held their office. Although the Belgian court did not cite its authorities, the court might well have been influenced by the February 2002 decision of the International Court of Justice, which held that Belgium could not apply its universal jurisdiction statute to Congo's Minister for Foreign Affairs because he was immune from arrest and prosecution under customary international law. The Court did not decide whether the Belgian statute was otherwise consistent with international law. (The ICJ decision is discussed in Chapter 6.)

In response to the growing controversy concerning its universal jurisdiction statute, Belgium adopted restricting amendments to the statute in May 2003 to allow the Belgian prosecutor and courts to dismiss cases when the act did not occur on Belgian territory, the alleged offender is not Belgian nor found on Belgian territory, and the victim is not Belgian or has not resided on Belgian territory in the last three years. The amendment also gives the Belgian government the authority to reject cases in situations, among others, where the accused person is a national of a country with courts that are "competent, independent, impartial and fair."

6. In listing the offenses of "universal concern," the Restatement, published in 1987, listed "piracy, slave trade, attacks on or hijacking of aircraft, genocide, war crimes, and perhaps certain acts of terrorism." Section 404. Do you think that "[u]niversal condemnation of those activities and general interest in cooperating to suppress them, as reflected in widely-accepted international agreements and resolutions of international organizations" (id. at cmt. *a*), now make it clear that the "perhaps" can be dropped from the Restatement's statement? That is to say, is it now clear that many acts of terrorism are subject to the principle of universal jurisdiction — for example large-scale killing of civilians?

7. Should murder, rape, torture and/or robbery be included as universal crimes? Why or why not? If these crimes are not considered universal crimes, can they not still be embodied in national laws and supported, as appropriate, by other principles of jurisdiction — both on a national and an international level?

B. JURISDICTION TO ENFORCE AND ADJUDICATE PUBLIC LAW

1. *Jurisdiction to Enforce*

Just because a state's statute is legitimately applicable (on one of the grounds described in Section A above) to a particular person or act, it does not follow that the state may take any action it wants to enforce that law. For example, until recently at least, the FBI did not run around the world arresting people without the consent of the host government, even if the criminal had committed an offense entirely within the United States. And a federal district court may not be able to subpoena all the evidence it believes it needs in a particular case where that evidence is located abroad. Enforcement jurisdiction is said to be territorial, and the limits seem much more strictly observed than with prescriptive jurisdiction. There are also limits on the power of courts or agencies to serve process across national boundaries as well. The limits may be set by international law, constitutional law, statute, or regulation. The Restatement summarizes its view of the international law:

Restatement

Section 431. Jurisdiction to Enforce

(1) A state may employ judicial or nonjudicial measures to induce or compel compliance or punish noncompliance with its laws or regulations, provided it has jurisdiction to prescribe in accordance with §§402 and 403.

(2) Enforcement measures must be reasonably related to the laws or regulations to which they are directed; punishment for noncompliance must be preceded by an appropriate determination of violation and must be proportional to the gravity of the violation.

(3) A state may employ enforcement measures against a person located outside its territory

(a) if the person is given notice of the claims or charges against him that is reasonable in the circumstances;

(b) if the person is given an opportunity to be heard, ordinarily in advance of enforcement, whether in person or by counsel or other representative; and

(c) when enforcement is through the courts, if the state has jurisdiction to adjudicate.

Comment

a. Relation of jurisdiction to enforce to jurisdiction to prescribe and to adjudicate. Under international law, a state may not exercise authority to enforce law that it has no jurisdiction to prescribe. Such assertion of jurisdiction, whether carried out through the courts or by nonjudicial means, may be objected to by both the affected person directly and by the other state concerned. A state that has jurisdiction to prescribe may enforce its law through its courts if it also has jurisdiction to adjudicate, but the fact that it cannot effectively exercise judicial jurisdiction with respect to a person does not preclude enforcement through nonjudicial means, such as those illustrated in Comment *c*. A state that does not have jurisdiction to prescribe is not barred from cooperating in law enforcement by appropriate means with a state that has jurisdiction to prescribe. . . .

b. Judicial enforcement measures. For purposes of this section, judicial enforcement measures include the imposition of criminal sanctions, such as fines and imprisonment, as well as other measures that may be ordered by a court in connection with a judicial proceeding, whether civil, criminal, or administrative, such as an order to produce a document, or a sanction for failure to comply with such an order. A judgment or decree ordering a person to do (or to refrain from doing) an act may have aspects both of prescription and of enforcement. Some measures taken by executive agencies subject to judicial confirmation or annulment, such as seizure of goods by the customs service, freezing of assets by revenue authorities, or execution of a warrant for arrest, have aspects of both judicial and nonjudicial enforcement. A judgment of a court awarding or denying damages in a civil action would generally not be seen as enforcement.

c. Nonjudicial enforcement measures. For purposes of this section, enforcement measures comprise not only the orders of a court, such as those mentioned in Comment *b*, but also measures such as the following, when used to induce compliance with or as sanctions for violation of laws or regulations of the enforcing state:

— denial of the right to engage in export or import transactions;
— removal from a list of persons eligible to bid on government contracts;
— suspension, revocation, or denial of a permit to engage in particular business activity;
— prohibition of the transfer of assets;

and comparable denial of opportunities normally open to the person against whom enforcement is directed.

This section deals with the imposition of executive, administrative or police sanctions against persons for violations of law, and is concerned with decisions by officials applying legal standards, both in determining that a violation has occurred and in pursuing procedures leading to the imposition of sanctions. It is not concerned with measures of state policy denying benefits to another state nor with application of general rules, such as a law that refuses entry visas to persons convicted of specified crimes in other states. Imposition of an embargo on trade with a foreign state is not within this section; placing an individual on an export blacklist as a sanction for violation of a law or regulation is an assertion of jurisdiction to enforce covered by this section.

d. *Reasonableness as limitation on enforcement jurisdiction.* Under Subsection (1), any exercise of jurisdiction to enforce is subject to the principle of reasonableness. For example, it might be reasonable for the United States to deny to a foreign company export privileges, i.e., the right to participate in transactions involving export of United States goods, because the company had knowingly reexported a strategic product of United States origin to country *X* in violation of United States law. It normally would be unreasonable for the United States to deny such export privileges to the same firm simply because it traded with country *X* in goods not of United States origin, since ordinarily the United States would not have jurisdiction to prescribe with respect to such trade.

There may be a greater limitation on the exercise of jurisdiction to enforce in respect of activity in another state than there is with respect to activity on the high seas.

e. *Nonjudicial enforcement measures and fair procedure.* Nonjudicial enforcement measures, such as those listed in Comment *c*, need not meet all the requirements associated with exercise of criminal jurisdiction, but exercise of nonjudicial enforcement jurisdiction is consistent with international law only if it is not arbitrary. The procedures associated with measures of nonjudicial enforcement need not parallel in all respects procedures in courts, but Subsection (3) requires that basic elements of fairness be observed. . . .

Section 432. Measures in Aid of Enforcement of Criminal Law

. . . (2) A state's law enforcement officers may exercise their functions in the territory of another state only with the consent of the other state, given by duly authorized officials of that state.

Comment

. . . b. *Territoriality and law enforcement.* It is universally recognized, as a corollary of state sovereignty, that officials of one state may not exercise their functions in the territory of another state without the latter's consent. Thus, while a state may take certain measures of nonjudicial enforcement against a person in another state, §431, its law enforcement officers cannot arrest him in another state, and can engage in criminal investigation in that state only with that state's consent. Within a state's own territory, the rules governing arrest and other steps in criminal law enforcement generally apply regardless of the nationality, residence, or domicile of the person accused or investigated, subject only to defined exceptions for persons enjoying diplomatic or consular immunity and to the obligation to observe basic human rights.

c. Consequences of violation of territorial limits of law enforcement. If a state's law enforcement officials exercise their functions in the territory of another state without the latter's consent, that state is entitled to protest and, in appropriate cases, to receive reparation from the offending state. If the unauthorized action includes abduction of a person, the state from which the person was abducted may demand return of the person, and international law requires that he be returned. If the state from which the person was abducted does not demand his return, under the prevailing view the abducting state may proceed to prosecute him under its laws. . . .

Section 433. External Measures in Aid of Enforcement of Criminal Law: Law of the United States

(1) Law enforcement officers of the United States may exercise their functions in the territory of another state only

(a) with the consent of the other state and if duly authorized by the United States; and

(b) in compliance with the laws both of the United States and of the other state.

a. Direct Enforcement Action

Occasionally a state or some of its citizens may undertake to enforce its laws through direct action in the territory of another state. Consider the following case involving the activities of alleged U.S. agents in Mexico and another recent episode involving the United States and Canada.

United States v. Alvarez-Machain

U.S. Supreme Court
504 U.S. 655 (1992)

REHNQUIST, C.J., delivered the opinion of the Court, in which WHITE, SCALIA, KENNEDY, SOUTER, and THOMAS, JJ., joined.

The issue in this case is whether a criminal defendant, abducted to the United States from a nation with which it has an extradition treaty, thereby acquires a defense to the jurisdiction of this country's courts. We hold that he does not, and that he may be tried in federal district court for violations of the criminal law of the United States.

Respondent, Humberto Alvarez-Machain, is a citizen and resident of Mexico. He was indicted for participating in the kidnap and murder of United States Drug Enforcement Administration (DEA) special agent Enrique Camarena-Salazar and a Mexican pilot working with Camarena, Alfredo Zavala-Avelar. The DEA believes that respondent, a medical doctor, participated in the murder by prolonging agent Camarena's life so that others could further torture and interrogate him. On April 2, 1990, respondent was forcibly kidnapped from his medical office in Guadalajara,

Mexico, to be flown by private plane to El Paso, Texas, where he was arrested by DEA officials. The District Court concluded that DEA agents were responsible for respondent's abduction, although they were not personally involved in it.[1]

Respondent moved to dismiss the indictment, claiming that his abduction constituted outrageous governmental conduct, and that the District Court lacked jurisdiction to try him because he was abducted in violation of the extradition treaty between the United States and Mexico. Extradition Treaty, May 4, 1978, [1979] United States-United Mexican States, 31 U.S.T. 5059, T.I.A.S. No. 9656 (Extradition Treaty or Treaty). The District Court rejected the outrageous governmental conduct claim, but held that it lacked jurisdiction to try respondent because his abduction violated the Extradition Treaty. The District Court discharged respondent and ordered that he be repatriated to Mexico.

The Court of Appeals affirmed the dismissal of the indictment and the repatriation of respondent. . . . Although the Treaty does not expressly prohibit such abductions, the Court of Appeals held that the "purpose" of the Treaty was violated by a forcible abduction, which, along with a formal protest by the offended nation, would give a defendant the right to invoke the Treaty violation to defeat jurisdiction of the district court to try him. The Court of Appeals further held that the proper remedy for such a violation would be dismissal of the indictment and repatriation of the defendant to Mexico.

In the instant case, the Court of Appeals affirmed the district court's finding that the United States had authorized the abduction of respondent, and that letters from the Mexican government to the United States government served as an official protest of the Treaty violation. Therefore, the Court of Appeals ordered that the indictment against respondent be dismissed and that respondent be repatriated to Mexico. We granted certiorari, and now reverse.

Although we have never before addressed the precise issue raised in the present case, we have previously considered proceedings in claimed violation of an extradition treaty, and proceedings against a defendant brought before a court by means of a forcible abduction. We addressed the former issue in United States v. Rauscher, 119 U.S. 407 (1886); more precisely, the issue of whether the Webster-Ashburton Treaty of 1842, 8 Stat. 572, 576, which governed extraditions between England and the United States, prohibited the prosecution of defendant Rauscher for a crime other than the crime for which he had been extradited. Whether this prohibition, known as the doctrine of specialty, was an intended part of the treaty had been disputed between the two nations for some time. Justice Miller delivered the opinion of the Court, which carefully examined the terms and history of the treaty; the practice of nations in regards to extradition treaties; the case law from the states; and the writings of commentators, and reached the following conclusion: "[A] person who has been brought within the jurisdiction of the court by virtue of proceedings under an extradition treaty, can only be tried for one of the offences described in that treaty, and for the offence with which he is charged in the proceedings for his extradition, until a reasonable time and opportunity have been

---

1. Apparently, DEA officials had attempted to gain respondent's presence in the United States through informal negotiations with Mexican officials, but were unsuccessful. DEA officials then, through a contact in Mexico, offered to pay a reward and expenses in return for the delivery of respondent to the United States.

given him, after his release or trial upon such charge, to return to the country from whose asylum he had been forcibly taken under those proceedings." In addition, Justice Miller's opinion noted that any doubt as to this interpretation was put to rest by two federal statutes which imposed the doctrine of specialty upon extradition treaties to which the United States was a party. Unlike the case before us today, the defendant in Rauscher had been brought to the United States by way of an extradition treaty; there was no issue of a forcible abduction.

In Ker v. Illinois, 119 U.S. 436 (1886), also written by Justice Miller and decided the same day as *Rauscher,* we addressed the issue of a defendant brought before the court by way of a forcible abduction. Frederick Ker had been tried and convicted in an Illinois court for larceny; his presence before the court was procured by means of forcible abduction from Peru. A messenger was sent to Lima with the proper warrant to demand Ker by virtue of the extradition treaty between Peru and the United States. The messenger, however, disdained reliance on the treaty processes, and instead forcibly kidnapped Ker and brought him to the United States. We distinguished Ker's case from *Rauscher,* on the basis that Ker was not brought into the United States by virtue of the extradition treaty between the United States and Peru, and rejected Ker's argument that he had a right under the extradition treaty to be returned to this country only in accordance with its terms. We rejected Ker's due process argument more broadly, holding in line with "the highest authorities" that "such forcible abduction is no sufficient reason why the party should not answer when brought within the jurisdiction of the court which has the right to try him for such an offence, and presents no valid objection to his trial in such court."

The only differences between Ker and the present case are that Ker was decided on the premise that there was no governmental involvement in the abduction, and Peru, from which Ker was abducted, did not object to his prosecution. Respondent finds these differences to be dispositive, as did the Court of Appeals contending that they show that respondent's prosecution, like the prosecution of Rauscher, violates the implied terms of a valid extradition treaty. The Government, on the other hand, argues that *Rauscher* stands as an "exception" to the rule in *Ker* only when an extradition treaty is invoked, and the terms of the treaty provide that its breach will limit the jurisdiction of a court. Therefore, our first inquiry must be whether the abduction of respondent from Mexico violated the extradition treaty between the United States and Mexico. If we conclude that the Treaty does not prohibit respondent's abduction, the rule in *Ker* applies, and the court need not inquire as to how respondent came before it.

In construing a treaty, as in construing a statute, we first look to its terms to determine its meaning. The Treaty says nothing about the obligations of the United States and Mexico to refrain from forcible abductions of people from the territory of the other nation, or the consequences under the Treaty if such an abduction occurs. Respondent submits that Article 22(1) of the Treaty which states that it "shall apply to offenses specified in Article 2 [including murder] committed before and after this Treaty enters into force," evidences an intent to make application of the Treaty mandatory for those offenses. However, the more natural conclusion is that Article 22 was included to ensure that the Treaty was applied to extraditions requested after the Treaty went into force, regardless of when the crime of extradition occurred.

More critical to respondent's argument is Article 9 of the Treaty which provides:

1. Neither Contracting Party shall be bound to deliver up its own nationals, but the executive authority of the requested Party shall, if not prevented by the laws of that Party, have the power to deliver them up if, in its discretion, it be deemed proper to do so.

2. If extradition is not granted pursuant to paragraph 1 of this Article, the requested Party shall submit the case to its competent authorities for the purpose of prosecution, provided that Party has jurisdiction over the offense.

According to respondent, Article 9 embodies the terms of the bargain which the United States struck: if the United States wishes to prosecute a Mexican national, it may request that individual's extradition. Upon a request from the United States, Mexico may either extradite the individual, or submit the case to the proper authorities for prosecution in Mexico. In this way, respondent reasons, each nation preserved its right to choose whether its nationals would be tried in its own courts or by the courts of the other nation. This preservation of rights would be frustrated if either nation were free to abduct nationals of the other nation for the purposes of prosecution. More broadly, respondent reasons, as did the Court of Appeals, that all the processes and restrictions on the obligation to extradite established by the Treaty would make no sense if either nation were free to resort to forcible kidnapping to gain the presence of an individual for prosecution in a manner not contemplated by the Treaty.

We do not read the Treaty in such a fashion. Article 9 does not purport to specify the only way in which one country may gain custody of a national of the other country for the purposes of prosecution. In the absence of an extradition treaty, nations are under no obligation to surrender those in their country to foreign authorities for prosecution. Extradition treaties exist so as to impose mutual obligations to surrender individuals in certain defined sets of circumstances, following established procedures. The Treaty thus provides a mechanism which would not otherwise exist, requiring, under certain circumstances, the United States and Mexico to extradite individuals to the other country, and establishing the procedures to be followed when the Treaty is invoked.

The history of negotiation and practice under the Treaty also fails to show that abductions outside of the Treaty constitute a violation of the Treaty. As the Solicitor General notes, the Mexican government was made aware, as early as 1906, of the *Ker* doctrine, and the United States' position that it applied to forcible abductions made outside of the terms of the United States-Mexico extradition treaty.[11] Nonetheless, the current version of the Treaty, signed in 1978, does not attempt to establish a rule

---

11. In correspondence between the United States and Mexico growing out of the 1905 Martinez incident, in which a Mexican national was abducted from Mexico and brought to the United States for trial, the Mexican chargé wrote to the Secretary of State protesting that as Martinez' arrest was made outside of the procedures established in the extradition treaty, "the action pending against the man can not rest [on] any legal foundation." Letter of Balbino Davalos to Secretary of State reprinted in Papers Relating to the Foreign Relations of the United States, H.R. Doc. No. 1, 59th Cong., 2d Sess., pt. 2, p.1121 (1906). The Secretary of State responded that the exact issue raised by the Martinez incident had been decided by *Ker*, and that the remedy open to the Mexican government, namely a request to the United States for extradition of Martinez' abductor had been granted by the United States. Letter of Robert Bacon to Mexican Chargé, reprinted in Papers Relating to the Foreign Relations of the United States, H.R. Doc. No. 1, 59th Cong., 2d Sess., pt. 2, at 1121-1122 (1906). . . .

that would in any way curtail the effect of *Ker*. Moreover, although language which would grant individuals exactly the right sought by respondent had been considered and drafted as early as 1935 by a prominent group of legal scholars sponsored by the faculty of Harvard Law School, no such clause appears in the current treaty.[12]

Thus, the language of the Treaty, in the context of its history, does not support the proposition that the Treaty prohibits abductions outside of its terms. The remaining question, therefore, is whether the Treaty should be interpreted so as to include an implied term prohibiting prosecution where the defendant's presence is obtained by means other than those established by the Treaty.

Respondent contends that the Treaty must be interpreted against the backdrop of customary international law, and that international abductions are "so clearly prohibited in international law" that there was no reason to include such a clause in the Treaty itself. The international censure of international abductions is further evidenced, according to respondent, by the United Nations Charter and the Charter of the Organization of American States. Respondent does not argue that these sources of international law provide an independent basis for the right respondent asserts not to be tried in the United States, but rather that they should inform the interpretation of the Treaty terms. . . .

More fundamentally, the difficulty with the support respondent garners from international law is that none of it relates to the practice of nations in relation to extradition treaties. In *Rauscher*, we implied a term in the Webster-Ashburton Treaty because of the practice of nations with regard to extradition treaties. In the instant case, respondent would imply terms in the extradition treaty from the practice of nations with regards to international law more generally. Respondent would have us find that the Treaty acts as a prohibition against a violation of the general principle of international law that one government may not "exercise its police power in the territory of another state." There are many actions which could be taken by a nation that would violate this principle, including waging war, but it cannot seriously be contended an invasion of the United States by Mexico would violate the terms of the extradition treaty between the two nations.

In sum, to infer from this Treaty and its terms that it prohibits all means of gaining the presence of an individual outside of its terms goes beyond established precedent and practice. In *Rauscher*, the implication of a doctrine of specialty into the terms of the Webster-Ashburton Treaty which, by its terms, required the presentation of evidence establishing probable cause of the crime of extradition before extradition was required, was a small step to take. By contrast, to imply from the terms of this Treaty that it prohibits obtaining the presence of an individual by means outside of the procedures the Treaty establishes requires a much larger inferential leap, with only the most general of international law principles to support it. The general principles cited by respondent simply fail to persuade us that we should imply in the United States-Mexico Extradition Treaty a term prohibiting international abductions.

---

12. In Article 16 of the Draft Convention on Jurisdiction with Respect to Crime, the Advisory Committee of the Research in International Law proposed: "In exercising jurisdiction under this Convention, no State shall prosecute or punish any person who has been brought within its territory or a place subject to its authority by recourse to measures in violation of international law or international convention without first obtaining the consent of the State or States whose rights have been violated by such measures." Harvard Research in International Law, 29 Am. J. Intl. L. 442 (Supp. 1935).

Respondent and his amici may be correct that respondent's abduction may be in violation of general international law principles. Mexico has protested the abduction of respondent through diplomatic notes, and the decision of whether respondent should be returned to Mexico, as a matter outside of the Treaty, is a matter for the Executive Branch. We conclude, however, that respondent's abduction was not in violation of the Extradition Treaty between the United States and Mexico, and therefore the rule of Ker v. Illinois is fully applicable to this case. The fact of respondent's forcible abduction does not therefore prohibit his trial in a court in the United States for violations of the criminal laws of the United States.

The judgment of the Court of Appeals is therefore reversed, and the case is remanded for further proceedings consistent with this opinion.

So ordered.

Justice STEVENS, with whom Justice BLACKMUN and Justice O'CONNOR join, dissenting.

. . . The case is unique for several reasons. It does not involve an ordinary abduction by a private kidnaper, or bounty hunter, as in Ker v. Illinois, 119 U.S. 436, nor does it involve the apprehension of an American fugitive who committed a crime in one State and sought asylum in another, as in Frisbie v. Collins, 342 U.S. 519 (1952). Rather, it involves this country's abduction of another country's citizen; it also involves a violation of the territorial integrity of that other country, with which this country has signed an extradition treaty.

A Mexican citizen was kidnaped in Mexico and charged with a crime committed in Mexico; his offense allegedly violated both Mexican and American law. Mexico has formally demanded on at least two separate occasions that he be returned to Mexico and has represented that he will be prosecuted and punished for his alleged offense. It is clear that Mexico's demand must be honored if this official abduction violated the 1978 Extradition Treaty between the United States and Mexico. In my opinion, a fair reading of the treaty in light of our decision in United States v. Rauscher, and applicable principles of international law, leads inexorably to the conclusion that the District Court, and the Court of Appeals for the Ninth Circuit, correctly construed that instrument.

I

The Extradition Treaty with Mexico is a comprehensive document containing 23 articles and an appendix listing the extraditable offenses covered by the agreement. The parties announced their purpose in the preamble: The two Governments desire "to cooperate more closely in the fight against crime and, to this end, to mutually render better assistance in matters of extradition." From the preamble, through the description of the parties' obligations with respect to offenses committed within as well as beyond the territory of a requesting party, the delineation of the procedures and evidentiary requirements for extradition, the special provisions for political offenses and capital punishment, and other details, the Treaty appears to have been designed to cover the entire subject of extradition. Thus, Article 22, entitled "Scope of Application" states that the "Treaty shall apply to offenses specified in Article 2 committed before and after this Treaty enters into force," and Article 2 directs that "[e]xtradition shall take place, subject to this Treaty, for willful acts which fall within any of [the extraditable offenses listed in] the clauses of the Appendix." Moreover, as noted by the Court, Article 9 expressly provides that neither Contracting Party is bound to deliver up its own nationals, although it may do so in its discretion, but if it does not do so, it "shall submit the case to its competent authorities for purposes of prosecution."

Petitioner's claim that the Treaty is not exclusive, but permits forcible governmental kidnaping, would transform these, and other, provisions into little more than verbiage. For example, provisions requiring "sufficient" evidence to grant extradition (Art. 3), withholding extradition for political or military offenses (Art. 5), withholding extradition when the person sought has already been tried (Art. 6), withholding extradition when the statute of limitations for the crime has lapsed (Art. 7), and granting the requested State discretion to refuse to extradite an individual who would face the death penalty in the requesting country (Art. 8), would serve little purpose if the requesting country could simply kidnap the person. . . .

It is true, as the Court notes, that there is no express promise by either party to refrain from forcible abductions in the territory of the other Nation. Relying on that omission, the Court, in effect, concludes that the Treaty merely creates an optional method of obtaining jurisdiction over alleged offenders, and that the parties silently reserved the right to resort to self help whenever they deem force more expeditious than legal process. If the United States, for example, thought it more expedient to torture or simply to execute a person rather than to attempt extradition, these options would be equally available because they, too, were not explicitly prohibited by the Treaty. That, however, is a highly improbable interpretation of a consensual agreement, which on its face appears to have been intended to set forth comprehensive and exclusive rules concerning the subject of extradition. In my opinion, "the manifest scope and object of the treaty itself," plainly imply a mutual undertaking to respect the territorial integrity of the other contracting party. That opinion is confirmed by a consideration of the "legal context" in which the Treaty was negotiated. . . .

Although the Court's conclusion in *Rauscher* was supported by a number of judicial precedents, the holdings in these cases were not nearly as uniform as the consensus of international opinion that condemns one Nation's violation of the territorial integrity of a friendly neighbor. It is shocking that a party to an extradition treaty might believe that it has secretly reserved the right to make seizures of citizens in the other party's territory. Justice Story found it shocking enough that the United States would attempt to justify an American seizure of a foreign vessel in a Spanish port: "But, even supposing, for a moment, that our laws had required an entry of the Apollon, in her transit, does it follow, that the power to arrest her was meant to be given, after she had passed into the exclusive territory of a foreign nation? We think not. It would be monstrous to suppose that our revenue officers were authorized to enter into foreign ports and territories, for the purpose of seizing vessels which had offended against our laws. It cannot be presumed that Congress would voluntarily justify such a clear violation of the laws of nations." The Apollon, 9 Wheat. 362, 370-371 (1824).

The law of Nations, as understood by Justice Story in 1824, has not changed. Thus, a leading treatise explains: "A State must not perform acts of sovereignty in the territory of another State. . . .

"It is . . . a breach of International Law for a State to send its agents to the territory of another State to apprehend persons accused of having committed a crime. Apart from other satisfaction, the first duty of the offending State is to hand over the person in question to the State in whose territory he was apprehended."

1 Oppenheim's International Law 295, and n.1 (H. Lauterpacht 8th ed. 1955). Commenting on the precise issue raised by this case, the chief reporter for the American Law Institute's Restatement of Foreign Relations used language reminiscent of Justice Story's characterization of an official seizure in a foreign jurisdiction as "monstrous:" "When done without consent of the foreign government, abducting a person from a foreign country is a gross violation of international law and gross disrespect for a norm high in the opinion of mankind. It is a blatant violation of the territorial integrity of another state; it eviscerates the extradition system (established by a comprehensive network of treaties involving virtually all states)." . . .

III

A critical flaw pervades the Court's entire opinion. It fails to differentiate between the conduct of private citizens, which does not violate any treaty obligation, and conduct expressly authorized by the Executive Branch of the Government, which unquestionably constitutes a flagrant violation of international law, and in my opinion, also constitutes a breach of our treaty obligations.

The importance of the distinction between a court's exercise of jurisdiction over either a person or property that has been wrongfully seized by a private citizen, or even by a state law enforcement agent, on the one hand, and the attempted exercise of jurisdiction predicated on a seizure by federal officers acting beyond the authority conferred by treaty, on the other hand, [was recognized] in Cook v. United States, 288 U.S. 102 (1933). . . .

The objection to the seizure is not that it was wrongful merely because made by one upon whom the Government had not conferred authority to seize at the place where the seizure was made. The objection is that the Government itself lacked power to seize, since by the Treaty it had imposed a territorial limitation upon its own authority. . . . To hold that adjudication may follow a wrongful seizure would go far to nullify the purpose and effect of the Treaty. . . .

The Court's failure to differentiate between private abductions and official invasions of another sovereign's territory also accounts for its misplaced reliance on the 1935 proposal made by the Advisory Committee on Research in International Law. As the text of that proposal plainly states, it would have rejected the rule of the *Ker* case. The failure to adopt that recommendation does not speak to the issue the Court decides today. The Court's admittedly "shocking" disdain for customary and conventional international law principles, is thus entirely unsupported by case law and commentary.

IV

As the Court observes at the outset of its opinion, there is reason to believe that respondent participated in an especially brutal murder of an American law enforcement agent. That fact, if true, may explain the Executive's intense interest in punishing respondent in our courts. Such an explanation, however, provides no justification for disregarding the Rule of Law that this Court has a duty to uphold. That the Executive may wish to reinterpret the Treaty to allow for an action that the Treaty in no way authorizes should not influence this Court's interpretation. Indeed, the desire for revenge exerts "a kind of hydraulic pressure . . . before which even well settled principles of law will bend," Northern Securities Co. v. United States, 193 U.S. 197, 401 (1904) (Holmes, J., dissenting), but it is precisely at such moments that we should remember and be guided by our duty "to render judgment evenly and dispassionately according to law, as each is given understanding to ascertain and apply it." The way that we perform that duty in a case of this kind sets an example that other tribunals in other countries are sure to emulate.

The significance of this Court's precedents is illustrated by a recent decision of the Court of Appeal of the Republic of South Africa. Based largely on its understanding of the import of this Court's cases — including our decision in Ker v. Illinois — that court held that the prosecution of a defendant kidnaped by agents of South Africa in another country must be dismissed. S v. Ebrahim, S. Afr. L. Rep. (Apr.-June 1991). The Court of Appeal of South Africa — indeed, I suspect most courts throughout the civilized world — will be deeply disturbed by the "monstrous" decision the Court announces today. For every Nation that has an interest in preserving the Rule of Law is affected, directly or indirectly, by a decision of this character. As Thomas Paine warned, an "avidity to punish is always dangerous to liberty" because it leads a Nation "to stretch, to misinterpret, and to misapply even the best of laws." To counter that tendency, he reminds us: "He that would make his own liberty secure must guard even his enemy from oppression; for if he violates this duty he establishes a precedent that will reach to himself."

I respectively dissent.

Notes and Questions

1. Did the United States have prescriptive jurisdiction over Alvarez-Machain for his alleged activities? If so, what is international jurisdictional authority that is at issue in this case? Is it the United States' right to adjudicate the legality of his conduct?

2. Why does the Court not apply the "general principles of international law" in this case? (See the reference to them in the paragraph near the very end of the majority opinion.) Is this case like *Garcia-Mir*, excerpted in Chapter 3, where the Executive Branch had acted? (Of course, many believe that *Garcia-Mir* was wrongly decided.)

3. What advice would you give Mexico as to its remedies following the *Alvarez-Machain* decision?

4. The Chief Justice is correct that the Extradition Treaty literally does not prohibit official kidnapping. But doesn't the Treaty assume that such acts are prohibited? Otherwise there would be no need for a treaty. Or would there?

5. Alan J. Kreczko, the Deputy Legal Adviser of the Department of State, testified to a House Judiciary Subcommittee:

Reactions of Foreign Governments

The Supreme Court's decision has caused considerable concern among a wide range of governments, particularly in the Americas, but elsewhere as well. Many governments have expressed outrage that the United States believes it has the right to decide unilaterally to enter their territory and abduct one of their nationals. Governments have informed us that they would regard such action as a breach of international law. They have also informed us that they would protect their nationals from such action, that such action would violate their domestic law, and that they would vigorously prosecute such violations. Some countries, as well, have told us that they believe that such actions would violate our extradition treaties with them. Some have also suggested that they will challenge the lawfulness of such abductions in international forums. Some have indicated that the decision could affect their parliaments' review of pending law enforcement agreements with the United States. At the same time, some have noted in private that the decision will cause narcotics traffickers to have an increased fear of apprehension by the United States. . . .

- The Presidents of Argentina, Bolivia, Brazil, Chile, Paraguay, and Uruguay issued a declaration on June 26 expressing their concern with the U.S. Supreme Court decision and requesting that the Inter-American Juridical Committee of the Organization of American States (OAS) issue an opinion on the "international juridical validity" of the *Alvarez-Machain* decision. That request was made formally to the Permanent Council of the OAS on July 15, which adopted a resolution referring this matter to the Juridical Committee. . . .
- On June 15, the Government of Colombia stated that it "energetically rejects the judgment issued by the United States Supreme Court. . . ." Although recognizing that the decision dealt only with a treaty between the United States and Mexico, the government felt that "its substance threatens the legal stability of [all] public treaties."
- The Minister of Security and Justice of Jamaica criticized the decision as based on the principle that "might makes right." He said the ruling was "an atrocity that would disturb the world," and called on the United States to come "back to its senses."

The reaction has not been confined, of course, to official government statements. Political leaders in and out of government, and commentaries in the media, have generally criticized the decision and the attitude of the U.S. Government that that decision is supposed to represent. . . .

The Supreme Court's decision led to a rigorous debate in the Canadian Parliament. The Canadian Minister of External Affairs told the Canadian Parliament that any attempt by the United States to kidnap someone in Canada would be regarded as a criminal act and a violation of the US-Canada Extradition Treaty. Spain's President publicly criticized the decision as "erroneous." And the media in Europe generally has been critical of the decision.

These negative reactions reflect a concern that the *Alvarez-Machain* decision constitutes a "green light" for international abductions. The reactions are grounded in the desire of countries to preserve their sovereignty and territorial integrity and to reassure their nationals. We expect that countries will continue to press this concern with us, bilaterally and multilaterally. . . .

The U.S. Government has moved actively to isolate the question of whether domestic legal authority exists from the separate question of whether the President will, in fact, exercise that authority. We have reassured other countries that the United States has not changed its policies toward cooperation in international law enforcement, and that the *Alvarez-Machain* case does not represent a "green light" for the United States to conduct operations on foreign territory.

Specifically, immediately following the Supreme Court's decision, the White House issued a public statement reaffirming that:

. . . The United States strongly believes in fostering respect for international rules of law, including, in particular, the principles of respect for territorial integrity and sovereign equality of states. U.S. policy is to cooperate with foreign states in achieving law enforcement objectives. Neither the arrest of Alvarez-Machain, nor the . . . Supreme Court decision reflects any change in this policy. . . .

At the same time, we are not prepared categorically to rule out unilateral action. It is not inconceivable that in certain extreme cases, such as the harboring by a hostile foreign country of a terrorist who has attacked U.S. nationals and is likely to do so again, the President might decide that such an abduction is necessary and appropriate as a matter of the exercise of our right of self-defense. This necessary reservation of right for extreme cases does not, however, detract from our strong support for the principles of sovereignty and territorial integrity generally. To reinforce this point, the White House statement also noted the Administration has in place procedures designed to ensure that U.S. law enforcement activities overseas fully take into account foreign relations and international law. These procedures require that decisions as to extraordinary renditions from foreign territories be subject to full inter-agency coordination and that they be considered at the highest levels of the government. . . .

In the aftermath of the *Alvarez-Machain* decision, the Mexican Foreign Minister gave a press conference with the following highlights:

- Mexico repudiates as invalid and illegal the decision of the Supreme Court;
- Mexico will consider as a criminal act any attempt by foreign persons or governments to apprehend in Mexican territory any person suspected of a crime;
- Mexico demands the return of Alvarez-Machain;
- Mexico declares that the only legal means for moving persons from one nation to face trial in another are treaties and mechanisms of extradition established under international law; [and]
- Foreign law enforcement officials of any country who operate in Mexican territory will be asked to observe updated rules that the Government of Mexico will establish.

Mexico sought assurances that further abductions will not take place on Mexican territory and stated that collaboration by Mexicans with foreign governments in criminal acts that violate Mexican sovereignty would be classified as acts of treason against Mexico.

The United States has responded to these Mexican concerns as follows:

- President Bush sent a letter to President Salinas containing unequivocal assurances that his Administration will "neither conduct, encourage nor condone" such trans-border abductions from Mexico.
- The two governments agreed to review the U.S.-Mexico Extradition Treaty . . . in order to analyze the implications of the recent Supreme Court decision and to avoid any possible repetitions of events such as the abduction of Alvarez-Machain.
- There was an exchange of letters between Secretary Baker and Foreign Secretary Solana of Mexico recognizing that trans-border abductions by so-called "bounty hunters" and other private individuals will be considered extraditable offenses by both nations. . . .

[3 U.S. Dept. of State Dispatch 614 (1992).]

6. In January 1993, President-elect Clinton apparently assured Mexican President Salinas that his administration, like his predecessor's, would not conduct or condone such trans-border abductions. In 1994, the Clinton Administration negotiated with Mexico a modification to the bilateral extradition treaty that would explicitly forbid "trans-border abductions" like the Alvarez-Machain kidnapping. For

reasons that are unclear, the treaty amendment was never submitted to the Senate for its advice and consent.

In 1995, President Clinton signed a directive that stated, "If we do not receive cooperation from a state that harbors a terrorist we are seeking, we shall take appropriate measures to induce cooperation." This policy would seem to permit law enforcement abductions, at least in certain circumstances.

7. Turning the clock back to before the 1990 seizure of Alvarez-Machain and the Supreme Court's decision in 1992, the U.S. government had formally determined in 1989 that it was legally permissible for its law enforcement agencies, such as the FBI and DEA, to apprehend individuals who are accused of violating U.S. criminal law in foreign states without the consent of the foreign state in which they are apprehended.

Shortly after the U.S. policy to apprehend individuals abroad appeared in the news, Iran reacted. Members of the Iranian Parliament passed a draft law giving the president of Iran the right to arrest anywhere Americans who take action against Iranian citizens or property anywhere in the world and bring them to Iran for trial. The bill provided that the U.S. citizen would be tried by Iranian courts under Islamic law.

The bill "aims at preserving the prestige and territorial integrity of the Islamic Republic, safeguarding the lives and properties of Iranian nationals abroad and defending the interests of the Islamic Republic."

The Iranian representatives who introduced the bill said it was in response to the U.S. policy and said that they wanted the Iranian law to remain in force for as long as the U.S. law. If you support the 1989 U.S. policy, should the Iranians be allowed a similar policy? It would presumably include seizing U.S. citizens in, say, Chicago for alleged acts against Iranians and spiriting the U.S. citizens back to Iran for trial. If Iran should not be allowed a similar policy as the United States, how does one distinguish between the rights of the two countries? Is the possibility of such reciprocal response by other states a good reason for the United States to curtail its own claims about seizing individuals abroad?

8. After the Supreme Court's ruling in *Alvarez-Machain*, the case was remanded to the district court for a judgment on the merits. Ironically, the case was dismissed for lack of evidence on December 14, 1992. The district judge said the prosecution's case was nothing but the "wildest speculation" that failed to support the charge that Alvarez had participated in Camarena's torture and death. (An informant indicated that a different doctor may have been the culprit.) Alvarez returned to his home in Guadalajara a few days later after having been imprisoned for two and a half years.

In July 1993, Alvarez brought an action under the Federal Tort Claims Act (FTCA) and the Alien Tort Statute (or Alien Tort Claims Act) against the United States, several DEA agents, and several Mexican citizens, alleging that he had been kidnapped, tortured, and wrongfully imprisoned. A three-judge panel of the Ninth Circuit Court of Appeals upheld in 2001 the district court's decision that Alvarez could receive damages for the abduction and imprisonment only up to the period prior to indictment, which broke the chain of "arbitrary" detention. It upheld the Alien Tort Statute award of $25,000 against the Mexican police officer who performed the abduction. It also upheld the ruling that Alvarez's only remedy against the DEA officers was an FTCA claim against the United States, but reversed the district court's dismissal of that claim and remanded the case for further proceedings.

The other Mexican defendants had earlier been dismissed from the lawsuit. In March 2002, however, the Ninth Circuit agreed to rehear the case en banc.

9. Even after *Alvarez-Machain,* where the defendant was abducted and brought to the United States by foreigners, there still might be a possible "outrageous conduct" limitation on actions by U.S. agents. A 1974 U.S. court of appeals decision held that a federal court must "divest itself of jurisdiction over the person of a defendant where it had been acquired as a result of the Government's deliberate, unnecessary, and unreasonable invasion" of the accused's constitutional rights. In that case, the defendant alleged that the U.S. court had acquired jurisdiction over him through the actions of U.S. agents, who had kidnapped him in Uruguay, used electronic surveillance and torture, and then brought him to the United States for prosecution. United States v. Toscanino, 500 F.2d 267 (2d Cir), *reh'g denied,* 504 F.2d 1380 (2d Cir. 1974); see M. Cherif Bassiouni, International Extradition: United States Law and Practice 229-246 (3d ed. 1996).

b. Extradition

The more common alternative to direct law enforcement abroad is through extradition treaties. Only treaties create an obligation to extradite under international law, although some nations will voluntarily extradite suspects as a matter of comity. The procedures a country uses to meet its extradition obligations under a treaty are typically established by its domestic laws. Extradition treaties typically establish a legally binding obligation to extradite fugitives, define the crimes covered by the extradition obligation, specify exceptions, and set forth the procedures and requisite evidence to activate the extradition obligation.

While some states have granted extradition of a fugitive even when no treaty exists, the modern trend is not to allow it in the absence of a treaty. In the United States the law does not allow extradition without a treaty or a statute. See 18 U.S.C. §3194. Moreover, U.S. procedures for extradition are governed by the relevant treaty, as supplemented by or a statute. See 18 U.S.C. §§3184-3195. Although this means that procedures may vary depending on the relevant treaty, almost all U.S. treaties correlate with the procedures described by U.S. statutes.

A complaint made under oath before an authorized U.S. judge or magistrate initiates extradition proceedings. If the relevant treaty requires the United States to represent the requesting state, the complaint is filed by the U.S. attorney for the district in which the fugitive is believed to reside. The U.S. attorney acts pursuant to a requisition to surrender (a formal extradition request) made to the U.S. Department of State by the requesting state via diplomatic channels. When the Department of State receives the requisition, it reviews it for sufficiency and transmits it to the Department of Justice.

Absent a specific agreement by the United States to represent the requesting state, the requesting state must engage a private attorney to prosecute its requisition. This does not relieve the requesting state from also transmitting a formal requisition to the State Department, but the requisition then needs only to be filed prior to the final disposition of the case.

Upon filing the complaint, an arrest warrant is issued for the fugitive. When he is apprehended, he is returned to the issuing magistrate. A public hearing follows.

The scope of the hearing is limited. The magistrate must determine that (1) the fugitive sought is the person detained; (2) a valid extradition treaty exists between the United States and the requesting state; (3) the treaty allows extradition; and (4) the standard of proof of criminality established by the treaty is met. If any of these fail, the detainee is released.

The first two issues are usually straightforward. The third and fourth issues are frequently contested. All U.S. extradition treaties contain a number of exceptions. One common exception is that for political offenses. It is especially troublesome when dealing with terrorism. The exempted political offenses have generally not been defined or enumerated in extradition treaties. The exception is usually provided for in the general language. A distinction may be made between a purely political offense (such as treason) and a relative political offense (a common crime, such as murder, politically motivated and committed during a revolt), but both categories are usually excepted from extradition. For example, Article V of the extradition treaty between the United States and Italy provides: "Extradition shall not be granted when the offense for which extradition is requested is a political offense, or if the person whose surrender is sought proves that the request for surrender has been made in order to try or punish him or her for a political offense. . . ."

Another common exception is that many foreign countries will not agree to extradite to the United States persons who are subject to the death penalty in the United States. This reflects the view, common in Europe, that capital punishment is not an appropriate penalty. During 2001-2002, this exception created obstacles to the United States extraditing terrorist suspects apprehended by foreign officials in Spain and elsewhere. (See the earlier *Soering* case in Chapter 8.) One approach that has sometimes allowed extradition is for the U.S. or state prosecutors to stipulate that they will not seek the death penalty against the persons they are seeking to have extradited.

Yet another common exception is that some treaties provide that the foreign state (e.g., Germany) will not extradite its own nationals to the United States. (The United States, however, will extradite its own nationals, as long as the extradition treaty with the requesting nation allows for such extradition. See Charlton v. Kelly, 229 U.S. 447, 467 (1913).) As for other examples of exceptions, if prosecution of the offense charged is time-barred in the requesting state, extradition is often not allowed. Another common exception is "dual criminality": the offense charged must be a crime both in the requesting and requested state.

Magistrates do not determine the guilt or innocence of the fugitive, only whether the standard of proof of criminality established by the treaty is met. There are a number of different formulations for this standard; however, most have been defined as the equivalent of probable cause in domestic criminal cases.

If the magistrate determines that extradiction is appropriate, she certifies her decision to the Secretary of State, along with a record of the proceedings. The Secretary of State makes the final determination on extradition. While no statute specifically limits the Secretary's discretion, he is bound by the relevant treaty. In other words, if he decides not to extradite, his decision must be based on a treaty exception. In addition, the Secretary customarily limits his consideration to the record certified by the magistrate.

If the Secretary approves extradition, he issues a warrant of surrender to the appropriate U.S. marshal. The requesting state then has two months to take custody of the fugitive. If it does not, the fugitive can petition for release.

Because the magistrate's decision is not final, there is no direct appeal from the decision. However, the fugitive can institute habeus corpus proceedings if the magistrate decides extradition is appropriate. Final disposition of the extradition is usually not made while habeus corpus proceedings are pending.

Judicial application of the political offense exemption,*both in magistrate's hearings and in habeus corpus proceedings, has created controversy. This was particularly true with U.K. extradition requests for Provisional Irish Republican Army (IRA) terrorists who fled to the United States, where the IRA had many supporters. For instance, in Matter of Doherty by Gov. of United Kingdom, 599 F. Supp. 270 (S.D.N.Y. 1984), the court found that the then-existing political offense exception to the U.S.-U.K. extradition treaty applied, and, consequently, that Doherty could not be extradited. Doherty had been convicted of a number of crimes, including the murder of a British Army officer and membership in the IRA. In addition, Doherty was wanted for crimes committed during his escape from prison.

The U.S. judiciary's refusal to allow extradition in *Doherty* and similar cases led to the British government asking that a supplementary treaty be negotiated, which narrowed the political offense exception, so that violent offenders such as Doherty could not escape extradition. A U.S.-U.K. Supplementary Extradition Treaty was signed and ratified in 1985-1986. It explicitly provided that a number of offenses involving killing, seriously injuring a person, using explosives, or using firearms were not to be regarded as an "offense of a political character." (The U.S.-U.K. Extradition Treaty and the Supplementary Treaty are excerpted in the Documentary Supplement.) In 1992, the U.S. Supreme Court agreed that Doherty could be deported to the United Kingdom. The Justice Department deported him in secret and without comment in February 1992, and British courts sentenced him to serve at least ten years, with no credit for his nine years in U.S. prisons. In 1999, as part of the President Clinton-sponsored peace deal for Northern Ireland, Doherty was released from prison.

If the person is extradited to the United States, the specialty doctrine requires that he "shall be tried only for the offence with which he is charged in the extradition proceedings and for which he was delivered up, and that if not tried for that, or after trial and acquittal, he shall have a reasonable time to leave the country before he is arrested upon the charge of any other crime committed previous to his extradition." United States v. Rauscher, 119 U.S. 407, 424 (1886). Although the Court found in *Rauscher* that the doctrine prevailed even if not specified in the extradition treaty, many extradition treaties today expressly refer to the specialty doctrine.

Although extradition procedures vary widely, the basic framework is nearly universal. Almost every country requires a judicial determination on requisitions. And almost every country allows its executive some discretion in the final determination of extradition requests.

The procedures for extradition from the United Kingdom almost mirror those in the United States. A formal requisition must be made via diplomatic channels to the Secretary of State. The Secretary of State transmits it to a police magistrate, who issues an arrest warrant. At the hearing the magistrate determines essentially the same issues as his American counterpart. If extradition is allowed, the magistrate's decision is transmitted to the Secretary of State, who makes the final determination.

The major difference between the procedures of the United States and United Kingdom derives from the role of the relevant treaty. In the United States, the procedures and standards of proof are governed by the treaty, as supplemented by domestic statutes. In the United Kingdom, all extradition proceedings and standards of proof are governed by the Extradition Act of 1870, 33 & 34 Vict., ch. 52, 17 Halsbury's Statutes of England and Wales 475 (4th ed. 1986). In the United States, proceedings may vary according to treaty; in the United Kingdom, the procedure does not vary.

In France, extradition proceedings are governed by Title II of the Law of March 10, 1927. The French procedures are also similar to United States practice. The law supplements valid treaties. Proceedings are initiated by a formal requisition to the Minister for Foreign Affairs, who confirms the "regularity" of the requisition. The Minister for Foreign Affairs transmits the requisition to the Minister for Justice, who takes the necessary steps to apprehend the fugitive. An interrogation and hearing follow the arrest.

Unlike proceedings in the United States or the United Kingdom, the French judiciary does not pass on the sufficiency of evidence of criminality, only on the evidence that there have been charges or a conviction. Evidence of pending prosecution or punishment is all that is required. The court's decision is not appealable. An affirmative extradition opinion is transmitted to the Minister of Justice. The Minister of Justice may either decline the extradition or obtain the signature for extradition from the president of the republic. The requesting state then has to take custody of the fugitive.

Questions

1. Why should there be a tougher test for enforcement than for prescription (or application) of law?

2. Should there be old-fashioned territorial limits on enforcement? Why shouldn't states increasingly expand their law enforcement extraterritorially, as in effects jurisdiction, to take account of increased international interdependence and easier transportation and communication?

3. Are extradition treaties a viable alternative to extraterritorial criminal enforcement? Why not an international criminal law and tribunal?

2. *Jurisdiction to Adjudicate*

As you recall, the Restatement asserts that there are limits imposed by customary international law on the right of a state to apply its law (§403). The Restatement also asserts that there are limits on the power of a court to extend its authority abroad:

Restatement

Section 421. Jurisdiction to Adjudicate

(1) A state may exercise jurisdiction through its courts to adjudicate with respect to a person or thing if the relationship of the state to the person or thing is such as to make the exercise of jurisdiction reasonable.

(2) In general, a state's exercise of jurisdiction to adjudicate with respect to a person or thing is reasonable if, at the time jurisdiction is asserted:

   (a) the person or thing is present in the territory of the state, other than transitorily;

   (b) the person, if a natural person, is domiciled in the state;

   (c) the person, if a natural person, is resident in the state;

   (d) the person, if a natural person, is a national of the state;

   (e) the person, if a corporation or comparable juridical person, is organized pursuant to the law of the state;

   (f) a ship, aircraft or other vehicle to which the adjudication relates is registered under the laws of the state;

   (g) the person, whether natural or juridical, has consented to the exercise of jurisdiction;

   (h) the person, whether natural or juridical, regularly carries on business in the state;

   (i) the person, whether natural or juridical, had carried on activity in the state, but only in respect of such activity;

   (j) the person, whether natural or juridical, had carried on outside the state an activity having a substantial, direct, and foreseeable effect within the state, but only in respect of such activity; or

   (k) the thing that is the subject of adjudication is owned, possessed, or used in the state, but only in respect of a claim reasonably connected with that thing.

(3) A defense of lack of jurisdiction is generally waived by any appearance by or on behalf of a person or thing (whether as plaintiff, defendant, or third party), if the appearance is for a purpose that does not include a challenge to the exercise of jurisdiction.

Notes and Questions

1. The factors are largely drawn from the due process jurisprudence of U.S. constitutional law, except that the Restatement seems to disallow "tag" jurisdiction (i.e., basing jurisdiction on the transitory presence of the defendant). Other states may recognize different tests for adjudicatory jurisdiction, such as the principal place of management of a corporation. Are the problems that could result from an expansive extension of adjudicative jurisdiction by the United States likely to be as severe as those encountered in the extraterritorial application of securities or antitrust law?

2. Even when jurisdiction to adjudicate might be reasonable as a matter of due process, there are some reasons why a U.S. court might choose not to exercise its jurisdiction. Among these are the doctrines of comity, forum non conveniens, and the rule of customary international law that a litigant must exhaust the available remedies provided by the local (or host) state before he may bring suit in a foreign or international court.

The doctrine of comity permits a court to decline to exercise jurisdiction in certain circumstances in deference to the laws and interests of a foreign country.

Declining jurisdiction under this doctrine is not obligatory, and the question does not arise until the court has already established that it has subject matter and personal jurisdiction. See the discussion above concerning Restatement section 403 and *Hartford Fire Insurance.*

A similar but distinct doctrine is forum non conveniens, which permits a court to dismiss a case where an adequate, alternative forum exists and public and private interests favor having the trial in that forum. Forum non conveniens is available only where the alternate forum provides a real opportunity to be heard, and only in certain circumstances. It is for the court to weigh the factors for and against dismissal and it is within the judge's discretion to deny the motion.

The threshold inquiry of a forum non conveniens analysis is to determine whether the alternate forum is adequate. This includes (1) whether the defendant is amenable to process in the alternate forum, and (2) whether the subject matter of the lawsuit is cognizable there, so as to afford the plaintiff the possibility of relief. The first element is sometimes met by making the dismissal contingent on the defendant's consent to jurisdiction in the alternate forum. The second depends on both the law and procedural safeguards of the alternate forum and the adequacy of the remedy available — although the remedy need not be identical to that available in the U.S. system.

If the court determines that the alternate forum is adequate, it must then balance the public and private interests of trying the case in each forum. Factors to consider are the ease of access to evidence in each forum, the ability to obtain witnesses, the enforceability of a judgment rendered, the interest of each forum in hearing the case and in not filling its docket with unrelated cases, and the interest in having a forum apply its own law where possible. None of these factors is dispositive, but the presumption in U.S. courts is in favor of the plaintiff's choice of forum where that forum is reasonable. In practice, however, the imprecision of the above analysis means that use of the doctrine varies widely from court to court. See, for example, Piper Aircraft Co. v. Reyno, 454 U.S. 235 (1981); In re Union Carbide Corp. Gas Plant Disaster at Bhopal, India, 809 F.2d 195 (2d Cir.), *cert. denied,* 484 U.S. 871 (1987) (affirming dismissal of personal injury claims from industrial disaster in Bhopal, India because India was the more appropriate forum to litigate such claims); but see Wiwa v. Royal Dutch Petroleum Co., 226 F.3d 88 (2d. Cir), *cert denied,* 121 S. Ct. 1402 (2001) (reversing district court's *forum non conveniens* dismissal of a Torture Victim Protection Act case where many of the events had occurred in Nigeria because, in part, two of the plaintiffs were U.S. residents and a policy of the TVPA in favor of U.S. jurisdiction).

A third doctrine is sometimes called the "exhaustion of local remedies" rule. As a principle of customary international law, it provides that a foreign court or international court should not hear a case unless the plaintiff has exhausted its possible remedies available in the local forum. This includes bringing any action authorized by local law and may include nonjudicial remedies. A court may dismiss an action for lack of jurisdiction where the plaintiff has failed to do so. However, under international law, a plaintiff is not obligated to pursue remedies where "such remedies are clearly sham or inadequate, or their application is unreasonably prolonged." (Restatement, at section 713, cmt. f.); see also Malcolm Shaw, International Law 202-203, 567 (4th ed. 1997); Ian Brownlie, Principles of Public International Law 496-497, 506 (5th ed. 1998).

International court and arbitral decisions have regularly supported the principle of exhaustion of local remedies. As summarized in the *Restatement (Third)*, at §713, Reporters' Notes:

5. *Exhaustion of domestic remedies.* In the Interhandel Case (Switzerland v. United States), [1959], I.C.J. Rep. 6, 26-27, the International Court of Justice noted that "[t]he rule that local remedies must be exhausted before international proceedings may be instituted is a well-established rule of customary international law". . . . The Court added that "[b]efore resort may be had to an international court in such a situation, it has been considered necessary that the State where the violation occurred should have an opportunity to redress it by its own means, within the framework of its own domestic legal system."

In that case, the United States had vested the assets of Interhandel during the Second World War, claiming that Interhandel, though incorporated in Switzerland, was controlled by a German company and therefore could properly be considered an enemy alien. Interhandel brought suit in the United States district court in 1946 to recover its assets; a judgment dismissing Interhandel's suit was affirmed in the court of appeals. While a petition for certiorari by Interhandel was pending before the United States Supreme Court in 1959, Switzerland brought a proceeding against the United States in the International Court of Justice.

The Supreme Court of the United States granted Interhandel's petition for certiorari and reversed and remanded the case to the district court. . . . The International Court of Justice dismissed the proceeding before it. The Court said that the exhaustion of local remedies must be observed *a fortiori* when the domestic proceedings are still pending, especially when both the domestic and the international actions are designed to obtain the same result, i.e., the restitution of Interhandel's assets.

As was stated in the Ambatielos Case (Greece v. United Kingdom), 1951, 12 R. Int'l Arb. Awards 91, 120, 122, the phrase "local remedies" should be interpreted broadly, including "the whole system of legal protection, as provided by municipal law," not only the courts and tribunals but also "the use of procedural facilities which municipal law makes available to litigants." There, the claimant lost the case in the lower court because he failed to call a crucial witness, and the Court of Appeals refused "to give leave to adduce [this] evidence." The tribunal held that the claimant had failed to exhaust local remedies, as it was due to his own action that the appeal became futile.

A more recent decision by the International Court of Justice (ICJ or Court), again involving the United States, reaffirmed the rule of exhaustion of local remedies. In Case Concerning Elettronica Sicula S.p.A. (ELSI) (United States of America v. Italy), 1989 I.C.J. 15, the United States instituted proceedings against Italy, alleging that the requisition by the Government of Italy of the plant and related assets of ELSI, a wholly owned subsidiary of a U.S. company (Raytheon), was a violation of a treaty and agreement between the two countries. Prior to concluding on the merits that Italy's actions did not constitute breaches of the treaty or agreement, the Court considered Italy's contention that Raytheon had failed to exhaust it local remedies in Italy. The Court found that the trustee in bankruptcy for ELSI brought a suit against Italian officials in the Court of Palermo, Italy, then the trustee appealed to the Court of Appeal of Palermo, and then appealed to the Court of Cassation which upheld the decision of the Court of Appeal. (Id. at para. 57.) The Court concluded that "Italy has not been able to satisfy the Chamber [of the ICJ] that there clearly remained some remedy which Raytheon . . . ought to have pursued and exhausted." (Id. at para. 63.)

Similarly, the U.S. courts have on occasion recognized and applied this rule of customary international law. Examples include Millicom International Cellular v.

Republic of Costa Rica, 995 F. Supp. 14, 23 (D.D.C. 1998) (action by three foreign corporations against Costa Rica for alleged unlawful competitive activity; the court cited, among other authorities, *Interhandel*); Greenpeace, Inc. (USA) v. State of France, 916 F. Supp. 773, 783 (C.D. Cal. 1996) (suit by U.S. entities and nationals, among others, against France for seizure of vessels which allegedly constituted a taking or expropriation; the court cited *Interhandel*). And, the U.S. Supreme Court observed in the seminal case of Banco Nacional de Cuba v. Sabbatino, 376 U.S. 398, 422-23 (1964) (decided on other grounds): "Because of its peculiar nation-to-nation character the usual method for an individual to seek relief is to exhaust local remedies and then repair to the executive authorities of his own state to persuade them to champion his claim in diplomacy or before an international tribunal."

3. It is important to distinguish between the assertion by a court of its jurisdiction over a person and the application of the forum's law (state or federal) to the dispute. It may be less offensive to hale a Swiss defendant into court if the court applies Swiss law to the case. Nevertheless, what reasons would foreign defendants cite as objections to U.S. judicial process? (And, conversely, why would a foreign plaintiff prefer to sue in a U.S. court?)

4. Do you think it would be appropriate to have a treaty establishing rules for adjudicatory jurisdiction? Or would it be preferable to harmonize national laws?

Restatement

Part IV Chapter 2 — Introductory Note

Traditionally, public international law dealt with judicial jurisdiction only when exercised on government initiative, and treated such jurisdiction as ancillary to jurisdiction to prescribe. The jurisdiction of courts in relation to private controversies was not an important concern of public international law, even when its exercise had transnational implications. In the early development of United States law, both public international law and the conflict of laws between nations were considered part of "the law of nations," as seen, for example, by Marshall and Story. Later, however, the law governing conflict between laws of different nations became a small part of the domestic law of conflict of laws, which primarily focused on conflict between laws of the several States of the United States. In Europe and Latin America the conflict of laws — usually called private international law — was seen as closer to the concerns of public international law, but even there was, until recently, a subject for coordination and harmonization more than for binding international agreements and norms.

The exercise of jurisdiction by courts of one state that affects interests of other states is now generally considered as coming within the domain of customary international law and international agreement. States have long maintained the right to refuse to give effect to judgments of other states that are based on assertions of jurisdiction that are considered extravagant; increasingly, they object to the improper exercise of jurisdiction as itself a violation of international principles. Long before the developments concerning jurisdiction to prescribe, the international law governing the jurisdiction of courts began to give less emphasis to territoriality and nationality. States exercise jurisdiction to adjudicate on the basis of various links, including the defendant's presence, conduct, or, in some cases, ownership of property within the state; conduct outside the state producing certain kinds of injury within the state; or the defendant's nationality, domicile, or residence in the state. Exercise of judicial jurisdiction on the basis of such links is on the whole accepted as "reasonable"; reliance on other bases, such as the nationality of the plaintiff or the presence of property unrelated to the claim, is generally considered "exorbitant."

The development from national law to norms of international law has left the transition incomplete and boundaries blurred. In the United States, and perhaps elsewhere, it is not always clear whether the principles governing jurisdiction to adjudicate are applied as requirements of public international law or as principles of national law. This Restatement sets forth some international rules and guidelines for the exercise of jurisdiction to adjudicate in cases having international implications, applicable to courts both in the United States and in other states. Some of these rules are relevant as well to recognition and enforcement of foreign judgments.

C. CHOICE OF LAW IN PRIVATE DISPUTES

In Sections A and B we examined the application and enforcement of criminal law and "public" law, such as antitrust and export controls. Comparable problems of allocation of governmental authority in the international system, with similar sources of legal limitation of that authority, can be found in more traditional areas of private law, which we take up in this section.

As indicated above, there are limits to the power of courts to adjudicate with respect to a person or controversy. The rules described in section 421 (Jurisdiction to Adjudicate) of the Restatement are derived from U.S. constitutional law, and they relate to in personam jurisdiction. After a court determines that it has in personam jurisdiction over the defendant (or "jurisdiction to adjudicate" in the Restatement and international law sense), the court must then decide *what law* to apply to the controversy. Thus, in U.S. domestic law if a New York plaintiff injures a New York defendant in an automobile crash in Michigan, the court must decide whether New York or Michigan rules apply on such questions as the standard of liability, the effect of contributory negligence, punitive damages, spousal immunity, and so on. Similarly, in a case involving a contract negotiated in Illinois and concluded in South Dakota by parties from New York and California, the court must decide whether to apply Illinois, South Dakota, New York, or California rules, on such matters as parol evidence, validity, etc. The same problem can arise in an international context. United States courts have normally applied the same rules regarding choice of law among different countries as the choice-of-law rules among the 50 states.

William M. Richman & William L. Reynolds, Understanding Conflict of Laws

157-158 (3d ed. 2002)

A court called upon to resolve a dispute with multi-state aspects must choose a law to apply to the problem. That choice often is not easy to take, and the task is further complicated by the need to select a process to use in choosing the appropriate law. It is not surprising, therefore, that the search for a system for choice of law has occupied a great deal of judicial and academic time and effort. The discussion, especially among the scholars, sometimes seems as though it were being conducted by Byzantine theologians.

Choice of law as a discipline in this country began with the monumental treatise by Justice Joseph Story published in 1834. Story, heavily influenced by the territorial concepts of earlier Dutch thinkers, emphasized the right of a state to control what went on in its courts, subject to notions of comity. American conflicts law in the first half of this century centered on the work of Professor Joseph Beale of the Harvard Law School, an effort culminating in the Restatement (First) of Conflict of Laws in 1934 and Beale's own treatise published in the following year. A territorial imperative lies at the core of Beale's theory, for it is based on the idea that at the moment a cause of action arises, rights vest according to the law of the place where the crucial event occurred. In tort law, for example, *lex loci delicti* ("the law of the place of the wrong") held sway, on the theory that the victim's cause of action had vested according to the law of the place where the injury occurred. . . .

The seeds of the demise of Beale's Restatement, however, had been planted even before it was written. Beginning at the turn of the century Sociological Jurisprudence, and then Legal Realism, had taught that law was and should be functional, and that legal rules should be tailored to serve societal goals. Because Beale's territorial system did not inquire into the purposes behind the competing substantive law rules, the system did not satisfy the mandate of twentieth-century jurisprudence. This problem was recognized by a young Harvard professor, David Cavers, in a path-breaking article in 1933, as well as by Walter Wheeler Cook in a series of articles. . . .

The approach advocated by those and other writers led to the drafting of the Restatement (Second). Work on the project began in 1952 and was essentially complete by 1963, although publication did not occur until 1971. The Reporter was Professor Willis Reese of Columbia. The Restatement (Second) generally eschews hard-and-fast rules in favor of the general principle that the law of the state with the "most significant relationship" to a transaction should control. The goal of that formula is to ensure that the law of the state most concerned with the problem will be applied and lead thereby to a sensible outcome to the litigation. . . .

While work progressed on the Second Restatement, Professor Brainerd Currie of Duke argued that the choice-of-law process should focus on the policies behind state substantive law rules; whether a rule should be applied should depend upon whether the policy underlying that rule would be advanced by its application. Currie's approach, known as "interest analysis," has appeared in various forms and has been incorporated . . . by the Restatement (Second). Some combination of the two systems has been adopted by most courts and commentators in the third of a century since Currie's first articles appeared.

Recent years have seen a partial withdrawal from interest analysis. The specific worry is that the indefinite, almost formless nature of Currie's process has led — perhaps ineluctably — to ad hoc decision-making. To counter that problem, some judges and scholars have suggested that our experience with modern forms of choice of law analysis is broad enough to permit the promulgation of new "rules" that will be both functional and certain.

One way to look at alternative methods of choosing the applicable law is to distinguish between jurisdiction-selecting systems on the one hand, and content- or policy-selecting systems on the other. Jurisdiction-selecting systems choose a state whose law will be applied, regardless of its content or motivating policy. By contrast, content-selecting systems focus on the content and motivating policy of competing substantive laws in making the choice-of-law decision. The First Restatement used jurisdiction-selecting rules. The rules prescribed a jurisdiction whose law was to be invoked once the problem had been properly characterized (as, say, one sounding in tort). The many varieties of interest analysis, by contrast, are content-selecting systems. Choice of law decisions in those systems are functional, in that they seek to assess the impact of a choice on the goals of the substantive law. Of course, the First Restatement and interest analysis are the polar opposites; intermediate positions also exist. An illustration is the Second Restatement, which combines presumptive jurisdiction-selecting rules with tools which can be used to focus on policy considerations. . . .

Under the First Restatement approach the law applicable to a tort claim was the law where the last act necessary to create the cause of action occurred (the "place of the wrong"). If a product is manufactured (but not negligently) in Alberta, Canada, and injures an Alberta resident while that person is visiting Montana, Montana law would apply under the First Restatement approach.

Under interest analysis, on the other hand, the court would analyze the case in terms of the policies underlying the conflicting rules. Thus, if Alberta law provided for strict product liability, while Montana law allowed recovery only for negligence, the court would apply Alberta law. The analysis would be that the policy underlying Alberta's rule of strict liability would seem to be to offer maximum protection to Alberta victims (interest analysis usually asumes that state legislators are only interested in legislating to protect their own constituents, and that state law should run to the benefit, or detriment, of only local residents). The policy behind Montana's law, on the other hand, would perhaps be characterized as subsidizing Montana manufacturers and sellers of manufactured products in Montana, or perhaps assuring Montana residents of reduced product prices (because Montana manufacturers and sellers would not be saddled with strict liability). In this hypothetical case, applying Montana law would not advance either Montana policy because the plaintiffs and defendants are from Alberta, not Montana, and hence are not within the class of intended beneficiaries of the Montana negligence rule. Applying Alberta law, on the other hand, would advance Alberta's policy of giving maximum protection to its residents. Hence, under interest analysis, the Alberta law of strict liability would apply. In this kind of case (sometimes called a "false conflict"), interest analysis offers a sensible, policy-oriented way to avoid application of the First Restatement approach that would mechanically apply the law of the place of injury, which may seem wholly fortuitous. Nevertheless, interest analysis provides an easy answer only to the relatively few cases that present false conflicts, where it is clear that choosing one rule over another advances the policies underlying the former and does not defeat the policies underlying the latter.

As fact situations are varied, and as the characterizations of "policy" become more complex, the cases become much more difficult. If the injured plaintiff in the hypothetical were a Montana resident, what result would follow? If the policy behind Alberta's strict liability rule is characterized as intended to benefit Alberta residents, that policy would not be advanced by applying Alberta law. But if the Montana policy is characterized as intended to protect Montana manufacturers, applying Montana law won't advance that policy either. Neither state's policy would be advanced, and interest analysis gives no guidance as to how to resolve such a case. Professor Currie, the founder of interest analysis, said the forum should apply its own law in such cases, but of course that exposes the potential of forum shopping (but what else is new?). In this hypothetical, however, punishing a Montana plaintiff does seem unjust. Why should a Montana plaintiff have to prove negligence while an Alberta plaintiff gets the benefit of strict liability?

Increasingly, U.S. courts adjudicate disputes having an international dimension. United States plaintiffs may feel that they might get a more sympathetic hearing from a local court (and jury). And foreign plaintiffs may believe that U.S. court procedure — for example, discovery rules — may be more favorable, and U.S. law may offer easier or more generous recovery. The last advantage, of course, should be mitigated by application of choice-of-law rules, especially under the First Restatement approach. Consider, however, the following case:

Pancotto v. Sociedade de Safaris de Mozambique, S.A.R.L.

U.S. District Court
422 F. Supp. 405 (N.D. Ill. 1976)

MEMORANDUM DECISION

MARSHALL, District Judge.

The plaintiff, Rosemary Pancotto, has brought this diversity action to recover damages for a personal injury she sustained in 1973 while on a hunting safari in Mozambique. Pending for decision is the motion of defendant Sociedade de Safaris de Mozambique (Safrique), to apply the law of Mozambique to the substantive issues in the action, and for a determination of the relevant Mozambique law. Defendant has complied with the notice provisions of Fed. R. Civ. P. 44.1. Under the rule of Klaxon v. Stentor Electric Mfg. Co., 313 U.S. 487 (1941), a federal court sitting in diversity applies the conflicts law of the state in which it sits. Thus our task regarding the first part of defendant's motion is to determine and apply the Illinois choice of law rule.

Illinois modified its choice of law rules for tort cases in Ingersoll v. Klein, 46 Ill. 2d 42 (1970). "In our opinion, the local law of the State where the injury occurred should determine the rights and liabilities of the parties, unless Illinois has a more significant relationship with the occurrence and the parties, in which case, the law of Illinois should apply."

The first step in the choice of law analysis is to isolate the substantive legal issues and determine whether the various states' tort rules conflict. If a potential conflict is discovered, the next step is to examine the contacts with the states, evaluating the importance of each contact in relation to the legal issues of the case. Finally, under the Illinois choice of law rule, the law of the state or country of the place of injury is followed, unless Illinois is more significantly interested in the resolution of a particular legal issue.

I. The Defendant's Liability

Defendant's motion identifies the two substantive legal issues to be addressed by this choice of law analysis, each of which will be considered in turn: (1) the defendant's liability; and (2) the appropriate measure of damages. A cursory look at the defendant's materials outlining Mozambique law indicates that the standard of care there was different from Illinois.[1] Briefly, the Mozambique standard of care upon which defendant relies was the "diligence with which a law abiding male head of a family would act." Portuguese Civil Code, Art. 487(2). Although this standard of care bears an analytical similarity to Illinois' reasonable man standard, it may be more or less demanding of an alleged wrongdoer. This putative difference could lead to a different result if Mozambique rather than Illinois law is applied. Consequently, we are faced with a true conflict of laws and must evaluate the parties' contacts with the two states to determine which law should control.

Ingersoll refers us to what is now Restatement (Second) of Conflicts of Laws §145 (1971), for a listing of the contacts to be evaluated in determining which jurisdiction is most significantly concerned with the liability of the alleged tortfeasor. The first of these is the place where the injury occurred. The parties do not dispute that plaintiff sustained her injuries in Mozambique. Mrs. Pancotto accompanied her husband and sons on a hunting safari directed by defendant. She was taking pictures of other members of the hunting party when a swamp buggy driven by a Safrique employee ran into her.

The place of injury has an interest in applying its own tort principles to discourage harmful behavior within its borders. This interest in controlling the tortfeasor's conduct is strongest when the alleged tort is intentional. If the harmful contact is unintentional, however, the interest of the place of injury is attenuated. Realistically, the negligent tortfeasor is not affected by a state's civil liability laws because he does not premeditate before he acts. Nonetheless, to the extent that such conduct is shaped by legal standards, Mozambique was, at the time of the alleged wrong, interested in the choice of the standard of care to be imposed upon the defendant.

The second contact listed in the Restatement is the place of the conduct which caused injury, which is again clearly Mozambique. The interest of the jurisdiction where the conduct occurred is similar if not identical to that of the place of injury. Again, however, Mozambique's valid interest in controlling harmful conduct assumes less importance when the alleged tortfeasor was not governed by conscious reference to a behavioral standard.

The Restatement's third contact is the domicile or place of business of the parties. This consideration refers us to both Illinois law and that of Mozambique. The

---

1. At the time of plaintiff's injury in 1973, Mozambique was a territory of Portugal and applied the Portuguese Civil Code. See Affidavit of Marcel Molines. We take judicial notice that Mozambique in 1975 became an independent nation, with its own law. However, to the extent that Mozambique law is controlling, it is the law as it existed at the time of the alleged wrong.

plaintiff's domicile, Illinois, is interested in compensating both the victim and her creditors. Mozambique, on the other hand, as the defendant's domicile and principal place of business, is concerned that defendant's conduct conforms to its standards, and may also have an interest in insulating a domiciliary from liability.

The Restatement's final contact point is the place where the parties' relationship is centered. The relationship here has an international flavor. The safari was arranged in large part by intercontinental telephone calls and cables. In addition, certain employees of the defendant visited the plaintiff's husband in Illinois approximately three times prior to the safari, although the parties dispute the business as opposed to personal significance of the visits. Regardless of the nature of the Illinois contacts, they obviously were preparatory to an extended, well-planned interaction in Mozambique. . . . In short, although the relationship had international aspects, it can fairly be characterized as centering in Mozambique.

These contacts and the state interests evoked by them indicate that both Illinois and Mozambique are interested in the resolution of the liability issue. Both jurisdictions' interests are significant. The numerous Mozambique contacts highlight that government's interest in controlling the conduct of those who take action within its borders, and the interest in affording the protection of its laws to its domiciliaries. Illinois, on the other hand, has a strong interest in seeing that its residents are adequately compensated for tortious injuries. The Illinois interest, although based upon a single contact, cannot for that reason be automatically dismissed as less significant. A contact assumes significance only in view of the legal issue to which it relates. Our evaluation of the contacts indicates that both Illinois and Mozambique are validly interested in the resolution of the issue of defendant's liability, and we hesitate to characterize either jurisdiction's interest as more significant.

In general, the Illinois courts have chosen their own law rather than the law of the place of injury only if the majority of the significant contacts were in Illinois, and the tort's occurrence in the foreign state was fortuitous. See e.g., *Ingersoll,* supra. Given that both states here may assert significant although distinct interests in the outcome of the liability issue, the Illinois choice of law rule directs the application of the law of the place of injury, Mozambique.

We now turn to a determination of the Mozambique law governing liability for the acts of misconduct alleged in the complaint.

Rule 44.1 gives district courts wide discretion in the materials to which they may resort to determine the content of foreign law. The defendant has provided copies of the relevant sections of the Portuguese Civil Code, both in that language and in translation. In addition, defendant offers the affidavit of Mr. Marcel Molins, an expert witness conversant with the law of Portugal, who comments upon the law pertinent to the issues of liability and damages. Regarding liability, these combined resources indicate that Portuguese law sets out two standards for liability, either of which might apply to the facts alleged in the complaint. The first standard seems to be a rough equivalent, allowing for cultural differences, of the common law reasonable man standard. Under this standard, "[f]ault is judged, in the absence of another legal criterion, by the diligence with which a law-abiding male head of a family would act in the face of the circumstances of each case." Art. 487(2). The injured person carries the burden of proving that the opposing party was at fault as measured by this standard, unless there is a legal presumption of fault. Art. 487. . . .

. . . We also need edification on the question whether the common law reasonable man standard and the Mozambique "male head of a family" standard are equivalents or whether the latter imposes a greater or lesser standard of care than does the former. Therefore, in preparation for trial the parties are directed to submit supplemental materials addressing these issues.

II. The Measure of Damages

A brief look at Mozambique's and Illinois' laws on recoverable damages reveals an acute conflict. Illinois permits recovery for medical expenses due to the injury, and, inter alia, compensation for the injury itself, for disfigurement, and for pain and suffering. In contrast, Art. 508 of the Portuguese Civil Code limits liability for travel accidents to 600 contos, or approximately $6,600 in United States dollars. This limit is not inflexible, however. A Mozambique court may apparently, in its discretion, award damages to the full extent of the plaintiff's out-of-pocket loss, although the typical recovery is less generous. And, under Mozambique law, the plaintiff recovers nothing for pain and suffering, disfigurement, or loss of enjoyment of life as she might under Illinois law.

The defendant argues that the Illinois choice of law rule dictates the application of Mozambique law to this issue also. And, in fact, the analysis of the two jurisdictions' interests in the measure of damages leads to such a result. As the place of conduct, injury, defendant's domicile, and the place where the parties' relationship centered, Mozambique has a strong interest in the resolution of this issue. As plaintiff's domicile and the place where the consequences of the injury are felt, Illinois is concerned that plaintiff receives compensation. Plaintiff, however, contends that the application of Mozambique's damage limitation would be so grossly repugnant to Illinois' public and constitutional policy of providing a remedy for all injuries that an Illinois court would refuse to follow Mozambique law, even if the *Ingersoll* rule would normally dictate its application.

With no Illinois cases in point, the parties discuss certain cases in which the New York courts have faced similar contentions. Of these, Rosenthal v. Warren, 475 F.2d 438 (2d Cir. 1973), is the closest factually to the case here. As a federal court sitting in New York, the *Rosenthal* court was concerned with the proper application of New York's choice of law rule, which differs from the Illinois rule.[3] Despite this difference in orientation, *Rosenthal* points out the important factors to consider in determining whether the forum state's public policy should overrule the law of a foreign jurisdiction.

The plaintiff's decedent in *Rosenthal* was domiciled in New York. Accompanied by the plaintiff, his wife and later his executrix, the decedent traveled to Boston for

___

3. New York employs the "interest analysis" approach to conflicts of law, and applies the law of the jurisdiction which because of its relationship to the parties or the occurrence has the greatest concern with the specific issues raised in the case. Rosenthal v. Warren, 475 F.2d 438 (2d Cir. 1973). Applying this rule, the New York courts have attached heavy weight to their state's vital concern that injured domiciliaries are compensated for their loss. E.g., Miller v. Miller, 22 N.Y.2d 12 (1969). In contrast, Illinois follows the approach of the Second Restatement, and applies the law of the place of injury unless Illinois has a more significant interest in the outcome of a specific issue.

medical treatment by a physician domiciled in Massachusetts. The decedent died while recuperating in a Massachusetts hospital after surgery performed by the physician. The decedent's wife subsequently sued the physician and the hospital in a New York state court.

The defendants argued that the Massachusetts wrongful death statute, with its $50,000 limit on damages, should apply. The court rejected Massachusetts' statute in favor of New York's full compensation policy. Before doing so, the court confronted and thoroughly analyzed the factors militating against the forum's application of its own public policy. First, the court considered whether the defendants had patterned their conduct upon the Massachusetts statute. A doctor does not, however, ordinarily think of wrongful death limitations before performing surgery; consequently the doctor could not claim he acted in reliance upon a Massachusetts behavioral standard. Second, the court considered whether the defendants would be unfairly surprised by the application of New York law. Neither the doctor nor the hospital had a strictly local clientele or practice. Consequently it could not be said that they justifiably expected to be affected only by Massachusetts law. Third, the court considered whether defendants had purchased insurance in reliance upon the Massachusetts limitation. The defendants' policies, however, made no distinction between recoveries for personal injuries and recoveries for wrongful death. As a result, the defendants could not convincingly argue that they relied upon the Massachusetts limit. Finally, the court evaluated the policy behind the Massachusetts limitation to determine whether application of the New York law would frustrate an important Massachusetts interest. Finding that the few remaining wrongful death limitations are vestiges of the mistaken view that a common law action for wrongful death did not exist, the court declined to apply an archaic and unjust policy, particularly in view of its own policy to assure just and fair compensation for the victims of tortious conduct.

In short, *Rosenthal* indicates that the defendant's reliance, and principles of fundamental fairness and governmental policy should be balanced in determining whether the forum's measure of damages, grounded upon a strong public policy, may be applied against a foreign defendant.

Applying these principles to the factual context here yields some similar conclusions. The tort alleged in the complaint is unintentional, rendering any argument of behavioral reliance untenable. And, as in *Rosenthal*, the defendant here anticipated and welcomed, if not solicited, business contacts with persons outside the jurisdiction. The last two *Rosenthal* considerations, however, are not so easily dismissed. Defendant's counsel has submitted an affidavit attesting that defendant told him it carries no insurance. The competency of this affidavit is questionable as counsel has no personal knowledge of this fact. He has assured us, however, that competent evidence will be forthcoming before trial. If we place aside the question of the competency of the affidavit, the lack of insurance suggests that defendant relied upon Mozambique's damage limitation. . . . [W]e have no knowledge of the status of damage limitations for personal injury actions in the world community of nations.

Despite these countervailing considerations, our educated prediction is that the Illinois courts would refuse to enforce the Portuguese limitation as unreasonable and contrary to Illinois public policy. Illinois public policy is found in its Constitution, laws, judicial decisions, and also in its customs, morals, and notions of justice. Marchlik v. Coronet Ins. Co., 40 Ill. 2d 327 (1968). There is perhaps no more compelling Illinois public policy than one expressed in the state's Constitution, which provides that every person should find a certain remedy in the law for injuries to his person. Ill. Const. Art. I, §12. On occasion, the Illinois courts have accepted reasonable limits on recoveries for personal injuries, as for example in the Dram Shop Act and the Wrongful Death Act. Ill. Rev. Stat. (1973). But as the Illinois Supreme Court noted in its recent decision invalidating Illinois' medical malpractice law, these statutes created actions unknown at common law. Thus, the courts were not disturbed when the newly created right was accompanied by a limited remedy. But if the right existed at common law, damage limitations without a *quid pro quo* have been disfavored. Id. Moreover, the damage limitations incorporated into Illinois legislation have been more consistent with potential out-of-pocket loss. The Dram Shop Act limits damages to $20,000. Ill. Rev. Stat. ch. 43, §135, the recently voided malpractice act carried a $500,000 limit.

Of course, we are not dealing here with a law of Illinois, but one from a foreign country. Recently liberated from foreign rule, the economic and social conditions in Mozambique are quite different from those in Illinois. Recognizing such international disparities, the court in Ciprari v. Servicos Aereos Cruzeiro, 245 F. Supp. 819 (S.D.N.Y. 1965), applied the Brazilian Code, which limited damages to an amount less than $100. The court, however, emphasized the unique justifications for the limitation, which applied only to accidents involving Brazil's national airline. In particular, the court cited Brazil's public policy of protecting the financial integrity of an infant national industry, and the overtones of national security in Brazil's special interest in the national airline. On the contrary, no exceptional national concern is asserted here. Instead, the damage limitation is general. . . .

In the absence of an articulated national policy, the final inquiry is whether the application of the Illinois law would unfairly prejudice the defendant. Although the defendant is a Mozambique corporation, its trade is international in scope. Safrique allows travel agencies to use its name in advertisements for sporting magazines with national circulation. If Safrique induces residents of other countries to visit Mozambique and profits from the excursions, it is hardly unfair to require Safrique to compensate its clients for tortious injuries inflicted by Safrique employees. Concomitantly, Safrique cannot claim that its clients' residencies take it by surprise. Indeed, Safrique deliberately engages in a business which thrives on international tourism.

A final aspect of the question of prejudice involves counsel's allegation that defendant carries no liability insurance. Safrique's failure to obtain insurance, however, is not alleged to have been motivated by the Mozambique damage limitation. Without supplemental affidavits, this neglect is as easily attributed to oversight as to a calculated business decision that it might cost more in premiums than to directly compensate a victim to the statutory limit.

In conclusion, although the Illinois choice of law rule indicates the application of Mozambique's law to the substantive issues in this action, we feel the Illinois courts would refuse to enforce the Mozambique policy of providing a remedy for personal injuries. Foreign substantive law is not unenforceable simply because it differs from our own law, but because the differences are against public policy. The refusal to enforce a foreign law should not be lightly made. But when no justification is offered for a policy which contravenes a sound public policy of the forum, and the defendant is not unfairly surprised, we believe that the Illinois courts would decline to apply the foreign limitation.

Notes and Questions

1. In *Pancotto,* where did the U.S. district court look for its choice-of-law rules?

2. Applying the selected choice-of-law approach, did the *Pancotto* court then use Illinois's or Mozambique's substantive tort law? Which jurisdiction's law did the court employ for determining damages?

3. As Professors Richman and Reynolds report, "The Second Restatement is the dominant conflicts methodology in American courts today. Twenty-two jurisdictions follow the Restatement's approach in tort conflicts, and twenty-four do so in contract cases. Additionally several other jurisdictions follow the similar 'significant contacts' approach thus yielding a majority of American jurisdictions. The next most popular American choice-of-law methodology, the traditional First Restatement approach, can claim less than half as many adherents." Understanding Conflict of Laws 213-214 (3d ed. 2002).

4. What law would the *Pancotto* court apply if it followed the First Restatement view? Would it be desirable to prevent forum shopping?

5. Do you see similarities between section 403 of the Restatement, which describes limits on a state's right to apply its law to conduct having connections with more than one state (or its jurisdiction to prescribe), and interest analysis on the Second Restatement approach? Is there any reason that a state should be more or less limited in its right to apply criminal law, regulatory law like the Sherman Act, or normal tort or contract law?

6. Section 403 assumes that more than one state may have jurisdiction to prescribe law to the same conduct. Section 421 sets forth expansive rules for asserting adjudicatory jurisdiction. Would you expect a U.S. judge ever to decide that the U.S. interest in litigation was less than the competing foreign interest? (See the discussion above after *Hartford Fire.*) Did the holding in *Pancotto* vindicate U.S. or Mozambique policy?

7. In an international setting, is a vested rights (or territorial) approach better than an interest analysis (section 403-like) approach? At least for potential conflicts of public law? Or is it better in all settings?

8. If it is sometimes illegitimate for the United States to apply sanctions when it applies public law extraterritorially, as suggested by section 403 and *Sensor* (supra at pages 659 and 676), should the result be different in the case of the application of U.S. tort law, procedural (discovery) law, or toxic pesticides rules? Why was the distinction drawn between public and private law? Is that distinction still viable?

9. Should a U.S. court have adjudicated the liability of Union Carbide Corporation for the gas leak disaster that occured at its foreign subsidary in Bhopal, India? (See discussion of forum non conveniens earlier.) If the U.S. court kept the case, what law should apply? Could Congress pass an antipollution law applicable to foreign subsidiaries of U.S. corporations anywhere in the world? Should it?

8

State Responsibility: Injuries to Aliens and International Human Rights

Chapter 5 introduced the concept of the "state," and in that chapter and in Chapter 6 we explored some of the more important consequences of statehood in the context of United States litigation. Chapter 7 examined the rights conferred by international law on a state to regulate private conduct, both inside and outside the state's territory, and the limitations imposed by international law on that authority. That chapter focused on the limitations of state authority in the event of conflicts of legitimate state claims to regulate, especially those occurring when a state asserts authority to regulate conduct *outside* its own territory. This chapter explores the limitations imposed by international law on the exercise of a state's authority to regulate private conduct *inside* its territory.

Traditionally, international law applied only to a state's treatment of *aliens* within its territory, not to the state's treatment of its own nationals. Since World War II, however, international human rights law has changed that framework. Now international law standards are increasingly brought to bear on the conduct of a state within its territory vis-à-vis its own nationals. Section A explains the traditional background of state responsibility for injuries to aliens and explores the question of international responsibility for injury to alien property. Section B covers international human rights law and the ways in which it is implemented and enforced.

A. STATE RESPONSIBILITY FOR INJURIES TO ALIENS

1. Historical Background

The following excerpt from a classic text on public international law summarizes the traditional rules of state responsibility (and the deeply entrenched Latin American opposition to those rules).

743

J. L. Brierly, The Law of Nations

276-287 (6th ed. 1963)

No state is legally bound to admit aliens into its territory, but if it does so it must observe a certain standard of decent treatment towards them, and their own state may demand reparation for an injury caused to them by a failure to observe this standard. The legal basis of such a demand, in the words of the Permanent Court [of International Justice], is that

> in taking up the case of one of its nationals, by resorting to diplomatic action or international judicial proceedings on his behalf, a state is in reality asserting its own right, the right to ensure in the person of its nationals respect for the rules of international law. This right is necessarily limited to the intervention on behalf of its own nationals because, in the absence of a special agreement, it is the bond of nationality between the state and the individual which alone confers upon the state the right of diplomatic protection, and it is as a part of the function of diplomatic protection that the right to take up a claim and to ensure respect for the rules of international law must be envisaged.*

There is a certain artificiality in this way of looking at the question. No doubt a state has in general an interest in seeing that its nationals are fairly treated in a foreign country, but it is an exaggeration to say that whenever a national is injured in a foreign state, his state as a whole is necessarily injured too. In practice, as we shall see, the theory is not consistently adhered to; for instance, the logic of the theory would require that damages should be measured by reference to the injury suffered by the state, which is obviously not the same as that suffered by the individual, but in fact the law allows them to be assessed on the loss to the individual, as though it were the injury to him which was the cause of action. The procedure, too, is far from satisfactory from the individual's point of view. He has no remedy of his own, and the state to which he belongs may be unwilling to take up his case for reasons which have nothing to do with its merits; and even if it is willing to do so, there may be interminable delays before, if ever, the defendant state can be induced to let the matter go to arbitration. Delay, besides being unjust to the claimant, creates difficulties in securing satisfactory evidence, and also often leads to the original claim being exaggerated beyond all recognition. It has been suggested that a solution might be found by allowing individuals access in their own right to some form of international tribunal for the purpose, and if proper safeguards against merely frivolous or vexatious claims could be devised, that is a possible reform which deserves to be considered. For the time being, however, the prospect of states accepting such a change is not very great.

[I]n the absence of a regular procedure for dealing with them the rules by which they ought to be determined have been obscured, both by the tendency of the stronger powers to press the claims of their nationals without much regard to legal justification, and by that of the weaker powers to try to avoid responsibilities for corrupt or incompetent administration by exaggerated emphasis on the rights supposed to be inherent in their independent status.

In general a person who voluntarily enters the territory of a state not his own must accept the institutions of that state as he finds them. He is not entitled to

---

* Pansvezys-Saldutiskis Railway Case, Seriès A/B 76, p. 16.

demand equality of treatment in all respects with the citizens of the state; for example, he is almost always debarred from the political rights of a citizen; he is commonly not allowed to engage in the coasting trade, or to fish in territorial waters; he is sometimes not allowed to hold land. These and many other discriminations against him are not forbidden by international law. On the other hand, if a state has a low standard of justice towards its own nationals, an alien's position is in a sense a privileged one, for the standard of treatment to which international law entitles him is an objective one, and he need not, even though nationals must, submit to unjust treatment. This statement of the law is denied by certain Latin-American states, which hold that if a state grants equality of treatment to nationals and non-nationals it fulfils its international obligation; but such a view would make each state the judge of the standard required by international law, and would virtually deprive aliens of the protection of their own state altogether. Facts with respect to equality of treatment of aliens and nationals may be important in determining the merits of a complaint of mistreatment of an alien. But such equality is not the ultimate test of the propriety of the acts of the authorities in the light of international law. That test is, broadly speaking, whether aliens are treated in accordance with ordinary standards of civilization.

This international standard cannot be made a matter of precise rules. It is the standard of the "reasonable state," reasonable, that is to say, according to the notions that are accepted in our modern civilization. It was thus described by the U.S.-Mexican Claims Commission [in the *Neers* case]:

> the propriety of governmental acts should be put to the test of international standards, and . . . the treatment of an alien, in order to constitute an international delinquency, should amount to an outrage, to bad faith, to wilful neglect of duty, or to an insufficiency of governmental action so far short of international standards that every reasonable and impartial man would readily recognize its insufficiency. Whether the insufficiency proceeds from deficient execution of an intelligent law or from the fact that the laws of the country do not empower the authorities to measure up to international standards is immaterial.

The standard therefore is not an exacting one, nor does it require a uniform degree of governmental efficiency irrespective of circumstances; for example, measures of police protection which would be reasonable in a capital city cannot fairly be demanded in a sparsely populated territory, and a security which is normal in times of tranquillity cannot be expected in a time of temporary disorder such as may occasionally occur even in a well-ordered state. But the standard being an international one, a state cannot relieve itself of responsibility by any provision of its own national law. Thus the central government of a federal or other composite state may be *constitutionally* unable to secure that justice is rendered to an alien by the authorities of a member state or of a colony, but if the central government is the only government which has relations with other states its *international* responsibility is not affected by the domestic limitation of its own powers.

It is ordinarily a condition of an international claim for the redress of an injury suffered by an alien that the alien himself should first have exhausted any remedies available to him under the local law. A state is not required to guarantee that the person or property of an alien will not be injured, and the mere fact that such an injury has been suffered does not give his own state a right to demand reparation on his behalf. If a state in which an alien is injured puts at his disposal apparently effective and sufficient legal remedies for obtaining redress, international law requires that he should have had recourse to and exhausted these remedies before his own state becomes entitled to intervene on his behalf. The principle of this rule is that a state is entitled to have a full and proper opportunity of doing justice in its own way before international justice is demanded of it by another state. The local remedies which must be exhausted include administrative remedies of a legal nature but not extra-legal remedies or remedies as of grace. . . .

Although . . . the local remedies rule is applied with a certain strictness, it does not mean that it is necessary for the individual to exhaust remedies which, though theoretically available, would be ineffective or insufficient to redress the injury of which he complains; for example, if the case or statute law binding upon the local courts was such as must compel them to reject his claim, or if, his claim having been lost in a lower court, it was useless to appeal because the critical point was one of fact and the higher court had no power to alter findings of fact. If the local tribunals are notoriously corrupt or notoriously discriminate against foreigners, the individual is not required "to exhaust justice when there is no justice to exhaust." Again, if the wrong has been committed by the legislature itself or by some high official, it not infrequently happens that the local law provides no remedy and in that case there are no local remedies to exhaust. In general, therefore, the prior exhaustion of local remedies is a condition of presenting an international claim unless it can be shown that either there were no local remedies to exhaust or that it was obviously futile to have recourse to those that were available.

Another condition of presenting an international claim is that there should be a bond of nationality between the claimant state and the person injured. So much is the bond of nationality a condition of an international claim that it must not only exist at the date of the original injury but must also continue until the date of the judgment or award. Thus, if the beneficial interest in the claim has meanwhile passed, by death or by assignment, from the person originally injured to a person of a different nationality, the right to bring an international claim will lapse. In principle, international law leaves it to each state to settle by its own laws the rules determining the persons whom it considers to be its own nationals. The International Court, however, has laid down in the *Nottebohm* case that the provisions of a state's municipal laws are not necessarily conclusive to establish its right to exercise diplomatic protection under international law, if the bond of nationality between the person injured and the claimant state is not a real and effective one. . . .

A state may incur responsibility by the act or omission of any of its organs, legislative, executive, or judicial. . . .

In certain circumstances the wrongful act of an official may involve his state in responsibility to the state of an injured alien. In the first place the official must have acted within the scope of his office; otherwise his act would be like that of a private individual. Secondly, a state has a higher responsibility for the acts of superior officials than for those of subordinates. . . .

The term "denial of justice" is sometimes loosely used to denote *any* international delinquency towards an alien for which a state is liable to make reparation. In this sense it is an unnecessary and confusing term. Its more proper sense is an injury involving the responsibility of the state committed by a court of justice, and on the question what acts of this kind do involve the state in responsibility there are two views. Most Latin-American states insist on a very narrow interpretation, and contend in effect that if the courts give a decision of any kind there can be no denial of justice and consequently no responsibility of the state for their conduct. Nothing but the denial to foreigners of access to the courts can be properly regarded as a denial of justice. This view, which involves the virtual rejection of the principle of an international standard applicable to the action of courts of law towards foreigners, cannot be accepted. There are many possible ways in which a court may fall below the standard fairly to be demanded of a civilized state without literally closing its doors. Such acts cannot be exhaustively enumerated, but corruption, threats, unwarrantable delay, flagrant abuse of judicial procedure, a judgment dictated by the executive, or so manifestly unjust that no court which was both competent and honest could have given it, are instances. Possibly it is convenient also to include in the term certain acts or omissions of organs of government other than courts, but closely connected with the administration of justice, such as execution without trial, inexcusable failure to bring a wrongdoer to trial, long imprisonment before trial, grossly inadequate punishment, or failure to enforce a judgment duly given. But no merely erroneous or even unjust judgment of a court will constitute a denial of justice, except in one case, namely where a court, having occasion to apply some rule of international law, gives an incorrect interpretation of that law, or where it applies, as it may be bound by its municipal law to do, a rule of domestic law which is itself contrary to international law.

It will be observed that even on the wider interpretation of the term "denial of justice" which is here adopted, the misconduct must be extremely gross. The justification of this strictness is that the independence of courts is an accepted canon of decent government, and the law therefore does not lightly hold a state responsible for their faults. It follows that an allegation of a denial of justice is a serious step which states, as mentioned above, are reluctant to take when a claim can be based on other grounds.

Restatement

Section 711. State Responsibility for Injury to Nationals of Other States

A state is responsible under international law for injury to a national of another state caused by an official act or omission that violates

(a) a human right that . . . a state is obligated to respect for all persons subject to its authority;

(b) a personal right that, under international law, a state is obligated to respect for individuals of foreign nationality; or

(c) a right to property or another economic interest that, under international law, a state is obligated to respect for persons, natural or juridical, of foreign nationality, as provided in §712.

Reporters' Notes

1. Injury to aliens and human rights standards. In the early decades of the 20th century, there was substantial agreement among the countries of Europe and North America on basic rules as to the protection to be afforded to foreign nationals. The countries of Latin America, most of which were recipients of foreign persons and capital, rejected these rules. After the Second World War, with the emergence of many new

importing states, and with the development of the law of human rights, opposition to special protection for aliens increased. It is generally accepted that states may invoke recognized international human rights standards on behalf of their nationals; attempts to invoke protections going beyond international human rights standards, as in clauses (b) and (c) of this section, might be resisted by some states.

2. Rights of foreign nationals recognized under customary law. Before the development of the contemporary law of human rights, states were held responsible for injury to aliens consisting of, or resulting from, various acts or omissions deemed to violate an international standard of justice or other standards accepted in customary international law. The law of responsibility for such injuries was largely developed by claims practice, by negotiation and agreement concerning liability and compensation, and by decisions of arbitral tribunals and claims commissions established pursuant to international agreement. . . .

This body of state practice and decision may be summarized as follows:

A. States have been held responsible for injury due to various actions that have since been accepted as violations of human rights in the Universal Declaration on Human Rights or the Covenant on Civil and Political Rights:

— Denials of due process in criminal proceedings:
  — arbitrary arrest
  — unlawful or prolonged detention or interrogation
  — prolonged arbitrary imprisonment
  — excessive bail
  — delayed trial
  — unfair trial
  — being tried twice for the same offense
  — failure to render a decision
  — tribunal manipulated by the executive
  — denial of right to defend oneself and confront witnesses
  — conviction without diligent and competent counsel
  — denial of an interpreter
  — denial to accused of communication with representatives of his government
— Arbitrary use of force by officials:
  — arbitrary or excessive use of force by state officials
  — inhuman treatment
  — arbitrary molestation of the person; torture to elicit "confession"
— Other violations of recognized rights: Claims were also made on behalf of aliens for other actions violating rights later recognized in the Universal Declaration, such as freedom of speech, freedom of religion, freedom to travel within a country, and the right to marry. There is some authority in international law to support such claims, but these freedoms might be restricted to resident aliens, and might be denied in time of national emergency.

There were also claims for injury due to denial to foreign nationals of benefits enjoyed by nationals, such as social security or aid to indigents or incompetents, or due to other discrimination between aliens and nationals or against aliens of particular nationality. International law forbids some such discriminations, but others are permitted. Compare the corresponding jurisprudence under the "equal protection" clause of the Fourteenth Amendment to the United States Constitution. . . .

B. State practice and arbitral decisions have supported state responsibility for several kinds of injury to aliens that have not been recognized as violations of human rights, clause (b) of this section. They include:

— Failure to protect foreign nationals. The rule that developed out of the arbitral awards before World War II was that a state was responsible for injuries inflicted upon aliens by private individuals only if the state failed, by intention or neglect, to provide adequate police protection for those aliens. A state incurs no liability for injury to aliens by acts of revolutionary forces if the state is unable to protect the aliens from such injury. If the revolutionary forces succeed, the state may become liable for their actions during the struggle for power. A state has greater and more specific duties under customary law and under some international agreements to protect certain classes of aliens, such as diplomatic or consular personnel. The seizure of the United States Embassy and the taking of United States hostages in Iran in 1979-80 may have been initially the act of a mob which the authorities could not prevent, but was soon ratified and became state policy for which Iran was responsible. See Case Concerning United States Diplomatic and Consular Staff in Tehran (United States v. Iran), [1980] I.C.J. Rep. 3.

— Failure to punish offenses against aliens. There is support for a rule obligating a state to act vigorously and diligently to punish crimes against aliens. It is argued that failure to punish shows contempt for the alien's state and increases the possibility of harm befalling other nationals of that state. . . .

— Failure to provide aliens a legal remedy. It is a wrong under international law for a state to deny a foreign national access to domestic courts. That is the central meaning of "denial of justice." Treaties of friendship, commerce, and navigation generally provide that each party shall give to nationals of the other party access to its courts on the same basis as to its own nationals. However, states reserve the right to deny access to their courts to corporations that have not registered or qualified to do business in the state although they in fact do business within the jurisdiction.

United States law generally affords aliens access to courts even in the absence of international agreement, although in respect of some claims against the United States, the right is conditioned on reciprocity by the alien's country of nationality.

C. States have been deemed not responsible under international law for
— Certain alleged procedural insufficiencies:
— witness did not take oath
— reasonable security for costs was required
— court incorrectly but in good faith applied or interpreted the law
— case dismissed for lack of jurisdiction (when another forum was available)
— "technical objections" or "minor irregularities"
— Such restrictions on aliens as:
— exclusion from public employment
— limiting access to certain professions and occupations
— denying access to public facilities or resources
— denying right to own or inherit certain property or interests in property
— requiring aliens to register or be otherwise identified
— deporting or expelling aliens pursuant to law
— requiring aliens to serve on juries or testify as witnesses or experts.

Notes and Questions

1. How would you articulate the international law standard? What is the "standard of the 'reasonable state'"? What seemed to have been required by the United States-Mexican Claims Commission, quoted in the Brierly excerpt? What is the meaning of a "denial of justice"?

2. Why do you think Latin American states resisted the idea of an objective minimum standard for the treatment of aliens?

3. To what extent are nations responsible for a failure to act? Does their obligation to act depend on their resources? See generally Gordon A. Christenson, Attributing Acts of Omission to the State, 12 Mich. J. Intl. L. 312 (1991).

4. Historically, the law of state responsibility was primarily reflected in customary international law rather than treaties. How was this customary international law ascertained? If an arbitral commission were adjudicating an alleged violation of the law of state responsibility, what materials would it look to in order to determine the content of this law?

5. As noted in the Brierly excerpt, normally the injured alien must exhaust local remedies before a claim may be brought for a violation of the law of state responsibility. What does exhaustion of local remedies entail? Are there circumstances under which exhaustion will not be required?

Problem. Suppose you have been asked by Singapore's ambassador to the United States to give advice on the options available to his government and the Singapore nationals injured in the following incident that occurred in southern California in January 1986: A family from Singapore rented a car at Los Angeles airport and drove down to San Diego. While returning that evening to Disneyland, they were detained by the Immigration and Naturalization Service (INS) at a routine immigration checkpoint. The INS officer demanded their passports, which they had left in their hotel in Los Angeles. They produced Singapore identity cards and driving licenses and explained the situation in English (the official language of Singapore). They pointed out that they were driving a car rented in Los Angeles. Nevertheless, apparently thinking they were illegal Hispanic immigrants, the officer threw them in a cell and threatened to deport them. Let us assume that they were held overnight (a family of five in a room without sanitation facilities), and then taken to the Mexican border where, although unable to speak Spanish, they were physically deported.

(a) Outline the options available — diplomatic and judicial — and what remedies would be available. How much would a lawsuit cost? Can you get compensation some other way?

(b) As Legal Adviser to the State Department how would you respond to a diplomatic claim by Singapore? Would you invoke the doctrine of exhaustion of local remedies? (See Brierly.) If not, could you authorize an agreement between the United States and Singapore, settling the claim for an agreed amount of compensation? Or agree to arbitrate the dispute? Is *Dames & Moore,* page 215, distinguishable? What if the compensation to be paid was nominal? Could you offer a formal apology?

(c) What if, on their return to the United States, the Singapore family was surrounded by an angry mob of detained aliens who attacked and beat them while the INS and local police officers looked on? Suppose instead that the police jailed them, knowing that they would almost certainly be beaten and raped. Would either be a violation of international law?

(d) Assume a U.S. court refused to permit recovery because of domestic constitutional law doctrines regarding official immunity. Would that refusal be a denial of justice and therefore a violation of international law?

(e) Could your clients use the Alien Tort Statute (discussed in Chapter 3) to sue federal and local officials for damages for violating international human rights law?

2. *Attribution of Conduct to the State*

The following excerpt discusses the circumstances under which conduct is attributed to the state for purposes of state responsibility.

Gordon A. Christenson, Attribution Issues in State Responsibility

1990 Proc. Am. Socy. Intl. L. 51, 52-57

The separation of conduct of the state from that of private or nonstate persons became almost universal once feudal collective responsibility receded. The central function of international law in determining this separation has remained unquestioned. Three principles, reflected in all recent codifications and restatements, summarize the tradition. *Three gendly principles*

The first principle says that a state acts through people exercising the state's machinery of power and authority. Acts or omissions of official organs, agents or political subdivisions, including those of successful revolutionary regimes, necessarily are those of the state. These include acts of de facto agents under direct control of those in power in a state or those acting as a government. . . .

The second principle is that international law does not attribute conduct of a nonstate character, such as acts or omissions of private persons, mobs, associations, corporations, trade unions or unsuccessful insurgents, to a state as such. The Harvard Draft emphasizes the independent duty of the state to protect aliens and distinguishes between state conduct from failure of duty and the actual acts of nonstate parties. . . .

The third principle is that a state may act through its own independent failure of duty or inaction when an international obligation requires state action in relation to nonstate conduct. This principle properly is a corollary to the first. . . . For example, a state has a duty to take reasonable care to protect aliens from harm and to punish offenders with due diligence. Inaction in the face of this duty is conduct attributable to the state quite independently of the actual wrongful acts. An example, as articulated in the Restatement (Third), of this duty is "to provide aliens reasonable police protection; the state is not responsible for injuries caused by private persons that result despite such police protection. . . ."

Nicaragua claimed U.S. responsibility for the contra insurgency in Nicaragua, for the mining of Nicaraguan harbors, and for other acts of intervention including the distribution of a guerrilla manual on psychological warfare. The acts of the contras during their insurgency in Nicaragua, though supported by U.S. military and other assistance, were not attributable to the United States. According to the opinion [of the International Court of Justice, pages 1010-1015 below], Nicaragua did not present sufficient evidence that the United States controlled the specific military operations of the insurgency. The Court also found insufficient evidence of U.S. involvement in the financing and tactical and strategic planning of contra attacks. Even if the United States "generally controlled" the contras, and the contras were "highly dependent" on the United States, this fact in itself would not mean that contra acts were attributable to the United States.

In order for contra conduct to be attributable, the U.S. Government would have had to possess effective control of the contras at the time the disputed activities occurred. . . .

The trend toward strictness in attributing conduct may be seen especially in recent decisions of the Iran-United States Claims Tribunal dealing with whether allegedly coercive expulsion was attributable to Iran for purposes of responsibility under the Algiers Accords. . . .

Four cases from the Tribunal confirm . . . using attribution doctrine to cut back the scope of a successful revolution's obligation to protect aliens from mob action or chaos during the revolution. . . .

Nongovernmental death squads in some countries have systematically eliminated political opposition by the tragic terror of torture and disappearances, not directed by any formal state action but instead allowed by responsible government officials averting their eyes, if not by outright collusion. Tacit approval or complicity by officials would unquestionably be conduct attributable to the state as a breach of human rights or as a crime of state against its own citizens. . . .

Suppose, however, that the link to government is much more difficult to show, that the wink and the nod denoting approval cannot be traced, and that the work of the death squads is seen more as the work of vigilantes or private terrorists. When such action is directed against aliens, the state has a clear affirmative duty under customary international law to protect against criminal acts, and may be held responsible. More often, the victims are nationals of the country as well as foreigners. . . . Failure to protect citizens from "private" death squads in these disappearances by failure to exercise due diligence should be attributable to the state. . . .

If, however, all governments have this affirmative duty to all persons within their jurisdiction, then the central power of a legitimate government to control private vigilante groups and death squads must be strengthened. This is a curious dilemma for all modern liberal governments.

In 2001, after decades of study and drafting, the International Law Commission (the principal law development arm of the United Nations) adopted a set of nonbinding Draft Articles on the Responsibility of States for Internationally Wrongful Acts. The UN General Assembly adopted a resolution on December 12, 2001, that "[t]akes note of the articles" and "commends them to the attention of Governments without prejudice to the question of their future adoption or other appropriate action." The following articles address the issue of attribution:

Article 4

Conduct of organs of a State

1. The conduct of any State organ shall be considered an act of that State under international law, whether the organ exercises legislative, executive, judicial or any other functions, whatever position it holds in the organization of the State, and whatever its character as an organ of the central government or of a territorial unit of the State.

2. An organ includes any person or entity which has that status in accordance with the internal law of the State.

Article 5

Conduct of persons or entities exercising elements of governmental authority

The conduct of a person or entity which is not an organ of the State under article 4 but which is empowered by the law of that State to exercise elements of the governmental authority shall be considered an act of the State under international law, provided the person or entity is acting in that capacity in the particular instance.

Article 6

Conduct of organs placed at the disposal of a State by another State

The conduct of an organ placed at the disposal of a State by another State shall be considered an act of the former State under international law if the organ is acting in the exercise of elements of the governmental authority of the State at whose disposal it is placed.

Article 7

Excess of authority or contravention of instructions

The conduct of an organ of a State or of a person or entity empowered to exercise elements of the governmental authority shall be considered an act of the State under international law if the organ, person or entity acts in that capacity, even if it exceeds its authority or contravenes instructions.

Article 8

Conduct directed or controlled by a State

The conduct of a person or group of persons shall be considered an act of a State under international law if the person or group of persons is in fact acting on the instructions of, or under the direction or control of, that State in carrying out the conduct.

Article 9

Conduct carried out in the absence or default of the official authorities

The conduct of a person or group of persons shall be considered an act of a State under international law if the person or group of persons is in fact exercising elements of the governmental authority in the absence or default of the official authorities and in circumstances such as to call for the exercise of those elements of authority.

Article 10

Conduct of an insurrectional or other movement

1. The conduct of an insurrectional movement which becomes the new government of a State shall be considered an act of that State under international law.

2. The conduct of a movement, insurrectional or other, which succeeds in establishing a new State in part of the territory of a pre-existing State or in a territory under its administration shall be considered an act of the new State under international law.

3. This article is without prejudice to the attribution to a State of any conduct, however related to that of the movement concerned, which is to be considered an act of that State by virtue of articles 4 to 9.

Article 11

Conduct acknowledged and adopted by a State as its own

Conduct which is not attributable to a State under the preceding articles shall nevertheless be considered an act of that State under international law if and to the extent that the State acknowledges and adopts the conduct in question as its own.

Notes and Questions

1. Based on the Christenson excerpt and the ILC Draft Articles, when is a state responsible for the conduct of non-state actors? For example, when would a state be responsible for the actions of a terrorist organization that operated from within the state's borders?

2. In its decision involving the 1979-1980 hostage situation at the U.S. embassy in Iran (discussed in Chapter 4), the International Court of Justice found that the student militants who stormed the embassy and seized the U.S. hostages were not initially acting on behalf of Iran, because Iranian authorities had not specifically instructed them to do what they did. Nevertheless, the Court found Iran liable for failing to take appropriate steps both to prevent the attack and to end the hostage situation. Later on, Iranian authorities officially approved the occupation and declared that the U.S. personnel at the embassy were "under arrest." At that point, reasoned the Court, "The militants, authors of the invasion and jailers of the hostages, had now become agents of the Iranian State for whose acts the State itself was internationally responsible." Case Concerning United States Diplomatic and Consular Staff in Tehran (United States v. Iran), 1980 I.C.J. 4, ¶74 (May 24).

3. In the *Nicaragua* case, discussed above by Professor Christenson and also discussed in Chapter 4, the International Court of Justice considered whether the United States was responsible for violations of international humanitarian law allegedly committed by the *contra* rebel forces in Nicaragua. Although the Court found that the United States had provided substantial assistance to the *contras*, and that this assistance violated international law (regarding intervention in the affairs of another state), the Court concluded that the United States was not responsible for the specific acts of the *contras*. The Court reasoned:

Despite the heavy subsidies and other support provided to them by the United States, there is no clear evidence of the United States having actually exercised such a degree of control in all fields as to justify treating the *contras* as acting on its behalf. . . . [The United States would not be responsible for the conduct of the *contras*] without further evidence, that the United States directed or enforced the perpetration of the acts contrary to human rights and humanitarian law alleged by the applicant State. Such acts could well be committed by members of the *contras* without the control of the United States. For this conduct to give rise to legal responsibility of the United States, it would in principle have to be proved that that State had effective control of the military or paramilitary operations in the course of which the alleged violations were committed. [Military and Paramilitary Activities In and Against Nicaragua (Nicaragua v. United States of America), Merits, I.C.J. Reports 1986, ¶¶109, 115.]

The Appeals Chamber of the International Criminal Tribunal for the Former Yugoslavia adopted a somewhat broader approach to attribution in its 1999 decision, Prosecutor v. Tadic. In that case, the Appeals Chamber had to decide whether the actions of the defendant, a Bosnian Serb, had occurred in the context of an international armed conflict, which turned on whether the Federal Republic of Yugoslavia was responsible for the actions of the Bosnian Serb forces. The Chamber criticized the *Nicaragua* court's adoption of a single "effective control" test:

The requirement of international law for the attribution to States of acts performed by private individuals is that the State exercises control over the individuals. The *degree of control* may, however, vary according to the factual circumstances of each case. The Appeals Chamber fails to see why in each and every circumstance international law should require a high threshold for the test of control. [Prosecutor v. Tadic, Judgment, ICTFY Appeals Chamber, ¶117 (July 15, 1999).]

The Chamber distinguished between state responsibility for the actions of individuals and state responsibility for the actions of organized groups. With respect to the latter, the Chamber concluded that it is sufficient for attribution "that the Group as a whole be under the overall control of the State." Id., ¶120. If the group is under the overall control of the State, the Chamber reasoned, "it must perforce engage the *responsibility of that State* for its activities, *whether or not each of them was specifically* imposed, requested or directed by the State." Id., ¶122. Under this analysis, in order for a state to be responsible for the actions of a military or paramilitary group, "it must be proved that the State wields overall control over the group, not only by equipping and financing the group, but also by coordinating or helping in the general planning of its military activity." Id., ¶131. How does the test for attribution in *Tadic* differ from the one in *Nicaragua*? Which test do the ILC Draft Articles adopt?

4. In a federal state (such as the United States), is the national government responsible for the conduct of sub-national officials? What if the national government lacks the constitutional authority to stop the sub-national officials from engaging in the allegedly wrongful conduct? In its initial order in the *LaGrand Case* (discussed in Chapters 3 and 4), the International Court of Justice made clear that the United States was responsible for violations of the Vienna Convention on Consular Relations by state or local authorities in the United States, stating that "the international responsibility of a State is engaged by the action of the competent organs and authorities acting in that State, whatever they may be." Case Concerning the Vienna Convention on Consular Relations (Germany v. United States of America), 38 I.L.M. 308, 313 (1999). See also Ronan Doherty, Note, Foreign Affairs v. Federalism: How

State Control of Criminal Law Implicates Federal Responsibility Under International Law, 82 Va. L. Rev. 1281 (1996).

5. To what extent is a nation responsible under international law for the decisions of its courts? What if the political branches of the nation had no role in the litigation? In a recent arbitration case brought against the United States under Chapter 11 of the North American Free Trade Agreement (NAFTA), the arbitration panel held that a U.S. judicial decision could constitute an expropriation for purposes of the Agreement. Chapter 11 applies to "measures adopted or maintained by a party" that relate to investors or investment, and NAFTA defines "measure" to include "any law, regulation, procedure, requirement or practice." The panel noted that this is a broad definition that contains no exclusion for judicial decisions and that the term "measure" has been construed by other tribunals to encompass judicial decisions. The panel also reasoned that interpreting the word "measure" in this way "accords with the general principle of State responsibility." See The Loewen Group, Inc. v. United States, ICSID Case No. ARB(AF)/98/3. (As of January 2003, the panel had not yet issued a decision on the merits of this case.)

6. For additional discussion of the issue of attribution, see Gordon A. Christenson, The Doctrine of Attribution in State Responsibility, in International Law of State Responsibility for Injuries to Aliens 321 (Richard B. Lillich ed., 1983); Gregory Townsend, State Responsibility for Acts of De Facto Agents, 14 Ariz. J. Intl. & Comp. L. 635 (1997). For additional discussion of the ILC Draft Articles, see Symposium, The ILC's State Responsibility Articles, 96 Am. J. Intl. L. 773-890 (2002).

3.   Property Rights

One of the most hotly debated issues in the area of state responsibility focuses on property rights. During the 1960s and 1970s, developing countries waged a vigorous attack on multinational corporate behavior and the international economic system in general, in part through advocating in the U.N. General Assembly the declaration of a "New International Economic Order" (NIEO). Their attempts were equally vigorously opposed by the United States and other capital-exporting states. One focus of the debate concerned expropriation of property. Although the asserted right to expropriate property without meeting international law-based standards of compensation now seems to have faded in the current wave of global market liberalism, the debates over the NIEO have contributed to customary law that continues to be applied — and will be applied in the future — by arbitral tribunals and courts. Customary law, of course, may also serve as a basis for advocacy and diplomatic protest.

In recent years, the scope of the debate has in some ways expanded. In response to expropriations of tangible real property like oil fields and copper mines (and in light of developing countries' rhetorical dedication to a state's "permanent sovereignty over its natural resources"), many corporations shifted their approach to "investment" by relying on contracts instead of relying on property rights. The U.S. government in turn added repudiation of contracts to its list of actions, along with expropriation of property, that U.S. policy opposed. In addition, the concept of "expropriation" itself has been adapted to the more sophisticated tactics of host governments such as driving an investor out of the country by raising taxes, increasing labor costs, or strengthening environmental or other regulation. The Restatement describes the traditional U.S. position and some of the challenges to that position.

Restatement

Section 712.   State Responsibility for Economic Injury to Nationals of Other States

A state is responsible under international law for injury resulting from:

(1) a taking by the state of the property of a national of another state that

    (a) is not for a public purpose, or

    (b) is discriminatory, or

    (c) is not accompanied by provision for just compensation;

For compensation to be just under this Subsection, it must, in the absence of exceptional circumstances, be in an amount equivalent to the value of the property taken and be paid at the time of taking, or within a reasonable time thereafter with interest from the date of taking, and in a form economically usable by the foreign national;

(2) a repudiation or breach by the state of a contract with a national of another state (a) where the repudiation or breach is (i) discriminatory; or (ii) motivated by noncommercial considerations, and compensatory damages are not paid; or

    (b) where the foreign national is not given an adequate forum to determine his claim of repudiation or breach, or is not compensated for any repudiation or breach determined to have occurred; or

(3) other arbitrary or discriminatory acts or omissions by the state that impair property or other economic interests of a national of another state.

Reporters' Notes

1. Subsection (1) restates the traditional principles of international law on expropriation. Early in this century these principles were settled law. . . .

The first major challenge to these principles was posed by the U.S.S.R., which rejected the traditional rule, claiming that an alien enters the territory of another state or acquires property there subject wholly to local law. The principles were challenged also by Latin American governments. In 1938, in a famous exchange between Secretary of State Hull and the Minister of Foreign Relations of Mexico, the United States insisted that property of aliens was protected by an international standard under which expropriation was subject to limitations, notably that there must be "prompt, adequate and effective compensation." In contrast, the Government of Mexico insisted that international law required only that foreign nationals be treated no less favorably than were nationals, at least in the case of "expropriations of a general and impersonal character like those which Mexico has carried out for the purpose of redistribution of land." 3 Hackworth, Digest of International Law 655-61 (1942).

After the Second World War, with the coming of many new states and the rise of the "Third World" to influence, opposition to the traditional view received widespread support. For the new majority of states, a people's right to dispose of its national resources became "economic self-determination," and was designated a "human right" and placed at the head of both the International Covenant on Civil and Political Rights and the International Covenant on Economic, Social and Cultural Rights. . . . In 1962, however, the United Nations General Assembly declared that in cases of expropriation of natural resources "the owner shall be paid appropriate compensation . . . in accordance with international law." G.A. Res. 1803, Permanent Sovereignty over Natural

Resources, 17, U.N. GAOR, Supp. 17, at 15. [The vote on that resolution was 87-2, with 12 abstentions. The United States voted for it.] . . .

Divisions became sharper in 1974 when the United Nations General Assembly adopted the Charter of Economic Rights and Duties of States, which dealt with the subject without making any reference to international law. The Charter declared that every state has the right

> to nationalize, expropriate or transfer ownership of foreign property, in which case appropriate compensation should be paid by the State adopting such measures, taking into account its relevant laws and regulations and all circumstances that the State considers pertinent. In any case where the question of compensation gives rise to a controversy, it shall be settled under the domestic law of the nationalizing State and by its tribunals . . . [unless otherwise agreed].

The Charter was adopted by 120 in favor, 6 against, and 10 abstentions, the vote reflecting the views of the majority as developing states, with the United States among the dissenters and the other developed Western states either dissenting or abstaining. . . .

The United States and other capital exporting states have rejected the challenge by developing states, have refused to agree to any change in the traditional principles, and have denied that these have been replaced or modified in customary law by state practice. . . . Those states have taken the position that the traditional requirements are solidly based on both the moral rights of property owners and on the needs of an effective international system of private investment. Moreover, they argued, whatever objections might be made to the traditional rules as applied to investments established during the colonial era, the traditional rules should clearly apply to arrangements made between investors and independent governments negotiated on a commercial basis. . . .

Both before and after the adoption of the Charter of Economic Rights and Duties of States, many states, including many developing states that supported the Charter (though not generally states in Latin America), concluded bilateral agreements that included provisions for compensation in the case of expropriation. Some of those provisions are contained in treaties of friendship, commerce, and navigation, as part of broader accommodations for foreign trade and investment. . . . . Others appear in agreements aimed particularly at the security of foreign investment . . . . Some provisions for compensation appear in arrangements whereby a state guarantees the investments of its nationals against loss due to expropriation, after agreement with the state host to the investment. . . .

U.N. General Assembly Resolution 1803 and the Charter of Economic Rights and Duties of States, referred to by the Restatement, are excerpted below.

U.N. General Assembly Resolution 1803
(adopted Dec. 14, 1962)

[The General Assembly] Declares that:

1. The right of peoples and nations to permanent sovereignty over their natural wealth and resources must be exercised in the interest of their national development and of the well-being of the people of the State concerned.

2. The exploration, development and disposition of such resources, as well as the import of the foreign capital required for these purposes, should be in

conformity with the rules and conditions which the peoples and nations freely consider to be necessary or desirable with regard to the authorization, restriction or prohibition of such activities.

3. In cases where authorization is granted, the capital imported and the earnings on that capital shall be governed by the terms thereof, by the national legislation in force, and by international law. The profits derived must be shared in the proportions freely agreed upon, in each case, between the investors and the recipient State, due care being taken to ensure that there is no impairment, for any reason, of that State's sovereignty over its natural wealth and resources.

4. Nationalization, expropriation or requisitioning shall be based on grounds or reasons of public utility, security or the national interest which are recognized as overriding purely individual or private interests, both domestic and foreign. In such cases the owner shall be paid appropriate compensation, in accordance with the rules in force in the State taking such measures in the exercise of its sovereignty and in accordance with international law. In any case where the question of compensation gives rise to a controversy, the national jurisdiction of the State taking such measures shall be exhausted. However, upon agreement by sovereign States and other parties concerned, settlement of the dispute should be made through arbitration or international adjudication.

Charter of Economic Rights and Duties of States
(adopted Dec. 12, 1974)

Each State has the right:

(a) To regulate and exercise authority over foreign investment within its national jurisdiction in accordance with its laws and regulations and in conformity with its national objectives and priorities. No State shall be compelled to grant preferential treatment to foreign investment;

(b) To regulate and supervise the activities of transnational corporations within its national jurisdiction and take measures to ensure that such activities comply with its laws, rules and regulations and conform with its economic and social policies. Transnational corporations shall not intervene in the internal affairs of a host State. Every State should, with full regard for its sovereign rights, co-operate with other States in the exercise of the right set forth in this subparagraph;

(c) To nationalize, expropriate or transfer ownership of foreign property, in which case appropriate compensation should be paid by the State adopting such measures, taking into account its relevant laws and regulations and all circumstances that the State considers pertinent. In any case where the question of compensation gives rise to a controversy, it shall be settled under the domestic law of the nationalizing State and by its tribunals, unless it is freely and mutually agreed by all States concerned that other peaceful means be sought on the basis of the sovereign equality of States and in accordance with the principle of free choice of means.

As noted in the Restatement, the United States has entered into numerous Friendship, Commerce, and Navigation (FGN) treaties and Bilateral Investment Treaties (BITs) that contain provisions protecting property rights. As an example, consider the excerpt of the BIT between the United States and the Republic of the Ukraine that is in the Documentary Supplement. Among other things, that treaty provides, in Article III:

> Investments shall not be expropriated or nationalized either directly or indirectly through measures tantamount to expropriation or nationalization ("expropriation") except: for a public purpose; in a nondiscriminatory manner; upon payment of prompt, adequate and effective compensation.
>
> . . . Compensation shall be equivalent to the fair market value of the expropriated investment immediately before the expropriatory action was taken or became known, whichever is earlier; be calculated in a freely usable currency on the basis of the prevailing market rate of exchange at that time; be paid without delay; include interest at a commercially reasonable rate. . . .

Notes and Questions

1. What are the important differences between Resolution 1803 and the Charter of Economic Rights and Duties of States? Why do you think the United States voted for the first but not the second?

2. What was the basis for Soviet and developing country opposition to the traditional international law rules governing expropriation? Recall that in its 1964 decision in *Sabbatino,* excerpted in Chapter 6, the Supreme Court stated that "there are few if any issues in international law today on which opinion seems to be so divided as the limitations of a state's power to expropriate the property of an alien."

3. Why do you think there is less controversy today over the international law rules governing property rights?

4. What investment protections are contained in the United States-Ukraine BIT excerpted in the Documentary Supplement? Note that, as of June 2002, the United States had concluded 45 BITs, 2 of which were still awaiting the advice and consent of the Senate and 6 of which were awaiting ratification by the other party. These treaties are with a variety of Eastern European, Latin American, Middle Eastern, and African countries.

5. Congress has adopted a number of measures designed to induce compliance with U.S. views of appropriate property guarantees. These statutory directives purport to require denial of U.S. foreign development assistance (the Hickenlooper Amendment, 22 U.S.C. §2370(e)(1)) as well as revocation of duty-free tariff treatment for those states (19 U.S.C. §2462(b)(4)) that expropriate American property without paying just compensation. Recall also the congressional limitation on the act of state doctrine for some of these situations. (See Chapter 6.) In addition, Congress has directed the President to vote against loans for those countries by international financial institutions, such as the World Bank, the Inter-American Development Bank, and the Asian Development Bank.

6. As part of the resolution of the 1979-1980 Iranian hostage crises, an Iran-United States Claims Tribunal was established in the Hague to resolve, among other things, claims of U.S. nationals against Iran and of Iranian nationals against the United States, which arise out of debts, contracts, expropriations, or other measures affecting property rights. As of June 2002, the Tribunal had resolved almost 4,000 claims and had issued almost 600 awards, the majority of which were in favor of U.S.

claimants. In resolving the claims, the Tribunal has issued numerous opinions addressing a wide variety of international law issues. For additional discussion of the Tribunal and its jurisprudence, see George H. Aldrich, The Jurisprudence of the Iran-United States Claims Tribunal (1996); Charles H. Brower & Jason D. Brueschke, The Iran-United States Claims Tribunal (1998); The American Society of International Law, The Iran-United States Claims Tribunal and the Process of International Claims Resolution (David D. Caron & John R. Crook eds., 2000); and The American Society of International Law, The Iran-United States Claims Tribunal: Its Contribution to the Law of State Responsibility (Richard B. Lillich & Daniel Barstow Magraw eds., 1998).

7. Following the defeat of Iraq in the Gulf War in 1991, the United Nations Security Council established a Compensation Commission to adjudicate claims against Iraq arising out of its invasion and occupation of Kuwait. See S.C. Resolution 687 in the Documentary Supplement. Compensation is paid to successful claimants out of a fund that receives a percentage of the proceeds from sales of Iraqi oil. Approximately 2.6 million claims were filed with the Commission and, as of January 2003, most of these claims had been resolved. However, some of the largest claims were still pending. The procedures used by this Commission are less formal (and less costly to administer) than those of the Iran-United States Claims Tribunal. See Status of Claims Processing, at http://www.unog.ch/uncc/status.htm.

8. Frequently, expropriation claims asserted by the United States under international law have been settled by an international agreement in which the expropriating state pays a "lump sum," often equal to the amount of that state's assets in the United States that had earlier been frozen under IEEPA or similar legislation in response to the nationalization, in exchange for a "discharge" of all claims the United States has against that state under international law. Such a lump-sum agreement was involved in the *Pink* case excerpted in Chapter 3. Since 1992, the United States has signed lump-sum claims settlement agreements with Germany, Albania, Cambodia, and Vietnam. The lump sum typically translates into an amount far less than the fair value of the claim. In 1990, the United States and Iran agreed to settle the remaining small claims (under $250,000) arising out of the 1979 revolution. As in the case of other lump-sum settlements, the claims involved were then referred for adjudication to the domestic U.S. Foreign Claims Settlement Commission (FCSC), an adjudicative body established by U.S. law to process claims of U.S. nationals against foreign governments. See 22 U.S.C. §§1645 et seq. Its work has normally involved adjudicating claims against governments that have agreed to lump-sum settlements under which a government pays an agreed sum in discharge of all U.S. international law-based claims against that government. The FCSC then adjudicates the various claims of U.S. nationals who in turn are paid out of the lump sum received for that purpose by the U.S. government. In the case of the small claims against Iran, the FCSC adjudicated approximately 3,100 claims, awarded over $41 million to 1,075 claimants, and denied or dismissed for procedural reasons the rest. See Richard B. Lillich & David J. Bederman, Jurisprudence of the Foreign Claims Settlement Commission: Iran Claims, 91 Am. J. Intl. L. 436 (1997).

The Iran-U.S. Tribunal in the *Sedco* case (25 I.L.M. 629 (1986)) intimated that lump-sum settlements were of "questionable evidentiary value for customary international law" because they "can be so greatly inspired by non-judicial considerations — e.g., resumption of diplomatic or trading relations — . . . and often include factors other than elements of law." Would that not be true of most state practice? Or is the point that the payments are made to get political advantages and therefore are not made "out of a sense of legal obligation," so that "opinio juris" is lacking? Aren't both political and legal elements present? The Tribunal said that treaty provisions, such as those in BITs, are better evidence of state practice. But why shouldn't actions speak louder than words? Is this situation analogous to the law versus practice question raised by *Filartiga* (excerpted in Chapter 3)? Isn't the expropriation situation significantly different than torture?

9. Another way to deal with the risk of expropriation is through insurance. Both the U.S. government, through the Overseas Private Investment Corporation (OPIC), and the World Bank, through the Multilateral Investment Guaranty Agency (MIGA), have sponsored insurance programs under which, for a fee, an investor can be protected against war and expropriation risk, as well as against currency inconvertibility. Some similar coverage may also be available in the private market.

Problem. If you were counsel to a corporation considering the establishment of a factory to manufacture aspirin in Indonesia, what legal protections, if any, regarding expropriation would you seek? What issues could be more important than expropriation, and how could you deal with them? How would you describe to your board of directors the relative value of a guarantee of no expropriation (or no currency controls) in (a) the Indonesia constitution, (b) a U.S.-Indonesia treaty, (c) customary international law, (d) insurance from OPIC or MIGA, (e) an individually negotiated agreement between your company and the government of Indonesia, or (f) the threat of U.S. retaliation?

10. As discussed in Chapter 4, the North American Free Trade Agreement contains provisions designed to protect cross-border investors in Canada, the United States, and Mexico. Under Chapter 11 of NAFTA, each of the three NAFTA countries is prohibited from discriminating against investors from the other two countries and from expropriating the property of those investors except in accordance with international law. With respect to expropriation, Chapter 11 provides in relevant part:

> 1. No Party may directly or indirectly nationalize or expropriate an investment of an investor of another Party in its territory or take a measure tantamount to nationalization or expropriation of such an investment ("expropriation"), except:
> (a) for a public purpose;
> (b) on a nondiscriminatory basis;
> (c) in accordance with due process of law . . . and
> (d) on payment of compensation. . . .
> 2. Compensation shall be equivalent to the fair market value of the expropriated investment immediately before the expropriation took place ("date of expropriation"), and shall not reflect any change in value occurring because the intended expropriation had become known earlier. Valuation criteria shall include going concern value, asset value including declared tax value of tangible property, and other criteria, as appropriate, to determine fair market value. [NAFTA, Article 1110.]

Investors who believe that the Chapter 11 protections have been violated are allowed to initiate an arbitration against the NAFTA country in question. For a list of the arbitration cases that have been brought against each of the three NAFTA countries, see the State Department's Web site on NAFTA State-Investor Arbitrations, http://www.state.gov/s/l/c3439.htm.

4.   The Law of Diplomatic Protection

Under traditional international law doctrine, when a state injured an alien, that injury was viewed as an injury to the state of which the injured person was a national. The resulting claim was therefore made by the injured national's state. In the vocabulary of international law, the injured national's state provides its "diplomatic protection." This somewhat artificial theory raises the question of what it takes to be a national of a state in order to enable that state to present a claim or provide its diplomatic protection. For most purposes a state itself determines who are its nationals (e.g., persons born in the country, or persons born of parents who are its nationals, or persons who are duly "naturalized"). That determination confers rights (e.g., to vote) and, as we saw in Chapter 7, responsibilities (e.g., the duty to respond to a subpoena) as a matter of domestic law. However, just because a person is a national for purposes of domestic law does not necessarily mean that the person is a national entitled to diplomatic protection. Consider the following excerpts from the Restatement.

Restatement

Section 713.   Remedies for Injury to Nationals of Other States

(1) A state whose national has suffered injury under §711 or §712 has, as against the state responsible for the injury, the remedies generally available between states for violation of customary law . . . as well as any special remedies provided by any international agreement applicable between the two states.

Comments

a. *Remedies under international law.* A state whose national has suffered injury under §711 or §712 may resort to any of the remedies usually available to a state that has been the victim of a breach of international law, including international claims procedures and other diplomatic measures or permissible international responses. The offended state may also invoke any special measures applicable by agreement between the two states, including arbitration or adjudication. Treaties of friendship, commerce, and navigation and other bilateral agreements commonly provide for resort to the International Court of Justice or to arbitration to resolve a claim that rights protected under the agreement have been violated. . . .

In principle, the responsibility of a state under §§711 and 712 is to the state of the alien's nationality and gives that state a claim against the offending state. The claim derives from injury to an individual, but once espoused it is the state's claim, and can be waived by the state. However, the derivative character of the claim has practical consequences: for example, damages are often measured by the damage to the individual, not by the loss to the state or the affront to its honor.

The derivative character of the claim is reflected also in the traditional rule that the accused state can reject an international claim if the individual victim has not exhausted domestic remedies . . . or if the individual has reached a voluntary settlement with the respondent state. . . .

Section 211. Nationality of Individuals

For purposes of international law, an individual has the nationality of a state that confers it, but other states need not accept that nationality when it is not based on a *genuine link* between the state and the individual. [Emphasis added.]

Comment

a. Nationality and international law. Although international law has been conferring some rights and obligations directly on individuals, international law impinges on individuals principally through the state with which they are linked, and the principal relationship that links an individual to the state is nationality. An individual's nationality is relevant in international law in various ways. A state has jurisdiction to prescribe with respect to activities of its nationals outside its territory in circumstances where it could not do so with respect to aliens. A state may afford diplomatic protection to its nationals, and make formal claims on their behalf. International agreements such as treaties of friendship, commerce, and navigation often confer rights on nationals of the contracting parties. Extradition treaties often provide that a state need not extradite its own nationals.

b. Nationality and diplomatic protection. International law recognizes the right of a state to afford diplomatic protection to its nationals and to represent their interests. Such formal diplomatic protection is generally limited to nationals, but international practice accepts informal intercessions by states on behalf of individuals who are not their nationals. Moreover, a state party to an international human rights agreement has the right to enforce the agreement on behalf of an alien, indeed even a national of the alleged violator-state. . . .

c. "Genuine link." A state is free to establish nationality law and confer nationality as it sees fit. However, under international law other states need not recognize a nationality that is involuntary or that is not based on an accepted "genuine link." The precise contours of this concept, however, are not clear. Laws that confer nationality on grounds of birth in a state's territory *(ius soli)* or of birth to parents who are nationals *(ius sanguinis)* are universally accepted as based on genuine links. Voluntary naturalization is generally recognized by other states but may be questioned where there are no other ties to the state, e.g., a period of residence in the state. The comparative "genuineness" and strength of links between a state and an individual are relevant also for resolving competing claims between two states asserting nationality, or between such states and a third state. . . .

Reporters' Notes

1. *"Genuine link."* The Nottebohm Case (Liechtenstein v. Guatemala), [1955] I.C.J. Rep. 4, ruled that because there was no genuine link between Nottebohm and

Liechtenstein, Guatemala did not have to recognize his Liechtenstein nationality and Liechtenstein could not bring proceedings before the International Court of Justice on his behalf against Guatemala. Nottebohm, originally of German nationality, was a long-time resident of Guatemala. He had taken a brief trip to Liechtenstein during which he complied with its requirements for naturalization and then returned to Guatemala. Although Liechtenstein's naturalization law required a showing of loss of prior nationality, and German law provided for loss of German nationality upon acquisition of another nationality, Guatemala, at war with Germany, treated Nottebohm as an alien enemy. Liechtenstein objected and brought a proceeding before the International Court of Justice. The Court referred to international arbitral decisions holding that the state to which a dual national has stronger ties is the one entitled to extend protection against third states. It is not clear from the opinion whether a third country would have been entitled to ignore Liechtenstein's naturalization of Nottebohm, since the court stressed the comparative ties of Nottebohm to Liechtenstein and to Guatemala. Nothing in the case suggests that a state may refuse to give effect to a nationality acquired at birth, regardless of how few other links the individual had at birth or maintained later. . . .

Section 213.   Nationality of Corporations

For purposes of international law, a corporation has the nationality of the state under the laws of which the corporation is organized.

Comment

a. Corporation defined. The term "corporation" as used in this Restatement means any organization or association formed for commercial, charitable, or other purposes under the private law of a state or of a subdivision of a state and given status as a legal entity by that law. . . .

b. Relevance of corporate nationality under international law. The nationality of a corporation is relevant under international law for various purposes. A state is responsible for injury to an alien corporation and the state of the corporation's nationality may make a claim for the injury. A state may exercise jurisdiction to prescribe laws for acts of its corporate nationals committed outside of its territory. Corporate nationality is relevant when states claim treaty rights for their nationals.

c. Nationality and state of incorporation. The traditional rule stated in this section, adopted for certainty and convenience, treats every corporation as a national of the state under the laws of which it was created. It has been suggested that the place of the *siège social,* or principal place of management is an alternative basis for corporate nationality under international law. In practical effect it is an additional requirement, since jurisdictions using that standard require that a firm be incorporated in the state where it has its *siège.* States generally treat the *siège social* not as conferring nationality, but as creating an equivalent connection. See Comment *d.*

As in the case of an individual, a state may refuse to treat a corporation as a national of the state that created it, and reject diplomatic protection by that state, where there is no "genuine link" between them.

d. Significant connections other than nationality. Since a corporation has the nationality of the state that created it, a corporation usually does not have the nationality of more than one state. But connections other than nationality may be significant for the purposes indicated in Comment *b*. In some circumstances, other states may treat as analogous to nationality the fact (i) that the shares of a corporation are substantially owned by nationals of that state; (ii) that the corporation is managed from an office within the state, or (iii) that the corporation has a principal place of business in that state. For example, in time of war, a state may treat a corporation having such ties to the enemy state as an enemy national even though it was incorporated in a non-belligerent state.

The state having such links to a corporation may treat the corporation as its national at least for some purposes. In some circumstances, the state may prescribe law for the corporation even in regard to acts committed outside the state's territory. For a state's limited jurisdiction to prescribe for foreign branches or subsidiaries of its corporations, see §414. . . . The United States has provided diplomatic protection for such companies in case of expropriation or other injury, particularly where the act was directed at the corporation because of its links with the United States. See §713.

e. Special definitions of corporate nationality by international agreement. States are free to depart from the rule of this section by international agreement. Different definitions of corporate nationality are sometimes found in tax treaties, treaties of establishment, treaties of friendship, commerce, and navigation, and in claims settlement agreements.

f. Multinational corporations. The multinational enterprise or corporation (sometimes referred to as a transnational or global corporation) is an established feature of international economic life, but it has not yet achieved special status in international law or in national legal systems. A multinational corporation generally consists of a group of corporations, each established under the law of some state, linked by common managerial and financial control and pursuing integrated policies. (Some writers reserve the term for enterprises that also meet some standard of size in assets, sales, or similar indicator.) In general, the rule stated in this section applies both to the parent company and to its subsidiaries.

Reporters' Notes

1. *Corporate and individual nationality distinguished.* This section applies to corporations the concept of nationality that was developed for individuals, but rules about nationality of individuals can be applied to corporations only with caution. Whereas the individual exists and represents a single mind and body, corporations are a juridical construct and may unite large numbers of individuals having different nationalities. Corporate nationality, moreover, is peculiarly subject to manipulation.

2. *Diplomatic protection of corporations.* A state is entitled to represent and afford diplomatic protection to corporations having its nationality as to individual nationals. However, as indicated in Comment *c*, a respondent state is entitled to reject representation by the state of incorporation where that state was chosen solely for legal convenience, for example as a tax haven, and the corporation has no substantial links with that state, such as property, an office or commercial or industrial establishment, substantial business activity, or residence of substantial shareholders. Compare the Nottebohm Case, §211, Reporters' Note 1.

In the Barcelona Traction Case (Belgium v. Spain), [1970] I.C.J. Rep. 3, the International Court of Justice held that Belgium could not bring proceedings against Spain for injury to a corporation incorporated and having its headquarters in Canada, although most of the company's shares were owned by Belgian nationals, at least where Canada had in the past extended diplomatic protection to the corporation and retained the legal capacity to do so. Id. at 43-45.

3. *Protection of shareholders or subsidiaries against state of incorporation.* Barcelona Traction, Reporters' Note 2, gave preference to the state of incorporation over a state with other significant links, in representing a company against a third state. The decision does not preclude representation of the company by a state with significant links against the state of incorporation itself. A state cannot, by requiring a foreign enterprise to incorporate locally, compel the enterprise to surrender in advance its right to protection by the state of its parent corporation or of the parent's shareholders. States have asserted the right to protect the interest of their nationals as shareholders in such a corporation, particularly when the corporation itself is disabled from acting on their behalf, e.g., when the state has dissolved it or placed it in receivership, perhaps because the corporation had claims against the state. The United States and other countries sometimes seek to protect the subsidiary corporation itself rather than its shareholders. The Claims Settlement Declaration of 1981 establishing the Iran-United States Claims Tribunal defines a "national" of Iran or of the United States to include, respectively, a corporation "organized under the laws of Iran or the United States or any of its states . . . , if, collectively, national persons who are citizens of such country hold, directly or indirectly an interest in such corporation or entity equivalent to fifty percent or more of its capital stock."

As indicated in Chapter 7, the question of corporate nationality is highly controversial in the context of a state's right to regulate corporate conduct based on the nationality principle. A state's right to formally espouse a corporate national's claim, which was construed narrowly in *Barcelona Traction,* seems somewhat less controversial. Governments regularly intercede on behalf of foreign subsidiaries owned by their domestic corporations.

Notes and Questions

1. What connection must an individual have to a state to satisfy the "genuine link" requirement? What connection must a corporation have?

2. Which states can raise a claim on behalf of an individual or corporation that has more than one nationality? What if the claim is against one of the states of which the individual or corporation is a national? Can any state raise a claim on behalf of a "stateless" individual — that is, an individual who does not have citizenship in any state?

3. The International Law Commission is currently working on draft articles on the law of diplomatic protection. At its Fifty-Fourth Session, in 2002, the Commission approved the first seven articles on this topic prepared by its Drafting Committee. For further information, see the Commission's Web site, http://www.un.org/ law/ilc.

B. INTERNATIONAL HUMAN RIGHTS

1. Background

The Nazi atrocities and World War II caused world leaders to reject the traditional assumption that a state's international responsibility is limited to aliens. The treatment by a state of its own nationals has now become a matter of international concern. International human rights law is the vehicle for expression of that concern. The following excerpt describes some of the pre-World War II antecedents of international human rights law.

Louis Henkin, The Age of Rights

13-15 (1990)

The internationalization of human rights, the transformation of the idea of constitutional rights in a few countries to a universal conception and a staple of international politics and law, is a phenomenon of the middle of our century. But it did not spring full-blown.

Historically, how a state treated persons in its territory was indeed its own affair, implicit in its territorial sovereignty. International law developed one early exception when it recognized that how a country treats a national of another state is the proper concern of that state. That exception might be seen as essentially political, not humanitarian, in motivation: if a citizen of the United States is abused elsewhere, the United States is offended. It was widely accepted, therefore, that injustice to a stateless person was not a violation of international law since no state was offended therey; surely, there was no state that could invoke a remedy for such injustice. But assuming that the doctrine developed because the offended state was concerned for its own rather than for human dignity, it is significant that governments were offended by violations of the "human rights" of their nationals.

In order to determine whether a state could properly claim that its national had been denied "justice," international law developed an international standard of justice. There was no accepted philosophical foundation for such a standard, and no agreed definition of its content; doubtless, it was redolent of "natural rights" and tantamount to a notion of "fairness." Whatever its underpinnings, whatever its substance, the standard for the treatment of foreign nationals that was invoked by their governments and acquiesced in by host governments was often higher than that — if any — applied by these countries to their own citizens at home. The international standard, then, was not a universal human standard, and governments that invoked or accepted it did not suggest that it applied also to how governments treated their own citizens. The treatment accorded by a state to its own citizens was not the concern of international law or the business of other governments, and in fact governments rarely concerned themselves with domestic injustice elsewhere. The few major-power intercessions — for example, that of the United States in the nineteenth century in response to Russian pogroms — did not invoke international law and occurred only when violations were egregious and dramatic. This was usually the case when there was a demand for intercession by a domestic constituency with special affinity for the victims in the other country (as in the United States, for example, the Irish, the Jews, and others).

International political considerations inspired other exceptions to the principle that how a government acts toward individuals at home is a matter of domestic concern only. Beginning in the seventeenth century, Catholic and Protestant princes (and others) concluded agreements according freedom of worship and wider toleration to each other's coreliginists. Later, governments assumed international obligations to respect freedoms for ethnic minorities, even those who as a matter of law were nationals of the country in which they lived; in the late

nineteenth and early twentieth century, such minority treaties were virtually imposed by the major powers on smaller ones in Central and Eastern Europe because
it was believed that violation of minority rights led to intervention by countries that
identified with them, and thus to war. Again, the basis for international concern in
these cases was some special affinity on the part of some government for some inhabitants of other countries, and concern for international peace, not concern by
governments generally for the basic dignity of all human beings, including their own
inhabitants. In a different context, the mandate system of the League of Nations following World War I required a commitment by the mandatory power to promote the
welfare of the local population. It has been argued that such clauses, too, did not
reflect bona fide concern for human rights but were only a "sop" to justify keeping
"the natives" in continued tutelage in disregard of commitments to the principle of
self-determination. There were authentic humanitarian motivations in the development of "humanitarian law" to mitigate the horrors of war by outlawing certain
weapons, protecting the sick and wounded and prisoners of war, and safeguarding
civilian populations, but that humanitarian law probably derived from concern by
states for their own soldiers and citizens, not for all human beings equally.

The International Labor Organization was an early and noteworthy contributor to international human rights. The ILO was organized after World War I to promote common basic standards of labor and social welfare. In the intervening seventy
years, the ILO has promulgated more than a hundred international conventions,
which have been widely adhered to and fairly well observed. Again, some might find
political-economic rather than humanitarian motivations for what the ILO
achieved. The ILO, it is said, was the West's fearful answer to socialism, which had
gained its first bridgehead in the USSR; perhaps the conventions reflected also a desire by developed states to reduce "unfair competition" from countries with sub-
standard labor conditions.

A less ambiguous example of early international concern for human rights was
the movement in the nineteenth century, after major powers abolished slavery in
their countries, to outlaw slavery and slave trade by international agreement. Perhaps slavery was sufficiently egregious that no state could be allowed to claim to contain it within its domestic jurisdiction. Moreover, the products of slave labor were
sold abroad at a competitive advantage with goods produced by societies that had
abolished slavery. Slave trade, surely, was not an internal matter only, involving as it
did international trade and colonial competition.

In all, international relations before our time were not impervious to the human condition inside countries, but concern for individual welfare was framed and
confined within the state system. That concern could not spill over state borders except in ways and by means that were consistent with the assumptions of that system,
that is, when a state identified with inhabitants of other states on recognized
grounds, and that identification threatened international order; when the condition of individuals inside a country impinged on the economic interests of other
countries. Whatever the reasons, primitive human rights provisions appeared in international instruments, and the seeds of international human rights were planted.

The Nuremberg trials after World War II, in which German officials were tried
for war crimes and crimes against humanity, were also important precedent in

establishing the responsibility of government officials for human rights abuses, even human rights abuses committed against their own population. The Charter authorizing those trials defined crimes against humanity as encompassing "murder, extermination, enslavement, deportation, and other inhumane acts committed against any civilian population, before or during the war; or persecutions on political, racial or religious grounds in execution of or in connection with any crime within the jurisdiction of the Tribunal, whether or not in violation of the domestic law of the country where perpetrated." The Charter also made clear that "[t]he official position of defendants, whether as Heads of State or responsible officials in Government Departments, shall not be considered as freeing them from responsibility or mitigating punishment," and that "[t]he fact that the Defendant acted pursuant to order of his Government or of a superior shall not free him from responsibility, but may be considered in mitigation of punishment if the Tribunal determines that justice so requires." The Nuremberg trials are discussed in Chapter 11.

2.   *U.N. Charter and Universal Declaration*

Article 1 of the United Nations Charter, excerpted in the Documentary Supplement, lists a variety of "purposes" for the United Nations. These purposes include the following:

> To achieve international cooperation in solving international problems of an economic, social, cultural, or humanitarian character, and in promoting and encouraging respect for human rights and for fundamental freedoms for all without distinction as to race, sex, language, or religion. [Article 1(3).]

Consistent with these purposes, Article 55 of the Charter provides for specific promotion of human rights by the United Nations:

> With a view to the creation of conditions of stability and well-being which are necessary for peaceful and friendly relations among nations based on respect for the principle of equal rights and self-determination of peoples, the United Nations shall promote:
>   a. higher standards of living, full employment, and conditions of economic and social progress and development;
>   b. solutions of international economic, social, health, and related problems; and international cultural and educational cooperation; and
>   c. universal respect for, and observance of, human rights and fundamental freedoms for all without distinction as to race, sex, language, or religion.

In addition, Article 56 of the Charter states that all members of the United Nations "pledge themselves to take joint and separate action in cooperation with the Organization for the achievement of the purposes set forth in Article 55."

The Charter provisions reflect a commitment to promoting human rights, but they do not themselves define those rights. In 1948, the United Nations General Assembly adopted a Universal Declaration of Human Rights that attempted to set forth "a common standard of achievement for all peoples and all nations." The Declaration (which is also excerpted in the Documentary Supplement) lists a variety of political, social, economic, and cultural rights. The Declaration was adopted by the

General Assembly without dissent. The vote was 48-0, with eight abstentions, primarily by the Soviet Union and the Communist nations of Eastern Europe. The Soviet bloc nations subsequently accepted the Declaration when they agreed to the 1975 Final Act on the Conference on Security and Cooperation, also known as the Helsinki Accords. The Helsinki Accords state, among other things, that "the participating States will act in conformity with the purposes and principles of the Charter of the United Nations and the Universal Declaration of Human Rights."

Although not a binding document per se, the Universal Declaration helped give content to the U.N. Charter's general human rights provisions. Together, the U.N. Charter and the Universal Declaration laid the groundwork for a revolutionary change in the focus of international law.

Louis B. Sohn, The New International Law: Protection of the Rights of Individuals Rather than States

32 Am. U. L. Rev. 1, 14-17 (1982)

As nature abhors a vacuum, constitutional documents abhor strait-jackets. Great ideas cannot be imprisoned; they must be able to move freely from one part of the earth to another. The U.N. Charter contains several such ideas, which revolutionized the world, although no one knew in 1945 how successful the drafters of the Charter would be in planting in that document the seeds from which many mighty trees would grow.

The most influential of these ideas are that human rights are of international concern, and that the United Nations has the duty to promote "universal respect for, and observance of, human rights and fundamental freedoms for all without distinction as to race, sex, language and religion." Although these two ideas were born out of the disasters of the Second World War, they are even more meaningful today than at the time they were first formulated. It is our common duty not only to respect human rights ourselves but also to promote their "universal respect" and to ensure that they are observed throughout the globe. All members of the United Nations — not only the original 50, but the more than 150 members today — have pledged to "take joint and separate action," in cooperation with the United Nations for the achievement of these great purposes. In the Charter's preamble, the peoples of the United Nations as well as their governments, have reaffirmed their "faith in fundamental human rights, in the dignity and worth of the human person, in the equal rights of men and women and of nations large and small." In that statement the authors of the Charter anticipated not only the racial revolution, but also the feminist revolution and the need to provide for equality notwithstanding gender. They did not anticipate, however, that more than one hundred nations, most of them small, would clamor for equality with the fifty nations that dominated the world in 1945. . . .

Although the U.N. Charter mentions human rights in many places, time constraints at the San Francisco conference made it impossible to prepare a more detailed document paralleling the national bills or declarations of the rights of man and of the citizen. It was promised at that time, however, that the United Nations would commence the drafting of an International Bill of Rights as one of the first items of business. The Commission on Human Rights was established in 1946, only a few months after the Charter came into force, and was asked to prepare such a document. It soon became obvious that the task could take a long time and, in view of the urgency of the matter, that the first step should be a declaration of general principles, to be followed later by a document containing more precise obligations.

Two years later the first document — the Universal Declaration of Human Rights — was ready. On December 10, 1948, the General Assembly, after some amendments, approved it unanimously, with eight abstentions: the Soviet bloc, Saudi Arabia, and the Union of South Africa. Although some delegations emphasized that the Universal Declaration of Human Rights was not a treaty imposing legal obligations, others more boldly argued that it was more than an ordinary General Assembly resolution, that it was a continuation of the Charter and shared the dignity of that basic document. It merely expressed more forcefully rules that already were recognized by customary international law. Under the latter view, the Declaration would possess a binding character. . . . The Declaration itself proclaims that it is "a common standard of achievement for all peoples and all nations." It exhorts every individual and every organ of society to strive, "by progressive measures, national and international, to secure . . . universal and effective recognition and observance [of the rights and freedoms therein]." . . .

The Declaration thus is now considered to be an authoritative interpretation of the U.N. Charter, spelling out in considerable detail the meaning of the phrase "human rights and fundamental freedoms," which Member States agreed in the Charter to promote and observe. The Universal Declaration has joined the Charter of the United Nations as part of the constitutional structure of the world community.

Notes and Questions

1. The United Nations Charter is a binding treaty that has been ratified by almost all nations of the world. In light of that fact, what is the legal significance of Articles 55 and 56? What obligations do those Articles impose? How, if at all, can these Articles be enforced? Should individuals have the right to invoke those Articles in domestic courts? We return to this last question below when we consider the relationship between international human rights law and U.S. law.

2. The Universal Declaration is not a treaty and, at least originally, was considered nonbinding. As we discuss below, many of the rights set forth in the Declaration have now been codified in treaties. In addition, many commentators have argued that at least some of the provisions of the Declaration reflect customary international law and are therefore binding even on nations that have not ratified the relevant treaties. Read through the Declaration. Which rights do you think should be binding on nations even in the absence of a treaty?

3. Do the rights in the Declaration reflect Western values? In a diverse world of over 190 nations, is it possible to have one universal set of human rights? For a critical perspective, consider these comments by Professor Makau Matua:

> The adoption in 1948 by the United Nations of the Universal Declaration of Human Rights — the foundational document of the human rights movement — sought to give universal legitimacy to a doctrine that is fundamentally Eurocentric in its construction. Sanctimonious to a fault, the Universal Declaration underscored its arrogance by proclaiming itself the "common standard of achievement for all peoples and

nations." The fact that half a century later human rights have become a central norm of global civilization does not vindicate their universality. It is rather a telling testament to the conceptual, cultural, economic, military, and philosophical domination of the European West over non-European peoples and traditions.

The fundamental texts of international human rights law are derived from bodies of domestic jurisprudence developed over several centuries in Western Europe and the United States. The dominant influence of Western liberal thought and philosophies is unmistakable. No one familiar with Western liberal traditions of political democracy and free market capitalism would find international human rights law unusual. Its emphasis on the individual egoist as the center of the moral universe underlines its European orientation. The basic human rights texts drew heavily from the American Bill of Rights and the French Declaration of the Rights of Man. There is virtually no evidence to suggest that they drew inspiration from Asian, Islamic, Buddhist, Hindu, African, or any other non-European traditions. [Makau Matua, Human Rights: A Political and Cultural Critique 154 (2002).]

By contrast, Professor Mary Ann Glendon argues that the Universal Declaration of Human Rights reflects non-Western, as well as Western, values:

It is true that the Declaration's provisions were derived from provisions of the world's existing and proposed constitutions and rights instruments – that is, mostly from countries with well-developed legal traditions. But the label "Western" obscures the fact that the Declaration's acceptance in non-Western settings was facilitated by the very features that made it seem "foreign" to a large part of the West: Britain and the United States.

The Declaration . . . was far more influenced by the modern dignitarian rights tradition of continental Europe and Latin America than by the more individualistic documents of Anglo-American lineage. . . .

Dignitarian rights instruments, with their emphasis on the family and their greater attention to duties, are more compatible with Asian and African traditions [than Anglo-American conceptions of rights]. In these documents, rights bearers tend to be envisioned within families and communities; rights are formulated so as to make clear their limits and their relation to one another as well as to the responsibilities that belong to citizens and the state. . . .

In the spirit of the latter vision, the Declaration's "Everyone" is an individual who is constituted, in important ways, by and through relationships with others. "Everyone" is envisioned as uniquely valuable in himself (there are three separate references to the free development of one's personality), but "Everyone" is expected to act toward others "in a spirit of brotherhood." "Everyone" is depicted as situated in a variety of specifically named, real-life relationships of mutual dependency: families, communities, religious groups, workplace associations, societies, cultures, nations, and an emerging international order. Though its main body is devoted to basic individual freedoms, the Declaration begins with an exhortation to act in a "spirit of brotherhood" and ends with community, order, and society. [Mary Ann Glendon, A World Made New: Eleanor Roosevelt and the Universal Declaration of Human Rights (2001).]

3. The International Covenants

Immediately following the passage of the Declaration, the United Nations Commission on Human Rights began drafting a human rights covenant aimed at converting the nonbinding provisions of the Declaration into binding treaty obligations. This process eventually led to the promulgation of a number of human rights treaties, including the International Covenant on Civil and Political Rights (ICCPR) and the International Covenant on Economic, Social and Cultural Rights (ICESCR), both of which are excerpted in the Documentary Supplement. Along with the Universal Declaration, these Covenants are sometimes described as forming an "international bill of rights." The ICCPR took effect in 1976 and, as of January 2003, had been ratified by 149 nations, including the United States. The ICESCR also took effect in 1976 and, as of January 2003, had been ratified by 146 nations. The United States signed the ICESCR in 1977 but, as of January 2003, had not ratified it.

The ICCPR includes a wide array of civil and political rights, including a right of self-determination, protection against discrimination, a right to life, prohibitions on torture and slavery, procedural rights concerning arrest, trial, and detention, a right of privacy, and rights of association and assembly. The ICESCR also contains a broad list of rights, including rights to work, to trade join unions, to obtain social security, to have an adequate standard of living, and to education. The ICESCR, however, is phrased in more gradual terms than the ICCPR. It provides, for example, that each party "undertakes to take steps . . . to the maximum of its available resources, with a view to achieving progressively the full realization of the rights recognized in the present Covenant by all appropriate means."

As called for by the terms of the ICCPR, a Human Rights Committee was established to monitor state compliance with the treaty. The Committee has eighteen members, who are nominated and elected by the parties to the ICCPR, and they serve in their individual capacities rather than as government representatives. Parties to the ICCPR are obligated to submit periodic reports to the Committee describing the measures they have taken to give effect to the rights recognized in the treaties. The Committee studies these reports and is authorized to issue "such general comments as it may consider appropriate." The Committee typically issues "concluding observations" about the country reports, including suggestions of ways in which the country can improve its human rights practices.

Under Article 41 of the ICCPR, parties may declare that they recognize a broader role for the Committee, whereby it will "receive and consider communications to the effect that a State Party claims that another State Party is not fulfilling its obligations under the present Covenant." If the parties cannot resolve the matter on their own, the Committee has the authority to "submit a report" on the matter. Over 40 nations, including the United States, have issued declarations accepting this role for the Committee, but, as of January 2003, no complaints had actually been made pursuant to Article 41.

In 1976, a First Optional Protocol to the ICCPR took effect, whereby the committee was given the authority to consider communications from individuals concerning alleged violations of the ICCPR. As of January 2003, 104 nations (but not the United States) had ratified this Protocol.* Unlike the state complaint process under Article 41, the individual communication process under this Protocol has been very active, and the Committee has developed an extensive jurisprudence through its issuance of opinions addressing these communications. (These opinions can be

---

*A second Optional Protocol to the ICCPR took effect in 1991. This Protocol calls for abolition of the death penalty. It also disallows reservations, except for a reservation allowing for the death penalty for certain crimes during wartime. As of January 2003, 49 nations (but not the United States) had ratified the Second Optional Protocol.—EDS.

found on the University of Minnesota's excellent human rights Web site, see http://www1.umn.edu/humanrts/undocs/allundocs.html.)

In addition to commenting on country reports and addressing communications under the First Optional Protocol, the Committee has issued a number of general comments interpreting the ICCPR. Many of these comments have been useful in clarifying the ICCPR's scope and have been relatively uncontroversial. Probably its most controversial general comment was the one excerpted below.

General Comment 24(52)

U.N. Doc. CCPR/C/21/Rev.1/Add.6 (1994)

6. The absence of a prohibition [in the ICCPR] on reservations does not mean that any reservation is permitted. The matter of reservations under the Covenant and the first Optional Protocol is governed by international law. Article 19(3) of the Vienna Convention on the Law of Treaties provides relevant guidance. It stipulates that where a reservation is not prohibited by the treaty or falls within the specified permitted categories, a State may make a reservation provided it is not incompatible with the object and purpose of the treaty. Even though, unlike some other human rights treaties, the Covenant does not incorporate a specific reference to the object and purpose test, that test governs the matter of interpretation and acceptability of reservations.

7. In an instrument which articulates very many civil and political rights, each of the many articles, and indeed their interplay, secures the objectives of the Covenant. The object and purpose of the Covenant is to create legally binding standards for human rights by defining certain civil and political rights and placing them in a framework of obligations which are legally binding for those States which ratify; and to provide an efficacious supervisory machinery for the obligations undertaken.

8. Reservations that offend peremptory norms would not be compatible with the object and purpose of the Covenant. Although treaties that are mere exchanges of obligations between States allow them to reserve *inter se* application of rules of general international law, it is otherwise is human rights treaties, which are for the benefit of persons within their jurisdiction. Accordingly, provisions in the Covenant that represent customary international law (and a fortiori when they have the character of peremptory norms) may not be be the subject of reservations. . . .

11. . . . The Committee's role under the Covenant, whether under article 40 or under the Optional Protocols, necessarily entails interpreting the provisions of the Covenant and the development of a jurisprudence. Accordingly, a reservation that rejects the Committee's competence to interpret the requirements of any provisions of the Covenant would also be contrary to the object and purpose of that treaty. . . .

17. As indicated above, it is the Vienna Convention on the Law of Treaties that provides the definition of reservations and also the application of the object and purpose test in the absence of other specific provisions. But the Committee believes that its provisions on the role of State objections in relation to reservations are inappropriate to address the problem of reservations to human rights treaties. Such treaties, and the Covenant specifically, are not a web of inter-State exchanges of mutual obligations. They concern the endowment of individuals with rights. The principle of inter-State reciprocity has no place, save perhaps in the limited context

of reservations to declarations on the Committee's competence under article 41. And because the operation of the classic rules on reservations is so inadequate for the Covenant, States have often not seen any legal interest in or need to object to reservations. The absence of protest by States cannot imply that a reservation is either compatible or incompatible with the object and purpose of the Covenant. Objections have been occasional, made by some States but not others, and on grounds not always specified; when an objection is made, it often does not specify a legal consequence, or sometimes even indicates that the objecting party nonetheless does not regard the Covenant as not in effect as between the parties concerned. In short, the pattern is so unclear that it is not safe to assume that a non-objecting State thinks that a particular reservation is acceptable. In the view of the Committee, because of the special characteristics of the Covenant as a human rights treaty, it is open to question what effect objections have between States inter se. However, an objection to a reservation made by States may provide some guidance to the Committee in its interpretation as to its compatibility with the object and purpose of the Covenant.

18. It necessarily falls to the Committee to determine whether a specific reservation is compatible with the object and purpose of the Covenant. This is in part because, as indicated above, it is an inappropriate task for States parties in relation to human rights treaties, and in part because it is a task that the Committee cannot avoid in the performance of its functions. In order to know the scope of its duty to examine a State's compliance under article 40 or a communication under the first Optional Protocol, the Committee has necessarily to take a view on the compatibility of a reservation with the object and purpose of the Covenant and with general international law. Because of the special character of a human rights treaty, the compatibility of a reservation with the object and purpose of the Covenant must be established objectively, by reference to legal principles, and the Committee is particularly well placed to perform this task. The normal consequence of an unacceptable reservation is not that the Covenant will not be in effect at all for a reserving party. Rather, such a reservation will generally be severable, in the sense that the Covenant will be operative for the reserving party without benefit of the reservation. . . .

As noted in Chapter 3, the United States vigorously objected to General Comment 24(52). Britain and France also filed objections. In addition, the United Nations' International Law Commission criticized General Comment 24(52) in a 1997 preliminary report. The following is an excerpt of the U.S. objections.

Observations by the United States on General Comment No. 24(52)

3 Intl. Hum. Rts. Rep. 265 (1996)

1.   ROLE OF THE COMMITTEE

The last sentence of paragraph 11 states that "a reservation that rejects the Committee's competence to interpret the requirements of any provisions of the Covenant would also be contrary to the object and purpose of that treaty."

This statement can be read to present the rather surprising assertion that it is contrary to the object and purpose of the Covenant not to accept the Committee's views on the interpretation of the Covenant. This would be a rather significant departure from the Covenant scheme, which does not impose on States Parties an obligation to give effect to the Committee's interpretations or confer on the Committee the power to render definitive or binding interpretations of the Covenant. The drafters of the Covenant could have given the Committee this role but deliberately chose not to do so.

In this respect, it is unnecessary for a State to reserve as to the Committee's power or interpretive competence since the Committee lacks the authority to render binding interpretations or judgments. . . .

In this regard, the analysis in paragraphs 16-20, regarding which body has the legal authority to make determinations concerning the permissibility of specific reservations, is of considerable concern. Here the Committee appears to reject the established rules of interpretation of treaties as set forth in the Vienna Convention on the Law of Treaties and in customary international law. The General Comment states, for example, that the established provisions of the Vienna Convention are "inappropriate to address the problem of reservations to human rights treaties . . . [as to which] [t]he principle of inter-State reciprocity has no place, save perhaps in the limited context of reservations to declarations on the Committee's competence under article 41."

Moreover, the Committee appears to dispense with the established procedures for determining the permissibility of reservations and to divest States Parties of any role in determining the meaning of the Covenant, which they drafted and joined, and of the extent of their treaty obligations. In its view, objections from other States Parties may not "specify a legal consequence" and States with genuine objections may not always voice them, so that "it is not safe to assume that a non-objecting State thinks that a particular reservation is acceptable." Consequently, because "the operation of the classic rules on reservations is so inadequate for the Covenant, . . . [i]t necessarily falls to the Committee to determine whether a specific reservation is compatible with the object and purpose of the Covenant."

The Committee's position, while interesting, runs contrary to the Covenant scheme and international law.

2. ACCEPTABILITY OF RESERVATIONS: GOVERNING LEGAL PRINCIPLES

The question of the status of the Committee's views is of some significance in light of the apparent lines of analysis concerning the permissibility of reservations in paragraphs 8-9. Those paragraphs reflect the view that reservations offending peremptory norms of international law would not be compatible with the object and purpose of the Covenant, nor may reservations be taken to Covenant provisions which represent customary international law.

It is clear that a State cannot exempt itself from a peremptory norm of international law by making a reservation to the Covenant. It is not at all clear that a State cannot choose to exclude one means of enforcement of particular norms by reserving against inclusion of those norms in its Covenant obligations.

The proposition that any reservation which contravenes a norm of customary international law is per se incompatible with the object and purpose of this or any other convention, however, is a much more significant and sweeping premise. It is, moreover, wholly unsupported by and is in fact contrary to international law. . . .

With respect to the actual object and purpose of this Covenant, there appears to be a misunderstanding. The object and purpose was to protect human rights, with an understanding that there need not be immediate, universal implementation of all terms of the treaty. Paragraph 7 (which forms the basis for the analysis in para. 8 and subsequently) states that "each of the many articles, and indeed their interplay, secures the objectives of the Covenant." The implied corollary is, of course, that any reservation to any substantive provision necessarily contravenes the Covenant's object and purpose.

Such a position would, of course, wholly mistake the question of the object and purpose of the Covenant insofar as it bears on the permissibility of reservations. In fact, a primary object and purpose of the Covenant was to secure the widest possible adherence, with the clear understanding that a relatively liberal regime on the permissibility of reservations should therefore be required. . . .

5.   EFFECT OF INVALIDITY OF RESERVATIONS

It seems unlikely that one can misunderstand the concluding point of this general comment, in paragraph 18, that reservations which the Committee deems invalid "will generally be severable, in the sense that the Covenant will be operative for the reserving party without benefit of the reservation." Since this conclusion is so completely at odds with established legal practice and principles and even the express and clear terms of adherence by many States, it would be welcome if some helpful clarification could be made.

The reservations contained in the United States instrument of ratification are integral parts of its consent to be bound by the Covenant and are not severable. If it were to be determined that any one or more of them were ineffective, the ratification as a whole could thereby be nullified.

Articles 20 and 21 of the Vienna Convention set forth the consequences of reservations and objections to them. Only two possibilities are provided. Either (i) the remainder of the treaty comes into force between the parties in question or (ii) the treaty does not come into force at all between these parties. In accordance with article 20, paragraph 4 (c), the choice of these results is left to the objecting party. The Convention does not even contemplate the possibility that the full treaty might come into force for the reserving State.

The general view of the academic literature is that reservations are an essential part of a State's consent to be bound. They cannot simply be erased. This reflects the fundamental principle of the law of treaties: obligation is based on consent. A State which does not consent to a treaty is not bound by that treaty. A State which expressly withholds its consent from a provision cannot be presumed, on the basis of some legal fiction, to be bound by it. It is regrettable that General Comment 24 appears to suggest to the contrary.

A monitoring committee also was established (in the late 1980s) to administer the ICESCR. Although this committee has issued a number of general comments, as well as "concluding observations" about the practices of specific countries, its juris-prudence has been less extensive than that of the ICCPR's committee.

Notes and Questions

1. Read through the ICCPR. Should any of these rights be controversial? Is the scope of some of these rights unclear? Does Article 6(1) have any relevance to abortion? What is encompassed by Article 7's reference to "cruel, inhuman or degrading treatment or punishment"? What does the word "promptly" mean in Article 9(3)? What constitutes an "arbitrary. . . interference with . . . privacy," referred to in Article 17(1)? Does the "equal protection of the law," referred to in Article 26, have the same scope as the equal protection of the law guaranteed under U.S. constitutional law?

2. Article 4 of the ICCPR allows parties to take measures derogating from their obligations under the treaty "[i]n time of public emergency which threatens the life of the nation." Why do you think the ICCPR contains this derogation clause? Should any derogation from human rights obligations be permitted? Who decides whether there is the requisite public emergency? Note that no derogation is permitted with respect to certain provisions of the ICCPR, such as the provisions governing the right to life and the prohibitions on torture and slavery. See Article 4(2).

In 2001, the ICCPR's Human Rights Committee issued a general comment designed to "assist States parties to meet the requirements of article 4." The Committee stated, among other things, that (a) "[m]easures derogating from the provisions of the Convenant must be of an exceptional and temporary nature"; (b) "even during an armed conflict measures derogating from the Covenant are allowed only if and to the extent that the situation constitutes a threat to the life of the nation"; (c) parties are required to "provide careful justification not only for their decision to proclaim a state of emergency but also for any specific measures based on such a procloamation"; (d) Article 4 may never be invoked as a basis for "acting in violation of international humanitarian law or peremptory norms of international law, for instance, by taking hostages, by imposing collective punishments, through arbitrary deprivations of liberty or by deviating from fundamental principles of fair trial, including the presumption of innocence"; (e) elements of certain rights in the Covenant, even though not specifically listed as non-derogable in Article 4, cannot be subject to lawful derogation — for example, there can be no derogation from the prohibitions on taking of hostages, abductions, or secret detentions; and (f) a state availing itself of the right of derogation "must immediately inform the other States parties, through the United Nations Secretary-General, of the provisions it has derogated from and of the reasons for such measures." Are these statements proper interpretations of the ICCPR? Do they go beyond mere interpretation?

3. Read through the ICESCR. How does this treaty compare with current U.S. law? Should the United States ratify this treaty? If so, are there any provisions that it should decline to accept (through reservations)? Why is the ICESCR phrased in more gradual terms than the ICCPR? Note that the monitoring committee for the ICESCR issued a general comment in 1990 observing that, "while the Covenant provides for progressive realization and acknowledges the constraints due to the limits of available resources, it also imposes various obligations which are of immediate effect." These obligations include, said the committee, the obligation to "take steps"

to implement the ICESCR and the obligation to guarantee that the rights under the ICESCR will be exercised without various forms of discrimination. The Committee further explained that, despite the "progressive realization" language in the ICE-SCR, there is an obligation "to move as expeditiously and effectively as possible to-wards" realizing the rights in the treaty and that "any deliberatively retrogressive measures in that regard would require the most careful consideration and would need to be fully justified by reference to the totality of the rights provided for in the Covenant and in the context of the full use of the maximum available resources."

4. Should the United States ratify the ICCPR's First Optional Protocol? What would be the advantages of doing so? The disadvantages?

5. In General Comment 24(52), what basis did the Committee have (in para-graph 17) for concluding that the rules concerning reservations set forth in the Vi-enna Convention on Treaties do not necessarily apply to the ICCPR? Do you agree with the Committee's statement (in paragraph 18) that "[i]t necessarily falls to the Committee to determine whether a specific reservation is compatible with the ob-ject and purpose of the Covenant"? What basis did the Committee have for con-cluding (also in paragraph 18) that an invalid reservation ordinarily will be "sever-able," such that "the Covenant will be operative for the reserving party without benefit of the reservation"? Are the U.S. objections to the General Comment 24(52) persuasive?

6. As noted in Chapter 2, the Human Rights Committee concluded in a general comment issued in 1998 that parties to the ICCPR do not have the right to withdraw from the treaty. The Committee reasoned that the rights under the ICCPR "belong to the people living in the territory of the State party" and that "once the people are accorded the protection of the rights under the Covenant, such protection devolves with territory and continues to belong to them, notwithstanding change in Govern-ment of the State party, including dismemberment in more than one State or State succession or any subsequent action of the State party designed to divest them of the rights guaranteed by the Covenant." General Comment 26(61), ¶4, U.N. GAOR Hum. Rts. Comm., 53d Sess., Supp. No. 40, U.N. Doc. A/53/40 (1998). Is this per-suasive? As a practical matter, can the Committee stop nations from withdrawing from the ICCPR?

7. For additional discussion of the ICCPR's Human Rights Committee, see Thomas Buergenthal, The U.N. Human Rights Committee, 5 Max Planck U.N.Y.B. 341 (2001). For access to the Committee's general comments and other docu-ments, see the University of Minnesota's Human Rights Library, at www1. umn.edu/humanrts/index.html.

4.   Other Human Rights Treaties

There are a number of other multilateral treaties focused on human rights issues. The most prominent treaties include the following (all of which are excerpted in the Documentary Supplement):

The Convention on the Prevention and Punishment of the Crime of Genocide, which took effect in 1951 and, as of January 2003, had been ratified by 134 coun-tries. The United States ratified this treaty in 1988. The Convention provides that genocide, "whether committed in time of peace or in time of war, is a crime under international law which they undertake to prevent and to punish." Genocide is defined in the Convention as "any of the following acts committed with intent to destroy, in whole or in part, a national, ethnical, racial or religious group; as such: (a) Killing members of the group; (b) Causing serious bodily or mental harm to members of the group; (c) Deliberately inflicting on the group conditions of life calculated to bring about its physical destruction in whole or in part; (d) Imposing measures intended to prevent births within the group; (e) Forcibly transferring children of the group to another group."

The Convention Against Torture and Other Cruel, Inhuman or Degrading Treatment or Punishment, which took effect in 1987 and, as of January 2003, had been ratified by 132 countries. The United States ratified this treaty in 1994. The Convention provides that the parties to the Convention "shall take effective legislative, administrative, judicial or other measures to prevent acts of torture in any territory under its jurisdiction." It also provides that "[n]o exceptional circumstances whatsoever, whether a state of war or a threat of war, internal political instability or any other public emergency, may be invoked as a justification of torture." In addition, the Convention obligates parties to prosecute or extradite individuals who are alleged to have committed torture within their jurisdiction.

The Convention on the Elimination of All Forms of Racial Discrimination, which took effect in 1969 and, as of January 2003, had been ratified by 168 countries. The United States ratified this treaty in 1994. The Convention obligates parties "to prohibit and to eliminate racial discrimination in all its forms and to guarantee the right of everyone, without distinction as to race, color, or national or ethnic origin, to equality before the law." It defines racial discrimination as "any distinction, exclusion, restriction or preference based on race, color, descent, or national or ethnic origin which has the purpose or effect of nullifying or impairing the recognition, enjoyment or exercise, on an equal footing, of human rights and fundamental freedoms in the political, economic, social, cultural or any other field of public life." As of January 2003, a draft protocol had been proposed for this Convention, which would "establish a system of regular visits undertaken by independent international and national bodies to places where people are deprived of their liberty, in order to prevent torture and other cruel, inhuman or degrading treatment or punishment."

The Convention on the Elimination of All Forms of Discrimination Against Women (CEDAW), which took effect in 1981 and, as of January 2003, had been ratified by 170 countries. The United States signed this treaty in 1980, but, as of January 2003, had not ratified it. The Convention requires parties to grant equal rights to women, and to take appropriate measures to eliminate discrimination against women, in a variety of areas, including political life, employment, education, health care, and marriage. It defines discrimination against women as "any distinction, exclusion or restriction made on the basis of sex which has the effect or purpose of impairing or nullifying the recognition, enjoyment or exercise by women, irrespective of their marital status, on a basis of equality of men and women, of human rights and fundamental freedoms in the political, economic, social, cultural, civil or any other field." An Optional Protocol to this Convention took effect in 2000, whereby parties to the Protocol recognize the competence of the monitoring committee for this Convention to receive and comment on individual complaints (similar to the First Optional Protocol to the ICCPR). As of January 2003, 49 countries had ratified the Optional Protocol.

The Convention on the Rights of the Child, which took effect in 1990 and, as of January 2003, had been ratified by 191 countries. The United States signed this treaty in 1995, but, as of January 2003, had not ratified it. The Convention sets forth a variety of rights for children, and defines "child" to mean anyone under the age of eighteen. The rights in the Convention relate to, among other things, freedom of expression and religion, access to information, adoption, standard of living, health care, education, and criminal punishment. The Convention provides that parties "shall undertake all appropriate legislative, administrative, and other measures for the implementation of the rights recognized in the present Convention," although it also states that, "[w]ith regard to economic, social and cultural rights, States Parties shall undertake such measures to the maximum extent of their available resources and, where needed, within the framework of international co-operation." There are currently two Optional Protocols to the Convention on the Rights of the Child, one prohibiting the use of children in armed conflict and the other prohibiting the sale of children, child prostitution, and child pornography. As of January 2003, these protocols had been ratified by 48 countries (including the United States, even though it had not ratified the Convention itself).

Like the ICCPR and ICESCR, all of these treaties, except for the Genocide Convention, have monitoring committees that issue reports and comments.

Notes and Questions

1. Is the widespread codification of human rights norms a positive development? Do you think this codification has improved human rights practices around the world? Are there other rights that should be codified?

2. Like the ICCPR, the Convention Against Torture prohibits the use of torture under all circumstances. Should there be any exceptions to this prohibition? What if a suspect had information concerning the location of a bomb that, if not discovered, would kill thousands of people?

3. Look at Article 1(4) of the Convention on the Elimination of All Forms of Racial Discrimination. What implications, if any, does it have for affirmative action programs?

4. Skim the Convention on the Rights of the Child. What are the implications of Article 13(1) of the Convention, which provides that "[t]he child shall have the right to freedom of expression; this right shall include freedom to seek, receive and impart information and ideas of all kinds, regardless of frontiers, either orally, in writing or in print, in the form of art, or through any other media of the child's choice"? How about Article 16, which provides that "[n]o child shall be subjected to arbitrary or unlawful interference with his or her privacy, family, home or correspondence, nor to unlawful attacks on his or her honor and reputation"? Are you surprised that 191 nations have ratified this treaty? Do you think all 191 nations comply with the treaty's requirements? Even if they do not, might their ratification of the treaty nevertheless be a positive development? Would it be a good idea to provide for expulsion of countries from human rights treaty regimes if they failed to comply with the treaties?

5. A recent controversial article finds that ratification of human rights treaties may not be correlated with an increase in human rights protections in the ratifying

countries. Using a database encompassing the experiences of 166 nations over a nearly 40-year period in 5 areas of human rights law, the author finds that

> Although the ratings of human rights practices of countries that have ratified interna-
> tional human rights treaties are generally better than those of countries that have not,
> noncompliance with treaty obligations appears to be common. More paradoxically,
> when I take into account the influence of a range of other factors that affect countries'
> practices, I find that treaty ratification is not infrequently associated with worse human
> rights ratings than otherwise expected. [Oona Hathaway, Do Human Rights Treaties
> Make a Difference?, 111 Yale L.J. 1935, 1940 (2002).]

If these findings are correct (and they likely will be contested), what could be the explanation? What is the appropriate solution? Can you think of ways in which enforcement of human rights treaties could be improved?

5.   U.N. Human Rights System

The United Nations has been the principal international forum for the promotion of international human rights. Article 68 of the U.N. Charter directs the U.N.'s Economic and Social Council (ECOSOC) to "set up commissions . . . for the promotion of human rights." Pursuant to this directive, ECOSOC established the U.N. Human Rights Commission in 1946. The Commission examines, monitors, and publicly reports on human rights situations in specific countries and on major phenomena of human rights violations worldwide. Each year it issues numerous resolutions on a wide variety of human rights issues.

As of January 2003, 53 nations were represented in the Commission. The United States has been represented on the Commission every year that it has been in operation, except during 2002, when the United States was controversially voted off the Commission. The Commission meets each year in regular session in March and April for six weeks in Geneva. Over 3,000 delegates from member nations, from observer nations, and from non-governmental organizations participate in those sessions. At these sessions, the Commission adopts about 100 resolutions, decisions, and Chairperson's statements. The Commission can also meet exceptionally between its regular sessions in special session, provided that a majority of the member nations agree. In 2000, for example, it held a special session to address alleged violations of the human rights of the Palestinians by Israel.

As noted, the Commission has procedures for examining and reporting on human rights situations in specific countries (known as country mechanisms or mandates) as well as on major phenomena of human rights violations around the world (known as thematic mechanisms or mandates). The Commission has had country mandates with respect to a variety of countries, including Afghanistan, Cambodia, Haiti, and Iraq. Its thematic mandates have included topics such as arbitrary detention, violence against women, and child prostitution. The Commission's reporting can place pressure on regimes to improve human rights practices. The Commission also sometimes establishes working groups to address the legal standards relating to particular issues. For example, a working group of the Commission was involved in developing a draft protocol to the Torture Convention that would authorize visits to places of detention to address and deter torture and other forms of cruel or inhuman treatment that might occur in such places.

In 1947, the Commission, under the authority of ECOSOC, established a subsidiary commission — the Sub-Commission on Prevention of Discrimination and Protection of Minorities. The name of this subsidiary commission was changed in 1999 to the Sub-Commission on the Promotion and Protection of Human Rights. The Sub-Commission undertakes studies and makes recommendations to the Commission concerning the prevention of discrimination relating to human rights and the protection of racial, religious, and linguistic minorities. The Sub-Commission is composed of 26 experts who act in their personal capacity. The Sub-Commission holds an annual session in Geneva, which ran for four weeks until 1999 but has been reduced to three weeks since 2000. In addition to the members and alternates, it is attended by observers from nations, U.N. bodies and specialized agencies, other intergovernmental organizations, and non-governmental organizations.

In late 1993, the United Nations established the post of the High Commissioner for Human Rights. This High Commissioner is the United Nations official with principal responsibility for United Nations human rights activities. The High Commissioner is appointed by the U.N. Secretary-General with the approval of the General Assembly for a fixed term of four years with the possibility of renewal for a further term of four years. The High Commissioner directs the U.N.'s Office of the High Commissioner for Human Rights, which has an extensive array of responsibilities relating to the promotion of human rights. As of January 2003, the High Commissioner was Sergio Vieira de Mello of Brazil, who succeeded Mary Robinson of Ireland in 2002.

Do you think the United Nations, with its great diversity of members (who vary substantially in their own human rights practices), can be an effective champion of human rights? Can you think of ways in which the U.N. human rights system could be improved — for example, in terms of enforcement? For additional discussion of this system, see Henry J. Steiner & Philip Alston, International Human Rights in Context, Ch. 8 (2000).

6. Customary International Human Rights Law

In addition to human rights treaties, nations are obliged to comply with customary international law with respect to the protection of human rights. The content of the customary international law of human rights is more difficult to discern, however, than the content of treaties. The Restatement (Third) of the Foreign Relations Law of the United States, published in 1987, contains the following list of human rights protections that are governed by customary international law.

Restatement

Section 702. Customary International Law of Human Rights

A state violates international law if, as a matter of state policy, it practices, encourages, or condones

(a) genocide,

(b) slavery or slave trade,

     (c) the murder or causing the disappearance of individuals,

     (d) torture or other cruel, inhuman, or degrading treatment or punishment,

     (e) prolonged arbitrary detention,

     (f) systematic racial discrimination, or

     (g) a consistent pattern of gross violations of internationally recognized human rights.

The Restatement notes that it is including "only those human rights whose status as customary law is generally accepted (as of 1987) and whose scope and content are generally agreed." It further notes that its list "is not necessarily complete, and is not closed: human rights not listed in this section may have achieved the status of customary law, and some rights may achieve that status in the future."

Although originally considered non-binding, the Universal Declaration of Human Rights is thought by many today as reflecting binding obligations as a matter of customary international law. The late Professor Lillich explained this development.

Richard B. Lillich, The Growing Importance of Customary International Human Rights Law

25 Ga. J. Intl. & Comp. L. 1 (1995–1996)

The original "game plan" of the Founding Fathers of the United Nations international human rights program was, first, to spell out in a non-binding Universal Declaration of Human Rights the general principles falling within the phrase "human rights and fundamental freedoms" found in the UN Charter, and then to draft a covenant (which later became two covenants) and various specific conventions relating to particular human rights that would contain legally binding obligations together with implementation provisions for those states that ratified such treaties. Thus, they intended international human rights law to be primarily, perhaps even exclusively, conventional law. That substantial portions of the Universal Declaration of Human Rights, adopted in 1948, eventually might become customary international law, and therefore binding on all states, was beyond the comprehension and vision of all but a few of the participants.

Over the years, however, the Universal Declaration took on a life of its own, aided in no small measure by the fact that the two International Covenants on Civil and Political Rights and Economic, Social and Cultural Rights took until 1966 to draft and entered into force only in 1976. "The process of creating an international law of human rights by the traditional method of concluding international treaties" having been so prolonged, the legal equivalent of the law of physics — that nature abhors a vacuum — came into play and, as the late Professor Schwelb noted in 1964, "the Declaration took over the function originally contemplated for the International Bill of Rights as a whole." Thus as early as 1965 the late Judge Waldock, perhaps a bit prematurely, concluded that the Universal Declaration had become, in toto, a part of binding, customary international law. Three years later the non-governmental Assembly for Human Rights adopted the Montreal Statement, which included the assertion that the "Universal Declaration of Human Rights . . . has over the years become a part of customary international law." Also in 1968, designated by the United Nations as Human Rights Year, the UN-sponsored International Conference on Human Rights adopted the Proclamation of Teheran stating that "the Universal Declaration of Human Rights . . . constitutes an obligation for members of the international community."

Of course, these statements that the Universal Declaration had become legally binding did not make it so; they did, however, constitute important indications that an international consensus to the effect that it reflected customary international law was evolving. Thus in 1976 Professor Humphrey, who as the first Director of the UN Secretariat's Division of Human Rights played a major role in drafting the Declaration, observed that in the course of over a quarter of a century "the Declaration has been invoked so many times both within and without the United Nations that lawyers now are saying that, whatever the intention of its authors may have been, the Declaration is now part of the customary law of nations and therefore is binding on all states." The following year Professor Sohn opined that he believed the Universal Declaration to be not only "an authoritative interpretation of the Charter obligations but also a binding instrument in its own right. . . ." In 1980 Professor McDougal and his colleagues, after describing "the evolution of the Universal Declaration of Human Rights from its first status as mere common aspiration to its present wide acceptance as authoritative legal requirement," also reached the conclusion that it had become "established customary international law, having the attributes of jus cogens and constituting the heart of a global bill of rights."

Evidence of state practice confirming that at least some norms found in the Universal Declaration were thought to have become customary international law was provided in dramatic fashion by the United States in two exceptionally significant cases — one international, one domestic — decided in 1980. In its Memorial to the International Court of Justice in the Hostages case, the United States argued that Iran had violated "certain fundamental human rights" of the hostages "now reflected, inter alia, in the Charter of the United Nations, the Universal Declaration of Human Rights and corresponding portions of the International Covenant on Civil and Political Rights. . . ." The Court subsequently endorsed this argument in its Judgment:

> Wrongfully to deprive human beings of their freedom and to subject them to physical constraint in conditions of hardship is in itself manifestly incompatible with the principles of the Charter of the United Nations, as well as with the fundamental principles enumerated in the Universal Declaration of Human Rights.

While the above passage can be read narrowly to single out the prohibition against torture or cruel, inhuman or degrading treatment or punishment and the right to liberty and security of person for special status, Professor Rodley's more convincing interpretation, with which the present writer agrees, "is that the Court was simply stating that the Universal Declaration as a whole propounds fundamental principles recognized by general international law."

Also in 1980, in the case of Filartiga v. Pena-Irala, the United States, pursuant to a request by the U.S. Court of Appeals for the Second Circuit at the end of oral argument, submitted an important amicus curiae brief further explaining its views on the customary international law of human rights. *Filartiga* involved an action by two Paraguayan plaintiffs against another Paraguayan citizen for the torture and death of their son and brother. The case was brought under the Alien Tort Statute, which provides that "the district courts shall have original jurisdiction of any civil action by an alien for a tort only, committed in violation of the law of nations or a treaty of the United States." Since the United States had yet to ratify the International Covenant on Civil and Political Rights, Article 7 of which prohibits torture, the plaintiffs could not rely upon it to establish jurisdiction under the Statute, but instead had to show that torture violated "the law of nations," i.e., customary international law.

In its brief the United States contended that customary international law now guarantees individuals "certain fundamental human rights," including the right to be free from torture. This universal condemnation [of torture], the brief concluded after an extensive canvass of the evidence demonstrating the existence of such an international norm, "is made explicit in the Universal Declaration of Human Rights, which declares that 'No one shall be subjected to torture. . . .' "The Court of Appeals, which undertook its own thorough examination of the sources from which customary international law is derived, endorsed the government's views when it unanimously held that the prohibition against torture "has become part of customary international law, as evidenced and defined by the Universal Declaration of Human Rights. . . ." Thus state practice, confirmed by a judicial decision, again affirmed that certain fundamental human rights contained in the Universal Declaration now have acquired the status of customary international law.

The *Filartiga* case was almost unanimously lauded by the many legal commentators appraising it. It has spawned a flurry of Alien Tort Statute litigation that, coupled with the occasional instance where customary international human rights law has been invoked in other contexts, has produced a sizeable body of U.S. case law affirming that a number of the norms found in the Universal Declaration have achieved customary international law status. In addition to the prohibition against torture, they include the prohibitions against arbitrary detention, summary execution or murder, "causing the disappearance" of individuals, cruel, inhuman or degrading treatment, and genocide.

All these core human rights — along with prohibitions against slavery or the slave trade, systematic racial discrimination, and a consistent pattern of gross violations of internationally recognized human rights — are listed in the blackletter of Section 702 of the American Law Institute's Restatement (Third) of the Foreign Relations Law of the United States, which purports to state the generally accepted "Customary International Law of Human Rights" as of 1987. As was to have been expected, however, human rights not specifically enumerated in Section 702's blackletter have not been held by U.S. courts to have achieved customary international law status, even when found in the Universal Declaration. They include the right to education, the right to property, and the right of free speech. Arguments that these and other human rights, whether contained in the Declaration or not, now are part of customary international law can be expected to be made in courts in the United States with increasing frequency.

As suggested in the excerpt from the Lillich article, the customary international law of human rights is formed somewhat differently than traditional customary international law. Among other things, it tends to be derived more from the verbal pronouncements of nations and international institutions, such as the adoption of the Universal Declaration of Human Rights and the widespread ratification of certain human rights treaties, than from nations' actual human rights practices. The following excerpt expresses some concern about this change in emphasis.

Bruno Simma & Philip Alston, The Sources of Human Rights Law: Custom, *Jus Cogens*, and General Principles

1988–1989 Austl. Y.B. Intl. L. 82, 82-90, 107

In many situations treaty law provides a solid and compelling legal foundation. But despite a steady increase in the number of States Parties to international treaties in recent years, reliance upon treaties alone provides an ultimately unsatisfactory patchwork quilt of obligations and still continues to leave many States largely untouched. Thus treaty law on its own provides a rather unsatisfactory basis on which to ground the efforts of international institutions whose reach is truly universal, such as the General Assembly and the Commission on Human Rights. The prospects for developing an effective and largely consensual international regime depend significantly on the extent to which those institutions are capable of basing their actions upon a coherent and generally applicable set of human rights norms. Reliance upon treaty law is likely to be even less rewarding in relation to domestic legal argumentation in the courts, legislatures and executives of countries which have ratified few if any of the major international treaties.

There is thus a strong temptation to turn to customary law as the formal source which provides, in a relatively straight-forward fashion, the desired answers. In particular, if customary law can be construed or approached in such a way as to supply a relatively comprehensive package of norms which are applicable to all States, then the debate over the sources of international human rights law can be resolved without much further ado. Given the fundamental importance of the human rights component of a just world order, the temptation to adapt or reinterpret the concept of customary law in such a way as to ensure that it provides the "right" answers is strong, and at least to some, irresistible. It is thus unsurprising that some of the recent literature in this field, especially but not exclusively that coming out of the United States, is moving with increasing enthusiasm in that direction

But while largely endorsing the result that is thereby sought to be achieved, we have considerable misgivings about the means being used. In particular, we believe it to be important to pose two questions. The first is whether this effort to revise or "update" custom does fundamental and irreparable violence to the very concept? As Jennings noted almost a decade ago, much of what many modern commentators characterize as custom "is not only not customary law: it does not even faintly resemble a customary law." The second is whether it is a necessary step in order to reach the desired goal, or whether there are other approaches to the issue of sources which enable us to achieve the same objective while maintaining the integrity of the concept of custom relatively intact? . . .

Caution is far from being a characteristic of much of the contemporary human rights literature. Perhaps this has to do with the fact that "human rights lawyers are notoriously wishful thinkers," as John Humphrey once observed. However this may be, it appears that a majority of authors today take the view that international human rights obligations incumbent upon States may, and actually do, also derive from customary international law. This thesis is presented with varying degrees of sophistication. There are writers who state flatly that the entire *corpus* of international human rights law, or, to be slightly more specific, the substance of the 1948 Universal

Declaration of Human Rights, is now to be regarded as customary law in its entirety. A recent variation on this approach is that, in order to accommodate all of the desired human rights principles, a "modernized view of customary international law" should be applied. That view would accord "the ability to create custom" to nonstate actors such as international organizations and "certain nongovernmental organizations [that] have a distinct, measurable impact on international affairs."

Then there are more moderate, "middle-of-the-road" views, like those of the new Restatement or of Oscar Schachter (if this distinction makes sense, given the important contribution of the latter to the former), according to which something like a "hard core" of human rights obligations exists as customary law today. . . .

Perhaps at this point one might ask what is the practical relevance of all this? In view of the paramount importance of human rights treaties, does it really matter whether, beyond these treaty instruments, there exists an extensive customary, or some other general, international law of human rights?

The answer is, of course, that it matters a great deal — for reasons probably more closely related to domestic law than to international legal issues proper. With regard to domestic law implications, a growing number of modern constitutions not only incorporate customary international law automatically as part of the law of the land but also grant it a rank superior to that of domestic statutes. On the other hand, with very few exceptions, contemporary constitutions put treaties on the same footing as statutes in this respect. As a consequence, international human rights prescriptions derived from customary law, or, in the language of Art. 25 of the German Basic Law, from a general rule (or principle) of international law, would be protected against derogation by a conflicting domestic statute much more effectively than provisions of human rights treaties. Apart from such worst-case scenarios, customary or general international law is allowed by modern constitutions to have a persuasive normative impact on municipal law. . . .

In an important Australian High Court case, in which state action aimed at preventing expanded Aboriginal land ownership was struck down as being contrary to the applicable international human rights norms, three of the four judges in the majority were prepared to rely upon customary international law as the source of the relevant norms. In the United States, we have witnessed the emergence of the famous *Filartiga* jurisprudence — one of the few more likeable facets of the omnipresent tendency of U.S. courts to usurp jurisdiction beyond limits — or at least, what most lawyers abroad would consider to be such limits.

For a foreign observer not accustomed to having to squeeze unwritten international law through a constitutional needle's eye, as prescribed in the *Paquete Habana* case, in order to prepare it for consumption by domestic courts, the readiness of U.S. courts — as well as of the Carter Administration and many American international lawyers serving as *amici curiae*— to view official torture, arbitrary detentions, disappearances and summary executions as violations of customary international law without feeling any particular need to engage in much serious debate about the prerequisites of that source, is striking, to say the least. Given the highly desirable nature of the policy goal of the *Filartiga* jurisprudence, and in view of the formidable array of authorities apparently accepting its approach with respect to custom (or lack of it) as now reflecting the received wisdom, one inevitably hesitates to tamper with it on more or less "academic" grounds. In many respects, what we observe in action here is essentially a concerted effort by American judges and activist human rights lawyers to compensate for the abstinence of the United States *vis-à-vis* ratification of international human rights treaties . . . .

In addition to its important domestic law ramifications, the question of the existence *vel non* of human rights obligations arising from customary international law is also of considerable relevance on the plane of inter-State relations. Thus for example, less than two-thirds of the U.N. Member States are parties to the two International Human Rights Covenants; and participation in most other human rights treaties is even more limited. With only a limited number of ratifications or accessions being added to that list every year in the case of the Covenants, a certain plateau seems to have been reached. The existence of a wide range of customary law obligations (or, let us say, obligations under general international law) *erga omnes* in this field would mitigate the negative significance of this fact. The existence of such obligations would probably entitle all States — not just the parties to human rights treaties *inter se* — to apply remedies or countermeasures at least in cases of gross and persistent breaches of such obligations. It may appear doubtful, however, whether States which prefer to abstain from joining human rights treaties will, at the same time, pursue activist international human rights policies going so far as to resort to effective countermeasures. But again, the practice of the United States is said to provide examples to the contrary Perhaps this is another reason why the thesis endorsing the existence of a customary law of human rights is so popular among American international lawyers.

In any case, the purpose of this brief analysis has been to demonstrate that a discussion of whether such obligations do indeed exist, amounts to more than an exercise in esoterics. Let us turn, then, to the question of the viability, so to speak, of a *customary* law of human rights. What makes this issue so controversial and confused is, in our view, the fact that the international human rights movement's quest for additional sources finds its favorite candidate, customary international law, in the midst of a profound identity crisis. . . .

According to the traditional understanding of international custom, the emphasis was clearly on the material, or objective, of its two elements, namely State *practice*. Customary international law was generally considered to come about through the emergence of a general (or extensive), uniform, consistent and settled practice, more or less gradually joined by a sense of legal obligation, the *opinio juris.* However, practice had priority over *opinio juris;* deeds were what counted, not just words. What international courts and tribunals mainly did in fact was to trace the subjective element by way of discerning certain recurrent patterns within the raw material of State practice and interpreting those patterns as resulting from juridical considerations. . . .

Rules of customary law thus firmly established through inductive reasoning based on deeds rather than words may have been, and still are, limited in scope, but they had, and continue to have, several undoubted advantages. They are hard and solid; they have been carefully hammered out on the anvil of actual, tangible interaction among States; and they allow reasonably reliable predictions as to future State behavior. . . .

So much then for the old-style of practice-based custom, *la coutume sage.* Then followed the stage of *la coutume sauvage:* a product grown in the hothouse of parliamentary diplomacy and all too often "sold" as customary law before actually having stood the test of time. What is customary about this cultured pearl version of customary law is not (at least, not necessarily) its consistent application in actual State practice but the fertilizing role it plays through proclamation, exhortation, repetition, incantation, lament. For some writers, practice no longer has any constitutive role to play in the establishment of customary law; rather it serves a purely evidentiary function. After all, the only task practice ever had to perform, "modernists" would say, was to bring consent or *opinio juris* to the fore; and now that we have all these international bodies, and above all the U.N. General Assembly, generating an almost permanent, intensive flow of communications, consent and *opinio juris* can manifest themselves more or less instantly and without the help of a vehicle as cumbersome and demanding as actual State practice.

For other writers, it is the notion of "practice" itself which has undergone a dubious metamorphosis. It has changed from something happening out there in the real world, after the diplomats and the delegates have had their say, into paper practice: the words, texts, votes and excuses themselves. The process of customary law-making is thus turned into a self-contained exercise in rhetoric. The approach now used is *deductive:* rules or principles proclaimed, for instance, by the General Assembly, as well as the surrounding ritual itself, are taken not only as starting points for the possible development of customary law in the event that State practice eventually happens to lock on to these proclamations, but as a law-making process which is more or less complete in itself, even in the face of contrasting "external" facts. This new, radical customary law has lost the element of retrospection; if its protagonists look back at the past it is a look back in anger, full of impatience with the imperfections and gaps of the old rules. Such impatience also extends to the processes of treaty-making, a field in which delay or a lack of consent simply cannot be argued away by theoretical constructs. Thus the flight into a new, "progressive," more or less instant custom.

The elevation of the Universal Declaration of 1948 and of the documents that have built upon its foundations to the status of customary law, in a world where it is still customary for a depressingly large number of States to trample upon the human rights of their nationals, is a good example of such an approach. . . .

To sum up then, the international protection of human rights has extended the scope of international law beyond hitherto accepted "natural" boundaries. In the development of this new human rights law, international treaties certainly play the most obvious role and give rise to the least jurisprudential difficulties. However, in human rights as in any other branch of the law, participation in treaties is at the discretion of States, the substance of the relevant treaties is often unsatisfactory and sometimes there simply is no treaty around. Thus the need for additional sources of international human rights law.

The mainstream position, particularly in the United States, satisfies its appetite by resorting to a progressive, streamlined theory of customary law, more or less stripped of the traditional practice requirement, and through this dubious operation is able to find a customary law of human rights wherever it is needed.

Questions

1. What rights, if any, should be added to the Restatement's list?

2. If the Universal Declaration of Human Rights has assumed the status of binding customary international law, how did this happen? What evidence does

Professor Lillich cite? Are there any dangers with allowing non-binding resolutions to become binding in this fashion?

3. How is the modern customary international law of human rights different from traditional customary international law? How persuasive are the Simma/Alston criticisms of this new customary international law? To what extent are customary human rights norms supported by state practice? *Opinio juris?*

4. For additional discussion of these issues, and responses to the Simma/Alston critique, see Symposium, Customary International Human Rights Law: Evolution, Status and Future, 25 Ga. J. Intl. & Comp. L. 1-426 (1995-1996).

7.   Role of NGOs

States and international institutions are not the only participants in the process of fashioning and enforcing international human rights law. Non-governmental organizations (NGOs) also play an important role. (They also play a prominent role with respect to other international law issues, as discussed in Chapter 1.) Prominent human rights NGOs include Amnesty International, Human Rights Watch, and the Lawyers Committee for Human Rights. There are also local human rights NGOs in numerous countries. The role of human rights NGOs, and some of the challenges they face, are described below.

**Kenneth Roth, Human Rights Organizations:
A New Force for Social Change, in Realizing Human
Rights: Moving from Inspiration to Impact**
228-237, 242-243 (Samantha Power & Graham Allison eds., 2000)

The expanded scope of human rights protection has been driven largely by a third major development since the adoption of the Universal Declaration: the growth of the human rights movement itself, that is, of nongovernmental organizations (NGOs) devoted to developing and applying international standards on human rights. The human rights movement did not begin with the Declaration. Precursors can be found in the campaigns to abolish slavery, to grant women the right to vote, and to alleviate suffering in time of war. Among the earliest human rights groups were the British and American Anti-Slavery the earliest human rights groups were the British and American Anti-Slavery Societies of the nineteenth century, the International Woman Suffrage Alliance of the early twentieth century, and the International Committee of the Red Cross; established in 1863. Following World War II, NGOs lobbied for the inclusion of language on human rights in the UN Charter and for the adoption of the Universal Declaration, but there was as yet little in the way of a formal human rights movement.

Since then, however, there has been a veritable explosion in the number and breadth of organizations devoted to human rights, particularly since the 1970s. That is when human rights groups began to emerge in Asia in reaction to repressive governments in Korea, Indonesia, and the Philippines. The Helsinki Accord of 1975, affirming "the right of the individual to know and act upon his rights," helped launch the human rights movement in the Soviet Bloc. Human rights groups emerged throughout Latin America in the 1970s and 1980s in opposition to death squads and "disappearances" under right-wing dictatorships. Much of Asia in the 1990s has seen a stunning proliferation of human rights groups. While growth has been slower in Africa and the Middle East, human rights organizations have established a firm presence in all but the most repressive countries. In many places human rights defenders still face persecution, often serve. Ten were killed for their work in 1999 alone, and in one of these cases, two family members were killed as well. Yet despite the danger, this growing movement has become a powerful new source of pressure to uphold human rights. It is the major reason why today the Universal Declaration has so much greater practical breadth and significance than it did fifty years ago.

Over time, the human rights movement has helped create a new kind of NGO. Many human rights organizations today serve not just to amplify the voice of their members but also to collect and deploy information strategically. This role would not have been possible if human rights ideals did not speak so directly to the people of the world. It is only against the backdrop of popular values that human rights information has an impact. Because of these widely shared values, the human rights movement has an influence far beyond its numbers: By uncovering human rights crimes, it can expose their authors to public condemnation.

Moreover, in the 1990s, new communications technologies such as the Internet helped human rights organizations go beyond addressing countries on by one, enabling them to launch global campaigns such as those to ban land mines, establish an International Criminal Court (ICC), end the use of child soldiers, and curb the tranfer of small arms. The coalitions thus assembled have transcended national boundaries and built a genuinely worldwide movement for human rights.

The reality that people around the globe now assert their rights has helped to undercore the universality of the rights proclaimed in the Universal Decalration. As the "interference in our internal affairs" argument loses its punch, many governments have sought to take refuge in the claim that human rights are a concept that is alien to their cultures. Variations of this argument can be found in the assertion of an "Asian concept of human rights," the appeal for "African solutions to African problems," the argument that Islam provides the only true basis for human rights, and the U.S. government's distrust of international standards. The emergence of human rights organizations in all parts of the world undercuts these arguments. It shows that rights are not a "foreign imposition" but that people everywhere aspire to the same basic dignity and respect that the rightsof the Universal Declaration protect. . . .

Despite its growing strength, the human rights movement has hardly ended serious human rights abuse. Thre has been much improvement in the last fifty years in most countries of the former Soviet bloc, Latin America, and southern Africa, as well as parts of Asia. But serious problems persist: many governments still resist applying the Universal Declaration to all their people. Repressive governments continue to run such countries as Burma, China, Iraq, North Korea, Saudi Arabia, and Turkmenistan. Abusive warfare is carried out in such places as Afghanistan, Algeria, Colombia, Kosovo, and Sudan. Even genocide, that most universally condemned crime, has been committed in the last decade of the twentieth century, in Bosnia and Rwanda.

It is a sad truth that governments and warring parties always will be tempted to violate human rights as a means to secure power. Why tolerate a nettlesome opposition when it can be jailed? Why suffer criticism of poor political performance when it is possible to divert public attention by attacking an unpopular minority? Why risk losing social or economic privilege if discrimination can keep challengers down? Why spare civilians the hazards of war it slaughtering them might weaken the enemy's will tŏ fight? The human rights movement cannot promise to end such abuse, but it can generate pressure on governments and insurgents to resist the temptation ot violate rights. The goal is to increase the cost of abuse and thus to alter the political calculations that might lead to human rights violations. . . .

In the last half of the twentieth century, seven factors have enabled the human rights movement to become such a substantial force: the human rights ideal, better communications technology, the press, the policies of influential governments, the development of international standards, the partnership between local and international human rights groups, and the growing professionalism of the human rights movement itself.

The strength of the human rights ideal is a necessary strating point in analyzing the power of the human rights movement. The values codified in the Universal Declaration are at the core of what it means to lead a complete and fulfilled human life. People fortunate enough to live in countries that respect the Universal Declaration in all its dimensions enjoy the freedom and means to live life to its fullest. They are able to speak their minds, practice the religions of their choosing, meet with their compatriots, be treated fairly by their government, and enjoy access to the neccesities of life. These ideals are universally sought.

Second, modern communications technology is essential for human rights activists to be able to inform the public of events in farway places. Earlier human rights movements needed decades to build public consciousness of even such a broadly condemned evil as slavery. It would have been imposible to mobilize public outrage against isolated atrocities, such as a massacre on distant shores, if word could travel no faster than the speed of a sailing ship. Technological developments such as the telegraph, the telephone, radio, television, fax machines, and the Internet have successfully enhanced the ability of human rights activists to scrutinize distant conduct and generate a popular response quickly enough to make a difference.

New communications technology also has rendered governmental efforts to restrict the flow of information increasingly futile. Just a decade ago, Western human rights group were smuggling primitive fax machines to Soviet dissidents who wanted to disseminate their reports more efficiently. Today the Internet is rendering traditional forms of censorship obsolete. For example, in September 1998 Human Rights Watch put a bulletin on its Web site about the political crackdown in Malaysia, including information that was not widely available in the Malaysian Press. In the next two weeks 28,000 people visited the page, mostly from Malaysia itself. By allowing cheap and efficient communication, the Internet also enhances cooperation among human rights activists worldwide, a key factor in the global campaigns to ban antipersonnel land mines and to establish an International Criminal Court.

Third, an related, growing press interest has played a significant role in advancing the human rights cause. It is a sign of the strength of the human rights movement that, today, no government wants to be known as a human rights violator. That is hardly to say that no government violates human rights, but every government does try to hide it abuse. Being seen to respect human rights has become an important part of a government's legitimacy before its own people and the international community. Press coverage of abuses can stigmatize and delegitimize a government before its public and peers. Governments willl go to great lengths to avoid that fate.

The press is also important for mobilizing action to curtail human rights violations. It does little good for activists to learn of serious abuse if they cannot disseminate that information widely to stimulate action by the general public and sympathetic governments. When the press covers attrocities, the exposure tends to elicit demands from the public that its representatives in government use their influence to end those attrocities. Indeed, government officials often treat press coverage as a surrogate for the public's reaction and may be moved to action even before the public itself actually demands it. . . .

A fourth key asset in the fight for human rights has been the willingness of many influential governments to make the protection of human rights an important part of their foreign policy. For example, in part in response to U.S. support for the brutal 1973 coup in Chile, the U.S. Congress enacted laws in the 1970s requiring many forms of government-to-government assistance (other than those serving basic human needs) to be cut off or redirected if a government engages in a systematic pattern of gross violations of human rights. These laws have been honored more often in the breach than in the observance, as is evinced by the fact that Israel, Egypt, and Turkey are among the largest recipients of U.S. aid, despite their systematic practice of torture and other serious abuses. Nonetheless, the laws set standards by which U.S. aid policy can be judged. At times campaigns by human rights organizations have led the United States to end aid relationship with abusive governments or to exert pressure on governments to curtail abuses in order to maintain their aid. The gradual diminution of U.S. aid to various African tyrants in the 1990s — Mohamed Siad Barre of Somalia, Samuel Doe of Liberia, Mobutu Sese Seko of Zaire — was due at least in part of pressure from human rights groups. So was the gradual cutoff of U.S. aid to the UNITA rebel group in Angola. Even when U.S. aid to an abusive government persisted, as it did to EI Salvador in the 1980s, pressure from human rights groups to comply with U.S. law forced the U.S. government to put pressure on the Salvadoran government to curtail abuses in order to minimize the political scandal in the United States surrounding El Salvador's receipt of military assistance.

In addition, the U.S. State Department's *Country Reports on Human Rights Practices,* a global survey of human rights conditions produced under congressional mandate, has been a useful tool for putting the U.S. government on record about human rights abuses and stigmatizing offending governments (although these reports have been too little heeded in making U.S. policy). The European Union, too, has adopted the practice of making its aid and cooperation agreements formally conditional on the beneficiary's respect for human rights, while the Japanese government's declared policy is that human rights are a factor in determining its overseas development assistance . . .

A fifth factor in the effectiveness and credibility of the human rights movement has been the elaboration of international human rights law and standards. Why, one might ask, should an abusive government listen to the demands of an international human rights organization that may be located a continent or an ocean away? What legitimacy does an international human rights organization have to address distant human rights concerns? The answer lies in the movement's application of internationally recognized human rights standards.

While the Universal Declaration of Human Rights speaks in nonbinding language, its principles have been codified in two binding treaties introduced by the United Nations in 1966: the International Covenant on Civil and Political Rights and the International Covenant on Economic, Social and Cultural Rights. These Covenants entered into force ten years later, making many of the provisions of the Universal Declaration of Human Rights binding on the scores of countries that have ratified them. Regional treaties also have been adopted for Africa, Europe, and the Americas, as have specialized treaties addressing the rights of women, children, refugees, and workers, and the problems of torture, racial discrimination, and wartime abuses. This legal framework enables international human rights organizations to point not just to their own values but to standards that have broad international endorsement.

Human rights groups deserve some credit for the development of international human rights law. They have helped to draft treaties and have been instrumental in interpreting them and giving them life. Because international law is relatively underdeveloped in comparison with most domestic systems, its violation does not yet always carry the same stigma: Whereas a domestic criminal offense usually is regarded as cause for opprobrium, violation of international law may seem less wrong because of the complexity and novelty of the international legal order. By portraying publicly the devastation caused to individual victims of abuse, however, human rights groups add a human dimension that gives flesh and urgency to the legal abstractions of international law.

Human rights organizations also have helped to extend moral judgments beyond the obvious original meaning of a law. For example, the drafters of the Universal Declaration probably would have said that common crime falls outside it scope. However, human rights organizations, looking at the problem of domestic violence against women, saw a link. While an act of domestic violence might not itself violate human rights standards, official indifference to the problem on the part of police, prosecutors, and judges can be said to violate international standards against discrimination on grounds of gender. By suggesting that this official indifference amounted to complicity in the abuse, the human rights movement helped to expand the meaning of international law to embrace this important but neglected problem. Similarly, years of campaigning by the human rights movement has promoted acceptance of the view that the right to an "effective remedy" for human right violations requires not simply granting the victim the opportunity to purse civil damages but, for the most serious abuses, official investigation of the crime, followed by punishment of the perpetrators.

The human rights movement has also led the lawmaking effort by bringing humanitarian problems to international attention and proposing new laws to address them. The successful campaign to ban antipersonnel land mines and the current campaign to end the use as soldiers of children under eighteen years of age are good examples. The tremendous strides made in recent years in convincing the public that multinational corporations should respect human rights standards — although the relevant international standards apply formally only to governments, not to the corporations themselves — illustrate the human rights movement's capacity to build moral consensus even in the absence of law.

A sixth key factor in the growing success of the human rights cause has been the effective partnerships forged in dozens of countries between international and local human rights organizations. Local organizations are best positioned to mobilize local opposition to human right abuse and to insist on change. Given governments' preoccupation with maintaining power, these local voices tend to have the greatest resonance. An abusive government wants to avoid being denounced before its citizens or having its disregard for human rights spark demonstrations and public protests. For that reason, however, many local activists have themselves become targets of abuse and repression: Many have been killed, and many more have faced persecution.

Because of this danger, international human rights organizations place their highest priority on trying to protect the local human rights activists who are on the front line. Any attack on a human rights monitor gives rise to fierce denunciations and intense pressure on the offending government. In this way international human rights organizations work to create and maintain the political space that local activists need to function.

As local organizations are able to operate more freely, they, in turn, provide invaluable assistance to international groups, ranging from logistical assistance in identifying witnesses and navigating difficult terrain, to strategic assistance in selecting topics for inquiry, shaping investigations, fashioning recommendations for policymakers, and planning advocacy campaigns. The partnership between local groups, with their superior knowledge of local conditions, and international groups, with their global perspective and access to the international press and policymakers, has been a powerful one. . . .

As powerful as the human rights movement has become, it is hardly assured of victory in any given case. Certain countries and issues remain stubbornly resistant to the human rights methodology. Some governments are so powerful economically that classic forms of pressure have little impact; Saudi Arabaia is an example. Sometimes the human rights movement faces powerful political antagonists, such as the oppositions of much of the international business community to forceful advocacy of human rights in China. Geopolitical calculations still lie behind the tolerance of abuses in certain countries, such as the U.S. government's lenient attitude toward persistent attrocities in Rwanda. A cultural tradition of certain forms of abuse can make it difficult to stigmatize a government as in the case of the repression of women in some Muslim countries. Certain highly repressive governments, such as that of Burma, have prevented the emergence of the local partners that the international human rights movement needs to be most effective. Some elected governments, such as that of Colombia, successfully deflect international opprobrium in part because they are viewed as "democracies" and hence assumed, however falsely, not to commit serious human rights violations. Certain issues are more resistant to the tools of the human rights community — for example, ending repression in Iraq may ultimately require military force — while other issues, such as those involving certain economic and social rights, have complicated causes and solutions and cannot be solved easily even where public pressure creates political will to do so.

Of course, steps still can be taken to overcome these obstacles, but they are not easy. In some cases, efforts at public stigmatization can be stepped up. In other cases, new sources of economic or diplomatic pressure can be generated. New allies can be found and innovative partnerships built. But even with such heightened efforts, the human rights methodology is not foolproof. Indeed, we should not expect it to be. The methodology was developed as a way of enforcing rights when traditional resort to a legal system fails. Given the fallibility of many legal systems in protecting rights, even with the coercive power of the state at their disposal, one would hardly expect the less direct methodology of human rights organizations to guarantee success. But it does greatly increase the likelihood that, even in the absence of a functionating legal system, people will have some prospect of securing their rights.

Notes and Questions

1. What are the advantages to NGO participation in the development and enforcement of international human rights law? Are there any disadvantages? Whose interests do the NGOs represent? Does their participation make international human rights law more or less democratic?

2. What obstacles do human rights NGOs face? How can these obstacles be overcome? What are the most effective tools of human rights NGOs?

3. Kenneth Roth, the author of the first excerpt above, is the Executive Director of Human Rights Watch, which is now the largest human rights NGO based in the United States. (Amnesty International is based in Great Britain.) As explained on the Web site for Human Rights Watch:

> Human Rights Watch researchers conduct fact-finding investigations into human rights abuses in all regions of the world. Human Rights Watch then publishes those findings in dozens of books and reports every year, generating extensive coverage in local and international media. This publicity helps to embarrass abusive governments in the eyes of their citizens and the world. Human Rights Watch then meets with government officials to urge changes in policy and practice — at the United Nations, the European Union, in Washington and in capitals around the world. In extreme circumstances, Human Rights Watch presses for the withdrawal of military and economic support from governments that egregiously violate the rights of their people. In moments of crisis, Human Rights Watch provides up-to-the-minute information about conflicts while they are underway. Refugee accounts, which were collected, synthesized and cross-corroborated by our researchers, helped shape the response of the international community to recent wars in Kosovo and Chechnya. [http://www.hrw.org/about/whoweare.html.]

4. For additional discussion of the role of NGOs in international human rights law, see Henry J. Steiner, Diverse Partners: Non-Governmental Organizations in the Human Rights Movement (1991); and David Weissbrodt, The Contribution of International Nongovernmental Organizations to the Protection of Human Rights, in 2 Human Rights in International Law: Legal and Policy Issues 403 (Theodor Meron ed., 1984).

8.   The United States and International Human Rights Law

The United States played a leading role in establishing the United Nations and drafting the Universal Declaration of Human Rights. It also frequently expresses concern about human rights violations around the world, and it sometimes uses economic and even military pressure to induce nations to improve their human rights practices. Further, U.S. law reflects a substantial commitment to domestic human rights protections — through, for example, the Bill of Rights. And, as we saw in Chapter 3, U.S. courts have shown a willingness to adjudicate cases involving alleged human rights abuses in other countries, especially in cases (such as *Filartiga*) brought under the Alien Tort Statute. Nevertheless, since the 1950s, the United States has had an uneasy relationship with human rights treaties and institutions, and it is frequently accused of having a double standard, whereby it seeks to enforce international human rights norms against other countries but is unwilling to have its own practices subjected to international regulation.

a.   Ratification of Human Rights Treaties

The excerpt below describes the history of U.S. ratification of human rights treaties.

Curtis A. Bradley & Jack L. Goldsmith, Treaties, Human Rights, and Conditional Consent

149 U. Pa. L. Rev. 399, 410-416 (2000)

Before World War II, international law primarily regulated interactions among nations, and it did not contain extensive protections for individual rights. Soon after the War, with the experience of the Holocaust and other atrocities fresh in mind, the international community began to develop a comprehensive body of international human rights law. The seeds of this human rights law revolution were sown in the 1940s. The United Nations Charter, which came into force in 1945, contained general commitments to protect human rights. Three years later, the United Nations General Assembly adopted the Convention on the Prevention and Punishment of the Crime of Genocide and opened it for national ratifications. That same year, the General Assembly issued its nonbinding, but nonetheless influential, Universal Declaration of Human Rights. The Universal Declaration, which aspired to be a "common standard of achievement for all peoples and all nations," contained broadly worded civil, political, economic, social, and cultural rights. Immediately following the passage of the Declaration, the United Nations Commission on Human Rights began drafting a human rights covenant that aimed to convert the nonbinding provisions of the Declaration into binding treaty obligations.

United States officials played a prominent role in creating the emerging international regime of human rights law. Nonetheless, there were intense debates in the United States during the 1950s over whether and to what extent the nation should participate in this regime. These debates focused principally on the domestic implications of ratifying the human rights treaties. Some people were concerned that the U.N. Charter's human rights provisions would give Congress the power to enact civil rights legislation otherwise beyond its constitutional powers. This was a plausible belief in light of the Supreme Court's decision in Missouri v. Holland, which held that, when implementing a treaty, Congress is not subject to the federalism limitations applicable to the exercise of its Article I powers. A related concern was that the U.N. Charter would preempt state laws by virtue of the Supremacy Clause. In fact, this argument was seemingly endorsed by one lower California court and four justices of the U.S. Supreme Court in their consideration of the validity of a California alien land ownership statute. The potentially self-executing nature of the Charter was particularly worrisome to some in the early days of the anticommunist Cold War period because the Universal Declaration, including its very progressive provisions concerning economic, social, and cultural rights, was described by its proponents as giving content to the vague human rights provisions of the U.N. Charter.

Another event that triggered concerns in the United States was President Truman's submission of the Convention on the Prevention and Punishment of the Crime of Genocide to the Senate in 1948. Although the United States had helped to draft the Convention and supported an international prohibition on genocide, many senators and others worried about the domestic consequences of ratifying the treaty. One of their central concerns was the vagueness of the Convention's definition of "genocide." The Convention defined genocide to include certain acts "committed with intent to destroy" covered groups, including the act of causing "mental harm" to members of covered groups. The unease over these definitional provisions related to their possible inconsistency with the First Amendment, their potential use as a basis for prosecuting U.S. military officials abroad, and their foreseeable use in support of a claim that U.S. policies toward African-Americans and Native Americans constituted genocide. There was also a more general concern about the erosion of U.S. sovereignty and independence.

These various concerns led to proposals in the 1950s to amend the Constitution to limit the treaty powers of the United States. Along with leaders of the American Bar Association, a key proponent of such an amendment was Senator John Bricker of Ohio, and the various proposed amendments are commonly referred to jointly as the "Bricker Amendment." In general, the proposed amendments were intended to preclude treaties from being self-executing and to make clear that treaties would not override the reserved powers of the states. Some versions also would have restricted the use of executive agreements. There was substantial consideration of these proposals during the 1950s. In fact, one of the proposed amendments fell only one vote short of obtaining the necessary two-thirds vote in the Senate.

To help defeat the Bricker Amendment, the Eisenhower administration made a commitment that it would not seek to become a party to any more human rights treaties. Secretary of State John Foster Dulles announced during the Bricker Amendment hearings in 1953 that the administration had no intention of becoming a party to the then-proposed human rights treaties. In 1955, Dulles reaffirmed that "the United States will not sign of become a party to the covenants on human rights, the convention on the political rights of women, and certain other proposed multilateral agreements." In the same year, the State Department published a circular stating, in obvious reference to the Bricker Amendment debate, that "treaties are not to be used as a device for the purpose of effecting internal social changes or to try to circumvent the constitutional procedures established in relation to what are essentially matters of domestic concern." For decades thereafter, presidents did not submit major human rights treaties to the Senate (although they did continue to seek the Senate's advice and consent for the Genocide Convention).

This reticence changed with the Carter administration, which submitted a package of human rights treaties to the Senate in the late 1970s. Since that time, every President has urged the Senate to approve the ratification of major human rights treaties, and the Senate has in fact given its advice and consent to four such treaties. With respect to the treaties to which the Senate has given its advice and consent, there has been a remarkable consensus across very different administrations and very different Senates about both the desirability of ratifying these treaties and the need to attach RUDs to the treaties as a condition of ratification to protect domestic prerogatives.

As for the desirability of ratifying human rights treaties, presidents and the Senate have agreed that a failure by the United States to ratify the major human rights treaties would result in at least two kinds of foreign policy costs. First, nonratification would preclude the United States from participating in the treaty-related institutions that, in turn, influence the course of international human rights law. Second, nonratification would create a "troubling complication" in U.S. diplomacy, namely, that the United States could not credibly encourage other nations to embrace human rights norms if it had not itself embraced those norms.

Presidents and the Senate have also agreed, however, that the modern human rights treaties implicate serious countervailing considerations reminiscent of the Bricker Amendment debates. These concerns are easiest to understand with respect to the most ambitious of these treaties, the International Covenant on Civil and Political Rights ("ICCPR"). The ICCPR contains dozens of vaguely worded rights guarantees that differ in important linguistic details from the analogous guarantees under U.S. domestic law. Some of these provisions arguably conflict with U.S. constitutional guarantees. In addition, the ICCPR, if self-executing, would have the same domestic effect as a congressional statute and thus would supersede inconsistent state law and prior inconsistent federal legislation. There was concern that, even if courts ultimately decided that each of the differently worded provisions in the ICCPR did not require a change in domestic law, litigation of these issues would be costly and would generate substantial legal uncertainty. These concerns also arose, although on a narrower scale, with respect to the other human rights treaties.

To address these concerns, President Carter and every subsequent President have included proposed RUDs with their submission of human rights treaties to the Senate. The Senate has given its advice and consent to, and the United States has ratified, four of these treaties: the Genocide Convention, ratified in 1988; the ICCPR, ratified in 1992; the Torture Convention, ratified in 1994; and the Convention on the Elimination of All Forms of Racial Discrimination, also ratified in 1994. The United States included RUDs in the ratification instruments for each of these treaties as a precondition of U.S. ratification. The Senate usually consented to the RUDs in the form proposed by the President, but sometimes the Senate modified them slightly or requested that the President modify them.

As indicated in the above excerpt, the United States finally began ratifying some of the major human rights treaties in the late 1980s. As of January 2003, however, the United States still had not ratified the ICESCR, the CEDAW, or the Convention on the Rights of the Child. Moreover, as discussed in the excerpt, the United States has conditioned its consent to the human rights treaties that it has ratified with an extensive array of reservations, understandings, and declarations (RUDs). (The RUDs that the United States attached to its ratification of the ICCPR are excerpted in the Documentary Supplement.)

The following excerpt (from the same article) summarizes the typical RUDs attached to U.S. ratification of human rights treaties, and the explanations given by the U.S. treatymakers for these RUDs.

Curtis A. Bradley & Jack L. Goldsmith, Treaties, Human Rights, and Conditional Consent

149 U. Pa. L. Rev. 399, 416-423 (2000)

RUDs are designed to harmonize the treaties with existing requirements of U.S. law and to leave domestic implementation of the treaties to Congress. They cover a variety of subjects and take a variety of forms. For purposes of analysis, they can be grouped into five categories:

Substantive Reservations. Some RUDs are reservations pursuant to which the United States declines to consent altogether to certain provisions in the treaties. These reservations are very much the exception to the rule; for each of the four human rights treaties under consideration, the United States consented to a large majority of the provisions. Some substantive reservations are based on potential conflicts between treaty provisions and U.S. constitutional rights. For example, First Amendment concerns led the United States to decline to agree to restrictions on hate speech in the Race Convention "to the extent that [such speech is] protected by the Constitution and laws of the United States." Similarly, the United States attached a reservations to its ratification of the ICCPR, stating that the ICCPR's restriction on propaganda for war and hate speech "does not authorize or require legislation or other action by the United States that would restrict the right of free speech and association protected by the Constitution and laws of the United States."

Other substantive reservations are based not on a constitutional conflict but rather on a political or policy disagreement with certain provisions of the treaties. For example, the United States attached to its ratification of the ICCPR reservations allowing it to impose criminal punishment consistent with the Fifth, Sixth, and Eighth Amendments, including capital punishment of juvenile offenders, notwithstanding limitations on such punishment in the ICCPR. The United States attached a similar reservation with respect to limitations on punishment in the Torture Convention. It also attached a condition to its ratification of the Race Convention making clear that it was not agreeing to modify the traditional public/private distinction irr U.S. civil rights law.

Interpretive Conditions. Some RUDs set forth the United States's interpretation of vague treaty terms, thereby clarifying the scope of United States consent. For example, Articles 2(1) and 26 of the ICCPR prohibit discrimination not only on the basis of "race, colour, sex, language, religion, political or other opinion, national or social origin, property, [and] birth," but also on the basis of any "other status." The United States attached an understanding stating that this open-ended prohibition on discrimination did not preclude legal distinctions between persons "when such distinctions are, at minimum, rationally related to a legitimate governmental objective." It also attached a reservation to both the ICCPR and the Torture Convention stating that the United States considers itself bound by the prohibitions in those treaties on "cruel, inhuman, or degrading treatment or punishment" only to the extent that such treatment or punishment is prohibited by the U.S. Constitution. The

United States similarly attached understandings to its ratification of the Genocide and Torture Conventions clarifying the circumstances under which conduct will fall within the terms of these treaties.

Non-Self-Execution Declarations. U.S. treatymakers also have included, when ratifying human rights treaties, declarations stating that the substantive provisions of the treaties are not self-executing. These declarations are designed to preclude the treaties from being enforceable in U.S. courts in the absence of implementing legislation. As the State Department explained in submitting the proposed treaties to President Carter for his transmission to the Senate, "with such declarations, the substantive provisions of the treaties would not of themselves become effective as domestic law."

The treatymakers have given several reasons for these declarations. First, they believe that, taking into account the substantive reservations and interpretive conditions, U.S. domestic laws and remedies are sufficient to meet U.S. obligations under human rights treaties. There is thus no additional need, in their view, for domestic implementation. Second, there is concern that the treaty terms, although similar in substance to U.S. law, are not identical in working and thus might have a destabilizing effect on domestic rights protections if considered self-executing. Third, there is disagreement about which treaty terms, if any, would be self-executing. The declaration is intended to provide certainty about this issue in advance of litigation. Finally, the treatymakers believe that if there is to be a change in the scope of domestic rights protections, it should be done by legislation with the participation of the House of Representatives. . . .

Federalism Understandings. RUDs for human rights treaties typically contain an understanding or other statement relating to federalism. The RUDs attached to the ICCPR, for example, provide that "the United States understands that this Covenant shall be implemented by the Federal Government to the extent that it exercises legislative and judicial jurisdiction over the matters covered therein, and otherwise by the state and local governments." The Bush Administration explained that this understanding "serves to emphasize domestically that there is no intent to alter the constitutional balance of authority between the State and Federal governments or to use the provisions of the Covenant to 'federalize' matters now within the competence of the States." And the Clinton Administration similarly explained that "there is no disposition to preempt these state and local initiatives or to federalize the entire range of anti-discriminatory actions through the exercise of the constitutional treaty power. . . . In some areas, it would be inappropriate to do so." . . .

ICJ Reservations. U.S. RUDs, like the reservations of many other nations, also typically decline to consent to "ICJ Clauses" in the human rights treaties, pursuant to which claims under the treaties could be brought against the United States in the International Court of Justice. The United States attached a reservation to its ratification of the Genocide Convention, for example, stating that "before any dispute to which the United States is a party may be submitted to the jurisdiction of the International Court of Justice under [Article IX of the Convention], the specific consent of the United States is required in each case." The U.S. treatymakers have explained that the ICJ reservations are designed "to retain the ability of the United States to decline a case which may be brought for frivolous or political reasons." They also have expressed the view that the reservations will not significantly affect the resolution of disputes under the treaties "because the [ICJ] has not played an important implementation role and because the Convention provides other effective means. . . . for dispute settlement."

The RUDs have generated significant criticism. Consider, for example, Professor Henkin's comments, excerpted below.

Louis Henkin, U.S. Ratification of Human Rights Conventions: The Ghost of Senator Bricker

89 Am. J. Intl. L. 341, 344, 345-349 (1995)

By adhering to human rights conventions subject to these reservations, the United States, it is charged, is pretending to assume international obligations but in fact is undertaking nothing. It is seen as seeking the benefits of participation in the convention (e.g., having a U.S. national sit on the Human Rights Committee established pursuant to the Covenant) without assuming any obligations or burdens. The United States, it is said, seeks to sit in judgment on others but will not submit its human rights behavior to international judgment. To many, the attitude reflected in such reservations is offensive: the conventions are only for other states, not for the United States. . . .

The "federalism" clause attached to U.S. ratifications of human rights conventions has been denominated an "understanding," a designation ordinarily used for an interpretation or clarification of a possibly ambiguous provision in the treaty. The federalism clause in the instruments of ratification of the human rights conventions is not an understanding in that sense, but may be intended to alert other parties to United States intent in the matter of implementation. . . .

The United States has proposed "federalism" clauses in the past, presumably to assuage "states' rights" sensibilities. At one time, the United States sought to limit its obligations under particular treaties to those matters that were "within the jurisdiction" of the federal Government, and to exclude any international obligation as to matters subject to the jurisdiction of the states. Some early versions of the federal-state clause reflected a misapprehension about "the jurisdiction" of the federal Government, as regards the reach of both its treaty power and congressional legislative power. There are no significant "states' rights" limitations on the treaty power. There is little that is not "within the jurisdiction of the United States," i.e., within the treaty power, or within the legislative power of Congress under the Commerce Power, under its authority to implement the Fourteenth Amendment, or under its power to do what is necessary and proper to carry out its treaty obligations. In time, recognizing that virtually any matter governed by treaty was "within the jurisdiction" of the United States, the executive branch took to declaring that the convention shall be implemented by the federal Government to the extent that it "exercises jurisdiction" over matters covered by the treaty, leaving to the states implementation of matters over which the states exercise jurisdiction.

Such a statement is deeply ambiguous. The federal Government exercises jurisdiction over all matters covered in a human rights convention, if only by making the treaty. It exercises jurisdiction over such matters because Congress has the power to legislate, and has legislated, in respect of them. In any event, as a matter of international treaty law, such a statement is not an "understanding" or a reservation, and raises no international difficulties. International law requires the United States to carry out its treaty obligations but, in the absence of special provision, does not prescribe how, or through which agencies, they shall be carried out. As a matter of international law, then, the United States could leave the implementation of any treaty provision to the states. Of course, the United States remains internationally responsible for any failure of implementation. ·

The "federalism" declarations that have been attached to human rights conventions thus serve no legal purpose. But some see such declarations as another sign that the United States is resistant to international human rights agreements, setting up obstacles to their implementation and refusing to treat human rights conventions as treaties dealing with a subject of national interest and international concern.

The United States [also] has been declaring the human rights agreements it has ratified to be non-self-executing.

The U.S. practice of declaring human rights conventions non-self-executing is commonly seen as of a piece with the other RUDs. As the reservations designed to deny international obligations serve to immunize the United States from external judgment, the declaration that a convention shall be non-self-executing is designed to keep its own judges from judging the human rights conditions in the United States by international standards. To critics, keeping a convention from having any effect as United States law confirms that United States adherence remains essentially empty.

The non-self-executing declaration has been explained — and justified — as designed to assure that changes in U.S. law will be effected only by "democratic processes" — therefore, by legislation, not by treaty. That argument, of course, impugns the democratic character of every treaty made or that will be made by the President with the consent of the Senate.

Whatever may be appropriate in a special case, as a general practice such a declaration is against the spirit of the Constitution; it may be unconstitutional. Article VI of the Constitution provides expressly for lawmaking by treaty: treaties are declared to be the supreme law of the land. The Framers intended that a treaty should become law ipso facto, when the treaty is made; it should not require legislative implementation to convert it into United States law. In effect, lawmaking by treaty was to be an alternative to legislation by Congress.

Nothing in the Constitution or in the history of its adoption suggests that the Framers contemplated that some treaties might not be law of the land. That was a later suggestion by John Marshall, because he found that some promises by their character could not be "self-executing": when the United States undertook to do something in the future that could be done only by legislative or other political act, the treaty did not — could not — carry out the undertaking. Marshall did not contemplate that treaty undertakings that could be given effect as law by the Executive and the courts, or by the states, should not be carried out by them, but might be converted into promises that Congress would legislate. Surely, there is no evidence of any intent, by the Framers (or by John Marshall), to allow the President or the Senate, by their ipse dixit, to prevent a treaty that by its character could be law of the land from becoming law of the land. . . .

Whatever might be said for amending the Constitution to require consent to a treaty by both Houses of Congress, that is not what the Constitution (unamended) provides. In any event, declaring a treaty — here a human rights convention — non-self-executing achieves the worst of both systems. A human rights convention, like other treaties, goes to the Senate for its consent, where — "undemocratically" — a third of the members (plus one) can reject the convention. But unlike treaties generally, human rights conventions would later, after Senate consent and U.S. ratification, require going to the Senate again, as well as to the House, for implementing legislation, involving additional, often extended delays and obstacles to carrying out United States international obligations.

There is more at issue in the United States RUDs than their effect on a particular treaty; at stake in United States human rights reservation policy is the integrity of the constitutional system for concluding treaties. I recall some background. . . . [Professor Henkin discusses the Bricker Amendment debates from the 1950s.]

In retrospect, the Bricker Amendment, if adopted, would have damaged the treaty power by making all treaties not self-executing, but it would not have prevented adherence to human rights treaties or their implementation by Congress. Limiting the power of Congress to implement treaties would not have proved to be serious for human rights: In 1954 the Constitution itself was interpreted as forbidding segregation, and the courts enforced desegregation without any human rights treaty or act of Congress. Within a few years it became clear that the powers of Congress apart from its power to implement treaties — notably the Commerce Power and the power to implement the Fourteenth Amendment — were broad enough to support civil rights legislation. The civil rights campaign in the United States became entirely domestic, and any thought of effecting change in United States law by treaty was abandoned. The Bricker Amendment campaign became ancient history.

It soon appeared, however, that — apart from the condition of human rights in the United States — United States foreign policy required U.S. support for, if not leadership in, the international human rights movement, and required U.S. adherence to international human rights conventions. Successive administrations slowly abandoned President Eisenhower's commitment. But Senator Bricker's ghost has proved to be alive in the Senate, and successive administrations have become infected with his ideology.

Senator Bricker lost his battle, but his ghost is now enjoying victory in war. For the package of reservations, understandings and declarations achieves virtually what the Bricker Amendment sought, and more. In pressing his amendment, Senator Bricker declared: "My purpose in offering this resolution is to bury the so-called Covenant on Human Rights so deep that no one holding high public office will ever dare to attempt its resurrection." By its package of RUDs, the United States effectively fulfilled Senator Bricker's purpose, leaving the Covenant without any life in United States law. . . .

U.S. ratification practice threatens to undermine a half-century of effort to establish international human rights standards as international law. Lawyers (and others) committed to the international human rights movement should be on guard to ensure that U.S. ratification policy not set an unfortunate example to other states contemplating adherence, that it not encourage states that have ratified to take their obligations under the conventions lightly. Lawyers in the United States should take arms against the anticonstitutional practice of declaring human rights conventions non-self-executing.

Notes and Questions

1. Should the United States ratify additional human rights treaties, such as the ICESCR, the CEDAW, and the Convention on the Rights of the Child? If so, should it condition its ratification with RUDs? How persuasive are Professor Henkin's criticisms of the RUDs? Do the RUDs make the U.S. ratification of human rights treaties meaningless? Would the United States have ratified the ICCPR and other human rights treaties without the RUDs?

2. Note that, despite its limited embrace of international human rights treaties, the United States has enacted legislation implementing some of the human rights treaties it has ratified. In connection with its ratification of the Genocide Convention, the United States enacted the Genocide Convention Implementation Act, 18 U.S.C. §1091, which makes genocide a federal crime if it is committed in the United States or the alleged offender is a U.S. national. In connection with its ratification of the Torture Convention the United States enacted a provision making torture outside the United States a federal crime, 18 U.S.C §2340A. Before ratifying the convention, the United States had also enacted a civil cause of action allowing for the recovery of damages for foreign torture, 28 U.S.C. §1350 note. (The latter statute, known as the Torture Victim Protection Act, is discussed in Chapter 3.) The United States also amended its immigration law to take account of Article 3 of the Torture Convention, which bars the return of a person to another nation "where there are substantial grounds for believing that he would be in danger of being subjected to torture." See P.L. 105-277, 112 stat. 2681-822 (Oct. 21, 1998).

3. In 1998, President Clinton promulgated the following executive order concerning U.S. compliance with human rights treaties:

> By the authority vested in me as President by the Constitution and the laws of the United States of America, and bearing in mind the obligations of the United States pursuant to the [ICCPR], the Convention Against Torture and Other Cruel, Inhuman or Degrading Treatment or Punishment (CAT), the Convention on the Elimination of All Forms of Racial Discrimination (CERD), and other relevant treaties concerned with the protection and promotion of human rights to which the United States is now or may become a party in the future, it is hereby ordered as follows:
>
> Section 1. Implementation of Human Rights Obligations. (a) It shall be the policy and practice of the Government of the United States, being committed to the protection and promotion of human rights and fundamental freedoms, fully to respect and implement its obligations under the international human rights treaties to which it is a party, including the ICCPR, the CAT, and the CERD.
>
> (b) It shall also be the policy and practice of the Government of the United States to promote respect for international human rights, both in our relationships with all other countries and by working with and strengthening the various international mechanisms for the promotion of human rights, including, inter alia, those of the United Nations, the International Labor Organization, and the Organization of American States.
>
> Sec. 2. Responsibility of Executive Departments and Agencies. (a) All executive departments and agencies . . . shall maintain a current awareness of United States international human rights obligations that are relevant to their functions and shall perform such functions so as to respect and implement those obligations fully. The head of each agency shall designate a single contact officer who will be responsible for overall coordination of the implementation of this order. Under this order, all such

agencies shall retain their established institutional roles in the implementation, interpretation, and enforcement of Federal law and policy.

(b) The heads of agencies shall have lead responsibility, in coordination with other appropriate agencies, for questions concerning implementation of human rights obligations that fall within their respective operating and program responsibilities and authorities or, to the extent that matters do not fall within the operating and program responsibilities and authorities of any agency, that most closely relate to their general areas of concern.

Sec. 3. Human Rights Inquiries and Complaints. Each agency shall take lead responsibility, in coordination with other appropriate agencies, for responding to inquiries, requests for information, and complaints about violations of human rights obligations that fall within its areas of responsibility or, if the matter does not fall within its areas of responsibility, referring it to the appropriate agency for response. . . .

Sec. 6. Judicial Review, Scope, and Administration. (a) Nothing in this order shall create any right or benefit, substantive or procedural, enforceable by any party against the United States, its agencies or instrumentalities, its officers or employees, or any other person.

(b) This order does not supersede Federal statutes and does not impose any justiciable obligations on the executive branch. . . . [Implementation of Human Rights Treaties, Exec. Order No. 13107, 63 Fed. Reg. 68,991 (1998)].

What legal effect, if any, does this order have? Is it binding on subsequent presidential administrations?

b. Economic Sanctions

Despite its limited and conditional embrace of international human rights law, the United States has frequently exerted pressure on other nations to improve their human rights practices. Economic aid is sometimes targeted with human rights issues in mind. In addition, starting essentially in the 1970s, many U.S. laws have been enacted and Executive Branch decisions made that authorize or impose economic sanctions against target countries for a variety of foreign policy reasons. These reasons can include changing the behavior of a country or its nationals in order to combat human rights abuses and/or promoting democracy. (The sanctions might also be intended to oppose terrorism, sanction drug-producing and drug-transit countries, oppose the acquisition of weapons of mass destruction, or protect the environment.)

The range of possible U.S. actions can and has included sanctions that limit exports from the United States, imports to the United States, investment in the target country, and private financial transactions between U.S. citizens and the target country's government or citizens. The sanctions can also involve restrictions on U.S. government programs, such as foreign aid and government credit and insurance programs. They can also include directions for the United States to vote against loans in international financial institutions (IFIs), such as the World Bank and IMF.

The International Emergency Economic Powers Act (IEEPA), passed in 1977, provides the President with broad powers over exports, imports, and financial transactions whenever the President has declared a national emergency. Presidents have increasingly declared such emergencies, sometimes for human rights reasons. For example, President Reagan invoked IEEPA in 1985 when the United States imposed trade and investment sanctions as well as limits on U.S. government programs against South Africa because of its apartheid policy. A 1986 law then reinforced those sanctions. Similarly, President Clinton cited IEEPA as well as new discretionary authority under a specific 1996 law to ban new U.S. investment in Myanmar (formerly Burma) in 1997. (IEEPA is analyzed in some detail in Chapter 3.)

The following excerpt discusses some of the specific laws that have been passed, ranging from limits on military aid and foreign assistance to directing U.S. votes in the international financial institutions.

Barry E. Carter, International Economic Sanctions: Improving the Haphazard U.S. Legal Regime

47-48, 169-173 (1988) [updated through 2002]

U.S. GOVERNMENT PROGRAMS . . .

2. *Abuse of human rights.*   Usually enacted at the initiative of Congress, several laws have attempted to limit foreign assistance to countries that are in gross violation of internationally recognized human rights. The primary legislative efforts have focused on military aid and arms sales, but there have also been efforts to limit economic assistance to these countries.

The first law was passed in 1973. A nonbinding sense of Congress resolution, it was openly ignored by the Nixon and Ford Administrations. Congress responded with several progressive amendments to tighten the law and reduce the President's discretion.

For military assistance and arms sales, the key provision is amended section 502B [22 U.S.C. §2304], which has changed little since 1978. The critical subsection provides that "no security assistance may be provided to any country the government of which engages in a consistent pattern of gross violations of internationally recognized human rights." An exception is permitted if the President certifies in writing to Congress that "extraordinary circumstances exist warranting provision of such assistance." . . .

For economic assistance, the primary provision is amended section 116 [22 U.S.C. §2151n]. Like section 502B, it prohibits assistance to any country that engages in a consistent pattern of gross violations of internationally recognized human rights. It has an important exception — when "such assistance will directly benefit the needy people in such country." . . .

Congress has also sought to encourage the Executive Branch to apply human rights criteria to U.S. action in various international financial institutions. The following statute is illustrative.

22 U.S.C. §262d

(a) Policy goals. The United States Government, in connection with its voice and vote in the International Bank for Reconstruction and Development, the International Development Association, the International Finance Corporation, the Inter-American Development Bank, the African Development Fund, the Asian Development Bank, the African Development Bank, the European Bank for Reconstruction and Development, and the International Monetary Fund, shall advance the cause of human rights, including by seeking to channel assistance toward countries other than those whose governments engage in —

(1) a pattern of gross violations of internationally recognized human rights, such as torture or cruel, inhumane, or degrading treatment or punishment, prolonged detention without charges, or other flagrant denial to life, liberty, and the security of person. . . .

(d) . . . The United States Government, in connection with its voice and vote in the institutions listed in subsection (a), shall seek to channel assistance to projects which address basic human needs of the people of the recipient country. . . .

(e) . . . In determining whether a country is in gross violation of internationally recognized human rights standards as defined by the provisions of subsection (a) [of this section], the United States Government shall give consideration to the extent of cooperation of such country in permitting an unimpeded investigation of alleged violations of internationally recognized human rights by appropriate international organizations including, but not limited to, the International Committee of the Red Cross, Amnesty International, the International Commission of Jurists, and groups or persons acting under the authority of the United Nations or the Organization of American States.

(f) . . . The United States Executive Directors of the institutions listed in subsection (a) [of this section] are authorized and instructed to oppose any loan, any extension of financial assistance, or any technical assistance to any country described in subsection (a)(1) [of this section] unless such assistance is directed specifically to programs which serve the basic human needs of the citizens of such country. . . .

[In the international financial institutions (IFIs) the] United States can raise . . . foreign policy considerations through its formal votes and by lobbying other member countries and the institution's staff. The decision-making structures at the IMF, World Bank, and regional banks are all similar.

With respect to formal voting, each institution has a board of executive directors, which votes on requests for financial assistance and oversees other operations. . . .

Most decisions on loan requests, however, are made by the executive boards through informal consensus rather than through formal voting procedures. This practice makes it difficult to discern behind-the-scenes maneuvering on loan requests, since records of informal meetings are usually confidential. As a result, it is often difficult to determine when political pressure by one country is instrumental in a loan request being approved, rejected, or never even receiving formal consideration.

. . . Generally, a simple majority of the votes cast is sufficient to resolve a financial request by a member. . . .

[T]he United States lacks the unilateral voting clout to stop assistance from the regular fund of the IBD or from the IMF, World Bank, or . . . regional banks. [The U.S. voting percentages are far less than a majority in each case. Except for the Inter-American Development Bank where the U.S. voting percentage is about 30 percent, the U.S. percentage in the other international financial institutions is 20 percent or less.] . . .

The United States has, then, only limited ability to use the IFIs to impose economic sanctions for its specific foreign policy reasons. This situation results from the nonpolitical purposes and charter provisions of the IFIs and from the limited U.S. voting power. Because U.S. influence is weak in terms of formal voting power, there is greater potential to operate informally through persuasion and coalition building.

There has been considerable debate about the effectiveness of U.S. economic sanctions in combating human rights abuses (or for other foreign policy purposes). There does seem to be considerable agreement among experts that sanctions taken in conjunction with other major countries or with the United Nations (i.e., multilateral sanctions) are more likely to have an impact and come closer to achieving their intended purpose than U.S. unilateral sanctions. For example, probably the most successful economic sanctions for human rights purposes were the fairly comprehensive sanctions imposed by many countries against South Africa.

The South Africa sanctions started with a non-binding resolution of the U.N. General Assembly in 1962 calling for some sanctions. The progressive adoption of increasingly broad measures by countries gained considerable momentum when the United States and most European Community members imposed sanctions in 1985. After South Africa then released Nelson Mandela and others from prison and repealed some apartheid laws, the United States lifted its sanctions in 1991, followed by other countries and the United Nations in 1991-1994. In a recent major analytical study of 170 cases of economic sanctions imposed since World War I, the authors concluded on South Africa:

> Overall, economic and political conditions inside South Africa were clearly the most important factors influencing the outcome in [the South Africa apartheid] case and economic sanctions can be credited with, at best, a modest contribution. The sanctions were obviously useful to the opposition, both as symbolic support and as a lever that the ANC [African National Congress] could use in its negotiations with the government. . . .
>
> In sum, the sanctions added to the already mounting costs of maintaining apartheid. Sanctions clearly did not cause the [governing] National Party to decide to abandon apartheid but they accelerated the inevitable. [Kimberly Ann Elliott, Jeffrey J. Schott, Gary Clyde Hufbauer & Barbara Oegg, case 85-1, in Economic Sanctions Reconsidered (3d ed. forthcoming 2003).]

In another situation, starting in 1988 and continuing into 2003, the United States, the European Community, and Japan progressively imposed sanctions against the government of Myanmar (which was formerly Burma and is still called that in some circles) for its harsh repression of political opponents, including the house arrest of Aung San Suu Kyi in 1990. Her opposition party nevertheless won a majority of the seats in the National Assembly in elections later that year, but the military regime refused to give up power. (Ms. Suu Kyi was awarded a Nobel Peace Prize in 1991 for her efforts to bring democracy to Myanmar.) In 1997 President Clinton, invoking IEEPA and a 1996 law, issued an executive order that bars new U.S. investment in Myanmar. About the same time, U.S. state and local governments also were imposing sanctions, though these were effectively stopped by the U.S. Supreme Court decision in Crosby v. National Foreign Trade Council, 530 U.S. 363 (2000).

(*Crosby* is considered in Chapter 3.) The recent major study on sanctions, cited above, made the following assessment:

> Although the military regime in Burma has steadfastly refused to honor the 1990 election results, the decision to hold the elections at all, as well as the decision to release Aung San Suu Kyi from house arrest appear to have been attributable at least in part to the international pressure, including economic sanctions. [Id. at Case 88-1.]

There also seems to be considerable support for the view that, while unilateral U.S. economic sanctions might highlight U.S. views and have symbolic value, these unilateral sanctions usually have only limited or negligible economic impact against target countries. This limited economic utility has become increasingly true because, with greater globalization and the industrial growth of a number of countries, a target country can usually find alternative sources of supplies or markets for its goods. Nevertheless, the United States has frequently imposed unilateral sanctions in the past two decades, as well as before.

For example, in 1989, in reaction to the brutal suppression by the Chinese government of students and others in Tiananmen Square in Beijing and elsewhere in China, President George H.W. Bush suspended U.S. arms sales, government-to-government contacts, and certain commercial sales of high-technology items, such as communications satellites. The U.S. sanctions have been steadily relaxed since then, but some limits on sales continue in 2003. The recent study mentioned above gives U.S. economic sanctions some credit for combating human rights abuses in China. The study comments: "Economic sanctions have prompted China to release a few individual dissidents and intermittently relax repressive policies. China's leadership, however, maintains the position that threats to the regime must be quelled." Id. at Case 89-2.

Notes and Questions

1. Given the broad powers provided to the President by IEEPA, why does Congress still pass specific, new legislation authorizing U.S. economic sanctions? For example, laws have been passed since 1995 authorizing various sanctions against Myanmar, against countries committing religious persecution, against countries practicing female genital mutilation, against countries supporting terrorists, and against countries harboring war criminals. Possibly these laws might be intended to fill any potential gaps in the President's authority, such as over foreign aid funds. However, the specific laws often overlap the broad IEEPA authorities. It would seem that sometimes those backing the legislation in Congress are using it to call attention to the objectionable activity. Also, the new laws might provide for specific Executive Branch procedures and reporting requirements that the congressional supporters would like to see followed.

2. Assume that a proposed unilateral U.S. economic sanction against, say, a small Asian or African country for egregious abuse of internationally recognized human rights is likely to have only a limited economic impact on that target country because the country could find other suppliers and markets. Should the United States still announce and impose the economic sanction as a symbolic way to

emphasize U.S. policies? Should such a sanction be pursued only in conjunction with other countries sanctioning the target country, or at least only after strenuous efforts are made to enlist other countries?

3. Assume you were advising a U.S. senator or representative who wanted to support imposing at least one economic sanction against a country that was seriously violating internationally recognized human rights. Although the impact of various types of economic sanctions obviously depends on the specific circumstances in real cases, assume for now that the economic impact on the target country would be the same whether the sanction were a limit on U.S. exports, a limit on imports from the target country, or a limit on financial transactions between the two countries (e.g., new U.S. loans or investment there). Which type of sanction should the senator or representative prefer? Consider the likely impact on U.S. jobs and on U.S. trade flows.

4. Besides the materials above, for additional discussion of economic sanctions and the related U.S. laws and actions, see USA*Engage, Study of U.S. Unilateral Sanctions 1997-2001 (April 2002) (research by Barry E. Carter), at www.USAEngage.org; Dianne E. Rennack, CRS Report to Congress: Economic Sanctions: Legislation in the 106th Congress (updated December 15, 2000); Richard Haas, Economic Sanctions and American Diplomacy (1998).

c.   Diplomatic Pressure

In addition to sanctions, the United States often uses diplomatic pressure in an effort to induce changes in human rights practices. Every year, for example, the U.S. State Department is required to prepare and send to Congress a report on each country's human rights record. Here is a brief history of these country reports:

> The first edition of the Country Reports was a product of its times. While the United States had been at the forefront of the international human rights movement since the end of World War II and the creation of the United Nations, the Cold War and the gradual ending of colonialism dominated the first decades of that movement. However, the early 1970s gave rise in the Congress and throughout the country to new concepts and measures of accountability. An important force behind this changing environment was an ever-growing community of NGO's whose global outlook, commitment to human rights, and access to the media helped shape public opinion and government decision-making.
>
> In 1973 Representative Donald Fraser held hearings on human rights in the Committee on Foreign Affairs Subcommittee on International Organizations. That same year, a sense of Congress resolution was passed urging the Nixon Administration to link U.S. foreign assistance programs to respect for human rights within those recipient countries. The Congress amended the Foreign Assistance Act 3 years later to require the Secretary of State to transmit to Congress "a full and complete report" every year concerning "respect for internationally recognized human rights in each country proposed as a recipient of security assistance."
>
> Thus in March 1977, the first volume of Country Reports was submitted to Congress. The report covered 82 countries. Because it focused on nations with whom the United States had formal security assistance programs, most of them were longstanding allies and friends. The initial report was brief — only 143 pages — and at the end of

each entry was a rating, taken from Freedom House, judging whether the country was free, partly free, or not free.

Like any innovation, the new report had its critics. To some the very existence of such a document harmed relations with the very nations with which the United States had established the best ties. To others the report fell short of full disclosure. Such criticism has helped improve the reports ever since. They now cover virtually every country of the world and include a level of detail that would have stunned earlier readers.

For the 1978 report, 33 additional countries that received U.S. economic assistance were added to the original 82. The next year, the Foreign Assistance Act was amended again to require an entry on each member of the United Nations. The 1979 report thus expanded to 854 pages and covered 154 countries, including for the first time discussions of Cuba, the Soviet Union, and the People's Republic of China. [Michael E. Parmly, Acting Assistant Secretary of State, Bureau of Democracy, Human Rights, and Labor, Introduction to Country Reports on Human Rights Practices (February 2001), at http://www.state.gov/g/drl/rls/hrrpt/2000/648.htm.]

The State Department's country report for the year 2000 covered 195 countries. Here is a summary of some of the criticisms in that report:

China's poor human rights record worsened during the year, as the authorities intensified their harsh measures against underground Christian groups and Tibetan Buddhists, destroyed many houses of worship, and stepped up their campaign against the Falun Gong movement. China also sharply suppressed organized dissent. In Burma the military continued its severe repression, holding Aung San Suu Kyi under house arrest for much of the year, detaining her supporters, imprisoning many religious believers, and coercing numerous persons, including children, into forced labor. North Korea's situation remained among the worst in the world: The Government stifled all dissent and widely curtailed freedom of religion, political prisoners were held in forced labor camps, and malnutrition remained widespread. In Afghanistan the Taliban continued to be a major violator of human rights, severely restricting women's and girls' access to education, medical facilities, and employment. Iraq remained under the complete domination of one of the world's most repressive regimes, as security forces routinely executed, tortured, beat, raped, or otherwise intimidated and abused any perceived political opponents. Cuba's overall human rights record remained poor, as the Government retained tight surveillance over anyone considered a potential opponent. The human rights situation in Belarus worsened in a number of areas, as the Lukashenko regime took severe measures to neutralize political opponents and repressed all calls for democracy. Turkmenistan remained one of the most totalitarian countries in the world, as the Committee on National Security maintained tight control over the country, and a personality cult centered around President Saparmurat Niyazov continued. . . . [Parmly, supra.]

The preparation of these country reports can stimulate the U.S. government to take up a particular problem with the government involved. Once published, the reports also provide a basis for pressure from other sources, such as human rights NGOs. Critics have argued, however, that because of foreign policy concerns, the reports have sometimes been muted in their reporting of human rights abuses.

Diplomatic pressure can take other forms as well. For example, the U.S. government might limit or even terminate its diplomatic relations with a particular regime because of its human rights practices. Or it might decline to engage in cooperative projects with the regime until certain human rights issues are addressed.

Can diplomatic pressure be more effective than formal sanctions? Would it be appropriate to overlook human rights abuses because of a nation's allowance of a U.S. military base on its soil? Cooperation in arresting individuals suspected of international terrorism? Agreement not to develop nuclear weapons? Supply of oil or other resources to the United States? How should the U.S. government balance its commitment to human rights against other foreign policy interests?

d. Domestic Litigation

Since the *Filartiga* decision in 1980, U.S. courts have exercised jurisdiction over a variety of civil suits alleging violations of international human rights norms. As discussed in Chapter 3, one of the recent developments in this area has been the use of the Alien Tort Statute (or Alien Tort Claims Act) to sue private corporations for alleged involvement in human rights abuses in foreign countries. In these cases, courts have had to consider the extent to which governmental action is required for violations of international human rights law, and also the circumstances under which governmental action will be imputed to private actors.

One of the important cases in this area is Doe v. Unocal Corp., which has been the subject of long and complicated litigation. In that case, residents of a region in Myanmar alleged that various U.S. and foreign oil companies (including Unocal Corporation and its subsidiary, Union Oil Company of California), certain individuals (including senior Unocal officers), and the Myanmar military subjected them to forced labor, murder, rape, and torture when the oil companies constructed a gas pipeline through the region. The plaintiffs based their claims on, among other things, the Alien Tort Statute.

After many preliminary decisions below, the U.S. district court consolidated related cases and granted summary judgment to the defendants in 2000. Doe I v. Unocal Corp., 110 F. Supp. 2d 1294 (C.D. Cal. 2000). The plaintiffs then appealed to the Ninth Circuit, and also filed a very similar case under California law in the state court. As of March 2003, the state case was scheduled for trial later in 2003.

On the appeal to the Ninth Circuit, a three-judge panel in September 2002 reversed the district court in part and remanded the case. However, in February 2003, the Ninth Circuit voted to rehear *Unocal* en banc, and it stated that the three-judge panel opinion (discussed below) "shall not be cited as precedent by or to this court or any district court of the Ninth Circuit, except to the extent adopted by the en banc court." The rehearing was set for summer 2003.

In the vacated opinion, the three-judge panel concluded that all of the torts alleged in the case constituted violations of the law of nations for purposes of the Alien Tort Statute. The court explained:

> We have recognized that torture, murder, and slavery are *jus cogens* violations and, thus, violations of the law of nations. Rape can be a form of torture. . . . Moreover, forced labor is so widely condemned that it has achieved the status of a *jus cogens* violation. Accordingly, all torts alleged in the present case are *jus cogens* violations and, thereby, violations of the law of nations.

The court further held that the claims could be pursued against Unocal even though it is a private party rather than a state actor. Citing the Second Circuit's decision in *Kadic v. Karadzic* (which is excerpted in Chapter 3), the court reasoned that liability under international law for some torts, such as genocide, war crimes, and slavery, does not require state action. The court also noted that "under *Kadic*, even crimes like rape, torture, and summary execution, which by themselves require state action for [Alien Tort Statute] liability to attach, do *not* require state action when committed in furtherance of other crimes like slave trading, genocide or war crimes." The court further held that forced labor is a modern form of slavery and thus does not require state action to give rise to liability under the Statute.

In addition, the court held that a reasonable factfinder could conclude that Unocal and some of the other defendants aided and abetted the Myanmar military in subjecting the plaintiffs to forced labor. To establish aiding and abetting liability, the court reasoned, the plaintiffs not need show that Unocal's conduct amounted to "active participation" in the forced labor. Rather, the court's opinion (for two judges) purported to apply an international law standard for aiding and abetting liability, derived largely from decisions of the international criminal tribunals for former Yugoslavia and Rwanda. Under this standard, "knowing practical assistance or encouragement which has a substantial effect on the perpetration of the crime" is sufficient for aiding and abetting liability. In a subsequent part of its opinion, the court dismissed the claims against the Myanmar military and a Myanmar government-owned oil company pursuant to the Foreign Sovereign Immunities Act.

In a concurrence, Judge Reinhardt argued that the court should not have applied an international law test to determine Unocal's aiding and abetting liability. Rather, in his view, Unocal's liability "should be resolved by applying general federal common law tort principles, such as agency, joint venture, or reckless disregard." Judge Reinhardt reasoned that "courts should not substitute international law principles for established federal common law or other domestic law principles, as the majority does here, unless a statute mandates that substitution, or other exceptional circumstances exist." He also objected to the majority's reliance on the *jus cogens* concept, stating: "Because the underlying conduct alleged constitutes a violation of customary international law, the violation was allegedly committed by a governmental entity, and Unocal's liability, if any, is derivative of that government entity's, *jus cogens* is irrelevant to any issue before us."

Notes and Questions

1. Is U.S. domestic litigation an effective or desirable strategy to improve human rights compliance by other countries? How does it differ from other aspects of U.S. human rights policy, such as economic sanctions and diplomatic pressure?

2. In the *Unocal* decision described above, the claims against the Myanmar military were dismissed under the Foreign Sovereign Immunities Act. Is it appropriate for a U.S. court to adjudicate aiding and abetting liability when it cannot adjudicate the liability of the principal wrongdoer?

3. Should the Foreign Sovereign Immunities Act be amended to permit more human rights litigation directly against foreign governments? Should the U.S. government be subject to human rights suits in foreign courts?

4. How much guidance does the test for aiding and abetting liability adopted by the majority in *Unocal* give to corporations in determining what they can and cannot do in other countries? Should Congress address this issue?

5. Was it appropriate for the majority in *Unocal* to rely on the decisions of international criminal tribunals in ascertaining the test for aiding and abetting liability under the Alien Tort Statute? What is Judge Reinhardt's objection to this? How would the majority's analysis have differed if it had used the "federal common law" approach suggested by Judge Reinhardt?

6. How did the *jus cogens* concept affect the majority's analysis in *Unocal?* Was it necessary for the majority to invoke that concept, given that it had concluded that the conduct in question violated customary international law? What is Judge Reinhardt's objection to the majority's reliance on *jus cogens?*

7. In addition to the cases, such as *Unocal,* that allege corporate involvement in contemporary human rights abuses, there have been a number of cases brought against corporate and other defendants concerning their alleged involvement in human rights abuses committed many years ago. For example, cases have been brought against companies that benefited from slave labor during World War II. See, e.g., Frumkin v. JA Jones, Inc., 129 F. Supp. 2d 370 (D.N.J. 2001); Iwanowa v. Ford Motor Co., 67 F. Supp. 2d 424 (D.N.J. 1999); Burger-Fischer v. Degussa AG, 65 F. Supp. 2d 48 (D.N.J. 1999). Although these cases have not been particularly successful in the courts, they may have helped to influence the relevant parties and their governments to enter into World War II restitution agreements. Recently, suits have been filed by black South Africans against various companies for human rights violations in connection with South Africa's apartheid regime.

8. As Professor Stephens has noted, the United States is unique in the extent to which its courts are open to civil cases alleging violations of international human rights law. See Beth Stephens, Translating *Filartiga:* A Comparative and International Law Analysis of Domestic Remedies for International Law Violations, 27 Yale J. Intl. L. 1 (2002). As discussed in Chapters 6 and 7, however, some countries have exercised broad criminal jurisdiction with respect to human rights abuses — for example, Spain's effort to try Augusto Pinochet, and Belgium's use of its universal jurisdiction statute. What explains the openness of the U.S. civil litigation system to international human rights claims? Why has the United States been less open than some countries to using its criminal jurisdiction to adjudicate human rights violations?

9. Regional Human Rights Law

In addition to the United Nations human rights system, there are several regional international institutions focused on human rights. The European system, the Inter-American system, and the African system are all described below. The European system is regarded as the most "successful" of the three. Its court has been the most active and has successfully elaborated on the content of a variety of human rights norms. European governments have been quite accommodating to this highly legalized, court-based system, perhaps because of general respect for the rule of law, habitual compliance with the decisions of an independent judiciary, and general absence of major human rights problems. The Inter-American system has been less active, although in recent years its Commission and Court have produced a number of interesting decisions (including a number of decisions concerning human rights practices in the United States). The African system has done very little. Its Charter contains provisions that are at odds with other views of human rights, and its institutions are moribund.

a.   European System

The European Court of Human Rights, based in Strasbourg, France, is an active regional court. It is a judicial organ of the Council of Europe, a body that is distinct from the European Union (although all 15 members of the European Union are members of the Council of Europe). The Court was established pursuant to the European Convention on Human Rights, which entered into force in 1953. As of January 2003, all 44 members of the Council of Europe had ratified the Convention. The following materials describe the experience of the Court, the changes effected by its recent reorganization (in Protocol 11), and some basic issues now facing the Court. An excerpt of the Convention is in the Documentary Supplement.

Henry J. Steiner & Philip Alston, International Human Rights in Context

797-801, 804 (2d ed. 2000)

The European Convention on Human Rights (ECHR) provides for two procedures by which member states (referred to in the Convention as the High Contracting Parties) may be held accountable by the European Court of Human Rights ("the Court") for violations of the recognized rights: the individual petition procedure pursuant to Article 34, and the interstate procedure under Article 33.

The Convention makes clear that the primary responsibility for implementation rests with the member states themselves. The implementation machinery of the Convention comes into play only after domestic remedies are considered to have been exhausted. The great majority of complaints submitted are deemed inadmissible, frequently on the grounds that domestic law provides an effective remedy for any violation that may have taken place. Recall the obligations of member states under Articles 1 and 13 of the Convention to "secure to everyone" the Convention's rights and to provide "an effective remedy before a national authority" for violations of those rights.

The remedy given by, say, a domestic court may be pursuant to provisions of domestic law that stand relatively independently of the Convention, although perhaps influenced by it: a code of criminal procedure or a constitutional provision on free speech that are consistent with the Convention, for example. Or a remedy may be given pursuant to the substantive provisions of the Convention itself after the Convention has been incorporated into domestic law automatically or by special legislation. . . .

This preference for domestic resolution is also reinforced by the requirement to seek a friendly settlement wherever possible and by the procedures for full government consultation in the examination of complaints. The confidentiality of part of the proceedings, the role accorded to the Committee of Ministers, and the provision for there to be a judge from every state party again underscore the state-centred nature of many of the Convention's procedures. . . .

The entry into force, in November 1998, of Protocol No. 11 to the Convention produced a more streamlined and efficient system than had previously been in operation. Under the old system, the main (and very often the final) stage in the examination of a complaint was undertaken by the European Commission of Human

Rights, which ceased existence in October 1999 as a result of what has often been termed a merger or fusion of the old Court and Commission.

In the former system, the Commission included an expert elected from every state party to the Convention. Its findings as to whether a breach of the Convention had occurred were not per se legally binding on the states parties. Within three months of the Commission's report the case could have been referred to the Court by either the Commission or by a state concerned, but not by the complainant. If the case did not thereby reach the Court, the final verdict was pronounced by the Committee of Ministers. Rather than being able to determine which cases it would hear, the old Court was at the mercy of the Commission or the state concerned.

The Continuing Impetus for Reform

The impetus to reform the Convention system was essentially twofold, stemming from the inability of the old system to deal with the rapidly increasing workload and the need to accommodate a dramatic expansion in the Council's post-Cold War membership. The opportunity was also taken to strengthen the judicial rather than political character of the system.

Between 1980 and 1997, the annual number of applications received by the Commission rose from 2,000 to over 12,000, while the number accepted rose from below 500 to almost 5,000. The number of judgments handed down by the old Court went from less than 10 to over 200. In an effort to deal with the backlog of cases, Protocol No. 8 was adopted by which the Commission was permitted to meet in Committees of Three and in Chambers, rather than always in plenary. But the entry into force of this reform coincided with the large increase in the Council's membership in the early 1990s, and the pressure of applications grew steadily. In 1998, the last year of operation of the old system, references by the Commission to the Court rose from 157 to 190 and decisions handed down by the Court rose from 206 to 216. Linked to this explosion was a blow-out in the time taken to resolve applications. In 1993 it took, on average, five years and eight months for a case to be finally decided. This was especially ironical in view of the Court's case law, which has often found states whose courts take equivalent periods of time to decide a case to be in breach of the right to a hearing "within a reasonable time" under Article 6.

The new system has yet to radically change the picture. In 1999 the President of the new Court noted that:

> The continuing steep increase in the number of applications to the Court is putting even the new system under pressure. Today we are faced with nearly 10,000 registered applications and more than 47,000 provisional files, as well as around 700 letters and more than 200 overseas telephone calls a day. The volume of work is already daunting but is set to become more challenging still. . . . [21]

In its first year (to October 1999) the new system attracted 8,396 applications compared with 5,981 in the last year of the old system, 2,040 in 1993, and 404 in 1981. The Court delivered 177 judgments, declared inadmissible or struck off 3,489

---

21. President of the Permanent European Court of Human Rights, quoted in 20/3 Hum. Rts L.J. 114 (1999).

applications and declared admissible 658 applications. These figures will continue to fuel the need for further reforms in how the ECHR system functions.

The Principal Elements of the Reform

. . . The Court is now permanent or full-time, rather than part-time; the right of individual petition is now mandatory rather than optional for states parties; virtually all interstate cases will now be considered by the Court, rather than only those referred to it from the Commission; the political role played by the Committee of Ministers is now confined to matters of enforcement, rather than the merits of cases; and applicants now have unrestricted access to the Court.

Under the new system, applications that are registered are reviewed by a three-judge Committee which may, by unanimous vote, declare cases inadmissible. Cases that go forward will, in the great majority of instances, be considered by a seven-judge Chamber (of which four now exist). Exceptionally, some cases will go to a Grand Chamber of 17 judges. The latter procedure is a consequence of the need for compromise between different models of reform that were put forward in the negotiation of Protocol No. 11. Under Article 30, in a case which "raises a serious question affecting the interpretation of the Convention or the protocols thereto or where the resolution of a question . . . might have a result inconsistent with a judgment previously delivered by the Court," a Chamber may relinquish its jurisdiction to the Grand Chamber (unless one of the parties objects).

Under Article 43, any party to a case may request, within three months of a judgment by a Chamber, that the case be referred to the Grand Chamber. But this is said to apply only "in exceptional cases" and a five-judge panel of the latter can only accept the case if it "raises a serious question affecting the interpretation or application of the Convention or the protocols thereto, or a serious issue of general importance." These re-hearing provisions are unusual by judicial standards, even though the Grand Chamber is to look at the matter anew and the judges from the Chamber that delivered the initial judgment (excepting the President of the Chamber and the judge coming from the state concerned) are excluded from the new panel. The appropriateness of these arrangements has been questioned however, and in the view of some commentators they "should be repealed."[23] During the new Court's first year, no Article 43 referrals were made to the Grand Chamber.

The Judges

There are currently [44] judges, equal to the number of states parties. A state can nominate a national of another state party if it wishes, and the first Court saw a Swiss judge elected on the nomination of Liechtenstein and an Italian for San Marino. Each state is required to nominate three candidates, who are interviewed by a special sub-committee established for the purpose, before the Parliamentary Assembly of the Council of Europe proceeds to an election. Judges are elected for a

---

23. A. Drezemczewski. *The European Human Rights Convention: Protocol No. 11 Entry into Force and First Year of Application,* November 1999, p. 5, n.3.

six-year term, and cannot serve beyond their 70th birthday. Although the Committee of Ministers encouraged numerical gender equality, only eight (just under 20 per cent) of the judges are women.

The New System

Proceedings under the individual petitions procedure of Article 34 begin with a complaint by an individual, group or NGO against a state party. To be declared admissible a petition must not be anonymous, manifestly ill-founded, or constitute an abuse of the right of petition. Domestic remedies must have been exhausted, it must be presented within six months of the final decision in the domestic forum and it must not concern a matter which is substantially the same as one which has already been examined under the ECHR or submitted to another procedure of international investigation or settlement.

The first stage of the procedure is generally written, although the Chamber may decide to hold a hearing, in which case issues arising in relation to the merits will normally also be addressed. Hearings are adversarial in nature and usually public. Memorials and other documents filed in the case are also accessible to the public. Chamber decisions on admissibility, which are taken by majority vote, must contain reasons and be made public. Legal representation at all stages is recommended, and for hearings or once admissibility has been established, it is obligatory. The impact of this requirement is softened somewhat by the existence of a Council of Europe legal aid scheme for applicants who do not have sufficient means.

While the Court's official languages are English and French, applications may be drafted in any of the 21 official languages and, in practice, as many as 32 have been accepted. In hearings either English or French are used, unless exceptional authorization for the use of another language is given.

Decisions in Chambers are taken by a majority vote and each judge is entitled to give a separate opinion, whether concurring or dissenting. During the proceedings on the merits, negotiations aimed at securing a friendly settlement may be conducted. This technique was highly successful under the old system. Thus while only 15 such settlements were reached between 1980 and 1984, there were 242 between 1992 and 1997. The question arose in drafting Protocol No. 11 as to whether such a procedure was appropriate in the context of a wholly judicial system, in which the Chambers themselves would be required to give a provisional view on the merits in order to stimulate a settlement. Such proceedings are confidential and, in response to misgivings, the process has been defended both as historically very successful and as a "triumph of pragmatism over principle." . . .

Article 33 of the revised Convention contains a procedure by which one or more states may allege breaches of the Convention by another state party. Unlike the traditional approach to such cases under the international law of state responsibility for injury to aliens, . . . it is not necessary for an applicant state to allege that the rights of its own nationals have been violated.

The European Court of Human Rights has issued numerous important decisions, most of which concern human rights practices in Europe. Its *Soering* decision, excerpted below, concerned human rights practices in the United States and has therefore attracted considerable attention in this country.

The Soering Case

European Court of Human Rights
161 Eur. Ct. H.R. (ser. A) (1989)

12. The homicides in question were committed in Bedford County, Virginia, in March 1985. The victims . . . were the parents of the applicant's girlfriend, Elizabeth Haysom, who is a Canadian national. Death in each case was the result of multiple and massive stab and slash wounds to the neck, throat and body. At the time the applicant and Elizabeth Haysom, aged 18 and 20 respectively, were students at the University of Virginia. They disappeared together from Virginia in October 1985, but were arrested in England in April 1986 in connection with cheque fraud.

13. The applicant was interviewed in England between 5 and 8 June 1986 by a police investigator from the Sheriff's Department of Bedford County. In a sworn affidavit dated 24 July 1986 the investigator recorded the applicant as having admitted to killings in his presence and in that of two United Kingdom police officers. The applicant had stated that he was in love with Miss Haysom but that her parents were opposed to the relationship. He and Miss Haysom had therefore planned to kill them. [They did.]

On 13 June 1986 a grand jury of the Circuit Court of Bedford County indicted him on charges of murdering the Haysom parents. The charges alleged capital murder of both of them and the separate noncapital murders of each.

14. On 11 August 1986 the Government of the United States of America requested the applicant's and Miss Haysom's extradition under the terms of the Extradition Treaty of 1972 between the United States and the United Kingdom. . . .

15. On 29 October 1986 the British Embassy in Washington addressed a request to the United States' authorities in the following terms:

> Because the death penalty has been abolished in Great Britain, the Embassy has been instructed to seek an assurance, in accordance with the terms of . . . the Extradition Treaty, that, in the event of Mr. Soering being surrendered and being convicted of the crimes for which he has been indicted . . . , the death penalty, if imposed, will not be carried out.
>
> Should it not be possible on constitutional grounds for the United States Government to give such an assurance, the United Kingdom authorities ask that the United States Government undertake to recommend to the appropriate authorities that the death penalty should not be imposed or, if imposed, should not be executed. . . .

20. On 1 June 1987 Mr. Updike swore an affidavit in his capacity as Attorney for Bedford County, in which he certified as follows:

> I hereby certify that should Jens Soering be convicted of the offence of capital murder as charged in Bedford County, Virginia . . . a representation will be made in the name of the United Kingdom to the judge at the time of sentencing that it is the wish of the United Kingdom that the death penalty should not be imposed or carried out. . . .

During the course of the present proceedings the Virginia authorities have informed the United Kingdom Government that Mr. Updike was not planning to provide any further assurances and intended to seek the death penalty in Mr. Soering's case because the evidence, in his determination, supported such action. . . .

63. The size of a death row inmate's cell is 3m by 2.2m. Prisoners have an opportunity for approximately 7 1/2 hours' recreation per week in summer and approximately 6 hours' per week, weather permitting, in winter. The death row area has two recreation yards, both of which are equipped with basketball courts and one of which is equipped with weights and weight benches. Inmates are also permitted to leave their cells on other occasions, such as to receive visits, to visit the law library or to attend the prison infirmary. In addition, death row inmates are given one hour out-of-cell time in the morning in a common area. Each death row inmate is eligible for work assignments, such as cleaning duties. When prisoners move around the prison they are handcuffed with special shackles around the waist.

When not in their cells, death row inmates are housed in a common area called "the pod." The guards are not within this area and remain in a box outside. In the event of disturbance or inter-inmate assault, the guards are not allowed to intervene until instructed to do so by the ranking officer present.

64. The applicant adduced much evidence of extreme stress, psychological deterioration and risk of homosexual abuse and physical attack undergone by prisoners on death row, including Mecklenburg Correctional Center. This evidence was strongly contested by the United Kingdom Government on the basis of affidavits sworn by administrators from the Virginia Department of Corrections. . . .

68. A death row prisoner is moved to the death house 15 days before he is due to be executed. The death house is next to the death chamber where the electric chair is situated. Whilst a prisoner is in the death house he is watched 24 hours a day. He is isolated and has no light in his cell. The lights outside are permanently lit. A prisoner who utilizes the appeals process can be placed in the death house several times. . . .

80. The applicant alleged that the decision by the Secretary of State for the Home Department to surrender him to the authorities of the United States of America would, if implemented, give rise to a breach by the United Kingdom of Article 3 of the Convention, which provides:

> No one shall be subjected to torture or to inhuman or degrading treatment or punishment.

81. The alleged breach derives from the applicant's exposure to the so-called "death row phenomenon." This phenomenon may be described as consisting in a combination of circumstances to which the applicant would be exposed if, after having been extradited to Virginia to face a capital murder charge, he was sentenced to death. . . .

89. What amounts to "inhuman or degrading treatment or punishment" depends on all the circumstances of the case. . . .

105. The applicant submitted that the circumstances to which he would be exposed as a consequence of the implementation of the Secretary of State's decision to return him to the United States, namely the "death row phenomenon," cumulatively constitute such serious treatment that his extradition would be contrary to

Article 3. He cited in particular the delays in the appeal and review procedures following a death sentence, during which time he would be subject to increasing tension and psychological trauma; the fact, so he said, that the judge or jury in determining sentence is not obliged to take into account the defendant's age and mental state at the time of the offence; the extreme conditions of his future detention on "death row" in Mecklenburg Correctional Center, where he expects to be the victim of violence and sexual abuse because of his age, color and nationality; and the constant spectre of the execution itself, including the ritual of execution. . . .

106. The period that a condemned prisoner can expect to spend on death row in Virginia before being executed is on average six to eight years. . . . This length of time awaiting death is, as the Commission and the United Kingdom Government noted, in a sense largely of the prisoner's own making in that he takes advantage of all avenues of appeal which are offered to him by Virginia law. The automatic appeal to the Supreme Court of Virginia normally takes no more than six months. . . . The remaining time is accounted for by collateral attacks mounted by the prisoner himself in habeas corpus proceedings before both the State and Federal courts and in applications to the Supreme Court of the United States for certiorari review, the prisoner at each stage being able to seek a stay of execution. . . . The remedies available under Virginia law serve the purpose of ensuring that the ultimate sanction of death is not unlawfully or arbitrarily imposed.

Nevertheless, just as some lapse of time between sentence and execution is inevitable if appeal safeguards are to be provided to the condemned person, so it is equally part of human nature that the person will cling to life by exploiting those safeguards to the full. However well-intentioned and even potentially beneficial is the provision of the complex of post-sentence procedures in Virginia, the consequence is that the condemned prisoner has to endure for many years the conditions on death row and the anguish and mounting tension of living in the ever-present shadow of death. . . .

107. As to conditions in Mecklenburg Correctional Center, where the applicant could expect to be held if sentenced to death, the Court bases itself on the facts which were uncontested by the United Kingdom Government, without finding it necessary to determine the reliability of the additional evidence adduced by the applicant, notably as to the risk of homosexual abuse and physical attack undergone by prisoners on death row. . . .

108. At the time of the killings, the applicant was only 18 years old and there is some psychiatric evidence, which was not contested as such, that he "was suffering from [such] an abnormality of mind . . . as substantially impaired his mental responsibility for his acts". . . .

Unlike Article 2 of the Convention, Article 6 of the 1966 International Covenant on Civil and Political Rights and Article 4 of the 1969 American Convention on Human Rights expressly prohibit the death penalty from being imposed on persons aged less than 18 at the time of commission of the offence. Whether or not such a prohibition be inherent in the brief and general language of Article 2 of the European Convention, its explicit enunciation in other, later international instruments, the former of which has been ratified by a large number of States Parties to the European Convention, at the very least indicates that as a general principle the youth of the person concerned is a circumstance which is liable, with others, to put in question the compatibility with Article 3 of measures connected with a death sentence.

It is in line with the Court's case-law . . . to treat disturbed mental health as having the same effect for the application of Article 3.

109. Virginia law, as the United Kingdom Government and the Commission emphasized, certainly does not ignore these two factors. Under the Virginia Code account has to be taken of mental disturbance in a defendant, either as an absolute bar to conviction if it is judged to be sufficient to amount to insanity or, like age, as a fact in mitigation at the sentencing stage. . . . They do not however remove the relevance of age and mental condition in relation to the acceptability, under Article 3, of the "death row phenomenon" for a given individual once condemned to death.

Although it is not for this Court to prejudge issues of criminal responsibility and appropriate sentence, the applicant's youth at the time of the offence and his then mental state, on the psychiatric evidence as it stands, are therefore to be taken into consideration as contributory factors tending, in his case, to bring the treatment on death row within the terms of Article 3. . . .

(c) Conclusion

111. For any prisoner condemned to death, some element of delay between imposition and execution of the sentence and the experience of severe stress in conditions necessary for strict incarceration are inevitable. The democratic character of the Virginia legal system in general and the positive features of Virginia trial, sentencing and appeal procedures in particular are beyond doubt. The Court agrees with the Commission that the machinery of justice to which the applicant would be subject in the United States is in itself neither arbitrary nor unreasonable, but, rather, respects the rule of law and affords not inconsiderable procedural safeguards to the defendant in a capital trial. . . .

However, in the Court's view, having regard to the very long period of time spent on death row in such extreme conditions, with the ever present and mounting anguish of awaiting execution of the death penalty, and to the personal circumstances of the applicant, especially his age and mental state at the time of the offence, the applicant's extradition to the United States would expose him to a real risk of treatment going beyond the threshold set by Article 3. . . .

FOR THESE REASONS, THE COURT UNANIMOUSLY

1. *Holds* that, in the event of the Secretary of State's decision to extradite the applicant to the United States of America being implemented, there would be a violation of Article 3. . . .

Notes and Questions

1. The European Court of Human Rights has issued thousands of decisions. These decisions have addressed a wide range of human rights issues, including due process, freedom of expression, freedom of association, and the right to privacy. Some of its noteworthy recent decisions include a 1998 decision holding that Turkey had violated the European Convention by ordering the dissolution of the

United Communist Party of Turkey; a 1999 decision holding that Great Britain had violated the Convention by discharging members of the Royal Navy based on their sexual orientation; a 2001 decision holding that Great Britain had violated the rights of members of the Irish Republican Army; and a 2002 decision holding that France had violated the rights of a Nazi collaborator, Murice Papon, by denying him a right of appeal. Despite some occasional grumbling, the member states have generally accepted and complied with the Court's decisions. For access to the Court's case law, see http://www.echr.coe.int/Eng/Judgments.htm.

2. Why has the European human rights system been so successful? Would it be desirable for the United States to join such a system, either on a regional or worldwide basis?

3. Some of the provisions of the European Convention allow interference with protected rights when "necessary in a democratic society." In addition, the Convention allows nations to derogate from the rights specified in the Convention "in time of war or other emergency threatening the life of the nation." In applying these provisions, the European Court on Human Rights has applied what is called a "margin of appreciation"—that is, it has given some deference to national government determinations about what is necessary. Does this deference help explain the Court's success? See generally Howard C. Yourow, The Margin of Appreciation Doctrine in the Dynamics of European Human Rights Jurisprudence (1996); R. St. John Macdonald, The Margin of Appreciation, in European System for the Protection of Human Rights (R. St. John Macdonald et al. eds., 1993).

4. Are you persuaded by the *Soering* decision? Why is there often a long wait on death row in the United States? Could the United States have eliminated the human rights problem in *Soering* by abolishing all appeals, except perhaps one expedited appeal, before execution? Would such a change advance the cause of human rights?

5. After the *Soering* decision, the prosecutor in Virginia reluctantly agreed not to seek the death penalty against the fugitive. The United Kingdom then extradited him, and he was convicted of first-degree murder and sentenced to life in prison. For additional discussion of the case, see Richard B. Lillich, Case Report: The *Soering* Case, 86 Am. J. Intl. L. 128 (1991). The *Soering* decision has been cited by Justice Breyer of the U.S. Supreme Court in dissents from denial of certiorari in cases involving constitutional challenges based on long periods of detention on death row. See Foster v. Florida, 123 S. Ct. 470 (2002) (Breyer, J., dissenting from denial of certiorari); Knight v. Florida, 528 U.S. 990 (1999) (Breyer, J., dissenting from denial of certiorari).

6. The parties to the Council of Europe have adopted 11 protocols to the European Convention for the Protection of Human Rights and Fundamental Freedoms. These protocols address a variety of issues, including the expulsion of aliens, criminal procedure, and the death penalty. A 12th protocol, concerning nondiscrimination, was opened for signature in 2000. The parties to the Council also have adopted a number of other human rights treaties, including a convention against torture. In addition, they have adopted treaties outside the human rights area, such as an extradition convention. For access to these various treaties, see the Legal Affairs Web site for the Council of Europe, at http://conventions.coe.int.

7. In 2000, the institutions of the European Union (which are distinct from the Council of Europe) adopted a Charter of Fundamental Rights, which sets out a wide range of civil, political, economic, and social rights for European citizens and

residents of the European Union. (The Charter is excerpted in the Documentary Supplement.) The Charter was adopted as non-binding "soft law" rather than as a binding treaty, but there are plans to convert it into a binding instrument in the future. (See Chapter 2 for a discussion of soft law.) Even before it becomes formally binding, the Charter is likely to be influential because it sets out for the first time, in a single text, a comprehensive list of human rights protections for the EU. It also moves the EU closer to having a Constitution and a true political union.

How does the Charter compare with the U.S. Bill of Rights? With the European Convention on Human Rights? Consider, for example, the following provisions in the Charter: Article 2(2), which prohibits the death penalty; Article 21(1), which prohibits discrimination on a wide variety of grounds, including sexual orientation; Article 23, which requires equal treatment of men and women in all areas; Article 25, which concerns the rights of the elderly; and Articles 37 and 38, which require a high level of environmental protection and consumer protection.

The Convention on the Future of Europe, which is composed of representatives of governments, national parliaments, the European Parliament, and the European Commission, began considering in 2002 whether to recommend that the Charter be incorporated into a treaty that would replace or rewrite the Treaty Establishing the European Community and the Treaty on European Union. (See Chapter 5 for a discussion of those treaties.) The Convention will make its report and recommendations to the EU's Intergovernmental Conference (IGC) in 2004, which could agree to ask member states to adopt this major reform. Under the present EU expansion schedule, 10 more countries will have become members of the EU by the 2004 IGC, thereby making the potential geographic coverage of the Charter even broader.

8. For additional discussion of the European human rights system, see George A. Bermann et al., Cases and Materials on European Union Law ch. 6 (2d ed. 2002); Mark W. Janis et al., European Human Rights Law: Text and Materials (2d ed. 2000); and J.G. Merrills, The Development of International Law by the European Court of Human Rights (2d ed. 1993).

b. Inter-American System

In 1948, 21 nations in the Western Hemisphere (including the United States) agreed to adopt the Charter of the Organization of American States (excerpted in the Documentary Supplement). Among other things, the Charter established a regional international institution — the Organization of American States (OAS) — which has its headquarters in Washington, DC. Today, all 35 nations in the Americas have ratified the Charter. Also in 1948, American states adopted the American Declaration of the Rights and Duties of Man, a non-binding instrument that sets forth a variety of individual rights and duties.

The OAS Charter called for the establishment of an Inter-American Commission on Human Rights, "whose principal function shall be to promote the observance and protection of human rights and to serve as a consultative organ of the Organization in these matters." The Commission was established in 1959 and held its first session in 1960. Since then, it has carried out numerous visits to the member states to observe the human rights situation in those states and to investigate specific human rights practices. Since 1965, it has been authorized to examine complaints or petitions concerning specific cases of human rights violations, and it has processed thousands of such cases, including a number of cases concerning the United States.

The American Convention on Human Rights took effect in 1978. As of January 2003, it had been ratified by 25 nations (but not by the United States). The Convention is a binding treaty that lists a variety of rights that the parties are required to observe. Among other things, the Convention established an Inter-American Court of Human Rights, based in San Jose, Costa Rica.

The Inter-American human rights system is described in more detail below.

Henry J. Steiner & Philip Alston, International Human Rights in Context

786-801 (2d ed. 2000)

In May 1948 the ninth Inter-American Conference, held in Bogotá, established the Organization of American States (OAS). Its predecessor organizations date back to the International Union of American Republics of 1890. The 1948 Charter entered into force in December 1951 and has since been amended by the Protocol of Buenos Aires of 1967, the Protocol of Cartagena de Indias of 1985, the Protocol of Washington of 1992, and the Protocol of Managua of 1993. The purposes of the OAS are:

> to strengthen the peace and security of the continent; to promote and consolidate representative democracy, with due respect for the principle of nonintervention; to prevent possible causes of difficulties and to ensure the pacific settlement of disputes that may arise among the member states; to provide for common action on the part of those States in the event of aggression; to seek the solution of political, juridical and economic problems that may arise among them; to promote by cooperative action, their economic, social and cultural development, and to achieve an effective limitation of conventional weapons that will make it possible to devote the largest amount of resources to the economic and social development of the member states. (Annual Report of the Inter-American Commission on Human Rights 1994 (1995), at 347.)

Its principal organs are the General Assembly that meets annually and in additional special sessions if required, the Meeting of Consultation of Ministers of Foreign Affairs that considers urgent matters, the Permanent Council and the General Secretariat. The latter two organs are based in Washington DC.

The Bogotá Conference of 1948 also adopted the American Declaration of the Rights and Duties of Man. The Inter-American system thus had a human rights declaration seven months before the United Nations had adopted the Universal Declaration and two and a half years before the European Convention was adopted. Nevertheless, the development of a regional treaty monitored by an effective supervisory machinery was to take considerably longer. The Inter-American Commission on Human Rights was created in 1959 and the American Convention on Human Rights was adopted in 1969. It entered into force in 1978.

The development of the Inter-American system followed a different path from that of its European counterpart. Although the institutional structure is superficially very similar and the normative provisions are in most respects very similar, the conditions under which the two systems developed were radically different. Within the Council of Europe, military and other authoritarian governments have been rare and short-lived, while in Latin America they were close to being the norm until the changes that started in the 1980s.

The major challenges confronting the European system are epitomized by issues such as the length of pre-trial detention and the implications of the right to privacy. Cases involving states of emergency have been relatively few. The European Commission and Court have rarely had to deal with completely unresponsive or even antagonistic governments or national legal systems, or with deep structural problems that led to systematic and serious human rights violations. . . . By contrast, states of emergency have been common in Latin America, the domestic judiciary has often been extremely weak or corrupt, and large-scale practices involving torture, disappearances and executions have not been uncommon. Many of the governments with which the Inter-American Commission and Court have had to work have been ambivalent towards those institutions at best and hostile at worst.

Notes and Questions

1. Should the United States ratify the American Convention on Human Rights? Should it consent to the jurisdiction of the Inter-American Court?

2. Although the United States has not yet consented to the jurisdiction of the Court, the Court has sometimes issued advisory opinions that relate to the United States. For example, in 1999, the Court issued an advisory opinion concluding that the failure of a nation to comply with the consular notice provision of the Vienna Convention on Consular Relations when arresting a foreign national violates the due process rights of the arrested person and that, in that situation, imposition of the death penalty is a violation of the person's right not to be deprived of life arbitrarily. The opinion was issued in response to a request by Mexico after it had complained to the United States that a number of its nationals had been sentenced to death by state authorities without having been advised of their right under the Vienna Convention to seek consular assistance. See Inter-American Court of Human Rights, Advisory Opinion OC-16/99 (requested by the United Mexican States) (Oct. 1, 1999).

3. Although the American Declaration of the Rights and Duties of Man was not originally established as a binding treaty, the Inter-American Commission has asserted that it became binding when countries (including the United States) ratified a Protocol to the OAS Charter in 1968. See Case 2141 (United States), OEA/Ser.L/V/II.54, doc. 9, rev. 1, 25, 38, ¶16 (1981). Article 112 of the Protocol gave the Commission the "principal function" of promoting "the observance and protection of human rights" and serving as "a consultative organ of the organization in these matters," and Article 150 stated that, "[u]ntil the Inter-American Convention on Human Rights . . . enters into force, the present Inter-American Commission on Human Rights shall keep vigilance over the observance of human rights." In addition, Article 2 of the Statute of the Inter-American Commission provides that, "[f]or purposes of the present Statute, human rights are understood to be . . . The rights set forth in the American Declaration of the Rights and Duties of Man, in

relation to the other member states." Do these provisions make the Declaration binding? See Thomas Buergenthal, The Revised OAS Charter and the Protection of Human Rights, 69 Am. J. Intl. L. 828 (1975).

4. The Inter-American Commission has played an important role in gathering information about human rights practices in Central and South America and in issuing reports concerning these practices. Thus, for example, it made a factfinding visit to Argentina in 1979, while the country was under military rule, and then issued an extensive report that recommended that Argentina take a number of steps to improve its human rights practices. In this and other instances, the Commission's factfinding and reporting may have helped to pressure governments to make human rights reforms. For access to the Commission's country-specific reports, see the Commission's Web site, at http://www.cidh.org/pais.eng.htm.

5. The Inter-American Commission has issued a number of decisions concerning U.S. death penalty practices. In 1987, it ruled that there was a "regional *jus cogens*" norm against the "execution of children," and that the diversity of capital punishment standards throughout the United States "results in the arbitrary deprivation of life and inequality before the law," in violation of Articles I and II of the American Declaration. See Case 9647 (Roach & Pinkerton v. United States), Inter.-Am. C.H.R. 147, OEA/Ser.L/V/II.71, doc. 9, rev. 1 (1987). In 1989, it ruled that the U.S. death penalty did not violate the right to life set forth in the American Declaration of Human Rights, notwithstanding statistical evidence suggesting that the race of the defendant and victim affect the likelihood that the death penalty will be imposed. See Case 10.031 (Celestine v. United States), Inter.-Am. C.H.R., OEA/Ser.L/V/II.77 rev. 1, Resolution No. 23/89 (Sept. 28, 1989). In October 2002, the Commission ruled that the United States would violate a general *jus cogens* norm if it executed an individual who was under 18 years of age at the time of his offense. See Case 12.285 (Domingues v. United States), Report No. 62/02 (Oct. 22, 2002), at www.cidh.oas.org/annualrep/2002eng/USA.12285.htm. See also Richard J. Wilson, The United States' Position on the Death Penalty in the Inter-American Human Rights System, 42 Santa Clara L. Rev. 1159 (2002).

6. The Commission's rulings concerning the United States have not been limited to the death penalty. For example, in 2002, it issued "precautionary measures" urging the United States to "have the legal status of the detainees at Guantanamo Bay [which were being held in connection with the post-September 11 war on terrorism] determined by a competent tribunal." See Inter-American Commission on Human Rights: Decision on Request for Precautionary Measures (Detainees at Guantanamo Bay, Cuba) (March 12, 2002), reprinted at 41 I.L.M. 532 (2002).

7. Is the Inter-American Commission now acting like a court? If so, is that appropriate? Does the Commission reflect an inevitable tendency by international institutions to expand their jurisdiction?

8. For additional discussion of the Inter-American system, see J. Scott Davidson, The Inter-American Human Rights System (1997).

c.   African System

The African Charter on Human and Peoples' Rights was adopted in 1981 under the auspices of the Organization of African Unity, and it entered into force in 1986.

Among other things, the Charter established the African Commission on Human and People's Rights, which is charged with promoting and protecting human rights on the African continent. The Charter and the Commission are described below.

Henry J. Steiner & Philip Alston, International Human Rights in Context

920-923 (2d ed. 2000)

The newest, the least developed or effective (in relation to the European and Inter-American regimes), the most distinctive and the most controversial of the three established regional human rights regimes involves African states. In 1981 the Assembly of Heads of States and Government of the Organization of African Unity adopted the African Charter on Human and People's Rights. It entered into force in 1986. As of March 2000, 53 African states were parties.

[T]he Charter [is] an important illustration of a human rights regime that [is] more duty-oriented than the universal human rights system or the two other regional systems. . . . [The African] system's sole implementing organ, the Commission, has had only 15 years of experience, has few powers, and for the most part has been hesitant in exercising those powers or creatively interpreting and developing them. . . .

It follows that the African system has not yet yielded anywhere near the same amount of information and "output" of recommendations or decisions — state reports and reactions thereto, communications (complaints) from individuals about state conduct, studies of "situations" or investigations of particular violations — as have the other systems. In comparison with those systems, the states parties and Commission have taken few forceful or persuasive actions within the structure of the Charter to attempt to curb serious human rights violations, although recent years have shown promise of a more insistent and active stance. Moreover, recent years have seen peacekeeping actions within the Organization of African Unity or by individual African states, both outside the framework of the Human Rights Charter, to respond to violence and slaughter in states like Liberia. . . .

The OAU is the official regional body of all African states. It was inspired by the anti-colonial struggles of the late 1950s, and was primarily dedicated to the eradication of colonialism. The emergent African states created through it a political bloc to facilitate intra-African relations and to forge a regional approach to Africa's relationships with external powers. The OAU's Charter was adopted in 1963 by a conference of Heads of State and Government. Today, all African states are members of the OAU.

Unlike the UN Charter, that of the OAU makes no provision for the enforcement of its principles. It emphasizes cooperation among member states and peaceful settlement of disputes, and includes among its purposes in Article II(1) the promotion of the "unity and solidarity" of African states, as well as defence of "their sovereignty, their territorial integrity and independence." This inviolability of territorial borders, expressed through the principle of non-interference in the internal affairs of member states, has been one of the OAU's central creeds.

This creed has contributed to the reluctance of member states to promote human rights aggressively. The most visible failure in this regard has been the reluctance of member states to criticize one another about human rights violations. A prominent case in point was the failure of most African states, the single exception being Tanzania, to denounce the abusive regime of Ugandan dictator Idi Amin. Over the last decade, there have been several peacekeeping (as well as overtly aggressive) interventions by African states, independently or through a joint force, into states of systematic, serious human rights violations, particularly states caught up in insurgencies and civil war. Congo and the Great Lakes region offer recent illustrations.

The single prominent exception with respect to general human rights policy has been the adoption by the OAU in 1981 of the African Charter on Human and Peoples' Rights. The formal, legal basis for that act is found in Article II(1)(b) of the OAU Charter, which requires member states to "coordinate and intensify their collaboration and efforts to achieve a better life for the people of Africa," and Article II(1)(e), which asks member states to "promote international co-operation, having due regard to the Charter of the United Nations and the Universal Declaration of Human Rights." . . .

The 11 members of the Commission, elected by secret ballot by the Assembly of Heads of State and Government from a list of persons nominated by parties to the Charter, are to serve (Article 31) "in their personal capacity." Article 45 defines the mandate or functions of the Commission to be (1) to "promote Human and People's Rights" (2) to "ensure the protection of human and peoples' rights" under conditions set by the Charter, (3) to "interpret all the provisions of the Charter" when so requested by states or OAU institutions; and (4) to perform other tasks that may be committed to it by the Assembly. So the three dominant functions appear to be promotion, ensuring protection, and interpretation.

The Commission's task of "promotion" includes (Article 45) undertaking "studies and researches on African problems in the field of human and peoples' rights," as well as organizing seminars and conferences, disseminating information, encouraging "local institutions concerned with human and peoples' rights," giving its views or making recommendations to governments, and formulating principles and rules "aimed at solving legal problems related to human and peoples' rights . . . upon which African Governments may base their legislation." Article 46 states tersely that the Commission "may resort to any appropriate method of investigation." In general, the "Charter gives pre-eminence to the promotion of human rights and vests a wide range of responsibility on the Commission. In this regard, it has functions that are not directly vested in the . . . American Commission."[37] Several steps have been taken to implement the task of promotion — for example, resolutions by the Commission to the effect that states should include the teaching of human rights at all levels of the educational curricula, should integrate the Charter's provisions into national laws, and should establish committees on human rights.

Communications (complaints) and state reports are the most significant functions or processes involving the Commission that are identified in the Charter. Thus far, the procedures in the Charter involving communications by a state party concerning another state party have not been used. Individuals and national and international institutions can also send communications to the Commission, as provided

---

37. U.O. Umozurike, The African Commission on Human and Peoples' Rights, 1 Rev. Afr. Comm. Hum. & Peoples' Rts 5 (1991), at 8.

in Articles 55-59. These provisions recall, but differ significantly from, the First Optional Protocol of the ICCPR. . . .

The Charter refers tersely to reports. Under Article 62, each party "shall undertake to submit every two years . . . a report on the legislative or other measures taken with a view to giving effect to the rights" under the Charter. Compare the more elaborate provisions in Article 40 of the ICCPR about the role of the ICCPR Committee in reviewing states' reports under that Covenant.

Although there is some irony in the observation that the Commission, addressing a continent rife with state-imposed abuses, should have promotion as its primary function, that concentration of energy makes some sense in view of Africa's large uneducated population that is ignorant of its rights or lacks organization and capacity for mobilization to vindicate them. Creating a "rights awareness" could understandably be considered to be a primary function.

But in the long run, promotion alone will not be sufficient. This human rights regime governs states that have committed rampant violations, and that lack experience in and institutions for curbing the abuse of governmental power. Such a regime must depend on the effectiveness of intervention and protection of individuals, in order to effect long-term change. The African system — in part through the work of the Commission — must raise the costs to states of violations through one or another of the sanctions with which other human rights regimes are familiar.

Questions

1. Why hasn't the African system been more successful? What could be done to improve it?

2. How does the African Charter compare with other regional human rights conventions, such as the European Convention and the American Convention? What explains the differences? Should human rights be different in different regions of the world?

10. International Humanitarian Law

International law also protects human rights during times of armed conflict — for example, by giving certain rights to prisoners of war and by prohibiting intentional attacks on non-combatants. This body of international law, known as "international humanitarian law," is discussed in detail in Chapter 11. International humanitarian law is reflected in a variety of treaties, most notably the four Geneva Conventions developed after World War II and the subsequent protocols to those Conventions, as well as in customary international law. The requirements of international humanitarian law have been a significant point of discussion in connection with the war on terrorism following the September 11, 2001, terrorist attacks on the United States.

In addition to regulating the actions of nation-states, international humanitarian law imposes individual responsibility. At least since the Nuremberg and Tokyo trials after World War II, it has been recognized that individuals responsible for egregious violations of international humanitarian law can be criminally prosecuted. In the 1990s, ad hoc international tribunals were established to try individuals for violations of international humanitarian law committed during conflicts in the former Yugoslavia and Rwanda. More recently, a tribunal was established to address such violations committed during Sierra Leone's decade-long civil war. In addition to these ad hoc tribunals, a treaty has been approved that calls for the establishment of a permanent International Criminal Court, based in the Netherlands. This Court will have jurisdiction to adjudicate four types of international crimes: genocide, crimes against humanity, war crimes, and the crime of aggression. The Court's jurisdiction became effective as of July 1, 2002, and the Court is expected to begin operations sometime in 2003. Both the ad hoc tribunals and the International Criminal Court are discussed in Chapter 11.

Bibliography

For additional discussion of international human rights law, see Thomas Buergenthal, Dinah Shelton & David Stewart, International Human Rights in a Nutshell (3d ed. 2002); Richard Lillich & Hurst Hannum, International Human Rights: Problems of Law, Policy, and Practice (3d ed. 1995); and David Weissbrodt, Joan Fitzpatrick & Frank Newman, International Human Rights: Law, Policy, and Process (3d ed. 2001).

9

Law of the Sea

Approximately three-quarters of the world's surface is covered by water, much of it in oceans and seas. As use of the seas intensifies and as it becomes easier to extract oil and minerals from the seabeds, the laws for channeling these burgeoning activities become increasingly important.

This chapter introduces you to the international legal norms for the seas. Even in areas of the seas where countries claim sovereignty, their claims usually reflect generally accepted norms of international law. Moreover, there are vast expanses in the seas where it is generally agreed that no single state or group of states has sovereignty. Here, too, international law is important. Throughout this chapter, remember to keep asking: How well defined are the international legal rules? How did this law develop? Does it bind states that have not agreed to it? Who will enforce the law? How? What should the law be?

A. INTRODUCTION

Much of this chapter will focus on the U.N. Convention on the Law of the Sea (LOS Convention). The LOS Convention is a comprehensive and complicated document that covers issues ranging from the width of a state's territorial waters (and the state's rights there), to rights in zones beyond the territorial waters, to who controls minerals at the bottom of the ocean.

The LOS Convention was completed in 1982 after nine years of intensive multilateral negotiations. It actually came into force in November 1994 after 12 years of diplomatic maneuvering, in part to gain the support of major countries. A key element in the maneuvering was the negotiation in 1994 of a companion Agreement Relating to Implementation of Part IX of the LOS Convention. It effectively modified the controversial deep seabed mining provisions of the LOS Convention and made the Convention more acceptable to many industrialized countries. As of April 2003, there were 142 parties to the LOS Convention, and 113 of these countries had also become parties to the 1994 agreement.

The United States and Canada are now alone among major industrial countries in not ratifying the LOS Convention and agreement. Although the United States had actively participated in the negotiations leading up to the LOS Convention, President Reagan opposed the final document, in large part because of the deep seabed mining provisions. The changes made by the 1994 agreement led the Clinton Administration, supported by a broad coalition that included the U.S. Navy and major industrial groups (e.g., shipping, mining, petroleum, and telecommunications), to submit both the Convention and the agreement to the U.S. Senate in 1994 for its advice and consent. However, in large part because of conservative opposition led by Senator Jesse Helms, the U.S. Senate Foreign Relations Committee has yet to hold the necessary committee hearings that precede a Senate vote of advice and consent. With Senator Helms' retirement at the end of 2002, the Convention and agreement might move forward. However, as of early 2003, there remains the question whether it is worth the effort to obtain the Senate vote and then ratify the treaty in the face of some lingering domestic opposition and the fact, as discussed below, that the United States is already enjoying many of the benefits of the Convention without even ratifying it.

Starting even before the new provisions of the 1982 LOS Convention had come into force in 1994 for many other countries, President Reagan and succeeding U.S. administrations have selectively embraced many of the Convention's key provisions and made them part of U.S. law. The United States also remains a party to the four 1985 Geneva conventions, discussed below.

The LOS Convention is the successor not only to the four Geneva conventions, but also to a long line of customary international law and earlier conventions that progressively became more detailed and that reflected technological changes in ships and naval warfare; developments in fishing, oil exploration, and mining; and growing concern about the environment. It is important to have an appreciation of the historical development of the law of the sea to understand the provisions of the LOS Convention. Some of its provisions reflect the customary international law and treaties existing at the time; others represent major expansions or departures from the existing law. Morever, until the LOS Convention is accepted by all the remaining states (especially the United States), there will be situations in which customary international law and prior treaties still have some weight.

Until the twentieth century, almost all of the law of the sea consisted of customary law that was premised on freedom of the sea. The Justinian Code of 529 A.D., for instance, extended its authority only to the high-water mark and not into the oceans. While several nations, especially Spain and Portugal, purported to control all the world's oceans, these claims were not only short-lived but impossible to enforce. Perhaps the most famous commentary on freedom of the seas is Hugo Grotius's Mare Liberum, first published in 1609. Grotius argued that no nation could legitimately exercise sovereignty over any of the world's oceans, and he generally repudiated the notion of a *mare clausem* (closed sea) as an illegitimate extension of sovereignty.

While widely adhered to, the concept of freedom of the seas was in some conflict with the desires of a coastal state to control the waters immediately adjacent to its coast. For instance, the coastal state would be concerned about smuggling and armed attacks. Throughout recent centuries, this conflict continued, primarily in debates over the exact breadth of the "territorial sea," the area of adjacent water over which a state could exercise sovereignty. Except for disputes over the territorial sea, however, the freedom of the seas was almost universally accepted.

At the beginning of the twentieth century, there was a growing movement to codify the law of the sea. This was motivated by a number of factors, including the progressive depletion of fishery stocks and the possibility of greater technological exploitation of the oceans. In the 1920s the League of Nations recognized the law of the sea as an area of international law ripe for codification. A conference was called for this purpose in 1930 at The Hague. Unfortunately, the attending nations were unable to agree on a number of specifics, including the proper breadth of the territorial sea, and the convention disbanded without agreement.

After World War II, the pressures for codification increased. Exploitation of offshore mineral wealth, particularly oil, was a reality, and the depletion of fishery stocks was rapidly increasing. By 1956, the International Law Commission, under the auspices of the United Nations, had drafted a comprehensive report on the subject, and a United Nations Conference on the Law of the Sea was called at Geneva (UNCLOS I).

UNCLOS I produced four treaties in 1958:

1. Convention on the Territorial Sea and Contiguous Zone
2. Convention on the Continental Shelf
3. Convention on the High Seas
4. Convention on Fishing and Conservation of Living Resources of the High Seas

The United States ratified all four, and all four entered into force in the early to mid-1960s.* Each of the Conventions is discussed later.

Although UNCLOS I was considered a great success, a number of issues were left unresolved, including the vital issue regarding the breadth of the territorial sea. In addition, several issues were inadequately resolved due to lack of information, such as the limits of the continental shelf. Consequently, a second conference (UNCLOS II) was convened in 1960. UNCLOS II was not a success. It failed, by only one vote, to adopt a compromise formula that provided for a territorial sea of six nautical miles, plus a six-mile fishery zone.** No formal conventions emerged from the conference.

By 1967 the need for a new agreement was evident. The issues left inadequately resolved by UNCLOS I were increasingly put at issue. Over-fishing and pollution in parts of the ocean raised questions about the narrow jurisdictional limits in the 1958 treaty regime. Also, mining of the deep seabed, an issue too remote for UNCLOS I, was thought to be close to practical reality. The mineral wealth of the seabed was thought to be almost limitless, and many were concerned over how it would be developed.

---

*As of January 2003, there were 51 parties to the first Convention, 57 to the second Convention, 62 to the third, and 37 to the fourth. There was also an Optional Protocol of Signature Concerning the Compulsory Settlement of Disputes to the LOS Conventions of 1958. It extended the compulsory jurisdiction of the International Court of Justice to disputes over the interpretation or application of the Conventions. The Protocol entered into force in September 1962. As of April 2003, there were 37 parties to it. Although the United States signed the Protocol in 1958, it has yet to ratify it.—EDS.

**Unless indicated otherwise, references in this chapter to a "mile" or "miles" are to a nautical mile(s). One nautical mile is equal to 1.151 miles or 1.852 kilometers.—EDS.

Dr. Arvid Pardo, Malta's representative at the United Nations, was at the fore in calling for a third conference. One of his proposals, adopted as a U.N. resolution in 1967, established an important principle for the conference and the Convention. The resolution declared that the deep seabed and its resources were the "common heritage of mankind." This concept meant that, instead of allowing the deep seabed to be exploited by whoever got there first, the seabed would be developed for the benefit of all mankind. The concept also reinforced the need to define the limits of the territorial sea and national jurisdiction over the seabed.

Once UNCLOS III began in Caracas in 1974 and in Geneva in 1975, the same sense of common concern governed the proceedings. Rather than adopt provisions through a straight majority vote, the conference used a system of consensus. Although this undoubtedly lengthened the proceedings, it guaranteed that no single group of nations could force their will on a minority and thereby attempted to secure the ongoing participation of all nations.

From its inception, the Convention was conceived as a comprehensive agreement. The document, opened for signature in 1982, contains 320 articles and 9 annexes and covers widely divergent subjects, ranging from the nationality of vessels to deep seabed mining. Among other accomplishments, the Convention definitively outlines various zones in the sea where the coastal state and other states have varying rights, such as control of the resources or passage. The regime is divided into areas of descending authority for the coastal state: internal waters, territorial sea, contiguous zone, exclusive economic zone, continental shelf, and high seas. (See the charts at pages 845–847 for a sense of the location of these zones.)

The Convention and its annexes also established a complicated system for the exploitation of the mineral resources in the deep seabed, the so-called Area. (This system will be addressed in later sections.) It was the most controversial aspect of the Convention: while many of the Convention's provisions simply adopted customary international law or have become accepted as international law, the deep seabed mining regime caused considerable dissension. This was the major reason that the Reagan Administration announced in 1982 that the United States would not sign the Convention nor participate in any further negotiations. (President Reagan later said that the United States viewed many of the other LOS Convention provisions as codifying existing customary international law.)

The compromise agreement* reached in 1994 modified the controversial provisions of the deep seabed mining regime and led most hold-out countries, including all the remaining industrial countries except for the United States, to ratify the LOS Convention and the agreement. Given the widespread ratification of the documents and even the U.S. acceptance of some of the key provisions in them, the LOS Convention and the companion agreement are the cornerstone of international law governing the world's oceans.

However, some interesting questions still linger about the Convention and the 1994 agreement. What is the legal status of the 1994 agreement? Even though the United States has only selectively endorsed some of the provisions of the Convention and the 1994 agreement, do all their provisions now constitute customary international law because of their widespread acceptance? Is it now in the United States' interests to ratify the Convention and agreement? At the end of this chapter,

---

*It is entitled Agreement Relating to the Implementation of Part XI of 1982 United Nations Convention on the Law of the Sea. As of April 2003, there were 113 parties to the agreement.—EDS.

we will look for answers to these questions after examining both the U.S. objections to the LOS Convention's provisions on deep seabed mining and the agreement that was designed to overcome those objections.

A short final section of this chapter focuses on Antarctica. Larger than the combined area of the United States and Mexico but covered almost entirely with ice one mile thick, the development of Antarctica raises some of the same issues as the use of the high seas and the deep seabed. A bibliography concludes this chapter.

B. NATIONALITY OF VESSELS

Vessels create particular jurisdictional problems, which should be examined briefly. The rules conferring nationality are, helpfully, almost universally recognized. The excerpts that follow will introduce you to the "law of the flag," recurring problems, and the significance of nationality.

1. Customary Law

Lauritzen v. Larsen

U.S. Supreme Court
345 U.S. 571 (1953)

[Larsen, a Danish seaman, brought suit under the Jones Act[*] to recover for injuries sustained on the Danish ship, the *Randa,* while docked in Havana, Cuba. Larsen based his assertion of federal jurisdiction on a broad reading of the Jones Act that encompassed all sailors and on Lauritzen's significant New York business contacts. The trial court entered a verdict for Larsen, based on U.S. law. Lauritzen appealed, contending that Danish, not United States, law should apply.[**] By a vote of 7 to 1, the Supreme Court ruled that U.S. law should not apply. In his opinion for the Court, Justice Jackson addressed a number of factors important for determining choice-of-law questions in maritime tort cases. One of these is the law of the flag.]

Mr. Justice JACKSON delivered the opinion of the Court.

2. Law of the flag. — Perhaps the most venerable and universal rule of maritime law relevant to our problem is that which gives cardinal importance to the law of the flag. Each state under international law may determine for itself the conditions on which it will grant its nationality to a merchant ship, thereby accepting responsibility

---

* At the time of this decision and as of November 2002, the statute read, in part:

> Any seaman who shall suffer personal injury in the course of his employment may, at his election, maintain an action for damages at law, with the right of trial by jury, and in such action all statutes of the United States modifying or extending the common-law right or remedy in cases of personal injury to railway employees shall apply. . . . [46 U.S.C. §688(a).] —EDS.

In 1982, a subsection (b) was added to the statute that limited the right of action under the statute by a person who was not a U.S. citizen or permanent resident alien at the time of the incident.

** Under Danish law, seamen's injuries were addressed under a state-operated plan similar to workers' compensation. The Danish plan, unlike American law, did not consider negligence or allow for recovery for pain and suffering. —EDS.

for it and acquiring authority over it. Nationality is evidenced to the world by the ship's papers and its flag. The United States has firmly and successfully maintained that the regularity and validity of a registration can be questioned only by the registering state.[17]

This Court has said that the law of the flag supersedes the territorial principle, even for purposes of criminal jurisdiction of personnel of a merchant ship, because it "is deemed to be a part of the territory of that sovereignty [whose flag it flies], and not to lose that character when in navigable waters within the territorial limits of another sovereignty." On this principle, we concede a territorial government involved only concurrent jurisdiction of offenses aboard our ships. United States v. Flores, 289 U.S. 137, 155-159, and cases cited. Some authorities reject, as a rather mischievous fiction, the doctrine that a ship is constructively a floating part of the flag-state,[18] but apply the law of the flag on the pragmatic basis that there must be some law on shipboard, that it cannot change at every change of waters, and no experience shows a better rule than that of the state that owns her.

It is significant to us here that the weight given to the ensign overbears most other connecting events in determining applicable law. As this Court held in United States v. Flores, supra, at 158, and iterated in Cunard Steamship Co. v. Mellon, at 123:

> And so by comity it came to be generally understood among civilized nations that all matters of discipline and all things done on board which affected only the vessel or those belonging to her, and did not involve the peace or dignity of the country, or the tranquillity of the port, should be left by the local government to be dealt with by the authorities of the nation to which the vessel belonged as the laws of that nation or the interests of its commerce should require. . . .

This was but a repetition of settled American doctrine.[19]

These considerations are of such weight in favor of Danish and against American law in this case that it must prevail unless some heavy counterweight appears.

2. Flags of Convenience

"Flag of convenience" (FOC) is a term used to describe ships that bear the flags of countries other than those of the beneficial owners. The most common FOC countries are also often referred to as having "open" registries because their requirements for registration are so minimal.

Registering ships under a flag of convenience started in the 1920s and has expanded greatly since World War II. It has been estimated that by 1994 about half of

---

17. The leading case is The Virginius, seized in 1873 by the Spanish when en route to Cuba. President Grant took the position that "if the ship's papers were irregular or fraudulent, the crime was committed against the American laws and only its tribunals were competent to decide the question." The Attorney General took the same position. The ship was restored.

18. The theoretical basis used by this Court apparently prevailed in 1928 with the Permanent Court of International Justice in the case of The Lotus, P.C.I.J., Series A, No. 10. For criticism of it see Higgins and Colombos, International Law of the Sea (2d ed.), 193-195. We leave the controversy where we find it, for either basis leads to the same result in this case, though this might not be so with some other problems of shipping.

19. Wildenhus's Case, 120 U.S. 1; Brown v. Duchesne, 19 How. 183. . . .

the gross registered tonnage of ships was represented primarily by FOC ships. As of 2001, Panama is the leading FOC country, with an estimated 4,368 vessels and 162 million gross registered tons on its registry, with Liberia next with approximately 75 million tons. The primary beneficial owners of FOC ships, based on tonnage, are Greece, Japan, the United States, and Norway. (The U.S. registry itself has just under 12 million tons.)

Owners started to register their vessels in foreign countries as a way to reduce costs and escape regulations. As A.D. Couper highlights in Voyages of Abuse 11-12 (1999):

> The shift to FOC meant renting a foreign flag at a relatively low price. This gave freedom to recruit from any part of the world at reduced wages and conditions. It also allowed companies to escape from national taxation, and from some ship safety and onboard health and social requirements. Comparing wages alone, by 1996 a chief officer from north-western Europe would earn about $7500 per month, from India $3100 and from the Philippines $2000. . . . When all conditions of crew and ship were taken into account, the operating costs of a high-standard ship and crew could be three times greater than those of substandard vessels with deplorable crew conditions.
>
> It was now possible to compete hard on crew costs and to manipulate most costs on a global basis. A single vessel could be financed, mortgaged, built, registered, owned, managed and insured all in different countries. It could be chartered to yet another country, leased back to the country of beneficial ownership and engaged in trading world-wide. The world fleet through these processes changed in structure, flag, ownership, ship types and shipboard society.

In response, as one expert observed: "[T]he traditional maritime States began to question the validity of the link of nationality established by such 'flag of convenience' registration in 'open registries.' The claim, for which there was certainly some evidence in the early years of this practice, was that safety of shipping and the environment were being endangered by sub-standard ships, manned by ill-paid and inadequately qualified crews and that the flag States concerned had neither the experience nor the administrative machinery to implement shipping legislation in relation to such vessels." 1 Edward Duncan Brown, The International Law of the Sea 288 (1994).

Starting with UNCLOS I in 1958, there were multilateral efforts to deal with the problem of flags of convenience. The primary approach was to add to the long-standing principle that the nationality of a vessel depends on the flag that it is entitled to fly. The result in the LOS Convention was to carry over the key provision in the 1958 Geneva Convention on the High Seas that there must be a "genuine link" between the flag state and the ship. In addition, the LOS Convention began to provide some detail about the duties of the flag state.

Excerpts from the LOS Convention
21 I.L.M. 1261 (1982)

Article 91.   Nationality of Ships

1. Every State shall fix the conditions for the grant of its nationality to ships, for the registration of ships in its territory, and for the right to fly its flag. Ships have the

nationality of the State whose flag they are entitled to fly. There must exist a genuine link between the State and the ship. . . .

Article 92.   *Status of Ships*

1. Ships shall sail under the flag of one State only and, save in exceptional cases expressly provided for in international treaties or in this Convention, shall be subject to its exclusive jurisdiction on the high seas. . . .

Article 94.   *Duties of the Flag State*

1. Every State shall effectively exercise its jurisdiction and control in administrative, technical and social matters over ships flying its flag. . . .

3. Every State shall take such measures for ships flying its flag as are necessary to ensure safety at sea with regard, inter alia, to:

(a)   the construction, equipment and seaworthiness of ships;

(b)   the manning of ships, labour conditions and the training of crews, taking into account the applicable international instruments;

(c)   the use of signals, the maintenance of communications and the prevention of collisions. . . .

6. A State which has clear grounds to believe that proper jurisdiction and control with respect to a ship have not been exercised may report the facts to the flag State. Upon receiving such a report, the flag State shall investigate the matter and, if appropriate, take any action necessary to remedy the situation. . . .

Unfortunately, the LOS Convention does not offer a definition of "genuine link." A similar ambiguity, plus the economic benefits reaped by an open registry, led to the widespread abuse of the provision in the earlier High Seas Convention.

In 1986, the Convention on Conditions for Registration of Ships was adopted by a conference in Geneva, and was then opened for signature and ratification. The Convention attempts to define more thoroughly the "genuine link" that should exist between a ship and the state whose flag it flies. The Convention offers flag states the option of maintaining a genuine link, either through the manning of the vessel or through the ownership and management of the vessel. The Convention also mandates that a flag state establish "competent and adequate national maritime administration" in order to exercise effective control over the vessel. The administration is charged with several specific mandatory tasks, such as ensuring that the ship complies with the state's "laws and regulations concerning registration of ships and with applicable international rules and standards concerning, in particular, the safety of ships and persons on board and the prevention of pollution of the marine environment." The Convention, however, does not have any enforcement provisions if the flag state fails to carry out its obligations and responsibilities.

As of January 2003, the Convention lacked sufficient contracting parties to become effective.

Questions

1. How do Panama and Liberia benefit from making registration easy?

2. What should be the minimum requirement for a ship to fly a state's flag? Ownership by a national? A percentage of nationals on the crew?

3. What responsibilities should the flag state have? Should Panama be held responsible for the actions of one of its flag vessels? How should these obligations be enforced against a flag state?

4. In July 1998, the Carnival cruise ship *Ecstasy,* registered in Liberia, caught on fire near the port of Miami. Although no one was hurt, this accident raised questions about the safety standards of ships under the flags of countries with open registries. The International Maritime Organization (IMO), which was established under the United Nations in 1958 and now has 162 Member States, provides some safety and pollution standards for ships in international waters. Under the U.N. Convention on the Safety of Life at Sea, the IMO requires flag states to certify that the ships registered under its flag meet certain safety requirements such as sprinkler systems. The IMO also adopted an international safety code, which establishes mandatory safety requirements for shipowners. (See IMO's Web site: <http://www.imo.org>.)

5. The cruise ship industry presents challenging problems.

> Once the exclusive playground of the very wealthy, the cruise business has expanded over the last decade by appealing to the vast middle class, especially families and young adults. The polished mahogany decks and formal dinners of a bygone era have been replaced by glittering floating cities dedicated to carefree partying, gambling and drinking.
>
> But as the industry has boomed to more than five million passengers a year, it has presented new concerns for its ports of call, its passengers and the environment, in part because of the size of its giant liners, in part because the cruise lines operate largely outside the laws of any one country. [Douglas Frantz, *On Cruise Ships, Silence Shrouds Crimes,* N.Y. Times, November 16, 1998, at 1.]

For example, Carnival Cruise Lines and Renaissance Cruises are both foreign corporations and register some of their ships in Panama or Liberia. Some of the problems that have arisen in recent years have involved the cruise ships dumping their wastes in Alaskan territorial waters, allegations of sexual assaults committed by foreign crew members against passengers, and outbreaks of communicable diseases in the close quarters of the ships. See, for example, Douglas Frantz, supra; Douglas Frantz, Cruise Industry Plans to Report Crimes to F.B.I., N.Y. Times, July 27, 1999, at A1; Denise Grady, Practical Traveler: Staying Well While at Sea, N.Y. Times, Feb. 16, 2003, at E4.

In part because of passenger protests, the foreign cruise lines usually consent to jurisdiction in private lawsuits by U.S. passengers in a U.S. court specified on the ticket. Although this provides jurisdiction in the United States, it might not be a convenient court for the former passengers. For example, see Carnival Cruise Lines v. Shute, 499 U.S. 585 (1991) (discussed in Chapter 4).

As for crimes, individuals can be charged and convicted of certain crimes under U.S. law that they may have committed in international or foreign waters, if the act that occurred was within the "special maritime and territorial jurisdiction of the United States." This jurisdiction is defined as including, "[t]o the extent permitted by international law, any foreign vessel during a voyage having a scheduled departure from or arrival in the United States with respect to an offense committed by or against a national of the United States." 18 U.S.C. § 7(8); see United States v. Neil, 312 F.3d 419 (9th Cir. 2002). Moreover, the F.B.I. is authorized to investigate possible crimes within this special jurisdiction. This jurisdiction and the *Neil* case are discussed in Chapter 7 at 696.)

6. See generally David D. Caron, Choice and Duty in Foreign Affairs: The Reflagging of the Kuwaiti Tankers, in The Persian Gulf War: Lessons for Strategy, Law, and Diplomacy (Christopher C. Joyner ed., 1990).

C. INTERNAL AND TERRITORIAL WATERS

This section begins our detailed discussion of maritime boundaries and zones — that is, internal waters, the territorial sea, the contiguous zone, the exclusive economic zone, the continental shelf, and the high seas. Although these terms are undoubtedly still new to you and will be defined as we proceed, three charts that illustrate these terms are included on the next pages. It will be helpful to glance at the charts now, but you will probably only fully understand them as you read through the materials.

To start, the "internal waters" of a state include not only fresh water lakes and rivers, but also parts of the sea. These parts include certain bays and the belt of the sea adjacent to the coast that is within the "baselines." These internal waters are considered part of the territory of the state, and it is generally recognized that a state can exercise the same sovereignty over these waters as over its land area.

From the baselines outward to a now generally accepted distance of 12 nautical miles is the "territorial sea." The coastal state also exercises sovereignty over these waters. (These important rules are in Articles 2 and 3 of the LOS Convention.) Foreign ships, though, have a right of innocent passage.

Additional sea zones, such as the "contiguous zone" and the "exclusive economic zone," are also measured from the baselines. Obviously critical, then, is how and where the baselines are established, because so much else is measured from them.

1. Baselines

a. General Provisions

Read carefully the relevant provisions of the LOS Convention regarding baselines (Articles 5-10 and 13, set out in the Documentary Supplement). A discussion of the principal rules concerning baselines and the early historical development of these rules is provided in the following excerpt.

CHART 9-1.   LOS Convention: Sea Claims Structure

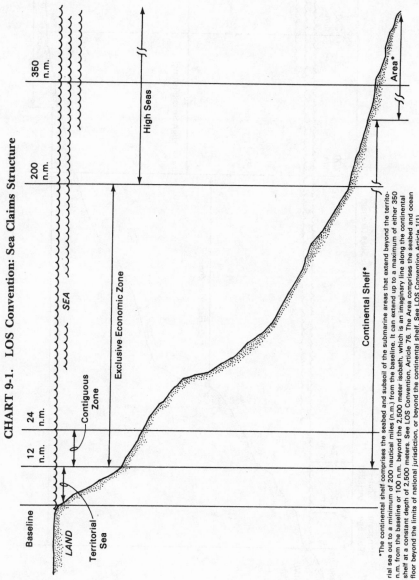

*The continental shelf comprises the seabed and subsoil of the submarine areas that extend beyond the territorial sea out to a minimum of 200 nautical miles (n.m.) from the baseline. It can extend up to a maximum of either 350 n.m. from the baseline or 100 n.m. beyond the 2,500 meter isobath, which is an imaginary line along the continental shelf at a constant depth of 2,500 meters. See LOS Convention, Article 76. The Area comprises the seabed and ocean floor beyond the limits of national jurisdiction, or beyond the continental shelf. See LOS Convention Article 1(1).

CHART 9-2. Uses

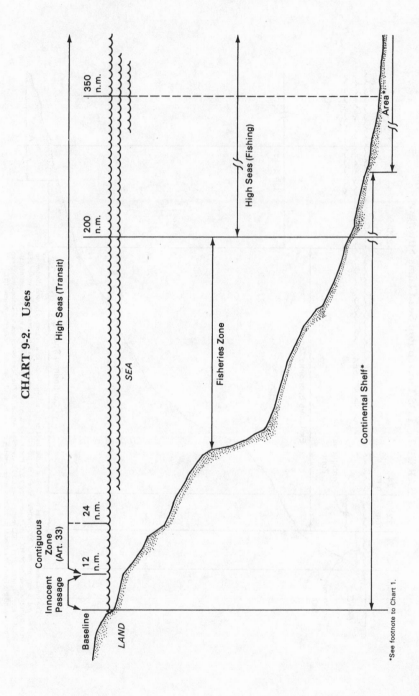

*See footnote to Chart 1.

CHART 9-3.
Land-based View: Distance from Shore

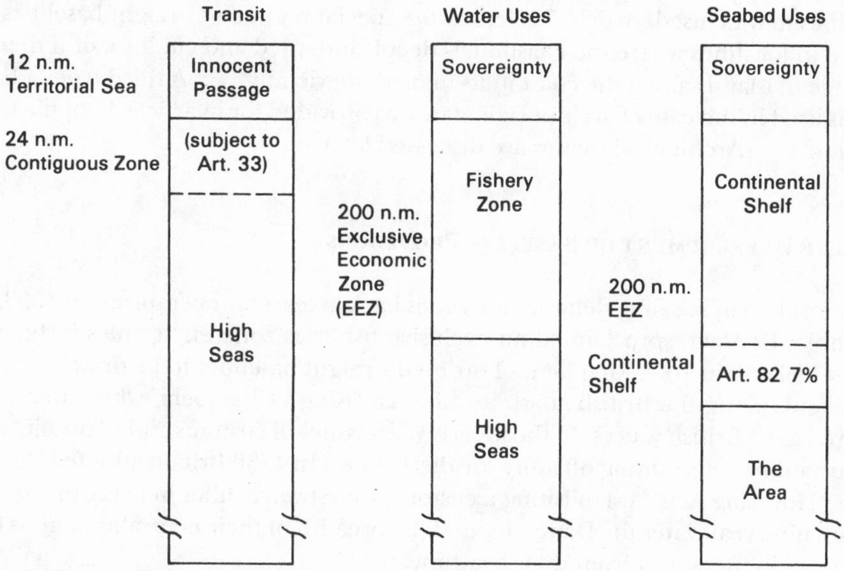

	Transit	Water Uses	Seabed Uses

12 n.m. Territorial Sea	Innocent Passage	Sovereignty	Sovereignty
24 n.m. Contiguous Zone	(subject to Art. 33)		Continental Shelf
	High Seas	200 n.m. Exclusive Economic Zone (EEZ) — Fishery Zone	
		200 n.m. EEZ — Continental Shelf	Art. 82 7%
		High Seas	The Area

Lewis M. Alexander, Baseline Delimitations and Maritime Boundaries

23 Va. J. Intl. L. 503 (1983)

The body of rules and regulations for establishing offshore jurisdictional zones involves three types of geographical issues. One type concerns the width of the various zones, a second issue pertains to the seaward and lateral limits of the zones, and the third involves the baselines along the coast from which the breadth of the zones is measured. The question of baselines is related to the physical nature of the coast itself, a phenomenon which varies greatly from place to place throughout the world. Some coasts are rugged and deeply indented; others are smooth and unbroken; still other coasts are the deltas of rivers where the low-water line can change significantly over short periods of time. Coasts may be fringed by islands, rocks or coral reefs. Given the wide variety of physical conditions which exist world wide, it is somewhat surprising that the 1982 Convention on the Law of the Sea (the Convention or the 1982 Convention) provides for baseline delimitations along almost all types of coastline in a relatively few articles.

The official baseline along the coast is an important juridical feature of the state. Waters landward of the baseline, such as bays and estuaries, are internal waters of the coastal state; waters seaward of the baseline are the territorial sea and, if claimed, the contiguous zone and the exclusive economic or fisheries zone. The baseline is also used in the delimitation of certain types of maritime boundaries between states with opposite or adjacent coasts.

The regulations for delimiting baselines are contained in articles 5 through 14 of the 1982 Convention, and reflect similar articles which appeared in the 1958

Convention on the Territorial Sea and the Contiguous Zone. Article 5 of the 1982 Convention refers to a "normal" baseline, one that follows the low-water line along the coast except for irregularities, such as bays or river mouths, where straight closing lines may be used. Article 7 refers to the special regime of straight baselines for use "[i]n localities where the coastline is deeply indented and cut into, or if there is a fringe of islands along the coast in its immediate vicinity. . . ." A third type of baseline is used in the case of archipelagic states, as provided for in article 47 of the Convention. . . . [Archipelagic states are discussed later.]

I.   THE DEVELOPMENT OF BASELINE PROVISIONS

The problem of baseline delimitations goes back at least four centuries. In 1598, for example, Denmark proclaimed an exclusive fisheries zone eight miles in breadth about Iceland; in 1604 King James I ordered straight baselines to be drawn between headlands along the British coast, forming 26 "King's Chambers" which were considered to be British waters. In those early years issues of customs and neutrality were important in determining offshore juridical zones. In 1736 Britain adopted the first of its "Hovering Acts," establishing a customs zone twelve miles in breadth along its coasts; nine years later the Danes defined the breadth of their neutrality zone as four miles, again measured from their coastline.

During the nineteenth and early twentieth centuries baselines tended to follow the sinuosities of the coast. The problem of bays, however, was seen as a special issue. The Anglo-French Fishing Treaty of 1839 stipulated that bays with entrances ten miles or less in width could be closed off by a straight line at their mouth; the breadth of the territorial sea was to be measured seaward of the closing line. The North Seas Fisheries Convention of 1882 for the first time permitted ten-mile closing lines within bays that were more than ten miles across at their mouth, and the closing line was to be drawn as close to the entrance of the bay as possible.

The first coordinated international attempt to develop rules and regulations for baseline delimitation occurred in the 1920s. In 1924 the Council of the League of Nations appointed a Committee of Experts for the Progressive Codification of International Law. One of a series of sub-committees appointed by the Committee concerned territorial waters and met in 1925 and in 1926. The sub-committee reports, issued in 1926, contained a number of recommendations on delimitation practices that, of course, had no binding effect on coastal states. . . .

The Second Committee of the 1930 Hague Conference on the Codification of International Law dealt with territorial waters. The United States delegation to the Conference presented a series of recommendations. . . . The Hague Conference adjourned without formally adopting any of the offshore delimitation proposals.

The issue of "true" (later termed "juridical") bays had become important prior to, and during, the 1930 Conference. As early as 1839, as noted earlier, ten-mile closing lines were permitted for bays, but problems arose in distinguishing indentations having the configuration of a bay from slight curvatures of the coast. . . .

The International Court of Justice grappled with the baseline issue and related questions in its 1951 decision in the Fisheries Case. The case illustrates some of the problems in drawing a baseline and stands as a statement of the existing customary international law at that time. It also provides a useful comparison with the rules that were developed only 30 years later in the LOS Convention.

Fisheries Case (United Kingdom v. Norway)

Intl. Court of Justice
[1951] I.C.J. 116 (Merits)

The facts which led the United Kingdom to bring the case before the Court are briefly as follows.

The historical facts laid before the Court establish that as the result of complaints from the King of Denmark and of Norway, at the beginning of the seventeenth century, British fishermen refrained from fishing in Norwegian coastal waters for a long period, from 1616-1618 until 1906.

In 1906 a few British fishing vessels appeared off the coasts of Eastern Finnmark. From 1908 onwards they returned in greater numbers. These were trawlers equipped with improved and powerful gear. The local population became perturbed, and measures were taken by the Norwegian Government with a view to specifying the limits within which fishing was prohibited to foreigners.

The first incident occurred in 1911 when a British trawler was seized and condemned for having violated these measures. . . . In 1932, British trawlers, extending the range of their activities, appeared in the sectors off the Norwegian coast west of the North Cape, and the number of warnings and arrests increased. On July 27th, 1933, the United Kingdom Government sent a memorandum to the Norwegian Government complaining that in delimiting the territorial sea the Norwegian authorities had made use of unjustifiable base-lines. On July 12th, 1935, a Norwegian Royal Decree was enacted delimiting the Norwegian fisheries zone north of 66° 28.8′ North latitude. . . .

In 1948, since no agreement had been reached, the Norwegian Government abandoned its lenient enforcement of the 1935 Decree. . . . A considerable number of British trawlers were arrested and condemned. It was then that the United Kingdom Government instituted the present proceedings. . . .

The Norwegian Royal Decree of July 12th, 1935, concerning the delimitation of the Norwegian fisheries zone sets out in the preamble the considerations on which its provisions are based. In this connection it refers to "well-established national titles of right," "the geographical conditions prevailing on the Norwegian coasts," "the safeguard of the vital interests of the inhabitants of the northernmost parts of the country"; it further relies on the Royal Decrees of February 22nd, 1812, October 16th, 1869, January 5th, 1881, and September 9th, 1889.

The Decree provides that "lines of delimitation towards the high sea of the Norwegian fisheries zone as regards that part of Norway which is situated northward of 66° 28.8′ North latitude . . . shall run parallel with straight base-lines drawn between fixed points on the mainland, on islands or rocks, starting from the final point of the boundary line of the Realm in the easternmost part of the Varangerfjord and going as far as Træna in the County of Nordland."

The subject of the dispute is clearly indicated under point 8 of the Application instituting proceedings: "The subject of the dispute is the validity or otherwise under international law of the lines of delimitation of the Norwegian fisheries zone laid down by the Royal Decree of 1935 for that part of Norway which is situated northward of 66° 28.8' North latitude." And further on: ". . . the question at issue between the two Governments is whether the lines prescribed by the Royal Decree of 1935 as the base-lines for the delimitation of the fisheries zone have or have not been drawn in accordance with the applicable rules of international law."

Although the Decree of July 12th, 1935, refers to the Norwegian fisheries zone and does not specifically mention the territorial sea, there can be no doubt that the zone delimited by this Decree is none other than the sea area which Norway considers to be her territorial sea. . . .

The coastal zone concerned in the dispute is of considerable length. It lies north of latitude 66° 28.8' N., that is to say, north of the Arctic Circle, and it includes the coast of the mainland of Norway and all the islands, islets, rocks and reefs, known by the name of the "skjærgaard" (literally, rock rampart), together with all Norwegian internal and territorial waters. The coast of the mainland, which, without taking any account of fjords, bays and minor indentations, is over 1,500 kilometres in length, is of a very distinctive configuration. Very broken along its whole length, it constantly opens out into indentations often penetrating for great distances inland: the Porsangerfjord, for instance, penetrates 75 sea miles inland. To the west, the land configuration stretches out into the sea: the large and small islands, mountainous in character, the islets, rocks and reefs, some always above water, others emerging only at low tide, are in truth but an extension of the Norwegian mainland. The number of insular formations, large and small, which make up the "skjærgaard," is estimated by the Norwegian Government to be one hundred and twenty thousand. From the southern extremity of the disputed area to the North Cape, the "skjærgaard" lies along the whole of the coast of the mainland; east of the North Cape, the "skjærgaard" ends, but the coast line continues to be broken by large and deeply indented fjords.

Within the "skjærgaard," almost every island has its large and its small bays; countless arms of the sea, straits, channels and mere waterways serve as a means of communication for the local population which inhabits the islands as it does the mainland. The coast of the mainland does not constitute, as it does in practically all other countries, a clear dividing line between land and sea. What matters, what really constitutes the Norwegian coast line, is the outer line of the "skjærgaard." . . .

Along the coast are situated comparatively shallow banks, veritable under-water terraces which constitute fishing grounds where fish are particularly abundant; these grounds were known to Norwegian fishermen and exploited by them from time immemorial. . . .

In these barren regions the inhabitants of the coastal zone derive their livelihood essentially from fishing. . . .

The Parties being in agreement on the figure of 4 miles for the breadth of the territorial sea, the problem which arises is from what base-line this breadth is to be reckoned. The Conclusions of the United Kingdom are explicit on this point: the base-line must be low-water mark on permanently dry land which is a part of Norwegian territory, or the proper closing line of Norwegian internal waters.

The Court has no difficulty in finding that, for the purpose of measuring the breadth of the territorial sea, it is the low-water mark as opposed to the high-water mark, or the mean between the two tides, which has generally been adopted in the

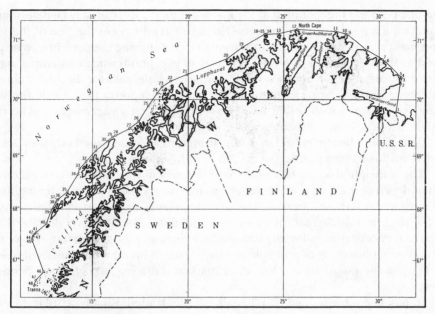

Straight baselines laid down by Norway along its skjærgaard coast under The Norway Royal Decree of 1935.*

practice of States. This criterion is the most favourable to the coastal State and
clearly shows the character of territorial waters as appurtenant to the land territory.
The Court notes that the Parties agree as to this criterion, but that they differ as to
its application.

The Parties also agree that in the case of a low-tide elevation (drying rock) the
outer edge at low water of this low-tide elevation may be taken into account as a
base-point for calculating the breadth of the territorial sea. . . .

The Court finds itself obliged to decide whether the relevant low-water mark is
that of the mainland or of the "skjærgaard." Since the mainland is bordered in its
western sector by the "skjærgaard," which constitutes a whole with the mainland,
it is the outer line of the "skjærgaard" which must be taken into account in delimiting the belt of Norwegian territorial waters. This solution is dictated by geographic
realities.

Three methods have been contemplated to effect the application of the low-
water mark rule. The simplest would appear to be the method of the *tracé parallèle*,
which consists of drawing the outer limit of the belt of territorial waters by following
the coast in all its sinuosities. This method may be applied without difficulty to an
ordinary coast, which is not too broken. Where a coast is deeply indented and cut
into, as is that of Eastern Finnmark, or where it is bordered by an archipelago such
as the "skjærgaard" along the western sector of the coast here in question, the

*The map appears as Figure 14 in Aaron Lewis Shalowitz, Shore and Sea Boundaries 69 (Vol. I,
1962).—Eds.

base-line becomes independent of the low-water mark, and can only be determined by means of a geometric construction. In such circumstances the line of the low-water mark can no longer be put forward as a rule requiring the coast line to be followed in all its sinuosities; nor can one speak of exceptions when contemplating so rugged a coast in detail. Such a coast, viewed as a whole, calls for the application of a different method. Nor can one characterize as exceptions to the rule the very many derogations which would be necessitated by such a rugged coast. The rule would disappear under the exceptions.

[The Court briefly considered and dismissed a second method, the "arc of circles" method. It then turned to the "straight base-lines method."]

The principle that the belt of territorial waters must follow the general direction of the coast makes it possible to fix certain criteria valid for any delimitation of the territorial sea; these criteria will be elucidated later. The Court will confine itself at this stage to noting that, in order to apply this principle, several States have deemed it necessary to follow the straight base-lines method and that they have not encountered objections of principle by other States. This method consists of selecting appropriate points on the low-water mark and drawing straight lines between them. . . .

It has been contended, on behalf of the United Kingdom, that Norway may draw straight lines only across bays. The Court is unable to share this view. If the belt of territorial waters must follow the outer line of the "skjærgaard," and if the method of straight base-lines must be admitted in certain cases, there is no valid reason to draw them only across bays, as in Eastern Finnmark, and not also to draw them between islands, islets and rocks, across the sea areas separating them, even when such areas do not fall within the conception of a bay. It is sufficient that they should be situated between the island formations of the "skjærgaard," *inter fauces terrarum.* . . .

In the opinion of the United Kingdom Government, Norway is entitled, on historic grounds, to claim as internal waters all fjords and sunds which have the character of a bay. She is also entitled on historic grounds to claim as Norwegian territorial waters all the waters of the fjords and sunds which have the character of legal straits (Conclusions, point 9), and, either as internal or as territorial waters, the areas of water lying between the island fringe and the mainland (point II and second alternative Conclusion II). . . .

The Court now comes to the question of the length of the base-lines drawn across the waters lying between the various formations of the "skjærgaard." Basing itself on the analogy with the alleged general rule of ten miles relating to bays, the United Kingdom Government still maintains on this point that the length of straight lines must not exceed ten miles.

In this connection, the practice of States does not justify the formulation of any general rule of law. The attempts that have been made to subject groups of islands or coastal archipelagoes to conditions analogous to the limitations concerning bays (distance between the islands not exceeding twice the breadth of the territorial waters, or ten or twelve sea miles), have not got beyond the stage of proposals.

Furthermore, apart from any question of limiting the lines to ten miles, it may be that several lines can be envisaged. In such cases the coastal State would seem to be in the best position to appraise the local conditions dictating the selection.

Consequently, the Court is unable to share the view of the United Kingdom Government, that "Norway, in the matter of base-lines, now claims recognition of an exceptional system." As will be shown later, all that the Court can see therein is the application of general international law to a specific case. . . .

Thus the Court, confining itself for the moment to the Conclusions of the United Kingdom, finds that the Norwegian Government in fixing the base-lines for the delimitation of the Norwegian fisheries zone by the 1935 Decree has not violated international law. . . .

It does not at all follow that, in the absence of rules having the technically precise character alleged by the United Kingdom Government, the delimitation undertaken by the Norwegian Government in 1935 is not subject to certain principles which make it possible to judge as to its validity under international law. The delimitation of sea areas has always an international aspect; it cannot be dependent merely upon the will of the coastal State as expressed in its municipal law. Although it is true that the act of delimitation is necessarily a unilateral act, because only the coastal State is competent to undertake it, the validity of the delimitation with regard to other States depends upon international law.

In this connection, certain basic considerations inherent in the nature of the territorial sea, bring to light certain criteria which, though not entirely precise, can provide courts with an adequate basis for their decisions, which can be adapted to the diverse facts in question.

Among these considerations, some reference must be made to the close dependence of the territorial sea upon the land domain. It is the land which confers upon the coastal State a right to the waters off its coasts. It follows that while such a State must be allowed the latitude necessary in order to be able to adapt its delimitation to practical needs and local requirements, the drawing of base-lines must not depart to any appreciable extent from the general direction of the coast.

Another fundamental consideration, of particular importance in this case, is the more or less close relationship existing between certain sea areas and the land formations which divide or surround them. The real question raised in the choice of base-lines is in effect whether certain sea areas lying within these lines are sufficiently closely linked to the land domain to be subject to the regime of internal waters. This idea, which is at the basis of the determination of the rules relating to bays, should be liberally applied in the case of a coast, the geographical configuration of which is as unusual as that of Norway.

Finally, there is one consideration not to be overlooked, the scope of which extends beyond purely geographical factors: that of certain economic interests peculiar to a region, the reality and importance of which are clearly evidenced by a long usage. . . . [The Court went on to discuss the Norwegian practice from 1812 to the present regarding delimitation of baselines.]

From the standpoint of international law, it is now necessary to consider whether the application of the Norwegian system encountered any opposition from foreign States. . . .

The general toleration of foreign States with regard to the Norwegian practice is an unchallenged fact.

The notoriety of the facts, the general toleration of the international community, Great Britain's position in the North Sea, her own interest in the question, and her prolonged abstention would in any case warrant Norway's enforcement of her system against the United Kingdom.

The Court is thus led to conclude that the method of straight lines, established in the Norwegian system, was imposed by the peculiar geography of the Norwegian coast; that even before the dispute arose, this method had been consolidated by a constant and sufficiently long practice, in the face of which the attitude of governments bears witness to the fact that they did not consider it to be contrary to international law.

For these reasons, the Court . . . Finds

by ten votes to two, that the method employed for the delimitation of the fisheries zone by the Royal Norwegian Decree of July 12th, 1935, is not contrary to international law; and

by eight votes to four, that the base-lines fixed by the said Decree in application of this method are not contrary to international law.

Questions

1. What was the basis for the Court's holding in the Fisheries Case? A multilateral treaty? A bilateral agreement? That Norway's claims represented customary international law? That Norway's claims were not inconsistent with customary international law?

2. Note that the Court accepts the parties' agreement that, in those circumstances, the territorial sea was four miles wide and that the issue was to delimit the baseline from which the breadth would be measured.

3. Compare the Court's conclusions in 1951 with the provisions in the LOS Convention for drawing baselines. Do they differ? On a general level, is customary international law now more defined? More specifically, how long a baseline does the LOS Convention allow across the mouth of a bay? Compared to the decision in the Fisheries Case, do the LOS Convention's baseline provisions expand or reduce the internal waters that a coastal state is likely to have?

b. Dealing with Islands

Islands create special problems in drawing baselines and in determining the territorial sea and other ocean zones. Article 121 of the LOS Convention provides:

LOS Convention

Article 121. Regime of Islands

1. An island is a naturally formed area of land, surrounded by water, which is above water at high tide.

2. Except as provided for in paragraph 3, the territorial sea, the contiguous zone, the exclusive economic zone and the continental shelf of an island are

determined in accordance with the provisions of this Convention applicable to other land territory.

3. Rocks which cannot sustain human habitation or economic life of their own shall have no exclusive economic zone or continental shelf.

Questions

1. Under Article 121, how should a coastal state draw the baselines of an island that is part of the state but is located at a distance of, say, 2 nautical miles from the mainland? 11 miles? 23 miles? 300 miles?

2. Does Article 121 mean that even a small island can provide an increase of ocean area that a state can claim for its territorial sea? Which is generally most useful for a state's territorial sea claim — an island 2 nautical miles off the coast, 11 miles, 23 miles, 300 miles, 800 miles? (We ask this question again later, after we have studied the other maritime boundaries and zones, including the exclusive economic zones.)

c. The Special Case of Archipelagic States

A state may be composed of a group of islands that are interrelated geographically, economically, politically, or historically. Important examples include Indonesia and the Philippines, each of which is composed of several thousand islands spread out over more than 1,000 miles. Such archipelagic states created special issues of how to draw baselines and to define the territorial sea and other zones. For example, would a baseline continue from one island to another if the distance between them were 3, 13, or 35 miles? The solution in the LOS Convention was to create a special regime for so-called archipelagic states. (See LOS Articles 46-54.) The key provisions regarding the drawing of the baselines are in Article 47.

LOS Convention

Article 47. Archipelagic Baselines

1. An archipelagic State may draw straight archipelagic baselines joining the outermost points of the outermost islands and drying reefs of the archipelago provided that within such baselines are included the main islands and an area in which the ratio of the area of the water to the area of the land, including atolls, is between 1 to 1 and 9 to 1.

2. The length of such baselines shall not exceed 100 nautical miles, except that up to 3 percent of the total number of baselines enclosing any archipelago may exceed that length, up to a maximum length of 125 nautical miles.

3. The drawing of such baselines shall not depart to any appreciable extent from the general configuration of the archipelago.

4. Such baselines shall not be drawn to and from low-tide elevations. . . .

Notes and Questions

1. Professors Churchill and Lowe provide a brief description of the significance of these archipelagic baselines.

> Archipelagic waters comprise all the maritime waters within archipelagic baselines. One qualification must, however, be made. *Within* archipelagic baselines an archipelagic State can draw closing lines across river mouths, bays and ports on individual islands in accordance with the normal rules on baselines. The waters so enclosed are internal waters, not archipelagic waters [LOS Convention, Article 50]. . . .
>
> The concept of archipelagic waters is a new one in international law. Such waters are neither internal waters nor territorial sea, although they bear a number of resemblances to the latter. An archipelagic State has sovereignty over its archipelagic waters, including their superjacent air space, subjacent sea bed and subsoil, and "the resources contained therein" [Article 49]. This sovereignty is, however, subject to a number of rights enjoyed by third States. . . .
>
> [M]ost important, there are the navigational rights of other States. [See discussion of rights of passage in section 4 below.] [R.R. Churchill & A.V. Lowe: The law of the sea 125-127 (3d ed. 1999).]

2. Do the baselines permitted for an archipelagic state potentially allow the state to claim sovereignty over a much larger ocean area?

2. Foreign Vessels in Internal Waters

Baselines are important not only because they set the landward limits of the territorial sea and the exclusive economic zone, but also because they set the outer limit of internal waters. Internal waters are also referred to as "inland" or "national" waters. As illustrated by Article 2 of the LOS Convention, it is generally accepted that a state may exercise the same sovereignty over these waters as it exercises over the land within its borders.

As a result, foreign vessels may only enter a state's inland waters (including its ports) with the state's consent. Usually this consent is freely given and is presumed from the lack of an express prohibition against ships of a foreign flag state, particularly commercial ships. A state can require specific notification, however. Foreign warships, for example, must usually send formal notification through appropriate channels. If no objection is received, the foreign warship is normally thought to have consent to enter the state's inland waters.

In the United States, a number of laws and regulations control access by foreign ships to U.S. ports, with the President being given broad discretion to decide on access. The United States has also entered into bilateral agreements with some countries that further define their rights and the procedures for gaining access. How access is controlled can be important for enforcing laws about drug traffic, customs, and immigration.

Once in the inland waters, a foreign vessel is subject to the sovereignty of the host state. All of that country's laws apply with equal force to the vessel. Violations of those laws can be prosecuted in the host state, absent treaty provisions to the contrary or the barrier of diplomatic immunity.

While host states are entitled to exercise jurisdiction over foreign vessels, they rarely do. Instead, most states abide by what is commonly known as the "French modification": host states, based on comity and reciprocity, decline to exercise their jurisdiction over foreign vessels unless activities threaten the "peace of the port" or the "public peace." This modification was adopted by the United States in the Wildenhus's Case, 120 U.S. 1 (1886). Chief Justice Waite, for the Court, said:

> From experience, however, it was found long ago that it would be beneficial to commerce if the local government would abstain from interfering with the internal discipline of the ship, and the general regulation of the rights and duties of the officers and crew towards the vessel or among themselves. And so by comity it came to be understood among civilized nations that all matters of discipline and all things done on board which affected only the vessel or those belonging to her, and did not involve the peace or dignity of the country, or the tranquillity of the port, should be left by the local government to be dealt with by the authorities of the nation to which the vessel belonged as the laws of that nation or the interests of its commerce should require. But if crimes are committed on board of a character to disturb the peace and tranquillity of the country to which the vessel has been brought, the offenders have never by comity or usage been entitled to any exemption from the operation of the local laws for their punishment, if the local tribunals see fit to assert their authority. [Id. at 12.]

The United States reaffirmed its adherence to the French modification during the Medvid Affair in 1985. Miroslav Medvid, a sailor on a Soviet freighter docked outside New Orleans, Louisiana, jumped ship on the night of October 24-25. United States Immigration and Naturalization Service (INS) officers determined that Medvid was not seeking political asylum and returned him to the freighter. After his initial return sparked a public protest, the United States demanded the opportunity to interview Medvid again to determine if he was being forced to return to the Soviet Union against his will. During the course of the affair, the Legal Adviser to the Department of State wrote Secretary of State Shultz that the United States was well within its rights to remove Medvid, by force if necessary, from the Soviet freighter. Concerning the Wildenhus's Case, the Legal Adviser wrote in part:

> Although *Wildenhus* is quite old, it is still good law and is cited as authority in contemporaneous U.S. court decisions. . . .
> Significantly, the foregoing principles are in accord with longstanding Department of State views: For example, in the 1910 case of *The Serak,* where the authorities of Corinto, Nicaragua, requested the captain of the American steamship *City of Panama* to permit removal of a German doctor from the vessel . . . [the State Department's position was] 1. Nations have, in general, the right to exercise, if they choose, civil and criminal jurisdiction over foreign merchant vessels entering their ports. . . . The duty of the ship's master is not to resist the proper arrest of persons in such cases.

Questions

1. What types of crimes do you believe disturb the "peace of the port"?
2. Should a state exercise its jurisdiction over public drunkenness? Over use of child labor? Over gambling among crew members? Over possession of heroin or cocaine on the vessel?

3. Breadth of the Territorial Sea

The LOS Convention provides that the territorial sea shall have a breadth of not more than 12 nautical miles from the baseline. This distance, which is being commonly accepted, is a recent development. Note, for example, the four-mile breadth that the parties agreed to in the Fisheries Case.

Sovereignty over oceans was unknown in the ancient world. The Romans restricted their sovereignty to the high-water mark along the shore. The first recorded exercise of sovereignty over the seas occurred in 1269, when Venice demanded fees for foreign use of the Adriatic Sea. Genoa soon followed by charging fees for the use of the present-day Ligurian Sea. By the end of the fifteenth century, several Papal Bulls and the Treaty of Tordesillas purported to divide most of the world's oceans between Spain and Portugal. England claimed all of the present-day English Channel, the North Sea, and all waters adjacent to France.

In contrast to state practice, many writers denied any legitimate sovereignty over the oceans. Hugo Grotius, apparently as an advocate for the Dutch East India Company, believed that neither the Papal Bulls nor the Treaty of Tordesillas could grant sovereignty over the open sea to either Spain or Portugal. While admitting that sovereignty might extend to waters adjacent to land, Grotius contended that no nation could own the oceans.

The practice of claiming sovereignty over adjacent waters flourished in the seventeenth and eighteenth centuries. Three different methods of delimitation became popular: the line-of-sight rule, the cannon-shot rule, and the marine league.

The "line-of-sight" rule was a vague criterion that was sometimes used in the sixteenth and seventeenth centuries. Because it included distances out to 20-30 miles or more and was also vague, countries came under pressure to adopt more precise and limited measures. The "cannon-shot" rule, as the name implies, held that a sovereign could exercise authority over the sea that fell within a cannon's range from the shore. Delimitation was easy, if somewhat varied, ranging from a few thousand feet to generally less than three miles.

The third method, the marine league, was the first consistent method of delimitation. Equal to three nautical miles, it had the advantage of being precise and relatively easy to determine. It also was related to the cannon-shot rule, because three miles was considered by some then as the maximum theoretical range of a cannon.

During the nineteenth century Great Britain, as the dominant naval power, proposed and repeatedly sought a three-mile limit. It concluded a number of treaties, beginning with the British-United States Convention of 1818, that called for three-mile delimitation. By the close of the nineteenth century, the three-mile limit was generally accepted by the major powers as the breadth of the territorial sea, but it was never unanimously accepted. The Scandinavian countries consistently claimed four miles, and several other states claimed larger zones for specific purposes.

The two World Wars and the period between undermined the three-mile limit. First, during the hostilities a number of countries declared vast "neutrality zones" in order to assure their security. For many purposes, these neutrality zones were the equivalent of territorial seas. Second, advances in technology made the three-mile limit economically and militarily too narrow for the waters of the developed states. Finally, the newly independent nations concluded that the three-mile limit was too narrow. Among other reasons, they resented the situation where developed states (and multinational corporations) exploited the resources just outside the three-mile limit.

At the 1958 Geneva Conference that led to the Convention on the Territorial Sea and Contiguous Zones, the negotiators could not agree on the breadth of the territorial sea, even though they developed careful rules regarding the drawing of baselines and other methods for measurements. There was still substantial support for a three-mile width but also considerable support for six miles. Lacking sufficient consensus, the Convention was silent on this fundamental issue. The 1960 Geneva Conference then came within one vote of approving a compromise that the United States and Canada proposed. It would have provided for a six-mile territorial sea plus a six-mile exclusive fisheries zone.

Pressures continued to increase for a breadth greater than three miles, and even greater than six miles. In 1970 the United States officially announced its support for the 12-mile limit in the LOS negotiations. (The Soviet Union had adopted such a limit soon after its Revolution of 1918.) By 1982, a majority of nations had acquiesced in the 12-mile limit for the territorial sea, which is what the LOS Convention provides.

In December 1988, President Reagan formally proclaimed that the United States was extending its territorial sea to 12 nautical miles. The proclamation said that the 12 miles were "the limits permitted by international law." Ironically, although Reagan had balked at signing the LOS Convention (for reasons discussed later), the proclamation cited the Convention as reflecting many rules of international law. Indeed, the 12-mile limit is now generally viewed throughout the world as customary international law.

Note

Although President Reagan issued a formal Proclamation and Executive Order in 1988 extending the territorial sea to 12 nautical miles, not all U.S. laws have been amended or interpreted to reflect this. In United States v. One Big Six Wheel, 166 F.3d 498 (2d Cir. 1999), the court denied the forfeiture of one Big Six Wheel, a gambling device on the *Liberty I,* a seagoing vessel that operates gambling cruises-to-nowhere from Brooklyn, New York. The owners operated the Big Six Wheel and other gambling devices while the *Liberty I* was situated more than 3, but fewer than 12, nautical miles from the U.S. shore. The court concluded that the Gambling Ship Act, as amended in 1994, did not clearly enough cover the area from 3 to 12 nautical miles that the criminal forfeiture provision was applicable. As for the 1988 Presidential Proclamation, the court noted that it explicitly limited its application by declaring that "nothing in this Proclamation . . . extends or otherwise alters existing Federal or State law or any jurisdiction, rights, legal interest, or obligations derived therefrom. . . ."

On the other hand, the same U.S. Court of Appeals ruled that meaning of "high seas" in the Death on the High Seas Act (DOSHA) of 1920 would be modified by the Presidential Proclamation to extend to 12 miles, rather than the 3 miles applicable when the law was passed. In In re Air Crash Off Long Island, 209 F.3d 200 (2d Cir. 2000), the plaintiffs were family members or administrators of the estates of some of the 230 passengers who died in the crash of TWA Flight 800 on July 17, 1996. The crash occurred approximately eight n.m. south of Long Island. Defendants TWA and Boeing contended that DOHSA is the exclusive law governing all damage claims because the deaths occurred over the high seas, meaning more than three miles from shore. The implication of DOHSA's application would be that nonpecuniary losses could not be recovered because DOHSA excludes damages from loss of society, survivor's grief, and any pre-death pain and suffering of a decedent as well as punitive damages.

The court reasoned that the impact of the Proclamation had to be assessed on a statute-by-statute basis. Analyzing the statutory language, legislative history, and relevant case law, the court concluded that the plaintiffs' interpretation that the "high seas" in the statute now only began beyond 12 n.m. better reflected the "meaning and purpose" of DOHSA.

4.   Rules for Passage

a.   Innocent Passage

The Corfu Channel Case (United Kingdom v. Albania)

Intl. Court of Justice
[1949] I.C.J. 1 (Merits)

[In May 1946 Albania fired on two British cruisers as they passed through the Corfu Channel. The British protested. Albania claimed that the British had failed to request Albanian permission for passage through the Channel, part of which included Albanian territorial waters. Consequently, Albania considered itself justified in firing. After a series of diplomatic notes, the British decided to reassert their right of innocent passage by sending a squadron of warships through the Channel. On October 22, 1946, while passing through the Channel, the squadron ran into a minefield, and two ships were damaged. In November the British Navy swept the Channel, including Albanian territorial waters, for mines.

The British government instituted this action to recover compensation for the ships. By special agreement, the Court considered only whether Albania was liable for the damage to the ships and whether British passage through Albanian territorial waters was a violation of Albanian sovereignty. After finding Albania liable for the mining of the Channel, the Court considered the various British passages.]

In the second part of the Special Agreement, the following question is submitted to the Court:

> (2) Has the United Kingdom under international law violated the sovereignty of the Albanian People's Republic by reason of the acts of the Royal Navy in Albanian waters on the 22nd October and on the 12th and 13th November 1946 and is there any duty to give satisfaction?

The Court will first consider whether the sovereignty of Albania was violated by reason of the acts of the British Navy in Albanian waters on October 22nd, 1946. . . .

It is, in the opinion of the Court, generally recognized and in accordance with international custom that States in time of peace have a right to send their warships through straits used for international navigation between two parts of the high seas without the previous authorization of a coastal State, provided that the passage is *innocent*. Unless otherwise prescribed in an international convention, there is no right for a coastal State to prohibit such passage through straits in time of peace.

The Albanian Government does not dispute that the North Corfu Channel is a strait in the geographical sense; but it denies that this Channel belongs to the class of international highways through which a right of passage exists, on the grounds that it is only of secondary importance and not even a necessary route between two parts of the high seas, and that it is used almost exclusively for local traffic to and from the ports of Corfu and Saranda.

It may be asked whether the test is to be found in the volume of traffic passing through the Strait or in its greater or lesser importance for international navigation. But in the opinion of the Court the decisive criterion is rather its geographical situation as connecting two parts of the high seas and the fact of its being used for international navigation. Nor can it be decisive that this Strait is not a necessary route between two parts of the high seas, but only an alternative passage between the Aegean and the Adriatic Seas. It has nevertheless been a useful route for international maritime traffic. . . . The Court is further informed that the British Navy has regularly used this Channel for eighty years or more, and that it has also been used by the navies of other States.

One fact of particular importance is that the North Corfu Channel constitutes a frontier between Albania and Greece, that a part of it is wholly within the territorial waters of these States, and that the Strait is of special importance to Greece by reason of the traffic to and from the port of Corfu.

Having regard to these various considerations, the Court has arrived at the conclusion that the North Corfu Channel should be considered as belonging to the class of international highways through which passage cannot be prohibited by a coastal State in time of peace.

On the other hand, it is a fact that the two coastal States did not maintain normal relations, that Greece had made territorial claims precisely with regard to a part of Albanian territory bordering on the Channel, that Greece had declared that she considered herself technically in a state of war with Albania, and that Albania, invoking the danger of Greek incursions, had considered it necessary to take certain measures of vigilance in this region. The Court is of opinion that Albania, in view of these exceptional circumstances, would have been justified in issuing regulations in respect of the passage of warships through the Strait, but not in prohibiting such passage or in subjecting it to the requirement of special authorization.

For these reasons the Court is unable to accept the Albanian contention that the Government of the United Kingdom has violated Albanian sovereignty by sending the warships through the Strait without having obtained the previous authorization of the Albanian Government.

In these circumstances, it is unnecessary to consider the more general question, much debated by the Parties, whether States under international law have a right to send warships in time of peace through territorial waters not included in a strait.

The Albanian Government has further contended that the sovereignty of Albania was violated because the passage of the British warships on October 22nd, 1946, was not an *innocent passage*. The reasons advanced in support of this contention may be summed up as follows: The passage was not an ordinary passage, but a political mission; the ships were manoeuvring and sailing in diamond combat formation with soldiers on board; the position of the guns was not consistent with innocent passage; the vessels passed with crews at action stations; the number of the ships and their armament surpassed what was necessary in order to attain their object and showed an intention to intimidate and not merely to pass; the ships had received orders to observe and report upon the coastal defences and this order was carried out.

It is shown by the Admiralty telegram of September 21st, cited above, and admitted by the United Kingdom Agent, that the object of sending the warships through the Strait was not only to carry out a passage for purposes of navigation, but also to test Albania's attitude. As mentioned above, the Albanian Government, on May 15th, 1946, tried to impose by means of gunfire its view with regard to the passage. As the exchange of diplomatic notes did not lead to any clarification, the Government of the United Kingdom wanted to ascertain by other means whether the Albanian Government would maintain its illegal attitude and again impose its view by firing at passing ships. The legality of this measure taken by the Government of the United Kingdom cannot be disputed, provided that it was carried out in a manner consistent with the requirements of international law. The "mission" was designed to affirm a right which had been unjustly denied. The Government of the United Kingdom was not bound to abstain from exercising its right of passage, which the Albanian Government had illegally denied.

It remains, therefore, to consider whether the *manner* in which the passage was carried out was consistent with the principle of innocent passage and to examine the various contentions of the Albanian Government in so far as they appear to be relevant.

When the Albanian coastguards at St. George's Monastery reported that the British warships were sailing in combat formation and were manoeuvring, they must have been under a misapprehension. It is shown by the evidence that the ships were not proceeding in combat formation, but in line, one after the other, and that they were not manoeuvring until after the first explosion. Their movements thereafter were due to the explosions and were made necessary in order to save human life and the mined ships. It is shown by the evidence of witnesses that the contention that soldiers were on board must be due to a misunderstanding probably arising from the fact that the two cruisers carried their usual detachment of marines.

It is known from the above-mentioned order issued by the British Admiralty on August 10th, 1946, that ships, when using the North Corfu Strait, must pass with armament in fore and aft position. That this order was carried out during the passage on October 22nd is stated by the Commander-in-Chief, Mediterranean, in a telegram of October 26th to the Admiralty. The guns were, he reported, "trained fore and aft, which is their normal position at sea in peace time, and were not loaded." It is confirmed by the commanders of *Saumarez* and *Volage* that the guns were in this position before the explosions. The navigating officer on board *Mauritius* explained that all guns on that cruiser were in their normal stowage position. The main guns were in the line of the ship, and the anti-aircraft guns were pointing outwards and up into the air, which is the normal position of these guns on a cruiser both in harbour and at sea. In the light of this evidence, the Court cannot accept the

Albanian contention that the position of the guns was inconsistent with the rules of innocent passage.

In the above-mentioned telegram of October 26th, the Commander-in-Chief reported that the passage "was made with ships at action stations in order that they might be able to retaliate quickly if fired upon again." In view of the firing from the Albanian battery on May 15th, this measure of precaution cannot, in itself, be regarded as unreasonable. But four warships — two cruisers and two destroyers — passed in this manner, with crews at action stations, ready to retaliate quickly if fired upon. They passed one after another through this narrow channel, close to the Albanian coast, at a time of political tension in this region. The intention must have been, not only to test Albania's attitude, but at the same time to demonstrate such force that she would abstain from firing again on passing ships. Having regard, however, to all the circumstances of the case, as described above, the Court is unable to characterize these measures taken by the United Kingdom authorities as a violation of Albania's sovereignty. . . .

In addition to the passage of the United Kingdom warships on October 22nd, 1946, the second question in the Special Agreement relates to the acts of the Royal Navy in Albanian waters on November 12th and 13th, 1946. This is the minesweeping operation called "Operation Retail" by the Parties during the proceedings. This name will be used in the present Judgment.

After the explosions of October 22nd, the United Kingdom Government sent a note to the Albanian Government, in which it announced its intention to sweep the Corfu Channel shortly. The Albanian reply, which was received in London on October 31st, stated that the Albanian Government would not give its consent to this unless the operation in question took place outside Albanian territorial waters. Meanwhile, at the United Kingdom Government's request, the International Central Mine Clearance Board decided, in a resolution of November 1st, 1946, that there should be a further sweep of the Channel, subject to Albania's consent. The United Kingdom Government having informed the Albanian Government, in a communication of November 10th, that the proposed sweep would take place on November 12th, the Albanian Government replied on the 11th, protesting against this "unilateral decision of His Majesty's Government." It said it did not consider it inconvenient that the British fleet should undertake the sweeping of the channel of navigation, but added that, before sweeping was carried out, it considered it indispensable to decide what area of the sea should be deemed to constitute this channel, and proposed the establishment of a Mixed Commission for the purpose. It ended by saying that any sweeping undertaken without the consent of the Albanian Government outside the channel thus constituted, i.e., inside Albanian territorial waters where foreign warships have no reason to sail, could only be considered as a deliberate violation of Albanian territory and sovereignty.

After this exchange of notes, "Operation Retail" took place on November 12th and 13th. Commander Mestre, of the French Navy, was asked to attend as observer, and was present at the sweep on November 13th. The operation was carried out under the protection of an important covering force composed of an aircraft carrier, cruisers and other war vessels. This covering force remained throughout the operation at a certain distance to the west of the Channel, except for the frigate *St. Bride's Bay*, which was stationed in the Channel south-east of Cape Kiephali. The sweep began in the morning of November 13th, at about 9 o'clock, and ended in the afternoon near nightfall. The area swept was in Albanian territorial waters, and within the limits of the channel previously swept.

The United Kingdom Government does not dispute that "Operation Retail" was carried out against the clearly expressed wish of the Albanian Government. It recognizes that the operation had not the consent of the international mine clearance organizations, that it could not be justified as the exercise of a right of innocent passage, and lastly that, in principle, international law does not allow a State to assemble a large number of warships in the territorial waters of another State and to carry out mine-sweeping in those waters. The United Kingdom Government states that the operation was one of extreme urgency, and that it considered itself entitled to carry it out without anybody's consent. . . . These explosions were suspicious; they raised a question of responsibility.

Accordingly, this was the ground on which the United Kingdom Government chose to establish its main line of defence. According to that Government, the *corpora delicti* must be secured as quickly as possible, for fear they should be taken away, without leaving traces, by the authors of the minelaying or by the Albanian authorities. This justification took two distinct forms in the United Kingdom Government's arguments. It was presented first as a new and special application of the theory of intervention, by means of which the State intervening would secure possession of evidence in the territory of another State, in order to submit it to an international tribunal and thus facilitate its task.

The Court cannot accept such a line of defence. The Court can only regard the alleged right of intervention as the manifestation of a policy of force, such as has, in the past, given rise to most serious abuses and such as cannot, whatever be the present defects in international organization, find a place in international law. Intervention is perhaps still less admissible in the particular form it would take here; for, from the nature of things, it would be reserved for the most powerful States, and might easily lead to perverting the administration of international justice itself.

The United Kingdom Agent, in his speech in reply, has further classified "Operation Retail" among methods of self-protection or self-help. The Court cannot accept this defence either. Between independent States, respect for territorial sovereignty is an essential foundation of international relations. The Court recognizes that the Albanian Government's complete failure to carry out its duties after the explosions, and the dilatory nature of its diplomatic notes, are extenuating circumstances for the action of the United Kingdom Government. But to ensure respect for international law, of which it is the organ, the Court must declare that the action of the British Navy constituted a violation of Albanian sovereignty.

This declaration is in accordance with the request made by Albania through her Counsel, and is in itself appropriate satisfaction. . . .

For these reasons, the Court,

by fourteen votes to two, gives judgment that the United Kingdom did not violate the sovereignty of the People's Republic of Albania by reason of the acts of the British Navy in Albanian waters on October 22nd, 1946; and

unanimously, gives judgment that by reason of the acts of the British Navy in Albanian waters in the course of the Operation of November 12th and 13th, 1946, the United Kingdom violated the sovereignty of the People's Republic of

Albania, and that this declaration by the Court constitutes in itself appropriate satisfaction.

Questions

1. Are the articles in the LOS Convention in general accord with the decision in The Corfu Channel Case? (See Articles 17-32 regarding innocent passage through a state's territorial sea, especially Articles 17-20.)

2. Under Articles 19-20 can a Russian surface warship traveling between Russia and Cuba sail along the Eastern seaboard of the United States at about ten miles from shore? Can a submerged Russian submarine accompany the surface warship? Can a North Korean "fishing trawler" loaded with electronic gear loiter at four miles off the U.S. naval base in Honolulu, Hawaii? At 14 miles?

3. Faced with the following proposed activities in its territorial sea, can the United States, under the LOS Convention, bar a Japanese ship carrying plutonium from Japan to another country; prevent a Liberian ship from cruising up and down the coast while it operates a gambling casino; require all tankers to have double-hulled bottoms; and prohibit ship captains and anyone else steering a ship from having more than .02 percent alcohol in their blood?

4. In September 1989, U.S. Secretary of State James A. Baker and Soviet Foreign Minister Eduard A. Shevardnadze signed a joint statement on a Uniform Interpretation of Rules of International Law Governing Innocent Passage. It provides, in part:

1. The relevant rules of international law governing innocent passage of ships in the territorial sea are stated in the 1982 United Nations Convention on Law of the Sea (Convention of 1982), particularly in Part II, Section 3.

2. All ships, including warships, regardless of cargo, armament or means of propulsion, enjoy the right of innocent passage through the territorial sea in accordance with international law, for which neither prior notification nor authorization is required.

3. Article 19 of the Convention of 1982 sets out in paragraph 2 an exhaustive list of activities that would render passage not innocent. A ship passing through the territorial sea that does not engage in any of those activities is in innocent passage.

4. A coastal State which questions whether the particular passage of a ship through its territorial sea is innocent shall inform the ship of the reason why it questions the innocence of the passage, and provide the ship an opportunity to clarify its intentions or correct its conduct in a reasonably short period of time.

5. Ships exercising the right of innocent passage shall comply with all laws and regulations of the coastal State adopted in conformity with relevant rules of international law as reflected in Articles 21, 22, 23 and 25 of the Convention of 1982. These include the laws and regulations requiring ships exercising the right of innocent passage through its territorial sea to use such sea lanes and traffic separation schemes as it may prescribe where needed to protect safety of navigation. In areas where no such sea lanes or traffic separation schemes have been prescribed, ships nevertheless enjoy the right of innocent passage.

6. Such laws and regulations of the coastal State may not have the practical effect of denying or impairing the exercise of the right of innocent passage as set forth in Article 24 of the Convention of 1982.

7. If a warship engages in conduct which violates such law or regulations or renders its passage not innocent and does not take corrective action upon request, the

coastal State may require it to leave the territorial sea, as set forth in Article 30 of the Convention of 1982. In such case the warship shall do so immediately.

8. Without prejudice to the exercise of rights of coastal and flag States, all differences which may arise regarding a particular case of passage of ships through the territorial sea shall be settled through diplomatic channels or other agreed means.

What seems to be the purpose of the joint statement? Is it relevant that it was signed along with other agreements at a major meeting between Baker and Shevardnadze and that both the United States and the Soviet Union were generally making efforts to improve their relations during this period and that there had been some tense encounters between the ships of the two countries' navies?

Note also the heavy reliance on the LOS Convention. Since neither country had ratified the Convention as the time of the joint statement, how do you explain this reliance on the Convention?

b. Passage Through International Straits and Archipelagic Sea Lanes

Besides the general rules for innocent passage in the territorial sea, the 1982 Convention recognized the need for special rules for passage through international straits and through the waters of the archipelagic states. These special rules allow less control by the coastal states over passing vessels than does innocent passage, but they do not give ships the same rights as they have on the high seas. As Professors Churchill and Lowe report:

> In the years between UNCLOS I and the close of UNCLOS III many States made claims to wider coastal jurisdiction. . . . While these claims were not inconsistent with the preservation of rights of passage through international straits, they signalled a growing reluctance to regard passing foreign ships as beyond the jurisdictional reach of coastal States whose security, environmental or economic interests these ships might adversely affect. The major maritime States, on the other hand, considered that their economic well-being and security — particularly in relation to the deployment, and pursuit, of submarines some of which now carried strategic nuclear missiles — depended upon continuing guarantees of passage through international straits such as Dover, Gibraltar, Hormuz, Bab el Mandeb and Malacca. A compromise was reached, based on the creation of two new legal rights of passage: "transit passage" through international straits [discussed above] . . . and "archipelagic sea lanes passage" through archipelagic waters. . . . Both new categories allow less coastal control over passing vessels than does innocent passage, but both also fall far short of granting the same freedom of navigation as would have existed had the waters of the straits constituted high seas.
>
> The regime of transit passage applies to "straits which are used for international navigation between one part of the high seas or an exclusive economic zone and another part of the high seas or an exclusive economic zone" [LOS Convention, Article 37]. . . .
>
> Transit passage is the exercise of freedom of navigation and overflight solely for the continuous and expeditious transit of the strait between one area of high seas or economic zone and another, or in order to enter or leave a State bordering the strait [Article 38(2)]. While there is no criterion of "innocence" to be satisfied, ships and aircraft exercising this right are bound to refrain from the threat or use of force . . . against States bordering the straits . . . [Article 39(1)(b)]. Moreover, there is an obligation to refrain from any activities other than those incidental to their normal modes of

continuous and expeditious transit unless rendered necessary by *force majeure* or distress [Article 39(1)(c)]....

... As far as submarines are concerned, their apparently common practice of transiting some international straits while submerged seems to be recognised in the requirement that passing vessels engage only in activities "incident to their *normal mode* of continuous and expeditious transit" [Article 39(1)(c); emphasis added]....

[Regarding archipelagic sea lanes,] [t]he ships of all States enjoy in archipelagic waters the same right of innocent passage as they enjoy in the territorial sea [Article 52(1)].... In addition, foreign ships and aircraft enjoy the rather more extensive right of "archipelagic sea lanes passage" in sea lanes and air routes designated by the archipelagic State: sea lanes must be designated in consultation with the "competent international organisation" (by which presumably is meant the [International Maritime Organization]) [Article 53].... Archipelagic sea-lanes passage is essentially the same as transit passage through straits.... [R.R. Churchill & A.V. Lowe, The law of the sea 104–107, 109, 127 (3d ed. 1999).]

D. CONTIGUOUS ZONES AND HOT PURSUIT

The existence of a contiguous zone is now generally accepted in international law. This is a zone adjacent to the territorial sea where the coastal state is allowed to enforce certain laws, such as customs and immigration. Article 33 of the LOS Convention provides that the contiguous zone may not extend more than 24 nautical miles from the baselines. (This actually makes the contiguous zone 12 miles wide because the territorial sea occupies the first 12 miles from the baselines, and because the contiguous zone is "contiguous," or adjacent, to the territorial sea.)

The historical development of this zone in international law and current questions about what activities are covered in the zone are worth examining. For example, Article 24 of the 1958 Convention on the Territorial Sea and the Contiguous Zone provided for a contiguous zone no wider than 12 miles from the baseline, with the width of the intervening territorial sea undefined.

A related concept that also has general international acceptance is the right of hot pursuit. This allows a coastal state to pursue into the high seas a foreign ship that the coastal state has reason to believe has violated its laws either within the contiguous zone or within its internal waters or territorial sea. The scope of this right is also worth examining.

While the existence of the contiguous zone was well established in international law, the present form of the zone is of recent origin.

Vaughan Lowe, The Development of the Concept of the Contiguous Zone

52 Brit. Y.B. Intl. L. 109 (1981)

[T]he modern contiguous zone is the result of the coming together of distinct kinds of claim to maritime jurisdiction identifiable in State practice. It was a gradual process, and it would be an oversimplification to ascribe a single date to the emergence of the concept or to its acceptance in customary international law. Stages in the development of the concept of the contiguous zone can, however, be identified. Thus, a jurisdictional zone distinct from the belt of maritime territory is clearly identifiable in nineteenth-century Latin American practice, and a rule of regional international law allowed the establishment of such zones. Most other States at that time either drew no clear distinction between territorial seas and other claims to maritime jurisdiction or, like Britain, drew the distinction but denied that such extended jurisdictional zones were permissible under customary international law. The distinction between the juridical status of the territorial sea and of the zones of limited jurisdiction was clarified during the 1920s, as first the enforcement of United States' "liquor laws" beyond the three-mile limit, and then the preparations for the Hague Conference, focused attention on the issue. By this time the contiguous zone had achieved a substantial degree of conceptual coherence, although there was still — and indeed there remains today — some uncertainty concerning the question of the extension of legislative, as opposed to enforcement, jurisdiction to the zone. . . .

In the years following the Hague Conference [1930] an increasing number of States either claimed contiguous zones of their own or abandoned their persistent objection to the zones of other States. In this way the concept, refined by the attentions of jurists and participants at the Hague Conference, developed into a rule of international law generally recognized among States. . . .

SUMMARY OF FOREIGN PRACTICE 1850-1930

To summarize this practice, it can be said that, apart from the generally accepted rights of hot pursuit and self-defence, and the doctrine of constructive presence, which afforded some extension of the *enforcement* jurisdiction of coastal States, there was no commonly adopted position. Some States adopted the same position as Great Britain, and held the three-mile limit to be the only limit of maritime jurisdiction. Others took a different view; some claimed contiguous zones beyond the territorial sea, yet others adopted a multiplicity of zones, but in both cases claims to jurisdiction for defence and customs purposes stood out as the most extensive *ratione loci*. While there was certainly no unanimity on the question of the contiguous zone, it was evident that a considerable number of States accepted the right to exercise control over foreign ships, at least for customs and defence purposes, beyond the marine league and beyond the limit within which general jurisdiction was exercised. . . .

. . . But in the years after the Second World War, no doubt under the joint impetus of the Truman proclamations, and the more general appreciation of the value of marine resources which had led to the conclusion of several international fishery agreements, many States started adding fisheries to the list of protected interests. There is no evidence to suggest that fishery zones were regarded as different in their juridical nature from other zones, although the exigencies of fishery management made it expedient to give fisheries separate treatment at the Geneva Conference. . . .

THE GENEVA CONFERENCE . . .

The final [1958] treaty text on the contiguous zone has a plain meaning when its words are read in their ordinary sense. This is that the "crimes" in relation to which the powers of prevention and punishment are given to the coastal State must be committed within the territory or territorial sea of the coastal State. . . .

Unfortunately, it is impossible to resolve any remaining doubts on this point by reference to the subsequent practice of States. That practice is divergent, and its analysis is complicated by the emergence of claims to pollution, defence and economic zones going beyond the scope of the 1958 contiguous zone article. . . .

That [1958] article has been incorporated verbatim, and without significant discussion, into successive texts prepared by the Third United Nations Conference on the Law of the Sea. Like many other formulae in international law, lack of agreement upon its meaning has not affected its durability. Whatever the shortcomings it might have as a treaty provision, the 1958 formula succeeded in bringing together a number of different approaches to maritime jurisdiction. Its development assisted both the crystallization of the territorial sea into a zone of sovereignty, and consequently of plenary jurisdiction, distinct from wider and more limited jurisdictional claims, and also the refinement of the concept of jurisdiction by drawing attention to the separability of enforcement and legislative jurisdiction. It remains a useful device, allowing a more sophisticated analysis and flexible accommodation of the competing interests of coastal and "maritime" States than could otherwise be achieved.

LOS Convention

Article 33. Contiguous Zone

1. In a zone contiguous to its territorial sea, described as the contiguous zone, the coastal State may exercise the control necessary to:
    (a) prevent infringement of its customs, fiscal, immigration or sanitary laws and regulations within its territory or territorial sea;
    (b) punish infringement of the above laws and regulations committed within its territory or territorial sea.
2. The contiguous zone may not extend beyond 24 nautical miles from the baselines from which the breadth of the territorial sea is measured.

Notes and Questions

1. In a major U.S. case on smuggling and jurisdictional issues, decided in 1925, the U.S. district court noted that the territorial sea then was a three-mile zone. It also relied on a U.S. statute that extended U.S. jurisdiction to 12 nautical miles from the coast for smuggling. The court then dismissed libels against a seized schooner and its cargo of whiskey, because the whiskey had been unloaded onto another vessel at about 19 miles away from the shore. The Over the Top (Schroeder v. Bissell), 5 F.2d 838 (D. Conn. 1925).

2. The language of Article 24 of the 1958 Geneva Convention on the Territorial Sea and Contiguous Zone (in the Documentary Supplement) is essentially identical to LOS Convention Article 33(1), quoted above. What, though, is an important difference between the two? What was the boundary on the landward side under the 1958 Convention?

3. What appear to be the principal purposes for states recognizing the existence of a contiguous zone? Why are some laws explicitly included?

4. Would you be for a wider or narrower contiguous zone? Why?

5. In August 1999, President Clinton extended the boundaries of the contiguous zone of the United States, a zone of waters "contiguous to the territorial sea of the United States," to 24 n.m. He specifically noted that this was "[i]n accordance with international law, reflected in the applicable provisions of the 1982 Convention on the Law of the Sea." See Presidential Proclamation No. 7219, 64 Fed. Reg. 48,701 (Aug. 2, 1999).

6. *The right of hot pursuit.* A ship engaged in illegal activities in the contiguous zone or even closer to the coast might try to flee to the high seas. As noted earlier, it is now generally recognized in international law that the coastal state can give chase under certain conditions. (See LOS Convention Article 111.) When can the coastal state pursue the foreign ship? When can it not?

E. THE EXCLUSIVE ECONOMIC ZONE AND THE CONTINENTAL SHELF

1. *Historical Background*

Under the regime established in the LOS Convention, a state exercises substantial sovereignty in the area known as the exclusive economic zone (EEZ). The EEZ is an area beyond and adjacent to the territorial sea, with a breadth of up to 200 miles from the baseline, in which the coastal state may exercise certain "sovereign rights" over living and nonliving resources. (See Articles 56-57 in the Documentary Supplement. Assuming a 12-mile-wide territorial sea, the EEZ could be up to 188 nautical miles wide.)

The EEZ is in many ways the merger of two previous concepts — the continental shelf regime and the fisheries regime — although the LOS Convention maintains a separate section concerning the continental shelf. The Convention also expands on the two concepts by granting the coastal state rights to exercise jurisdiction with respect to marine scientific research and preservation of the marine environment.

An important balance in the EEZ is granting to the coastal state a variety of rights to the resources in the zone, while protecting the rights of other states to navigate through and over the EEZ, to fish the surplus catch, and to conduct research subject to certain limits. Articles 56 and 57 are carefully balanced by Articles 58 and 87 and by the dispute settlement arrangements provided for in the Convention. (Dispute settlement is discussed in Section G, below.)

A brief history of the two concepts of the continental shelf and a fisheries zone helps explain the EEZ. Prior to World War II, there was no affirmative international law permitting states to claim jurisdiction over the resources of the seas or seabed outside their territorial seas. Several states, particularly in Latin America, had claimed wide "patrimonial" seas, which were essentially the equivalent of the territorial sea. In addition, the practice of the United Kingdom was that countries could claim seabed resources when there was an effective claim and actual exploitation. The customary international law, however, was that a state's sovereignty and jurisdiction almost always stopped at the outer edge of its territorial sea.

The Truman Proclamations of 1945 were the "first positive law on this subject," according to the ICJ in the North Sea Continental Shelf Cases ([1969] I.C.J. 3). President Truman claimed major new rights for the United States with regard to its continental shelf and fisheries. While similar or greater claims had been made by other countries, the Truman Proclamations were the first such unilateral claim by a major maritime power. Their immediate impact was great, with a number of countries following the U.S. example. By 1958, 20 countries had made similar unilateral claims to their continental shelves. Even more states claimed a right to manage fisheries outside their territorial waters.

The Truman Proclamations

White House Press Release of Sept. 29, 1945
13 Dept. of State Bull. 485-486 (July-Dec. 1945)

The President issued two proclamations on September 28 asserting the jurisdiction of the United States over the natural resources of the continental shelf under the high seas contiguous to the coasts of the United States and its territories, and providing for the establishment of conservation zones for the protection of fisheries in certain areas of the high seas contiguous to the United States. . . .

Policy of the United States with Respect to the Natural Resources of the Subsoil and Sea Bed of the Continental Shelf

By the President of the United States of America

A PROCLAMATION

Whereas the Government of the United States of America, aware of the long range world-wide need for new sources of petroleum and other minerals, holds the view that efforts to discover and make available new supplies of these resources should be encouraged; and

Whereas its competent experts are of the opinion that such resources underlie many parts of the continental shelf off the coasts of the United States of America, and that with modern technological progress their utilization is already practicable or will become so at an early date; and

Whereas recognized jurisdiction over these resources is required in the interest of their conservation and prudent utilization when and as development is undertaken; and . . .

Whereas it is the view of the Government of the United States that the exercise of jurisdiction over the natural resources of the subsoil and sea bed of the continental shelf by the contiguous nation is reasonable and just, since the effectiveness of measures to utilize or conserve these resources would be contingent upon cooperation and protection from the shore, since the continental shelf may be regarded as an extension of the land-mass of the coastal nation and thus naturally appurtenant to it, since these resources frequently form a seaward extension of a pool or deposit lying within the territory, and since self-protection compels the coastal nation to keep close watch over activities off its shores which are of the nature necessary for utilization of these resources . . . .

Now, therefore, I, Harry S Truman, President of the United States of America, do hereby proclaim the following policy of the United States of America with respect to the natural resources of the subsoil and sea bed of the continental shelf.

Having concern for the urgency of conserving and prudently utilizing its natural resources, the Government of the United States regards the natural resources of the subsoil and sea bed of the continental shelf beneath the high seas but contiguous to the coasts of the United States as appertaining to the United States, subject to its jurisdiction and control. In cases where the continental shelf extends to the shores of another State, or is shared with an adjacent State, the boundary shall be determined by the United States and the State concerned in accordance with equitable principles. The character as high seas of the waters above the continental shelf and the right to their free and unimpeded navigation are in no way thus affected.

Policy of the United States with Respect to Coastal Fisheries in Certain Areas of the High Seas

By the President of the United States of America

A PROCLAMATION

. . . Now, therefore, I, Harry S Truman, . . . do hereby proclaim the following policy of the United States of America with respect to coastal fisheries in certain areas of the high seas:

In view of the pressing need for conservation and protection of fishery resources, the Government of the United States regards it as proper to establish conservation zones in those areas of the high seas contiguous to the coasts of the United States wherein fishing activities have been or in the future may be developed and maintained on a substantial scale. Where such activities have been or shall hereafter be developed and maintained by its nationals alone, the United States regards it as proper to establish explicitly bounded conservation zones in which fishing activities shall be subject to the regulation and control of the United States. Where such activities have been or shall hereafter be legitimately developed and maintained jointly by nationals of the United States and nationals of other States, explicitly bounded conservation zones may be established under agreements between the United States and such other States; and all fishing activities in such zones shall be subject to regulation and control as provided in such agreements. The right of any State to establish conservation zones off its shores in accordance with the above principles is conceded, provided that corresponding recognition is given to any fishing interests of nationals of the United States which may exist in such areas. The character as high seas of the areas in which such conservation zones are established and the right to their free and unimpeded navigation are in no way thus affected.

The U.S. Congress also addressed these issues. Sections (1) and (2) below were enacted in 1953; section (3) was enacted in 1978.

43 U.S.C. §1332

Congressional Declaration of Policy

It is hereby declared to be the policy of the United States that —

(1) the subsoil and seabed of the outer Continental Shelf appertain to the United States and are subject to its jurisdiction, control, and power of disposition as provided in this subchapter;

(2) this subchapter shall be construed in such a manner that the character of the waters above the outer Continental Shelf as high seas and the right to navigation and fishing therein shall not be affected;

(3) the outer Continental Shelf is a vital national resource reserve held by the Federal Government for the public, which should be made available for expeditious and orderly development, subject to environmental safeguards, in a manner which is consistent with the maintenance of competition and other national needs. . . .

2.   *After the Truman Proclamations*

By 1958, unilateral continental shelf claims were common and well established in customary international law. The first U.N. Conference on the Law of the Sea drafted the 1958 Convention on the Continental Shelf (in the Documentary Supplement). By 1974, when the first substantive meeting of the Third U.N. Conference on the Law of the Sea convened, 53 nations were contracting parties to the 1958 Convention.

The Convention on the Continental Shelf recognizes "sovereign rights" of coastal states over the natural resources of the continental shelf. "Natural resources" are the "mineral and other non-living resources of the seabed and subsoil together with living organisms belonging to sedentary species." These sovereign rights did not change the juridical nature of the water above. (Articles 1-3 in the Documentary Supplement.)

Defining the boundaries of the continental shelf encountered some difficulties, however. According to the Convention, the continental shelf encompassed the seabed and subsoil of areas outside and adjacent to the territorial sea, to a depth of 200 metres or, beyond that, to "where the depth of the superjacent waters admits of the exploitation of the natural resources of said areas." (Article 1.) As improvements in technology made it possible to exploit the seabed out to greater and greater distances, it became clear that the outer boundary of the continental shelf needed better definition.

Although a substantial number of nations never signed the Convention, in the North Sea Continental Shelf Cases, [1969] I.C.J. 3, the ICJ recognized that certain articles of the Convention had become customary international law. This case basically recognized that the coastal state could claim jurisdiction over resources throughout the natural prolongation of the continental landmass.

The LOS Convention substantially adopted the provisions of the Convention on the Continental Shelf. (See Articles 76-85 of the LOS Convention in the Documentary Supplement.) It provided, however, more precise limits on the outer boundary. Whenever it extends beyond 200 nautical miles (n.m.), the outer edge shall not exceed 350 miles from the baseline or 100 n.m. from the 2500-meter iso-bath, with some qualifications.[4]

More controversy has surrounded coastal state claims over fisheries beyond their territorial waters. The period after World War II has witnessed great advances in fishing technology and rising concern over the depletion of fishing stock. After the Truman Proclamations, a number of states unilaterally claimed broader and broader fisheries jurisdiction. During the 1960s, such unilateral claims were often accompanied by bilateral agreements with nations who traditionally fished in the newly claimed waters. The agreements typically allowed the noncoastal state to grad-ually reduce its fishing in the newly created fishing zone, rather than having to stop operations immediately.

A consensus proved difficult to reach at both the 1958 and 1960 U.N. confer-ences on the law of the sea. The developing nations were anxious to maintain con-trol over the fisheries adjacent to their territorial seas, while distant-water fishing na-tions, such as Japan, were just as anxious to maintain the "high seas" nature of fisheries. The 1958 Convention on the Territorial Sea and the Contiguous Zone pro-vided that the coastal state's sovereignty over the territorial sea, whose breadth was undefined, included sovereignty over the sea (and hence the fish in it). And, al-though the 1958 Convention on the High Seas defined "freedom of the high seas" to include freedom of fishing, it did not elaborate. (Article 2.)

The 1958 Convention on Fishing and Conservation of Living Resources of the High Seas generally recognized that all states had the right for their nationals to en-gage in fishing on the high seas. (Article 1.) However, the Convention recognized a coastal state's special interest in the "maintenance of productivity of living resources" in areas of the high seas adjacent to its territorial sea. (Article 6.) The Convention went so far as to allow these interested states to impose temporary regulations on fishing the adjacent high seas in specific circumstances. (Article 7.) The Convention, however, was primarily directed toward fostering bilateral agreements and estab-lished a dispute resolution system in case agreement could not be reached. Of the four 1958 conventions, this particular one has been ratified by the fewest number of parties (37 as of January 2003) and is generally considered the least effective.

The issue of a fisheries regime was on the agenda of the UNCLOS III when it convened in Caracas in 1974. At the same time, the ICJ issued its decision in the Fisheries Jurisdiction Case, [1974] I.C.J. 3, discussed below.

D.P. O'Connell, The International Law of the Sea

Vol. 1, 539-541 (1982)

5. THE FISHERIES JURISDICTION CASE

On 25 July 1974, the International Court of Justice handed down its judgment in the cases of United Kingdom v. Iceland and Germany v. Iceland. The United Kingdom and Germany had asked the court to declare that there was no foundation in

---

4. Article 76, §§4-7. The 2500-meter isobath refers to an imaginary line along the continental shelf that is at a constant depth of 2500 meters.

international law for the claim by Iceland to be able to extend its fisheries jurisdiction to fifty miles from the baseline of the territorial sea and also to decide some ancillary questions to the effect that Iceland could not unilaterally conserve the fisheries within this area or exclude British fishing vessels from it outside the twelve-mile limit. . . .

The starting-point for the Court's analysis is the passage in the Anglo-Norwegian Fisheries Case of 1951 in which the Court then said that "the delimitation of sea areas has always an international aspect; it cannot be dependent merely upon the will of the coastal State as expressed in its municipal law." This brought international law into the matter. The court reinforced this point by referring to the Geneva Convention on the High Seas which includes fishing among the freedoms of the sea. It pointed out, however, that the freedoms of the high seas are to be exercised, according to the Geneva Convention, "with reasonable regard to the interests of other states in their exercise of the freedom of the high seas." From this the Court concluded that fishing was not an absolute right.

The Court then proceeded to say that two concepts had crystallized in customary law since the Geneva Conference, namely:

(a)   the concept of the fishery zone up to twelve miles limit, and
(b)   the concept of preferential rights of fishing in adjacent waters of the coastal state beyond the distance of twelve miles.

It regarded the coastal state's absolute right of fishing as restricted to twelve miles, but, at the same time, it did not deny that the coastal state had the right to preferential access to fisheries beyond that limit. The problem which the case presents is whether preferential rights are in practice really distinguishable from absolute rights, and whether the court altogether ruled out unilateral claims beyond twelve miles.

As to the concept of preferential rights, the court based its assertion that these have become part of customary international law upon the history of that proposal at the Geneva Conferences in 1958 and 1960; upon the widespread acceptance of the concept of preferential rights by a large majority at those two conferences, thus showing overwhelming support for the idea that in certain special situations it was fair to recognize that the coastal state had preferential fishing rights; and upon the recognition of preferential rights in various bilateral and multilateral international agreements entered into since 1960. The Court's conclusion on preferential rights is that they are

> not compatible with the exclusion of all fishing activities of other states. A coastal state entitled to preferential rights is not free, unilaterally and according to its own uncontrolled discretion, to determine the extent of those rights. The characterisation of the coastal state's rights as preferential implies a certain priority, but cannot imply the extinction of current rights of other states, and particularly of a state which, like the applicant, has for many years been engaged in fishing in the waters in question, such fishing activity being important to the economy of the country concerned. The coastal state has to take into account and pay regard to other states, particularly when they have established an economic dependence on the same fishing grounds.

The emphasis thus put upon traditional fishing rights led the Court to declare that Iceland's unilateral action constituted an infringement of the principle in the

Convention on the High Seas which requires that all States, including coastal states, in exercising their freedom of fishing, pay reasonable regard to the interests of other States. . . .

The Court then indicated that the appropriate method of resolving the dispute was by negotiation on the basis of the facts that Iceland had preferential rights in the fishing, but the United Kingdom had an historic interest. The negotiations between the parties should aim to bring about an equitable apportionment of fishing resources beyond the twelve-mile limit.

On the face of it, the majority judgment appears to rule out the validity of unilateral claims to exclusive jurisdiction beyond twelve miles from the baseline of the territorial sea, irrespective of the fact that a considerable number of states have made such claims. However, five of the ten judges who subscribed to the majority opinion appended a separate joint opinion. These judges, all representing countries with claims beyond twelve miles, concurred in the majority judgment only for special limited reasons. They said that they did not regard the judgment as declaring that the extension of Iceland's jurisdiction was without foundation in international law and invalid. They said that the judgment was based on special grounds confined to the circumstances and characteristics of the present case and was not based on the main British legal contention that a customary rule of international law exists today imposing a general prohibition on extensions by States of their exclusive fisheries jurisdiction beyond twelve miles from their baselines. This was because there was not "an international usage to that effect sufficiently widespread and uniform as to constitute" evidence. . . .

This decision by the ICJ was criticized for the imprecision of the concept of preferential rights. The decision also did not help the Court's reputation among many of the developing countries, who were advocating broad coastal state jurisdiction for fisheries in the ongoing Law of the Sea conference. These countries were later joined by some developed countries, including Canada, Australia, and New Zealand. As Churchill and Lowe recount in The law of the sea 288 (3d ed. 1999):

> The USA, and initially Canada, proposed [another] approach to fisheries management based on the migratory characteristics of different species. This proposal categorised fish into sedentary, coastal (i.e. non-sedentary species which inhabit nutrient-rich areas adjacent to the coast), anadromous and wide-ranging species. Access to and management of the first three of these would vest exclusively or primarily in the coastal State, but wide-ranging species would be regulated by international fishery organisations. . . .
>
> The Law of the Sea Convention's provisions on fisheries generally reflect the first of these approaches [i.e., that initially pushed by the developing countries], although elements of the species approach can also be seen.

3. The Law of the Sea Convention and the Current Status of the Exclusive Economic Zone and Continental Shelf

The key provisions in the LOS Convention for the EEZ and fisheries are found in Part V, especially Articles 55-58 and 61-62. The major provisions for the continental shelf are in Part VI, particularly Articles 76-78 and 82. (See Documentary Supplement.)

The countries that have become parties of the LOS Convention effectively adopted the LOS provisions for their EEZs and continental shelves. In addition, as noted earlier, various economic and fishery zones and continental shelves have been declared. For example, although the United States is not a party to the LOS Convention, the Truman Proclamations in 1945 had made claims about the U.S. continental shelf and fisheries. In 1983, President Reagan proclaimed a U.S. EEZ and announced that the United States would treat those portions of the Convention delimiting various coastal state rights as customary international law on a reciprocal basis. (His statement is excerpted below.)

To give you an appreciation of the substantial area that is included in the exclusive economic zones, some figures are useful. The 200-mile limit encloses 36 percent of the world's total ocean area, or over 37.7 million square nautical miles. Moreover, this area contains about 90 percent of the presently exploitable fishery stock, 87 percent of known oil deposits, and 10 percent of the seabed manganese nodules.

Okinotorishima provides an illustration of the importance of the EEZ and the critical land that provides a basis for drawing the 200 n.m. boundaries. Where is Okinotorishima? The following news article reports the valiant efforts to keep it above water.

Clyde Haberman, Japanese Fight Invading Sea for Priceless Speck of Land

N.Y. Times, Jan. 4, 1988, at 1, col. 2

TOKYO, Jan. 3 — Japan, always a bit self-conscious about its limited size, has taken a giant step to keep itself from shrinking.

With an initial $75 million budget outlay approved last week, the Government hopes to prevent an insignificant dot of a Pacific island, 1,300 miles southwest of Tokyo, from being swallowed up by the sea.

Actually, to call Okinotorishima an island is somewhat akin to describing a row-boat as a vessel — true but grandiose. This island has eroded so badly over the years that it now consists of two barren rocks, neither of them much bigger at high tide than a kingsize bed.

But Okinotorishima, which means Offshore Bird Island, happens to be this country's southernmost point. And if it disappears beneath the sullen Pacific, as it is almost certain to do unless remedial action is taken, Japan will lose exclusive fishing and mineral rights to 163,000 square miles of ocean.

That, as Japanese officials are painfully aware, is an area bigger than Japan itself.

Without Okinotorishima, Japan's exclusive economic zone, which extends 200 nautical miles in all directions from its coastline, would be pushed far back — to either Minami Iwo Jima, an island nearly 400 miles to the northeast, or to Oki Daitojima, another island about the same distance to the northwest.

"Our mission is to conserve Japanese territory," said Masashi Waki, a civil engineer who will oversee the island rescue project for the Construction Ministry.

What Mr. Waki and his colleagues plan to do is to encase Okinotorishima's protruding rocks in large steel-and-concrete blocks that can absorb waves and thereby

At high tide, Okinotorishima is
about the size of two big beds.

keep the Japanese outpost afloat. The process is not unlike a dentist putting a cap
on a crumbling tooth, only this job is expected to take three years and cost up to
$240 million altogether. . . .

It is a coral island, known on some maps as Douglas Reef or Parece Vela. While
never inhabited, it has long been considered potentially important for meteorological observation.

Japan claimed it in 1931, lost it to the United States in 1945 at the end of World
War II, then regained it in 1968 when the Americans returned the Bonin Islands,
500 miles to the northeast. Anomalously, like many minuscule Japanese islands stud-
ding the northern Pacific, Okinotorishima falls under the jurisdiction of the faraway
Tokyo Metropolitan Government.

Many years ago, Japan thought about putting a weather station there, but
the idea never got off the ground. Now, officials are more concerned about
Okinotorishima's fishing rights and the possibility that the surrounding waters
contain seabed deposits of manganese and cobalt.

But none of that will mean much if the island disappears.

In Storms' Path

Its main problem is that it lies in an area that the Japanese have dubbed
Typhoon Ginza, a center of relentless storms that send 60-foot waves pounding
against Okinotorishima's twin boulders. By now, they barely endure, two bumps lying
1,400 yards apart and sticking no more than two feet out of the water at high tide.

Beneath the water's surface, they are supported by spindly columns of rock that
Government officials fear can collapse at any moment.

Mr. Waki's task of keeping the island above water has persuaded him to build
two circular blocks, each 160 feet in diameter, which will surround the deteriorating
rocks with protective layers of steel and concrete. In effect, they will create artificial
land, designed to stay at least three feet above the water at all times.

It will not be easy, Mr. Waki says.

The most difficult part will be transporting the necessary materials to the site. "This coral reef is in very deep sea," he said, "and it is particularly hard to reach at low tide."

Then, too, Mr. Waki added, there is no way to guarantee the durability of his work. "This should last 50 to 100 years, like any other steel and concrete work," he said. "But I really can't be sure. Out there on the water, conditions are really rough."

Notes and Questions

1. Does saving Okinotorishima automatically provide Japan the exclusive economic zone around it? Consider Article 121 (regime of islands), discussed earlier. See also Article 13.

2. As noted in the article above, Japan's investment of over $75 million was the first installment on a total investment of over $240 million to keep the island above water. In addition, the Japanese government regularly conducted scientific experiments on Okinotorishima, including a four-year study of the durability of a concrete-carbon fiber compound that could be used for building offshore oil rigs.

The investment apparently paid off. As of November 2002, it appears well accepted that Okinotorishima is a Japanese island to which Japan claims not only a territorial sea, but an EEZ.

3. Given the control over large ocean areas that the LOS Convention gives to any island (unless there are overlapping boundary claims, which are discussed below), rival national claims to an island or island grouping takes on potentially huge economic importance. For example, the Spratley Islands are small, largely uninhabited islands in the South China Sea whose surrounding waters many contain vast deposits of natural gas and oil. The islands are claimed, in whole or part, by China, Taiwan, the Philippines, Brunei, Malaysia, and Vietnam. The Chinese military has occupied some of the islands over the objections of other countries and there have been armed confrontations in recent years. In August 2002, Vietnamese forces occupying one small island fired warning shots at Philippine military aircraft. In November 2002, at the summit of the Association of Southeast Asian Nations (ASEAN) (discussed in Chapter 5), China signed a declaration with ten other Southeast Asian countries in which all parties agreed to exercise self-restraint in the area and to hold future talks. No country, however, relinquished its territorial claims.

Similarly, just off Taiwan's northern coast, Japan occupied in the 1980s a group of tiny islands, which China and Taiwan also continue to claim. Japan calls the islands the Senkakus, while China and Taiwan call them the Diaoyu.

Closer to home, Haiti has protested U.S. control of Navassa, an uninhabited Caribbean island barely two miles square, that is 40 miles off Haiti's southwest peninsula. A U.S. environmental group returned from a trip there in the summer of 1998 with tales of finding "biological riches unimagined," including new species. See N.Y. Times, Oct. 19, 1998, at A4.

4. To help you review the various maritime zones under the LOS Convention, which would you consider generally most useful for a state's claims to ocean area for its territorial sea, contiguous zone, and EEZ — an island 2 nautical miles off the state's coast? 11 miles? 23 miles? 300 miles? 800 miles?

Turning to present U.S. policy, we again find the United States selectively adopting some of the legal norms in the LOS Convention.

President Reagan, U.S. Ocean Policy
19 Weekly Comp. Pres. Doc. 383 (Mar. 10, 1983)

The United States has long been a leader in developing customary and conventional law of the sea. Our objectives have consistently been to provide a legal order that will, among other things, facilitate peaceful, international uses of the oceans and provide for equitable and effective management and conservation of marine resources. The United States also recognizes that all nations have an interest in these issues.

Last July I announced that the United States will not sign the United Nations Law of the Sea Convention that was opened for signature on December 10. We have taken this step because several major problems in the Convention's deep seabed mining provisions are contrary to the interests and principles of industrialized nations and would not help attain the aspirations of developing countries. . . .

However, the convention also contains provisions with respect to traditional uses of the oceans which generally confirm existing maritime law and practice and fairly balance the interests of all states.

Today I am announcing three decisions to promote and protect the oceans interests of the United States in a manner consistent with those fair and balanced results in the convention and international law.

First, the United States is prepared to accept and act in accordance with the balance of interests relating to traditional uses of the oceans — such as navigation and overflight. In this respect, the United States will recognize the rights of other states in the waters off their coasts, as reflected in the convention, so long as the rights and freedoms of the United States and others under international law are recognized by such coastal states.

Second, the United States will exercise and assert its navigation and overflight rights and freedoms on a worldwide basis in a manner that is consistent with the balance of interests reflected in the convention. The United States will not, however, acquiesce in unilateral acts of other states designed to restrict the rights and freedoms of the international community in navigation and overflight and other related high seas uses.

Third, I am proclaiming today an Exclusive Economic Zone in which the United States will exercise sovereign rights in living and nonliving resources within 200 nautical miles of its coast. This will provide United States jurisdiction for mineral resources out to 200 nautical miles that are not on the continental shelf. Recently discovered deposits there could be an important future source of strategic minerals.

Within this Zone all nations will continue to enjoy the high seas rights and freedoms that are not resource related, including the freedoms of navigation and overflight. My proclamation does not change existing United States policies concerning the continental shelf, marine mammals, and fisheries, including highly migratory species of tuna which are not subject to United States jurisdiction. The United States will continue efforts to achieve international agreements for the effective management of these species. The proclamation also reinforces this government's policy of promoting the United States fishing industry. . . .

The Exclusive Economic Zone established today will also enable the United States to take limited additional steps to protect the marine environment. In this connection, the United States will continue to work through the International Maritime Organization and other appropriate international organizations to develop uniform international measures for the protection of the marine environment while imposing no unreasonable burdens on commercial shipping.

The policy decisions I am announcing today will not affect the application of existing United States law concerning the high seas or existing authorities of any United States Government agency. . . .

The administration looks forward to working with the Congress on legislation to implement these new policies.

Notes and Questions

1. Why is the Truman Proclamation viewed as so important for the development of customary international law? Was it a unilateral claim, unsupported at the time by any generally accepted principle of international law? Does it make a difference that the United States at that time was the most powerful maritime nation?

2. Compare the width of the EEZ and the continental shelf under the LOS Convention with what was generally accepted before. Wasn't this an expansion of the sea area that a coastal state had some control over?

3. Why do you think that such a change occurred in the area over which a state has some control? Who benefited the most? Do most states have some sea coasts? From the standpoint of a multinational corporation engaged in offshore drilling for oil and gas, was it that much of a setback that many states extended the outer boundaries of their claims, or did it provide more certainty?

4. For the issues that we have now covered regarding the law of the sea (e.g., the territorial sea, the contiguous zone, the EEZ, the continental shelf), is President Reagan's proclamation of March 1983 generally consistent with the LOS Convention? Where does it differ, if at all, on these issues?

5. The Magnuson Fishery Conservation and Management Act of 1976 asserted U.S. jurisdiction over a fishery conservation zone with a breadth of 200 nautical miles. Reflecting the influence of the LOS Convention, the concept of this zone was later dropped by amendment and the area of coverage was changed to the Exclusive Economic Zone. This area encompasses approximately 3 million square nautical miles off the coasts of the 50 states, Puerto Rico, and all U.S. territories and possessions. The exact outer limits of the zone had to be negotiated with many neighboring countries who have overlapping boundary claims.

The 1976 Act prohibited foreign fishing within this area unless certain conditions were met. Moreover, the principal fisheries policy of the United States, especially as the Act has been implemented since 1980, has been the "Americanization" of fisheries within the zone. The allocation to foreign countries of allowable catches within the zone was cut by over 90 percent between 1980 and 1989, at the same time that catches by U.S. fishermen within the zone rapidly increased.

In an evolving effort to conserve marine fishery resources, Congress passed several amendments to the Magnuson Fishery Conservation and Management Act. The 1996 amendments, collectively known as the Sustainable Fisheries Act, required national fishery conservation and management standards to provide for the sustained participation of fishery dependent communities and to minimize the economic impacts to those communities; mandated the Secretary of Commerce to identify overfished species and to take action to rebuild those stocks; also mandated the Secretary to promulgate guidelines for identification of essential fish habitat; and established a fishing capacity reduction program. (See Digest of Federal Resource Laws of Interest to the U.S. Fish and Wildlife Service, Fishery Conservation and Management Act of 1976, at http://laws.fws.gov/lawsdigest/fishcon.html.)

6. One effect of the limits on foreign fishing within the U.S. zone and within the EEZs of other countries has been to drive fishing fleets from Japan and other countries further offshore, where they often resort to the use of huge nets, which indiscriminately snare most marine life in their paths.

7. The decline in the world's fish stocks is approaching crisis proportions. Many of the 200 fisheries monitored by the U.N.'s Food and Agricultural Organization (FAO) are depleted or being overfished. One response is that nations, (like the United States, discussed above) have taken steps to protect the fish stocks within 200 miles of their shores. Fish, however, do not respect international boundaries. Overfishing on the high seas also is contributing toward this depletion of the world's fish stocks.

Besides national measures, some progress in managing the fish stocks can be made through international agreements. For example, 80 countries met in 1993-1995 for the U.N. Conference on Straddling Fish Stocks and Highly Migratory Fish Stocks. In August 1995, the conference reached an agreement to implement the provisions of the LOS Convention relating to the conservation and management of these fish stocks. The agreement provides minimum standards for such fish, which are overharvested by many countries. The agreement entered into force in December 2001.

For a bilateral example, in 1999, Canada and the United States signed a comprehensive agreement under the existing Pacific Salmon Treaty. The agreement provides a conservation-based approach to the management of the Pacific salmon fisheries, and also contains an equitable sharing of the salmon catch. This agreement came after several years of friction, which included temporary Canadian legislation in 1994 authorizing the seizure of U.S. and other foreign boats in certain cases beyond the 200-mile Canadian EEZ, as well as the actual seizure of three U.S. fishing boats off Vancouver Island in 1997.

4. Opposite and Adjacent States

Drawing the outer boundaries of either the EEZ or the continental shelf can encounter problems. These include the situation where the outer boundary would overlap with that of another coastal state or where drawing the outer boundary of a coastal state's continental shelf is unclear due to physical factors. These problems arise on a regular basis. For example, there are over 50 treaties in force delimiting continental shelves between opposite or adjacent states.

In the North Sea Continental Shelf Cases, [1969] I.C.J. 1, the ICJ was asked to state what international law mandated as the proper method for delimiting the continental shelf between the Federal Republic of Germany, Denmark, and the Netherlands. The continental shelf in that region is particularly shallow, never going below a depth of 200 meters. Most of the boundaries had already been settled between the parties, but the parties could not agree on the method to apply to the contested boundary. Denmark and the Netherlands contended that international law mandated the use of the "equidistance principle" in delimiting the boundary, essentially meaning that every point along the boundary is the same distance from two points chosen on either side of the boundary. Use of this principle, however, would have substantially reduced the German continental shelf. Germany argued that the equidistance principle was not mandated by international law and that more equitable principles should apply.

North Sea Continental Shelf Cases (Federal Republic of Germany v. Denmark; Federal Republic of Germany v. Netherlands)

Intl. Court of Justice
[1969] I.C.J. Rep. 1 (Judgment)

THE PRINCIPLES AND RULES OF LAW APPLICABLE

The legal situation was that the Parties were under no obligation to apply the equidistance principle either under the 1958 Convention or as a rule of general or customary international law. . . . It remained for the Court . . . to indicate to the Parties the principles and rules of law in the light of which delimitation was to be effected.

The basic principles in the matter of delimitation, deriving from the Truman Proclamation, were that it must be the object of agreement between the States concerned and that such agreement must be arrived at in accordance with equitable principles. The Parties were under an obligation to enter into negotiations with a view to arriving at an agreement and not merely to go through a formal process of negotiation as a sort of prior condition for the automatic application of a certain method of delimitation in the absence of agreement.

The Parties were under an obligation to act in such a way that in the particular case, and taking all the circumstances into account, equitable principles would be applied. There was no question of the Court's decision being *ex aequo et bono*. It was precisely a rule of law that called for the application of equitable principles, and in such cases as the present ones the equidistance method could unquestionably lead to inequity. Other methods existed and might be employed, alone or in combination, according to the areas involved. Although the Parties intended themselves to apply the principles and rules laid down by the Court some indication was called for of the possible ways in which they might apply them.

For all the foregoing reasons, the Court found in each case that the use of the equidistance method of delimitation was not obligatory as between the Parties; that no other single method of delimitation was in all circumstances obligatory; that delimitation was to be effected by agreement in accordance with equitable principles and taking account of all relevant circumstances, in such a way as to leave as much as possible to each Party all those parts of the continental shelf that constituted a natural prolongation of its land territory, without encroachment on the natural prolongation of the land territory of the other; and that, if such delimitation produced

overlapping areas, they were to be divided between the Parties in agreed proportions, or, failing agreement, equally, unless they decided on a régime of joint jurisdiction, user, or exploitation.

In the course of negotiations, the factors to be taken into account were to include: the general configuration of the coasts of the Parties, as well as the presence
of any special or unusual features; so far as known or readily ascertainable, the physical and geological structure and natural resources of the continental shelf areas involved; the element of a reasonable degree of proportionality which a delimitation
effected according to equitable principles ought to bring about between the extent
of the continental shelf areas appertaining to each State and the length of its coast
measured in the general direction of the coastline, taking into account the effects,
actual or prospective, of any other continental shelf delimitations in the same region.

[The vote was 11-6.]

The Court has built further on its general statements in the North Seas Continental Shelf Cases in several succeeding cases, such as the Maritime Delimitation
in the Area Between Greenland and Jan Mayen (Denmark v. Norway), [1993] I.C.J.
Rep. 38; Gulf of Maine Case (Canada v. United States), [1984] I.C.J. Rep. 246; and
the Continental Shelf (Libyan Arab Jamahiriya/Malta) Case, [1984] I.C.J. Rep. 1.

For both the EEZ and the continental shelf, the LOS Convention adopted essentially the same clause as the 1958 Convention on the Continental Shelf for the
delimitation of boundaries between the opposite or adjacent states. (See Article 74
for the EEZ and Article 83 for the continental shelf.)

Jonathan I. Charney, Progress in International Maritime Boundary Delimitation Law

88 Am. J. Intl. L. 227 (1994)

Judgments of the International Court of Justice (ICJ) and awards of ad hoc arbitration tribunals carry special weight in international maritime boundary law. On its
face, the international maritime boundary law codified in the 1982 Convention on
the Law of the Sea is indeterminate. For the continental shelf and the exclusive
economic zone, the legal obligation of coastal states is to delimit the boundary "by
agreement on the basis of international law, as referred to in Article 38 of the Statute of the International Court of Justice, in order to achieve an equitable solution."

The article on the delimitation of maritime boundaries in the territorial sea is
no more determinative despite the fact that it makes direct references to the equidistant line, special circumstances and historic title. In spite of this indeterminacy, if
not because of it, coastal states have found that third-party dispute settlement procedures can effectively resolve maritime boundary delimitation disputes. As a consequence, there are more judgments and awards on maritime boundary disputes
than on any other subject of international law, and this trend is continuing.

Owing to the relative scarcity of authoritative pronouncements, ICJ judgments
and even ad hoc arbitration awards generally assume considerable importance in international law. In international maritime boundary law, the judgments and awards
take on even greater salience. There are two reasons for this situation: first, the

existence of a unique line of jurisprudence made possible by a continuing series of decisions and, second, the absence of clearer guidance from codification efforts, *opinio juris* and state practice.

Jonathan I. Charney, International Maritime Boundaries
xlii-xlv (1993)

. . . In my opinion . . . no normative principle of international law has developed that would mandate the specific location of any maritime boundary line. The state practice varies substantially. Due to the unlimited geographic and other circumstances that influence the settlements, no binding rule that would be sufficiently determinative to enable one to predict the location of a maritime boundary with any degree of precision is likely to evolve in the near future. . . .

There are, however, trends and practices that are substantial. Surprisingly, it appears from the practice that the equidistant line has played a major role in boundary delimitation agreements, regardless of whether they concern boundaries between opposite or adjacent states. In the vast preponderance of the boundary agreements studied, equidistance had some role in the development of the line and/or the location of the line that was established. . . .

Despite the normative and theoretical uncertainties present in this area, the evidence brought out in this study suggests to me that states seeking to delimit their maritime boundaries ought to consider certain facts and options as they develop their positions and resolve them through negotiation and third party processes.

First, it is clear that primary attention will be placed upon the geography of the coastline.

Second, the equidistant line will be considered in most circumstances as a basis for analyzing the boundary situation. It may very well be used in some form or variant to generate the boundary line itself.

Third, the delimitation of a definitive maritime boundary is not the only option available to states. While different boundaries for different regimes or uses are rare, creative settlements that take certain matters out of contention for boundary delimitation purposes are possible. Thus, joint development or management zones that cross boundaries, revenue sharing, and management cooperation are all possible options which, in the appropriate cases, can facilitate settlement or even make settlement of the maritime boundary irrelevant.

Fourth, even if a definitive boundary cannot be established interim arrangements may be possible. . . .

Ninth, despite the relative indeterminacy of the maritime boundary law there are in state practice and in judicial decisions real limits to the geographical range in which a maritime boundary between two states will be located. These limits are primarily a function of the coastal geography, the size and location of islands, and the waters of the areas in question. What is ultimately considered to be fair or equitable will be largely dictated by a visual conception by the decision-makers of the maps and charts examined for this purpose. As a consequence, focus will be on the division of the water areas in question relative to the coastal states.

Finally, within the above considerations the law and practice permit states and tribunals a range of discretion that allows for the resolution of maritime boundaries in ways that no state need be characterized as a winner or a loser, unless a state were itself to stake out an unswervingly doctrinal position. Viewed in isolation, boundary making is a zero sum game. However, the options available to vary the line over extended distances and to resolve related issues on the basis of non-boundary solutions allows for the resolution of maritime boundaries to the maximum advantage of all the participants.

Questions

1. Does there seem to be too much "indeterminancy" to maritime boundary decisions? Should there be more reliance on one standard (e.g., equidistance or equitable standard)? Which standard?

2. How could disputes over the location of a boundary matter between two countries?

F. THE REGIME OF THE HIGH SEAS

The term "high seas" is defined in the LOS Convention as "all parts of the sea that are not included in the exclusive economic zone, in the territorial sea or in the internal waters of a State, or in the archipelagic waters of an archipelagic State." The LOS Convention substantially incorporated the provisions of the 1958 Convention on the High Seas. See Articles 86 and 58 of the LOS Convention. Together, the LOS Convention's provisions on the high seas and EEZ make the EEZ a "sui generis" zone that is neither high seas nor territorial sea. The provisions do preserve the rights of the high seas in the EEZ for states other than the coastal state, unless the Convention specifies to the contrary. A succinct discussion of the high seas provisions of the LOS Convention and the 1958 Convention is provided by the Restatement of Foreign Relations Law.

Restatement

Section 521.   Freedom of High Seas

(1) The high seas are open and free to all states, whether coastal or land-locked.
(2) Freedom of the high seas comprises, inter alia:
  (a) freedom of navigation;
  (b) freedom of overflight;
  (c) freedom of fishing;
  (d) freedom to lay submarine cables and pipelines;
  (e) freedom to construct artificial islands, installations, and structures; and
  (f) freedom of scientific research.
(3) These freedoms must be exercised by all states with reasonable regard to the interests of other states in their exercise of the freedom of the high seas.

Source Note

This section is based on Article 2 of the 1958 Convention on the High Seas, and Articles 87 and 89 of the LOS Convention.

Comment

a. Area in which high seas freedoms can be exercised. This section applies to all parts of the sea that are not included in the internal waters, the territorial sea, or the exclusive economic zone of any state, or in the archipelagic waters of an archipelagic state. Certain of these freedoms may be exercised also in the exclusive economic zone of other states. . . .

Section 522. Enforcement Jurisdiction over Foreign Ships on High Seas

(1) A warship, or other ship owned or operated by a state and used only on government noncommercial service, enjoys complete immunity on the high seas from interference by any other state.

(2) Ships other than those specified in Subsection (1) are not subject to interference on the high seas, but a warship or clearly-marked law enforcement ship of any state may board such a ship if authorized by the flag state, or if there is reason to suspect that the ship

(a) is engaged in piracy, slave trade, or unauthorized broadcasting;

(b) is without nationality; or

(c) though flying a foreign flag or refusing to show its flag, is in fact of the same nationality as the warship or law enforcement ship.

Source Note

This section follows with minor modifications Articles 8, 9 and 22 of the 1958 Convention on the High Seas, and Articles 95, 96 and 110 of the LOS Convention.

Comment . . .

b. Enforcement procedure. In cases under Subsection (2), the warship or law enforcement ship may proceed to verify a foreign ship's right to fly its flag by examining its documents and, if necessary, by an examination on board the ship. However, if the suspicions prove to be unfounded, and the boarded ship has committed no act justifying those suspicions, the inspecting state is obligated to pay compensation for any loss or damage. LOS Convention, Article 110.

In specified circumstances warships and law enforcement ships are entitled to engage in hot pursuit.

c. Piracy. Any state may seize a ship or aircraft on the high seas on reasonable suspicion of piracy, arrest the suspected pirates, seize the property on board, try the suspected pirates, and impose penalties on them if convicted. Where the seizure of a ship or aircraft on suspicion of piracy was effected without adequate grounds and the ship was found not to be a pirate ship, the state that made the seizure is liable to the flag state of the seized ship or aircraft for any loss or damage caused by the seizure. LOS Convention, Articles 105-106.

Not every act of violence committed on the high seas is piracy under international law. Only the following acts are considered piratical:

(i)   Any illegal acts of violence, detention, or depredation committed for private ends by the crew or the passengers of a private ship or a private aircraft, and directed against another ship or aircraft on the high seas, or against persons or property on board such other ship or aircraft; or against a ship, aircraft, persons, or property in a place outside the jurisdiction of any state;

(ii)   any act of voluntary participation in the operation of a ship or of an aircraft with knowledge of facts making it a pirate ship or aircraft;

(iii)   any act of inciting or of intentionally facilitating an act described in subparagraphs (1) or (2).

In addition, acts committed by a mutinous crew of a warship or other government ship or aircraft against another ship or aircraft, may also constitute piracy. LOS Convention, Articles 101-102.

d. Slave and drug traffic. Because of the general condemnation of slave trade, international law allows the boarding and inspection of vessels suspected of such trade; it does not permit seizure of the vessel or arrest of the crew unless the flag state has consented. Since slave trade is an offense subject to universal jurisdiction (see §404), the state that boarded the vessel could try members of the crew for violations of its laws, if the flag state consented, and any state could try them later if it obtained jurisdiction over them.

There is movement to extend these rules to illicit traffic in narcotic drugs and psychotropic substances. However, even states, such as the United States, that strongly condemn such traffic do not take steps on the high seas against suspected smugglers except when the ship is without nationality . . . or when permission has been obtained from the flag state (often granted by telegraph or radio) to board, search, and seize the vessel. . . .

Reporters' Notes

1. *Warships and other government ships.* A United States Coast Guard ship is considered a warship. . . . Some convention provisions grant immunity to "government ships operated for non-commercial purpose" (e.g., LOS Convention, Arts. 31-32); others provide immunity to "ships owned or operated by a State and used only on government non-commercial service" (e.g., LOS Convention, Art. 96). It is not clear that any difference was intended. As long as a ship is operated for noncommercial purposes, it is entitled to immunity if it is either owned or operated by the government, for instance, a government-owned ship operated by an oceanographic institute, and engaged on a government-sponsored hydrographic survey, or a private-owned ship chartered by the government for a meteorological service.

2. *Piracy and hijacking.* Acts indicated in Comment *c* are piracy only if they are by private ships and for private ends. Seizure of a ship for political purposes is not considered piracy. See the *Santa Maria* incident in 1961, 4 Whiteman, Digest of International Law 665 (1965). Crew members forced to assist the pirates are not, under the above definition, considered pirates. Wrongful acts by governmental ships are not included in the definition of piracy, but are addressed by general principles of international law governing state responsibility for violations of international obligations. See §§207 and 901. . . .

5. *Unauthorized broadcasting from high seas.* International law has accepted that any person or ship engaged in unauthorized broadcasting from the high seas may be arrested, and the broadcasting apparatus may be seized, by a law enforcement ship of any of the following states: the flag state of the broadcasting ship; the state of registry of the installation (as some of the broadcasts are made from abandoned platforms built on the continental shelf); the state of which the person is a national; a state where the transmission can be received; and the state where authorized radio communication is suffering interference. See LOS Convention, Art. 109. . . .

Questions

1. See United States v. Postal (5th Cir. 1979) in Chapter 3 at page 170. Was that case decided consistent with the Convention on the High Seas and the LOS Convention? Did either of those conventions influence the decision? If not, why not?

2. See United States v. Romero-Galue (11th Cir. 1985) in Chapter 7 at page 688. Was that case decided consistent with the Convention on the High Seas and the LOS Convention? Did either of those conventions influence the decision? If not, why not?

3. Professor Frederic L. Kirgis reports on and analyzes the implications of two Spanish naval vessels stopping and boarding a North Korean vessel on the high seas in December 2002. The boarding appeared to be part of sea patrols that the U.S., Spanish, and other ships were engaged in to intercept, among other things, Al Qaeda fighters fleeing from Afghanistan.

On December 10, two Spanish naval ships stopped and boarded a North Korean cargo vessel on the high seas about 600 miles from the coast of Yemen. The cargo vessel flew no flag. According to a Pentagon official, the vessel took evasive measures in order to avoid inspection. The boarding party found fifteen Scud missiles hidden under sacks of cement. The cargo vessel's manifest said that it was carrying 40,000 sacks of cement, and apparently mentioned no other cargo. The Spanish naval ships were participating in organized patrols of the Indian Ocean and nearby waters keeping watch for Al Qaeda fighters fleeing from Afghanistan. The United States and other countries also participate in the patrols . . .

Under the [LOS Convention], vessels on the high seas are subject to the exclusive jurisdiction of their flag state and ordinarily may not be boarded by anyone from a foreign naval ship. An exception exists, however, if the boarded ship is without nationality. A vessel that flies no flag and is not otherwise clearly identified with a state of registration is considered a ship without nationality. Consequently it appears that the boarding of the cargo vessel, in and of itself, did not violate international law.

There would still be questions relating to the purpose and consequences of the boarding. The Convention on the Law of the Sea says that when an exception to the no-boarding rule exists, the naval ship may verify the boarded vessel's right to fly its flag or may check its documents and further examine the ship if "suspicion remains." In the context of the Convention, though, the suspicion would have to relate to certain enumerated offenses, which do not include the carrying of weapons. The carrying of weapons at sea, even on a merchant ship, is not a violation of international law unless the carriage is in violation of a treaty obligation of the transporting state. Such does not appear to have been the case here . . .

The missiles obviously would have military uses, but they appear to have been destined for use by the government of Yemen, which could not reasonably be considered a belligerent despite any terrorist incidents that have occurred there. Nor is there currently a war in the normal sense between the United States (or Spain) and any state involved in the carriage of the missiles.

On December 11, the United States government confirmed that the missiles were destined for the government of Yemen, and released the cargo vessel to complete its voyage. White House spokesperson Ari Fleischer was quoted as saying that "In this instance there is no clear authority to seize the shipment of Scud missiles from North Korea to Yemen." He added, "There is no provision under international law prohibiting Yemen from accepting delivery of missiles from North Korea." Thus the U.S. government appears to have conceded that any justification it might offer under international law for detaining the vessel or seizing the missiles would be unconvincing.

Mr. Fleischer's statements reflect a willingness of the United States government to respect international law under the circumstances currently prevailing. Among those circumstances presumably are the need for cooperation by the government of Yemen in U.S. efforts to contain terrorism and in the event of war with Iraq. Nevertheless, the government's expression of respect for international law as the motivation for releasing the vessel is significant as a recognition by the world's superpower of relevant legal norms restricting the confiscation on the high seas of cargo with obvious military uses, even when the military cargo is being transported clandestinely from an unfriendly state into a volatile part of the world. [Frederic L. Kirgis, Board of North Korean Vessel on the High Seas, ASIL Insight (Dec. 12, 2002), at http://www.asil.org/insights.htm.]

G. DISPUTE SETTLEMENT UNDER THE LOS CONVENTION

One of the many accomplishments of the LOS Convention is the establishment of a comprehensive dispute settlement system. This system is incorporated in Part XV of the Convention.

Louis B. Sohn, Peaceful Settlement of Disputes in Ocean Conflicts: Does UNCLOS III Point the Way?

46 Law & Contemp. Probs. 195 (1983)

I. INTRODUCTION

One of the important accomplishments of the Third United Nations Law of the Sea Conference is the development of a veritable code for the settlement of the disputes which may arise with respect to the interpretation and application of the Law of the Sea Convention. It was recognized early in the negotiations that if the parties to the Convention had retained the right of unilateral interpretation, then the complex text drafted by the Conference would have lacked stability, certainty, and predictability. It is one of the prerogatives of sovereign equality that in the absence of an agreement on impartial third-party adjudication, the view of one state with respect to the interpretation of the Convention cannot prevail over the views of other member states. . . .

The only effective remedy in such a situation is to provide in advance in the Convention itself for an effective method of settling future interpretation disputes. . . .

II.   THE GENERAL FRAMEWORK FOR DISPUTE SETTLEMENT

The resulting system for the settlement of law of the sea disputes is at the same time simple and complex. Its simplicity is due to the fact that the Convention accepts as its guiding principle that in general the will of the parties to a dispute shall prevail and that the parties may by agreement select any dispute settlement method they wish.[6] The more complex provisions apply only if the parties do not agree upon a dispute settlement method.[7]

Even after a dispute has arisen, and even if one of the procedures provided for in the Convention has been started, the parties can agree "at any time" to adopt a special method for settling their dispute.[8] Similarly, if the parties to a dispute have previously agreed, in a bilateral, regional, or general international agreement, to settle disputes (including those relating to the interpretation of international agreements between them) by a procedure entailing a binding decision, this procedure supersedes the procedures provided for in the Law of the Sea Convention.[9]

For example, if the two parties to the dispute have agreed unconditionally to accept the jurisdiction of the International Court of Justice, either of them can refer the dispute to that forum. . . .

Flexibility does not stop at this stage. Unlike most other international instruments, the Law of the Sea Convention does not provide for a unitary system of dispute settlement. Various groups of states have expressed preferences for different methods of settling Convention disputes. Some states have argued for conferring the jurisdiction to interpret the Convention on the International Court of Justice;[13] others have expressed preferences for arbitration;[14] while some have supported special technical commissions;[15] a large group of states has opted for a permanent International Tribunal for the Law of the Sea.[16] After many other solutions were rejected, it was agreed that a state can choose any one of these four methods, but if the two states concerned have chosen different methods, the dispute may be submitted

---

6. See Convention, art. 280.
7. Id. art. 281(1).
8. Id. art. 280.
9. Id. art. 282.
13. E.g., Japan and the Netherlands.
14. E.g., France, the United Kingdom, and the United States.
15. E.g., the Soviet Union and other Eastern European states.
16. Most African states and several Latin American states have supported this idea.

"only to arbitration."[17] All states agreed that if they cannot have the tribunal of their choice they would be willing to go to arbitration. To ensure that this solution will work, an annex to the Convention provides an effective method for selecting the arbitral tribunal.[18]

III. SETTLEMENT OF SPECIFIC CATEGORIES OF DISPUTES

Three categories of cases are subject, however, to different procedures: (a) Article 297 governs disputes relating to the exercise by a coastal state of its sovereign rights or jurisdiction in the Exclusive Economic Zone (EEZ); (b) Article 298 governs disputes relating to sea boundary delimitations, to military or law enforcement activities, or to disputes submitted to the Security Council of the United Nations; and (c) Articles 186-91 govern disputes relating to seabed mining. The simplicity of the other provisions of the Convention is matched by the complexity of these three exceptions. . . .

[T]he dispute settlement provisions will be available only to parties to the Convention. Should a dispute arise between a state party to the Convention and a state not a party thereto, such a dispute would have to be resolved in accordance with procedures available to the parties to the dispute outside the Convention. At present, such procedures are seldom available. . . . On the other hand, for disputes between parties to the Convention the system of dispute settlement provided by the Convention, though it appears extremely flexible and provides several options, in the great majority of cases can lead to a binding decision likely to be accepted and complied with by the parties to the dispute. This is the way to the rule of law and to ensuring that the peace of the world will not be jeopardized by a dangerous escalation of law of the sea controversies.

Notes and Questions

1. As noted above, the LOS Convention allows the parties to choose among different dispute settlement forums. What do you think are the pros and cons of this approach? Did it seem to help obtain the support of the negotiating countries? Does it provide flexibility to the parties? Is it optimal for ensuring consistency in the international law of the sea?

2. Note that when the parties cannot agree on a particular dispute settlement forum the "default function" (in computer terms) is arbitration. Does this suggest that international arbitration among states is now widely accepted?

3. As noted above, the LOS Convention did provide for the creation of a new dispute body for at least some of the disputes arising out of the interpretation and application of the Convention. The International Tribunal for the Law of the Sea is an independent judicial body seated in Hamburg, Germany. It is composed of 21 independent members elected by the state parties, with no two members being nationals of the same state and with no fewer than three members from each geographical group.

17. Convention, art. 287(1), (5).
18. Id. annex VII.

Disputes over activities in the International Seabed Area are submitted to the Seabed Disputes Chamber of the Tribunal, which consists of 11 judges. Any party to such a dispute may ask the Seabed Disputes Chamber to form an ad hoc chamber composed of three members of the Seabed Disputes Chamber.

The Tribunal has an excellent Web site at http://www.itlos.org.

4. As of January 2003, eleven cases had been filed with the Tribunal since its inception in 1996, with most of the cases dealing with disputes over seized vessels. For example, the Tribunal's first case involved the government of Saint Vincent and the Grenadines instituting proceedings against the government of Guinea because of Guinea's alleged seizure and arrest in October of the *M/V Saiga* and its crew and cargo off the coast of West Africa. Moving expeditiously, the Tribunal ruled on December 4, 1997, that it had jurisdiction and that Guinea should promptly release the ship and its crew from detention upon the posting of a reasonable bond of some of petroleum cargo and $400,000.

In the Tribunal's tenth case, Ireland sought provisional measures against the United Kingdom over the proposed operation of a nuclear reprocessing plant, with Ireland arguing that the plant would contribute to the pollution of the Irish Sea and that there were dangers in the transportation of radioactive material to and from the plant. Ireland had requested that the dispute be submitted to an arbitral tribunal established under the Convention, but it sought provisional measures under Article 290 pending the constitution of the arbitral tribunal. In December 2001 the International Tribunal for the Law of the Sea prescribed provisional measures, including that the two countries should exchange information and devise appropriate measures to prevent marine pollution from the plant.

H.   THE DEEP SEABED MINING REGIME AND THE 1994 AGREEMENT

One of the most controversial parts of the LOS Convention was the deep seabed mining regime it envisioned. In 1958, when the Convention on the High Seas was concluded, the U.N.'s International Law Commission considered the prospect of deep seabed mining to be so remote that it was not material to the agreement.

The rapid advance of technology and the depletion of land-based mineral deposits, however, made deep seabed mining increasingly attractive.

The discovery of rich deposits of nickel and manganese at the bottom of the oceans, and the development of technologies capable of harvesting such valuable ores in the near future, inaugurated an international legal debate . . . over the rights of the individual states to mine the world's untapped mineral wealth. Specifically, one block, represented by most developing nations, maintain[ed] that the natural resources of the deep oceans [were] the common heritage of mankind, and their exploitation as a consequence, should take place under a communal regime. Conversely, another faction, headed by the United States, and including the most developed nations, argue[d] that the high economic value of the seabed minerals, and their strategic value to the First-World states, require[d] free access by the technologically and financially richer countries as a matter of economic interest. . . . [Arcangelo Travaglini, Reconciling Natural Law and Legal Positivism in the Deep Seabed Mining Provisions of the Convention on the Law of the Sea, 15 Temp. Intl. & Comp. L.J. 313, 313 (2001).]

Given the controversy over the deep seabed mining, there ensued a great deal of international debate, diplomatic maneuvering, and steps by individual states. While negotiations on the LOS Convention were ongoing, Congress in 1980 passed the Deep Seabed Hard Mineral Resources Act, 94 Stat. 553, codified at 30 U.S.C. §§1401-1471 (1982). The expressed purpose of the Act was to establish an interim deep seabed regime pending successful completion and entry into force of the Convention. Apparently, passage of the Act was also quietly supported by the then U.S. ambassador to the LOS Convention as a way to pressure the developing countries into agreeing to certain U.S. positions in the negotiations. In addition to licensing and safety provisions, section 118 of the Act called for the negotiation of "reciprocating states" agreements.

This unilateral action was quickly condemned by a number of Convention participants, especially by the Group of 77. The Group of 77, which now numbers more than 120 countries, primarily includes developing countries seeking to protect the interests of the Third World. (See Chapter 5, Section C.) During the Law of the Sea negotiations, the Group often worked out an agreed position in its caucus and then pushed for that position as a bloc in the negotiating sessions. Given its many members, the Group's voice was very influential. Unanimity on deep seabed mining issues was relatively easy to achieve because the members' interests were generally similar.

Although criticized, the 1980 U.S. statute regarding reciprocating states was followed by similar legislation in like-minded developed mining states, such as the United Kingdom, West Germany, and Japan. In September 1982, France, West Germany, the United Kingdom, and the United States signed the Interim Arrangements Relating to Polymetalic Nodules of the Deep Seabed.

In December 1982, the LOS Convention was signed by 115 countries and the ratification process began in these countries and in some other countries that signed soon afterward. Essentially because of the deep seabed provisions, however, President Reagan refused to sign the Convention, as did the governments of several other major industrial countries. (The details of these provisions, as they were "interpreted" or changed by a 1994 agreement, are discussed after some further history.)

When the United States rejected the 1982 Convention, what had previously been thought of as only an interim regime became the potential basis for the permanent U.S. statutory system. The United States moved further toward an alternative to the Convention's deep seabed regime through bilateral and multilateral agreements. This alternative was commonly referred to as the "reciprocating states regime" or the "mini-treaty." In 1984, Belgium, France, West Germany, Italy, the Netherlands, the United Kingdom, and the United States concluded the Provisional Understanding Regarding Deep Seabed Mining, 23 I.L.M. 1354 (1984). Japan joined later. The Provisional Understanding attempted to ensure respect for mining rights granted by reciprocating states and to avoid overlapping mining sites.

Needless to say, many signatories to the LOS Convention condemned this alternative approach. However, a number of the early assumptions underlying the provisions for deep seabed mining changed after the LOS Convention was drafted. First, the end of the Cold War brought a global focus on the advantages of free market economies. Aspects of the Convention taken from the centrally planned economy model were in sharp contrast to ongoing free market reforms. Second, commercial interest in deep seabed mining decreased due to a period of relatively low mineral prices. Industry experts revised their predictions that the mining sites would be fully operational from the mid-1980s to the second decade of the twenty-first century. These factors combined to make supporters and opponents of the LOS Convention's provisions on mining more open to accommodation.

In October 1990, consultations among a representative group of countries began under U.N. auspices to determine whether there was enough common ground between the developing and developed countries to seek more generally acceptable arrangements for the governance of deep seabed mining. After the Reagan Administration had consistently refused during 1982-1988 to engage in multilateral discussions about how to deal with the LOS Convention, representatives of the U.S. Department of State participated in these new consultations. These consultations led to an agreement on "interpreting" or implementing the LOS Convention provisions. This agreement will be examined below.

First, however, it is useful to appreciate what the U.S. concerns had been over the deep seabed mining provisions.

Statement of Ambassador David A. Colson, Deputy Assistant Secretary of State for Oceans

The Law of the Sea Treaty and Reauthorization of the Deep Seabed
Hard Mineral Resources Act: Hearings before the Subcomm. on
Oceanography, Gulf of Mexico, and the Outer Continental Shelf
Deep Seabed Mining, 103rd Cong., 1st Sess. 37 (1994)

The basic flaws of t[he] deep seabed mining regime are manifold. But stated simply, it failed to provide the United States, and other states with major economic interests, a voice commensurate with those interests in decision-making relating to management of deep seabed resources, and it was based on a highly interventionist central economic planning model that was overly bureaucratic and would have preempted private investment in deep seabed mineral resource development, thus, preventing the development of those resources when economic conditions warrant.

In 1982, the Reagan Administration, in its ocean policy statement, reaffirmed support for the rest of the Convention while identifying the specific U.S. objections concerning deep seabed mining. They fell into two broad categories: institutional issues and economic and commercial issues. On the institutional front, we objected to the fact that the U.S. was not guaranteed a seat on the executive council of the international seabed authority (the organization that would administer the deep seabed regime); and we objected that developing countries would dominate the organization based on the rules for decision making and the relationship between the executive council and the plenary assembly. In addition, we objected to the fact that the convention's provisions on seabed mining could in the future be amended and bind the U.S. without our consent; and we objected to the possibility that future revenues from deep seabed mining might be distributed to national liberation movements over our objections.

On the economic and commercial front we objected to the requirement that commercial enterprises, as a condition to the awarding of mining rights, must undertake to transfer their mining technology to a competing operating arm of the regime known as the Enterprise, or possibly to developing countries. We also objected to the Enterprise benefitting from discriminatory and competitive advantages over commercial enterprises. . . . We also objected to the regime's production control arrangements that limited the level of production from the seabed so as to protect land-based producers of deep seabed minerals. We also objected to the regime's onerous system of financial payments that would have been made by commercial miners, in particular a U.S. $1 million annual fee payable beginning with the exploration stage.

These features made the regime non-viable and led the United States, the United Kingdom and Germany not to sign the convention. Other major industrial countries that signed the convention did not move to ratify, for these same reasons. . . .

The 1994 agreement was specifically negotiated and designed to cure the defects, indicated above, that the United States and certain other industrialized countries saw in the LOS Convention. What follows is a description of the deep seabed mining regime as it stands presently under the LOS Convention as interpreted or implemented by the 1984 agreement, entitled Agreement Relating to the Implementation of Part XI of the United Nations Convention on the Law of the Sea of 10 December 1982.

R.R. Churchill & A.V. Lowe, The Law of the Sea
238–253 (3d ed. 1999)

The international law of the deep sea bed has a complexity which readers could be forgiven for thinking is out of proportion to its current practical importance. Given the purpose of this book, and the plethora of detailed treatments of the subject, we will do no more than outline the regime as it stands at present under the 1982 Convention as modified by the 1994 Implementation Agreement.

PRINCIPLES OF THE LAW OF THE SEA CONVENTION REGIME

The regime governs all activities connected with exploration and exploitation of mineral resources in the Area (LOSC, art. 134(2)). The latter is defined as the "sea bed and ocean floor and subsoil thereof beyond national jurisdiction" (LOSC, art. 1). . . . "[N]ational jurisdiction" for these purposes extends, broadly speaking, to the outer edge of the continental margin, or to a distance of 200 miles from the baseline where the margin does not extend up to that distance. Both the Area itself, which comprises about sixty per cent of the whole sea bed, and its resources (limited by article 133 to mineral resources)[49] are the "common heritage of mankind." As such they are not susceptible of unilateral national appropriation. Rights in the Area and to its resources can be obtained only in accordance with the provisions of the Convention, which is to say, only with the authorisation of the International Sea Bed Authority established by the 1982 Convention (LOSC, arts. 136, 137).

---

49. Living resources and other non-mineral resources (e.g., thermal energy) remain subject to the regime of the high seas.

All activites in the Area, which in principle may be conducted both by the Authority itself through its mining arm, the "Enterprise," and by commercial operators, are to be carried out for the benefit of mankind as a whole, taking into particular consideration the interests of developing States and peoples who have not attained self-governing status (LOSC, art. 140). Furthermore, since the superjacent waters and air space remain high seas, reasonable regard must be had to other legitimate uses of those waters and of the Area itself. A succinct (if ungrammatical) account of the core of the regime can be found in article 155(2), which states that any revision of Part XI

> shall ensure the maintenance of the principle of the common heritage of mankind, the international régime designed to ensure equitable exploitation of the resources of the Area for the benefit of all countries, especially the developing States, and an Authority to organize, conduct and control activities in the Area. It shall also ensure the maintenance of the principles laid down in this Part with regard to the exclusion of claims or exercise of sovereignty over any part of the Area, the rights of States and their general conduct in relation to the Area, and their participation in activities in the Area in conformity with this Convention, the prevention of monopolization of activities in the Area, the use of the Area exclusively for peaceful purposes, economic aspects of activities in the Area, marine scientific research, transfer of technology, protection of the marine environment, protection of human life, rights of coastal States, the legal status of the waters superjacent to the Area and that of the air space above those waters and accommodation between activities in the Area and other activities in the marine environment. . . .

THE INTERNATIONAL SEA BED AUTHORITY[50]

It would be wrong to say that the Area is "governed" by the Authority, because many uses of the Area, such as pipeline and cable laying and scientific research unconnected with the exploitation of sea-bed resources, may be carried out without the need for the Authority's permission. But the Authority is the body through which States Parties are to organise and control all activities concerned with sea-bed minerals beyond national jurisdiction.

Part XI of the 1982 Convention provides that the Authority has three principal organs: the plenary Assembly, the thirty-six-State Council, and the Secretariat (LOSC, art. 158). The Authority is served by two specialised bodies, the Legal and Technical Commission (LOSC, art. 163) and the Finance Committee (1994 IA, Annex, Section 1, paragraph 4, and Section 9). In addition, there is the Authority's mining arm, the Enterprise. Each component of this system has a particular role to play, but it is the Council that is the most important organ, particularly after the amendments effected by the 1994 Implementation Agreement.

The Assembly

All States Parties to the Convention are *ipso facto* members of the Authority and so, too, of the Assembly, wherein each State has one vote. The Assembly is said to be "the supreme organ of the Authority to which the other principal organs shall be

---

50. Documents concerning the Authority, and lists of current members of its various organs, are set out on its web site: http://www.isa.org.jm.

accountable," but by depriving it of the power to act alone in crucial areas the 1994 Implementation Agreement has significantly reduced the power of the Assembly, and increased that of the Council, as we explain below when we discuss the decision-making process. The Assembly formally elects members of the Council, the Governing Body of the Enterprise, and other subsidiary organs of the Authority, and is the forum within which Authority decisions are formally adopted on matters such as the budget and sharing of the costs of the Authority, the rules governing sea-bed mining, and the distribution of the economic benefits of sea-bed mining.

The Council

The Council is responsible for the implementation of the Convention regime within the limits set by the Convention and the general policies established by the Authority, and the establishment of the specific policies of the Authority. Its main specific tasks, listed in article 162, include the supervision of the implementation of Part XI of the Convention; the approval of plans of work submitted by sea-bed miners; the making of recommendations on economic assistance to developing countries which suffer serious adverse effects on their export earnings or economies resulting from a reduction in the price of an affected mineral or in the volume of exports of that mineral, to the extent that such reduction is caused by activities in the Area; the recommendation of rules concerning the equitable sharing of economic benefits of sea-bed mining; and the adoption and provisional application (pending Assembly approval) of rules for the Authority.

The Council has thirty-six members. Its membership is carefully designed both to be representative of the main interest groups concerned with sea-bed mining and to establish a broadly equitable geographical distribution of Council members. According to Section 3, paragraph 15 of the Implementation Agreement (which complements LOSC, art. 161), members of the Council are to be elected by the Assembly in the following order:

(a) Four members from among those States Parties which during the last five years for which statistics are available, have either consumed more than 2 per cent in value terms of total world consumption or have had net imports of more than 2 per cent in value terms of total world imports of the commodities produced from the categories of minerals to be derived from the Area, provided that the four members shall include one State from the Eastern European region having the largest economy in that region in terms of gross domestic product and the State, on the date of entry into force of the Convention, having the largest economy in terms of gross domestic product, if such States wish to be represented in this group;

(b) Four members from among the eight States Parties which have made the largest investments in preparation for and in the conduct of activities in the Area, either directly or through their nationals;

(c) Four members from among States Parties which on the basis of production in areas under their jurisdiction, are major net exporters of the categories of minerals to be derived from the Area, including at least two developing States whose exports of such minerals have a substantial bearing upon their economies;

> (d) Six members from among developing States Parties, representing special in-
> terests. The special interests to be represented shall include those of States
> with large populations, States which are land-locked or geographically dis-
> advantaged, States which are major importers of the categories of minerals
> to be derived from the Area, States which are potential producers of such
> minerals and least developed States;
>
> (e) Eighteen members elected according to the principle of ensuring an equi-
> table geographical distribution of seats in the Council as a whole, provided
> that each geographical region shall have at least one member elected under
> this subparagraph. For this purpose, the geographical regions shall be Africa,
> Asia, Eastern Europe, Latin America and the Caribbean and Western Europe
> and Others. . . .

Seats for Russia and the USA are guaranteed under the "largest economy" provisions
of sub-paragraph (a). Each of the groups in sub-paragraphs (a), (b) and (c) is referred to as a "chamber" of the Council; and the developing States members of the
groups in sub-paragraphs (d) and (e) together form the fourth "chamber" of the
Council (1994 IA, Annex, Section 3, paragraph 9).[55] The significance of the chambers relates to decision-making in the Council, as will be explained below.

The Secretariat

The Secretariat of the Authority has the responsibility for the administration of the
Authority and the maintenance of contacts with other international and non-
governmental organisations. . . . The first Secretary General, Mr Satya N. Nandan
(Fiji), was elected in 1996 for four years.

The Legal and Technical Commission

The Legal and Technical Commission has a wide competence, including the supervision (at the request of the Council) of activities in the Area; the making of recommendations to the Council on such matters as the acceptance of applications for
sea-bed mining, environmental protection, the establishment of an inspectorate for
day-to-day supervision of sea-bed mining, the institution of cases before the Sea Bed
Disputes Chamber, and measures to enforce decisions of the Chamber (LOSC, arts
163, 165). In addition, the Commission drafts the rules and regulations of the Authority (LOSC, art. 165.). . . .

However, while the Council is to endeavour to ensure that the Commission includes all necessary skills, it is also required to take due account of the need for equitable geographical distribution and the representation of special interests when
electing members. According to LOSC, article 163(2), the Commission should have
fifteen members, but its size may be increased "having due regard to economy and
efficiency." In fact, all twenty-two candidates nominated to the Commission were
elected in the first election in 1996.[56] . . .

55. States may be eligible for election in a number of categories. . . .
56. The first members came from the following States: Bahamas, Cameroon, China, Costa Rica,
Côte d'Ivoire, Cuba, Egypt, Fiji, Finland, France, Gabon, Germany, India, Italy, Japan, Namibia, Norway,
Poland, Republic of Korea, Russia, Ukraine, USA.

The Finance Committee

The 1994 Implementation Agreement (Annex, Section 9) established a Finance Committee, for which the 1982 Convention had made no specific provision. As in the case of the other organs, the election of its fifteen members, who must have appropriate financial qualifications, must take due account of the need for equitable geographical distribution and the representation of special interests. Each of the Council groups in sub-paragraphs (a), (b), (c) and (d) (see above under "The Council") must have at least one member. . . . The Committee is responsible for making recommendations concerning the drafting of the financial rules of the Authority, the Authority's budget and the contributions of Member States to it, and the equitable sharing of the economic benefits of sea-bed mining activities.

The Enterprise

In the early days of UNCLOS III it was hoped by many that the mining of the riches of the deep sea bed would be primarily the privilege and responsibility of an international mining corporation, the Enterprise, to be established under the auspices of the Authority. The 1982 Convention provided for the establishment of the Enterprise as a separate organ of the Authority, and empowered it to engage in prospecting and mining the Area. . . . Subject to obligations to comply with the Assembly's general policies and the Council's directives and to report to the Authority, the Enterprise was an autonomous organisation, and so would have stood in much the same relationship to the Authority as would commercial operators. Thus mining by the Enterprise would have been dependent upon authorisation by the Authority, following applications made by the Governing Board. The intention was that the Enterprise would gain the necessary mining technology by buying it from commercial operators, or entering into joint ventures with them. Its "profits" would then be distributed, as part of the "common heritage of mankind," by the Authority (LOSC, art. 170 and Annex IV).

That plan has been radically revised in the face of the commercial realities of sea-bed mining. No commercial mining of the Area is likely in the near future, and there is therefore no immediate need to establish the Enterprise. Moreover, the Enterprise is required by the 1994 Implementation Agreement to conduct its initial mining operations through joint ventures, not as an independent mining operator. Accordingly, the Secretariat will perform the functions of the Enterprise until the Council decides that the Enterprise should begin to operate independently of the Secretariat. Those functions are, in the first instance, extremely modest: they include the monitoring of sea-bed mining trends and developments, the assessment of research and prospecting data, and the assessment of approaches to joint-venture arrangements. Sea-bed mining is, conspicuously, not made a priority (1994 IA, Annex, Section 2).

Decision-making in the International Sea Bed Authority

The provisions on the composition of the Authority's organs go some way towards safeguarding the interests of the various constituencies concerned with sea-bed mining. It was, however, thought necessary to provide safeguards for the interests of those who might find themselves in a minority in those organs. The powers of the various organs are therefore closely defined, and a complex decision-making procedure has been established. The Council "chambers" are given a crucial role in that procedure, which prevents simple majorities in the Authority from overriding the interests of the special groups. Broadly speaking, the more important a decision is for sea-bed mining interests the more it is insulated from simple majority decision-making within the Authority.

The Assembly was initially given "the power to establish general policies in conformity with the relevant provisions of this Convention on any question or matter within the competence of the Authority." That position was, in theory, fundamentally changed by the 1994 Implementation Agreement, which brought the law into line with the political realities of the situation by stipulating that "the general policies of the Authority shall be established by the Assembly in collaboration with the Council" (Annex, Section 3, paragraph 1). The implication of that is spelled out:

> Decisions of the Assembly on any matter for which the Council also has competence or on any administrative, budgetary or financial matter shall be based on the recommendations of the Council. If the Assembly does not accept the recommendation of the Council on any matter, it shall return the matter to the Council for further consideration. (1994 IA, Annex, Section 3, paragraph 4)

The practical result is that the Council is given the pivotal role in the formation of Authority policy. . . .

The Implementation Agreement stipulates that "as a general rule, decision-making in the organs of the Authority should be by consensus" (Annex, Section 3, paragraph 2). Consensus means the absence of formal objection. In cases where a consensus cannot be achieved, the organ may have to fall back on a majority vote.[59] The Assembly, for example, decides questions of substance by a two-thirds majority, and questions of procedure by simple majority, in such circumstances. But the hope, and expectation, is that consensus will be the norm. . . .

Some substantive decisions to be taken by the Council *must* be taken by consensus: they cannot be taken by majority vote. These include the adoption of measures to protect the economies of developing countries from adverse effects of sea-bed mining; recommendations to the Assembly on the sharing of the benefits of sea-bed mining; the adoption of rules concerning sea-bed mining; and the adoption of amendments to Part XI of the Convention.[60] The necessity for proceeding in these four cases by consensus, and the veto power possessed by each State that it implies, creates a danger that the Authority may be unable to act. Accordingly a "conciliation procedure" was built in to facilitate progress. . . . (LOSC, art. 161(8)).

The risk of dissent precluding Council action in the case of the decisions requiring consensus is further reduced by other procedural devices. . . .

Council decisions on other questions of substance require a two-thirds majority. In addition, it is necessary that the decision be not opposed by a majority in any one of the four chambers into which the members of the Council are divided (1994

---

59. Subject to the exceptional cases, described below, in which decisions *must* be taken by consensus.
60. LOSC, art. 161(8)(d). On the amendment procedure, see also LOSC, arts 316–16.

IA, Annex, Section 3, paragraph 5). The latter requirement offers added protection to the interests of the major consumers, investors and land-based exporters who, as has been seen, constitute chambers (a) to (c) of the Council. . . . Council decisions on procedural questions are taken by a simple majority of members present and voting (1994 IA, Annex, Section 3, paragraph 5).

These procedural safeguards were important in winning the confidence of the developed States and assuaging their fears that the developing States, with their large majority in the Assembly, might override the developed States' interests. . . .

Financing the Authority

Up to the end of 1997 the Authority was funded out of the regular UN budget. Thereafter it will be funded by contributions from its members until it is able to fund itself from "other soruces"— the payments received from deep-sea-bed miners (LOSC, arts 171, 173; 1994 IA, Annex, Section 1, paragraph 14). The Secretary General submits a draft annual budget to the Finance Committee, which then reports to the Council, which passes it on to the Assembly for approval. Contributions are raised from member States in accordance with a scale based on that used for the regular UN budget. . . . The intention is that as sea-bed mining gets under way the Authority should move steadily towards being self-financing. Funding will come from the payments made to the Authority by commercial operators and the Enterprise.

The financing of the Enterprise is quite distinct from that of the Authority. . . . The present intention . . . that the Enterprise should become an independent mining operator only when it is able to do so on a self-supporting commercial basis.

THE SYSTEM OF EXPLOITATION

Attention can now be turned from the institutions to the substantive provisions of the deep-sea-bed mining regime. They are based on the "parallel system," under which the Area may be exploited both by the Enterprise and by commercial operators.

Prospecting is the first stage of exploitation under this system. Although the term is not defined, it seems to connote general searches for sea-bed resources, rather than the detailed pre-production surveying which appears to be covered by the term "exploration." Prospecting is essentially free. . . . Two or more prospectors may be active in the same area simultaneously. . . .

Exploration and exploitation, in contrast, require specific authorisation by the Authority, which authorisation carries with it exclusive rights. Qualified applicants may submit plans of work for the approval of the Authority. Applicants are "qualified" if they are entities possessing the nationality of a State Party . . . and effectively controlled by them or by their nationals. . . . The applicants must also be sponsored by those States, and meet the qualification standards set out by the Authority. . . . Applicants are also obliged to undertake to comply with the Convention and rules made under it, to accept the control of the Authority over activities in the Area, and to give a written assurance of good faith in fulfilling contractual obligations (LOSC, art. 153, and Annex III, arts. 3, 4; 1994 IA, Annex, Section 1, paragraph 12).

Applicants were formerly required to accept the Convention provisions concerning the mandatory transfer of technology. Those provisions were one of the main obstacles to ratification by certain western States, which considered them an unacceptable undermining of the principles of intellectual property ownership. The provisions stipulated that the applicant had to undertake to make available to the Enterprise and developing States wishing to engage in sea-bed mining, on fair and reasonable commercial terms and conditions, any technology which it used in sea-bed activities which it was legally entitled to transfer, if the Enterprise could not obtain such technology or equally efficient and useful technology on reasonable commercial terms on the open market. Those provisions were disapplied by the 1994 Implementation Agreement, and replaced with a much simpler provision. It amplifies the general exhortation in article 144 of the 1982 Convention to promote technology transfer and obliges contractors and their sponsoring States to co-operate with the Authority in obtaining technology for the Enterprise and developing States "on fair and reasonable commercial terms and conditions, consistent with the effective protection of intellectual property rights" (1994 IA, Annex, Section 5).

The plans of work submitted by qualified applicants (not by the Enterprise) must specify two sites of equal estimated commercial value which may or may not be contiguous, each large enough to support a mining operation. Data concerning both sites and their resources must also be submitted. The Authority may then approve a plan of work relating to one of the two sites, and enter into a contract with the applicant incorporating that plan. If it does so, it must designate the other site as a "reserved site." There is an initial period of fifteen years from the date of the site's "reservation" (or, if that is later, fifteen years from the time that the Enterprise becomes independent of the Secretariat) during which reserved sites are available only for development by the Authority, acting through the Enterprise or in association with developing States. . . . Where joint ventures are sought (as they must be by the Enterprise in its early days) the contractor that "contributed" the reserved area has the right of first refusal to enter the joint venture arrangement (1994 IA, Annex, Section 2, paragraph 2). If the Enterprise does not submit a plan for a reserved site within the fifteen-year period the contractor that contributed the reserved area may submit a plan of work for it, as long as it offers in good faith to include the Enterprise as a joint-venture partner.

Applications are to be dealt with by the Authority in order of receipt. To preclude any possibility of the Authority unreasonably impeding development of the sea bed, it is provided that approval of plans can be refused only in certain specified circumstances. . . .

In all cases it is the Legal and Technical Commission which first reviews the proposed plan (1994 IA, Annex, Section 1, paragraph 6; LOSC, Annex III). The policies that it is to adopt have been spelled out in the 1994 Implementation Agreement. Deep-sea-bed resources are to be developed in accordance with sound commercial principles; there is to be no subsidisation of sea-bed mining (a provision backed up by the linking of the LOSC regime to the GATT/World Trade Organisation regime and its provisions on subsidies, procurement, and so on);[65] and there must be no

---

65. 1994 IA, Annex, Section 6, paragraph 1. Sea-bed mining is thus brought within the GATT/WTO dispute settlement procedures, on which see E.-U. Petersmann, The GATT/WTO Dispute Settlement System (London, Kluwer), 1997.

discrimination, such as preferential access to markets, between minerals derived from the deep sea bed and those from other sources (1994 IA, Annex, Section 6, paragraphs 1 to 6).

Plans must indicate the maximum mineral production expected, year by year. Under the original 1982 provisions the Authority was required to limit production authorisations to levels that would permit sea-bed minerals to meet a certain proportion of the growth in world nickel demand. That elaborate production ceiling, and the preferential treatment enjoyed by the Enterprise under it, was regarded as objectionable in principle by many western States. It was abandoned in the 1994 Implementation Agreement (Annex, Section 6, paragraph 7): regulation of production is left to the market. . . .

The financial terms of contracts concluded pursuant to approved plans of work and production authorisations were very complicated in the 1982 text (LOSC, Annex III, art. 13), and have been greatly simplified by the 1994 Implementation Agreement. There is an initial fee of $250,000 payable for the processing of the plan application. There will also be an annual fee payable by the contractor once commercial exploitation begins; and the Authority is required to devise a payment system, of which the annual fee is a part, that "should not be complicated". . . .

Throughout the contract period the Authority will supervise operations, and may require operators to transfer to it any data necessary for the performance of its functions. In cases of non-compliance the Authority may impose monetary penalties, and, in serious cases, suspend or terminate the contract, although in all cases the contractor has the right to take the matter through the dispute settlement procedure (LOSC, arts 186–91, and Annex III, arts 14–19; see also chapter nineteen). That procedure ensures that rights and duties provided for in the Convention are enforced. Neither the Authority nor the contractor has the right to modify the terms of a contract without the other's consent. . . .

THE COMMON HERITAGE

The "common heritage" will be exploited for the benefit of "mankind as a whole," and not simply of the industrialised States, in a number of ways. The collection and distribution among States — in particular, developing States and peoples — of payments made to the Authority by the commercial operators and perhaps later by the Enterprise is the most obvious. The Convention does not stipulate the manner in which the financial benefits are to be shared out; only that the sharing should be "equitable" (LOSC, art. 140). Precise rules will be decided upon by the Authority. In fact some States will, in effect, have a preferential claim on the monies. These are the developing States that suffer adverse effects on their export earnings or economies as a result of falls in mineral prices caused by sea-bed mining, for whose benefit the Convention requires the Authority to establish a system of economic assistance. But it seems clear that the financial benefits of sea-bed exploitation are likely to be modest and not immediate. Commercial mining is still some way off; and the discoveries of substantial new land-based reserves of nickel, copper and cobalt in Canada and elsewhere and of manganese nodules within the coastal waters of Papua New Guinea are likely to postpone even further resort to the complex, expensive technologies for recovering minerals from the abyssal depths. The claims made in the 1960s of unimaginable wealth seem unlikely ever to be realised. Certainly, for the foreseeable future the most concrete dividend from the deep sea bed is likely to be in the form of knowledge and expertise channelled through the databases and training programmes organized by the Authority and the mining companies.

Notes and Questions

Although the 1994 agreement may have resolved the problems with the LOS Convention's provisions on deep seabed mining, the debate illustrates fundamental questions regarding the balancing of competing ideologies in international agreements.

1. Do you agree with the fundamental assumption of the Convention that the Area and its resources "are the common heritage of mankind"? (Article 136.) If not, what principle do you support?

2. The Outer Space Treaty, which came into effect in 1967 and has over 100 parties (including the United States), provides that: "The exploration and use of outer space, including the moon and other celestial bodies, shall be carried out for the benefit and in the interests of all countries . . . , and shall be the province of all mankind. . . ." Outer Space Treaty, January 27, 1967, art. 1, 18 U.S. T. 2410, 610 U.N.T.S. 205. Is this similar to the "common heritage of mankind" in the LOS Convention? See also the discussion of Antarctica at the end of this chapter.

3. As for the institutions for the Area, does the Convention establish a fair arrangement from the standpoint of most countries? From the standpoint of the United States? If not, why not?

4. Prior to the 1994 agreement, how significant were the provisions about the Area in the overall importance of the Convention? Were problems with those provisions worth opposing the entire Convention?

5. In the absence of an agreement addressing the U.S. objections, would it have been sound policy for the United States to support as customary international law the provisions of the Convention that it liked and disregard the other provisions? Are there any dangers to such a policy?

I. WIDESPREAD ACCEPTANCE OF THE CONVENTION

The successful negotiation of the 1994 agreement led many countries to move forward with the ratification process for the Convention and the 1994 agreement. The Convention came into force in November 1994. The agreement came into force on a provisional basis at the same time and then it acquired the necessary ratifications to come definitively into force in July 1996.

Promptly after the 1994 agreement had been reached, the Clinton Administration announced that the United States would sign the agreement and that it would submit the agreement and the Convention to the U.S. Senate for its advice and consent.

Letter of Submittal from the State Department to the President

Message from the President of the United States Transmitting United Nations Convention on the Law of the Sea and the Agreement Relating to the Implementation of Part XI of the United Nations Convention on the Law of the Sea, S. Treaty Doc. No. 103-39 (Oct. 7, 1994)

THE AGREEMENT

The achievement of a widely accepted and comprehensive law of the sea convention — to which the United States can become a Party — has been a consistent objective of successive U.S. administrations for the past quarter century. However, the United States decided not to sign the Convention upon its adoption in 1982 because of objections to the regime it would have established for managing the development of seabed mineral resources beyond national jurisdiction. While the other Parts of the Convention were judged beneficial for U.S. ocean policy interests, the United States determined the deep seabed regime of Part XI to be inadequate and in need of reform before the United States could consider becoming Party to the Convention.

Similar objections to Part XI also deterred all other major industrialized nations from adhering to the Convention. However, as a result of the important international political and economic changes of the last decade — including the end of the Cold War and growing reliance on free market principles — widespread recognition emerged that the seabed mining regime of the Convention required basic change in order to make it generally acceptable. As a result, informal negotiations were launched in 1990, under the auspices of the United Nations Secretary-General, that resulted in adoption of the Agreement on July 28, 1994.

The legally binding changes set forth in the Agreement meet the objections of the United States to Part XI of the Convention. The United States and all other major industrialized nations have signed the Agreement.

The provisions of the Agreement overhaul the decision-making procedures of Part XI to accord the United States, and others with major economic interests at stake, adequate influence over future decisions on possible deep seabed mining. The Agreement guarantees a seat for the United States on the critical executive body and requires a consensus of major contributors for financial decisions.

The Agreement restructures the deep seabed mining regime along free market principles and meets the U.S. goal of guaranteed access by U.S. firms to deep seabed minerals on the basis of reasonable terms and conditions. It eliminates mandatory transfer of technology and production controls. It scales back the structure of the organization to administer the mining regime and links the activation and operation of institutions to the actual development of concrete commercial interest in seabed mining. A future decision, which the United States and a few of its allies can block, is required before the organization's potential operating arm (the Enterprise) may be activated, and any activities on its part are subject to the same requirements that apply to private mining companies. States have no obligation to finance the Enterprise, and subsidies inconsistent with GATT are prohibited.

The Agreement provides for grandfathering the seabed mine site claims established on the basis of the exploration work already conducted by companies holding U.S. licenses on the basis of arrangements "similar to and no less favorable than" the best terms granted to previous claimants; further, it strengthens the provisions requiring consideration of the potential environmental impacts of deep seabed mining.

The Agreement provides for its provisional application from November 16, 1994, pending its entry into force. Without such a provision, the Convention would enter into force on that date with its objectionable seabed mining provisions unchanged. . . . Further, the Agreement provides flexibility in allowing States to apply it provisionally in accordance with their domestic laws and regulations.

In signing the agreement on July 29, 1994, the United States indicated that it intends to apply the agreement provisionally pending ratification. Provisional application by the United States will permit the advancement of U.S. seabed mining interests by U.S. participation in the International Seabed Authority from the outset to ensure that the implementation of the regime is consistent with those interests, while doing so consistent with existing laws and regulations. . . .

The U.S. Senate has yet to act on the Convention and agreement. Primarily because of conservative opposition led by Senator Jesse Helms, the U.S. Senate Foreign Relations Committee (which he chaired during much of the 1994-2002 period) has yet to hold the committee hearings that are required to precede a Senate vote of advice and consent. This was in spite of the efforts of the Clinton Administration as well as a coalition of groups spearheaded by the U.S. Navy and oil, mining, shipping, and telecommunication industries that supported ratification.

Senator Helms retired at the end of 2002. However, as of early 2003, it is unclear whether the Republican-controlled Senate will move forward with hearings and a vote in the near future on the Convention and the agreement. There is still some lingering domestic opposition to the Convention, even after the 1994 agreement, essentially because of somewhat undefined concerns that the agreement was insufficient. Moreover, as discussed above, the United States has already selectively adopted many of the provisions of the Convention through laws, executive orders, and presidential proclamations. As a result, it is already enjoying many of the benefits of the Convention without having ratified it.

While the United States hesitated, the 1994 agreement led most other countries to ratify the Convention and the agreement, if they were not already parties to the Convention. By April 2003, there were 142 parties to the LOS Convention and 113 parties to the 1994 agreement. The parties to the Convention now include all the major industrial nations, except for the United States and Canada. (See the full list in the Documentary Supplement.)

Notes and Questions

1. What are some of the more important provisions of the agreement?

2. Overall, does the agreement further the U.S. objective of a widely ratified, comprehensive law of the sea treaty that protects and promotes U.S. ocean interests?

3. What major U.S. bureaucracies, constituencies, or interest groups in the United States do you expect would support U.S. ratification of the LOS Convention and the 1994 agreement? Who was likely to oppose ratification? For example, on which side would you expect to find the U.S. Navy? American fishermen? U.S. deep seabed mining companies? U.S. oil companies?

4. The U.S. Congress passed the Oceans Act of 2000, which went into effect on January 20, 2001. The Act established a 16-member Commission on Ocean Policy to undertake an 18-month study and to make recommendations to the President and Congress for a national ocean policy for the United States. As indicated on the Commission's Web site:

> The Act charges the Commission to conduct a detailed review of existing and planned U.S. ocean and coastal programs and activities. The Commission is to provide recommendations for a coordinate and comprehensive national ocean policy on a broad range of issues, ranging from the stewardship of marine resources and pollution prevention to enhancing and supporting marine science, commerce, and transportation.

President George W. Bush appointed the 16 members to the Commission, based on a process that included nominations by both Congress and the President. Admiral James D. Watkins, USN (Ret.), the former Chief of Naval Operations (the Navy's highest uniformed position), was named chairman. The appointments were not finalized until July 3, 2001. As one of the Commissioners' first public actions, they unanimously passed the following resolution on November 14, 2001:

United Nations Law of the Sea Convention

> The National Commission on Ocean Policy unanimously recommends that the United States of America immediately accede to the United Nations Law of the Sea Convention. Time is of the essence if the United States is to maintain its leadership role in ocean and coastal activities. Critical national interests are at stake and the United States can only be a full participant in upcoming Convention activities if the country proceeds with expedition expeditiously. [See the Commission Web site: <http:www.oceancommission.gov>].

5. Do you agree with the Commission's recommendation? Is it preferable for the United States not to ratify the Convention and the 1994 agreement, but continue to select which provisions it will adopt and follow by relying on customary international law, domestic laws, presidential proclamations, and executive orders? What about the Commission's argument that the United States needs to become a full participant in upcoming Convention activities?

6. If a state that was already a party to the LOS Convention refused to approve the 1994 agreement, would the Convention apply between that state and another state (such as the United States) that ratified the Convention and the agreement? Would the Convention apply in all respects — as interpreted with or without the agreement? (See earlier discussion in Chapter 2 at pages 114-119.)

J. ANTARCTICA

Antarctica is the southernmost continent. Its area of 5.5 million square miles is larger than the United States and Mexico combined, but 98 percent of it is covered with ice an average one-mile thick. Antarctica is colder than any other continent and is a virtual desert, with annual precipitation of less than 3 inches; yet its snow and ice hold [about 70] percent of the world's fresh water. Except for a few bacteria, moss, and insects, the land is lifeless — in contrast with the teeming bird and marine life that includes penguins, seals, whales, fish, and krill (small Antarctic shrimp). [Antarctica Today, Environment, Sept. 1985, at 17.]

For over a quarter of a century, Antarctica has been a model of international cooperation, though disputes over possible future exploitation of the continent's mineral resources threaten the harmony. The accomplishments of the past were achieved largely as a result of the Antarctic Treaty System. This system includes the Antarctic Treaty, recommendations adopted pursuant to the Treaty, and separate agreements negotiated under the Treaty.

The Antarctic Treaty was negotiated in 1959 after a year of successful international scientific cooperation by 12 countries. The participants reached this agreement despite the cold war and conflicting land claims. Seven of the countries (Argentina, France, Norway, Britain, Australia, New Zealand, and Chile) claim territorial sovereignty, with some of these claims overlapping. The other five countries (United States, Belgium, Japan, South Africa, and Russia) neither recognize these claims nor assert claims, although the United States and Russia maintain a basis for a claim if they choose to make one. The treaty suspends all the claims and establishes Antarctica as a zone of peace, demilitarized, denuclearized, and subject to unannounced on-site inspections.

The Antarctic Treaty has a two-tiered status for Member States: "contracting status" and "consultative power." Any U.N. member or any unanimously approved state may accede to the Treaty and achieve contracting status. The consultative powers are the decision-makers in Antarctica. They include the 12 original signatories and any other state that can show sufficient interest in Antarctica by conducting "substantial scientific research activity." As of January 2003, there were 45 contracting members, 27 of which were also consultative powers.

As the main channel of negotiations for Antarctica, the consultative powers meet regularly to adopt new measures. These resolutions, which require unanimous approval, provide the flexibility necessary to manage changing interests in Antarctica. The requirement of unanimity assures commitment to the measure by all involved countries. As a result of these meetings, two additional treaties were negotiated: the Convention on the Conservation of Antarctic Marine Living Resources and the Convention for the Conservation of Antarctic Seals.

A problem came to the fore in late 1989, when environmental concerns led two of the consultative powers, France and Australia, to announce that they could no longer support an agreement that would have allowed exploitation, although strictly regulated, of Antarctica's mineral resources.

In 1991, the Antarctic Treaty states approved the Protocol on Environmental Protection to the Antarctic Treaty (the Madrid Protocol). The agreement bans all prospecting, exploration, or commercial exploitation of natural resources on the continent of Antarctica for the next 50 years.

As the Department of State explained:

The new protocol builds on the Antarctic Treaty to provide improved environmental protection measures that can be strengthened in the future as necessary. The protocol sets forth basic principles on the protection of the Antarctic environment, establishes an advisory body, and provides for a system of annexes to incorporate detailed mandatory rules for environmental protection.

The annexes establish legally binding measures on the conservation of Antarctic flora and fauna, waste disposal, marine pollution, and environmental impact assessment procedures that will be subject to compulsory and binding dispute settlement. Future annexes could be added following entry into force of the protocol.

The protocol also prohibits any activities other than scientific research that relate to Antarctic mineral resources. The prohibition can be reviewed at any time after 50 years following entry into force of the protocol.

After 50 years, an amendment to lift the mining ban would have to be approved by three-fourths of the 26 current voting nations to the Antarctic Treaty. The ban may be lifted prior to the 50-year window only if all the parties to the Treaty agree to do so.

The Protocol went into effect in 1998, after all consultative parties (26 at the time) had ratified it. Obviously, a 50-year moratorium puts a long halt on exploitation of Antarctica.

Notes and Questions

1. Should individual states be allowed to make territorial claims to Antarctica? If so, on what basis? If not, should the continent remain subject to international control? What states should have a voice in the control?

2. Should the mineral and oil resources of Antarctica be considered part of the "common heritage of mankind"? If not, what system for exploitation would be appropriate? If so, how should the states determine whether, and how, exploitation should proceed?

Bibliography

There is an extensive literature on the Law of the Sea and Antarctica, some excerpted or already cited in this chapter. In addition, for the Law of the Sea, see A Handbook on the New Law of the Sea (R.-J. Dupuy & D. Vignes eds., 1991); E.D. Brown, Sea-Bed Energy and Minerals: The International Legal Regime (1992); Lee A. Kimball, Treaty Implementation: Scientific and Technical Advice Enters a New Stage (1996); Law of the Sea (Hugo Caminos ed., 2001); Law of the Sea: The Common Heritage and Emerging Challenges (Harry N. Scheiber, ed. 2000); Jonathan I. Charney, The Implications of Expanding International Dispute Settlement Systems, The 1982 Convention on the Law of the Sea, 90 Am. J. Intl. L. 69 (1996); John E. Noyes, International Law of the Sea, 31 Intl. Law. 703 (1997). For the latest developments in the Law of the Sea, see Web site: <http://www.un.org/Depts/los>.

On Antarctica, see, for example, Christopher C. Joyner, Governing the Frozen Commons: The Antarctic Regime and Environmental Protection (1998); Lee A. Kimball, Southern Exposure: Deciding Antarctica's Future (1990); Protecting the Polar Environment (Davor Vidas ed., 2000). For the latest developments in Antarctica, see the following Web sites: <http://www.antdiv.gov.au/information/treaty> and <http://www.asoc.org>.

10

International
Environmental Law

Until recently, environmental problems were normally considered to be local or national problems. In the past three decades, however, the pace of industrialization and urbanization, together with an enhanced consciousness of the interconnections of the biosphere, have made environmental issues a matter of international concern. As with human rights, the development of international rules concerning the environment has been hotly contested. Some developing countries regard environmental concerns as problems for the rich and environmental regulation as another impediment to economic development. And in this area, too, the United States has sometimes attempted to apply its laws and procedures extraterritorially in ways that other states may find objectionable. Finally, environmental regulation may strike at the economic well-being of important industries and states and can even challenge cultural and social attitudes (as with attempts to ban commercial whaling). In part because the issues are so contentious, there is no general treaty dealing comprehensively with environmental issues. As was the case in human rights, however, concerned organizations and states have used the United Nations as a forum to heighten consciousness of the scope of the problem and to try to lay a foundation for the development of customary international law.

In this chapter we start by examining the historical background, learning about the many, and somewhat diffuse, efforts to deal with international environmental problems. We look at the possible foundations for the development of customary law, including the work of the United Nations and a key arbitral decision.

Most of the law in this area, however, is treaty law. In the last twenty years, several quite revolutionary multilateral treaties have been negotiated that go well beyond previous treaty regimes. These treaties deal with global problems such as ozone depletion, global warming, biodiversity, and toxic waste disposal on a widely accepted multilateral basis. The creation of these new regimes involves important developments in international law-making (such as the role of NGOs) and offers general lessons in law-making for other areas of international law. We will focus particularly on two treaties dealing with "global commons" problems, ozone depletion and global warming, and will extract from those regimes the general techniques employed. You should of course also think about how these international obligations are implemented domestically, again with a view to understanding the most effective techniques to maximize treaty compliance.

A.   BACKGROUND AND CUSTOMARY LAW

The relatively recent development of international environmental law is illustrated by the *Trail Smelter* arbitration between the United States and Canada. Many commentators consider the decision as one of the early bases of customary international law in the environmental area.

The history leading up to the arbitration is summarized by the Restatement section 601, Reporters' Note 1:

> The *Trail Smelter* case resulted from injuries caused in the State of Washington by large amounts of sulphur dioxide emitted since 1925 by a smelter plant at Trail, British Columbia. Claims for the injury could not be brought in the courts of British Columbia under a doctrine of nuisance since under the law of that province such claims were "local" and could be brought only in the jurisdiction where the injured property was located.... The State of Washington, on the other hand, had no jurisdiction over the polluter, a Canadian company, as it was not engaged in any business in that State. (At that time long-arm jurisdiction was not yet available....) In 1928, the matter was referred to the International Joint Commission established under the Boundary Waters Treaty of 1909, 36 Stat. 2448, T.S. No. 548, 12 Bevans 319, but the Commission's report was rejected by the United States. Further negotiations led to a Convention in 1935 submitting to arbitration two questions: reparation for past injuries and arrangements for the future.

Trail Smelter Case (United States v. Canada)

Arbitral Tribunal, 1941
III U.N. Rep. Intl. Arb. Awards 1905, 1907 (1949)

CONVENTION FOR SETTLEMENT OF DIFFICULTIES ARISING FROM OPERATION OF SMELTER AT TRAIL, B.C. ...

Article III

The Tribunal shall finally decide the questions, hereinafter referred to as "the Questions," set forth hereunder, namely:

(1) Whether damage caused by the Trail Smelter in the State of Washington has occurred since the first day of January, 1932, and, if so, what indemnity should be paid therefor?

(2) In the event of the answer to the first part of the preceding Question being in the affirmative, whether the Trail Smelter should be required to refrain from causing damage in the State of Washington in the future, and if so, to what extent? ...

Article IV

The Tribunal shall apply the law and practice followed in dealing with cognate questions in the United States of America as well as international law and practice, and shall give consideration to the desire of the high contracting parties to reach a solution just to all parties concerned. . . .

DECISION

Reported on March 11, 1941, to the Government of the United States of America and to the Government of the Dominion of Canada, Under the Convention Signed April 15, 1935.

Tribunal answered Question No. 1 as follows:

Damage caused by the Trail Smelter in the State of Washington has occurred since the first day of January, 1932, and up to October 1, 1937, and the indemnity to be paid therefor is seventy-eight thousand dollars ($78,000), and is to be complete and final indemnity and compensation for all damage which occurred between such dates. Interest at the rate of six per centum per year will be allowed on the above sum of seventy-eight thousand dollars ($78,000) from the date of the filing of this report and decision until date of payment. . . .

In 1896, a smelter was started under American auspices near the locality known as Trail, B.C. [British Columbia]. In 1906, the Consolidated Mining and Smelting Company of Canada, Limited, obtained a charter of incorporation from the Canadian authorities, and that company acquired the smelter plant at Trail as it then existed. Since that time, the Canadian company, without interruption, has operated the Smelter, and from [time] to time has greatly added to the plant until it has become one of the best and largest equipped smelting plants on the American continent. In 1925 and 1927, two stacks of the plant were erected to 409 feet in height and the Smelter greatly increased its daily smelting of zinc and lead ores. This increased production resulted in more sulphur dioxide fumes and higher concentrations being emitted into the air. In 1916, about 5,000 tons of sulphur per month were emitted; in 1924, about 4,700 tons; in 1926, about 9,000 tons — an amount which rose near to 10,000 tons per month in 1930. In other words, about 300-350 tons of sulphur were being emitted daily in 1930. (It is to be noted that one ton of sulphur is substantially the equivalent of two tons of sulphur dioxide or SO_2.)

From 1925, at least, to 1937, damage occurred in the State of Washington, resulting from the sulphur dioxide emitted from the Trail Smelter. . . .

The second question under Article III of the Convention is as follows:

In the event of the answer to the first part of the preceding question being in the affirmative, whether the Trail Smelter should be required to refrain from causing damage in the State of Washington in the future and, if so, to what extent? . . .

The first problem which arises is whether the question should be answered on the basis of the law followed in the United States or on the basis of international law. The Tribunal, however, finds that this problem need not be solved here as the law followed in the United States in dealing with the quasi-sovereign rights of the States of the Union, in the matter of air pollution, whilst more definite, is in conformity with the general rules of international law.

Particularly in reaching its conclusions as regards this question as well as the next, the Tribunal has given consideration to the desire of the high contracting parties "to reach a solution just to all parties concerned."

As Professor Eagleton puts it (Responsibility of States in International Law, 1928, p. 80): "A State owes at all times a duty to protect other States against injurious acts by individuals from within its jurisdiction." A great number of such general pronouncements by leading authorities concerning the duty of a State to respect other States and their territory have been presented to the Tribunal. These and many others have been carefully examined. International decisions, in various matters, from the Alabama case onward, and also earlier ones, are based on the same general principle, and, indeed, this principle, as such, has not been questioned by Canada. But the real difficulty often arises rather when it comes to determine what . . . is deemed to constitute an injurious act. . . .

No case of air pollution dealt with by an international tribunal has been brought to the attention of the Tribunal nor does the Tribunal know of any such case. The nearest analogy is that of water pollution. But, here also, no decision of an international tribunal has been cited or has been found.

There are, however, as regards both air pollution and water pollution, certain decisions of the Supreme Court of the United States which may legitimately be taken as a guide in this field of international law, for it is reasonable to follow by analogy, in international cases, precedents established by that court in dealing with controversies between States of the Union or with other controversies concerning the quasi-sovereign rights of such States, where no contrary rule prevails in international law and no reason for rejecting such precedents can be adduced from the limitations of sovereignty inherent in the Constitution of the United States.

In the suit of the State of Missouri v. the State of Illinois (200 U.S. 496, 521) concerning the pollution, within the boundaries of Illinois, of the Illinois River, an affluent of the Mississippi flowing into the latter where it forms the boundary between that State and Missouri, an injunction was refused. "Before this court ought to intervene," said the court, "the case should be of serious magnitude, clearly and fully proved, and the principle to be applied should be one which the court is prepared deliberately to maintain against all considerations on the other side." The court found that the practice complained of was general along the shores of the Mississippi River at that time, that it was followed by Missouri itself and that thus a standard was set up by the defendant which the claimant was entitled to invoke. . . .

In the more recent suit of the State of New York against the State of New Jersey (256 U.S. 296, 309), concerning the pollution of New York Bay, the injunction was also refused for lack of proof. . . . ". . . Before this court can be moved to exercise its extraordinary power under the Constitution to control the conduct of one State at the suit of another, the threatened invasion of rights must be of serious magnitude and it must be established by clear and convincing evidence."

What the Supreme Court says there of its power under the Constitution equally applies to the extraordinary power granted this Tribunal under the Convention. What is true between States of the Union is, at least, equally true concerning the relations between the United States and the Dominion of Canada.

In another recent case concerning water pollution (283 U.S. 473), the complainant was successful. The City of New York was enjoined, at the request of the State of New Jersey, to desist, within a reasonable time limit, from the practice of disposing of sewage by dumping it into the sea, a practice which was injurious to the coastal waters of New Jersey in the vicinity of her bathing resorts.

In the matter of air pollution itself, the leading decisions are those of the Supreme Court in the State of Georgia v. Tennessee Copper Company and Ducktown Sulphur, Copper and Iron Company, Limited. Although dealing with a suit against private companies, the decisions were on questions cognate to those here at issue. Georgia stated that it had in vain sought relief from the State of Tennessee, on whose territory the smelters were located, and the court defined the nature of the suit by saying: "This is a suit by a State for an injury to it in its capacity of quasi-sovereign. In that capacity, the State has an interest independent of and behind the titles of its citizens, in all the earth and air within its domain."

On the question whether an injunction should be granted or not, the court said (206 U.S. 230):

> It (the State) has the last word as to whether its mountains shall be stripped of their forests and its inhabitants shall breathe pure air. . . . It is not lightly to be presumed to give up quasi-sovereign rights for pay and . . . if that be its choice, it may insist that an infraction of them shall be stopped. This court has not quite the same freedom to balance the harm that will be done by an injunction against that of which the plaintiff complains, that it would have in deciding between two subjects of a single political power. Without excluding the considerations that equity always takes into account . . . it is a fair and reasonable demand on the part of a sovereign that the air over its territory should not be polluted on a great scale by sulphurous acid gas, that the forests on its mountains, be they better or worse, and whatever domestic destruction they may have suffered, should not be further destroyed or threatened by the act of persons beyond its control, that the crops and orchards on its hills should not be endangered from the same source. . . . Whether Georgia, by insisting upon this claim, is doing more harm than good to her own citizens, is for her to determine. The possible disaster to those outside the State must be accepted as a consequence of her standing upon her extreme rights.

Later on, however, when the court actually framed an injunction, in the case of the Ducktown Company (237 U.S. 474, 477) (an agreement on the basis of an annual compensation was reached with the most important of the two smelters, the Tennessee Copper Company), they did not go beyond a decree "adequate to diminish materially the present probability of damage to its (Georgia's) citizens."

Great progress in the control of fumes has been made by science in the last few years and this progress should be taken into account.

The Tribunal, therefore, finds that the above decisions, taken as a whole, constitute an adequate basis for its conclusions, namely, that, under the principles of international law, as well as of the law of the United States, no State has the right to use or permit the use of its territory in such a manner as to cause injury by fumes in or to the territory of another or the properties or persons therein, when the case is of serious consequence and the injury is established by clear and convincing evidence. . . .

Considering the circumstances of the case, the Tribunal holds that the Dominion of Canada is responsible in international law for the conduct of the Trail Smelter. Apart from the undertakings in the Convention, it is, therefore, the duty of the Government of the Dominion of Canada to see to it that this conduct should be in conformity with the obligation of the Dominion under international law as herein determined.

The Tribunal, therefore, answers Question No. 2 as follows: (2) So long as the present conditions in the Columbia River Valley prevail, the Trail Smelter shall be required to refrain from causing any damage through fumes in the state of Washington. . . .

In 1972, the U.N. sponsored the Stockholm Conference, which adopted, among other items, the non-binding Stockholm Declaration of guiding general principles. Of particular relevance to the development of general principles of customary international law are Principles 21 and 22:

Stockholm Declaration (1972)

Principle 21

States have, in accordance with the Charter of the United Nations and the principle of international law, the sovereign right to exploit their own resources pursuant to their own environmental policies, and the responsibility to ensure that activities within their jurisdiction or control do not cause damage to the environment of other States or of areas beyond the limits of national jurisdiction.

Principle 22

States shall co-operate to develop further the international law regarding liability and compensation for the victims of pollution and other environmental damage caused by activities within the jurisdiction or control of such states to areas beyond their jurisdiction.

Professor Phillipe Sands provides more detail and analysis of the Stockholm Conference and its Declaration in an excerpt below. (The Stockholm Declaration itself is in the Documentary Supplement.) Next, however, is the 1987 Restatement's key section about the then evolving principles of customary international law.

Restatement

Section 601. State Obligations with Respect to Environment of Other States and the Common Environment

(1) A state is obligated to take such measures as may be necessary, to the extent practicable under the circumstances, to ensure that activities within its jurisdiction or control

(a) conform to generally accepted international rules and standards for the prevention, reduction, and control of injury to the environment of another state or of areas beyond the limits of national jurisdiction; and

(b) are conducted so as not to cause significant injury to the environment of another state or of areas beyond the limits of national jurisdiction.

(2) A state is responsible to all other states

(a) for any violation of its obligations under Subsection (1)(a), and

(b) for any significant injury, resulting from such violation, to the environment of areas beyond the limits of national jurisdiction.

(3) A state is responsible for any significant injury, resulting from a violation of its obligations under Subsection (1), to the environment of another state or to its property, or to persons or property within that state's territory or under its jurisdiction or control.

Comment

a. Application of general principles of state responsibility. This Part applies to environmental questions the general principles of international law relating to the responsibility of states for injury to another state or its property or to persons within its territory or their property, or for injury to interests common to all states. A state is responsible under Subsections (2) and (3) for breach of any of its obligations under Subsection (1). It is responsible under Subsection (2) to all states, and any state may request that it abate a threat of pollution and make arrangements to prevent future violations. Under Subsection (3), it is responsible to an injured state for any significant injury and is required to make reparation for the injury. The conditions of responsibility and the remedies available may differ with the circumstances and with the interests affected.

b. "Generally accepted international rules and standards." This phrase is adopted from the law of the sea; the obligation under Subsection (1)(a) refers to both general rules of customary international law (see, e.g., the *Trail Smelter* case, Reporters' Note 1) and those derived from international conventions, and from standards adopted by international organizations pursuant to such conventions, that deal with a specific subject, such as oil pollution or radioactive wastes. A state is also obligated to comply with an environmental rule or standard that has been accepted by both it and an injured state, even if that rule or standard has not been generally accepted.

Where an international rule or standard has been violated, any state can object to the violation; where a state has been injured in consequence of such violation, it is entitled to damages or other appropriate relief from the responsible state; where there is a threat of injury, the threatened state, or any state acting on behalf of threatened common interests, is entitled to have the dangerous activity terminated. . . .

d. Conditions of responsibility. A state is responsible under Subsections (2) and (3) for both its own activities and those of individuals or private or public corporations under its jurisdiction. The state may be responsible, for instance, for not enacting necessary legislation, for not enforcing its laws against persons acting in its territory or against its vessels, or for not preventing or terminating an illegal activity, or for not punishing the person responsible for it. In the case of ships flying its flags, a state is responsible for injury due to the state's own defaults under Subsection (1) but is not responsible for injury due to fault of the operators of the ship. In both cases, a state is responsible only if it has not taken "such measures as may be necessary" to comply with applicable international standards and to avoid causing injury outside its territory, as required by Subsection (1). In general, the applicable international rules and standards do not hold a state responsible when it has taken the necessary and practicable measures; some international agreements provide also for responsibility regardless of fault in case of a discharge of highly dangerous (radioactive, toxic, etc.) substances, or an abnormally dangerous activity (e.g., launching of space satellites). . . . In all cases, however, some defenses may be available to the state; e.g., that it had acted pursuant to a binding decision of the Security Council of the United Nations, or that injury was due to the failure of the injured state to exercise reasonable care to avoid the threatened harm. A state is not responsible for injury due to a natural disaster such as an eruption of a volcano, unless such disaster was triggered or aggravated by a human act, such as nuclear explosion in a volcano's vicinity. But a state is responsible if after a natural disaster has occurred it does not take necessary and practicable steps to prevent or reduce injury to other states.

Under Subsections (2)(b) and (3), responsibility of a state for a significant injury entails payment of appropriate damages if the complaining state proves the existence of a causal link between an activity within the jurisdiction of the responsible state and the injury to the complaining state. Determination of responsibility raises special difficulties in cases of long-range pollution where the link between multiple activities in some distant states and the pollution in the injured state might be difficult to prove. Where more than one state contributes to the pollution causing significant injury, the liability will be apportioned among the states, taking into account, where appropriate, the contribution to the injury of the injured state itself.

A state is responsible under this section for environmental harm proximately caused by activity under its own jurisdiction, not for activity by another state. . . .

Although there has been no authoritative consideration of the issue, international environmental law has apparently not extended responsibility beyond the state directly responsible for the activities causing injury, under principles analogous to "product liability" which apply in some national legal systems. Thus, under this section, state A is responsible for a radioactive emission from a nuclear reactor operated in its territory that causes injury to state B, but there is no recognized responsibility to B by state C in which the defective reactor was manufactured or from which it was sold to state A. There may, however, be such responsibility pursuant to an international agreement between state A and state C, and in special circumstances under general principles of state responsibility. Also, there may be liability by the manufacturer or seller of the defective reactor, whether it is a state or a private person, under principles of national law applicable to the transaction.

Under this section, a state is obligated to take all necessary precautionary measures where an activity is contemplated that poses a substantial risk of a significant transfrontier environmental injury; if the activity has already taken place, the state is obligated to take all necessary measures to prevent or reduce pollution beyond its borders. Similarly, where a violation of international environmental rules and standards has already occurred, the violating state is obligated to take promptly all necessary preventive or remedial measures, even if no injury has yet taken place. . . .

Reporters' Notes

1. *General principles of state responsibility for environmental injury.* Principle 21 of the 1972 Stockholm Declaration on the Human Environment provides [see excerpt above]. . . . Report of the United Nations Conference on the Human Environment . . . (1973). According to Principle 22 of the Stockholm Declaration [see excerpt above]. . . . In 1973, the Council of the European Communities issued a statement of principles and objectives of Community environmental policy including the following: "In accordance with the Declaration of the United Nations Conference on Human Environment adopted in Stockholm, care should be taken to ensure that activities carried out in one state do not cause any degradation of the environment in another state." . . .

The 1963 Treaty banning certain nuclear weapon tests prohibits underground explosions that cause "radioactive debris to be present outside the territorial limits of the State under whose jurisdiction or control such explosion is conducted." The Soviet Union complained when nuclear explosions in Nevada vented and resulted in radioactive debris over Canada, Mexico, and the Eastern Pacific. Similarly, the United States complained when explosions in the Soviet Union resulted in radioactive debris in the air over Japan and the Western Pacific.

The Convention on Long-Range Transboundary Air Pollution was adopted in Geneva on November 13, 1979, by which more than 30 European states, as well as Canada and the United States, agreed to "endeavour to limit and, as far as possible, gradually reduce and prevent air pollution including long-range transboundary air pollution." Such pollution was defined as air pollution that originates "within the area under the national jurisdiction of one State and which has adverse effects in the area under the jurisdiction of another State at such a distance that it is not generally possible to distinguish the contribution of individual emission sources or groups of sources." The main emphasis of the Convention is on research and exchange of information. T.I.A.S. No. 10541; 18 Intl. Leg. Mat. 1442 (1979). . . . For a 1984 protocol to the Convention, providing more adequate financing for the program, see 24 Intl. Leg. Mat. 484 (1985). As to the implementation by the United States of the Convention, see Benedick, "Transboundary Air Pollution," U.S. Dept. of State, Current Policy No. 723 (1985). . . .

Two cases involving the United States and Canada illustrate the difficulties that have arisen in dealing with transfrontier injuries to the environment and the development of international law rules on this subject: the *Trail Smelter* case [excerpted above] and the *Gut Dam* case. . . .

In 1972, Canada invoked the *Trail Smelter* principle against the United States when an oil spill at Cherry Point, Washington, resulted in a contamination of beaches in British Columbia. . . . For a recent application of the *Trail Smelter* principle by a Dutch court, see Lammers, Pollution of International Watercourses 198 (1984).

The Gut Dam, which was built by Canada across the international boundary on the St. Lawrence River with the consent of the United States . . . , raised the water levels of Lake Ontario between 1947 and 1952 and caused injury by erosion and inundation to property owners on the United States shore of the lake. Their attempts to sue Canada in United States courts, and to sue the United States Government, proved unsuccessful. A United States statute authorized the investigation of the Gut Dam claims by the Foreign Claims Settlement Commission, but, before any decisions were rendered, the United States and Canada agreed to establish an international arbitral tribunal to dispose finally of the claims of United States citizens. . . .

After the tribunal rendered several preliminary decisions in favor of the United States, Canada agreed to pay to the United States $350,000 in full settlement of all claims. The tribunal recorded the settlement and terminated the proceedings.

In 1992, after the 1987 Restatement, the U.N. sponsored the 1992 Rio Conference, formally called the United Nations Conference on Environment and Development (UNCED). The conference adopted a comprehensive set of principles that built on or perhaps changed those adopted at Stockholm. Below is the important Rio Principle 2.

Rio Declaration

Principle 2

States have, in accordance with the Charter of the United Nations and the principles of international law, the sovereign right to exploit their own resources pursuant to their own environmental and development policies, and the responsibility to ensure that activities within their jurisdiction or control do not cause damage to the environment of other States or of areas beyond the limits of national jurisdiction.

The excerpts below from Professor Phillipe Sands and from Professor David Wirth further discuss the Rio Conference and Principle 2. We start with Professor Sands, who provides an overview of the historical development of international environmental law and also describes some of the law's generally accepted norms.

Phillipe Sands, Environmental Protection in the Twenty-First Century: Sustainable Development and International Law

The Global Environment: Institutions, Law, and Policy 123-137 (Norman J. Vig & Regina S. Axelrod eds., 1999)

The "greening" of international law has occurred over four periods, responding to particular factors that influenced legal developments. Until recently it was evident that international environmental law had arisen without a coordinated legal and institutional framework. The 1972 Stockholm conference and then UNCED [in 1992 at Rio] attempted to create such a framework.

To 1945. The first distinct period in the greening process began with nineteenth-century bilateral fisheries treaties and the [1893] Pacific Fur Seal Arbitration and concluded with the creation of the new UN family of international institutions in 1945. . . .

. . . [T]here was no international forum in which to raise environmental concerns, and most of the agreements adopted in this initial period did not create arrangements to ensure that legal obligations were complied with or enforced. Many initiatives grew from private activities by private citizens, an early harbinger of the more intensive activism of nongovernmental organizations that marks international negotiations today.

The Creation of the United Nations: 1945-1972. The establishment of the UN introduced a second period in the development of international environmental law, which culminated with the 1972 UN Conference on the Human Environment. During this period many international organizations with competence in environmental matters were created, and legal instruments were adopted to address particular sources of pollution and the conservation of general and particular environmental resources. These included oil pollution, nuclear testing, wetlands, the marine environment and its living resources, freshwaters, and the dumping of waste at sea.

The UN provided a forum for the discussion of the consequences of technical progress and introduced a period characterized by international organizations, involvement with environmental issues, and the addressing of the causes of pollution and environmental degradation. The relationship between economic development and environmental protection began to be understood. However, the UN Charter did not, and still does not, explicitly address environmental protection or the conservation of natural resources.

In 1949 the UN convened its first environmental conference, entitled the Conservation and Utilization of Resources. . . . The conference was significant also because it recognized the UN's competence in regard to environmental and natural resource issues. In 1954 the UN General Assembly convened its first major conference, the Conference on the Conservation of the Living Resources of the Sea, which led to the conservation rules adopted in the 1958 Geneva Conventions. The following year the General Assembly adopted the first of many resolutions on atomic energy and the effects of radiation, which led to the 1963 Nuclear Test Ban Treaty and, ultimately, the political context for Australia and New Zealand to bring to the International Court of Justice [in 1974] a case calling on France to stop all atmospheric nuclear tests.

Stockholm and Beyond. The third period began with the 1972 Stockholm conference and concluded with UNCED in 1992. In this twenty-year span the UN attempted to put in place a system to address a growing range of environmental issues in a more coordinated and coherent way. A raft of regional and global conventions addressed new issues, and new techniques of regulation were employed.

The 1972 conference, convened by the General Assembly, adopted three non-binding instruments: a resolution on institutional and financial arrangements; the Declaration of Twenty-six Guiding Principles; and an Action Plan setting forth 109 recommendations for more specific international action. These represented the international community's first effort at constructing a coherent strategy for the development of international policy, law, and institutions to protect the environment.

For international law the significant developments proved to be the creation of the United Nations Environment Programme (UNEP); the establishment of coordinating mechanisms among existing institutions; the definition of a framework for future actions to be taken by the international community; and the adoption of a set of general principles to guide such action, including Principle 21. UNEP has subsequently been responsible for the establishment and implementation of its Regional Seas Programme, including some thirty regional treaties, as well as important global treaties addressing ozone depletion, trade in hazardous waste, and biodiversity.

Stockholm catalyzed other global treaties adopted under the UN's auspices. The most important agreement, over time, may be the 1982 United Nations Convention on the Law of the Sea (UNCLOS). This established a unique, comprehensive framework for the establishment of global rules for the protection of the marine environment and marine living resources, including detailed institutional arrangements and provisions on environmental impact assessment, technology transfer, and liability. Its provisions have provided an influential basis for the language and approach of many other environmental agreements. Stockholm was followed by other new regional agreements. Also in this period economic and financial institutions began for the first time to address environmental issues.

By 1990, when preparations for UNCED formally began, there existed a solid body of rules of international environmental law. States were increasingly subject to limits on the right to allow or carry out activities that harmed the environment. New standards were in place and a range of techniques were sought to implement those standards. Environmental issues, moreover, had begun to intersect with economic matters, especially trade and development lending. But in spite of these relatively impressive achievements, environmental matters remained on the periphery of the international community's agenda and the activities of most institutions.

UNCED and Beyond. UNCED launched a fourth period for international environmental law, which might be characterized as the period of integration, requiring environmental concerns to be integrated into all international activities. In this period international environmental law was merged into international law in the field of sustainable development.

In December 1987 the UN General Assembly endorsed the Brundtland Report, and the following year it called for a global conference on environment and development. . . . [A]fter four preparatory negotiating sessions 176 states, several dozen international organizations, and several thousand NGOs converged on Rio de Janeiro for two weeks in June 1992. The purpose of the conference was to elaborate strategies and measures to halt and reverse the effects of environmental degradation in the context of strengthened national and international efforts to promote sustainable and environmentally sound development in all countries. UNCED adopted three nonbonding instruments: the Rio Declaration on Environment and Development (the Rio Declaration); a Non-legally Binding Authoritative Statement of Principles for a Global Consensus on the Management, Conservation, and Sustainable Development of All Types of Forest (the Forest Principles); and Agenda 21. Two treaties were also opened for signature at UNCED: the Convention on Biological Diversity and the United Nations Framework Convention on Climate Change.

It is still too early to fully assess UNCED's contribution to the progressive development of international law. . . .

INTERNATIONAL ENVIRONMENTAL LAW: GENERAL PRINCIPLES . . .

Despite impressive achievements, there is reason to doubt the impact of this body of law on actual governmental and human behavior. Limited implementation and enforcement suggests that international environmental law remains in its formative stages. Lawmaking is decentralized, with legislative initiatives being developed in literally dozens of different intergovernmental organizations at the global, regional, and subregional levels. Coordination between the initiatives is inadequate, leading to measures that are often duplicative and sometimes inconsistent. Moreover, the lawmaking process tends to be reactive and somewhat ad hoc in nature, often vulnerable to the vagaries of political, economic, and scientific events and findings. . . .

This part describes international environmental law as it currently stands — the general principles, the basic rules, and the emerging legal techniques for their implementation and enforcement. Although no single international legal instrument establishes binding rules or principles of global application, the pattern of state behavior has given rise to an emerging set of guiding principles and minimum standards of acceptable behavior in relation to particular environmental resources . . .

Principles of General Application

Several general principles and rules of international law have emerged, or are emerging, specifically in relation to environmental matters, as reflected in treaties, binding acts of international organizations, state practice, and soft law commitments. They are general in the sense that they are potentially applicable to all members of the international community across the range of activities that they carry out or permit to be carried out and that they address the protection of all aspects of the environment.

Sovereignty and Responsibility for the Environment. The rules of international environmental law have developed in pursuit of two principles that pull in opposing directions: that states have sovereign rights over their natural resources and that states must not cause damage to the environment. These objectives are now reflected in Principle 21 of the Stockholm Declaration and Principle 2 of the Rio Declaration and provide the foundation of international environmental law.

The first element (sovereignty) reflects the preeminent position of states as primary members of the international legal community. It is tempered by the second element (environmental protection), however, which places limits on the exercise of sovereign rights. In an environmentally interdependent world, activities in one state almost inevitably produce effects in other states or in areas beyond national jurisdiction (such as the high seas).

In the form presented by Principle 21 and Principle 2, the responsibility not to cause damage to the environment of other states or of areas beyond national jurisdiction has been accepted as an obligation by all states. . . . [T]he International Court of Justice has now confirmed that the second element reflects customary international law.[24]

The emergence of the responsibility of states not to cause environmental damage in areas outside their jurisdiction has historical roots that predate the Stockholm conference. These relate to the . . . principle endorsed by the arbitral tribunal in the much-cited *Trail Smelter* case, which stated that "no state has the right to use or permit the use of territory in such a manner as to cause injury by fumes in or to the territory of another of the properties or persons therein, when the case is of serious consequence and the injury is established by clear and convincing evidence."

Good Neighborliness and International Cooperation. The principle of "good neighborliness," as enunciated in Article 74 of the UN Charter, concerning social, economic, and commercial matters, has been extended to environmental matters by rules promoting international environmental cooperation. It applies particularly

---

24. *Legality of the Threat or Use of Nuclear Weapons,* ICJ Reports 1996, para. 29. See also "Case Concerning the Gabcikovo-Nagymaros Project" (Hungary/Slovakia), ICJ Reports 1997, paras. 53 and 112.

where activities carried out in one state might have adverse effects on the environment of another state or in areas beyond national jurisdiction. The commitment to environmental cooperation is reflected in many international agreements and is supported by state practice. . . . Specifically, the obligation can require information sharing, notification, consultation or participation rights in certain decisions, the conduct of environmental impact assessments, and cooperative emergency procedures, particularly where activities might be ultrahazardous. The construction of nuclear power plants on borders is an example where cooperative obligations are reasonably well developed, at least in some regions. . . .

Sustainable Development. Another emerging principle requires states to ensure that they develop and use their natural resources in a manner that is sustainable. Although the ideas underlying the concept of "sustainable development" have a long history in international law, the term has only recently begun to be used in international agreements. It has also been confirmed as having a role in international law by the International Court of Justice in the Gabcikovo-Nagymaros Case. The ideas underlining "sustainability" date at least to the Pacific Fur Seal Arbitration in 1893, when the United States asserted a right to ensure the legitimate and proper use of seals and to protect them, for the benefit of humankind, from wanton destruction.

What "sustainable development" means in international law today is, however, a more complicated matter. Where it has been used it appears to refer to at least four separate but related objectives that, taken together, might comprise the legal elements of the concept of "sustainable development". . . . First, as invoked in some agreements, it refers to the commitment to preserve natural resources for the benefit of present and future generations. Second, in other agreements sustainable development refers to appropriate standards for the exploitation of natural resources based upon harvests or use; examples include use that is "sustainable," "prudent," "rational," "wise," or "appropriate." Third, yet other agreements require an "equitable" use of natural resources, suggesting that the use by any state must take account of the needs of other states and people. And a fourth category of agreements require that environmental considerations be integrated into economic and other development plans, programs, and projects, and that development needs are taken into account in applying environmental objectives.

The instruments adopted at UNCED reflect each of these four objectives, and translate them in Agenda 21 and the Rio Declaration into more specific proposals and principles to govern human activity.

Common but Differentiated Responsibility. This principle has emerged from the application of the broader principle of equity in general international law, and from the recognition that the special needs of developing countries must be taken into account in the development, application, and interpretation of rules of international environmental law if they are to be encouraged to participate in global environmental agreements. The principle is reflected in a handful of international environmental agreements and is applicable in the Climate Change convention to require parties to protect the climate system "on the basis of equity and in accordance with their common but differentiated responsibilities and respective capabilities."

The principle of common but differentiated responsibility includes two important elements. The first expresses the common responsibility of states to protect certain environmental resources. The second element relates to the need to take account of differing circumstances, particularly in relation to each state's contribution to the creation of a particular environmental problem and its ability to respond to, prevent, reduce, and control the threat. . . .

Precautionary Principle. The precautionary principle emerged in international legal instruments only in the mid-1980s, though it had previously been relied upon in some domestic legal systems. It aims to provide guidance to states and the international community in the development of international environmental law and policy in the face of scientific uncertainty and is, potentially, the most radical of environmental principles, generating considerable controversy. Some of its supporters invoke it to justify preemptive international legal measures to address potentially catastrophic environmental threats such as ozone depletion or climate change. Opponents, however, have decried the principle for allowing overregulation of a range of human activities. The core of this emerging legal principle, which has now been endorsed in a number of agreements, is reflected in Principle 15 of the Rio Declaration, one part of which provides that "[w]here there are threats of serious or irreversible damage, lack of full scientific certainty shall not be used as a reason for postponing cost-effective measures to prevent environmental degradation."

Polluter-Pays Principle. The polluter-pays principle refers to the requirement that the costs of pollution be borne by the person or persons responsible for causing the pollution and the consequential costs. The precise meaning, international legal status, and effect of the principle remains open to question, since international practice based upon the principle is limited. It is doubtful whether it has achieved the status of a generally applicable rule of customary international law, except perhaps in relation to states in the European Union (EU), the UN Economic Commission for Europe (UNECE), and the OECD. It has nevertheless attracted broad support and relates closely to the development of rules on civil and state liability for environmental damage, on the permissibility of state subsidies, and the growing acknowledgment by developed countries of the "responsibility that they bear in the international pursuit of sustainable development in view of the pressures their societies place on the global environment," as well as the financial and other consequences that flow from this acknowledgment. Supporting instruments include Principle 14 of the Rio Declaration, OECD Council Recommendations, the EC Treaty of Rome (as amended) and related instruments. . . .

BASIC RULES AND EMERGING LEGAL STANDARDS

As international environmental law has developed, standards have been adopted to address a widening range of environmental resources. These standards tend to address particular resources, of which the most important have been flora and fauna, water quality, air quality, hazardous substances, and waste. Agenda 21 identifies the priority environmental issues and divides them into two categories. The first category addressed the priority needs for the protection and conservation of particular environmental media. These needs are

- the protection of the atmosphere, in particular by combating climate change, depletion of the ozone layer, and ground level and trans-boundary air pollution;
- protection of land resources, including farmlands, by, for example, combating desertification and drought and protecting mountain ecosystems;

- halting deforestation;
- the conservation of biological diversity;
- the protection of freshwater resources; and
- the protection of oceans and seas (including coastal areas) and marine living resources.

The second category of major issues identified the products of human technological and industrial innovation that are considered to be particularly harmful to the environment and that require international regulation. These are

- the management of biotechnology;
- the management of toxic chemicals, including their international trade;
- agricultural practice;
- the management of hazardous wastes, including their international trade;
- the management of solid wastes and sewage-related issues; and
- the management of radioactive wastes.

The difficulty with an approach that regulates sector by sector is that it tends to transfer harm from one environmental medium to another, or to substitute one form of harm for another. Thus, the prohibition on the dumping of radioactive wastes at sea may result in harm to land-based resources resulting from long-term storage. Efforts to address this problem have led to the emergence of the concept of integrated pollution control, which requires states and other persons to consider and minimize the impact of activities on all environmental resources at each stage of the processes that contribute to that activity.

Although Professor Sands and others view Stockholm Principle 21 and Principle 2 of the Rio Declaration as essentially the same, some commentators have noted that Rio Principle 2 might differ from the Stockholm principle.

David A. Wirth, The Rio Declaration on Environment and Development: Two Steps Forward and One Back, or Vice Versa?

29 Ga. L. Rev. 599, 603-610, 618-624 (1995)

Transboundary pollution — the transmission of a physical agent from the territory of one state that causes harm in the territory of another or in the areas beyond national jurisdiction — was one of the principal issues addressed at Stockholm. . . .

The Stockholm Declaration addresse[d] transboundary pollution in Principle 21. . . . At the Stockholm Conference, both the United States and Canada stated that they regarded Principle 21 as a codification of then-existing customary international law. Although it was framed as a nonbinding exhortation, over time Principle 21 acquired the force of a substantive rule of customary international law and is the only component of the Stockholm Declaration widely regarded to have achieved that status.

Since 1972, Stockholm Principle 21 has been alluded to and incorporated by reference in innumerable international authorities. While most of these instruments reference or quote the text as adopted in Stockholm, some authorities go further than Principle 21 in articulating a "pure" or "clean" formulation of a substantive obligation to prevent transboundary pollution, omitting the qualifying language asserting states' "sovereign right to exploit their own resources." By contrast, Rio Principle 2 restates Stockholm Principle 21 with an embellishment that expands this clause, authorizing states "to exploit their own resources pursuant to their own environmental *and developmental* policies."

The addition of the phrase "and developmental" might be interpreted as disrupting and skewing the already delicate balance between the twin clauses juxtaposed in Stockholm Principle 21, and in a manner inconsistent with at least some post-Stockholm sources. Alternatively, one observer commented that the drafters of Rio Principle 2 "simply updated" the Stockholm formulation by clarifying rights of states that are implicit in the earlier text and, indeed, in the international legal regime. After all, a state's right to exploit its resources does not derive from a United Nations-sponsored conference or even the Stockholm Declaration, but instead is an inherent attribute of sovereignty. The Rio Declaration, moreover, preserved the second clause, which addresses a state' "responsibility" not to cause damage outside its own territory, suggesting that the obligation to refrain from transboundary pollution has not changed.

However this modification might be interpreted, the Rio Declaration clearly altered the text of the earlier principle. And if Stockholm Principle 21 codified customary international law on the day before the Rio conference began, what was customary law on the day after its conclusion? Some might characterize Rio Principle 2 as "instant custom," a controversial approach whose application to Rio Principle 2 is not entirely clear. In this view, representatives of virtually every state on Earth, including more than a hundred heads of state or government, might be thought to have redirected the development of the international customary law of transboundary pollution when they adopted the Rio Declaration at UNCED. . . . Whatever the legal effect of this change, given the widespread acceptance and reaffirmance of Principle 21 and, indeed, the numerous documents that have recited it verbatim in the years following the Stockholm Declaration, the only plausible motivation for this modification is a purposeful shift on the part of the drafters of the Rio Declaration in the direction of the development side of the environment/development debate.

Questions

1. Where did the U.S.-Canada arbitral tribunal find the precedential support for its decision in the *Trial Smelter* case? In previous international tribunal decisions? In U.S. case law?

2. Given the precedents used by the *Trial Smelter* tribunal, how persuasive is that decision for the assertion of a rule of customary international law? Do the other authorities summarized in the Reporters' Notes to the Restatement contribute to finding that there are customary international law norms here?

3. Assuming that Principles 21 and 22 of the Stockholm Declaration (excerpted above at p. 916) have become customary international law, what is the exact obligation of a state under these principles? Is there a lack of specificity here?

4. Consider the provisions of Section 601 of the 1987 Restatement of Foreign Relations Law. Does the Restatement formulation closely follow the Stockholm principles? What about the Restatement's requirement for "significant injury"?

5. How useful for actual situations are the Stockholm Principles or the Restatement? Note the Restatement's qualifier, "to the extent practicable under the circumstances."

6. Rio Principle 2 includes the additional phrase that takes into account a state's "developmental" policies. Could this be interpreted, as Professor Wirth suggests above, as a modification of the *Trial Smelter* result and Stockholm Principle 21? What are the arguments pro and con? What is required for the formation and change of customary international law? What political forces might be reflected in the language change in the Rio principle?

7. Is the kind of damage involved in the *Trial Smelter* arbitration normally compensable under domestic law? Should domestic law, including nuisance law and remedies, be used in the development of customary international law?

8. What remedies besides monetary compensation should be available when there are international environmental harms? What were the remedies provided in *Trail Smelter*? What entity might impose and administer any continuing remedies?

9. What are the weaknesses of customary international environmental law? What are the strengths?

10. In Beanal v. Freeport-McMoran, 197 F.3d 161 (5th Cir. 1999), an Indonesian sued U.S. mining companies under the Alien Tort Statute and the Torture Victim Protection Act for a variety of alleged human rights violations, including environmental abuses, in its operation of an open pit copper, gold, and silver mine situated in Irian Jaya, Indonesia. (Both laws are discussed in Chapter 3.) Although plaintiff's pleadings apparently were not very specific, Beanal did refer to the Rio Declaration and to writings by Phillipe Sands (excerpted above). Analyzing the sources cited, including the specific language of the Rio Declaration's Principle 2, the court concluded (at 167) that the "sources of international law cited by Beanal and the amici merely refer to a general sense of environmental responsibility and state abstract rights and liberties devoid of articulable or discernable standards and regulations to identify practices that constitute international environmental abuses or torts."

B. TREATY LAW: GLOBAL APPROACHES

The following materials describe further the evolution of international environmental law since the 1972 Stockholm Conference, with the focus turning toward the development of treaty law. Even more specifically, the materials focus on treaties designed to deal with two major international problems, ozone depletion and global warming. Considerable progress has been made internationally in limiting ozone depletion, while global warming appears to be a growing problem.

Michael Faure & Jurgen Lefevere, Compliance with International Environmental Agreements

The Global Environment: Institutions, Law, and Policy 138-153
(Norman J. Vig & Regina S. Axelrod eds., 1999)

The United Nations Conference on the Human Environment, held in Stockholm in 1972, set off an unprecedented development of new international environmental treaties. Before 1972 only a dozen international treaties with relevance to the environment were in force; twenty-five years later more than a thousand such instruments could be counted.

With the intensified use of international treaties as a means to combat environmental degradation, concerns have arisen regarding the compliance of states with the commitments to which they agreed. Even within relatively strong regional organizations such as the European Union, compliance problems are more and more overshadowing successes in the adoption of new instruments. . . .

In recent decades new approaches to the drafting, adoption, implementation, operation, and enforcement of international environmental treaties have been attempted in an effort to improve the compliance of states with international environmental treaties. This chapter will give a brief overview of the problems experienced with treaty compliance and the solutions sought, both in theory and in practice. The findings of this chapter will be related to [two] international treaty regimes, the Montreal Protocol on Substances That Deplete the Ozone Layer [and] the United Nations Framework Convention on Climate Change (FCCC)[, which addresses global warming]. . . . In addition, other examples of environmental treaties will be given as well. . . .

THEORY OF COMPLIANCE

The term *compliance* is often not used in a consistent way, but confused with related terminology such as *implementation, effectiveness,* or even *enforcement.* To avoid unnecessary confusion, however, one should be careful in using these terms. *Implementation, compliance, enforcement,* and *effectiveness* refer to different aspects of the process of achieving international political and legal cooperation.

Implementation refers to the specific actions (including legislative, organizational, and practical actions) that states take to make international treaties operative in their national legal system. Implementation therefore establishes the link between the national legal system and the international obligations. The aim of establishing this link should be compliance. *Compliance* is generally defined as the extent to which the behavior of a state, party to an international treaty, actually conforms to the conditions set out in this treaty. . . . The third term, *enforcement,* indicates the methods that are available to force states to implement but also to comply with treaty obligations. Where compliance and implementation concern the actions of the states themselves, *effectiveness* is more concerned with, as the term indicates, the effect of the treaty as a whole. *Effectiveness* addresses the question whether treaties that are correctly complied with actually achieve the objectives stated in the treaty, or whether the treaty actually helped to reach the environmental goal for which it was designed. . . .

SOURCES OF COMPLIANCE AND NONCOMPLIANCE

Having discussed the theory of compliance in general, we will now address a few factors that may affect compliance with environmental agreements and possible sources of noncompliance.

Country Characteristics

The chances of compliance with international environmental accords will first of all depend to a large extent upon the characteristics of the parties involved in negotiating and adopting international environmental treaties, that is, the states concerned. . . .

There may be many reasons why states sign treaties but nevertheless do not comply. States may sign an agreement because of international pressure or to serve domestic interests. Domestic interests, however, may also oppose compliance. Hence, it may well be in the states' interest to sign the agreement but not to comply. . . .

Other factors that may play a role are, for example, the cultural traditions, the political system, and the administrative capacities of the country concerned, as well as economic factors. Also the strength of nongovernmental organizations (NGOs) . . . may influence compliance.

An important question is whether a country has a democratic form of government. Many features of democratic governments contribute to improved implementation and compliance. There may be more transparency and hence easier monitoring by citizens who can bring pressure to improve the implementation record. Also NGOs generally have more freedom to operate in democratic countries. . . .

A considerable role can also be played by individuals, such as the heads of state. In many cases the personal enthusiasm of a particular head of state has facilitated compliance, usually during the treaty negotiating process. . . .

Number of States and the "International Environment"

[Another] aspect relates to the number of states involved in the treaty and the pressure that other signatory states can exercise toward compliance of all. The greater the number of countries that have ratified an accord, and the greater the extent of their implementation and compliance, the greater also the probability will be of compliance by any individual country. Non-compliance would then run counter to international public opinion. . . .

Primary Rule System

The most important factor determining the likelihood of compliance is probably the primary rule system. The primary rule system is the actual contents of the treaty that is agreed upon by the parties. This primary rule system defines the behavior that is required by the specific treaty, or in other words, the duties imposed upon the participatory states under the specific treaty. The primary rules are directly related to the activity that the environmental accord is supposed to regulate. . . .

A first important aspect of the design of the primary rule system relates to whether it requires any behavioral change, what the costs of this change will be, and by whom this behavioral change is required. It is easier to achieve compliance if the degree of behavioral change and the costs of this change are low. It is therefore argued that, for instance, compliance with the FCCC might be harder to achieve than compliance with the Montreal Protocol, since more people and industries must make bigger behavioral changes. The Montreal Protocol mainly requires behavioral changes by the producers of a limited number of regulated substances. The goals of the FCCC, however, require large-scale behavioral changes, not only by industry, but also by individuals. . . .

The amount of detail or specificity of a treaty may affect future compliance. States can facilitate their own compliance by negotiating vague and ambiguous rules, for example, if they agree to provisions that seem to be in the environmental interest on paper but are sufficiently vague to allow business as usual. However, primary rules can also often increase compliance through greater specificity. Specific obligations make compliance easier by reducing the uncertainty about what states need to do to comply. . . .

When discussing the country characteristics, we indicated that one source of noncompliance may be the incapacity of states to fulfill the treaty obligations due to a lack of resources or a lack of technological abilities. Hence, when these problems are recognized during the drafting stage, noncompliance may be prevented by designing the primary rules in such a manner that differing capacities are taken into account. This can either take the form of a differentiation of the treaty obligations, related to the various capacities or of a transfer of resources or technologies. This is, again, an example of a managerial approach, where instead of blunt sanctions instruments are developed that take into account the varying capacities and thus prevent noncompliance in the treaty design stage. . . .

One concept used in the area of climate change, which also takes into account differing abilities of states, is joint implementation. When a treaty contains specific obligations (for example, concerning emissions reduction), joint implementation implies that one state can fulfill its emission reduction goals by investing in pollution reduction in a second state, in which the marginal costs of emission reduction are lower. Joint implementation is somewhat similar to the economic concept of "tradeable emission rights" to the extent that it causes a flow of "emission rights" to industrial states in exchange for financial aid and technologies to developing countries. Hence, this can also remedy the incapacity problem. Instruments such as financial or technology transfer mechanisms all should facilitate compliance. . . .

Reporting and Information

The likelihood of compliance will also depend upon informational issues. Information plays a role at several stages. First, accurate information on the environmental risks concerned seems important both for the chances of adoption of a treaty on the specific subject and to the likelihood of compliance. Second, information plays a role in increasing the transparency of implementation and compliance records of states through monitoring or reporting systems. . . .

Transparency can be achieved through an effective compliance information system that is laid down in the treaty. To a large extent treaties rely on self-reporting by states. . . . [I]n a regime system with often delicate political links and pressures, the "status" of a state is often very important. States are generally careful about "losing face" toward other states and toward their own population. This fear of losing face has traditionally been used in many treaties, including those outside the field of the environment, by imposing a requirement for the state to report on its compliance with the treaty. . . . Although reporting procedures can be found in most environmental treaties, they are often vaguely formulated and the reports are badly drafted. Hence the reporting procedure is often criticized for its "weak" character and the absence of sanctions in case of noncompliance with the reporting requirements. . . .

Compliance can be improved through monitoring by an independent third party. The likelihood of compliance will indeed to a large extent be influenced by the possibilities provided for in the treaty to monitor compliance effectively. This in turn also depends on the contents of the primary rules. The Montreal Protocol, for instance, regulated the production of chlorofluorocarbons (CFCs) because it was easier to monitor a few producers than thousands of consumers. . . .

The problems with reporting procedures have led to the development of *compliance information systems*. Such compliance information systems contain elaborate procedures for the provision of information by member states, the possible review of this information by independent experts, and the availability of this information to the general public. By developing a more elaborate and transparent system for the provision of information on the compliance of member states with a treaty, the accountability of member states automatically increases.

This increased attention to compliance information systems and to reporting procedures is part of the transformation from an enforcement to a managerial approach to compliance. Traditionally, the incentives for states to report their own noncompliance were low, since such an admission could only lead to "bad news," such as the imposition of sanctions. The situation totally changes, however, when noncompliance is not necessarily considered as the intentional act of a sovereign state, but may be due, for example, to incapacity. In that case, reporting this capacity problem may lead the other partners in the regime to look for remedies to overcome the capacity problems of the state concerned, for example, through a transfer of finance or technology. In this managerial approach to compliance, reporting noncompliance should not be threatening but may well be in the state's interest. . . . Thus, the reporting of noncompliance under the Montreal Protocol leads the Implementation Committee to investigate the possibilities of financial and technical assistance instead of threatening with traditional sanctions.

RESPONSES TO NONCOMPLIANCE

Finally, the likelihood of compliance with an environmental treaty will depend upon the possibilities of coercive or other measures being imposed in reaction to violations.

. . . [T]raditional treaty mechanisms for noncompliance were restricted to adversarial dispute settlement procedures (DSPs). Traditional dispute settlement procedures, used generally under international environmental law, mostly involve a sequence of diplomatic and legal means of dispute settlement. Diplomatic settlement procedures usually involve negotiation and consultation in a first instance. If this negotiation and consultation does not lead to a solution, often some form of mediation or conciliation is prescribed. This mediation or conciliation involves third parties or international institutions. In case of deeper conflicts parties often can have recourse to legal means of dispute settlement, either arbitration or the International Court of Justice. In July 1993 the International Court of Justice even set up a special chamber for environmental matters.

This standard sequence of dispute resolution — negotiation, mediation, and finally arbitration or submission to the International Court of Justice — can still also be found in more recent treaties, such as the Vienna Convention for the Protection of the Ozone Layer, 1985, and the FCCC. Article 11 of the Vienna Convention prescribes negotiation as the first means of dispute resolution (para. 1). If this fails, parties must seek mediation by a third party (para. 2). As an ultimate remedy, arbitration or submission to the International Court of Justice, or in absence of agreement over this remedy a conciliation committee, is prescribed (paras. 3 to 5). Article 14 of the FCCC contains similar wording.

Although the number of cases brought under dispute settlement proceedings has increased in the last few years, they are still very rare, especially considering the compliance problems with most environmental treaties. The International Court of Justice has so far never dealt with a purely environmental conflict. Conflicts under dispute settlement proceedings mostly involve either trade relationships or territorial disputes. One of the reasons for the small use of dispute settlement instruments is the fact that these procedures are characterized by an adversarial relationship between the parties, and are only used as a last resort. States are rarely willing to risk their relationship with other "sovereign" international actors by openly challenging them. . . . [T]raditional dispute settlement procedures . . . are also considered less effective and appropriate in environmental treaties. The result of noncompliance with environmental treaties is often damage to the global commons in general, affecting all states, rather than several well-identifiable parties.

The ineffectiveness of dispute settlement proceedings in international environmental agreements has led to the development of a new system of responding to noncompliance, called noncompliance procedures (NCPs). Such procedures, rather than "punishing" noncompliance, are aimed at finding ways to facilitate compliance by the state that is in breach of its obligations. They provide a political framework for "amicable" responses to noncompliance that cannot be considered "wrongful." This tendency toward NCPs reflects the new managerial approach, which no longer assumes that noncompliance is the result of a willful desire to violate.

One of the consequences of shifting from an adversarial approach to a more managerial approach is that sanctions play only a minor role in the noncompliance response system. Three categories of sanctions can be distinguished: the treaty-based sanctions, membership sanctions, and unilateral sanctions. The latter category of unilateral sanctions is now severely restricted under international law. As we have discussed above, resort to the use of military force is exceptional. Trade sanctions are increasingly difficult to invoke under the rapidly developing international trade regimes. Treaty-based sanctions have also not proven very effective. . . . Sanctions against states party to an international treaty, including expulsion or suspension of rights and privileges, are also not considered an effective response in the case of noncompliance with an environmental treaty, since one of the aims of environmental treaties is to achieve global membership. . . .

TOWARD COMPREHENSIVE NONCOMPLIANCE RESPONSE SYSTEMS

. . . Increasingly, more recent treaties have included a comprehensive combination of different instruments for responding to noncompliance. These systems, also referred to as comprehensive noncompliance response systems, contain not only methods to sanction violations but, more important, methods to facilitate compliance, improve transparency, improve reporting procedures, and prevent violations.

. . . Although the managerial approach is proving very successful in treaties such as the Vienna Convention and the Montreal Protocol, one should not forget that we are only at the beginning of new efforts to find solutions to compliance problems. The instrument of joint implementation under the FCCC, for instance, is still to be tested. In many other areas it remains difficult to reach any international consensus at all on the protection of our global environment.

International environmental law is still in a phase in which the adoption of standards is more of a concern than the actual compliance with these standards. One should not forget, however, that it is especially in the phase of adoption that a well-designed noncompliance response system can prove decisive in getting states to agree to new commitments.

1.   Protecting the Ozone Layer

Reacting to a growing body of scientific discovery and analysis as well as pressures from NGOs about the dangers of ozone depletion in the world's stratosphere, most states demonstrated a commendable ability and willingness to act. They negotiated relatively quickly the 1985 Vienna Convention for the Protection of the Ozone Layer, and then the 1987 Montreal Protocol on Substances That Deplete the Ozone Layer, followed by successive amendments and adjustments tightening the Protocol's provisions. A rapidly developing situation that could have led to worldwide catastrophic effects has been for the most part contained. The following materials provide more details about the problem and the resulting agreements. They also highlight some of the agreements' characteristics that contributed to the generally successful outcome.

Edith Brown Weiss et al., International Environmental Law and Policy

641-642 (1998)

In the stratosphere, high above Earth, a layer of ozone filters ultraviolet radiation from sunlight, protecting Earth and its inhabitants. In recent years the ozone layer has been threatened by human-made chemicals, such as chlorofluorocarbons, which are used in air conditioners and refrigerators. . . . These chemicals can migrate into the stratosphere and destroy the ozone layer. In the Antarctic, a large hole . . . developed in the ozone layer, and . . . very significant thinning of the ozone layer over the Arctic has developed. Holes in the ozone layer or even depletion of the density of the ozone layer means more ultraviolet radiation reaches Earth. This can cause skin cancer and cataracts in humans and damage flora and fauna.

The depletion of the stratospheric ozone layer must be distinguished from the problem of ozone pollution in the lower atmosphere (the troposphere). In the air we breathe, large quantities of ozone — emitted by cars, for example — damage human health. Thus, ozone is an air pollutant that the United States and other countries regulate. This problem must not be confused with the problem of depletion of the stratospheric ozone layer that protects Earth from ultraviolet radiation.

Depletion of the ozone layer is an inherently long-term, intergenerational issue. Chlorine chemicals we produce today drift up to the stratosphere over time and remain there to deplete the ozone layer. They dissipate only over time. Chlorine chemical emissions today cause damage decade in the future.

Concern about the health of the ozone layer led to a historic agreement in 1985, the Vienna Convention for the Protection of the Ozone Layer negotiated under the auspices of the United Nations Environment Programme. The agreement provided a framework for monitoring and learning about the ozone layer but did not provide specific controls on substance believed to deplete the ozone layer. In 1987 countries adopted a protocol to the agreement that does provide such controls: the Montreal Protocol on Substances That Deplete the Ozone Layer. Since it is a protocol, countries wishing to join the agreement must become parties to the Vienna Convention as well as to the Protocol.

Since 1987, scientific evidence . . . suggested that the problem of ozone depletion may be more serious than had been believed, and additional chemicals [were] reducing the ozone layer. This . . . led to amendments to the Protocol in June 1990 and in November 1992, which . . . added chemicals to the list of controlled substances, and to adjustments in 1990, 1992, 1994, 1995, and 1997 such that some chemicals [were] to be phased out even well before the year 2000.

The chief U.S. negotiator for the Montreal Protocol, Richard Benedick, provides some background on the evolving scientific understanding of the ozone problem and the impact of that on the treaty negotiations.

Richard Elliot Benedick, Ozone Diplomacy

9-22 (1991)

The Montreal Protocol was the result of research at the frontiers of science combined with a unique collaboration between scientists and policy makers. Unlike any previous diplomatic endeavor, it is based on continually evolving theories, on state-of-the-art computer models simulating the results of intricate chemical and physical reactions for decades into the future, and on satellite-, land-, and rocket-based monitoring of remote gases measured in parts per trillion. An international agreement of this nature could not, in fact, have occurred at any earlier point in history.

DISTURBING THEORIES

The existence of ozone was unknown before 1839. An unstable form of oxygen composed of three, rather than the customary two, atoms of oxygen, ozone has been characterized as "the single most important chemically active trace gas in the earth's atmosphere." This significance derives from two singular properties. First, certain wavelengths of ultraviolet radiation are absorbed by the very thin "layer" of ozone molecules surrounding Earth, particularly in the upper part of the atmosphere known as the stratosphere, approximately 6 to 30 miles above the surface. If these biologically active ultraviolet (UV-B) lightwaves were to reach the planet's surface in excessive quantities, they could damage and cause mutations in human, animal, and plant cells. Second, the distribution of ozone throughout different altitudes could influence the temperature structure and circulation patterns of the stratosphere and thus have major implications for climate around the world. It is no exaggeration to conclude that the ozone layer, as currently constituted, is essential to life as it has evolved on Earth.

In 1973 two University of Michigan scientists, Richard Stolarski and Ralph Cicerone, were exploring the effects of possible chemical emissions from National Aeronautics and Space Administration rockets. Their research, published in 1974, indicated that chlorine released in the stratosphere could unleash a complicated chemical process that would continually destroy ozone for several decades. A single chlorine atom, through a catalytic chain reaction, could eliminate tens of thousands of the ozone molecules. This theory, though interesting, did not at first seem alarming, because the potential release of chlorine from space rocketry would be inconsequential.

In 1974 Mario Molina and Sherwood Rowland at the University of California, Irvine, became intrigued with some peculiar properties of a family of widely used anthropogenic chemicals, the chlorofluorocarbons [CFCs]. Molina and Rowland discovered that, unlike most other gases, CFCs are not chemically broken down or rained out quickly in the lower atmosphere but rather, because of their exceptionally stable chemical structure, persist and migrate slowly up to the stratosphere. Depending on their individual structure, different CFCs can remain intact from many decades to several centuries. The two researchers concluded that CFCs are eventually broken down by solar radiation and in the process release large quantities of chlorine into the stratosphere. The combined implications of these two independently-arrived-at hypotheses were deeply disturbing. The researchers had not anticipated any link between CFCs and ozone depletion. There had been no prior suspicion that CFCs were harmful to the environment. Indeed, following their invention in the 1930s, CFCs had seemed an ideal chemical. They had been thoroughly tested by customary standards and found to be safe. The possibility that dangers could originate many miles above Earth's surface was never considered.

CFCs are unusually stable, nonflammable, nontoxic, and noncorrosive — qualities that make them extremely useful in many industries, where they often replaced other chemicals, such as ammonia in refrigerators and air conditioners, as well as effective propellants in spray containers for cosmetics, household products, pharmaceuticals, and cleaners. They are also excellent insulators and are standard ingredients in the manufacture of a wide range of rigid and flexible plastic-foam materials. Their nonreactive properties make them seemingly perfect solvents for cleaning microchips and telecommunications equipment and for use in a myriad of their industrial applications. And, as an added bonus, CFCs are inexpensive to produce.

The 1974 theories came, therefore, as an economic as well as environmental bombshell. Because new uses had continually been found for CFCs, their production had soared from 150,000 metric tons in 1960 to over 800,000 metric tons by 1974. Because of their long lifetimes, as much as nine-tenths of all CFCs ever emitted was still in the atmosphere. Millions of tons of prior-year CFC production were thus already en route, so to speak, to their fatal stratospheric rendezvous with ozone. Even if CFC emissions were to level off or decline, chlorine would continue to accumulate in the stratosphere for decades. If the chlorine-ozone break-down process actually occurred in the stratosphere, as indicated by the laboratory results, some future depletion of the vitally important ozone layer seemed inescapable. . . .

THE ANTARCTIC OZONE HOLE

British scientists in 1985 published astonishing findings based on a review of land-based measurements of stratospheric ozone made at their Halley Bay station in the Antarctic. . . . They . . . concluded that ozone levels recorded during the Antarctic springtime (September-November) had fallen to about 50 percent lower than they had been in the 1960s. Although concentrations recovered by mid-November, the amount of the seasonal ozone loss had apparently accelerated sharply beginning in 1979. The "ozone hole" (that is, a portion of the stratosphere in which greatly diminished ozone levels were measured) had also expanded by 1985 to cover an area greater in size than the United States.

This unexpected revelation was quickly confirmed by Japanese and U.S. scientists rechecking their own data sets. . . .

The ozone hole did not, however, provide any clear signal for policymakers at that time. Scientists in 1986 and 1987 were far from certain that CFCs were involved in Antarctica. Nor could they confirm whether the hole was a localized phenomenon peculiar to unusual polar conditions or an ominous precursor of future ozone losses elsewhere over the planet. . . .

There were several credible theories, besides the role of CFCs, to account for the ozone hole, including polar winds, volcanic activity, and sunspots. . . .

The hole over Antarctica did attract additional public attention to the ozone issue (though more in the United States than in Europe and Japan, where greater public pressure on governments was most needed). It may also have influenced some participants in the negotiations as evidence of the fragility of Earth's atmosphere. Significantly, however, Antarctica was never discussed at the negotiations, which were based solely on the global models. . . .

EFFECTS OF OZONE LOSS

Definitive evidence concerning harmful effects of ozone modification was even more sparse than proof of the atmospheric theories. Existing research, however, though tentative in many respects, did indicate a potential for extremely serious and wide-ranging damage to humans, animals, plants, and materials.

In June 1986, EPA [the U.S. Environmental Protection Agency] sponsored with UNEP [U.N. Environmental Programme] a weeklong international conference on risks to human health and the environment from ozone loss and climate change. This conference produced a large compendium of scientific papers, later supplemented by a multivolume EPA risk assessment, which together represented the most thorough study of the subject up to that time. The scholarly work stimulated by EPA exerted a considerable influence on the subsequent diplomatic negotiations.

The link between ultraviolet radiation and skin cancer had been well established. . . .

. . . [F]uture ozone depletion would have serious consequences. EPA estimated that there could be over 150 million new cases of skin cancer in the United States alone among people currently alive or born by the year 2075, resulting in over 3 million deaths (with an uncertainty range of 1.5 to 4.5 million). . . .

For other theoretical effects of excessive radiation, quantitative predictions proved difficult. For example, evidence from animal research indicated that UV-B could suppress the immune system. . . .

Major damage to agriculture was also suspected. Laboratory tests indicated that some two-thirds of 200 plant species (including peas, cabbage, melons, and cotton) were sensitive to UV-B radiation, although this had not been confirmed under field conditions. . . .

Ultraviolet radiation was also implicated in costly accelerated weathering of polymers and in increased formation of low-level ozone (urban smog), injurious both to human health and to crops.

The potential effect of CFCs on global climate was related both to the redistribution of ozone at different altitudes and to the action of CFCs themselves as heat-trapping gases. Quantitative assessments were crude, but there was growing scientific consensus that greenhouse warming would have far-reaching implications for rainfall and agriculture, sea levels, and the survival of many animal and plant species whose habitat would be seriously modified.

All of these possible effects were known to the negotiators of the Montreal Protocol, and they were never seriously contested. It was generally accepted that changes in the ozone layer would pose serious risks to human health and the environment. The point of contention among the participating governments was the extent of international action necessary to provide a reasonable degree of protection.

These scientific discoveries and the growing governmental and public concern about the depletion of the ozone layer led to the Vienna Convention, the Montreal Protocol, and successive amendments and adjustments tightening the Protocol's provisions. (Excerpts of both agreements are in the Documentary Supplement.) Professor Weiss and her colleagues briefly describe the two agreements in the first excerpt below. Further analysis is then provided by Professors Faure and Lefevere, whose general ideas on treaty compliance were presented above.

Edith Brown Weiss et al., International Environmental Law and Policy

650-651 (1998)

In March 1985, the Vienna Convention for the Protection of the Ozone Layer established a framework system for addressing the multilateral environmental problems of ozone depletion. Division between representatives wanting a phaseout of CFCs and those wanting production caps prevented the adoption of any formal commitments to limit the substances, but the groundwork was laid for further work.

By 1987, the two groups were able to reach a compromise, and the Montreal Protocol placed quantitative limits on both the production and the consumption of CFCs and halons. As of January 2003, the Vienna Convention on the Ozone Layer had 185 parties. The Montreal Protocol had 184 parties. The 1990 London Amendment to the protocol had 164 parties: the 1992 Copenhagen Amendment had 144 parties.

The Montreal Protocol is based on consumption levels of countries. Consumption is determined by calculating production of the chemicals minus exports plus imports. Exports to nonmember countries may not be included in the calculation. Thus, there is an incentive not only to limit production but also to trade only with states party to the agreement.

The Protocol makes special provision in Article V for developing countries: a ten-year delay in required compliance with targets and timetables, a separate consumption limit of 0.3 kilograms per capita, access to a Multilateral Fund (1990 Amendment) to assist with the costs of compliance, and the promotion of bilateral technical assistance programs. The classification of a country as qualifying under Article V(1) to deserve special treatment is not permanent but is subject to the recommendations of an Open-Ended Working Group of the Parties. Some countries have been declassified, such as Singapore and Saudi Arabia; others have been reclassified to become Article V countries, such as Georgia.

The Protocol gives certain countries flexibility in meeting their obligations. . . .

The Protocol prohibits exports and imports of controlled substances with countries that are not party to the treaty (although an exception for nonparties that are determined to be in full compliance with the control measures in Article 2 of the Protocol). In a second phase, the trade ban with nonparties would extend to products containing the controlled substances. . . .

While trade in bulk CFCs is small in value relative to world merchandise trade, trade in CFC-containing products (heating and cooling equipment, passenger cars, airplanes, ships and boats with air conditioners and/or heat pumps) amounts to approximately 12 percent of world trade. Products currently produced with, but not containing, CFCs (semiconductors and products with electronic components) amount to an additional 16 percent of world trade. . . .

Besides the quantitative limits on chemicals that deplete the ozone layer, the protocol contains an innovative financial assistance mechanism to allow developing countries to pursue environmentally sound policies and comply with the protocol. Under the protocol, countries have established a general multilateral fund administered by the World Bank, the United Nations Environment Programme (UNEP), the United Nations Development Programme (UNDP), and, since 1993, the United Nations Industrial Development Organization (UNIDO). Initiated in the 1990 London meeting . . . the "Interim Multinational Fund" was made permanent by an amendment passed in Copenhagen. . . . The most notable characteristic of this fund is that it is specifically not for economic development. Instead, countries contribute to help offset the costs of Article V countries complying with the protocol. The fund "shall meet all agreed incremental costs of Parties in order to enable their compliance with the control measures of the Protocol." . . .

The fund secretariat has worked with OZONAction, a UNEP-industry group in Paris, France, to help develop and review country programs and proposed projects under the fund. By 1996, most but not all Article V countries had developed country programs or were in the process of doing so. The review process for the programs and projects is stringent.

As part of the country program, each country must designate an ozone action officer. These officers meet regularly on a regional basis to discuss implementation problems and to exchange views.

Michael Faure & Jurgen Lefevere, Compliance with International Environmental Agreements

The Global Environment: Institutions, Law, and Policy 138-153
(Norman I. Vig & Regina S. Axelrod eds., 1999)

THE MONTREAL PROTOCOL . . . A "MANAGERIAL" PRIMARY RULE SYSTEM

The approach to international environmental treaty design has changed in the past decades, mainly because of the new, more realistic "managerial" approach. Prime examples of this new approach are the Vienna Convention for the Protection of the Ozone Layer and, more important, its subsequent Montreal Protocol on Substances That Deplete the Ozone Layer, adopted under this convention, are used.

The Vienna Convention . . . did not contain any substantive commitments for the states but provided for a general framework, including the possibility of adopting protocols in the Conference of the Parties, the main institution set up under the convention. Only two years after the adoption of the convention the 1987 Montreal Protocol . . . was adopted under the Vienna Convention. The Vienna Convention and more particularly its Montreal Protocol surprised the international community by their swift adoption, their specific goals, their effectiveness, and the large and still increasing number of states party to it. . . . One of the main reasons given for this effectiveness is the design of the treaty system. This system has several "modern" characteristics that make it very suitable for dealing with environmental problems in the modern international context. In many of the more recent international environmental treaties the Vienna/Montreal system is used as a model. One of the main reasons is the flexibility of its primary rule system.

The Vienna Convention establishes the Conference of the Parties (Article 6), which is to meet "at regular intervals," in practice every three to four years. The Montreal Protocol adds to this Conference of the Parties a Meeting of the Parties. These meetings now are held annually to discuss the implementation of the commitments and possible improvements to or adoption of new commitments. They are organized by the Ozone Secretariat, set up under Article 7 of the Vienna Convention and Article 12 of the Montreal Protocol. The regular convening of the Conference of the Parties has proven very useful in keeping the treaty goals and standards. The continuous updating of the treaty goals and standards was made possible by the framework structure chosen by the Vienna Convention. Although this framework structure was not new . . . it proved particularly effective. Whereas the Vienna Convention only lays down the framework for further negotiations, the real commitments are laid down in the Montreal Protocol. . . . At the meetings of the parties to the conference unexpected agreement could be reached on a regular updating of the protocol. The Montreal Protocol has in its short existence already seen three adjustments and amendments, in 1990 at the London meeting, in 1992 at the

Copenhagen meeting (at which the timetable for a total phase-out of ozone depleting substances was accelerated), and most recently in September 1997 at the Montreal meeting. This shows how the likelihood of compliance can be influenced in the treaty design stage, by adopting primary rules that allow for flexibility.

The Montreal Protocol also provides an example of how the individual capacities of states may determine this willingness to accept treaty obligations in the first place. India and China would not become parties to the Montreal Protocol until the agreement about compensatory financing had been adopted at the London meeting in 1990. This agreement provided for financial support to developing states in return for and in order to allow these states to become party to the protocol and actually be financially capable of complying with its obligations.

Under the Montreal Protocol various instruments have been developed to remedy the incapacity problem: a Multilateral Fund was set up (Article 10) in order to provide this financial assistance. The implementing agencies of this fund — the International Bank for Reconstruction and Development (World Bank), the United Nations Environment Programme, and the United Nations Development Programme — draw up "country programmes" and "country studies" consisting of a combination of financial support, assistance, and training. Furthermore, the Montreal Protocol provides for the transfer of technology under its Article 10A. On the basis of this article all states party to the protocol "shall take every practicable step" to ensure that "the best available, environmentally safe substitutes and related technologies are expeditiously transferred" to developing countries (as defined in Article 5[1] of the protocol) and that those transfers "occur under fair and most favourable conditions."

NONCOMPLIANCE PROCEDURES: MONTREAL PROTOCOL

In the more recent environmental treaties one can observe new noncompliance procedures, often side by side with the traditional dispute settlement procedures. A prime example of a well-functioning noncompliance procedure is the procedure set up under Article 8 of the Montreal Protocol. This article states that the parties to the protocol "shall consider and approve procedures and institutional mechanisms for determining noncompliance with the provisions of this Protocol and for treatment of Parties found to be in noncompliance."

At the Copenhagen meeting in November 1992 the Meeting of the Parties adopted the procedure under this article. Under this noncompliance procedure an Implementation Committee is set up. The committee consists of ten representatives elected by the Meeting of the Parties based on equitable geographical distribution. . . . The focus has . . . been put on the nonadversarial functions. The procedure allows states, when they believe they are unable to comply with their obligations, to report this inability to the Secretariat and the Implementation Committee. The Implementation Committee also discusses the general quality and the reliability of the data contained in the member states' reports. The Implementation Committee, meeting three to four times a year, has in fact assumed a very active role in improving the quality and reliability of the data reported by the member states and by seeking in a cooperative sphere solutions for parties with administrative structural and financial difficulties.

The noncompliance procedure under the Montreal Protocol operates independently from the dispute settlement procedure laid down in Article 11 of the Vienna Convention. Although it is tempting to see the noncompliance procedures as a prelude to the heavier dispute settlement procedure, the international community has so far been very hesitant to take this approach. . . . The resistance against linking the two procedures can be explained by the fear of states that linking them will reduce the use of the noncompliance procedure, and thus that it might be followed by an "uncomfortable" dispute settlement proceeding.

Notes and Questions

1. When considering the treaty regime governing ozone, you should examine the Vienna Convention and the Montreal Protocol in the Documentary Supplement. You should extract in general terms what the treaties actually do — for example, establish goals, set substantive standards (or "primary rules"), monitor compliance, and enforce its norms. Look particularly at Articles 2-7, 10, and 11 of the Vienna Convention and Articles 4, 5, 6-10, 10A, 11, and 12 of the Montreal Protocol.

2. What are the objectives of the treaties and how do the treaties provide for updating their goals and standards?

3. What are the actual substantive obligations that a state assumes under the Montreal Protocol? Use as examples the United States and a developing country such as Indonesia.

4. How will the meaning of ambiguous provisions be ascertained?

5. What role do trade restrictions play in the treaty regime?

6. How is compliance monitored? What other alternatives are there for monitoring compliance?

7. What happens if a state does not comply? What enforcement techniques can be used? Note the Faure & Lefevere excerpts above about the treaty regime and compliance under it. See also the excellent empirical analysis, Engaging Countries: Strengthening Compliance with International Environmental Accords (Edith Brown Weiss & Harold K. Jacobson eds., 1998).

8. What are the major advantages and disadvantages of the Protocol from the point of view of the United States? How might democratic accountability exist in the treaty decision-making process? Does this result from the way treaties are ratified in the United States? Should the Montreal Protocol be a self-executing treaty?

9. Is the Protocol excessively favorable to developing countries? If you think so (or not), what values and assumptions are implicit in your view?

10. As an alternative to the Vienna Convention and the Montreal Protocol, would the general norms enunciated in the *Trail Smelter* case, Principle 21 of the Stockholm Declaration, or Principle 2 of the Rio Declaration be sufficient to deal with the problem of ozone depletion?

2.   Global Warming

Another major problem in the "global commons" is the phenomenon of global warming, which is an important aspect of global climate change. Global warming (or "greenhouse warming") is much more complicated and controversial than the problem of ozone depletion discussed above. Although there is an emerging consensus among scientists that global warming is in fact occurring, there is still considerable debate about the likely rate of future warming and the relative importance of various causes. There is also considerable debate about how to deal with the problem, with most policymakers recognizing that the costs of action could be substantial (as would be the costs of inaction).

At the Rio Conference in 1992, the participants negotiated a Framework Convention on Climate Change (FCCC). At the third conference of the parties to the Framework Convention, held in Kyoto, Japan, in December 1997, the parties adopted a controversial Protocol that established some legally binding obligations to reduce greenhouse gas emissions. In these negotiations, the role of NGOs has been especially prominent. (The FCCC went into effect on March 21, 1993. As of January 2003, 188 countries were parties to the convention, including the United States. The Kyoto Protocol had not yet gone into effect, though 104 countries had become parties. Although the United States signed the Protocol in November 1998, the Bush Administration made clear in 2001 that it was opposed to the Protocol for several reasons, discussed below.) Excerpts of the Convention and the Protocol are in the Documentary Supplement.

The following materials provide some background to the problem of global warming and outline the key provisions of the Framework Convention and the Kyoto Protocol. The first excerpt provides a helpful introduction to the basic science and the beginning efforts to deal with global warming.

Edith Brown Weiss et al., International Environmental Law and Policy
677-678, 701 (1998)

"Climate" is the general term for the seasonal interactions of air and water in the atmosphere. Climate consists of the elements of temperature, precipitation, wind, and cloud cover, and it affects every substance on the planet, whether organic or inorganic. In turn, any substance that affects the climate has other effects on the globe.

. . . Climate change is an inherently intergenerational problem. The actions we take today will cause effects for several decades or more. Climate change, by its very nature, is a common global concern of all countries, for climate respects no political boundaries. . . .

Climate change differs considerably from other global environmental concerns, such as ozone depletion, because it involves complex interactions between air, land, and water; the human-induced causes go the heart of countries' economies; and there are large economic costs associated both with the effects of climate change and measures to prevent and mitigate it. Internationally there is still considerable disagreement about what to do about the threat of global warming. . . .

In Geneva, in November 1988, 35 nations founded the Intergovernmental Panel on Climate Change (IPCC) to assess the effects of human activities on climate change and to analyze science, policy implications, and response strategies to the greenhouse effect in three working groups. This body met periodically over the next 20 months and produced a consensus document indicating that the global temperature could be expected to rise significantly in response to human activities. This was technically a scientific panel, but governments sent other officials as well as scientists. Many have called the result "negotiated science"; in the end the process was essential for providing the international consensus necessary to open negotiations on a convention on climate change.

[Ed.—Returning to page 677 of the Weiss book.] In June 1992, at the United Nations Conference on Environment and Development [UNCED], countries opened for signature the United Nations Framework Convention on Climate Change (FCCC). The FCCC sets forth a framework for addressing climate change, although it does not contain binding targets and timetables for controlling emissions of gases that cause global warming. . . . In 1997, the Kyoto Protocol to the FCCC was finalized and adopted. It contains binding targets and timetables for industrialized countries.

The next excerpt reports what the IPCC was concluding in the mid-1990s and provides details about the 1997 Kyoto Protocol.

Peter G.G. Davies, Current Developments — Public International Law — Global Warming and the Kyoto Protocol

47 Intl. & Comp. L.Q. 446 (1998)

A.   The "Greenhouse Effect"

The Intergovernmental Panel on Climate Change (IPCC) . . . recently concluded that "the balance of evidence suggests that there is a discernible human influence on global climate," and that an increase in global surface temperature of between 1 and 3.5 degrees Celsius by 2100 is expected in comparison with 1990 temperatures, a "rate of warming [which] would probably be greater than any seen in the last 10,000 years" Average sea levels are expected to rise by approximately 50 centimetres by 2100, affecting island and low-lying countries globally, including areas within Europe; the European Commission has indicated that such a rise

> would affect large stretches of the Netherlands, certain marshlands in England, the length of the German North Sea coast, coastal areas on the Black Sea, around the Po flood plain in Italy and the tidal flats (the Wadden Sea) on the west coast of Jutland in Denmark.

In addition, an increase in the number of violent storms and floods is projected, and "climate zones (and thus ecosystems and agricultural zones) could shift towards the poles by 150-550 km in the mid-latitude regions. As a result, many ecosystems may decline or fragment, and individual species will become extinct."

The so-called "greenhouse effect" is in part a quite natural phenomenon. Radiation emanating form the sun reaches the Earth's atmosphere and, with the exception of certain harmful ultra-violet radiation which is filtered out in the stratospheric ozone layer, eventually reaches the surface of the Earth. Some of this energy is reflected back from the Earth's surface to the Earth's atmosphere where it is trapped by so-called "greenhouse gases" and brings about a warming effect. Since the Industrial Revolution this natural process has been intensified as a consequence of certain human activities: atmospheric concentration of the main greenhouse gas, carbon dioxide, has increased by 30 per cent since 1750, largely as a result of the burning of fossil fuels and forest clearance; methane and nitrous oxide concentrations have increased by 145 and 15 per cent respectively in the same period. . . . Whilst certain States, most notably members of the Organisation of Petroleum Exporting Countries (OPEC), have shown reluctance in accepting these IPCC findings, or see no reason to reduce emissions even if the findings are accurate, most States accept the Panel's general conclusions.

B. International Action to Combat Global Warming Prior to the Kyoto Conference . . .

3. The Kyoto Protocol

. . . The Protocol addresses the following eight issues. . . .

(a) Implementation of policies and measures by industrialised countries.   In achieving the greenhouse gas emissions reductions specified in the Protocol Annex I parties will implement and/or elaborate policies and measures, such as energy efficiency programmes, measures to protect carbon sinks and reservoirs, afforestation and reforestation activities, sustainable forms of agriculture, the promotion of research and development of technology limiting carbon dioxide emissions, and programmes that will reduce greenhouse gas emissions in the transport sector. . . .

(b) Emission reductions.   Reduction commitments have been established for developed countries to be met by the period 2008-2012 representing a total reduction of greenhouse gas emissions from industrialised countries of at least 5 per cent when compared to their 1990 emission levels. The commitment period stretches over five years and is intended to provide greater flexibility for States parties than a single target year. This flexibility applies in particular to those countries with annual emission levels of a highly variable nature.

Emission reductions attributable to afforestation and reforestation projects since 1990 will be taken into account in the emissions reduction equation, in addition to emission reductions initiated by action in the energy, industrial, agricultural and waste sectors. Emission reductions cover six greenhouse gases. Individual States' commitments to reductions are differentiated with a view to meeting the 5 per cent overall target; the European Community and all its member States are committed to 8 per cent reductions, the United States to 7 per cent and Japan and Canada to 6 per cent. New Zealand, the Russian Federation and Ukraine will stabilise emissions at 1990 levels, whilst some States negotiated an actual increase in emissions.

Once the Protocol has entered into force, Annex I parties must submit an annual inventory of emissions to the Convention Secretariat, enabling expert review teams to provide a full assessment of such parties' compliance with the Protocol. These expert assessments will be reviewed by the Conference of the Parties serving as the meeting of the parties to the Protocol which will adopt decisions on implementation. . . .

... [I]t is significant that the Protocol includes a review clause which requires the Conference to the Parties to the Protocol to undertake a general review of the Protocol at its second session and subsequently to review obligations at regular intervals. Specifically on the issue of emissions, the Conference of the Parties to the Protocol must begin to give consideration to the adoption of further reductions by the end of 2006. The Protocol makes reference to the period 2008-2012 as being the *first* commitment period, Article 3(9) indicating that further commitments to emission reductions by industrialised countries "shall be established."

(c) The "EC Bubble": joint action by the EC member States.   Annex I parties may agree to take joint action to fulfil their emission reduction targets. For instance, if two Annex I parties, State A and State B, decide to act jointly, and have notified the Secretariat to that effect, they will be deemed to have fulfilled their emission reduction obligations if State A's and State B's joint emissions do not exceed the level of emissions assigned to both States under the Protocol. . . .

These provisions are of particular relevance to the European Community and have been referred to as the "EC Bubble." The Community has indicated that its member States will take advantage of this ability to burden-share. . . . This burden-sharing process will allow the wealthier member States to accept much of the burden of reaching the overall EC target. . . .

(d) Joint implementation by industrialised countries (Annex I parties).   Annex I countries are able to acquire "emission reduction units" from participation in joint projects with other Annex I parties which reduce emissions or enhance natural carbon sinks. Such reduction units can be used to contribute to their emission reduction targets under the Protocol. The United States was a strong advocate of this system as it introduces greater flexibility into the process of making emission cuts. It is important to stress that any such joint implementation must supplement domestic action to reduce greenhouse gases, and that therefore an Annex I country would not be able to depend solely on joint action taken in another industrialised country. . . .

(e) Commitments by all parties to the Protocol.   It is important to stress that the Protocol introduces no new commitments for developing States. . . . However, Article 10 of the Protocol reaffirms existing commitments in the Climate Change Convention on the part of both Annex I and non-Annex I parties. As such it includes the obligation periodically to update national inventories of greenhouse gases, to formulate and implement national programmes to reduce the effects of climate change, to co-operate on scientific and technical research, and to develop education and training programmes. In addition, the Protocol reaffirms the existing commitment on parties to co-operate in the transfer of environmentally friendly technology to developing States, many developing countries had stressed the critical importance of the transfer of environmentally sound technology from Annex I parties on preferential terms to the Third World.

Several Annex I parties, including Australia, Canada, Japan and the United States, strongly supported a proposal by New Zealand that reference to a process to establish new commitments in the form of emission limitation objectives on the part of the wealthier developing States should be included in the Protocol. The proposal noted that any emission limitation objectives adopted in this process would not have been applicable in the 2008-2012 commitment period. This proposal was rejected by developing countries as . . . capable of hindering social and economic development in the Third World. Developing countries have long taken the view that they should not be made either to take on commitments to reduce emissions to a specified level within a given time frame or to begin a process which could lead to the adoption of such commitments, until the developed world has taken effective action to reduce greenhouse gas emissions. The New Zealand proposal was dropped and, as such, no new commitments on the part of non-Annex I parties are included in the Protocol.

(*f*) *The Clean Development Mechanism (CDM)*. The concept of joint implementation by a developed country and a clear developing country is endorsed through this new mechanism. The advantage in joint implementation of this nature is that projects to reduce greenhouse gases in developing countries are often cheaper to finance than in Annex I States. The CDM has a dual purpose in that it enables developing countries to operate projects which result in emission reductions and thus to contribute to the objective of the Convention, and also allows Annex I countries which finance such projects through the CDM to use emission reductions attributable to such projects to reduce their own emissions totals. The private sector will be encouraged to participate in such projects. . . .

The introduction of the CDM was supported by the G77 group of developing States despite long-standing fears that this type of joint implementation between Annex I parties and developing States would allow rich developed States to finance projects in the Third World, gain credit for doing so, and reduce the need on the part of Annex I parties involved in such projects to take action at a domestic level. The Protocol seeks to allay this fear by stressing that Annex I parties may gain credit through CDM projects, but that such projects will only contribute to "part" of their emission reduction targets.

An executive board will supervise the CDM, and the Conference of the Parties to the Protocol must establish procedures to ensure appropriate verification of projects. Emission reductions from such jointly implemented projects in the period 2000-2008 can be used by Annex I countries to contribute to their own emission reduction targets under the Protocol. . . .

. . . [T]he introduction of the CDM is to be welcomed as a way in which financial investment from the North can bring about the transfer of environmentally sound technology and contribute to the global reduction of harmful emissions. . . .

(g) *Emissions trading*. The Protocol endorses the establishing of an emissions trading system which will allow developed countries to buy and sell emissions credits. If, for instance, Canada was in danger of exceeding its emission quota under the Protocol, it would have the option of purchasing some or all of the unused quota of another industrialised country. Canada would then be able to use this emission credit to increase its total allowable emissions under the Protocol.

The details of this emissions trading system must be defined by the Conference of the Parties to the Protocol. . . .

Studies in recent years have advocated the introduction of some sort of tradeable permit system for *all* parties to the Climate Change Convention which would allow the purchasing of permits by those States in excess of their emission quotas. It is to be stressed that the system of emissions trading endorsed by the Protocol is limited to the buying and selling of credits among industrialised countries which are party to the Protocol and, as such, have bound themselves to limiting emissions of greenhouse gases with a view to ensuring emissions are collectively reduced by at least 5 per cent by 2008-2012. . . . [T]he United States remains a supporter of a system which includes both developed and developing countries. . . .

(h) *Non-compliance procedure.* The first Conference of the Parties to the Protocol will establish an "appropriate and effective" non-compliance procedure and, in doing so, draw up an "indicative list of consequences, taking into account the cause, type, degree and frequency of non-compliance." It is important to note that if the non-compliance mechanism provides for the possible imposition of binding penalties on parties, the introduction of such a mechanism can be made only by formally amending the Protocol and not simply by decisions of the Conference of the Parties to the Protocol. It is therefore possible for a party which objects to the implementation of binding penalties to signify such disapproval by failing to ratify the amendment to the Protocol, in which case the amendment would not apply as far as that party is concerned.

After the adoption of the Kyoto Protocol in 1997, the details of its implementation had to be worked out and the necessary number of states needed to ratify it.

David A. Wirth, The Sixth Session (Part Two) and Seventh Session of the Conference of the Parties to the Framework Convention on Climate Change

96 Am. J. Intl. L. 648, 648-649, 656 (2002)

The FCCC . . . specifies an annual meeting of the parties to the instrument. The Third Conference of the Parties (COP-3) adopted the Kyoto Protocol. . . .

The Fourth Conference of the Parties (COP-4), held in Buenos Aires in 1998, adopted a plan of action to address remaining unfinished business that included a call for rules to implement key provisions of the Kyoto Protocol. Because of the need for technical elaboration of the protocol's broad-gauge requirements, agreement on the terms of the implementing rules is critical to the ratification of the protocol by most, if not all, states with substantive emission-reduction obligations under it. As of the end of COP-6, held in The Hague in November 2000 while the outcome of the U.S. presidential election was still uncertain, agreement still had not been reached on decisions to implement the protocol. Consequently, parties to the Convention agreed to convene a resumed sixth session in Bonn, the seat of the Convention's secretariat, in 2001.

In late March 2001, the prospects for progress on rules implementing the Kyoto Protocol darkened considerably when President Bush announced that the United States would not ratify the protocol, which had been signed by the Clinton administration. As a condition precedent for entry into force, the protocol requires fifty-five ratifications representing 55 percent of total carbon dioxide emissions from industrialized countries in 1990; emissions of carbon dioxide from the United States account for slightly more than 36 percent of that year's total. The support of Japan, with somewhat more than 8 percent of 1990 emissions, was consequently essential in order to salvage the protocol after the U.S. withdrawal. . . .

An additional factor affecting the climate negotiations . . . was the release of the Third Assessment Report of the Intergovernmental Panel on Climate Change (IPCC). That report, which concluded that the "Earth's climate system has demonstrably changed on both global and regional scales since the pre-industrial era, with some of these changes attributable to human activities," reinforced the seriousness of the global-warming problem. Notwithstanding the IPCC's broadly international character, its consensus-based decision-making process, and its high degree of international respect, the Bush administration requested the U.S. National Academy of Sciences to review the IPCC's work product. Instead of contradicting the panel's conclusions, the National Academy reaffirmed them. . . .

The review requested by President Bush was undertaken by an expert committee for the National Research Council, which is administered by the National Academy of Sciences, the National Academy of Engineering, and the Institute of Medicine.

Committee on the Science of Climate Change of the National Research Council, Climate Change Science: An Analysis of Some Key Questions

1-3, 20 (2001)

Greenhouse gases are accumulating in Earth's atmosphere as a result of human activities, causing surface air temperatures and subsurface ocean temperatures to rise. Temperatures are, in fact, rising. The changes observed over the last several decades are likely mostly due to human activities, but we cannot rule out that some significant part of these changes is also a reflection of natural variability. Human-induced warming and associated sea level rises are expected to continue through the 21st century. Secondary effects are suggested by computer model simulations and basic physical reasoning. These include increases in rainfall rates and increased susceptibility of semi-arid regions to drought. The impacts of these changes will be critically dependent on the magnitude of the warming and the rate with which it occurs.

The mid-range model estimate of human induced global warming by the Intergovernmental Panel on Climate Change (IPCC) is based on the premise that the growth rate of climate forcing[1] agents such as carbon dioxide will accelerate. The predicted warming of 3°C (5.4°F) by the end of the 21st century is consistent with the assumptions about how clouds and atmospheric relative humidity will react to global warming. This estimate is also consistent with inferences about the sensitivity[2] of climate drawn from comparing the sizes of past temperature swings between ice ages and intervening warmer periods with the corresponding changes in the climate forcing. . . . Because there is considerable uncertainty in current understanding of how the climate system varies naturally and reacts to emissions of greenhouse gases and aerosols, current estimates of the magnitude of future warming should

---

1. A climate forcing is defined as an imposed perturbation of Earth's energy balance. Climate forcing is typically measured in watts per square meter (W/m²).

2. The sensitivity of the climate system to a prescribed forcing is commonly expressed in terms of the global mean temperature change that would be expected after a time sufficiently long for both the atmosphere and ocean to come to equilibrium with the change in climate forcing.

be regarded as tentative and subject to future adjustments (either upward or downward). . . .

Of the greenhouse gases that are directly influenced by human activity, the most important are carbon dioxide, methane, ozone, nitrous oxide, and chlorofluorocarbons (CFCs). Aerosols released by human activities are also capable of influencing climate. . . .

Weather station records and ship-based observations indicate that global mean surface air temperature warmed between about 0.4 and 0.8°C (0.7 and 1.5°F) during the 20th century. . . .

By how much will temperatures change over the next 100 years and where?

Climate changes simulations for the period of 1990 to 2100 based on the IPCC emissions scenarios yield a globally-averaged surface temperature increase by the end of the century of 1.4 to 5.8°C (2.5 to 10.4°F) relative to 1990. . . .

Even the mid-range scenarios considered in the IPCC result in temperatures that continue to increase well beyond the end of this century, suggesting that assessments that examine only the next 100 years may well underestimate the magnitude of the eventual impacts. For example a sustained and progressive drying of the land surface, if it occurred, would eventually lead to desertification of regions that are now marginally arable, and any substantial melting or breaking up of the Greenland and Antarctic ice caps could cause widespread coastal inundation.

Just prior to the National Research Council report, President George W. Bush wrote in a March 13, 2001, letter to four Republican senators that "My Administration takes the issue of global climate change very seriously." However, he indicated that "I oppose the Kyoto Protocol because it exempts 80 percent of the world, including major population centers such as China and India from compliance, and would cause serious harm to the U.S. economy." He called the Protocol "an unfair and ineffective means of addressing global climate change concerns." He went on to note "the incomplete state of scientific knowledge of the causes of, and solutions to, global climate change and the lack of commercially available technologies for removing and storing carbon dioxide."

Shortly after the NRC report and without denying the seriousness of the global warming problem, a Cabinet-level working group issued a report spelling out in more detail the reasons for the Bush Administration's opposition to the Kyoto Protocol.

Cabinet-Level Climate Change Working Group, Review of U.S. Climate Change Policy

13-14 at http://www.whitehouse.gov (June 2001)

AN ANALYSIS OF THE KYOTO PROTOCOL

The Kyoto Protocol is fundamentally flawed. The Kyoto Protocol fails to establish a long-term goal based on science, poses serious and unnecessary risks to the U.S. and world economies, and is ineffective in addressing climate change because it excludes major parts of the world.

The Kyoto Protocol is ineffective in addressing climate change because it excludes developing countries. The Kyoto Protocol's emission reduction requirements apply only to industrialized countries. Developing countries can continue business as usual under the Kyoto Protocol, despite their rapidly growing emissions:

- Current data indicate that developing countries' net emissions (including emissions and uptake from land use activities) have *already* exceeded those of the developed world.[10]
- Moreover, annual developing country emissions of CO_2 will double between 1990 and 2010 — an increase that represents over twice as many tons as all of the reductions the United States would be required to take under the Kyoto Protocol.

The Kyoto Protocol's targets are not based on science. Its targets and timetables were arrived at arbitrarily as a result of political negotiations, and are not related to any specific scientific information or long-term objective.

The Kyoto Protocol's targets are precipitous. Under the Kyoto Protocol, the emission reduction target for the United States is 7% from 1990 levels for each year from 2008-2012. However, the figure of 7% is misleading, because it does not take into account growth in emissions between 1990 and 2012. The actual reduction from the U.S. current emissions trajectory for this period is over 30% . . . The Kyoto Protocol also does not allow countries to count legitimate mitigation activities. In fact, it restricts the use of carbon sequestration as a means of achieving its objectives . . .

The Kyoto Protocol risks significantly harming the U.S. and global economies. The Kyoto Protocol would require the United States to meet its target no matter what the cost, which could be substantial:

- Most models suggest a reduction in U.S. GDP of 1% to 2% by 2010 as a result of Kyoto without emissions trading.[13] A 2% reduction is comparable to the impact of the oil shock of the 1970s.
- A U.S. Department of Energy model suggests a reduction of as much as 4%[14] in GDP under a scenario in which the United States does not establish implementing regulations before 2005 and does not engage in emissions trading. . . .

The Kyoto Protocol would leave the United States dangerously dependent on other countries to meet its emission targets. Under the Kyoto Protocol's emissions trading system, countries are allowed to buy and sell part of their emissions allowances. Most economic models indicate that achieving reductions through emissions trading with other countries may cost about half of what it would cost to achieve the same reductions domestically under the Kyoto Protocol.

10. IPCC Special Report on Emission Scenarios, International Energy Agency data (www.iea.org) and Land-use data from Oak Ridge Laboratory Carbon dioxide Information Analysis Center (cdiac.esd.ornl.gov).

13. Energy Modeling Forum results reported in IPCC Working Group III Third Assessment Report, Ch. 18, p. 70 (Final Government Distribution version).

14. Impacts of the Kyoto Protocol on U.S. Energy Markets and Economic Activity, US Energy Information Administration, 2000.

Many analysts have pointed to trading as the only way that the United States could meet its Kyoto target. . . .

Professor Wirth responds to the Bush Administration's arguments against the Kyoto Protocol and reports on the climate change conferences in 2001. Professor Armin Rosencranz of Stanford University then picks up the story in 2002 and provides his prognosis for the future.

David A. Wirth, The Sixth Session (Part Two) and Seventh Session of the Conference of the Parties to the Framework Convention on Climate Change

96 Am. J. Intl. L. 648, 655-657, 648, 658, 658-660 (2002)

The . . . decision of the Bush administration on behalf of the United States not to ratify the Kyoto Protocol sent shock waves through the negotiating process at a critical juncture, but ultimately did not derail adoption of the implementing rules. The United States — the single largest national emitter of carbon dioxide (the principal greenhouse gas) and a major economic power — remains an important component of any international effort to control global warming. . . . Moreover, under the Clinton administration, the United States was a principal architect of the trading scheme, the protocol's major structural innovation. . . .

. . . The Bush administration's June 2001 critique of the protocol labeled it as "fundamentally flawed" and identified five themes that were familiar from earlier debate on the greenhouse issue, but that until that time had not precluded executive branch support for the protocol. The subsequent adoption of the Marrakesh Accords can likewise be taken as an implied rejection of these objections by the rest of the states. . . .

The Kyoto Protocol reduction targets — 7 percent for the United States and an average of roughly 5 percent for the industrialized world — are said to be "precipitous" because of the increase in U.S. emissions during the last decade of the twentieth century, thereby necessitating actual reductions of 30 percent from current emissions in order to reach the protocol's target for the United States. This position ignores the fact that the FCCC, adopted nearly a decade earlier, had already established the goal of limiting greenhouse gas emissions to 1990 levels. The U.S. share of the reduction goal is disproportionately small by reference to its current emissions, which amounted to nearly a quarter of the global annual total of carbon dioxide emissions from fuel combustion in the late 1990s.

From the broader perspective of environmental necessity, the protocol's goals can hardly be said to be precipitous. Because of the long atmospheric lifetimes of the gases concerned, significant reductions in emissions would be necessary merely to stabilize concentrations at their current levels, let alone reverse the warming phenomenon. . . .

Yet another Bush administration criticism is that the Kyoto Protocol is ineffective in addressing climate change because it excludes developing countries. This objection mirrors one presented in a 1997 Senate resolution. Developing countries are, to be sure, an important component of a long-term strategy for protecting the global climate. Greenhouse gases from this group of states are expected to constitute the largest source of future increases in emissions. Nevertheless, industrialized countries represent the bulk of current and past greenhouse gas emissions — a situation that has led most of the developing countries to object on equity grounds to including substantive reduction obligations for them in the FCCC or the protocol. Consequently, at the time of this writing, a nonnegotiable requirement for quantified reductions from developing countries would amount to a "poison pill," impeding even the modest first steps represented by the Kyoto Protocol. By contrast, a phased integration of developing countries into a global regime to limit greenhouse gas emissions is a reasonable goal that would be simultaneously responsive both to the environmental imperative and to equity constraints.

It would be wrong to infer that developing countries are merely free riders under the current international regime consisting of the FCCC and its protocol. The Convention includes obligations for all parties to adopt programs to control greenhouse gas emissions and to address emissions issues in specific sectors, such as energy, transport, industry, agriculture, forestry, and waste management. Although the protocol does not contain substantive reduction obligations for developing countries, the CDM is designed to facilitate reductions in emissions from those countries. Moreover, some developing countries, such as India and China, have already begun to take voluntary steps to control emissions. The protocol anticipates the adoption of reduction obligations that have yet to be negotiated for a second and subsequent commitment periods — which might well include quantified emissions limitations for developing countries. Further, the Kyoto Protocol and Marrakesh Accords, by limiting participation in the trading scheme to those parties . . . that have accepted emissions limitations, contain incentives for parties to take on quantified targets.

Alleged economic harm to the U.S. and global economies, amounting to as much as 4 percent of U.S. GDP, is another stock criticism reiterated in the Bush announcement. Other analyses . . . suggest that concerns about the cost of implementation may be overstated. The United States' final objection, namely, that the protocol would leave it "dangerously dependent on other countries to meet its emission targets," is disingenuous at best. The protocol's flexible mechanisms were originally adopted at the insistence of the United States, over the objections of the EU, as a strategy for controlling the costs of reductions.

SUBSEQUENT DEVELOPMENTS . . .

The reconvened sixth session of the Conference of the Parties (COP-6bis) . . . took place in Bonn from July 16 to 27, 2001. . . . The meeting was noteworthy as the occasion for adopting the Bonn Agreements on the Kyoto Protocol rules, a crucial juncture for entry into force of the principal international instrument for reducing emissions of greenhouse gases. The rules were adopted in final form as the Marrakesh Accords at the seventh session of the Conference of the Parties (COP-7), held in Marrakesh, Morocco, from October 29 to November 9, 2001. . . .

More so perhaps than for most international pacts, the Bonn Agreements are distinguished by the very fact that they exist. After the disappointing and inconclusive end to COP-6 in The Hague, followed by the United States' announcement that it would not ratify the Kyoto Protocol, it was widely reported that the protocol was doomed never to enter into force. Consequently, although there might be some dispute as to whether the Bonn Agreements should be considered . . . the most important international environmental instrument ever, there is little doubt that the high drama associated with the genuine uncertainty about the likelihood of reaching a consensus has rarely been equaled.

Had the outcome of the Bonn and Marrakesh negotiations been other than what it was, the prospects for the protocol would likely have been grim indeed. As things turned out, however, the outlook for the protocol's success is considerably better than it was before Bonn and Marrakesh. . . .

The Bonn Agreements have also been widely cited as emblematic of the EU's capacity to exercise global leadership in the absence of U.S. support for multilateral initiatives. Dubbed by some participants "The Mission to Rescue the Kyoto Protocol," COP-6bis has since become a larger metaphor for the potential of multilateral cooperation, as juxtaposed against a go-it-alone unilateralism embodied by the United States. . . .

One important question that has yet to be answered is the long-term compatibility or convergence between the Kyoto Protocol, on the one hand, and unilateral U.S. policies, on the other . . .

Overall, there is a sense of optimism that an agreement of this immense technical complexity can be agreed upon by a consensus of the representatives of nearly two hundred states. Simultaneously, the Bonn Agreements and Marrakesh Accords are very much a political deal, characterized by an enormous network of interlaced linkages and trade-offs. As with any process involving compromise, the result is less satisfying than some would like. Realistic expectations focus on the Kyoto Protocol's future promise, as to which the forecast, though now brighter, is still clouded by uncertainty.

Armin Rosencranz, U.S. Climate Change Policy

Climate Change Policy: A Survey 221, 228-231 (Stephen H. Schneider,
Armin Rosencranz & John O. Niles eds., 2002)

On February 14, 2002, President Bush announced his long-awaited strategy to address climate change. His target is to cut the rate of annual domestic carbon emissions through voluntary corporate action from 183 metric tons per million dollars of GDP to 151 metric tons by 2012. His aim is to slow the *growth* of emissions rather than reducing them — thereby avoiding harm to the U.S. economy. . . .

The Bush climate change strategy included a proposed $4.6 billion in tax credits over five years, averaging $900 million per year, to stimulate investments in clean energy sources, hybrid and fuel cell vehicles, and emissions reducing technologies. Notwithstanding much talk by Bush administration officials and the Council of Economic Advisers about market based initiatives, there is nothing in the new strategy about carbon emissions trading — one of the flexibility mechanisms of the Kyoto Protocol contributed by the U.S. delegation to COP-3 in 1997. . . .

President Bush observed that, under the Kyoto Protocol, the U.S. would have had to "make deep and immediate cuts in our economy to meet an arbitrary target. It would have cost our economy up to $400 billion and we would have lost 4.9 million jobs." He also noted that "developing countries such as China and India already account for a majority of the world's greenhouse gas emissions," but failed to acknowledge that China and India *together* contain 2.3 billion people and produce fewer carbon emissions than the U.S. with 280 million people.

President Bush's budget allocations to address climate change are on the same order and roughly the same tiny percentage of GDP that President Clinton allocated. Like the Bush-Cheney energy policy, there is scant emphasis in the new climate change strategy on energy conservation, renewable energy, or fuel efficiency standards. An editorial in the *New York Times* concluded that President Bush does not regard global warming as a problem: "There seems no other way to interpret a policy that would actually increase the gases responsible for heating the earth's atmosphere. . . . By his own figures, actual emissions . . . could rise by 14 percent, which is exactly the rate at which they have been rising for the last 10 years." [N.Y. Times, Feb. 16, 2002]. . . .

PROGNOSIS

Stanford Senior Fellow David Victor has argued that the Kyoto targets were "symbolically high but hopelessly unrealistic, and should be abandoned." *The Economist* believes that Bush's formal repudiation of Kyoto contains some good news and some bad news. The bad news is that President Bush has retrogressed by alleging continued uncertainties about the science of climate change (in the face of an overwhelming consensus among climate scientists) that global warming and its damaging effects are real and are caused by human activity. Additionally, President Bush's team has argued that developing countries get a "free ride" by not being required to cut carbon emissions, while developed countries suffer economic loss. But developing countries' per capita carbon emissions are now a small fraction of per capita emissions in the United States and other developed countries; the developed countries' emissions account for the bulk of the greenhouse effect, so it is fair that they act first and all climate negotiations envision a carbon emission role for developing countries at a later stage.

The good news, according to *The Economist,* is that the Bush administration is focusing on the costs of complying with Kyoto targets. An international climate change treaty could be implemented in a flexible way that gives broad play to market forces and encourages innovation and development of clean technologies. Europeans seem to be unreasonably skeptical of market approaches, and the Bush repudiation may get them to rethink their position. *The Economist* cites with approval Victor's argument that the cause of the Kyoto Protocol's collapse is its cap-and-trade system, which allows ambitious targets but puts no limits on compliance costs.

Michael Grubb, a scholar at London's Imperial College, believes that the EU must take the lead and act boldly in international climate negotiations. Contrary to conventional wisdom among economists, he believes that technical change driven by corporate research and development in response to market conditions will tend to accelerate carbon abatement to induce cost reductions, rather than deferring abatement to await cost reductions. Grubb's model encourages early action to accelerate the development of cost-effective technologies.

Moreover, Grubb seems to have accurately predicted that with the EU, eager to accommodate its environmentalists, taking the lead, and with flexible policies and mechanisms, the Kyoto Protocol would come into force without the United States. Russia would be motivated to ratify because it could sell its unused emission credits to other industrialized countries, and Japan would not scuttle a treaty bearing the name *Kyoto*. With the EU, Russia, Australia, Japan, and a scattering of other signatory states, the protocol would come into force during this decade with the required ratification of 55 signatory states representing 55 percent of global carbon emissions. With such a demonstration of serious purpose and without an "elephant" (the United States) in the room, developing countries might voluntarily commit to reduction targets. This commitment, together with flexible market-based mechanisms developed in tandem with Bush policy advisors and with growing pressure from Democrats, scientists, environmentalists, and progressive U.S. industrialists, could eventually bring the United States back into global climate change negotiations.

The declaration that the Kyoto Protocol is dead seems premature in light of its adoption by 178 nations in Bonn in July 2001. In fact, the EU agreed to compromises in Bonn that well exceed those they were unwilling to consider only eight months earlier in The Hague.

CONCLUSIONS

Benefiting from the international shock over President Bush's withdrawal from the Kyoto negotiating process, the EU went along with sweeping compromises in July 2001 (COP-6bis) that they had not considered in November 2000 at COP-6. In the wake of Bush's repudiation and unilateralism, the EU was willing to accept a partial deal rather than a continued stalemate. Thus, U.S. policy has had a major, though obviously unintended, influence on the entire climate change negotiation.

The major challenge for U.S. climate change advocates seems to be to persuade the Bush administration to act now to reduce carbon dioxide domestically and to collaborate in shaping carbon reduction policies, strategies, and mechanisms with fellow member states of the Framework Convention on Climate Change, all sharing the same carbon-loaded atmosphere.

The Conferences of the Parties to the FCCC continued with the eighth session taking place in New Delhi, India, from October 23 to November 1, 2002. Progress was made on a number of issues for implementing the Kyoto Protocol. The resulting Ministerial Declaration noted the continuing danger of climate change and called on all the states that had ratified the Kyoto Protocol to encourage other states to do so. The Declaration also encouraged countries to promote sustainable development.

In February 2003, the importance of dealing with global warming was underscored by another expert panel of the National Academies' National Research Council, as well as by Prime Minister Tony Blair of Britain. (See earlier report of National Research Council at page 949 above.) The new expert panel issued a report that politely criticized President Bush's proposals for further research into climate change. As the panel noted: "[President Bush's] draft plan lacks most of the basic elements of a strategic plan: a guiding vision, executable goals, clear timetables and criteria for measuring progress." The panel also found that the President's 2004 budget request "appears to leave funding relatively unchanged" for the administration's initiatives, despite past pledges to increase it. Eric Pianin, Report Gives Bush's Global Warming Efforts Mixed Rating, Washington Post, February 26, 2003, at A9.

Even as he was backing President Bush on Iraq, Mr. Blair made clear that environmental problems generally and climate change in particular could be "just as devastating in their potential impact" as the damage that might be caused by weapons of mass destruction and terrorism. Mr. Blair pledged a 60 percent cut in Britain's emissions of greenhouse gases by mid-century, which exceeded the Kyoto Protocol's goal for industrialized nations of an average 5 percent reduction by 2012. Editorial, Rebuked on Global Warming, N.Y. Times, March 1, 2003, at A32.

Notes and Questions

1. In considering the treaty regime governing global warming, you should examine the Framework Convention and the Kyoto Protocol, which are excerpted in the Documentary Supplement. You should extract in general terms what the treaties actually do — for example, establish goals, set substantive standards, monitor compliance, and enforce norms. Look particularly at Articles 2, 3, and 4 of the Framework Convention and Articles 2-8, 12, 13, 17, and 19 of the Kyoto Protocol. Consider Questions 2-7 pertaining to the ozone treaty regime (at page 942).

2. Should the United States ratify the Kyoto Protocol as it now stands, and why or why not? If not, should the United States try to obtain changes in the Kyoto Protocol or seek another multilateral protocol? If so, what would be the key differences from the present Kyoto Protocol? If the United States should not try to proceed multilaterally, what alternative approach would you recommend for the United States to deal with the apparent problem of global warming? For other perspectives on the Kyoto Protocol, see, for example, John K. Setear, Learning to Live with Losing: International Environmental Law in the New Millennium, 20 Va. J. Intl. L. 129 (2001).

3. The Clinton Administration was one of the major proponents of the provisions in the Kyoto Protocol allowing states to buy and sell emissions rights. (See Wirth excerpt above on the Protocol.) Many economists justified this on efficiency grounds. However, does it favor wealthy countries that can afford to buy additional emissions rights? How might the system be made a fair one?

4. With complicated problems such as global warming, is the better approach to seek one convention or protocol to solve the problem or to negotiate a framework convention and a series of protocols and agreements (as was done with the ozone depletion problem)?

5. What should be the role of NGOs in these negotiations? To whom are they accountable?

6. Why do you think that it has been more difficult to obtain international agreement on the problem of global warming versus ozone depletion? Might it be a result of the dangers of inaction? Or, might it reflect the complexity of the problem and the difficulties of solutions?

7. Besides the problems of ozone depletion and global warming, what other international environmental problems do you consider the most serious?

8. In August 2002, ten years after the Rio Conference and the Rio Declaration, world leaders met at the World Summit on Sustainable Development in Johannesburg, South Africa. At the Johannesburg Summit, governments, NGOs, and private sector participants worked together to address the slow progress in implementing the sustainable development goals that emerged from the 1992 Earth Summit. Although the Johannesburg Summit did not result in any new agreements or treaties, the negotiations did produce new energy and sanitations targets. Moreover, the Summit led to the formation of more than 300 voluntary partnerships among governments, organizations, and private businesses. Through these partnerships, governments will gain access to additional resources to implement sustainable development. For more information on the Johannesburg Summit, visit the U.N. Web site at <http://www.un.org>.

9. Now that you have read a bit about international environmental law, we offer some concluding thoughts from two thoughtful professors who conducted empirical studies in an effort to evaluate the elements that might be relevant to the success of an international agreement on the environment. As you read, think about whether the agreements you have studied satisfy these proscriptions.

Harold K. Jacobson & Edith Brown Weiss, Assessing the Record and Designing Strategies to Engage Countries

Engaging Countries: Strengthening Compliance with International Environmental Accords, 552-554 (Edith Brown Weiss & Harold K. Jacobson eds., 1998)

As we sought to explain the difference in levels of compliance across treaties and among countries, and the overall trend toward strengthened compliance, and then developed and analyzed broad legal and institutional strategies to strengthen compliance, we implicitly and explicitly offered several prescriptions. Some of the prescriptions apply to the way accords are drafted; others, to essential institutional features; and still others, to actions that should be taken after the accords come into effect. The more important of the prescriptions that we have covered can be summarized briefly in three categories.

NEGOTIATING THE ACCORD

- Ensure that the obligations of the accord are perceived as equitable by parties and potential parties.
- If clearly assessing compliance is a primary concern, make the obligations as precise as possible.
- Try to ensure that the obligations are reinforced rather than contradicted by economic forces.
- Craft the treaty so that the burden of compliance is placed on a manageable number of actors. Target the major actors.
- Ensure that there are leader countries in the negotiations and that early on, they take measures to implement and comply with the agreement.

INSTITUTIONAL ARRANGEMENTS ASSOCIATED WITH THE ACCORD

- Provide for regular meetings of parties, so that national and international bureaucracies will be mobilized regularly.
- Ensure that secretariats are strong enough to identify cases of noncompliance, advise various actors on how to comply, propose measures (through governments) to address issues of noncompliance, and seek support from various institutions, and other actors in which parties have confidence, to help countries.
- Include means, in which parties have confidence, for ongoing scientific assessments of problems targeted by the accord.
- Involve the international financial institutions, including the Global Environmental Facility, in building local capacity to comply with the accords.
- Link access to financial support for projects to compliance with obligations that might affect the implementation of the project.
- Involve nongovernmental organizations in helping to carry out accords.
- Develop standardized forms for reporting data, which should contribute to the effectiveness of reporting. Data required should be frugal, and perceived as equitable and essential.
- Inform the public about the agreement through the media and new information technology. This can build support for implementation and compliance.

MEASURES DIRECTED AT COUNTRIES

- Focus strategies for strengthening compliance on individual countries, and differentiate them according to their intention and capacity to comply.
- Make it possible for low- and middle-income countries to participate meaningfully in all agreements they may be expected to join.
- Assist countries, when necessary, in drafting implementing legislation and in initiating the steps required by the agreement for compliance.
- Make available technical assistance and capacity-building programs at the national and local levels. Regional networks of relevant national officers who have responsibility for implementation and compliance may encourage learning how to address shared compliance problems.
- Strengthen coordination among relevant ministries and departments, and between national and provincial or municipal units of government. Strengthen domestic institutions concerned with compliance.
- Build a culture of compliance by engaging both the public sector and the private sector in determining domestic needs and setting priorities.

These prescriptions are in effect tactical suggestions. They can be employed singly and in combination, and to varying degrees at various times.

In the end, engaging countries means engaging all relevant actors to promote compliance. While we speak of countries as separate political entities, the international system is a very complex web of transnational networks and local actors, joined in dynamic ways. A strategy of compliance must look beyond governments to provide incentives and pressures for all relevant actors to comply with the environmental accords.

While national compliance may be easier for countries that intend, and have the capacity, to comply, even they will need external pressures upon relevant actors, if only in the form of sunshine, and incentives at least to the private sector, to ensure compliance. For countries lacking the capacity, external incentives to relevant actors are essential, and external pressures are needed to maintain or to develop the intention to comply. Engaging states and all relevant actors from the beginning and keeping them engaged are the essential steps that must be taken to strengthen national compliance with international environmental accords.

11

Use of Force and Arms Control

The legal principles for regulating the use of military force is a subject that has fascinated, and frustrated, those interested in international law. It has fascinated because the use of force or the threat to use force has often had important and highly visible results in international relations, affecting the fate of nations and individuals. Moreover, the great destructiveness of modern weaponry has made it increasingly important for the world to develop limits on the use of military force. At least nine states are believed to possess nuclear weapons or can quickly fabricate them, and more states are likely to have that capability in the near future. Even non-nuclear, or conventional, weapons are much improved in their ability to kill and maim.

Developing limits on the use of force has also frustrated international law scholars and practitioners. A state's leaders and citizens are particularly hesitant to circumscribe the state's ability to use its military to protect its perceived vital interests — indeed, in some cases its very existence. These strongly felt concerns have meant that progress toward an international legal regime limiting the use or threat to use force has been uneven at best.

Nevertheless, the issues are so fundamentally important that we need to examine what has happened in the past, where the law stands at present, and what might be reasonable goals for the future. To do this, this chapter will address five areas.

The first section explores international legal norms regarding the use of force, especially as they have evolved since World War II. We will analyze what the legal principles are and how well they have worked.

The second section addresses the role of collective intervention, notably U.N. and regional peacekeeping efforts, including a study of the U.N. and U.S. response to Iraq since its 1990 invasion of Kuwait through the war in early 2003, as well as a study of NATO's actions against the Federal Republic of Yugoslavia for its repression of Albanians in Kosovo. The third section will consider the question of individual responsibility for military actions, both under international and U.S. law. The fourth section then examines other relevant U.S. domestic law, such as the War Powers Resolution.

Finally, we look at efforts to combat the proliferation of nuclear, chemical, and biological weapons — efforts that have created important constraints under both international and domestic law. This last section includes a discussion of past measures and the recent case of North Korea.

A. INTERNATIONAL LEGAL NORMS REGARDING THE USE OF FORCE

International legal principles regarding the use of force began to emerge in a systematic fashion after the searing experience of the Second World War. Prior to that, there were centuries of sporadic development and decline. The first decade after World War I witnessed some seminal efforts, such as the League of Nations and the Kellogg-Briand Pact, but these efforts failed, and many states found themselves fighting World War II barely 20 years after the end of the previous War.

1. Legal Norms Prior to World War II

a. Developments Before the First World War

The following two excerpts trace the development of international legal norms from the Roman Empire to the start of World War I. First, Malcolm Shaw provides a brief overview of the period up to the Treaty of Westphalia in 1648. The doctrine of the "just war" was at its peak.

Malcolm Shaw, International Law

777-779 (4th ed. 1997)

The doctrine of the just war arose as a consequence of the Christianisation of the Roman Empire and the ensuing abandonment by Christians of their pacificism. Force could be used provided it complied with the divine will. The concept of the just war embodied elements of Greek and Roman philosophy and was employed as the ultimate sanction for the maintenance of an ordered society. St. Augustine (354-430) defined the just war in terms of avenging of injuries suffered where the guilty party has refused to make amends. War was to be embarked upon to punish wrongs and restore the peaceful status quo but no further. Aggression was unjust and the recourse to violence had to be strictly controlled. . . .

St. Thomas Aquinas in the thirteenth century took the definition of the just war a stage further by declaring that it was the subjective guilt of the wrongdoer that had to be punished rather than the objectively wrong activity. He wrote that war could be justified provided it was waged by the sovereign authority, it was accompanied by a just cause (i.e. the punishment of wrongdoers) and it was supported by the right intentions on the part of the belligerents.

With the rise of the European nation-states, the doctrine began to change. It became linked with the sovereignty of states and faced the paradox of wars between Christian states, each side being convinced of the justice of its cause. This situation tended to modify the approach to the just war. The requirement that serious attempts at a peaceful resolution of the dispute were necessary before turning to force began to appear. This reflected the new state of international affairs, since there now existed a series of independent states, uneasily co-existing in Europe in a primitive balance of power system. The use of force against other states, far from strengthening the order, posed serious challenges to it and threatened to undermine it. Thus the emphasis in legal doctrine moved from the application of force to suppress wrongdoers to a concern (if hardly apparent at times) to maintain the order by peaceful means. The great Spanish writer of the sixteenth century, Vitoria, emphasised that "not every kind and degree of wrong can suffice for commencing war," while Suarez noted that states were obliged to call the attention of the opposing side to the existence of a just cause and request reparation before action was taken. The just war was also implied in immunity of innocent persons from direct attack and the proportionate use of force to overcome the opposition.

Gradually it began to be accepted that a certain degree of right might exist on both sides, although the situation was confused by references to subjective and objective justice. Ultimately, the legality of the recourse to war was seen to depend upon the formal processes of law. This approach presaged the rise of positivism with its concentration upon the sovereign state, which could only be bound by what it had consented to. Grotius, in his systematising fashion, tried to exclude ideological considerations as the basis of a just war, in the light of the destructive seventeenth century religious conflicts, and attempted to redefine the just war in terms of self-defence, the protection of property and the punishment for wrongs suffered by the citizens of the particular state.

But with positivism and the definitive establishment of the European balance of power system after the Peace of Westphalia, 1648, the concept of the just war disappeared from international law as such. States were sovereign and equal, and therefore no one state could presume to judge whether another's cause was just or not.

Professor Brownlie picks up the story from the Treaty of Westphalia to the start of World War I.

Ian Brownlie, International Law and the Use of Force by States

14-50 (rev. ed. 1981)

EUROPE AFTER WESTPHALIA, 1648-1815: POSITIVISM AND THE BALANCE OF POWER

Not long after Grotius's death the European states reached a general settlement in the treaties constituting the Peace of Westphalia. This marked the end of a period of violent religious wars and the disappearance of the Papacy and Holy Roman Empire as effective instruments for regulating the affairs of Europe. The intention was to create a system which would be stable and permanent, resting on a concept of a European public peace and public law. This juridical order was to rest on the political status quo which was assumed to represent a "Balance of Power" or *principe d'équilibre* between the various states or groups of states. . . . The Balance of Power and the public law of Europe were to last until 1914. . . .

The period 1648 to 1815 is characterized by the relegation of the just war doctrine to the realms of morality or propaganda since in deference to public opinion governments frequently took pains to advance reasons for declaring war which would give the action some colour of righteousness. . . .

The doctrine which appears in the seventeenth century of a society of European states subject to no *de facto* or legal superior bound by a law they can make themselves, declaring war when the ruler or his advisers think it expedient, may seem incompatible with a legal order between states. And yet it was a prerequisite for the appearance of an international legal order to replace the universal system of the Holy Roman Empire and Pre-Reformation Europe. There could be no Law of Nations without a society of state units with formal equality.

Positivist thought on the Law of Nations flourished in the eighteenth century and the maintenance of the Balance of Power continued to be the *ultima ratio* of diplomacy, although it was constantly disturbed by ambitious despots, dynastic problems, and commercial rivalries in other parts of the world. State practice reflected the . . . doctrine in various ways, not least in the growth of the law of neutrality based on the assumption that the war was lawful on both sides. . . .

MAJOR FEATURES OF STATE PRACTICE IN THE PERIOD 1815 TO 1914

The next century was still dominated by an unrestricted right of war and the recognition of conquests, qualified by the political system of the European Concert. In the latter part of the period new trends in favour of peaceful settlement of disputes appeared, trends which, although they left the customary law basically unchanged, deserve notice as a preparation for the Covenant of the League of Nations and as the beginnings of the process of eroding the "right of war."

The European settlement of 1814 and 1815 and the Final Act of the Congress of Vienna re-established the public law of Europe and the principle of the Balance of Power. Maintenance of the status quo against the rising tide of liberalism and national sentiment necessitated close co-operation in support of legitimism and the repression of rebellion. . . . European society and the public law became heavily institutionalized. The concept of the Concert of Europe and the Congress system raised a strong presumption against unilateral changes in the status quo. Thus the Treaty of Paris, signed on 30 March 1856, was signed not only by the belligerents in the Crimean War but also by the other Great Powers, Austria and Prussia. To some extent territorial changes depended for their permanence and validity under the public law upon collective recognition. . . . European states with interests which conflicted with those of the Great Powers, and states outside the European Concert, were liable to various forms of forcible interference.

Apart from the functioning of the public law of Europe, which had some characteristics of a constitutional law, the right of states to go to war and to obtain territory by right of conquest was unlimited although some qualifications to this position had appeared by 1914. Situations resulting from resort to force were regarded as legally valid as in the case of the Prussian annexation of the Danish duchies and the annexation of Alsace-Lorraine by the German Empire. Great Britain, France, and Russia made numerous incursions in Asia and Africa, many of which resulted in annexations or the imposition of a protectorate. The United States fought wars in 1846 and 1898 resulting in the annexation of Texas, the Philippines, Cuba, and Puerto Rico. . . . Many contemporary works of authority stated the position by saying that the right to resort to war was a question of morality and policy outside the sphere of law or that it was a means of change aiding the evolution of international society. A large number of writers described war as a judicial procedure involving also execution and punishment; it was looked upon as the "litigation of nations," a means of obtaining redress for wrongs in the absence of a system of international justice and sanctions.

In the latter part of the nineteenth century there appeared a corollary of this view in the form of war as a judicial procedure, a means of settling a dispute. War was stated to be a means of last resort after recourse to available means of peaceful settlement had failed. In state practice this sometimes appeared as a substantial though perhaps somewhat formal qualification of the right to resort to war. . . .

In the course of the century governments began to give more attention to the justification of resort to force. For various reasons public opinion had become a force to be reckoned with. There was an extension of constitutional government and ideas of democratic control. Improvements in the technology of war brought a heavier toll of the population and economic resources of nations. Cheap newspapers with mass circulation increased the flow of ideas and discussion of policy. War had ceased to be the affair of despots and professional armies. . . .

State practice reacted to the new circumstances in two ways. First, the practice of states evolved various forms of coercion which did not constitute "war" in the formal sense but which were justifiable under the Law of Nations: reprisals, pacific blockades, certain justifiable interventions, and naval demonstrations. These lesser measures had certain advantages; inter alia, they avoided constitutional checks on resort to "war" and the stigma of "declaring war." Secondly, more care was taken to indicate the necessity for the war and the justice of the cause. "Unprovoked aggression" became a familiar term in diplomacy and pleas of provocation, self-defence, self-preservation, defence of vital interests, and necessity were advanced. The legal significance of these two developments will now be considered.

THE STATE OF WAR DOCTRINE

The practice of states since the early nineteenth century has developed a doctrine which might be considered so absurd as not to merit discussion if it were not for the circumstances that governments have frequently used the doctrine and that it has been resorted to even in more recent times. State practice has emphasized that war is not a legal concept linked with objective phenomena such as large-scale hostilities between the armed forces of organized state entities but a legal status the existence of which depends on the intention of one or more of the states concerned. Thus hostilities resulting in considerable loss of life and destruction of property may not result in a state of war, the term commonly applied to this legal status, if the parties contending do not regard a "state of war" as existing. This technical concept is also referred to variously in the sources as "war," "*de jure* war," "war in the legal sense," and "war in the sense of international law." As a legal status it depended on subjective determination by governments of the legal significance of their own actions. . . . [T]he determination did not depend on any objective criteria. In the period between 1798 and 1920 military occupations, invasions, bombardments, blockades, and lesser forms of conflict took place in the absence of any state of war, at least in the opinion of the governments concerned. War became such a subjective concept in state practice that to attempt a definition was to play with words.

In the view of most of the governments there were substantial reasons of policy for avoiding a state of war while at the same time using the desired amount of coercion. In the era of constitutional government the executive was usually bound to observe time-consuming and politically embarrassing procedures before recourse to "war." The process involved preparation of public opinion and the rallying of sufficient support in the legislative assembly. Recourse to "war" incurred a certain odium; "war" was a term which had acquired a deep psychological and emotional significance. "War" implied a full-scale combat which offended pacific sentiment and was wasteful of lives and a nation's resources. Furthermore, if a government admitted the existence of a state of war third states could, without embarrassment, demand observance of neutral rights and were themselves under various legal duties. The "state of war" involved a termination of commercial intercourse between the contending states and the invalidation or suspension of treaties. In the more modern period, the appearance of restrictions on the right to resort to war in the League Covenant and other instruments was to provide a further reason for avoiding "war." The extreme subjectivity of what may be called the state of war doctrine was tolerable in the period before the League when war was still viewed to some extent as a private duel and not a matter automatically of concern to the community of states. . . .

States often considered that it was desirable to avoid the disruption and embarrassment of full-scale hostilities and war in the legal sense by recourse either to some restricted use of force with a limited object or to extensive operations without any admission of the existence of a "state of war." The constant use in the nineteenth century of various restricted forms of coercion gave rise to a body of legal doctrine on reprisals, pacific blockade, and intervention to protect nationals and their property in foreign states. . . . It is sufficient for the present to notice that, in theory at least, states had to pay for the luxury of avoiding the consequences of a state of war by submitting to some measure of legal regulation of the lesser means of coercion as a reprisal, pacific blockade, or justified intervention. Reprisals and the justified forms of intervention were bounded by the requirement of proportionality to the danger threatened and the restricted object of the use of force. [See materials at the end of this excerpt regarding the *Naulilaa* arbitration.]

In most of the cases of resort to force . . . considerations of internal and external policy have played a major role in determining whether or not a "state of war" should be admitted to exist. The state of war doctrine must not, however, be dismissed as selfish and anarchic on that account. At a time when legal controls of the use of force were not conspicuous it had perhaps one useful function. The absence of any admission that a state of war existed indicated that the action might be intended as a reprisal or justified intervention. And even if there were no obvious justification for reprisal or intervention, its absence nearly always signified the use of force for a limited purpose, either to settle a grievance or to punish wrongdoers or to provide warning or preventive action. In such a case there is no intention to conquer or annex. . . .

The most important conclusion to be drawn from the nineteenth-century experience is the unsatisfactory nature of "war" as a term of art in view of the freedom which the concept conferred on states in characterizing their own actions. It might include situations in which no hostilities were taking place but fail to cover conflicts which though perhaps limited in scope were nevertheless serious threats to peace. . . .

Legal Justifications for the Use of Force in the Classical Law: Customary Rules of the Nineteenth Century

The customary law shows greater complexity than is commonly assumed. The complexity springs in part from the contradiction between the assertion of a sovereign right to resort to war and to gain title by conquest on the one hand and a tendency in spite of this to provide theoretical and moral bases for resort to war on the other. A lack of a coherent terminology contributes to the confusion.

The right of war, as an aspect of sovereignty, which existed in the period before 1914, subject to the doctrine that war was a means of last resort in the enforcement of legal rights, was very rarely asserted either by statesmen or works of authority without some stereotyped plea to a right of self-preservation, and of self-defence, or to necessity or protection of vital interests, or merely alleged injury to rights or national honour and dignity. Unilateral interference with the status quo was regarded as a *casus belli*. The great variety of *casus belli* admitted in state practice indicates the unreality of any theoretical justification on the ground of a right of self-preservation or on the basis of a doctrine of necessity. Moreover, the essential subjectivity of such concepts was reinforced by the right assumed of individual determination of the factual prerequisites for the resort to war. . . .

Even during the nineteenth century there were some attempts to restrict the right to go to war to cases of direct and immediate danger. [Further information regarding the following incident is provided at the end of this excerpt.] The *Caroline* incident on the night of 29-30 December 1837 was the subject of a letter, dated 6 February 1838, from the British Ambassador in Washington, Fox, to the American Secretary of State, Forsyth, in which Fox justified the British action:

> The piratical character of the steamboat "Caroline" and the necessity of self-defence and self-preservation, under which Her Majesty's subjects acted in destroying that vessel, would seem to be sufficiently established. . . .

In a letter of 24 April 1841 from the Secretary of State, Webster, to Fox, later incorporated in a Note to Lord Ashburton of 27 July 1842, Webster required the British Government to show the existence of:

> . . . necessity of self-defence, instant, overwhelming, leaving no choice of means, and no moment for deliberation. It will be for it to show, also, that the local authorities of Canada, even supposing the necessity of the moment authorised them to enter the territories of the United States at all, did nothing unreasonable or excessive; since the act justified by the necessity of self-defence, must be limited by that necessity, and kept clearly within it.

Lord Ashburton in his letter of 28 July 1842 did not dispute Webster's statement of principle. The formula used by Webster has proved valuable in recent years but the correspondence made no difference to the legal doctrine, such as it was, of the time. Self-defence was regarded either as synonymous with self-preservation or as a particular instance of it. Webster's Note was an attempt to describe its limits in relation to the particular facts of the incident. The statesmen of the period used self-preservation, self-defence, necessity, and necessity of self-defence as more or less interchangeable terms and the diplomatic correspondence was not intended to restrict the right of self-preservation which was in fact reaffirmed. . . .

HOSTILE MEASURES SHORT OF WAR

By perhaps the year 1880 it had become recognized in the practice of states that certain legal conditions were to be observed if resort to force was not to be regarded as creating a formal war and the application of the rights and duties of belligerency and neutrality. Reprisals, pacific blockade, and various types of intervention appeared as institutions of customary law. . . . In theory they created a legal régime for the use of force which did not involve a state of war and modern writers refer to them as though they were highly formalized and well defined. The position was in practice affected by the artificiality of the state of war doctrine and both writers and governments failed to provide any adequate means of distinguishing between the various "hostile measures short of war," or between these, the right of self-preservation and self-defence, and the category of "intervention."

Thus the hostilities against the Boxers and Chinese troops in 1900 and 1901 were variously categorized by contemporary statesmen, diplomats, and governments inter alia, as "war," "intervention," and an "expedition." The practice of states was in this case concerned with the question as to whether a state of war existed. Writers have nevertheless been intrepid in forcing these events into the legal mould of "hostile measures short of war," or in classifying the action as a joint punitive expedition, or acts of self-preservation. The United States occupation of Cuba in 1898 was not related to the distinctions drawn by the writers and the writers themselves failed to agree on its correct characterization. The Joint Resolution of Congress approved on 20 April 1898 justified the intervention in terms of American interests. Writers have nevertheless described it as a case of humanitarian intervention, intervention to protect the property of nationals, action dictated by a variety of motives, or abatement of a nuisance.

THE CLOSE OF THE PERIOD 1815 TO 1914: RETROSPECT AND PROSPECT

The world on the eve of the First World War had more of the attributes of a community of states than at any previous period. The formal unit of the nation state on the European and American model had become the common mould, either as a result of European imperialism and influence or as a result of the voluntary adoption of Western forms of state organization. The "public law of Europe" was extended to non-European states. The railway and steamship and an international banking system and cartels tended to create a universal economic system. In such conditions international law became a world system for the first time and this legal order could cease to depend for its efficacy on the dominance of a group of states which to some extent made and enforced the law in their own interest by means of the various forms of intervention and by reprisals. Thus the concept and fact of a world legal order was comparatively new and the League of Nations established in 1920 was not far removed in point of time from an era when the Powers were chary of conceding even a formal equality to states such as Turkey and China.

Moreover, the legacies of the state practice in the nineteenth century were of somewhat dubious value for any future development of an effective legal régime relating to resort to force. Trends in state practice toward peaceful settlement of disputes provide a positive feature of the period but it was nevertheless dominated by the right to go to war as an attribute of the sovereign state. It is true that in the latter part of the period between the Congress of Vienna and the world war the doctrine that war was an *ultimate* means of enforcing legal rights, peaceful modes of settlement having failed, had developed in the practice of states. But this is not to assert that the "ultimate means" doctrine in any way superseded the assumption that resort to war was a sovereign right of states. There was simply a partial development of the former doctrine and the two doctrines existed side by side in the somewhat contradictory practice of states. The evidence points to a continued dominance of the view that resort to war was a sovereign right. . . . The existence of the technical state of war doctrine with its dependence on the formal admissions of the interested states imported an undesirable artificiality into the law; but most unfortunate of all was the confusion both in legal doctrine and state practice attendant on the categories of hostile measures short of war, intervention, self-defence, self-preservation, and necessity, and the relations between them.

Two examples that help illustrate the excerpt from Professor Brownlie are the *Caroline* incident and the *Naulilaa* arbitration case. The correspondence in the *Caroline* incident has already been discussed above, but additional facts and other materials are useful.

Destruction of the "Caroline"

2 Moore, A Digest of International Law 409-414 (1906)

[During the insurrection in Canada in 1837, the insurgents found refuge, recruits, and other private support from the United States, particularly along the border. The U.S. government "adopted active measures for the enforcement of the neutrality laws," but effective enforcement was difficult. In late December 1837, about 1,000 armed insurgents were encamped at Navy Island on the Canadian side of the Niagara River. There was another camp at Black Rock, on the American side.

The *Caroline* was a small steamer used by the men on Black Rock and Navy Island to travel between the camps and other locations, including the port of Schlosser on the New York side. On December 29, 1837, 23 U.S. citizens were on board the ship in Schlosser when it was boarded at midnight by about 70 or 80 armed men. They attacked the persons on board, who merely tried to escape.

The attackers also "set the steamer on fire, cut her loose, and set her adrift over the Niagara Falls." It was generally reported at the time of the incident that 12 of the U.S. citizens had been wounded on the steamer and "were sent with her over the falls." There were also reports of celebrations by the British forces at Chippewa on the Canadian side. (Canada was still a British colony at the time.) As a result, the incident generated considerable public outcry in the United States.

A later investigation revised the casualty estimates. It determined that one of the U.S. citizens was killed on the dock, several others were wounded, and one person was missing. The rest of the people were accounted for. The investigation also determined that the insurgents on Navy Island had fired some shots into Canada the day of the incident and that the force that attacked the *Caroline* was under the command of a British officer.

The 1838 letter of Mr. Fox, the British ambassador in Washington, justifying the attack was quoted above in the Brownlie excerpt. In response, the United States demanded reparations, which the British said were under consideration.

In 1841 the incident gained new notoriety when Alexander McLeod was arrested in New York on a charge of murder, after he had boasted (apparently while intoxicated) of having taken part in the destruction of the *Caroline*.]

Lord Palmerston then avowed responsibility, on the part of Her Majesty's government, for the destruction of the steamer, as a public act of force, in self-defense, by persons in her Majesty's service, and on this ground demanded McLeod's release. [Instead,] McLeod was ultimately tried, and was acquitted on proof of an alibi.

The case was finally disposed of by [U.S. Secretary of State Daniel] Webster and Lord Ashburton, in the course of their negotiations in 1842, Mr. Webster admitting that the employment of force might have been justified by the necessity of self-defense, but denying that such necessity existed, while Lord Ashburton, although he maintained that the circumstances afforded excuse for what was done, apologized for the invasion of United States territory. . . .

[In his August 6, 1842 letter to Lord Ashburton, Webster stated:]

"The President sees with pleasure that your Lordship fully admits those great principles of public international law, applicable to cases of this kind, which this government has expressed; and that on your part, as on ours, respect for the inviolable character of the territory of independent states is the most essential foundation of civilization. . . . [W]hile it is admitted that exceptions growing out of the great law of self-defense do exist, those exceptions should be confined to cases in which the 'necessity of that self-defence is instant, overwhelming, and leaving no choice of means, and no moment for deliberation.'"

Requirement of proportionality. In an earlier letter to the British, Webster wrote:

It will be for [Her Majesty's government] to show, also, that the local authorities of Canada, even supposing the necessity of the moment authorized them to enter the [U.S.] territories . . . at all, did nothing unreasonable or excessive; since the act, justified by the necessity of self-defense, must be limited by that necessity, and kept clearly within it. [Webster to Fox (April 24, 1841), 29 British & Foreign State Papers 1129, 1138 (1937), as quoted in Louis Henkin, International Law 663-664 (1987).]

Reprisals. The next excerpt briefly discusses reprisals in general and then reports on the *Naulilaa* case.

Sir Humphrey Waldock, The Regulation of the Use of Force by Individual States in International Law

81 Recueil des Cours 455, 458-460 (1952, vol. II), as excerpted in 12
Whiteman, Digest of International Law 148-149 (1963)

The legal institution of international reprisals goes back to mediaeval times. It has its roots in a system of private reprisals which was in operation from the 14th-18th centuries. An individual, who had suffered injustice abroad and been unable to obtain redress in the State concerned, would obtain his own Sovereign's authority to take reprisals against the nationals of the foreign sovereign. The basis of this form of reprisals was a communal responsibility for injuries done to foreigners. The system was, of course, open to grave abuse and at sea was apt to deteriorate into licensed piracy. Nevertheless, in the absence of other means of redressing injuries to foreigners, it served a purpose and played an important part in the development of the modern right possessed by States of protecting their nationals abroad. By the 19th century all reprisals are public reprisals taken by the State itself and any international wrong done to the State or its nationals is a just cause for reprisals. Again, reprisals having become State acts, they take more often than not the drastic forms of pacific blockade, bombardment or military occupation. . . . There is, in fact, more legal doctrine surrounding the institution of reprisals than is sometimes appreciated. The institution was derived from the old law of private reprisals for denial of justice from which it acquired certain principles. Thus reprisals were not considered legitimate unless the reprisals-taker had previously attempted to obtain redress from the wrongdoer. . . .

The best account of the customary law of reprisals is to be found in the *Naulilaa* case decided in 1928 by a special arbitral tribunal. When Portugal was neutral in the first World War, a small German party crossed the frontier of Portuguese South-West Africa. Owing to a misunderstanding, the Portuguese fired a few shots which killed 3 Germans. Germany immediately sent a punitive force which invaded Portuguese territory, defeated the Portuguese and then withdrew. A native rising followed causing considerable loss to Portugal. The Tribunal, which was established under the Versailles Treaty to hear Portugal's claim, defined reprisals as follows:

> Reprisals are acts of self-help by the injured State, acts in retaliation for acts contrary to international law on the part of the offending State, which have remained unredressed after a demand for amends. In consequence of such measures, the observance of this or that rule of international law is temporarily suspended, in the relations between the two States. They are limited by considerations of humanity and the rules of good faith, applicable in the relations between States. They are illegal unless they are based upon a previous act contrary to international law. They seek to impose on the offending State reparation for the offence, the return to legality and the avoidance of new offences.

It then rejected Germany's pleas of legitimate reprisals saying:

> (1) The *sine qua non* of a legitimate resort to reprisals is that there should have been a previous violation of international law by the other party and in this case the previous act had been not a breach of international law but an accident.

(2) Reprisals are only legitimate when they have been preceded by an unsuccessful demand for redress and in this case there had been no attempt to obtain satisfaction by legal means. The employment of force is only justifiable by a necessity to use it.

(3) Reprisals, when taken, must be reasonably proportionate to the injury suffered and in this case they were out of all proportion to the injury.

This award by three independent Swiss arbitrators is generally accepted as giving a correct interpretation of the customary law of reprisals.

Notes and Questions

1. Consider the circumstances enunciated by Webster in the *Caroline* incident that justify self-defense and incursions into another country's territory. Do you believe that they encompass all the likely cases for allowing self-defense? If the necessity to react is not "instant, overwhelming, and leaving no choice of means, and no moment for deliberation," then is a country barred from using its military force to respond to another country's use of force — for example, a small border incursion, an attack on its military forces abroad, or an attack on its commercial shipping? If a country cannot use its force in response, what other alternatives should it be allowed? The use of economic sanctions? Resort to the International Court of Justice (discussed in Chapter 4)?

2. Do you agree with the conditions for reprisals announced by the arbitral panel in the *Naulilaa* incident? Based on your reading of the historical excerpt from Professor Brownlie, how did reprisals differ traditionally from the use of force in self-defense? Were reprisals more limited in scope? Could some modern theory of reprisals provide a good basis for reacting to attacks by terrorists who are based in another country?

3. When there was a state of war between belligerent states, there could also be neutrality for certain third states. As Professor Oppenheim has written,

> Neutrality may be defined as the attitude of impartiality adopted by third States towards belligerents and recognised by belligerents, such attitude creating rights and duties between the impartial States and the belligerents. Whether or not a third State will adopt an attitude of impartiality at the outbreak of war is not a matter for International Law but for international politics. [2 L. Oppenheim, International Law 653 (7th ed. 1952).]

The neutral state was accorded freedom from belligerent acts and respect for its territory. The traditional rules of neutrality were based on two principles: (1) nonparticipation and (2) nondiscrimination. The nonparticipation requirement was a guarantee to the belligerents that the neutral state would not assist one of the belligerents against the opposing side. Nondiscrimination required the neutral state to deal impartially with all belligerents. The neutral state could continue to interact with the belligerent states in nonmilitary matters, but no belligerent would have trading advantages over the other.

In 1907, the laws of neutrality were codified in the Hague Convention and were then further elaborated in later conventions. Article 6 of Hague Convention No. XIII, for example, forbade neutral states from furnishing military supplies to a belligerent. Other rules, such as the movement of troops, military equipment, or prizes of war across neutral land, waters, or airspace, were also codified.

Under the neutrality rules of the Hague Convention, neutral states could continue trading with belligerent states in two ways: first, the neutral state could trade in any nonmilitary supplies; second, the neutral state could allow private individuals to supply military goods. A neutral state was not obligated to deter private intervention but was still bound by the nondiscrimination principle. As a result, a neutral state could either impose a total embargo on exports of military goods by private individuals or, alternatively, it could allow the exports but without any discrimination among the belligerents.

b. Developments from World War I to World War II

The scope and carnage of World War I had a considerable impact on the attitude of states toward the use of force. As Professor Brownlie relates:

> In the period of the First World War and of the peace settlement and conferences of 1919-1920 there were several indications of the development of increased sensitivity on the part of states to the use of force. The dramatic results of the failure to maintain peace by a system of alliances, the geographical extent of the war, and the enormous loss of life, the chaos which followed, all these tended to create a climate favourable to a new approach. During the currency of the war numerous peace plans appeared and the creation of the League of Nations was an integral part of the peace settlement. [Ian Brownlie, International Law and the Use of Force by States 51 (rev. 1981).]

(1) The League of Nations

The major institutional result of the war was the creation of the League of Nations. President Woodrow Wilson was one of the leading figures at the peace conferences and championed the idea of the League, but the United States failed to join because of opposition in the U.S. Senate. Malcolm Shaw provides a brief analysis of the significance of the League and how it was designed to stop aggression:

> The First World War marked the end of the balance of power system and raised anew the question of unjust war. It also resulted in efforts to rebuild international affairs upon the basis of a general international institution which would oversee the conduct of the world community to ensure that aggression could not happen again. The creation of the League of Nations reflected a completely different attitude to the problems of force in the international order.
>
> The Covenant of the League declared that members should submit disputes likely to lead to a rupture to arbitration or judicial settlement or inquiry by the Council of the League. In no circumstances were members to resort to war until three months after the arbitral award or judicial decision or report by the Council. This was intended to provide a cooling-off period for passions to subside and reflected the view that such a delay might well have broken the seemingly irreversible chain of tragedy that linked the assassination of the Austrian Archduke in Sarajevo with the outbreak of general war in Europe.
>
> League members agreed not to go to war with members complying with such an arbitral award or judicial decision or unanimous report by the Council.
>
> The League system did not, it should be noted, prohibit war or the use of force, but it did set up a procedure designed to restrict it to tolerable levels. It was a constant challenge of the inter-war years to close the gaps in the Covenant in an effort to achieve the total prohibition of war in international law and this resulted ultimately in the

signing in 1928 of the General Treaty for the Renunciation of War (the Kellogg-Briand Pact [discussed below]). [International Law 780 (4th ed. 1997).]

Professor John Murphy notes one other unique feature of the League, and then relates what happened in the next two decades.

> The most important of the novel features were the principle of the guarantee by member states of the political independence and territorial integrity of each member against external aggression, and the use of collective measures — economic, financial, and, perhaps, military — to defeat aggression. . . .
>
> During its first decade the League enjoyed a substantial measure of success in spite of the failure of the United States to become a member. The years 1924 to 1929 were a period of apparent general prosperity, relative peace, and promising cooperative efforts in the economic and social fields. But this veneer of prosperity contributed to the failure of governments to take steps necessary to deal with the basic problems of economic maladjustment and imbalance resulting from the war. The bubble burst in 1929, and the years 1930 to 1936 saw a worldwide depression of unprecedented breadth and depth. The depression helped to bring to power expansionistic, authoritative regimes in Germany, Italy, and Japan. These regimes challenged the peace-keeping capabilities of the League, and the League proved unequal to the challenge.
>
> More properly put, the Great Powers, on whose support the peace-keeping capabilities of the League depended, declined to meet the threat. The United States, as a nonmember, gave only limited support; Great Britain and France, for a variety of political, economic, and social reasons, failed to fulfill their responsibilities as League members. As a result, the League was unable to check Japanese aggression in Manchuria in the early thirties or to sanction Italy effectively after its attack on Ethiopia in October 1935. No attempt whatsoever was made to use League machinery and procedures to prevent German remilitarization of the Rhineland in March 1936 in clear violation of the Treaty of Versailles and the Locarno Pact or the outbreak of war when it became imminent as the result of the Czechoslovakian crisis and the threat to Poland. The expulsion of the Soviet Union in 1939 following its attack on Finland was, in a sense, the League's last gesture as an institution designed to prevent and punish aggression. [The United Nations and the Control of International Violence 10-11 (1982).]

(2)   *The Kellogg-Briand Pact*

Among the many agreements and conferences that occurred during the inter-War years, the Kellogg-Briand Pact was one of the most publicized, generating considerable hope. It contained two brief, substantive articles.

The General Treaty for the Renunciation of War

(commonly called the Kellogg-Briand Pact)
Aug. 27, 1928, 46 Stat. 2343, 94 L.N.T.S. 57

ARTICLE I

The High Contracting Parties solemnly declare in the names of their respective peoples that they condemn recourse to war for the solution of international controversies, and renounce it as an instrument of national policy in their relations with one another.

ARTICLE II

The High Contracting Parties agree that the settlement or solution of all disputes or conflicts of whatever nature or of whatever origin they may be, which may arise among them, shall never be sought except by pacific means.

Notes and Questions

1. Did the Covenant of the League of Nations outlaw war? Outlaw the use of force? What about aggression by one Member State against another?

2. The Kellogg-Briand Pact became effective in July 1929 and is still in force. As of January 2003, it had been ratified by over 60 parties, including the United States.

3. Consider the text of the pact. It renounces war. What about the use of military force without calling it war? Is that prohibited? Is this a major loophole? (See the discussion in the first Brownlie excerpt in this chapter about the state of war doctrine and its subjective use.) Are uses of force short of war prohibited by the agreement of the parties in Article II "that the settlement or solution of all disputes or conflicts . . . shall never be sought except by pacific means"? What if pacific means fail?

4. The Kellogg-Briand Pact does not include any enforcement mechanisms, except the general language of Article II. Why do you think it did not? How effective can such an agreement be without an enforcement mechanism?

5. The following are two different assessments of the Pact. As you continue through this chapter, decide which assessment you consider more accurate. First, Malcolm Shaw concludes:

> In view of the fact that this treaty has never been terminated and in the light of its widespread acceptance, it is clear that prohibition of the resort to war is now a valid principle of international law. It is no longer possible to set up the legal relationship of war in international society. However, this does not mean that the use of force in all circumstances is illegal. Reservations to the treaty by some states made it apparent that the right to resort to force in self-defence was still a recognised principle in international law. Whether in fact measures short of war such as reprisals were also prohibited or were left untouched by the treaty's ban on war was unclear and subject to conflicting interpretations. [International Law 780-781 (4th ed. 1997).]

On the other hand, historian Arnold Toynbee concluded in a dismissive way:

> The Kellogg-Briand Pact . . . was . . . a brief afterglow of Wilsonian optimism on the darkening horizon of European politics at the close of the period of fulfillment. Calling for the renunciation of aggressive war, but without establishing means of enforcement, the . . . Pact was almost universally subscribed. It stands as an ironic preface to the supervening decades of blood and steel, the 1930's and 1940's. [Essay by Toynbee in 2 Major Peace Treaties of Modern History: 1648-1967, at 1232 (F. Israel ed., 1967).]

2.   World War II to the Present

Two of the most important developments for limiting the use of force that emerged from the cataclysm of World War II were (1) the Nuremberg Charter and Trials and (2) the United Nations Charter.

a.   The Nuremberg Charter and Trials

The International Military Tribunal was established at Nuremberg, Germany, in August 1945 by the four major powers — the United States, France, the United Kingdom, and the U.S.S.R. — who defeated Nazi Germany. The Tribunal was "for the trial of war criminals whose offenses have no particular geographical location whether they be accused individually or in their capacity as members of organizations or groups or in both capacities." (Article 1 of the Agreement among the four countries.)

The Charter of the Tribunal and the ensuing war crime trials before the Tribunal, as well as the trials of the International Military Tribunal for the Far East and a host of other trials and proceedings before other civilian and military tribunals, established important precedents both for the general norms limiting a state's use of force and for the responsibility of individuals. (Section C, below, provides a description of the various proceedings and addresses the issue of individual responsibility.)

For present purposes, it should be noted that the Charter defined certain crimes and authorized the Tribunal to try people for them and to impose judgment and sentence. Article 6 of the Charter defined the crimes while Articles 26 through 29 dealt with judgment and sentence.

The Charter of the International Military Tribunal

Article 6

. . . The following acts, or any of them, are crimes coming within the jurisdiction of the Tribunal for which there shall be individual responsibility:

(a) *Crimes against peace:* namely, planning, preparation, initiation or waging of a war of aggression, or a war in violation of international treaties, agreements or assurances, or participation in a common plan or conspiracy for the accomplishment of any of the foregoing;

(b) *War crimes:* namely, violations of the laws or customs of war. Such violations shall include, but not be limited to, murder, ill-treatment or deportation to slave labor or for any other purpose of civilian population of or in occupied territory, murder or ill-treatment of prisoners of war or persons on the seas, killing of hostages, plunder of public or private property, wanton destruction of cities, towns or villages, or devastation not justified by military necessity;

(c) *Crimes against humanity:* namely, murder, extermination, enslavement, deportation, and other inhumane acts committed against any civilian population, before or during the war, or persecutions on political, racial or religious grounds in execution of or in connection with any crime within the jurisdiction of the Tribunal, whether or not in violation of the domestic law of the country where perpetrated.

Leaders, organizers, instigators and accomplices participating in the formulation or execution of a common plan or conspiracy to commit any of the foregoing crimes are responsible for all acts performed by any persons in execution of such plan.

VI.   JUDGMENT AND SENTENCE

Article 26

The Judgment of the Tribunal as to the guilt or the innocence of any Defendant shall give the reasons on which it is based, and shall be final and not subject to review.

Article 27

The Tribunal shall have the right to impose upon a Defendant, on conviction, death or such other punishment as shall be determined by it to be just.

Article 28

In addition to any punishment imposed by it, the Tribunal shall have the right to deprive the convicted person of any stolen property and order its delivery to the Control Council for Germany.

Article 29

In case of guilt, sentences shall be carried out in accordance with the orders of the Control Council for Germany, which may at any time reduce or otherwise alter the sentences, but may not increase the severity thereof.

In short, the Charter made it, for example, a serious crime against peace to engage in "planning, preparation, initiation or waging of a war of aggression, or a war in violation of international treaties." Likewise, "killing of hostages [and] wanton destruction of cities, towns or villages" was a war crime. Punishment could include death.

The creation of these crimes, and then finding people guilty of them during the war crimes trials, obviously added a new element to the traditional norms regarding the use of force. In response to challenges about how the Tribunal could uphold the 1945 Charter's criminalization of wars of aggression, the Tribunal relied heavily on the renunciation of war in the Kellogg-Briand Pact. (We will consider the bases for the Tribunal's authority further at page 1085 below.)

b.   The U.N. Charter

The United Nations was created in 1945 primarily to prevent military conflict among its members and to settle international disputes. (See discussion of the

United Nations in Chapter 5, Section C.) The key provisions of the U.N. Charter regarding the use of force are Articles 2(4) and 51.

Article 2(4)

All Members shall refrain in their international relations from the threat or use of force against the territorial integrity or political independence of any state, or in any other manner inconsistent with the Purposes of the United Nations.

Article 51

Nothing in the present Charter shall impair the inherent right of individual or collective self-defense if an armed attack occurs against a Member of the United Nations, until the Security Council has taken the measures necessary to maintain international peace and security. . . .

Note also that Article 2(3) provides that "[a]ll Members shall settle their international disputes by peaceful means in such a manner that international peace and security, and justice, are not endangered."

See also Articles 39-51 regarding the role of the U.N. Security Council, and Articles 52-54 regarding the role of regional arrangements (such as the North Atlantic Treaty Organization or NATO). Article 42 provides in part: "Should the Security Council consider that measures provided for in Article 41 [not involving the use of force] would be inadequate or prove to be inadequate, it may take such action by air, sea, or land forces as may be necessary to maintain or restore international peace and security." (The U.N. Charter is in the Documentary Supplement.)

What has been the impact of these Charter provisions? What is the international law today on the use of force? Professor Thomas Franck provides his point of view in the following excerpt. As you read this excerpt and the other materials in this section, it might be helpful analytically to separate the use of force into three categories: (1) a major use of a state's own military forces against another state; (2) a state's support of armed bands (be they called guerrillas, insurgents, or contras) that are attacking another state or fighting within it; and (3) a use of a state's force against terrorists who are located in another state. Although the materials do not always make these distinctions, should the legal norms differ?

Thomas M. Franck, Recourse to Force

1-5, 9, 11, 16-17, 45, 48-52, 69-70, 76-77, 96-99, 107-110, 131-139, 171-173 (2002)

After the Second World War, . . . the Nuremberg tribunal was called upon to draw a much brighter line than hitherto against aggression. So, too, at Dumbarton Oaks and San Francisco, a UN Charter was written that makes absolute the obligation of states not to resort to force against each other and to resist collectively any breach of this prohibition.

New remedies, as we know from medicine, tend to produce unexpected side effects. Article 2(4) of the Charter seemingly cures the . . . normative ambiguities [in the League of Nations' Covenant] regarding states' "threat or use of force" against each other. It plugs the loopholes. But did it intend to prevent a state — one facing imminent and overwhelming attack — from striking first in anticipatory self-defense? Did it intend also to immunize against foreign intervention a state whose government is engaged in genocide against a part of its own population? Are there circumstances in which the prohibition on recourse to force in effect endorses that which itself is wholly unconscionable? Did the Charter try to plug too many loopholes? Has the pursuit of perfect justice unintentionally created conditions of grave injustice?

The Use of Force under the UN Charter System

On its face, the UN Charter, ratified by virtually every nation, is quite clear-eyed about its intent: to initiate a new global era in which *war* is forbidden as an instrument of state policy, but *collective security* becomes the norm. Collective security is to be achieved by use of international military police forces and lesser but forceful measures such as diplomatic and economic sanctions. Recourse to such measures is to be the exclusive prerogative of the United Nations, acting in concert. . . .

The Charter text embodies these two radical new concepts: it absolutely prohibits war and prescribes collective action against those who initiate it. We are thereby ushered into the "post-war" era through Charter text: Articles 2(4), 42, and 43.

Article 2(4) essentially prohibits states from using force against one another. Instead, Articles 42 and 43 envisage the collective use of force at the behest of the Security Council upon its determination — Article 39 — that there exist what Article 2(4) forbids, a threat to the peace, breach of the peace, or act of aggression: one that must therefore be met by concerted police action. Article 42 sets the parameters for collective measures, including the deployment of military forces. Under Article 43, such forces are to be committed by member states to the service of the Security Council.

In the idealized world of the Charter, no state would ever again attack another: and if one did, its aggression would be met by a unified and overwhelming response made under the authority and control of the Security Council.

Even in 1945, however, there were doubts as to whether this idealized world order was as imminent as the post-San Francisco euphoria predicted. Thus, two articles of the Charter provide alternatives, just in case. Article 51 authorizes states to act alone or with their allies in self-defense against any military aggression ("armed attack") that the Security Council might have failed either to prevent or to repel. Article 106 makes further provision for "transitional security arrangements" by the five permanent Council members (Britain, China, France, Russia, and the US). These may "consult with one another" on "joint action," if the Security Council is disabled, "for the purpose of maintaining international peace and security." They are licensed to act in concert until such time as the Council can "begin the exercise of its responsibilities."

In this way, the Charter establishes a two-tiered system.

- The upper tier consists of a normative structure for an ideal world — one in which no state would initiate armed conflict, but in which any acts of aggression that did occur would be met by effective armed force deployed by the United Nations or, for a transitional period, by the Security Council's five permanent members.

- A lower tier is to operate whenever the United Nations is unable to respond collectively against aggression. Subject to certain conditions, states may invoke an older legal principle: the sovereign right of self-defense. Acting alone or with allies, the Charter authorizes members to use force to resist any armed attack by one state on another until UN collective measures come to the victim's rescue. But they may do so only after an actual armed attack. . . .

Both tiers, almost immediately, were seen to fail to address adequately four seismic developments that, even as the Charter was being signed, were beginning to transform the world.

One was the advent of the Cold War, which, because of the veto, froze the Security Council's ability to guarantee collective security under Articles 42 and 43 of the Charter and precluded operation of Article 106's interim Big Power protectorate.

Another was the ingenuity with which states effectively and dangerously substituted indirect aggression — the export of insurgency and covert meddling in civil wars — for the sort of traditional frontal military aggression the Charter system was designed to prohibit by Article 2(4) and to repress by Article 42.

The third development was the technological transformation of weaponry (nuclear, chemical, and biological) and of delivery systems (rocketry). These "improvements" tended to make obsolete the Charter's Article 51 provision for states' "inherent" right of self-defense. . . . Article 51 limits "self-defence" to situations where an "armed attack" has occurred. However, the acceleration and escalation of means for launching an attack soon confounded the bright line drawn by the law, effecting a *reductio ad absurdum* that, literally, seems to require a state to await an actual attack on itself before instituting countermeasures. Inevitably, states responded to the new dangers by claiming a right of "anticipatory self-defence." That claim, however, is not supported by the Charter's literal text. And "anticipatory self-defence," too, is vulnerable to *reductio ad absurdum*. If every state were free to determine for itself when to initiate the use of force in "anticipation" of an attack, there would be nothing left of Articles 2(4) and 51. . . .

The fourth development was a rising global public consciousness of the importance of human freedom and the link between the repression of human rights and threats to the peace. . . . [T]he text of the Charter puts human rights rather at its periphery while focusing on the prevention of aggression. That deliberate drafting choice reflected the concerns of some states that the cause of human rights might be used to justify intervention in their sovereign affairs. The drafters, of course, did not anticipate the imminent end of colonialism and communism, the rise of a democratic entitlement, and a tectonic shift in public values during the 1990s, each of which altered perceptions of sovereignty and its limits.

All four of these developments might have been (and to some extent were) foreseen, but the Charter's text is not facially responsive to the challenge of change. It, like other grand instruments written for the long term, has had to meet the threat of obsolescence with adaption. . . .

The UN Charter is a treaty, one to which almost every state adheres. This universality, alone, distinguishes it from the general run of international agreements.

That the drafters of the Charter recognized its special quality is evidenced by Article 103, which purports to establish an unusual principle of treaty law:

> In the event of a conflict between the obligations of the Members of the United Nations under the present Charter and their obligations under any other international agreement, their obligations under the present Charter shall prevail.

This legal primacy of the Charter over subsequent agreements can only be construed as a "quasi-constitutional" feature. Clearly, it illustrates that the drafters intended to create a special treaty different from all others. This difference becomes relevant when we consider the instrument's capacity for adaption through the interpretative practice of its organs and members. . . .

The Charter's Constraints on Violence

The Charter's absolute prohibition on states' unilateral recourse to force, Article 2(4), is deliberately located in Chapter I, entitled "Purposes and Principles." The drafters considered these enumerated principles of transcendent importance, elucidating all other provisions of the Charter. . . .

Thus it becomes apparent that, even before the Charter was signed, ratified, and implemented, there was unease, at least in some quarters, that states were being asked to renounce recourse to violence in return for a community-based system of collective measures that would be geared primarily to averting threats to, or breaches of, the peace rather than to preserving justice and redressing injustice: a concept for which the Charter made little provision. . . .

In practice, the problem of injustice in the operation of the Charter has turned out to be manifest less in unconscionable actions of the Council than in its inaction owing to the veto. Otherwise, however, time has not abated the problem. The very same paradoxical juxtaposition between the Charter's insistence on order (non-violence) and the common moral instinct (justice) was posed . . . by Secretary General Kofi Annan . . . in his [2000] report to the Millennium Assembly of the United Nations:

> Few would disagree that both the defence of humanity and the defense of sovereignty are principles that must be supported. Alas that does not tell us which principle should prevail when they are in conflict.

What it may tell us, nevertheless, is that there cannot be an absolute priority either for the claim of sovereignty (in the name of peace) or of humanity (in the name of justice). . . . If this is so, then the claims of sovereignty and humanity must, whenever possible, be reconciled and, when impossible, be weighed against one another in accordance with a widely agreed, situationally specific system of weights and measures. . . .

THE ORIGINAL PARAMETERS OF SELF-DEFENSE

[T]he Charter's primary thrust [was] the prohibition of aggression and enforcement of that ban by collective military measures taken in the name of the new

Organization. Only as a secondary, fail-safe resort did the drafters permit members to deploy force in their individual, sovereign capacity, and then only in self-defense against an actual armed attack. Under pressure of changing circumstances, however, this exception to the general prohibition on nations' unilateral recourse to force has also undergone adaption and expansion through institutional practice. . . .

The new language [of Article 51] did more than open the door to states' autonomous recourse to force. By adding the term "collective" to a provision that essentially licenses victims to defend themselves, it was also intended to accommodate regional or other mutual defense arrangements. One of these, in the Americas, was already in existence. Although essentially collateral to the Charter system, it was designed to do what the Charter does not: legally oblige member states to defend one another against attack. Another, establishing the North Atlantic Treaty Organization (NATO), soon followed suit. . . .

Article 51 is not quite a *carte blanche*. It extends the right of individual and collective self-defense only "until the Security Council has taken measures necessary to maintain international peace and security." Asked by [a] US Senator . . . whether this would not require states to stop defending themselves once the Council acted, John Foster Dulles assured him that "states were not obliged to discontinue their countermeasures taken in self-defence. In other words . . . there was concurrent power" as between the Council and the states acting under Article 51. That interpretation is not evident from the text, but it does correctly foresee its actual implementation, notably during the crisis following Iraq's invasion of Kuwait, and, again, after Al Qaeda's terrorist strike against Washington, DC and New York City. In both instances, the Security Council recognized the right of the attacked state to defend itself with the help of its allies and specifically reaffirmed that right after the Council began to order the taking of collective measures against the attackers.

Nevertheless, Article 51 as drafted does not sanction continuation of the use of force by states in self-defense after the Council has taken measures. It is only by subsequent practice that the potential coexistence of collective measures with the continued measures in self-defense has become accepted practice. . . .

. . . At San Francisco . . . , it is beyond dispute that the negotiators deliberately closed the door on any claim of "anticipatory self-defence," a posture soon to become logically indefensible by the advent of a new age of nuclear warheads and long-range rocketry. . . .

The decision to limit the right of self-defense to situations where there had been an "armed attack" also sadly failed to anticipate, let alone address, the imminent rise in surrogate warfare prompted by rogue states and international terrorists. . . .

Analyzing Practice of Collective Self-Defense

. . . The Charter does not even begin to define its key terms: "inherent right," "self-defence" or "armed attack." All this was left, perforce, to interpretation: primarily by the United Nations' political organs and by the actual practices of members and regional groupings. . . .

The practice of these organs consists of members' speaking and voting. Faced with one or more of their number seeking to justify resort to armed force, members register their response: positive, negative, or noncommittal. In fifty-five years of practice, a pattern of justifications has emerged, sometimes explicitly spelled out, sometimes implicit in the situation. . . .

Five kinds of justifications stand out, each based on a "creative" interpretation of Article 51:

1.   The claim that a state may resort to armed self-defence in response to attacks by terrorists, insurgents or surrogates operating from another state;
2.   The claim that self-defence may be exercised against the source of ideological subversion from abroad;
3.   The claim that a state may act in self-defence to rescue or protect its citizens abroad.
4.   The claim that a state may act in self-defence to anticipate and preempt an imminent armed attack;
5.   The claim that the right of self-defence is available to abate an egregious, generally recognized, yet persistently unredressed wrong, including the claim to exercise a right of humanitarian intervention.

These five kinds of claims will be examined [below, with the terrorist justification dealt with in a later section]. In practice, some are now routinely vindicated, others not. . . .

SELF-DEFENSE AGAINST IDEOLOGICAL SUBVERSION . . .

The response of states and international institutions to this justification has been entirely and resoundingly negative. However, the same justification is recently beginning to be heard again, this time in the theological–ideological conflict between forces of Islamic fundamentalism and more tolerant societies, including other more liberal Islamic states, secular India, and the Western societies in which religions have been disestablished. It is too early to judge whether the claim of a right to use force in self-defense against the export of militant theocratic ideology, or of liberal democracy and religious pluralism, will encounter greater acceptance in the practice of states and international organizations than did the Cold War claim to a right to use force against the export of ideological subversion. . . .

SELF-DEFENSE AGAINST ATTACKS ON CITIZENS ABROAD . . .

[Such "humanitarian interventions"] are criticized as a subterfuge used by the strong to interfere in the domestic affairs of the weak. This criticism arises equally whether the intervention is, or is not, approved by the government of the place where it occurs. When undertaken with consent, "humanitarian intervention" incurs the suspicion that its real purpose is less to rescue endangered persons than to save unpopular regimes from their domestic critics. When it occurs without consent, the intervenor is likely to be accused of undermining a regime it does not like.

It is the latter, non-consensual interventions that have been most common in practice and most controversial in modern law. . . . Nevertheless, such interventions continue, usually justified by the intervening state as permissible under a flexible reading of Charter Article 51's right of "self-defence." The actual practice of UN organs has tended to be more calibrated, manifesting a situational ethic rather than doctrinaire consistency either prohibiting or permitting all such actions. [Professor Franck proceeds to consider several examples ranging from the U.S. intervention in the Dominican Republic in 1965 in part to protect U.S. citizens there, the Israeli rescue of hostages aboard a hijacked aircraft at Entebbe, Uganda, in 1976, and the U.S. missile attack against a training camp of Osama bin Laden in Afghanistan after two U.S. embassies were bombed in Africa, with hundreds killed.]

. . . When the facts and their political context are widely seen to warrant a preemptive or deterrent intervention on behalf of credibly endangered citizens abroad, and if the UN itself, for political reasons, is incapable of acting, then some use of force by a state may be accepted as legitimate self-defense within the meaning of Article 51. Military action is more likely to be condoned if the threat to citizens is demonstrably real and grave, if the motive of the intervening state is perceived as genuinely protective, and if the intervention is proportionate and of short duration and likely to achieve its purpose with minimal collateral damage. In practice, whether an action is deemed lawful or not has come to depend on the special circumstances of each case, as demonstrated to, and perceived by, the political and legal institutions of the international system. . . .

. . . Narrowly, recourse to armed force in order to protect nationals abroad may be said to have been condoned as legitimate in specific mitigating circumstances, even though that recourse is still recognized as technically illegal. Or, in a broader interpretation of practice, the system may be said to have adapted the concept of self-defense, under Article 51, to include a right to use force in response to an attack against nationals, providing there is clear evidence of extreme necessity and the means chosen are proportionate.

Anticipatory Self-Defense . . .

Anticipatory self-defense has a long history in customary international law. As early as 1837, it was canvassed by US Secretary of State Daniel Webster in the *Caroline* dispute. In a classical attempt to define but also to limit it, Webster concluded that such a right arises only when there is a "necessity of self-defence . . . instant, overwhelming, leaving no choice of means and no moment for deliberation." He cautioned that it permits "nothing unreasonable or excessive."

Has recourse to such anticipatory self-defense in circumstances of extreme necessity been preserved, or repealed, by the Charter? Common sense, rather than textual literalism, is often the best guide to interpretation of international legal norms. Thus, Bowett concludes that "no state can be expected to await an initial attack which, in the present state of armaments, may well destroy the state's capacity for further resistance and so jeopardise its very existence." In 1996, the International Court of Justice indirectly touched on this question in its *Advisory Opinion on the Legality of the Use of Nuclear Weapons in Armed Conflict*. A majority of judges was unable to conclude that first-use of nuclear weapons would invariably be unlawful if the very existence of a state were threatened. Despite its ambiguity, the Court appears to have recognized the exceptional nature and logic of a state's claim to use means necessary to ensure its self-preservation. The same reasoning can lead to the logical deduction that no law — and certainly not Article 51 — should be interpreted to compel the *reductio ad absurdum* that states invariably must await a first, perhaps decisive, military strike before using force to protect themselves.

On the other hand, a general relaxation of Article 51's prohibitions on unilateral war-making to permit unilateral recourse to force whenever a state feels potentially threatened could lead to another *reductio ad absurdum*. The law cannot have intended to leave every state free to resort to military force whenever it perceived itself grievously endangered by actions of another, for that would negate any role for law. In practice, the UN system has sought, with some success, to navigate between these two conceptual shoals. Three instances may be indicative: the US (and OAS) blockade against Cuba during the 1962 missile crisis, Israel's attack on its Arab neighbors in 1967, and Israel's raid on the Iraqi nuclear reactor in 1981. . . .

The problem with recourse to anticipatory self-defense is its ambiguity. In the right circumstances, it can be a prescient measure that, at low cost, extinguishes the fuse of a powder-keg. In the wrong circumstances, it can cause the very calamity it anticipates. The 1967 Israeli "first strike" against Egypt's air force was widely seen to be warranted in circumstances where Cairo's hostile intention was evident and Israel's vulnerability patently demonstrable. In the end, the UN system did not condemn Israel's unauthorized recourse to force but, instead, sensibly insisted on its relinquishing conquered territory in return for what was intended to be a securely monitored peace. The system balanced Egypt's illegitimate provocations against Israel's recourse to illegal preventive measures. Most states understood that a very small, densely populated state cannot be expected to await a very probable, potentially decisive attack before availing itself of the right to self-defense.

In the case of the Cuba missile crisis, the international system appears to have been less than convinced that the Soviets' introduction of nuclear-armed missiles — albeit stealthy — genuinely and imminently threatened the US. It was apparent, for example, that deployment of nuclear-armed missiles on US and Russian submarines off each other's coasts had not engendered similar claims to act in "anticipatory self-defence." Still, the covert way Soviet missiles were introduced in Cuba and the disingenuousness with which their deployment had at first been denied, strengthened the US claim to be responding to an imminent threat. That claim was so strongly supported by other states in the Americas as to impede the usual third world rush to judgment against the US. Most important, the forceful countermeasures taken, although probably an act of war in international law and a violation of the literal text of Articles 2(4) and 51, was also seen as cautious, limited, and carefully calibrated. No shots were fired by the ships implementing the blockade. In the end, the outcome — the withdrawal of Soviet missiles from Cuba in return for a reciprocal dismantling of US missiles on the Turkish–Soviet border, together with Washington's promise not again to attempt an invasion of Cuba — was seen by most states (except Cuba) as a positive accomplishment.

Only in the instance of Israel's aerial strike against the Iraqi nuclear plant did the system categorically condemn and deny both the legality and legitimacy of recourse to anticipatory self-defense. In doing so, however, even vociferous critics of Israel made clear that they were not opposed to a right of anticipatory self-defense in principle but, rather that they did not believe that Iraq's nuclear plant was being used unlawfully to produce weapons and that a nuclear attack on Israel was neither probable nor imminent. In this conjecture they may have been wrong, but they were surely right in subjecting to a high standard of probity any evidence adduced to support a claim to use force in anticipation of, rather than as a response to, an armed attack.

COUNTERMEASURES AND SELF-HELP . . .

When a right is denied, it is natural to turn to the authority that is the source of that right in the expectation that it will be enforced. When that expectation is not met, there is moral force to the argument that those aggrieved by the failure should themselves be allowed to enforce their legal entitlement as best they can.

In international law, the issue of the legality of countermeasures and self-help arises when, a state having refused to carry out its legal responsibilities and the international system having failed to enforce the law, another state, victimized by that failure, takes countermeasures to protect its interests. "Its interests" in this context denotes the peaceful enjoyment of rights accruing to a state, of which it is deprived by the continuing wrongful acts of another state. It may also be, however, that the notion of a transgressed state interest has expanded to include not only violations of its rights as a sovereign, but also of rights held derivatively as a member of the international system. Thus, for example, every state may enjoy the right *erga omnes* not to have the earth's "commons"— the seas, the air — polluted in violation of globally applicable norms. Along similar lines, every state may have a right to act to prevent a genocide that, even if not directed at its own people, violates the treaty-based common conscience of humanity. Some recognition has been given to this more extended notion of a state's self-interest by the International Law Commission's Restatement of the Law of State Responsibility.[1] That there are such *erga omnes* norms in international law which, if violated, give rise to a claim by any or all states does not of course resolve the vexed issue of what remedial steps states may take to protect their violated rights against further breaches. Normally, redress would have to be sought through the peaceful means provided by the treaty establishing the violated right or by general international law. The Draft Articles on State Responsibility, in Article 49, permits countermeasures "against a State which is responsible for an internationally wrongful act in order to induce that State to comply with its obligations" but, it adds, such countermeasures "shall not affect (a) The obligation to refrain from the threat or use of force as embodied in the United Nations Charter . . .".

What, exactly, is that "obligation . . . as embodied in the . . . Charter"? Is there an inexorable obligation "to refrain from . . . use of force," when does it arise and what countermeasures are precluded by it? How relevant is the practice of UN organs in construing this limitation on the right to take countermeasures?

These questions are all too relevant because of severe imperfections in the capacity of the international legal system to ensure compliance with its norms and to

---

1. Text of Articles, State Responsibility, 31 May 2001, International Law Commission, article 48: "Any State other than an injured State is entitled to invoke the responsibility of another State . . . if: (a) The obligation breached is owed to a group of States including that State, and is established for the protection of a collective interest of the group." The Convention on the Prevention and Punishment of the Crime of Genocide, 78 U.N.T.S. 277 of 1951 is the leading example of a wrong *erga omnes* that accords a right to all states *qua* any violation.

guarantee a remedy for violations. Reason suggests that self-help and countermeasures remain necessary remedies of last resort. Nevertheless, the text and context of the UN Charter seem to indicate otherwise. . . .

The UN Charter makes no exception to the rule barring states' recourse to violence, not even in situations where an evident and serious wrong has been done that the system, over a protracted period, has failed to redress. The Charter makes no provision for individual or collective military enforcement of legal rights of states and peoples, as such. In this sense, the Charter may be said to have abrogated states' historic right to deploy force in self-help and to have restricted countermeasures to actions not involving "the threat or use of force" prohibited by Charter Article 2(4). It thus seems to have tilted the balance in the direction of peace and away from justice or, alternatively, in favor of the enunciation of rights but away from their muscular implementation.

On the other hand, a limited right to self-help has long been recognized in customary international law and practice. This has not been specifically repealed by the Charter. It can be argued that, in the absence of new ways to defend or effectuate legal rights, the Charter should not be read to prohibit countermeasures as the remedy of last resort. Indeed, UN practice seems to offer some latitude for states' resort to countermeasures in self-help. In some instances this tolerance has been manifest in UN passivity when faced with actual recourse to force. Israel's capture of Eichmann in Argentina, India's invasion of Goa, as well as Turkey's intervention in Cyprus were met with comparative equanimity, the specific circumstances of each case lending an aura of legitimacy to a recourse to unilateral force and mitigating the system's judgment of self-help in those instances.

On the other hand, those instances in which the UN organs rejected claims of a right to self-help demonstrate that the system mitigates or acquiesces only reluctantly. Self-help may be acknowledged as a remedy of last resort in a situation in which all alternatives for the peaceful vindication of a recognized legal right have been exhausted and the law and the facts indisputably support a plea of extreme necessity. It has not been recognized when used to press less legally convincing claims such as those solely based on geographic contiguity and historic title, especially when the claimed rights are opposable by rights of equal or greater weight, such as that of self-determination.[141]

Nevertheless, in exception cases the use of force in self-help, while prohibited by the Charter text, may be justified by the evident legitimacy of the cause in which self-help is deployed; and a widespread perception of that legitimacy is likely to mitigate, if not actually to exculpate, the resort to force. . . . The practice of UN organs demonstrates that while the prohibition on forcible self-help is absolute in theory, the principle is more textured in practice. . . .

Obviously, the law of countermeasures and self-help is in flux. . . . Like the [ICJ], the political organs of the United Nations have carefully avoided giving a broad, dogmatic answer to the issues posed by states' recourse to armed countermeasures. Doctrine and principle, here, too, appear subservient to narrower reasons

---

141. Instances include the resistance of a population to their absorption by a neighboring state. These include territories such as Gibraltar, Kaliningrad, Nagoro-Karabakh, St. Helena, St. Pierre et Miquelon, St. Martin/St. Maartens, St. Thomas, Western Samoa, and numerous other Pacific and Caribbean territories. In none of these instances has practice justified a right on the part of neighbors to liberate these "dependent territories."

of contextual justice and legitimacy, with the specific facts being given appropriate weight. The invasion of Goa was perceived as the democratic liberation of a part of geographic and cultural India long ruled by a remote and stubborn Iberian dictatorship. The Turkish military occupation of Northern Cyprus in 1974 at first seemed a legitimate reaction to the subterfuge of a despised and expansionist Greek military junta. In the Eichmann case, the strength of Israel's justification was generally acknowledged. The Israelis had argued that a great wrong may sometimes have to be redressed by a much smaller one, and that definition of mitigating circumstances found considerable resonance.

Other arguments based on self-help have fallen on stonier ground. This is exemplified by the rejection of efforts by Argentina's junta to legitimize its invasion of the Falklands, of Indonesia's occupation of East Timor, and of Morocco's suppression of self-determination in the Western Sahara. Each of these cases is different. . . . Each demonstrates the importance of facts, evidence and sensitivity to political context in shaping the systemic response to a claim of self-help, whether that claim is advanced as a legal right or in mitigation of the consequences of a technical wrong.

A larger conclusion may also be teased from this evidence of practice. In interpreting the normative principles of the Charter, the principal organs have made an effort to act as a sort of jury: determining the probative value of alleged facts, assessing claims of extreme necessity, and weighing the proportionality of specific action taken by a party that might otherwise be deprived of any remedy for a serious delict committed against it. This quasi-jury has demonstrated concern to apply the United Nations' quasi-constitution as a "living tree." And, like juries everywhere, the principal organs have tried to bridge the gap, when it appears, between legality and legitimacy, so that the legal order is not seen to suffer from the deficiency that arises when that gap becomes too wide.

This approach encounters its most difficult test when a state or group of states engages in an unauthorized military action that is sought to be justified by evidence of extreme humanitarian necessity. . . .

THE "PURELY HUMANITARIAN" INTERVENTION . . .

When a government turns viciously against its own people, what may or should other governments do? The events of the recent past do not permit this to be dismissed as an "academic question."

If the wrong being perpetrated within a state against a part of its own population is of a kind specifically prohibited by international agreement (e.g., the Genocide Convention and treaties regarding racial discrimination, torture, the rights of women and children, and the International Covenant on Civil and Political Rights, as well as agreements on the humanitarian law applicable in civil conflict), humanitarian intervention against those prohibited acts may be thought of as a subspecies of self-help. This is conceptually more persuasive if the wrongful acts have been characterized explicitly or implicitly by the applicable universal treaties as offenses *erga omnes:* that is, against any and all states party to the agreement defining and prohibiting the wrong. In such circumstances, it is possible to argue that every state may claim a right of self-help as a vicarious victim of any violation, at least after exhaustion of institutional and diplomatic remedies. Analogous universal rights to self-help might also arise in the event of violations of certain rules of customary international law. . . .

It is . . . difficult conceptually to justify in Charter terms the use of force by one or several states acting without prior Security Council authorization, even when such action is taken to enforce human rights and humanitarian values. The Charter's Article 2(4), strictly construed, prohibits states' unilateral recourse to force. The text makes no exception for instances of massive violation of human rights or humanitarian law when these occur in the absence of an international aggression against another state. In the strict Charter scheme, states are not to use force except in self-defense and regional organizations may not take "enforcement action . . . without the authorization of the Security Council . . .".

A state using military force without Council authorization against another in "humanitarian intervention" is thus engaging in an action for which the Charter text provides no apparent legal authority. . . .

However, . . . the institutional history of the United Nations — as distinct from the Charter's text — and record of state practice, neither categorically precludes nor endorses humanitarian intervention. Rather, the history and practice support a more nuanced reconciling of the pursuit of peace (as evidenced by Charter Article 2(4)) and of justice through the protection of human and humanitarian rights (as evidenced by the canon of rights-creating universal agreements). In this practical reconciliation we can detect a pragmatic range of systemic responses to unauthorized use of force, depending more on the circumstances than on strictly construed text. This patterned practice suggests *either* a graduated reinterpretation by the United Nations itself of Article 2(4) or the evolution of a subsidiary adjectival international law of mitigation, one that may formally continue to assert the illegality of state recourse to force but which, in ascertainable circumstances, mitigates the consequence of such wrongful acts by imposing no, or only nominal, consequences on states which, by their admittedly wrongful intervention, have demonstrably prevented the occurrence of some greater wrong.

[Franck then examined] eight instances of states' use of force in overtly or implicitly humanitarian interventions. In four of these, an individual state used force without prior Security Council authorization: (India–Pakistan, 1971, Tanzania–Uganda, 1978-79, Vietnam–Kampuchea, 1978-79, France–Central African Empire, 1979). In one, several states jointly participated in such enforcement (France, UK, US–Iraq, 1991-93). In three instances it was regional or collective security organizations that used force in humanitarian crises without prior Council authorization (ECOMOG [Economic Community of West Africa's Cease-Fire Monitoring Group]–Liberia, 1989, ECOMOG–Sierra Leone, 1991, NATO–Yugoslavia (Kosovo), 1999).

[W]hile the UN system aims to substitute its collective security for traditional state reliance on unilateral force, it has had some success in adjusting to a harsher reality. In particular, it has acquiesced, sometimes actively, at other times passively, in the measured expansion of the ambit for discretionary state action and has done so without altogether abandoning the effort evident in Article 2(4) to contain unilateral recourse to force. It has sought balance, rather than either absolute prohibition or license.

This balance is difficult to achieve. If the use of force by NATO in Kosovo is seen as a precedent for a reinterpretation of Article 2(4)'s absolute prohibition on the discretionary use of force by states, the substitution of a more "reasonable" principle, one that accommodates use of force by any government to stop what it believes to be an extreme violation of fundamental human rights in another state, could launch the international system down the slippery slope into an abyss of anarchy. . . .

[T]he law cannot hope to secure acquiescence in a norm that permits its violation at the sole discretion of a party to which it is addressed. Law is strengthened when it avoids absurdly rigid absolutes — for example, by requiring passivity in the face of destruction of entire populations — but only if exceptions intended to prevent such *reductio ad absurdum* are clearly understood and applied in a manner consonant with agreed notions of procedural and evidentiary fairness.

Finally, the instances in which a state or group of states has intervened for humanitarian purposes without incurring significant opposition from the international system may indicate a certain willingness on the part of that community to brook some violation of the law in instances of clearly demonstrated necessity. It does not, however, indicate a fundamental change in the law to give wholesale permission to states to do that which is textually prohibited. Even less does it suggest that conduct which is textually prohibited has, through practice, become legally obligatory. It cannot, on the broadest interpretation of the legal significance of practice, be argued that the law now *requires* states to intervene with or without Security Council authorization, wherever and whenever there is evidence of a massive violation of humanitarian law or human rights. As a former British Foreign Secretary has recently pointed out:

> There is room for much argument about the nature of the cruelties which have been or are being inflicted in Chechnya, Tibet and the Occupied Territories of Palestine. But however great and unwarranted such cruelties, the international community will certainly prove unable or unwilling to intervene to stop them. The distribution of power in the world makes such intervention impossible. . . . The fact that the international community cannot intervene everywhere to protect human rights need not be an argument against helping where we can. . . . It is . . . a reason for not trying to confuse decisions of policy with obligations under international law.

Or, put in lawyers' terms, it is important not to confuse what the law *in some limited circumstances may condone* or excuse with what is *required* by law in every circumstance.

Notes and Questions

Before analyzing in detail a few of the past uses of U.S. military forces as well as reviewing the ICJ judgment in the *Nicaragua* case, some notes and questions are helpful in analyzing the various rationales offered by states for the use of force. Many of these were discussed in the excerpt by Professor Franck above, including his comments regarding "creative" interpretations of Article 51.

1. *The Brezhnev Doctrine.* The so-called Brezhnev Doctrine, named after Premier Leonid Brezhnev, asserted the right of the Soviet Union and other socialist states to intervene in support of any socialist government threatened by antisocialist forces.

The Soviet Union relied on this justification when it sent forces into Hungary in 1956 and into Czechoslovakia in 1968. The Soviet Union eventually disavowed the Doctrine, in the end allowing its European satellite states to choose their own paths. Premier Gorbachev's spokesman, Gennady Gerasimov, called this position the "Sinatra Doctrine," referring to Sinatra's song "My Way" and allowed that "Hungary and Poland are doing it their way." (Newsweek, Nov. 6, 1989, at 48.)

Could the Brezhnev Doctrine have been justified as individual or collective self-defense under Article 51? Or could it have been justified under any of the exceptions or interpretations discussed by Professor Franck above? Note that Professor Franck concludes that the "creative" interpretation of Article 51 that would allow self-defense against the source of ideological subversion from abroad has met a strong negative response from other states and from international institutions.

2. *The Monroe Doctrine.* U.S. leaders and others have often claimed a Monroe Doctrine for the United States. When first enunciated by President Monroe in his message to Congress on December 9, 1823, the U.S. concern was the possibility that European powers would try to extend their control over some of the countries and lands in the Western Hemisphere. Several colonies existed at the time, but the Doctrine was aimed at new colonization. President Monroe's message stated in part:

> The occasion has been judged proper for asserting as a principle in which the rights and interests of the United States are involved, that the American continents, by the free and independent condition which they have assumed and maintain, are henceforth not to be considered as subjects for future colonization by any European powers. . . . The political system of the allied powers is essentially different in this respect from that of America. . . . We owe it, therefore, to candor, and to the amicable relations existing between the United States and those powers, to declare that we should consider any attempt on their part to extend their system to any portion of this hemisphere as dangerous to our peace and safety.

The Monroe Doctrine has undergone several interpretations and transformations since 1823. (For historical materials through 1941, see Abram Chayes, The Cuban Missile Crisis 116-132 (1974).)

In 1965, for example, President Lyndon Johnson used a version of the Monroe Doctrine to justify his sending U.S. military units into the Dominican Republic when it was in the midst of a revolution. Besides saying that the troops were sent to protect the lives of thousands of U.S. citizens and other foreign citizens, Johnson also said that there was a danger that communist elements would gain the ascendancy. He declared in a speech carried nationwide on May 2: "The American nations cannot, must not, and will not permit the establishment of another Communist government in the Western Hemisphere." Johnson tied this declaration to a 1962 resolution of the Organization of American States (OAS) and to a 1963 statement of President Kennedy that were both objecting to the communist government in Cuba.

3. *The Reagan Doctrine.* Although the Reagan Administration never formally proclaimed a "Reagan Doctrine," champions and opponents of the administration's policies often cited or criticized it. In some of its more expansive versions, the Reagan Doctrine appears to have claimed the right generally to use military force or provide other assistance to impose or restore "democracy," particularly where communism existed or threatened.

President Reagan frequently stated U.S. solidarity with victims of totalitarianism. In a 1985 speech in West Germany he declared that

> today freedom-loving people around the world would say: I am a Berliner, I am a Jew in a world still threatened by anti-Semitism. I am an Afghan, and I am a prisoner of the Gulag. I am a refugee in a crowded boat foundering off the coast of Vietnam. I am a Laotian, a Cambodian, a Cuban, and a Miskito Indian in Nicaragua. I, too, am a potential victim of totalitarianism. [Remarks at Bitburg Air Base, May 5, 1985.]

Reagan further expressed a U.S. willingness to help and even acknowledged the popular name given to the doctrine.

In fact, the Reagan Administration provided U.S. assistance (sometimes including weapons) to "freedom fighters" in Afghanistan, Angola, and Cambodia, as well as to the Nicaraguan Contras. The Reagan Doctrine was also cited as one justification for the U.S. invasion of Grenada in 1983.

Some have said that the Reagan Doctrine is a version of the Monroe Doctrine, but it would appear to be a much expanded version both in terms of the geographic coverage and triggering causes.

Can the Reagan Doctrine be justified as individual or collective self-defense under Article 51? Can it be justified under any of the exceptions to or interpretations of Article 51 discussed by Professor Franck? Should the United States be able to overthrow a totalitarian government (e.g., Iraq or Syria) to bring democracy to another country? Should it matter whether the other country is in the Western Hemisphere?

If the United States can intervene to oppose totalitarianism or protect democracy abroad, can other countries with democratic governments (e.g., Brazil, France, or India) use force to bring about democratic governments in other countries, such as neighbors or former colonies? Can Russia use force to reassert its preferred form of government on some of its neighbors (e.g., Ukraine, Kazakhstan, or Georgia)? Can Islamist regimes (e.g., Iran or Saudi Arabia) use some principle of self-defense against ideological subversion to justify their support of Islamist insurgencies in more moderate Islamic countries such as Pakistan, Indonesia, and Malaysia?

4. *Self-defense to rescue or protect citizens abroad.* Should there be an exception to Article 2(4) to allow a state to use military intervention to free its citizens who are being held hostage if the territorial state will not intervene or cannot do so? If so, under what circumstances? Should an action such as the successful Israeli mission to free Israeli hostages on a hijacked plane in Entebbe, Uganda, be permissible? Was the abortive U.S. rescue mission in 1980 to free U.S. hostages in Iran justifiable? (The U.S. mission is discussed in more detail at page 1005.)

Professor Franck and many other experts agree that there should be some ability for a state to rescue its own citizens. In his excerpt above, Franck concludes that this activity might be viewed as legitimate in specific circumstances, though technically illegal under the U.N. Charter, or it is more frequently justified as an adaptation of the Article 51 concept of self-defense. Franck does note that the justification is sometimes a pretext for a strong state to help a friendly regime or to undermine a regime that it does not like.

Professor Yoram Dinstein of Tel Aviv University and Germany's Max Planck Institute distinguishes between a country's efforts on behalf of its own nationals, which he considers a form of self-defense, and efforts on behalf of other people, which he does not think permissible. He writes:

[T]he use of force by [B] within its own territory, against [A's] nationals, is considered by many to constitute an armed attack against [A]. If that is the case, forcible counter-measures employed by [A] may rate as self-defence, provided that the usual conditions of necessity, proportionality and immediacy are complied with. Sir Humphrey Waldock reiterated these conditions in somewhat different wording, fitting better the specific circumstances of protection of nationals abroad: "There must be (1) an imminent threat of injury to nationals, (2) a failure or inability on the part of the territorial sovereign to protect them and (3) measures of protection strictly confined to the object of protecting them against injury." [War, Aggression and Self-Defense 202-203 (3d ed 2001).]

Dinstein also notes that

[T]he exponents of the putative right of "humanitarian intervention" minimize the link of nationality. . . . Most commentators who favour "humanitarian intervention" studiously avoid the terminology of self-defense and insist that the forcible measures taken are legitimate, not by virtue of compatibility with Article 51 . . . but as a result of being compatible with Article 2(4). . . .

This is a misreading of the Charter. No individual State (or group of States) is authorized to act unilaterally, in the domain of human rights or in any other sphere, as if it were the policeman of the world. [Dinstein at 85.]

By contrast, Professor Henkin believes that the justification to rescue or protect individuals need not be restricted to actions by a state to protect its own nationals. He, however, would limit the exception to efforts to liberate hostages by rescue missions. He writes: "It has not been accepted . . . that a state has a right to intervene by force to topple a government or occupy its territory even if that were necessary to terminate atrocities or liberate detainees. Entebbe was acceptable, but the occupation of Cambodia by Vietnam was not." Louis Henkin, Use of Force: Law and U.S. Policy, in Right v. Might 42 (Louis Henkin et al. eds., 1989).

How broad do you think the right to rescue individuals should be for a state? Should it include a right to act on behalf of nationals of other states? Does it depend on whether you consider it a category of self-defense or an independent justification for use of force? Which is the better justification for this right to rescue? (Note 9 discusses Professor Franck's possible broader justification of "purely humanitarian" intervention.)

5. *Anticipatory or preemptive self-defense.* By its terms, Article 51 permits a state to use force in self-defense "if an armed attack occurs." However, Article 51 also purports to preserve the inherent right of self-defense, which Professor Franck notes has a long history in customary international law. This includes the *Caroline* incident, discussed earlier, where U.S. Secretary of State Daniel Webster had sought to limit the right to only where there is a "necessity of self-defense . . . instant, overwhelming, leaving no choice of means and no moment for deliberation." This customary international law also included the requirement of proportionality.

In his excerpt above, Professor Franck notes the impracticability in today's world of insisting in all circumstances that a country must await an initial attack that may well defeat or even destroy that country, but also the dangers of permitting "unilateral recourse to force whenever a state feels potentially threatened." Professor Henkin and other scholars have argued for a narrow reading of the circumstances where force might be used in anticipation of a threatened attack by the other country. Professor Dinstein offers a more nuanced approach:

> [I]t is important to pinpoint the exact moment at which an armed attack begins to take place. . . .
>
> In many instances, the opening of fire is an unreliable test of responsibility for an armed attack. . . .
>
> As Sir Humphrey Waldock phrased it: "Where there is convincing evidence not merely of threats and potential danger but of an attack actually mounted, then an armed attack may be said to have begun to occur, though it has not passed the frontier."
>
> Had the Japanese carrier striking force been destroyed on its way to Pearl Harbor, this would have constituted not an act of preventive war but a miraculously early use of counter-force. To put it in another way, the self-defence exercised by the United States (in response to an incipient armed attack) would have been not anticipatory but interceptive in nature. Interceptive, unlike anticipatory, self-defence takes place after the other side has committed itself to an armed attack in an ostensibly irrevocable way. Whereas a preventive strike anticipates an armed attack which is merely "foreseeable" (or even just "conceivable"), an interceptive strike counters an armed attack which is "imminent" and practically "unavoidable." It is the opinion of the present writer that interceptive, as distinct from anticipatory, self-defence is legitimate even under Article 51 of the Charter. [Dinstein at 169-172.]

How should the language of Article 51 ("if an armed attack occurs") be interpreted? Should it require that the attacking state has actually fired a weapon or crossed a border? Should the Article include Dinstein's concept of interceptive self-defense? Should a more expansive version of preemptive or anticipatory self-defense be allowed — that is, even when the attacking state has not committed itself in any irrevocable way? For example, what evidence should Israel need before it can invoke the right of self-defense and attack its traditional enemies, say, Syria or Iraq? What evidence of state-supported terrorist activity should the United States need before it attacks, say, Iraq or Iran? (You might also consider here the Cuban missile crisis and the U.S. decision not to rely on a self-defense justification. See pages 1072-1076 below, especially Note 3.)

In September 2002, the Bush Administration issued a new document, "The National Security Strategy of the United States of America." In the section on preventing U.S. enemies from threatening the United States or its friends with nuclear, chemical, or biological weapons (often called weapons of mass destruction or WMD), the Bush Administration announced:

> We must be prepared to stop rogue states and their terrorist clients before they are able to threaten or use weapons of mass destruction against the United States and our allies and friends. . . .
>
> For centuries, international law recognized that nations need not suffer an attack before they can take actions to defend themselves against forces that present an imminent danger of attack. Legal scholars and international jurists often conditioned the legitimacy of preemption on the existence of an imminent threat — most often a visible mobilization of armies, navies, and air forces preparing to attack.
>
> We must adapt the concept of imminent threat to the capabilities and objectives of today's adversaries.
>
> The United States has long maintained the option of preemptive actions to counter a sufficient threat to our national security. The greater the threat, the greater

the risk of inaction — and the more compelling the case for taking anticipatory action to defend ourselves, even if uncertainty remains as to the time and place of the enemy's attack. To forestall or prevent such hostile acts by our adversaries, the United States will, if necessary, act preemptively.

The United States will not use force in all cases to preempt emerging threats, nor should nations use preemption as a pretext for aggression. Yet in an age where the enemies of civilization openly and actively seek the world's most destructive technologies, the United States cannot remain idle while dangers gather.

We will always proceed deliberately, weighing the consequences of our actions. To support preemptive options, we will:

- build better, more integrated intelligence capabilities to provide timely, accurate information on threats, wherever they may emerge;
- coordinate closely with allies to form a common assessment of the most dangerous threats; and
- continue to transform our military forces to ensure our ability to conduct rapid and precise operations to achieve decisive results.

The purpose of our actions will always be to eliminate a specific threat to the United States or our allies and friends. The reasons for our actions will be clear, the force measured, and the cause just.

Do you believe that the new strategy of possible preemptive actions is justified on a policy basis? Can it be supported in international law? How precise are the parameters of this policy?

Does the new policy provide a legitimate justification for the U.S. and allied attack on Iraq in spring 2003? (See the discussion of the Iraq situation below at page 1040.) When, if ever, would this new strategy have provided a legitimate justification for attacking North Korea in 2003 because it restarted a nuclear reactor, a reprocessing plant, and other facilities that would enable it to soon begin making a new nuclear weapon every month or so? (See the section on nonproliferation and North Korea below at page 1125.)

6. In a crisis between two countries, should the armed attack requirement be different if one of the countries believes that the imminent attack will be with nuclear weapons rather than with conventional ones? A nuclear attack would be much more destructive in most circumstances than one with non-nuclear forces, but wouldn't a preemptive nuclear strike also be much more destructive — and hence an act that requires greater caution than a conventional strike? Also, in one major study of numerous conventional conflicts, the analysis revealed that there were considerable advantages to being able to strike first. The conventional attacker could take advantage of massing its forces and hopefully benefitting from surprise. See Richard Betts, Surprise Attack (1982).

As for a nuclear conflict, doesn't it matter if the attacker has many nuclear weapons or not and how vulnerable they are to a preemptive strike? For example, the United States has thousands of nuclear warheads, which are deployed in different ways, and some are relatively invulnerable to an initial attack. On the other hand, India, Pakistan or North Korea might have only a few weapons, and they might be vulnerable to a preemptive attack. Would it make sense for an opponent of, say, India to strike first if the opponent thought a nuclear attack by India were "imminent" or "practically unavoidable"?

7. *Reprisals and other self-help countermeasures.* In the absence of an effective enforcement mechanism in international law, the question necessarily arises as to

whether a state may have a limited right to use force in self-help if it is unable to remedy a violation of its rights under international law through peaceful means. As Professor Franck indicated in the excerpt above, "a limited right to self-help has long been recognized in customary international law and practice." This right is illustrated by the *Naulilaa* incident discussed above. Franck goes on to note: "This [limited right] has not been specifically repealed by the Charter. . . . Indeed, UN practice seems to offer some latitude for states' resort to countermeasures in self-help." Franck concludes that this right of self-help is only acknowledged as a remedy of last resort and is sometimes viewed as mitigating, if not exculpating, the resort to force.

Professor Dinstein envisions a role for reprisals, albeit under the umbrella of Article 51.

> Generally speaking, reprisals constitute "counter-measures that would be illegal if not for the prior illegal act of the State against which they are directed." While most reprisals are non-forcible, we shall focus on armed reprisals. . . .
>
> Armed reprisals are measures of counter-force, short of war, undertaken by one State against another in response to an earlier violation of international law. Like all other instances of unilateral recourse to force by States, armed reprisals are prohibited unless they qualify as an exercise of self-defence under Article 51. Only defensive armed reprisals are allowed. They must come in response to an armed attack, as opposed to other violations of international law, in circumstances satisfying all the requirements of legitimate self-defence. . . .
>
> The choice of the time and place for putting into operation defensive armed reprisals . . . is made by the victim State. . . . The decision obviously depends on considerations of where, when and how to deal a blow that would be most advantageous to that State. The actions taken "need not mirror offensive measures of the aggressor." . . .
>
> The view expressed here, whereby armed reprisals can be a permissible form of self-defence (in response to an armed attack) under Article 51, is supported by some scholars. It must be conceded, however, that most writers deny that self-defence pursuant to Article 51 may ever embrace armed reprisals. The International Law Commission, too, neatly separated the concepts of armed reprisals and self-defence.
>
> Those denying the possibility of armed reprisals ever earning the seal of legitimacy of self-defence do so on the ground that armed reprisals take place "after the event and when the harm has already been inflicted," so that their purpose is always punitive rather than defensive. In the present writer's opinion, this is a narrow approach influenced, to some extent, by nomenclature. The legal analysis might benefit if the term "armed reprisals" were simply abandoned. . . .
>
> Armed reprisals do not qualify as legitimate self-defence if they are impelled by purely punitive, nondefensive, motives. But the motives driving States to action are usually multifaceted, and a tinge of retribution can probably be traced in every instance of response to force. . . . To be defensive, and therefore lawful, armed reprisals must be future-oriented, and not limited to a desire to punish past transgressions. . . .
>
> In the final analysis, defensive armed reprisals are post-attack measures of self-defence short of war. The availability of such a weapon in its arsenal provides the victim State with a singularly important option. If this option were to have been eliminated from the gamut of legitimate self-defence, the State upon which an armed attack is inflicted would have been able to respond only with either on-the-spot reaction or war. On-the-spot reaction is dissatisfactory because it is predicated on employing counter-force on the spur of the moment, meaning that hostilities (i) erupt without any (or, at least, any serious) involvement of the political branch of the Government; and (ii) take

place at a time as well as a place chosen by the attacking State, usually at a disadvantage for the defending State. War, for its part, requires a momentous decision that may alter irreversibly the course of history. Defensive armed reprisals enable the target State to fine-tune its response to an armed attack by relying on an intermediate means of self-defence. . . .

Since the entry into force of the UN Charter, the record is replete with measures of defensive armed reprisals implemented by many countries (including the Permanent Members of the Security Council), although statesmen frequently shy away from the expression "reprisals." Thus, in 1986, American air strikes were launched against several targets in Libya, in exercise of the right of self-defence, in response to Libyan State-sponsored terrorist attacks (especially, a bomb explosion in Berlin killing two American servicemen and wounding many others). In substance, these were acts of defensive armed reprisals. . . .

[I]t is interesting to note that the Judgment of the [International Court of Justice in the *Nicaragua* case in 1986] . . . refrained from ruling that all armed reprisals are automatically unlawful. [Dinstein at 194-195, 198-202.]

Do you think that defensive armed reprisals, as Dinstein defines them, should be a permissible use of force? If so, should they be a calibrated form of Article 51 self-defense, or how else would you justify them? If you oppose these reprisals, how do you deal with Dinstein's argument that they allow a victim state to fine-tune its response, rather than to react immediately and at the time and place of the attacker's choosing? Is there a danger that allowing reprisals will infact allow more uses of force?

Returning to Professor Franck's analysis, what about a state's persistent violation of its international obligations? Professor Franck suggests that a state may be permitted to enforce obligations accruing to it directly or indirectly under international law, but also notes that the international system has in practice been ambivalent about recourse to force in such enforcement actions.

Do you believe that the use of force in self-help, as described by Franck, is a permissible use of force under international law today? If it is permissible, is it justified under Article 51 as Dinstein suggests, or it is sometimes justified on less defined grounds of "extreme necessity" or "last resort," as Franck and state practice would imply? Further, should measures of self-help in these circumstances be viewed as legitimate, or as technically illegal but where the illegality is mitigated by the circumstances?

8. *1993 U.S. attack on Iraq.* On June 26, 1993, the United States launched a limited strike against Baghdad, Iraq in response to what U.S. officials had concluded was a plot to assassinate former President Bush while he was in Kuwait in April 1993. President Clinton chose one of the most limited options available in order to minimize civilian casualties and to make the response proportionate to the assassination attempt. The attack was also limited because there was no evidence that Saddam Hussein was directly involved.

U.S. officials said the attack was consistent with Article 51 of the U.N. Charter. The United States regarded the attempted assassination as a direct attack on the United States that warranted a direct response. (Even if so, can a measure by the United States two months later be justified as self-defense?) The United States also warned that any retaliation by Iraq "would be met with a direct and overwhelming response."

Administration officials said that they had suspected as early as mid-May that Iraq had plotted to kill former President Bush and that the United States might very well have responded with military force. But the United States refrained from retaliating until it had more proof that Iraq had been involved. (The proof included bomb components that had been linked to earlier instances of known Iraqi terrorist attacks.)

9. *"Purely humanitarian" intervention.* The need for (and collaterally, the right to) humanitarian intervention by a state, a group of states, or the U.N. has become an increasingly relevant topic in recent years.

One issue is to what degree the United Nations itself can intervene in the domestic affairs of a country wracked by internal violence, genocide, or civil war. The Charter makes no provision for Security Council involvement except where it determines the existence of a "threat to peace" under Article 39. Until the 1990s, with a few exceptions, the Cold War paralyzed the Security Council, and prevented this issue from arising, but this paralysis began to dissolve with the breakup of the Soviet Union. In 1991, concerned with Iraq's suppression of its Kurds and other civilians after Operation Desert Storm, the Security Council passed Resolution 688. Read broadly, its provisions indicate that concern for widespread human rights abuses may justify U.N. intervention in the domestic affairs of a country. Although some member States were hesitant to expand the role of the Security Council into conflicts they viewed as primarily domestic, a majority was willing to act in response to repression when it resulted in substantial flows of refugees across borders, which arguably constituted a threat to international peace and security. This theory was accepted reluctantly in 1991, but its acceptance grew during the 1990s, partly because of strong support by Secretary General Kofi Annan for the idea that humanitarian concerns could supersede territorial sovereignty in certain egregious cases, such as in the former Yugoslavia.

As Professor Franck observes:

> It is much more difficult conceptually to justify in [U.N.] Charter terms the use of force by one or several states acting without prior Security Council authorization even when such action is taken to enforce human rights and humanitarian values. . . . In the strict Charter scheme, states are not to use force except in self-defense and regional organizations may not take "enforcement action. . . without the authorization of the Security Council."
>
> A state using military force without Council authorization against another in "humanitarian intervention" is thus engaged in an action for which the Charter provides no apparent legal authority. . . .
>
> However, the institutional history of the United Nations . . . neither categorically precludes nor endorses humanitarian intervention. Rather, the history and practice support a more nuanced reconciling of the pursuit of peace (as evidenced by Charter Article 2(4)) and of justice through the protection of human and humanitarian rights (as evidenced by the canon of rights-creating universal agreements).
>
> [In his conclusions excerpted earlier, Franck notes:] Finally, the instances in which a state or group of states has intervened for humanitarian purposes without incurring significant opposition from the international system may indicate a certain willingness on the part of that community to brook some violation of the law in instances of clearly demonstrated necessity. It does not, however, indicate a fundamental change in the law to give wholesale permission to states to do that which is textually prohibited. Even less does it suggest that conduct which is textually prohibited has, through practice,

become legally obligatory." [Franck at 137-139, 172; see the more complete Franck excerpt earlier].

Under what circumstances should the international community condone or excuse a state or group of states that intervene, without U.N. authorization, in another state for humanitarian purposes? Should the international community's acceptance of some interventions be limited to instances of demonstrated necessity? Can the circumstances be defined more specifically in advance? To the extent that some circumstances for intervention are found acceptable, doesn't this mean that a state's territorial integrity and political independence does not now extend to, say, the state committing mass murder or engaging in wholesale repression of its own citizens in its own territory. (The question of collective responses by the U.N. and regional organizations is discussed in a separate section below.)

10. At this point, what exceptions do you think should now be allowed to the Article 2(4) prohibition on the use of force? Should the exceptions be limited to self-defense under Article 51? What do you interpret that self-defense to allow — anticipatory self-defense? Reprisals? Humanitarian intervention? Do you think that other exceptions should be allowed either under an expansive reading of Article 51 or beyond Article 51? If so, which uses of force?

More broadly, turning back to the long excerpt from Professor Franck, recall his view that the U.N. "Charter's text is not facially responsive to the challenge of change. It, like other grand instruments written for the long term, has had to meet the threat of obsolescence with adaptation." Do you agree? If not, how do you otherwise explain U.N. and international practice in apparently accepting, or at least acquiescing in, some uses of force that do not fit within the terms of the Charter — for example, for humanitarian interventions? Reprisals? Anticipatory self-defense? In the future, would you support strict construction of the Charter, or continued, limited adaptation, or what other approach to regulating the use of force?

11. What has happened to the pre-World War I customary law of neutrality, discussed above at page 972? As one commentator observed:

> Since the signing of the United Nations Charter, the customary law of neutrality has been caught between an international legal order which purports to outlaw war and hence make neutrality obsolete, and an international political environment characterized by frequent armed conflicts in which there is a need to regulate the relations of belligerent and nonbelligerent states. The results have been confused, if not chaotic. With the juridical status of armed conflicts uncertain, third states have most often refrained from taking a formal stance of neutrality. But where the need for *some* legal rule has been acute and where the particular rule of the customary law has suited their interests, states have invoked that customary law. . . . Neutrality has . . . led a sort of "juridical half-life," suspended between an ideology which denies its premises and a reality which finds it useful, if not necessary. [Patrick M. Norton, Between the Ideology and the Reality: The Shadow of the Law of Neutrality, 17 Harv. Intl. L.J. 249, 249 (1976).]

During the Iran-Iraq war in the 1980s, the United States and several other countries with important shipping interests in the Persian Gulf often emphasized their neutral status as a basis for arguing that their ships should not be attacked by either Iran or Iraq. This did not always deter the belligerents from attacking neutral shipping, but it did provide nonbelligerents with an argument in international organizations. (See Maxwell Jenkins, Air Attacks on Neutral Shipping in the Persian Gulf: The Legality of the Iraqi Exclusion Zone and Iranian Reprisals, 8 B.C. Intl. & Comp. L. Rev. 517 (1985).) One of the grounds used by the Reagan Administration to justify the need for U.S. Navy escorts for American and other commercial ships going to and from neutral ports in the Gulf was that the Iranians and, to a lesser extent, the Iraqis were illegally attacking neutral shipping.

12. Before turning to analyze some other U.S. uses of force, the intervention by the former Soviet Union in Afghanistan during 1979-1989 is worth noting. The Soviets moved large military units there starting in December 1979. At the time, the Soviet Union claimed that its action was prompted by armed intervention by other foreign powers, including the United States. The Soviet Union said that its troops entered Afghanistan at the repeated invitation of the Afghanistan government, headed by Hafizullah Amin.

In fact, there was no evidence of armed intervention by other countries. Moreover, as the U.S. ambassador to the United Nations observed in a speech on January 12, 1980, "no reasonable man could possibly believe that the Government of President Amin issued such a deadly invitation." Shortly after the Soviet troops entered the country, they "surrounded the presidential palace in Kabul, the President of Afghanistan [Amin] was summarily executed, and a puppet leader" (Babrak Karmal, of Afghan descent) was brought in from the Soviet Union to be installed in Amin's place.

The Soviet intervention was almost universally condemned by all states other than the Soviet Union and its close allies. A General Assembly resolution "strongly deplore[d]" the action as a violation of Article 2(4). The resolution passed by a vote of 104 for and 18 against, with 18 abstentions and 12 absent or not voting.

The continued opposition of Afghan guerrilla groups, labeled freedom fighters by President Reagan, exacted a heavy toll on the Soviet and Afghan government forces. The opposition was aided by substantial covert aid from the United States, including a supply of Stinger missiles. This shoulder-fired missile proved relatively effective against Soviet aircraft and helicopters.

In 1989 the Soviet Union withdrew its military forces. In October 1989, in a speech to the Supreme Soviet, Foreign Minister Eduard A. Shevardnadze acknowledged that the Soviet Union had been wrong in intervening in Afghanistan. He said: "When more than 100 U.N. members for a number of years were condemning our action, what other evidence did we need to realize that we had set ourselves against all of humanity, violated norms of behavior, ignored universal human values?"

c.   Vietnam: The Controversy Continues

The U.S. actions in Vietnam had a traumatic effect on Americans during the late 1960s and early 1970s. Many U.S. citizens opposed the war as it dragged on and as U.S. involvement increased. Opposition to the war and the fact that the Executive Branch had taken the lead in embroiling the United States in the war were major causes of a resurgence of congressional activity in foreign affairs in the 1970s. The War Powers Resolution, discussed below in Section D was a direct result of the new congressional activism. In the following excerpt, Professor Henkin addresses the question of the legality of the war under principles of international law.

Louis Henkin, Vietnam: The Uncertain Trumpet of Uncertain Law

How Nations Behave: Law and Foreign Policy 303-308 (2d ed. 1979)

"Vietnam" appears deeply etched in American history as one of the few great national tragedies. At home, it was a cause of unprecedented malaise and dissension; internationally, it meant near-defeat in war, loss of prestige and credibility, damage to "image" and leadership, friction even with allies. Both in the United States and abroad there was common agreement that the United States had made a big mistake. Both in the United States and abroad there was a disposition to assume that what was deemed stupid or immoral must also be illegal. . . . The executive branch, however, . . . rejected charges that the United States committed any violation of international law, insisting, rather, that U.S. involvement was dictated by international undertakings in the spirit of the U.N. Charter to assist victims of aggression.

Accusations of violations of law are common weapons in political controversy, often with little warrant. For their part, on the other hand, those who in fact violate the law, commonly plead "not guilty." As regards Vietnam, however, even . . . the judiciously-minded and the impartial were hard put to reach a clear judgment as to the merits of the legal claims of the two sides.

The legal uncertainties about Vietnam revealed uncertainties in the law of the U.N. Charter; they revealed, too, the importance of facts and their characterizations in legal determinations. The legality of the actions of the United States (and those of other parties to the war) turned on difficult issues as to the status and character of the territory and the government of South Vietnam, and their relation to the Vietcong, to North Vietnam, and to the North Vietnamese government. Was the war in Vietnam civil war or international war, and what was the status of the United States in that war? Of course, if the facts were confused, if what they amounted to was disputable, and the governing legal principles uncertain, they were less likely to exercise restraining influence on the policies of governments.

Even the barest, briefest narrative of American involvement in Indochina must go back at least to 1954. At a political conference in Geneva following years of fighting, France signed a cease-fire and agreed to transfer sovereignty to a "State of Vietnam." The Final Declaration of the Conference affirmed the unity of Vietnam and envisioned holding elections in July 1956. But while the rival governments in North and South Vietnam committed themselves to unifying the country, the South Vietnamese government did not accept the Geneva Conference and the United States did not sign the Final Declaration, although it announced that it would abide by the Declaration's terms.

It soon appeared that the South Vietnam government would not agree to general elections, claiming that the elections could not be free in the Communist-controlled North. The United States supported that view. Instead, it led in the establishment of the South-East Asia Collective Defense Treaty (SEATO), and a protocol to that treaty made its provisions applicable to Cambodia, Laos, and "the free territory under the jurisdiction of the state of Vietnam."

General elections were not held in 1956, and in the years that followed Communist-led dissident groups (known as the Vietcong, or later, the National

Liberation Front) [engaged] in terroristic activities, rebellion and war against the South Vietnamese government. Supported by Southern Communists trained in North Vietnam, the Vietcong made important headway and by the end of 1960 controlled substantial areas of South Vietnam.

United States support for the South began early and increased slowly. In the early years it helped build up the South Vietnamese army; in 1961 it began to send combat advisers to accompany combat-support units, and by 1963 there were some 16,000 U.S. military personnel in South Vietnam. Following a coup d'état, apparently with U.S. knowledge if not support, President Johnson concluded that stronger U.S. support was necessary. In August 1964 a North Vietnamese attack on two U.S. destroyers in the Gulf of Tonkin led to a resolution by Congress authorizing the President to "take all necessary measures to repel any armed attack against the forces of the United States and to prevent further aggression," and to assist any member or protocol State of SEATO "requesting assistance in defense of its freedom." In October 1964 American aircraft began to attack supply trails in Laos; in March 1965 they began to bomb in North Vietnam; in April 1965 President Johnson sent combat troops. Beginning in the latter months of 1965, North Vietnamese troops entered the South to support the Vietcong. In 1967 the United States began to bomb in Laos, and in 1970 in Cambodia, claiming that the Communists were using those territories to support their aggression, and the local governments were unwilling or unable to prevent them. Despite intermittent efforts by both sides and by third parties to end the war, it continued for years more, terminating finally with the Paris agreements of 1973.

THE LAW AND THE FACTS

What international law would say about U.S. involvement in Vietnam depends on disputed questions of fact, even more on debatable characterizations of those facts. The lawyer seeking to apply norms needs first to decide what was going on. He might begin by asking which side was responsible for the failure of a political solution and the resort to arms. It seems agreed that the South refused to go along with elections; was it legally obligated to do so? If so, was it excused by the fact that elections would probably not be "free" in the North? Assuming the South was responsible for the failure of general elections, was the North justified in responding by supporting the Vietcong in the South and helping it achieve control by force?

It is difficult to conclude that the United States breached international obligations by supporting the South in its refusal to proceed with elections, since the United States was not party to the 1954 Declaration. But was it permitted by law to support the South Vietnam regime, build its army, advise its troops in combat? Political and auxiliary military support to the South Vietnam government was probably seen by the North as intervention in the internal affairs of Vietnam, but the United States was free to treat the government of South Vietnam as a legitimate government and to support it accordingly. More serious allegations against the United States came after the Tonkin Gulf incident with direct U.S. participation in hostilities, particularly by bombing in North Vietnam and by committing ground troops to combat.

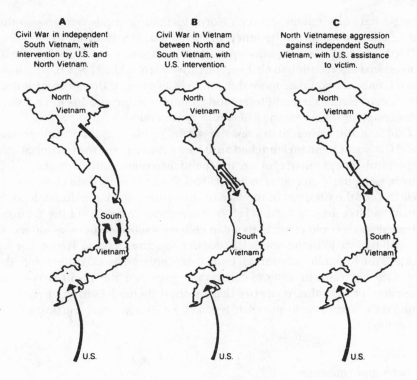

A

Civil War in independent
South Vietnam, with
intervention by U.S. and
North Vietnam.

North
Vietnam

South
Vietnam

U.S.

B

Civil War in Vietnam
between North and
South Vietnam, with
U.S. intervention.

North
Vietnam

South
Vietnam

U.S.

C

North Vietnamese aggression
against independent South
Vietnam, with U.S. assistance
to victim.

North
Vietnam

South
Vietnam

U.S.

There are at least three possible models to characterize the Vietnam War and the U.S. role in it, and the judgment of international law will largely depend on which characterization it accepts.

Model A saw the war as civil war within an independent South Vietnam, with North Vietnam an outside state helping one side, the United States another outside state helping the other. Military intervention in civil war was not acceptable under traditional international law, but that law may never have recovered from the wounds it suffered at many hands during the Spanish Civil War [in 1936-39]. On its face at least, such external intervention is not obviously a violation of Article 2(4) of the U.N. Charter as a use of force against the political independence or territorial integrity of another state, if the support was bona fide and the intervenor was not seeking to dominate the side it supported and establish a puppet regime.

On this view of the Vietnam War, neither the United States nor North Vietnam violated a vital contemporary norm of international law, as long as both confined themselves to supporting activity. But U.S. bombing of North Vietnam added an unacceptable dimension, converting an essentially civil war into an international war. (In the Spanish Civil War, intervenors did not, nor claimed the right to, attack each other's territory.) Indeed, world reaction to U.S. participation appeared to harden appreciably after the United States began to bomb in the North, in part perhaps because the world saw the war as an internal affair in South Vietnam and held the United States responsible for expanding it.

A second view (Model B) also saw the war as civil war, not between the Vietcong and the Saigon government in a separate independent South Vietnam, but within the single state of Vietnam, between North Vietnam and the Vietcong on the one hand and Saigon forces on the other. In such a war, U.S. intervention, even bombing North Vietnam, was — again — perhaps a violation of traditional international norms against intervention in civil war, but not clearly of the U.N. Charter. Bombing Laos or Cambodia would be more difficult to justify, even if they were viewed as tacit supporters of North Vietnam; toleration of mutual interventions in civil war does not contemplate attacks by one intervenor against another.

Officially, the United States saw the war in Vietnam in yet a third perspective (Model C). North Vietnam launched an armed attack against the territorial integrity and political independence of an independent country, the Republic of South Vietnam, using the Vietcong as its agent. This was a use of force in clear violation of Article 2(4) of the Charter. In the face of this armed attack, the Republic of South Vietnam had its inherent right of self-defense under Article 51 of the Charter, and the United States could come to its aid in collective self-defense — as indeed, it had obligated itself to do in the South East Asian Collective Defense Treaty. The United States and the Republic of South Vietnam had every right to carry the war to the territory of the aggressor in order to defeat the aggression; they could carry the war to the territory of any other countries that involved themselves in the aggression, or permitted the aggressor to use their territory for its aggressive purposes, i.e., Laos and Cambodia.

Notes and Questions

1. Are any of the three models above a more accurate statement of the Vietnam situation than the others? Does an answer depend on facts that were genuinely in dispute during the time of the U.S. intervention?

2. Under any of the three models, what legal justification is there for the U.S. bombing of Laos and Cambodia? Did it matter whether Laos or Cambodia agreed to the Vietcong and North Vietnamese use of their territory or whether they lacked the power to oust them?

In two insightful articles analyzing the legality under the U.S. Constitution of the U.S. involvement in Indochina, Professor John Ely undertook an impressive factual analysis of the actual U.S. involvement in Laos and Cambodia. He concludes that much of the U.S. bombing of Laos from 1964 on was to help protect the Laotian government, not just to cut off the North Vietnamese supply routes to South Vietnam. Similarly, the U.S. bombing of parts of Cambodia, which began secretly in March 1969, apparently had at least the acquiescence of Prince Sihanouk, the Cambodian leader. (See John Hart Ely, The American War in Indochina, Part II: The Unconstitutionality of the War They Didn't Tell Us About, 42 Stan. L. Rev. 1093, 1093-1099, 1137-1141 (1990); and Ely, The American War in Indochina, Part I: The (Troubled) Constitutionality of the War They Told Us About, 42 Stan. L. Rev. 877 (1990).) Do Ely's conclusions make it easier to justify the bombings under international law?*

---

*Under U.S. law, Ely concludes that the secret bombing of Cambodia between March 1969 through April 1970 raised very serious constitutional questions, because the Nixon Administration made major efforts to hide what was happening from Congress and the American public. Ely concludes: "I'd have impeached [President Nixon] for it. Surely it would have been a more worthy ground than the combination of a third-rate burglary and a style the stylish couldn't stomach." Id. at 1148. — Eds.

Does it matter whether the governments of Laos and Cambodia had requested U.S. military assistance?

3. If you believe under one theory or another that the U.S. bombing of Laos or Cambodia was justified under international law, would the then-Soviet Union have been justified to attack Afghan refugee camps in Pakistan during the Soviet intervention in Afghanistan — on the grounds that these refugee camps were acting as training and support bases for the Afghan guerrillas? Would Nicaragua be justified in attacking Honduras because the Contras maintained base camps there? Were there important factual differences between the three cases?

4. Professor Viet Dinh, who escaped from Vietnam by boat with some of his family after the war, recently took a broad historical look at U.S.–Vietnamese relations. He found that the war should be understood as part of the continuing U.S. fight for democracy and capitalism. See Viet D. Dinh, How We Won in Vietnam, Policy Review 51 (Dec. 2000-Jan. 2001). Other attempted explanations abound, including that the U.S. decision makers on Vietnam were overly focused on containing communism worldwide and viewed it as monolithic, rather than appreciating the domestic revolutionary character of the Vietnamese opposition. Another explanation was that the U.S. decision makers were operating from the lessons of World War II, when they had come of age and when early British and French attempts to pacify an aggressive country, Nazi Germany, had failed.

d.   The Unsuccessful Mission to Rescue U.S. Hostages in Iran

During political turmoil in Iran after the fall of the Shah, Iranians occupied the U.S. Embassy in Tehran on November 4, 1979, and held 53 Americans, mainly diplomatic personnel, as hostages. The events marked a sharp blow to the already deteriorating relations between Iran and the United States, a deterioration that followed decades of close ties. The crisis dominated the news in the United States and often in the rest of the world as well.

The United States responded in a number of ways — with economic sanctions, protests in the United Nations, and proceedings before the International Court of Justice. After these efforts had failed over five months to obtain the peaceful release of the hostages — or even to offer much hope for success — President Carter gave the go-ahead for a rescue mission. The planning for the mission had begun as a contingency soon after the seizure of the hostages.

The daring U.S. rescue mission failed on April 25, 1980. A small, specially trained force had been scheduled to rendezvous in the Iranian desert with eight helicopters and fly to a location close to Tehran. The force would then travel by trucks to the U.S. Embassy compound where the hostages were held and, using surprise and force, try to free the hostages. The rescuers and the hostages would then move to a nearby field and be flown by helicopters and then aircraft out of Iran.

After three of the eight helicopters developed troubles, the mission was scrubbed at the first rendezvous. As the evacuation began, one of the remaining helicopters collided with a tanker plane. In the ensuing explosion and fire, eight members of the rescue team were killed, and others were injured. The survivors quickly flew back to Egypt.

The President made the following report to Congress:

President Carter, Message to Congress
Apr. 26, 1980, 1 Pub. Papers 777–779 (1980-1981)

Because of my desire that Congress be informed on this matter and consistent with the reporting provisions of the War Powers Resolution of 1973 (Public Law 93-148), I submit this report.

On April 24, 1980, elements of the United States Armed Forces under my direction commenced the positioning stage of a rescue operation which was designed, if the subsequent stages had been executed, to effect the rescue of the American hostages who have been held captive in Iran since November 4, 1979, in clear violation of international law and the norms of civilized conduct among nations. The subsequent phases of the operation were not executed. Instead, for the reasons described below, all these elements were withdrawn from Iran and no hostilities occurred.

The sole objective of the operation that actually occurred was to position the rescue team for the subsequent effort to withdraw the American hostages. The rescue team was under my overall command and control and required my approval before executing the subsequent phases of the operation designed to effect the rescue itself. No such approval was requested or given because, as described below, the mission was aborted.

Beginning approximately 10:30 A.M. EST on April 24, six U.S. C-130 transport aircraft and eight RH-53 helicopters entered Iran airspace. Their crews were not equipped for combat. Some of the C-130 aircraft carried a force of approximately 90 members of the rescue team equipped for combat, plus various support personnel.

From approximately 2 to 4 P.M. EST the six transports and six of the eight helicopters landed at a remote desert site in Iran approximately 200 miles from Tehran where they disembarked the rescue team, commenced refueling operations and began to prepare for the subsequent phases.

During the flight to the remote desert site, two of the eight helicopters developed operating difficulties. . . . Of the six helicopters which landed at the remote desert site, one developed a serious hydraulic problem and was unable to continue with the mission. The operational plans called for a minimum of six helicopters in good operational condition able to proceed from the desert site. . . . When the number of helicopters available to continue dropped to five, it was determined that the operation could not proceed as planned. Therefore, on the recommendation of the force commander and my military advisers, I decided to cancel the mission and ordered the United States Armed Forces involved to return from Iran.

During the process of withdrawal, one of the helicopters accidentally collided with one of the C-130 aircraft, which was preparing to take off, resulting in the death of eight personnel and the injury of several others. . . . Altogether, the United States Armed Forces remained on the ground for a total of approximately three hours. . . .

Our rescue team knew, and I knew, that the operation was certain to be dangerous. We were all convinced that if and when the rescue phase of the operation had been commenced, it had an excellent chance of success. They were all volunteers; they were all highly trained. . . .

The mission on which they were embarked was a humanitarian mission. It was not directed against Iran. It was not directed against the people of Iran. It caused no Iranian casualties.

This operation was ordered and conducted pursuant to the President's powers under the Constitution as Chief Executive and as Commander-in-Chief of the United States Armed Forces, expressly recognized in Section 8(d)(1) of the War Powers Resolution. In carrying out this operation, the United States was acting wholly within its right, in accordance with Article 51 of the United Nations Charter, to protect and rescue its citizens where the government of the territory in which they are located is unable or unwilling to protect them. . . .

Many believed that the rescue mission was too little, too late. Others questioned the wisdom and scope of the mission. Believing that the plan was too risky and that the Iranians could easily seize new hostages, Secretary of State Cyrus Vance had opposed it. He secretly submitted his resignation to President Carter on April 21, after the President had decided to proceed but before the mission had occurred.

While President Carter called the abortive effort a "humanitarian mission," there were later news reports that major U.S. forces would have been thrown into the effort if the rescuers had met opposition in Tehran.

Notes and Questions

1. Do you think that the planned U.S. rescue mission should be acceptable under international law? If so, under what theory? If not, why not?

2. Was President Carter correct in relying on Article 51, the self-defense provision, of the U.N. Charter? If so, what should be the limits on this justification? Should there be requirements of necessity and proportionality? Do you think the Article 51 justification would allow the larger military operation that was waiting if troubles developed?

Could Russia intervene in Poland if Polish crowds threw rocks at two Russian diplomats who were peacefully watching a parade in Warsaw? Should the United States be able to bomb Iran for its apparent support of terrorists (a) who set off a car bomb next to a U.S. embassy in another country or (b) who kill two American tourists in Egypt because they are Americans?

3. President Carter referred to the mission as a "humanitarian mission." Should this be a separate theory (humanitarian intervention) from self-defense or a variant on self-defense? In either event, what should be the limits on a humanitarian mission? Should it be confined to missions to protect a country's own citizens, as Professor Dinstein argued earlier? Or, on its own initiative, could the United States have gone to the aid of the hostages if the Iranian government had held New Zealand diplomats as hostages? Or could the United States have mounted the rescue mission to help the New Zealand diplomats if the government of New Zealand had asked for U.S. help because it did not have the military resources to conduct a rescue mission in Iran? What if the hostages in Iran were 30 students from a Catholic high school in New Zealand who were on a round-the-world tour?

4. What if U.S. citizens are held hostage by terrorists in Lebanon and the Lebanese government would like to get them released, but does not have the resources to force their release in a nonrisky way? Does the U.S. government have to wait for Lebanon to request its aid, or can the U.S. President send in a rescue mission on his own initiative?

5. Two excellent books on the 1979-1981 hostage crisis in Iran are American Hostages in Iran (Paul Kreisberg ed., 1985) (with chapters by several of the major U.S. policy-makers in the crisis), and Gary Sick, All Fall Down (1985) (Sick was a key member of the National Security Council staff).

e.   The U.S. Invasion of Panama: Where Does It Fit In?

On December 20, 1989, the United States invaded Panama with a large force that eventually totalled about 25,000 troops and vastly outnumbered and outgunned the Panama Defense Force. The U.S. force encountered some initial resistance and then sporadic sniper fire. Within a few days, however, all resistance had ended. Twenty-three U.S. military and three U.S. civilians died, and over 200 more were wounded. Panamanian deaths, mainly civilian, probably exceeded 400. The property destruction was substantial because of the U.S. firepower and especially because of looting by Panamanians that went unchecked for several days.

The Panamanian leader, General Manuel Antonio Noriega, took refuge in the Vatican's embassy, but surrendered after several days to the U.S. military. He was immediately transported to the United States to face trial on outstanding indictments against him for drug smuggling and money laundering. He was convicted and given a long prison sentence. (See Chapter 6 regarding head-of-state immunity.)

The invasion might usefully be put in historical context. United States-Panamanian relations date back to the founding of Panama in November 1903, when it broke away from Colombia. President Teddy Roosevelt ordered U.S. naval forces to stand offshore, helping to deter any action by the Colombian government. Within two weeks, Panama signed a treaty granting the United States sweeping rights over a ten-mile wide strip of land, to be called the Canal Zone.

The construction and operation of the Panama Canal, a major engineering feat when it was opened in 1914, and its perceived strategic importance led the United States to stay closely involved in Panamanian politics through the ensuing decades.

The later Panama Canal Treaties, signed in 1977 and effective in 1979, provided for the gradual transfer of the Canal to Panama and the withdrawal of U.S. troops from what had been the Canal Zone. (The process was completed in 1999.)

The on-again, off-again relations between the United States and Panama took a definite downturn in early 1988 when General Noriega was indicted in Miami and Tampa on charges of drug smuggling and money laundering. Although it appears that the prosecution might have been initiated by a local U.S. attorney rather than Washington, relations with Noriega had been souring and no one in Washington wanted to block the U.S. prosecutor. It was quite a turnaround from earlier, close U.S. ties to Noriega.

Shortly after the drug indictments, the then president of Panama, Eric Arturo Delvalle, tried to oust Noriega from his position as head of the Panama Defense Force (PDF). Noriega, however, refused and quickly convened a meeting of the

Panamanian National Assembly, which voted to oust Delvalle instead and install a new president acceptable to Noriega. Delvalle went into hiding on a U.S. military base in Panama. Many Panamanians participated in a general strike, backing Delvalle. The United States recognized the Delvalle government as the government of Panama, and it also imposed selective economic sanctions against the Noriega regime, although it never resorted to cutting off imports from Panama. Through strong-arm tactics and the backing of his PDF, Noriega survived the challenges.

Matters between the two countries became even more difficult when Panama held elections to select a new president on May 7, 1989. Foreign observers reported that the opposition, led by Guillermo Endara, had won overwhelmingly. Noriega, however, refused to release any official results, and voided the election on May 10. He continued to tighten his grip on the country, in spite of diplomatic efforts by a few Latin American countries and the Organization of American States (OAS) to have him step down.

A military coup attempt on October 3, 1989, presented the next challenge to Noriega. The insurgents actually captured Noriega, but troops loyal to him rescued him after a firefight. Some of the coup leaders were killed.

On December 15, the Panamanian National Assembly adopted a resolution "To declare the Republic of Panama in a state of war for the duration of the aggression unleashed against the Panamanian people by the United States government." The declaration gave additional powers to the "Maximum Leader." On December 16, PDF forces killed a U.S. Marine officer at a checkpoint in Panama. Other PDF forces beat a U.S. naval officer and detained and abused his wife. At this point, apparently, President Bush gave the go-ahead for the invasion. It achieved the military results detailed above. Some of the U.S. forces began withdrawing within a few days, but some combat forces remained in Panama for about 60 days.

The immediate political effect of the invasion was to install a civilian government under Guillermo Endara, the apparent victor of the May election. "I have political power," declared Endara after he swore himself in at a U.S. base in Panama as the invasion began.

On December 22, the OAS voted 20 to 1 to express "regret" over the intervention and to urge the United States to withdraw its invasion forces. On December 29, the U.N. General Assembly voted 75-20, with 39 countries abstaining, in favor of a resolution that "[s]trongly deplores" the U.S. invasion as a "flagrant violation of international law" and demanding an immediate cease-fire and troop withdrawal. The United States, Britain, and France had used their vetoes to block the adoption of a similarly worded resolution in the Security Council. Most nonaligned countries, Spain, Austria, Sweden, and Soviet bloc countries supported the General Assembly resolution. Some of the countries that opposed the resolution, such as Italy, said that they objected because the resolution failed to criticize Noriega and not because they were endorsing the U.S. action.

Panama also voted against the resolution. The representative of the new government of President Endara explained that the government's legitimacy rested on Endara's presumed victory in the May 1989 elections. He said that the U.S. invasion was the price that Panama had accepted to pay for the restoration of its democracy.

The U.S. invasion was very popular in the United States, many of whose citizens had come to see Noriega as a devil incarnate. Although accurate measures of opinion in Panama were difficult, the invasion was also apparently supported by the majority of the Panamanian citizens because of their unhappiness with Noriega and the economic plight of the country.

On the day after the invasion, "[i]n accordance with [his] desire that Congress be fully informed on this matter, and consistent with the War Powers Resolution" (which will be discussed later at page 1121), President Bush put forward several justifications for U.S. intervention in his Report to Congress. These included the killing of a U.S. Marine and brutal treatment of at least two other U.S. citizens in Panama, a threat to U.S. rights under the Canal Treaties and the continued safe operation of the Canal, an invitation from the Endara government of Panama, and a so-called declaration of war by the Noriega regime. Although the President's report did not explicitly cite the Reagan Doctrine, it did characterize its invasion, in part, as a defense of democracy in Panama. Bush Administration sources suggested that the two primary legal justifications were the right to protect the lives of U.S. citizens and U.S. rights under the Panama Canal Treaties.

Notes and Questions

Are acts of violence such as those directed at U.S. citizens in 1989 justification for the major use of military force in a foreign country? What about the invitation of a government that does not have control of any part of the country? The apparent declaration of war by Noriega's government appears to have been a domestic measure, akin to a state of emergency, rather than an actual declaration. In any event, is a declaration of war an "armed attack" for the purposes of Article 51?

What about the Canal Zone Treaties? They included provisions that allowed both countries to protect the operation of the Canal. However, the United States attached reservations to its ratification of the Treaties stating that any U.S. action in Panama would be "only for the purpose of assuring that the Canal shall remain open, neutral, secure, and accessible" and it specifically disavowed a "right of intervention in the internal affairs of the Republic of Panama or interference with its political independence . . .". No immediate threat to the Canal was established, and the United States already had over 13,000 U.S. troops stationed in the Canal Zone or otherwise near the Canal. Can toppling of the Noriega regime be justified under the Treaties?

If none of these reasons individually amounts to justification for the U.S. use of force, does the combination of reasons help? Or does it highlight the lack of a justification? Finally, why do you think President Bush did not assert the Reagan Doctrine?

f. Intervention and Counterintervention

One area of recent importance that seems to suffer from considerable legal ambiguity deals with intervention and counterintervention.

The Nicaragua Case. As the International Court of Justice's first and still primary opinion addressing the customary international law regarding the use of force and the U.N. Charter provisions, its 1986 judgment in the *Nicaragua* case offers some important conclusions as well as raising or ignoring a number of other issues.* The background to the *Nicaragua* case is discussed in Chapter 4, Section B, where we consider the 1984 ICJ decision on the jurisdictional issues. The ICJ judgment broadly interpreted Article 2(4) to impose strict constraints on the use of force and narrowly interpreted Article 51 to limit the situations where force could be used in self-defense. However, there is much more in the very long and wide-ranging opinion. In the excerpt below, after providing some historical background on intervention and counterintervention, Professor Henkin summarizes the ICJ opinion and then goes on to address the issues and legal ambiguities in the area.

Louis Henkin, Use of Force: Law and Policy

Right v. Might: International Law and the Use of Force 47-65 (1991)

Before the UN Charter, the law [regarding intervention and counterintervention] seemed to be that a state may provide military assistance to the government of another state, even to help it suppress rebellion, but a state could not assist rebels against the incumbent government of another state. If rebellion succeeded sufficiently to achieve the status of "belligerent" and constitute a civil war, the law probably forbade assistance to either side. That law . . . was battered during the Spanish Civil War as states intervened on both sides. The United States, however, honored the principle of nonintervention, helping neither side.

   The United Nations Charter did not expressly address intervention in civil wars. Nothing in article 2(4) forbids sending military assistance to an incumbent government, but the use of force in support of rebels against an incumbent government would be a use of force against the territorial integrity of the state and, presumably, against its political independence. Under the Charter, a state probably may not send troops into the territory of another state to support either side in a civil war, since that too would violate the latter's territorial integrity and compromise its political independence. Assistance not involving the use of force, however — for example, providing advice, selling arms, or giving financial assistance to one (or both) sides in a civil war — seems not to be covered by article 2(4), but may violate norms against nonintervention that predate the Charter and have been strongly restated in numerous General Assembly resolutions.

AUTHORITATIVE CONSTRUCTION OF THE LAW: THE NICARAGUA CASE . . .

In 1986, in the *Nicaragua* case, the International Court of Justice issued what is in effect its first judgment construing key elements in the law of the Charter.[22] It construed the prohibition in article 2(4) broadly (as imposing strict limitations on the

---

   *Case Concerning Military and Paramilitary Activities In and Against Nicaragua (Nicaragua v. United States of America), [1986] I.C.J. Rep. 14 (Judgment).—EDS.

   22. The court concluded that it could not decide the case under the Charter because of a reservation by the United States, and would therefore decide it only under customary international law. But the Court held that customary law and the law of the Charter were essentially congruent in relevant respects, in effect construing the Charter.

use of force) and the exception in article 51 narrowly (as limiting the circumstances in which force may be used in self-defense). . . .

[T]he court held (or said) the following:

- The only exception to article 2(4) is article 51: Force against another state that is not justified by a right of self-defense under Article 51 is in violation of Article 2(4) (paragraph 211).
- Whether self-defense is individual or collective, "the exercise of this right is subject to the State concerned having been the victim of an armed attack" (paragraphs 195, 232).
- Armed attack may include acts by armed bands where such acts occur on a significant scale, but "assistance to rebels in the form of the provision of weapons or logistical or other support is not an armed attack justifying the use of force in self-defense" (paragraph 195). . . .
- "States do not have a right of 'collective' armed response to acts which do not constitute an 'armed attack'" (paragraphs 210-11). If no armed attack has occurred, collective self-defense is unlawful, even if "carried on in strict compliance with the canons of necessity and proportionality" (paragraph 237).
- The court could not "contemplate the creation of a new rule opening up a right of intervention by one State against another on the ground that the latter has opted for some particular ideology or political system." And "to hold otherwise would make nonsense of the fundamental principle of State sovereignty, on which the whole of international law rests, and the freedom of choice of the political, social, economic and cultural system of a State" (paragraph 263).
- There is no "general right of intervention, in support of an opposition within another state" (paragraph 209).
- The "use of force could not be the appropriate method to monitor or ensure" respect for human rights (paragraph 268).

The court did not resolve important questions as to the law of the Charter. In particular, the *Nicaragua* judgment gave only partial guidance on the difficult issues of intervention and counterintervention. The court denied any right to intervene by force in another state for purposes other than collective self-defense against armed attack; it denied any right to use force against another state in response to the latter's intervention in a third state by means that do not constitute an armed attack. But the court did not address the victim's right of armed response to "less than an armed attack," or what means other than force can be used in response to such interventions by either the victim or its friends (see paragraph 210). The court did not address whether when a state supports one side in a civil war in another country, a third state may "counterintervene" on the other side and, if so, subject to what limitations.

The *Nicaragua* case did not bring other current issues in the law of the Charter before the court. Thus, the court did not decide whether a target state (and its allies) may use force in anticipation of an armed attack (see paragraph 194). Its opinion gives no guidance as to whether a state responsible for terrorist activities may have committed an armed attack either against the state in whose territory such activities took place or against a state whose nationals were the targets or the victims of those activities.

A decision of the International Court of Justice is not binding on states other than the parties to the case, but judicial decisions are "subsidiary means for the determination of rules of law" (article 38 of the Statute of the Court), and decisions of the court are highly authoritative. . . .

The court's opinion is not the last word. The Reagan administration in the United States may not have been alone in rejecting some of its implications. But it is important to sort out the different conclusions. The court's declaration that force may be used only in self-defense against an armed attack reaffirms the original intent of the Charter and the positions commonly held by states (other than the few that have sought to justify their own uses of force). . . .

Less clear, more likely to be reexamined, and requiring much refinement are the court's definition of "armed attack" and its statement of the law as to what is permitted to a victim state (and its friends) in response to violations that do not constitute an armed attack. . . .

In the main, hostilities in our times have taken the form of "interventions" and "counterinterventions." From the lawyer's perspective, some of these have been cases of "indirect aggression"—notably those involving the USSR in Czechoslovakia (twice), in Hungary, and more recently in Afghanistan. Some have been cases of support for rebels against incumbent governments, sometimes followed by "counterintervention" by other states—in Vietnam, El Salvador, Nicaragua, Chad, and Angola, among others. . . . Terrorism has spread its own terrors and has occasionally evoked uses of force by states on the territory of other states, as when the United States dropped bombs in Libya or when Israel attack[ed] targets in Lebanon linked to the Palestine Liberation Organization. . . .

The difficult legal issues for the future continue to be those of military intervention and counterintervention. They are not resolved by the court's opinion in the *Nicaragua* case, and there is need—and room—to develop norms within the spirit and the letter of the Charter.

The attempt to regulate military intervention has suffered from asymmetries that are inherent when an international system, consisting of states represented by incumbent governments, is compelled to address internal change and from the difficulties of definition and drawing lines in complex, confused internal and international situations. The governing principles should not be controversial. The international system favors voluntary cooperation between states and between their governments. International law does not forbid one state to sell arms to another state, and upon authentic invitation, a state may introduce military forces into the territory of another to assist the government for various purposes, including maintaining internal order. On the other hand, a state may not introduce arms or armed forces into a country without the consent of its government, surely not to support any groups hostile to the government. . . .

That asymmetry, however, begins to erode as rebellion succeeds or moves to civil war. At some stage, the law's partiality to the incumbent government ceases, and it is no longer lawful for another state to help either the incumbent or its adversaries by military force (perhaps even by sale of arms). The Charter's fundamental commitment to state autonomy requires that states allow internal developments in another country to have their way. External forces must not significantly affect the territorial integrity of the receiving country or its political independence. Hence, external forces may not be introduced to help effect or prevent secession or to assist either side in civil war. The difficulty is that one cannot measure when aid to a government stops being that and becomes intervention in civil war.

That is the command of the law of the Charter. It has often been flouted. Inevitably, especially in an ideologically divided world, unlawful military intervention on one side has invited counterinterventions. Some commentators have supported the view that if a state has unlawfully intervened on one side of an internal struggle, another state should be permitted to counter that intervention. . . . Above all, the right to counterintervene does not include the right to attack the third-state intervenor. . . .

Like the law of the Charter on the use of force generally, the law on intervention does not make ideological distinctions. . . . A state may not intervene to help rebels, whether against a totalitarian or a democratic regime. If external forces intervene on one side of a civil war, perhaps other states may intervene on the other, but again regardless of the ideology of either side. . . .

The law of the Charter needs clarification and perhaps modest modification in regard to counterintervention.

Notes and Questions

1. In its judgment in *Nicaragua,* the ICJ decided that the United States had, among other things, violated the customary international law not to invervene in the affairs of another state "by training, arming, equipping, financing and supplying the *contra* forces or otherwise encouraging, supporting and aiding military and paramilitary activities in and against Nicaragua." (The vote was 12-3 on this.) The ICJ also found that the United States had violated its 1956 Treaty of Friendship, Commerce, and Navigation (FCN) with Nicaragua by laying mines in the internal or territorial waters of Nicaragua (14-1) and by declaring a general embargo on trade with Nicaragua (12-3). The ICJ further decided that the United States was under an obligation to make reparation to Nicaragua for the violations of customary international law and for the breaches of the FCN treaty. (For more history of the case before and after this judgment, see Chapter 4 at page 296.)

2. In his discussion of the present legal issues regarding military intervention and counterintervention, does Professor Henkin sometimes fail to distinguish between generally accepted principles of international law and what he presumably would want them to be? For example, Henkin writes that "a state may not introduce arms . . . into a country without the consent of its government, surely not to support any groups hostile to the government." Is that statement consistent with the ICJ's judgment in the *Nicaragua* case regarding "the provision of arms to the opposition in another State"? In paragraph 230 of the judgment, the Court said:

> As regards El Salvador, the Court has found . . . that it is satisfied that between July 1979 and the early months of 1981, an intermittent flow of arms was routed via the territory of Nicaragua to the armed opposition in the country. . . . Even assuming that the supply of arms to the opposition of El Salvador could be treated as imputable to the Government of Nicaragua, to justify invocation of the right of collective self-defense in customary international law, it would have to be equated with an armed attack by Nicaragua on El Salvador. . . . [T]he Court is unable to consider that,

in customary international law, the provision of arms to the opposition in another State constitutes an armed attack on the State. Even at a time when the arms flow was at its peak, and again assuming the participation of the Nicaraguan Government, that would not constitute such armed attack.

See also paragraph 195.

3. Professor Henkin also says that "external forces may not be introduced . . . to assist either side in civil war." How clear an international law principle is that at present? Is intervention in a civil war prohibited by the U.N. Charter? As for customary international law, Henkin recognizes that it was abused during the Spanish civil war of the 1930s. Moreover, intervention in a civil war was one of the models for viewing U.S. intervention in Vietnam. (See the Henkin excerpt on Vietnam above.)

4. Are there even more ambiguities in today's international law norms than Professor Henkin suggests?

g. Dealing with Terrorists

International law principles also seem less than precise when it comes to dealing with terrorists. An initial question is, Who is a terrorist (versus, say, a freedom fighter)? A further question is, What are the responsibilities of the "host" country (where the terrorist organization or individual is located) to take action? Then there is the issue of what actions another country whose officials or citizens are the target of a terrorist action might take unilaterally against terrorists located in the host country. The Sept. 11 attacks and U.S. and world response to them has provided possible answers to some of these questions, while further complicating the issues raised by others. (A case study regarding September 11 and its aftermath appears at Chapter 1.E.)

The initial obstacle to creating a coherent international approach for combating terrorism is the absence of an agreed definition. This obstacle is sometimes expressed by the saying, "One person's terrorist is another person's freedom fighter." This statement has been applied to such groups as Palestinian militants in the Middle East, Kashmiri resistance groups in India and Pakistan, and pro- or anti-Communist rebel groups all over the world during the Cold War.

As a result, none of the 12 multilateral treaties on terrorism adopted by the United Nations since 1963 contains an explicit definition of terrorism, but usually fall back to the next best alternative, the functional approach of outlawing specific acts, such as airplane hijacking, assaults on diplomats, and taking hostages. The definition of these prohibited activities sometimes includes the element that the act be done for the purpose of influencing political authorities in a country. (The United States is a party to all 12 conventions.) Attempts to be more specific have foundered on the insistence of certain countries and blocs on excluding particular groups from the definition. Despite the world's reaction to the events of September 11, 2001, there seems little chance that a comprehensive convention on terrorism will emerge from the United Nations in the near future.

In September 2001, President Bush declared that any state harboring terrorists would be held accountable for the acts of the terrorists. This policy justified the attacks on and destruction of the Taliban regime in Afghanistan in response to the

Sept. 11 attacks. The idea of punishing a host state for sponsoring terrorism goes back further, however. In 1986, the Reagan Administration sent U.S. planes to bomb targets in Libya in response to a discotheque bombing in Germany that killed two and injured several other U.S. soldiers. Abraham Sofaer was Legal Adviser to the Department of State when the United States bombed Libya. The following is an excerpt of his 1989 speech taking an assertive view toward U.S. actions against terrorists.

Abraham Sofaer, Terrorism, the Law, and National Defense
126 Mil. L. Rev. 89, 90-122 (1989)

In the realm of international law, several legal concepts have been invoked that would impose serious limits on strategic flexibility. The most significant of these is the narrow view of self defense recently espoused by the International Court of Justice (ICJ) in *Nicaragua v. United States*. Narrow views of self defense give terrorists and their state sponsors substantial advantages. . . .

. . . The United States has long assumed that the inherent right of self defense potentially applies against any illegal use of force, and that it extends to any group or State that can properly be regarded as responsible for such activities.

These assumptions are supported in customary practice. A substantial body of authority exists, however, which advocates positions that, if adhered to by the U.S., would largely undermine this or any other nation's capacity to defend itself against state-sponsored terrorism. The principal limitations proposed in these sources are: (a) an unrealistically limited view of the meaning of "armed attack"; (b) artificially restrictive views of necessity and proportionality; (c) restrictions on the situations in which terrorist groups or States can be held responsible for terrorist actions; and (d) absolute deference to the principle of territorial integrity. . . .

. . . The limitations of necessity and proportionality are traditional, civilizing constraints on the use of force. Respect for such traditional doctrine is undermined, however, when States are expected to accept too high a degree of risk of substantial injury before being allowed to defend themselves or to accept a continuation of unlawful aggression because of a tit-for-tat limit on military response. The law should not be construed to prevent military planners from implementing measures they reasonably consider necessary to prevent unlawful attacks. . . .

The principle of territorial integrity is a major — and proper — legal constraint to taking actions against terrorists or States that support terrorism. World-class terrorists need bases in which to live and work, to train, to store their weapons, to make their bombs, and to hold hostages. The States in which they locate are almost invariably unable or unwilling to extradite them. An extradition request in such cases will do nothing more than reveal that we know their location, an advantage that would thereby be squandered. The only possible remedies against such terrorists often would require infringement of the territorial integrity of the State in which they are located.

Breaches of territorial integrity are always serious. Control over territory is one of the most fundamental attributes of sovereignty. . . .

Nonetheless, territorial integrity is not entitled to absolute deference in international law, and our national defense requires that we claim the right to act within the territory of other States in appropriate circumstances, however infrequently we may choose for prudential reasons to exercise it. Territorial integrity is not the only principle of international law that deserves protection. All States are obliged to control persons within their borders to ensure that they do not utilize their territory as a base for criminal activity. Most States have also voluntarily undertaken to prosecute or to extradite persons for the most common terrorist crimes, such as air piracy and sabotage. When States violate these obligations, and especially when they are implicated in the conduct of the terrorists involved, other States are seriously affected. These States are left in some cases with no option for ending the threat from such terrorists short of violating in some manner the territorial integrity of the State that has violated its own international responsibilities. . . .

The United States also supports the right of a State to strike terrorists within the territory of another State where the terrorists are using that territory as a location from which to launch terrorist attacks and where the State involved has failed to respond effectively to a demand that the attacks be stopped. . . .

. . . We are not struggling against the rule of law, but for a rule of law that reflects our values and methods: the values of custom, tolerance, fairness, and equality; and the methods of reasoned, consistent, and principled analysis. . . .

Judge Sofaer's view was not commonly accepted in the 1980s and 1990s. While U.S., British, and French vetoes blocked a Security Council resolution, the General Assembly voted 79 to 28 to condemn the U.S. attack on Libya. By contrast, the 2001-2002 campaign in Afghanistan was accepted by nearly every U.N. member, including Libya. Jack Beard, a law professor and a senior lawyer in the Department of Defense, analyzes the difference.

Jack M. Beard, America's New War on Terror: The Case for Self-Defense Under International Law

25 Harv. J.L. & Pub. Poly. 559, 563-564, 573-589 (2002)

Previous military actions by the United States against terrorist-supporting states elicited varying responses from the international community and the United Nations. In the case of the 1986 raid on Libya, the United States action was not widely supported. A resolution condemning the U.S. action was introduced in the U.N. Security Council but was vetoed by the United States, France, and the United Kingdom. The U.N. General Assembly adopted a resolution condemning the United States for the attack by a vote of seventy-nine to twenty-eight, with thirty-three abstentions. . . .

. . . While a significant part of the reaction of the United Nations to America's raid on Libya can be explained by Cold War politics, serious legal questions were also raised. A perceived lack of evidence tying the West Berlin discotheque bombing and other terrorist activities to Libya, questions regarding the propriety under Article 51 of an armed response against a state for the actions of terrorists, the suggestion of retaliatory motives, related arguments against the necessity and proportionality of U.S. actions, and absence of an "armed attack" owing in part to an isolated murder of American servicemen abroad, all contributed to criticism by states and scholars of the raid on Libya as an illegitimate act of self-defense. The unprecedented response of the U.N. Security Council and the international community in general to the September 11 terrorist attacks on the United States provides a stark contrast to the reaction to the raid on Libya. Assessing a number of factual and legal distinctions between the circumstances surrounding the September 11 attacks and previous terrorist attacks giving rise to the use of force by the United States helps to demonstrate the propriety of the most recent exercise of self-defense under Article 51 and customary international law. . . .

. . . Before the September 11 terrorist attacks, the U.N. Security Council had never approved a resolution explicitly invoking and reaffirming the inherent right of individual and collective self-defense in response to a particular terrorist attack. . . .

VII. FACTS AND LAW: DISTINGUISHING BETWEEN THE SEPTEMBER 11 ATTACKS AND PREVIOUS TERRORIST ATTACKS

The actions of the U.N. Security Council and the decisive, widespread, and unprecedented actions and statements by states supporting the U.S. right of self-defense against the September 11 terrorist attacks are compelling evidence of the international community's assessment of the applicability of Article 51 of the U.N. Charter to America's new war on terror. These state actions also highlight various factual and legal distinctions between the September 11 terrorist attacks and previous terrorist attacks that resulted in more widely criticized uses of force by the United States against terrorist-supporting states.

A.   Location of the Attack

Opponents of the United States's previous resorts to force in the face of terrorist acts argued that states may only respond to terrorist attacks within their own territory and that attacks on nationals overseas cannot meet the "armed attack" requirement of Article 51. This . . . is much debated among scholars, yet it is clearly not at issue with regard to the September 11 attacks. . . .

B.   Magnitude of the Attack and Sustained and Continuing Terrorist Campaign

Another objection to the 1986 action against Libya was that isolated or "sporadic or minor attacks do not warrant such a serious and conspicuous response as the use of force in self-defence." Such a criticism does not appear to be applicable with regard to the September 11 attacks. . . . [E]ven the U.N. General Assembly has taken the unusual step of meeting in a special session to condemn the "heinous acts of terrorism, which have caused enormous loss of human life, destruction and damage in the cities of New York and Washington, D.C., and in Pennsylvania.". . .

C.   Evidentiary Support

Another criticism of previous American uses of force against states supporting terrorists is the perceived lack of evidence tying the terrorists to a particular organization and tying that organization to a particular state. Some critics have argued that the U.S. Government has shown "consistent disregard of evidentiary showings" in such previous uses of force and that it has effectively taken the position that the factual premises of these actions were unreviewable. Evidentiary concerns about the identity of the bombers of the West Berlin discotheque and their ties to Libya were aggravated by the inability of the Reagan Administration to fully disclose the compelling records of intercepted communications between Tripoli and the Libyan Embassy in East Berlin. . . .

In contrast to some previous uses of force against terrorists, the U.S. Government made presentations of relevant sensitive and classified information about the attacks of September 11 to a number of foreign governments and subjected this evidence to considerable scrutiny. The result was decisive. . . .

Any denials of responsibility by Osama bin Laden have also been undermined by his own remarks. His statements alone have been persuasive evidence of his guilt to some government leaders. . . .

Even clearer is the evidentiary link between the Al Qaeda organization and the Taliban Regime, a link explicitly recognized by the U.N. Security Council in its imposition of economic sanctions on the Taliban Regime. Statements by the British Government that Osama bin Laden's Al Qaeda and the Taliban have a "close and mutually dependent alliance" were further demonstrated to be true by discoveries of Al Qaeda facilities and infrastructure throughout Afghanistan after the Taliban's retreat from these areas.

VIII. ATTRIBUTING STATE RESPONSIBILITY FOR TERRORIST ACTIONS UNDER INTERNATIONAL LAW

While a link between the Taliban Regime and the Al Qaeda terrorists who launched the September 11 attacks is well established, the issue of attributing state responsibility for these terrorist actions raises a number of international legal questions. This is particularly true in finding that the Taliban Regime's support, protection, or sponsorship of terrorists constitutes an "armed attack" under Article 51 of the U.N. Charter or that it violates Article 2(4) of the U.N. Charter. . . . [I]t is . . . fairly well established that a state that directly supports and sends out armed bands or groups to carry out serious acts of armed force against another state is itself responsible for an act of aggression. It is not difficult to maintain the integrity of the U.N. Charter by applying these concepts to states that are closely affiliated with terrorist organizations, directly support their activities, and assist them in orchestrating devastating attacks against other states. International practice now increasingly confirms state responsibility for such terrorist actions against other states.

While the extent of affiliation, tolerance, or support of terrorist organizations can be a source of debate in holding states accountable for terrorist acts, the international community appears to be increasingly willing to apply international legal prohibitions, including Article 2(4) of the U.N. Charter, to states that sponsor or support terrorists, and even to apply these prohibitions to states that merely acquiesce in their organized activities on their territory. The attitude of states in this area has been evolving towards stricter standards of state responsibility and imposition of clearer obligations. . . .

[A]cting in the wake of the September 11 terrorist attacks, the U.N. Security Council . . . clearly established state responsibility for terrorist acts and decisively imposed related obligations on the members of the United Nations under Chapter VII of the U.N. Charter. . . . U.N. Security Council Resolution 1373 requires all states to undertake a wide range of measures to prevent, suppress, and criminalize the financing, planning, preparation, and execution of terrorist acts. The Council further *decided* that all states shall, *inter alia:*

> Refrain from providing any support, active or passive, to entities or persons involved in terrorist acts, including by suppressing recruitment of members of terrorist groups and eliminating the supply of weapons to terrorists; . . . Deny safe haven to those who finance, plan, support, or commit terrorist acts, or provide safe havens; . . . Prevent those who finance, plan, facilitate or commit terrorist acts from using their respective territories for those purposes against other States or their citizens. . . .

IX. NECESSITY AND PROPORTIONALITY

A final legal issue that has given rise to substantial debate among scholars regarding previous uses of force against terrorism is the requirement of necessity and proportionality. It is a well established rule of customary international law that even when a state is lawfully engaged in the exercise of its inherent right of self-defense, its use of force must be limited to that force necessary to defend against the attack and must be proportionate. Striking back against an enemy without a necessity for self-defense in a punitive act of retaliation is another matter; prevailing scholarly opinion now holds that acts of armed reprisal are not permitted under the U.N. Charter or customary international law, although this is a much debated proposition in the context of responding to, and deterring, terrorist attacks. In fact, the distinction between reprisal and self-defense may sometimes be difficult to discern in responding to specific acts of terror.

It is clear, however, that legal arguments regarding necessity, proportionality, and reprisal figured prominently in criticism of the U.S. raid on Libya in 1986. In criticizing that and other uses of force, some commentators have argued that the doctrine of necessity in self-defense requires "immediacy.". . . In this regard, some writers are fond of citing Secretary of State Daniel Webster and his statement to Lord Ashburton . . . in the *Caroline* dispute. . . .

Webster's comments in the *Caroline* dispute were, however, related to the standards applicable to a state launching a preemptive strike or engaging in a form of anticipatory self-defense and cannot be relied on to establish a rule prohibiting a state from responding with force to repulse and end on-going acts of aggression after that state has been the target of repeated attacks and faces a near certainty that more attacks will follow. In fact, an unnecessarily strict or overly broad reading of the necessity requirement could prohibit almost all "after the fact" acts of self-defense except those that are immediately necessary to repel an attack or prevent being overwhelmed. Such a strict and self-defeating version of necessity expansively based on the *Caroline* test does not appear to be consistent with the right of self-defense under customary international law . . .

The use of force by the United States in response to the September 11 terrorist attacks seems, however, to involve facts which make the exercise of the inherent right of self-defense under the U.N. Charter less vulnerable to the criticism that U.S. actions are not necessary and proportionate or that they constitute prohibited acts of retaliation, revenge, or reprisal. . . . [The September 11 attacks] were part of an on-going terrorist campaign over many years that has been directed by the Al Qaeda terrorist network against the United States, and it is a campaign which Al Qaeda and Taliban leaders have insisted must and will continue until America capitulates or is destroyed. . . .

In this context, the United States and its allies seem to have had little choice but to act forcefully in self-defense and defeat the Al Qaeda network and its sponsor, the Taliban Regime, particularly after having given the Taliban several opportunities to avoid an armed response. . . . In the context of a genuine armed attack, even noted writers that argue for strict limits on the use of force and a narrow interpretation of self-defense under Article 51 concede that . . . self-defense, while subject to limitations of necessity and proportionality, "includes a right both to repel the armed attack and to take the war to the aggressor State in order effectively to terminate the attack and prevent a recurrence."

Notes and Questions

1. Who is a terrorist? Do you agree with the functional approach that has emerged that focuses on the activities that individuals or organizations undertake? If so, which activities should be considered terrorist actions? For example, should suicide bombings of civilians always be considered terrorism?

If a group is oppressed by an authoritarian government or a foreign occupying power, should it have some ability to resist with force? If so, what are the limits of this ability? For example, during the Saddam Hussein regime, should an Iraqi Kurd have had the right to plant a bomb in a civilian part of Baghdad or is that terrorism? Should the Iraqi Kurd have had the right to attack an isolated Iraqi military outpost or is this terrorism? Moving to another part of the world, if a member of a splinter group of the Irish Republican Army bombs a British army base in Northern Ireland, should he be considered a terrorist? If he explodes a bomb in a public market in a Protestant town in Northern Ireland?

2. If the host country does not take action against terrorists found within its borders, should it be required to turn these people over to another country for prosecution for acts committed in the other country or against the target country's citizens?

3. The U.N. Security Council criticized Libya for not complying with requests for the extradition of suspected bombers of Pan Am flight 103 that blew up in 1988 over Lockerbie, Scotland, killing 270 people, including 189 U.S. citizens. The Security Council also imposed sanctions against Libya in 1992 and 1993, pending Libya's renunciation of terrorism and extradition of the suspects to either the United States or the United Kingdom, both of which had sought their extradition.

Libya then filed a case in the International Court of Justice, claiming that the United States and the United Kingdom did not have the right to compel it to extradite the bombing suspects under the applicable treaties. In 1998, the International Court of Justice decided, over the objections of the United States and Britain, that it had jurisdiction to hear the case.

In response, at least in part, to the world pressure reflected in the U.N. resolutions and economic sanctions, President Qaddafi turned over the two accused Libyans in a carefully negotiated arrangement whereby they would be tried by a Scottish court applying Scottish law (because the plane blew up over Scotland), but meeting on more neutral ground in The Hague, Netherlands. (See further developments in Chapter 4 at p. 109 note.)

4. The United States has a number of laws that can provide jurisdiction to U.S. courts for terrorist acts abroad against U.S. citizens and sometimes even for acts against non-U.S. citizens. (See the Alien Tort Statute and Torture Victim Protection Act, discussed in Chapter 3, and 18 U.S.C. §2333, which is discussed in Chapter 7.) Also, for certain acts, the Foreign Sovereign Immunities Act denies sovereign immunity to those foreign states (or their officials, employees, or agents) who have been designated as supporting terrorists (see Chapter 6 at page 588). Note that terrorist acts occurring in the United States would also be subject to U.S. federal and state law regarding the various acts — for example, murder and destruction of property.

5. Should Article 51 require that self-defense be a response to an armed attack against the "territorial integrity or political independence" of a state?

6. What should be the standard for holding the host state liable for the activities of terrorists? In an analogous area, what was the ICJ's standard in the *Nicaragua* case for finding the United States responsible or not for the activities of the contras?

7. On August 20, 1998, the United States fired several dozen Tomahawk cruise missiles against targets in Afghanistan and Sudan. The Afghanistan target was an Al Qaeda training complex. Al Qaeda was believed to be responsible for the simultaneous bombings of U.S. embassies in Kenya and Tanzania on August 7, which resulted in about 225 people being killed (including 12 Americans) and thousands more being injured. There was also evidence that a meeting of high-level terrorists was scheduled at the Afghan site around the time of the missile attack.

The target destroyed in Sudan was a factory that U.S. officials said made a precursor element used in the production of a potent nerve gas and that the factory owner had financial ties to Osama bin Laden. Sudan denied this, saying that the factory was a pharmaceutical plant. Later news reports indicated that the U.S. planning for the attack had been very closely held within the Administration and that some of the evidence used for the Sudan attack might not have been fully vetted by the U.S. intelligence community.

After touring the seriously damaged U.S. embassy facilities in Africa, but before the U.S. strikes, Secretary of State Albright had said: "It is like being in a war. . . . I think we are embarked on a venture in which we have to deal over the long run with what is a very serious threat to our way of life." After the U.S. military response, President Clinton described them as acts of self-defense and of retribution.

Do you believe that the U.S. attack on the Afghanistan training complex was justified under Article 51 of the U.N. Charter? How much should the U.S. be required to try to work with Afghan officials in advance to get the Afghan government to take action against the terrorists within its borders, before the United States launches its own strikes? Does the U.S. attack meet the criteria for necessity and proportionality? Can it also be justified under the customary international law theory of reprisals?

Turning to the attack on the Sudan plant, how definite must the evidence be that the plant is being used for terrorist activities before an attack is justified? The

Sudanese owner of the plant later filed suits in the United States against the U.S. government for wrongful destruction of the plant. In March 2003, the U.S. Court of Federal Claims dismissed the suit that alleged a taking. As for the validity of the U.S. reasons for the attack, the court noted that "the legitimacy . . . of the [U.S.] Government's action must be conceded in takings proceedings before this Court," so that the Sudanese owner could not question there President Clinton's justification. El-Shifa Pharmaceutical Industries Co. v. United States, No. 00-443L, 2003 U.S. Claims LEXIS 47, at *49 (Fed. Cl. March 14, 2003). On the other hand, the U.S. government, which had earlier frozen some of the Sudan owner's bank accounts, lifted that freeze possibly to avoid trying to defend its action in court, though there was no U.S. admission of error. On a different issue of U.S. compensation rather than the reasons for the attack, the *El-Shifa* court explained that "[t]he Constitutional protection afforded by the Takings Clause is not intended to compensate for destruction of enemy war-making property through the exercise of military force." Id. at *41.

8. The case study at Chapter 1.E. addresses in some detail the September 11 terrorist attacks and the U.S. and world response to them. Now that you have read and thought more about the international law governing the use of force, was the U.S. campaign in Afghanistan justified under Article 51? Could it be justified under a theory of reprisal? Does the removal of the Taliban and installation of a new government meet the requirement of proportionality?

Despite the loss of Afghanistan, Al Qaeda remains a threat, although perhaps a reduced one. The United States and its allies have continued to hunt down and arrest or kill terrorist leaders and operatives around the world, although many remained at large as of February 2003, including apparently bin Laden himself. Does the doctrine of self-defense permit the United States to keep forces in Afghanistan to prevent Al Qaeda from re-establishing itself there? What if Hamid Karzai or a future Afghan president asked the United States to withdraw? Does Article 51 permit the United States to send forces (ranging from small highly trained units to larger groups) into Yemen, Pakistan, Malaysia, or Indonesia if Al Qaeda operatives are located there, but the government in that country tells the United States to keep its forces out?

In November 2002, an unmanned Predator aircraft, controlled by U.S. government operators nearby, fired its missile and killed six Al Qaeda members in Yemen, including one who may have helped to plan the attack in 2000 on the U.S.S. Cole warship when it was in a Yemeni port as well as one person who may have been a U.S. citizen. Is this use of force justified under Article 51? Is it necessary and proportionate?

9. On a more general level, what should U.S. policy be toward the principles in the U.N. Charter and customary international law limiting the use of force? Should the United States embrace them wholeheartedly? As Professor Franck discussed above, should the United States emphasize that the U.N. Charter is an instrument with a "capacity for adaption through the interpretative practice of its organs and members"? Hence, could the United States argue that the meaning of some of the provisions of the Charter have evolved through practice? If so, how should the United States now interpret the text of Articles 2(4) and 51? Should the United States formally espouse the Reagan Doctrine, as described above? Should the United States continue to assert the right to take preemptive actions against some emerging threats, as the Bush Administration announced in September 2002?

10. If the United States seeks to clarify or change the principles (e.g., regarding terrorism or regarding intervention and counterintervention), what is the best way

to do this? Should the United States seek actual amendments in the U.N. Charter? Should the United States seek resolutions in the Security Council or General Assembly? should the United States act unilaterally?

11. At least one scholar takes a pessimistic view of countries either trying to live within the U.N. Charter's provisions or even trying to amend them at present. Professor Michael Glennon writes that, to the degree that states use force in circumstances not permitted under the U.N. Charter, it is their practice and not the Charter that governs. As determined by state practice, he argues, international law is far more permissive of force than the Charter would indicate.

Michael J. Glennon, The Fog of Law: Self-Defense, Inherence, and Incoherence in Article 51 of the United Nations Charter

25 Harv. J.L. & Pub. Poly. 539, 540, 557-558 (2002)

[I]nternational "rules" concerning use of force are no longer regarded as obligatory by states. Between 1945 and 1999, two-thirds of the members of the United Nations — 126 states out of 189 — fought 291 interstate conflicts in which over 22 million people were killed. This series of conflicts was capped by the Kosovo campaign in which nineteen NATO democracies representing 780 million people flagrantly violated the Charter. [The Kosovo campaign is discussed below at page 1077.] The international system has come to subsist in a parallel universe of two systems, one *de jure*, the other *de facto*. The *de jure* system consists of illusory rules that would govern the use of force among states in a platonic world of forms, a world that does not exist. The *de facto* system consists of actual state practice in the real world, a world in which states weigh costs against benefits in regular disregard of the rules solemnly proclaimed in the all-but-ignored *de jure* system. The decaying *de jure* catechism is overly schematized and scholastic, disconnected from state behavior, and unrealistic in its aspirations for state conduct.

The upshot is that the Charter's use-of-force regime has all but collapsed. This includes, most prominently, the restraints of the general rule banning use of force among states, set out in Article 2(4). The same must be said, I argue here, with respect to the supposed restraints of Article 51 limiting the use of force in self-defense. Therefore, I suggest that Article 51, as authoritatively interpreted by the International Court of Justice, cannot guide responsible U.S. policy-makers in the U.S. war against terrorism in Afghanistan or elsewhere. . . .

In one sense, the conclusion that Article 51 has no practical force follows *a fortiori* from my earlier argument: If there is no authoritative general prohibition of use of force, it makes no sense to consider the breadth of a possible exception. Yet an examination of Article 51 reveals a measure of inconsistency, illogic, and, indeed, incoherence that provides independent grounds for questioning its importuned restraints in decisions concerning use of force. The received interpretation of Article 51 consists in hopelessly unrealistic prescriptions as to how states should behave. Its more concrete sub-rules illustrate why policymakers have come to ignore the Charter's use-of-force regime in fashioning how states behave. . . .

. . . No rules will work that do not reflect underlying geopolitical realities. The use-of-force regime set out in the U.N. Charter failed because the Charter sought to impose rules that are out-of-sync with the way states actually behave. A new use-of-force regime that does work will have to rest far more firmly upon actual patterns of practice that reveal, with solid empirical evidence, what regulation of force is possible and what is not. . . . There is no use in telling ghost stories, Holmes said, to people who do not believe in ghosts.

At this point, the consensus within the international community on underlying values is not sufficient to sustain an authentic legalist regime that would subordinate the use of force to pre-agreed limits. One person's terrorist remains another's freedom fighter. What is considered justified humanitarian intervention in one part of the world is a seen as a violation of state sovereignty in another. What is self-defense to one state is aggression, armed reprisal, armed attack, intervention, or forcible counter-measures to another. No advance in the art of legal drafting can bridge the enormous gulf that divides the international community over what constitutes acceptable use of force. Any linguistic formula that purported to do so would necessarily consist of a chain of endlessly contested weasel words. Perhaps that chasm will narrow as more active phases of the war against terrorism wind down. The conclusion of great conflicts of the past presented possibilities at Vienna, Versailles, and San Francisco to re-shape the contours of international legalist institutions.

Even if no comprehensive re-integration or formal revision of the legalist order occurs, patterns of cooperation that develop in prosecuting the war on terrorism can still congeal gradually and incrementally into post-war legalist regimes. In the meantime, however, states will continue to judge for themselves what measure of force is required for their self-defense — action that is appropriate, it must always be borne in mind, not because defense is permitted by the U.N. Charter, but because defense is necessary for survival and survival is intrinsic in the very fact of statehood.

For a fuller exposition of Professor Glennon's views, see Michael J. Glennon, Why the Security Council Failed, 82 For. Aff. 16 (May/June 2003).

His thesis has encountered considerable criticism. While states have often interpreted the legal norms for their own purposes, no responsible state has been willing to argue that the rules do not apply. Indeed, states and others feel the need to explain how their steps are consistent with international legal norms. For example, when the Bush Administration announced its new policy of preemptive options in September 2002, the analysis included the observation that: "For centuries, international law recognized that nations need not suffer an attack before they can take actions to defend themselves against forces that present an imminent danger of attack." The government's analysis moved from this historical and legal discussion to say, "We must adapt the concept of imminent threat to the capabilities and objectives of today's adversaries." (See Note 5 above at page 994.)

Most scholars argue that the Charter remains international law. Some, like Professor Mary Ellen O'Connell, make the point that, even if a rule is violated, it is still the rule if the international community accepts it as the rule.

As long as inconsistent state practice is treated as law violation and not as practice moving toward a new customary rule, the rules remain viable. If the international community continues to express support for the rules — another form of state practice — the rules remain. This is particularly pertinent with regard to the United States. The United States has not heretofore argued for new rules. It has not stated that the existing rules are out-moded, or that its practice is aiming at developing new law. Until the Kosovo intervention, the United States justified its uses of force in terms of the Charter. And even after Kosovo, American officials have not sought a general rule-change. [The Myth of Preemptive Self Defense 15 (2002).]

Professor Franck takes the more nuanced approach that the principles of the U.N. Charter have adapted to the interpretative practice of states and the U.N. organs. (See discussion at 981.) What position do you support?

B. COLLECTIVE INTERVENTION: U.N. AND REGIONAL PEACEKEEPING EFFORTS

Besides enunciating principles regarding the use of force, the U.N. Charter allows for the use of force and peacekeeping operations by the U.N. itself, and it also recognizes the possibility of efforts by regional organizations such as NATO and the Organization of American States. The U.N. efforts have been more frequent in recent years and there have also been activities by the regional groups. Overall, collective intervention has increasingly occurred or been actively considered for internal conflicts.

This section first analyzes the U.N.'s efforts, including with respect to Iraq from the time of its invasion of Kuwait in 1990 through 2003. The section then turns to the activities of regional organizations, especially NATO's bombing campaign against the former Republic of Yugoslavia over its repression of Albanians in Kosovo.

1. *U.N. Use of Force and Peacekeeping Efforts*

Chapter VII of the U.N. Charter has several articles dealing with U.N. action with respect to threats to the peace and acts of aggression. Among the key ones are Articles 39-42.

Chapter VII.   Action with Respect to Threats to the Peace, Breaches of the Peace, and Acts of Aggression

Article 39

The Security Council shall determine the existence of any threat to the peace, breach of the peace, or act of aggression and shall make recommendations, or decide what measures shall be taken in accordance with Articles 41 and 42, to maintain or restore international peace and security.

Article 40

In order to prevent an aggravation of the situation, the Security Council may, before making the recommendations or deciding upon the measures provided for in Article 39, call upon the parties concerned to comply with such provisional measures as it deems necessary or desirable. Such provisional measures shall be without prejudice to the rights, claims, or position of the parties concerned. The Security Council shall duly take account of failure to comply with such provisional measures.

Article 41

The Security Council may decide what measures not involving the use of armed force are to be employed to give effect to its decisions, and it may call upon the Members of the United Nations to apply such measures. These may include complete or partial interruption of economic relations and of rail, sea, air, postal, telegraphic, radio, and other means of communication, and the severance of diplomatic relations.

Article 42

Should the Security Council consider that measures provided for in Article 41 would be inadequate or have proved to be inadequate, it may take such action by air, sea, or land forces as may be necessary to maintain or restore international peace and security. Such action may include demonstrations, blockade, and other operations by air, sea, or land forces of Members of the United Nations.

Article 25 makes a Security Council decision to use force binding on all Members, which are obliged "to accept and carry out decisions of the Security Council. . . ."

Chapter VII also includes Article 43, which envisioned that the U.N. itself would have the military forces to implement the Security Council decisions to use force. Article 43 provides that all Members shall "undertake to make available to the Security Council, on its call and in accordance with a special agreement or agreements, armed forces, assistance, and facilities . . . necessary for the purpose of maintaining international peace and security." The special agreement(s) "shall govern the numbers and types of forces, their degree of readiness and general location. . . ."

For a variety of reasons, probably including each Member's concerns about maintaining control over its military forces and the start of the Cold War soon after 1945, the U.N. has entered into no such special agreements. However, as Professor Thomas Franck notes, "the adaptive capacity of the Charter has functioned dramatically and controversially to fill the vacuum created by Article 43's nonimplementation." Professor Franck then goes on to explain how.

Thomas M. Franck, Recourse to Force
24-40 (2002)

Faced with its failure to establish a police militia under Article 43, the Security Council has adapted by using, or authorizing states to use, *ad hoc* forces put together for the purpose of responding to a specific crisis. . . .

The Korean War is the first example of the Security Council's authorizing *ad hoc* collective measures in the absence of Article 43 forces. On June 25, 1950,

Secretary-General Trygve Lie reported the previous night's attack by North Korea on the South. Qualifying the-situation as a threat to international peace, he called on the Security Council as the "competent organ" to act at once by determining that the attack was a breach of the peace, calling for a cessation of hostilities, embargoing all "assistance to the North Korean authorities," and calling "upon all Members to render every assistance to the United Nations in the execution of this resolution." This was precisely the response voted by the Council. Its resolution determined that there had been a "breach of the peace" and thereby invoked Article 39, the prerequisite for collective measures under the Charter's Chapter VII.

. . . Resolution 83 of June 27 (passed with only Yugoslavia opposed and with the Soviet Union absent)* recommended . . . "that the Members of the United Nations furnish such assistance to the Republic of Korea as may be necessary to repel the armed attack and to restore international peace and security in the area." On July 7, with the Soviets still absent . . ., the Council recommended that all members providing military assistance make such forces available to a unified military command headed by the US, authorized that command to use the United Nations flag, and requested the US to report "as appropriate" to the Security Council.

Since the Charter makes no provision for a UN military response except with Article 43 forces, the Council's authorization of action in its named by *ad hoc* national contingents — what has since become known as a "coalition of the willing" — represented a creative adaption of the text. The practice of Security Council authorization of action by such coalitions of the willing subsequently became a firmly established part of the UN collective security system. In this first experience, the UN force was constituted by ground forces volunteered by ten states, naval units from eight nations, and air units from five. . . .**

In 1960, the Security Council authorized another coalition of the willing to respond to an appeal by the Government of the Republic of the Congo to restore order and facilitate the removal of Belgian troops from that newly-independent state (see below). Six years later, the Council authorized the British navy to enforce UN sanctions against the break-away white-supremacist regime of Ian Smith in the self-governing Crown Colony of Rhodesia.

Forty year after the Korean episode, the Security Council — still lacking an Article 43-based military capability of its own — once again authorized a massive coalition of the willing: this time to undertake operation "Desert Storm" after Iraq's invasion of Kuwait. As in the earlier instances, the Council, in accordance with Charter Article 39, began by determining that Iraq's actions constituted a breach of the peace to which a collective military response was warranted. That finding was made by a vote of 14-0 with only Yemen abstaining. The resolution as a whole, invoking Chapter VII and requesting member states to "use all necessary means" to reverse Iraqi aggression, passed with only Cuba and Yemen opposed and with China abstaining but not claiming to have cast a veto. [The Iraq situation is discussed in more detail below.]

---

* The Soviet Union was absent because it was boycotting the Council over another issue at the time. — EDS.

** The international force was under the initial command of General Douglas MacArthur, numbered in the tens of thousands, and engaged in major battles. — EDS.

The drafters of the Charter . . . did not envisage such Council-mandated use of force in the absence of an Article 43-based military capability. There is no reason, however, why the Council's responses to aggression cannot be understood as a creative use of Article 42. . . . Textually, Article 42 can stand on its own feet and it now may be said to do so as a result of Council practice. . . .

Article 39 . . . empowers the Council to "take measures" under Article 42 without reference to Article 43, thereby creating room for the Council to order — or, more probably, to call for — states' participation in collective security measures. . . .

If the Council were to *order* states to use force, Article 25 would require all members to "agree and carry out" that decision. To date, however, all the resolutions authorizing *ad hoc* military forces have merely "called on" or "authorized" states to use force. While participation in military action has thus been voluntary, the authority and objectives of *ad hoc* forces have usually been formulated in mandatory terms. For example, in resolution 678, the Security Council speaks of Iraq's "obligation" to "comply" with its demands to restore Kuwaiti sovereignty and authorizes the use of force "to implement" those demands. . . .

There have been several subsequent occasions on which the Security Council has authorized the use of force by states in coalitions of the willing: national military contingents assembled *ad hoc* for a particular task. The Council has also authorized a single state or a regional organization to lead a specified military operation. . . . Thus, on November 30, 1992, the Secretary-General informed the Council that "the situation in Somalia has deteriorated beyond the point at which it is susceptible to peace-keeping treatment." . . . He concluded that "the Security Council now has no alternative but to decide to adopt more forceful measures to secure the humanitarian operations. . . . It would therefore be necessary for the Security Council to make a determination under Article 39 of the Charter that a threat to the peace exists. . . . Promptly, the Security Council made the requisite finding under Chapter VII and authorized the US, and any others "willing," to "use all necessary means" through and *ad hoc* Unified Task Force (UNITAF) to achieve the specified objectives. . . .

It is notable that the Council, in authorizing military intervention in Somalia, followed precisely the requisites of Article 42. . . .

These were not trivial operations. UNITAF engaged 37,000 (primarily American) forces. Its multinational successor, UNOSOM II, deploying 30,000 military personnel, was placed by the Council under the control of the UN Secretary-General and charged with enforcement powers and the task of creating peace, democracy and unity in that riven land. All the more significant is it to note that both operations — engaging the United Nations in an essentially humanitarian intervention with *ad hoc* forces and doing so even in the absence either of a clearly *international* crisis or the consent of Somalia — should have received the unopposed consent of the members of the Security Council. Although few members of the Council thought it prudent to spell out general principles of Charter-interpretation underpinning this use of collective force — and, indeed, in Resolution 794 states took care to note the "unique character" of the crisis to which they were responding — the actions of the Council cannot but be seen as precedent-setting.

Another example of the expansion of the practice of deploying coalitions of the willing is the Council's — again, expressly "exceptional" — authorization, in 1994, of a multinational force under "unified command and control" to "use all necessary means" to facilitate the ouster from Haiti of the military leadership that had overthrown its democratically elected government. On this occasion the resolution was passed by 13-0 with Brazil and China abstaining. Yet another instance is the mandate given by the Security Council to another *ad hoc* force, UNPROFOR, in the former Yugoslavia and the gradual extension of that military mandate to include the defense of Bosnian "safe areas." When those safe areas and the UN personnel in them came under attack, the Security Council authorized air strikes by NATO against Serb heavy weapons. This UN cooperation with NATO, the "double key" approach to air strikes, was later extended by the Council to UNPROFOR operations in Croatia. These resolutions, too, were adopted with the unanimous assent of Council members and widespread approval from states outside the Council. Despite *pro forma* protest from the Russian Federation, the ensuing "bombs of August" constituted the first effective military partnership between a regional military organization and the United Nations' own *ad hoc* multinational force, one that ultimately led to the defeat of Serb forces and, in turn, to the Dayton peace negotiations. . . .

There are other, even more recent examples of coalitions of the willing or individual states being authorized by the Security Council to use force as necessary, usually but not always under Chapter VII. Thus, the Security Council in 1994 authorized France to use "all necessary means" for security and humanitarian ends during the civil turmoil in Rwanda and in 1997 authorized Italy, with others, to deploy forces to prevent civil war in Albania and created INTERFET under Australian leadership to establish security in East Timor. In an effort to contain the civil war in Sierra Leone the Council, in 1999, created UNAMSIL, a force of 11,000 with authority, under Chapter VII, to use force "to afford protection to civilians under imminent threat of physical violence" as well as to "assist . . . the Sierra Leone law enforcement authorities in the discharge of their responsibilities."

It may thus be concluded that the failure to implement Article 43 has not seriously hampered the United Nations in carrying out its mission to provide collective security. On the contrary, *ad hoc* coalitions of the willing, in various logistical configurations, or designated surrogates . . . have been deployed with mandates, including interventions in essentially domestic conflicts for primarily humanitarian purposes. . . . It was the intention of the founders at San Francisco to create a living institution, equipped with dynamic political, administrative, and juridical organs, competent to interpret their own powers under a flexible constituent instrument in response to new challenges. The United Nations has fulfilled that mandate.

The Role of the General Assembly: Original Intent

Another issue left largely uncontemplated and wholly unresolved at Dumbarton Oaks and at San Francisco was this: what would happen if a palpable threat to the peace were to arise but the Security Council (either for lack of a majority or by exercise of the veto) were unable to act? . . . [T]his soon became the principal challenge to the effectiveness of the Charter system.

At Dumbarton Oaks some consideration had been given to allotting a secondary role to the General Assembly for the maintenance of international peace and security, but this was rejected. . . .

. . . Nevertheless, its power, set out in Article 11(2) of the Charter, does permit the Assembly to make recommendations as to "questions relating to the maintenance of international peace and security" as long as it refrains from doing so while "the Security Council is exercising in respect of any dispute or situation the functions assigned to it in the . . . Charter." [Article 12(1).] . . .

This makes all the more remarkable the evolutionary growth of Assembly jurisdiction in matters requiring collective action, including the deployment of military forces. This adaption has occurred through two developments: the adoption of the "Uniting for Peace Resolution" and the invention of "Chapter 6 1/2."

Adapting General Assembly Powers: "Uniting for Peace"

After being absent from the Security Council in June 1950 at the inception of North Korea's aggression, the Soviet Union resumed its participation in August. This presaged renewed deadlock in that organ. Accordingly, in October, at the beginning of the General Assembly's annual meeting, the US introduced an agenda item entitled "United Action for Peace." . . .

. . . Responding to those who thought the proposal distorted the drafters' allocation of functions, US Ambassador Benjamin Cohen reasoned that the Charter should be interpreted flexibly to allow new responses to unanticipated changes of circumstance. He cited US constitutional practice in allowing the making of "executive agreements" supplementing the formal treaty power, and the recognition of "implied powers" of Congress by the Supreme Court's decision in McCulloch v. Maryland. . . .

Whatever Assembly delegates may have made of these references to US constitutional practice, they endorsed the "Uniting for Peace" resolution by a resounding vote of 52-5 with only the Soviet bloc in opposition, and 2 abstentions (India and Argentina). The resolution:

> 1. *Resolves* that if the Security Council, because of lack of unanimity of the permanent members, fails to exercise its primary responsibility for the maintenance of international peace and security in any case where there appears to be a threat to the peace, breach of the peace, or act of aggression, the General Assembly shall consider the matter immediately with a view to making appropriate recommendations to Members for collective measures, including in the case of a breach of the peace or act of aggression the use of armed force when necessary, to maintain or restore international peace and security. . . .

. . . Canadian Secretary of State for External Affairs, Lester B. Pearson conceded that "some honest doubts have been expressed about [the resolution's] constitutionality and . . . the sponsors . . . respect them. Nevertheless . . . [w]e believe that the General Assembly has the power to make recommendations on the subjects dealt with [in the Charter], although it would not have the power to make decisions which would automatically impose commitments or enforce obligations on the Members of the United Nations."

Left unexamined in this explanation, however, is the difference between the effect of a General Assembly resolution on the entire membership—which could only be recommendary—and its potential effect on parties affected by the recommended action, which might well be dispositive. For example . . . [c]ould the Assembly recommend that states deploy force against an aggressor or a genocidal government? . . . While this was scarcely touched upon during the debate, both advocates and opponents of "Uniting for Peace" understood that its effect, in some unspecified instances, would be to empower the Assembly to deploy military force.

The resolution had its first full-scale test in 1956, during the Suez crisis. Israel
having invaded the Sinai, and with Britain and France bombing Suez Canal cities in
anticipation of an expeditionary landing, the US, on October 30, convened the Security Council demanding that it determine that there had been a breach of the
peace and order Israeli forces back to the armistice lines established by the Council's cease-fire order of 11 August 1949.

With the UN Truce Supervisory Organization (UNTSO) already deployed in
the area, the Secretary-General . . . rejected Israel's claim to be acting in self-defense
against an Egyptian attack. The US then introduced a draft resolution calling for
withdrawal of Israeli forces and insisting that Britain and France not intervene. It received 7 votes in favor, with 2 opposed and 2 abstentions. The two negative votes
having been cast by Britain and France, the resolution was vetoed.

Immediately, Yugoslavia . . . offered a resolution which, "taking into account"
that the Council had been prevented "from exercising its primary responsibility for
the maintenance of international peace and security" called for an emergency session of the General Assembly. . . .

The Assembly quickly adopted a resolution that "urged" a ceasefire. As fighting
continued, Canada [successfully] submitted a resolution . . . urgently requesting the
Secretary-General to propose a plan for an international emergency force (UNEF)
to secure and supervise a cease-fire. Such a proposal . . . was adopted by 57-0 with
19 abstentions. It appointed a Chief of Staff . . . and authorized recruitment of a military force "from member states other than the permanent members of the Security
Council." The same day the Secretary-General received Israel's unconditional agreement to a cease-fire, followed one day later by French and British acquiescence.

In his second and final report to the Assembly on the establishment of the new
force, the Secretary-General emphasized that it had been authorized by, and would
operate under, the "Uniting for Peace" resolution. He noted that it was being deployed with the consent of the countries concerned and would be stationed on
Egyptian territory with that country's agreement as "required under generally recognized international law." . . .

. . . The moment, clearly, had been seized. The Organization, adapting to the circumstances of Cold War stasis in the Security Council, had found a new way to authorize, recruit, and deploy the military force necessary to allow it to fulfill its mission.

Less than four years later, the Assembly once again stepped forward to authorize UN military action in the face of Security Council deadlock. The force deployed
in the Congo (ONUC) by the Security Council in July 1960 had become mired in a
dispute between the West and the Soviet Union. . . . On September 17, the US invoked "Uniting for Peace" to convene another emergency session of the General Assembly, which, by a large majority, voted new instructions for the Secretary-General
to "assist the Central Government of the Congo in the restoration and maintenance
of law and order throughout the territory of the Republic of the Congo and to safeguard its unity, territorial integrity and political independence in the interests of international peace and security." This became an important extension of ONUC's
mandate, leading to military operations against the secessionist regime of Katanga
province. Only a year later was the Council again able to assume operational control
over ONUC.

Large expenses were incurred by the United Nations to maintain ONUC's 25,000 military and support personnel. France and Russia, however, refused to pay their share, arguing that ONUC operations authorized by the Assembly were *ultra vires* the Charter. To test the legality of that proposition, the Assembly asked the International Court for an advisory opinion as to whether these expenditures constituted "expenses of the organization" that, under Article 17(2) of the Charter, must "be borne by the Members as apportioned . . .". Since Paris and Moscow were also refusing to pay their share of the cost of UNEF's Sinai operation, the Court was also asked to consider the legality of that earlier Assembly-authorized deployment.

In responding, the Court had to decide on the legality of the General Assembly's role in military operations — UNEF and ONUC — under "Uniting for Peace." The judges, by a majority of 9 to 5, confirmed the *vires* of both.

Article 24 of the Charter states:

> In order to ensure prompt and effective action by the United Nations, its members confer on the Security Council primary responsibility for the maintenance of international peace and security. . . .

The Court reasoned that, while the text was clear in giving the Council "primary" responsibility, that term itself implied a "secondary" responsibility which the Assembly could exercise when the Council was stymied by a veto. In the majority's view, the Assembly has the right "by means of recommendations . . . [to] organize peace-keeping operations" although only "at the request or with the consent, of the States concerned."

In this opinion, the International Court both endorsed and shaped the "Uniting for Peace" Resolution, deeming it a lawful means by which the Assembly could exercise at least some of the Organization's responsibility for maintaining international peace and security when the Security Council was unable to do so. What the opinion leaves undefined is the circumference of the category of "states concerned" whose consent must be obtained. Logically, if there appears a likelihood of conflict between states *A* and *B*, the Assembly, following upon consent by state *B*, could position a peacekeeping force on its territory even without the consent of state *A* as it would have no lawful cause to be "concerned" with that peaceable deployment.

Inventing "Chapter 6 1/2"

"Uniting for Peace" established a new procedure expanding General Assembly jurisdiction over peacekeeping operations. Concurrently, the United Nations began also to expand the kinds of such operations and their missions. Thus, the large UNEF military deployment in 1956 was a new venture both in scale and kind. "Blue helmets," lightly armed but in persuasive numbers, were deployed to observe a truce and to interpose themselves between hostile parties. They were not to engage in combat but, if attacked or hindered, were authorized to defend themselves and their mission. Thirty-eight peacekeeping operations based on this innovative precedent were deployed during the United Nations' first fifty years.

Most of these operations, unlike UNEF, have been authorized by the Security Council, but the resolutions creating them usually do not invoke the Council's unique Chapter VII enforcement powers. Yet, neither do they quite fit the parameters of

United Nations peacekeeping operations, 2000

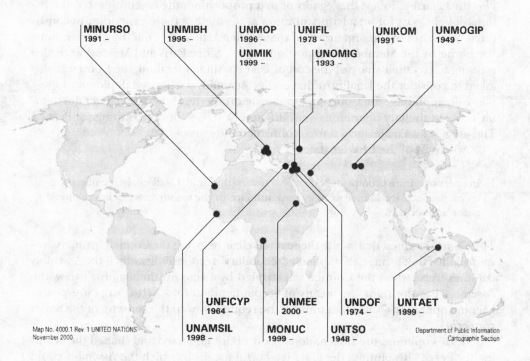

MINURSO 1991 –
UNMIBH 1995 –
UNMOP 1996 –
UNMIK 1999 –
UNIFIL 1978 –
UNOMIG 1993 –
UNIKOM 1991 –
UNMOGIP 1949 –

UNFICYP 1964 –
UNAMSIL 1998 –
UNMEE 2000 –
MONUC 1999 –
UNDOF 1974 –
UNTSO 1948 –
UNTAET 1999 –

Map No. 4000.1 Rev 1 UNITED NATIONS
November 2000

Department of Public Information
Cartographic Section

Chapter VI, which deals only with "negotiation, enquiry, mediation, conciliation, arbitration, judicial settlement, resort to regional agencies or arrangements . . ." (Article 33). Hence, the blue helmets are commonly said to be authorized by "Chapter 6 1/2." This is yet another illustration of the Charter's adaption in practice.

. . . .The space occupied by the fictive Chapter 6 1/2 is fluid, being defined by practice rather than Charter text. A Chapter 6 1/2 operation may begin by the parties' acquiescence in deployment of a peacekeeping force. Over time, however, the operation may incur the hostility of one or several of the parties, requiring either its withdrawal (as in the instance of UNEF in the Sinai) or its difficult and risky transformation into a peace enforcement operation (as with ONUC in the Congo and UNPROFOR in the former Yugoslavia). This phenomenon of "mission-creep" . . . illustrates the ambiguity which may arise in conducting UN "blue helmet" military operations which, although initially not authorized or armed to engage in Chapter VII-based enforcement actions, are assigned new tasks that may involve them in combat operations. Nevertheless, the concept has proven to be of immense utility. . . .

The number of U.N. peacemaking and peacekeeping activities increased exponentially during the 1990s, but has recently declined somewhat. The activities reached a peak in 1994-1995, when over 70,000 civilian and military personnel were serving in 17 peacekeeping missions worldwide. The estimated cost in 1994 was

Current peacekeeping operations*

- United Nations Truce Supervision Organization (UNTSO, established 1948), in the Middle East (strength: military 150; civilian 218);
- United Nations Military Observer Group in India and Pakistan (UNMOGIP, 1949) (military 46; civilian 62);
- United Nations Peacekeeping Force in Cyprus (UNFICYP, 1964) (military 1,213; civilian police 33; civilian 187);
- United Nations Disengagement Observer Force (UNDOF, 1974), in the Syrian Golan Heights (military 1,034; civilian 124);
- United Nations Interim Force in Lebanon (UNIFIL, 1978) (military 5,802; civilian 483);
- United Nations Iraq-Kuwait Observation Mission (UNIKOM, 1991) (military 1,096; civilian 208);
- United Nations Mission for the Referendum in Western Sahara (MINURSO, 1991) (military 230; civilian police 31; civilian 398);
- United Nations Observer Mission in Georgia (UNOMIG, 1993) (military 103; civilian 240);
- United Nations Mission in Bosnia and Herzegovina (UNMIBH, 1995) (military 5; civilian police 1,808; civilian 1,772);
- United Nations Mission of Observers in Prevlaka (UNMOP, 1996), in Croatia (military 27; civilian 9);
- United Nations Interim Administration Mission in Kosovo (UNMIK, 1999) (military 39; civilian police 4,411; civilian 3,920);
- United Nations Mission in Sierra Leone (UNAMSIL, 1999) (military 10,386; civilian police 34; civilian 399);
- United Nations Transitional Administration in East Timor (UNTAET, 1999) (military 7,889; civilian police 1,398; civilian 2,655);
- United Nations Observer Mission in the Democratic Republic of the Congo (MONUC, 1999) (military 207; civilian 358; authorized strength of 5,537 military when conditions allow);
- United Nations Mission in Ethiopia and Eritrea (UNMEE, 2000) (military 1,777; civilian 183; authorized strength of 4,400 military).

*As of December 2000. Source: Basic Facts About the United Nations 74-75 (2000).

about $3.3 billion. The largest operation was Protection Force for the Former Yugoslavia (UNPROFOR), with over 34,000 troops.

As of October 2002, the United Nations had 43,000 civilian and military personnel serving in 15 peacekeeping missions worldwide in the Congo, Ethiopia and Eritrea, Sierra Leone, Western Sahara, East Timor, India-Pakistan, Bosnia and Herzegovina, Cyprus, Georgia, Kosovo, Prevlaka Peninsula, Golan Heights, Iraq-Kuwait, Lebanon, and the Middle East. The approved budget for these efforts for 2002-2003 was about $2.6 billion. Fiscal constraints put a damper on new peacekeeping efforts and created pressures to scale back ongoing activities.

U.S. policy on U.N. peacekeeping missions.   To clarify the U.S. position regarding U.N. peacekeeping efforts, the Clinton Administration established a policy governing U.S. participation in multilateral peacekeeping operations. The policy, known as Presidential Decision Directive (PDD) 25 and completed in May 1994, sets forth several preconditions for U.S. involvement, which are designed to make U.S. involvement in international peacekeeping operations "more selective and more effective."

Under the policy, before the United States agrees to participate in a U.N. operation, the following conditions should be met:

> An identifiable U.S. interest must be at stake; the U.N. mission must be clearly defined in size, scope and duration; there must be sufficient resources and political will to carry out the mission; and there must be an identifiable "exit strategy" for ending U.S. involvement. Clear lines of command must be in place, and Congress and the American people must support U.S. involvement. [Broder, U.S. Completes Policy on Peacekeeping, L.A. Times, May 6, 1994, at A4.]

U.N. Intervention in "Internal" Matters.   There has been an expansion of U.N.-authorized military intervention in events occurring within an individual state. Professor Franck raised this in an earlier excerpt (at page 989), and he expands on this development below.

Thomas M. Franck, Recourse to Force

40-44 (2002)

Of particular significance is the gradual expansion of UN military intervention to meet threats to peace arising not out of aggression by one state against another but from events occurring within one nation.

The US legal justification for the deployment of ONUC military force to vanquish the Katanga separatists in the Congo was explained in February 1963 . . . as follows:

> First, the Government of the Congo asked the United Nations to come in.
> Second, the Security Council authorized the U.N. to go in with a mandate to maintain law and order — a mandate which was subsequently expanded into a mandate to prevent civil war, protect the Congo's territorial integrity, and remove the foreign mercenaries.
> Third, the military actions of the U.N. Force were taken in pursuit of these mandates and in self-defense.

[The United States] added that "this was not an internal matter — there was a clear threat to international peace and security because of the actual involvement or potential involvement of outside powers."

Despite this explanation, it is clear from the drafting history of the Charter's Articles 39, 42, 43, and 51 that the representatives at San Francisco had not intended to authorize a role for the United Nations in civil wars. Rather, Charter Articles 2(4) and 2(7) appear to forbid such intervention. In practice, however, the Congo was but the first of several UN military involvements in precisely those sorts of conflict: in

Yemen, Iraq, the former Yugoslavia, Somalia, Haiti, and Sierra Leone. It is worth emphasizing in this connection that the Charter's prohibition on UN intervention in matters "essentially . . . domestic" is not, textually, suspended even when a government asks for help in suppressing a domestic insurgency. Indeed, a literal reading of Article 2(7) precludes a positive response to such a request. The practice, however, has been much more flexible, treating an "invitation" from the government of a state as suspending the obligation not to intervene: or, alternatively, construing civil conflict, at least when it exceeds certain levels of virulence, as no longer "primarily . . . domestic."

The Charter also makes no provision for UN intervention in cases of gross violations of human rights, destruction of democracy, the disintegration of effective governance, or mass starvation and environmental degradation. The literal Charter text would appear to preclude any international action unless such "domestic" crises begin to threaten international peace. That threshold, however, has been gradually lowered in the practice of the United Nations' principal organs. In 1999, UN Secretary-General Kofi Annan stated that gross violations of human rights and denials of democratic fundamentals can no longer be regarded as purely "domestic" matters. He boldly called on the United Nations to "forge unity behind the principle that massive and systematic violations of human rights — wherever they may take place — should not be allowed to stand." . . .

The Secretary-General's observation . . . is based solidly on practice. Both the General Assembly and the Security Council have invoked Chapter VII measures, in 1966 against the white minority regime in Rhodesia and in 1977 against its equivalent in South Africa, in an effort to end those governments' gross racism. Chapter VII was also invoked in 1994 and military enforcement measures were authorized to reverse the military coup against the democratically elected government of Haiti. In 1998, Chapter VII was again used to threaten the Federal Republic of Yugoslavia with collective measures if it continued to repress its Kosovar minority. On September 28, 2001, the Security Council invoked Chapter VII to impose mandatory sanctions on terrorist groups, thereby extending the Council's enforcement powers to reach non-state actors.

It is increasingly apparent that, in practice, both the Security Council and the General Assembly now regard themselves as entitled to act against oppressive and racist regimes, and, in situations of anarchy, to restore civil society, order, and legitimate governance where these have unraveled. In some instances the United Nations has deployed military force (Congo, Somalia, Haiti, East Timor) or police (Namibia, Cambodia, Mozambique, Haiti) to neutralize or disarm factions or reintegrate them into a cohesive national army and otherwise to help recreate a civil society and establish democratic governance. . . .

The gradual attrition, in UN practice, of states' monopoly over matters of "domestic jurisdiction" has occurred in tandem with an expansion of activities and conditions seen to constitute "threats to the peace." Aggravated instances of racism, colonial repression, massive violations of human rights, tactical starvation, genocide, the overthrow by military juntas of democratically elected governments, and the "harbouring of terrorists" have all begun to be regarded as potentially constituting "threats to the peace" even if they are not instances of "aggression" in the traditional international legal sense.

This expansion of global jurisdiction has not happened at once and, like much legal reform, tends to occur in the guise of "legal fictions." We have noted . . . the US Government[] defending ONUC's use of force to subdue Katanga secessionists in the Congolese civil war, by reference to the "potential involvement of outside powers" which threatened to turn "an internal matter" into "a clear threat to international peace and security." In 1977, the Security Council, invoking Chapter VII, found that the racist policies of the Government of South Africa "are fraught with danger to international peace and security," thereby opening the way for its first exercise of enforcement powers against a member. Later, the Secretary-General persuaded the Security Council to find a threat to the peace in the Somali civil war because of its "repercussions . . . on the entire region." . . .? In determining in 1994 that the rule of the Haitian military junta constituted a threat to peace and security in the region and authorizing military intervention by a coalition of the willing, the Council referred to "the desperate plight of Haitian refugees" as evidence of a threat to the peace. This has rightly been called "unprecedented in authorizing the use of force to remove one regime and install another." . . . In reaction to the destruction of the New York World Trade Center, "international terrorism" was classified by the Council "as a threat to international peace and security" and subjected to Chapter VII mandatory sanctions.

These somewhat artificial "international" dimensions of what, in 1945, would have been seen as lamentable but primarily domestic tragedies or criminal matters subject to domestic police enforcement have not been advanced fraudulently or cynically. Rather, the meaning of "threat to the peace, breach of the peace and act of aggression" is gradually being redefined experientially and situationally. For the present, those doing this redefining understandably seek to contain it within familiar, or at least non-threatening, parameters. For example, an intervention to respond to the "inducing of massive flows of refugees" is as yet more acceptable to many governments than intervention to stop a government's slaughter of its own ethnic or political minorities, its subordination of women, or its failure to control calamitous domestic starvation and civil war.

. . . Nevertheless, the more remarkable fact is that the global system is responding, tentatively and flexibly, through *ad hoc* actions rather than by systematic implementation, to new facts and threats that are redefining the threshold of what is seen to constitute a threat to peace, requiring a powerful collective response.

Notes and Questions

1. Some emphasize the traditional distinction between U.N. peacekeeping and U.N. enforcement actions. As a U.N. website indicates:

> UN peacekeeping has traditionally relied on the consent of the opposing parties and involves the deployment of peacekeepers to implement an agreement approved by those parties. In the case of enforcement action [also sometimes called peacemaking action], the Security Council gives Member States the authority to take all necessary measures to achieve a stated objective. Consent of the parties is not necessarily required.
>
> Enforcement action has been used in very few cases. Examples include the Gulf war, Somalia, Rwanda, Haiti, Bosnia and Herzegovina, Albania and East Timor. [http://www.un.org/Depts/dpko/dpko/ques.htm].

As Professor Franck notes above, though, what begins as a peacekeeping force (or, as he also calls it, a Chapter 6 1/2 operation) can sometimes "incur the hostility of one or several of the parties, requiring either its withdrawal (as in . . . the Sinai) or its difficult and risky transformation into a peace enforcement operations (as with ONUC in the Congo and UNPROFOR in the former Yugoslavia)."

2. Should the U.N. General Assembly have a say in the implementation of U.N. peacekeeping forces? Will General Assembly decisions on U.N. peacekeeping forces necessarily always be in U.S. interests?

3. Should U.N. peacekeeping efforts continue to increase in number and scope as new crises or problems arise in the world? When are U.N. peacekeeping efforts most appropriate? When should they not be used? What are the limitations on the U.N. peacekeeping process?

4. Based on your reading of the materials above, what improvements, if any, should be made in the arrangements for peacekeeping forces? Should a standby peacekeeping fund be established? Should national forces be designated for call-up by the Council? Should there be joint training exercises by designated national forces?

5. To strengthen the U.N.'s peacekeeping efforts, there have been proposals for the creation of standing U.N. armies and rapid deployment forces that could be quickly sent to crisis areas around the world. These steps have generally been rejected by many nations, including the United States. What is your reaction to the proposal for the creation of a small, highly trained, and mobile U.N. force that is all-volunteer and recruited globally? Why do you think similar proposals have not received much support from major countries in the past?

6. Is the trend toward the U.N. Security Council authorizing the sending of military forces into situations occurring in an individual state a positive development? When should such intervention be allowed? When the government is committing genocide? Repressing a particular group or a large segment of the population? When there is a civil war or civil strife is rampant?

7. What are the rationales that are used in support of collective intervention into internal matters? "Threats to peace"? "Consent"? Are these rationales presently clear in the U.N. Charter? In other international documents, such as the Convention on the Prevention and Punishment of the Crime Against Genocide? What weight should be given to Article 2(7) of the U.N. Charter, which provides that "[n]othing contained in the present Charter shall authorize the United Nations to intervene in matters which are essentially within the domestic jurisdiction of any state?" (See the Franck discussion at page 989.)

8. Should there be some international codification of the expanded rationales for collective intervention? How could this be done? An amendment to the U.N. Charter? A new treaty among major powers? Formal U.N. General Assembly resolutions adopted by consensus? Can one realistically expect that the international community will accept codification in a reasonable period of time?

9. As you read some of the following materials about specific cases and regional organizations, consider which institution or institutions are best suited for collective intervention. Is it always the United Nations? Established regional organizations, such as the Organization of American States, the North Atlantic Treaty Organization (NATO), the Organization on Security and Cooperation in Europe? Ad hoc regional groups?

2.   U.N. and U.S. Response to Iraq

Now that you have read about the principles regarding U.N. use of force and peace-keeping, it may be useful to see how these principles apply in a contemporary situation. In this section we recount the 1990 Iraqi invasion of Kuwait and the international responses to Iraqi aggression and intransigence through the fall of Saddam Hussein in April 2003. We start with the history of Iraq and the events leading up to the 1990 invasion. The case study then addresses the international reactions to the invasion, Operation Desert Storm in 1991, and the problems afterwards with Saddam Hussein. Finally we discuss the intensifying pressures on Iraq in 2002-2003, sometimes accomplished through the U.N., and close with the successful toppling of the Saddam Hussein regime by U.S., British, and other coalition forces in 2003 and with questions about the implications of this regime change.

a.   Historical Background

Although Iraq has been a country only since the end of World War I, the area it covers has a long history. This is briefly summarized in the following two excerpts.

Avigdor Levy, The Gulf Crisis in Historical Perspective

14 Suffolk Transnatl. L.J. 23, 24-26 (1990)

The term "Iraq," throughout history, was a loose geographical term used to designate the area between the Tigris and Euphrates Rivers, but there never existed a state by that name. Iraq was created by the British after the First World War. . . . The area which constitutes present day Iraq was, until the First World War, part of the Ottoman Empire. The Ottoman Empire . . . had ruled most of the Middle East. During the First World War, the Ottoman Empire was allied with Germany and the Central Powers. It was defeated and disintegrated, and from its ruins emerged present day Turkey and most of the Arab countries of the Middle East. The British, who controlled the Middle East between the World Wars, joined three Ottoman provinces — Basra, Baghdad and Mosul — whose populations had little in common with each other, and created Iraq. . . .

Unlike Iraq, . . . Kuwait has been a separate political entity since the middle of the eighteenth century. . . . Between 1899 and 1961 Kuwait was a British protectorate. It became independent in 1961 and was admitted as a member state to the United Nations and the League of Arab States. . . .

Congressional Quarterly, The Middle East

228-234 (8th ed. 1995)

GEOGRAPHY

Iraq is located at the northern end of the Persian Gulf. The country's only access to the high seas is a thirty-mile coastline with two major ports, Umm Qasr on the Gulf

itself and Basra, which is inland on the confluence of the Tigris and Euphrates rivers. The confluence is called the *Shatt al-Arab,* or "the river of the Arabs." South of Basra the Shatt al-Arab forms the international border between Iraq and Iran. . . . In this case the [boundary] line was drawn down the Iranian bank of the river, giving control of the Shatt al-Arab entirely to Iraq. [See the accompanying map.] Over the years the placement of the boundary has been a source of dispute between the two countries, eventually contributing to the outbreak of the Iran-Iraq War in 1980.

A vast alluvial plain lies between Basra, Baghdad (the capital), and the Tigris and Euphrates rivers. This area is interlaced with irrigation canals and small lakes, and much of the land is fertile. Most Iraqis live on these plains near the two cities. The area east and north of where the Shatt al-Arab begins is a large, six-thousand-square-mile marshland that extends into Iran. West of the Euphrates River lies the Syrian desert, which extends into Jordan and Saudi Arabia. The Iraqi highlands cover the region between the cities of Mosul and Kirkuk north to the Turkish and Iranian borders. . . . Rainfall in this area, unlike most of the country, is sufficient to support agriculture.

Iraq's most valuable national resource is oil. The largest and most productive fields are around Mosul and Kirkuk. A series of smaller fields are located around Basra in the south. When its oil facilities are fully operational, Iraq has the capacity to produce as much as 3.5 million barrels per day (bpd) for limited periods. In 1988 Iraq's petroleum export earnings were $11.8 billion, second among the members of the Organization of Petroleum Exporting Countries (OPEC) to Saudi Arabia's. . . .

Aside from oil, Iraq has few natural resources. . . . Iraq's potential for agricultural production is greater than that of most nations in the Middle East, but this potential has yet to be developed fully. . . .

DEMOGRAPHY

Iraq's cultural, ethnic, linguistic, and religious diversity stems in part from its history of foreign domination. Once known as *Mesopotamia* or "the land between rivers," Iraq served as a frontier province for the Persian, Greek, Roman, Arab, Mongol, and Turkish empires. It was the Arab invasion in the seventh century A.D. that brought Islam and the Arabic language to Iraq. *Iraq* means "to take root" in Arabic. . . . As each empire fell it left a cultural residue that survived succeeding invasions.

One consequence of Iraq's heterogeneous population has been that some subnational groups have never been assimilated into the mainstream of Iraqi society. One-quarter of Iraq's population speaks a language other than Arabic or an Arabic dialect that is unintelligible to the rest of the population. Illiteracy, estimated to be nearly 45 percent in urban areas and as high as 75 percent in the countryside, compounds the problem. . . .

Religious heresies and schisms added to the already-complex cultural makeup of the region. In the seventh century A.D. the Islamic faith split into the *Sunni* and *Shi'ite* branches. The Shi'ite movement actually began in Iraq and spread rapidly among new converts to Islam who felt excluded from the Arab-dominated faith. Shi'ites can now be found all through the Middle East, and they represent a majority of the population in Iran. . . .

Kurds, an estimated 20 percent of the population, predominate in the isolated mountains of the north and are found in large numbers around the oil fields near Kirkuk. Arab Sunni Muslims generally live in the center of the country. Shi'ite Muslims, who make up about 60 percent of Iraq's population, are concentrated in the south around the oil fields near Basra.

HISTORY

Foreign influences have shaped both the modern and ancient history of Iraq. British interests wanted protection for trade routes from India and, after 1903, the Baghdad Railroad. In 1912, while Iraq was still under Ottoman domination, British, Dutch, and German entrepreneurs obtained a concession to explore for oil in the vicinity of Basra. Two years later the Ottoman Empire allied with Germany in World War I, and the British dispatched an expeditionary force to Iraq from India to maintain control. The British presence continued after the war. . . . In 1921 the British created a constitutional monarchy in Iraq and placed at its head a Meccan prince, Faisal ibn Hussein (Faisal I), whose acceptance by the people derived from his being a descendant of the Prophet Muhammad. In 1932 Iraq became independent, but British influence over the ruling elite continued for another twenty-eight years.

The concept of nation was an alien one to most Iraqis, who identified more readily with ancient local orientations. . . .

During and after World War II, anti-imperialist sentiments began to grow. Opposition groups demanded the reduction of British influence in the country, the liberalization of politics, and land reform. On July 14, 1958, a group of officers led by Brig. Gen. Abdul Karim Kassim overthrew the Hashemite monarchy. . . .

The new regime reversed Iraq's international orientation and declared that Iraq was now part of the movement of nonaligned nations. Iraq's foreign policy became controlled by the drive to destroy Israel. . . .

Iraq's domestic policies changed dramatically as well. The new Kassim government enacted land reform laws and greatly liberalized the political system. . . . As a result, ancient local enmities increased as a factor in national politics. . . . Turks clashed with Kurds, Persians with Arabs, Shi'ite Muslims with Sunnis.

Out of this confusion emerged a group that eventually dominated Iraq's politics. A pan-Arab faction, opposed to the narrow nationalist policies of the Kassim government and in favor of union with Syria, formed the Arab Socialist Resurrection party, better known as the *Ba'ath* party. Aided by sympathetic members of Iraq's officer corps, the Ba'ath party seized power in February 1963. It lost control nine months later. . . .

A coup in July 1968 brought the Ba'athists back to power. Officers aligned with the Ba'ath party were led by Maj. Gen. Ahmed Hassan al-Bakr. . . . He assumed the presidency and set a harsh authoritarian tone for his regime by directing that "all spies for the United States, Israel, imperialism, and Zionism" be arrested. A former president, two former prime ministers, numerous high-ranking officers, and prominent members of the Shi'ite Muslim and Kurdish communities were executed.

Many analysts have theorized that the driving force behind the new regime was al-Bakr's second in command and distant cousin, Saddam Hussein. Saddam's organization of a secret police force had been an important factor in the relatively easy Ba'ath seizure of power. Saddam began to enhance his personal position through contacts outside the party. His ties to the military resulted in his amassing supreme military rank and honors and even obtaining advanced degrees in military science. Saddam was able to gain the loyalty of key officers, in part by sponsoring a military build-up unparalleled in the Arab world.

Authoritarianism soon became the norm inside Iraq. Party and nonparty purges were routine. Saddam had experience in these matters; he allegedly had served as a Ba'ath party executioner in his early days and reportedly killed his brother-in-law because of his Communist party activities.

In 1979 Saddam eliminated all pretenses of power by placing al-Bakr under arrest and assuming the presidency himself. Saddam then embarked on a campaign to establish his own cult. Young Iraqis were taught Ba'ath party doctrine, and Saddam was extolled in literature, music, and film. . . .

Ba'athism

Ba'athism is first and foremost a pan-Arab movement with broad appeal to the diverse sectarian interests in Iraq. The party regards existing national borders as West-imposed artificial barriers that must one day be eliminated if Arab unity is to be achieved. . . .

The philosophy of the Ba'ath party is central to Iraq's political organization and policies. . . . Its basic tenets were pan-Arab, secular, and Socialist. . . . Their national Socialist approach was meant to include all Arabs as a single indivisible political unit; that is, the Arab nation. . . .

A major factor in the Iraqi Ba'ath party's survival has been its capacity to control all the important functions of organized society. At each echelon of the state structure, beginning with local governments, there is a functionally parallel party organization that oversees the performance of the bureaucracy, sometimes even performing the bureaucratic service itself. . . .

Iran-Iraq War

The war with Iran overshadowed all other issues in Iraq from September 22, 1980, when Iraq attacked Iran, until Iran agreed to a cease-fire on July 18, 1988. Saddam Hussein's objective was to regain total control over the Shatt al-Arab. In addition, he hoped that an Iranian military defeat would cause the fall of the Ayatollah Khomeini.

At the time of the Iraqi attack the Iranian government appeared to be vulnerable. Eighteen months after the revolution in Iran, individuals and groups were still struggling for influence within the government, and the military was in total disarray following the purges of officers who had supported the shah.

A year after the war began, however, it became obvious that the Iraqi government had miscalculated. Initial success quickly turned to failure as a combination of poor strategy and equally bad tactical execution brought the invasion to a halt. By June 1982 Iran had driven the Iraqi army back to its own borders. . . . [T]he war degenerated into a bloody stalemate on Iraqi territory.

In the first years of the war, Iraq had few international supporters. . . .

As the war dragged on, however, and as Iran's foreign policy became more aggressive, the Arab states and some nations in the West backed Iraq in the conflict. . . .

Fearing the consequences of an Iranian victory, Western and most Arab nations continued supporting Iraq, despite internal repression by Saddam's regime, Iraq's attacks on neutral ships doing business with Iran, and Iraq's use of brutal tactics, including air strikes against Iranian cities and poison gas attacks against Iranian troops. In part because of the war, Iraq and the United States restored diplomatic relations on November 26, 1984. Iraq had severed ties in June 1967 because of U.S. support for Israel in the Six-Day War. In 1986 the renewed U.S.-Iraqi relationship was hurt by the disclosure that the administration of President Ronald Reagan had sold arms to Iran in an effort to build contacts among Iranian moderates and win the release of American hostages held in Lebanon. Iraq also accused the United States of providing it with false intelligence information. In May 1987 an Iraqi jet mistakenly fired a missile at the USS *Stark,* killing thirty-seven crew members. The United States accepted Iraq's explanation that the attack was an accident. The relationship improved that summer when the United States began naval patrols in the Persian Gulf to halt Iranian attacks on Kuwaiti ships. . . .

After several Iranian offensives in 1986 and 1987 failed to capture Basra, Iraqi forces pushed the exhausted Iranians back across the border in the spring and summer of 1988, causing Iran finally to accept a cease-fire. . . .

The outcome of the war with Iran had both strengthened and weakened Saddam's position. Iraqi society was exhausted by the war, and its debts totaled a staggering $80 billion. Yet as the leader of the nation that had turned back the Iranian threat, Saddam's prestige among other Arab leaders was enhanced. The war also had resulted in a larger, battle-hardened Iraqi military, and Saddam took advantage of the end of the war to crush domestic opposition. Given these advantages and Saddam's perceptions that Iraq was owed a debt of gratitude by the rest of the Arab world, he was not content to preside over a quiet period of rebuilding.

b. The Iraqi Invasion of Kuwait

On the morning of August 2, 1990, an Iraqi force of over 100,000 troops equipped with several hundred tanks invaded neighboring Kuwait. Kuwaiti forces, which totaled about 20,000 personnel and 250 tanks, put up a scattered resistance, but they were greatly outnumbered and were soon routed. The Emir of Kuwait fled to Saudi Arabia.

The disparity between the two military forces reflected the significant difference in size between the two countries, accentuated by the very large military establishment in Iraq. Iraq was a country of about 19 million people and a military force of over 1 million. Kuwait's population was about 2 million people, with over 1 million of these being foreign workers and their dependents.

The Iraqi invasion came less than 24 hours after talks between Iraq and Kuwait had collapsed, apparently following Iraq's demand that Kuwait accept without further discussion Baghdad's financial and territorial claims.

Iraq's announced reasons for invading Kuwait varied over time. On the day of the invasion, an Iraq communique claimed that a "temporary and free" government had been established. The communique accused the Sabah family — descendants of a dynasty that had ruled Kuwait for 234 years — of corruption and of violating Kuwaiti peoples' rights. It reported that Iraq was "dismissing" the Emir and the Crown Prince, who was also the prime minister, and that it would help "organize free, honest elections." Iraq announced on August 8, however, that it was annexing Kuwait and that its decision was irreversible. Moreover, the Iraqis systematically set about to loot Kuwait and to brutalize its people.

Experts estimated that with Kuwait in its grasp, Iraq had come to control 10 percent of the world's oil production. Moreover, the combined Iraqi/Kuwait proved reserves were exceeded only by those of Saudi Arabia. (While increased production by other countries from unused capacity was expected to be sufficient to offset an embargo against Iraqi/Kuwaiti oil, the margin was slim.)

The invasion and claimed annexation of Kuwait had the effect of substantially reducing Iraq's foreign debt, which was a heavy burden on Iraq even with its revenues from oil exports. About $15-20 billion of the debt (or about 20 percent) was owed to Kuwait. Iraq also might have hoped to help itself to the estimated $100 billion in Kuwaiti government assets spread around the world in investments and bank deposits, plus some of the $50 billion in assets owned by individual Kuwaitis.

c. Initial Reactions

In the rest of the world, only the leadership of Yemen, King Hussein of Jordan (where a majority of the population is Palestinian), and Yasir Arafat of the Palestine Liberation Front openly expressed much sympathy for Saddam's arguments.

The response elsewhere was generally hostile, and the reactions swift. These initial responses were reinforced by serious concerns that the Iraqi military would continue on its drive and try to seize all, or part, of the even more oil-rich Saudi Arabia. While the Saudis had a larger army than Kuwait and a significant air force, alone they were probably no match for Iraq.

On the day of the invasion of Kuwait, President George H.W. Bush promptly imposed very comprehensive economic sanctions against Iraq. He declared a national emergency and invoked the International Emergency Economic Powers Act (IEEPA). (IEEPA is discussed in detail in Chapter 3.)

Besides cutting off trade and business with Iraq, the Executive Order froze Iraqi funds in U.S. banks or in the possession of U.S. corporations—whether located in the United States or abroad—or on account with the U.S. government for purchases yet to be completed. Although there was considerable uncertainty at the time of the Executive Order about the exact amount of assets involved, later estimates indicated that this order froze over $1.6 billion in Iraqi funds, about $420 million of which was in U.S. bank branches abroad.

To prevent Iraq from drawing on Kuwaiti assets, President Bush also issued on August 2 another Executive Order freezing Kuwaiti assets within the possession or control of U.S. persons.

At least as important as the U.S. sanctions, the European Community, Japan, the Soviet Union, and other countries also quickly imposed sanctions. As a result, Iraq's trade was largely cut off, and Iraqi and Kuwaiti assets abroad were frozen. (The Kuwaiti government in exile and individual Kuwaiti exiles were later permitted by the United States and other countries to regain control of their assets outside Kuwait.)

d. The United Nations Gets Involved

The United Nations quickly became involved in reacting to the Iraqi invasion. With the thawing of the cold war and the general reaction to the Iraqi invasion, the Security Council began cooperating in an unprecedented way. It began passing a series of increasingly forceful and detailed resolutions.

On August 2, the day of the Iraqi invasion, the Security Council determined that "there exists a breach of international peace and security." It "condemn[ed]" the invasion and demanded that Iraq "withdraw immediately and unconditionally all its forces." The vote was 14 to 0, with Yemen abstaining. (S.C. Res. 660. See the Documentary Supplement for this resolution and others cited in the section.)

On August 6, affirming and reinforcing under U.N. auspices the economic sanctions that many countries had already imposed individually, the Security Council ordered a comprehensive trade and financial boycott against Iraq and occupied Kuwait. The vote on Resolution 661 was 13-0, with Cuba and Yemen abstaining.

The embargo imposed by the Security Council was binding on U.N. Member States under the Charter. (See Articles 48 and 25.) The Resolution also helped provide a domestic legal basis in some countries allowing them to undertake the U.N.-mandated actions. In the United States, for example, the Resolution allowed the United States to invoke the U.N. Participation Act, initially passed in 1945, as another legal ground for the sanctions that President Bush had ordered on August 2. (Excerpts of the Act are in the Documentary Supplement.)

The Security Council continued to demonstrate its solidarity in response to Iraqi intransigence. On August 9, the Council voted 15-0 to declare Iraq's purported annexation of Kuwait on August 8 null and void. (S.C. Res. 662.) On August 18, the Council again voted 15-0 to demand that Iraq free all detained foreigners. (S.C. Res. 664.)

On October 30, the Security Council tightened the pressure on Baghdad by approving a resolution that laid the groundwork for seizing Iraqi assets that had been frozen around the world and for paying compensation to victims. Resolution 674 was passed 13-0, with Cuba and Yemen abstaining. It declared Iraq responsible for all damage and personal injuries resulting from its invasion and illegal occupation of Kuwait. This was a very significant statement regarding liability. The Resolution then requested states to collect relevant information regarding their claims and those of their nationals and corporations "for restitution or financial compensation by Iraq."

Notes and Questions

1. Why was there a near-unanimous condemnation of Iraq's invasion of Kuwait? Was it in part the fear of countries, particularly the industrialized ones, that Iraq was gaining too much control over the world's oil supplies, especially if Iraq added Saudi Arabia to its conquests? Was it some sense of fair play that a relatively large country like Iraq should not invade a smaller country?

Could international law be part of the reason? Did any of Iraq's reasons for the invasion have much legitimacy under international law? Review the U.N. Charter's Articles 2(4) and 51. Other international treaties and declarations enshrine the territorial integrity and political independence of a state. Is this an example of where international law norms contributed to the intensity of the world's reaction to the Iraqi invasion?

In large parts of Africa the states were created after World War II out of former colonies. The boundaries often cut across tribal areas or did not take into account important geographical features. Why is it, though, that not only the United Nations but also regional organizations do not support any redrawing of the boundaries along more "rational" lines?

2. What was the legal basis for the U.N. Security Council's comprehensive economic sanctions under Resolution 661? Are the sanctions pursuant to Article 41 of the U.N. Charter? Could the Council have been more explicit? Why do you think the Council was not as explicit as it could have been?

3. Prior to the Iraqi case, U.N. economic sanctions had been explicitly imposed under Article 41 in two situations—against Rhodesia and South Africa. White Rhodesians had made a "unilateral declaration of independence" from Great Britain in 1965, and initial British efforts to resolve the dispute failed. In December 1966, the Security Council passed Resolution 232, calling for selective mandatory sanctions. That was followed by Resolution 253 in 1968, which called for comprehensive sanctions.

Relying on the U.N. Participation Act, President Lyndon Johnson issued executive orders implementing the U.N. resolutions and controlling transactions with Rhodesia. The U.S. and U.N. sanctions were terminated in December 1979, when an arrangement was reached for majority rule in Rhodesia, soon to be called Zimbabwe.

As for South Africa, in 1977 the Security Council called for an embargo on shipments of arms, munitions, and military equipment to or from that country. (S.C. Res. 418.) The United States, however, had already taken the required actions pursuant to its arms export laws. Indeed, U.S. sanctions against South Africa were more thoroughgoing than mandated by the Security Council resolutions. The U.N. and

U.S. sanctions against South Africa helped pressure the government of F.W. de Klerk to concede power in 1994 to Nelson Mandela.

Since 1990, the U.N. Security Council has also imposed economic sanctions of varying comprehensiveness in the conflicts in the former Yugoslavia, Somalia, and Rwanda. For further discussion of economic sanctions, including unilateral U.S. sanctions, see Chapter 8 at page 808.

4. After Iraq announced that it was annexing Kuwait on August 8, it told all states with diplomatic missions in Kuwait that they had to close their missions by August 24 and that Iraq was withdrawing the diplomatic immunity of the missions' personnel. The U.N. Security Council rejected Iraq's purported annexation and demanded that Iraq rescind its orders for the closure of the missions and the withdrawal of immunity for the missions' personnel. (See S.C. Res. 664, and also 667 and 662.) On August 24, Iraqi troops surrounded the diplomatic missions that had not been evacuated. Several countries, including the United States, said they would keep their missions open as long as food and water held out.

Why did the United Nations, United States, and others object to Iraq's actions? Cannot Iraq withdraw diplomatic immunity from those within its territory? For example, see Articles 2 and 9 of the Vienna Convention on Diplomatic Relations (in the Documentary Supplement). In protest over Iraqi's action, could the United States legally demand that, say, 10 Iraqi diplomats in the United States leave within 72 hours?

5. Review Resolution 674. Does the Security Council have the authority under Articles 39–42 of the U.N. Charter to order that the Iraqi assets frozen in other countries be used to pay reparations to Kuwait or to other states injured by the Iraqi actions? How could Iraq's obligation to pay damages, and presumably an exact amount, "be established in accordance with international law"? (Para. 9.) By the U.N. Security Council? By the International Court of Justice? By a domestic court, like a U.S. federal court? By an international claims tribunal? In the last situation, who could establish such a tribunal?

e. Military Buildup: Operation Desert Shield

While the Security Council was taking these steps to implement and enforce the economic sanctions, there was a dramatic military build up in the region. Shortly after the Iraqi invasion, President Bush dispatched thousands of U.S. troops plus combat aircraft and naval ships to Saudi Arabia and the Persian Gulf. (King Fahd of Saudi Arabia explicitly requested the U.S. deployments, and the Emir of Kuwait also asked for assistance.) Britain, France, Italy, Spain, and other European nations sent detachments, as did Canada, Argentina, and various other states.

Very important militarily and diplomatically was the bitterly divided but favorable vote on August 10 by the 21-member Arab League, which urged Arab participation in the military deployments to protect Saudi Arabia and other Arab states against Iraq. Moreover, Egypt and Syria each sent sizable contingents of over 20,000 troops to Saudi Arabia.

By the end of November 1990, over 250,000 U.S. military personnel had been rapidly sent to the region as part of a planned deployment of over 400,000 by mid-January 1991. Non-American deployments amounted to about 200,000 to 250,000 troops, including the Saudi forces. Despite the suggestions by some countries that the various forces arrayed against Iraq be coordinated under a single U.N. command, the United States argued successfully for continued national control over each country's own forces and worked instead to develop less formal methods of coordination.

In the meantime, Iraq built up its forces in Kuwait and southern Iraq. U.S. officials estimated that these forces swelled from 100,000 on August 2 to about 450,000 by the end of October. After the United States announced in November that it would increase U.S. forces in the area to over 400,000, Saddam Hussein said that he would send to the Kuwaiti area another 250,000 personnel, in part by calling up his reserves, to join the 450,000 Iraqi soldiers already there.

The economic embargo and the military build-up against Iraq created a host of economic problems for other countries. For example, the "front line" states, such as Jordan and Turkey, suffered from a cutoff of their traditional trade with Iraq and found themselves, especially Jordan, burdened with the tens of thousands of foreign workers and their dependents fleeing Kuwait and Iraq. Not only did the U.N. Security Council take steps to consider recommendations to help states with special problems (see S.C. Res. 669), but Saudi Arabia, the Kuwaiti government in exile, the United States, and other major industrial countries began providing substantial financial assistance.

Saudi Arabia and the Kuwaiti government in exile also made multi-billion dollar payments to the United States to help offset the costs of its military deployments to the Persian Gulf. The United States also asked Germany, Japan, and other industrial countries that were not making major deployments themselves for various reasons to help share the burden of the deployments. Germany and Japan did make financial commitments.

f.   The Authorization for Use of Force and the U.N. Ultimatum

In November 1990, the Bush Administration steered a difficult course among divisive pressures on the coalition against Iraq and competing views regarding whether force might soon be necessary and under what circumstances. After intensive diplomacy, the Security Council adopted on November 29 the important Resolution 678 by a vote of 12-2, with Cuba and Yemen opposed and permanent member China abstaining.

U.N. Security Council Resolution 678
(Nov. 29, 1990)

The Security Council . . .
Mindful of its duties and responsibilities under the Charter of the United Nations for the maintenance and preservation of international peace and security,
Determined to secure full compliance with its decisions,
Acting under Chapter VII of the Charter of the United Nations,
1. *Demands* that Iraq comply fully with Resolution 660 (1990) and all subsequent relevant resolutions and decides, while maintaining all its decisions, to allow Iraq one final opportunity, as a pause of good will, to do so;

2. *Authorizes* member states cooperating with the Government of Kuwait, unless Iraq on or before Jan. 15, 1991, fully implements, as set forth in paragraph 1 above, the foregoing resolutions, to use all necessary means to uphold and implement the Security Council Resolution 660 and all subsequent relevant Resolutions and to restore international peace and security in the area;

3. *Requests* all states to provide appropriate support for the actions undertaken in pursuance of paragraph 2 of this resolution; and

4. *Requests* the states concerned to keep the Council regularly informed on the progress of actions undertaken pursuant to paragraphs 2 and 3 of this resolution. . . .

The Resolution's reference to "all necessary means" was understood to authorize the possible use of force after January 15, 1991. This was only the second time the Security Council had authorized the use of force. The first situation was the response 40 years before to the invasion of Korea. (See page 1027.)

g.   Operation Desert Storm

Passage of Resolution 678 with its deadline helped trigger some new diplomatic attempts to resolve the crisis. However, after those efforts failed, Saddam Hussein ignored the ultimatum to withdraw from Kuwait by January 15.

On January 12, after a thoughtful debate, Congress passed a resolution authorizing President Bush to use U.S. armed forces to achieve Iraqi compliance with the applicable U.N. resolutions. (See H.R.J. Res. 77 in the Documentary Supplement.) On January 16, allied warplanes bombed targets in Iraq and occupied Kuwait, thus beginning the Persian Gulf War and upgrading the U.S. involvement from Operation Desert Shield to Operation Desert Storm. At that time, there were 425,000 U.S. troops stationed in the region, the result of the largest and quickest mobilization in U.S. military history. American troops were joined by an additional 265,000 troops from 27 other countries, and faced an estimated Iraqi force of 545,000.

The first phase of the air attack consisted of targeting Iraqi air defenses, command and control centers, and Iraqi Scud missiles. One objective of this phase was to separate Iraqi troops in Kuwait from the central government and military control in Baghdad. Tomahawk cruise missiles, fired from U.S. warships in the Gulf, and F-117 stealth fighters were used in the initial attack. Iraq retaliated by launching Scud missiles at targets in Israel and Saudi Arabia.

Six weeks of allied air attacks followed. They were designed to isolate Iraqi forces by demolishing roads, railroads, and supply lines. On February 26, 1991, an allied ground offensive was unleashed. More than 700,000 allied troops faced an entrenched but severely depleted Iraqi force. The coalition forces, who had created a decided tactical advantage (e.g., the air support of 2,000 warplanes and a combined warfleet of over 100 ships), made rapid progress.

Relying on a major flanking movement, mobility, and firepower, the allied forces completely drove the Iraqi forces from Kuwait and began to penetrate deep into Iraq. Although their forces were encountering diminished resistance, the allied countries suspended their offensive at midnight on February 28, exactly 100 hours after ground operations had commenced. President Bush and his key military and civilian advisers called a halt apparently for humanitarian and public relations reasons. Also, after Kuwait had been liberated, some of the U.S. allies questioned what the allied force's authority was to continue deep into Iraq and try to oust Saddam Hussein.

The war was over. The allies had destroyed or captured an estimated 3,700 of 4,230 Iraqi tanks and 2,140 of 3,110 pieces of artillery. Allied casualties were very low, though 79 Americans died. Iraqi casualties were estimated at over 100,000.

Notes and Questions

1. Were the allied attacks on Iraqi command and control centers and weapons production facilities authorized by Resolution 678? With what language? What about nuclear reactors and other sites where nuclear weapons might be constructed in future years? If such steps were included in the language "all necessary means," who decides what means are "necessary"?

2. Assume that Iraq refused to withdraw from Kuwait and the Security Council had been unable to pass a resolution authorizing any offensive military action against Iraq. Could the United States (possibly with the British) have then decided under Article 51 to conduct a major offensive against Iraq in an effort to dislodge Iraqi forces from Kuwait? Does it matter if the Emir of Kuwait requests the U.S. action, possibly in cooperation with a small contingent of Kuwaiti exiles? What if Saudi Arabia requested the U.S. action in cooperation with its forces in order to ensure that Iraq did not invade Saudi Arabia? Do Articles 52–54 provide another basis for the action?

3. Continue the assumptions of the preceding question. Could the United States undertake a military offensive if the Emir requests it, and if Iraqi aircraft fire for unknown reasons at U.S. aircraft that are over the Persian Gulf and not in Iraqi airspace? And if an Iraqi military aircraft launches an air-to-surface missile that hits a U.S. naval ship outside of Iraqi territorial waters, killing ten crewmen? Would the U.S. response have to be proportional?

h. Gulf War Cease-Fire Resolutions

Although the allied offensive was successful in restoring sovereignty to Kuwait, the allies did not drive Saddam Hussein from power. However, in the spring of 1991, the U.N. Security Council passed two major resolutions setting forth required conditions for Iraq. Resolutions 687 and 688 also stipulated that the U.N. sanctions originally imposed upon Iraq would remain in place until Iraq fully complied with the terms of the cease-fire. (Both resolutions are in the Documentary Supplement.) A U.S. Department of State publication briefly explains the general provisions of these resolutions as follows:

> On April 3, 1991, at the end of the Gulf War, the U.N. Security Council adopted its famous "cease-fire resolution," numbered 687, which established a cease-fire on the basis of Iraq's acceptance of conditions deemed essential to the restoration of peace and stability in the area. This resolution required Iraq to give up its weapons of mass destruction, return Kuwaiti property, account for detainees, and renounce terrorism,

as well as accept the U.N. demarcation of the Iraq-Kuwait border. It also set up UNIKOM—a U.N. peace-keeping force on the border. [Also established by the resolution were the U.N. Special Commission (UNSCOM), designed to dismantle Iraq's weapons of mass destruction and to provide long-term monitoring of Iraq's weapons systems; the Iraq-Kuwait Boundary Demarcation Commission, created to mark and restore the Iraq-Kuwait boundary to the position agreed to by the two countries in 1963; and the U.N. Compensation Commission (UNCC), which would provide reimbursement to those individuals who suffered damages as a result of the war.]

Shortly after Resolution 687 was passed, a surge of repression [in Iraq] led to the passage of Resolution 688, demanding an end to Iraqi repression and cooperation with humanitarian efforts. Under this resolution [the United States] also led in setting up Operation Provide Comfort to extend protection in northern Iraq. Various other resolutions have built on these resolutions. Of these, two of the most significant are UNSCR 715, which spelled out in detail 687's demand for long-term monitoring of Iraq's weapons of mass destruction, and Resolution 833, which reaffirmed the finality and inviolability of the boundary as demarcated by the U.N. Boundary Demarcation Commission, as well as the Security Council's guarantee of that border. [Dept. St. Dispatch, Feb. 7, 1994, at 66.]

Iraqi noncompliance with these conditions led the Security Council to continue applying sanctions to Iraq. However, as discussed below, international pressure succeeded in achieving at least partial Iraqi compliance on some issues—for example, boundary demarcation, compensation, human rights, and (at times) weapons destruction and monitoring.

(1)   Boundary Demarcation

Iraq ceased to attend the sessions of the Iraq-Kuwait Boundary Demarcation Commission, established by Resolution 687, in December 1992. The Commission, however, continued to meet without Iraq's involvement. In Resolution 833, passed in May 1993, the U.N. Security Council approved the boundary recommendation of the Demarcation Commission, and reminded both Iraq and Kuwait to recognize the inviolability of international boundaries. Finally, in November 1994, Iraq's National Assembly voted to recognize the sovereignty and territorial integrity of Kuwait.

(2)   Claims Before the U.N. Compensation Commission

Resolution 687 says that Iraq "is liable under international law for any direct loss, damage, including environmental damage and the depletion of natural resources, or injury to foreign Governments, nationals and corporations, as a result of Iraq's unlawful invasion and occupation of Kuwait."

The Security Council later established the U.N. Compensation Commission (UNCC) to compensate eligible victims of the Iraqi invasion. Funds were originally expected to come from a 30 percent charge on the export sale of Iraqi oil. Iraq, however, refused to make such oil sales in protest over this 30 percent charge, even though this meant that Iraq was not earning the rest of the revenues to purchase food and other commodities for its population.

The Security Council then passed Resolution 778, which established a mechanism for countries to loan to the fund Iraqi assets that had been frozen in response to the Iraq invasion of Kuwait. The countries that made such loans were to be repaid, with interest, from the 30 percent charge on Iraqi oil export revenues as soon as those exports began. The UNCC released its first reparations payments of $2.7 million in June 1994. The Kuwaiti government received $1.4 million, which it then dispersed to 303 claimants whose relatives had died or been injured as a result of the Iraqi invasion. Each family member was eligible to receive between $2,500 and $10,000.

After Iraq had subjected some of its population to starvation and malnutrition for years, it finally agreed to begin exporting oil. Pursuant to Security Council Resolution 986 (April 14, 1995), Iraq was allowed to sell $1 billion worth of oil on the world market every 90 days, provided that the revenue was dispersed according to U.N. conditions, which included funds being allocated to humanitarian supplies, with part specifically directed to the northern Kurdish population. The UNCC and the U.N. Special Commission (UNSCOM) for weapons inspection also received funds. In February 1998, the Security Council increased the amount of oil Iraq could sell every six months to $5.25 billion, though Iraq claimed that its old equipment could not produce that much oil.

The UNCC has received about 2.6 million claims seeking compensation in excess of $300 billion for claimants in Kuwait and nearly 100 other countries. United States claims numbered about 3,000, with a total value of over $200 million. The UNCC's Governing Council ruled in early 1994 that the military costs incurred by the allied forces during Operation Desert Storm were not eligible for compensation from the fund. As of March 2003, approximately 99 percent of the 2.6 million claims have been resolved, with 1.5 million of these claims being awarded compensation of $44 billion. Some large claims were still pending resolution.

(3)   U.N. Justifications for Resolution 688 and Iraqi Human Rights Violations

Jane Stromseth, Iraq's Repression of Its Civilian Population: Collective Responses and Continuing Challenges

Enforcing Restraint 83-90 (Lori F. Damrosch ed., 1993)

The coalition forces' defeat of Saddam Hussein created temporary chaos in Iraq, a development that both rebel Kurdish groups in northern Iraq and Shi'ite opposition forces in southern Iraq viewed as a fortuitous opening. . . .

In early March [1991] Kurds in northern Iraq and Shi'ites in the south engaged in popular uprisings against the regime of Saddam Hussein. The rebels initially had considerable success in taking control of cities and territory. Republican guard troops loyal to Saddam Hussein quickly responded with military force against the rebels, however, using helicopter gunships, tanks, and artillery against unarmed civilians. . . . Despite his earlier remarks encouraging revolt against Saddam Hussein, President Bush initially characterized the Kurdish and Shi'ite uprisings and the Iraqi response as an "internal matter" that did not warrant a U.S. military response. . . .

By the end of March, Iraqi forces had effectively crushed the rebellion and retaken rebel-held areas first in southern Iraq and then in the Kurdish north, brutally slaughtering captured rebels and unarmed civilians. Thousands of Shi'ites in the south fled to the allied-occupied areas along the Iraq-Kuwait border or to Iran. The

Kurds in the north fled into the mountains by the thousands, toward neighboring Turkey and Iran, where they were stranded without food or medicine and were vulnerable to attacks by Iraqi helicopter gunships. As television reports brought their suffering into homes around the world, Western governments could no longer characterize the situation in Iraq as a strictly "internal" matter.

Just as the United Nations served as the umbrella legitimizing collective action to expel Iraq from Kuwait, so too the Security Council became the central forum for articulating a collective response to the situation unfolding in Iraq. . . .

THE INTERNATIONAL RESPONSE

Security Council Resolution 688

. . . On April 5, 1991, the UN Security Council adopted resolution 688 by a vote of 10-3, with two abstentions. That resolution did several things: First, it condemned Iraq's repression of its civilian population, including most recently the Kurdish population. Second, it characterized the consequences of that repression—"a massive flow of refugees towards and across international frontiers" and "cross border incursions"—as a threat to international peace and security. Third, it demanded that Iraq stop the repression. Fourth, it expressed hope for an open dialogue to "ensure that the human and political rights of all Iraqi citizens are respected." Fifth, it insisted that Iraq allow international humanitarian organizations immediate access to those needing assistance. Sixth, it requested the secretary-general to pursue humanitarian efforts in Iraq, using all the resources at his disposal to respond to the needs of displaced Iraqis, and it demanded that Iraq cooperate with the secretary-general. Finally, it appealed to member states and to humanitarian organizations "to contribute to these humanitarian relief efforts."

The Security Council debate preceding passage of resolution 688 was both a response to urgent human needs and a wide-ranging philosophical discussion of the purpose and limits of the Security Council. The participants understood that the resolution would establish a precedent that would shape perceptions of the proper role of the Security Council in future crises growing out of internal conflict. Under article 39 of the UN Charter, the Security Council has broad authority to take action in response to threats to the peace. But at the heart of the debate over resolution 688 was the meaning and contemporary significance of article 2(7), which provides that nothing in the Charter authorizes the UN "to intervene in matters which are essentially within the domestic jurisdiction of any state." . . .

The ten states that supported resolution 688 relied on three types of arguments. The predominant argument was fully consistent with a traditional state-centric view: namely, that the massive flow of refugees *across international borders* that Iraq's actions caused was a threat to international peace and security in the region. . . .

A second, more human rights-oriented argument was advanced by several members of the Security Council, most notably France and Britain. These states contended that Iraq's violation of its citizens' human rights was itself a matter of international concern and thus not within Iraq's "domestic" jurisdiction.

The third type of argument made in support of Security Council action to protect the Kurds and Shi'ites was that the UN had a special responsibility to respond to developments growing out of its own decision to authorize the use of force to expel Iraq from Kuwait. . . . On April 6, the day after the Security Council adopted resolution 688, the U.S. air force began dropping food, blankets, and clothing to Kurdish refugees. The United States also warned Iraq against undertaking military operations, including any air operations, north of the 36th parallel. . . .

Operation Provide Comfort

Concerted pressure from Britain, France, and Turkey soon persuaded the United States to contribute military forces to a joint operation to create and protect refugee camps within Iraq's northern border. In mid-April troops from the United States, Britain, and France entered northern Iraq and began to establish refugee camps in the Zakho region, creating a de facto safe haven zone for Iraqi Kurds guarded by allied forces.

American and allied officials argued that the purpose of Operation Provide Comfort was humanitarian, not political, and that resolution 688 provided authority for the operation. UN Secretary-General Pérez de Cuéllar cautioned, however, that a foreign military presence on Iraqi territory required Iraqi consent or the express authorization of the Security Council. Iraq denounced the allied operation as an intervention in its internal affairs and insisted that the UN operate any relief centers on Iraqi territory. In light of Saddam Hussein's violence against the Kurds, the allies persisted in their efforts to create a protected safe haven, despite the legal reservations of the secretary-general and the opposition of Iraq.

In April 1991, Iraq consented to a U.N. humanitarian presence where needed and agreed to facilitate the establishment of U.N. Humanitarian Centers (UN-HUCs), which would return refugees to their homes. In the fall of 1991, however, Iraq instituted an embargo against the Kurd-inhabited northern regions. This occurred after the Kurds had unsuccessfully attempted to negotiate and gain autonomy from Saddam Hussein.

Iraq also challenged the no-fly zones that were established by the allies to protect the Kurds and Shi'ites in the northern and southern regions as illegal and unprecedented intrusions on its sovereignty. The Iraqi government's refusal to respect these no-fly zones led to U.S. bombing strikes against Iraq in January and June 1993. U.N. and U.S. monitoring of the northern no-fly region deterred any Iraqi military offensives in the region.

Through March 2003, the United States and its coalition partners continued to enforce the no-fly zones under Operation Northern Watch and Operation Southern Watch (the successor missions to Operation Provide Comfort). (The need for these zones ended with the downfall of the Saddam Hussein regime.)

(4)   Weapons Monitoring and Destruction

U.N. Security Council Resolution 687 included a number of provisions regarding Iraq's weapons systems. It required full Iraqi disclosure of its weapons of mass destruction (WMD) and ballistic missile programs. It authorized the U.N. to dismantle these weapons systems and establish a monitoring regime to ensure that Iraq could not reacquire banned weapons. To implement these provisions, the U.N. Special Commission (UNSCOM) was established by the Security Council to eliminate and verify the destruction of Iraq's biological, chemical, and ballistic missile programs. The International Atomic Energy Agency (IAEA) assumed responsibility for dismantling Iraq's nuclear program.

A U.S. Government White Paper concluded in February 1998 that "UNSCOM and IAEA inspections and monitoring activities have severely curtailed Iraq's WMD programs." However, for years, Iraq followed a policy of concealment and delay, which on occasion had led to diplomatic disputes.

A serious confrontation occurred in October 1997, when Iraq escalated its harassment of U.N. inspection teams by announcing the expulsion of all American inspectors. Richard Butler, the Australian executive chairman of UNSCOM, then said that he would suspend all inspections until all the Americans were allowed to participate rather than let the Iraqis pick and choose the inspectors.

A last-chance diplomatic effort in February 1998 by U.N. Secretary General Kofi A. Annan resulted in a Memorandum of Understanding between Iraq and the United Nations. The U.N. Security Council affirmed the agreement in Resolution 1154 (Mar. 2, 1998). As summarized by UNSCOM Chairman Butler: "The Memorandum of Understanding reconfirmed Iraq's acceptance of all relevant resolutions of the Security Council and reiterated Iraq's undertaking to cooperate fully with the Commission and the [IAEA]. It also established special procedures to apply to the initial and subsequent entries by the Commission and IAEA for the performance of the tasks mandated at the eight presidential sites in Iraq, which were defined in the annex to the Memorandum. It also provided that all other areas of Iraq and facilities, equipment, records and means of transportation would be subject to the Commission's procedures. . . ." (Resolution 1154 is in the Documentary Supplement.)

Another serious situation arose in August 1998, when Iraq decided to cut off field inspections by UNSCOM. The situation became even more severe when Iraq announced on October 31 that it was suspending all cooperation with UNSCOM, preventing even the monitoring that had still been going on. UNSCOM inspectors and other U.N. personnel began to evacuate Iraq.

Iraq's new actions troubled even countries that had been among the more sympathetic to it. On November 5, 1998, the U.N. Security Council adopted unanimously Resolution 1205, which formally condemned Iraq for halting cooperation with the weapons inspections and warned that the sanctions against Iraq could not be lifted unless Iraq reversed its decision "immediately and unconditionally."

The Resolution's language does not specifically authorize military action. Although most Council members apparently contended that any military strike would require further specific authorization, the United States and Britain said that further Council permission was not needed. (The Resolution is in the Documentary Supplement.)

On Friday night, November 15, President Clinton approved a major attack on Iraq. The attack would have relied heavily on cruise missiles but would also have involved aircraft and naval ships—both U.S. and British. The Pentagon had made an estimate that about 10,000 Iraqis would be killed in a medium case scenario.

Long-range B-52 warplanes, laden with cruise missiles, actually began their flights. However, possibly tipped off by another country, Iraq sent a letter to the United Nations pledging that Iraq would allow the resumption of the weapons inspections. When President Clinton and his advisers learned of this on Saturday morning, the President put the attack on hold, apparently just an hour or two before the first cruise missiles would have been launched. The initial decision was to delay the attack, and it could have occurred the next day if some questions about the Iraqi letter were not cleared up. However, on Sunday, President Clinton then called off the attack for the time being.

The U.N. inspectors returned to Iraq and resumed their inspections. However within days, the inspectors met new resistance from Iraq over the production of certain documents and then over visits to certain sites. On December 15, UNSCOM Chairman Butler reported to the U.N. Secretary General that Iraq continued to block the inspections called for by the Security Council.

That was enough for President Clinton, British Prime Minister Tony Blair, and others. U.S. and British forces began an attack on Iraq on December 17. The Clinton Administration explained that the principal purpose of the attack was to reduce or "degrade" Iraq's ability to develop nuclear arms, poison gas, biological weapons, or the means to deliver them. (They denied that the imminent vote in the House of Representatives regarding the impeachment of President Clinton affected the President's decision to strike. The decision had been unanimously recommended by all his senior national security advisors, including General Henry H. Shelton, chairman of the Joint Chiefs of Staff.)

During the next 70 hours, U.S. and British forces struck nearly 100 targets with 415 cruise missiles and hundreds of bombs. While there was some uncertainty about the full effect of the strikes, Secretary of Defense William S. Cohen and General Shelton said that the bombing had set back Iraq's plans to develop longer-range missiles by at least a year.

Secretary of State Albright indicated that the United States and Britain had received strong expressions of support from Canada, the European Union, Japan, Korea, Australia, New Zealand, and Norway. As for criticism from Russia and China, Albright noted: "The Russians and Chinese are critical, of course, but over the past year they have failed to provide any viable alternative."

At the conclusion of the strikes, President Clinton and his senior advisers emphasized that the United States would repeat the strikes if necessary to prevent Iraq from developing or deploying weapons of mass destruction or the missiles to deliver them. President Clinton also indicated that the United States would intensify its engagement with Iraqi opposition groups.

Nevertheless, for the next several years, Hussein remained defiant, and U.N. weapons inspections were not resumed.

Notes and Questions

1. What should be the extent of Iraq's liability for its invasion and occupation of Kuwait? Do you agree with Resolution 687? Do you agree with the U.N. Commission's decision that the war-fighting costs of the United States and its allies should

not be compensated out of the fund? Could this conclusion stem in part from the realization that the claims against Iraq far exceeded any reasonable estimates of the funds that would be obtained through the 30 percent charge on Iraqi oil exports for decades to come?

2. Review Resolution 688. Professor Stromseth notes in her article:

> Resolution 688 was an attempt to respond collectively to the urgent humanitarian needs of displaced Iraqis in the aftermath of the Gulf War and to halt Iraq's repression of its civilian population through diplomatic pressure and the involvement of humanitarian relief agencies under UN coordination. Thus, the resolution demanded that Iraq stop repressing its civilian population and—contrary to standard UN practice requiring host country consent—obliged Iraq to allow international humanitarian organizations immediate access to its territory. [Stromseth, supra, at 88.]

Does Resolution 688's characterization of the response as a humanitarian effort, rather than intervention against Iraq's political leadership, matter under international law? (See, e.g., Articles 2(4) and 2(7) in the U.N. Charter.) Why was no Iraqi government consent needed for the U.N. humanitarian effort? Because the Resolution was passed as part of the U.N. response to Iraq's invasion of Kuwait and later events? Could the Security Council (assuming it was not vetoed) pass a similar resolution (complete with sanctions) against, say, Turkey or a former Soviet republic, such as Georgia, if that state was repressing an ethnic minority in its territory?

3. Iraq's refusal in late 1997 and early 1998 to permit the UNSCOM inspectors full access was a violation of its obligations regarding weapons of mass destruction under Resolution 687. If Iraq had not reached an agreement with Secretary General Annan, and if the Security Council could not agree on a military response because of vetoes by, say, Russia or China, what legal justification(s) would the United States and a few other countries (e.g., Britain) have had for carrying out military strikes against Iraq, as these countries were on the verge of doing? Was Resolution 678 of pre-Operation Desert Storm days still in effect? See also Resolution 1137 in the Documentary Supplement—by citing Resolution 678, does the Security Council indicate that Resolution 678 is still in effect, or does the Security Council's stated intention in Resolution 1137 to take further measures indicate that a new resolution would be necessary?

4. Were the actual U.S.-British strikes in mid-December 1998 justified, legally or otherwise? In any case, what should have been the policies of the United States toward Iraq after the attacks? Should the United States have taken additional steps to overthrow Saddam Hussein beyond further support of Iraqi opposition groups? If so, what steps?

5. What should have been the U.N. policies after the December attacks? Should the U.N. sanctions have been continued? Should there have been a continuing insistence that Iraq accept the UNSCOM inspections?

6. Resolution 687 after Desert Storm also required Iraq to refrain from supporting international acts of terrorism. However, most reports indicate that since the end of the war, Iraq has continued to support and conduct terrorist acts abroad. For many years up through March 2003, the U.S. Secretary of State designated Iraq as one of seven states that support international terrorism. This designation triggers various sanctions under U.S. law. (The other states are Cuba, Iran, Libya, North

Korea, Sudan, and Syria.) (For examples of these other laws, see the discussion of section 1605(a)(7) and the so-called Flatow amendment in Chapter 6 at page 588.)

7. In general, up until the end of 1998, how effective was the U.N. response to the Iraqi invasion of Kuwait? To the longer-term problems on human rights and nonproliferation that Saddam Hussein and Iraq presented? Did the Security Council seem more effective in certain activities than in others?

8. From the standpoint of the United States through 1998, was the U.N. Security Council a help or a hinderance in reacting to the Iraqi invasion of Kuwait? To dealing with Iraq and Saddam Hussein on human rights and nonproliferation? Is there another international or regional organization that the United States should have sought the assistance of rather than the United Nations? Should the United States have "done it alone" or with a handful of allies from 1990 on? Is there anything that you think the United States should have done differently? If so, would these other steps be consistent with international law as you now know it?

i. Iraq Returns to the Forefront: 2002-2003

From the end of 1998 into 2003, Saddam Hussein remained hostile to U.N. sanctions and he refused to readmit the U.N. weapons inspectors. Iraq did continue exporting oil under the supervision of the U.N., which levied the 30 percent charge. The U.N. used these revenues for humanitarian purposes and to help finance the U.N. Compensation Commission, as discussed earlier. However, there was also considerable evidence that Iraq was smuggling some oil out of the country through Jordan, Syria, and coastal waterways in order to evade the U.N. levy.

In spite of Iraq's opposition to weapons inspections and its smuggling, continued Iraqi diplomatic pressure — supported in part by Russia, France, and some other countries — led to repeated discussion in the U.N. Security Council in 1999-2001 about the possibility of relaxing the U.N. sanctions. However, strong resistance from the United States and, to some degree, Britain and others, blocked a dismantling of the sanctions regime.

The terrorist attacks of September 11, 2001, caused some analysts in the United States and elsewhere to suspect Iraqi involvement with Al Qaeda and the attacks, but no persuasive evidence could apparently be unearthed in the months right after September 11.

Nevertheless, the Bush Administration began to focus more on Iraq in early 2002. In President George W. Bush's State of the Union speech on January 29, 2002, he wove together the war of terrorism with efforts to combat the proliferation of weapons of mass destruction. He set out as a goal the prevention of "regimes that sponsor terror from threatening America or our friends and allies with weapons of mass destruction." He specifically listed Iraq, Iran, and North Korea and said that they "and their terrorist allies, constitute an axis of evil, arming to threaten the peace of the world." He went on to explain:

> By seeking weapons of mass destruction, these regimes pose a grave and growing danger. They could provide these arms to terrorists, giving them the means to match their hatred. They could attack our allies or attempt to blackmail the United States. In any of these cases, the price of indifference would be catastrophic.

... [A]ll nations should know: America will do what is necessary to ensure our nation's security.

We'll be deliberate, yet time is not on our side. I will not wait on events, while dangers gather. I will not stand by, as peril grows closer and closer. The United States of America will not permit the world's most dangerous regimes to threaten us with the world's most destructive weapons.

President Bush's speech was generally well received at that time in the United States, which was still focused on the implications of the September 11 attacks. However, questions were raised abroad about his lumping the three countries together and about the implications of his promise "not to wait on events."

Over the next few months, particularly accelerating in August 2002, the Bush Administration's attention seemed to shift increasingly from rooting out Al Qaeda and finding Osama bin Laden toward changing the regime of Saddam Hussein. Speeches by Vice President Richard Cheney and Secretary of Defense Donald Rumsfeld in August strongly suggested that the Bush Administration, in conjunction with the British and a few other countries, was preparing to use military force to oust Hussein. There were even arguments that past congressional and U.N. Security Council resolutions gave the United States all the authority it needed to act, and that there was no need to return to Congress or the U.N. Security Council.

President Bush, however, decided to seek both congressional and U.N. support. In a powerful speech to the U.N. General Assembly on September 12, President Bush focused on Iraq and its failure to comply with numerous past Security Council resolutions. He listed ongoing acts of defiance by the Iraqi regime, including its efforts to obtain biological, chemical, and nuclear weapons as well as missiles, its human rights violations, its continued support of international terrorists, its refusal to account for missing individuals from the Gulf War, its refusal to return Kuwaiti property, and its efforts to undermine U.N. economic sanctions.

President Bush squarely challenged the U.N.: "Are Security Council resolutions to be honored and enforced, or cast aside without consequence? Will the United Nations serve the purpose of its founding, or will it be irrelevant?" He then committed the United States to work with the U.N. Security Council in drafting new resolutions. However, he also warned that the resolutions needed to be enforced or "action will be unavoidable."

Shortly after this, President Bush released his National Security Strategy for the United States, which he had foreshadowed in his 2002 State of the Union speech and in comments during the summer of 2002. The new strategy took a proactive stance against potential threats to the United States. The following excerpt explains some of the key concepts.

The gravest danger our Nation faces lies at the crossroads of radicalism and technology. Our enemies have openly declared that they are seeking weapons of mass destruction, and evidence indicates that they are doing so with determination.... We will cooperate with other nations to deny, contain, and curtail our enemies' efforts to acquire dangerous technologies. And, as a matter of common sense and self-defense, America will act against such emerging threats before they are fully formed. We cannot defend America and our friends by hoping for the best....

We must be prepared to stop rogue states and their terrorist clients before they are able to threaten or use weapons of mass destruction against the United States and our allies and friends....

The United States has long maintained the option of preemptive actions to counter a sufficient threat to our national security. The greater the threat, the greater the risk of inaction — and the more compelling the case for taking anticipatory action to defend ourselves, even if uncertainly remains as to the time and place of the enemy's attack. To forestall or prevent such hostile acts by our adversaries, the United States will, if necessary, act preemptively. . . .

The purpose of our actions will always be to eliminate a specific threat to the United States or our allies and friends. The reasons for our actions will be clear, the force measured, and the cause just.

(See the discussion of this new strategy of possible preemptive actions to page 994 above.)

As the world awaited U.N. action on Iraq, President Bush sought and obtained a strong Joint Resolution from the U.S. Congress on October 16 that authorized the President to "use the Armed Forces of the United States as he determines to be necessary and appropriate in order to defend the national security of the United States against the continuing threat posed by Iraq. . . ." (The resolution is in the Documentary Supplement.)

On November 9, after effective diplomacy by the United States and Britain, the U.N. Security Council unanimously passed Resolution 1441. The Resolution declared that Iraq was in "material breach of its obligations under relevant [past] resolutions" and that Iraq was being afforded a "final opportunity" to comply with its disarmament obligations imposed by the previous resolutions. The Resolution established a rigorous inspection regime and demanded that Iraq provide "immediate, unimpeded, unconditional, and unrestricted access to any and all" places and persons that the U.N. inspectors wished to investigate. The Resolution concluded by recalling "that the Council has repeatedly warned Iraq that it will face serious consequences as a result of its continued violations of its obligations."

U.N. Security Council Resolution 1441
(Nov. 8, 2002)

The Security Council,

Recalling all its previous relevant resolutions . . . ,

Recognizing the threat Iraq's non-compliance with Council resolutions and proliferation of weapons of mass destruction and long-range missiles poses to international peace and security,

Recalling that its resolution 678 (1990) authorized Member States to use all necessary means to uphold and implement its resolution 660 (1990) of 2 August 1990 and all relevant resolutions subsequent to resolution 660 . . . ,

Further recalling that its resolution 687 (1991) imposed obligations on Iraq . . .

Deploring the fact that Iraq has not provided an accurate, full, final, and complete disclosure, as required by resolution 687 (1991), of all aspects of its programmes to develop weapons of mass destruction and ballistic missiles with a range greater than one hundred and fifty kilometres . . . ,

Deploring further that Iraq repeatedly obstructed immediate, unconditional, and unrestricted access to sites designated by the United Nations Special Commission (UNSCOM) and the International Atomic Energy Agency (IAEA), failed to cooperate fully and unconditionally with UNSCOM and IAEA weapons inspectors, as required by resolution 687 (1991), and ultimately ceased all cooperation with UNSCOM and the IAEA in 1998, . . .

Deploring also that the Government of Iraq has failed to comply with its commitments pursuant to resolution 687 (1991) with regard to terrorism, pursuant to resolution 688 (1991) to end repression of its civilian population and to provide access by international humanitarian organizations to all those in need of assistance in Iraq, and pursuant to resolutions 686 (1991), 687 (1991), and 1284 (1999) to return or cooperate in accounting for Kuwaiti and third country nationals wrongfully detained by Iraq, . . .

Recalling that in its resolution 687 (1991) the Council declared that a ceasefire would be based on acceptance by Iraq of the provisions of that resolution, including the obligations on Iraq contained therein,

Determined to ensure full and immediate compliance by Iraq without conditions or restrictions with its obligations under resolution 687 (1991) and other relevant resolutions. . . ,

Determined to secure full compliance with its decisions,

Acting under Chapter VII of the Charter of the United Nations,

1. *Decides* that Iraq has been and remains in material breach of its obligations under relevant resolutions, including resolution 687 (1991), in particular through Iraq's failure to cooperate with United Nations inspectors and the IAEA, and to complete the actions required under paragraphs 8 to 13 of resolution 687 (1991);

2. *Decides,* while acknowledging paragraph 1 above, to afford Iraq, by this resolution, a final opportunity to comply with its disarmament obligations under relevant resolutions of the Council; and accordingly decides to set up an enhanced inspection regime with the aim of bringing to full and verified completion the disarmament process established by resolution 687 (1991) and subsequent resolutions of the Council;

3. *Decides* that . . . the Government of Iraq shall provide to UNMOVIC, the IAEA, and the Council, not later than 30 days from the date of this resolution, a currently accurate, full, and complete declaration of all aspects of its programmes to develop chemical, biological, and nuclear weapons, ballistic missiles, and other delivery systems such as unmanned aerial vehicles and dispersal systems designed for use on aircraft, including any holdings and precise locations of such weapons, components, sub-components, stocks of agents, and related material and equipment, the locations and work of its research, development and production facilities, as well as all other chemical, biological, and nuclear programmes . . . ,

4. *Decides* that false statements or omissions in the declarations submitted by Iraq pursuant to this resolution and failure by Iraq at any time to comply with, and cooperate fully in the implementation of, this resolution shall constitute a further material breach of Iraq's obligations . . . ,

5. *Decides* that Iraq shall provide UNMOVIC and the IAEA immediate, unimpeded, unconditional, and unrestricted access to any and all, including underground, areas, facilities, buildings, equipment, records, and means of transport which they wish to inspect, as well as immediate, unimpeded, unrestricted, and private access to all officials and other persons whom UNMOVIC or the IAEA wish to interview in the mode or location of UNMOVIC's or the IAEA's choice pursuant to

any aspect of their mandates; further decides that UNMOVIC and the IAEA may at their discretion conduct interviews inside or outside of Iraq, . . . and that, at the sole discretion of UNMOVIC and the IAEA, such interviews may occur without the presence of observers from the Iraqi Government; and instructs UNMOVIC and requests the IAEA to resume inspections no later than 45 days following adoption of this resolution and to update the Council 60 days thereafter; . . .

10. *Requests* all Member States to give full support to UNMOVIC and the IAEA in the discharge of their mandates, including by providing any information related to prohibited programmes or other aspects of their mandates, including on Iraqi attempts since 1998 to acquire prohibited items, and by recommending sites to be inspected, persons to be interviewed, . . . the results of which shall be reported to the Council by UNMOVIC and the IAEA;

11. *Directs* the Executive Chairman of UNMOVIC and the Director-General of the IAEA to report immediately to the Council any interference by Iraq with inspection activities, as well as any failure by Iraq to comply with its disarmament obligations, including its obligations regarding inspections under this resolution;

12. *Decides* to convene immediately upon receipt of a report in accordance with paragraphs 4 or 11 above, in order to consider the situation and the need for full compliance with all of the relevant Council resolutions in order to secure international peace and security;

13. *Recalls*, in that context, that the Council has repeatedly warned Iraq that it will face serious consequences as a result of its continued violations of its obligations;

14. *Decides* to remain seized of the matter.

U.N. weapons inspectors arrived in Iraq in mid-November and soon began their inspections. Moreover, pursuant to U.N. Resolution 1441, Iraq submitted a voluminous report on December 7. Secretary of State Colin Powell quickly condemned the Iraqi report as incomplete. National Security Adviser Condoleezza Rice authored an op-ed article in January 2003 in which she concluded that: "[I]nstead of full cooperation and transparency, Iraq has filed a false declaration to the United Nations that amounts to a 12,200 page lie." The chief U.N. weapons inspector, Hans Blix, and the head of the International Atomic Energy Agency (IAEA), Mohamed ElBaradei, were more mixed in their comments on the report, saying essentially that the report contained much information, but that there were important gaps and questions. Inspections continued at an accelerating pace into March 2003, especially after the inspectors obtained helicopters and also arranged for U-2 surveillance plane flights.

As the inspections were proceeding, so were the major deployments of military forces from the United States and Britain, along with some support from Australia and other countries. By early March, over 200,000 U.S. troops had arrived in the area around Iraq, mainly in Kuwait or on ships offshore. The U.S. forces included Marines, combat Army units, naval ships, and hundreds of aircraft that would operate from land bases and from aircraft carriers. About 45,000 British troops and their combat equipment had also been deployed. More forces were on the way. Possibly for its psychological value, the U.S. military also tested with considerable publicity the largest conventional bomb ever, a 21,000 pound behemoth, in Florida, and noted that it could be used against hardened targets in Iraq.

During this winter of 2002-2003, the Bush Administration and Blair government continued their harsh criticism of Saddam Hussein. They emphasized that Iraq was not disarming (e.g., eliminating its weapons of mass destruction and delivery systems), but "deceiving." Also, in part possibly because of the mixed reports about the success of the ongoing inspections, President Bush, Prime Minister Blair, and other U.S. or U.K. officials emphasized additional reasons for regime change. For example, they said that the Iraqi government had links to Al Qaeda or "Al Qaeda-type" terrorist groups, and provided some evidence, though most of the evidence regarding Al Qaeda appeared to involve activities after September 11. President Bush and Prime Minister Blair both highlighted Saddam Hussein's human rights abuses. In his State of the Union speech on January 28, 2003, President Bush was graphic, describing how the Iraqis were "torturing children while their parents are made to watch" and reporting that they used "electric shock, burning with hot irons, dripping acid on the skin, mutilation with electric drills, cutting out tongues, and rape."

In late February 2002, in part reacting to questions about what would happen if the United States and its allies forced a regime change in Iraq, President Bush promised a "sustained commitment from many nations, including our own," to rebuilding Iraq. He envisioned that: "The nation of Iraq — with its proud heritage, abundant resources and skilled and educated people — is fully capable of moving toward democracy and living in freedom."

Nevertheless, the governments of many other countries and, judging from the opinion polls and demonstrations, many people abroad were not persuaded in early 2003 of the need to invade Iraq. Indeed, the Turkish government declined to allow the United States to deploy over 60,000 troops there (as a prelude to opening a northern front against Iraq) apparently because of strong popular opposition to being involved in a war with Iraq. Even in Britain, public opinion polls were strongly against Britain being involved in an attack against Iraq without a new Security Council resolution, with the opposition being especially intense in Prime Minister Blair's own Labor Party.

Led by France and Germany, a coalition emerged that wanted, at a minimum, to allow the inspectors more time. Russia and China were more cautious, but in early March 2003, they appeared to be leaning against supporting a new U.N. resolution that could be interpreted as allowing soon the use of force against Iraq.

The debate was sharpened in early March when, on March 6, President Bush flatly said at a rare press conference that the United States would force a vote on a new resolution the week of March 9. He implied that Saddam Hussein had missed his final opportunity and that the U.N. should authorize the use of force by member states.

Then, on March 7, Hans Blix and ElBaradei made new reports to the Security Council. Blix found new cooperation from the Iraqis, including their start in destroying some of their al-Samoud missiles whose range he had determined exceeded the permitted limit. Blix was cautiously optimistic about the possibility of further progress through the use of inspections. ElBaradei indicated that his IAEA inspectors had not found evidence of new Iraqi efforts to make nuclear weapons. Indeed, he specifically refuted one of the U.K. and U.S. claims that Iraq had sought to buy 500 tons of uranium from Niger. He said that the relevant documents had been forged, creating an embarrassment for the U.S. and U.K. intelligence agencies, who had obtained the documents from a third country and had somehow continued to cite them even after serious questions had been raised about their authenticity.

With a vote on a new resolution called for, efforts by the different sides to obtain support intensified, particularly directed at the countries with seats on the 15-member Security Council. Among the five veto-wielding members, the United States and Britain were obviously accounted for, as was France on the other side, with Russia and China cautious. Bulgaria and Spain announced their support for the U.S.-U.K. position, but Germany was opposed. Syria was also likely opposed and other countries hesitated to commit publicly, including Angola, Cameroon, Chile, Guinea, Mexico, and Pakistan.

Although France made it increasingly clear that it would not only vote against but also veto any resolution that might be interpreted as authorizing the use of force, the United States, Britain, and many observers seemed to believe that it would nevertheless be very helpful for the United States and Britain to obtain the required majority of nine votes. The apparent undecideds found themselves being wooed in private and sometimes threatened in public statements by officials from the committed countries. The French Foreign Minister personally flew to the three countries in Africa that were on the Security Council (Angola, Cameroon, and Guinea) in hopes of persuading them to oppose a new U.S.-U.K. resolution. President Bush made many telephone calls and some administration officials made veiled threats about remembering those who voted against the United States.

Lacking their goal of nine votes during the week of March 9, Bush and Blair delayed any voting, opting for a weekend summit with the Spanish and Portuguese leaders in the Azores islands on March 15. Although the participants called for a last diplomatic effort over the next 24 hours, it apparently became clear to the U.S. and U.K. governments that they did not have the nine votes and also faced a certain French veto. Rather than seeking another vote, President Bush and Prime Minister Blair stopped their diplomacy in the U.N.

On Monday evening, March 16, President Bush went on television briefly. He recounted how the Iraqi regime had refused to disarm and that it had trained and harbored terrorists. He noted the danger from "chemical, biological, or, one day, nuclear weapons." He then assured the audience: "Before the day of horror can come, before it is too late to act, this danger will be removed. The United States of America has the sovereign authority to use force in assuring its own national security." However, he went on to cite specifically U.N. Resolutions 678 and 687, saying "both [were] still in effect," as well as Resolution 1441. He observed that today "no nation can possibly claim that Iraq has disarmed." Noting opposition from "some permanent members of the Security Council" to a new resolution, he concluded: "The United Nations Security Council has not lived up to its responsibilities, so we will rise to ours."

President Bush gave a specific ultimatum: "Saddam Hussein and his sons must leave Iraq within 48 hours. Their refusal to do so will result in military conflict, commenced at a time of our choosing." He did offer a message to Iraqi citizens, though: "If we must begin a military campaign, it will be directed against the lawless men who rule our country and not against you."

The next day, Saddam Hussein's spokesman said that Saddam rejected the ultimatum and another Iraqi called on President Bush to resign. The ultimatum ended on the evening of March 19 (and early on March 20 in Iraq). For several days before this, U.S. and British aircraft protecting the no-fly zones had already increased their attacks on Iraqi targets and The Washington Post had reported that U.S. special forces were already operating in Iraq, working with the Kurdish opposition and preparing the battlefield. However, hostilities were about to escalate sharply with a major U.S. missile strike against Baghdad.

Notes and Questions

1. Look carefully at the language of Resolution 1441, especially the closing paragraphs. Does the text of the resolution authorize the use of force if Iraq does not fully comply with the renewed weapons inspections? Why might the language on possible consequences be intentionally vague? If there is a clear-cut Iraqi violation (such as hiding weapons of mass destruction), what is the next step under the resolution?

2. Note how President Bush just before the attack cited Resolutions 678, 687, and 1441, and made clear that Iraq had not complied. Did the existing resolutions provide legal grounds for the U.S. and other coalition forces to mount a major attack on Iraq and force a change in the government? If not, what additional facts might be sufficient to justify these attacks on Iraq on legal grounds? Or, was another resolution required?

3. How important was it to the coalition's position whether or not it actually found in Iraq any weapons of mass destruction that were prohibited under the earlier U.N. resolutions?

4. For more detailed justifications by the U.S. and British governments for their actions under existing U.N. resolutions, see the March 20 letter from the U.S. Ambassador to the U.N. and the statement from Britain's Attorney General. President Bush also made an important statement in his letter of March 18 to Congressional leaders reporting on the diplomatic efforts with regard to Iraq. (All these documents are in the Documentary Supplement.) In his letter, President Bush wrote:

> Consistent with section 3(b) of the Authorization for Use of Military Force Against Iraq Resolution of 2002 (Public Law 107-243) . . . , I determine that: (1) reliance by the United States on further diplomatic and other peaceful means alone will neither (A) adequately protect the national security of the United States against the continuing threat posed by Iraq nor (B) likely lead to enforcement of all relevant United Nations Security Council resolutions regarding Iraq; and (2) acting pursuant to the Constitution and Public Law 107-243 is consistent with the United States and other countries continuing to take the necessary actions against international terrorists and terrorist organizations. . . .

5. Did the U.S. and British governments weaken their position that the existing U.N. resolutions gave the coalition sufficient authority to attack when the U.S. and Britain sought another resolution in March 2003, only to drop that effort when it appeared that they did not have a nine-vote majority?

6. In his speech to the American people on March 17, President Bush said that: "The United States has the sovereign authority to use force in assuring its own national security." He had earlier discussed continued Iraqi actions to "possess and conceal" weapons of mass destruction and the danger that terrorists, "with the help of Iraq" might one day use these weapons against the United States or other countries. In his letter of March 18, the President referred to the "continuing threat posed by Iraq." Although the President did not use the term "self-defense" either in

his speech or letter, were the statements cited above a reliance on "the inherent right or individual or collective self-defense"? (The State Department's Legal Adviser explicitly invoked U.N. Charter Article 51.)

Did the President's arguments fit within the exact language of Article 51 — i.e., "if an armed attack occurs"? Or did his justifications appear to rely on a theory of anticipatory self-defense? Or was President Bush relying, in part, on the U.S. national security strategy of possible preemptive actions that had been announced in September 2002 as part of the new U.S. national security strategy? (See earlier discussion of the doctrine of self-defense and variants on it pages 981 and 993.)

If you were a senior U.S. official, what is the justification or justifications that you would use to support the attacks by U.S. and other coalition forces in March 2003?

One senior Bush Administration lawyer said privately that the U.S. government had purposely not adopted anticipatory self-defense or the possibility of preemptive actions as one of its justifications for the March 2003 actions. Rather, the Bush Administration had intended to rely on the breach of the U.N. resolutions and Article 51, while "reserving" the anticipatory self-defense and preemptive strike justifications.

Whatever the intent of the Bush Administration, possibly because of the new U.S. national security strategy or because of the understandably large number of statements by various Bush Administration officials during March and April 2003, some observers interpreted the March 2003 attacks as based on the strategy of preemptive attacks.

At least some of the leadership in one country — India — interpreted the attack that way. Moreover, India's minister of external affairs said that India had a "better case" for a preemptive strike against Pakistan than America did against Iraq. As a New York Times article reporting on the minister's interview began: "[T]he argument is seductive: if America can strike out at a suspect sponsor of terrorism and hugely destructive weapons thousands of miles away, why can't India hit out at one next door?" Amy Waldman, India Pressed on Kashmir Attacks, N.Y. Times, April 9, 2003, at A6. India and Pakistan have had a long-standing feud over Kashmir, which is within India, with militants crossing from Pakistan into Kashmir. In March 2003, another of a string of incidents had occurred there when 24 Hindus were massacred. India blamed Pakistan for supporting the perpetrators. Does India have a "better case" or as good a case as the United States for a preemptive attack?

7. From 1999 on, how effective was the U.N.'s handling of the situation in Iraq generally? How effective was it on issues involving human rights and nonproliferation in Iraq?

8. From the standpoint of the United States, from 1999 on, was the U.N. Security Council a help or a hindrance in reacting to Saddam Hussein on nonproliferation? On support of terrorists? On human rights? Is there anything that you think the United States should have done differently? If so, would these other steps be consistent with international law as you now know it?

9. In a thoughtful op-ed article on March 18, 2003, Dean Anne-Marie Slaughter observed that the world was witnessing "an unruly process of pushing and shoving toward a redefined role for the United Nations." She noted that NATO had earlier decided to go ahead with its intervention in Kosovo (see below at page 1077) without U.N. Security Council authorization because of Russian opposition. She noted that neither those for intervention in Iraq nor those against it could command

a majority on a new resolution. She acknowledged that the U.S. course of action might now be "illegal but legitimate," but concluded that the U.N. rules might well evolve "so that what is legitimate is also legal." The New York Times, March 18, 2003, at A31. Do you agree? Why or why not? (Note the earlier discussion by Professor Franck about the U.N. Charter being an adaptive instrument, at page 981.)

j. The War Begins

At 5:33 A.M. in Baghdad on March 20, less than two hours after the end of President Bush's 48-hour ultimatum, many loud explosions broke the tense quiet. Operation Iraqi Freedom had begun. Rather than initial strikes against a large number of targets in Iraq, the first coalition attack was aimed at a location where Saddam Hussein and his senior aides were thought to be meeting. The CIA had apparently received what it considered reliable information and, after hurried discussions among President Bush and his senior civilian and military advisers, it was decided to seize the opportunity. Two F-117A stealth fighters each dropped a one-ton bomb guided by satellite and dozens of cruise missiles were launched from ships at this "leadership target." Whether this strike or at least two other major missile and bombing strikes in the next two weeks against senior leadership targets killed or injured Saddam Hussein or his two sons was still unclear as of May 30. However, at a minimum, it appears that these strikes did help disrupt Iraqi command and control because other Iraqi officials had questions about the fate of Saddam Hussein, thus weakening their loyalty and/or fear of the regime, and the tactics of Iraqi military units did not seem well coordinated.

Fierce airstrikes soon followed on March 20 throughout the rest of Iraq. Moreover, rather than waiting for several days of airstrikes, U.S. and British ground forces were pouring into Iraq from Kuwait by that evening. In part, this rapid ground attack was designed to protect the more than 1,000 oil wells in the south before they could be destroyed.

The British forces moved to seize the southern port of Umm Qasr. The sporadic, but sometimes substantial, resistance that the British encountered in Umm Qasr and then Faw presaged the occasional resistance that the coalition forces were to encounter. While most Iraqi regular forces surrendered or defected, British marines found themselves in a long standoff at Basra with Iraqi irregulars, sometimes called the fedeyeen, who were loyal to Saddam Hussein and who had occupied Iraq's second largest city.

The U.S. Marines quickly began moving north, but ran into heavy fire outside Nasiriyah, which cost 26 U.S. lives and slowed the advance. Further to the west, the U.S. Army's 3rd Infantry Division moved rapidly northward toward Baghdad, covering 200 miles in the first 36 hours. On the other hand, in northern Iraq, the coalition had not been able to launch a major ground attack because Turkey had not allowed the use of its country as a staging and jumping off point. However, small U.S. Special Force units worked with Iraqi Kurdish fighters, called the pesh merga, to move against Iraqi military positions. U.S. and British special units also operated in the west and other parts of Iraq to attack specific targets and disrupt the Iraqi defenses.

The battle took a turn for the worse on March 23, when a U.S. Army supply convoy made a wrong turn and ran into opposition that led to 12 U.S. soldiers being killed or captured. Also, the continuing persistence of the fedeyeen opposition made supply lines vulnerable and slowed progress. Then, a large attack by Apache helicopters, the Army's major deep strike weapon, was thwarted by widespread small arms fire from the ground, with two helicopters downed and many of the others seriously damaged. Also, the advancing coalition forces had begun to reach areas where Iraqi use of chemical weapons seemed most likely.

March 24 then was the start of three days of difficult weather with sandstorms that grounded most close air support and made even ground transportation difficult. Rather than stopping the advance and regrouping, however, the coalition pushed forward to the outskirts of Baghdad as the weather cleared. U.S. forces soon began encircling the capital. Although the U.S. military was hesitant to engage in prolonged street fights with its often heavy casualties, U.S. armored columns began making forays into the city. Sooner than many people expected, the Iraqi opposition began to crumble. Possibly because of another strike against the Iraqi leadership, Saddam Hussein (if he still lived) and his senior leadership all but disappeared. On April 9, the U.S. Marines, with help from the Iraqis, pulled down a prominent statute of Saddam in the center of Baghdad.

Sporadic opposition still continued in the capital, and the major northern towns had yet to be taken. However, on April 10, Kurdish pesh merga fighters occupied the oil center of Kirkuk. Mosul surrendered on the 11th without much of a fight. On April 13 Saddam Hussein's home town, Tikrit, fell without any organized opposition and the Pentagon announced that the "major combat operations" in Iraq had ended. On April 16, in a symbolic act of victory less than a month after the start of the war, General Tommy R. Franks, commander of the U.S.-led forces in Iraq, met with his senior generals in one of the presidential palaces in Baghdad. However, because of the occasional firefights and continuing lawlessness (discussed further below), his short visit to Baghdad was accompanied by very heavy security. As of April 24, the reported casualties during the hostilities were less than 120 Americans killed and about 30 British dead. Iraqi casualties were in the many thousands, but accurate estimates were not possible.

It was still unclear in May 2003 how much the swift victory was the result of the coalition's military prowess, how much was the result of an internal breakdown of the Iraqi leadership and its senior military, or what other factors might have been significant. Nevertheless, it was clear that this war was like no others in its use of new twenty-first-century weapons and tactics. Compared to 1991 Operation Desert Storm, when only nine percent of the bombs dropped were precision-guided, most of the bombs and all the cruise missiles used in 2003 were precision ammunitions. Moreover, thanks to new surveillance methods, including low-flying drones as well as high-altitude aircraft and satellites, targets could be identified quickly day and night. Then, though rapid communications, bombs might be dropped or missiles launched against the targets within minutes or even less.

k.   The Aftermath of the War

Even as Saddam Hussein's statute was toppling over in Baghdad on April 9, widespread looting by Iraqis began to break out in Baghdad and in other cities as the Iraqi government essentially disappeared. The looting quickly spread to encompass not only office buildings that had harbored the most disliked elements of the Iraqi government, but also stores, banks, and even homes. Among the most regrettable incidents was the looting of the Iraqi National Museum of Antiquities, a repository of treasures from 7,000 years of world history starting with Mesopotamia, one of civilization's first societies, and including artifacts from early Islamic culture.

On April 9 and for several days afterwards, coalition forces were still focused on defeating the remaining Iraqi military forces and taking control of the northern towns. However, the lawlessness in Baghdad and elsewhere was to be expected from the past experience of other repressive governments collapsing, such as in the recent Yugoslav struggles. Moreover, American archaeologists and other scholars had warned the U.S. government about the danger to the museums before the war had begun.

As a result, there was widespread international criticism when the coalition forces seemed unprepared for trying to maintain civil order. Retired Lt. Gen. Jay Garner, picked by the Bush Administration to run postwar Iraq, first entered Iraq and met in Nasirya with 70 Iraqis on April 14. He did not arrive in Baghdad until April 21. U.S. and international humanitarian assistance (including medical supplies) had still not entered Baghdad in any noticeable quantities by April 21.

Outside of Iraq, there was international debate on what should be the relative roles of the coalition countries and the U.N. in the post-war reconstruction of Iraq. Meeting on April 8, President Bush and Prime Minister Blair acknowledged that the U.N. should have a "vital role" in the reconstruction, but President Bush apparently meant this only to encompass the provision of humanitarian aid. In contrast, France, Germany, and Russia called for the U.N. to play the "central" role in Iraq's reconstruction. Moreover, on April 18-19, the foreign ministers of the six countries bordering Iraq (i.e., Iran, Jordan, Kuwait, Syria, and Saudi Arabia, and Turkey) met in Saudi Arabia and urged the "occupying powers" to quickly stabilize Iraq and withdraw.

In the streets of Baghdad and elsewhere, Iraqis began exercising their new freedom by resuming some religious services and demonstrating on various matters, including against the coalition's presence. Some Iraqis began assuming roles as mayors or other positions on their own initiative. Trying to maintain stability and the coalition's role, the commander of U.S. ground forces in Iraq issued a proclamation, saying, "The coalition alone retains absolute authority within Iraq."

The first issue that required U.N. Security Council attention was the removal or at least relaxation of the wide-ranging economic sanctions against Iraq. The United States and Britain said that was essential for Iraqi reconstruction to go forward.

Notes and Questions

1. During the fighting, a handful of U.S. soldiers were captured by Iraqi forces and coalition forces captured thousands of Iraqi prisoners. What are a country's obligations under international law for prisoners of war (POWs)? These and other questions regarding the laws of war are discussed below in Section C.

2. After the collapse of the Saddam government and the coalition's military victories in Iraq, what should have been the coalition's post-war responsibilities in the separate though overlapping areas of restoring and maintaining order, providing humanitarian relief, and helping the Iraqis establish their new government? What should have been the role of the U.N.?

3. Note that some critics of a large U.N. role pointed to its past experience during the troubles in Yugoslavia, most recently in Kosovo, when the U.N. had appeared to move slowly and very bureaucratically. The U.N. has recently been involved, to mixed reviews, in the efforts to reconstruct Afghanistan after the major fighting ended there in 2001. (See case study in Chapter 1.E.) On the other hand, the United States had done commendably in its reconstruction efforts in Germany, Italy, and Japan after World War II, but that was over 50 years ago. The United States had not played the leading role in reconstruction efforts in any important situation since.

Part of the struggle over roles, though not admitted publicly by the various countries, revolved around which countries would be deciding what companies would receive contracts for hundreds of millions, and possibly billions, of dollars for various reconstruction efforts, including helping repair and modernize the Iraqi oil fields. The major French and Russian oil companies were reportedly very concerned that their past good commercial relations with Iraq under Saddam Hussein would be jeopardized by their countries' opposition to the coalition's attack on Iraq.

4. On May 22, 2003, the U.N. Security Council adopted an important post-war resolution regarding Iraq, which was submitted by the coalition after some discussions with other countries. Resolution 1483 passed by a vote of 14-0, with Syria not present, and was adopted under Chapter VII of the U.N. Charter, which makes the resolution binding on all U.N. member states.

The detailed provisions of the resolution include, among other matters: an explicit recognition that the United States and the U.K. were "occupying powers" as a unified command (the "Authority"); the appointment of a U.N. Special Representative for Iraq with various coordinating responsibilities: support for the formation of an "Iraqi interim administration . . . run by Iraqis, until an internationally recognized, representative government is established by the people of Iraq and assumes the responsibility of the Authority"; the end of the U.N. economic sanctions against Iraq, except those related to weapons sales; the creation of a Development Fund for Iraq with an initial $1 billion from the U.N.'s expiring Oil for Food Program and further funds to come from the export sales of Iraqi petroleum products. (Excerpts of the resolution are in the Documentary Supplement.)

5. Given the events leading up the regime change in Iraq in 2003 (including the coalition's inability to obtain a U.N. resolution in March, but its decision to proceed anyway), what is the future role of the U.N. Security Council in cases of countries that might be harboring terrorists? Developing weapons of mass destruction? Brutally repressing large segments of their population?

Is it likely that there will be more "coalitions of the willing" that proceed without U.N. Security Council authorization? When, if ever, are countries likely even to seek Security Council approval in future situations that might involve the use of military force against another country[ies]? What reforms, if any, should the U.N. Security Council itself undertake?

3.   Regional Peacekeeping Efforts

Regional peacekeeping efforts have occurred sporadically in the Western Hemisphere, Africa, and Europe. There have been several such efforts in the Western Hemisphere in the past century and an African regional group has recently become active. However, as detailed at the end of this section, the recent peacekeeping effort with possibly the greatest precedential value was NATO's bombing campaign against the former Yugoslavia over the repression of Albanians in Kosovo.

The principal vehicle for peacekeeping in the Western Hemisphere has been the Organization of American States (OAS), working through the Rio Treaty. Its effectiveness, however, has declined in the past decade after its major successes with the quarantine of Cuba in 1962 and sending peacekeeping forces to the Dominican Republic in 1965. The Organization of Eastern Caribbean States (OECS) was involved to a disputed extent in the Grenada invasion in 1983, but that group's membership and geographic scope are limited for purposes of future peacekeeping operations. (See Chapter 5, Section C, regarding the OAU and the OAS. The Cuba operation is analyzed below.)

Some commentators suggested in the early 1990s that regional groups might have less of a peacekeeping role to play in the future. It was the United Nations that created in 1989 a peacekeeping force for Central America, the first U.N. peacekeeping operation in the Western Hemisphere, then sent a U.N. observer mission to monitor Nicaraguan elections, and then authorized the creation of a U.S.-led multinational force for Haiti in 1994. However, other events indicate a possible growing trend in the opposite direction. As described further below, starting in 1990, a West African regional group began peacekeeping operations in Liberia and its forces have since operated in Sierra Leone and the Ivory Coast. Moreover, the NATO air strikes against the Federal Republic of Yugoslavia over Kosovo in 1999 were undertaken by NATO forces without explicit Security Council authorization. Although U.N. resolutions and, eventually, U.N. peacekeepers played a role in the aftermath, the primary actor in the Kosovo intervention was NATO, possibly indicating an increased role for regional organizations.

a. The Cuban Quarantine

The Cuban missile crisis of 1962 involved a dramatic, direct, and potentially deadly confrontation between the United States and the Soviet Union. Both countries' military forces went on alert, and the possibility of nuclear warfare was not insignificant. The result was a clear success for the United States and President Kennedy. Indeed, the crisis is frequently studied as a model for U.S. diplomacy in the nuclear age.

The crisis also involved a regional peacekeeping force, though some questions have been raised about whether the U.N. Charter was complied with regarding the linkage between the OAS action and the U.N. Security Council. Professor Henkin provides a succinct description and analysis of the crisis.

Louis Henkin, How Nations Behave: Law and Foreign Policy

279-302 (2d ed. 1979)

On October 22, 1962, President Kennedy addressed the people of the United States by television in an atmosphere of crisis. He announced that the United States had clear evidence that the Soviet Union was in the process of installing in Cuba "large, long-range, and clearly offensive weapons of sudden mass destruction." These weapons constituted "an explicit threat to the peace and security of all the Americas," and their introduction was "a deliberately provocative and unjustified change in the status quo which cannot be accepted by this country." The President announced that the United States would impose a defensive maritime quarantine to prevent the further introduction into Cuba of offensive missiles, and to induce the Soviet Union to withdraw the missiles already there.

On the same day, the United States placed the Cuban situation before the United Nations Security Council and asked for an urgent meeting of the Council. The Council met on the following day, October 23, and discussed the crisis and the proposed quarantine but took no action. On that day, the Organization of American States, acting under the Rio Treaty of 1947, adopted a resolution recommending that the members

> take all measures, individually and collectively, including the use of armed force, which they may deem necessary to ensure that the Government of Cuba cannot continue to receive from the Sino-Soviet powers military material and related supplies which may threaten the peace and security of the Continent and to prevent the missiles in Cuba with offensive capability from ever becoming an active threat to the peace and security of the Continent.

In the evening of October 23, after the action of the OAS, President Kennedy proclaimed the quarantine to take effect on the following day. Under the quarantine all vessels, of whatever nationality, in defined zones would be intercepted but would be allowed to continue to Cuba if they were not carrying prohibited materials.

Pursuant to the quarantine, vessels of the Soviet Union and of other nations were trailed, boarded, inspected. Soviet submarines were located, tracked, surfaced, and photographed. Other vessels apparently destined for Cuba changed course and proceeded elsewhere. No vessels were forcefully seized or diverted, and military force was not actually used.

The outcome is well known. The Soviet Union agreed to discontinue bringing missiles into Cuba; it agreed to discontinue building its missile bases in Cuba and to dismantle and remove missiles that had already been installed. The United States agreed to end the quarantine and gave assurances against an invasion of Cuba. . . .

THE LEGAL JUSTIFICATIONS . . .

Principally, United States lawyers based their case on the authorization from the Organization of American States. The OAS is a regional organization contemplated by Chapter VIII of the United Nations Charter; indeed, it was the inter-American system which the framers of the Charter had principally in mind. As the later embodiment of the inter-American system, the OAS can take collective action, or can authorize action by its members, in defense of the hemisphere. Just as the United Nations Charter was interpreted as permitting the General Assembly to act in support of international peace and security when the Security Council proved ineffective, so, argued the lawyers for the United States, the Charter should be interpreted to allow a similar role to such regional organizations when the organs of the United Nations cannot be effective.

It is true that Article 53 of the Charter provides that "no enforcement action shall be taken under regional arrangements or by regional agencies without the authorization of the Security Council." But the resolution of October 23, it was argued, was not "enforcement action"; it was only a recommendation. Also, the authorization required from the Security Council need not be prior authorization nor need it be expressed. The Security Council was informed of the OAS resolution and of the proposed action of the United States thereunder, and, in the words of the Deputy Legal Adviser of the State Department, "did not see fit to take action in derogation of the quarantine. Although a resolution condemning the quarantine was laid before the Council by the Soviet Union, the Council subsequently, by general consent, refrained from acting upon it." . . .

THE JUSTIFICATIONS WHICH THE UNITED STATES AVOIDED

What the United States did not say about Cuba — just as what it did not do — may have been more significant than what the United States did and said. . . . Although the President and others invoked the needs of American defense and security in political justifications, no responsible spokesman mentioned Article 51, even as possible alternative legal support for the quarantine. Repeatedly, the Legal Adviser and the Deputy Legal Adviser stressed that the United States "did not rest its case" on that ground. Report has it that reference to Article 51 was several times proposed for insertion in statements by the President and others, and every time alert and insistent lawyers succeeded in eliminating it.

The temptation must have been great. Pressed to justify the action of the United States, the lawyers relied on the authorization of the OAS, although some may have found that authorization flimsy and the argument under it strained. They eschewed Article 51, although, as some would interpret it, that article would have handsomely justified the quarantine, as well as bombing and perhaps even invasion of Cuba, without need of OAS authorization. But spokesmen for the United States apparently recognized the dangers which the argument entailed.

Notes and Questions

1. Under Article 53 of the U.N. Charter, was the quarantine an "enforcement action," which should have required the authorization of the U.N. Security Council? Did the Security Council provide authorization by its inaction? If you believe that the quarantine was an enforcement action requiring affirmative authorization by the Security Council, doesn't that view seriously weaken the possible role of regional organizations because the Security Council might be deadlocked because of a veto by a permanent power? Shouldn't strong regional organizations be encouraged? (See Chapter VIII of the Charter.)

Besides the argument for strong regional organizations, there is the historical evidence of the U.N. General Assembly playing a role when the Security Council is paralyzed. For example, as discussed earlier, because of Security Council inaction, during the Suez crisis in 1956 a U.N. Emergency Force was established pursuant to resolutions of the U.N. General Assembly.

2. The Cuban missile crisis of 1962 is generally viewed as a success for U.S. foreign policy and for OAS regional peacekeeping efforts. Why doesn't the United States or other countries in the Western Hemisphere resort to the OAS more often?

One reason is that Article 6 of the Rio Treaty requires a two-thirds vote of the countries that have ratified the Treaty. (The United States and over 20 other countries in the Western Hemisphere have ratified the Treaty.) The foreign policies of the United States and many of the Latin American countries often differ. For example, how likely is it that the United States could have obtained in 1989 a two-thirds vote supporting a recommendation for peacekeeping actions (such as a naval quarantine) against the Sandinista government of Nicaragua? Or even a recommendation for a peacekeeping action against General Noriega's government in Panama in 1989? (Indeed, there was the 22-1 OAS vote against the U.S. invasion of Panama.)

3. Why do you think that U.S. officials avoided invoking the Article 51 justification of self-defense in the Cuban missile crisis? What is the explicit condition in the Article for resort to self-defense? Was it met here?

In his excellent book about the crisis, the Legal Adviser to the Department of State at the time, Professor Abram Chayes, gives his perspective on why he thought self-defense should not have been invoked:

> [I]t was inconsistent with the effort to obtain O.A.S. endorsement and would be unnecessary if that effort were successful.
>
> Intra-office discussions at the time emphasized that it would set a bad precedent if the United States were to rely on a self-defence theory. . . . [T]he normative atmosphere in which states act, though tenuous and impalpable perhaps, is affected by the earlier actions of others and their accompanying statements of what they take the governing law to be. An official United States position endorsing a latitudinarian construction of "armed attack" could not help but weaken those normative checks. To this extent there was something in the idea that a claim of self-defence would set a dangerous precedent.
>
> In retrospect, however, I think the central difficulty with the Article 51 argument was that it seemed to trivialize the whole effort at legal justification. No doubt the phrase "armed attack" must be construed broadly enough to permit some anticipatory response. But it is a very different matter to expand it to include threatening deployments or demonstrations that do not have imminent attack as their purpose or probable outcome. To accept that reading is to make the occasion for forceful response essentially a question for unilateral national decision that would not only be formally unreviewable, but not subject to intelligent criticism, either. There is simply no standard against which this decision could be judged. Whenever a nation believed that interests, which in the heat and pressure of a crisis it is prepared to characterize as vital, were threatened, its use of force in response would become permissible. . . .
>
> In this sense, I believe an Article 51 defence would have signalled that the United States did not take the legal issues involved very seriously, that in its view the situation was to be governed by national discretion not international law. Some may regard that conclusion as inherently reprehensible; others as refreshingly candid. In either case, it would have meant that values other than law were being chiefly relied on as justification for action. If legitimation by law was needed or wanted, the Article 51 argument could not really carry the burden. [Abram Chayes, The Cuban Missile Crisis 63-66 (1974).]

Is the danger Professor Chayes identifies still a threat in today's post-9/11 world? As discussed above at page 994, the Bush Administration adopted in 2002 a national security strategy that included the limited use of preventive or preemptive attacks. Might this strategy weaken the restraints on other states' use of force?

4. President Kennedy spoke to the American people on October 22 and said that the United States would impose the quarantine on Cuba. The OAS voted in favor of its recommendation on October 23. What if the United States had not obtained the necessary two-thirds votes? Should the United States have proceeded with the quarantine anyway? Using what justification in international law?

5. For further discussion of the legal issues in the Cuban missile crisis and the role of the U.S. government lawyers, see Professor Chayes' book, The Cuban Missile Crisis (1974). For a seminal study on U.S. government decision-making that uses the Cuban crisis as its primary factual basis, see Graham Allison, The Essence of Decision: Explaining the Cuban Missile Crisis (2d ed 1991). International conferences in 1987 and 1989 brought together some of the former U.S., Soviet, and Cuban officials who had been governmental decision-makers during the 1962 crisis. See Raymond Garthoff, Reflections on the Cuban Missile Crisis (1989).

6. *Intervention in Grenada.* A much more controversial event was the intervention in Grenada on October 25, 1983, by 8,000 U.S. troops, along with 3,000 soldiers from six Caribbean countries. The allied force initially met stiff resistance from Cuban and Grenadian forces, but all U.S. combat forces were withdrawn by December 15 after stability had been restored.

The invasion followed the summary execution of Prime Minister Maurice Bishop and the surrounding confusion in October. The prime minister's government had been increasing ties with the Soviet Union and especially Cuba, but then he had a falling out with the rest of the leadership of his New Jewel Movement. In the turmoil, Bishop and several loyal colleagues were captured and killed by the Grenadian People's Revolutionary Army.

U.S. officials offered several justifications for the invasion, never relying on a single one. One of the reasons offered was that the lives of about 1,000 U.S. citizens living in Grenada were endangered as a result of the violent unrest. It is not clear, however, that the Americans' lives were actually at risk, nor whether that threat would justify the invasion force occupying the island for almost two months, long after any Americans who wanted to leave had been evacuated. The other major justification was that the invasion was a regional peacekeeping operation by the Organization of Eastern Caribbean States (OECS), with the OECS asking the United States to participate. However, there were several disputes regarding whether the OECS had the authority under its treaty to authorize the invasion of a member state, and if so, whether it had followed proper procedures.

A special committee to the American Bar Association submitted a report on the legal justifications for the invasion of Grenada. The report concluded that "the military action initiated October 25th rests upon an unsteady legal foundation." Edward Gordon (chairman), Richard B. Bilder, Arthur W. Rovine, and Don Wallace Jr., International Law and the United States Action in Grenada: A Report, in 18 Intl. Law. 331 (1984).

7. *Intervention in Liberia.* In August 1990, the Economic Community of West African States (ECOWAS) — a regional organization founded to promote economic integration — began peacekeeping operations in Liberia in response to a civil war. The 15,000-strong peacekeeping force, called ECOMOG, was arguably acting

outside the terms of its 1981 self-defense pact, but with the refusal of the United Nations and United States to get involved, regional action seemed necessary.

The ECOMOG fought rebel forces and bombed rebel strongholds as necessary to enforce the ceasefire. Finally, elections were held in 1997. ECOMOG withdrew a year later. The members of ECOWAS justified their intervention by citing the need to stop the slaughter of civilians, to protect foreign nationals, and to eliminate the threat posed by anarchy to peace in the region. The rebel leader, Charles Taylor, claimed it was an illegal intrusion into Liberian sovereignty. Today, ECOMOG is a permanent West African peacekeeping force. Since withdrawing from Liberia, it has operated in Sierra Leone and in the Ivory Coast.

b.   Intervention in Kosovo

At the conclusion of World War II, the leader of one of the guerilla groups that had resisted the German invasion, Tito (aka Josip Broz), became head of the newly created Federal People's Republic of Yugoslavia, which was made up of a mix of different ethnic groups that had long histories of wars and rivalries. The three major ethnic groups (Serbs, Croats, and Muslims) lived relatively peacefully under the iron grip of Marshall Tito until his death in 1980, and this peace continued a while under a rotating presidency arrangement whereby the heads of each of the then republics (Serbia, Montenegro, Croatia, Slovenia, Macedonia, and Bosnia-Herzegovina) took turns as president.

With the fall of communism in the Soviet Union and Eastern Europe in the late 1980s and early 1990s, tensions rapidly grew within Yugoslavia as the various republics went in different political directions. Croatia, Slovenia, Macedonia, and Bosnia-Herzegovina sought independence. Slovenia, the most northern of the republics and relatively distant from Serbia, declared its independence in 1991 and its militia won an important victory over the Yugoslav army. With the quick recognition of the European Union countries, Slovenia was standing on its own by the end of 1991.

It would take longer for the other republics to succeed in breaking away. A truly vicious civil war began, with Serbian President Slobodan Milosevic seeking to maintain Yugoslav control over all ethnically Serbian areas, including parts of Croatia and Bosnia-Herzegovina. The U.N. tried unsuccessfully to maintain the peace with its peacekeeping forces, including troops from NATO countries and Russia. After extensive diplomacy by the United States (with a leading role played by Ambassador Richard Holbrooke) and by European countries, the warring parties agreed in November 1995 to the Dayton Accords (named after the Ohio city where the key negotiations had occurred). This led to Milosevic agreeing to the independence of Bosnia-Herzegovina, Croatia, and Macedonia.

Peace, however, did not come to Kosovo. Ethnic Albanians stepped up a campaign of attacks against Serbians in their effort to split off from Serbia and become a part of Albania. The Serbs responded with much violence. In the winter of 1998-1999, the Serbs conducted a major attack against Kosovo, forcing some 700,000 ethnic Albanians from their homes. NATO warned Milosevic to stop his campaign, but the "ethnic cleansing" continued.

As described more fully below by Professor Mary Ellen O'Connell, the United States and other countries in NATO felt the compelling need to stop this violence against an ethnic group, but they met opposition from Russia in the U.N. Security Council. Nevertheless, NATO decided to proceed. On March 24, 1999, NATO forces began airstrikes against targets inside Serbia. The attacks continued for 78 days, until Serbia surrendered and Milosevic accepted NATO's terms under which Serbia would withdraw all its military forces from Kosovo and NATO would send 50,000 troops there.

Militarily and politically, NATO's military action was a success. However, by intervening inside a sovereign state without the explicit authorization of a Security Council resolution, the NATO campaign raised questions about the U.N. Charter's restrictions on the use of force by regional organizations and it created an important precedent regarding humanitarian intervention.

Mary Ellen O'Connell, The UN, NATO, and International Law After Kosovo

22 Hum. Rts. Q. 57, 73-82 (2000)

The first volley in the post-Cold War Balkan conflicts occurred when Slobodan Milosovic revoked the autonomy of Kosovo within the Federal Republic of Yugoslavia in 1988 as a demonstration of his brand of Serb nationalism. Despite this ominous event and the increasingly "miserable" conditions of life in Kosovo that followed it, the mostly ethnic Albanian population of the province did not take up arms to liberate themselves from Yugoslavia as did the populations of Slovenia, Croatia, and Bosnia-Herzegovina. They did proclaim independence but tried to realize it for many years through nonviolent resistance under the leadership of Ibrahim Rugova. Rugova's strategy had both moral and pragmatic underpinnings. It was clear that Serbs would not let go of Kosovo without a fight. . . . Even if Serbia lost a war over Kosovo, the struggle to regain it would likely never end. According to Milosevic, Kosovo is "the heart of Serbia . . . Kosovo is a holy [land]."

The Kosovo Albanians did not have even the minimal resources of the Bosnians at the start of their liberation struggle. Kosovo was the poorest region of the former Yugoslavia. Albania, the Kosovars' chief champion, is the poorest country in Europe and its own military is in shambles. Rugova depended, rather, on international support to eventually triumph. At first, he received it. . . . Yet when the Dayton Peace Accords of 1995 were signed, Kosovo was not mentioned. This omission severely undermined Rugova, triggering the rapid rise of the Kosovo Liberation Army (KLA). . . .

During 1997, the KLA claimed more than fifty attacks on Serbs in Kosovo and were labeled a terrorist organization by the United States. Serb police had retaliated — killing dozens. Then, over the weekend of 28 February to 1 March 1998, Serb police killed twenty-five ethnic Albanians, apparently in revenge for the killing of four Serb police by the KLA.

On 7 March, US Secretary of State Madeleine Albright announced in Rome that the United States would not stand idly by. On 9 March, Albright and Germany's Foreign Minister Klaus Kinkel announced in Bonn that they favored intervening in

Kosovo — at least diplomatically. . . . By 31 March, the Security Council had adopted Resolution 1160, which stated that the Council:

Acting under Chapter VII of the Charter of the United Nations,

1. *Calls upon* the Federal Republic of Yugoslavia immediately to take the further necessary steps to achieve a political solution to the issue of Kosovo through dialogue and to implement the actions indicated in the Contact Group* statements of 9 and 25 March 1998;

2. *Calls also upon* the Kosovar Albanian leadership to condemn all terrorist action, and *emphasizes* that all elements in the Kosovar Albanian community should pursue their goals by peaceful means only; . . .

8. *Decides* that all States shall, for the purposes of fostering peace and stability in Kosovo, prevent the sale or supply to the Federal Republic of Yugoslavia, including Kosovo, . . . arms and related *matériel* of all types. . . .

Economic sanctions, however, did not persuade the parties to develop a peaceful solution. . . . Discussion began to turn to military intervention, and to the Russian statement that any request for Security Council authorization to use force in Kosovo would be met by a Russian veto.

US Secretary of Defense William Cohen said in June 1998 that the United States took the position that NATO would not need a UN Security Council authorization to intervene in Kosovo. . . .

In September 1998, the Security Council did pass Resolution 1199, in which the Council, "*Affirming* that the deterioration of the situation in Kosovo, Federal Republic of Yugoslavia, constitutes a threat to peace and security in the region" and "*Acting* under Chapter VII of the Charter of the United Nations" demanded the parties agree to a cease-fire, that both sides end criminal acts and allow the diplomatic monitoring group, the OSCE, and the International Committee of the Red Cross to have access to the province. Finally, the resolution said the Security Council "*Decides,* should the concrete measures demanded in this resolution and resolution 1160 (1998) not be taken, to consider further action and additional measures to maintain or restore peace and stability in the region." The Resolution does not, however, refer to any parties being authorized to use "all necessary means" or other explicit formula to indicate the Council intended to authorize the use of force.

The Security Council took no further action. Nevertheless, on 13 October 1998, NATO members agreed to authorize the use of force in Yugoslavia. . . . NATO requires consensus to authorize such an operation, so all sixteen members had to favor the action order ("ACTORD"). . . . [M]ost of the NATO members involved made arguments quite similar to the United States in the Cuban Missile Crisis: even if NATO had not exactly met the requirements of the UN Charter, it was close, and the deviation would neither set a precedent nor harm the Charter regime. NATO had, after all, Security Council Resolution 1199, which came close to authorization. Winter was coming and people would die in the mountains if action was not taken. Some NATO members might have approved the action not really believing that force would actually be used, that a threat would be enough. Moreover, the Russians

* [The "Contact Group" was a name given to a group of countries that were especially interested in the developments in Yugoslavia and that met on an irregular basis and communicated frequently. The states included the United States, the United Kingdom, France, Germany, Italy, and Russia.— Eds.]

indicated to the United States that if no explicit resolution was requested, they would not protest the Action Order at the Security Council. . . .

Nor did NATO actually use force in October 1998. . . . [T]he United States succeeded in brokering an agreement with Yugoslavia's president, Slobodan Milosevic, which permitted the return of those who had fled their homes and the positing of a group of 2,000 unarmed human rights monitors. In the end, only 1400 monitors were deployed, but the vast majority of refugees returned to their homes. Still, it was an unstable peace. . . . More attacks [by Kosovo Albanians] did occur. . . .

In January 1999, about forty Kosovo Albanians were killed at Racak. The monitors were withdrawn and the Contact Group turned to discussions of a peacekeeping force for Kosovo. During these discussions, "French officials said the deployment of NATO peacekeepers in Kosovo needed to be backed by a United Nations Security Council resolution, a proposition that the Clinton Administration opposed. Washington, according to State Department officials, was sticking to its stand that NATO should be able to act independently of the United Nations."

Talks continued intermittently near Paris during February and March between the Contact Group, Yugoslavia, and representatives of the Kosovo Albanians. The aim was to get both sides to agree to a plan drafted by the United States, the "Rambouillet Accords." The Kosovo Albanians were finally persuaded to agree to the Accords. The Serbs were not, despite NATO's threats to use force if Yugoslavia did not agree to the Accords. In the meantime, the Serbs had massed 40,000 troops in Kosovo close to the international borders.

On 24 March 1999, NATO began a bombing campaign over Yugoslavia; it had no explicit Security Council authorization to do so. NATO issued no statement setting out the legal justification for the action, nor did the United States. The US President and Secretary of State made references to humanitarian disaster, though not to a right of humanitarian intervention. . . . The State Department press spokesperson, in answer to a direct question about the law, seemed to say that Yugoslavia's violation of international law, humanitarian catastrophe, and the threat to NATO members justified the use of force. Following the start of the bombing, Kosovo Albanians began streaming out of the province. Over 900,000 left, bringing with them reports of terror, destruction, and especially of young men being singled out and killed or taken away.

In April, Yugoslavia brought a case to the International Court of Justice (ICJ) against ten NATO members arguing that they had used force in violation of international law, including violation of the Genocide Convention. At the ICJ, the Legal Adviser to the US Department of State argued that "[m]embers of the NATO Alliance find their justification in a number of factors. These include: — [t]he humanitarian catastrophe . . . ; [t]he acute threat . . . to the security of neighbouring States . . . ; [t]he serious violation of international humanitarian law and human rights . . . ; and, . . . the resolutions of the Security Council. . . ." He did not, however, argue explicitly that a right of humanitarian intervention justified NATO's action nor that the Security Council resolutions were sufficient on their own to authorize a use of force.

Belgium, alone of the ten states responding to Yugoslavia's case, suggested that at least a nascent right of humanitarian intervention existed when NATO began bombing. Most of the other capitals involved in NATO's use of force argued that the bombing was a justifiable exception to the normal rules. Though their arguments appear related to the defenses of distress or necessity, none explicitly argued either.

Some argued that the Security Council Resolutions prior to NATO's 13 October decision and use of force provided sufficient authorization to use force. Adding to the lack of clarity of the legal situation, just two days after the start of the bombing, Russia introduced a resolution at the Security Council condemning NATO's bombing as a violation of the Charter and as a threat to international peace. Only Russia, China, and Namibia voted in favor. Even the Secretary General did not condemn NATO's use of force, saying only "normally a U.N. Security Council Resolution is required."

Given the circumstances of NATO's intervention over Kosovo, what legal justifications, if any, are available to NATO? Does Kosovo provide a precedent that might be followed in the future? As Professor O'Connell notes above, the United States refrained from offering an official legal justification, thought there were a series of statements from U.S. officials and from officials in other countries. In addition, as is consistent with the War Powers Resolution (discussed in a later section), President Clinton made a report to Congress shortly after the NATO bombing began, in which he said:

> The F[ederal] R[epublic] Y[ugoslavia] government has failed to comply with U.N. Security Council resolutions, and its actions are in violation of its obligations under the U.N. Charter and its other international commitments. The FRY government's actions in Kosovo are not simply an internal matter. The Security Council has condemned FRY actions as a threat to regional peace and security. The FRY government's violence creates a conflict with no natural boundaries, pushing refugees across borders and potentially drawing in neighboring countries. The Kosovo region is a tinderbox that could ignite a wider European war with dangerous consequences to the United States. . . .
>
> We cannot predict with certainty how long these operations will need to continue. Milosevic must stop his offensive, stop the repression, and agree to a peace accord based on the framework from Rambouillet. If he does not comply with the demands of the international community, NATO operations will seriously damage Serbia's military capacity to harm the people of Kosovo. NATO forces will also use such force as is necessary to defend themselves in the accomplishment of their mission. [Letter to Congressional Leaders, 35 Weekly Comp. Pres. Doc. 527 (March 26, 1999).]

Before turning to what are the best justifications, if any, for NATO's military intervention, it might be helpful to consider the analysis of Professor Jane Stromseth about the implications for the international law on humanitarian intervention in light of the Kosovo campaign.

Jane Stromseth, Rethinking Humanitarian Intervention: The Case for Incremental Change

in Humanitarian Intervention: Ethical, Legal and Political Dilemmas
232, 241-245 (J.L. Holzgrefe and Robert O. Keohane, eds. 2003)

For years to come, NATO's 1999 military intervention in Kosovo will shape international attitudes toward the use of force in response to human rights atrocities. In contrast to the U.S. military action in Afghanistan taken in self-defense against terrorist attacks, the legal basis for NATO's action in Kosovo remains contested. Whether "humanitarian intervention"—the use of force for humanitarian purposes—is lawful or otherwise justified in the absence of state consent or United Nations authorization is a question that has long vexed international lawyers and philosophers. . . .

Four distinct attitudes or approaches to humanitarian intervention in the absence of Security Council authorization can be identified. Each has pros and cons. First is the status quo approach. This view categorically affirms that military intervention in response to atrocities is lawful only if authorized by the UN Security Council or if it qualifies as an exercise of the right of self-defense. Proponents of this view regard NATO's intervention in Kosovo as a clear violation of Article 2(4) that should not be repeated in the future. Defenders of this position include a number of states, most notably Russia and China. . . .

Yet, after Kosovo, it is hard to take a rigid status quo approach. NATO responded to urgent humanitarian circumstances in a situation recognized as a threat to the peace by the Security Council. Furthermore, neither the Council nor the Secretary-General were prepared to condemn NATO's action. . . .

This leads to the "excusable breach" approach to humanitarian intervention. Under this second approach, humanitarian intervention without a UN mandate is technically illegal under the rules of the UN Charter but may be morally and politically justified in certain exceptional cases. In short, it is a violation of the Charter for which states are unlikely to be condemned or punished. . . .

The excusable breach approach has some distinct benefits. It highlights the truly exceptional nature of legitimate non-authorized humanitarian intervention. It contemplates no new legal rules governing the use of force. On the contrary, the existing legal framework, with its various benefits, is affirmed. Yet, in those extraordinary cases that produce a tension between the rules governing the use of force and the protection of fundamental human rights, a "safety valve" is opened. States intervening in such situations are unlikely to be condemned as law-breakers; but they act at their own risk in full awareness that they are violating the rules for a higher purpose.

This approach has evident drawbacks as well, however. For one thing, it is unsatisfying to label as "illegal" action that the majority of the UN Security Council views as morally and politically justified. . . . Second, the justifications offered by states — and the international responses to state action — are more nuanced than the "excusable breach" approach. NATO states did not argue "we are breaking the law but should be excused for doing so." Instead, NATO states, in sometimes differing ways, explained why they viewed their military action as "lawful"— as having *a legal basis within the normative framework of international law*. . . .

This leads to a third approach: customary law evolution of a legal justification for humanitarian intervention in rare cases. This approach looks to both Security Council and broader international responses to instances of non-authorized humanitarian intervention to ascertain patterns, consistency of rationales, and degrees of acceptance, reflected in practice, if certain conditions are met. This approach asks whether an emerging norm of customary international law can be identified under which humanitarian intervention should be understood not simply as ethically and politically justified but also as legal under the normative framework governing the use of force. The strong non-intervention presumption at the Charter's core is affirmed, but this approach allows for a narrow, evolving legal exception and justification for humanitarian intervention in light of concrete circumstances, and in light of the reasons that states and the UN Security Council find persuasive over time, rather than calling such action flatly illegal or an "excusable breach" of the UN Charter.

The advantages of this approach are considerable and, as I will argue, it offers a more promising path for the future than the alternatives. Nevertheless, the ambiguities inherent in this approach have led some to advocate a fourth, more explicit, approach to humanitarian intervention. Advocates of this fourth approach favor codification of a clear legal doctrine or "right" of humanitarian intervention. Proponents argue that such a "right" or "doctrine" should be established through some formal or codified means such as a UN Charter amendment or a UN General Assembly declaration. The idea is that humanitarian intervention should be a distinct legal basis for using force on a par with the right of self-defense, with fixed criteria or principles spelled out in advance governing legitimate appeal to the right. Although states have been extremely reluctant to advocate a legal right of humanitarian intervention in the absence of Security Council authorization, a number of scholars . . . have made the case for establishing such a right or doctrine with specified criteria to guide assessments of legality. The case for codifying a right of humanitarian intervention rests on a normative attitude towards such interventions, a view about the impact of codification on the legitimacy of international law, a position concerning the role of formalization in curbing abuses, and a view about the relative benefits of clarity versus open-endedness in the evolution of international legal norms.

5th Approach — Regional action under regional consent and notion of "responsibility to protect"

Notes and Questions

1. What do you believe are the best justifications, if any, for NATO's military intervention, including bombing attacks, against the Federal Republic of Yugoslavia over Kosovo? Consider the grievances that President Clinton listed against the FRY. Do any provide the legal justification for the use of force by NATO? What principles justifying the use of force can be found in this statement? President Clinton refers to the risk of a "wider European war," but no NATO member claimed that the Kosovo airstrikes were justified as self-defense under Article 51. Why not? Could any interpretation of Article 51 extend to an attack on a state threatening not an armed attack but merely a "threat to regional security"?

2. The principle that internal repression causing refugees to cross international borders could constitute a "threat to international peace and security" was established in the aftermath of the Gulf War. However, there had been Security Council resolutions authorizing the use of force against Iraq over its invasion of Kuwait. Nevertheless, does the precedent whereby the United States, Britain, and other countries used force against Iraq to prevent its repression of its own minorities after Operation Desert Storm provide helpful precedent for the NATO action against the FRY?

3. What about the Security Council resolutions regarding Kosovo? Resolutions 1160 and 1199, discussed in Professor O'Connell's article, invoked Chapter VII to require certain actions of Serbia and to impose multilateral economic sanctions. Neither resolution, however, explicitly authorized the use of force (which would have triggered a Russian veto). Do the resolutions nevertheless provide some support? (The resolutions are in the Documentary Supplement.)

4. Consider Articles 52-53 of the U.N. Charter regarding the role of regional organizations, such as the OAS and NATO. Article 53 does state that "no enforcement action shall be taken under regional arrangements or by regional agencies without the authorization of the Security Council," except for some specified situations not applicable here. However, could it be argued, as some did regarding the U.S. and OAS action regarding the quarantine of Cuba in 1962, that the NATO action over Kosovo was not an "enforcement action"?

Some NATO members likened the Kosovo situation to the Cuba quarantine, where the Security Council was paralyzed by the Soviet veto. Does it help the case under Articles 52-53 that, while Russia refused to allow the Security Council to authorize the use of military force against Serbia, Russia indicated in October 1998 that it would not protest NATO's Action Order? Can this be taken as tacit authorization for NATO's airstrikes? Did that authorization, if any, expire when Russia in fact introduced a resolution condemning the use of force, even though the resolution was defeated? What bearing does the tacit approval of Secretary General Kofi Annan have on the legality of the airstrikes?

5. What does Kosovo imply for the principle of humanitarian intervention? With the exception of Belgium's after-the-fact defense before the ICJ, no state claimed that an independent right of humanitarian intervention justified NATO's action. However, the U.S. and its allies relied heavily upon evidence of massacres and ethnic cleansing for political and moral justification for the airstrikes, and several offered it as a reason to regard the intervention as legitimate, though technically in violation of the Charter.

6. Eight of the ten ICJ cases brought by Yugoslavia against NATO members remain open as of January 2003 (the cases against Spain and the United States were dismissed for lack of jurisdiction). If the Court reaches a ruling on the merits in any of the remaining cases, it may help define the extent of the right of humanitarian intervention and the restrictions on the use of force by regional organizations in light of Security Council inaction. However, the court had extended the time for Yugoslavia to file responses to the objections of the eight NATO states, and changes to the Yugoslav government since 1999 may mean that the Court will never reach the merits of the case.

C. INDIVIDUAL RESPONSIBILITY AND INTERNATIONAL HUMANITARIAN LAW

Just as legal norms have developed about whether or when the United Nations, regional organizations or other groups of states, or an individual state might resort to the use of force, there are legal norms regarding the responsibilities of states and individuals during the conduct of war and other armed conflicts. These latter norms are sometimes referred to as international humanitarian law.

This section starts with the important law regarding individual responsibility that was developed under the Nuremberg Charter and international tribunals right after World War II, and that has been developed further in the more recent international criminal courts for Yugoslavia and Rwanda and by the new International

Criminal Court. The section then focuses on the international humanitarian law norms, often found in the Geneva Conventions, and examines how they apply to occupying powers and the treatment of prisoners of war. Finally, there is an analysis of the law that might be applicable to the treatment of terrorists — not only international humanitarian law, but also international criminal law and domestic law.

1. Nuremberg and Other World War II Precedents

Even before World War II ended, the United States, Great Britain, the Soviet Union, and France were considering how to deal after the war not only with the aggression of Nazi Germany and Japan, but also with the increasingly obvious atrocities that had occurred in the concentration camps and elsewhere. One central document accepted by the parties was the 1945 Charter of the International Military Tribunal that defined certain crimes — crimes against peace, war crimes, and crimes against humanity (discussed above at page 976). The Charter specified that an individual could be responsible for these crimes through his or her acts. It also provided that "[l]eaders, organizers, instigators, and accomplices participating in the formulation or execution of a common plan or conspiracy to commit any of the foregoing crimes are responsible for all acts performed by any persons in execution of such plan." (Article 6.) Article 7 provided further that: "The official position of defendants, whether as Heads of State or responsible officials in Government Departments, shall not be considered as freeing them from responsibility or mitigating circumstances."

The Charter specifically dealt with the question of who in the chain of command could be held responsible for illegal acts. Article 8 states: "The fact that the Defendant acted pursuant to order of his Government or of a superior shall not free him from responsibility, but may be considered in mitigation of punishment. . . ." The Tribunal was given the right to impose a sentence on the convicted of "death or such other punishment as shall be determined by it to be just." (Article 27.)

The following is an excerpt from the Judgment of the Tribunal, where the Tribunal addresses the basis for its jurisdiction.

Judgment of the International Military Tribunal for the Trial of German Major War Criminals
Nuremberg, Sept. 30 and Oct. 1, 1946

In Berlin, on the 18th October, 1945, in accordance with Article 14 of the Charter, an Indictment was lodged against the defendants named in the caption above, who had been designated by the Committee of the Chief Prosecutors of the signatory Powers as major war criminals. . . .

This Indictment charges the defendants with crimes against peace by the planning, preparation, initiation and waging of wars of aggression, which were also wars in violation of international treaties, agreements and assurances; with war crimes; and with crimes against humanity. The defendants are also charged with participating in the formulation or execution of a common plan or conspiracy to commit all these crimes. The Tribunal was further asked by the Prosecution to declare all the named groups or organisations to be criminal within the meaning of the Charter. . . .

THE LAW OF THE CHARTER

The jurisdiction of the Tribunal is defined in the Agreement and Charter, and the crimes coming within the jurisdiction of the Tribunal, for which there shall be individual responsibility, are set out in Article 6. The law of the Charter is decisive, and binding upon the Tribunal.

The making of the Charter was the exercise of the sovereign legislative power by the countries to which the German Reich unconditionally surrendered; and the undoubted right of these countries to legislate for the occupied territories has been recognised by the civilised world. The Charter is not an arbitrary exercise of power on the part of the victorious nations, but in the view of the Tribunal, as will be shown, it is the expression of international law existing at the time of its creation; and to that extent is itself a contribution to international law.

The Signatory Powers created this Tribunal, defined the law it was to administer, and made regulations for the proper conduct of the Trial. In doing so, they have done together what any one of them might have done singly; for it is not to be doubted that any nation has the right thus to set up special courts to administer law. With regard to the constitution of the court, all that the defendants are entitled to ask is to receive a fair trial on the facts and law.

The Charter makes the planning or waging of a war of aggression or a war in violation of international treaties a crime; and it is therefore not strictly necessary to consider whether and to what extent aggressive war was a crime before the execution of the London Agreement. But in view of the great importance of the questions of law involved, the Tribunal has heard full argument from the Prosecution and the Defence, and will express its view on the matter.

It was urged on behalf of the defendants that a fundamental principle of all law — international and domestic — is that there can be no punishment of crime without a pre-existing law. *"Nullum crimen sine lege, nulla poena sine lege."* It was submitted that ex post facto punishment is abhorrent to the law of all civilised nations, that no sovereign power had made aggressive war a crime at the time the alleged criminal acts were committed, that no statute had defined aggressive war, that no penalty had been fixed for its commission, and no court had been created to try and punish offenders.

In the first place, it is to be observed that the maxim *nullum crimen sine lege* is not a limitation of sovereignty, but is in general a principle of justice. To assert that it is unjust to punish those who in defiance of treaties and assurances have attacked neighbouring states without warning is obviously untrue, for in such circumstances the attacker must know that he is doing wrong, and so far from it being unjust to punish him, it would be unjust if his wrong were allowed to go unpunished. Occupying the positions they did in the government of Germany, the defendants, or at least some of them must have known of the treaties signed by Germany, outlawing recourse to war for the settlement of international disputes; they must have known that they were acting in defiance of all international law when in complete deliberation they carried out their designs of invasion and aggression. On this view of the case alone, it would appear that the maxim has no application to the present facts.

This view is strongly reinforced by a consideration of the state of international law in 1939, so far as aggressive war is concerned. The General Treaty for the Renunciation of War of 27th August, 1928, more generally known as the Pact of Paris or the Kellogg-Briand Pact, was binding on sixty-three nations, including Germany, Italy and Japan at the outbreak of war in 1939. . . .

The question is, what was the legal effect of this Pact? The nations who signed the Pact or adhered to it unconditionally condemned recourse to war for the future as an instrument of policy, and expressly renounced it. After the signing of the Pact, any nation resorting to war as an instrument of national policy breaks the Pact. In the opinion of the Tribunal, the solemn renunciation of war as an instrument of national policy necessarily involves the proposition that such a war is illegal in international law; and that those who plan and wage such a war, with its inevitable and terrible consequences, are committing a crime in so doing. War for the solution of international controversies undertaken as an instrument of national policy certainly includes a war of aggression, and such a war is therefore outlawed by the Pact. . . .

But it is argued that the Pact does not expressly enact that such wars are crimes, or set up courts to try those who make such wars. . . . The law of war is to be found not only in treaties, but in the customs and practices of states which gradually obtained universal recognition, and from the general principles of justice applied by jurists and practised by military courts. This law is not static, but by continual adaptation follows the needs of a changing world. Indeed, in many cases treaties do no more than express and define for more accurate reference the principles of law already existing. . . .

At the meeting of the Assembly of the League of Nations on the 24th September, 1927, all the delegations then present (including the German, the Italian and the Japanese), unanimously adopted a declaration concerning wars of aggression. The preamble to the declaration stated:

> The Assembly:
> Recognising the solidarity which unites the community of nations;
> Being inspired by a firm desire for the maintenance of general peace;
> Being convinced that a war of aggression can never serve as a means of settling international disputes, and is in consequence an international crime. . . .

The unanimous resolution of the 18th February, 1928, of twenty-one American Republics of the Sixth (Havana) Pan-American Conference, declared that "war of aggression constitutes an international crime against the human species."

All these expressions of opinion, and others that could be cited, so solemnly made, reinforce the construction which the Tribunal placed upon the Pact of Paris, that resort to a war of aggression is not merely illegal, but is criminal. The prohibition of aggressive war demanded by the conscience of the world, finds its expression in the series of pacts and treaties to which the Tribunal has just referred.

It is also important to remember that Article 227 of the Treaty of Versailles provided for the constitution of a special Tribunal, composed of representatives of five of the Allied and Associated Powers which had been belligerents in the first

World War opposed to Germany, to try the former German Emperor "for a supreme offence against international morality and the sanctity of treaties." . . . In Article 228 of the Treaty, the German Government expressly recognised the right of the Allied Powers "to bring before military tribunals persons accused of having committed acts in violation of the laws and customs of war."

It was submitted that international law is concerned with the actions of sovereign States, and provides no punishment for individuals; and further, that where the act in question is an act of state, those who carry it out are not personally responsible, but are protected by the doctrine of the sovereignty of the State. In the opinion of the Tribunal, both these submissions must be rejected. That international law imposes duties and liabilities upon individuals as well as upon States has long been recognised. In the recent case of Ex Parte Quirin (1942 317 US I), before the Supreme Court of the United States, persons were charged during the war with landing in the United States for purposes of spying and sabotage. The late Chief Justice Stone, speaking for the Court, said:

> From the very beginning of its history this Court has applied the law of war as including that part of the law of nations which prescribes for the conduct of war, the status, rights and duties of enemy nations as well as enemy individuals.

He went on to give a list of cases tried by the Courts, where individual offenders were charged with offences against the laws of nations, and particularly the laws of war. . . . Crimes against international law are committed by men, not by abstract entities, and only by punishing individuals who commit such crimes can the provisions of international law be enforced. . . .

The principle of international law, which under certain circumstances, protects the representatives of a state, cannot be applied to acts which are condemned as criminal by international law. The authors of these acts cannot shelter themselves behind their official position in order to be freed from punishment in appropriate proceedings. Article 7 of the Charter expressly declares:

> The official position of defendants, whether as Heads of State, or responsible officials in government departments, shall not be considered as freeing them from responsibility, or mitigating punishment.

On the other hand the very essence of the Charter is that individuals have international duties which transcend the national obligations of obedience imposed by the individual State. He who violates the laws of war cannot obtain immunity while acting in pursuance of the authority of the State if the State in authorising action moves outside its competence under international law.

It was also submitted on behalf of most of these defendants that in doing what they did they were acting under the orders of Hitler, and therefore cannot be held responsible for the acts committed by them in carrying out these orders. The Charter specifically provides in Article 8:

> The fact that the defendant acted pursuant to order of his Government or of a superior shall not free him from responsibility, but may be considered in mitigation of punishment.

The provisions of this Article are in conformity with the law of all nations. That a soldier was ordered to kill or torture in violation of the international law of war has never been recognised as a defence to such acts of brutality, though, as the Charter here provides, the order may be urged in mitigation of the punishment. The true test, which is found in varying degrees in the criminal law of most nations, is not the existence of the order, but whether moral choice was in fact possible.

Notes and Questions

1. Do you agree with the Nuremberg Tribunal's rejection of the defendants' argument that they were charged with some crimes (e.g., waging a war of aggression) that did not exist until after the acts occurred? What were the Tribunal's principal precedents for responding to the ex post facto defense? Did these precedents establish criminal liability?

2. Do you agree that the defense of "superior orders" should not free a defendant of individual responsibility but should only go to mitigation of punishment?

3. The U.N. General Assembly unanimously affirmed the principles of international law that were recognized in the Nuremberg Charter and Tribunal. (G.A. Res. 95 (1946).)

4. The Tribunal convicted 19 Germans, sentencing 12 to death and the rest to imprisonment.

5. The Allied nations also established the International Military Tribunal for the Far East. This tribunal was a result of the Potsdam Declaration of July 26, 1945, signed by China, Great Britain, and the United States, and later adhered to by the Soviet Union. The government of Japan accepted the provisions of the Potsdam Declaration on September 2, 1945, when it signed the Instrument of Surrender to the Allied Powers. Trials were conducted throughout the Far East. The most famous of these was the trial in Tokyo from 1946-1948, which resulted in the conviction of 25 major figures from the Japanese government, including General Tojo. For a complete account of the proceedings of this Tribunal, see R. John Pritchard & Sonia Magbanua Zaide, The Tokyo War Crimes Trial (1981).

6. In addition to the two international major military tribunals after World War II, there were a host of other trials and proceedings. The following excerpt provides a sense of the large number of these activities.

War Crimes, War Criminals, and War Crimes Trials
4-8 (Norman E. Tutorow ed., 1986)

There is no complete list of the thousands of war crimes trials held following World War II. Among them were trials conducted by the International Military Tribunal at Nuremberg (IMT), the International Military Tribunal for the Far East (IMTFE) at Tokyo, the United States Military Tribunal at Nuremberg (NMT), United States Military Commissions sitting in various places in Europe and Asia, the General Military Government Court and Intermediate Government Court of the American Zone of Germany, British military courts sitting in various places in Europe and Asia, the

French Permanent Military Tribunal sitting in various places in France, the French Court of Appeal and the General Military Government Tribunal of the French Occupation Zone of Germany, the Australian Military Court sitting at Rabaul, the Canadian Military Court sitting in Aurich, Germany, the Netherlands Temporary Court-Martial and Special Courts, the Norwegian Court of Appeal, the Supreme Court of Norway, the Chinese War Crimes Court, and the Supreme National Tribunal of Poland.

The two international military tribunals tried a small number of major war criminals, while other tribunals tried so-called minor war criminals, among them financiers, industrialists, high government officials, police authorities, members of enemy armed forces, and other civilians.

Some enemy combatants accused of war crimes were tried by military tribunals, while most minor war criminals and civilians were tried by civil courts. These were either national courts of the nation that had apprehended the defendants or to which the defendants owed some sort of allegiance other than by citizenship. There were also a number of trials conducted by nations against their own citizens. . . .

Estimates vary on the total number of war crimes trials held. . . . The following is an estimate of the number of war crimes trials held by major Allied nations as of 1963:

Country	Number of Sentences	Death Sentences
USA	1,814	450
UK	1,085	240
USSR	c. 10,000	?
West Germany	12,846	?

In addition to war crimes trials conducted by foreign tribunals, there were thousands of denazification proceedings in Germany. On March 5, 1946, the three Länder (states) in the American Zone enacted a denazification law designed primarily not to punish Germans who had been Nazis, but to remove them from or keep them out of positions of postwar leadership. The accused were classified as either major offenders, offenders, lesser offenders, or followers. Major offenders were subject to immediate removal or permanent exclusion from public office, confiscation of property, and to a maximum of ten years in prison.

Under this law, 13 million people in the American Zone of occupation had to register. Of them, approximately 3 million were found subject to classification under the denazification law. In all, 545 tribunals, employing 22,000 people, worked on this classification process. Despite amnesties granted by the Military Governor, over 930,000 defendants were eventually tried by denazification tribunals. Of them, 1549 were classified as major offenders, 21,000 as offenders, 104,000 as lesser offenders, and 475,000 as followers. Over 500,000 people were fined for various criminal offenses, 122,000 suffered restrictions on employment, 25,000 were subject to confiscation of property, 22,000 were declared ineligible to hold public office, 30,000 were required to perform special labor, and 9000 were given prison sentences.

German courts prosecuted thousands of war criminals either not tried by the Allies or tried by them and acquitted. According to one account, West Germany alone prosecuted 12,982 defendants between 1945 and 1963. . . .

Trials conducted by various occupational and national authorities are almost countless and records of them are not always easy to obtain. It is particularly difficult to secure reliable and verifiable information on those trials held by the Soviet Union. . . .

Many war criminals were tried for acts committed in concentration or extermination camps. There were seven so-called "parent cases" involving six concentration camps — Dachau, Mauthausen, Flossenburg, Nordhausen, Buchenwald, and Mühldorf — as well as 170 subsequent proceedings related to these trials.

2.   The Tribunals for Yugoslavia and Rwanda

The vicious civil war that broke out in the former Republic of Yugoslavia in the early 1990s (as discussed at page 1077 above) was replete with evidence of torture, incarceration, forced deportation, systematic rape, willful killing, and indiscriminate shelling of civilians. Appalled by these atrocities and encouraged by the U.S. Ambassador to the U.N., Madeleine K. Albright, the U.N. Security Council established the International Criminal Tribunal for Yugoslavia (ICTY) with Resolution 827 on May 25, 1993. It was the first international war crimes tribunal since the tribunals right after World War II. (Prior U.N. resolutions had responded to the atrocities in the former Yugoslavia with investigations and condemnations by a Commission of Experts.)

The Security Council relied on Chapter VII of the U.N. Charter to justify the Tribunal. Violations of international humanitarian law were found to be a threat to international peace and security. Resolution 827 gave the Tribunal subject matter jurisdiction over war crimes and crimes against humanity. The Resolution required every state to turn over indicted individuals. If a state refused, the Security Council was to respond, presumably with sanctions initially. The Resolution also addressed issues of individual responsibility and due process. (Excerpts of the Resolution are in the Documentary Supplement.)

In November 1993, the eleven judges of the Tribunal, elected by the U.N. General Assembly, took oaths enabling them to indict, try, and sentence suspects. The Tribunal initially consisted of two trial chambers of three judges and a single five-judge appellate chamber. As of January 2003, the ICTY consists of 16 judges — three trial chambers of three judges each and a seven-judge appellate chamber. The expansion was an effort to help alleviate a backlog of more than two years.

After 14 months of political wrangling, the U.N. Security Council selected Justice Richard Goldstone of South Africa as chief prosecutor in July 1994. He served in that capacity until 1996, followed by Louise Arbour of Canada. Since September 1999, Carla Del Ponte, a career prosecutor and former Swiss Attorney General, has served as chief prosecutor. The prosecutors had the benefit of the files and data bank of the earlier-created Commission of Experts to aid their investigations. The first indictments, however, did not come until the fall of 1994.

In May 1997, a three-judge panel convicted Busko Tadic, a Bosnian Serb, on 11 counts of persecution and maltreatment committed in several internment camps during the war. On appeal, Tadic was convicted of 9 additional counts. The Tadic trial was the Tribunal's first completed trial and represents the first-ever judicial condemnation of "ethnic cleansing." Tadic was sentenced to 20 years' imprisonment and transferred to Germany to serve his sentence.

The Tribunal began hearings in March 1997 against four defendants associated with atrocities committed at the Celebici camp. The Celebici case was the first international war crimes trial of a group of individuals since the Nuremberg and Tokyo trials. It was also the first case in which the ICTY considered the issue of command responsibility for failing to prevent atrocities, pursuant to Article 7(3) of the ICTY statute. The Tribunal convicted and sentenced Zdravko Mucic to nine years for his responsibility for the war crimes committed by soldiers under his command.

Nevertheless, especially in its early years, the Tribunal's work has been stymied by the lack of cooperation of some of the states involved and their refusal to surrender key suspects. In addition, many of the accused retained positions of power and influence. As one response, the Tribunal began issuing sealed indictments in 1996. By not disclosing the names of indictees, the Tribunal prosecutor hoped to halt the concealment of wanted suspects. In June 1997, Tribunal investigators made their first arrest of a secretly indicted defendant.

After NATO's bombing campaign in 1999 over Serbia's repression in Kosovo and in response to reports from Amnesty International and Human Rights Watch, the chief prosecutor Louise Arbour initiated a review of NATO's actions during the Kosovo bombing campaign in an effort to demonstrate the Tribunal's independence. Arbour's successor, Carla Del Ponte, permitted the investigation to continue, arguing that she had a responsibility not to reject allegations out of hand. In a report released to the public in June 2000, she concluded that, while some of its air strikes may have been "excessive," NATO had not committed war crimes.

In 2001, under economic and diplomatic pressure from the United States and other countries, Serbia turned over to the Tribunal its former president, Slobodan Milosovic, whom the ICTY had indicted for a wide range of war crimes. His well-publicized trial began in February 2002 and was continued through March 2003.

Through March 2003, about 85 accused individuals have appeared before the ICTY, 20 of them have received their final sentence, and five have been found not guilty. There are at least 23 arrest warrants pending against individuals at large, including top officials like Radovan Karadzic, the former Bosian Serb president, and military commander Ratko Mladic.

In one overview of the ICTY in 2001, Professor Steven Ratner and U.N. lawyer Jason Abrams observed:

> Even in its brief lifespan, the Tribunal has produced some significant advancements in the substance and implementation of international criminal law. For example, the indictments and jurisprudence have highlighted the role of sexual violence in the Balkan conflict and more clearly defined the status of such offenses in international criminal law. In the *Celibici* case, for example, the ICTY found that rape may constitute a form of torture. Additional holdings on the scope of command responsibility and the defense of duress* are quite significant.
>
> Nevertheless, for all its accomplishments, the ICTY remains far too remote from the population, whose need for justice and healing was the primary reason for its

---

* [See discussion of the *Erdemovic* case at page 152.—EDS.]

creation. Many elements in the region view the Tribunal as biased or ineffective and have exploited its work for their own political and propaganda purposes. [Steven R. Ratner & Jason S. Abrams, Accountability for Human Rights Atrocities in International Law 201 (2d ed. 2001).]

Rwanda. In November 1994, the U.N. Security Council provided for a tribunal to prosecute genocide and other war crimes in Rwanda after widespread killings and other crimes had occurred. To simplify getting the arrangement underway, the new tribunal had the same prosecutor and appeals judges as the ICTY.

The International Criminal Tribunal for Rwanda (ICTR) has had some success. As of January 2003, 55 persons were in the Tribunal's custody, and six more were serving sentences in Mali. The Tribunal had completed 13 cases. Many of those arrested were apparently the leaders of the genocide, including the president and vice president of the party that ruled Rwanda in 1994. Moreover, in 1998, former Rwandan Prime Minister Jean Kambanda pled guilty to genocide before the Tribunal, making the ICTR the first international court to announce a judgment concerning the crime of genocide.

Notes and Questions

1. Although progress has often seemed to be slow, why does it appear that the criminal tribunals for Yugoslavia and Rwanda have had at least some success? Might it help that their jurisdiction is limited? Does it help that they were both authorized by the U.N. Security Council, including the United States and the other four permanent members with vetoes?

2. Another approach is the Special Court for Sierra Leone, which is an independent institution established by an agreement between the United Nations and Sierra Leone. It was established in 2002 with a focus on prosecuting the individuals who organized and oversaw the atrocities that occurred starting in 1996 in Sierra Leone's civil war. These atrocities include hacking off the limbs and ears of victims, the mass use of rape as a weapon of terror, and the kidnapping of young children to be forced into combat. The structure of the court partly stems from concerns that the Yugoslav and Rwanda international tribunals were moving too slowly and were very expensive. Unlike the other tribunals, the new Sierra Leone court sits in the country and has eight judges (five appointed by the U.N. and three by Sierra Leone), a fixed and limited budget, and a three-year mandate. Direct contributions from individual U.N. members fund it, rather than the general U.N. budget. See Douglas Farah, Sierra Leone Court May Offer Model for War Crimes Cases, Wash. Post, April 15, 2000, at A21. The Special Court's Web site is http://www.sc-sl.org.

3. With all the accusations of war crimes by Saddam Hussein and others in his regime, should a specialized international criminal tribunal or a joint international-Iraqi tribunal be established for Iraq? Or should the reconstituted Iraqi national courts deal with these cases? As of April 2003, the U.S. government was supporting the use of the Iraqi courts, rather than an international tribunal. This might have reflected the Bush Administration's hesitancy to support an international tribunal when it was strongly opposing U.S. participation in the International Criminal Court, discussed below.

4. For more information on the Yugoslavia and Rwanda tribunals, see Paul Williams & Michael P. Scharf, Peace with Justice (2002). More generally, see Ratner & Abrams, supra. The Web site of the ICTY is http://www.un.org/icty and the ICTR's Web site is http://www.ictr.org.

5. Individuals can also be responsible under U.S. law for violations of the laws of war. For example, see Johnson v. Eisentrager, 339 U.S. 763 (1956) and Ex parte Quirin, 317 U.S. 1 (1942), the latter being cited above in the Judgment of the Nuremberg Tribunal. U.S. military are subject to the Uniform Code of Military Justice, which incorporates international war crimes as offenses and provides a comprehensive criminal justice system. See Evolving Military Justice (Eugene R. Fidell and Dwight H. Sullivan eds., 2002).

During the Vietnam era, 122 U.S. servicemembers were convicted for law of war-related crimes. One of the most publicized cases stemmed from the massacre of innocent civilians in My Lai during the Vietnam war. William Calley, a U.S. Army lieutenant, was convicted for the premeditated murder of 22 infants, children, women, and old men, and of assault with intent to murder a child of about two years of age. The sentence of dismissal from the Army and confinement to hard labor for 20 years was affirmed by the U.S. Court of Military Appeals. United States v. William L. Calley, 22 C.M.R. 534 (C.M.A. 1973). In a complicated litigation history after that, however, his prison sentence was reduced.

3. The International Criminal Court

In March 2003, the 18 judges of the International Criminal Court were sworn in and the ICC began business in The Hague, Netherlands, where the International Court of Justice is also located.* The ICC was established by the so-called Rome Treaty, which had finally been negotiated at a U.N. Conference in Rome in 1998, attended by delegates from 130 countries. The Rome Treaty, containing the ICC Statute, came into force on July 1, 2002, after the required 60 ratifications. (Excerpts of the ICC Statute are in the Documentary Supplement.)

Although the United States was a strong supporter of the ad hoc war crimes tribunals for the former Yugoslavia and Rwanda (discussed above), it did not join the 120 countries who approved the treaty. Instead, during the Rome Conference, the United States lobbied to amend the proposed treaty in order to reduce the power of the ICC. After its lobbying efforts failed, the United States voted with Iraq, Libya, Qatar, Yemen, China, and Israel to reject the establishment of the ICC.

Professor Leila Nadya Sadat provides an overview of the new ICC. After her analysis, we discuss the Bush Administration's firm position against participating in the ICC, and the reasons for and against this U.S. decision.

---

*The first group of 18 judges elected to the ICC in 2003 included judges from Bolivia, Ireland, Mali, the United Kingdom, Trinidad and Tobago, Germany, Canada, Finland, South Korea, Ghana, Cyprus, Latvia, Brazil, Samoa, France, Italy, Ghana, Costa Rica, and South Africa. The judges were to be sorted into three groups, serving three, six, and nine years respectively, to achieve a revolving succession of judges. The judges' terms began on March 11, 2003.—EDS.

Leila Nadya Sadat, The International Criminal Court and the Transformation of International Law

86-99, 132-142, 148-169 (2002)

B. Structural Framework

1. The Judiciary

The eighteen judges of the Court will be nominated and elected by secret ballot by the Assembly of States Parties. They are each to be persons "of high moral character, impartiality and integrity who possess the qualifications required in their respective states for appointment to the highest judicial offices." In choosing the judges, the Assembly is to "take into account" the need for gender balance, equitable geographical representation, and the representation of the principal legal systems of the world. In addition, the "States Parties shall also take into account the need to include Judges with legal expertise on specific issues, including, but not limited to, violence against women or children." Finally, at least nine of the judges must have "established competence [and experience] in criminal law and procedure," and five must have "established competence [and experience] in relevant areas of international law." The areas specifically mentioned as "relevant" to the work of the Court include international humanitarian law and the law of human rights. . . .

. . . [C]onsonant with the Framers' vision of a Court dispensing uniform and universal international justice, the Statute . . . does not automatically disqualify judges on the basis of their nationality, but adopts a more flexible approach, permitting a judge's disqualification on a case-by-case basis if his or her "impartiality might reasonably be doubted". . . .

. . . [T]he Rome Statute . . . provides that each of the judges elected to the Court will serve one, non-renewable, nine-year term. . . .

Apart from issues of personnel, developing consistency in its judgments will be critical to the Court's perceived legitimacy. The Rome Statute permits the issuance of majority and minority views by the Trial and Appeals Chambers, and allows the issuance of separate opinions (on questions of law only) by judges in the Appeals Chamber. This may not be an advantage to the Court in establishing either the credibility or authority of its decisions. Although many of the common law delegations present in Rome strongly advocated the right of dissent, it is not part of the judicial traditions of many parts of the world. . . .

Once elected, the judges of the Court are to organize themselves into divisions and elect the members of the Presidency. . . . [T]he Court will have an Appeals Division, consisting of one appeals chamber with five judges, including the President; a Trial Division, consisting of at least six judges, further divided into Trial Chambers of three judges each; and a Pre-Trial Division of not less than six judges that is further divided into Pre-Trial Chambers of one or three judges. . . . Judges will not rotate between the appellate and trial divisions, a feature of the ad hoc tribunals that has been criticized. . . .

. . . The Pre-Trial Division will oversee each case, from the initial decision whether to open an investigation until confirmation of the charges, after which time the accused will be committed to a Trial Chamber for trial. . . .

2.   The Presidency

. . . [T]he addition of the Pre-Trial Division eliminated many functions assigned to the Presidency by earlier drafts of the Statute. Nevertheless, the Presidency, composed of a President and two Vice-Presidents, still retains a certain importance. First, the judges composing the Presidency, who are elected by an absolute majority of their peers, are the only judges required by the Statute to serve full-time. The Presidency is responsible for the proper administration of the Court, with the exception of the Office of the Prosecutor. . . .

3.   The Office of the Prosecutor

Defining the powers of the Prosecutor was a highly contentious issue during the Preparatory Committee's meetings, specifically with respect to whether the Prosecutor should be able to act *proprio motu* or *ex officio,* that is, on his or her own motion, in bringing cases to the Court. This issue created a deep schism among the delegates to the Preparatory Committee, with many smaller nations, some European nations, and most NGOs strongly supporting a Prosecutor able to act independently of State referral, and many larger countries, including most of the permanent five members of the Security Council [such as the United States], opposing an independent Prosecutor. Many States were concerned that the independent prosecutor could become an "independent counsel for the universe," unaccountable to anyone and liable to file complaints against States on the basis of political prejudices rather than legal concerns. However, numerous procedural safeguards are built into the Statute to prevent the Prosecutor from abusing his or her power.

Pursuant to Article 42 of the Statute, the Office of the Prosecutor is to be independent from the other organs of the Court. The Statute also provides that no member of the Office shall seek or act on instruction from any external source. The Prosecutor is responsible for receiving referrals and substantiated information on crimes within the jurisdiction of the Court, for examining those referrals and for conducting investigations and prosecutions. Like the judges, the Prosecutor and Deputy Prosecutors will be elected by the Assembly of States Parties, and will serve one nonrenewable, nine-year term.

The Prosecutor and Deputy Prosecutors are to be of different nationalities. However, the Prosecutor and Deputy Prosecutors shall not automatically be disqualified from acting in respect of complaints involving a person of their own nationality. . . .

As a response to the concerns about the unchecked power of an independent Prosecutor, the Rome Statute contains a complex procedure by which the Pre-Trial Chamber is to closely supervise cases in which the Prosecutor exercises his or her *proprio motu* investigation powers. . . . [T]he Prosecutor may commence an investigation only if both he or she and the Pre-Trial Chamber (composed of three judges) have determined that a "reasonable basis" exists to initiate the investigation [Art. 15(3), (4)]. Reasonable basis is not a defined term, *per se,* in the Statute, but Article 53 suggests that a finding of reasonable basis has three elements: (a) there is a reasonable basis to believe that a crime within the jurisdiction of the Court has been or is being committed; (b) the case is or would be admissible under Article 17; (c) the investigation serves the interests of justice, taking into account the gravity of the crime and the interest of victims. . . .

If a State or the Security Council refers a situation, however, the matter is referred to the Court under Article 13(a) or under Article 13(b), respectively, and the Prosecutor is to initiate an investigation pursuant to Article 53, unless there is no reasonable basis to proceed under the Statute. The Statute permits the Pre-Trial Chamber to order an investigation or prosecution to proceed if the Prosecutor's decision not to do so is based solely on a determination that the prosecution would not serve the interests of justice. . . .

C.   The Assembly of States Parties

The Rome Statute adds another institution to the structure envisaged by the 1994 ILC Draft: the Assembly of States Parties. . . . Although not stated to be one of the four "official" organs of the Court, it is . . . extremely important as the Court's *organe plénier* charged with overseeing its operations and functioning. It will not only consider the work of the Preparatory Commission in establishing the Court, but will also provide management oversight, act on the budget, decide whether to alter the number of the judges, adopt the Elements of Crimes and the Rules of Procedure and Evidence, and take up amendments to the Statute. In addition, the Assembly of States Parties will elect the Judges, Prosecutor, and Deputy Prosecutors. It may remove them as well. . . .

I.   CRIMES WITHIN THE COURT'S JURISDICTION . . .

Aggression: The Supreme International Crime

The Nuremberg judgment declared aggression to be "not only an international crime; [but] the supreme international crime differing only from other war crimes in that it contains within itself the accumulated evil of the whole." Following World War II, this prohibition against aggressive war was embodied in Article 2(4) of the United Nations Charter, not as a matter of criminal law, but as a fundamental norm of international law binding all States. Yet, the Charter does not define the crime, and arriving at one has posed a seemingly intractable problem for the international community. . . .

It is thus unsurprising that criminalizing aggression in the Rome Statute proved difficult. Although the Statute reaffirms the illegality of aggression in principle, implementing jurisdiction over the crime was the source of significant disagreement. . . . In a clever compromise . . . the Statute includes aggression as one of the crimes within the Court's jurisdiction, but leaves it undefined. The Treaty specifies that the Court may not exercise jurisdiction over aggression until the Assembly of States Parties defines it, which cannot occur until seven years after the Statute enters into force. . . . Thus, for the time being, aggression, while illegal in principle, remains non-justiciable in practice. . . .

Genocide

Sometimes referred to as "the crime of crimes," genocide was established as a form of crime against humanity in order to criminalize the eradication of ethnic minorities. Its criminalization in the Rome State was a foregone conclusion. . . . [T]he Rome Statute incorporates wholesale Article II of the Genocide Convention, which has been generally accepted as part of customary international law. . . .

Crimes Against Humanity

Defining crimes against humanity presented one of the most difficult challenges at Rome, for no accepted definition existed, either as a matter of treaty or customary international law. Indeed, of the several definitions that have been "promulgated," no two are alike. . . .

The disparity in definitions underscores the two major problems in defining the scope of crimes against humanity: first, distinguishing the crime from war crimes and from crimes under domestic law; second, determining which acts are punishable under international law as a matter of individual criminal responsibility, as opposed to State responsibility for violations of human rights. The Rome Statute attempts to address both problems through an extensive *chapeau*. The text is quite restrictive in overall character, although two positive outcomes should be noted. First, the Rome Statute does not require any nexus to an "armed conflict."[98] . . .

Second, absent from the *chapeau* is any requirement that the crimes be committed as part of an attack based on political, philosophical, racial, ethnic, religious, or other grounds. . . .

Article 7 contains four separate preconditions that must be satisfied before jurisdiction attaches in a particular case in which crimes against humanity are charged. . . .

First, the Statute requires commission of the crimes as part of a "wide-spread *or* systematic attack." . . .

Second, the attack must be against a "civilian population." . . .

Third, the crime must be committed "with knowledge of the attack [directed against any civilian population]." This is clearly a material element of the offense. For not only must the Prosecutor demonstrate that the defendant committed the criminal act (such as murder or extermination) in the context of an attack on a civilian population, but also that the defendant must personally have known about the larger context in which the attack was occurring. . . .

Finally, the attack must involve "a course of conduct involving the multiple commission of acts . . . against any civilian population *pursuant to or in furtherance of a State or organizational policy to commit such attack.*" The Rome Statute thus takes a middle road between those who argue and the case law which suggests, that governmental action, and indeed a governmental policy, are necessary prerequisites to the commission of a crime against humanity, and authorities that require no such linkage. Although there does not appear to be a "State-action" requirement *per se*, there does need to be some plan on behalf of some entity. . . .

With respect to the list of criminal acts, the Rome Statute retained those offenses historically considered crimes against humanity under the IMT Charter and

---

98. In this way the Rome Statute is more liberal than the ICTY Statute, which retained the armed conflict nexus. In the *Tadić* case, the Appellate Chamber questioned the armed conflict nexus, pointing out that it was "settled" that "crimes against humanity do not require a connection to international armed conflict. Indeed . . . customary international law may not require a connection between crimes against humanity and any conflict at all." Prosecutor v. Tadić (Case No. IT-94-1-AR72). . . .

its successor instruments, and added several more: the forcible transfer of population; "severe deprivation of physical liberty in violation of fundamental rules of international law;" "sexual slavery, enforced prostitution, forced pregnancy, enforced sterilization, or any other form of sexual violence of comparable gravity;" and the crime of apartheid. The Statute also includes the residual category of "other inhumane acts" (which has been traditionally part of crime against humanity's various manifestations), but further qualifies it by specifying that these acts must be "of a similar character intentionally causing great suffering, or serious injury to body or to mental or physical health." The enforced disappearance of persons was also added as a crime, partly in response to the problem of the *desaparecidos* (political prisoners who are arrested and then disappeared). The inclusion of this provision further supports the decision of the Framers not to require any nexus to armed conflict from the definition of crimes against humanity, as these disappearances often occur in the absence of any conflict, whether internal or international. . . .

War Crimes

The war crimes section of the Statute is extensive, and the battle over which crimes should be included was protracted. The Rome Statute is much more detailed than any of the predecessor instruments, which has the virtue of making it more complete and the defect of expressly excluding certain very serious threats to international peace and security. . . .

. . . [I]n spite of some ambiguity in Article 8(2)(b), it appears that war crimes cannot be committed within the meaning of the Rome Statute unless an armed conflict exists. . . .

The Statute elaborates in four paragraphs the substance of the war crimes within the Court's jurisdiction. Article 8(2)(a) incorporates Grave Breaches of the Geneva Conventions of 12 August 1949, and is uncontroversial. As others have noted, the use of the formula "namely" suggests that the list of grave breaches in the Statute is exhaustive, not merely illustrative.

Article 8(2)(b) covers "other serious violations of the laws and customs applicable in international armed conflict, *within the established framework of international law.*" This phrasing . . . presumably requires that an international armed conflict exist before acts under Article 8(2)(b) can become criminal. . . .

Articles 8(2)(c) and 8(2)(e) address armed conflict not of an international character. Their inclusion, even if imperfect, represents a great success, for many States at the conference. . . . expressed a desire to completely exclude war crimes committed in internal conflict from the Statute. The International Committee of the Red Cross and the United States' delegation fought consistently for its inclusion, however, and ultimately prevailed, although the Statute is not as broad with regard to criminalizing offenses committed in internal armed conflicts as it is with regard to crimes committed in international armed conflict. . . .

II. PENALTIES . . .

The primary punishment envisioned by the Statute is imprisonment for a term of up to thirty years. No minimum sentences are suggested by the text, nor are specific sentences proposed for particular crimes. . . . Rather, the length of a given sentence is left to the discretion of the judges, subject to two qualifications. First, the maximum sentence of thirty years may only be extended to life imprisonment in cases of "extreme gravity." Second, because many delegations felt that life imprisonment was excessively severe, . . . article 110 of the Statute imposes a mandatory review (but not a mandatory reduction) of the sentence after twenty-five years to determine if the sentence should be reduced. Other sentences are to be reviewed by the Court after the person has served two-thirds of his or her time. . . .

In addition to imprisonment, the Court has the power to impose fines, or to order the forfeiture of proceeds, property and assets derived directly or indirectly from the crime. . . .

One punishment rejected by the Framers was the death penalty, despite strong support from many delegations for its inclusion. . . .

Opponents of the death penalty were vehement in their opposition on both legal and humanitarian grounds. . . .

In the final analysis, the availability of a sentence of life imprisonment won over those delegations that felt that application of the death penalty was a necessary deterrent; the absence of the death penalty no doubt persuaded those opposed even to life imprisonment on humanitarian grounds (as well as legal principles) to compromise on the issue of life imprisonment to reach a consensus. . . .

U.S. Participation in the International Criminal Court. President Clinton signed the Rome Treaty as one of the last acts of his administration on December 31, 2000, though "noting our concerns about significant flaws in the treaty." He pointed out, however, that under the terms of the Rome Treaty, the United States would only be able to work to change the treaty from within if it signed the treaty before January 1, 2001.

Under the new Bush Administration, the United States sent a letter to the U.N. Secretary-General, saying:

> This is to inform you, in connection with the Rome Statute of the International Criminal Court adopted on July 17, 1998, that the United States does not intend to become a party to the treaty. Accordingly, the United States has no legal obligations arising from its signature on December 31, 2000. The United States requests that its intention not to become a party, as expressed in this letter, be reflected in the depositary's status lists relating to this treaty. [Press Statement, International Criminal Court: Letter to U.N. Secretary General Kofi Annan, at http://www.state.gov/r/pa/prs/ps/2002/9968.htm.]

Why did the Bush Administration take this step in May 2002? Besides substantive objections to some of the treaty provisions as discussed below, the administration was apparently concerned that if it had remained a signatory to the treaty, the United States might be "obliged to refrain from acts which would defeat the object and purpose of the treaty." (Vienna Convention on Treaties, Art. 18; see discussion in Chapter 2 at page 100.) Congress then passed the American Servicemembers Protection Act of 2002, 107 Pub. L. 206, 116 Stat. 820 (2002). It barred the U.S. government from cooperating with the ICC. (Section 2004.) The law also, controversially, authorized the President to use "all means necessary and appropriate to bring about the release" of Americans held by or for the ICC. (Section 2008.)

A senior Bush official, Under Secretary of State Marc Grossman, provided the rationale for the administration's opposition to the Rome Treaty and its decision not to try to work to change the ICC from within.

Marc Grossman, American Foreign Policy and the International Criminal Court

Prepared Remarks to the Center for Strategic and International Studies, Washington, D.C. (May 6, 2002)

President Bush has come to the conclusion that the United States can no longer be a party to this [treaty] process. In order to make our objections clear, both in principle and philosophy, and so as not to create unwarranted expectations of U.S. involvement in the Court, the President believes that he has no choice but to inform the United Nations, as depository of the treaty, of our intention not to become a party to the Rome Statute of the International Criminal Court. This morning, at the instruction of the President, our mission to the United Nations notified the UN Secretary General in his capacity as the depository for the Rome Statute of the President's decision. These actions are consistent with the Vienna Convention on the Law of Treaties.

The decision to take this rare but not unprecedented act was not arrived at lightly. But after years of working to fix this flawed statute, and having our constructive proposals rebuffed, it is our only alternative. . . .

Like many of the nations that gathered in Rome in 1998 for the negotiations to create a permanent International Criminal Court, the United States arrived with the firm belief that those who perpetrate genocide, crimes against humanity, and war crimes must be held accountable — and that horrendous deeds must not go unpunished. . . .

But the International Criminal Court that emerged from the Rome negotiations, and which will begin functioning on July 1 will not effectively advance these worthy goals.

. . . [W]e believe the ICC is an institution of unchecked power. In the United States, our system of government is founded on the principle that, in the words of John Adams, "power must never be trusted without a check." . . .

But in the rush to create a powerful and independent court in Rome, there was a refusal to constrain the Court's powers in any meaningful way. . . . The treaty created a self-initiating prosecutor, answerable to no state or institution other than the Court itself. . . .

. . . [T]he treaty threatens the sovereignty of the United States. The Court, as constituted today, claims the authority to detain and try American citizens, even through our democratically-elected representatives have not agreed to be bound by the treaty. While sovereign nations have the authority to try non-citizens who have committed crimes against their citizens or in their territory, the United States has never recognized the right of an international organization to do so absent consent or a UN Security Council mandate. . . .

. . . [W]e believe that by putting U.S. officials, and our men and women in uniform, at risk of politicized prosecutions, the ICC will complicate U.S. military cooperation with many friends and allies who will now have a treaty obligation to hand over U.S. nationals to the Court — even over U.S. objections.

The United States has a unique role and responsibility to help preserve international peace and security. At any given time, U.S. forces are located in close to 100 nations around the world conducting peacekeeping and humanitarian operations and fighting inhumanity.

We must ensure that our soldiers and government officials are not exposed to the prospect of politicized prosecutions and investigations. Our President is committed to a robust American engagement in the world to defend freedom and defeat terror, we cannot permit the ICC to disrupt that vital mission. . . .

OUR EFFORTS

The President did not take his decision lightly.

After the United States voted against the treaty in Rome, the U.S. remained committed and engaged — working for two years to help shape the court and to seek the necessary safeguards to prevent a politicization of the process. . . .

While we were able to make some improvements during our active participation in the UN Preparatory Commission meetings in New York, we were ultimately unable to obtain the remedies necessary to overcome our fundamental concerns.

On December 31, 2000, the previous administration signed the Rome Treaty. In signing President Clinton reiterated "our concerns about the significant flaws in the treaty," but hoped the U.S. signature would provide us influence in the future and assist our effort to fix this treaty. Unfortunately, this did not prove to be the case.

On April 11, 2002, the ICC was ratified by enough countries to bring it into force on July 1 of this year. Now we find ourselves at the end of the process. Today, the treaty contains the same significant flaws President Clinton highlighted.

Many observers, including states that are parties to the ICC and human rights groups, have taken issue with the Bush Administration's objections to the Court. They argue that the U.S. complaints misrepresent the facts, and that the Court has a number of safeguards in place to prevent the problems that the United States claimed to exist. One critic is Dr. Gary Solis, a retired Marine lieutenant colonel and a law professor.

Gary D. Solis, The ICC and Mad Prosecutors

Remarks delivered at Georgetown University on March 27, 2003

Why is America opposed to the ICC? Every army, including ours, commits law of war violations, but few armies so strongly condemned them, or so religiously prosecute them. Witness our Vietnam-era court-martial convictions of 95 soldiers and 27 Marines for law of war related crimes.

Yet the ICC that the U.S. was instrumental in raising — that the U.S. urged on the world community — we now reject. In doing so we marginalize ourselves from the long march from impunity to personal responsibility for war crimes; we alienate ourselves from our allies and warfare coalition partners. By un-signing the ICC Charter, we ensured that we have no voice in selecting judges or prosecutors, and no influence in shaping the Court's jurisprudence.

Why?

Concern for our warfighters? "The Servicemens' Protection Act" . . . is a political fraud. Most accept that our real concern is for our political policy makers and senior generals, and those of our allies. American servicemen and women are already well-covered by prosecutorial options in the Uniform Code of Military Justice. But echoes of the 1999 Pinochet case[1] continue to resonate in the Pentagon's "E" Ring.

We can no more isolate ourselves from the ICC than we were able to insulate our armed forces from 1977 Geneva Convention Additional Protocol I, now ratified by 161 nations and said by the ICTY to represent customary international law. In any international combat we undertake with allies, when formulating operational plans they must conform to Protocol I and, perforce, so must we. Eventually, the same circumstance will prevail as to the ICC.

Eighty-nine states have ratified the ICC Charter. They include allies like the United Kingdom, Canada, Australia, New Zealand, Spain, the Netherlands, Denmark, Sweden, Finland, Norway, and South Korea — most of whom, no less than the U.S., contribute to international peace keeping forces in proportional numbers. We're not talking about "old Europe," or nations that are under water at high tide.

What are we afraid of? Thanks to complementarity,[2] a provision that we sponsored and insisted upon, the ICC is a court of last resort. Complementarity holds that the ICC may only exercise jurisdiction if a good-faith prosecution is not carried out by the accused's state. . . .

Some are shocked that the ICC suggests exercising jurisdiction over nationals of states that are not parties to the ICC Statute. This overlooks, for example, the 1970 Convention for Suppression of Unlawful Seizure of Aircraft, the 1971 Montreal Convention on Civil Aviation Safety, the 1988 Convention and Protocol on Maritime Navigation, and the 1979 Hostages Convention. These four, and several others — including the 1949 Geneva Conventions – all reach citizens of non-parties, a concept America embraced in prosecuting U.S. v. Yunis[7] when we tried a Lebanese national who hijacked a Jordanian plane carrying American passengers. Lebanon is not a party to the Hijacking Convention, and did not consent (or object) to jurisdiction. Nor is that the only case in which we have convicted a foreign national non-party, contrary to the accused's state's wishes.[8] Yet we complain of the possibility that the same shoe might be fit to us.

Familiar American trial rights are present in the ICC Statute: the presumption of innocence[9]; the guarantee against double jeopardy[10]; the right against self-incrimination[11]; right to remain silent[12]; to be informed of charges[13]; to have counsel, either of choice or appointed[14]; a public trial[15]; the prosecutorial burden

1. House of Lords, Regina v. Bartle, *Ex Parte* Pinochet and Regina v. Evans, *Ex Parte* Pinochet, Mar. 24, 1999, reprinted in 38 I.L.M. 581 (1999).

2. Art. 17.

7. 681 F. Supp. 896 (D.D.C., 1998).

8. See also, *U.S. v. Marino-Garcia*, 679 F.2d 1373 (11th Cir. 1982), a case involving the Law of the Sea Convention.

9. Art. 66.1.

10. Art. 20.

11. Art. 55.1.

12. Arts. 55.2 and 67.1.

13. Arts. 55.2, 61.3, 64.8, and 67.1.

14. Arts. 55.2 and 67.1.

15. Arts. 64.7 and 67.1.

of proof[16]; to present and challenge evidence[17]; to cross-examine witnesses[18]; proof of guilt beyond a reasonable doubt[19]; and the right of appeal.[20] There is even provision for the protection of national security information.[21]

It is true that there is no right to a jury trial — just as there is no such right in American courts-martial under our Uniform Code of Military Justice.

In discussing U.S. concerns, we have a model to look to: the International Criminal Court for the Former Yugoslavia — a court that has jurisdiction over U.S. servicemen and women *right now!* Have we seen out-of-control ICTY prosecutors, or ill-founded charges against U.S. commanders? Have the dark predictions of ICC opponents found substance in the ICTY Chief Prosecutor? Are they likely to find substance in the ICC's Chief Prosecutor, Argentine jurist Luis Moreno Ocampo, who currently teaches at Harvard Law School?

In 1999, a group led by professors from Osgoode Hall Law School, in Toronto, sought to charge President Clinton, Madeleine Albright, Gen. Wesley Clark, and other NATO officials and generals, with Yugoslav war crimes. Like the ICC Statute, the ICTY Statute *requires* an indictment upon a determination that a case exists. I hold a copy of Prosecutor del Ponte's letter to NATO's Secretary-General, relating her disposition of the allegations. An informal inquiry was conducted, but no investigation was undertaken, and no indictment considered. Despite this experience, ICC opponents predict the worst from an ICC Prosecutor. . . .

This does not mean that the actions of any given state could never become the subject of an ICC prosecution. It is possible — as possible as an American *failure* to prosecute, for example, the My Lai cases. There, twenty-five soldiers and officers were charged with war crimes, only six went to trial and only one of those, Calley, was convicted. Nineteen My Lai cases went unprosecuted, dismissed "for lack of evidence."

Let's consider the ICC's boogeyman, Chief Prosecutor Moreno. Presume that he will be as corrupt as, say, John Mitchell, and as politically devious as, say, Richard Nixon. Could [he] . . . unilaterally indict our President? Under the ICC Statute Moreno may initiate an investigation — but only with the authorization of a three-judge Pre-Trial Chamber.[22] That finding of jurisdiction, if confirmed, may be appealed to another Trial Chamber panel.[23] Even with both panels' authorizations, any prosecution may be delayed for a year by the UN Security Council, the year's delay being renewable.[24] Finally, the Prosecutor may be removed by simple majority vote. If this is a U.S. railroad job, it isn't the fast track. . . .

Finally, the ICC is a fledgling international body bearing the high hopes of many democratic nations. The Court's success, even its continued long-term existence, depends upon the good will of, and acceptance by, the international community. Is the ICC likely to facilitate its own marginalization through biased indictments and politically-motivated prosecutions?

Time will tell, but *my* money is on the Court.

16. Art. 67.1.
17. Art. 61.6.
18. Art. 67.1.
19. Art. 66.3.
20. Art. 81.
21. Art. 72.
22. Art. 15.
23. Art. 19.
24. Art. 16.

Notes and Questions

1. Is there a need for an International Criminal Court with broad geographic jurisdiction? What are the alternatives? Ad hoc international tribunals such as those for Yugoslavia and Rwanda? Or a mixed international-national tribunal, such as the new Sierra Leone tribunal discussed earlier? National courts?

2. Should the U.S. government resume efforts to try to obtain rules and interpretations from the ICC that would allow the United States to join, or should the United States keep its distance as the Bush Administration has been doing since 2002? If the United States should resume efforts, what seems to be the most important protections to seek?

3. The Bush Administration suggested that American men and women in uniform might be subject to ICC jurisdiction in certain situations and were concerned about "politicized prosecutions." If the ICC prosecutor decided to initiate a case against a U.S. service person in a foreign country that was a party to the ICC, what are the safeguards against that situation arising? Would the Court have jurisdiction if the U.S. government investigated and acted upon the case itself? Even if the United States did not act or there were questions about the U.S. investigation, would the ICC pre-trial chamber have a say about whether the ICC prosecutor could move forward? Could the Security Council call for a renewable delay of 12 months to a prosecution? Should the ability to initiate cases be limited to nations and the U.N. Security Council? For help in answering these questions, see the Sadat and Solis excerpts above as well as the Rome Statute in the Documentary Supplement. For a statement by the new ICC Prosecutor, Luis Moreno Ocampo, that he will proceed cautiously, see his speech to the ICC Assembly of States Parties on April 22, 2003. It can be found on the ICC Web site at http://www.un.org/law/icc.

4. To protect its soldiers, the United States asked in 2002 that the Security Council pass a resolution that protected U.N. peacekeepers from nonratifying states (e.g., the United States) from the jurisdiction of the Court. Under the Rome Treaty, the Security Council has the power to delay any prosecution for renewable 12-month periods. The United States, threatening to withdraw its peacekeepers from Bosnia, East Timor, and other regions, proposed a resolution that would automatically renew every year unless the Security Council affirmatively cancelled it — a decision the United States could veto. The United States finally settled for Resolution 1422 (2002). In it, the Security Council:

> 1. *Requests* . . . that the ICC, if a case arises involving current or former officials or personnel from a contributing State not a Party to the Rome Statute over acts or omissions relating to a United Nations established or authorized operation, shall for a twelve-month period starting 1 July 2002 not commence or proceed with investigation or prosecution of any such case, unless the Security Council decides otherwise;
>
> 2. *Expresses* the intention to renew the request in paragraph 1 under the same conditions each 1 July for further 12-month periods for as long as may be necessary. . . . [The Resolution is in the Documentary Supplement.]

As a second protection, the United States began seeking, as a condition of foreign aid, that other countries sign bilateral agreements promising immunity to U.S. troops on their territory. These so-called Article 98 Agreements, after the article in the Rome Treaty that the United States claims authorizes their use, have been signed by at least 15 countries, including some that are parties to the ICC. Other ICC member states, including Canada and Germany, have refused to sign such agreements, and the European Union has encouraged its members and applicant states to refuse U.S. requests. Still other groups, such as Human Rights Watch, assert that Article 98 cannot bear the interpretation that the United States has given it. (See Article 98 of the Rome Statute in the Documentary Supplement.)

5. In addition to the sources above, much has been written on the International Criminal Court. See, for example, The International Criminal Court: The Making of the Rome Statute (Roy S. Lee ed., 1999); The United States and the International Criminal Court: National Security and International Law (Sarah B. Sewall & Carl Kaysen eds., 2000).

4.   *The Geneva Conventions, Occupation, Prisoners of War, and Suspected Terrorists*

In the wake of the attacks of September 11, 2001, and the war in Iraq in 2003, there has been increased focus on the conduct of states as well as on their leaders and military personnel when engaged in hostilities. Questions have arisen on, among other matters, the role of an occupying power and on the classification and treatment of prisoners of war (POWs). Special questions have emerged about whether and how international humanitarian law — or other international law or domestic law — should apply to the treatment of terrorists.

A starting point for that analysis is understanding how the laws of war apply generally. The following excerpt by Frits Kalshoven and published by the International Committee of the Red Cross ("ICRC"), which supervises compliance with the Geneva Conventions, explains the history of the Conventions and those combatants to whom they apply. (Excerpts from the Third and Fourth Geneva Conventions are in the Documentary Supplement.)

Frits Kalshoven, Constraints on the Waging of War

7-11, 40-41, 71, 75 (1987)

The tendency to start the treaty-making process with respect to rules of warfare dates back to the 1860s, when on two entirely separate occasions an international conference convened to conclude a treaty dealing with one highly specific aspect of the law of war: one, in Geneva in 1864, on the fate of wounded soldiers on the battlefield, and the other, in St. Petersburg in 1868, prohibiting the use of explosive rifle bullets. From these modest beginnings there developed two distinct (though never entirely separate) trends in the law of armed conflict, each characterized by its particular perspective: one, the so-called law of Geneva, more particularly concerned with the condition of war victims who have fallen into enemy hands . . . , and the other, . . . the law of The Hague, relating to . . . proper and permissible means and methods of war. . . .

This first, modest step had to be followed by a good many others before the "law of Geneva" acquired its present scope and relative completeness. Further steps served either to expand the circle of protected persons, or to improve the rules in the light of acquired experience.

In 1899, a treaty was concluded rendering the principles of the treaty of 1864 applicable to the wounded, sick and shipwrecked at sea. . . .

In 1929, . . . a diplomatic conference convened in Geneva. The Conference adopted, first, a much improved treaty on the treatment of the wounded and sick on land, taking into account the experiences of the First World War. Secondly, it negotiated a separate Convention on the treatment of prisoners of war.

The latter treaty significantly expanded the circle of persons protected under the law of Geneva. Admittedly, rules relating to the status of prisoners of war did already exist: having initially developed as rules of customary law, they had been incorporated in 1899 in the Hague Regulations on Land Warfare. . . . Yet the First World War, with its long duration and huge numbers of prisoners of war on both sides, had brought to light the need for more detailed regulations for the protection of this category of war victims. . . . [P]articularly important improvements on the old law [include]: the far greater clarity and completeness of the rules and principles on capture and captivity of prisoners of war; introduction of a categorical ban on reprisals against such persons, and acceptance of the principle that application of the agreed rules would be open to international scrutiny.

The tragic events, successively, of the Spanish Civil War and the Second World War provided the incentive for yet another major revision and further development of the law of Geneva. To this end a diplomatic conference met in 1949 in Geneva. . . . The three Conventions in force . . . were substituted by new Conventions, giving improved versions of many existing rules. . . . To give just one example, the armed resistance in several European countries under German occupation during the Second World War led to the express recognition that members of organized resistance movements which fulfil a number of (severe) conditions would qualify as prisoners of war.

Then the law of Geneva was enriched by an entirely novel convention on the protection of civilian persons in time of war. This [Fourth] Convention serves to protect two categories of civilians in particular: enemy civilians in the territory of a belligerent party, and the inhabitants of occupied territory. . . . With this latest addition the law of Geneva had come to comprise four Conventions, dealing with the wounded and sick on land; the wounded, sick and shipwrecked at sea; prisoners of war; and protected civilians.

The law of Geneva serves to provide protection for all those who, as a consequence of an armed conflict, have fallen into the hands of the adversary. The protection envisaged here is, hence, not protection against the violence of war itself, but against the arbitrary power which one belligerent party acquires in the course of the war over persons belonging to the other party.

For a full enumeration of persons protected under Conventions I-III, the reader may be referred to Article 4 of the Third Convention. The following list is drawn from that Article:

1. members of the armed forces of a Party to the conflict, even if the Government or authority they profess allegiance to is not recognized by the adversary;

2.   members of other militias or volunteer corps, including those of organized resistance movements, which belong to a Party to the conflict and operate in or outside their own territory, even if this is occupied; provided always that the group they belong to fulfils . . . [four conditions]:

   (a)   to be commanded by a person responsible for his subordinates;
   (b)   to have a fixed distinctive sign recognizable at a distance;
   (c)   to carry arms openly;
   (d)   to conduct their operations in accordance with the laws and customs of war;

3.   participants in a *levée en masse*, provided they carry arms openly and respect the laws and customs of war; . . .

[R]esistance fighters, or, more generally, guerilla fighters, who do not meet all four conditions mentioned above cannot claim a right to be treated as prisoners of war; they may, on the other hand, be entitled to the (lesser) protection of the Civilians Convention [the Fourth Convention].

[Two Protocols Additional to the Geneva Conventions of 1949 were adopted in 1977.] One (Protocol I) is applicable in international armed conflicts, and the other (Protocol II) in non-international armed conflicts. . . .

[S]tatements of a number of delegations left no doubt that they still had more or less serious misgivings about certain parts of Protocol I, and some delegations even about the entire Protocol II. It remains therefore to be seen how many States will ultimately decide to ratify or accede to the Protocols.

In this respect, it is worth noting that a good part of the provisions in the Protocols, and notably in Protocol I, is simply a codification of pre-existing rules of customary international law. . . .

Part III, Section II, of Protocol I seeks to solve . . . problems [related to irregular armed forces not protected under the Third Geneva Convention] by providing an entirely novel approach to the question of defining the "armed forces" and "combatants". . . .

This definition does not make any distinction whatsoever between the highly organized regular armed forces of long established States on one hand, and on the other, the perhaps far more loosely organized fighting arm of a beginning resistance or liberation movement. The only requirements, for all armed forces without distinction, are a measure of organization, a responsible command, and an internal disciplinary system, designed in particular to ensure compliance with the written and unwritten rules of armed conflict.

---

a.   The Responsibilities of Occupying Powers

The successful outcome of the conflict in Iraq in 2003 toppled the Saddam Hussein regime and left the United States, Britain, and their coalition powers in military control of the country. Professor Jordan Paust addresses whether that made the United States an "Occupying Power" and, if so, what were its responsibilities.

Jordan J. Paust, The U.S. as Occupying Power over Portions of Iraq and Relevant Responsibilities under the Law of War

ASIL Insight (April 2003)

Is the United States an Occupying Power in Iraq? Some have argued that the United States is not an occupying power with respect to any portion of Iraq because the U.S. is on a "liberation" mission. . . . However, Article 42 of the Annex to the 1907 Hague Convention IV Respecting the Laws and Customs of War on Land affirms: "Territory is considered occupied when it is actually placed under the authority of the hostile army. The occupation extends . . . where such authority has been established and can be exercised." As recognized in a U.S. Army text addressing this provision, "Article 42 . . . emphasizes the primacy of FACT as the test of whether or not occupation exists."[3] . . .

Paragraph 2 of Article 2 of the [Fourth] Geneva Convention Relative to the Protection of Civilian Persons in Time of War reads: "The Convention shall . . . apply to all cases of partial or total occupation of the territory of a High Contracting Party, even if the said occupation meets with no armed resistance." . . .

Do U.S. military commanders and U.S. political leaders have legal responsibilities under the laws of war concerning occupied territory? If so, are there limitations on the extent of such responsibilities with respect to Iraqi territory? . . . In United States v. List[7] a military tribunal operating after World War II during the so-called subsequent Nuremberg proceedings affirmed:

> A commanding general of occupied territory is charged with the duty of maintaining peace and order, punishing crime, and protecting lives and property within the area of his command. His responsibility is coextensive with his area of command. He is charged with notice of occurrences taking place within that territory . . . dereliction of duty rests upon him"[8]. . . .

Would the looting of artifacts from the National Museum in Baghdad involve violations of the law concerning occupied territory? Important questions would include: When exactly did main looting take place? Was the museum within an area of Baghdad under effective control of U.S. military forces at that time? . . . Was the local commander in the area still engaged in combat actions? Were other commanders able to send in other U.S. military personnel for public order and protection of property in that particular sector at that time?

Generally, the responsibility of the United States to restore law and order and public life in areas under effective control of its military is reflected in Article 43 of the Annex to the Hague Convention of 1907, which requires that the occupying power "shall take all the measures in his power to restore, and ensure, as far as possible, public order and safety, while respecting, unless absolutely prevented, the laws in force in the country." . . .

Applicable portions of the laws of war include Hague Convention IV, portions of the Geneva Civilian Convention, and other customary international law concerning occupied territory. . . . Moreover, common Article 3 of the 1949 Geneva

---

[3] U.S. Dep't of Army Pam. 27-161-2, 2 International Law 159 (1962).
[7] United States v. List, et al., 11 Trials of War Criminals 757 (1948).
[8] Id. at 1270-71.

Conventions is customary international law providing a minimum set of rights not only during internal conflict, but also during an international armed conflict.[12] . . . Consequently, common Article 3 appears to provide minimum standards for an occupation during an armed conflict. . . .

Article 3 expressly recognizes the fundamental right, in all circumstances, to be treated humanely as well as specific prohibitions of: "(a) violence to life and person, in particular murder of all kinds, mutilation, cruel treatment and torture; (b) taking of hostages, (c) outrages upon personal dignity, in particular humiliating and degrading treatment; [and] (d) the passing of sentences and the carrying out of executions without previous judgment pronounced by a regularly constituted court, affording all the judicial guarantees which are recognized as indispensable by civilized peoples." Articles 27-34 of the Geneva Civilian Convention also contain several related rights and prohibitions. . . . Section III of Part III of the Convention adds several other specific rights and prohibitions concerning occupied territories as such. Specific rights and prohibitions concerning occupied territory can also be found in Articles 43-56 of the Annex to the 1907 Hague Convention IV.

2. SPECIAL CONCERNS

Can persons in Iraq who are not prisoners of war be transferred to Guantanamo Bay for detention, to the U.S. for trial, or to other countries? . . . Article 49 of the Geneva Civilian Convention prohibits "[i]ndividual or mass forcible transfers, as well as deportations of protected persons from occupied territory . . . regardless of their motive." . . . Can the United States prosecute persons who are reasonably accused of war crimes, genocide, and other crimes against humanity in Iraq? As an occupying power, the United States could set up a military commission for prosecution of war crimes and other crimes under international law. However, the military commission would have to follow rules of procedure and provide other due process rights guaranteed under human rights law and the 1949 Geneva Conventions.[20] The U.S. could also agree with other occupying forces and/or a new regime in Iraq to set up an international military commission or tribunal with proper procedures and rights to due process. Additionally, the U.S. could seek the creation by the United Nations Security Council of a new International Criminal Tribunal for Iraq (ICTI). . . .

[P]risoners of war could be transferred for trial. . . .

b.   Prisoners of War

Article 4 of the Third Geneva Convention defines prisoners of war as follows:

Prisoners of war, in the sense of the present Convention, are persons belonging to one of the following categories, who have fallen into the power of the enemy:

1. Members of the armed forces of a Party to the conflict as well as member of militias or volunteer corps forming part of such armed forces.

---

[12]See, e.g., . . . The Prosecutor v. Tadic, ICTY Trial Chamber (10 Aug. 1995), noting especially the same recognition by the ICJ in Nicaragua v. United States, 1986 I.C.J. 4, at paras. 218, 255), 814, 823, 829-31; The Prosecutor v. Tadic, ICTY Appeals Chamber (2 Oct. 1995), recognizing that common Article 3 violations, if serious, are war crimes.

[20]See, e.g., Paust, Antiterrorism Military Commissions: The Ad Hoc DOD Rules of Procedure, 23 Mich. J. Int'l L. 677 (2002); Antiterrorism Military Commissions: Courting Illegality, id. 1 (2001).

2. Members of other militias and members of other volunteer corps, including those of organized resistance movements, belonging to a Party to the conflict and operating in or outside their own territory, even if this territory is occupied, provided that such militias or volunteers corps, including such organized resistance movements, fulfil the following conditions:
>   (a) That of being commanded by a person responsible for his subordinates;
>   (b) That of having a fixed distinctive sign recognizable at a distance;
>   (c) That of carrying arms openly;
>   (d) That of conducting their operations in accordance with the laws and customs of war.

3. Members of regular armed forces who profess allegiance to a government or an authority not recognized by the Detaining Power. . . .

Article 5 of that Convention further provides that, "Should any doubt arise as to whether persons, having committed a belligerent act and having fallen into the hands of the enemy, belong to any of the categories enumerated in Article 4, such persons shall enjoy the protection of the present Convention until such time as their status has been determined by a competent tribunal."

The Convention proceeds to set forth a variety of rights for POWs. For example, Article 17 provides that POWs, when interrogated, are required to give only their name, rank, and a few other pieces of information. Article 71 gives POWs the right to send and receive letters and cards. Article 87 states that, "Prisoners of war may not be sentenced by the military authorities and courts of the Detaining Power to any penalties except those provided for in respect of members of the armed forces of the said Power who have committed the same acts." In effect, this means that POWs cannot be tried for merely having participated in the military conflict. In addition, Article 118 provides that POWs "shall be released and repatriated without delay after the cessation of active hostilities."

Notes and Questions

1. Most of the countries in the world are parties to the four Geneva Conventions of 1949 discussed above, including the United States, Afghanistan, Iraq, and Saudi Arabia. As of January 2003, 190 countries were parties to the Conventions. (See also Chapter 1 at page 86.) On the other hand, the United States is a not a party to the two Optional Protocols, though 161 countries were parties to Protocol I and 156 to Protocol II. (Excerpts of the Geneva Conventions are in the Documentary Supplement.)

2. Were the United States and other coalition countries "occupying powers" after the collapse of Saddam Hussein's regime and the coalition military victories? If there were any doubt about this, would it have been resolved by the April 23 proclamation by the commander of the U.S. ground forces in Iraq, which said that: "The coalition alone retains absolute authority within Iraq"?

3. As indicated above, Article 4 of the Third Geneva Convention states that "[m]embers of the armed forces of a Party to the conflict" qualify as prisoners of war (POWs). Irregular forces can qualify for POW status under Article 4(A)(2) of that Convention if they meet four conditions. Does the lack of additional requirements in Article 4(A)(1) mean that members of armed forces will qualify as POWs even if they do not, for example, wear a fixed distinctive sign? Alternatively, is satisfaction

of the four requirements inherent in the concept of regular armed forces? The United States has maintained that members of the Taliban's regular armed forces, whom the United States detained in conjunction with the Afghan conflict (see page 86 above) are not entitled to POW status, in part, because they failed to wear a fixed distinctive sign. See Fact Sheet: White House on Status of Detainees at Guantanamo (Feb. 7, 2002) at <http://usinfo.state.gov/topical/pol/terror/02020700.htm>. Human Rights Watch, on the other hand, has alleged that that interpretation "requires a strained reading of the plain language of the Third Geneva Convention." Human Rights Watch Letter to Donald Rumsfeld, May 29, 2002. Should a Taliban fighter captured in Afghanistan during the hostilities there be treated as a POW?

4. Although the United States is not a party to Protocol I or Protocol II of the Geneva Conventions, is there a situation in which the United States would be bound by Protocol I's broader definition of a combatant, and hence be required to treat an individual as a POW, even if the individual did not meet the definition of Article 4 of the Third Geneva Convention? Does the Protocol help establish norms of customary international law?

5. Besides losing the rights and protections provided by the Third Geneva Convention, those persons who took part in hostilities but do not satisfy the requirements for POW status are considered as illegal or unlawful combatants. The following excerpt describes the consequences of being deemed an unlawful combatant.

> As persons who were combatants in hostilities and are not entitled to POW status, they are entitled, under customary international law, to humane treatment of the same nature as that prescribed by Article 3 common to the four Geneva Conventions of 1949[1] and, in more detail, by Article 75 of the Additional Protocol I to those Conventions of 1977; but they may be lawfully prosecuted and punished under national laws for taking part in the hostilities and for any other crimes, such as murder and assault, that they may have committed. . . . This vulnerability to prosecution for simply taking part in an armed conflict and for injuries that may have been caused in that connection is the sanction prescribed by the law to deter illegal combatants. [George H. Aldrich, The Taliban, Al Qaeda, and the Determination of Illegal Combatants, 96 Am. J. Intl. L. 891, 893-894 (2002).]

---

1. Article 3 common to the Geneva Conventions of 1947 provides:

In the case of armed conflict not of an international character occurring in the territory of one of the High Contracting Parties, each Party to the conflict shall be bound to apply, as a minimum, the follow provisions:

(1) Persons taking no active part in the hostilities, including members of armed forces who have laid down their arms and those placed *hors de combat* by sickness, wounds, detention, or any other cause, shall in all circumstances be treated humanely, without any adverse distinction founded on race, colour, region or faith, sex, birth or wealth, or any other similar criteria.

To this end, the following acts are and shall remain prohibited at any time and in any place whatsoever with respect to the above-mentioned persons:

(a) violence to life and person, in particular murder of all kinds, mutilation, cruel treatment and torture; . . .

(c) outrages upon personal dignity, in particular, humiliating and degrading treatment:

(d) the passing of sentences and the carrying out of executions without previous judgment pronounced by regularly constituted court, affording all the judicial guarantees which are recognized as indispensable by civilized peoples.

Hence, if an Al Qaeda member captured in Afghanistan did not qualify as a POW but as an illegal combatant, could he be liable under Afghan laws for killing or attempting to kill a U.S. or Northern Alliance soldier?

c. The Scope of an "Armed Conflict" and the Treatment of Terrorists

The following excerpt addresses the scope of the Geneva Conventions beyond declared wars.

Steven R. Ratner & Jason S. Abrams, Accountability for Human Rights Atrocities in International Law
83-85 (2001)

[P]rior to the Geneva Conventions, legal protections applied only in the event of war, which had a clear definition in both treaties and custom. The Geneva Conventions, however, apply in the case of . . . "declared war or of any other armed conflict . . . even if the state of war is not recognized by one of them". . . . The term "armed conflict" is quite broad compared to the term "declared war." Neither party need recognize a state of war or sever diplomatic relations; only de facto hostilities are required.

The precise level of hostilities required to trigger the Conventions is subject to some debate. . . . [A]ccording to the ICRC's official commentary, they encompass "[a]ny difference arising between two States and leading to the intervention of members of the armed forces," regardless of the length of the conflict or the casualties on either side. . . . The Yugoslavia Tribunal offered the formulation of "a resort to armed force between States," noting that humanitarian law applies "from the initiation" of conflict. The traditional references to armed forces suggest a reluctance by states to consider many types of convert action as triggering the Conventions.

[There is a] lack of any "exact, objective criterion" defining "armed conflict." The applicability of the Conventions will turn upon the perspectives of the belligerents and states observing the situation. States, courts, and commentators agree that it involves the use of armed forces, as opposed to police, and involves the use of force, although that may not involve the actual firing of weapons. Border skirmishes would seem to qualify to invoke the Conventions; even if only sporadic, they ought to trigger the Conventions at least during the period when they are in progress. However, they render a determination as to the termination of armed conflict difficult.

A related important issue concerns the extent to which the Geneva Conventions are triggered in the absence of a classic state-to-state armed conflict, but when one state intervenes in the civil war of another. The Yugoslavia Tribunal Appeals Chamber addressed this matter in considerable detail in its review of the *Tadic* judgment. In determining that the conflict in Bosnia-Herzegovina was international at the time of the acts of the defendant, the court opted for a standard of "overall control" by the outside state of the armed forces of one side of the internal conflict, in this case, Serbia's control of the Bosnian Serb army. It defined such control as "going beyond the mere financing and equipping of such forces and involving also participation in the planning and supervision of military operations," but rejected the view that such control extend to the issuance of specific orders or instructions relating to individual military actions. Finally, the court stated that if individuals within a civil war became assimilated to foreign state organs based on their behavior, the war will have become internationalized.

Notes and Questions

1. Given the breadth of the term *armed conflict,* what is the outer limit of hostilities to which the Geneva Conventions would apply? In 1997, the Inter-American Commission on Human Rights determined that an "attack by 42 civilians, armed with civilian weapons, on the La Tablada military barracks in Argentina during peacetime" constituted an internal armed conflict to which common Article 3 of the Geneva Conventions applied. Michael P. Scharf, Defining Terrorism as the Peace Time Equivalent of War Crimes: A Case of Too Much Convergence Between International Humanitarian Law and International Criminal Law, 7 ILSA J. Intl. & Comp. L. 391, 393 (2001).

2. Did U.S. involvement in Afghanistan after September 11 constitute an international armed conflict? Given that an internal conflict already existed in Afghanistan, did U.S. aid to one party internationalize a civil war? Alternatively, was U.S. military action against Afghanistan's de facto government sufficient to trigger application of the Geneva Conventions? According to reports, President Bush initially determined that the Third Geneva Convention did not apply to the Taliban because "Afghanistan was not a functioning state during the conflict and the Taliban was not recognized as a legitimate government." Sean D. Murphy, Decision Not to Regard Persons Detained in Afghanistan as POWs, 96 Am. J. Intl. L. 475, 477 (2002). The President, however, later stated in a press release that the Third Geneva Convention applied to Taliban detainees, but that they did not qualify as POWs. See Fact Sheet: White House on Status of Detainees at Guantanamo (Feb. 7, 2002) at <http://usinfo.state.gov/topical/pol/terror/02020700.htm>. (See discussion in Chapter 1 at page 87.) What do you think caused the apparent shift in the President's interpretation? Concern for treatment of U.S. soldiers if the Geneva Conventions did not apply to the Taliban? Language in Article 4(A)(3) that covers regular armed forces of "an authority not recognized by the Detaining Power?" Public opinion, including the protests from abroad and home about the apparent harsh treatment in some cases of detainees at Guantanamo. If the Third Geneva Convention applies to Taliban detainees, does it also apply to Al Qaeda members who fought with the Taliban in Afghanistan?

3. Did an international armed conflict exist between the United States and Al Qaeda as of the September 11th attacks? George Aldrich argues that an international armed conflict within the meaning of the Geneva Conventions cannot exist.

Al Qaeda is evidently a clandestine organization consisting of elements in many countries and apparently composed of people of various nationalities; it is dedicated to advancing certain political and religious objectives by means of terrorist acts directed against the United States and other, largely Western, nations. As such, Al Qaeda does not in any respect resemble a state, is not a subject of international law, and lacks international legal personality. It is not a party to the Geneva Conventions, and it could not be a party to them or to any international agreement. Its methods brand it as a criminal organization under national laws and as an international outlaw. [George H. Aldrich, The Taliban, Al Qaeda, and the Determination of Illegal Combatants, 96 Am. J. Intl. L. 891, 893 (2002).]

Alternatively, was the nature of the attacks and the international response to those attacks such that an international armed conflict should be deemed to exist between the United States and Al Qaeda? For such a view, see Curtis A. Bradley & Jack L. Goldsmith, The Constitutional Validity of Military Commissions, 5 Green Bag 2d 249, 256-257 (2002).

Even if the laws of war do apply to the September 11th attacks, would they apply, for example, to an Al Qaeda member, who was a Spanish citizen, apprehended by the Spanish authorities in Spain for planning future terrorist acts and turned over to the United States? If not, what protections does that Spanish Al Qaeda member have? *ICCPR ?*

4. As noted earlier, Article 5 of the Third Geneva Convention states that "[s]hould any doubt arise as to whether persons, having committed a belligerent act and having fallen into the hands of the enemy, belong to any of the categories enumerated in Article 4, such persons shall enjoy the protection of the present Convention until such time as their status has been determined by a competent tribunal." Given the debate surrounding the status of detained Taliban and Al Qaeda members under international law, should the United States have provided them with a competent tribunal to determine their POW status instead of categorically denying them POW status? "The [U.S.] administration apparently was of the view that there was no 'doubt' regarding the status of any of the detainees, and consequently that the use of such tribunals was not necessary or required." Sean Murphy, Decision Not to Regard Persons Detained in Afghanistan as POWs, 96 Am. J. Intl. L. 475, 478-479 (2002). Is the United States the party that should decide whether a "doubt" exists? If the detaining state can make that determination without any limits, when will there ever be "doubt"?

5. Would there be negative ramifications from applying laws of war to Al Qaeda's terrorist acts? Professor Michael Scharf argues that one problem with applying the laws of war to terrorism

is that, under this approach, terrorists can rely on the "combatant's privilege" under which combatants are immune from prosecution for common crimes. For example, killing a combatant is justified homicide, not murder. This means that terrorist attacks on military, police, or other government personnel would not be prosecutable or extraditable offenses. . . . [G]overnment installations are a lawful target of war. Thus terrorist attacks on military, police, or government buildings would not be regarded as criminal. And the collateral damage doctrine would apply, such that injury or deaths to civilians would not be regarded as criminal so long as the target was a government installation, and reasonable steps were taken to minimize the risk to innocent civilians. [Michael P. Scharf, Defining Terrorism as the Peace Time Equivalent of War Crimes: A Case of Too Much Convergence Between International Humanitarian Law and International Criminal Law, 7 ILSA J. Intl. & Comp. L. 391, 396 (2001).]

Professor Jordan Paust further argues that the following problems would occur if the laws of war were applied to Al Qaeda's acts.

> [A]ny attempt to expand the concept of war beyond the present minimal levels of belligerency and insurgency would be extremely dangerous because certain forms of nonstate actor violence and targeting that otherwise remain criminal could become legitimate. Two such targetings would have been the September 11th attack on the Pentagon, a legitimate military target during armed conflict of war (except for the means used, an airliner with passengers and crew), and the previous attack on the U.S.S. Cole, another legitimate military target during armed conflict or war. [Jordan M. Paust, There Is No Need to Revise the Laws of War in Light of September 11th, at 3 (ASIL publication, 2002).

Should the combatant's privilege be available to terrorists?

If the laws of war do not apply, in what ways can international law address terrorism without extending the combatant's privilege to terrorists? The following excerpt suggests some alternative approaches.

Robert K. Goldman & Brian D. Tittemore, Unprivileged Combatants and the Hostilities in Afghanistan: Their Status and Rights Under International Humanitarian and Human Rights Law

33, 39-40, 44-46, 48-51, 53-55 (ASIL publication, 2002)

That the United States must afford certain minimum human rights protections to unprivileged enemy combatants who fall into its hands in the course of an international armed conflict is dictated by treaty and customary norms to which it is bound under international human rights and humanitarian law. . . .

It is well recognized that the international human rights commitments of states apply at all times, whether in times of peace or situations of armed conflict, to all persons subject to a state's authority and control. The [ICJ] has stated . . . that "the protection of the [ICCPR] does not cease in times of war, except by operation of Article 4 of the Covenant whereby certain provisions may be derogated from in a time of national emergency." International humanitarian law, on the other hand, generally does not apply in peacetime and its fundamental purpose is to place restraints on the conduct of warfare in order to diminish the effects of hostilities. . . . Consequently, in situations of armed conflict, both international human rights law and international humanitarian law apply concurrently, and a state that is a party to the conflict must afford the fundamental protections under these regimes of law to persons falling within its power. . . .

[T]here is no question that Taliban and Al Qaeda fighters captured by the United States in Afghanistan have fallen into and remain within the power of the United States and that the United States exercises full and effective authority and control over these individuals. Accordingly, the United States' fundamental obligations under conventional and customary international law . . . extend to these detainees. . . .

Drawing upon this framework of international human rights and humanitarian law rules and principles binding upon the United States, the minimum protections that must be afforded to unprivileged combatants will be reviewed in three areas: lawful detention, humane treatment, and fair trial guarantees.

DETENTION OF UNPRIVILEGED COMBATANTS

International human rights law addresses the protection of personal liberty principally in the context of the right not to be subjected to arbitrary arrest or detention, and only permits the detention of persons in cases or circumstances expressly provided by law and subject to strict adherence to the procedures defined thereunder. . . . While the right to personal liberty is not expressly included among the nonderogable rights in the ICCPR and similar treaties, it is widely considered that certain aspects of this right are so fundamental that the exigencies of a situation may never reasonably permit their suspension. . . . Nonderogable aspects of the right to personal liberty have been considered to include the rights:

- Not to be deprived of physical liberty except for the reasons and under conditions established by law;
- To be informed, at the time of the arrest and in a language they understand, of the reasons for their detention and to be promptly informed of any charges against them;
- To be brought promptly before a judge or other officer authorized by law . . . to determine the lawfulness of his or her arrest or detention and to order his or her release if the arrest or detention is unlawful; and
- To be tried within a reasonable time. . . .

As with all other international human rights protections, the right to personal liberty and security applies during times of armed conflict, except to the extent that it may be the subject of lawful derogation. At the same time, it must be recognized that, as international human rights treaties were not specifically designed to regulate international armed conflict situations, they do not contain specific rules governing such concepts as prisoner of war status and the detention of privileged and unprivileged enemy combatants in the course of hostilities and are devoid of rules addressing the detention or internment of such persons. Therefore, international human rights law may not be sufficient to determine whether the detention of a combatant during an armed conflict is arbitrary or otherwise unlawful and it may be necessary to have regard to the *lex specialis* of international humanitarian law.

International humanitarian law in turn, like international human rights law, permits the detention of persons based upon certain grounds and subject to certain conditions. Of particular significance in this regard is the fact that international humanitarian law has throughout its history recognized that enemy combatants in armed conflicts may, upon capture, continue to be held. . . . Further, the Third Geneva Convention permits the internment of prisoners of war by a Detaining Power until the cessation of active hostilities, when they must be released and repatriated. However, prisoners of war against whom criminal proceedings for an indictable offense are pending may be detained until the end of such proceedings and, if necessary, until the completion of the punishment. . . . [T]herefore, it appears that the United States may detain unprivileged combatants captured in the

Afghan hostilities at least until the cessation of active hostilities and, if such detainees are the subject of criminal proceedings for an indictable offense, until the end of such proceeding and, if necessary, until the completion of the punishment.

Can the prisoners in Guantanamo continue to be detained? are hostility ongoing?

HUMANE TREATMENT OF UNPRIVILEGED COMBATANTS

International human rights and humanitarian law exhibit perhaps their greatest convergence in the principles and standards of humane treatment, which in both fields are predicated on fundamental respect for human dignity. . . . The prohibition of torture and other cruel, inhuman, or degrading treatment or punishment under international human rights law has been further elaborated upon in the UN Torture Convention, to which the United States is also a party. . . .

It is therefore beyond question that the United States is subject to an absolute and nonderogable obligation under international human rights and humanitarian law to ensure that unprivileged combatants under its power are not subjected to torture or other cruel, inhuman or degrading treatment or punishment. This applies to all aspects of the detainees' treatment, including the transfer of detainees, methods of interrogation, conditions of detention, and any form of punishment imposed for disciplinary or penal offenses. . . .

UNPRIVILEGED COMBATANTS AND FAIR TRIAL PROTECTIONS

[T]here is marked convergence between international human rights and humanitarian law in minimum fair trial protections, including the standards applicable to unprivileged combatants. . . . [A] comparison of [Articles 14 and 15 of the ICCPR and Article 75(4) of Protocol I show] that they share a common nucleus of fair trial requirements. These include the following: *Geneve conventions do*

If the use of Military tribunals under the Geneve conventions do not apply, what does?

(a) The right to respect for fundamental principles of criminal law, including prohibition of retroactive criminal law, the presumption of innocence, and the *non-bis-in-idem* principle;

(b) The right to be tried by a competent, independent and impartial tribunal in conformity with applicable international standards. . . . In respect of prosecution of civilians, this requires trial by regularly constituted courts that are demonstrably independent from the other branches of government and comprised of judges with appropriate tenure and training, and generally prohibits the use of *ad hoc*, special, or military tribunals or commissions to try civilians. Military courts are, on the other hand, generally considered competent to prosecute members of a state's military for crimes relating to the functions that the law assigns to military forces and, during international armed conflicts, may try enemy combatants, provided the minimum requirements of due process are guaranteed. . . .

(c) The right to procedural guarantees. . . .

[I]t is broadly considered that the core fair trial protections, including those enumerated above, are so essential that their suspension can never be justified.

Indeed, no human rights supervisory body has yet found the exigencies of a genuine emergency situation sufficient to justify suspending even temporarily basic fair trial safeguards. . . .

Notes and Questions

1. The above excerpt concerns Taliban and Al Qaeda members captured in Afghanistan while fighting against the United States. In such a situation, the author argues that both international humanitarian law (designed for periods of hostilities) and international human rights law would provide a minimum of protections for the detainees even if they were deemed to be unlawful combatants. As of May 2003, the United States has not provided any type of hearing for those Taliban and Al Qaeda members detained in Guantanamo Bay. Does that failure violate international law? If the United States keeps the detainees without a hearing after all hostilities in Afghanistan have ceased, would that violate international law? Would the Taliban have a stronger claim because they are from an Afghan group?

2. The United States has allegedly turned over detainees who did not cooperate with CIA interrogation "to foreign intelligence services whose practice of torture has been documented by the U.S. government and human rights organizations." Dana Priest & Barton Gellman, U.S. Decries Abuse But Defends Interrogations, Wash. Post, Dec. 26, 2002, at 1. Would such a practice violate international law?

3. What protections would a detained Al Qaeda member have who had no relationship to the hostilities in Afghanistan? If no armed conflict exists between the United States and Al Qaeda in general, would that mean that international humanitarian law would not apply at all? Would human rights law, standing alone, entitle detained Al Qaeda members to a fair trail? Could detained Al Qaeda members who have no relationship to the hostilities in Afghanistan be detained indefinitely without a hearing? Human Rights Watch believes that such persons must be formally charged.

> When persons are apprehended outside areas of armed conflict and have no direct connection to the conflict, the Geneva Conventions are inapplicable. Instead, the protections of international human rights law apply. These include the requirements of being formally charged, informed of one's rights, and permitted access to legal counsel. [Human Rights Watch Letter to Donald Rumsfeld, May 29, 2002].

If an international conflict exists between the United States and Al Qaeda, is there any area outside of the armed conflict?

4. Is domestic criminal law the most appropriate way to deal with Al Qaeda members and other terrorists? The United States has already charged some apparent Al Qaeda members, such as Zacarias Moussaoui and Richard Reid, with crimes in federal court. Reid, who attempted unsuccessfully to explode a bomb in his shoe during a passenger flight over the Atlantic, pled guilty and was sentenced to life imprisonment in January 2003. After his sentencing during a hearing at a U.S. federal district court in Massachusetts, Reid proclaimed his allegiance to Osama bin Laden and said, "I am at war with your country."

D. U.S. DOMESTIC LAW REGARDING
THE USE OF FORCE

There are a host of U.S. treaties, laws, and regulations that affect the use of force. After the introduction, this section considers briefly one area — the War Powers Resolution, which attempts to impose some limits on the President's authority to deploy U.S. armed forces abroad in certain situations.

To begin, though, we should note some of the other, often noncontroversial, laws in order to provide a sense of the complex system that exists. First, there are laws that limit the export and sales of weapons abroad. Such activities are covered by the Arms Control Export Act, the Atomic Energy Act of 1948 (as amended by the Nuclear Non-Proliferation Act of 1978), and the Export Administration Act (though it has often lapsed in recent years because of congressional deadlocks lapsed and the President has resorted to the International Emergency Economic Powers Act to maintain the EAA's regulations). These laws effectively authorize the President to stop any and all arms exports unless he approves them. (As with other exports, the President often gives general approval for most sales to friendly countries, but requires specific approval by the Executive Branch for exports to certain countries or for sales of sensitive items.) Depending on the situation, Congress requires that the President must report to it in advance or within a certain period of time after approving certain arms sales, such as arms exports to countries that support terrorism or major arms sales to the Middle East.

Second, there are laws and executive orders limiting covert actions abroad by the U.S. government. "Covert action" can be roughly defined as an activity by an intelligence agency that is other than for the collection of intelligence. As a result, covert activities can range from secretly contributing to the election campaign of a political party in a foreign country, bribing a foreign cabinet officer to influence his or her country's policies, to attempting to blow up a terrorist base clandestinely. Although covert actions are usually conducted by the Central Intelligence Agency and not the Department of Defense, they sometimes involve the use of force. An existing executive order, however, provides that "[n]o person employed by or acting on behalf of the United States Government shall engage in, or conspire to engage in, assassination." (Exec. Order No. 12,333 (1981), reprinted in 50 U.S.C.A. §401.) One important set of laws are those requiring the President to notify certain committees or members of Congress of covert actions.

There is also a wide panoply of laws and international agreements that regulate the type, number, and location of U.S. military forces in peacetime. Congress regularly passes legislation setting ceilings on the number of military personnel, with some limits regarding the foreign deployment of these forces. . . . Some of these limits on forces are based on international agreements entered into with Russia or with several countries — for example, limits on nuclear arms and biological weapons. Some of these agreements will be considered in Section E below on nonproliferation.

There are also treaties, laws, and regulations limiting the actual conduct of U.S. forces when hostilities occur. Most publicized is the War Powers Resolution of 1973 (discussed below). The United States is also party to several treaties and conventions on such matters as the treatment of prisoners and the treatment of civilian populations in war zones. (See the preceding section on individual responsibility.) In addition, the military services have their own rules, which are often based on the international conventions or even customary international law.

The War Powers Resolution

The U.S. Constitution gives both Congress and the President important powers in foreign affairs and, more specifically, in the use of military force. Article I, Section 8 gives Congress numerous war-related powers, including the power to "declare War, grant Letters of Marque and Reprisal, and make Rules concerning Captures on Land and Water." Congress also is given important general powers, such as the power of the purse.

On the other hand, Article II of the Constitution makes the President the "Commander in Chief" and gives him the authority to make treaties, provided two-thirds of the Senate present concur. The Constitution also empowers him to nominate and appoint Ambassadors, with the advice and consent of a Senate majority. Article II also states that "[t]he executive Power" is vested in the President. The result is a less-than-clear allocation of powers between the President and Congress on many foreign policy matters, including the use of the military.

Since the Constitution, the relative roles that the President and Congress have played in foreign affairs has evolved and varied over time, with a trend generally toward an increased role for the President.

By the early 1970s, the President's growing predominance in foreign policy began to trouble many people in Congress and elsewhere. American foreign policy had usually been "achieved by a zealous patriotic rallying behind the Presidential colors" during the 30 years after World War II. (Thomas M. Franck & Edward Weisband, Foreign Policy by Congress 3 (1979).)

The Watergate mess and growing opposition to the war in Vietnam contributed to the Presidency coming under heavy fire. During 1972 to 1977, there was a renaissance of congressional influence in the making of U.S. foreign policy. The War Powers Resolution of 1973, discussed below, was one of the first major achievements during this period. Also, congressional oversight was increased over foreign assistance (on such issues as human rights), arms sales, the making of executive agreements, and the conduct of CIA operations. Included in this congressional activity was the passage of the National Emergencies Act of 1976 and the International Emergency Economic Powers Act (IEEPA) in 1977. (See Chapter 3 at page 222 regarding emergency powers.)

The War Powers Resolution is one of the most misunderstood and maligned statutes that Congress has passed in recent decades. Briefly, the War Powers Resolution provides that the President should "in every possible instance consult with Congress before introducing United States Armed Forces into hostilities, or into situations where imminent involvement in hostilities is clearly indicated by the circumstances." Moreover, in the absence of a declaration of war, in cases where the U.S. forces are introduced in specified circumstances (e.g., hostilities or imminent involvement in hostilities), the President shall report to Congress within 48 hours and regularly thereafter. (Section 4(a).) Within 60 calendar days after the 48-hour report is required to be submitted, the President should terminate any use of the U.S. armed forces in the situation requiring the report unless Congress has declared war, has enacted a specific authorization for this use, has extended the 60-day period by law, or is physically unable to meet because of an armed attack on the United States. The President can extend the initial 60-day period for another 30 days if he certifies to Congress that unavoidable military necessity requires the continued use of these forces in the course of removing them from the situation.

The Resolution does provide an early consultation and reporting requirement. However, as some observers have put it, the Resolution gives the President a "free" or unrestricted 60- or 90-day war before he needs any congressional approval. Moreover, once U.S. troops are engaged in combat or imminent danger thereof, how likely is it that Congress will not give the President the authority to continue the fight?

The statute is short. (The text is in the Documentary Supplement.) Note that the original section number in the Resolution is provided in brackets next to the section number in the U.S. Code. Except for the addition of section 1546a and minor procedural changes (none of which is of central importance), the law has not been amended since 1973.

The Resolution was passed over the veto of President Nixon who challenged, among other matters, the constitutionality of some of its provisions. No President since Nixon has supported the law's constitutionality, but many constitutional law scholars believe that its major provisions are constitutional and no U.S. court has ruled otherwise. At least as important is the experience under the statute.

In practice, particularly in recent years, the Resolution has meant that the congressional leadership is consulted before U.S. forces are sent into hostilities, though such consultation often occurred even before the Resolution. In several cases, however, where the U.S. military was sent into hostilities or the imminent threat of hostilities, Presidents have not reported as required under section 4(a) or they have failed to specify that the report is a section 4(a) report, thus avoiding the start of the 60-day clock. Moreover, even when they do report, Presidents do not say that it is "pursuant to" the Resolution, but only "consistent with" it.

In some of the most recent situations where the Resolution might be applicable, Presidents have sought approval from Congress for major uses of force through joint resolutions requiring a majority vote of both the House and Senate and the signature of the President. (By their wording, these resolutions are not declarations of war. The last U.S. declaration of war was after Pearl Harbor in 1941.) This alternative approach is probably to avoid disputes over the Resolution, as well as to marshal broad-based support before sending U.S. forces into dangerous and potentially disastrous situations, As indicated in sections above, President George H.W. Bush obtained such a resolution in 1991 before Operation Desert Storm and President George W. Bush obtained such congressional support to retaliate against the terrorists behind the September 11 attacks and then to invade Iraq. In each of these resolutions, passed in advance of U.S. military action, Congress has specifically declared that the resolution is intended to constitute specific statutory authorization within the meaning of the War Powers Resolution. President Clinton, however, did not seek such a resolution before the U.S. and NATO forces began bombing Yugoslavia over Kosovo in 1999.

Thomas M. Franck, Rethinking War Powers: By Law or by "Thaumaturgic Invocation"?*

83 Am. J. Intl. L. 766, 770 (1989)

The case for reform does not rest solely on the merit of that constitutional balance among the branches which the Act tried, but failed, to ensure. One undesired and undesirable side effect of the War Powers Resolution, as it has evolved in practice, is that it has enveloped foreign policy in a miasma of legalities. It has transformed argument about the political wisdom of being involved in military encounters — in the Gulf of Tonkin, or the Persian Gulf, or the Gulf of Sidra — into an arcane debate about the legality and constitutionality of various foreign policy initiatives. This change in emphasis impoverishes the marketplace of ideas and shrinks the dimensions of public comprehension and participation. It simply leaves most Americans bewildered and disaffected.

The purpose of the Resolution was to encourage serious dialogue on war/peace issues between the branches of government, and between the Government and the public. In any reform of the War Powers Resolution, that objective must be restored as its centerpiece. This does not mean that the legal and constitutional separation of powers issues do not matter. They most certainly do. But the effect of the Resolution on the public life of our nation should be to resolve the constitutional issues with sufficient simplicity, clarity and certainty to permit concentration on the policy debate about the wisdom or folly of any particular engagement of the armed forces. Only if the law can make clear what is legal can the political process concentrate on what is wise.

Notes and Questions

1. Does the War Powers Resolution require congressional approval in advance for the President to send U.S. military forces into combat abroad? Could the President invade Iraq or Iran without advance approval?

2. What does the Resolution tell the President to do in advance? In every case? How much consultation is required? (The relevant provisions are in section 1542. To experts, it is often referred to as section 3, since that was its section number in the original resolution.) What if some congressional leaders tell the President that his plans are a dumb and dangerous idea? Can the President still proceed? What might be the benefits of consultation?

3. The Resolution requires the President to report to Congress within 48 hours in "the absence of a declaration of war, in any case in which United States Armed Forces are introduced ..." into any of three situations. Compare the three situations. Which appears to be the most dangerous?

4. When does the Resolution require Congress to take action within 60 days (or 90 days in some cases)? In all three situations under section 4 (§1543)? (A time

[*"Thaumaturgy" is the "supposed working of miracles; magic." Webster's New World Dictionary (3rd ed. 1986).—Eds.]

limit on actions, such as the 60-day one here, is sometimes referred to as a "sunset" provision.)

5. Where a report was required under section 4(a)(1) (§1543(a)(1)) and the President has sent it to Congress, can the U.S. combat forces remain in a situation for 60 (or possibly 90 days) without any action by Congress?

6. Does the Resolution give the President a "free" 60- or 90-day war without requiring any congressional authorization? What exactly does the Resolution prevent the President from doing?

7. Section 5(c) (§1544(c)) provides that Congress can direct the President by a concurrent resolution to remove U.S. armed forces from situations where they are engaged in hostilities abroad. (A concurrent resolution can be passed by a majority vote of the House and Senate, and it does not need the signature of the President.) When the War Powers Resolution was passed, this concurrent resolution provision had been viewed as an important limit on the President's power, in addition to the 60-day limit in certain situations. However, it is likely that this legislative veto provision is now void under the Supreme Court's ruling in *Chadha* and other cases. (Immigration and Naturalization Service v. Chadha, 462 U.S. 919 (1983).) The Resolution does contain a severability clause — section 9 (§1548).

8. What if the President does not file a report under section 4 even though U.S. armed forces have been deployed in, say, the Persian Gulf and firefights have quickly occurred between the U.S. naval units and Iranian naval units. Does the 60-day period still begin to run? Who determines that the period has begun to run, and from what date? Is this clear in the Resolution?

9. Is it likely that a U.S. court will rule that the 60- (or 90-)day period has begun to run? Why not? What circumstances might be required?

10. So far, no court has upheld a challenge under the War Powers Resolution. Rather, these challenges have all been dismissed under limiting doctrines such as standing, ripeness, equitable discretion, and the political question doctrine. For example, see Campbell v. Clinton, 203 F.3d 19 (D.D.C. 2000) (lack of standing in suit over U.S. bombing campaign over Kosovo); Ange v. Bush, 752 F. Supp. 509 (D.D.C. 1990) (dismissing challenge to Gulf War on political question, equitable discretion, and ripeness grounds).

11. A book review by Professor Jane Stromseth provides a valuable analysis of the War Powers Resolution and its use. In it, she suggests that four major alternatives present themselves for reforming the Resolution: strengthen it, repeal it in part, repeal it completely, or essentially leave it as it. She notes the various advocates and the literature for and against these major alternatives. She adds: "Partial repeal of the resolution . . . is the reform most likely to succeed. Proposals to repeal the Resolution's 60-day time clock and concurrent resolution provisions and to turn it effectively into a consultation and reporting mechanism have circulated for some time." Jane Stromseth, Understanding Constitutional War Powers Today: Why Methodology Matters, 106 Yale L.J. 845, 913 n.344 (1996).

However, see also Michael J. Glennon, Too Far Apart: Repeal the War Powers Resolution, 50 U. Miami L. Rev. 17, 30-31 (1997). "I favor strengthening the Resolution over repealing it. But, if the alternatives are the current version of the Resolution versus no Resolution, a hardheaded cost-benefit analysis is required. . . . The War Powers Resolution should be repealed."

E.   COMBATING THE PROLIFERATION OF WEAPONS OF MASS DESTRUCTION

The world has witnessed a long and mixed history of efforts designed to limit and even eliminate weapons. These endeavors have become even more important in the post-September 11 world. Some of the past emphasis has shifted from bilateral agreements between the United States and Russia or other countries to multilateral arrangements designed to include large numbers of states. The frequent goal is to combat the proliferation of weapons of mass destruction — nuclear, chemical, and biological — and their delivery systems (WMD).

1.   A Brief History and the Present Threat

Attempts at arms control are in part an outgrowth of earlier efforts to develop rules of war. Two highlights of those earlier efforts were the 1864 Geneva Conference and the First Hague Peace Conference in 1899, where multilateral conventions were drafted to make binding rules of war in areas where there had been some development of customary international law.

The Geneva Conference concerned the fate of victims of hostilities and started a process that has produced a number of Geneva conventions, as discussed above at page 1106.

The Hague Conference concerned the regulation of weapons and permissible methods of war. The most basic rule was laid down in Article 22 of the Hague Regulations of 1907: "The right of belligerents to adopt means of injuring the enemy is not unlimited." A number of somewhat more specific prohibitions have been added to this general principle, such as prohibitions on the use of poisoned weapons and dum-dum bullets, weapons that cause much greater injuries than are necessary to put an adversary out of combat.

There have been other efforts at arms control. For example, the Washington Treaty of 1922 and the London Naval Treaty of 1930 included limitations on the number and type of naval ships that the participating countries were allowed, many of the limitations expressed in terms of ratios among the major countries. The London Treaty led to the destruction of several large naval ships that were under construction, including U.S. ships. Observance of these treaties was mixed. For example, Japan denounced them in 1934 and embarked on a major shipbuilding program, and the treaties became a dead letter by the eve of World War II.

The most immediate threat now to U.S. and international security comes from the possible use of weapons of mass destruction (WMD). Although the threat of nuclear attack from the former Soviet Union has diminished with the end of the Cold War, nuclear, chemical, and biological weapons are increasingly available to hostile states, terrorist groups, and even criminal organizations. The potential acquisition of WMD materials and technologies is more likely now than at any other time in history.

First, due to the dissolution of the former Soviet Union and the resulting economic and political turmoil in the successor states, there are more pressures and opportunities for groups or individuals to traffic in nuclear weapons, components, and technology (sometimes referred to as the "loose nukes" problem). Second, more and more countries have developed their own nuclear and other WMD programs in recent years — for example, India, Pakistan, North Korea, and Iran. Some of these countries face continuing friction with their neighbors, notably India and Pakistan over Kashmir, that could lead to the pressures to use the WMD weapons.

Third, the increasing diffusion of modern technology through the growth of the world trade and the information revolution make it harder to detect illicit diversions of materials and technologies relevant to building WMD programs. For example, many of the technologies and components associated with chemical and biological weapons programs also have legitimate commercial applications unrelated to creating WMD, with some items being called "dual use" because they have the potential for both peaceful and dangerous uses. For example, the 1995 chemical weapons attack by the Aum Shinrikyo cult in Japan demonstrated that the use of WMD was no longer restricted to sovereign states in the battlefield and revealed the ease of manufacturing chemical agents from legally supplied, commercial dual-use technology. The sect released sarin gas on the Tokyo subway using gas that the sect manufactured itself, killing 12 people and injuring over 5,000.

Further, the September 11, 2001, terrorist attacks on the World Trade Center demonstrated that terrorist groups are capable of organizing and conducting major attacks against civilians. And, as discussed below, North Korea's withdrawal from the Nuclear Nonproliferation Treaty in January 2003, along with a capability to produce a nuclear bomb a month and its apparently unbridled willingess to obtain much-needed funds from exports of dangerous goods, underscores the growing threats from weapons of mass destruction.

2. *Chemical and Biological Weapons*

The anthrax attacks in the United States in October 2001, the earlier Japanese cult attacks in Tokyo in 1995, and the horrific use of chemical weapons by Saddam Hussein against Iranians and against his own Kurdish population during the 1980s highlight the need for limiting, if not eliminating, chemical and biological weapons. For both types of weapons, there are treaties as well as an export control regime.

Three main multilateral treaties exist for banning the use of chemical and biological weapons. The Geneva Protocol of 1925 is the first important multilateral agreement regarding chemical and biological weapons. It explicitly bans the use in war of "asphyxiating, poisonous or other gases" and "bacteriological methods of warfare." However, it does not ban the possession of these chemical weapons, nor does it contain limits on their production or deployment. The Geneva Protocol also implicitly does not cover internal or civil conflicts, and lacks verification mechanisms. Further, several parties to the Protocol, including the United Kingdom and France, have reserved the right to retaliate in kind if chemical or biological weapons are first used against them, thus rendering the Protocol a no-first-use agreement for these states.

The second multilateral agreement in effect is the Biological and Toxins* Weapons Convention (BWC) of 1972. Unlike the Geneva Protocol, this agreement

*Toxins are substances that, in rough terms, fall between biologicals and chemicals because they act like chemicals but are ordinarily produced by biological or microbic processes.—EDS.

applies solely to biological weapons, which in general are those produced by use of living organisms. The practical differences between chemical and biological warfare are sometimes more important than this technical distinction. Some chemical weapons are easier to handle and control than biological weapons. In addition, chemical weapons have also been used in modern warfare, and many countries have maintained stocks for deterrence purposes.

Supplementing the prohibition on use in the Geneva Protocol, parties to the Biological Weapons Convention have agreed not to develop, produce, stockpile, or acquire biological agents or toxins "of types and in quantities that have no justification for prophylactic, protective, and other peaceful purposes." All such existing weapons were to be destroyed within nine months of the Convention's entry into force. The Convention contains no inspection or verification provisions. Instead, the parties are to "consult and cooperate" in solving any problems that arise. Complaints regarding a breach of obligation are to be lodged with the U.N. Security Council.

Parties review the operation of the BWC approximately every five years. They have affirmed that the scope of the Convention extends to new scientific and technological developments, and they have also enhanced transparency by instituting voluntary data-exchanges among states. In recognition of the Convention's gap on inspection and verification, the Parties have worked to establish international mechanisms necessary to strengthen the Convention. For example, at the most recent Review in 2002, the Parties set forth as their continued priorities the continued promotion of "necessary national measures to implement the prohibitions" and continuing efforts to "enhance international capabilities for responding to, investigating, and mitigating" potential illegal uses, including the recommendation for establishing a code of conduct for scientists. In any event, given the challenges of finding the relatively small facilities that might be used for developing biological weapons, it is clear that a stronger verification regime is needed, possibly like the substantial one for the more recent Chemical Weapons Convention (discussed below). As of January 2003, 146 states were parties to the BWC.

On a bilateral basis, in June 1990, President Bush and President Gorbachev signed the U.S.-U.S.S.R. Chemical Weapons Destruction Agreement. It provided for the destruction of the vast bulk of the United States' and Soviet's (and now Russia's) declared chemical weapons stockpiles, with on-site inspection to confirm that destruction has taken place. Destruction was to begin in 1992 and to proceed until each country had reached a declared stockpile of 500 tons — about 20 percent of the initial U.S. stockpile level — by the year 2002. Both countries were also to stop producing chemical weapons under this agreement, without waiting for a multilateral chemical weapons ban.

In December 1994, the Clinton Administration notified Congress that it had "concerns" and "questions" about Russia's willingness and ability to comply with this agreement and others restricting the development and use of chemical and biological weapons. Although Russia's leaders appeared committed to abolishing the weapons, bureaucratic resistance and shortage of funds meant that the Russian program for destroying chemical weapons was moving slowly and some data exchanges were not satisfactory. These problems are apparently continuing.

The third and most recent multilateral agreement in the area of biological and chemical weapons is the Chemical Weapons Convention (CWC). The Convention came into force in 1997. Shortly before this, the United States ratified the CWC after intense lobbying from the Clinton Administration, arms control advocates, and the U.S. chemical industry led the U.S. Senate to advise and consent to the treaty.

The CWC forbids all signatory states from developing, producing, stockpiling, or using chemical weapons, and requires all member nations to destroy any existing chemical weapons within ten years from the time the Convention enters into force. Like the BWC, the CWC parties must adopt measures to ensure that toxic chemicals and their precursors are only used for purposes not prohibited by the Convention. However, unlike the BWC, the CWC has detailed provisions for verifying compliance, including the creation of a new international organization, the Organization for the Prohibition of Chemical Weapons (OPCW). Verification procedures include both routine visits from international teams of inspectors and "challenge inspections," which may be requested by a member nation if it believes another state is not complying with the terms of the Convention.

As of January 2003, there were 148 parties to the CWC, but this did not include some countries that probably have active programs or stockpiled chemical weapons such as Iraq, Libya, North Korea, and Syria. The first CWC review conference is scheduled for May 2003 in The Hague, with subsequent review conferences every five years after that.

Besides the multilateral treaties above, 33 countries are members of the Australia Group (AG), a multilateral nonproliferation regime controlling chemical and biological weapons-related goods. In the wake of chemical weapons used during the Iran-Iraq war, the AG was established in 1984 to ensure that companies producing supplies and materials capable of building chemical weapons did not assist states seeking to acquire CBW capability. The dual-use nature of many CBW materials and technologies makes such controls critical. Although nonbinding, the AG works to harmonize participants' export controls, and provides a channel to discuss CBW threats and trends, as well as share experiences in implementing and enforcing CBW controls.

3. Nuclear Arms Control

The capability of nuclear weapons to wipe out whole societies has consistently stimulated efforts to reduce the risk of nuclear war. Since the end of the cold war and the breakup of the Soviet Union, negotiators have endeavored to reduce the number of existing weapons, ensure responsible control over the remaining weapons, and prevent the production of new weapons. Other efforts have focused on preventing additional states from acquiring nuclear weapons capability (nuclear proliferation).

What follows is a description of some of the most important nuclear arms agreements — the test ban treaties, U.S-Soviet/Russian agreements, and the Nonproliferation Treaty. This is followed by a section on the growing nuclear threat from North Korea.

a. The Test Ban Treaties

The first nuclear weapons test was in 1945 at Alamogordo, New Mexico. After the end of World War II, the United States resumed its testing and the Soviet Union conducted its first weapons test in 1949. Both countries continued to make major improvements in their weapons and continued testing. There were fitful efforts to reach a test ban moratorium and then an actual moratorium in the late 1950s, but the moratorium had failed by 1961. By this time both Great Britain and France had arrived on the scene as nuclear powers, and France's first nuclear tests in 1960 and 1961 were one of the reasons that the Soviet Union gave to resume testing in 1961.

With the encouragement of President Kennedy, relatively rapid negotiations among the United States, Great Britain, and the Soviet Union led to the Limited Test Ban Treaty (LTBT) in the summer of 1963. The LTBT banned all nuclear explosions except for underground tests. The three original signatories plus over 105 other states are now parties to the LTBT.

France refused to sign the Treaty but did stop atmospheric testing in 1974. China also refused to sign, conducting its first atmospheric test in 1964, although it has since stopped atmospheric testing. India is a party to the LTBT. It conducted testing of its "peaceful" nuclear devices underground.

Although the LTBT ended the severe environmental problems that were arising as a result of atmospheric testing, underground testing continued at a significant pace after 1963. In an effort to limit at least the size of underground nuclear tests, two further treaties were signed by the United States and the Soviet Union in the 1970s. The Threshold Test Ban Treaty (TTBT) of 1974 placed a limit of 150 kilotons on underground weapon tests. (The bomb that the United States dropped with devastating effects on Hiroshima in 1945 was approximately 13-15 kilotons, so the TTBT would allow tests up to ten times the size of that bomb. Nevertheless, the 150-kiloton limit is still much smaller than some of the weapons of 1,000 kilotons and more in the U.S. and Russian arsenals.) The Peaceful Nuclear Explosion Treaty (PNET) of 1976 then closed a loophole in the TTBT by extending the 150-kiloton limit to underground nuclear explosions for alleged peaceful purposes, such as diverting rivers or digging underground cavities for the storage of gas.

Active negotiations for a comprehensive test ban treaty (CTBT), which included strong support from the United States, began at the United Nations Conference on Disarmament (CD) in Geneva in January 1994. In September 1996, the CTBT was drafted and opened for signature. Also in 1996, a preparatory commission for the CTBT Organization was established to set up a verification regime, including the International Monitoring System, International Data Center, and capabilities for conducting on-site inspections. By January 2003, 97 countries had ratified the treaty. However, the treaty will not enter into force until sufficient countries have ratified it, including certain specified countries that have yet to do so, such as India, Pakistan, North Korea, and the United States. President Clinton submitted the CTBT to the U.S. Senate for its advice and consent, but the Senate dealt a severe blow to the near-term prospects for U.S. ratification when it refused by a 48-51 negative vote to provide its advice and consent in October 1999. No progress on U.S. ratification has been made since then.

In September 2002, representatives from 18 countries that have ratified the treaty, including France, Japan, Russia, and the United Kingdom, issued a declaration at the U.N. supporting the CTBT and noted that "international tensions . . . make entry into force of the treaty, within the broader framework of . . . nonproliferation efforts, even more urgent today." The statement also urged countries to continue not undertaking nuclear tests until the CTBT enters into force. See Arms Control Association, The Status of the Comprehensive Test Ban Treaty: Signatories and Ratifiers (October 2002), at http://www.armscontrol.org.

b.   U.S.-Soviet/Russian Nuclear Arms Control

Since the 1972 summit between President Nixon and General Secretary Leonid Brezhnev, where the SALT I agreements were signed, the bilateral efforts to limit the large nuclear arsenals of the United States and the Soviet Union/Russia have been the centerpiece of many of these two countries' summit meetings and they have been a critical part of efforts to limit nuclear weapons generally. Even with the series of agreements that these two countries have reached, the American and Russian nuclear weapons inventories still far exceed those of any other country, though China's nuclear inventory is apparently growing. What follows is a brief description of a selection of the various U.S.-Soviet/Russian agreements and attempted agreements.

Arms Control Association, U.S.-Soviet/Russian Nuclear Arms Control

Arms Control Today (June 2002)

According to the United States, the [2002] Strategic Offensive Reductions Treaty [(SORT) would reduce] the number of "operationally deployed strategic warheads," i.e., those warheads that are mated to their delivery vehicles and ready for launch. But the complete nuclear arsenals of the United States and Russia include many other weapons. In addition to those deployed strategic weapons, both countries deploy tactical nuclear weapons—which are designed for battlefield use, are generally less powerful, and have a shorter range—and store thousands of additional warheads.

Currently, the total U.S. nuclear stockpile is estimated to consist of almost 11,000 warheads, including almost 7,000 deployed strategic warheads; more than 1,000 operational tactical nuclear warheads; and almost 3,000 reserve strategic and tactical warheads, which are not mated to delivery vehicles. (The United States also maintains thousands of nuclear warhead components that could be reassembled into functional weapons.)

The current Russian nuclear stockpile is estimated to include about 5,000 deployed strategic weapons, about 3,500 operational tactical nuclear weapons, and more than 11,000 stockpiled strategic and tactical warheads, for a total arsenal of about 19,500 nuclear warheads. Unlike the United States, Russia possesses these reserves at least in part because dismantling the warheads has proven prohibitively expensive. And unlike the United States, Russia continues to produce limited numbers of new nuclear warheads, largely because its warheads are designed to have far shorter operational lives and therefore must be replaced more frequently.

STRATEGIC NUCLEAR ARMS CONTROL AGREEMENTS

SALT I

Begun in November 1969, the Strategic Arms Limitation Talks (SALT) had produced by May 1972 both the Anti-Ballistic Missile (ABM) Treaty, which bans

8

nationwide strategic missile defenses, and the Interim Agreement, an executive-legislative agreement that capped U.S. and Soviet ICBM and SLBM forces. [In December 2001, President Bush gave notice that the United States would withdraw from the ABM Treaty, effective June 2002. See page 120 above. The Interim Agreement was for a term of five years, though the two countries continued to observe its limits for several years after that. For background information, an ICBM is an intercontinental ballistic missile and is based on land. An SLBM is a submarine-launched ballistic missile and is fired from a submarine. Both have ranges in excess of 5,000 miles.] . . .

Because of NMD National Missle Defense Initiative

SALT II

In November 1972, Washington and Moscow agreed to pursue a follow-on treaty to SALT I. SALT II, signed in June 1979, initially limited U.S. and Soviet ICBM, SLBM, and strategic bomber-based nuclear forces to 2,400 delivery vehicles (defined as an ICBM silo, a submarine missile-launch tube, or a bomber) and placed a variety of other restrictions on deployed strategic nuclear forces. . . . However, President Jimmy Carter asked the Senate not to consider SALT II for its advice and consent after the Soviet Union invaded Afghanistan in December 1979, and the treaty was not taken up again. Both Washington and Moscow subsequently pledged to adhere to the agreement's terms despite its failure to enter into force. But on May 26, 1986, President Ronald Reagan said that future decisions on strategic nuclear forces would be based on the threat posed by Soviet forces and "not on standards contained in the SALT structure."

also failed

9

START I

The Strategic Arms Reduction Treaty (START I), first proposed in the early 1980s by President Ronald Reagan and finally signed in July 1991, required the United States and the Soviet Union to reduce their deployed strategic arsenals to 1,600 delivery vehicles, carrying no more than 6,000 warheads as counted using the agreement's rules. . . . The destruction was verified using an intrusive verification regime that involved on-site inspections and regular exchanges of information, as well as national technical means (i.e., satellites). The agreement's entry into force was delayed for several years because of the collapse of the Soviet Union. . . . START I reductions were completed in December 2001, and the treaty will remain in force until December 2009 unless extended by the parties.

10

START II

In June 1992, Presidents George H. W. Bush and Boris Yeltsin agreed to pursue a follow-on accord to START I. START II, signed in January 1993, called for reducing deployed strategic arsenals to 3,000-3,500 warheads and banned the deployment of destabilizing multiple-warhead land-based missiles. . . . The agreement's original

11

implementation deadline was January 2003, but a 1997 protocol extended the deadline until December 2007 because of Russia's concerns over its ability to meet the earlier date. Both the Senate and the Duma have approved START II, but the treaty [never took] effect because the Senate [did not approve] the 1997 protocol and several ABM Treaty amendments, whose passage the Duma established as a condition for START II's entry into force.

failed

START III Framework

12

In March 1997, Presidents Bill Clinton and Boris Yeltsin agreed to a framework for START III negotiations that included a reduction in deployed strategic warheads to 2,000-2,500. . . . Negotiations were supposed to begin after START II entered into force, which never happened.

SORT [Strategic Offensive Reduction Treaty]

13

On May 24, 2002, Presidents George W. Bush and Vladimir Putin signed a [relatively short] treaty under which the United States and Russia will reduce their strategic arsenals to 1,700-2,200 warheads each. Although the two sides have not agreed . . . on specific counting rules, the Bush administration has made clear that it will reduce only warheads deployed on strategic delivery vehicles in active service, i.e., "operationally deployed" warheads, and will not count warheads removed from service and placed in storage or warheads on delivery vehicles undergoing overhaul or repair. Russia disagrees with this interpretation of the treaty and hopes to negotiate stricter counting rules at a later date. The agreement's limits are similar to those envisioned for START III, but the treaty does not require the destruction of delivery vehicles, as START I and II did, or the destruction of warheads, as had been envisioned for START III. [The treaty was ratified by both countries in mid-2003 and is in force.]

NONSTRATEGIC NUCLEAR ARMS CONTROL MEASURES

Intermediate-Range Nuclear Forces (INF) Treaty

14

Signed December 8, 1987, the INF Treaty required the United States and the Soviet Union to verifiably eliminate all ground-launched ballistic and cruise missiles with ranges between 500 and 5,500 kilometers. Distinguished by its unprecedented, intrusive inspection regime, . . . [T]he INF Treaty entered into force June 1, 1988, and the two sides completed their reductions by June 1, 1991, destroying a total of 2,692 missiles. The agreement was multilateralized after the breakup of the Soviet Union, and current active participants in the agreement's implementation include the United States, Russia, Belarus, Kazakhstan, and Ukraine. . . . The ban on intermediate-range missiles is of unlimited duration.

Presidential Nuclear Initiatives

On September 27, 1991, President George H. W. Bush announced that the United States would remove almost all U.S. tactical nuclear forces from deployment so that Russia could undertake similar actions, reducing the risk of nuclear proliferation as the Soviet Union dissolved. Specifically, Bush said the United States would eliminate all its nuclear artillery shells and short-range nuclear ballistic missile warheads and remove all nonstrategic nuclear warheads from surface ships, attack submarines, and land-based naval aircraft. Soviet leader Mikhail Gorbachev reciprocated on October 5. . . . However, significant questions remain about Russian implementation of its pledges, and there is considerable uncertainty about the current state of Russia's tactical nuclear forces.

c.   The Nonproliferation Treaty

The dangers of the proliferation of nuclear weapons have been a threat ever since the atomic bomb was first developed. Progressively, more and more countries have acquired nuclear weapons or the technical capability to undertake a nuclear weapons program. As of March 2003, there were seven declared nuclear weapon states — the United States, Russia, Great Britain, France, China, India, and Pakistan. Israel and North Korea likely have nuclear weapons also. South Africa had nuclear weapons but dismantled them. Many other nations are technically capable of undertaking a nuclear weapons program, including Germany, Japan, and Iran.

An important objective is slowing the spread of these weapons. The key treaty here is the Nuclear Nonproliferation Treaty (NPT) of 1968. There are 188 states who are parties to the Treaty. The NPT essentially involved a bargain at the time: The non-nuclear-weapon states agreed to renounce the development and acquisition of nuclear weapons in exchange for pledges from the nuclear-weapons states to share peaceful nuclear technology, such as for producing energy, and to take steps toward nuclear disarmament.

Some states, however, with a nuclear weapons capability — such as India, Israel, and Pakistan — are not NPT members. Moreover, as discussed below, North Korea announced in January 2003 that it was withdrawing from the Treaty.

Arms Control Association, The Nuclear Nonproliferation Treaty at a Glance

Fact Sheet (January 2003)

[The treaty's] 188 states-parties are classified in two categories: nuclear-weapon states (NWS) — consisting of the United States, Russia, China, France, and the United Kingdom — and non-nuclear-weapon states (NNWS). Under the treaty, the five NWS commit to pursue general and complete disarmament, while the NNWS agree to forgo developing or acquiring nuclear weapons.

With its near-universal membership, the NPT has the widest adherence of any arms control agreement, with only India, Israel, and Pakistan remaining outside the treaty. In order to accede to the treaty, these states must do so as NNWS, since the treaty restricts NWS status to nations that "manufactured and exploded a nuclear weapon or other nuclear explosive device prior to 1 January 1967." For India, Israel, and Pakistan, all known to possess or suspected of having nuclear weapons, joining the treaty as NNWS would require that they dismantle their nuclear weapons and place their nuclear materials under international safeguards. South Africa followed this path to accession in 1991.

SELECT TREATY ARTICLES

Under Articles I and II of the treaty, the NWS agree not to help NNWS develop or acquire nuclear weapons, and the NNWS permanently forswear the pursuit of such weapons. To verify these commitments and ensure that nuclear materials are not being diverted for weapons purposes, Article III tasks the International Atomic Energy Agency with the inspection of the non-nuclear-weapon states' nuclear facilities. In addition, Article III establishes safeguards for the transfer of fissionable materials between NWS and NNWS.

Article IV acknowledges the "inalienable right" of NNWS to research, develop, and use nuclear energy for non-weapons purposes. It also supports the "fullest possible exchange" of such nuclear-related information and technology between NWS and NNWS. . . .

Article VI commits the NWS to "pursue negotiations in good faith on effective measures relating to cessation of the nuclear arms race at an early date and to nuclear disarmament, and on a treaty on general and complete disarmament under strict and effective international control." . . .

Article VIII requires a complex and lengthy process to amend the treaty, effectively blocking any changes absent clear consensus. Article X establishes the terms by which a state may withdraw from the treaty, requiring three month's advance notice should "extraordinary events" jeopardize its supreme national interests.

. . . The 1995 review conference extended the treaty indefinitely and enhanced the review process by mandating that the five-year review conferences review past implementation and address ways to strengthen the treaty.

Jan Lodal, a former senior official in the Pentagon and on the National Security Council staff, thoughtfully analyzes below the NPT's significance and how the NPT regime can be strengthened.

Jan Lodal, The Price of Dominance

87-91 (2001)

The Nuclear Nonproliferation Treaty has been the backbone of America's nuclear nonproliferation strategy. . . . The NPT not only prohibits the acquisition of nuclear weapons by nonnuclear signatories of the treaty, but it also prohibits the transfer of nuclear weapons technology by nuclear weapons states to nonnuclear weapons states. Since the end of the Cold War, all states except India, Israel, and Pakistan and the five declared nuclear powers have renounced plans to develop nuclear weapons and have joined the NPT. Brazil, Argentina, Taiwan, South Korea, and South Africa all had nuclear weapons programs during the Cold War but have now renounced them. South Africa had built an operational arsenal of, according to its own statements, seven nuclear weapons. It has announced that these weapons have been destroyed, although no outside third party has verified [this]. . . .

The NPT was the first significant multilateral arms control agreement that included built-in enforcement provisions. . . . [T]he International Atomic Energy Agency (IAEA) . . . is responsible for monitoring nuclear facilities of nonnuclear states party to the treaty. This monitoring is designed to ensure that no "peaceful" nuclear activities are used covertly to develop nuclear weapons. The IAEA model became the basis (with many differences in details) for the enforcement provisions later included in the Chemical Weapons Convention and proposed for the Biological Weapons Convention.

It is important to understand the NPT for what it is worth, acknowledging what it can and cannot accomplish. The NPT will not lead to the elimination of nuclear weapons, despite the provisions of Article VI calling for nuclear abolition (nor will it lead to general and complete disarmament, also called for by Article VI). The NPT has not been able to stop all proliferation — India, Israel, and Pakistan refused to join so they could develop their own nuclear weapons. The NPT's enforcement arm, the IAEA, cannot prevent a determined covert program. North Korea and Iraq joined the NPT, but both countries successfully carried out covert nuclear weapons programs under the nose of the IAEA. The NPT has also motivated considerable foot-dragging by nonnuclear states. These states have used the Article VI call for nuclear disarmament to criticize the nuclear states and to justify their covert nuclear programs. India, Pakistan, and Iran have been the most voluble of those states in this regard. . . .

But the NPT has one crucial achievement — it has established an accepted international norm against transferring nuclear weapons technology from nuclear weapons states to a nonnuclear state. After the Cold War, the NPT became the mechanism by which states that had equivocated about nuclear weapons could make a legally binding commitment to forego them. When Iraq and North Korea were caught cheating, the NPT became the rallying point for an international consensus to insist on compliance. When China and Russia were caught orchestrating (or at least condoning) prohibited exports of nuclear technology to rogue states, the NPT allowed the United States and its allies to raise the diplomatic stakes substantially and insist that the leakage be stopped. The NPT should remain the centerpiece of U.S. nonproliferation diplomacy, despite its weaknesses and contradictions. It should be strengthened, not undercut.

In strengthening the NPT regime, India and Pakistan present special problems. Pakistan will remain nuclear as long as India is nuclear, and India will remain nuclear as long as China is nuclear — which might be forever. India first detonated a "peaceful nuclear explosion" (i.e., a nuclear bomb) in 1974, so it has been a de facto nuclear power for a quarter of a century. But its decision to declare and test its nuclear weapons, highly popular with India's voters, eliminates the option of ambiguity concerning its intentions. Nuclear testing did the same for Pakistan.

Having two declared nuclear powers that are highly unlikely to roll back their nuclear programs leaves the NPT in a state of limbo. It is supposed to regulate the spread of nuclear weapons throughout the world, which is clearly impossible with two nuclear powers outside the treaty. It is not clear what rules govern them — are they bound by the export controls and commitment to work against further proliferation imposed by the NPT or not? To date, India has not been a major source of

WMD proliferation assistance, but India has done much less than is possible to help solve the WMD problem. Pakistan has extensive nuclear-related commerce with China, North Korea, and possibly Iran.

The NPT would be stronger with both India and Pakistan admitted as nuclear weapons states, a position completely contrary to current U.S. policy. A new "line in the sand" would be drawn at seven versus five nuclear powers. . . . The issue of who would be permitted by the international community to have nuclear weapons would be settled. Any state that refused to join the consensus could be treated as a rogue state and isolated. (Israel would remain ambiguous, but as discussed below, there will come a time when Israel must give up nuclear weapons.)

Notwithstanding the logic of bringing both India and Pakistan into the NPT, doing so will remain diplomatically infeasible for the foreseeable future. Their admission as nuclear weapons states would require obtaining the unanimous consent of the parties to the treaty, an almost impossible task. Many nations (including the United States) believe that it would be a major mistake to "reward" India for its proliferation by bringing it into the regime or to reward Pakistan for resisting the years of diplomatic pressure against its nuclear program. Others would remain concerned that admitting India and Pakistan would open the possibility of admitting other states that are today nonnuclear should they change their policies, such as Japan or Germany, notwithstanding the existing treaty commitment of all such states to remain nonnuclear.

For the moment, the best compromise would be for the United States to acknowledge openly India's and Pakistan's nuclear status and insist that they live by the nonproliferation provisions of both the NPT and its supporting institutions, even though they are not members. Both nations could be admitted to some of the supporting institutions (such as [export control groups]) if they agree to their strict provisions on technology transfer. Both states should be strongly pressured not to develop "hair trigger" nuclear weapons delivery systems, They each have land-based missile programs that could easily motivate a preemptive strike during a crisis. These programs should be rolled back. Finally, both states should be given whatever assistance is possible consistent with the NPT's prohibitions on technology transfer to improve their nuclear weapons safety, security, and control.

Israel has not and probably will not acknowledge its nuclear weapons program. Very strong historical and ideological reasons will prohibit Israel's giving up its program until there is a secure peace in the Middle East. When peace comes, there will be no further reason to keep it; Israel's conventional military dominance will be adequate for its security. In the interim, the ambiguity will remain the only option.

Perhaps the most important step related to the NPT would be to strengthen the capabilities of the IAEA. . . .[I]mprovements in intelligence cooperation . . . would help considerably. The recent challenge-inspection procedures, put in place in response to failures in Iraq and North Korea, must be implemented vigorously. Finally, the parties to the NPT must take a more realistic view of the limits of the IAEA. The IAEA can only indict; it can never give a state a clean bill of health. It will remain up to the member states to find hidden proliferation and to organize the international community to take action against the offending state.

The IAEA announced in 2002 a stronger global safeguards system. The new approach, called "integrated safeguards," provide the IAEA with more flexibility in deciding where to focus its efforts and limited resources. Inspectors were being given wider authority and advanced verification tools. As the IAEA Director General Mohamed ElBaradei said in briefing the IAEA's Board of Directors in March 2002, "The discoveries in Iraq [of secret programs as a result of the far-ranging inspections mandated by the U.N. Security Council after the 1991 Gulf War], as well as later revelations involving the Democratic People's Republic of Korea, shattered assumptions about the world's nuclear nonproliferation regime."

The Nuclear Nonproliferation Treaty and the IAEA are supplemented by the Nuclear Nonproliferation Treaty Exporters (Zangger) Committee. Its 35 members seek to harmonize implementation of the NPT's requirements in applying IAEA safeguards to nuclear exports. In addition, there are several multilateral nonproliferation arrangements or regimes that have as at least one of their objectives preventing the proliferation of nuclear weapons and the means to deliver them (or chemical or biological weapons). The two most important are the Nuclear Suppliers Group and the Missile Technology Control Regime (MCTR).

The Nuclear Suppliers Group was created in 1974 after India's nuclear explosion, which illustrated how nuclear technology and materials transferred for peaceful purposes could be used for other purposes. The group, which now includes 40 countries, has procedures for sensitive nuclear exports including requiring assurances from the recipient country. The Missile Technology Control Regime (MCTR) was created in 1987 to limit the proliferation of missiles capable of delivering WMD and related equipment and technology. The MCTR Guidelines and Annex include a list of controlled items whose transfer is restricted. This regulatory regime has 33 participating countries.

d. The Dangerous Case of North Korea

Although efforts to stop the nonproliferation of nuclear weapons have had some success, as noted above, the number of nuclear-weapons states has grown over the years and more states appear on the verge of developing these weapons. North Korea has become an especially difficult situation in recent years, both because of its potential for making several bombs quickly out of available plutonium and its past practice of selling for much-needed hard currency dangerous items (e.g., missiles) to dangerous countries and possibly other suspicious customers.*

The situation reached crisis proportions in most experts' minds in 2002-2003, but there had been problems on occasion in the past. In 1994, as recounted by Professor Ashton B. Carter, then a U.S. Assistant Secretary of Defense, "North Korea was planning to take fuel rods out of its research reactor at Yongbyon and extract the six or so bombs' worth of weapons-grade plutonium they contained." The United States actively explored possible military options, but pushed for a diplomatic solution. See Ashton B. Carter, Prepared Testimony before Senate Committee on Foreign Relations, February 4, 2003.

The United States and North Korea negotiated and signed the Agreed Framework in October 1994. It froze operations at Yongbyon, including a reactor, a fuel reprocessing plant, and two partially completed larger reactors. The freeze was to be

---

*There was also growing evidence in 2002-2003 that Iran was embarked on a program to develop nuclear weapons, but it was still years behind North Korea's. — EDS.

verified through IAEA on-site inspections. In return, through a multinational consortium, the Korean Peninsula Energy Development Organization (KEDO), the United States agreed to help build two nuclear power reactors of a type (light-water) whose byproducts cannot easily be used in the development of nuclear weapons. Moreover, the consortium would supply North Korea with 500,000 metric tons of heating oil each year while the reactors were under construction.

Events heated up again in 1998, when the launch by North Korea of a ballistic missile over Japan and into the Pacific Ocean caused concern in Japan and the United States, with some people calling for a halt to the oil shipments under the Framework Agreement. President Clinton asked former Secretary of Defense William Perry to lead a policy review, with Professor Carter assisting. After direct and frank talks between U.S. and North Korean officials, Carter reports:

> Over the next two years, North Korea took some small steps on the upward path. It agreed to a moratorium on tests of long-range missiles. It continued the freeze at Yongbyon. It embarked on talks with South Korea that led to the 2000 summit meeting of the leaders of North and South.
>
> The North also began the process of healings its strained relations with Japan, making the astonishing admission that it had kidnapped Japanese citizens in the 1970's and 1980's. [Carter, supra.]

The 1994 Agreed Framework did not provide for regular verification in North Korea outside of Yongbyon. In 2002, North Korea apparently admitted to a visiting senior U.S. official that it had a hidden uranium enrichment facility elsewhere and implied that North Korea would use it for building nuclear weapons. While it might take a while for there to be enough bomb-making material from that facility, there was a more immediate threat. "Way back in 1989 North Korea extracted some fuel rods. The amount is unknown but could have been as much as one or two bombs' worth. No one outside of North Korea knows where that plutonium is. No technical expert doubts that North Korea could make a bomb or maybe two out of it — a 'starter kit' towards a nuclear arsenal." (Carter, supra.)

The situation only became worse in late 2002 and early 2003. In reaction to North Korea's admission of its enrichment program, the U.S.-led consortium that was implementing the Framework Agreement announced in November that it was suspending the fuel oil deliveries to North Korea. Then, in December 2002, North Korea announced that it was restarting the small reactor at Yongbyon, allegedly to produce electricity. North Korea removed seals and monitoring equipment from the nuclear facilities and ordered IAEA inspectors, who were responsible for monitoring the freeze, out of the country.

On January 10, 2003, North Korea announced its withdrawal from the Nuclear Nonproliferation Treaty (NPT), saying it was effective immediately, and stated that this withdrawal freed it from its Safeguards Agreement with the International Atomic Energy Agency (IAEA). Also, because the 1994 Agreed Framework required that North Korea remain a party to the NPT, North Korea breached another of its obligations under that agreement.

If matters were not already serious enough, there were intelligence reports in January-February 2003 that North Korea was taking steps to move the fuel rods with plutonium away from Yongbyon to some unknown location. This led to calls for immediate steps by the U.S. government. Former Secretary of Defense Perry, former

Chairman of the Joint Chiefs of Staff Shalikashvili, and Professor Carter co-authored the followed article.

William J. Perry, Ashton B. Carter, & John M. Shalikashvili, A Scary Thought: Loose Nukes in North Korea

Wall Street Journal, February 6, 2003, at p. 18

While the world prepares to disarm Iraq of chemical and biological arms, by force if necessary, it does nothing as a larger disaster unfolds in North Korea — loose nukes.

News reports indicate that North Korea has begun to move fuel rods containing six bombs' worth of plutonium from its facility at Yongbyon. For eight years, since 1994, that plutonium has been stored at Yongbyon where it could be seen by on-site inspectors and, if necessary, entombed by an airstrike of precision bombs. Now it is being trucked away, perhaps to one of North Korea's many caves, where it will be difficult to find or destroy.

This development undermines global nonproliferation efforts that have been successful for decades, and represents an imminent danger to the security of the region. Even more, in an age of terrorism it poses the additional specter of putting nuclear weapons into the hands of parties even more threatening than the North Korean government. North Korea has few cash-generating exports other than ballistic missiles. Now nuclear weapons or fissile material could take their place in its shopping catalogue. Or North Korea's government might collapse, losing control of the nukes in the process. While hijacked airlines and anthrax-dusted letters are a dangerous threat to civilized society, it would change the way Americans were forced to live if it became an ever-present possibility that a city could disappear in a mushroom cloud.

North Korea has not been allowed to reprocess nuclear fuel rods to obtain weapons plutonium since 1989. In that period, North Korea obtained a quantity of plutonium that it did not declare honestly to the IAEA, as it was required to do. How much is uncertain, but estimates range as high as two bombs' worth. Whether it has had a bomb or two for the past 15 years is not known, but for sure it is now only a few months away from obtaining six bombs. The North Koreans might reckon that's enough to sell some and have some left over to threaten the U.S. and its allies, South Korea and Japan.

North Korea also admitted last October that it aims to produce the other metal from which nuclear weapons can be made — uranium. It will be years, however, before that effort produces anything like the amount of fissile material now being trucked from Yongbyon. The material at Yongbyon is the immediate threat.

Even if their nukes remain in the hands of the current government, a nuclear North Korea could prompt a domino effect of proliferation in East Asia. South Korea once had a nuclear weapons program that it stopped because it was persuaded its security could be assured without them. Will some in South Korea start to reconsider? Similar questions might be asked in Japan and Taiwan — questions no government wants asked.

We cannot wait for the Iraq situation to resolve itself while the North Korean government is taking actions that cross a dangerous "red line." The North Koreans have chosen, as many predicted, the most inconvenient time to take the wheel and drive out of Yongbyon. So far, they have been in the driver's seat. The U.S. needs to develop a policy that gets its hands back on the wheel.

First, we must make it clear that the concealment or reprocessing of those rods constitutes an unacceptable threat to our security and to the security of the region.

Second, we must repair our relations with South Korea, because no American strategy can succeed if it does not have the support of our allies. Their national interests and ours are not identical, but they overlap strongly. South Korea can provide vital assistance in persuading North Korea's leaders to change course — or it can undermine our position if it is not persuaded we are right. Above all, our troops must stand shoulder to shoulder to deter North Korean aggression.

Third, President Bush must begin now the diplomacy he has said will be his first resort for staving off a nuclear setback on the Korean peninsula. No one can say whether diplomacy will work. Perhaps the North Koreans are determined to attempt to get nuclear weapons despite our resolve and the world's condemnation. We can only ascertain that by beginning direct talks.

Our position in that diplomacy must be clear: We require the complete and verifiable elimination of North Korea's nuclear and missile programs. One thing we can offer in return is not something tangible, but something that North Korea might value highly: a formal pledge that the U.S. does not have hostile intent against North Korea. Much as we object to North Korea's treatment of its people, we do not plan to go to war to change it. We can live in peace. Only the U.S. can make this pledge, which is why direct talks are required.

We can argue that since North Korea has enough conventional firepower on the DMZ to make war a distinctly unpleasant prospect to us, it doesn't need nuclear weapons to safeguard its security. Far from guaranteeing security, pursuit of nuclear weapons will force a confrontation. Once the nuclear program is gone, the relative stability that will remain can provide the time and conditions for a relaxation of tensions, and, eventually, improved relations. . . .

The other thing the U.S. can offer is assistance with the process of dismantling the North's nuclear and missile weapons and facilities, in a version of the historic Nunn-Lugar program that dismantled the former Soviet Union's weapons of mass destruction.

The loose nukes disaster unfolding at Yongbyon touches the highest security interests of the U.S. and the world as we enter the 21st century. Delay is not an option.

Besides the national security and diplomatic considerations above, there were legal issues. Professor Frederic L. Kirgis identifies the issues under the Nonproliferation Treaty.

Frederic L. Kirgis, North Korea's Withdrawal from the Nuclear Nonproliferation Treaty

ASIL Insight (January 15, 2003)

North Korea became a party to the NPT in 1985 as a non-nuclear-weapon state. Article III of the NPT requires each non-nuclear-weapon state to accept safeguards in an agreement with the IAEA, in order to verify its compliance with its obligation under Article II to refrain from manufacturing or acquiring nuclear explosives. Article X, paragraph 1 of the NPT provides:

> Each party shall in exercising its national sovereignty have the right to withdraw from the Treaty if it decides that extraordinary events, related to the subject matter of this Treaty, have jeopardized the supreme interests of its country. It shall give notice of such withdrawal to all other Parties to the Treaty and to the United Nations Security Council three months in advance. . . .

In 1992, North Korea entered into its Safeguards Agreement with the IAEA under Article III of the NPT. The Safeguards Agreement provides for measurements and observations of North Korean nuclear material and facilities by IAEA inspectors. Article 26 of the Safeguards Agreement provides, "This Agreement shall remain in force as long as the Democratic People's Republic of Korea is party to the Treaty [the NPT]." Consequently, if North Korea has validly withdrawn from the NPT pursuant to its January 2003 announcement, the Safeguards Agreement would no longer be in force. . . .

Even if the withdrawal is proper under the strict terms of Article X and is effective immediately, the United Nations Security Council could decide that the withdrawal, considered in conjunction with North Korea's stated intent to resume missile testing, to begin reprocessing spent fuel rods and to reactivate its nuclear facilities, and its expulsion of IAEA inspectors, amount to a threat to the peace. The Security Council could make that determination on its own initiative, or on a referral from the IAEA Board of Governors based on North Korea's noncompliance with its obligations under the Safeguards Agreement. Acting under Chapter VII of the U.N. Charter, the Security Council could impose mandatory economic, diplomatic or even military sanctions on North Korea. Any proposed resolution to impose such sanctions, however, would be subject to a possible veto by any of the permanent Security Council members (China, France, Russia, the United Kingdom and the United States).

Indeed, the IAEA was active. Paul Kerr of the Arms Control Association reported the IAEA actions and the resulting diplomatic maneuvers through February 2003.

Paul Kerr, North Korea Restarts Reactor; IAEA Sends Resolution to UN

Arms Control Today (March 2003)

Responding to North Korea's rejection of two previous IAEA resolutions, the agency's Board of Governors adopted a resolution February 12 declaring Pyongyang in "further non-compliance" with its obligations under the NPT. The board decided to report the matter to the UN Security Council, in accordance with agency mandates.

The two previous resolutions, adopted in November and January, called for Pyongyang to provide details about its reported uranium-enrichment program, as well as reverse its recent decisions to expel IAEA monitors, remove monitoring equipment and seals from nuclear facilities, and withdraw from the NPT.

The new IAEA resolution "stresses" the board's "support" for a diplomatic solution to the crisis. According to a February 19 UN press statement, the Security

Council referred the matter to its group of experts, who are to study the resolution and make recommendations to the council.

A State Department official said in a February 25 interview that Washington is consulting with allies about future Security Council action, adding that it is "too soon to speculate" about specific measures. [White House Press Secretary Ari] Fleischer explained in a February 12 statement that the council's options ranged from a statement condemning North Korea's actions to imposing economic sanctions.

The IAEA board voted 31-0 to adopt the resolution, with Russia and Cuba abstaining. Fleischer expressed the Bush administration's approval, calling the resolution a "clear indication that the international community will not accept a North Korea nuclear weapons program."

U.S. allies, however, continued to resist the administration's approach, arguing that Washington should soon engage in bilateral talks with Pyongyang. . . .

Newly installed South Korean President Roh Moo-hyun condemned North Korea's nuclear activities during his February 25 inauguration speech, but he emphasized that the North Korean nuclear issue "should be resolved peacefully through dialogue," . . .

Chinese Foreign Minister Tang Jiaxuan stated February 24 that China wants the Bush administration to "begin dialogue as equals" with North Korea. . . .

Hatsuhisa Takashima, press secretary for Japan's Ministry of Foreign Affairs, said in a February 21 statement that Tokyo's priority is to "maintain unity and solidarity" among Japan, the United States, and South Korea, adding that the issue should be "addressed with good care and caution."

The many pressures for negotiations resulted in diplomatic representatives from China, North Korea, and the United States meeting in Bejing, China, on April 24-25, 2003. The meeting involved an initial exchange of views and was meant to a first step toward further talks, which might also include Japan and South Korea. The exchange of views included North Korea's claim that it already had at least one nuclear weapon and that it sought a security guarantee from the United States as a condition of dismantling its nuclear weapons program, though it suggested that it might not be willing to dismantle any existing weapon(s). (A North Korean statement before the meeting had indicated that the lesson North Korea had learned from the coalition's March 2003 attack on Iraq was the importance of having nuclear weapons to deter such attacks.) The United States apparently pushed hard for North Korea to dismantle its nuclear weapons program verifiably.

In a public speech at the time of the meeting, Secretary of State Colin Powell said: "The one thing that is absolutely clear . . . is that there is unity within the [Asia-Pacific] community that we must not allow the [Korean] peninsula to become nuclear." And in a TV interview aired on April 24, President Bush said that North Korea was "back to the old blackmail game," and he insisted that "we are not going to be threatened." Mr. Bush, however, did not indicate what the next U.S. steps would be.

Notes and Questions

1. Working with the benefit of hindsight, what should the U.N. Security Council have done with respect to North Korea in 2003? Should it have acted under

Chapter VII of the U.N. Charter and imposed economic sanctions against North Korea? Or even authorized the use of military force?

2. Do the statements by Russian and Chinese officials encouraging the United States to have a bilateral dialogue with North Korea, as described in the Kerr excerpt above, suggest that it might have been difficult to obtain Security Council approval for strong sanctions or, even more so, for military action?

3. Again, with the benefit of hindsight, what do you think the U.S. government should have done in early to mid-2003? Were the policies wise that the Bush Administration actually followed? If not, why not? Were the Bush Administration policies consistent with its approach toward Saddam Hussein and Iraq in 2002-2003?

4. More generally on combating proliferation, Representative John Spratt, a moderate Democrat who is a senior member of the House Armed Services Committee and the ranking member on the House Budget Committee, raised some warning flags. In a thoughtful article, he emphasized the importance of nonproliferation efforts and pointed out for particular praise the ongoing Nunn-Lugar program. It had already reduced the nuclear threat by working with Russia and other former Soviet countries "to deactivate 6,020 [former Soviet] warheads, destroy 486 intercontinental ballistic missiles, and eliminate 347 submarine-launched ballistic missiles and 97 strategic bombers." On the other hand, Rep. Spratt identified budget initiatives and other Pentagon steps that appeared to contemplate "a resumption of [U.S.] nuclear testing and the development of new 'bunker-busting' nuclear weapons." He concluded:

> We must . . . re-establish our credibility as an adherent to the Nuclear Nonproliferation Treaty. This means we should abandon any push for development of new nuclear weapons, low-yield or otherwise, and reaffirm our commitment to a moratorium on nuclear tests. Only in so doing can the United States credibly urge other nations to cease pursuit of nuclear weapons. [John M. Spratt, Jr., Stopping a Dangerous Drift in U.S. Arms Control Policy, Arms Control Today 1 (March 2003).]

5. The materials above describe a number of formal treaties and other agreements. There is also at least one example of an informal understanding between two countries — that is, the 1991 Presidential Nuclear Initiatives on tactical nuclear weapons between the United States and Russia. Also, there are occasional unilateral measures, such as a moratorium on nuclear testing or unilaterally giving up nuclear weapons (as South Africa apparently did). What are the relative advantages and disadvantages of formal agreements, informal understandings, and unilateral measures?

6. Might concerns over compliance and verification affect your answer to the preceding Note? Some of the more recent arms control agreements — for example, the Intermediate Nuclear Forces Agreement (INF), START I, and the CWC — have much more extensive verification provisions than earlier treaties, such as SALT I. On the other hand, the 2002 Strategic Offensive Agreement (SORT) has only limited verification provisions. Since there are ways to design detailed verification requirements, should a country prefer seeking those over more limited verification? Of course, verification applies to all countries.

7. Why might a state be more reluctant to bind itself in an agreement on arms control or related nonproliferation issues as compared to, say, an economic, environmental, or law of the seas agreement? Is an arms control/nonproliferation

agreement likely to involve more politically sensitive issues for a country than those other agreements? If so, what are the implications of this in terms of the ease with which a country might enter into an arms control/nonproliferation agreement or accept, for instance, a long-term arrangement?

8. Formal methods for resolving disputes about compliance in the area of arms control/nonproliferation are much less developed than in many other areas, such as international trade. Why do you think that is the case? Could it be related to the fundamental national security interests that are involved and each country's concern that it does not want to limit its flexibility?

9. If a country is willing to enter into an arms control/nonproliferation agreement, should it ensure that disputes will be handled in a way that will minimize the chances of unnecessarily jeopardizing the whole agreement? (See the discussion above at page 111 about the U.S.-Soviet dispute over the Krasnoyarsk radar and the ABM Treaty.)

Table of Cases

Index